Chapter	You Make the Call	Selected Highlights Current Happenings	Using the Information	Did You Know?
<16>	• Engineer • Farmer • Teacher • Director	• Declining dividends • Reporting income • Stock options • Online trading	• Earnings per share • Dividend yield • Price-earnings	• Buybacks explode • Earnings expectations
<17>	• Bond rater • Retailer • Bond investor	• Return of junk bonds • Convertible bonds • Amortization software	• Bond vs stock financing • Collateral agreements • Analyzing pledged assets	• Bond quotes • Rating bonds
<18>	• Money manager • Home builder • Retailer	• Classifying investments • International investments • Reporting investments	• Interpreting investments • Foreign exchange rates • Return on total assets	• Tinseltown securities
<19>	• Reporter • Community activist	• Measuring cash flows • Classifying cash flows • Reporting cash flows	• Cash vs net income • Analyzing sources & uses • Cash flow on total assets	• Cash valuation • E-cash • Cash flow
<20>	• Banker • Auditor	• Data from the Web • Building blocks of analysis • Reporting analysis results	• Horizontal analysis • Vertical analysis • Ratio analysis	• Chips and brokers • Ticker prices • Bears and bulls
<21>	• Division manager • Budget officer • Purchases manager • Salesperson	• Customer orientation • Global economy • Manuf. mgmt. principles	• Classifying costs • Quality management • Contribution margin	• Airline quality • Banished to overhead
<22>	• Mgmt. consultant • Sales director • Systems consultant	• Manufacturing activities • Job order manufacturing • Job order documents	• Applying overhead • Analyzing cost flows • Multiple overhead rates	• Build-to-order PCs • Software modules
<23>	• Process manager • General manager • Budget officer	• Customer-interaction software • Flexibility & standardization • Process cost summary	• Analyzing process cost • Cost per equivalent unit • Spoiled units	• Factory smarts • Service companies • Just-in-time
<24>	• Operations manager • Accounting Officer • Centre manager	• Responsibility accounting • Activity-based costing • Contribution reporting	• Assigning overhead • Allocating joint costs • Analyzing centres	• Overhead kills • Healthcare costing • Nonfinancial measures
<25>	• Trainee • Operations manager • Marketing manager	• Cost-volume-profit analysis • Cost behaviour • Multiproduct analysis	• Estimating costs • Break-even • Operating leverage	• Compaq's break-even • Price-cutting
<26>	• Environmental manager • Budget staffer • Sales manager	• Administering budgets • Master budgeting • Linking budgets	• Expense planning • Managing cash • Zero-based budgeting	• Budget calendar • Budgeting and acquisitions • Activity/Process budgeting
<27>	• Human Resource Mgr. • Sales manager • Internal auditor • Budget officer	• Standard costing • Management by exception • Performance reports	• Cost variances • Flexible budgeting • Revenue variances	• Setting standard costs • Strategic partnerships • Benchmarking
<28>	• Systems manager • Production supervisor • Investment manager • R & D manager	• Using payback • Analyzing rate of return • Net present value	• Capital budgeting • Relevant costs • Break-even time	• The winner is ... • Inadequate information • Outsourcing

NINTH CANADIAN EDITION

Fundamental Accounting Principles

Kermit D. Larson
University of Texas—Austin

John J. Wild
University of Wisconsin at Madison

Barbara Chiappetta
Nassau Community College

Morton Nelson
Wilfrid Laurier University

Ray F. Carroll
Dalhousie University

Michael Zin
Professor Emeritus
University of Windsor

**McGraw-Hill
Ryerson**

Toronto   Montreal   New York   Burr Ridge   Bangkok   Bogotá
Caracas   Lisbon   London   Madrid   Mexico City   Milan   New Delhi
Seoul   Singapore   Sydney   Taipei

McGraw-Hill
Ryerson Limited

A Subsidiary of The McGraw·Hill Companies

FUNDAMENTAL ACCOUNTING PRINCIPLES
Ninth Canadian Edition

ISBN: 0-07-560480-9

1 2 3 4 5 6 7 8 9 10 GTC 5 4 3 2 1 0 9 8 7 6

Printed and bound in Canada

Sponsoring Editor: *Jennifer Dewey/Lisa Feil*
Developmental Editor: *Denise McGuinness*
Senior Supervising Editor: *Margaret Henderson*
Production Editor: *Shirley Corriveau*
Production Co-ordinator: *Nicla Dattolico*
Interior Design: *Ellen Pentengell*
Cover Design: *Liz Harasymczuk*
Cover Illustration: *Dave Cutler/SIS©*
Page Make-up: *Valerie Bateman/ArtPlus Limited*
Typeface: *Times Roman*
Printer: *Transcontinental Printing Inc.*

Canadian Cataloguing in Publication Data

Main entry under title:

Fundamental accounting principles

9th Canadian ed.
Issued also as v. 1-2 of: Fundamental accounting principles. 9th Canadian ed.
Includes index.
ISBN 0-07-560480-9

1. Accounting.   I. Larson, Kermit D.   II. Title: Fundamental accounting principles.

HF5635.F455 1999   657   C99-930411-9

ontents in Brief

ontents

Chapter 4   Adjusting Accounts for Financial Statements   150

Appendix 4A—Alternatives in Accounting for Prepaids   178

Appendix 4B—Worksheet Format for Adjusted Trial Balance   181

Chapter 5   Completing the Accounting Cycle and Classifying Accounts   204

Appendix 5A—Reversing Entries and Account Numbering   231

Chapter 6 Accounting for Merchandising Activities 256

Appendix 6A—Periodic and Perpetual Inventory Systems: Accounting Comparisons 291

Chapter 7 Merchandise Inventories and Cost of Sales 316

Appendix 7A—Assigning Costs to Inventory—Periodic System 346

Chapter 11 Payroll Liabilities 520

Chapter 12 Capital Assets: Plant and Equipment, Natural Resources, and Intangible Assets 556

Chapter 16   Corporate Reporting: Dividends, Shares, and Income 730

Chapter 17   Bonds and Long-Term Notes Payable 778

Appendix 17A—Present Values of Bonds and Notes 812

Chapter 20   Analyzing Financial Statements 938

Appendix I—Financial Statement Information I-1

Appendix II—Present and Future Values II-1

Appendix III—Accounting Concepts and Alternative Valuations III-1

Code of Professional Conduct CPC-1

Chart of Accounts CH-1

Credits CR-1

Index IND-1

Preface

Let's Talk

Through extensive market-based surveys, focus groups, and reviews, we discovered several interests and needs in accounting education today. In a nutshell, these desires can be grouped into eight pedagogical areas: (1) motivation, (2) organization, (3) preparation, analysis, and use, (4) ethics, (5) technology, (6) real world, (7) active learning, and (8) flexibility. Our main goal in this edition of *Fundamental Accounting Principles* (F.A.P.) is to address these needs and create the most contemporary, exciting, relevant, and flexible principles book in the market. A quick summary of these areas follows.

Motivation. Motivation drives learning. From the chapter's opening article and its focus on young entrepreneurs to the decision-making prompted by You Make the Call, **F.A.P.** motivates readers. It brings accounting and business to life and demonstrates that this material can make a difference in your life.

Organization. Organization serves the learning process, and **F.A.P.'s** outstanding organization aids that process. From "Chapter Linkages" and learning objectives to chapter outlines and Flashbacks, **F.A.P.** is the leader in lending readers a helping hand in learning about accounting and business.

Preparation, Analysis, and Use. Accounting involves preparing, analyzing, and using information. **F.A.P.** balances each of these important roles in explaining and illustrating topics. From the unique Using the Information section to the creative Hitting the Road projects, **F.A.P.** shows all aspects of accounting.

Ethics. Ethics is fundamental to accounting. **F.A.P.** highlights the roles of ethics and social responsibility in modern businesses. From the Judgment and Ethics decision-making feature to its Ethics Challenge assignments, **F.A.P.** alerts readers to relevant and important ethical concerns.

Technology. Technology continues to change business and accounting, creating new and exciting accounting opportunities. **F.A.P.** is the leader in applying and showing technology in accounting. From the innovative Taking It to the Net projects to its Web-based assignments, **F.A.P.** pushes the accounting frontiers.

Real World. Accounting is important to the information age. From features and assignments that highlight companies like Alliance Communications Corporation, and Atlantis Communications Inc. to the Teamwork in Action and Communication in Practice activities, **F.A.P.** shows accounting in a modern, global context. It also engages both accountants and nonaccountants. From the exciting Did You Know? features to its Business Break, **F.A.P.** shows accounting is relevant to everyone.

Active Learning. Active learning implies active inquiry and interaction. The Teamwork in Action and Communicating in Practice are excellent starting points in developing an active learning environment.

Flexibility. **F.A.P.** is the undisputed leader in offering a strong pedagogical support package. Also, the *MHLA* service is a new, special addition to our support package.

This is just a sneak preview of **F.A.P.'s** new and exciting features. From communication, interpersonal, and critical thinking skills to the development of ethical and global awareness, **F.A.P.** is the leader. We invite you to take a complete look at these and other special features in the remainder of this preface to see why **F.A.P.** is the *first choice* in accounting principles books.

Motivation

Motivation is a main goal of **F.A.P.** We know information retention is selective—if it does not apply to the lives of readers, they typically are not motivated to learn. **F.A.P.** explains and illustrates how accounting applies to the reader. Here is a sampling of materials that motivate the reader.

The **Chapter Opening Article** sets the stage and shows how the chapter's contents are relevant to the reader. Articles often focus on young entrepreneurs in business who benefit from preparing, analyzing, and using accounting information. These articles bring the material to life in concrete terms.

Fizzling Inventory

Toronto, ON—By June 1997, 27-year-old Rob Stavos was living his dream. He'd just opened **Liquid Nectar,** a small retail outlet devoted to serving the quirky tastes of young and old alike. But within months, this young entrepreneur's dream had become a nightmare.

Liquid Nectar started out with a bang. Customers raved about its stock of exotic and unique beverage products. Profit margins on successful drinks far outweighed the costs of unsold products. "We were ready to take on the large producers," boasts Rob. Within two months, however, Rob lost control of inventory and margins were being squeezed. What happened? Was Liquid Nectar soon to be another flash-in-the-pan?

You Make the Call features develop critical thinking and decision-making skills by requiring decisions using accounting information. Each chapter contains two to four of these features. They are purposely chosen to reflect different kinds of users. Examples are investors, consultants, programmers, financial planners, engineers, appraisers, and political and community activists. Guidance answers are provided.

Entrepreneur
You are the owner of a small retail store. You are considering allowing customers to purchase merchandise using credit cards. Until now, your store only accepted cash and cheques. What form of analysis do you use to make this decision?

You Make the Call

Company Excerpts call attention to well-known organizations to illustrate accounting topics. These excerpts are often accompanied by text describing the nature of the business and its relevance to readers.

...the Company announced it was proceeding with the construction of a 375,000-tonne smelter at Alma, Quebec. Total cost is estimated at $1,600 [million], most of which will be incurred over the next three years. Approximately $220 [million] is expected to be spent in 1998.

ALCAN

Financial Statements of familiar companies are used to acquaint readers with the format, content, and use of accounting information. The financial statements for Alliance, and Atlantis are reproduced in an appendix at the end of the book and referenced often.

CONSOLIDATED STATEMENTS OF EARNINGS AND RETAINED EARNINGS
ALLIANCE COMMUNICATIONS CORPORATION

For the years ended March 31, 1997, March 31, 1996 and March 31, 1995
(In thousands of Canadian dollars, except per share data)

	1997	1996	1995
REVENUES	$ 282,599	$ 268,945	$ 233,811
DIRECT OPERATING EXPENSES	213,816	209,789	183,685
GROSS PROFIT	68,783	59,156	50,126
OTHER EXPENSES			
Other operating expenses	42,037	40,363	28,643
Amortization	5,160	5,038	5,164
Interest (note 10)	1,296	8	

Organization

Organization is crucial to effective learning. If it is not well-organized or linked with previous knowledge, learning is less effective. **F.A.P.** helps readers organize and link accounting concepts, procedures, and analyses. A **Preview** kicks off each chapter. It introduces the importance and relevance of the materials. It also links these materials to the opening article to further motivate the reader. Here are some additional materials to enhance learning effectiveness.

To Instructor

Use the learning objectives to help structure the course and assignment material to your instructional style.

To Student

Study each of these helpful organizational aids to increase your understanding and learning of accounting and business.

A Look Back

Chapter 1 began our study of accounting by considering its role in the information age. We described accounting for different organizations and identified users and uses of accounting. We saw that ethics and social responsibility are crucial to accounting.

A Look at This Chapter

In this chapter we describe financial statements and the accounting principles guiding their preparation. An important part of this chapter is transaction analysis using the accounting equation. We prepare and analyze financial statements based on transaction analysis.

A Look Forward

Chapter 3 explains the recording of transactions. We introduce the double-entry accounting system and show how T-accounts are helpful in analyzing transactions. Journals and trial balances are also identified and explained.

Chapter linkages launch a chapter and establish bridges between prior, current, and upcoming chapters. Linkages greatly assist readers in effectively learning the materials and help them link concepts across topics.

Learning Objectives

LO 1 Identify and explain the content and reporting aims of financial statements.

LO 2 Describe differences in financial statements across forms of business organization.

LO 3 Explain the roles of preparers, auditors and users of financial statements.

LO 4 Identify those responsible for setting accounting and auditing principles.

LO 5 Identify, explain and apply accounting principles.

LO 6 Analyze business transactions using the accounting equation.

Learning Objectives are shown at the beginning of the chapter to help focus and organize the materials. Each objective is repeated in the chapter at the point it is described and illustrated. Self-contained summaries for learning objectives are provided at the end of the chapter.

Flashback

10. Identify seven internal operating functions in organizations.
11. Why are internal controls important?

A series of **Flashbacks** in the chapter reinforce the immediately preceding materials. Flashbacks allow the reader to momentarily stop and reflect on the topics described. They give immediate feedback on the reader's comprehension before going on to new topics. Answers are provided.

Chapter Outline

► **Communicating with Financial Statements**
- Previewing Financial Statements
- Financial Statements and Forms of Organization

► **Transactions and the Accounting Equation**
- Transaction Analysis—Part I
- Transaction Analysis—Part II
- Summary of Transactions

A colour-coded **Chapter Outline** is provided for the chapter. This gives a mental and visual framework to help readers learn the material.

Preparation, Analysis, and Use

Accounting is a service focused on preparing, analyzing, and using information. **F.A.P.** presents a balanced approach to those three crucial aspects of accounting. The preparation aspect of **F.A.P.** is well established and highly regarded. A new progressive emphasis and use continues to put **F.A.P.** in the frontier of practice. Here's a sampling of new or revised textual materials on analysis and use:

The **Accounting Equation** (Assets = Liabilities + Equity) is used as a tool to evaluate a journal entry. The accounting equation is especially useful in learning and understanding the impacts of business transactions and events on financial statements. **F.A.P.** is a pioneer in showing this additional analysis tool.

Aug. 31	Cash	6,300			
	Sales		6,000	Assets = Liabilities + Equity	
	Sales Taxes Payable ($6,000 × 0.05) ..		300	+6,300 +300 +6,000	
	To record cash sales and 5% sales tax.				

The **Using the Information** section wraps up each chapter and emphasizes critical-thinking and decision-making skills. Each section introduces one or more tools of analysis. It applies these tools to actual companies and interprets the results. The section often focuses on use of ratio analyses to study and compare the performance and financial condition of competitors.

Return on Investment   USING THE INFORMATION

LO 10 Compute and interpret return on investment.

We introduced return on investment in assessing return and risk earlier in the chapter. Return on investment is also useful in evaluating management, analyzing and forecasting profits, and planning future activities. **Dell Computer** has its marketing department compute return on investment for *every* mailing. "We spent 15 months educating people about return on invested capital," says Dell's Chief Financial Offi-

Hitting the Road is a unique addition to the chapter's assignment material. This activity requires readers to work outside the book and often requires application of interpersonal and communication skills. Tasks range from visits to local merchandisers and government offices to conducting phone interviews and Web searches. These activities help readers understand and appreciate the relevance of accounting.

Select a company in your community which you may visit in person or interview on the telephone. Call ahead to the company to arrange a time when you can interview a member of the accounting department who helps in the preparation of the annual financial statements for the company. During the interview inquire about the following aspects of the company's accounting cycle:

Hitting the Road
LO 5

Business Break requires the reader to apply the chapter's material to read and interpret a business article. It also aids in developing reading comprehension skills and gives exposure to business happenings.

Read the article, "Car and Strive," in the September 1996 issue of *Canadian Business*.

Business Break
LO 11

Required

1. Contrast the profitability of **Magna** in the early 1990s to 1996.
2. What is the amount of revenue for Magna in the 1996 fiscal year?
3. What is the reason for Magna's success?
4. Despite its recent profitability what does the article identify as a possible problem for Magna?

Ethics

Ethics is the most fundamental accounting principle. Without ethics, information and accounting cease to be useful. **F.A.P.** is the leader in bringing ethics into accounting and demonstrating its importance. From the first chapter's article to the ethics codes at the end of the book, **F.A.P.** sets the standard in emphasizing ethical behaviour and its consequences. Here's a sampling of how we sensitize readers to ethical concerns and decision making:

The **Judgment and Ethics** feature requires readers to make accounting and business decisions with ethical consequences. It uses role-playing to show the interaction of judgment and ethics, the need for ethical awareness, and the impact of ethics. Guidance answers are provided.

Accountant

You are a public accountant consulting with a client. This client's business has grown to the point where its accounting system must be updated to handle both the volume of transactions and management's needs for information. Your client requests your advice in purchasing new software for its accounting system. You have been offered a 10% commission by a software company for each purchase of its system by one of your clients. Do you think your evaluation of software is affected by this commission arrangement? Do you think this commission arrangement is appropriate? Do you tell your client about the commission arrangement before making a recommendation?

A new **Ethics Challenge** is provided in the *Beyond the Numbers* section. It confronts ethical concerns based on material from the chapter. Many of these challenges involve actions where the ethical path is blurred.

Ethics Challenge

LO 2,3

Randy Meyer is the chief executive officer of a medium-sized company in Regina, Saskatchewan. Several years ago Randy persuaded the board of directors of his company to base a percent of his compensation on the net income the company earns each year. Each December Randy estimates year-end financial figures in anticipation of the bonus he will receive. If the bonus is not as high as he would like he offers several accounting recommendations to his controller for year-end adjustments. One of his favourite recommendations is for the controller to reduce the estimate of doubtful accounts. Randy has used this

Social Responsibility is a major emphasis of progressive organizations. **F.A.P.** is unique in introducing this important topic in Chapter 1. We describe social responsibility and accounting's role in both reporting on and assessing its impact. **F.A.P.** also introduces social audits and reports on social responsibility.

In Pursuit of Profit

How far can companies go in pursuing profit? Converse proposed to name a new footwear product Run N' Gun. This sparked debate on ethics, social responsibility and profits. Converse said Run N' Gun was a basketball and football term. Critics claimed it invited youth violence and links with the gun culture. To the credit of Converse, it changed the name from Run N' Gun to Run N' Slam prior to its sale to consumers.

To Instructor

PowerPoint presentation slides can be customized for your instructional style and are great visual aids to lecture materials.

To Student

Use **F.A.P.**'s Home Page for current updates, hot links to important sites, and much more . . .

Student Software provides several technology-assisted educational activities. These include (1) *Tutorial*—interactive review of topics, and (2) *SPATS*—instructional software to solve problems.

Technology

Technology and innovation can be exciting and fun. **F.A.P.** makes the transition to new technologies easy. It is the leader in demonstrating the relevance of technology and showing readers how to use it. To ensure easy access, all technology offerings are linked to the Larson booksite. The address is **www.mcgrawhill.ca/college/larson**. Here's a sampling of items pushing the technology frontier:

Accounting Web Community

The Financial Accounting Web Community is a place on the Internet designed and built with our adopters in mind. It is a place where instructors can quickly access teaching resources directly related to the text they are using. It is also a place where instructors can share ideas and information with each other.

The Financial Accounting Web Community is the starting point for accessing accounting and business resources on the Web. The book's Web site harnesses technology resources to provide the most up-to-date and powerful Web services available.

Taking It to the Net requires accessing a Web site and obtaining information relevant to the chapter. It aims to make readers comfortable with Web technology, familiar with information available, and aware of the power of Web technology.

Taking It to the Net
LO 1, 7

There is extensive accounting and business information available on the Internet. This includes the **TSE's** on-line address at **http://www.tse.com** and the Depository for Canadian Securities' database referred to as **SEDAR** (**http://www.sedar.com**) and numerous other Web sites offering access to financial statement information or related data.

Required

Access at least one of the Web sites selected by either you or your instructor and answer the following:

a. Write a brief report describing the types of relevant information available at this Web site.

b. How would you rate the importance of the information available at this Web site for accounting and business?

PowerPoint® Presentations and Supplements augment each chapter with colorful graphics, interesting charts, innovative presentations, and interactive activities. The PowerPoint® materials are flexible and can be customized for any use.

Real World

Showing readers that accounting matters is part of an effective learning package. **F.A.P.** is the leader in real world instructional materials. It offers unique assignments challenging the reader to apply knowledge learned in practical and diverse ways. These challenges include analytical problems, research requirements, comparative analysis, teamwork assignments, and communication exercises. They also allow greater emphasis on conceptual, analytical, communication, and interpersonal skills. Here's a sampling of these materials:

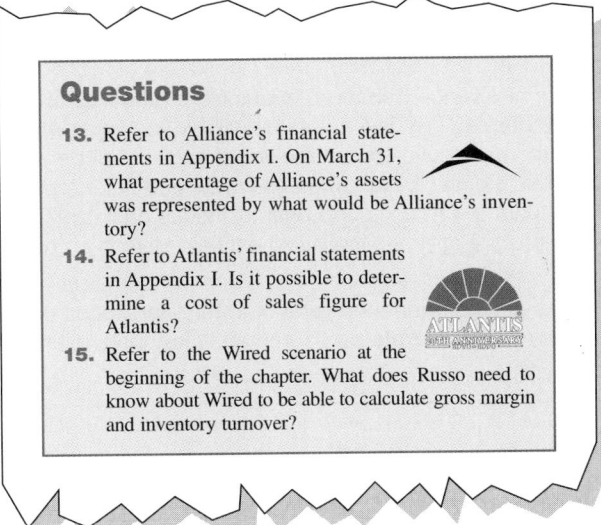

Questions

13. Refer to Alliance's financial statements in Appendix I. On March 31, what percentage of Alliance's assets was represented by what would be Alliance's inventory?

14. Refer to Atlantis' financial statements in Appendix I. Is it possible to determine a cost of sales figure for Atlantis?

15. Refer to the Wired scenario at the beginning of the chapter. What does Russo need to know about Wired to be able to calculate gross margin and inventory turnover?

Reporting in Action requires analysis and use of Alliance's annual report information.

Alliance Communication produces, markets and sells movies and television programs. Key financial figures for Alliance Communication's fiscal year ended March 31, 1997, are:

Key Figure	$ millions
Financing (liabilities + equity)	$353.7
Profit	18.2
Sales	282.6

Reporting in Action

LO 2, 6, 10

Required

1. What is the total amount of assets invested in Alliance Communication?

2. What is Alliance Communication's return on investment? Alliance Communication's assets at March 31, 1996, equal $238.9 (in millions).

3. How much are total expenses for Alliance Communication?

Analysis component:

4. Does Alliance Communication's return on investment seem satisfactory if competitors average a 5% return?

Comparative Analysis compares the performance and financial condition of Alliance and Atlantis using the accounting knowledge obtained from the chapter. These activities help develop analytical skills.

Both **Alliance Communications** and **Atlantis Communications** produce, market and sell movies and television programs. Key comparative figures ($ millions) for these two organizations follow:

	Alliance	Atlantis
Financing (liabilities + equity)	$353.7	$333.5
Profit	18.2	5.6
Sales	282.6	178.0

Source: Alliance figures are from its annual report for fiscal year-end March 31, 1997.
Atlantis figures are from its annual report for fiscal year-end December 31, 1997.

Comparative Analysis

LO 2, 6, 10

Note: In September 1998 shareholders of Alliance Communications Corp. and Atlantis Communications Inc. approved a merger of the two companies. The new company will be known as Alliance Atlantis Communications Inc. and will "be far more effective around the world and. . . will be positioned for further growth" according to Michael MacMillan, the newly appointed chairman and chief executive officer. Although it will not be possible to compare the Alliance and Atlantis results past 1997, it will be interesting to compare the new company's results to the previous individual entities. Here is an opportunity to see if expected synergies are realized.

Comprehensive and Serial Problems are included in several chapters and focus on multiple learning objectives from multiple chapters. They help integrate and summarize key principles.

Comprehensive Problem

Alpine Company

LO 1

(If the Working Papers that accompany this text are not available, omit this comprehensive problem.)

Assume it is Monday, May 1, the first business day of the month, and you have just been hired as the accountant for Alpine Company, which operates with monthly accounting periods. All of the company's accounting work has been completed through the end of April and its ledgers show April 30 balances. During your first month on the job, you record the following transactions:

May 1   Issued Cheque No. 3410 to S&M Management Co. in payment of the May rent, $3,710. (Use two lines to record the transaction. Charge 80% of the rent to Rent Expense, Selling Space and the balance to Rent Expense, Office Space.)

   2   Sold merchandise on credit to Essex Company, Invoice No. 8785, $6,100. (The terms of all credit sales are 2/10, n/30.)

   2   Issued a $175 credit memorandum to Nabors, Inc., for defective merchandise sold on April 28 and returned for credit. The total selling price (gross) was $4,725.

Problems often cover multiple learning objectives and usually require preparing, analyzing, and using information. They are paired with **Alternate Problems** for further review of the same topics. Problems are supported with software and other technology options. Many include an **Analytical Component** focusing on financial statement consequences and interpretations.

Problem 7-3A
Income statement comparisons and cost flow assumptions

LO 4, 9

The Denney Company sold 2,500 units of its product at $98 per unit during 19X1. Incurring operating expenses of $14 per unit in selling the units, it began the year with, and made successive purchases of, units of the product as follows:

January 1 beginning inventory . .	740 units costing $58 per unit
Purchases:	
April 2	700 units @ $59 per unit
June 14	600 units @ $61 per unit
August 29	500 units @ $64 per unit
November 18	800 units @ $65 per unit
	3,340 units

Required

Preparation component:

1. Prepare a comparative income statement for the company, showing in adjacent columns the net incomes earned from the sale of the product, assuming the company uses a periodic inventory system and prices its ending inventory on the basis of (a) FIFO, (b) LIFO, and (c) weighted-average cost.

Check Figure Net income (LIFO), $69,020

A **Demonstration Problem** is at the end of the chapter. It illustrates important topics and shows how to apply concepts in preparing, analyzing, and using information. A problem-solving strategy helps guide the reader. Most chapters also have a **Mid-Chapter Demonstration Problem** with solution.

Demonstration Problem

On July 14, 19X1, Truro Company paid $600,000 to acquire a fully equipped factory. The purchase included the following:

Asset	Appraised Value	Estimated Salvage Value	Estimated Useful Life	Amortization Method
Land	$160,000			Not amortized
Land improvements .	80,000	$ -0-	10 years	Straight line
Building	320,000	100,000	10 years	Double-declining balance
Machinery	240,000	20,000	10,000 units	Units of production*
Total	$800,000			

*The machinery is used to produce 700 units in 19X1 and 1,800 units in 19X2.

Required

1. Allocate the total $600,000 cost among the separate assets.

Infographics and Artwork aid in visual learning of key accounting and business topics. Photos, colour, highlighting, and authentic documents all help with visual learning.

Exhibit 12.2

Issues in Accounting for Capital Assets

Decline in book value over service life

Acquisition
1. Compute cost

Use
2. Allocate cost to periods benefited
3. Account for subsequent expenditures

Disposal
4. Record disposal

This chapter focuses on the decisions and factors surrounding these four important issues.

Active Learning

Active learning requires effective assignments. **F.A.P.** is the student-proven and instructor-tested leader in assignment materials. Proven and thoughtful assignments not only facilitate but motivate effective and active learning. many assignments include writing components. Here's a sampling of relevant assignment materials:

Teamwork in Action assignments require preparing, analyzing, and using information in teams. They can be completed in or outside of class. These active learning activities reinforce understanding of key topics and develop interpersonal skills.

Teamwork in Action

LO 5

A team will be called upon to personify the operation of a voucher system. Yet all teams must prepare for the potential to be selected by doing the following:

1. Each team is to identify the documents in a voucher system. The team leader will play the voucher, and each team member is to assume "the role" of one or more documents.

2. To prepare for your individual role you are to:
   a. Find an illustration for the document within the chapter.
   b. Write down your document function, where you originate, and how you flow through the voucher system.

3. Rehearse the role playing of operating the system. You may use text illustrations as props, and for visual effort you may wear a nametag identifying the part you play.

Communicating in Practice exercises aim at applying accounting knowledge to develop written and verbal communication skills.

Communicating in Practice

LO 12

The classroom should be divided into teams. Teams are to select an industry, and each team member is to select a different company in that industry. Each team member is to acquire the annual report of the company selected. Annual reports can be obtained in many ways including accessing this book's Web page or **http://www.sedar.com**. Use the annual report to compute total asset turnover. Communicate with teammates via a meeting, e-mail or telephone to discuss the meaning of this ratio, how different companies compare to each other, and the industry norm. The team must prepare a single memo reporting the ratios for each company and identify the conclusions or consensus of opinion reached during the team's discussion. The memo is to be duplicated and distributed to the instructor and all classmates.

Flexibility

Learning and instructing requires flexibility **F.A.P.** offers flexibility in meeting the unique demands of individual students and teachers. From the conventional classroom to the active learning environment, **F.A.P.'s** new edition and its pedagogical package give more flexibility and options for innovation in learning and instruction. It does this while maintaining the rich content that has made it the market-leading book in accounting principles.

Packaging Options

Unique **packaging options** support **F.A.P.** flexibility. Nobody matches McGraw-Hill Ryerson when it comes to packaging options for accounting principles. Discuss the flexible packaging options with your McGraw-Hill Ryerson sales representative.

To Instructor

F.A.P. supports all instructional and learning styles.
Additional Supporting Materials
Instructor's Resource Manual
Solutions Manual
Test Bank
Solutions Acetates
Teaching Acetates
PowerPoint Slides
Tutorial Software
SPATs
Videos (U.S.)

To Student

F.A.P. provides learning aids.
Additional materials that may be helpful in your accounting course include
Working Papers
Study Guide
GLAS (General Ledger Applications Software)
Essentials of Financial Accounting: A Multimedia Approach

Innovations and Enhancements

In preparing this edition, we asked questions of instructors and students. We asked what topics to add, or change in emphasis. We asked what pedagogical aids would help in teaching and learning. We wanted to know what innovations and enhancements would help them and maintain **F.A.P.** leadership in accounting principles. From these questions came several requests. We listened, and this edition is the result. We have already described major content and pedagogical changes. This section identifies many other chapter-by-chapter innovations and enhancements:

Chapter 1

- New focus on the information age and the relevance of accounting.
- Early introduction to income, revenues, and expenses using Alliance Communications.
- New discussion of return and risk as part of all business decisions.
- New descriptions of business activities: financing, investing, and operating.
- New and unique presentation of ethics and social responsibility.

Chapter 2

- *FASTForward,* an athletic service company, introduced as the new focus company for Chapters 2–5.
- New company transactions to add realism and interest.
- Revised discussion and presentation of accounting principles.
- Added analysis of each transaction using the accounting equation.
- New presentation and integration of cash flow statement with other financial statements.
- New description of reporting differences between proprietorships, partnerships, and corporations.

Chapter 3

- Revised presentation of transactions and source documents.
- New exhibits on the accounting equation and double-entry accounting.
- New exhibits and discussion linking transactions to financial statements, including the statement of cash flows.
- Revised discussion and exhibits for recording transactions.
- Expanded discussion of debt ratio with new comparative analysis.

Chapter 4

- New discussion of the accounting period and the motivation for adjusting accounts.

- New framework for preparing and analyzing adjustments.
- Several new exhibits and graphics illustrating adjusting accounts.
- New presentation linking adjustments to financial statements.
- Several new features highlighting current happenings in revenue recognition and the role of technology.
- Revised discussion of profit margin using Loblaw along with comparative analysis.

Chapter 5

- Revised presentation and new exhibits for the closing process.
- Revised presentation and discussion of the statement of cash flow as an integral part of the full set of financial statements.
- New exhibits presenting the accounting cycle.
- New presentation of the classified balance sheet.
- Revised current ratio discussion using Canadian Tire and industry analyses.

Chapter 6

- New discussion comparing a service company and a merchandiser.
- New presentation of the operating cycle of a merchandiser with credit or cash sales.
- New design of source documents including an invoice and debit and credit memoranda.
- Revised presentation of merchandising sales and purchases using the perpetual inventory system.
- Revised discussion on the transfer of ownership for inventory.
- New discussion and presentation of merchandising cost flows across periods.
- New comparison of cash and accrual measures of sales and costs.
- Revised acid-test ratio and gross margin discussion using Mitel and industry analyses.
- New appendix on accounting for merchandise sales and purchases under both the periodic and perpetual inventory systems.

Chapter 7

- Revised presentation of assigning costs to inventory using the perpetual inventory system.
- Revised discussion of inventoriable items and costs.
- New exhibits illustrating statements effects of inventory errors.
- Revised presentation of alternative inventory valuation methods.
- New appendix presentation assigning costs to inventory using the periodic system.
- Expanded merchandise turnover and days' sales in inventory ratio discussion and industry analyses.

Chapter 8

- New section on fundamental system principles.
- Contemporary and streamlined presentation on components of accounting systems.
- Revised discussion of hardware and software for systems.
- Contemporary presentation of Special Journals.
- Revised discussion of technology-based accounting systems.
- Revised layout for Special Journals reflecting current practice.
- New discussion of *enterprise-application software*, including SAP and Oracle.
- New analysis of business segments using a contribution matrix and Bombardier data.

Chapter 9

- New sections on the purpose of internal control and its limitations.
- Revised discussion on the principles of internal control.
- New feature boxes involving current technological developments.
- Revised discussion on control of cash.
- New presentation and exhibits on the voucher system of control.
- New depictions of important source documents.
- New presentation on using banking activities as controls, including the bank reconciliation.
- Revised discussion of days' sales uncollected using comparative analyses of Oshawa Group and George Weston.

Chapter 10

- New organization focuses on receivables first and short-term investments second.
- Revised discussion of credit sales, including use of credit cards.

- New presentation on accounting for accounts receivables.
- New ordering of (simpler) write-off method before (more complex) allowance method.
- New presentation and exhibits for estimating bad debts.
- Revised presentation and exhibits for notes receivable.
- Streamline accounting for investments including unrealized lower of cost and market.
- Revised discussion of accounts receivable turnover using comparative analyses of Imperial Oil and Ocelot Energy.

Chapter 11

- New exhibits including introducing computerized payroll systems.
- Excerpts from Revenue Canada forms.

Chapter 12

- New introduction and motivation on accounting for capital assets.
- New discussion to describe and illustrate amortization.
- Revised presentation and exhibits for disposals of capital assets.
- New discussion on natural resources and intangible assets.
- New discussion on the cash flow impacts of long-term assets.
- Revised total asset turnover illustration using George Weston and Oshawa Group.

Chapter 13

- New introduction on accounting for liabilities.
- Revised presentation of known (determinable) liabilities.
- New exhibits and discussion on promissory notes.
- Revised discussion of accounting for long-term liabilities.
- Transfer of present value discussion of liabilities to Chapter 16.
- Revised presentation of times interest earned with application to Best Buy.

Chapter 14

- New discussion of partnerships, including financial statements, admission/withdrawal, and liquidation.

Chapter 15

- Revised corporation coverage to focus on its characteristics and both common and preferred shares.
- New summary exhibit highlighting differences across alternative forms of organization.

- New exhibits including share certificate.
- Streamlined coverage of share subscriptions.
- Transfer of cash dividends discussions to Chapter 16.
- Revised book value per share discussion with references to Royal Bank.

Chapter 16

- Reorganization into four main sections: dividends; treasury shares; reporting income; and retained earnings.
- New dividends presentation with new exhibits.
- Revised and streamlined discussion on treasury shares.
- Streamlined presentation on reporting income information.
- Revised earnings per share discussion.
- New section on accounting for share options.
- Revised presentation of reporting retained earnings.
- New presentation of dividends yield and price-earnings ratios using Viceroy Homes, Nova Scotia Power, Noranda and CIBC.

Chapter 17

- New introduction to bond (long-term debt) financing.
- Revised bond presentation with new exhibits.
- New layout for effective interest amortization tables.
- Revised presentation of accounting for bond retirements.
- Revised presentation for notes payable.
- New explanation of present value concepts.
- New discussion of present values using interest tables.
- New discussion of collateral agreements for bonds and notes.
- Revised presentation of pledged assets to secured liabilities.

Chapter 18

- Streamlined coverage of investments and international accounting.
- Reorganized into three sections: Classification of investments; long-term investments in securities; and international investments.
- New presentation on the components of return on total assets with real company application.

Chapter 19

- New presentation on the motivation for cash flow reporting.
- New exhibits on the format of the statement of cash flows replacing the statement of changes in financial position.

- Revised discussion on cash from operating activities—both direct and indirect methods.
- New flexible presentation allows coverage of either or both direct or indirect methods.
- New exhibits summarize adjustments for both the direct and indirect methods.
- Revised discussion of cash flows from investing activities.
- Revised discussion of cash flows from financing activities.
- Revised presentation of analysis of cash sources and uses.

Chapter 20

- New discussion on the basics of financial statement analysis.
- New explanation of the building blocks of analysis.
- Revised discussion on analysis tools and standards for comparisons.
- Revised presentation of horizontal and vertical analysis.
- Revised summary exhibit of financial statement analysis ratios.
- New section on analysis reporting.

Chapter 21

- New introduction to managerial accounting.
- New section and exhibit on the purpose of managerial accounting.
- Revised presentation of reporting manufacturing activities.
- New section on cost accounting concepts emphasizing cost identification and classification.
- New discussion of manufacturing management principles.
- New introduction to important managerial topics including prime, conversion, product, and period costs.
- New infographics augment many new and revised topics.
- Transfer of discussion of a manufacturing statement and a general accounting system to Chapter 22.
- New presentation on unit contribution margin with illustrations using a bike manufacturer.

Chapter 22

- New focus on manufacturing and job order cost accounting.
- Revised presentation of manufacturing activities and reporting.

- Revised discussion of the job order cost accounting system.
- Streamlined discussion of underapplied and overapplied overhead.
- New presentation on multiple overhead allocation rates.
- Revised discussion of general accounting system (periodic) in a new appendix.

Chapter 23

- Revised introduction with discussion of motivation for a process manufacturing system.
- New exhibit and discussion comparing job order and process manufacturing systems.
- New exhibit to explain process manufacturing operations.
- Revised discussion of computing and using equivalent units.
- New discussion on the physical flow of units and preparation of a cost reconciliation.
- New presentation on spoilage in process costing and its effects on costs per equivalent unit.

Chapter 24

- New section and exhibits on two-stage allocation.
- New presentation and exhibits for activity-based costing.
- Transfer of activity-based costing upfront to link with Chapter 23.
- Revised discussion of decision-making relevance of cost allocation and performance measurement.
- Revised discussion of department expense allocation.
- New exhibit and presentation of joint costs.
- New presentation of return on assets by investment centres.
- Transfer of discussion of "eliminating an unprofitable department" to Chapter 28.

Chapter 25

- Revised discussion on describing and identifying cost behaviour.
- Revised presentation and comparison of the high-low, scatter diagram, and regression methods.

- Revised presentation on applying cost-volume-profit analysis.
- New presentation of operating leverage and its role in determining income.

Chapter 26

- New presentation of the budget calendar.
- New exhibit showing the master budget sequence.
- Expanded discussion and new exhibits of production and manufacturing budgets.
- Revised discussion motivated by new material on planning objectives.
- New presentation on zero-based budgeting.

Chapter 27

- New discussion and exhibit on the process of budgetary control.
- Revised emphasis on a decision making role for budgets and standard costs.
- New presentation of standard costs and the standard cost card.
- Revised organization of variance analysis.
- New presentation of and visual orientation to variance analysis.
- New separate analysis of variable and fixed overhead variances.
- New presentation on sales variances with illustrations.

Chapter 28

- Revised presentation of capital budgeting.
- New exhibits illustrating capital budgeting and its computations.
- New presentation of the internal rate of return for capital budgeting.
- New section comparing methods of analyzing investments using capital budgeting.
- New section on managerial decision making, information, and relevant costs.
- Revised presentation of short-term managerial decision tools.
- New section on qualitative factors in managerial decisions.
- New presentation of break-even time with illustrations.

Supplements

Instructor's Resource Manual

This manual contains materials for managing an active learning environment and provides new instructional visuals. Each chapter provides a Lecture Outline, a chart linking Learning Objectives to end-of-chapter material, and transparency masters. For instructor's convenience, student copies of these visuals are provided in the *Study Guide*. If students do not acquire the study guide, adopters are permitted to duplicate these visuals for distribution.

Solutions Manual

The manuals contain solutions for all assignment materials. Transparencies in large, boldface type are also available.

Test Bank

The Test Bank contains a wide variety of questions, including true-false, multiple-choice, matching, short essay, quantitative problems, and completion problems of varying levels of difficulty. All Test Bank materials are grouped according to learning objective. A computerized version is also available in Windows.

PowerPoint Slides

This is a package of multimedia lecture enhancement aids that uses PowerPoint® software to illustrate chapter concepts. It includes a viewer so that they can be shown with or without Microsoft PowerPoint® software.

McGraw-Hill Learning Architecture

This Web-based Class Management System distributes product course materials for viewing with any standard Web Browser. This online learning centre is packed with dynamically generated pages of text, graphics, PowerPoint® slides, exercises, and more. Customization possibilities are easily implemented.

PageOut

PageOut is a McGraw-Hill online tool that enables instructors to create and post class-specfic Web pages simply and easily. No knowledge of HTML is required.

Online Learning Centre

A body of online content to augment the text and provide students with interactive quizzing features.

Videos (U.S.)

Lecture Enhancement Video Series. These short, action-oriented videos provide the impetus for lively classroom discussion. There are separate *Financial Accounting and Managerial Accounting* libraries. Available upon adoption.

SPATS (Spreadsheet Applications Template Software).

Excel templates for selected problems and exercises from the text. The templates gradually become more complex, requiring students to build a variety of formulas. What-if questions are added to show the power of spreadsheets and a simple tutorial is included. Instructors may request a free master template for students to use or copy, or students can buy shrinkwrapped versions at a nominal fee.

Tutorial Software

Windows version of multiple-choice, true-false, journal entry review and glossary review questions are randomly assessed by students. Explanations of right and wrong answers are provided and scores are tallied. Instructors may request a free master template for students to use or copy, or students can buy shrinkwrapped versions for a nominal fee.

Solutions Manual to accompany the practice sets.

Student

Working Papers

These new volumes match end-of-chapter assignment material. They include papers that can be used to solve all quick studies, exercises, serial problems, comprehensive problems, and Beyond the Numbers activities. Each chapter contains one set of papers that can be used for either the problems or the alternate problems.

Study Guide

For each chapter and appendix, these guides review the learning objectives and summaries, outline the chapter, and provide a variety of practice problems and solutions. Several chapters also contain visuals to illustrate key chapter concepts.

Additional Software (U.S.)

Essentials of Financial Accounting: A Multimedia Approach
GLAS (General Ledger Applications Software) by Jack E. Terry, ComSource Associates, Inc.

Practice Sets

Student's Name CD Centre, by Harvey C. Freedman of Humber College of Applied Arts and Technology. A manual, single proprietorship practice set covering a one-month accounting cycle. The set includes business papers and can be completed manually and/or using computer data files for use with *Simply Accounting for Windows.* The problem set can be assigned after Chapter 8.

Adders 'N Keyes, Fourth Edition by Brenda Mallouk. *Adders 'N Keyes* is a sole proprietorship practice set that gives students exposure to a real life business setting.

Barns Bluff Equipment, by Barrie Yackness of British Columbia Institute of Technology and Terrie Kroshus. A manual, single proprietorship practice set with business papers that may be assigned after Chapter 9.

Computerized Practice Set

Interactive Financial Accounting Lab by Ralph Smith, Rick Birney and Alison Wiseman.

Acknowledgments

We are thankful for the encouragement, suggestions, and counsel provided by the many instructors, professionals, and students in preparing the Ninth Canadian edition. This new edition reflects the pedagogical needs and innovative ideas of both instructors and students of accounting principles. If has been a team effort and we recognize the contributions of many individuals. We especially thank and recognize individuals who provided valuable comments and suggestions to further improve this edition, including:

Reviewers:

John Glendinning	Centennial College
Allen McQueen	Grant MacEwan Community College
Peter Woolley	BCIT
Ann Paterson	Humber College
Bob Holland	Kingstec Community College
David Bopara	Toronto School of Business
Donna Grace	Sheridan College Brampton
Aziz Rajwani	Langara College
Margaret Tough	Seneca College
Neill Nedohin	Red River Community College
Peter Norwood	Langara College
Tony McGowan	Lambton College
Jim Chambers	St. Clair College
Jack Castle	SIAST—Palliser
Cecile Ashman	Algonquin College
Shawn P. Thompson	Algonquin College
Micheal S. Sirtonski	Assiniboine Community College
George Duquette	Canadore College
Denis Woods	Centennial College—Progress Campus
Robin Hemmingsen	Centennial College
Harold J. Keller	College of the Rockies
Joe Pidutti	Durham College
Robert Bryant	Durham College
Ralph Sweet	Durham College
Paul Hurley	Durham College
Bill Rice	Fairview College
Elaine Hales	Georgian College
Don Smith	Georgian College
G. D. McLeod	Humber College—Lakeshore Campus
Gordon Holyer	Malaspina University College
Jeffrey Rudolph	Marianopolis College
Wayne Larson	Northern Alberta Institute of Technology
John Daye	New Brunswick Community College
Brad MacDonald	Nova Scotia Community College—Annapolis Campus
Heather Martin	Nova Scotia Community College—I.W. Akerley Campus
Louise Conners	Nova Scotia Community College—I.W. Akerley Campus
Carol Derksen	Red River Community College
Randy Ross	Ridgetown College, University of Guelph
Greg Fagan	Seneca College
Michael A. Perretta	Sheridan College—Brampton Campus
Don Thibert	Toronto School of Business—Windsor
Pamela Hamm	New Brunswick Community College—Saint John

Problem checkers:

Connie Hahn	Southern Alberta Institute of Technology
Albert Ferris	UPEI
Dirk VanVoorst	Sheridan College—Oakville
Richard Wright	Fanshawe College
Elaine Hales	Georgian College
Maria Belanger	Algonquin College
Karen Matthews	SIAST—Palliser
Neill Nedohin	Red River Community College
Bonnie Martel	Niagara College

Students input plays an important role in the new edition. Over 300 students from the schools below contributed to Student Focus Groups and Student Surveys.

Acadia University	Nova Scotia Community College
Algonquin College	Saskatchewan Institute of Applied Science and Technology
British Columbia Institute of Technology	(Palliser Campus)
Kwantlen College	Simon Fraser University
Northern Alberta Institute of Technology	Souther Alberta Institute of Technology

We also want to recognize the contribution of Dennis Wilson of Centennial College who prepared the updates of the payroll liabilities chapter and solutions for this edition and also our final accuracy checker, Elaine Hales of Georgian College. Special thanks also go to Matthew Carroll and Marife Abella for their research assistance.

Morton Nelson   *Ray Carroll*   *Michael Zin*
Kermit D. Larson *Barbara Chiappetta*   *John J. Wild*

1

Accounting in the Information Age

Winning at Giving

Winnipeg, MN—In August of 1997, Stephanie Williams was working as a salesclerk. She hated her job, and spent most of her time dreaming about getting a degree and a better position. In September of that year, her dreams came true. She quit her job and returned to school, never dreaming that by the age of 28 she would be living her dream.

Williams signed up for her first accounting course with no idea of what to expect. "I took accounting because people I trusted said it would be useful," says Williams. "What I got in return was a career, lots of friends, and a partner!" Her accounting course included a community service requirement. Students had to pair up and help less advantaged individuals. "My partner, Brett Fulwood, and I volunteered our services to a senior citizens' community."

Williams and Fulwood first visited the seniors community in September 1997 and never looked back. On that visit, they helped more than a dozen senior citizens, fielding questions on reading bank statements, interpreting pension cheques, and analyzing the financial reports of companies in which a few had invested their modest savings. "It was unbelievable," says Williams. "I saw the relevance of accounting and I was able to give something to others."

In the weeks that followed, Williams and Fulwood answered several follow-up questions. "We even got a call from a woman's nephew in Brandon asking if we could help with recordkeeping in the family trucking business," says Williams. "He offered to pay us a decent fee if we'd do it," added Fulwood. "That's when we knew we were onto something." Within sixteen months, Williams and Fulwood were running their own business, **W&F Financial Services**. "We still visit the community on the second Saturday of every month with free accounting advice," says Williams. "It is the most rewarding work I do."

Learning Objectives

LO 1 Explain the goals and uses of accounting in the information age.

LO 2 Describe profit and its two major components.

LO 3 Explain the relation between return and risk.

LO 4 Identify forms of organization and their characteristics.

LO 5 Identify and describe the three major activities in organizations.

LO 6 Explain and interpret the accounting equation.

LO 7 Identify users and uses of accounting.

LO 8 Explain why ethics and social responsibility are crucial to accounting.

LO 9 Identify opportunities in accounting and related fields.

LO 10 Compute and interpret return on investment.

CHAPTER PREVIEW

Accounting in the information age is about people like Stephanie Williams and Brett Fulwood. Today's world is one of information—its preparation, communication, analysis and use. Accounting is at the heart of the information age. Knowledge of accounting principles gives us a leg up on our competition. It gives us more opportunities and the insight to benefit from them. Through your studies in this course and this book, you will learn about many concepts, procedures and analyses that are useful in everyday life. This knowledge will reduce your reliance on hunches, guesses and intuition, and in turn improve your decision-making ability.

In this chapter we describe accounting in the information age, the users and uses of accounting information, the forms and activities of organizations, and the importance of ethics and social responsibility. We also explain several important accounting concepts, procedures and analyses. This chapter should provide a foundation for those students who have little or no understanding of business. Chapter 2 will build on this foundation when we consider transactions and financial statements.

Living in the Information Age

We live in the **information age**. The information age is a period of communication, data, news, facts, access and commentary. It encourages timeliness, independence and freedom of expression. Access to and understanding of information affect how we live, whom we associate with, and the opportunities we have. We use information to pick and choose among products and services like cars, bikes, clothes, computers, hotels, and restaurants. We pay people for analyzing information for us. Examples of information we pay for and sources that provide it include product quality (*Consumer Reports*), medicinal advice (Canadian Medical Association), and credit rating (Dun & Bradstreet).

Communication and access to data is a major part of the information age and is part of the information superhighway. The information superhighway is redefining all communication, especially business communication. Global computer networks and telecommunications equipment allow us access to all types of business information. Like Stephanie Williams and Brett Fulwood, information provides us with powerful tools and opportunities. To take advantage of these, we need knowledge of the information system.

Knowing the information system means real increases in job opportunities. Between 1990 and 1996, the number of jobs for those with a high school diploma or less fell by 910,000; employment for those with a degree or diploma increased by more than 1.4 million.[1] This increased employment opportunity is due in large part to an ability to understand and process information. Understanding and processing information is the *core* of accounting. To get the most from your education and your opportunities in life, you must know accounting. Your instructor will provide you with many assignments from this book and related materials to help you master it. We also encourage you to join us on the information superhighway to explore some of the wonderful opportunities awaiting you.

Power of Accounting

LO1 Explain the goals and uses of accounting in the information age.

One of the most important purposes of the information superhighway is the reporting of business activities. Information that reports what businesses own, what they owe, and how they perform is the aim of accounting. **Accounting** is an information and measurement system that identifies, records and communicates relevant,

---

[1] *The Globe and Mail*, November 24, 1997, p. A14.

reliable and comparable information about an organization's economic activities. Its objective is to help people make better decisions. It also helps people better assess opportunities, products, investments, and social and community responsibilities. Accounting opens our eyes to new and exciting possibilities.

This book and course can be part of an important learning experience. Both will help you apply accounting information in a way you can use it in your everyday life. You do not have to be an accountant to use accounting information. You don't even have to be in business. Often the greatest benefits from understanding accounting come to those outside of accounting and business. This is because an improved understanding of accounting gives you a head start. You can use accounting to get a loan for a house or to start your own business. You can use accounting to make better investment decisions with your hard-earned money. You can use accounting knowledge wherever you go and in whatever career you choose.

Business and Investment

A **business** is one or more individuals selling products or services for profit. Products like athletic apparel (**CCM, Bauer, NIKE, Reebok**), computers (**Dell, Hewlett-Packard, Apple**) and clothing (**Tilley, Levis, GAP**) are part of our lives. Services like information communication (**Sympatico, AOL Canada, CompuServe, Microsoft**), dining (**Tim Hortons, Harvey's, McDonald's, Burger King**) and car rental (**Tilden, Hertz, Budget**) make our lives easier. A business can be as small as an in-home child care service or as massive as **The Bay.** Nearly one hundred thousand new businesses are started in Canada each year, no different from **W&F Financial Services.** Most of these are started by people who want freedom from ordinary jobs, a new challenge in life, or the advantage of extra money.

 Describe profit and its two major components.

Business Profit

A common feature of all businesses is the desire for profit. **Profit,** also called **net income** or **earnings,** is the amount a business earns after subtracting all expenses necessary for its sales. **Sales,** also called **revenues,** are the amounts earned from selling products and services. **Expenses** are the costs incurred to generate (or produce) sales. For **W&F Financial Services,** profit equals the amounts earned from consulting with clients less expenses incurred like travel, meals, advertising and promotion. Not all businesses make profits. A **loss** arises when expenses are more than sales. Many new businesses incur losses in their first several months or years of business. Yet no business can continually experience losses and stay in business.

Let's look at the **Bank of Montreal's** profit breakdown in Exhibit 1.1. If we pay $100 in interest to the bank, $8.99 is profit to the Bank of Montreal and the rest goes to cover expenses like salaries ($17.00) and interest charges ($52.93).

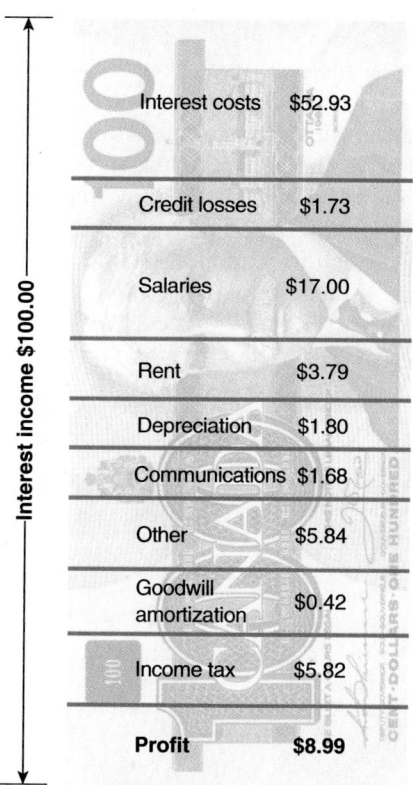

Interest costs	$52.93
Credit losses	$1.73
Salaries	$17.00
Rent	$3.79
Depreciation	$1.80
Communications	$1.68
Other	$5.84
Goodwill amortization	$0.42
Income tax	$5.82
Profit	**$8.99**

Interest income $100.00

Exhibit 1.1

Bank of Montreal 1997 Income Statement Breakdown

The Bank of Montreal also pays $5.82 in income taxes. One question confronting our society today is what is the "right" amount of profit. Should business pay more for charitable giving or community services? Are taxes too high or too low? For us to even begin considering important questions like these we must understand accounting.

L03 Explain the relation between return and risk.

Return and Risk

Profit is often referred to as **return.** The term "return" derives from the idea of getting something back from an investment. Return also derives from the concept of return on investment. **Return on investment** is often stated in ratio form as *profit divided by amount invested.* For example, banks or trust companies often report our return from a savings account in the form of an interest rate of return on investment (for example we might have a 3% savings account or invest our college money in a 6% money market fund).

We can invest our money in many ways. If we invest it in a bank savings account or in Canada Savings Bonds, it will probably give us a return of around 3% to 6%. We could also invest in a company's shares, or even start our own business like Williams and Fulwood. How do we decide among these investment options? Our answer rests on the trade-off between return and risk.

Did You Know?

Celebrity Investment
How do fame and fortune translate into return and risk? Ask people which celebrity would be the best investment. Similar to business investments, people would most likely name relatively young performers with years of earning power ahead, such as Celine Dion, Ross Rebagliati, Wayne Gretzky, and Elvis Stojko.

Did you know? is a feature that extends throughout the book. This feature highlights important and interesting cases from practice.

Risk is the amount of uncertainty about the return we expect to earn. All business decisions involve risk. But some decisions involve more risk than others. The lower the risk of an investment, the lower the expected return. The reason why savings accounts pay a low return is the small degree of risk of the funds not being repaid with interest. Indeed the government guarantees most savings accounts from default. Similarly, the reason why Canada Savings Bonds pay a low return is the low risk of default by the Canadian government. However, if we buy a share of **Canadian Tire,** there is no guarantee of return. There is even a risk of loss. The bar graph in Exhibit 1.2 shows the returns for bonds with different risks. **Bonds** are written promises by organizations to repay amounts borrowed plus interest.

Exhibit 1.2

Returns for Bonds with Different Risks

Canadian treasury bonds provide us a low expected return of 4.47%, but they also offer low risk since they are backed by the Canadian government. High-risk corporate bonds offer a much larger expected return (11.31%) but with much greater risk. But expected return is not actual return. The difference between expected and actual return is the primary source of risk.

The trade-off between return and risk is a normal part of business. Higher expected return offsets higher risk. We must remember that *actual* return usually differs from *expected* return. Higher risk implies higher, but more risky expected returns. To help us make better business decisions, we use accounting information in measuring both return and risk. We decide on our desired level of return and risk, and use accounting information to achieve it.

Answer—p. 30

Programmer
You are considering two job offers. Both require your computer programmer skills. One is with a new start-up Internet provider at an annual salary of $31,000: the other is with an established medical supply company for $25,500 a year. Which offer do you accept? (Note: Solutions to You Make the Call are at the end of the chapter.)

You Make the Call

You Make the Call are role-playing exercises extending throughout the book. These exercises stress the relevance of accounting for people in and outside of business.

Accounting Information

Factors of production are the means businesses use to make profit. *Land, labour, buildings* and *equipment* are the traditional factors of production. Today's information age suggests we add accounting information to these traditional factors of production. Accounting information gives us knowledge to make better decisions, and good decision making is key to business success. If we analyze recent business performance, we see that it is not the traditional factors driving success. For example, we see **Semi-Tech** with its factors of production worth $3.5 billion reporting a 1996 loss of more than $24 million. We see **Rogers Communications** which has more than ten thousand employees, reporting a 1996 loss of $278 million. Other giants like **Northern Telecom, George Weston** and **Dofasco** struggle to consistently yield a 5% or 10% return on investment. Yet smaller companies may yield 20% or greater. One common denominator in the success stories is relevant and reliable information. Accounting information is what makes or breaks many businesses. Those who can understand and use accounting information have an advantage in today's job market.

Focus of Accounting

We need to guard against a narrow view of accounting. Accounting affects many parts of life and is crucial to modern society. The most obvious contacts with accounting are often through credit approvals, chequing accounts, tax forms and payroll. Yet these experiences are limited and tend to focus on the recordkeeping, or bookkeeping, parts of accounting. **Recordkeeping, or bookkeeping,** is the recording of financial transactions and events, either manually or electronically. While recordkeeping is essential to data reliability in the information age, accounting is this and much more.

The primary objective of accounting is to provide useful information for decision making as shown in Exhibit 1.3. Accounting activities include identifying, measuring, reporting and analyzing economic events and transactions. Accounting also involves interpreting information, and designing information systems to provide useful reports that monitor and control an organization's activities. All of these services demand special expertise and judgment. Whatever your career path, accounting is part of it. You can benefit by understanding how accounting

Exhibit 1.3

Accounting Activities

Identifying and measuring

Recording

Reporting and analyzing

information is prepared and used. To gain this understanding you need to know certain recordkeeping skills and this book provides opportunities for you to learn these skills. This knowledge helps you read and interpret financial data. Yet it is crucially important for you to learn to analyze and interpret this information. Opportunities are greater if you understand accounting and are able to use information effectively.

Accounting and Technology

Technology is a key part of modern society and business practice. It also plays a major role in accounting. Computing technology reduces the time, effort and cost of recordkeeping while improving clerical accuracy. Although some smaller organizations continue to perform various accounting tasks manually, they are nevertheless impacted by information technology. Because technology changes the way we store, process and summarize large masses of data, accounting has been freed to expand its field. Major consulting, planning and other financial services are quickly becoming part of accounting. Now more than ever there is a need for people who can quickly sort through masses of data, interpret their meaning, identify key factors, and analyze their implications. Community leaders of today and tomorrow require accounting skills and support. This book starts you on the path to opportunity and success.

Did You Know?

Accounting Web
Technology is changing the face of business and accounting. Many organizations maintain their own Web pages that include substantial accounting information. You might want to visit **Bell Canada Enterprise (www.bce.com)** or the **Hummingbird** Web site **(www.hummingbird.com)** to see for yourself. You can also search the on-line database called **SEDAR (http://www.sedar.com)**. SEDAR has accounting information for thousands of public companies.

Setting Accounting Rules

There are rules for reporting on an organization's performance and current condition. These rules increase the usefulness of reports including their reliability and comparability. The rules that make up acceptable accounting practices are determined by many individuals and groups and are referred to as **generally accepted accounting principles,** or **GAAP.** Since accounting is a service activity, these rules reflect our society's needs and not those of accountants or any other single constituency. This is reinforced by the federal and provincial governments who regulate organizations that sell shares of ownership to the public. Provincial securities commissions, such as the **Ontario Securities Commission (OSC),** have the authority to set reporting rules for these public companies. For the most part, the OSC passes authority to set accounting rules to professionals in practice.

The **Accounting Standards Board (AcSB),** supported by a research staff, is currently responsible for setting accounting rules. It has issued an accounting recommendation[2] of accounting concepts to help guide accounting standard setting. Still many interested groups and individuals involve themselves in setting accounting rules, and provide the AcSB with their views. They include unions, investors, government agencies, lenders, politicians, and other business and nonbusiness organizations. Individuals and leaders in these organizations must understand accounting information and any proposed rules to chart and defend a position in their best interests.

Flashback

1. What is the aim of accounting?
2. Can you describe profit, sales and expenses?
3. Can you explain the trade-off between return and risk?
4. What is the relation between accounting and recordkeeping?
5. Who sets accounting rules?

Flashbacks give you a chance to stop and reflect on key points in the book. Brief answers to Flashbacks are given at the end of the chapter.

Answers—p. 30

Forms of Organization

There are many forms of organization in society (see Exhibit 1.4). These organizations can be classified as either business or nonbusiness. Typically, businesses are organized for profit, while nonbusiness organizations serve society in ways that are not always measured by profit.

Most organizations engage in economic activities. These can include the usual business activities of purchasing materials and labour, and selling products and services. These can also involve nonbusiness activities like collecting money through taxes, dues, contributions, investments or borrowings. A common feature in all organizations is the power and use of accounting.

LO4 Identify forms of organization and their characteristics.

 Exhibit 1.4

Forms of Organizations

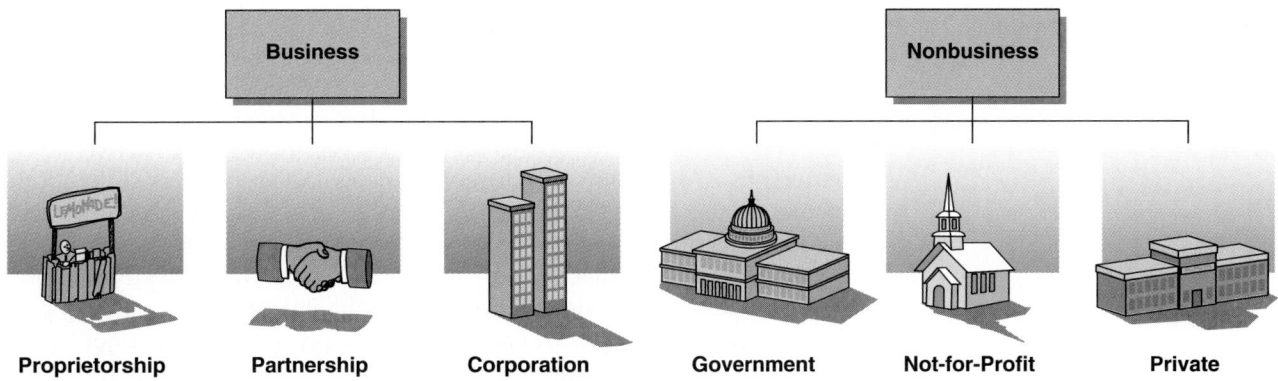

Business			Nonbusiness		
Proprietorship	Partnership	Corporation	Government	Not-for-Profit	Private

---

[2] Canadian Institute of Chartered Accountants, *CICA Handbook*, Section 1000, "Financial Statement Concepts," (Toronto).

Business Organization

A business is organized and operated to make profit. Because of this, a business is often called a profit-oriented organization. One principle that must be followed in accounting for organizations is the **business entity principle**. The business entity principle is also known as the *accounting entity principle* or simply the *entity principle*. This principle means that every organization is accounted for separately from its owner's personal activities. It also means that a set of accounting records and reports refers only to the transactions and events of that one organization. We discuss this and other important accounting principles in the next chapter. Businesses take one of three forms: a *sole proprietorship,* a *partnership* or a *corporation*. For some of the characteristics of business organizations, see Exhibit 1.5.

Exhibit 1.5

Characteristics of Business Organizations

	Proprietorship	Partnership	Corporation
Business entity	yes	yes	yes
Legal entity	no	no	yes
Limited liability	no	no	yes
Unlimited life	no	no	yes
Business taxed	no	no	yes
One owner allowed	yes	no	yes

Sole Proprietorship

A **sole proprietorship,** or **single proprietorship,** is a business owned by one person. No special legal requirements must be met to start this form of business. While it is a separate entity for accounting purposes, it is *not* a separate legal entity from its owner. This means, for example, a court can order an owner to sell personal belongings to pay a proprietorship's debt. An owner is even responsible for debts that exceed the resources of the proprietorship. This *unlimited liability* of a proprietorship is sometimes a disadvantage. Also, tax authorities do not separate a proprietorship from its owner. This means that the profits of a proprietorship are not subject to a business income tax but these profits must be reported and taxed on the owner's personal income tax return. The rate of tax on a proprietorship's income depends on the level of total income from all sources that the owner had for the year. Small retail stores and service businesses often are organized as proprietorships. Sole proprietorships are by far the most common form of business organization in our society.

Partnership

A **partnership** is owned by two or more persons, called *partners*. Like a proprietorship, no special legal requirements must be met in starting a partnership. All that is required is an agreement between partners to run a business together. The agreement can be either oral or written and usually indicates how profits and losses are shared. A written agreement is preferable because it can help partners avoid or resolve disputes. A partnership, like a proprietorship, is not legally separate from its owners. This means that each partner's share of profits is reported and taxed on that partner's tax return. Usually, it also means *unlimited liability* for its partners.

There are two types of partnerships that limit liability. A **limited partnership** includes a *general partner(s)* with unlimited liability and a *limited partner(s)* with liability restricted to the amount invested. A **limited liability partnership** restricts partners' liabilities to their own acts and the acts of individuals under their control. This protects an innocent partner from the negligence of another partner. Yet all partners remain responsible for partnership debts. There are about one-tenth as many partnerships as proprietorships. **W&F Financial Services** described in the opening article is set up as a partnership between Stephanie Williams and Brett Fulwood.

Corporations

A **corporation** is a business that is a separate legal entity under provincial or federal laws with owners that are called *shareholders* or *stockholders*. This means a corporation is responsible for its own acts and its own debts. It can enter into its own contracts, and it can buy, own and sell property. It can also sue and be sued. Separate legal status means a corporation can conduct business with the rights, duties and responsibilities of a person. A corporation acts through its managers, who are its legal agents. Separate legal status also means its shareholders are not personally liable for corporate acts and debts. Shareholders are legally distinct from the business and their loss is limited to their net investment in shares purchased. This *limited liability* is a key to why corporations can raise resources from shareholders who are not active in managing the business. It also encourages more risky investment with higher expected returns. A corporation is legally chartered (or *incorporated*) under provincial and/or federal laws. Separate legal status results in a corporation having unlimited life. Ownership, or equity, of all corporations is divided into units called **shares** or **stock.** Owners of shares are called **shareholders** or **stockholders.** A shareholder can sell or transfer shares to another person without affecting the operations of a corporation. When a corporation issues only one class of shares, we call it **common shares** or *capital stock.* **Canadian Airlines Corp.,** or **CA,** is incorporated and sells its shares to the public. It had 39,400,000 shares of common share capital outstanding as of its 1996 year-end. This means Canadian's Airline's ownership is divided into 39,400,000 units. A shareholder who owns 394,000 shares of CA owns 1% of the company.

A corporation is subject to *double taxation*. This means a corporation is taxed on its net income, and any distribution of corporate earnings (i.e., dividends) to its owners is also taxed as part of their personal income.

Other Organizations

Not-for-profit organizations plan and operate for other than profit. Goals often include security, health, education, transportation, judicial and religious services, cultural and social activities. These goals are often met by government or not-for-profit organizations. Examples are public schools meeting the needs of citizens, and community care groups meeting the needs of the poor. Not-for-profit organizations lack an identifiable owner. Still the demand for accounting information in these organizations is high since they are accountable to their sponsors. Governments need to report receipts and expenditures of tax money, and universities and colleges need to explain tuition increases. These organizations are accountable to taxpayers, donors, lenders, legislators, regulators and other constituents. Accounting for these organizations is usually a *fund*-based system, but the basic principles are similar to accounting for business organizations. Exhibit 1.7 lists a wide range of government and not-for-profit organizations affected by the power of accounting. This list is but a sampling of the roughly one-third of Canadian economic activity done by this type of organization. Some of these organizations, such as hospitals, are often run as private, not-for-profit or government operations. In all of these organizations, accounting captures key information about their activities and makes it available to users, both internal and external to the organization.

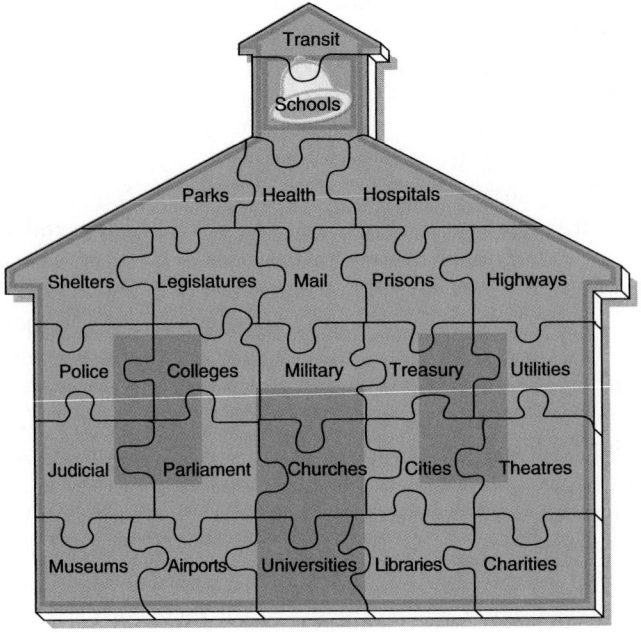

Exhibit 1.6

Partial List of Government and Not-for-Profit Organizations

You Make the Call

Entrepreneur
You and a friend have developed a new design for mountain bikes that improves speed and performance by a remarkable 25% to 40%. You are planning to form a small business to manufacture and market these bikes. You and your friend want to minimize taxes, but your prime concern is potential lawsuits from individuals who will "push the limit" on these bikes and be injured. What form of organization do you set up?

Answer—p. 30

Activities in Organizations

LO 5 Identify and describe the three major activities in organizations.

Organizations carry out their activities in many different ways. These differences extend to their products, services, goals, organization form, management style, worker compensation, and community giving. Yet the major activities of organizations are similar. We discuss three major types of activities—financing, investing and operating—each of which requires a planning phase. These activities are portrayed graphically in Exhibit 1.7

Planning

All organizations begin with planning. **Planning** involves defining the ideas, goals and actions of an organization. Strategies and tactics need to be laid out. Employees must be informed and motivated. Managers must be credible and display leadership and vision. All of these tasks are part of planning and are the duty of *executive management*. Executive management sets the organization's strategic goals and policies that are captured in an *organization plan*. The owner or owners take on this duty in most organizations. In others, key employees take it on. Responsibility for this duty often carries with it the title of presi-

Exhibit 1.7

Activities in Organizations

dent, chief executive officer, or chair of the board of directors. In not-for-profit organizations the title for top managers is often executive director.

Planning assists an organization in focusing its efforts and identifying opportunities. External users benefit from knowledge of an organization's plans. They look for clues on tactics, market demands, competitors, promotion, pricing, innovations, and projections. Much of this information, both for internal and external users, is obtained through accounting reports. In the case of **Alliance Communications Corporation** (and most public corporations) we look to the Management Discussion and Analysis section in its annual report (see Appendix I):

> The Company will continue to pursue its long term strategy of expanding its libraries and increasing its direct distribution reach. The Company's proven ability to deliver and distribute high quality product combined with its strong financial position, makes it well positioned to achieve its aggressive growth strategy.

It is important we remember that planning involves change and reacting to it. It is not cast in stone. This adds *risk* to both the development and analysis of an organization's plans. Accounting information can reduce this risk through more informed and better decision making. Both internal and external accounting reports affect the plans, decisions and actions of management. While accounting does not give us all the answers, it helps us evaluate an organization's plans and activities.

Financing

An organization requires financing to begin to operate according to its plans. **Financing activities** are the means organizations use to pay for resources like land, buildings, and machines to carry out its plans. Organizations are careful in acquiring and managing financing activities because of their potential to determine success or failure. There are two main sources of financing: owner and nonowner. *Owner financing* refers to resources contributed by the owner and any profits that the owner chooses to leave in the organization. *Nonowner (or creditor) financing* refers to resources contributed by creditors or lenders. Creditors can include banks, or other financial institutions. *Financial management* is the task of planning how to obtain these resources and how to set the right mix between the amounts of owner and nonowner financing. Government organizations can also acquire resources with taxes and fees, while not-for-profit organizations can acquire resources from contributions by donors. **Alliance Communication's** total 1997 financing equals $353.7 (in millions). It is comprised of owner ($150.4) and nonowner financing ($203.3). We describe in the next chapter how these figures are communicated using financial statements.

Investing

Investing activities refer to the buying and selling of resources that an organization uses to sell its products or services. These resources or assets are funded by an organization's financing. **Assets** are economic resources that are expected to produce future benefits. They include land, buildings, equipment, inventories, licences, supplies, cash, and all investments needed for operating an organization. **Alliance's** 1997 assets total $353.7 (in millions). Organizations differ on the amount and makeup of their assets. Some organizations require land and factories to operate. Others might only need an office. Determining the amount and type of assets needed for an organization to operate is called *asset management*.

LO 6 Explain and interpret the accounting equation.

It is important for us to see that an organization's investing and financing totals are *always* equal (investing = financing). Since invested amounts are referred to as *assets,* and financing is made up of owner and nonowner financing (commonly called *equity*), we can expand this equality and write this as:

$$\text{Assets} = \text{Nonowner's Equity} + \text{Owner's Equity}$$

Creditors and owners hold claims or rights in the assets. Creditors' claims are called **liabilities** and the owner's claim is called **owner's equity.** This equality can then be written as:

$$\textbf{Assets} = \textbf{Liabilities} + \textbf{Owner's Equity}$$

This equality is called the **accounting equation.** Notice that **Alliance's** 1997 assets of $353.7 equal its liabilities of $203.3 plus its owners' equity of $150.4 (in millions):

$$\text{Assets} = \text{Liabilities} + \text{Equity}$$
$$\$353.7 = \$203.3 + \$150.4$$

The accounting equation works for all organizations. It is an important part of accounting. We will return to and use the accounting equation in our analysis of transactions in the next chapter.

Operating

An organization's main purpose is its operating activities. **Operating activities** are the carrying out of an organization's plans and involve using assets to research, develop, purchase, produce, distribute and market products and services. They also include management activities like supervising workers and ensuring compliance with law. Operating activities aim at selling the organization's products and services. **Sales and revenues** are the inflow of assets from selling products and services. **Costs and expenses** are the outflow of assets necessary to support operating activities. Examples of costs and expenses are salaries, rent, electricity and supplies. *Strategic management* is the process of determining the right mix of operating activities for the type of organization, its plans and its market. How well the organization carries out its operating activities determines its success and return (or profit).

Exhibit 1.7 summarizes these activities. Planning is part of every activity and is the common link between all activities. Planning gives the activities meaning and focus. You should note that investing (assets) and financing (liabilities and equity) are set opposite each other to stress their balance. Operating activities are shown below investing and financing activities. This is to emphasize that operating activities are the result of investing and financing activities. The planning, financing, investing, and operating activities are constantly changing to reflect the actions of an organization.

Flashback

6. What are the three common forms of business organizations?

7. Can you identify examples of nonbusiness organizations?

8. What are the four major activities in organizations?

Answers—p. 31

Use the accounting equation to determine the missing values in each case.

Case	a	b	c	d
Assets	$175,000	$195,000	?	$240,000
Liabilities	?	120,000	$140,000	?
Equity	68,000	?	95,000	93,000

Mid-Chapter Demonstration Problem

Since assets = liabilities + equity, the missing values can be determined as follows:

a. $175,000 − $68,000 = $107,000
b. $195,000 − $120,000 = $75,000
c. $140,000 + $95,000 = $235,000
d. $240,000 − $93,000 = $147,000

Solution to Mid-Chapter Demonstration Problem

Organizations set up accounting information systems to help them and others make better decisions. Every organization uses some type of information system to report on their activities. The accounting information system is a service activity. It serves the information needs of many kinds of users including managers, lenders, suppliers, customers, directors, auditors, employees, and current and potential investors. Knowledge of accounting and the power to use it improves their decisions. Exhibit 1.8 outlines some users of accounting information.

Users of Accounting Information

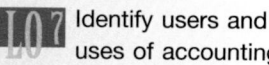 **LO7** Identify users and uses of accounting.

 **Exhibit 1.8**

Users of Accounting Information

Internal users	External users

• Managers	• Sales managers	• Lenders	• Labour unions
• Officers	• Budget officers	• Shareholders	• External auditors
• Internal auditors	• Controller	• Government	• Customers

External Information Users

External users of accounting information are *not* directly involved in running the organization. They include shareholders, lenders, directors, customers, suppliers, regulators, lawyers, brokers and the press. Yet these users are affected by, and sometimes affect, the organization in monetary and nonmonetary ways. All of these external users rely on accounting information to make better and more informed decisions in pursuing their own goals. For example, highly profitable organizations might be expected by regulators to increase worker and product safety, reduce pollution, and pay more taxes. In addition, a consumer advocate is likely to have more success attacking the poor working conditions for employees of an organization earning high profits than of those barely hanging on. Also a lender is less likely to make a bad loan or a shareholder a bad investment when knowing current and past profits of a business.

External Reporting

Financial accounting is the area of accounting aimed at serving external users. Its primary objective is to provide external reports called *financial statements* to help users analyze an organization's activities. External users have limited access to an organization's valuable information. Their own success depends on getting external reports that are reliable, relevant and comparable. Some governmental and regulatory agencies have the power to get reports in specific forms. But most external users must rely on *general-purpose financial statements*. The term *general-purpose* refers to the broad range of purposes for which external users rely on these statements. Generally accepted accounting principles are important in increasing the usefulness of financial statements to users. We discuss these principles along with the financial statements in the next chapter.

External Users

There are many different kinds of *external users*. Each user has special information needs depending on the kinds of decisions one must make. These decisions involve getting answers to key questions, answers that are often available in accounting reports. This section describes several external users and the questions they confront. Your accounting course will provide you with many insights into where answers can be found.

Lenders (Creditors)

Lenders lend money or other resources to an organization. Lenders include banks, trust companies, co-ops, and mortgage and finance companies. Lenders look for information to help them assess whether an organization is likely to repay its loan with interest. External reports help them answer questions about organizations such as:

■ Has it promptly paid past loans?

■ What are its current risks?

■ Can it repay current loans?

■ What is its profit outlook?

These questions can change between short- and long-term lending decisions. The more long-term a loan, the more a lender's questions look like those of an owner.

Shareholders (Owners)

Shareholders have legal control over part or all of a corporation. They are the owners of corporations, and in many cases are not part of management. Owners are exposed to the greatest return and risk. Risk is high because there is no promise of either repayment or a return on investment. They can lose their entire investment. Yet owners have a claim on profits after a business pays its debts. Many businesses do not give all or most of their profits back to owners but invest them in more assets to enable the company to grow. External reports aim to help answer shareholder (owner) questions such as:

■ What is net income for current and past periods?

■ Are assets adequate to meet business plans?

■ Do expenses fit the level and type of sales?

■ Are customers' bills collected promptly?

■ Do loans seem large or unusual?

Corporations typically have a board of directors. *Directors* are elected representatives of shareholders and are charged to oversee their interests in an organization. Because directors are responsible to shareholders, their questions are similar. **Alliance Communication's** 1997 board of directors had 13 members.

External Auditors

External auditors examine and provide assurance that financial statements are prepared according to generally accepted accounting principles. External reports of competing organizations are used by auditors to help assess the reasonableness of a client's reports. **Alliance's** external auditor is **Coopers & Lybrand.**

Employees

Employees, or their union representatives, have a special interest in an organization. They are interested in judging the fairness of their wages and in assessing their future job prospects. External reports provide information useful in addressing these needs. External reports are also used in bargaining for better wages when an organization is successful.

Regulators

Regulators often have legal authority or significant influence over the activities of organizations. Revenue Canada and other provincial and municipal tax authorities require organizations to use various reports in computing taxes. These taxes extend to income, employment, pension, sales, and excise taxes. Tax reports usually require special forms and supporting records. Government and nongovernment agencies also use financial reports. Examples include utility boards using accounting information to set utility rates and securities regulators that require special filings for businesses with publicly traded securities.

Other Important External Users

Accounting serves the needs of many other important external users. Voters, legislators and elected officials use accounting information to monitor and evaluate a government's receipts and expenses. Contributors to not-for-profit organizations use accounting information to evaluate the use and impact of their donations. Suppliers use accounting information to judge the soundness of a business before making sales on credit. Customers use external reports to assess the staying power of potential suppliers.

Internal Information Users

Internal users of accounting information are those individuals directly involved in managing and operating an organization. They include managers, officers, and other important internal decision makers. Internal users make the strategic and operating decisions of an organization. The internal role of accounting is to provide information to help improve the efficiency or effectiveness of an organization in delivering products or services. In this way, accounting helps businesses reach their goals. Internal users are also affected by external reports. For example, management's compensation is often based on profits as reported in external reports. In addition, loans sometimes restrict managers' from taking on further loans.

Internal Reporting

Management accounting is the area of accounting aimed at serving the decision-making needs of internal users. Management accounting provides internal reports to help internal users improve an organization's activities. Internal reports are not subject to the same rules as external reports. This is because decisions of internal users are not constrained by the need to keep certain information private from external users (for example, because of competitive concerns) nor by the need to quickly analyze a number of different organizations. Internal users often have access to a lot of private and valuable information. Costs in preparing internal reports are usually the only constraint on internal reporting. Internal reports aim to answer questions like:

- What are the manufacturing costs per product?
- What is the most profitable mix of services?
- What level of sales is necessary to break even?
- Which service activities are most profitable?
- What costs vary with sales?

Information to help answer these questions is very important for success. This book provides many tools to help in this task.

Internal Operating Functions

Exhibit 1.9

Internal Operating Functions

The responsibilities and duties of internal users extend to every function of an organization. There are at least seven functions common to most organizations. Accounting is essential to the smooth operation of each of these functions. The internal operating functions are shown in Exhibit 1.9 and include: research and development, purchasing, human resources, production, distribution, marketing and servicing. The larger the business, the more likely these operating functions are separate units in the business. Each unit often has its own internal manager who is responsible for decisions. Depending on the type of business, not all of these operating functions are necessary. For example, publishing companies usually don't require separate research and development units, and banks don't require production units. Sometimes less frequently used functions are combined in one unit. We briefly describe these operating functions:

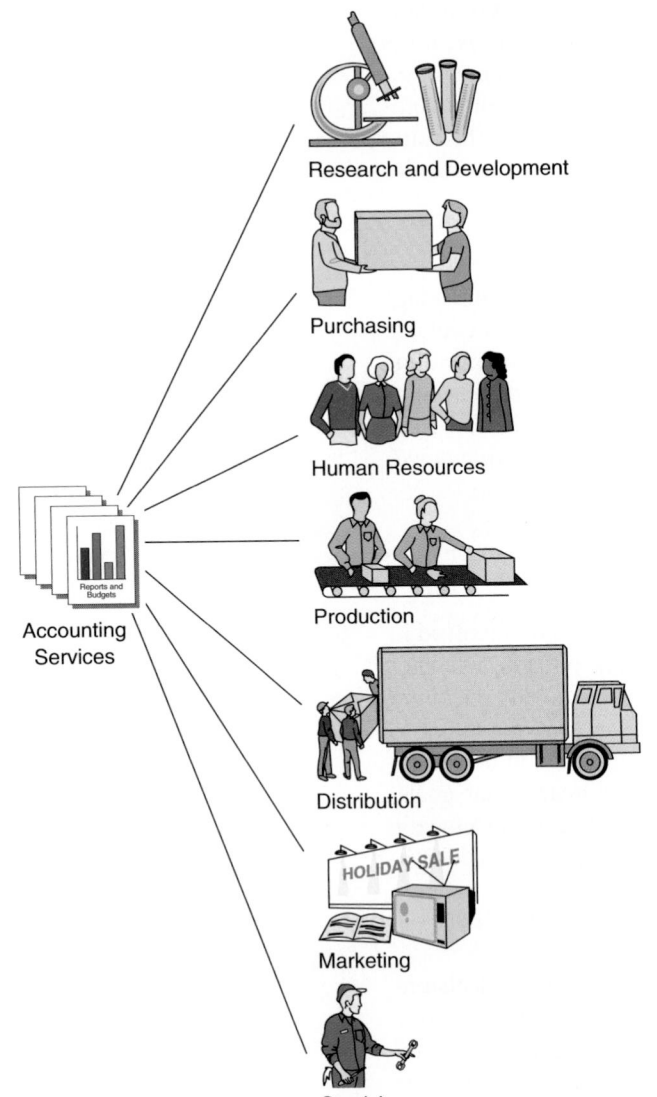

- **Research and Development** Research and development is aimed at creating or improving a company's products or services. It can be as basic as testing a new recipe for pizza or as complex as creating genetically altered plants. It is directed to meet the needs of customers. Managers need information about current and projected costs and potential sales to decide whether to pursue or continue research and development projects.

- **Purchasing** Purchasing involves acquiring and managing materials needed for operations. Managers need to know what, when, and how much to purchase. Information on both quality and quantity of purchases is needed.

- **Human Resources** Human resource management ensures that labour is available to carry out the business plan. Employees must be located, screened, hired, trained, compensated, promoted and counselled. Managers can perform this task more effectively if there is information about current and potential employees, payroll costs, employee benefits, and other performance and compensation data.

- **Production** Production is the mix of the factors of production to produce products and services. Good production methods depend on information to monitor costs and ensure quality. It requires planning and coordinating the factors to best meet customer needs, and it requires process design.
- **Distribution** Distribution involves timely and accurate delivery of products and services. Relevant information is often key to quality distribution. Cost information is also very important for distribution decisions.
- **Marketing** Marketing is the promotion and advertising of products and services. Marketing managers use accounting reports about sales and costs to effectively target consumers and set pricing. Marketing also uses accounting to monitor consumer needs, tastes and price concerns. It includes distributing products or services when and where customers want them. These activities are sometimes referred to as the four P's of marketing—*p*roduct (design), *p*romotion, *p*ricing and *p*lace (distribution).
- **Servicing** Servicing customers after selling products or services is often key to success in business. This includes training, assistance, installation, warranties and maintenance. Information is important to maintaining this bridge between seller and buyer, and often crucial to developing "permanent customers."

Managers rely on internal controls to monitor operating functions. **Internal controls** are procedures set up to protect assets, ensure reliable accounting reports, promote efficiency, and encourage adherence to company policies. For example, certain actions require verification such as a manager's okay before materials enter production. Internal controls are crucial if accounting reports are to provide relevant and reliable information.

Ethics and Social Responsibility

LO8 Explain why ethics and social responsibility are crucial to accounting.

We know ethics and ethical behaviour are important. We are reminded of this when we run across disappointing stories in the media or witness wrongful actions by individuals. These include cheating, harassing, misconduct, bribery, and other wrongful behaviour. Such cases make it more difficult for people to trust one another. If trust is missing, our lives are more difficult, inefficient and unpleasant.

This section explains the meaning of ethics and describes how ethics affect organizations. We take up ethics early in our study because of their importance to organizations, accounting and everyday living. The goal of accounting is to provide useful information for decision making. For information to be useful it must be trusted. This demands ethics in accounting. This section also discusses social responsibility for organizations.

Understanding Ethics

Ethics are beliefs that separate right from wrong. They are known as accepted standards of good and bad behaviour. Ethics and laws often coincide, with the result that many unethical actions (such as theft and physical violence) are also illegal. Yet other actions are not against the law but are considered unethical, such as not helping people with certain needs. Because of differences between laws and ethics, we cannot look to laws to keep people ethical.

Identifying the ethical path is sometimes difficult. The preferred ethical path is to take a course of action that avoids casting doubt on one's decision. For example, accounting users are less likely to trust an auditor's report on the fairness of the accounting if the auditor's pay depends on the issuance of a favourable report. To avoid questions and concerns of this type, ethics rules are often set. Auditors are indeed banned from any direct investment in their client, regardless of amount.[3] Auditors also cannot accept pay that depends on figures reported in a client's accounting reports.[4] These ethics rules are aimed to prevent conflicts of interest or even the appearance that an auditor is not independent. Exhibit 1.10 gives us guidelines for making ethical decisions.

Exhibit 1.10

Guidelines for Ethical
Decision Making

Identify ethical issues	Analyze options	Make ethical decision
Use personal ethics to recognize ethical issue.	Consider both good and bad consequences for all affected.	Choose best option after weighing all consequences.

Throughout our lives we will continue to face decisions with ethical aspects. These arise in our school, our workplace and our personal lives. They are a part of life. A commitment to ethical behaviour requires us to think carefully before we act, to be certain we are making ethical choices. Our success in making these choices affects how we feel about ourselves and how others feel about us. Ethics is not a personal matter. Our combined individual choices affect the quality of our community and the experiences of others.

Did You Know?

In Pursuit of Profit

How far can companies go in pursuing profits? **Converse's** Run'N Gun shoe has sparked debate on ethics, social responsibility and profits. **Converse** claims Run'N Gun refers only to fastbreaking basketball. Critics claim it invites youth violence and links with the gun culture. Whatever one's view, it is important that companies balance profits with ethics and social responsibility.

Organizational Ethics

Organizational ethics are likely learned through example and leadership. Companies like **Shell Canada,** the **Body Shop, Northern Telecom** and **Bank of Montreal** work hard to convey the importance of ethics to employees. Yet we still hear people express concern about what they see as low ethics in organizations. A survey of more than eleven hundred executives, educators and legislators showed that 94% of the participants agreed with the comment that "the business community is troubled by ethical problems." This survey revealed that the vast majority of participants believe high ethical standards are followed by organizations that are successful over the long run. This finding confirms an old saying: "*Good ethics is good business.*" Ethical practices build trust, which promotes loyalty and long-term relationships with customers, suppliers and employees. Good ethics add to an organization's reputation and its success. Because of this and the public interest in ethics, many organization's have their own codes of ethics. These codes set standards for internal activities and for relationships with customers, suppliers, regulators, the public and even competitors. Companies often use their codes as public promises of their commitment to ethical practices. More importantly, they serve as guidance for employees in their work.

---

[3] Institute of Chartered Accountants of Ontario, *ICAO Rules of Professional Conduct,* Rule 204.

[4] Ibid., Rule 215.

Accounting Ethics

Ethics are crucial in accounting. Providers of accounting information often face ethical choices as they prepare financial reports. Their choices can affect both the use and receipt of money, including taxes owed and money shared with owners. It can affect the price a buyer pays and the wages paid to workers. It can even affect the success of products, services and divisions. Misleading information can lead to a wrongful closing of a division where workers, customers and suppliers are seriously harmed.

Because of the importance of accounting ethics, codes of ethics are set up and enforced. These codes include those of the Provincial Institutes of Chartered Accountants, the Provincial Societies of Management Accountants, and the Provincial Certified General Accountants' Associations. Samples from these codes are presented in Appendix III near the end of the book, and can help us when confronting ethical dilemmas. For example, organizations often pay managers bonuses based on the amount of income reported. Managers can benefit from using accounting in ways to increase their pay. These choices can reduce the money available for employee wages, training programs, community giving and other charities.

Ethics codes can also help in dealing with confidential information. For example, auditors have access to confidential salaries and an organization's strategies. Organizations can be harmed if auditors pass this information to others. To prevent this, auditors' ethics codes require them to keep information confidential. Internal accountants are also not to use confidential information for personal gain. These examples show the practical value of ethical codes. They provide guidance in knowing what action to take and the power to do it. They also tell clients what they can expect in services and give users confidence in accounting reports. In many ways our economy depends on trustworthy accounting information.

Ethical Challenge

In our lives we encounter many situations needing ethical decisions. You will face many such situations in this book. We need to remember that accounting must be done ethically if it is to be useful. Ethics is the most fundamental of accounting principles. We are all in control of our ethics and the ethical decisions we make. It is our choice—a choice that matters—and is the ethical challenge we face.

Social Responsibility

Social responsibility is a concern for the impact of our actions on society as a whole, and is a concern for all of us. Organizations too are increasingly concerned with their social responsibility. As **George Weston** proclaims in its annual report:

> George Weston Limited is committed to improving quality of life in the communities it serves, and believes that business should participate with its employees in supporting our community organizations.

Our society is increasing the pressure on organizations to give something back. Socially conscious employees, customers, investors, and others see to it that organizations back up rhetoric with actions. There are several ways that organizations give something back. This section describes some of these programs. We also discuss social auditing as a means to monitor social responsibility.

Social Programs

An organization's social responsibility extends in many directions. It can include donations to not-for-profit organizations such as hospitals, colleges, community programs and law enforcement. It can also include programs to reduce pollution, increase product safety, improve worker conditions, support continuing education, and better use our natural resources. Yet most organizations are more likely to invest in their own social programs. For example, **Canadian Tire** is committed to active participation in cities and towns across Canada primarily through the Canadian Tire Child Protection Foundation which is dedicated to helping kids live happier and healthier lives through education and awareness. We are aware of hundreds of businesses that offer social programs to their employees to pursue community service activities. **Moore Corporation** citizenship is described in its annual report as follows:

> The Corporation and its employees continue to be involved in community activities as well as providing support to the charitable and non-profit sector. Moore focuses contributions in four areas: children and families, education, community services, and arts and culture.

A more detailed social responsibility report is that of **NOVA's** shown in Exhibit 1.11. These programs are not limited to large companies. For example, many independently owned movie theatres and leisure sports businesses offer discounts to students and senior citizens. Still others help sponsor events such as the Special Olympics and summer reading programs with the local library.

Exhibit 1.11

"Social Responsibility" Report

> In an era when nonprofit organizations increasingly look to the corporate sector to support the survival of vital public programs and services, NOVA is taking a leadership role. "Lending a Hand" is the guiding principle behind NOVA's corporate contributions program. The program's mission is to "invest in the growth, diversity and well-being of the communities we share in by lending a hand to organizations dedicated to improving the overall quality of life in our communities." During 1996, we reinforced our social commitment by establishing the NOVA Corporation Charitable Foundation. The foundation allows us to more effectively fulfil our responsibilities by stabilizing the amount we give, rather than having contributions fluctuate with earnings. Using the Canadian Centre for Philanthropy's "Imagine 1% Commitment" formula, NOVA established its $4-million annual corporate contributions budget which is targeted to education, Aboriginals, women and people at risk. In addition, NOVA encourages employees in their dedication towards community volunteer efforts by actively supporting them through public recognition and support.

Support for all of these types of social programs by organizations is not universal. Some argue that organizations are not unbiased in supporting social programs. There is a concern that an organization's interests might be quite different from its workers, customers, or the public. It is sometimes argued that organizations should increase pay to its workers so that they can contribute to their own community concerns. Yet it is clear that social responsibility is now part of our culture. While there will be continuing debate and disagreement with the charitable giving of organizations, the new era of social responsibility is here to stay.

Did You Know?

Returns on Social Responsibility
Virtue isn't always its only reward. **Investors Group** Summa Equity Fund invests in common shares of socially responsible, environmentally sound and ethically managed Canadian Companies. Compare their 1997 return of 23.04% to that of the Toronto Stock Exchange return for 1997 of 14.9%.

Social Auditing

How do we measure and evaluate an organization's activities aimed at social responsibility? **Imperial Oil** declares in its annual report:

> Imperial remains committed to protecting the health and safety of its employees, contractors, customers and the public, and to environmental responsibility in its business and operating activities.

While it is difficult to compute a net social contribution measure for declarations like these, we can use social auditing to help us out. A **social audit** is an analysis of an organization's success in carrying out programs that are socially responsible and responsive. But how do we measure socially responsible and responsive? Can we measure the activities' effects on society? Do we measure the expenditures and ignore the effects? How do we measure time contributed by employees? There are different approaches in practice. Organizations that report these activities stick with disclosing *positive* actions (contributions, pollution reduction, minority business). But we might also want to assess *negative* actions like layoffs, discrimination, and forced retirement. Social auditing must also face ethical issues. For example, is it right for a Canadian company to refuse to buy materials from a small family business in a less developed country because it disagrees with that country's political agenda? Does it matter if that company's decision drives this small family out of business and they must return to work in low-paying government run factories? These are difficult but all too common questions. Social auditing is slowly coming to grips with these difficult questions.

Flashback

9. Who are the external and internal users of accounting information?
10. Identify seven internal operating functions in organizations.
11. Why are internal controls important?
12. What are the guidelines in helping us make ethical decisions?
13. Why are ethics and social responsibility valuable to organizations?
14. Why are ethics crucial to accounting?

Answers—p. 31

Accounting information affects many aspects of our lives. The organizations we work for, the work we do, and the lives we live are impacted by accounting. When we pay taxes, earn money, invest savings, budget earnings, and plan for the future, we are influenced by accounting. Accounting helps us live better lives. It enables us to better perform and compete in society. To help us understand the opportunities for us in accounting, this section discusses four areas: financial, managerial, taxation and accounting-related. These areas differ by the kinds of information provided to and demanded by decision makers. Exhibit 1.12 lists selected opportunities for each of these areas. We also discuss unique aspects of these areas by business and nonbusiness organizations when appropriate. These activities demand the work of millions of individuals employed in accounting or accounting-related areas.

Opportunities in Practice

LO9 Identify opportunities in accounting and related fields.

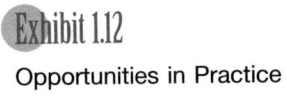

Exhibit 1.12

Opportunities in Practice

The Types of Accountants

One way to classify accountants is to identify the kinds of work they perform. In general, accountants work in these four broad fields:

- Financial accounting
- Managerial accounting
- Tax accounting
- Accounting-related

These fields provide a variety of information to different users. We describe the activities of accountants in these fields later in this chapter.

Another way to classify accountants is to identify the kinds of organizations in which they work. Most accountants are private accountants. A **private accountant** works for a single employer, which is often a business. A large business might employ a hundred or more private accountants, but most companies have fewer.

Many other accountants are public accountants. Public accountants provide their services to many different clients. They are called **public accountants** because their services are available to the public. Some public accountants are self-employed. Many others work for public accounting firms that may have thousands of employees or only a few. Canada's leading public accounting firms as of 1997 are:

	Revenue ($000's)
KPMG	$607,000
Deloitte & Touche	570,000
Ernst & Young	449,000
Coopers & Lybrand	368,180
Price Waterhouse	352,000
Doane Raymond Grant Thornton	207,600
Arthur Andersen	146,000
BDO Dunwoody	136,000

Source: *The Bottom Line,* April 1998, p. 18.

Government accountants work for local, provincial, and federal government agencies. Some government accountants perform accounting services for their own agencies. Other government accountants are involved with business regulation. Still others investigate violations of laws.

Accounting is a profession like law and medicine because accountants have special abilities and responsibilities. The professional status of an accountant is often indicated by one or more certificates.

Financial Accounting

Financial accounting provides information to decision makers who are not involved in the day-to-day operations of an organization. As we described earlier, these external decision makers include investors, creditors, and others. The information is distributed primarily through general-purpose financial statements. Financial statements describe the condition of the organization and the events that happened during the year. Chapter 2 explains the form and contents of financial statements.

Financial statements are prepared by the company's private accountants as shown in Exhibit 1.12. However, many companies issue their financial statements only after an audit. An audit is an independent review and test of an organization's accounting systems and records; it is performed to add credibility to the financial statements.[5] For example, banks require audits of the financial statements of companies applying for large loans. Also, federal and provincial laws require companies to have audits before their securities (shares and bonds) can be sold to the public. Thereafter, their financial statements must be audited as long as the securities are traded.

To perform an **audit,** auditors examine the financial statements and the accounting system. Their objective is to decide whether the statements reflect the company's financial position and operating results in agreement with generally accepted accounting principles (GAAP). These principles are rules adopted by the accounting profession as guides for measuring and reporting the financial condition and activities of a business. You will learn more about GAAP in Chapter 2 and in many of the following chapters.

When an audit is completed, the auditors prepare a report that expresses their professional opinion about the financial statements. The auditors' report must accompany the statements when they are distributed.

Financial accountants also work for government and prepare financial statements. These statements describe the financial status of government agencies and results of events occurring during the year. The financial statements of governmental bodies are usually audited by the auditor general (federal), provincial auditors, and/or independent accountants.

Other government accountants are involved with regulating financial accounting practices used by businesses. For example, some accountants work for the provincial securities commissions which regulate securities markets, including the flow of information from companies to the public. Securities commission accountants review companies' financial reports that are distributed to the public to be sure that the reports comply with the appropriate regulations.

As we mentioned briefly, some government accountants investigate possible violations of laws and regulations. For example, accountants who work for the provincial securities commissions (e.g., the Ontario Securities commission) investigate crimes related to securities. Other accountants investigate financial frauds and white-collar crimes in their capacity as officers of the RCMP and provincial police forces.

---

[5] To achieve this result, audits are performed by independent professionals who are public accountants. Little or no credibility would be added to statements if they were audited by a company's own employees.

Managerial Accounting

The field of managerial accounting involves providing information to an organization's managers. Managerial accounting reports often include much of the same information used in financial accounting. However, managerial accounting reports also include a great deal of information that is not reported outside the company.

General Accounting

The task of recording transactions, processing the recorded data, and preparing reports for managers is called **general accounting.** General accounting also includes preparing the financial statements that executive management presents to external users. An organization's own accountants usually design the accounting information system, often with help from public accountants. The general accounting staff is supervised by a chief accounting officer, who is often called the **controller.** This title stems from the fact that accounting information is used to control the organization's operations.

Cost Accounting

To plan and control operations, managers need information about the nature of costs incurred. **Cost accounting** is a process of accumulating the information managers need about operating costs. It helps managers identify, measure, and control these costs. Cost accounting may involve accounting for the costs of products, services, or specific activities. Cost accounting information is also useful for evaluating each manager's performance. Large companies usually employ many cost accountants because cost accounting information is so important.

Budgeting

Budgeting is the process of developing formal plans for an organization's future activities. A primary goal of budgeting is to give managers from different areas in the organization a clear understanding of how their activities affect the entire organization. After the budget has been put into effect, it provides a basis for evaluating actual performance.

Internal Auditing

Just as independent auditing adds credibility to financial statements, **internal auditing** adds credibility to reports produced and used within an organization. Internal auditors not only examine recordkeeping processes but also assess whether managers are following established operating procedures. In addition, internal auditors evaluate the efficiency of operating procedures. Almost all large companies and government agencies employ internal auditors.

Management Advisory Services

Public accountants participate in managerial accounting by providing **management consulting** or management advisory services to their clients. Independent auditors gain an intimate knowledge of a client's accounting and operating procedures when they conduct their examinations. As a result, auditors are in an excellent position to offer suggestions for improving the company's procedures. Most clients expect these suggestions as a useful by-product of the audit. For example, public accountants often help companies design and install new accounting and internal control systems. This effort includes offering advice on selecting new computer systems. Other advice might relate to budgeting procedures or employee benefit plans.

Tax Accounting

Income taxes raised by federal and provincial governments are based on the income earned by taxpayers. These taxpayers include both individuals and corporate businesses. The amount of taxes is based on what the laws define to be income. In the field of **tax accounting,** tax accountants help taxpayers comply with these laws by preparing their tax returns. Another tax accounting activity involves planning future transactions to minimize the amount of tax to be paid. The Taxation column of Exhibit 1.12 identifies the activities of accountants in this field.

Large companies usually have their own private accountants who are responsible for preparing tax returns and doing tax planning. However, large companies may consult with public accountants when they need special tax expertise. Most small companies rely on public accountants for their tax work.

Many accountants are employed on the government side of the tax process. For example, Revenue Canada employs numerous tax accountants. **Revenue Canada** has the duty of collecting federal taxes and otherwise enforcing tax laws. Most Revenue Canada accountants review tax returns filed by taxpayers, while others offer assistance to taxpayers and help write regulations. Still others investigate possible violations of tax laws.

Accounting-Related Opportunities

Accounting-related opportunities are great. Accounting is the common language of financial communications. It spans professionals, continents, and economies. Exhibit 1.12 lists several accounting-related opportunities including leaders, consultants, managers, and planners. Less traditional ones include community activist, political consultant, reporter, salesperson, union official, entrepreneur, programmer, engineer, and mechanic. All of these professions are made easier with a working knowledge of accounting. This course provides that knowledge.

Professional Certification

In Canada, there are a number of accounting organizations providing education and professional training. Provincially, these include the Institute of Chartered Accountants, the Certified General Accountants' Association, and the Society of Management Accountants. Successful completion of the prescribed courses of instruction and practical experience lead to the following designations:

> **Chartered Accountant (CA)**
> **Certified General Accountant (CGA)**
> **Certified Management Accountant (CMA)**

Activities of the three accounting organizations that have shaped accounting thought have been their education and their publication programs. Each has an extensive educational program and has maintained the publication of journals which enjoy wide readership.

In the past decade reliance on postsecondary accounting education has become a significant part of the educational process and complements the extensive correspondence, university degree completion through distance study, and lecture programs of the Certified General Accountants' Association of Canada (CGAAC). Most provincial bodies of the Canadian Institute of Chartered Accountants (CICA) require a university degree with specified courses. A university degree is required also by some of the provincial bodies of the Society of Management Accountants of Canada (SMAC).

Accountancy is still one of the fastest growing of the professions. This growth is in response to the expansion and complexity of the economy, the increasing involvement of the accountant in the process of management decision making, and a growing number of financial reporting activities.

Summary

The preceding discussion shows how important accounting is for most organizations. Regardless of your career goals, you will surely use accounting information and work with accountants. The discussion also shows the variety of opportunities available if you find accounting to be enjoyable and challenging.

Flashback

15. What services are performed by public accountants?

16. What are the four broad fields of accounting?

17. What is the purpose of an audit? Describe what public accountants do when they perform an audit.

Answers—p. 31

Return on Investment　　　　　　　　　USING THE INFORMATION

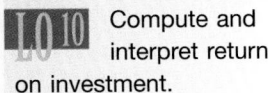
LO 10 Compute and interpret return on investment.

We described return on investment and its use in assessing return and risk earlier in the chapter. Return on investment is also useful in evaluating management, analyzing and forecasting profits, and in planning future activities. **Dell Computer** has its marketing department compute return on investment for every mailing. "We spent 15 months educating people about return on invested capital," says Dell's chief financial officer, T. J. Meredith. This section describes return on investment and how it can help us with these tasks.

Return on investment (ROI), also commonly called return on assets (or ROA), measures performance independent of its financing sources. It is viewed as an indicator of operating efficiency. Exhibit 1.13 shows how we compute return on investment:

Exhibit 1.13

Return on Investment

$$\text{Return on investment} = \frac{\text{Net income}}{\text{Average total assets}}$$

Average total assets is usually computed by adding beginning and ending year amounts and dividing by two. For illustrative purposes, let's consider **Alliance Communications.** Alliance reports net income of $18.2 in 1997 (in millions). At the beginning of 1997, Alliance's total assets are $238.9 and at the end of 1997 they total $353.7 (in millions). Alliance's return on investment for 1997 is:

$$\text{Return on investment} = \frac{\$18.2}{(\$238.9 + \$353.7)/2} = 6.14\%$$

Is a 6.14% return on investment good or bad for Alliance? To help answer this question and others like it, we can compare Alliance's return on investment with its prior performance, the returns of similar companies (such as **Atlantis Communications** and **Paragon Entertainment Corp.**), and with returns from alternative investments. Alliance's return on investment for each of the prior four years is reported in the second column of Exhibit 1.14.

Exhibit 1.14

Alliance, Atlantis and Industry Returns

Year	Alliance's Return on Investment (%)	Atlantis' Return on Investment (%)	Industry Return on Investment (%)
1997	6.1	1.7	
1996	4.3	2.1	2.0
1995	6.3		5.1
1994	5.2		3.6

Alliance's return on investment for this period ranges from 4.3% to 6.3%. The pattern suggests a make or break pattern in its efficiency in using its assets. We can also compare Alliance to a similar company such as Atlantis whose return on investment is shown in the third column above. In the two years available Alliance has a higher return for this period. We can also compare Alliance's return to the normal return for motion picture production and allied industry. Industry averages are available from services like Dun & Bradstreet's (D&B) *Canadian Industry Norms and Key Business Ratios*. Ratios computed from a select group of similar manufacturers are shown in the fourth column. When compared to their competitors, Alliance performs well unlike Atlantis.

Another useful analysis is to compare returns to alternative investments. Exhibit 1.15 shows recent returns for five familiar companies. None of the companies performed as well as Alliance although **Monarch** came closest. Atlantis' performance was worse than all of the others. Using this information, Alliance's performance appears rather "good," as it is better than the norm as judged by the returns of competitors both in and outside its industry.

Exhibit 1.15

Return on Investment

Source: Recent annual reports.

Summary

LO1 **Explain the goals and uses of accounting in the information age.** Accounting is an information and measurement system that aims to identify, record and communicate relevant, reliable and comparable information about economic activities. It helps us better assess opportunities, products, investments, and social and community responsibilities. The power of accounting is in opening our eyes to new and exciting opportunities. The greatest benefits from understanding accounting often come to those outside of accounting. This is because an improved understanding of accounting helps us better to compete in today's world.

LO2 **Describe profit and its two major components.** Profit is the amount a business earns after subtracting all expenses necessary for its sales (revenues − expenses = profit). Sales (revenues) are the amounts earned from selling products and services. Expenses are the costs incurred with sales. A loss arises when expenses are more than sales.

LO3 **Explain the relation between return and risk.** Return refers to profit, and risk is the uncertainty about the return we hope to make. All business decisions involve risk. The lower the risk of an investment, the lower is its expected return. For example, savings accounts pay a low return because of the low risk of the bank not returning the principal with interest. Also, higher expected return offsets higher risk. Actual return can differ from

expected return. Higher risk means higher, but more risky expected return.

LO4 **Identify forms of organization and their characteristics.** Organizations can be classified as either businesses or nonbusinesses. Businesses are organized for profit, while nonbusinesses serve us in ways not always measured by profit. Businesses take one of three forms: sole proprietorship, partnership or corporation. These forms of organization have characteristics that hold important implications for legal liability, taxation, continuity, number of owners, and legal status.

LO5 **Identify and describe the three major activities in organizations.** Organizations carry out three major activities: financing, investing and operating. These activities are tied together by an organization's plans, including its ideas, goals and strategies. Financing is the means used to pay for resources like land, buildings and machines. Investing refers to the buying and selling of resources used in selling products and services. Operating activities are the carrying out of the organization's plans.

LO6 **Explain and interpret the accounting equation.** Investing activities are funded by an organization's financing activities. An organization cannot have more or less assets than its financing and, similarly, it cannot have more or less nonowner (liabilities) and owner (equity) financing than its total assets. This basic relation gives us the accounting equation: assets = liabilities + owner's equity.

 Identify users and uses of accounting. There are both internal and external users of accounting. Some users and uses of accounting include: (a) management for control, monitoring and planning; (b) lenders for measuring the risk and return of loans; (c) shareholders for assessing the return and risk in acquiring shares; (d) directors for overseeing management; and (e) employees for judging employment opportunities. Other users are auditors, consultants, officers, regulators, analysts, unions, suppliers and appraisers.

Explain why ethics and social responsibility are crucial to accounting. The goal of accounting is to provide useful information for decision making. For information to be useful it must be trusted. This demands ethics and socially responsible behaviour in accounting. Without these, accounting information loses its reliability.

Identify opportunities in accounting and related fields. Opportunities in accounting and related

fields are numerous. They include traditional ones like financial, managerial and tax accounting. They also include accounting related fields such as lending, consulting, managing and planning. We can even identify nontraditional opportunities with accounting knowledge including careers as a community activist, political consultant, reporter, salesperson, union official, entrepreneur, programmer, engineer and mechanic. There are millions of individuals employed in accounting and accounting-related fields.

Compute and interpret return on investment. Return on investment is commonly computed as profit, also called net income or earnings, divided by the amount invested. For example, if we have an average balance in our savings account of $100 and it earns interest of $5 for the year, then our return on investment is $5/$100 or 5%. Return on investment is also called return on assets, where the amount invested is measured by the average assets for the period. This return measure tells us how successful an organization is at earning a profit with a given amount of investment called assets.

Guidance Answers to **You Make the Call**

Programmer

The computer programmer is confronting a trade-off between return (salary) and risk (dependable employment). The new start-up company has an uncertain future and is willing to increase your pay to balance the added risk you have in working for them (this company could fail). The established medical supply company pays less, but you are assured of long-term employment. If you or others are totally dependent on your income, the risk of the start-up company might be too high. Yet if you and others do not depend on your salary, the increased pay might be worth the risk.

Entrepreneur

You should probably form your business as a corporation if potential lawsuits are of prime concern. The corporate form of organization would protect your personal property from lawsuits directed at the business, and would place only the corporation's resources at risk. A downside of the corporate form is "double taxation"—the corporation must pay taxes on earnings and you must pay taxes on any money distributed to you from the business (even though the corporation already paid taxes on this money). You should also examine the ethical and socially responsible aspects of starting a business where you anticipate injuries to others.

Guidance Answers to

1. Accounting is an information and measurement system that identifies, records and communicates relevant information to people that helps them make better decisions. It helps people in business identify and react to investment opportunities. It also helps us better assess opportunities, products, investments, and social and community responsibilities.

2. Profit is the money a business earns after paying for all expenses necessary for its sales. Sales, also called revenues, are the amounts earned from selling products and services. Expenses are the costs incurred with sales.

3. The trade-off between return and risk is a normal part of business. The lower the risk of an investment, the lower is our expected return. Similarly, higher expected return offsets higher risk. Remember that *actual* return usually

differs from expected return. Higher risk implies higher, but more risky *expected* returns.

4. Recordkeeping is the recording of financial transactions and events, either manually or electronically. While recordkeeping is essential to data reliability, accounting is this and much more. Accounting includes identifying, measuring, reporting and analyzing economic events and transactions. It involves interpreting information, and designing information systems to provide useful reports that monitor and control an organization's activities.

5. The rules are determined by many individuals and groups. Since accounting is a service activity, these rules reflect our society's needs and not those of accountants or any other single constituency. Major participants in setting rules include the various securities commissions

(eg., the Ontario Securities Commission), and the Accounting Standards Board (AcSB) of the Canadian Institute of Chartered Accountants (CICA).

6. The three common forms of business organizations are sole proprietorships, partnerships and corporations.

7. Nonbusiness organizations often include airports, libraries, museums, religious institutions, cities, police, mail, colleges, universities, bus lines, utilities, highways, shelters, parks, hospitals and schools.

8. Organizations pursue financing, investing and operating activities. These three major activities are organized under planning activities.

9. External users of accounting information are not directly involved in running the organization and include lenders, shareholders, directors, customers, suppliers, regulators, lawyers, brokers and the press. Internal users of accounting information are those individuals directly involved in managing and operating an organization. They include managers, officers, and other important internal decision makers involved with the strategic and operating decisions.

10. The internal operating functions are: research and development, purchasing, human resources, production, distribution, marketing and servicing.

11. Internal controls are procedures set up to protect assets, ensure reliable accounting reports, promote efficiency, and encourage adherence to company policies. Internal controls are crucial if accounting reports are to provide relevant and reliable information.

12. The guideline are threefold: (1) Identify ethical issues using personal ethics, (2) analyze options considering both good and bad consequences for all individuals affected, and (3) make ethical decision choosing the best option after weighing all consequences.

13. We know ethics and social responsibility are important for us because without them our lives are more difficult, inefficient and unpleasant. They are equally important to organizations for these same reasons. In addition, they often translate into higher profits and a better working environment.

14. Accounting aims to provide useful information for decision making. For information to be useful it must be trusted. Trust of information demands ethics in accounting.

15. The services performed by public accountants generally include: (a) income tax services, management advisory services, and independent auditing; (b) general accounting, independent auditing, and budgeting; and (c) government accounting, private accounting, and independent auditing.

16. Financial accounting, managerial accounting, taxation, and accounting-related careers.

17. The purpose of an audit is to add credibility to the financial statements. Public accountants perform an independent review and test of an organization's accounting systems and records.

Glossary

Accounting An information and measurement system that identifies, records and communicates relevant information to people to help them make better decisions. (p. 4)

Accounting Equation The equality where Assets = Liabilities + Owner's Equity. (p. 14)

AcSB The Accounting Standards Board; the authoritative committee of the CICA that identifies generally accepted accounting principles. (p. 9)

Assets Economic resources that are expected to produce future benefits. (p. 13)

Audit A check of an organization's accounting systems and records using various tests. (p. 25)

Bond Written promises by organizations to repay amounts loaned with interest. (p. 6)

Bookkeeping The part of accounting that involves recording economic transactions and events, either electronically or manually; also called *recordkeeping*. (p. 7)

Budgeting The process of developing formal plans for future activities, which often serve as a basis for evaluating actual performance. (p. 26)

Business One or more individuals selling products or services for profit. (p. 5)

Business entity principle Every business is accounted for separately from its owner's personal activities. (p. 10)

CA Chartered Accountant; an accountant who has met the examination, education and experience requirements of the Institute of Chartered Accountants for an individual professionally competent in accounting. (p. 27)

CGA Certified General Accountant; an accountant who has met the examination, education and experience requirements of the Certified General Accountants' Association for an individual professionally competent in accounting. (p. 27)

CMA Certified Management Accountant; an accountant who has met the examination, education and experience requirements of the Society of Management Accountants for an individual professionally competent in all areas of accounting and specializing in management accounting. (p. 27)

Common share capital The name for a corporation's shares when only one class of share capital is issued; also called *capital stock* (p. 11)

Controller The chief accounting officer of an organization. (p. 26)

Corporation A business that is a separate legal entity under provincial or federal laws with owners that are called shareholders or stockholders. (p. 11)

Cost accounting A managerial accounting activity designed to help managers identify, measure and control operating costs. (p. 26)

Costs See *expenses*.

Earnings The amount a business earns after subtracting all expenses necessary for its sales; also called *net income* or *profit*. (p. 5)

Expenses The costs incurred to earn sales (or revenues). (p. 5)

External auditors Examine and provide assurance that financial statements are prepared according to generally accepted accounting principles. (p. 17)

External users Persons using accounting information who are not directly involved in the running of the organization; examples include shareholders, customers, regulators, and suppliers. (p. 15)

Ethics Beliefs that separate right from wrong. (p. 19)

Factors of production The means businesses use to make profit; land, labour, buildings and equipment are the traditional factors of production. (p. 7)

Financial accounting The area of accounting aimed at serving external users. (p. 16)

Financing activities The means organizations use to pay for resources like land, building, and machines. (p. 13)

GAAP Generally accepted accounting principles are the rules that indicate acceptable accounting practice. (p. 8)

General accounting The task of recording transactions, processing data, and preparing reports for managers; includes preparing financial statements for disclosure to external users. (p. 26)

Government accountants Work for local, provincial and federal government agencies. (p. 25)

Information age A time period which emphasizes communication, data, news, facts, access and commentary. (p. 4)

Internal auditing Activity conducted by employees within organizations to assess whether managers are following established operating procedures and to evaluate the efficiency of operating procedures. (p. 26)

Internal controls Procedures set up to protect assets, ensure reliable accounting reports, promote efficiency, and encourage adherence to company policies. (p. 19)

Internal users Persons using accounting information who are directly involved in managing and operating an organization; examples include managers and officers. (p. 17)

Investing activities The buying and selling of resources that an organization uses to sell its products or services. (p. 13)

Liabilities Creditors' claims on an organization's assets. (p. 14)

Limited liability partnership Restricts partners' liabilities to their own acts and the acts of individuals under their control. (p. 10)

Limited partnership Includes both general partner(s) with unlimited liability and a limited partner(s) with liability restricted to the amount invested. (p. 10)

Loss Arises when expenses total more than sales (revenues). (p. 5)

Management accounting The area of accounting aimed at serving the decision-making needs of internal users. (p. 17)

Management consulting Activity in which suggestions are offered for improving a company's procedures; the sug-gestions may concern new accounting and internal control systems, new computer systems, budgeting, and employee benefit plans; also called *advisory services*. (p. 26)

Net income The amount a business earns after subtracting all expenses necessary for its sales; also called *profit* or *earnings*. (p. 5)

Operating activities The use of assets to carry out an orga-nization's plans in the areas of research, development, pur-chasing, production, distribution, and marketing. (p. 14)

OSC Ontario Securities Commission; the Ontario agency that sets reporting rules for organizations that sell owner-ship shares to the public in Ontario through the Toronto Stock Exchange. (p. 8)

Owner's equity The owner's claim on an organization's assets. (p. 14)

Partnership A business that is owned by two or more peo-ple that is not organized as a corporation. (p. 10)

Planning The term for defining the ideas, goals, and actions of an organization. (p. 12)

Private accountants Accountants who work for a single employer other than the government. (p. 24)

Profit The amount a business earns after subtracting all expenses necessary for its sales; also called *net income* or *earnings*. (p. 5)

Public accountants Aacountants who provide their ser-vices to many different clients. (p. 24)

Recordkeeping The recording of financial transactions and events, either manually or electronically; also called *book-keeping*. (p. 7)

Return Derives from the idea of getting something back from an investment in a business; also called *profit*. (p. 6)

Return on investment A financial ratio serving as an indi-cator of operating efficiency; net income divided by aver-age total assets. (p. 6)

Revenues The amounts earned from selling products or services; also called *sales*. (pp. 5, 14)

Revenue Canada The federal agency that has the duty of collecting federal taxes and otherwise enforcing tax laws. (p. 27)

Risk The amount of uncertainty about the return to be earned. (p. 6)

Sales The amounts earned from selling products or ser-vices; also called *revenues*. (pp. 5, 14)

Shareholders The owners of a corporation; also called *stockholders*. (p. 11)

Shares A unit of ownership in a corporation; also called *stock*. (p. 11)

Single proprietorship A business owned by one individ-ual that is not organized as a corporation; also called a *sole proprietorship*. (p. 10)

Social audit An analysis of an organization's success in carrying out programs that are socially responsible and responsive. (p. 23)

Social responsibility Involves considering the impact and being accountable for the effects that actions might have on society. (p. 21)

Sole proprietorship A business owned by one person that is not organized as a corporation; also called *single proprietorship.* (p. 10)

Stock Equity of a corporation divided into units called shares. (p. 11)

Stockholders The owners of a corporation. (p. 11)

Tax accounting The field of accounting that includes preparing tax returns and planning future transactions to minimize the amount of tax; involves private, public, and government accountants. (p. 26)

Questions

1. Identify four external users and their uses of accounting information.
2. Identify three types of organizations that can be formed as either profit-oriented businesses, government units, or not-for-profit establishments.
3. What type of accounting information might be useful to those who carry out the marketing activities of a business?
4. Explain return and risk. Discuss the trade-off between return and risk.
5. What is the purpose of accounting in society?
6. Describe the internal role of accounting for organizations.
7. Explain business profit and its computation.
8. What are three questions that business owners might answer by looking at accounting information?
9. Technology is increasingly used to process accounting data. Why should we study accounting?
10. Define and explain return on investment (assets).
11. Why do organizations license and monitor accounting and accounting-related professionals?
12. What is the relation between accounting and the information superhighway?
13. Identify three types of services typically offered by accounting professionals.
14. Describe three forms of business organizations and their characteristics.
15. An organization's chief accounting officer is often called the "controller." Why?
16. Identify four managerial accounting tasks performed by both private and government accountants.
17. Describe three important activities in organizations.
18. Identify two management advisory services offered by public accounting professionals.
19. Explain why investing (assets) and financing (liabilities and equity) totals are always equal.
20. List three examples of the types of tasks performed by government accounting professionals.
21. Identify three businesses that offer services and three businesses that offer products.
22. What work do tax accounting professionals perform in addition to preparing tax returns?
23. Why is accounting described as a service activity?
24. What is a social responsibility report?
25. What ethical issues might accounting professionals face in dealing with confidential information?
26. Identify the chief financial officer for **Alliance Communications** from its financial statements in Appendix I? How many directors does Alliance have?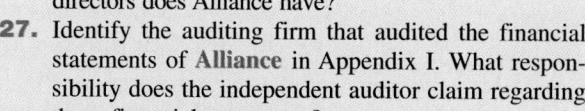
27. Identify the auditing firm that audited the financial statements of **Alliance** in Appendix I. What responsibility does the independent auditor claim regarding these financial statements?
28. The chapter's opening article discussed **W&F Financial Services.** This business is organized as a partnership. Identify important characteristics of partnerships and their implications.

Quick Study exercises give readers a brief test of many key elements in every chapter.

Accounting provides information about an organization's economic transactions and events. Identify examples of economic transactions and events.

Quick Study

QS 1-1

Identifying transactions and events

LO 5

Identify four responsibilities in the internal *marketing* function of organizations. Identify three responsibilities in the overall *executive management* (planning) activity of organizations.

QS 1-2

Identifying internal operating functions

LO 7

QS 1-3

Explaining internal control

An important responsibility of many accounting professionals is to design and implement internal control procedures for organizations. Explain the purpose of internal control procedures.

QS 1-4

Accounting and accounting related opportunities

Identify at least three main areas of accounting for accounting professionals. For each accounting area identify at least three accounting-related opportunities in practice.

QS 1-5

Identifying ethical matters

Accounting professionals must sometimes choose between two or more acceptable methods of accounting for certain transactions and events. Explain why these situations can involve difficult matters of ethical concern.

QS 1-6

Identifying and working with assets, liabilities and equity

Use **Atlantis Communication's** 1997 annual report printed in Appendix I near the end of the book to answer the following:

a. Identify the dollar amounts of Atlantis Communication's 1997 (1) assets, (2) liabilities, and (3) equity.

b. Using Atlantis Communication's amounts from part a of this question, verify that: assets = liabilities + equity.

Exercises

Exercise 1-1

Distinguishing business organizations

Presented below are descriptions of several different business organizations. Determine whether the situation described refers to a sole proprietorship, partnership, or corporation.

a. Ownership of Cola Company is divided into 1,000 shares.

b. Text Tech is owned by Kimberly Fisher, who is personally liable for the debts of the business.

c. Jerry Forrentes and Susan Montgomery own Financial Services, a financial and personal services provider. Neither Forrentes nor Montgomery has personal responsibility for the debts of Financial Services.

d. Nancy Kerr and Frank Levens own Runners, a courier service. Both Kerr and Levens are personally liable for the debts of the business.

e. MRS Consulting Services does not have separate legal existence apart from the one person who owns it.

f. Biotech Company has one owner and does not pay taxes.

g. Torby Technologies has two owners and pays its own taxes.

Exercise 1-2

Determining internal operating functions

Select the internal operating function from the two identified that is most likely to regularly use the information described. While the information is likely used in both functions, the information is most obviously relevant to one.

a. What internal operating function is most likely to use payroll information: marketing or human resources?

b. Which internal operating function is most likely to use sales report information: marketing or research and development?

c. Which internal operating function is most likely to use cash flow information: finance or human resources?

d. Which internal operating function is most likely to use financial statement, budget, and performance report information: research and development or executive management?

e. Which internal operating function is most likely to use product quality information: finance or production?

Identify at least three external users of accounting information and indicate some questions they might seek to answer through their use of accounting information.

Exercise 1-3

Identifying accounting
users and uses

LO 7

Many accounting professionals work in one of the following three areas:

A. Financial accounting

B. Managerial accounting

C. Tax accounting

For each of the following responsibilities, identify the area of accounting most involving that responsibility:

_____ **1.** Auditing financial statements.

_____ **2.** Planning transactions to minimize taxes paid.

_____ **3.** Cost accounting.

_____ **4.** Preparing financial statements.

_____ **5.** Reviewing financial reports for compliance with provincial securities commissions requirements.

_____ **6.** Budgeting.

_____ **7.** Internal auditing.

_____ **8.** Investigating violations of tax laws.

Exercise 1-4

Describing accounting
responsibilities

LO 9

Assume the following role and describe a situation where ethical considerations play an important part in guiding your action:

a. You are a student in an accounting principles course.

b. You are a manager with responsibility for several employees.

c. You are an accounting professional preparing tax returns for clients.

d. You are an accounting professional with audit clients that are competitors in business.

Exercise 1-5

Identifying ethical
decisions

LO 8

Indicate which description best depicts each of the following important terms:

A. Audit

B. Controller

C. Cost accounting

D. GAAP

E. Ethics

F. General accounting

G. Budgeting

H. Tax accounting

_____ **1.** An accounting area that includes planning future transactions to minimize taxes paid.

_____ **2.** A managerial accounting process designed to help managers identify, measure and control operating costs.

_____ **3.** Principles that determine whether an action is right or wrong.

_____ **4.** An examination of an organization's accounting system and records that adds credibility to financial statements.

_____ **5.** The task of recording transactions, processing recorded data, and preparing reports and financial statements.

_____ **6.** The chief accounting officer of an organization.

Exercise 1-6

Learning the language of
business

LO 1, 9

Indicate which description best depicts each of the following important terms:

A. Government accountants

B. Internal auditing

C. Revenue Canada

D. OSC

E. CIA

F. Profit

G. Risk

H. Public accountants

I. CICA

J. CMA

Exercise 1-7

Learning the language of
business

LO 2, 3, 7, 9

_____ **1.** Responsibility of an organization's employees involving examining the organization's recordkeeping processes, assessing whether managers are following established operating procedures, and appraising the efficiency of operating procedures.

_____ **2.** Amount of uncertainty associated with an expected return.

_____ **3.** Money a business earns after paying for all expenses associated with its sales.

_____ **4.** Federal department responsible for collecting federal taxes and enforcing tax law.

_____ **5.** Accounting professionals who provide services to many different clients.

_____ **6.** Accounting professionals employed by federal, provincial, or local branches of government.

Exercise 1-8

Using the accounting equation

 6

Answer the following questions.

a. Doug Stockton's medical supplies business has assets equal to $123,000 and liabilities equal to $53,000 at the end of the year. What is the total of the owner's equity for Stockton's business at the end of the year?

b. At the beginning of the year ParFour Company's assets are $200,000, and its owner's equity is $150,000. During the year assets increase $70,000 and liabilities increase $30,000. What is the owner's equity at the end of the year?

c. At the beginning of the year, Niagara Company's liabilities equal $60,000. During the year assets increase by $80,000 and at year-end they equal $180,000. Liabilities decrease $10,000 during the year. What are the beginning and ending amounts of owner's equity.

Exercise 1-9

Calculating return on investment

 10

Java Jimmies reports net income of $20,000 for 1999. At the beginning of 1999, Java Jimmies had $100,000 in assets. By the end of 1999 assets had grown to $140,000. What is Java Jimmies return on investment?

Exercise 1-10

Using the accounting equation

 6

Determine the amount missing from each accounting equation below.

	Assets	=	Liabilities	+	Equity
a.	?	=	$30,000	+	$65,000
b.	$ 89,000	=	$22,000	+	?
c.	$132,000	=	?	+	$20,000

Problems

Problem 1-1

Determining profits, sales, expenses and returns

 2, 6, 10

Bell Systems manufactures, markets and sells cellular telephones. The average amount invested, or average total assets, in Bell Systems is $250,000. In its most recent year, Bell earned a profit of $55,000 on sales of $455,000.

Required

1. What is Bell Systems' return on investment?

2. Does return on investment seem satisfactory for Bell Systems when its competitors average a 12% return on investment?

3. What are the total expenses for Bell Systems in its most recent year?

4. What is the average total amount of financing (liabilities plus equity) for Bell Systems?

Problem 1-2

Computing and interpreting return on investment

 10

PC Company and Sprite Inc. both produce and market beverages and are direct competitors. Key financial figures (in $ millions) for these businesses over the past four years follow:

Key Figures	PC Company	Sprite Inc.
Sales	$400	$250.7
Profit	50	37.5
Average invested (assets)	625	312.5

Required

1. Compute return on investment for (a) PC Company and (b) Sprite Inc.
2. Which company is more successful in sales to consumers?
3. Which company is more successful in earning profits from its amount invested?

Analysis component:

4. Write a brief memo explaining in which company you would invest your money.

All business decisions involve risk and return. Identify the risk and return in the following activities:

1. Investing $1,000 in a 4% saving account.
2. Placing a $1,000 bet on your favourite sports team.
3. Investing $10,000 in **AOL Canada** shares.
4. Taking a $10,000 student loan to study accounting.

Problem 1-3
Identifying risk and return
LO 3

Write a description of an organization's three major activities.

Problem 1-4
Describing organizational activities
LO 5

A new company often engages in the following activities during their first year of operations. Identify these activities within one of the four major categories of an organization's activities:

A. Planning
B. Financing
C. Investing
D. Operating

_____ 1. Deciding on organizational tactics.
_____ 2. Owner chooses to leave profits in the business.
_____ 3. Obtaining necessary licences.
_____ 4. Purchasing land.
_____ 5. Use of credit at bank.
_____ 6. Goal setting.
_____ 7. Purchasing supplies.
_____ 8. Distributing products.
_____ 9. Conducting an advertising campaign.

Problem 1-5
Describing organizational activities.
LO 5

Klondike Company manufactures, markets, and sells snowmobile equipment. The companies that comprise the recreational vehicle industry earn an average return on investment of 9.5%. The average amount invested, or average total assets, in Klondike Company is $2,000,000. In its most recent year, Klondike earned a profit of $100,000 on sales of $1,200,000.

Required

1. What is Klondike Company's return on investment?
2. Does return on investment seem satisfactory for Klondike given competitors' return on investment?
3. What are the total expenses for Klondike Company in its most recent year?
4. What is the average total amount of financing (liabilities and equity) for Klondike Company?

Alternate Problems
Problem 1-1A
Determining profits, sales, expenses and returns
LO 2, 6, 10

Problem 1-2A

Computing and
interpreting return on
investment

 LO 10

Bell Canada and Cantel produce and market telecommunications products and are direct competitors. Key financial figures (in $ millions) for these businesses over the past year follow:

Key Figures	Bell	Cantel
Sales	$79,609	$19,957
Profit	139	2,538
Average invested (assets)	87,261	37,019

1. Compute return on investment for (a) Bell and (b) Cantel.
2. Which company is more successful in sales to consumers?
3. Which company is more successful in earning profits from its amount invested?

Analysis component:

4. Write a brief memo explaining in which company you would invest your money.

Problem 1-3A

Identifying risk and return

 LO 3

All business decisions involve risk and return. Identify the risk and return in the following activities:
1. Stashing $1,000 under your mattress.
2. Placing a $500 bet on the Calgary Flames.
3. Investing $10,000 in Corel shares.
4. Investing $10,000 in Canada Savings Bonds.

Problem 1-4A

Describing organizational
activities

 LO 5

Prepare an outline of an organization's major activities.

Problem 1-5A

Describing organizational
activities.

 LO 5

A new company will engage in the following activities during their first year of operation. Categorize the activities listed by the following letters:
A. Planning
B. Financing
C. Investing
D. Operating
_____ **1.** Checking compliance with local laws.
_____ **2.** Obtaining a bank loan.
_____ **3.** Defining the goals of the organization.
_____ **4.** Procuring inventory.
_____ **5.** Researching products.
_____ **6.** Worker supervision.
_____ **7.** Owner contributes personal savings to the business.
_____ **8.** Setting policies.
_____ **9.** Renting office space.

BEYOND THE NUMBERS

Alliance Communication produces, markets and sells movies and television programs. Key financial figures for Alliance Communication's fiscal year ended March 31, 1997, are:

Key Figure	$ millions
Financing (liabilities + equity)	$353.7
Profit	18.2
Sales	282.6

Reporting in Action

LO 2, 6, 10

Required

1. What is the total amount of assets invested in Alliance Communication?

2. What is Alliance Communication's return on investment? Alliance Communication's assets at March 31, 1996, equal $238.9 (in millions).

3. How much are total expenses for Alliance Communication?

Analysis component:

4. Does Alliance Communication's return on investment seem satisfactory if competitors average a 5% return?

Both **Alliance Communications** and **Atlantis Communications** produce, market and sell movies and television programs. Key comparative figures ($ millions) for these two organizations follow:

	Alliance	Atlantis
Financing (liabilities + equity)	$353.7	$333.5
Profit	18.2	5.6
Sales	282.6	178.0

Source: Alliance figures are from its annual report for fiscal year-end March 31, 1997.
Atlantis figures are from its annual report for fiscal year-end December 31, 1997.

Comparative Analysis

LO 2, 6, 10

Required

1. What is the total amount of assets invested in (a) Alliance and (b) Atlantis?

2. What is the return on investment for (a) Alliance and (b) Atlantis? Alliance's beginning of year assets equal $238.9 (in millions) and Atlantis' beginning of year assets equal $334.8 (in millions).

3. How much are costs for (a) Alliance and (b) Atlantis?

Analysis component:

4. Is return on investment satisfactory for (a) Alliance and (b) Atlantis when competitors average a 5% return?

5. What can you conclude about Alliance and Atlantis from these computations?

Rupert Jones works in a public accounting firm and hopes to eventually be a partner. The management of ShadowTech Company invited Jones to prepare a "bid" to audit ShadowTech's financial statements. In discussing the audit's fee, ShadowTech's management suggests a fee range where the fee amount depends on the reported profit of ShadowTech. The higher its profit, the higher the audit fee paid to Jones' firm.

Ethics Challenge

LO 8

Required

1. Identify the parties potentially affected by this situation.
2. What are the ethical factors in this situation?
3. Would you recommend that Jones accept this audit fee arrangement? Why?
4. Describe some of the factors guiding your recommendation.

Communicating in Practice
LO 3, 4

Refer to this chapter's opening article about **W&F Financial Services.** Before establishing the business, Williams and Fulwood met with a loan officer of a Winnipeg bank to discuss a loan.

Required

1. Prepare a brief report outlining the information you would request from Williams and Fulwood if you were the loan officer.
2. Indicate whether the information you request, and your loan decision, are affected by the form of business organization for **W&F Financial Services.**

Taking It to the Net
LO 1, 7

There is extensive accounting and business information available on the Internet. This includes the **TSE's** on-line address at **http://www.tse.com** and the Depository for Canadian Securities' database referred to as **SEDAR (http://www.sedar.com)** and numerous other Web sites offering access to financial statement information or related data.

Required

Access at least one of the Web sites selected by either you or your instructor and answer the following:

a. Write a brief report describing the types of relevant information available at this Web site.
b. How would you rate the importance of the information available at this Web site for accounting and business?

Teamwork in Action
LO 1

Effectively implementing a team approach in both business and education requires scheduling team meetings and maintaining ongoing communication between team members. Cooperation and support are key elements in effective teams. As part of a team you have the right to receive assistance from your teammates when you need or request it and you have the responsibility to provide it when possible. This activity is designed to open channels of communication to provide ongoing opportunities to fulfill team rights and responsibilities.

Required

1. Open a team discussion and determine a regular time and place where your team will meet between each scheduled class meeting.
2. Develop a list of telephone numbers and/or e-mail addresses of your teammates.
3. Notify your instructor, via a memo or e-mail message, as to when and where your team will hold regularly scheduled meetings.

Hitting the Road
LO 4

You are to interview a local business owner; this can be a friend or relative. Opening lines of communication with members of the business community can provide personal benefits of business networking. If you do not know the owner, you should call ahead to introduce yourself and explain your position as a student and your assignment requirements. You should request an appointment for a face-to-face or phone discussion to discuss the form of organization and operations of the business. Be prepared to make a good impression.

Required

1. Identify and describe the primary operating activity and the form of organization for this business.
2. Determine and explain why the owner(s) chose this particular form of organization.
3. Identify any special advantages and/or disadvantages the owner(s) generally experience in operating with this form of business organization.

Report on Business publishes an annual ranking of the top one thousand businesses based on market performance. This issue is called the "The Top 1000." Obtain the most recent publication of this issue. *Report on Business* also maintains a Web site with access to past articles at **http://www.theglobeandmail.com**.

Required

1. What are the top 10 performing businesses?
2. What are the bottom 10 performing businesses?
3. What industries are more frequently seen in the top 10? Bottom 10?
4. How does *Report on Business* rank businesses?

2

CHAPTER

Financial Statements and Accounting Transactions

▶ A Look Back

Chapter 1 began our study of accounting by considering its role in the information age. We described accounting for different organizations and identified users and uses of accounting. We saw that ethics and social responsibility are crucial to accounting.

▶ A Look at This Chapter

In this chapter we describe financial statements and the accounting principles guiding their preparation. An important part of this chapter is transaction analysis using the accounting equation. We prepare and analyze financial statements based on transaction analysis.

▶ A Look Forward

Chapter 3 explains the recording of transactions. We introduce the double entry accounting system and show how T-accounts are helpful in analyzing transactions. Journals and trial balances are also identified and explained.

Chapter Outline

▶ **Communicating with Financial Statements**
- Previewing Financial Statements
- Financial Statements and Forms of Organization
- Financial Statements, Auditing and Users

▶ **Generally Accepted Accounting Principles**
- Setting Accounting Principles
- International Accounting Principles
- Fundamental Principles of Accounting

▶ **Transactions and the Accounting Equation**
- Transaction Analysis—Part I
- Transaction Analysis—Part II
- Summary of Transactions

▶ **Financial Statements**
- Income Statement
- Statement of Changes in Owner's Equity
- Balance Sheet
- Statement of Cash Flows

▶ **Using the Information— Return on Equity**

▶ **Appendix 2A—Developing Accounting Standards**

Shoes on Trial

Vancouver, BC—Tucked along a harbourside street, **FastForward** could be another trendy sports shop. But its small back lot, where Chuck Taylor runs up grassy mounds, through sand pits, and in mud, makes clear this is something far different. These obstacles are product research tools.

FastForward consults on athletic footwear, a potentially hot, new service. In just one year, Chuck Taylor has become a sought-after consultant by sports clubs, schools and athletes. In the first six months of 1998, the company's profits are rising at a 35% rate.

FastForward's story is the envy of every entrepreneur. Taylor, 29, loved sports—but he hated his shoes. He never seemed to have the right shoes for the right conditions. Independent tests of shoe performance were either nonexistent or outdated. So in September 1997, Taylor had an idea. He went out and purchased 21 pair of the best basketball shoes on the market. He ran the shoes through a battery of tests under many different court conditions. The results shocked even him. Many lower-priced, less known shoes performed on par or better than many big ticket, big name shoes. He carried his findings to athletic teams and athletes. He got a welcome reception and payment for his services.

In November of 1997, Taylor quit his job to devote full time to his new business. "I instantly needed accounting skills to keep track of receipts, bills, everything," says Taylor. "When I later applied for a loan, the bank couldn't believe my poor accounting records. But what do you expect from a jock!" Taylor eventually cleaned up his accounting and got the loan. To boost growth, FastForward is now moving into testing of soccer, track and football shoes. "We are meeting a market need and making people happy," added Taylor. And you can count Taylor as one of the happy.

Learning Objectives

LO 1 Identify and explain the content and reporting aims of financial statements.

LO 2 Describe differences in financial statements across forms of business organization.

LO 3 Explain the roles of preparers, auditors and users of financial statements.

LO 4 Identify those responsible for setting accounting and auditing principles.

LO 5 Identify, explain and apply accounting principles.

LO 6 Analyze business transactions using the accounting equation.

LO 7 Prepare financial statements from business transactions.

LO 8 Compute the return on equity and use it to analyze company performance.

CHAPTER PREVIEW

Financial statements are one of the most important products of accounting. They are useful to both internal and external decision makers. Chuck Taylor of **FastForward** recognized the importance of accounting reports when running his own business and in applying for a loan. Financial statements are the way business people communicate. Knowledge of their preparation, organization and analysis is important.

In this chapter we describe the kind of information captured and revealed in financial statements. We also discuss the principles and assumptions guiding their preparation. This discussion includes the organizations that regulate and influence accounting. An important part of this chapter is to illustrate how transactions are reflected in financial statements and their implications for our analysis. This helps us see the immediate usefulness of financial statements. Special attention is devoted to a discussion of FastForward, whose first month's transactions are the focus of our analysis. We also explain return on equity, which is helpful in evaluating a company's operating success.

Communicating with Financial Statements

 Identify and explain the content and reporting aims of financial statements.

We discussed in Chapter 1 how accounting provides useful information to help people make better decisions. These decision makers include investors, lenders, managers, suppliers, customers and others. Many organizations report their accounting information to internal and external users in the form of financial statements. These statements are useful in revealing an organization's financial health and performance in a summarized and easy-to-read format. They give an overall view of an organization's financing, investing and operating activities. They also are the primary means of financial communication. Financial statements, however, are the end result of a process, or cycle, which begins with a business transaction, like a sale. These transactions are recorded, classified, sorted and summarized in order to produce the statements. In this chapter we follow this process in an informal manner so that you become familiar with the accounting cycle. In Chapter 3 we present the formal development of the accounting records that are used by businesses.

Previewing Financial Statements

There are four major financial statements: income statement, balance sheet, statement of changes in owner's equity, and statement of cash flows. We begin our study of these statements with a brief description of these statements. We cover all four statements in detail by the end of this chapter. The links in time among these statements is captured in Exhibit 2.1:

Exhibit 2.1

Links between Financial Statements

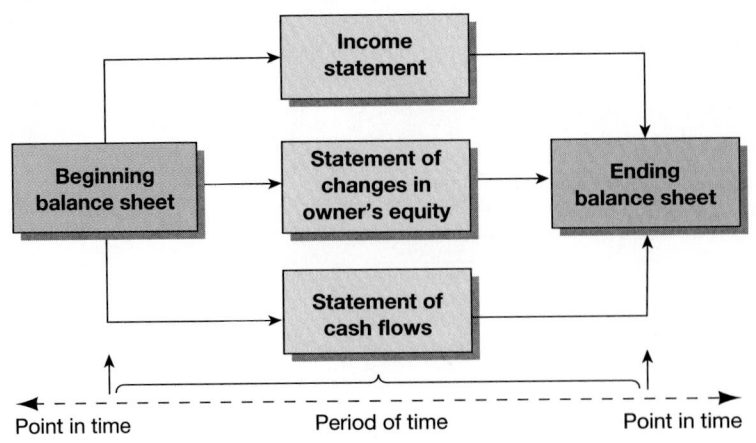

A balance sheet reports on an organization's financial position at a *point in time*. The income statement, statement of changes in owner's equity, and statement of cash flows report on performance over a *period of time*. These three statements in the middle column of the above diagram link balance sheets from the beginning to the end of a reporting period. They explain how the financial position of an organization changes from one point to another.

Selection of a reporting period is up to preparers and users (including regulatory agencies). A one-year, or annual, reporting period is common, as are semiannual, quarterly and monthly periods. Most large corporations issue quarterly statements, which investors eagerly await, as they impact on share prices. The one-year reporting period is also known as the accounting or *fiscal year.* Businesses whose accounting year begins on January 1 and ends on December 31 are known as *calendar year* companies. But many companies choose a fiscal year ending on other than December 31. **Alliance Communications** is a *non*calendar year company as reflected in the headings of its March 31st year-end financial statements. Some companies choose a fiscal year-end when sales and inventory are low. For example, **Suzy Shier's** fiscal year-end is February 1, after the holiday season.

Income Statement

An **income statement** reports revenues earned and expenses incurred by a business over a period of time. Expenses are subtracted from revenues on the income statement to show whether the business earns a profit, also called net income. A **net income** means revenues exceed expenses. A **net loss,** or simply loss, means expenses exceed revenues. An income statement tells us how well a company performs over a period of time.

The income statement for FastForward's first month of operations is shown in Exhibit 2.2. Notice an income statement does not simply report net income or net loss. It lists the types and amounts of both revenues and expenses. This is crucial information for users as it helps in understanding and predicting company performance. For example, **Laidlaw** classifies its revenues and expenses in three categories: passenger services, health-care transportation services and hazardous waste services. Also **Rogers** separates its revenues into three groups: cable television, wireless communications and multimedia. This information is more useful for making decisions than simply a profit or loss number.

FASTFORWARD Income Statement For Month Ended December 31, 1997		
Revenues:		
Consulting revenue	$3,800	
Rental revenue	300	
Total revenues		$4,100
Expenses:		
Rent expense	$1,000	
Salaries expense	700	
Total expenses.		1,700
Net income		$2,400

Exhibit 2.2

Income Statement for FastForward

Revenues

Revenues are inflows of assets in exchange for products and services provided to customers as part of the primary operations of a business.[1] Revenues also can arise from decreases in liabilities.[2] We can think of assets as economic resources owned by a business and liabilities as amounts owed. Later in the chapter, we will define these terms more precisely. The income statement in Exhibit 2.2 shows that Fast-

---

[1] Canadian Institute of Chartered Accountants *CICA Handbook* (Toronto), "Financial Statement Concepts," par. 1000.37.

[2] For example, a customer may pay for a product or service in advance which creates a liability for the firm to provide the product or service at a later date. When the product or service is delivered the liability is satisfied and the revenue is recognized.

Forward earned total revenues of $4,100 during December from consulting services and rental revenue. Examples of revenues for other businesses include sales of products and amounts earned from dividends and interest.

Expenses

Expenses are outflows or the using up of assets that result from providing products and services to customers.[3] Expenses also can arise from increases in liabilities.[4] The income statement in Exhibit 2.2 shows FastForward used up some of its assets in paying for rented store space. The $1,000 cost for store space is reported in the income statement as rent expense. FastForward also paid for an employee's wages at a cost of $700. This is reported on the income statement as salaries expense. Notice that the income statement heading in Exhibit 2.2 identifies the business, names the type of statement, and indicates the time period covered. Knowledge of the time period is important for us in judging whether the business' performance is satisfactory. In assessing whether FastForward's $2,400 net income is satisfactory, we must remember that it earned this amount during a one-month period.

You Make the Call

Employee
You are working at a restaurant and feel your wages are too low. You decide to ask the owner for a raise. How can you use the income statement of the business to justify your request?

Answer—p. 70

Exhibit 2.3

Statement of Changes in Owner's Equity for FastForward

Statement of Changes in Owner's Equity

The **statement of changes in owner's equity** reports on changes in equity over the reporting period. This statement starts with beginning equity and adjusts it for events that (1) increase it such as investments by the owner and net income, and (2) decrease it such as net loss and owner withdrawals.

FASTFORWARD Statement of Changes in Owner's Equity For Month Ended December 31, 1997		
C.Taylor, capital, December 1, 1997		$ -0-
Add: Investment by owner	$30,000	
Net income	2,400	32,400
Total		$32,400
Less: Withdrawal by owner		(600)
C.Taylor, capital, December 31, 1997		$31,800

The statement of changes in owner's equity for FastForward's first month of operations is shown in Exhibit 2.3. This statement describes events that changed owner's equity during the month. It shows $30,000 of equity created by Taylor's initial investment. It also shows $2,400 of net income earned during the month. The statement also reports Taylor's $600 withdrawal and FastForward's $31,800 equity balance at the end of the month.

Balance Sheet

The **balance sheet** reports the financial position of a business at a point in time (similar to a snapshot), often at the end of a month or year. Because of its emphasis on financial position it is also called the **statement of financial position.** The balance sheet describes financial position by listing the types and dollar amounts of assets, liabilities and equity for the business. Exhibit 2.4

---

[3] *CICA Handbook,* "Financial Statement Concepts," par. 1000.38

[4] The wages which employees earn are not usually paid until the end of the week or month. However, their labour is an expense and their wages owed, a liability.

shows the balance sheet for FastForward as of December 31, 1997. Unlike the income statement that refers to a period of time, the balance sheet describes conditions that exist at a point in time. The balance sheet heading lists the business, the statement, and the specific date on which assets and liabilities are identified and measured. The amounts in the balance sheet are measured as of the close of business on that specific date.

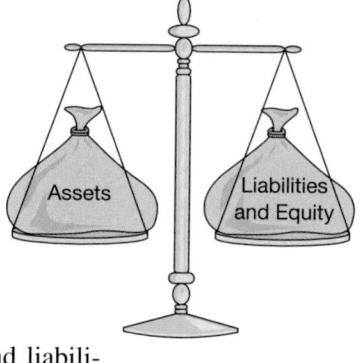

The balance sheet for FastForward shows it owns three different assets at the close of business on December 31, 1997. The assets are cash, supplies and equipment. The total dollar amount for these assets is $38,000. The balance sheet also shows total liabilities of $6,200. Owner's equity is $31,800. Equity is the difference between assets and liabilities. Notice the total amounts on each side of the balance sheet are equal. This equality is why the statement is named a *balance sheet*. This name also reflects the reporting of asset, liability and equity *balances* in the statement.

FASTFORWARD Balance Sheet December 31, 1997			
Assets		**Liabilities**	
Cash	$ 8,400	Accounts payable	$ 200
Supplies	3,600	Note payable	6,000
Equipment	26,000	Total liabilities	$ 6,200
		Owner's Equity	
		C. Taylor, capital	31,800
		Total liabilities and owner's equity	$38,000
Total assets	$38,000		

Exhibit 2.4

Balance Sheet for FastForward

Assets

Assets are the properties or economic resources owned by a business. A common characteristic of assets is their ability to provide future benefits to the business.[5] Assets are of many types. A familiar asset is *cash*. Another is accounts receivable. An **account receivable** is an asset created by selling products or services on credit. It reflects amounts owed to a business by its credit customers. These customers, and other individuals and organizations, who owe amounts to a business are called its **debtors.** Other common assets owned by businesses include merchandise held for sale, supplies, equipment, buildings and land. Assets also can be intangible rights, such as those granted by a patent or copyright.

Household Financial Assets		
Percent of Total	**1980**	**1996**
Savings	25%	17%
Stock	15	21
Mutuals	1	7
Pensions	15	25
Bonds	7	9
Insurance/Trusts	8	9
Farms/Businesses	29	12
Source: *Bank of Canada Review*, 1997.		

Personal Assets

Assets of Canadian households have more than tripled since 1980. But as Bay Street soars and inflation has cooled, the asset mix has changed. Where we once saw savings and money market accounts, we now see shares, mutual funds and pension assets.

Did You Know?

---

[5] *CICA Handbook*, "Financial Statement Concepts," par. 1000.29.

Liabilities

Liabilities are obligations of a business. They are claims of others against the assets of the business. A common characteristic of liabilities is their capacity to reduce future assets or to require future services or products.[6] Liabilities take many forms. Common liabilities are accounts payable and notes payable. An **account payable** is a liability created by buying products or services on credit. It reflects amounts owed to others. A **note payable** is a liability expressed by a written promise to make a future payment at a specific time. Other common liabilities are salaries and wages owed to employees, and interest payable.

Individuals and organizations who own the right to receive payments from a business are called its **creditors.** From a creditor's view, a business' liability is a creditor's asset. Creditors own the right to be paid by a business. One entity's payable is another entity's receivable. If a business fails to pay its obligations, the law gives creditors a right to force sale of its assets to obtain the money to meet their claims. When assets are sold under these conditions, creditors are paid first but only up to the amount of their claims. Any remaining money, or the residual, goes to the owner of the business. Creditors often use a balance sheet to help decide whether to loan money to a business. They compare the amounts of liabilities and assets. A loan is less risky if liabilities are small in comparison to assets. This is because there are more resources than claims on resources. A loan is more risky if liabilities are large compared to assets.

Equity

Equity is the owner's claim on the assets of a business. It is the *residual interest* in the assets of a business that remains after deducting liabilities.[7] Equity also is called **net assets.** Since FastForward is a sole proprietorship, the equity heading of its balance sheet in Exhibit 2.4 is *owner's equity*. If it was organized as a corporation, then its owners are shareholders and equity is called *shareholders' (or stockholders') equity*.

We explained that net income is the difference between revenues and expenses of a business over a period of time. Net income is also equal to the change in owner's

Exhibit 2.5

Flow of Money In and Out of Owner's Equity

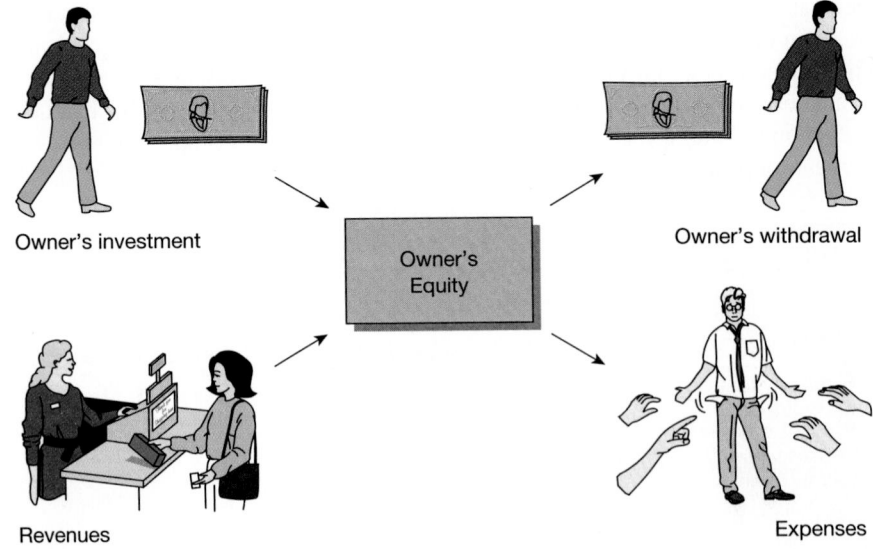

Owner's investment

Revenues

Owner's Equity

Owner's withdrawal

Expenses

---

[6] Ibid., par. 1000.32.

[7] Ibid., par. 1000.35.

equity due to operating activities over a period of time. In this way an income statement links balance sheets from the beginning and the end of a reporting period.

Owner's equity is increased by owner's investments and revenues. It is decreased by owner's withdrawals and expenses. Exhibit 2.5 shows these important relations. Owner's investments are assets put into the business by the owner. Owner's withdrawals are assets taken from the business by the owner. These changes in owner's equity are reported in the statement of changes in owner's equity and give us the ending balance of owner's equity. This ending balance is also reported in the balance sheet.

Statement of Cash Flows

The **statement of cash flows** describes the sources and uses of cash for a reporting period. It also reports the amount of cash at both the beginning and end of a period. The statement of cash flows is arranged by an organization's major activities: operating, investing and financing. Since a company must carefully manage cash if it is to survive and prosper, cash flow information is important.

FastForward's statement of cash flows for December is shown in Exhibit 2.6. The first section shows net cash outflows from operating activities equal to $100. This is the result of $4,100 of cash received from customers less $4,200 paid for supplies, rent and salaries. The second section reports on investing activities and shows a $20,000 cash outflow for purchase of equipment. The third section reports a $28,500 net cash inflow from financing activities. FastForward's financing activities included an owner investment, a loan repayment, and an owner withdrawal.

FASTFORWARD Statement of Cash Flows For Month Ended December 31, 1997		
Cash flows from operating activities:		
Cash received from clients	$4,100	
Cash paid for supplies	(2,500)	
Cash paid for rent	(1,000)	
Cash paid for employee salary	(700)	
Net cash used by operating activities		$ (100)
Cash flows from investing activities:		
Purchase of equipment	$(20,000)	
Net cash used by investing activities		(20,000)
Cash flows from financing activities:		
Investment by owner	$ 30,000	
Partial repayment of note	(900)	
Withdrawal by owner	(600)	
Net cash provided by financing activities		28,500
Net increase in cash		$ 8,400
Cash balance, December 1, 1997		-0-
Cash balance, December 31, 1997		$ 8,400

Exhibit 2.6

Statement of Cash Flows for FastForward

Financial Statements and Forms of Organization

There are three different forms of business organizations: proprietorships, partnerships, and corporations. Chapter 1 described many important differences between these forms of business organizations. Despite these differences, the financial statements for these organizations are very similar.

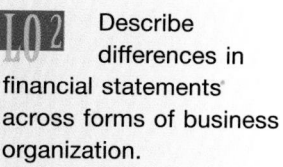

LO2 Describe differences in financial statements across forms of business organization.

Exhibit 2.7

Equity Section of a
Partnership Balance Sheet

FASTFORWARD
Partial Balance Sheet
December 31, 1997

Owner's Equity	
Chuck Taylor, Capital	$15,900
Jane Taylor, Capital	15,900
Total owner's equity	$31,800

Exhibit 2.8

Equity Section of a
Corporation Balance Sheet

FASTFORWARD
Partial Balance Sheet
December 31, 1997

Shareholder's Equity	
Contributed Capital:	
Common Shares	$30,000
Retained Earnings	1,800
Total shareholder's equity	$31,800

One important difference in financial statements is in the equity section of the balance sheet. A proprietorship's balance sheet lists the equity balance beside the owner's name as in Exhibit 2.4. Partnership balance sheets use the same approach, unless there are too many owners for their names to fit in the available space. For example, if Chuck Taylor is part of an equal partnership with his sister Jane in all aspects, then the equity section of the balance looks like Exhibit 2.7.

The names of a corporation's shareholders, however, are not listed in a balance sheet. Instead, equity is divided into **contributed capital** (also called **paid-in capital**) and retained earnings. Contributed capital reflects shareholders' investments. **Retained earnings** are the corporation's profits that have not been distributed to shareholders. For example, assume Chuck Taylor had set up FastForward as a corporation where he was the sole shareholder. If he is issued common shares for his $30,000 investment (called contributed capital), then the equity section of the balance would look as in Exhibit 2.8.

Retained earnings refers to a corporation's net income (loss) for all years' operations that is not distributed to shareholders. For FastForward, it earns $2,400, of which $600 is distributed to Taylor as a dividend, leaving $1,800 in retained earnings.

Notice the difference in the term used to describe distributions by a business to its owners. When an owner of a proprietorship or a partnership takes cash or other assets from a company, the distributions are called **withdrawals.** When owners of a corporation receive cash or other assets from a company, the distributions are called **dividends.** Withdrawals and dividends are not reported as part of an income statement because they are *not* expenses incurred to generate revenues.

Recording payments to managers when managers are also owners is another difference. When the owner of a proprietorship is its manager, no salary expense is reported on the income statement for these services. The same is true for a partnership. But since a corporation is a separate legal entity, salaries paid to its managers are always reported as expenses on its income statement. This different treatment of owners' salaries requires special consideration when analyzing an income statement. We explain one special adjustment for analysis purposes near the end of this chapter.

The emphasis in the early chapters of this book is on sole proprietorships. This allows us to focus on important measurement and reporting issues in accounting without getting caught up in the complexities of additional forms of organization. We do discuss other forms of organization and provide examples when appropriate. Chapters 14, 15 and 16 return to this topic and provide additional detail about the financial statements of partnerships and corporations.

Flashback

1. What are the four major financial statements?
2. Describe revenues and expenses.
3. Explain assets, liabilities and equity.
4. What are three differences in financial statements for different forms of organization?

Answers—p. 70

Financial Statements, Auditing and Users

Generally accepted accounting principles (GAAP) are developed in response to the needs of users. They also can change as users' needs change. We separate users into three groups in showing how people are affected by financial statements: preparers, auditors and decision makers. While accounting professionals prepare financial statements, independent auditors often examine them and prepare an audit report to give decision makers more assurance with the statements. Statements along with an audit report then are distributed to decision makers.

Exhibit 2.9 shows how accounting principles and auditing standards relate to the three groups comprising this reporting process. First, notice that GAAP are applied in preparing financial statements. Preparers use GAAP to decide what procedures are most appropriate in accounting for business transactions and events, and for proper reporting of statements. Second, notice that audits are performed in accordance with **generally accepted auditing standards (GAAS)**. GAAS are the accepted rules for conducting audits of financial statements. GAAS guide auditors in deciding on the audit procedures useful in determining whether financial statements comply with GAAP. Applying both GAAP and GAAS help assure users that financial statements include relevant, reliable and comparable information. An audit does not ensure that a user can safely invest in or loan to a business. It is not assurance of success, and does not reduce the risk that a company's products and services will be unsuccessful or that adverse factors will cause it to fail. Rather, it tells us that the statements are prepared using accepted accounting principles. **Price Waterhouse** says the following in its audit report of **Imperial Oil**:

> In our opinion, these consolidated financial statements present fairly, in all material respects ... in accordance with generally accepted accounting principles in Canada

LO 3   Explain the roles of preparers, auditors and users of financial statements.

AcSB   GAAP

Preparers   Financial statements

Auditors   Audit report

ASB   GAAS

Decision makers

Exhibit 2.9

Accounting, Auditing and Decision Makers

Generally Accepted Accounting Principles

We explained in Chapter 1 how financial accounting practice is governed by rules called *generally accepted accounting principles,* or *GAAP.* For us to use and interpret financial statements effectively, we need an understanding of these principles. A primary purpose of GAAP is to make information in financial statements relevant, reliable and comparable. Information that is relevant can affect decisions made by users. Reliable information is necessary for decision makers to depend on it. Information that is comparable allows users to compare companies. Comparisons are more likely to be useful if companies use similar practices. GAAP impose limits on the range of accounting practices companies can use. We describe in this section the current process for setting GAAP and some of the important accounting principles.

Setting Accounting Principles

LO 4 Identify those responsible for setting accounting and auditing principles.

GAAP were historically developed through common usage. A principle was acceptable if it was permitted by most professionals. This history is reflected in the phrase *generally accepted.* As business transactions became more complex, users were less satisfied with the lack of more concrete guidance. Many of these users desired more uniformity in practice. Authority for developing accepted principles was eventually assigned to a select group of professionals in the field. These committees or boards have authority to establish GAAP. The authority of these groups has increased over time. The **CICA Handbook** establishes GAAP in Canada.

We show two organizations in Exhibit 2.9 that are the primary authoritative sources of GAAP and GAAS. The CICA's Accounting Standards Board (AcSB) is the primary authoritative source of GAAP. We describe the present arrangement for establishing GAAP in Appendix 2A at the end of this chapter.

Authority for generally accepted auditing standards (GAAS) belongs to the CICA's **Auditing Standards Board (ASB).**[8]

International Accounting Principles

Today's global economy means that people in different countries increasingly do business with each other. It is common for companies in Canada to sell products and services around the world. We also see examples of companies in other countries such as Singapore selling their shares to Canadian, American and Japanese investors, and borrowing from lenders in places such as Saudi Arabia and Germany. **Novatel** is a Canadian company that designs and markets a broad range of products that determine precise geographic locations using the Global Positioning System (GPS). While most of Novatel's sales are in Canada and the U.S., they also sell to distributors in 30 different countries in Asia, Australia and Europe

Despite our growing global economy, countries continue to maintain their unique set of acceptable accounting practices. Consider one of the Singapore companies cited above. Should it prepare financial statements that comply with Singapore accounting standards or with the standards of Canada, the United States, Japan, Saudi Arabia or Germany? Should it prepare five different sets of reports to gain access to financial markets in all six countries? This is a difficult and pressing problem.

---

[8] Many other professional organizations support the CICA's Standards Boards and include the: Canadian Academic Accounting Association (CAAA), Canadian Council of Financial Analysts (CCFA), Certified General Accountants' Association of Canada (CGAAC), Financial Executives Association of Canada (FEAC), and Society of Management Accountants of Canada (SMAC).

World Prospects

Investors continue to increase their international investments. Nearly one-third of mutual fund investors now hold international securities. What do they see as the world regions that are the best bets for the future? A survey of investors shows that Europe is expected to do as well or better than domestic investments. The Pacific Basin, China and Japan are all being approached with caution but are attractive for the longer term. Africa and the Middle East fare the worst.

Source: Ross Laver, *Maclean's* (January 26, 1998).

Did You Know?

One response has been to create an **International Accounting Standards Committee (IASC).** The IASC issues *International Accounting Standards* that identify preferred accounting practices and it encourages their worldwide acceptance. By narrowing the range of alternative practices, the IASC hopes to create more harmony among accounting practices of different countries. If standards are harmonized, a single set of financial statements can be used by one company in all financial markets. Many countries' standard setters support the IASC. The CICA, SMAC and CGAAC provide support and technical assistance. Yet the IASC does not have authority to impose its standards on companies. While interest is growing in moving Canadian GAAP toward the IASC's preferred practices, authority to make such changes rests with the CICA.

Flashback

5. What organization sets GAAP and from where does it draw authority?

6. What is GAAS? What organization sets GAAS?

7. How are Canadian companies with international operations affected by International Accounting Standards?

Answers—p. 70

Fundamental Principles of Accounting

Accounting principles are both general and specific. General principles are the basic assumptions, concepts and guidelines for preparing financial statements. Specific principles are detailed rules used in reporting on business transactions and events. General principles stem from long-used accounting practices. Specific principles arise more often from the rulings of authoritative groups.

We need an understanding of both general and specific principles for effectively using accounting information. Because general principles are especially crucial in using accounting information, we emphasize them in the early chapters of this book. The general principles described in this chapter include: business entity, objectivity, cost, going-concern, monetary unit, and revenue recognition. General principles described in later chapters (with their relevant chapter in parentheses) include: time period (4), matching (4), materiality (9), full-disclosure (9), consistency (10), and conservatism (10). The specific principles are especially important for understanding individual items in financial statements and are portrayed as the "building blocks" for the "House of GAAP" illustrated in Exhibit 2.10. They are described throughout the book as we come to them.

LO 5 Identify, explain and apply accounting principles.

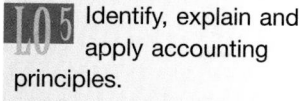 **Exhibit 2.10**

Building Blocks for the House of GAAP

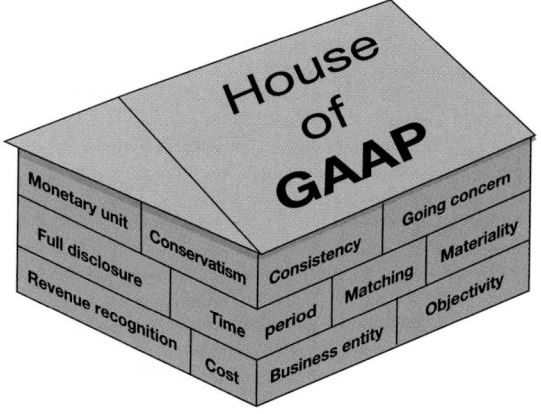

PRINCIPLE APPLICATION—
Business Entity Principle
George Weston Limited owns about 71% of **Loblaw Companies Limited** equity. Yet Loblaw Companies Limited accounts for its operations as a separate entity and prepares its own financial statements.

Business Entity Principle

The **business entity principle** means that a business is accounted for separately from its owner or owners. It also means we account separately for all businesses that are controlled by the same owner. The reason for this principle is that separate information about each business is relevant to the decisions of its users.

We use **FastForward** to illustrate the importance of the business entity principle. Suppose Chuck Taylor, the owner, wants to know how well the business is doing. For financial statements to address his need, FastForward's transactions must not be mixed with Taylor's personal transactions. For example, Taylor's personal expenses (such as a stereo or clothes) must not be subtracted from FastForward's revenues on its income statement because they are not incurred as part of FastForward's business. More generally, a company's statements must not reflect its owner's *personal* transactions, assets and liabilities. It also must not reflect the transactions, assets and liabilities of *another business*. Effective reports and decision making depend on businesses following the entity principle.

Did You Know?

Investment Ethics
Abuse of the business entity principle brought down a prominent fund manager at **AGF**. Veronica Hirsch was forced to resign over the issue of investing on behalf of herself instead of or in addition to the fund she was managing. The question is whether fund managers should be allowed to invest for their own account.
Source: *The Globe and Mail,* November 12, 1996, p. B2.

Objectivity Principle

The **objectivity principle** means that financial statement information is supported by independent, unbiased evidence. It involves more than one person's opinion. Information is not reliable if it is based only on what a preparer thinks might be true. A preparer can be too optimistic or pessimistic. An unethical preparer might even try to mislead users by intentionally misrepresenting the truth. The objectivity principle is intended to make financial statements useful by ensuring they report reliable and verifiable information.

Cost Principle

The **cost principle** means financial statements are based on actual costs incurred in business transactions. Business transactions are exchanges of economic consideration between two parties. Sales and purchases are examples of business transactions. Economic consideration can include products, services, money and rights to collect money. Cost is measured on a cash or cash equivalent basis. If cash is given for an asset or service, its cost is measured as the entire amount of cash paid. If something other than cash is exchanged (such as an older car traded for a new one), cost is measured as the cash equivalent value of what is given up or received, whichever is more evident.[9]

The cost principle is accepted by users because of its emphasis on reliability and relevance. Cost is the amount sacrificed to purchase an asset or service. It also approximates the market value of an asset or service when it is acquired. Most users consider information about the amount sacrificed and the initial market value of what is received as relevant. The cost principle also is consistent with *objectivity*. Most users consider information based on cost as objective. For example, reporting purchases of assets and services at cost is more objective than reporting a manager's estimate of their value.

We use FastForward to illustrate this principle. Suppose FastForward pays $5,000 for used equipment at an auction. The cost principle tells us to record this purchase at $5,000. It would make no difference if Chuck Taylor thinks this equipment is

---

[9] *CICA Handbook,* "Non-monetary Transactions," par. 3830.05.

really worth $7,000. The cost principle requires this purchase be recorded at a cost of $5,000. Later in this book we describe some cases where an *objective estimate* of value is reported instead of cost to improve the usefulness of information.

Going-Concern Principle

The **going-concern principle,** also called the **continuing-concern principle,** means financial statements reflect an assumption that the business continues operating instead of being closed or sold. This means that a balance sheet does not report liquidation values of operating assets held for long-term use. Instead, these assets are reported at cost. Many users believe the going-concern principle leads to reporting relevant information because many of their decisions about a business assume it continues to operate. Applying both the cost and going-concern principles implies that a balance sheet seldom reflects a company's exact worth. If a company is to be bought or sold, buyers and sellers are advised to obtain additional information from other sources.[10] Neither the going-concern principle nor the cost principle is appropriate if a company is expected to fail or be liquidated. Instead, estimated market values are relevant.

Monetary Unit Principle

The **monetary unit principle** means we can express transactions and events in monetary, or money, units. Money is the common denominator in business. Expressing transactions and events in money helps us communicate with financial statements in business. Examples of monetary units are the dollar in Canada, the United States, Australia and Singapore, pound sterling in the United Kingdom, and peso in Mexico, Philippines and Chile. An *exchange rate* expresses the value of one currency relative to another. Exhibit 2.11 is a partial listing of exchange rates in terms of Canadian dollars (as of July 1998):

Country	Canadian $ Equivalent	Country	Canadian $ Equivalent
United States (dollar)	.6782	Japan (yen)	94.607
Taiwan (dollar)	.0430	Mexico (peso)	6.053
United Kingdom (pound)	.4144	France (franc)	4.134

Exhibit 2.11

Exchange Rates

The monetary unit used by an organization usually depends on the country where it operates. But we are seeing more companies expressing financial statements in more than one monetary unit. For example, Microsoft, on its Web page (**http://www.microsoft.com**) provides its financial statements in several local languages, currencies and accounting conventions including those of Australia, Canada, France, Germany, the United Kingdom and the United States.

Accounting generally assumes a *stable* monetary unit. This means we expect the value of a currency to not change. The greater the changes in the monetary unit, the more difficult it is for us to use and interpret financial statements, especially across time.

Flashback

8. Why is the business entity principle important?

9. How are the objectivity and cost principles related?

Answers—p. 70

---

[10] *CICA Handbook,* "Financial Instruments" requires that the fair (market) value of financial assets and liabilities be disclosed as supplemental information, par. 3860.78.

Transactions and the Accounting Equation

 Analyze business transactions using the accounting equation.

Exhibit 2.12

The Accounting Equation

We know that financial statements reflect the business activities of a company. We also know that many of these activities, such as purchases and sales, involve business transactions. For us to fully reap the benefits of information in financial statements, we need to know how an accounting system captures relevant data about transactions, classifies and records data, and reports data in financial statements. This section begins us on an important path that continues through Chapter 5.

Exhibit 2.12 shows the basic tool of modern accounting systems, the accounting equation:

$$\text{Assets} = \text{Liabilities} + \text{Owner's Equity}$$

The **accounting equation** is also called the **balance sheet equation** because of its link to the balance sheet. Like any mathematical equation, the accounting equation can be modified by rearranging terms. Moving liabilities to the left side of the equality gives us an equation for owner's equity in terms of assets and liabilities:

$$\text{Assets} - \text{Liabilities} = \text{Owner's Equity}$$

We next show how to use the accounting equation to keep track of changes in a company's assets, liabilities and owner's equity in a way that provides us useful information.

Transaction Analysis—Part I

A **business transaction** is an economic event that changes the financial position of an organization. It often is an exchange of economic consideration between two parties. Examples of economic considerations include products, services, money and rights to collect money. Because two different parties exchange assets and liabilities, transactions affect the components of the accounting equation. It is important for us to realize that every transaction leaves the equation in balance. Assets *always* equal the sum of liabilities and equity. We show how this equality is preserved by looking at the transactions of **FastForward** in its first month of operations.

Transaction 1: Investment by Owner

On December 1, 1997, Chuck Taylor formed his athletic shoe consulting business. He set it up as a proprietorship. Taylor is the manager of the business as well as its owner. The marketing plan for the business is to primarily focus on consulting with schools, sports clubs and other groups who place relatively large orders of athletic shoes with manufactures. Taylor invested $30,000 cash in the new company and deposits it in a bank account opened under the name of Fast-Forward. After this transaction, the cash (an asset) and the owner's equity (called *C. Taylor, Capital*) each equal $30,000. The effect of this transaction on the accounting equation is:

Assets	=	Liabilities	+	Owner's Equity
Cash	=			**C. Taylor, Capital**
(1) +$30,000	=			+$30,000 Investment

Notice the accounting equation is in balance. The equation reveals that FastForward has one asset, cash, equal to $30,000. It also reveals no liabilities and an owner's equity of $30,000. The source of increase in equity is also identified as an investment to distinguish it from revenues.

Transaction 2: Purchase Supplies for Cash

FastForward uses $2,500 of its cash to purchase supplies of brand name athletic shoes for testing. This transaction is an exchange of cash, an asset, for another kind of asset, supplies. The transaction produces no expense because no value is lost. It merely changes the form of assets from cash to supplies. The decrease in cash is exactly equal to the increase in supplies. The equation remains in balance.

	Assets			=	Liabilities	+	Owner's Equity
	Cash	+	Supplies	=			C. Taylor, Capital
Old Bal.	$30,000			=			$30,000
(2)	−$2,500		+$2,500				
New Bal.	$27,500	+	$2,500	=			$30,000
		$30,000		=		$30,000	

Transaction 3: Purchase Equipment for Cash

FastForward spends $20,000 to acquire equipment for testing athletic shoes. Like transaction 2, transaction 3 is an exchange of one asset, cash, for another asset, equipment. It is not an expense because no value is lost. This purchase changes the makeup of assets but does not change the asset total. The equation remains in balance.

	Assets					=	Liabilities	+	Owner's Equity
	Cash	+	Supplies	+	Equipment	=			C. Taylor, Capital
Old Bal.	$27,500		$2,500			=			$30,000
(3)	−$20,000				+$20,000				
New Bal.	$7,500	+	$2,500	+	$20,000	=			$30,000
			$30,000			=		$30,000	

Transaction 4: Purchase Equipment and Supplies on Credit

Taylor decided he needed more testing equipment and supplies of brand name athletic shoes. These purchases total $7,100. But as we see from the accounting equation in transaction 3, FastForward has only $7,500 in cash. Concerned that these purchases would use nearly all of FastForward's cash, Taylor arranges to purchase them on credit from CanTech Supply Company. This means FastForward acquires these items in exchange for a promise to pay for them later. Supplies of athletic shoes cost $1,100, the new testing equipment costs $6,000, and the total liability to CanTech Supply is $7,100. The effects of this purchase on the accounting equation are:

	Assets					=	Liabilities			+	Owner's Equity
	Cash	+	Supplies	+	Equipment	=	Accounts Payable	+	Note Payable	+	C. Taylor, Capital
Old Bal.	$7,500		$2,500		$20,000	=					$30,000
(4)		+	1,100	+	6,000		+$1,100	+	6,000		
New Bal.	$7,500	+	$3,600	+	$26,000	=	$1,100	+	$6,000	+	$30,000
			$37,100			=		$37,100			

Notice this purchase increases assets by $7,100 while liabilities (called *accounts payable* and *note payable*) increased by the same amount. Both of these payables are promises by Taylor to repay its debt, where the note payable reflects a more formal agreement. We will discuss these liabilities in detail in later chapters.

Transaction 5: Services Rendered for Cash

A primary objective of a business is to increase its owner's wealth. This goal is met when a business produces a profit, also called *net income*. Net income is reflected in the accounting equation as an increase in owner's equity. FastForward earns revenues by consulting with clients about their test results on athletic shoes. FastForward earns a net income only if its revenues are greater than the expenses incurred in earning them. As we would expect, the process of earning consulting revenues and incurring expenses affects the accounting equation.

We see how the accounting equation is affected by earning consulting revenues in transaction 5. FastForward provided consulting services to a Vancouver athletic club on December 10 and immediately collects $2,200 cash. The accounting equation reveals this event increased cash by $2,200 and owners' equity by $2,200. This increase in equity is identified in the far right column as a revenue because it is earned by providing services. These explanations are useful in preparing and understanding a statement of changes in owner's equity and an income statement.

	Assets			=	Liabilities		Owner's Equity	
	Cash	+ Supplies	+ Equipment	=	Accounts Payable	+ Note Payable	+ C. Taylor, Capital	Explanation
Old Bal.	$7,500	+ $3,600	+ $26,000	=	$1,100	+ $6,000	+ $30,000	
(5)	+2,200						+ 2,200	Consulting Revenue
New Bal.	$9,700	+ $3,600	+ $26,000	=	$1,100	+ $6,000	+ $32,200	
		$39,300				$39,300		

Transactions 6 and 7: Payment of Expenses in Cash

FastForward paid $1,000 rent on December 10 to the landlord of the building where its store is located. Paying this amount allowed FastForward to occupy the space for the entire month of December. The effects of this event on the accounting equation are shown below as transaction 6. On December 12, FastForward paid the $700 salary of the company's only employee. This event is reflected in the accounting equation as transaction 7.

	Assets			=	Liabilities		Owner's Equity	
	Cash	+ Supplies	+ Equipment	=	Accounts Payable	+ Note Payable	+ C. Taylor, Capital	Explanation
Old Bal.	$9,700	+ $3,600	+ $26,000	=	$1,100	+ $6,000	+ $32,200	
(6)	−1,000						−1,000	Rent Expense
Bal.	$8,700	+ $3,600	+ $26,000	=	$1,100	+ $6,000	+ $31,200	
(7)	−700						−700	Salary Expense
New Bal.	$8,000	+ $3,600	+ $26,000	=	$1,100	+ $6,000	+ $30,500	
		$37,600				$37,600		

Both transactions 6 and 7 produce expenses for FastForward. They use up cash for the purpose of providing services to clients. Unlike the asset purchases in transactions 2 and 3, the cash payments in transactions 6 and 7 acquired services. The benefits of these services do not last beyond the end of this month. The accounting equation shows that both transactions reduce cash and Taylor's equity. The accounting equation remains in balance after each event. The far right column identifies these decreases as expenses. This information is valuable when the income statement is prepared and analyzed.

Summary of Part I Transactions

FastForward has net income when its revenues exceed its expenses. Net income increases owner's equity. If expenses exceed revenues, a net loss occurs and equity is decreased. Net income or loss is not affected by transactions between a business and its owner. This means Taylor's initial investment of $30,000 is not income to FastForward, even though it increased equity.

To stress that revenues and expenses yield changes in equity, we add revenues directly to owner's equity and subtract expenses directly from owner's equity. In practice and in later chapters, information about revenues and expenses is kept compiled separately and these amounts are added to or subtracted from owner's equity. We describe this process in Chapters 3 through 5. We now need to examine some important revenue transactions of FastForward. Because of the importance of properly recognizing revenues for a business, we interrupt our analysis of FastForward's transactions to describe the revenue recognition principle.

Flashback

10. How can a transaction not affect liability and equity accounts?

11. Describe a transaction increasing owner's equity and one decreasing it.

Answers—p. 70

Revenue Recognition Principle

Preparers need guidance in deciding when to recognize revenue. *Recognize* means to record a transaction or event for the purpose of reporting its effects in financial statements. If revenue is recognized too early, the income statement reports net income sooner than it should and the business looks more profitable than it is. If revenue is recognized late, the earlier income statement shows lower amounts of revenue and net income than it should and the business looks less profitable than it is. In both cases the income statement does not provide decision makers with the most useful information about company success.

The **revenue recognition principle** provides guidance on when revenue should be recognized on the income statement. Recognition is also sometimes called *realization*. The recognition principle includes three important guidelines:

1. *Revenue is recognized when earned.* The process of preparing to provide services, finding customers, and promoting sales contributes to earning revenue. Yet the revenue earned at any point in the process usually cannot be determined reliably until the process is complete. This does not occur until the business acquires the right to collect the selling price. This means revenue is usually not recognized on the income statement until the earnings process is complete. The earnings process is normally complete when services are rendered or the seller transfers ownership of products sold to the buyer. Suppose that a customer pays in advance of taking delivery of a product or service. Because the earnings process is not complete, the seller must not recognize revenue. The seller must complete the earnings process before recognizing revenue.[11] This practice is called *sales basis of revenue recognition*.

---

[11] *CICA Handbook*, "Revenue," par. 3400.06.09.

2. *Assets received from selling products and services do not have to be in cash.* A common noncash asset acquired by the seller in a revenue transaction is a customer's promise to pay at a future date. The seller views the customer's promise as an account receivable. These transactions are called *credit sales* and are often convenient for customers in purchasing products or services and paying for them later. FastForward did this in transaction 4 when it bought supplies and equipment on credit. If objective evidence shows that a seller has earned the right to collect from a customer, this seller should recognize an account receivable as an asset and record revenue earned. When cash is collected later, no additional revenue is recognized. Collecting the cash simply changes the makeup of assets from a receivable to cash.

3. *Revenue recognized is measured by cash received plus the cash equivalent (market) value of other assets received.* This means, for example, if a transaction creates an account receivable, the seller recognizes revenue equal to the value of the receivable which usually is the amount of cash expected to be collected.

Notes to financial statements should include an explanation of the revenue recognition method used by a company. **Canadian Tire** reports in its 1997 annual report that "the Corporation's shipments of merchandise to Associate Dealers (retail store owner-operators) are recorded as revenue when delivered."

Transaction Analysis—Part II

We return to the transactions of FastForward to show how revenue recognition works in practice.

Transaction 8: Services and Rental Rendered for Credit

FastForward provided consulting services of $1,600 and rental of test facilities for $300 to a college sports team. The rental involved allowing selected team members to try recommended shoes at FastForward's testing grounds. The sports team is billed for $1,900. This transaction results in a new asset, account receivable from client. The $1,900 increase in assets produces an equal increase in owner's equity. Notice the increase in equity is identified as two revenue components in the far right column of the accounting equation:

		Assets				=	Liabilities			+	Owner's Equity	
	Cash	+ Accounts Receivable	+	Supplies	+ Equipment	=	Accounts Payable	+ Note Payable	+	C. Taylor, Capital	Explanation
Old Bal.	$8,000		+	$3,600	+ $26,000	=	$1,100	+ $6,000	+	$30,500	Consulting
(8)		+ $1,900							+	1,600	Revenue
									+	300	Rental Revenue
New Bal.	$8,000	+ $1,900	+	$3,600	+ $26,000	=	$1,100	+ $6,000	+	$32,400	
			$39,500					$39,500			

Transaction 9: Receipt of Cash on Account

The amount of $1,900 is received from the client 10 days after being billed for consulting services in transaction 8. Transaction 9 does not change the amount of assets and does not affect liabilities or equity. It converts the receivable to cash. It does not create new revenue. Revenue was recognized when FastForward rendered the services, not when the cash is now collected. This emphasis on the earnings process instead of cash flows is a goal of the revenue recognition principle and provides relevant information to users. The new balances are:

		Assets			=	Liabilities		+	Owner's Equity
	Cash	+ Accounts Receivable	+ Supplies	+ Equipment	=	Accounts Payable	+ Note Payable	+	C. Taylor, Capital
Old Bal.	$8,000	+ $1,900	+ $3,600	+ $26,000	=	$1,100	+ $6,000	+	$32,400
(9)	+1,900	−1,900							
New Bal.	$9,900	+$ -0-	+ $3,600	+ $26,000	=	$1,100	+ $6,000	+	$32,400
			$39,500				$39,500		

Transaction 10: Payment of Note Payable

FastForward pays $900 to CanTech Supply on December 24. The $900 payment is for the earlier $6,000 purchase of testing equipment from CanTech, leaving $5,100 unpaid. The $1,100 amount due CanTech for supplies remains unpaid. The accounting equation shows this transaction decreases FastForward's cash by $900 and decreases its liability to CanTech Supply by the same amount. As a result, owner's equity does not change. This event does not create an expense even though cash flowed out of FastForward.

		Assets			=	Liabilities		+	Owner's Equity
	Cash	+ Accounts Receivable	+ Supplies	+ Equipment	=	Accounts Payable	+ Note Payable	+	C. Taylor, Capital
Old Bal.	$9,900	+ $ -0-	+ $3,600	+ $26,000	=	$1,100	+ $6,000	+	$32,400
(10)	− 900						− 900		
New Bal.	$9,000	+ $ -0-	+ $3,600	+ $26,000	=	$1,100	+ $5,100	+	$32,400
			$38,600				$38,600		

Transaction 11: Withdrawal of Cash by Owner

Taylor withdrew $600 in cash from FastForward for personal living expenses. A proprietorship's distribution of cash, or other assets, to its owner is called a *withdrawal*. This decrease in owner's equity is not an expense. Withdrawals are not expenses because they are not part of the company's earnings process. Since withdrawals are not expenses, they are not used in calculating net income.

		Assets			=	Liabilities		+	Owner's Equity	Explanation
	Cash	+ Accounts Receivable	+ Supplies	+ Equipment	=	Accounts Payable	+ Note Payable	+	C. Taylor, Capital	
Old Bal.	$9,000	+ $ -0-	+ $3,600	+ $26,000	=	$1,100	+ $5,100	+	$32,400	
(11)	− 600								− 600	Withdrawal
New Bal.	$8,400	+ $ -0-	+ $3,600	+ $26,000	=	$1,100	+ $5,100	+	$31,800	
			$38,000				$38,000			

Summary of Transactions

FastForward engaged in transactions with five major entities: the owner, suppliers, an employee, customers and the landlord. We identify the specific transactions by number with the specific entity in Exhibit 2.13.

Exhibit 2.13

FastForward's Transactions
Grouped by Entities

We also summarize in Exhibit 2.14 the effects of all 11 transactions of FastForward using the accounting equation. Three points should be noted. First, the accounting equation remains in balance after every transaction. Second, transactions can be analyzed by their effects on components of the accounting equation. For example, total assets and equity increased by equal amounts in transactions 1, 5 and 8. In transactions 2, 3 and 9, one asset increased while another decreased by equal amounts. For transaction 4, we see equal increases in assets and a liability. Both assets and equity decrease by equal amounts in transactions 6, 7 and 11. In transaction 10, we see equal decreases in an asset and a liability. Third, the equality of effects in the accounting equation is fundamental to the double entry accounting system. We discuss this system in the next chapter.

FAST Forward

Exhibit 2.14

Summary
Analysis of
Transactions of
FastForward
Using the
Accounting
Equation

			Assets			=	Liabilities		+	Owner's Equity	
		Cash	+ Accounts Receivable	+ Supplies +	Equipment =		Accounts Payable	+ Note Payable	+	C. Taylor, Capital	Explanation
(1)		$ 30,000								$30,000	Investment
(2)		− 2,500		+ $ 2,500							
Bal.		$ 27,500		$2,500						$30,000	
(3)		−20,000			+ $20,000						
Bal.		$ 7,500		$ 2,500	$20,000					$30,000	
(4)				+ 1,100	+ 6,000		+ $1,100	+ $6,000			
Bal.		$ 7,500		$ 3,600	$26,000		$1,100	$6,000		$30,000	Consulting
(5)		+ 2,200								+ 2,200	Revenue
Bal.		$9,700		$ 3,600	$26,000		$1,100	$6,000		$32,200	
(6)		− 1,000								− 1,000	Rent Expense
Bal.		$8,700		$ 3,600	$26,000		$1,100	$6,000		$31,200	
(7)		− 700								− 700	Salary Expense
Bal.		$8,000		$ 3,600	$26,000		$1,100	$6,000		$30,500	Consulting
(8)			+ $1,900							+ 1,600	Revenue
										+ 300	Rental Revenue
Bal.		$8,000	$1,900	$ 3,600	$26,000		$1,100	$6,000		$32,400	
(9)		+ 1,900	− 1,900								
Bal.		$9,900	$ -0-	$ 3,600	$26,000		$1,100	$6,000		$32,400	
(10)		− 900							− 900		
Bal.		$9,000	$ -0-	$ 3,600	$26,000		$1,100	$5,100		$32,400	
(11)		− 600								− 600	Withdrawal
Bal.		$8,400 +	$ -0-	+ $ 3,600 +	$26,000	=	$1,100 +	$5,100 +		$31,800	
				$38,000				$38,000			

Flashback

12. Why is the revenue recognition principle important?

13. Identify a transaction decreasing both assets and liabilities.

14. When is the accounting equation in balance and what does it mean?

Answers—p. 70

Mid-Chapter Demonstration Problem

Bob Delgado began a new moving firm on May 1. The accounting equation showed the following balances after each of the company's first four transactions. Analyze the equations and describe each of the four transactions with their amounts.

Transaction	Cash	+	Accounts Receivable	+	Truck	+	Office Furniture	=	Accounts Payable	+	B. Delgado, Capital
A	$10,000		$ -0-		$45,000		$ -0-		$ -0-		$55,000
B	10,000		-0-		45,000		5,000		5,000		55,000
C	10,000		4,000		45,000		5,000		5,000		59,000
D	14,000		-0-		45,000		5,000		5,000		59,000

Solution to Mid-Chapter Demonstration Problem

A. Started the business by investing $10,000 cash and a $45,000 truck.

B. Purchased office furniture for $5,000 on account.

C. Billed a customer $4,000 for services.

D. Collected $4,000 from the customer in C.

Financial Statements

We described the major financial statements at the beginning of this chapter. These statements are required under GAAP. In this section we show how financial statements are prepared from business transactions. Recall that the four major financial statement and their purposes are:

1. *Income statement.* It describes a company's revenues and expenses along with the resulting net income or loss over a period of time. It helps explain how owner's equity changes during a period due to earnings activities.

2. *Statement of changes in owner's equity.* It explains changes in equity due to items such as net income, and investments and withdrawals by an owner over a period of time.

3. *Statement of cash flows.* It identifies cash inflows (receipts) and outflows (payments) over a period of time. It explains how the cash balance on the balance sheet changed from the beginning to the end of a period.

4. *Balance sheet.* It describes a company's financial position (assets, liabilities and equity) at a point in time.

We show how to prepare these financial statements using the transactions of Fast-Forward in the next chapter.

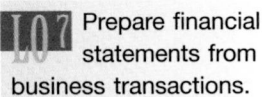

Prepare financial statements from business transactions.

Income Statement

FastForward's income statement is shown at the top of Exhibit 2.15. It is prepared from the December transactions of FastForward. These transactions and information about revenues and expenses are conveniently taken from the owner's equity column of Exhibit 2.14.

Exhibit 2.15

FastForward Financial Statements

FASTFORWARD Income Statement For Month Ended December 31, 1997		
Revenues:		
Consulting revenue	$3,800	
Rental revenue	300	
Total revenues		$4,100
Expenses:		
Rent expense	$1,000	
Salaries expense	700	
Total expenses		1,700
Net income		$2,400

FASTFORWARD Statement of Changes in Owner's Equity For Month Ended December 31, 1997		
C.Taylor, capital, December 1, 1997		$ -0-
Plus: Investment by owner	$30,000	
Net income	2,400	32,400
Total		$32,400
Less: Withdrawal by owner		600
C.Taylor, capital, December 31, 1997		$31,800

FASTFORWARD Balance Sheet December 31, 1997			
Assets		**Liabilities**	
Cash	$ 8,400	Accounts payable . . . . $	1,100
Supplies	3,600	Note payable	5,100
Equipment	26,000	Total liabilities	$6,200
		Owner's Equity	
		C.Taylor, capital	31,800
		Total liabilities and	
Total assets	$38,000	owner's equity	$38,000

FASTFORWARD Statement of Cash Flows For Month Ended December 31, 1997		
Cash flows from operating activities:		
Cash received from clients.	$4,100	
Cash paid for supplies	(2,500)	
Cash paid for rent	(1,000)	
Cash paid to employee	(700)	
Net cash used by operating activities		$ (100)
Cash flows from investing activities:		
Purchase of equipment	$(20,000)	
Net cash used by investing activities.		(20,000)
Cash flows from financing activities:		
Investment by owner.	$30,000	
Partial repayment of note.	(900)	
Withdrawal by owner.	(600)	
Net cash provided by financing activities		28,500
Net increase in cash.		$8,400
Cash balance, December 1, 1997		-0-
Cash balance, December 31, 1997		$8,400

Revenues of $4,100 are reported first on the income statement. They include consulting revenues of $3,800 resulting from transactions 5 and 8, and rental revenue of $300 from transaction 8. If FastForward earned other kinds of revenues, they would be listed separately to help users better understand the company's activities. Expenses follow revenues. We can list expenses in different ways. For convenience in this chapter, we list larger amounts first. Rent and salaries expenses are from transactions 6 and 7. Expenses help users interpret events of the time period. Net income is reported at the bottom and is the amount earned during December. Owner's investments and withdrawals are *not* part of measuring income.

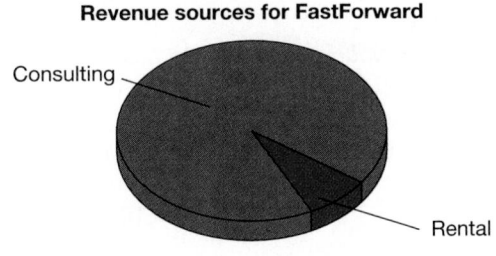

Revenue sources for FastForward

Consulting

Rental

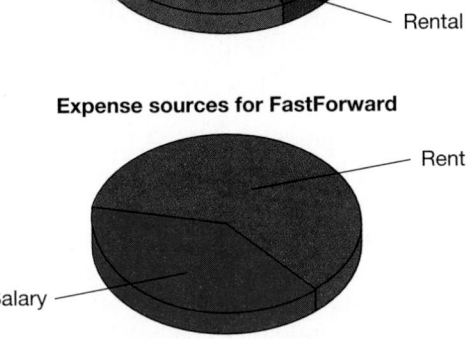

Expense sources for FastForward

Rent

Salary

Exhibit 2.16

Pie Chart Analysis of Revenues and Expenses

Pie charts shown in Exhibit 2.16 are often helpful in analyzing the make up of revenues and expenses.

Statement of Changes in Owner's Equity

The statement of changes in owner's equity reports information about changes in equity over the reporting period. This statement shows beginning equity, events that increase it (such as investments by owner and net income), and events that decrease it (such as withdrawals and net loss). Ending owner's equity is computed from this statement and is carried over and reported on the balance sheet.

The second report in Exhibit 2.15 is the statement of changes in owner's equity for FastForward. Its heading lists the month of December 1997 because this statement describes events that happened during that month. The beginning balance of equity is measured as of the start of business on December 1. It is zero because FastForward did not exist before then. An existing business reports the beginning balance as of the end of the prior reporting period (such as November 30 for a continuing business). FastForward's statement shows $30,000 of equity is created by Taylor's initial investment. It also shows the $2,400 of net income earned during the month. This item links the income statement to the statement of changes in owner's equity. The statement also reports Taylor's $600 withdrawal and FastForward's $31,800 equity balance at the end of the month.

Balance Sheet

FastForward's balance sheet is the third report listed in Exhibit 2.15. This is the same statement we described in Exhibit 2.4. Its heading tells us the statement refers to FastForward's financial condition at the close of business on December 31, 1997.

The left side of the balance sheet lists FastForward's assets: cash, supplies and equipment. The right side of the balance sheet shows FastForward owes $6,200 to creditors. This is made up of $1,100 for accounts payable and $5,100 for a note payable. If any other liabilities had existed (such as a bank loan) they would be listed here. The equity section shows an ending balance of $31,800. Note the link between the ending balance from the statement of changes in owner's equity and the equity balance of the capital account. Also, note that the balance sheet equation, Assets = Liabilities + Owner's Equity, is still true ($38,000 = $6,200 + $31,800).

Supplier
You open your own wholesale business selling home entertainment equipment to small retail outlets. You quickly find that most of your potential customers demand to buy on credit. How can you use the customers' balance sheets in deciding to which customers you wish to extend credit?

Answer—p. 70

Statement of Cash Flows

The final report in Exhibit 2.15 is FastForward's statement of cash flows. This statement describes where FastForward's cash came from and where it went during December. It also shows the amount of cash at the beginning of the period, and how much is left at the end. This information is important for users because a company must carefully manage cash if it is to survive and grow. **Canadian Airlines** reported net losses of $378.7 million for the two-year period ending December 31, 1996. But Canadian has avoided bankruptcy by carefully managing its cash by delaying spending, increasing borrowings, and issuing shares. Canadian Airlines earned a 1997 third quarter profit of $106.4 million and a net income of $39.2 million for the nine months ended September 30, 1997.

Cash Flows from Operating Activities

The first section of the statement of cash flows reports cash flows from *operating* activities. The $4,100 of cash received from customers equals total revenue on the income statement only because FastForward collected all of its revenues in cash. If credit sales are not collected, or if credit sales from a prior period are collected this period, the amount of cash received from customers does not equal the revenues reported on the income statement for this period.

This first section also lists cash payments for supplies, rent and salaries. These cash flows are from transactions 2, 6 and 7. We put these amounts in parentheses to indicate they are subtracted. Amounts for rent and salaries equal the expenses on FastForward's income statement only because it paid expenses in cash.

The payment for supplies is an operating activity because they are expected to be used up in short-term operations. We explain this idea more completely in Chapter 19. Cash used by operating activities for December is $100. If cash received exceeds cash paid for operating activities, we would call it "cash from operating activities." Decision makers are especially interested in the operating section of the statement of cash flows. This information allows users to answer questions such as how much of operating income is in the form of cash.

Cash Flows from Investing Activities

The second section of the statement of cash flows describes *investing activities.* Investing activities involve the buying and selling of assets such as land and equipment that are held for long-term use in the business. FastForward's only investing activity is the $20,000 purchase of equipment in transaction 3. Notice no cash flows are reported for transaction 4, which is a credit purchase.

Decision makers are interested in the investing section of the statement because it describes how a company is preparing for its future. If it is spending cash on productive assets, it should be able to grow. But a user is also concerned that a company does not spend too much on productive assets and face a cash shortage. If a company is selling its productive assets, it is downsizing its operations. Information in the investing section helps users answer these and other questions.

Cash Flows from Financing Activities

The third section of this statement shows cash flows related to *financing activities.* Financing activities include borrowing and repaying cash from lenders, and cash investments or withdrawals by the owner. The statement of cash flows in Exhibit 2.15 shows FastForward received $30,000 from Chuck Taylor's initial investment in transaction 1. If the business had borrowed cash, its amount would appear here as an increase in cash. The financing section also shows $900 paid to CanTech Supply for the note from transaction 10 and the $600 owner withdrawal in transaction 11. The total effect of financing activities was a $28,500 net inflow of cash.

The information in the financing section shows us why FastForward did not run out of cash even though it spent $20,000 on assets and used $100 in its operating activities. Namely, it used the owner's investment and a note from a supplier. Decision makers are interested in the financing section. This is because financing sources of cash can affect future profits. Excessive borrowing can burden a company with too much debt and reduce its potential for growth.

The final part of the statement of cash flows is the net increase or decrease in cash. It shows FastForward increased its cash balance by $8,400 in December. Because it started with no cash, the ending balance is also $8,400. This end amount is the link from the statement of cash flows to the balance sheet. We give a more detailed explanation of the statement of cash flows in Chapter 19.

Flash back

15. Explain the link between an income statement and the statement of changes in owner's equity.

16. Describe the link between a balance sheet and the statement of changes in owner's equity.

17. Discuss the three major sections of the statement of cash flows.

Answers—p. 71

Return on Equity

USING THE INFORMATION

LO 8 Compute return on equity and use it to analyze company performance.

An important reason for recording and reporting information about assets, liabilities, equity and income is to help an owner judge the company's success compared to other opportunities or investments. One measure of success is the **return on equity ratio** (see Exhibit 2.17). This ratio is computed by taking net income for a period and dividing it by the average owner's equity:

$$\text{Return on equity} = \frac{\text{Net income}}{\text{Average owner's equity}}$$

Chuck Taylor's return on equity is computed by taking the $2,400 of net income and dividing by average owner's equity of $30,900.[12] This shows Taylor earned a return on equity of 7.8% for the month of December.

Taylor's return for December is very high compared to most investments, especially for the first month of operations. But we must remember that net income for a proprietorship does not include an expense for the effort exerted by the owner in managing its operations. Because of this we can compute a

Exhibit 2.17

Return on Equity

---

[12] A simple average equals the sum of beginning and ending balances divided by two, or ($30,000 + $31,800)/2. Since this is FastForward's first month of operations, we use the owner's initial investment as its beginning balance.

modified return on equity for proprietorships and partnerships. This modified return on equity reduces net income by the value of the owner's efforts and is computed as shown in Exhibit 2.18.

Exhibit 2.18
Modified Return on Equity

$$\text{Modified return on equity} = \frac{\text{Net income} - \text{Value of owner's efforts}}{\text{Average owner's equity}}$$

Other employment opportunities suggest that Taylor's efforts are valued at $1,800 per month. Taylor's modified return on equity is then computed as $600 divided by average owner's equity of $30,900, or 1.9%. The $600 is calculated from $2,400 less $1,800. This modified return for Taylor of 1.9% per month is quite different from the 7.8% above.

Taylor should compare his return with other investment alternatives to determine whether this return is adequate. Examples of investment alternatives are savings accounts, government bonds, company stock, and other business ventures. Because 1.9% per month is more than 20% per year, it is likely Taylor will continue to operate FastForward. For further comparison, we graph in Exhibit 2.19 the return on equity for seven different industries. FastForward's return exceeds each of these.

Three further points need mentioning. First, an evaluation of returns should also recognize risk. Risk can differ considerably across investment alternatives. Second, income can fluctuate from month to month. This income fluctuation is related to risk. Third, because of company, business and economic fluctuations, we often get a better measure of return by computing it over a longer period such as one year. Finally, we have not yet captured all the earnings activities of FastForward for December. Chapters 3 and 4 identify additional revenues and expenses for the month.

Exhibit 2.19
Return on Equity for Selected Industries

Flash back

18. Explain how the owner of a sole proprietorship uses return on equity.

19. How do we assess whether a return is adequate?

Answers—p. 71

Summary

LO1 **Identify and explain the content and reporting aims of financial statements.** The major financial statements are: income statement, balance sheet, statement of changes in owner's equity, and statement of cash flows. An income statement shows a company's profitability including revenues, expenses and net income (loss). A balance sheet reports on a company's financial position including assets, liabilities and owner's equity. A statement of changes in owner's equity explains how owner's equity changes from the beginning to the end of a period, and the statement of cash flows identifies all cash inflows and outflows for the period.

LO2 **Describe differences in financial statements across forms of business organization.** One important difference is in the equity section of the balance sheet. A proprietorship's and partnership's balance sheet lists the equity balance beside the owner's name. Names of a corporation's shareholders are not listed in a balance sheet. Another difference is with the term used to describe distributions by a business to its owners. When an owner of a proprietorship or a partnership takes cash or other assets from a company, the distributions are called withdrawals. When owners of a corporation receive cash or other assets from a company, the distributions are called dividends. Recording payments to managers when managers are also owners is another difference. When the owner of a proprietorship or partnership is its manager, no salary expense is reported. But since a corporation is a separate legal entity, salaries paid to its managers are always reported as expenses on its income statement.

LO3 **Explain the roles of preparers, auditors and users of financial statements.** Accounting professionals prepare financial statements, independent auditors often examine them and prepare an audit report, and users rely on them for making important decisions. Preparers use GAAP to decide what procedures are most appropriate in accounting for business transactions and events, and for proper reporting of statements. GAAS guide auditors in deciding on the audit procedures useful in determining whether financial statements comply with GAAP. Applying both GAAP and GAAS help assure users that financial statements include relevant, reliable and comparable information to the users.

LO4 **Identify those responsible for setting accounting and auditing principles.** The CICA's AcSB is the primary authoritative source of GAAP. The AcSB draws its authority from the Canada Business Corporations Act. Authority for GAAS belongs to the ASB. The OSC is an important source of the ASB's authority.

LO5 **Identify, explain and apply accounting principles.** Accounting principles aid in producing relevant, reliable and comparable information. The general principles described in this chapter include: business entity, objectivity, cost, going-concern, monetary unit, and revenue recognition. We will discuss others in later chapters. The business entity principle means that a business is accounted for separately from its owner. The objectivity principle means information is supported by independent, objective evidence. The cost principle means financial statements are based on actual costs incurred in business transactions. The monetary unit principle assumes transactions and events can be captured in money terms and that the monetary unit is stable over time. The going-concern principle means financial statements reflect an assumption that the business continues operating. The revenue recognition principle means revenue is recognized when earned, that assets received from selling products and services do not have to be in cash, and that revenue recognized is measured by cash received plus the cash equivalent (market) value of other assets received.

LO6 **Analyze business transactions using the accounting equation.** A transaction is an exchange of economic consideration between two parties. Examples of economic considerations include products, services, money and rights to collect money. Because two different parties exchange assets and liabilities, transactions affect the components of the accounting equation. The accounting equation is: Assets = Liabilities + Owner's Equity. Business transactions always have at least two effects on the components of the accounting equation. The equation is always in balance when business transactions are properly recorded.

LO7 **Prepare financial statements from business transactions.** Business transactions can be summarized using the accounting equation. Once transaction data are organized by the accounting equation we can readily prepare the financial statements. The balance sheet uses the ending balances in the accounting equation at a point in time. The statement of changes in owner's equity and the income statement use data from the owner's equity account for the period. The statement of cash flows uses the numbers in the cash account for the period.

LO8 **Compute the return on equity and use it to analyze company performance.** Return on equity is computed as net income divided by average owner's equity. A modified return on equity for proprietorships and partnerships, that values the owner's efforts, is often useful and is computed as net income less the value of the owner's efforts and this quantity divided by average owner's equity. We should compare return with other investment alternatives and opportunities to determine whether it is adequate. We should also remember that income can fluctuate and is related to risk.

Guidance Answers to **You Make the Call**

Employee

An employee's efforts are often reflected in the income statement. This statement reports information on the revenues and expenses associated with operating activities. If operating activities are successful and the employee can point to specific contributions such as increased sales or reduced expenses, then the employee is much more likely to be successful in getting a wage increase.

Supplier

We can use the accounting equation to help us identify risky customers to whom we would not want to extend credit. The accounting equation is: Assets − Liabilities = Owner's Equity. A balance sheet provides us with amounts for each of these key components. The lower the owner's equity, the less likely you should be to extend credit. A low owner's equity means there is little value in the business that does not already have claims on it from other creditors. Note that any decision to grant credit would normally include an examination of the complete financial statements.

Guidance Answers to **Flash backs**

1. The four major financial statements are: income statement, balance sheet, statement of owner's equity, and statement of cash flows.

2. Revenues are inflows of assets in exchange for products or services provided to customers as part of the primary operations of a business. Revenues also can arise from decreases in liabilities. Expenses are outflows or the using up of assets that result from providing products or services to customers. Expenses also can arise from increases in liabilities.

3. Assets are the properties or economic resources owned by a business. Liabilities are the obligations of a business, representing the claims of others against the assets of a business. Equity is the owner's claim on the assets of the business. It is the owner's residual interest in the assets of a business after deducting liabilities.

4. Three differences are: (i) A proprietorship's balance sheet lists the equity balance beside the owner's name. Partnerships use the same approach, unless there are too many owners for listing purposes. Names of a corporation's owners, or shareholders, are not listed in the balance sheet. (ii) Distributions of cash or other assets to owners of a proprietorship or partnership are called withdrawals. Distributions of cash or other assets to owners of a corporation are called dividends. Neither withdrawals nor dividends are reported as part of an income statement. (iii) When the owner of a single proprietorship is also its manager, no salary expense is reported on the income statement. The same is true for a partnership. But salaries paid to a corporation's managers are always reported as expenses on its income statement.

5. The AcSB sets GAAP. Its recommendations are reported in the *CICA Handbook*. The AcSB draws authority from two main sources: Canada Business Corporations Act and the provincial bodies that license public accountants.

6. GAAS refer to generally accepted auditing standards and are the guidelines for performing audits of financial statements. GAAS are set by the Auditing Standards Board (ASB).

7. Canadian companies with international operations are not directly affected by International Accounting Standards. International standards are put forth as preferred accounting practices. However, there is growing pressure by stock exchanges and other parties to narrow differences in worldwide accounting practices. International Accounting Standards are playing an important role in that process.

8. Users desire information about the performance of a specific entity. If information is mixed between two or more entities, its usefulness decreases. It is important for the usefulness of accounting that the business entity principle be followed.

9. The objectivity principle means that financial statement information is supported by independent, unbiased evidence. The cost principle means financial statements are based on actual costs incurred in business transactions. The objectivity and cost principles are related in that most users consider information based on cost as objective. Information prepared using both principles is considered highly reliable and often relevant.

10. A transaction that changes the makeup of assets would not affect any liability and equity accounts. Both transactions 2 and 3 offer examples. Each involve changing the form of one asset for another asset.

11. Performing services for a customer such as in transaction 5 increases the owner's equity (and assets). Incurring expenses while servicing clients such as in transactions 6 and 7 decrease the owner's equity (and assets). Other examples include owner investments that increase equity, and owner withdrawals that decrease equity.

12. The revenue recognition principle give preparers guidelines on when to recognize (record) revenue. This is important since if revenue is recognized too early, the income statement reports net income sooner than it should and the business looks more profitable than it is. If revenue is recognized too late, the income statement shows lower amounts of revenue and net income than it should and the business looks less profitable than it is. In both cases the income statement is less useful to users.

13. Payment of a liability with an asset reduces both asset and liability totals. An example is transaction 10 where an account payable is settled by paying cash.

14. The accounting equation is: Assets = Liabilities + Owner's Equity. This equation is always in balance, both

before and after every transaction. Balance refers to the equality in this equation and it is always maintained.

15. An income statement describes a company's revenues and expenses along with the resulting net income or loss. A statement of changes in owner's equity describes changes in equity that include net income. Also, both statements report transactions occurring over a period of time.

16. A balance sheet describes a company's financial position (assets, liabilities and equity) at a point in time. The owner's equity account in the balance sheet is obtained from the statement of changes in owner's equity.

17. The statement of cash flows reports cash inflows and outflows in three sections involving operating, investing and financing activities. Cash flows from operating activities include revenues and expenses from the primary business the company is engaged in. Cash flows from investing activities involve transactions from the buying and selling of assets. Cash flows from financing activities include borrowing cash or other assets from lenders and the investments or withdrawals of the owner. The net figure in the statement of cash flows is the increase or decrease in cash for the business over the period. This net figure links the statement of cash flows to the balance sheet.

18. An owner of a proprietorship uses return on equity to measure the success of the business. This return is compared to alternative investment opportunities an owner could engage in. If the owner also works in the business, a modified return on equity is appropriate. This modified return subtracts the value of the owner's effort from net income in the numerator of the return on equity formula.

19. The return should be compared with other investment alternatives to determine whether it is adequate. Investment alternatives include savings accounts, government bonds, stocks, and other business ventures. These alternatives should be compared on the basis of both return and risk.

Demonstration Problem

After several months of planning, Barbara Schmidt started a haircutting business called The Cutlery. The following events occurred during its first month:

a. On August 1, Schmidt put $3,000 cash into a chequing account in the name of The Cutlery. She also invested $15,000 of equipment that she already owned.

b. On August 2, paid $600 cash for furniture for the shop.

c. On August 3, paid $500 cash to rent space in a strip mall for August.

d. On August 4, furnished the shop by installing the old equipment and some new equipment that was purchased on credit for $1,200. This amount is to be repaid in three equal payments at the end of August, September, and October.

e. On August 5, The Cutlery opened for business. Receipts from services provided for cash in the first week and a half of business (ended August 15) were $825.

f. On August 15, Schmidt provided haircutting services on account for $100.

g. On August 17, Schmidt received a $100 cheque in the mail for services previously rendered on account.

h. On August 17, paid $125 to an assistant for working during the grand opening.

i. Cash receipts from services provided during the second half of August were $930.

j. On August 31, Schmidt paid a $400 installment on the account payable.

k. On August 31, withdrew $900 cash for her personal use.

Required

1. Arrange the following asset, liability, and owner's equity titles in a table similar to the one in Exhibit 2.14: Cash, Accounts Receivable, Furniture, Store Equipment, Accounts Payable, and Barbara Schmidt, Capital. Show the effects of each transaction on the equation. Explain each of the changes in owner's equity.

2. Prepare an income statement for August.

3. Prepare a statement of changes in owner's equity for August.

4. Prepare a balance sheet as of August 31.

5. Prepare a statement of cash flows for August.

6. Determine the return on equity ratio for August.

7. Determine the modified return on equity ratio for August, assuming that Schmidt's management efforts were worth $1,000.

Planning the Solution

■ Set up a table with the appropriate columns, including a final column for describing the events that affect owner's equity.

■ Analyze each transaction and show its effects as increases or decreases in the appropriate columns. Be sure that the accounting equation remains in balance after each event.

■ To prepare the income statement, find the revenues and expenses in the last column. List those items on the statement, calculate the difference, and label the result as *net income* or *net loss*.

■ Use the information in the Explanation of Change column to prepare the statement of changes in owner's equity.

■ Use the information on the last row of the table to prepare the balance sheet.

■ To prepare the statement of cash flows, include all events listed in the Cash column of the table. Classify each cash flow as operating, investing, or financing. Follow the example in Exhibit 2-15.

■ Calculate the return on equity by dividing net income by the beginning equity. Calculate the modified return by subtracting the $1,000 value of Schmidt's efforts from the net income, and then dividing the difference by the beginning equity.

Solution to Demonstration Problem

1.

	Assets				= Liabilities +	Owner's Equity	
	Cash +	Accounts + Receivable	Furni- + ture	Store = Equip- ment	Accounts + Payable	Barbara Schmidt, Capital	Explanation of Change
a.	$3,000			$15,000		$18,000	Investment
b.	− 600		+$600				
Bal.	$2,400		$600	$15,000		$18,000	
c.	− 500					− 500	Rent Expense
Bal.	$1,900		$600	$15,000		$17,500	
d.				+ 1,200	+$1,200		
Bal.	$1,900		$600	$16,200	$1,200	$17,500	
e.	+ 825					+ 825	Haircutting Services Revenue
Bal.	$2,725		$600	$16,200	$1,200	$18,325	
f.		+$100				+ $100	Haircutting Services Revenue
Bal.	$2,725	$100	$600	$16,200	$1,200	$18,425	
g.	+ 100	−$100					
Bal.	$2,825	$-0-	$600	$16,200	$1,200	$18,425	
h.	− 125					− 125	Salaries Expense
Bal.	$2,700		$600	$16,200	$1,200	$18,300	
i.	+ 930					+ 930	Haircutting Services Revenue
Bal.	$3,630		$600	$16,200	$1,200	$19,230	
j.	− 400				− 400		
Bal.	$3,230		$600	$16,200	$800	$19,230	
k.	− 900					− 900	Withdrawal
Bal.	$2,330 +		$600 +	$16,200 =	$800 +	$18,330	

2.

THE CUTLERY Income Statement For Month Ended August 31		
Revenues:		
Haircutting Services Revenue		$1,855
Operating expenses:		
Rent expense	$500	
Salaries expense	125	
Total operating expenses		625
Net income		$1,230

3.

THE CUTLERY Statement of Changes in Owner's Equity For Month Ended August 31		
Barbara Schmidt, capital, August 1		$ -0-
Plus: Investments by owner	$18,000	
Net income	1,230	19,230
Total		$19,230
Less: Withdrawals by owner		(900)
Barbara Schmidt, capital, August 31		$18,330

4.

THE CUTLERY Balance Sheet August 31			
Assets		**Liabilities**	
Cash	$ 2,330	Accounts payable	$ 800
Furniture	600	**Owner's Equity**	
Store equipment	16,200	Barbara Schmidt, capital	18,330
		Total liabilities and	
Total assets	$19,130	owner's equity.	$19,130

5.

THE CUTLERY
Statement of Cash Flows
For Month Ended August 31

Cash flows from operating activities:		
Cash received from customers	$1,855	
Cash paid for rent	(500)	
Cash paid for wages	(125)	
Net cash provided by operating activities . . .		$1,230
Cash flows from investing activities:		
Cash paid for furniture		(600)
Cash flows from financing activities:		
Cash received from owner	$3,000	
Cash paid to owner	(900)	
Repayment of debt	(400)	
Net cash provided by financing activities . . .		1,700
Net increase in cash		$2,330
Cash balance, August 1		-0-
Cash balance, August 31		$2,330

6.

$$\text{Return on equity } = \frac{\text{Net income}}{\text{Average owner's equity}} = \frac{\$1,230}{\$18,165} = 6.77\%$$

Average owner's equity is ($18,000 + $18,330)/2 = $18,165

7.

$$\text{Modified return on equity} = \frac{\text{Net income} - \text{Owner's efforts}}{\text{Average owner's equity}} = \frac{\$1,230 - \$1,000}{\$18,165} = 1.27\%$$

Developing Accounting Standards

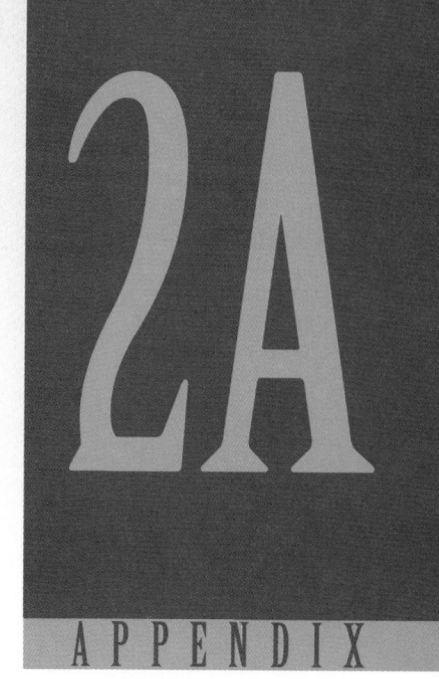

Generally accepted accounting principles are not natural laws like the laws of physics or other sciences. Instead, GAAP are identified in response to the needs of users and others affected by accounting. Thus, GAAP are subject to change as needs change.

Three groups of people are most directly affected by financial reporting: preparers, auditors, and users. Exhibit 2A.1 shows the relationship between the financial statements and these groups.

Private accountants prepare the financial statements. To give users more confidence in the statements, independent auditors usually examine the financial statements and develop an audit report. The statements and the audit report are then distributed to the users.

Learning Objective

LO 9 Describe the process by which generally accepted accounting principles are established.

Accounting Principles, Auditing Standards, and Financial Accounting

Exhibit 2A.1

The Relationship between Financial Statements and the Three Groups Affected by Them

How Accounting Principles Are Established

Exhibit 2A.2 expands this diagram to show how accounting principles and auditing standards relate to the financial reporting process. First, in Exhibit 2A.2, we show that GAAP are applied in preparing the financial statements. Preparers use GAAP to decide what procedures to follow as they account for business transactions and put the statements together.

Second, in Exhibit 2A.2, we show that audits are performed in accordance with generally accepted auditing standards (GAAS) which are developed by the CICA's Auditing Standards Board (ASB). GAAS are the rules adopted by the accounting profession as guides for conducting audits of financial statements. GAAS provide a framework for auditors to properly assess whether the financial statements comply with GAAP.

Applying both GAAP and GAAS assures users that financial statements include relevant, reliable, and comparable information. The audit does not, however, ensure that users can safely invest in or lend to the company. The audit

Exhibit 2A.2

Generally Accepted
Accounting Principles
(GAAP), Generally Accepted
Auditing Standards (GAAS),
and the Groups That
Participate in Financial
Accounting

does not reduce the risk that the company's products and services will not be successfully marketed or that other internal or external factors, such as the loss of a key executive, could cause it to fail.

In Exhibit 2A.2, we also identify the two organizations that are the primary authoritative sources of GAAP and GAAS. The primary authoritative source of GAAP is the Accounting Standards Board (AcSB). The board members, supported by a research staff, use their collective knowledge to identify problems in financial accounting and to find ways to solve them. The board also seeks advice from groups and individuals affected by GAAP. The advice comes via comments on the board's "exposure drafts" on specific issues. The finalized recommendations are published as part of the *CICA Handbook*.

The Accounting Standards Board gains its authority from both law and the members of the Canadian Institute of Chartered Accountants. Under the regulations of the Canada Business Corporations Act, the accounting standards for external reporting set out in the *CICA Handbook* have the force of law. Also, in 1969 the CICA adopted paragraph 1500.06, which states:

> Where the accounting treatment or statement presentation does not follow the recommendations of this Handbook, the practice used should be explained in notes to the financial statements with an indication of the reason why the recommendation concerned was not followed.

A number of other professional organizations support the Accounting Standards Board's process by providing input. In summary, the Accounting Standards Board's job is to improve financial reporting while balancing the interests of the affected groups.

International Accounting Standards

In today's world, people in different countries engage in business with each other more easily than in the past. A company in Canada might sell its products all over the world. Another company in Singapore might raise cash by selling shares to Canadian and Japanese investors. At the same time, it might borrow from creditors in Saudi Arabia and Germany.

An increasing number of companies have international operations. For example, **Four Seasons Hotels Inc.,** is a Canadian company with operations in lodging and contract services. Most of the company's operations are in the United States. However, the company also manages properties in the West Indies, New Zealand, Thailand, Hong Kong, Malaysia, England, Australia, Fiji, Singapore, and Taiwan. It also has properties under construction or development in Germany, Hawaii, and the Czech Republic.

Accounting organizations from around the world responded to this problem of internationalizing accounting standards by creating the International Accounting Standards Committee (IASC) in 1973. With headquarters in London, the IASC issues International Accounting Standards that identify preferred accounting practices and then encourages their worldwide acceptance. By narrowing the range of alternative practices, the IASC hopes to create more harmony among the accounting practices of different countries. If standards could be harmonized, a single set of financial statements could be used by one company in all financial markets.

In many countries, the bodies that set accounting standards have encouraged the IASC to reduce the differences. The CICA's Accounting Standards Committee has provided this encouragement and technical assistance. However, the IASC does not have the authority to impose its standards on companies. Although progress has been slow, interest is growing in moving Canadian GAAP toward the IASC's preferred practices.

Flashback

20. Which body currently establishes generally accepted accounting principles in Canada? (a) the Ontario Securities Commission, (b) Parliament, (c) the AcSB, or (d) The IASC.

21. What is the difference between GAAP and GAAS?

22. Is it true that Canadian companies with operations in foreign countries are required to prepare their financial statements according to the rules established by the IASC?

Answers—p. 77

Summary of Appendix 2A

LO 9 **Describe the process by which generally accepted accounting principles are established.** Specific accounting principles for financial accounting are established in Canada by the Accounting Standards Board (AcSB), with input from various interested parties. Auditing standards are established by the Auditing Standards Board (ASB), another committee of the Canadian Institute of Chartered Accountants (CICA). The International Accounting Standards Committee (IASC) identifies preferred practices and encourages their adoption throughout the world.

Guidance Answers to Appendix Flashbacks

20. *c*

21. GAAP are the Generally Accepted Accounting Principles and GAAS are the Generally Accepted Auditing Standards.

22. Although companies are not required to adhere to the International Accounting Standards, the AcSB encourages companies to provide financial statements which do comply with the IASs.

Glossary

Accounting equation A description of the relationship between a company's assets, liabilities, and equity; expressed as Assets = Liabilities + Owner's Equity; also called the *balance sheet equation*. (p. 56)

Account payable A liability created by buying goods or services on credit. (p. 48)

Account receivable An asset created by selling products or services on credit. (p. 47)

Auditing Standards Board (ASB) The authoritative committee of the CICA that identifies generally accepted auditing standards. (p. 52)

Assets Properties or economic resources owned by the business; more precisely, resources with an ability to provide future benefits to the business. (p. 47)

Balance sheet A financial statement that reports a position of a business at a point in time; lists the types and dollar amounts of assets, liabilities, and equity as of a specific date; also called the *statement of financial position*. (p. 46)

Balance sheet equation Another name for the *accounting equation*. (p. 56)

Business entity principle The principle that requires every business to be accounted for separately from its owner or owners; based on the goal of providing relevant information about each business to users. (p. 54)

Business transaction An economic event that changes the financial position of an organization; often takes the form of an exchange of economic consideration (such as goods, services, money, or rights to collect money) between two parties. (p. 56)

CICA Handbook The publication of the CICA that establishes generally accepted accounting principles in Canada. (p. 52)

Continuing-concern principle Another name for the *going-concern principle*. (p. 55)

Contributed capital The category of equity created by the shareholders' investments; also called *paid-in capital*. (p. 50)

Cost principle The accounting principle that requires financial statement information to be based on actual costs incurred in business transactions; it requires assets and services to be recorded initially at the cash or cash equivalent amount given in exchange. (p. 54)

Creditors Individuals or organizations entitled to receive payments from a company. (p. 48)

Debtors Individuals or organizations that owe amounts to a business. (p. 47)

Dividends Distributions of assets by a corporation to its owners. (p. 50)

Equity The owner's claim on the assets of a business; more precisely, the residual interest in the assets of an entity that remains after deducting its liabilities; also called *net assets*. (p. 48)

Expenses Outflows or the using up of assets as a result of the major or central operations of a business; also, liabilities may be increased. (p. 46)

Financial statements The most important products of accounting; include the balance sheet, income statement, statement of changes in owner's equity, and the statement of cash flows. (p. 44)

Generally accepted auditing standards (GAAS) Rules adopted by the accounting profession as guides for conducting audits of financial statements. (p. 51)

Going-concern principle The rule that requires financial statements to reflect the assumption that the business will continue operating instead of being closed or sold, unless evidence shows that it will not continue; also called *continuing-concern principle*. (p. 55)

International Accounting Standards Committee (IASC) A committee that attempts to create more harmony among the accounting practices of different countries by identifying preferred practices and encouraging their worldwide acceptance. (p. 53)

Income statement The financial statement that shows whether the business earned a profit by subtracting expenses from revenues; it lists the types and amounts of revenues earned and expenses incurred by a business over a period of time. (p. 45)

Liabilities The obligations of a business; claims by others which will reduce the future assets of a business or require future services or products. (p. 48)

Modified return on equity The ratio of net income minus the value of owner's effort to average owner's equity. (p. 68)

Monetary unit principle The expression of transactions and events in money units; examples include units such as the dollar, peso, and pound sterling. (p. 55)

Net assets Another name for *equity*. (p. 48)

Net income The excess of revenues over expenses for a period. (p. 45)

Net loss The excess of expenses over revenues for a period. (p. 45)

Note payable A liability expressed by a written promise to make a future payment at a specific time. (p. 48)

Objectivity principle The accounting guideline that requires financial statement information to be supported by independent, unbiased evidence rather than someone's opinion; objectivity adds to the reliability, verifiability, and usefulness of accounting information. (p. 54)

Paid-in capital Another name for *contributed capital*. (p. 50)

Retained earnings The shareholders' equity that results from a corporation's profits that have not been distributed to shareholders. (p. 50)

Return on equity ratio The ratio of net income to average owners' equity; used to judge a business's success compared to other activities or investments. (p. 67)

Revenue recognition principle Provides guidance on when revenue should be reflected on the income statement; the rule includes three guidelines (1) requires revenue to be recognized at the time it is earned, (2) allows the inflow of assets associated with revenue to be in a form other than cash, and (3) measures the amount of revenue as the cash plus the cash equivalent value of any noncash assets received from customers in exchange for goods or services. (p. 59)

Revenues Inflows of assets received in exchange for goods or services provided to customers as part of the major or primary operations of the business; may occur as inflows of assets or decreases in liabilities. (p. 45)

Statement of cash flows A financial statement that describes the sources and uses of cash for a reporting period, i.e., where a company's cash came from (receipts) and where it went during the period (payments); the cash

flows are arranged by an organization's major activities: operating, investing, and financing activities. (p. 49)

Statement of changes in owner's equity Reports the changes in equity over the reporting period; beginning equity is adjusted for increases such as owner investment or net income and for decreases such owner withdrawals or a net loss. (p. 46)

Statement of financial position Another name for the *balance sheet*. (p. 46)

Withdrawal The distribution of cash or other assets from a proprietorship or partnership to its owner or owners. (p. 50)

Questions

1. What information is presented in an income statement?
2. What do accountants mean by the term *revenue*?
3. Why does the user of an income statement need to know the time period that it covers?
4. What information is presented in a balance sheet?
5. Define (a) assets, (b) liabilities, (c) equity, and (d) net assets.
6. Identify two categories of generally accepted accounting principles.
7. What CICA publication identifies generally accepted accounting principles?
8. What does the objectivity principle require for information presented in financial statements? Why?
9. A business shows office stationery on the balance sheet at its $430 cost, although it cannot be sold for more than $10 as scrap paper. Which accounting principle justifies this treatment?
10. Why is the revenue recognition principle needed? What does it require?
11. What events or activities change owner's equity?
12. Identify four financial statements that a business presents to its owners and other users.

13. What should a company's return on equity ratio be compared with to determine whether the owner has made a good investment?
14. Find the financial statements of **Alliance Communications Corp.**, in Appendix I. To what level of significance are the dollar amounts rounded? What time period does the income statement cover?
15. Review the balance sheet of **Atlantis Communications Inc.** in Appendix I. What is the amount of total assets reported at December 31, 1997? Prove the accounting equation for Atlantis for December 31, 1997.
16. Review FastForward's financial statements presented in the chapter for the year ended December 31, 1997. Review the balance sheet and determine the business form Chuck Taylor has chosen to organize his business. How much cash did FastForward generate from the total of its operating, investing, and financing activities in 1997?

Name the financial statement on which each of the following items appears:

a. Office supplies
b. Service fees earned
c. Cash received from customers
d. Owner, withdrawals

e. Office equipment
f. Accounts payable
g. Repayment of bank loan
h. Utilities expense

Quick Study

QS 2-1
Identifying financial statement items

Identify which broad accounting principle describes most directly each of the following practices:

a. Tracy Regis owns Second Time Around Clothing and also owns Antique Accents, both of which are sole proprietorships. In having financial statements prepared for the antique store, Regis should be sure that the revenue and expense transactions of Second Time Around are excluded from the statements.

b. In December, 19X1, Classic Coverings received a customer's order to install carpet and tile in a new house that would not be ready for completion until March 19X2. Classic Coverings should record the revenue for the order in March 19X2, not in December 19X1.

c. If $30,000 cash is paid to buy land, the land should be reported on the purchaser's balance sheet at $30,000 although the purchaser was offered $35,000 the following week.

QS 2-2
Identifying accounting principles

QS 2-3

Applying the accounting equation

LO 6

Determine the missing amount for each of the following equations:

	Assets	=	Liabilities	+	Owner's Equity
a.	$ 75,000		$ 40,500		?
b.	$300,000		?		$ 85,500
c.	?		$187,500		$ 95,400

QS 2-4

Applying the accounting equation

LO 6

Use the accounting equation to determine:

a. The owner's equity in a business that has $374,700 of assets and $252,450 of liabilities.

b. The liabilities of a business having $150,900 of assets and $126,000 of owner's equity.

c. The assets of a business having $37,650 of liabilities and $112,500 of owner's equity.

QS 2-5

Computing Return on equity

LO 8

In its 1996 financial statements, Air Canada reported the following:

Sales and other operating revenues	$4,880 million
Net earnings (net income)	149 million
Total assets	5,386 million
Total beginning-of-year shareholders' equity	833 million
Total end-of-year shareholders' equity	985 million

Calculate the return on equity.

Exercises

Exercise 2-1

Effects of transactions on the accounting equation

LO 5,6

The following equation shows the effects of five transactions on the assets, liabilities, and owner's equity of Pace Design. Write short descriptions of the probable nature of each transaction.

	Cash	+	Accounts Receivable	+	Office Supplies	+	Land	=	Accounts Payable	+	C. Pace Capital
	$7,500				$2,500		$14,500				$24,500
a.	−3,000						+3,000				
	$4,500				$2,500		$17,500				$24,500
b.					+ 400				+$400		
	$4,500				$2,900		$17,500		$400		$24,500
c.			+$1,050								+ 1,050
	$4,500		$1,050		$2,900		$17,500		$400		$25,550
d.	− 400								−400		
	$4,100		$1,050		$2,900		$17,500		$ -0-		$25,550
e.	+1,050		−1,050								
	$5,150	+	$ -0-	+	$2,900	+	$17,500	=	$ -0-	+	$25,550

Carter Stark began a new consulting firm on January 3. The accounting equation showed the following balances after each of the company's first five transactions. Analyze the equations and describe each of the five transactions with their amounts.

Exercise 2-2
Analyzing the accounting equation

LO 6

Trans-action	Cash	+	Accounts Receivable	+	Office Supplies	+	Office Furniture	=	Accounts Payable	+	C. Stark, Capital
a.	$30,000		$ -0-		$ -0-		$ -0-		$ -0-		$30,000
b.	29,000		-0-		1,750		-0-		750		30,000
c.	21,000		-0-		1,750		8,000		750		30,000
d.	21,000		2,000		1,750		8,000		750		32,000
e.	20,500		2,000		1,750		8,000		750		31,500

A business had the following amounts of assets and liabilities at the beginning and end of a recent year:

Exercise 2-3
Determining net income

LO 1, 5

	Assets	Liabilities
Beginning of the year	$ 75,000	$30,000
End of the year	120,000	46,000

Determine the net income earned or net loss incurred by the business during the year under each of the following unrelated assumptions:

a. The owner made no additional investments in the business and withdrew no assets during the year.

b. The owner made no additional investments in the business during the year but withdrew $1,750 per month to pay personal living expenses.

c. The owner withdrew no assets during the year but invested an additional $32,500 cash.

d. The owner withdrew $1,750 per month to pay personal living expenses and invested an additional $25,000 cash in the business.

Linda Champion began a professional practice on May 1 and plans to prepare financial statements at the end of each month. During May, Champion completed these transactions:

Exercise 2-4
The effects of transactions on the accounting equation and return on equity

LO 6, 8

a. Invested $50,000 cash and equipment that had a $10,000 fair market (cash equivalent) value.

b. Paid $1,600 rent for office space for the month.

c. Purchased $12,000 of additional equipment on credit.

d. Completed work for a client and immediately collected $2,000 cash.

e. Completed work for a client and sent a bill for $7,000 to be paid within 30 days.

f. Purchased $8,000 of additional equipment for cash.

g. Paid an assistant $2,400 as wages for the month.

h. Collected $5,000 of the amount owed by the client described in transaction *e*.

i. Paid for the equipment purchased in transaction *c*.

j. Withdrew $500 for personal use.

Required

Create a table like the one in Exhibit 2.14, using the following headings for the columns: Cash; Accounts Receivable; Equipment; Accounts Payable; and L. Champion, Capital. Then, use additions and subtractions to show the effects of the transactions on the elements of the equation. Show new totals after each transaction. Determine the modified return on Champion's initial investment, assuming that her management efforts during the month have a value of $3,000.

Check Figure Net income, $5,000

Exercise 2-5
The effects of
transactions on the
accounting equation

LO 6

Following are seven pairs of changes in elements of the accounting equation. Provide an example of a transaction that creates the described effects:

a. Decreases a liability and increases a liability.
b. Increases an asset and decreases an asset.
c. Decreases an asset and decreases equity.
d. Increases a liability and decreases equity.
e. Increases an asset and increases a liability.
f. Increases an asset and increases equity.
g. Decreases an asset and decreases a liability.

Exercise 2-6
Income statement

LO 1,7

On November 1, Joseph Grayson organized a new consulting firm called The Grayson Group. On November 30, the company's records showed the following items. Use this information to prepare a November income statement for the business.

Cash..................	$12,000	Owner's withdrawals.......	$ 3,360
Accounts receivable.......	15,000	Consulting fees earned.....	15,000
Office supplies...........	2,250	Rent expense............	2,550
Automobiles.............	36,000	Salaries expense	6,000
Office equipment	28,000	Telephone expense........	660
Accounts payable........	7,500	Miscellaneous expenses	680
Owner's investments	84,000		

Check Figure Net income,
$5,110

Exercise 2-7
Statement of changes in
owner's equity

LO 1,7

Use the facts in Exercise 2-6 to prepare a November statement of changes in owner's equity for The Grayson Group.

Exercise 2-8
Balance sheet

LO 1,7

Use the facts in Exercise 2-6 to prepare a November 30 balance sheet for The Grayson Group.

Exercise 2-9
Information in financial
statements

LO 1

Match each of these numbered items with the financial statement or statements on which it should be presented. Indicate your answer by writing the letter or letters for the correct statement in the blank space next to each item.

A. Income statement
B. Statement of changes in owner's equity
_____ 1. Cash received from customers
_____ 2. Office supplies
_____ 3. Rent expense paid in cash
_____ 4. Consulting fees earned and received as cash

C. Balance sheet
D. Statement of cash flows
_____ 5. Accounts payable
_____ 6. Investments of cash by owner
_____ 7. Accounts receivable
_____ 8. Cash withdrawals by owner

Exercise 2-10
Missing information

LO 1

Calculate the amount of the missing item in each of the following independent cases:

	a	b	c	d
Owner's equity, January 1	$ -0-	$ -0-	$ -0-	$ -0-
Owner's investments during the year ...	120,000	?	63,000	75,000
Owner's withdrawals during the year ...	?	(54,000)	(30,000)	(31,500)
Net income (loss) for the year	31,500	81,000	(9,000)	?
Owner's equity, December 31	102,000	99,000	?	85,500

Match each of these numbered descriptions with the term it best describes. Indicate your answer by writing the letter for the correct principle in the blank space next to each description.

A. Broad principle

B. Cost principle

C. Business entity principle

D. Revenue recognition principle

E. Specific principle

F. Objectivity principle

G. Going-concern principle

_____ **1.** Requires every business to be accounted for separately from its owner or owners.

_____ **2.** Requires financial statement information to be supported by evidence other than someone's opinion or imagination.

_____ **3.** Usually created by a pronouncement from an authoritative body.

_____ **4.** Requires financial statement information to be based on costs incurred in transactions.

_____ **5.** Derived from long-used accounting practices.

_____ **6.** Requires financial statements to reflect the assumption that the business will continue operating instead of being closed or sold.

_____ **7.** Requires revenue to be recorded only when the earnings process is complete.

Exercise 2-11
Accounting principles

LO 5

Use the information for each of the following independent cases to calculate the company's return on equity and its modified return on equity:

	a	b	c	d
Average equity	$50,000	$800,000	$300,000	$572,800
Net income	10,800	216,000	91,500	177,930
Value of owner's efforts	4,400	100,000	66,000	150,000

Exercise 2-12
Return on equity

LO 8

Classify the following cash flows to the appropriate section in which they would appear on the statement of cash flows.

A. Cash flow from operating activity

B. Cash flow from investing activity

C. Cash flow from financing activity

_____ **1.** Cash paid to suppliers

_____ **2.** Withdrawal by owner

_____ **3.** Cash paid to employee

_____ **4.** Purchase of equipment

_____ **5.** Cash paid for rent

_____ **6.** Investment by owner

_____ **7.** Repayment of note

_____ **8.** Cash received from customers

Exercise 2-13
Statement of cash flows

LO 1

George Hemphill started a new business called Hemphill Enterprises and incurred the following transactions during its first month of operations:

a. Hemphill invested $60,000 cash and office equipment valued at $30,000 in the business.

b. Paid $300,000 for a small building to be used as an office. Paid $50,000 in cash and signed a note payable promising to pay the balance over several years.

c. Purchased $4,000 of office supplies for cash.

d. Purchased $36,000 of office equipment on credit.

e. Completed a project on credit and billed the client $4,000 for the work.

f. Paid a local newspaper $1,000 for an announcement that the office had opened.

g. Completed a project for a client and collected $18,000 cash.

h. Made a $2,000 payment on the equipment purchased in transaction *d*.

i. Received $3,000 from the client described in transaction *e*.

j. Paid $2,500 cash for the office secretary's wages.

k. Hemphill withdrew $1,800 cash from the company bank account to pay personal living expenses.

Problems
Problem 2-1
Analyzing the effects of transactions and calculating return on equity

LO 5, 6, 8

Required

Preparation component:

1. Create a table like the one in Exhibit 2.14, using the following headings for the columns: Cash; Accounts Receivable; Office Supplies; Office Equipment; Building; Accounts Payable; Notes Payable; and George Hemphill, Capital. Leave space for an Explanation column to the right of the Capital column. Identify revenues and expenses by name in the Explanation column.

2. Use additions and subtractions to show the transactions' effects on the elements of the equation. Show new totals after each transaction. Also, indicate next to each change in the owner's equity whether it was caused by an investment, a revenue, an expense, or a withdrawal.

3. Once you have completed the table, determine the company's net income.

Analysis component:

4. Determine the return on Hemphill's equity for the period. Next, assume that Hemphill could have earned $6,000 for the period from another job and determine the modified return on equity for the period. State whether you think the business is a good use of Hemphill's money if an alternative investment would have returned 9% for the same period.

Problem 2-2
Balance sheet, income statement, and statement of changes in owner's equity

LO 1, 6, 7

Kelly Young started a new business called Resource Consulting Co. and began operations on April 1. The following transactions were completed during the month:

Apr. 1 Young invested $60,000 cash in the business.
  1 Rented a furnished office and paid $3,200 cash for April's rent.
  3 Purchased office supplies for $1,680 cash.
  5 Paid $800 cash for the month's cleaning services.
  8 Provided consulting services for a client and immediately collected $4,600 cash.
  12 Provided consulting services for a client on credit, $3,000.
  15 Paid $850 cash for an assistant's salary for the first half of the month.
  20 Received payment in full for the services provided on April 12.
  22 Provided consulting services on credit, $2,800.
  23 Purchased additional office supplies on credit, $1,000.
  28 Received full payment for the services provided on April 22.
  29 Paid for the office supplies purchased on April 23.
  30 Purchased advertising for $60 in the local paper. The payment is due May 1.
  30 Paid $200 cash for the month's telephone bill.
  30 Paid $480 cash for the month's utilities.
  30 Paid $850 cash for an assistant's salary for the second half of the month.
  30 Purchased insurance protection for the next 12 months (beginning May 1) by paying a $3,000 premium. Because none of this insurance protection had been used up, it was considered to be an asset called Prepaid Insurance.
  30 Young withdrew $1,200 cash from the business for personal use.

Required

1. Arrange the following asset, liability, and owner's equity titles in an equation like Exhibit 2.14: Cash; Accounts Receivable; Prepaid Insurance; Office Supplies; Accounts Payable; and Kelly Young, Capital. Include an Explanation column for changes in owner's equity. Identify revenues and expenses by name in the Explanation column.

2. Show the effects of the transactions on the elements of the equation by recording increases and decreases in the appropriate columns. Do not determine new totals for the items of the equation after each transaction. Next to each change in owner's equity, state whether it was caused by an investment, a revenue, an expense, or a withdrawal. Determine the final total for each item and verify that the equation is in balance.

3. Prepare an income statement for April, a statement of changes in owner's equity for April, and an April 30 balance sheet.

The accounting records of Goodall Delivery Services show the following assets and liabilities as of the end of 19X1 and 19X2:

	December 31	
	19X1	19X2
Cash	$ 52,500	$ 18,750
Accounts receivable	28,500	22,350
Office supplies	4,500	3,300
Trucks	54,000	54,000
Office equipment	138,000	147,000
Building		180,000
Land		45,000
Accounts payable	7,500	37,500
Notes payable		105,000

Late in December 19X2 (just before the amounts in the second column were calculated), Travis Goodall, the owner, purchased a small office building and moved the business from rented quarters to the new building. The building and the land it occupies cost $225,000. The business paid $120,000 in cash and a note payable was signed for the balance. Goodall had to invest $35,000 cash in the business to enable it to pay the $120,000. The business earned a satisfactory net income during 19X2, which enabled Goodall to withdraw $3,000 per month from the business for personal expenses.

Required

1. Prepare balance sheets for the business as of the end of 19X1 and the end of 19X2. (Remember that owner's equity equals the difference between the assets and the liabilities.)
2. By comparing the owner's equity amounts from the balance sheets and using the additional information presented in the problem, prepare a calculation to show how much net income was earned by the business during 19X2.
3. Calculate the 19X2 return on equity for the business. Also, calculate the modified return on equity, assuming that Goodall's efforts were worth $40,000 for the year.

Problem 2-3
Calculating and interpreting net income, preparing a balance sheet, and calculating return on equity
LO 1, 7, 8

Check Figure Modified return on equity, 6.3%

Problem 2-4
Analyzing transactions, preparing financial statements, and calculating return on equity
LO 1, 6, 7, 8

Stan Frey started a new business and incurred these transactions during November:

Nov. 1 Transferred $56,000 out of a personal savings account to a chequing account in the name of Frey Electrical Co.
1 Rented office space and paid cash for the month's rent of $800.
3 Purchased electrical equipment from an electrician who was going out of business for $14,000 by paying $3,200 in cash and agreeing to pay the balance in six months.
5 Purchased office supplies by paying $900 cash.
6 Completed electrical work and immediately collected $1,000 for doing the work.
8 Purchased $3,800 of office equipment on credit.
15 Completed electrical work on credit in the amount of $4,000.
18 Purchased $500 of office supplies on credit.
20 Paid for the office equipment purchased on November 8.
24 Billed a client $600 for electrical work; the balance is due in 30 days.
28 Received $4,000 for the work completed on November 15.
30 Paid the assistant's salary of $1,200.
30 Paid the monthly utility bills of $440.
30 Withdrew $700 from the business for personal use.

Required

Preparation component:

1. Arrange the following asset, liability, and owner's equity titles in an equation like Exhibit 2.14: Cash; Accounts Receivable; Office Supplies; Office Equipment; Electrical Equip-

ment; Accounts Payable; and Stan Frey, Capital. Leave space for an Explanation column to the right of Stan Frey, Capital. Identify revenues and expenses by name in the Explanation column.

2. Use additions and subtractions to show the effects of each transaction on the items in the equation. Show new totals after each transaction. Next to each change in owner's equity, state whether the change was caused by an investment, a revenue, an expense, or a withdrawal.

3. Use the increases and decreases in the last column of the equation to prepare an income statement and a statement of changes in owner's equity for the month. Also prepare a balance sheet as of the end of the month.

4. Calculate the return on equity for the month, using the initial investment as the beginning balance of equity.

Analysis component:

5. Assume that the investment transaction on November 1 had been $40,000 instead of $56,000, and that Frey obtained the $16,000 difference by borrowing it from a bank. Explain the effect of this change on total assets, total liabilities, owner's equity, and return on equity.

Check Figure Ending owner's equity, $58,460

Problem 2-5
Missing information
LO 1, 2

The following financial statement information is known about five unrelated companies:

	Company A	Company B	Company C	Company D	Company E
December 31, 19X1:					
Assets	$45,000	$35,000	$29,000	$80,000	$123,000
Liabilities	23,500	22,500	14,000	38,000	?
December 31, 19X2:					
Assets	48,000	41,000	?	125,000	112,500
Liabilities	?	27,500	19,000	64,000	75,000
During 19X2:					
Owner investments	5,000	1,500	7,750	?	4,500
Net income	7,500	?	9,000	12,000	18,000
Owner withdrawals	2,500	3,000	3,875	-0-	9,000

Required

1. Answer the following questions about Company A:
   a. What was the owner's equity on December 31, 19X1?
   b. What was the owner's equity on December 31, 19X2?
   c. What was the amount of liabilities owed on December 31, 19X2?
2. Answer the following questions about Company B:
   a. What was the owner's equity on December 31, 19X1?
   b. What was the owner's equity on December 31, 19X2?
   c. What was the net income for 19X2?
3. Calculate the amount of assets owned by Company C on December 31, 19X2.
4. Calculate the amount of owner investments in Company D made during 19X2.
5. Calculate the amount of liabilities owed by Company E on December 31, 19X1.

Check Figure Company C, Dec. 31, 19X2 assets, $46,875

Problem 2-6
Identifying the effects of transactions on the financial statements
LO 1, 6

Identify how each of the following transactions affects the company's financial statements. For the balance sheet, identify how each transaction affects total assets, total liabilities, and owner's equity. For the income statement, identify how each transaction affects net income. For the statement of cash flows, identify how each transaction affects cash flows from operating activities, cash flows from financing activities, and cash flows from investing activities. If there is an increase, place a "+" in the column or columns. If there is a decrease, place a "−" in the column or columns. If there is both an increase and a decrease, place a "+/−" in the column or columns. The line for the first transaction is completed as an example.

		Balance Sheet			Income Statement	Statement of Cash Flows		
	Transaction	Total Assets	Total Liab.	Equity	Net Income	Operating	Financing	Investing
1	Owner invests cash	+		+			+	
2	Sell services for cash							
3	Aquire services on credit							
4	Pay wages with cash							
5	Owner withdraws cash							
6	Borrow cash with note payable							
7	Sell services on credit							
8	Buy office equipment for cash							
9	Collect receivable from (7)							
10	Buy asset with note payable							

A new business, Do You Copy, has the following cash balance and cash flows for the month of December:

Cash Balance, December 1	$ -0-
Withdrawals by owner	500
Cash received from customers	4,000
Repayment of debt	1,000
Cash paid for store supplies.	2,600
Purchase of equipment	21,000
Cash paid for rent	2,000
Cash paid to employee	800
Investment by owner	32,000

Required

Prepare a statement of cash flows for Do You Copy for the month of December.

Problem 2-7
Preparing a statement of cash flows

LO 1

Check Figure Cash bal., Dec. 31, $8,100

Alternate Problems

Problem 2-1A

Analyzing the effects of transactions on the accounting equation and calculating return on equity

LO 5, 6, 8

Judith Grimm started a new business called Southwest Consulting and incurred the following transactions during its first year of operations:

a. Grimm invested $50,000 cash and office equipment valued at $5,000 in the business.

b. Paid $120,000 for a small building to be used as an office. Paid $10,000 in cash and signed a note payable promising to pay the balance over several years.

c. Purchased $9,000 of office equipment for cash.

d. Purchased $2,000 of office supplies and $3,200 of office equipment on credit.

e. Paid a local newspaper $1,500 for an announcement that the office had opened.

f. Completed a financial plan on credit and billed the client $3,000 for the service.

g. Designed a financial plan for another client and collected a $5,400 cash fee.

h. Grimm withdrew $2,750 cash from the company bank account to pay personal expenses.

i. Received $1,200 from the client described in transaction *f*.

j. Made a $900 payment on the equipment purchased in transaction *d*.

k. Paid $1,900 cash for the office secretary's wages.

Required

Preparation component:

1. Create a table like the one presented in Exhibit 2.14, using the following headings for the columns: Cash; Accounts Receivable; Office Supplies; Office Equipment; Building; Accounts Payable; Notes Payable; and Judith Grimm, Capital. Leave space for an Explanation column to the right of the Capital column. Identify revenues and expenses by name in the Explanation column.

2. Use additions and subtractions to show the effects of the above transactions on the elements of the equation. Show new totals after each transaction. Also, indicate next to each change in the owner's equity whether it was caused by an investment, a revenue, an expense, or a withdrawal.

3. Once you have completed the table, determine the company's net income.

Analysis component:

4. Determine the return on Grimm's equity for the period. Next, assume that Grimm could have earned $3,000 for the period from another job and determine the modified return on equity for the period. State whether you think the business is a good use of Grimm's money if an alternative investment would have returned 10% for the same period.

Problem 2-2A

Preparing a balance sheet, income statement, and statement of changes in owner's equity

LO 1, 6, 7

Andrew Martin began a new business called Universal Maintenance Co. and began operations on June 1. The following transactions were completed during the month:

June 1 Martin invested $120,000 in the business.

1 Rented a furnished office of a maintenance company that was going out of business and paid $4,500 cash for the month's rent.

4 Purchased cleaning supplies for $2,400 cash.

6 Paid $1,125 cash for advertising the opening of the business.

8 Completed maintenance services for a customer and immediately collected $750 cash.

14 Completed maintenance services for First Union Centre on credit, $6,300.

16 Paid $900 cash for an assistant's salary for the first half of the month.

20 Received payment in full for the services completed for First Union Centre on June 14.

21 Completed maintenance services for Skyway Co. on credit, $3,500.

22 Purchased additional cleaning supplies on credit, $750.

24 Completed maintenance services for Comfort Motel on credit, $825.

29 Received full payment from Skyway Co. for the work completed on June 21.

29 Made a partial payment of $375 for the cleaning supplies purchased on June 22.

30 Paid $120 cash for the month's telephone bill.

30 Paid $525 cash for the month's utilities.

30 Paid $900 cash for an assistant's salary for the second half of the month.

30 Purchased insurance protection for the next 12 months (beginning July 1) by paying a $3,600 premium. Because none of this insurance protection had been used up, it was considered to be an asset called Prepaid Insurance.

30 Martin withdrew $2,000 from the business for personal use.

Required

1. Arrange the following asset, liability, and owner's equity titles in an equation like Exhibit 2.14: Cash; Accounts Receivable; Cleaning Supplies; Prepaid Insurance; Accounts Payable; Andrew Martin, Capital. Include an Explanation column for changes in owner's equity. Identify revenues and expenses by name in the Explanation column.

2. Show the effects of the transactions on the elements of the equation by recording increases and decreases in the appropriate columns. Do not determine new totals for the items of the equation after each transaction. Next to each change in owner's equity, state whether it was caused by an investment, a revenue, an expense, or a withdrawal. Determine the final total for each item and verify that the equation is in balance.

3. Prepare a June income statement, a June statement of changes in owner's equity, and a June 30 balance sheet.

The accounting records of Stiller Co. show the following assets and liabilities as of the end of 19X1 and 19X2:

	December 31	
	19X1	**19X2**
Cash	$ 14,000	$ 10,000
Accounts receivable	25,000	30,000
Office supplies	10,000	12,500
Office equipment	60,000	60,000
Machinery	30,500	30,500
Building		260,000
Land		65,000
Accounts payable	5,000	15,000
Notes payable		260,000

Problem 2-3A
Calculating and interpreting net income, preparing a balance sheet, and calculating return on equity
LO 1, 7, 8

Late in December 19X2 (just before the amounts in the second column were calculated), Joseph Stiller, the owner, purchased a small office building and moved the business from rented quarters to the new building. The building and the land it occupies cost $325,000. The business paid $65,000 in cash and a note payable was signed for the balance. Stiller had to invest an additional $25,000 to enable it to pay the $65,000. The business earned a satisfactory net income during 19X2, which enabled Stiller to withdraw $1,000 per month from the business for personal use.

Required

1. Prepare balance sheets for the business as of the end of 19X1 and the end of 19X2. (Remember that owner's equity equals the difference between the assets and the liabilities.)

2. By comparing the owner's equity amounts from the balance sheets and using the additional information presented in the problem, prepare a calculation to show how much net income was earned by the business during 19X2.

3. Calculate the 19X2 return on equity for the business. Also, calculate the modified return on equity, assuming that Stiller's efforts were worth $25,000 for the year.

Problem 2-4A

Analyzing transactions, preparing financial statements, and calculating return on equity

LO 1, 6, 7, 8

Cantu Excavating Co., owned by Robert Cantu, began operations in July and incurred these transactions during the month:

July 1 Cantu invested $60,000 cash in the business.
1 Rented office space and paid the month's rent of $500.
1 Purchased excavating equipment for $4,000 by paying $800 in cash and agreeing to pay the balance in six months.
6 Purchased office supplies by paying $500 cash.
8 Completed work for a customer and immediately collected $2,200 for doing the work.
10 Purchased $3,800 of office equipment on credit.
15 Completed work for a customer on credit in the amount of $2,400.
17 Purchased $1,920 of office supplies on credit.
23 Paid for the office equipment purchased on July 10.
25 Billed a customer $5,000 for completed work; the balance is due in 30 days.
28 Received $2,400 for the work completed on July 15.
31 Paid an assistant's salary of $1,260.
31 Paid the monthly utility bills of $260.
31 Cantu withdrew $1,200 from the business to pay personal expenses.

Required

Preparation component:

1. Arrange the following asset, liability, and shareholders' equity titles in an equation like Exhibit 2.14: Cash; Accounts Receivable; Office Supplies; Office Equipment; Excavating Equipment; Accounts Payable; and Robert Cantu, Capital. Leave space for an Explanation column to the right of Robert Cantu, Capital. Identify revenues and expenses by name in the Explanation column.

2. Use additions and subtractions to show the effects of each transaction on the items in the equation. Show new totals after each transaction. Next to each change in owner's equity, state whether the change was caused by an investment, a revenue, an expense, or a withdrawal.

3. Use the increases and decreases in the last column of the equation to prepare an income statement and a statement of changes in owner's equity for the month. Also, prepare a balance sheet as of the end of the month.

4. Calculate the return on the equity for the month, using the initial investment as the beginning balance of equity.

Analysis component:

5. Assume that Cantu invested $4,000 cash in the business to obtain the excavating equipment on July 1 instead of the purchase conditions described in the transaction. Explain the effect of this change on total assets, total liabilities, owner's equity, and return on equity.

Problem 2-5A

Missing information

LO 1, 2

The following financial statement information is known about five unrelated companies:

	Company V	Company W	Company X	Company Y	Company Z
December 31, 19X1:					
Assets	$45,000	$70,000	$121,500	$82,500	$124,000
Liabilities	30,000	50,000	58,500	61,500	?
December 31, 19X2:					
Assets	49,000	90,000	136,500	?	160,000
Liabilities	26,000	?	55,500	72,000	52,000
During 19X2:					
Owner investments ...	6,000	10,000	?	38,100	40,000
Net income	?	30,000	16,500	24,000	32,000
Owner withdrawals ...	4,500	2,000	-0-	18,000	6,000

Required

1. Answer the following questions about Company V:
   a. What was the owner's equity on December 31, 19X1?
   b. What was the owner's equity on December 31, 19X2?
   c. What was the net income for 19X2?
2. Answer the following questions about Company W:
   a. What was the owner's equity on December 31, 19X1?
   b. What was the owner's equity on December 31, 19X2?
   c. What was the amount of liabilities owed on December 31, 19X2?
3. Calculate the amount of owner investments in Company X made during 19X2.
4. Calculate the amount of assets owned by Company Y on December 31, 19X2.
5. Calculate the amount of liabilities owed by Company Z on December 31, 19X1.

You are to identify how each of the following transactions affects the company's financial statements. For the balance sheet, you are to identify how each transaction affects total assets, total liabilities, and shareholders' equity. For the income statement, you are to identify how each transaction affects net income. For the statement of cash flows, you are to identify how each transaction affects cash flows from operating activities, cash flows from financing activities, and cash flows from investing activities. If there is an increase, place a "+" in the column or columns. If there is a decrease, place a "−" in the column or columns. If there is both an increase and a decrease, place "+/−" in the column or columns. The line for the first transaction is completed as an example.

Problem 2-6A
Identifying the effects of transactions on the financial statements
LO 1, 6

	Transaction	Balance Sheet			Income Statement	Statement of Cash Flows		
		Total Assets	Total Liab.	Equity	Net Income	Operating	Financing	Investing
1	Owner invests cash	+		+			+	
2	Pay wages with cash							
3	Aquire services on credit							
4	Buy store equipment for cash							
5	Borrow cash with note payable							
6	Sell services for cash							
7	Sell services on credit							
8	Buy rent with cash							
9	Owner withdraws cash							
10	Collect receivable from (7)							

Problem 2-7A
Constructing a statement
of cash flows

LO 1

A new business , Surfnet, has the following cash balance and cash flows for the month of December:

Cash Balance, December 1	$ -0-
Withdrawals by owner	1,000
Cash received from customers	7,800
Repayment of debt	1,800
Cash paid for store supplies.	5,000
Purchase of equipment	40,000
Cash paid for rent	2,000
Cash paid to employee	1,400
Investment by owner	60,000

Required
Prepare a statement of cash flows for the month of December.

Analytical and Review Problems
A & R Problem 2-1

Jack Tasker began his Auto Repair Shop the first part of this month. The balance sheet, prepared by an inexperienced part-time bookkeeper is shown below:

Required
1. Prepare a correct balance sheet.
2. Explain why the incorrect balance sheet can be in balance.

TASKER AUTO REPAIR SHOP
Balance Sheet
November 30,1999

Assets		Liabilities and Owner's Equity	
Cash	$ 6,300	Parts and supplies.	$11,025
Accounts payable	34,650	Accounts receivable.	47,250
Equipment	22,050	Prepaid rent	3,150
Jack Tasker, capital . .	26,775	Mortgage payable	28,350
Total income	$89,775	Total equities	$89,775

A & R Problem 2-2

Susan Huang began the practice of law the first day of October with an initial investment of $10,500 in cash. After completing the first month of practice, the financial statements were being prepared by Ryan Player, the secretary/bookkeeper Ms. Huang had hired. The statements were completed, and Ms. Huang almost burst out laughing when she saw them. She had completed a course in legal accounting in law school and knew the statements prepared by Mr. Player left much to be desired. Consequently, she asks you to revise the statements. The Player version is presented below:

Required
Prepare the corrected financial statements for Susan Huang.

SUSAN HUANG, LAWYER
Balance Sheet
October 31,1999

Assets		Liabilities and Owner's Equity	
Cash	$3,780	S. Huang, capital	$7,350
Prepaid rent	2,100		
Supplies expense	420		
Accounts payable	1,050		
	$7,350		$7,350

SUSAN HUANG, LAWYER
Income Statement
For Month Ended October 31, 1999

Revenues:		
Legal fees	$11,550	
Accounts receivable	2,100	$13,650
Expenses:		
Salaries expense	$ 2,940	
Telephone expense	210	
Rent expenses	2,100	
Supplies	1,050	
Law libary	8,400	14,700
Loss		$ 1,050

BEYOND THE NUMBERS

Alliance Communications Corporation is a fully integrated supplier of entertainment products with interests in television, motion pictures, broadcasting, computer-generated animation facilities, music publishing and financing services. The financial statements and other information from Alliance's March 31, 1997, annual report are included in Appendix I at the end of the book. Use information from that report to answer the following questions:

Reporting in Action

1. Examine Alliance's consolidated balance sheet. To what level of significance are the dollar amounts rounded?
2. What is the closing date of Alliance's most recent annual reporting period?
3. What amount of net income did Alliance earn for the fiscal year ended March 31, 1997?
4. How much cash (and cash equivalents) did Alliance hold at fiscal year-end March 31, 1997?
5. What was the net amount of cash provided by the company's operating activities during the fiscal year ended March 31, 1997?
6. Did the company's investing activities for the fiscal year ended March 31, 1997, create a net cash inflow or outflow? What was the amount of the net flow?
7. Compare fiscal year-end 1997's results to 1996's results to determine whether the company's total revenues increased or decreased. If so, what was the amount of the increase or decrease?
8. What was the change in the company's net income between fiscal year-end 1997 and 1996?
9. What amount was reported as total assets at fiscal year-end 1997?
10. Calculate the return on equity that Alliance achieved for the fiscal year ended 1997.

Both **Alliance** and **Atlantis** design, produce, distribute and broadcast television programs. Key comparative figures ($ millions) for these two organizations follow:

Comparative Analysis

	Alliance	Atlantis
Beginning equity	$ 95.4	$68.8
Ending equity	150.4	97.1
Net income	18.2	5.6

Required

1. What is the return on equity for (a) Alliance and (b) Atlantis?
2. Is return on equity satisfactory for (a) Alliance and (b) Atlantis when competitors average a 15% return?
3. Would it be appropriate to calculate the modified return on equity for Alliance and Atlantis?
4. What can you conclude about Alliance and Atlantis from these computations?

Ethics Challenge
LO 5

BJ Crist is a new entry-level accountant for a mail order company that specializes in supplying skateboards and accessories for the sport. At the end of the fiscal period, Crist is advised by a supervisor to include as revenue for the period any orders that have been charged by phone but not yet fulfilled by shipping the product. Crist is also advised to include as revenue any orders received by mail with cheques enclosed that are also pending fulfillment.

Required

1. Identify relevant accounting principles that Crist should be aware of in view of the supervisor's instructions.
2. What are the ethical factors in this situation?
3. Would you recommend that Crist follow the supervisor's directives?
4. What alternatives might be available to Crist if deciding to not follow the supervisor's directions?

Communicating in Practice

Understanding and using financial information is important in a wide range of careers. You are to obtain a copy of the article, "Why Neil Simon Decided to Turn His Back on Broadway" by Donald G. McNeil, Jr., *The New York Times*. November 21, 1994, pp. C9 and C13. After reading the article, prepare a brief written report that includes responses to the following questions/issues:

1. How does this article illustrate the importance for Neil Simon, a playwright, to understand financial statements?
2. Summarize and explain the financial considerations that brought Neil Simon and his producer to the conclusion it was a financially wise decision to produce Off Broadway. Do you agree with their conclusion? Why?
3. Using the figures in the article, at what point does the decision to produce Off Broadway prove less profitable than the alternative one? Explain.

Taking It to the Net
LO 1

Access the **Alliance Communication Corporation** Web site (**http://www.alliance.ca**). After your arrive at Alliance's home page click on the "Corporate Highlights" hotlink.

Required:

a. What are some of the awards that Alliance has won?
b. Using your knowledge of accounting principles write a brief memo listing reasons why Alliance has not included these awards as assets on their balance sheet.

Teamwork in Action
LO 5

This activity is aimed at generating a team discussion of basic business transactions. Understanding transactions provides the necessary background for dealing with more complex transactions later in the book.

Required:

1. Each team member should write down as many different transactions they can think of that fall into one of the following categories:
   a. Transactions affecting assets.
   b. Transactions affecting liabilities.
   c. Transactions affecting owner's equity but not affecting revenues and expenses.
   d. Transactions affecting revenues and/or expenses.
2. Team members should exchange lists, analyze the transactions, and write down the accounts affected by each transaction on the list.
3. Each team member is to report the results of part 2. If all members of the team agree with the analysis presented, they should proceed to other transactions and team members' reports. If there is disagreement, team members should discuss differences and consult the book in reaching a decision. If the discussion does not result in agreement, consult your instructor.

Use the **SEDAR** database (**http://www.sedar.com**) and obtain the toll-free 800 number of a company that you are interested in learning more about. Once you have obtained the 800 number call the company and ask to speak to the Investor Relations' department. Request a copy of that company's most recent annual report from the Investor Relations' phone representative. Or, you may use *The Globe and Mail's* annual report request service. You should receive the requested report within one to three weeks time. Once you have received your report consult it throughout the term to see the principles you are learning in the classroom applied in practice.

Hitting the Road
LO 1

Report on Business periodically publishes a ranking of the top one thousand Canadian businesses based on size of profit. Obtain the most recent publication of this issue.

Business Break
LO 8

Required

1. What company is ranked first?
2. Of the top five businesses, how many are from the same industry?
3. What is the return on equity for the number one company?
4. What is the industry of the number one company?

3

CHAPTER

Analyzing and Recording Transactions

▶ A Look Back

We explained the value of accounting in the information age. We saw how financial statements communicate useful information and how accounting principles guide their preparation. We also analyzed and prepared financial statements from transactions.

▶ A Look at This Chapter

This chapter focuses on the accounting process. We describe transactions and source documents as inputs for analysis. We explain analysis and recording of transactions for preparing financial statements. T-accounts, postings, ledgers and trial balances are shown as useful tools in carrying out these important steps.

▶ A Look Forward

Chapter 4 extends our focus on processing information. We explain the importance of adjusting accounts and procedures in preparing financial statements.

Chapter Outline

Spinning an Accounting Web

Kitchener, ON—Maria Sanchez's second year on the job was nearly her last. She was working as a staff accountant for a shoe manufacturer where she was assigned to payroll and accounts receivable. In late December of her second year, she was instructed to add 1% to all employees' end-of-year paycheques as a bonus. Instead, she keyed an extra zero and gave everyone a 10% bonus. "The controller was furious," says Sanchez. "To top it off, the employees were so happy that the controller and board couldn't do anything but keep quiet, accept the error and thank everyone."

Today, Sanchez takes blame for the error. But, it wasn't always that way. "I still partly blame our accounting technology. It was awful," says Sanchez. It was this experience that led Sanchez to add technology to her accounting. While taking evening classes in computing, Sanchez became convinced that accounting packages could be more user friendly. She also foresaw the power of the Web.

Sanchez, now 31, is today owner of **RecordLink.** It is an accounting software firm aimed at recordkeeping services for small business. It is unique in that it relies on the Web. This means there is no need for software purchases or special computing hardware requirements for small business. Clients link into her Web servers for their computing needs.

The convenience and power of clients having access to their accounting information anytime, anywhere, are attracting new clients. "We offer 24-hour accounting and computing advice, and we are expanding our software options to include strategic planning, budget analyses and other sophisticated programs that few small businesses can individually afford." RecordLink spreads these costs over all its clients.

Sanchez sees recordkeeping services for small business as a lucrative and underserved market. She plans to expand her business to Guelph and London by year-end. So far, her creativity has been a hit with clients. Last year, RecordLink's revenues went over $250,000. Adds Sanchez, "Not bad for a high-tech recordkeeper!"

Learning Objectives

LO 1   Explain the steps in processing transactions.

LO 2   Describe source documents and their purpose.

LO 3   Describe an account and its use in recording information about transactions.

LO 4   Describe a ledger and a chart of accounts.

LO 5   Define debits and credits and explain their role in double-entry accounting.

LO 6   Analyze the impact of transactions on accounts and financial statements.

LO 7   Record transactions in a journal and post entries to a ledger.

LO 8   Prepare and explain the use of a trial balance.

LO 9   Compute the debt ratio and describe its use in analyzing company performance.

CHAPTER PREVIEW

The accounting process is crucial to producing useful financial information. We explained in Chapter 2 how the accounting equation (*assets = liabilities + equity*) helps us understand and analyze transactions and events. Because most businesses have numerous transactions, we need a more sophisticated system than that used in Chapter 2. In this chapter we describe how transactions are processed and how their effects are recorded in accounts. All accounting systems use procedures similar to those described here. These procedures are important steps leading to financial statements. Maria Sanchez of **RecordLink** uses a Web-based system, but the accounting procedures are essentially identical for manual systems.

We begin by describing how source documents provide crucial information about transactions. We then describe accounts and explain their purpose. A valuable tool in helping us to understand and process transactions is introduced. It is the use of debits and credits. This background enables us to describe the process of recording events in a journal and posting them to a ledger. We return to transactions of **FastForward,** first introduced in Chapter 2, to illustrate many of these procedures. We conclude the chapter by describing how to use a company's debt ratio to assess its risk.

Transactions and Documents

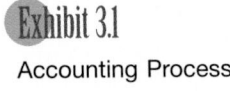 Explain the steps in processing transactions.

We explained in Chapter 1 how accounting provides useful information to help people make better decisions. This information is the result of an accounting process that captures business transactions and events, analyzes and records their effects, and summarizes and prepares information in reports and financial statements. These reports and statements are used for making investing, lending, and other important decisions. We describe the steps in the accounting process in Exhibit 3.1

Transactions and events are the starting points in the accounting process. Relying on the original documents, we analyze transactions and events using the accounting equation to understand how they affect organization performance and financial position. These effects are recorded in accounting records, informally referred to as the *accounting books* or simply the *books*. Additional processing steps such as posting and preparing a trial balance help us summarize and classify the effects of transactions and events. A final step in the accounting process is to provide information in useful reports or financial statements to decision makers. This section and much of the chapter focus on many important parts of the accounting process.

Exhibit 3.1

Accounting Process

Transaction or Event → Source Document → Analysis → Recording → Posting → Trial Balance → Reporting

Transactions and Events

Business activities can be described in terms of transactions and events. We know from Chapter 2 that business transactions are exchanges of economic consideration between two parties. We also know that the accounting equation is affected by transactions and events. Transactions and events are the beginning points in the accounting process.

External transactions are exchanges between an organization and some other person or organization. A sale to a customer or the purchase of merchandise for resale would be examples of external transactions. These external transactions yield changes in the accounting equation. **Internal transactions** are exchanges within an organization. Internal transactions can also affect the accounting equation. An example is a company using equipment in its operating activities. As the equipment is used, its remaining benefits decrease. This using up of an equipment's economic benefits is an event that decreases assets and decreases owner's equity.

Many events can affect an organization's performance and financial position. These include financial events such as changes in the market value of certain assets and liabilities. They also include natural events such as floods and fires that destroy assets and create losses. The analysis and recording of events are explained in the next chapter.

Source Documents

Organizations use various documents and papers when doing business. **Source documents,** or *business papers,* identify and describe transactions and events entering the accounting process. They are the source of accounting information, and can be in either paper or electronic form. Examples are sales invoices, cheques, purchase orders, charges to customers, bills from suppliers, employee earnings records, and bank statements.

LO 2   Describe source documents and their purpose.

When we buy an item on credit the store usually prepares at least two copies of a sales invoice. One copy is given to you. Another is sent to the store's accounting department and gives rise to an entry in the information system to record a sale. This copy is often sent electronically. If you pay cash for an item, the sale is usually rung up on a cash register that records and stores the amount of each sale. Many cash registers record this information for each sale on a paper tape or electronic file locked inside the register. Total cash sales for a day or for any time period can be obtained immediately from these registers. This total is used as a source document for recording sales in the accounting records.

These procedures when buying an item are part of an information system designed to ensure the accounting records include all transactions. They also help prevent mistakes and theft. To encourage employees to follow procedures such as these, stores may give discounts or free goods if a customer is not provided an invoice. This is part of internal control procedures which are put in place to ensure adherence to company policies.

Cashier
You are a cashier at a retail convenience store. When hired, the assistant manager explained to you the policy of immediately ringing up each sale. Recently, lunch hour traffic has increased dramatically and the assistant manager asks you to take customers' cash and make change without ringing up sales to avoid delays. The assistant manager says she will add up cash and ring up sales equal to the cash amount after lunch. She says that in this way the register will always be accurate when the manager arrives at three o'clock. What do you do?

Judgment and Ethics

Answer—p. 127

Both buyers and sellers use sales invoices as source documents. Sellers use them for recording sales and for control purposes. Buyers use them for recording purchases and for monitoring purchasing activity. In both cases, a copy of the invoice is a source document.

Source documents, especially if obtained from outside the organization, provide objective evidence about transactions and their amounts for recording. As we explained in Chapter 2, objective evidence is important because it makes information more reliable and useful.

There are still many accounting systems that require manual (pencil and paper) recording and processing of transaction data. But these are mostly limited to small businesses. In today's information age, computers assist us in recording and processing data. Yet computers are only part of the process, and modern technology still demands human insight and understanding of transactions. In our discussion of the steps making up the accounting process, we use a manual system for presentation. The fundamental concepts of the manual system are identical to those of a computerized information system. More importantly, our understanding of how information proceeds through an accounting system is made clear through studying a manual system.

Flashback

1. Describe external and internal transactions.
2. Identify examples of accounting source documents.
3. Explain the importance of source documents.

Answer—p. 127

Accounts and Double-Entry Accounting

This section explains an *account* and its importance to accounting and business. We also describe several crucial elements of an accounting system. These include ledgers, T-accounts, debits and credits, and double-entry accounting.

The Account

LO3 Describe an account and its use in recording information about transactions.

An **account** is a detailed record of increases and decreases in a specific asset, liability, equity, revenue or expense. Information is taken from accounts, analyzed, summarized, and presented in useful reports and financial statements for users. A separate account is maintained for items of importance to information users. This means that separate accounts are kept for each type of asset, liability, and equity items. It also means separate accounts are kept for important revenue and expense items. Important changes in owner's withdrawals and contributions are also captured in separate accounts.[1]

A **ledger** is a record containing all accounts. This is often in electronic form and is what we mean when we refer to the *books*. While most companies' ledgers contain similar accounts, there are often several accounts that are unique to a company because of its individual type of operations. Accounts are arranged into three general categories using the accounting equation as shown in Exhibit 3.2.

Exhibit 3.2

Accounting Equation

| Assets | = | Liabilities | + | Equity |

These accounts directly flow into the preparation of financial reports and statements. The remainder of this section describes accounts that are important to most organizations.

---

[1] As an example of an account, Exhibit 3.5 shows the cash account for FastForward.

Asset Accounts

Assets are resources controlled by an organization and that hold current and future benefits. Most accounting systems include separate accounts for the assets described here.

Cash

Increases and decreases in the amount of cash are recorded in a *Cash* account. A cash account includes money and any medium of exchange that a bank accepts for deposit. Examples are coins, currency, cheques, money orders, and chequing account balances.

Accounts Receivable

Products and services are often sold to customers in return for promises to pay in the future. These transactions are called *credit sales* or *sales on account.* The promises from buyers are called the seller's *accounts receivable.* Accounts receivable are increased by new credit sales and are decreased by customer payments. A company needs to know the amount currently due from each customer to send monthly statements. A separate record for each sale to a customer and cash receipts is necessary for this purpose. We describe the system for maintaining these records in Chapter 7. For now, we use the simpler practice of recording all increases and decreases in receivables in a single account called *Accounts Receivable.* The importance of accounts receivable, like many other accounts, depends on the nature of a company's operations as shown in this excerpt from practice:

> At the end 1996, **Loblaw's** accounts receivable amounted to less than 4.5% of its assets. In comparison, **Mark's Work Warehouse's** accounts receivable amounted to more than 18% of its assets.

Notes Receivable

A **note receivable,** or **promissory note,** is an unconditional written promise to pay a definite sum of money on demand or on a defined future date(s). A company holding a promissory note signed by another party has a valuable asset. This asset is recorded in a *Notes Receivable* account.

Prepaid Insurance

Insurance contracts provide us with protection against losses caused by fire, theft, accidents and other events. The insurance policy often requires the fee, called *premium,* to be paid in advance. Protection can be purchased for almost any time period, including monthly, yearly, or even several years. When an insurance premium is paid in advance, the cost is typically recorded in an asset account called *Prepaid Insurance.* Over time the expiring portion of the insurance cost (the amount "used up") is removed from this asset account and reported in expenses on the income statement. The unexpired portion remains in Prepaid Insurance and is reported on the balance sheet as an asset.

Office Supplies

All companies use office supplies such as stationery, paper, and pens. These supplies are assets until they are used. When they are used up, their cost is reported as an expense. The cost of unused supplies is an asset and is recorded in an *Office Supplies* account.

Store Supplies

Many stores keep supplies for wrapping and packaging purchases for customers. These include plastic and paper bags, gift boxes, cartons, and ribbons. The cost of these unused supplies is recorded in a *Store Supplies* account. Supplies are reported as expenses as they are being used.

Prepaid Expenses

Prepaid Expenses is an asset account containing payments made for assets that are not used until later. As these assets are used up, the costs of the used assets become expenses. Common examples of prepaid expenses include office supplies, store supplies, prepaid insurance, prepaid rent, and advance payments for legal and accounting services. Prepaid expenses that are more crucial to the business are often accounted for in separate asset accounts as described above. An asset's cost can be initially recorded as an expense *if* it is used up before the end of the period when statements are prepared. If an asset will not be used before the end of the reporting period, then its cost is recorded in an asset account.

Equipment

Most organizations own computers, printers, desks, chairs, and other office equipment. Costs incurred to buy this equipment are recorded in an *Office Equipment* account. The costs of assets used in a store such as counters, showcases, and cash registers are recorded in a *Store Equipment* account.

Buildings

A building owned by an organization can provide space for a store, an office, a warehouse, or a factory. Buildings are assets because they provide benefits, and their costs are recorded in a *Buildings* account. When several buildings are owned, separate accounts are sometimes used for each of them. Buildings wear out and their costs are *amortized* or allocated to expense.

Land

A *Land* account records the cost of land owned by a business. The cost of land is separated from the cost of buildings located on the land to provide more useful information in financial statements. Land does not normally wear out, and its cost is not allocated to expense.

Liability Accounts

Liabilities are obligations to transfer assets or provide services to other entities. An organization often has several different liabilities each represented by a separate account. The more common liability accounts are described here.

Accounts Payable

Purchases of merchandise, supplies, equipment, or services made by an oral or implied promise to pay later produce liabilities called *accounts payable*. Accounting systems keep separate records about purchases from and payments to each creditor. We describe these individual records in Chapter 7. For now, we use the simpler practice of recording all increases and decreases in payables in a single account called *Accounts Payable*.

Notes Payable

When an organization formally recognizes a promise to pay by signing a promissory note, the resulting liability is a *note payable*. Its recording in either a *Short-Term Notes Payable* account or a *Long-Term Notes Payable* account depends on when it must be repaid. We explain details of account classification in Chapter 5.

Unearned Revenues

Chapter 2 explained that the *revenue recognition principle* requires that revenues be reported on the income statement when earned. This principle means we must be careful with transactions where customers pay in advance for products or services. Because cash from these transactions is received before revenues are earned, the seller considers them **unearned revenues.** Unearned revenue is a liability that is satisfied by delivering products or services in the future. Examples of unearned revenue include magazine subscriptions collected in advance by a publisher, sales of gift certificates by stores, rent collected in advance by a landlord and airline tickets sold in advance.

Air Canada reported unearned revenues of $270 million as of December 31, 1996.

When cash is received in advance for products and services, the seller records it in a liability account such as *Unearned Subscriptions, Unearned Rent,* or *Unearned Professional Fees.* When products and services are delivered, the now earned portion of the unearned revenues is transferred to revenue accounts such as *Subscription Fees, Rent Earned* or *Professional Fees.*[2]

Accrued Liabilities

Common accrued liabilities include wages payable, taxes payable, and interest payable. Each of these is often recorded in a separate liability account. If they are not large in amount, one or more of them may be added and reported as a single amount on the balance sheet.

The liabilities section of **Canadian Tire's** balance sheet at the end of 1996 included *accrued liabilities* of $190 million.

Equity Accounts

We described four types of transactions in the prior chapter that affect owner's equity. They are (1) investments by the owner, (2) withdrawals by the owner, (3) revenues and (4) expenses. We entered all equity transactions in a single column under the owner's name in Chapter 2. When we later prepared the income statement and the statement of changes in owner's equity, we had to review the items in that column to properly classify them in financial statements.

A better approach is to use four separate accounts. They are: owner's capital, owner's withdrawals, revenues, and expenses. In Exhibit 3.3 we show this visually by expanding the accounting equation.

Exhibit 3.3

Expanded Accounting Equation

---

[2] There are variations in account titles in practice. As one example, *Subscription Fees* is sometimes called *Subscription Fees Revenue, Subscription Fees Earned,* or *Earned Subscription Fees.* As another example, *Rent Earned* is sometimes called *Rent Revenue, Rental Revenue,* or *Earned Rent Revenue.* We must use our good judgment when reading financial statements since titles can differ even within the same industry. For example, product sales are called *Revenues* at **Alliance** and **Atlantis,** but *Sales* at **Scott's Restaurants** and **Cangene.** Yet *Revenues* or *Sales* are the most commonly used terms.

Information in these separate accounts is readily used to prepare financial statements without further analysis. We describe these four accounts below.

Owner's Capital

When a person invests in a proprietorship the invested amount is recorded in an account identified by the owner's name and the title *Capital*. An account called *Chuck Taylor, Capital* can be used to record Taylor's original investment in FastForward. Any further investments by the owner also are recorded in the owner's capital account.

Owner's Withdrawals

Owner's equity increases when a business earns income. The owner can leave this equity intact or can withdraw assets from the business. When the owner withdraws assets, perhaps to cover personal living expenses, the withdrawal decreases both the company's assets and owner's equity.

It is common for owners of proprietorships to withdraw regular weekly or monthly amounts of cash. The owners may even think of these withdrawals as "salaries." We know that owners of proprietorships cannot receive salaries because they are not legally separate from their companies. They cannot enter into salary (or any other) contracts with themselves. These withdrawals are neither income to the owners nor expenses of the business. They are simply the opposite of investments by owners.

Most accounting systems use an account with the name of the owner and the word *Withdrawals* in recording withdrawals by the owner. An account called *Chuck Taylor, Withdrawals* is used to record Taylor's withdrawals from FastForward. The owner's withdrawals account also is sometimes called the owner's *Personal* account or *Drawing* account.

NHL Accounting

The Vancouver Canucks report the following major revenue and expense accounts:

Revenues:	**Expenses:**
Game ticket sales	Hockey operations
Radio and television	Merchandise & programs
Merchandise & programs	Administrative & marketing
Advertising & promotions	

Source: Orca Bay Hockey Holdings' Financial Statements.

Revenues and Expenses

Decision makers often want information about revenues earned and expenses incurred for a period. Businesses use a variety of revenue and expense accounts to report this information on income statements. Different companies have different kinds of revenue and expense accounts reflecting their own important activities. Examples of revenue accounts are *Sales, Commissions Earned, Professional Fees Earned, Rent Earned* and *Interest Earned*. Examples of expense accounts are *Advertising Expense, Store Supplies Expense, Office Salaries Expense, Office Supplies Expense, Rent Expense, Utilities Expense* and *Insurance Expense*.

We can get an idea of the variety of revenues looking at the chart of accounts in Appendix I. It lists accounts needed to solve some of the exercises and problems in this book.[3]

---

[3] Different companies can use different account titles than those in the list. For example, a company might use *Interest Revenue* instead of *Interest Earned,* or *Rental Expense* instead of *Rent Expense.* It is only important that an account title describe the item it represents.

Ledger and Chart of Accounts

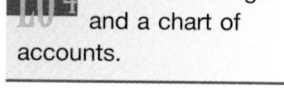

LO 4 Describe a ledger and a chart of accounts.

The actual recording of accounts can differ depending on the system. Computerized systems store accounts in files on electronic storage devices. Clients of RecordLink, as explained in the opening article, store their accounts online at another location. Manual systems often record accounts on separate pages in a special booklet or on separate cards in a tray of cards. The collection of all accounts for an information system is called a ledger. If accounts are in files on a hard disk, those files are the ledger. If the accounts are pages in a booklet or cards in a tray, then the book or file is the ledger. A ledger simply refers to the group of accounts.

A company's size and diversity of operations affect the number of accounts needed in its accounting system. A small company may get by with as few as 20 or 30 accounts, while a large company may need several thousand. The **chart of accounts** is a list of all accounts used by a company. The chart includes an *identification number* assigned to each account. Companies assign account identification numbers in an orderly manner. A typical small business might use the numbering system here for its accounts:

101 – 199	Asset accounts
201 – 299	Liability accounts
301 – 399	Owner's equity accounts
401 – 499	Revenue accounts
501 – 699	Expense accounts

While this particular system provides for 99 asset accounts, a company may not use all of them. The numbers provide a three-digit code that is useful in record-keeping. In this case the first digit assigned to asset accounts is a 1, while the first digit assigned to liability accounts is a 2, and so on. The first digit of an account's number also shows whether the account appears on the balance sheet or the income statement. The second and third digits may also relate to the accounts' categories. A partial chart of accounts is shown below for FastForward.

Account Number	Account Name	Account Number	Account Name
101	Cash	301	C. Taylor, Capital
106	Accounts receivable	302	C. Taylor, Withdrawals
125	Supplies	403	Consulting revenue
128	Prepaid insurance	406	Rental revenue
167	Equipment	641	Rent expense
201	Accounts payable	622	Salaries expense
236	Unearned consulting revenue	690	Utilities expense
240	Note payable		

Ledger Bytes

What does technology mean for information processing? **Sears** provides an answer. For its annual financial plan, Sears at one time used a 100-square-foot flow chart with more than 300 steps. Using computing technology, this plan is now 25 steps on one $8\frac{1}{2}$-by-11-inch sheet of paper! Technology also allows Sears' analysts to view and analyze budgets and financial plans on their PCs. Sears says it has slashed $100 million in costs. [Source: *Business Week,* October 28, 1996.]

Did You Know?

T-Account

A **T-account** is a helpful tool in showing the effects of transactions and events on specific accounts. The T-account gets its name from its shape. Its shape looks like the letter T and is shown in Exhibit 3.4 below:

Exhibit 3.4

The T-Account

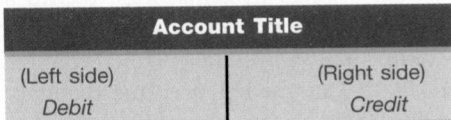

Account Title	
(Left side)	(Right side)
Debit	*Credit*

The format of a T-account includes (1) the account title on top, (2) a left or debit side, and (3) a right or credit side. A T-account provides one side for recording increases in the account and the other side for decreases. As an example, the T-account for FastForward's cash account after recording the transactions in Chapter 2 is in Exhibit 3.5:

Exhibit 3.5

Cash T-Account for
FastForward

Cash			
Investment by owner	30,000	Purchase of supplies	2,500
Consulting services revenue received	2,200	Purchase of equipment	20,000
Collection of account receivable	1,900	Payment of rent	1,000
		Payment of salary	700
		Payment of note payable	900
		Withdrawal by owner	600

Balance of an Account

An **account balance** is the difference between the increases and decreases recorded in an account. For example, the balance of an asset account equals the cost of that asset on the date the balance is computed. The balance of a liability account is the amount owed on the date the balance is computed.

Putting increases on one side of an account and decreases on another helps in computing an account's balance. To determine the balance, we (1) compute the total increases shown on one side (including the beginning balance), (2) compute the total decreases shown on the other side, and (3) subtract the sum of the decreases from the sum of the increases. The total increases in FastForward's Cash account are $34,100, the total decreases are $25,700, and the account balance is $8,400. The T-account in Exhibit 3.6 shows how we calculate the $8,400 balance:

Exhibit 3.6

Computing the Balance of a
T-Account

Cash			
Investment by owner	30,000	Purchase of supplies	2,500
Consulting services revenue earned	2,200	Purchase of equipment	20,000
Collection of account receivable	1,900	Payment of rent	1,000
		Payment of salary	700
		Payment of note payable	900
		Withdrawal by owner	600
Total increases	**34,100**	Total decreases	**25,700**
Less decreases	**−25,700**		
Balance	8,400		

Debits and Credits

LO 5 Define debits and credits and explain their role in double-entry accounting.

The left side of a T-account is called the **debit** side, often abbreviated *Dr.* The right side is called the **credit** side, abbreviated *Cr.*[4] To enter amounts on the left side of an account is to *debit* the account. To enter amounts on the right side is to *credit* the account. The difference between total debits and total credits for an account is the account balance. When the sum of debits exceeds the sum of credits, the account has a *debit balance*. It has a *credit balance* when the sum of credits exceeds the sum of debits. When the sum of debits equals the sum of credits, the account has a *zero balance*.

We must guard against the error of thinking that the terms debit and credit mean increase or decrease. Rather, whether a debit is an increase or decrease depends on the account. Similarly, whether a credit is an increase or decrease depends on the account. But in every account a debit and a credit have opposite effects. In an account where a debit is an increase, a credit is a decrease. And, in an account where a debit is a decrease, a credit is an increase. Knowing the account is the key to understanding the effects of debits and credits.

We must remember in working with T-accounts that a debit means an entry on the left side and a credit means an entry on the right side. To emphasize this, Exhibit 3.7 shows how Taylor's initial investment in FastForward is recorded in the Cash and Capital T-accounts:

Cash		C. Taylor, Capital	
Investment 30,000			Investment 30,000

Exhibit 3.7

Debits and Credits in T-Accounts

Notice the cash increase is recorded on the *left side* of the Cash account with a $30,000 debit entry. Also notice the corresponding increase in owner's equity is recorded on the *right side* of the capital account with a $30,000 credit entry. This dual method of recording transactions on both the left and right sides is an essential feature of *double-entry accounting,* and is the topic of the next section.

Flash back

4. Classify the following accounts as either assets, liabilities, or equity: (1) Prepaid Rent, (2) Unearned Fees, (3) Buildings, (4) Owner's Capital, (5) Wages Payable, and (6) Office Supplies.

5. What is an account? What is a ledger?

6. What determines the quantity and types of accounts used by a company?

7. Does debit always mean increase and credit always mean decrease?

Answers—p. 127

Double-Entry Accounting

Double-entry accounting means every transaction affects and is recorded in at least two accounts. *The total amount debited must equal the total amount credited* for each transaction. Since each transaction is recorded with total debits equal to total credits, the sum of the debits for all entries must equal the sum of the credits for all entries. The sum of debit account balances in the ledger must

---

[4] These abbreviations are remnants of eighteenth-century English recordkeeping practices where the terms *Debitor* and *Creditor* were used instead of *debit* and *credit*. The abbreviations use the first and last letters of these terms, just as we still do for *Saint* (St.) and *Doctor* (Dr.).

"Each action yields an equal and opposite reaction."

"Each entry yields equal and opposite total debits and total credits."

equal the sum of credit account balances. The only reason the sum of debit balances would not equal the sum of credit balances is an error has occurred. Double-entry accounting helps prevent errors by assuring that debits and credits for each transaction are equal.

The system for recording debits and credits follows from the accounting equation in Exhibit 3.8.

Exhibit 3.8

Accounting Equation

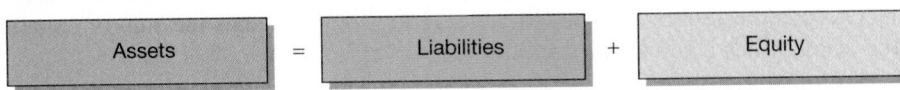

Assets = Liabilities + Equity

Assets are on the left side of this equation. Liabilities and equity are on the right side. Two points are important here. First, like any mathematical relation, increases or decreases on one side have equal effects on the other side. For example, the net increase in assets must be accompanied by an identical net increase in the liabilities and equity side. Recall that some transactions only affect one side of the equation. This means that two or more accounts on one side are affected, but their net effect on this one side is zero. Second, we treat the left side of an account as the *normal balance* side for assets, and the right side of an account as the *normal balance* for liabilities and equity. This matches their layout in the accounting equation.

The normal debit balances of asset accounts and the normal credit balances of liability and equity accounts again follow from the accounting equation. This means that increases in asset accounts are recorded with debits, while increases in liability and equity accounts are recorded with credits. These important relations are captured in Exhibit 3.9.

Exhibit 3.9

Debit and Credit Effects for Accounts

Three important rules for recording transactions in a double-entry accounting system follow from this diagram:

1. Increases in assets are debited to asset accounts. Decreases in assets are credited to asset accounts.

2. Increases in liabilities are credited to liability accounts. Decreases in liabilities are debited to liability accounts.

3. Increases in owner's equity are credited to owner's equity accounts. Decreases in owner's equity are debited to owner's equity accounts.

We explained in Chapter 2 how owner's equity increases from owner's investments and revenues. We also described how owner's equity decreases from expenses and withdrawals. These important owner's equity relations are conveyed by expanding the accounting equation in Exhibit 3.10.

Exhibit 3.10

Components of Accounting Equation

Assets = Liabilities + Owner's capital − Owner's withdrawals + Revenues − Expenses

We can extend the above diagram to include debits and credits in double-entry form in Exhibit 3.11.

Exhibit 3.11

Debit and Credit Effects for Component Accounts

Assets		=	Liabilities		+	Owner's Capital		–	Owner's Withdrawals		+	Revenues		–	Expenses	
Dr. for increases +	Cr. for decreases –		Dr. for decreases –	Cr. for increases +		Dr. for decreases –	Cr. for increases +		Dr. for increases +	Cr. for decreases –		Dr. for decreases –	Cr. for increases +		Dr. for increases +	Cr. for decreases –

Notice that increases in capital or revenues *increase* owner's equity, while increases in withdrawals or expenses *decrease* owner's equity. These relations are reflected in the following important rules:

4. Investments are credited to owner's capital because they increase equity.

5. Withdrawals are debited to owner's withdrawals because they decrease equity.

6. Revenues are credited to revenue accounts because they increase equity.

7. Expenses are debited to expense accounts because they decrease equity.

Our understanding of these diagrams and rules is crucial to analyzing and recording transactions. This also helps us prepare and analyze financial statements.[5]

Marketing Manager
You are a company's marketing manager and you want to know your company's revenues for the current period. Financial statements are not yet available. Where do you direct your search for this information? Would the general journal or the ledger be more useful to you in knowing revenues?

You Make the Call

Answer—p. 127

Indicate whether the following transactions increase or decrease the relevant account.
a. A liability account is debited for $500.
b. A revenue account is credited for $1,000.
c. An asset account is debited for $300.
d. An expense account is credited for $75.
e. Owner's capital is credited for $1,000.

_____

a. decrease; b. increase; c. increase; d. decrease; e. increase

Mid-Chapter Demonstration Problem

Solution to Mid-Chapter Demonstration Problem

---

[5] We can use good judgment to our advantage in applying double-entry accounting. For example, revenues and expenses normally (but not always) accumulate in business. This means they increase and rarely decrease during an accounting period. Accordingly, we should be alert to decreases in these accounts (debit revenues or credit expenses) to be certain this is our intent.

Analyzing Transactions

LO 6 Analyze the impact of transactions on accounts and financial statements.

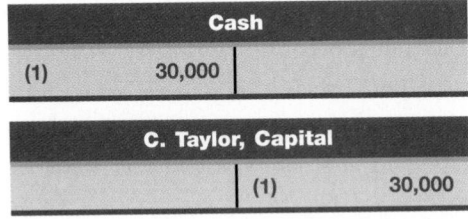

We return to the activities of FastForward to show how debit and credit rules and double-entry accounting are useful in analyzing and processing transactions. We analyze FastForward's transactions in two steps. *Step one* analyzes a transaction and its source document(s). *Step two* applies double-entry accounting to identify the impact of a transaction on account balances. We include in step two an analysis of "statement links" to identify the financial statements impacted by a transaction. Exhibit 3.13 shown later in this chapter makes these links clear.

We should study each transaction thoroughly before going on. The first 11 transactions are familiar to us from Chapter 2. We expand our analysis of these transactions and consider five new transactions (numbered 12 through 16) of FastForward that were earlier omitted.

1. Investment by Owner

Cash	
(1) 30,000	

C. Taylor, Capital	
	(1) 30,000

Transaction. Chuck Taylor invested $30,000 in FastForward on December 1.

Analysis. Assets increase. Owner's equity increases.

Double-entry. Debit the Cash asset account for $30,000. Credit Taylor's Capital account in owner's equity for $30,000.

Ledger Statements.[6] BS, SCF and SCOE

2. Purchase Supplies for Cash

Supplies	
(2) 2,500	

Cash	
(1) 30,000	(2) 2,500

Transaction. FastForward purchases supplies by paying $2,500 cash.

Analysis. Assets increase. Assets decrease. This changes the composition of assets, but does not change the total amount of assets.

Double-entry. Debit the Supplies asset account for $2,500. Credit the Cash asset account for $2,500.

Ledger Statements. BS and SCF

3. Purchase Equipment for Cash

Equipment	
(3) 20,000	

Cash	
(1) 30,000	(2) 2,500
	(3) 20,000

Transaction. FastForward purchases equipment by paying $20,000 cash.

Analysis. Assets increase. Assets decrease. This changes the composition of assets, but does not change the total amount of assets.

Double-entry. Debit the Equipment asset account for $20,000. Credit the Cash asset account for $20,000.

Ledger Statements. BS and SCF

4. Purchase Equipment and Supplies on Credit

Supplies	
(2) 2,500	
(4) 1,100	

Transaction. FastForward purchases $1,100 of supplies and $6,000 of equipment on credit. FastForward signs a promissory note for the $6,000 of equipment.

Analysis. Assets increase. Liabilities increase.

---

[6] We use abbreviations for the statements: Income Statement (IS); Balance Sheet (BS); Statement of Cash Flows (SCF); and Statement of Changes in Owner's Equity (SCOE).

Equipment	
(3) 20,000	
(4) 6,000	

Accounts Payable	
	(4) 1,100

Note Payable	
	(4) 6,000

Double-entry. Debit two asset accounts: Supplies for $1,100 and Equipment for $6,000. Credit two liability accounts: Accounts Payable for $1,100 and Note Payable for $6,000.

Ledger Statements. BS

5. Services Rendered for Cash

Cash			
(1)	30,000	(2)	2,500
(5)	2,200	(3)	20,000

Consulting Revenue		
		(5) 2,200

Transaction. FastForward provided consulting services to a customer and immediately collected $2,200 cash.

Analysis. Assets increase. Owner's equity increases from Revenue.

Double-entry. Debit the Cash asset account for $2,200. Credit the Consulting Revenue account for $2,200 (this increases owner's equity).

Ledger Statements. BS, IS, SCF and SCOE

6. Payment of Expense in Cash

Rent Expense	
(6) 1,000	

Cash			
(1)	30,000	(2)	2,500
(5)	2,200	(3)	20,000
		(6)	1,000

Transaction. FastForward pays $1,000 cash for December rent.

Analysis. Assets decrease. Owner's equity decreases from Expense.

Double-entry. Debit the Rent Expense account for $1,000 (this decreases owner's equity). Credit the Cash asset account for $1,000.

Ledger Statements. BS, IS, SCF and SCOE

7. Payment of Expense in Cash

Salaries Expense	
(7) 700	

Cash			
(1)	30,000	(2)	2,500
(5)	2,200	(3)	20,000
		(6)	1,000
		(7)	700

Transaction. FastForward pays $700 cash for employee's salary for the pay period ending on December 12.

Analysis. Assets decrease. Owner's equity decreases from Expense.

Double-entry. Debit the Salaries Expense account for $700 (this decreases owner's equity). Credit the Cash asset account for $700.

Ledger Statements. BS, IS, SCF and SCOE

8. Services and Rental Revenues Rendered on Credit

Accounts Receivable		
(8)	1,900	

Consulting Revenue		
	(5)	2,200
	(8)	1,600

Rental Revenue		
	(8)	300

Transaction. FastForward provided consulting services of $1,600 and rented test facilities for $300 to a customer. The customer is billed $1,900 for the services and FastForward expects to collect this money in the near future.

Analysis. Assets increase. Owner's equity increases from Revenue.

Double-entry. Debit the Accounts Receivable asset account for $1,900. Credit two revenue accounts: Consulting Revenue for $1,600 (this increases owner's equity) and Rental Revenue for $300 (this increases owner's equity).

Ledger Statements. BS, IS and SCOE

9. Receipt of Cash on Account

Cash			
(1)	30,000	(2)	2,500
(5)	2,200	(3)	20,000
(9)	1,900	(6)	1,000
		(7)	700

Accounts Receivable			
(8)	1,900	(9)	1,900

Transaction. An amount of $1,900 is received from the client in transaction 8 on the tenth day after being billed for the services and facilities provided.

Analysis. Assets increase. Assets decrease. This changes the composition of assets, but does not change the total amount of assets.

Double-entry. Debit the Cash asset account for $1,900. Credit Accounts Receivable asset account for $1,900.

Ledger Statements. BS and SCF

10. Partial Payment of Note Payable

Note Payable			
(10)	900	(4)	6,000

Cash			
(1)	30,000	(2)	2,500
(5)	2,200	(3)	20,000
(9)	1,900	(6)	1,000
		(7)	700
		(10)	900

Transaction. FastForward pays $900 cash toward the note payable of $6,000 owed from the purchase of equipment in transaction 4.

Analysis. Assets decrease. Liabilities decrease.

Double-entry. Debit the Note Payable liability account for $900. Credit the Cash asset account for $900.

Ledger Statements. BS and SCF

11. Withdrawal of Cash by Owner

C. Taylor, Withdrawals	
(11) 600	

Cash			
(1)	30,000	(2)	2,500
(5)	2,200	(3)	20,000
(9)	1,900	(6)	1,000
		(7)	700
		(10)	900
		(11)	600

Transaction. Chuck Taylor withdraws $600 from FastForward for personal living expenses.

Analysis. Assets decrease. Owner's equity decreases.

Double-entry. Debit the owner's equity Withdrawal account for $600. Credit the Cash asset account for $600.

Ledger Statements. BS, SCF and SCOE

12. Receives Cash for Future Services

Cash			
(1)	30,000	(2)	2,500
(5)	2,200	(3)	20,000
(9)	1,900	(6)	1,000
(12)	3,000	(7)	700
		(10)	900
		(11)	600

Unearned Consulting Revenue		
	(12)	3,000

Transaction. FastForward enters into (signs) a contract with a customer to provide future consulting. FastForward receives $3,000 cash in advance of rendering these consulting services.

Analysis. Assets increase. Liabilities increase. Accepting the $3,000 cash obligates FastForward to perform future services, and is a liability. No revenue is earned until services are rendered.

Double-entry. Debit the Cash asset account for $3,000. Credit an Unearned Consulting Revenue liability account for $3,000.

Ledger Statements. BS and SCF

13. Pays Cash for Future Insurance Coverage

Prepaid Insurance	
(13) 2,400	

Cash			
(1)	30,000	(2)	2,500
(5)	2,200	(3)	20,000
(9)	1,900	(6)	1,000
(12)	3,000	(7)	700
		(10)	900
		(11)	600
		(13)	2,400

Transaction. FastForward pays $2,400 cash (premium) for a two-year insurance policy. Coverage begins on December 1.

Analysis. Assets increase. Assets decrease. This changes the composition of assets from cash to a "right" of insurance coverage. This does not change the total amount of assets. Expense will be incurred as insurance coverage is provided.

Double-entry. Debit the Prepaid Insurance asset account for $2,400. Credit the Cash asset account for $2,400.

Ledger Statements. BS and SCF

14. Purchase Supplies for Cash

Supplies	
(2)	2,500
(4)	1,100
(14)	120

Cash			
(1)	30,000	(2)	2,500
(5)	2,200	(3)	20,000
(9)	1,900	(6)	1,000
(12)	3,000	(7)	700
		(10)	900
		(11)	600
		(13)	2,400
		(14)	120

Transaction. FastForward purchases supplies by paying $120 cash.

Analysis. Assets increase. Assets decrease. This changes the composition of assets.

Double-entry. Debit the Supplies asset account for $120. Credit the Cash asset account for $120.

Ledger Statements. BS and SCF

15. Payment of Expense in Cash

Utilities Expense	
(15)	230

Cash			
(1)	30,000	(2)	2,500
(5)	2,200	(3)	20,000
(9)	1,900	(6)	1,000
(12)	3,000	(7)	700
		(10)	900
		(11)	600
		(13)	2,400
		(14)	120
		(15)	230

Transaction. FastForward pays $230 cash for December utilities.

Analysis. Assets decrease. Owner's equity decreases from Expense.

Double-entry. Debit the Utilities Expense account for $230 (this decreases owner's equity). Credit the Cash asset account for $230.

Ledger Statements. BS, IS, SCF and SCOE

16. Payment of Expense in Cash

Salaries Expense	
(7)	700
(16)	700

Cash			
(1)	30,000	(2)	2,500
(5)	2,200	(3)	20,000
(9)	1,900	(6)	1,000
(12)	3,000	(7)	700
		(10)	900
		(11)	600
		(13)	2,400
		(14)	120
		(15)	230
		(16)	700

Transaction. FastForward pays $700 cash for employee's salary for the two-week pay period ending on December 26.

Analysis. Assets decrease. Owner's equity decreases from Expense.

Double-entry. Debit the Salaries Expense account for $700 (this decreases owner's equity). Credit the Cash asset account for $700.

Ledger Statements. BS, IS, SCF and SCOE

Accounting Equation Analysis

Exhibit 3.12 lists the accounts of FastForward after all sixteen transactions are recorded and the balances computed. The accounts are grouped into three major columns. These columns represent the terms in the accounting equation: assets, liabilities and owners' equity.

Exhibit 3.12 highlights several important points. First, as with each transaction, the totals for the three columns must obey the accounting equation: assets = liabilities + equity. Specifically, assets equal \$40,070 (\$7,950 + \$0 + \$2,400 + \$3,720 + \$26,000). Total liabilities are \$9,200 (\$1,100 + \$3,000 + \$5,100) and total equity is \$30,870 (\$30,000 − \$600 + \$3,800 + \$300 − \$1,000 − \$1,400 − \$230). These numbers obey the accounting equation: \$40,070 = \$9,200 + \$30,870. Second, the withdrawals, revenue and expense accounts reflect the events that change owner's equity. Their ending balances make up the statement of changes in owner's equity. Third, the revenue and expense account balances are summarized and reported in the income statement. Fourth, components of the cash account make up the elements reported in the statement of cash flows.

Exhibit 3.12

Ledger for FastForward

Assets			=	Liabilities		+	Owner's Equity		
Cash				**Accounts Payable**			**C. Taylor, Capital**		
(1)	30,000	(2) 2,500			(4) 1,100			(1)	30,000
(5)	2,200	(3) 20,000							
(9)	1,900	(6) 1,000		**Unearned Consulting Revenue**			**C. Taylor, Withdrawls**		
(12)	3,000	(7) 700			(12) 3,000	(11)	600		
		(10) 900							
		(11) 600		**Note Payable**			**Consulting Revenue**		
		(13) 2,400		(10) 900	(4) 6,000			(5)	2,200
		(14) 120			Balance 5,100			(8)	1,600
		(15) 230						Bal.	3,800
		(16) 700							
Total	37,100	Total 29,150					**Rental Revenue**		
Balance	7,950							(8)	300

Accounts Receivable		
(8)	1,900	(9) 1,900
Balance	-0-	

Prepaid Insurance	
(13)	2,400

Supplies	
(2)	2,500
(4)	1,100
(14)	120
Balance	3,720

Equipment	
(3)	20,000
(4)	6,000
Balance	26,000

Rent Expense	
(6)	1,000

Salaries Expense	
(7)	7000
(16)	700
Balance	1,400

Utilities Expense	
(15)	230

Accounts in this shaded area reflect increases and decreases in owner's equity. Their balances are reported on the income statement or the statement of changes in owner's equity.

\$40,070		=	**\$9,200**		+	**\$30,870**

Financial Statement Links

Exhibit 3.13 extends the statement links analysis to summarize how transactions and their related accounts impact financial statements. Some transactions such as purchasing supplies on credit (no. 4) only impact one statement. Others such as receiving cash for services performed (no. 5) impact all of the statements. We should review this exhibit and understand how transactions link with financial statements. We return to explain the details of these links in Chapter 5, including the adjusting and closing processes required.

Flash back

8. What kinds of transactions increase owner's equity? What kinds decrease owner's equity?

9. Why are most accounting systems called *double-entry*?

10. Double-entry accounting requires that:

a. All transactions that create debits to asset accounts must create credits to liability or owner's equity accounts.

b. A transaction that requires a debit to a liability account also requires a credit to an asset account.

c. Every transaction must be recorded with total debits equal to total credits.

Answers—p. 127

Exhibit 3.13

Financial Statement Links with Transactions

		Balance Sheet (BS)									
Transactions		**Assets**					**=**	**Liabilities**			**+ Equity**
No.	**Description**	**Cash**	**Accts. Rec.**	**Prepd. Insur.**	**Supp.**	**Equip.**	**= Accts. Pay**	**Unear. Rev.**	**Note Pay.**	**+**	**Cap.**
1	Owner Investment	30,000					=			+	30,000
2	Purch. supp.	(2,500)			2,500		=			+	
3	Purch. equip.	(20,000)				20,000	=			+	
4	Credit Purch.				1,100	6,000	= 1,100		6,000	+	
5	Services for cash	2,200					=			+	2,200
6	Rent exp.	(1,000)					=			+	(1,000)
7	Sal. exp.	(700)					=			+	(700)
8	Services for credit		1,900				=			+	1,600 300
9	Cash rec'd. on Acct. Rec.	1,900	(1,900)				=			+	
10	Payment of Note Pay	(900)					=		(900)	+	
11	Owner Withdrawal	(600)					=			+	(600)
12	Cash for future Service	3,000					=	3,000		+	
13	Payment of future Insur.	(2,400)		2,400			=			+	
14	Purch. Supp.	(120)			120		=			+	
15	Util. exp.	(230)					=			+	(230)
16	Salary exp.	(700)					=			+	(700)
	Total	7,950	-0-	2,400	3,720	26,000	= 1,100	3,000	5,100	+	30,870

We used double-entry accounting in the prior section to show how transactions affect accounts. This process of analyzing transactions (*step one*) and recording their effects directly in accounts (*step two*) is useful in understanding the double-entry accounting system.

Yet accounting systems rarely record transactions directly in accounts. Instead, the accounting process includes a *third step* where we record transactions in a record called a **journal** before recording them in accounts. This is to avoid the potential for error and the difficulty in tracking mistakes. This practice gives us a complete record of each transaction in one place. It also links directly the debits and credits for each transaction. The process of recording transactions in a journal is called **journalizing.**

Step four of the accounting process is to transfer (or *post*) entries from the journal to the ledger. This step occurs only after debits and credits for each transaction are entered into a journal. This process leaves a helpful trail in checking for accuracy. It also helps us avoid errors. The process of transferring journal entry information to the ledger is called **posting.** This section describes both journalizing and posting of transactions. *Step five,* preparing a trial balance, is explained in the next section. Each of these steps in processing transactions is depicted in Exhibit 3.14.

Recording and Posting Transactions

LO7 Record transactions in a journal and post entries to a ledger.

Income Statement (IS)			Statement of Cash Flows (SCF)				Transactions	
Rev. −	Exp. =	Net Inc.	Oper.	Inv.	Fin.	Net Cash Flow	No.	Description
−	=				30,000	30,000	1	Owner Investment
−	=		(2,500)			(2,500)	2	Purch. supp.
−	=			(20,000)		(20,000)	3	Purch. equip.
−	=						4	Credit Purch.
2,200 −	=	2,200	2,200			2,200	5	Services for cash
−	1,000 =	(1,000)	(1,000)			(1,000)	6	Rent exp.
−	700 =	(700)	(700)			(700)	7	Sal. exp.
1600 −	=	1600					8	Services for credit
300		300						
−	=		1,900			1,900	9	Cash rec'd. on Acct. Rec.
−	=				(900)	(900)	10	Payment of Note Pay
−	=				(600)	(600)	11	Owner Withdrawal
−	=		3,000			3,000	12	Cash for future Service
−	=		(2,400)			(2,400)	13	Payment of future Insur.
−	=		(120)			(120)	14	Purch. Supp.
−	230 =	(230)	(230)			(230)	15	Util. exp.
−	700 =	(700)	(700)			(700)	16	Salary exp.
4,100 −	2,630 =	1,470	(550)	(20,000)	28,500	7,950		Total

Exhibit 3.14

Steps in Processing
Transactions

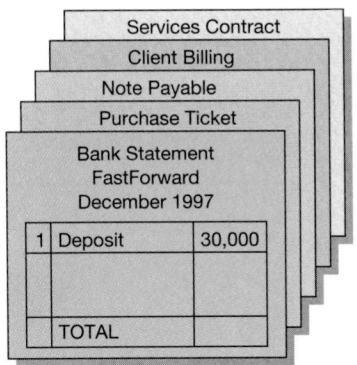

Step 1: Analyze transactions and
source documents.

Step 2: Apply double-entry accounting.

General Journal		
Dec. 1 Cash	30,000	
Taylor, Capital		30,000
Dec. 2 Supplies	2,500	
Cash		2,500

Step 3: Record journal entry.

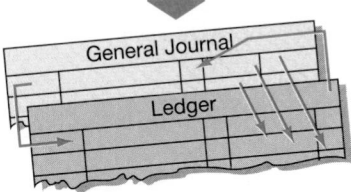

Step 4: Post entry to ledger.

FastForward Trial Balance		
December 31, 1997		
	Debit	Credit
Cash	$7,950	
Accounts Receivable	-0-	
Prepaid Insurance	$2,400	

Step 5: Prepare trial balance.

The Journal Entry

The **general journal** is flexible in that it can be used to record any transaction. A general journal entry includes the following information about each transaction:

1. Date of transaction.
2. Titles of affected accounts.
3. Dollar amount of each debit and credit.
4. Explanation of transaction.

Exhibit 3.15 shows how the first four transactions of FastForward are recorded in a general journal. A journal is often referred to as the *book of original entry*. The accounting process is similar for manual and computerized systems. Many computer programs even copy the look of a paper journal.

   The fourth entry in Exhibit 3.15 uses four accounts. There are debits to the two assets purchased, supplies and equipment. There are also credits to the two sources of payment, accounts payable and note payable. A transaction affecting three or more accounts yields a **compound journal entry.**

Journalizing Transactions

There are regular procedures when recording entries in a general journal. We can identify nine steps in journalizing the entries in Exhibit 3.15. It is helpful to review the entries when studying these steps.

1. Enter the year on the first line at the top of the first column.
2. Enter the month in column one on the first line of the journal entry. Later entries for the same month and year on the same page of the journal do not require reentering the same month and year.
3. Enter the day of the transaction in column two on the first line of each entry.
4. Enter the titles of accounts debited. Account titles are taken from the chart of accounts and are aligned with the left margin of the Account Titles and Explanation column.
5. Enter the debit amounts in the Debit column on the same line as the accounts to be debited.
6. Enter the titles of accounts credited. Account titles are taken from the chart of accounts and are indented from the left margin of the Account Titles and Explanation column to distinguish them from debited accounts (an inch is common).
7. Enter the credit amounts in the Credit column on the same line as the accounts to be credited.
8. Enter a brief explanation of the transaction on the line below the entry. This explanation is indented about half as far as the credited account titles to avoid confusing an explanation with accounts. For illustrative purposes, we italicize explanations so they stand out. This is not normally done.
9. Skip a line between each journal entry for clarity.

A complete journal entry gives us a useful description of the transaction and its effects on the organization.

   The **posting reference (PR) column** is left blank when a transaction is initially recorded. Individual account numbers are later entered into the PR column when entries are posted to the ledger. The PR column is also called the *folio column*. This follows from past recordkeeping procedures where each account took up a page in a book, and an old word for page is *folio*.

| General Journal | | | | Page 1 |
Date	Account Titles and Explanation	PR	Debit	Credit
1997				
Dec. 1	Cash		30,000	
	C. Taylor, Capital			30,000
	Investment by owner.			
2	Supplies		2,500	
	Cash			2,500
	Purchased store supplies for cash.			
3	Equipment		20,000	
	Cash			20,000
	Purchased testing equipment for cash.			
6	Supplies		1,100	
	Equipment		6,000	
	Accounts Payable			1,100
	Note Payable			6,000
	Purchased supplies and equipment on credit.			

Exhibit 3.15

Partial General Journal for FastForward

Computerized Journals

Journals in computerized and manual systems serve the same purposes. Computerized journals are often designed to look like a manual journal page like in Exhibit 3.15. Maria Sanchez of RecordLink in the opening article designed her Web-based system to look exactly like the paper-based system. Computerized systems typically include error-checking routines that ensure debits equal credits for each entry. Shortcuts often allow recordkeepers to enter account numbers instead of names, and to enter account names and numbers with pull-down menus.

Balance Column Ledger

T-accounts are simple and direct means to show how the accounting process works. They allow us to omit less relevant details and concentrate on main ideas. Accounting systems in practice need more structure such as a running balance and use **balance column ledger accounts.** Exhibit 3.16 is an example.

| Cash | | | | | Account No. 101 | |
Date		Explanation	PR	Debit	Credit	Balance
1997	1		G1	30,000		30,000
Dec.	2		G1		2,500	27,500
	3		G1		20,000	7,500
	10		G1	2,200		9,700

Exhibit 3.16

Cash Account in Balance Column Ledger

The balance column ledger account format is similar to a T-account in having columns for debits and credits. It is different in having a transaction's date and explanation. It also has a third column with the balance of the account after each entry is posted. This means the amount on the last line in this column is the account's current balance. For example, FastForward's Cash account in Exhibit 3.16 is debited on December 1 for the $30,000 investment by Taylor. The account then shows a $30,000 debit balance. The account is credited on December 2 for $2,500, and its new $27,500 balance is shown in the third column. On December 3, it is credited again, this time for $20,000, and its balance is reduced to $7,500. The Cash account is debited for $2,200 on December 10, and its balance increases to $9,700.

When a balance column ledger is used, the heading of the Balance column does not show whether it is a debit or credit balance. This omission is no problem because every account has a *normal balance*. The normal balance of each account (asset, liability, owner's equity, revenue or expense) refers to the left or right (debit or credit) side where increases are recorded. The earlier diagrams in this chapter highlight this. Exhibit 3.17 shows normal balances for accounts to emphasize their importance.

Exhibit 3.17

Normal Balances for Accounts

Assets		=	Liabilities		+	Owner's Capital		–	Owner's Withdrawals		+	Revenues		–	Expenses	
Dr. for increases + **Normal**	Cr. for decreases –		Dr. for decreases –	Cr. for increases + **Normal**		Dr. for decreases –	Cr. for increases + **Normal**		Dr. for increases + **Normal**	Cr. for decreases –		Dr. for decreases –	Cr. for increases + **Normal**		Dr. for increases + **Normal**	Cr. for decreases –

Abnormal Balance

Unusual events can sometimes give an abnormal balance for an account. An *abnormal balance* refers to a balance on the side where decreases are recorded. For example, a customer might mistakenly overpay a bill. This gives that customer's account receivable an abnormal (credit) balance. An abnormal balance is often identified by circling it or by entering it in red or some other unusual colour. Computerized systems often provide a code beside a balance such as *dr.* or *cr.* to identify what kind of balance.

Zero Balance

A zero balance for an account is usually shown by writing zeros or a dash in the Balance column. This practice avoids confusion between a zero balance and one omitted in error.

Did You Know?

The Next Generation

What are likely duties for the next generation of accounting professionals? A recent article on professional management accountants gives us a peek. Accountants were once perceived as: bean counters; nonplayers in corporate strategy; narrowly focused; and preoccupied with costs. Management accountants are now major players in: long-term planning; revenue strategies; using technology; and interpreting accounting information. This suggests the next generation of accounting professionals will require more analytical and conceptual skills. [Source: *CMA Magazine*, July–August, 1996.]

Posting Journal Entries

Exhibit 3.16 showed us that journal entries are posted to ledger accounts. To ensure that the ledger is up to date, entries are posted as soon as possible. This might be daily, weekly, or when time permits. All entries must be posted to the ledger by the end of a reporting period. This is so that account balances are current when financial statements are prepared. It also indicates why the ledger is referred to as the *book of final entry*.

When posting entries to the ledger, the debits in journal entries are copied into ledger accounts as debits, and credits are copied into the ledger as credits.

Exhibit 3.18 lists six steps of manual systems to post each debit and credit from a journal entry.

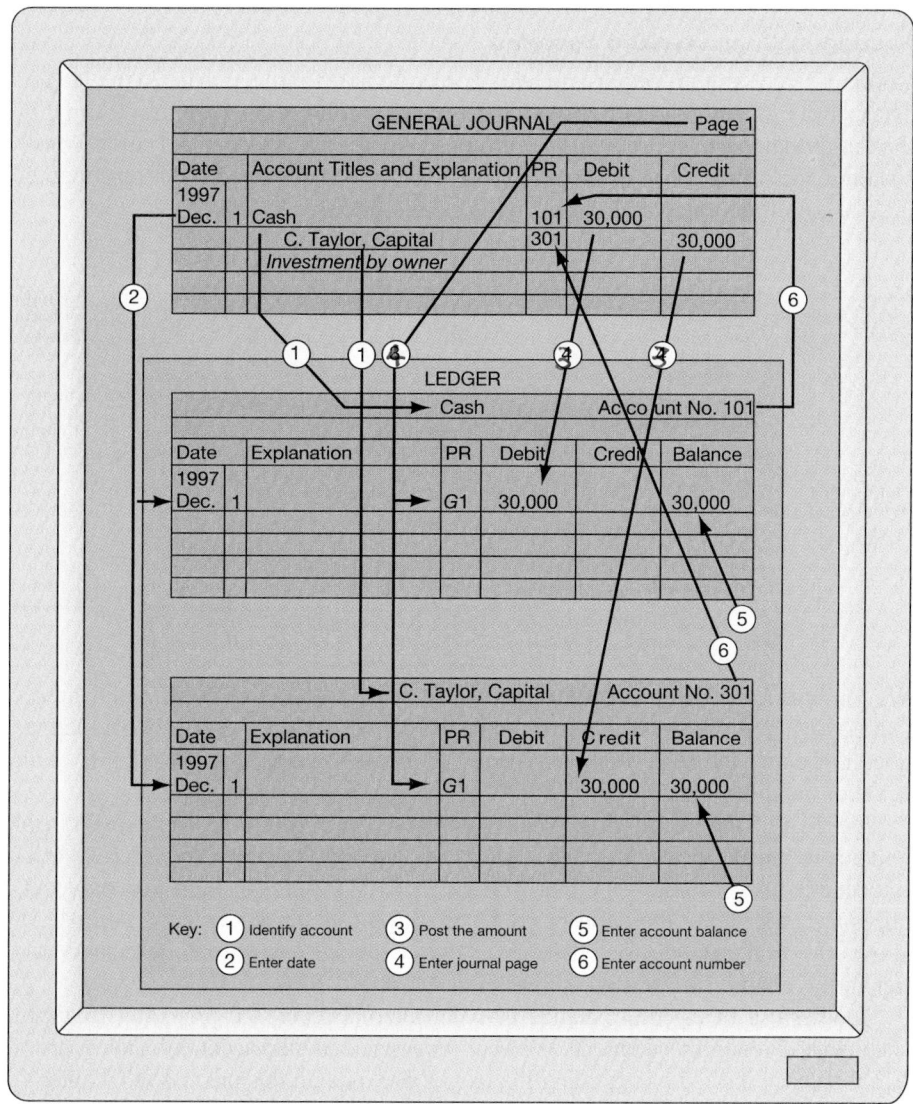

Exhibit 3.18

Posting an entry to the ledger

The usual process is to post in order debits and then credits. The steps in posting are:

1. Identify the ledger account that was debited in the journal entry.
2. Enter the date of the journal entry in this ledger account.
3. Enter the amount debited from the journal entry into the Debit column of the ledger account.
4. Enter the source of the debit in the PR column, both the journal and page. The letter *G* shows it came from the general journal.[7]
5. Compute and enter the account's new balance in the Balance column.
6. Enter the ledger account number in the PR column of the journal entry.

Repeat the six steps for credit amounts and Credit columns.

Step 6 in the posting process for both debit and credit amounts of an entry inserts the account number in the journal's PR column. This creates a link between the ledger and the journal entry. This link is a useful cross-reference for tracing

---

[7] Other journals are identified by their own letters. We discuss other journals later in the book.

an amount from one record to another. It also readily shows the stage of completion in the posting process. This permits one to easily start and stop the posting process without losing one's place.

Posting in Computerized Systems

Computerized systems require no added effort to post journal entries to the ledger. These systems automatically transfer debit and credit entries from the journal to the ledger database. Journal entries are posted directly to ledger accounts. Many systems, including those of **RecordLink,** have programs testing the reasonableness of a journal entry and the account balance when recorded.

Flash back

11. When Maria Sanchez set up RecordLink, she invested $15,000 cash and equipment with a market value of $23,000. RecordLink also took responsibility for an $18,000 note payable issued to finance the purchase of equipment. Prepare the journal entry to record Sanchez's investment.

12. Explain what a compound journal entry is.

13. Why are posting reference numbers entered in the journal when entries are posted to accounts?

Answers—p. 127

Trial Balance

LO8 Prepare and explain the use of a trial balance.

We know double-entry accounting records every transaction with equal debits and credits. We also know an error exists if the sum of debit entries in the ledger does not equal the sum of credit entries. This also means that the sum of debit account balances must equal the sum of credit account balances.

Step five of the accounting process explained in Exhibit 3.14 is using a trial balance to check on whether debit and credit account balances are equal. A **trial balance** is a list of accounts and their balances at a point in time. Account balances are reported in the debit or credit column of the trial balance. Exhibit 3.19 shows the trial balance for FastForward after the sixteen entries described earlier in the chapter are posted to the ledger.

Another use of the trial balance is as an internal report for preparing financial statements. Preparing statements is easier when we can take account balances from a trial balance instead of searching the ledger. We explain this process in Chapter 4.

Preparing a Trial Balance

Preparing a trial balance involves five steps:

1. Identify each account balance from the ledger.
2. List each account and its balance. Debit balances are entered in the Debit column and credit balances in the Credit column.[8]
3. Compute the total of debit balances.
4. Compute the total of credit balances.
5. Verify that total debit balances equal total credit balances.

Notice that the total debit balances equal the total credit balances for the trial balance in Exhibit 3.19. If these two totals were not equal, we would know that one or more errors exist. We should also realize that equality of these two totals does not guarantee us no errors were made.

---

[8] If an account has a zero balance, it can be listed in the trial balance with a zero in the column for its normal balance.

Using a Trial Balance

We know one or more errors exist when a trial balance does not balance (when its columns are not equal). When one or more errors exist they often arise from one of the following steps in the accounting process: (1) preparing journal entries, (2) posting entries to the ledger, (3) computing account balances, (4) copying account balances to the trial balance, or (5) totalling the trial balance columns.

Exhibit 3.19

Trial Balance

FASTFORWARD Trial Balance December 31, 1997		
	Debit	**Credit**
Cash	$7,950	
Accounts receivable	-0-	
Prepaid insurance	2,400	
Supplies	3,720	
Equipment	26,000	
Accounts payable		$1,100
Unearned consulting revenue . . .		3,000
Note payable		5,100
C. Taylor, Capital		30,000
C. Taylor, Withdrawals	600	
Consulting revenue		3,800
Rental revenue		300
Rent expense	1,000	
Salaries expense	1,400	
Utilities expense	230	
Total	$43,300	$43,300

When a trial balance does balance, the accounts are likely free of the kind of errors that create unequal debits and credits. Yet errors can still exist. One example is when a debit or credit of a correct amount is made to a wrong account. This can occur when either journalizing or posting. The error would produce incorrect balances in two accounts but the trial balance would balance. Another error is to record equal debits and credits of an incorrect amount. This error produces incorrect balances in two accounts but again the debits and credits are equal. We give these examples to show that when a trial balance does balance, it does not prove all journal entries are recorded and posted correctly.

Searching for Errors

At least one error exists if the trial balance does not balance. The error (or errors) must be found and corrected before preparing financial statements. Searching for the error is more efficient if we check the journalizing, posting and trial balance preparation process in *reverse order*. Otherwise we would need to look at every transaction until the error is found.

Several steps are involved. Step one is to verify that the trial balance columns are correctly added. If step one fails to find the error, then step two is to verify that account balances are accurately copied from the ledger. Our third step to identify the error is to see if a debit or credit balance is mistakenly listed in the trial balance as a credit or debit. A clue to this kind of error is when the difference between total debits and total credits in the trial balance equals twice the amount of the incorrectly listed account balance.

If the error is still undiscovered, our fourth step is to recompute each account balance. Our fifth step if the error remains is to verify that each journal entry is properly posted to ledger accounts. Our sixth step is to verify that the original journal entry has equal debits and credits.

One frequent error is called a *transposition*. This error is when two digits are switched or transposed within a number. If transposition is the only error, then it yields a difference between two trial balance columns that is evenly divisible by nine. For example, assume a $691 debit in a journal entry is incorrectly posted to the ledger as $619 instead of the correct $691. Total credits in the trial balance are then larger than total debits by $72 ($691 − $619). The $72 error is evenly divisible by 9 ($72/9 = 8). Also, the quotient or result (in our example it is 8) equals the difference between the two transposed numbers (91 vs. 19, that is, 9 − 1 = 8). The number of digits in the quotient also tells the location of the transposition. Because the quotient in our example had only one digit (8), it tells us the transposition is in the first digit of the transposed numbers, starting from the right.[9]

---

[9] Consider another example where a transposition error involves posting $961 instead of the correct $691. The difference in these numbers is $270, and its quotient is $30 ($270/9). Because the quotient has two digits, it tells us to check the second digits from the right for a transposition of two numbers that have a difference of 3.

Correcting Errors

If errors are discovered in either the journal or the ledger, they must be corrected. Our approach to correcting errors depends on the kind of error and when it is discovered.

If an error in a journal entry is discovered before the error is posted, it can be corrected in a manual system by drawing a line through the incorrect information. The correct information is written above it to create a record of change for the auditor. Many computerized systems allow the operator to replace the incorrect information directly. If a correct amount in the journal is posted incorrectly to the ledger, we can correct it the same way.

Another case is when an error in a journal entry is not discovered until after it is posted. We usually do not strike through both erroneous entries in the journal and ledger. Instead, the usual practice is to correct the error in the original journal entry by creating *another* journal entry. This *correcting entry* removes the amount from the wrong account and records it to the correct account. As an example, suppose we recorded a purchase of office supplies in the journal with an incorrect debit to Office Equipment:

Assets = Liabilities + Equity
+1,600
−1,600

Oct. 14	Office Equipment	1,600	
	Cash		1,600
	To record the purchase of office supplies.		

We then post this entry to the ledger. The Office Supplies ledger account balance is understated by $1,600 and the Office Equipment ledger account balance is overstated by the same amount. When we discover the error three days later, the following correcting entry is made:

Assets = Liabilities + Equity
+1,600
−1,600

Oct. 17	Office Supplies	1,600	
	Office Equipment		1,600
	To correct the entry of October 14 that incorrectly debited Office Equipment instead of Office Supplies.		

The credit in the correcting entry removes the error from the first entry. The debit correctly records the supplies. The explanation reports exactly what happened.

Computerized systems often use similar correcting entries. The exact procedure depends on the system used and management policy. Yet nearly all systems include controls to show when and where a correction is made.

Did You Know?

Window on Accounting
Manual and computerized accounting systems mirror each other. Computerized systems often take on many routine tasks in accounting. They also give regular updating (batch time) or continuous (real time) processing of information. Many programs point out errors like unequal debits and credits or the transposing of numbers. They usually look like the paper-based ledger and general journal. Computerized systems have freed accounting professionals to spend more time and effort on analyzing and interpreting information for users. [Source: *Computing Canada*, June 6, 1996.]

Formatting Conventions

Dollar signs are not used in journals and ledgers. They do appear in financial statements and other reports, including trial balances. This book follows the usual practice of putting a dollar sign beside the first amount in each column of numbers and the first amount appearing after a ruled line indicating that an addition or subtraction has been performed. The financial statements in Exhibit 2.15 demonstrate how dollar signs are used in this book. Different companies use various conventions for dollar signs. For example, dollar signs are usually printed beside only the first and last numbers in columns of the financial statements for **Alliance**.

When amounts are entered manually in a journal, ledger or trial balance, commas are not needed to indicate thousands, millions and so forth. Also, decimal points are not needed to separate dollars and cents. If an amount consists of even dollars without cents, a convenient shortcut uses a dash in the cents column instead of two zeros. However, commas and decimal points are used in financial statements and other reports. An exception is when this detail is not important to users.

It is common for companies to round amounts to the nearest dollar, and even to a higher level for certain accounts. Alliance is typical of many companies in that it rounds its financial statement amounts to the nearest thousand dollars. But it continues to report its income per share amount in dollars with cents. Alliance's decision is usually linked with the perceived importance of the rounding for users' decisions.

Debt Ratio

USING THE INFORMATION

LO 9 Compute the debt ratio and describe its use in analyzing company performance.

Accounting records are designed to provide useful information for users of financial statements. One important objective for many users is gathering information to help them assess a company's risk of failing to pay its debts when they are due. This section describes the debt ratio and how it can help in this task.

Most companies finance a portion of their assets with liabilities and the remaining portion with equity. A company that finances a relatively large portion of its assets with liabilities is said to have a high degree of *financial leverage*. While we will discuss more about financial leverage in Chapter 16, we should understand that higher financial leverage involves greater risk. This is because liabilities must be repaid and often require regular interest payments. The risk is that a company may not be able to meet required payments. This risk is higher if a company has more liabilities (more highly leveraged).

One way to assess the risk associated with a company's use of liabilities is to compute and analyze the debt ratio. The **debt ratio** describes the relation between the amounts of a company's liabilities and assets, and is defined in Exhibit 3.20.

$$\text{Debt ratio} = \frac{\text{Total liabilities}}{\text{Total assets}}$$

Exhibit 3.20

Debt Ratio

To see how we apply the debt ratio, let's look at **Loblaw's** liabilities and assets (in millions) for 1992–1996. Loblaw is Canada's largest retail and wholesale food distributor. Using these data, we compute in Exhibit 3.21 the debt ratio for Loblaw at the end of each year.

	1996	1995	1994	1993	1992
a. Total liabilities	2,220	2,037	1,937	1,758	1,588
b. Total assets	3,531	3,197	3,042	2,743	2,504
c. Debt ratio (a ÷ b)	.629	.637	.637	.641	.634

Exhibit 3.21

Computation and Analysis of Debt Ratio

Evaluating a company's debt ratio depends on several factors such as the nature of its operations, its ability to generate cash flows, its industry and economic conditions. It is not possible to say that a specific debt ratio is good or bad for all companies. As we discussed in the prior chapters, we need to compare performance over time and across companies both in and outside of the industry.

We should note that Loblaw's debt ratio is stable over recent years, ranging from a low of .629 to a high of .641. This is average for most companies when compared to industry figures.

You Make the Call

Investor
You are considering buying shares in Canadian Tire. As part of your analysis you compute the debt ratio of Canadian Tire for 1994, 1995 and 1996: .57, .54 and .50, respectively. Based on these debt ratios, is Canadian Tire a low-risk investment? Has the risk of buying Canadian Tire shares increased or decreased over 1994 to 1996?

Answer—p. 127

Flash back

14. Explain a chart of accounts.

15. When are dollar signs typically used in accounting reports?

16. If a $4,000 debit to Equipment in a journal entry is incorrectly posted to the ledger as a $4,000 credit, and the ledger account has a resulting debit balance of $20,000, what is the effect of this error on the trial balance column totals?

17. Does a higher or lower debt ratio imply more risk?

Answers—p. 128

Summary

LO1 Explain the steps in processing transactions.
The accounting process captures business transactions and events, analyzes and records their effects, and summarizes and prepares information useful in making decisions. Transactions and events are the starting points in the accounting process. Source documents help in analyzing them. The effects of transactions and events are recorded in the accounting books. Postings and the trial balance help summarize and classify these effects. The final step is providing this information in useful reports or financial statements to decision makers.

LO2 Describe source documents and their purpose.
Source documents are business papers that identify and describe transactions and events. Examples are sales invoices, cheques, purchase orders, bills, and bank statements. Source documents help ensure accounting records include all transactions. They also help prevent mistakes and theft, and are important to internal control. Source documents provide objective evidence making information more reliable and useful.

LO3 Describe an account and its use in recording information about transactions. An account is a detailed record of increases and decreases in a specific asset, liability, equity, revenue, or expense item. Information is taken from accounts, analyzed, summarized, and presented in useful reports and financial statements for users.

LO4 Describe a ledger and a chart of accounts. A ledger is a record containing all accounts used by a company. This is what is referred to as the books. The chart

of accounts is a listing of all accounts and usually includes an identification number assigned to each account.

LO5 Define debits and credits and explain their role in double-entry accounting. Debit refers to left, and credit refers to right. Debits increase assets, withdrawals and expenses, while credits decrease them. Credits increase liabilities, capital and revenues, while debits decrease them. Double-entry accounting means every transaction affects at least two accounts. The total amount debited must equal the total amount credited for each transaction. The system for recording debits and credits follows from the accounting equation. The left side is the normal balance for assets, and the right side is the normal balance for liabilities and equity.

LO6 Analyze the impact of transactions on accounts and financial statements. We analyze transactions using the concepts of double-entry accounting. This analysis is performed by determining a transaction's effects on accounts. These effects are recorded in journals and posted to ledgers.

LO7 Record transactions in a journal and post entries to a ledger. We record transactions in a journal to give a record of their effects. Each entry in a journal is posted to the accounts in the ledger. This provides information in accounts that is used to produce financial statements. Balance column ledger accounts are widely used and include columns for debits, credits and the account balance after each entry.

LO8 Prepare and explain the use of a trial balance. A trial balance is a list of accounts in the ledger showing their debit and credit balances in separate columns. The trial balance is a convenient summary of the ledger's contents and is useful in preparing financial statements. It reveals errors of the kind that produce unequal debit and credit account balances.

LO9 Compute the debt ratio and describe its use in analyzing company performance. A company's debt ratio is computed as total liabilities divided by total assets. It tells us how much of the assets are financed by creditor (nonowner) or liability financing. The higher this ratio, the more risk a company faces in using liabilities to finance assets. This is because liabilities must be repaid.

Guidance Answers to **You Make the Call**

Marketing Manager

You direct your search toward individuals working with the accounting information system. The general journal contains all the revenue information you desire. The difficulty in working with the journal is that you must go through all entries, identify revenues and compute the total. Assuming entries are posted, the ledger would also contain the information you desire. The ledger is a preferred source as it keeps a running balance of each account and would directly answer your question.

Investor

The debt ratio suggests the shares of Canadian Tire are of lower risk than normal and that this risk is decreasing. Industry ratios reported along with Loblaw's debt ratios in the chapter further support the conclusion that Canadian Tire is of lower risk. In particular, the debt ratio for Canadian Tire has been steadily decreasing and is now 20% below that of Loblaw.

Guidance Answer to **Judgment and Ethics**

Cashier

There are advantages to the process proposed by the assistant manager. They include improved customer service, less delays, and less work for you. However, you should have serious concerns about control and the potential for fraud. In particular, there is no control over the possibility of embezzlement by the assistant manager. The assistant manager could steal cash and simply ring up less sales to match the remaining cash. You should reject her suggestion without approval by the manager. Moreover, you should have an ethical concern about the assistant manager's suggestion to ignore store policy.

Guidance Answers to

1. External transactions are exchanges between an organization and some other person or organization. Internal transactions are exchanges within an organization; for example, a company that uses equipment in its operating activities.

2. Examples of source documents are sales invoices, cheques, purchase orders, charges to customers, bills from suppliers, employee earnings records, and bank statements.

3. Source documents serve many purposes including recordkeeping and internal control. Source documents, especially if obtained from outside the organization, provide objective evidence about transactions and their amounts for recording. Objective evidence is important because it makes information more reliable and useful.

4.

Assets	Liabilities	Equity
1,3,6	2,5	4

5. An account is a record in an accounting system where increases and decreases in a specific asset, liability, owner's equity, revenue, or expense item are recorded and stored. A ledger is a collection of all accounts used by a business.

6. A company's size and diversity affects the number of accounts needed in its accounting system. The types of accounts used by a business depend on information the business needs to both effectively operate and report its activities in financial statements.

7. No. Debit and credit both can mean increase or decrease. The particular meaning in a circumstance depends on the type of account and its position in the accounting equation. For example, a debit increases the balance of asset and expense accounts but decreases the balance of liability, equity and revenue accounts.

8. Owner's equity is increased by revenues and owner's investments in the company. Owner's equity is decreased by expenses and owner's cash withdrawals.

9. The name double-entry is used because all transactions affect and are recorded in at least two accounts. There must be at least one debit in one account and at least one credit in another.

10. Answer is (*c*).

11. The entry is:

Cash	15,000	
Equipment	23,000	
Note Payable		18,000
Sanchez, Capital		20,000

12. A compound journal entry is one that affects three or more accounts.

13. Posting reference numbers are entered in the journal when posting to the ledger as a control over the posting process. They provide a cross-reference that allows the bookkeeper or auditor to trace debits and credits from journals to ledgers and vice versa. They also create a marker in case the posting process is interrupted.

14. A chart of accounts is a listing of all of a company's accounts and their identifying numbers.

15. Dollar signs are used in financial statements and other reports to identify the kind of currency being used in the reports. At a minimum, they are placed beside the first and last numbers in each column. Some companies place dollar signs beside any amount that appears after a ruled line to indicate that an addition or subtraction has taken place.

16. The effect of this error is to understate the trial balance's debit column total by $8,000. This results in an $8,000 difference between the two totals.

17. A higher debt ratio implies more risk (assuming other factors are similar).

Demonstration Problem

This demonstration problem is based on the same facts as the demonstration problem at the end of Chapter 2. The following events occurred during the first month of Barbara Schmidt's new haircutting business called The Cutlery:

a. On August 1, Schmidt put $3,000 cash into a chequing account in the name of The Cutlery. She also invested $15,000 of equipment that she already owned.

b. On August 2, paid $600 cash for furniture for the shop.

c. On August 3, paid $500 cash to rent space in a strip mall for August.

d. On August 4, furnished the shop by installing the old equipment and some new equipment that was bought on credit for $1,200. This amount is to be repaid in three equal payments at the end of August, September, and October.

e. On August 5, The Cutlery opened for business. Cash receipts from haircutting services provided in the first week and a half of business (ended August 15) were $825.

f. On August 15, provided haircutting services on account for $100.

g. On August 17, received a $100 cheque in the mail for services previously rendered on account.

h. On August 17, paid $125 to an assistant for working during the grand opening.

i. Cash receipts from haircutting services provided during the second half of August were $930.

j. On August 31, paid a $400 installment on the accounts payable.

k. On August 31, withdrew $900 cash for personal use.

Required

1. Prepare general journal entries for the preceding transactions.

2. Open the following accounts: Cash, 101; Accounts Receivable 102; Furniture, 161; Store Equipment, 165; Accounts Payable, 201; Barbara Schmidt, Capital, 301; Barbara Schmidt, Withdrawals, 302; Haircutting Services Revenue, 403; Wages Expense, 623; and Rent Expense, 640.

3. Post the journal entries to the ledger accounts.

4. Prepare a trial balance as of August 31, 19X1.

Extended Analysis

5. In the coming months The Cutlery will experience an even greater variety of business transactions. Identify which accounts will be debited and credited for the transactions that follow. (Hint: You may have to use some accounts that are not listed in 2 above.)

   a. Purchases of supplies with cash.

   b. Pays cash for future insurance coverage.

   c. Receives cash for a service to be provided in the future.

Planning the Solution

■ Analyze each transaction to identify the accounts affected by the transaction and the amount by which each account is affected.

■ Use the debit and credit rules to prepare a journal entry for each transaction.

■ Post each debit and each credit in the journal entries to the appropriate ledger accounts and cross-reference each amount in the Posting Reference columns in the journal and account.

■ Calculate each account balance and list the accounts with their balances on a trial balance.

■ Verify that the total debits in the trial balance equal total credits.

■ Analyze future transactions to identify the accounts affected and apply debit and credit rules.

Solution to Demonstration Problem

1. General journal entries:

	General Journal			
Date	Account Titles and Explanations	PR	Debit	Credit
Aug. 1	Cash	101	3,000	
	Store Equipment	165	15,000	
	Barbara Schmidt, Capital	301		18,000
	Owner's initial investment.			
2	Furniture	161	600	
	Cash	101		600
	Purchased furniture for cash.			
3	Rent Expense	640	500	
	Cash	101		500
	Paid rent for August.			
4	Store Equipment	165	1,200	
	Accounts Payable	201		1,200
	Purchased additional equipment on credit.			
15	Cash	101	825	
	Haircutting Services Revenue	403		825
	Cash receipts from 10 days of operations.			
15	Accounts Receivable	102	100	
	Haircutting Services Revenue	403		100
	To record revenue for services provided on account.			
17	Cash	101	100	
	Accounts Receivable	102		100
	To record cash received as payment on account.			
17	Wages Expense	623	125	
	Cash	101		125
	Paid wages to assistant.			
31	Cash	101	930	
	Haircutting Services Revenue	403		930
	Cash receipts from second half of August.			
31	Accounts Payable	201	400	
	Cash	101		400
	Paid an installment on accounts payable.			
31	Barbara Schmidt, Withdrawals	302	900	
	Cash	101		900
	Owner withdrew cash from the business.			

2. & 3. Accounts in the ledger:

Cash					Account No. 101	
Date	Explanation	PR	Debit	Credit	Balance	
Aug. 1		G1	3,000		3,000	
2		G1		600	2,400	
3		G1		500	1,900	
15		G1	825		2,725	
17		G1	100		2,825	
17		G1		125	2,700	
31		G1	930		3,630	
31		G1		400	3,230	
31		G1		900	2,330	

Accounts Receivable					Account No. 102	
Date	Explanation	PR	Debit	Credit	Balance	
Aug. 15		G1	100		100	
17		G1		100	-0-	

Furniture					Account No. 161	
Date	Explanation	PR	Debit	Credit	Balance	
Aug. 2		G1	600		600	

Store Equipment					Account No. 165	
Date	Explanation	PR	Debit	Credit	Balance	
Aug. 1		G1	15,000		15,000	
4		G1	1,200		16,200	

Accounts Payable					Account No. 201	
Date	Explanation	PR	Debit	Credit	Balance	
Aug. 4		G1		1,200	1,200	
31		G1	400		800	

Barbara Schmidt, Capital					Account No. 301	
Date	Explanation	PR	Debit	Credit	Balance	
Aug. 1		G1		18,000	18,000	

Barbara Schmidt, Withdrawals					Account No. 302	
Date	Explanation	PR	Debit	Credit	Balance	
Aug. 31		G1	900		900	

Haircutting Services Revenue					Account No. 403	
Date	Explanation	PR	Debit	Credit	Balance	
Aug. 15		G1		825	825	
15		G1		100	925	
31		G1		930	1,855	

Date		Wages Expense Explanation	PR	Debit	Account No. 623 Credit	Balance
Aug.	17		G1	125		125

Date		Rent Expense Explanation	PR	Debit	Account No. 640 Credit	Balance
Aug.	3		G1	500		500

4. Trial Balance

THE CUTLERY
Trial Balance
August 31, 19X1

	Debit	Credit
Cash	$ 2,330	
Accounts receivable	0	
Furniture	600	
Store equipment	16,200	
Accounts Payable		$ 800
Barbara Schmidt, capital		18,000
Barbara Schmidt, withdrawals	900	
Haircutting services revenue		1,855
Wages expense	125	
Rent expense	500	
Totals	$20,655	$20,655

5a. Supplies debited
   Cash credited
5b. Prepaid Insurance debited
   Cash credited
5c. Cash debited
   Unearned Service Revenue credited

Glossary

Account A place or location within an accounting system in which the increases and decreases in a specific asset, liability, equity, revenue, or expense are recorded and stored. (p. 100)

Account balance The difference between the increases (including the beginning balance) and decreases recorded in an account. (p. 106)

Balance column ledger account An account with debit and credit columns for recording entries and a third column for showing the balance of the account after each entry is posted. (p. 119)

Chart of accounts A list of all accounts used by a company; includes the identification number assigned to each account. (p. 105)

Compound journal entry A journal entry that affects at least three accounts. (p. 118)

Credit An entry that decreases asset and expense accounts or increases liability, owner's equity, and revenue accounts; recorded on the right side of a T-account. (p. 107)

Debit An entry that increases asset and expense accounts or decreases liability, owner's equity, and revenue accounts; recorded on the left side of a T-account. (p. 107)

Debt ratio The ratio between a company's total liabilities and total assets; used to describe the risk associated with the company's debts. (p. 125)

Double-entry accounting An accounting system where every transaction affects and is recorded in at least two accounts; the sum of the debits for all entries must equal the sum of the credits for all entries. (p. 107)

External transactions Exchanges between the entity and some outside person or organization. (p. 99)

General Journal The most flexible type of book of original entry; can be used to record any kind of transaction. (p. 118)

Internal transactions Exchanges within an organization that can also effect the accounting equation. (p. 99)

Journal A record where transactions are recorded before they are recorded in accounts; amounts are posted from the journal to the ledger; also called the *book of original entry*. (p. 117)

Journalizing The process of recording transactions in a journal. (p. 117)

Ledger A record containing all accounts used by a business. (p. 100)

Note Receivable An unconditional written promise to pay a definite sum of money on demand or on a defined future date(s); also called promissory note. (p. 101)

Posting The process of transferring journal entry information to the ledger. (p. 117)

Posting Reference (PR) column A column in journals and ledgers where individual account numbers are entered when entries are posted to the ledger. (p. 118)

Promissory Note An unconditional written promise to pay a definite sum of money on demand or on a defined future date(s); also called *note receivable*. (p. 101)

Source documents Another name for *business papers*; these documents are the source of information recorded with accounting entries and can be in either paper or electronic form. (p. 99)

T-account A simple account form used as a helpful tool in showing the effects of transactions and events on specific accounts. (p. 106)

Trial balance A list of accounts and their balances at a point in time; the total debit balances should equal the total credit balances. (p. 122)

Unearned revenues Liabilities created when customers pay in advance for products or services; created when cash is received before revenues are earned; satisfied by delivering the products or services in the future. (p. 101)

Questions

1. What are the three fundamental steps in the accounting process?
2. What is the difference between a note receivable and an account receivable?
3. If assets are valuable resources and asset accounts have debit balances, why do expense accounts have debit balances?
4. Why does the bookkeeper prepare a trial balance?
5. Should a transaction be recorded first in a journal or the ledger? Why?
6. Are debits or credits listed first in general journal entries? Are the debits or the credits indented?
7. What kinds of transactions can be recorded in a general journal?
8. If a wrong amount was journalized and posted to the accounts, how should the error be corrected?
9. Review the **Alliance** balance sheet for fiscal year-end March 31, 1997, in Appendix I. Identify three accounts on the balance sheet that would carry debit balances and three accounts on the balance sheet that would carry credit balances.
10. Review the **Atlantis** balance sheet for fiscal year-end December 31, 1997, in Appendix I. Identify four different liability accounts that include the word "payable" in the account title.
11. Reread the chapter's opening scenario describing Maria Sanchez's company named RecordLink. Last year RecordLink's revenues exceeded $850,000. Suggest an appropriate account title for RecordLink's revenue account.

Quick Study

QS 3-1
Identifying source documents

LO 2

Select the items from the following list that are likely to serve as source documents:

a. Income statement.
b. Trial balance.
c. Telephone bill.
d. Invoice from supplier.
e. Owner's withdrawals account.
f. Balance sheet.
g. Bank statement.
h. Sales invoice.

Indicate the financial statement on which each of the following accounts appears, using IS for income statement, SCOE for the statement of changes in owner's equity, and BS for balance sheet:

a. Buildings.
b. Interest Earned.
c. Owner, Withdrawals.
d. Owner's Equity.
e. Prepaid Insurance.

f. Interest Payable.
g. Accounts Receivable.
h. Salaries Expense.
i. Office Supplies.
j. Repair Services Revenue.

QS 3-2
Classifying accounts in financial statements
LO 6

Indicate whether a debit or credit is necessary to *decrease* the normal balance of each of the following accounts:

a. Buildings.
b. Interest Earned.
c. Owner, Withdrawals.
d. Owner, Capital.
e. Prepaid Insurance.

f. Interest Payable.
g. Accounts Receivable.
h. Salaries Expense.
i. Office Supplies.
j. Repair Services Revenue.

QS 3-3
Linking credit or debit with normal balance
LO 5

Identify whether a debit or credit entry would be made to record the indicated change in each of the following accounts:

a. To increase Notes Payable.
b. To decrease Accounts Receivable.
c. To increase Owner, Capital
d. To decrease Unearned Fees.
e. To decrease Prepaid Insurance.

f. To decrease Cash.
g. To increase Utilities Expense.
h. To increase Fees Earned.
i. To increase Store Equipment.
j. To increase Owner, Withdrawals

QS 3-4
Analyzing debit or credit by account
LO 5

Prepare journal entries for the following transactions:

a. On January 15, Stan Adams opened a landscaping business by investing $60,000 cash and equipment having a $40,000 fair value.
b. On January 20, purchased office supplies on credit for $340.
c. On January 28, received $5,200 in return for providing landscaping services to a customer.

QS 3-5
Preparing journal entries
LO 6

A trial balance has total debits of $21,000 and total credits of $25,500. Which one of the following errors would create this imbalance? Explain.

a. A $4,500 debit to Salaries Expense in a journal entry was incorrectly posted to the ledger as a $4,500 credit, leaving the Salaries Expense account with a $750 debit balance.
b. A $2,250 credit to Consulting Fees Earned in a journal entry was incorrectly posted to the ledger as a $2,250 debit, leaving the Consulting Fees Earned account with a $6,300 credit balance.
c. A $2,250 debit to Rent Expense in a journal entry was incorrectly posted to the ledger as a $2,250 credit, leaving the Rent Expense account with a $3,000 debit balance.

QS 3-6
Identifying a posting error
LO 8

Exercises

Exercise 3-1
Increases, decreases, and normal balances of accounts

LO 3, 5

Complete the following table by (1) identifying the type of account listed on each line, (2) entering *debit* or *credit* in the blank spaces to identify the kind of entry that would increase or decrease the account balance, and (3) identifying the normal balance of the account.

	Account	Type of Account	Increase	Decrease	Normal Balance
a.	Land				
b.	H. Cooper, capital				
c.	Accounts receivable				
d.	H. Cooper, withdrawals				
e.	Cash				
f.	Equipment				
g.	Unearned revenue				
h.	Accounts payable				
i.	Postage expense				
j.	Prepaid insurance				
k.	Wages expense				
l.	Fees earned				

Exercise 3-2
Analyzing the effects of a transaction on the accounts

LO 6

Jan Garret recently notified a client that he would have to pay a $48,000 fee for accounting services. Unfortunately, the client did not have enough cash to pay the entire bill. Garret agreed to accept the following items in full payment: $7,500 cash and computer equipment worth $75,000. Garret also had to assume responsibility for a $34,500 note payable related to the equipment. The entry Garret would make to record this transaction would include which of the following:

a. $34,500 increase in a liability account.
b. $7,500 increase in the Cash account.
c. $7,500 increase in a revenue account.
d. $48,000 increase in the Jan Garret, Capital account.
e. $48,000 increase in a revenue account.

Exercise 3-3
Recording the effects of transactions directly in T-accounts

LO 6

Open the following T-accounts: Cash; Accounts Receivable; Office Supplies; Office Equipment; Accounts Payable; Steve Moore, Capital; Steve Moore, Withdrawals; Fees Earned; and Rent Expense. Next, record these transactions of the Moore Company by recording the debit and credit entries directly in the T-accounts. Use the letters beside each transaction to identify the entries. Finally, determine the balance of each account.

a. Steve Moore invested $12,750 cash in the business.
b. Purchased $375 of office supplies for cash.
c. Purchased $7,050 of office equipment on credit.
d. Received $1,500 cash as fees for services provided to a customer.
e. Paid for the office equipment purchased in transaction *c*.
f. Billed a customer $2,700 as fees for services.
g. Paid the monthly rent with $525 cash.
h. Collected $1,125 of the account receivable created in transaction.
i. Steve Moore withdrew $1,000 cash from the business.

Exercise 3-4
Preparing a trial balance

LO 8

After recording the transactions of Exercise 3-3 in T-accounts and calculating the balance of each account, prepare the trial balance for the ledger. Use May 31, 19X1, as the date.

Complete the following table by filling in the blanks. For each of the listed posting errors, enter in column (1) the amount of the difference that the error would create between the two trial balance columns (show a zero if the columns would balance). If there would be a difference between the two columns, identify in column (2) the trial balance column that would be larger. Identify the account(s) affected in column (3) and the amount by which the account(s) is under- or overstated in column (4). The answer for the first error is provided as an example.

Exercise 3-5
Effects of posting errors
on the trial balance

LO 6, 8

	Description	(1) Difference between Debit and Credit Columns	(2) Column with the Larger Total	(3) Identify Account(s) Incorrectly Stated	(4) Amount That Account(s) Is Over- or Understated
a.	A $2,400 debit to Rent Expense was posted as a $1,590 debit.	$810	Credit	Rent Expense	Rent Expense is understated by $810
b.	A $42,000 debit to Machinery was posted as a debit to Accounts Payable.				
c.	A $4,950 credit to Services Revenue was posted as a $495 credit.				
d.	A $1,440 debit to Store Supplies was not posted at all.				
e.	A $2,250 debit to Prepaid Insurance was posted as a debit to Insurance Expense.				
f.	A $4,050 credit to Cash was posted twice as two credits to the Cash account.				
g.	A $9,900 debit to the owner's withdrawals account was debited to the owner's capital account.				

As the bookkeeper for a company, you are disappointed to learn that the column totals in your new trial balance are not equal. After going through a careful analysis, you have discovered only one error. Specifically, the balance of the Office Equipment account has a debit balance of $23,400 on the trial balance. However, you have figured out that a correctly recorded credit purchase of a computer for $5,250 was posted from the journal to the ledger with a $5,250 debit to Office Equipment and another $5,250 debit to Accounts Payable. Answer each of the following questions and present the dollar amount of any misstatement for each:

Exercise 3-6
Analyzing a trial balance
error

LO 6, 8

a. Is the balance of the Office Equipment account overstated, understated, or correctly stated in the trial balance?

b. Is the balance of the Accounts Payable account overstated, understated, or correctly stated in the trial balance?

c. Is the debit column total of the trial balance overstated, understated, or correctly stated?

d. Is the credit column total of the trial balance overstated, understated, or correctly stated?

e. If the debit column total of the trial balance is $360,000 before correcting the error, what is the total of the credit column?

Exercise 3-7
Preparing a corrected trial balance

LO 8

On January 1, Jan Taylor started a new business called The Party Place. Near the end of the year, she hired a new bookkeeper without making a careful reference check. As a result, a number of mistakes have been made in preparing the following trial balance:

THE PARTY PLACE Trial Balance December 31		
	Debit	**Credit**
Cash	$ 5,500	
Accounts receivable		$7,900
Office supplies	2,650	
Office equipment	20,500	
Accounts Payable		9,465
Jan Taylor, capital	16,745	
Services revenue		22,350
Wages expense		6,000
Rent expense		4,800
Advertising expense		1,250
Totals	$45,395	$52,340

Taylor's analysis of the situation has uncovered these errors:

a. The sum of the debits in the Cash account is $37,175 and the sum of the credits is $30,540.

b. A $275 payment from a credit customer was posted to Cash but was not posted to Accounts Receivable.

c. A credit purchase of office supplies for $400 was completely unrecorded.

d. A transposition error occurred in copying the balance of the Services Revenue account to the trial balance. The correct amount was $23,250.

Other errors were made in placing account balances in the trial balance columns and in taking the totals of the columns. Use all this information to prepare a correct trial balance.

Exercise 3-8
Analyzing account entries and balances

LO 6

Use the information in each of the following situations to calculate the unknown amount:

1. During October, Ridgeway Company had $97,500 of cash receipts and $101,250 of cash disbursements. The October 31 Cash balance was $16,800. Determine how much cash the company had on hand at the close of business on September 30.

2. On September 30, Ridgeway had a $97,500 balance in Accounts Receivable. During October, the company collected $88,950 from its credit customers. The October 31 balance in Accounts Receivable was $100,500. Determine the amount of sales on account that occurred in October.

3. Ridgeway had $147,000 of accounts payable on September 30 and $136,500 on October 31. Total purchases on account during October were $270,000. Determine how much cash was paid on accounts payable during October.

Exercise 3-9
Analyzing transactions from T-accounts

LO 6

Seven transactions were posted to these T-accounts. Provide a short description of each transaction. Include the amounts in your descriptions.

Cash			
(a)	7,000	(b)	3,600
(e)	2,500	(c)	600
		(f)	2,400
		(g)	700

Office Supplies	
(c)	600
(d)	200

Prepaid Insurance	
(b)	3,600

Equipment	
(a)	5,600
(d)	9,400

Automobiles	
(a)	11,000

Accounts Payable			
(f)	2,400	(d)	9,600

Jerry Steiner, Capital			
		(a)	23,600

Delivery Services Revenue			
		(e)	2,500

Gas and Oil Expense	
(g)	700

Use the information in the T-accounts in Exercise 3-9 to prepare general journal entries for the seven transactions.

Exercise 3-10
General journal entries

LO 6

Prepare general journal entries to record the following transactions of a new business called PhotoFinish Co.

Exercise 3-11
General journal entries

LO 6

Aug.	1	Hannah Young, the owner, invested $7,500 cash and photography equipment with a fair value of $32,500.
	1	Rented a studio, paying $3,000 for the next three months in advance.
	5	Purchased office supplies for $1,400 cash.
	20	Received $2,650 in photography fees.
	31	Paid $875 for August utilities.

Use the information provided in Exercise 3-11 to prepare an August 31 trial balance for PhotoFinish Co. First, open these T-accounts: Cash; Office Supplies; Prepaid Rent; Photography Equipment; Hannah Young, Capital; Photography Fees Earned; and Utilities Expense. Then post the general journal entries to the T-accounts. Finally, prepare the trial balance.

Exercise 3-12
T-accounts and the trial balance

LO 8

Examine the following transactions and identify those that created revenues for Jarrell Services, a sole proprietorship owned by John Jarrell. Prepare general journal entries to record those transactions and explain why the other transactions did not create revenues.

a. John Jarrell invested $38,250 cash in the business.

b. Provided $1,350 of services on credit.

c. Received $1,575 cash for services provided to a client.

d. Received $9,150 from a client in payment for services to be provided next year.

e. Received $4,500 from a client in partial payment of an account receivable.

f. Borrowed $150,000 from the bank by signing a promissory note.

Exercise 3-13
Analyzing and journalizing revenue transactions

LO 6

Examine the following transactions and identify those that created expenses for Jarrell Services. Prepare general journal entries to record those transactions and explain why the other transactions did not create expenses.

a. Paid $14,100 cash for office supplies purchased 30 days previously.

b. Paid the $1,125 salary of the receptionist.

c. Paid $45,000 cash for equipment.

d. Paid utility bill with $930 cash.

e. John Jarrell withdrew $5,000 from the business account for personal use.

Exercise 3-14
Analyzing and journalizing expense transactions

LO 6

1. Calculate the debt ratio for each of the following cases:

Exercise 3-15
Calculating the debt ratio

LO 8

Case	Assets	Liabilities	Owner's Equity
1	$88,500	$11,000	$77,500
2	62,000	46,000	16,000
3	30,500	25,500	5,000
4	145,000	55,000	90,000
5	90,000	30,000	60,000
6	102,500	50,500	52,000

2. Of the six cases which business relies most heavily on creditor financing?

3. Of the six cases which business has the most equity financing?

4. Which three companies indicates the greatest risk?

Problems

Problem 3-1
Recording transactions in T-accounts; preparing a trial balance

LO 6, 8

Following are business transactions completed by Kevin Smith during the month of November:

a. Kevin Smith invested $80,000 cash and office equipment with a $30,000 fair value in a new sole proprietorship named Apex Consulting.
b. Purchased land and a small office building. The land was worth $30,000, and the building was worth $170,000. The purchase price was paid with $40,000 cash and a long-term note payable for $160,000.
c. Purchased $2,400 of office supplies on credit.
d. Kevin Smith transferred title of his personal automobile to the business. The automobile had a value of $18,000 and was to be used exclusively in the business.
e. Purchased $6,000 of additional office equipment on credit.
f. Paid $1,500 salary to an assistant.
g. Provided services to a client and collected $6,000 cash.
h. Paid $800 for the month's utilities.
i. Paid account payable created in transaction c.
j. Purchased $20,000 of new office equipment by paying $18,600 cash and trading in old equipment with a recorded cost of $1,400.
k. Completed $5,200 of services for a client. This amount is to be paid within 30 days.
l. Paid $1,500 salary to an assistant.
m. Received $3,800 payment on the receivable created in transaction k.
n. Kevin Smith withdrew $6,400 cash from the business for personal use.

Required

1. Open the following T-accounts: Cash; Accounts Receivable; Office Supplies; Automobiles; Office Equipment; Building; Land; Accounts Payable; Long-Term Notes Payable; Kevin Smith, Capital; Kevin Smith, Withdrawals; Fees Earned; Salaries Expense; and Utilities Expense.
2. Record the effects of the listed transactions by entering debits and credits directly in the T-accounts. Use the transaction letters to identify each debit and credit entry.
3. Determine the balance of each account and prepare a trial balance as of November 30.

Check Figure Total debits in trial balance, $305,200

Problem 3-2
Recording transactions in T-accounts, preparing a trial balance, and calculating debt ratio

LO 6, 8, 9

Forest Engineering, a sole proprietorship, completed the following transactions during the month of July:

a. Stephen Forest, the owner, invested $105,000 cash, office equipment with a value of $6,000, and $45,000 of drafting equipment in the business.
b. Purchased land for an office. The land was worth $54,000, which was paid with $5,400 cash and a long-term note payable for $48,600.
c. Purchased a portable building with $75,000 cash and moved it onto the land.
d. Paid $6,000 cash for the premiums on two one-year insurance policies.
e. Completed and delivered a set of plans for a client and collected $5,700 cash.
f. Purchased additional drafting equipment for $22,500. Paid $10,500 cash and signed a long-term note payable for the $12,000 balance.
g. Completed $12,000 of engineering services for a client. This amount is to be paid within 30 days.
h. Purchased $2,250 of additional office equipment on credit.
i. Completed engineering services for $18,000 on credit.
j. Received a bill for rent on equipment that was used on a completed job. The $1,200 rent must be paid within 30 days.
k. Collected $7,200 from the client described in transaction g.
l. Paid $1,500 wages to a drafting assistant.
m. Paid the account payable created in transaction h.
n. Paid $675 cash for some repairs to an item of drafting equipment.
o. Stephen Forest withdrew $9,360 cash from the business for personal use.
p. Paid $1,500 wages to a drafting assistant.
q. Paid $3,000 cash to advertise in the local newspaper.

Required

1. Open the following T-accounts: Cash; Accounts Receivable; Prepaid Insurance; Office Equipment; Drafting Equipment; Building; Land; Accounts Payable; Long-Term Notes Payable; Stephen Forest, Capital; Stephen Forest, Withdrawals; Engineering Fees Earned; Wages Expense; Equipment Rental Expense; Advertising Expense; and Repairs Expense.

2. Record the transactions by entering debits and credits directly in the accounts. Use the transaction letters to identify each debit and credit. Prepare a trial balance as of July 31.

3. Calculate the company's debt ratio. Use $236,265 as the ending total assets. Are the assets of the company financed more by debt or equity?

Check Figure Total debits in trial balance, $253,500

Problem 3-3
Preparing and posting general journal entries and preparing a trial balance

LO 6, 7, 8

Hector Mendez opened a computer consulting business called Capital Consultants and completed the following transactions during May:

May	1	Mendez invested $100,000 in cash and office equipment that had a fair value of $24,000 in the business.
	1	Prepaid $7,200 cash for three months' rent for an office.
	2	Made credit purchases of office equipment for $12,000 and office supplies for $2,400.
	6	Completed services for a client and immediately received $2,000 cash.
	9	Completed an $8,000 project for a client, who will pay within 30 days.
	10	Paid the account payable created on May 2.
	19	Paid $6,000 cash for the annual premium on an insurance policy.
	22	Received $6,400 as partial payment for the work completed on May 9.
	25	Completed work for another client for $2,640 on credit.
	31	Mendez withdrew $6,200 cash from the business for personal use.
	31	Purchased $800 of additional office supplies on credit.
	31	Paid $700 for the month's utility bill.

Required

1. Prepare general journal entries to record the transactions. Use page 1 for the journal.

2. Open the following accounts (use the balance column format): Cash (101); Accounts Receivable (106); Office Supplies (124); Prepaid Insurance (128); Prepaid Rent (131); Office Equipment (163); Accounts Payable (201); Hector Mendez, Capital (301); Hector Mendez, Withdrawals (302); Services Revenue (403); and Utilities Expense (690).

3. Post the entries to the accounts and enter the balance after each posting.

4. Prepare a trial balance as of the end of the month.

Check Figure Cash account balance, $73,900

Problem 3-4
Interpreting journals, posting, and analyzing trial balance errors

LO 6, 7, 8

Art Platt started a business called Able Movers and began operations in July. His accounting and bookkeeping skills are not well polished, and he needs some help gathering information at the end of the month. He recorded the following journal entries during the month:

July	1	Cash	60,000	
		Trucks	44,000	
		Art Platt, Capital		104,000
	2	Office Supplies	1,292	
		Cash		1,292
	4	Moving Equipment	12,800	
		Accounts Payable		12,800
	8	Cash	2,000	
		Accounts Receivable	10,000	
		Moving Fees Earned		12,000
	12	Cash	1,600	
		Moving Fees Earned		1,600

		Debit	Credit
15	Prepaid Insurance	2,700	
	Cash		2,700
21	Cash	10,000	
	Accounts Receivable		10,000
23	Accounts Payable	12,800	
	Cash		12,800
25	Office Equipment	18,800	
	Art Platt, Capital		18,800
29	Office Supplies	2,908	
	Accounts Payable		2,908
31	Art Platt, Withdrawals	4,912	
	Cash		4,912
31	Wages Expense	6,280	
	Cash		6,280

Based on these entries, Platt prepared the following trial balance:

ABLE MOVERS
Trial Balance
For Month Ended July 31

	Debit	Credit
Cash	$ 45,616	
Accounts receivable ..	-0-	
Office supplies	2,400	
Prepaid insurance	2,700	
Trucks	44,000	
Office equipment	18,800	
Moving equipment		$12,800
Accounts payable		29,080
Art Platt, capital		122,800
Art Platt, withdrawals ..	491	
Moving fees earned ...		13,600
Wages expense	6,280	
Totals	$120,287	$178,280

Required

Preparation component:

Platt remembers something about trial balances and realizes that the preceding one has at least one error. To help him find the mistakes, set up the following balance column accounts and post the entries to them: Cash (101); Accounts Receivable (106); Office Supplies (124); Prepaid Insurance (128); Trucks (153); Office Equipment (163); Moving Equipment (167); Accounts Payable (201); Art Platt, Capital (301); Art Platt, Withdrawals (302); Moving Fees Earned (401); and Wages Expense (623).

Analysis component:

Although Platt's journal entries are correct, he forgot to provide explanations of the events. Analyze each entry and present a reasonable explanation of what happened. Then, prepare a correct trial balance and describe the errors that Platt made.

Check Figure Total credits in trial balance, $139,308

Problem 3-5
Analyzing account balances

LO 6, 8

Carlos Young started an engineering firm called Young Engineering. He began operations in March and completed seven transactions, including his initial investment of $17,000 cash. After these transactions, the ledger included the following accounts with their normal balances:

Cash	$26,660
Office supplies	660
Prepaid insurance	3,200
Office equipment	16,500
Accounts payable	16,500
Carlos Young, capital	17,000
Carlos Young, withdrawals	3,740
Engineering fees earned	24,000
Rent expense	6,740

Required

Preparation component:

Prepare a trial balance for the business.

Analysis component:

Analyze the accounts and balances and prepare narratives that describes each of the seven most likely transactions and their amounts. Also, present a schedule that shows how the transactions resulted in the $26,660 Cash balance.

Travis McAllister operates a surveying company. For the first few months of the company's life (through April), the accounting records were maintained by an outside bookkeeping service. According to those records, McAllister's owner's equity balance was $75,000 as of April 30. To save on expenses, McAllister decided to keep the records himself. He managed to record May's transactions properly, but was a bit rusty when the time came to prepare the financial statements. His first versions of the balance sheet and income statement follow. McAllister is bothered that the company operated at a loss during the month, even though he had been very busy. Using the information contained in the original financial statements, prepare revised statements, including a statement of changes in owner's equity, for the month of May.

Problem 3-6
Analyzing Financial
Statement Errors

LO 6

McALLISTER SURVEYING
Income Statement
For Month Ended May 31, 2000

Revenue:		
Investments by owner		$ 3,000
Unearned surveying fees		6,000
Total		$ 9,000
Operating expense:		
Rent expense	$3,100	
Telephone expense	600	
Surveying equipment	5,400	
Advertising expense	3,200	
Utilities expense	300	
Insurance expense	900	
Withdrawals by owner	6,000	
Total operating expense		19,500
Net income (loss)		$(10,500)

McALLISTER SURVEYING
Balance Sheet
May 31

Assets			Liabilities		
Cash	$ 3,900		Accounts payable	$ 2,400	
Accounts receivable . .	2,700		Surveying fees earned	18,000	
Prepaid insurance . . .	1,800		Short-term notes payable. . . .	48,000	
Prepaid rent	4,200		Total liabilities	$ 68,400	
Office supplies	300				
Buildings	81,000		**Owner's Equity**		
Land	36,000		Travis McAllister, capital	64,500	
Salaries expense	3,000		Total liabilities and		
Total assets	$132,900		owner's equity.	$132,900	

West Consulting completed these transactions during June:

a. Susan West, the sole proprietor, invested $23,000 cash and office equipment with a $12,000 fair value in the business.

b. Purchased land and a small office building. The land was worth $8,000 and the building was worth $33,000. The purchase price was paid with $15,000 cash and a long-term note payable for $26,000.

c. Purchased $600 of office supplies on credit.

d. Susan West transferred title of her personal automobile to the business. The automobile had a value of $7,000 and was to be used exclusively in the business.

**Alternate
Problems**

Problem 3-1A
Recording transactions in
T-accounts; preparing a
trial balance

LO 6,8

e. Purchased $1,100 of additional office equipment on credit.

f. Paid $800 salary to an assistant.

g. Provided services to a client and collected $2,700 cash.

h. Paid $430 for the month's utilities.

i. Paid account payable created in transaction c.

j. Purchased $4,000 of new office equipment by paying $2,400 cash and trading in old equipment with a recorded cost of $1,600.

k. Completed $2,400 of services for a client. This amount is to be paid within 30 days.

l. Paid $800 salary to an assistant.

m. Received $1,000 payment on the receivable created in transaction k.

n. Susan West withdrew $1,050 cash from the business for personal use.

Required

1. Open the following T-accounts: Cash; Accounts Receivable; Office Supplies; Automobiles; Office Equipment; Building; Land; Accounts Payable; Long-Term Notes Payable; Susan West, Capital; Susan West, Withdrawals; Fees Earned; Salaries Expense; and Utilities Expense.

2. Record the effects of the listed transactions by entering debits and credits directly in the T-accounts. Use the transaction letters to identify each debit and credit entry.

3. Determine the balance of each account and prepare a trial balance as of June 30.

Problem 3-2A
Recording transactions in T-accounts; trial balance; debt ratio

LO 6, 8, 9

At the beginning of June, Avery Wilson created a custom computer programming company called Softouch Co. The company had the following transactions during the month:

a. Avery Wilson invested $45,000 cash, office equipment with a value of $4,500, and $28,000 of computer equipment.

b. Purchased land for an office. The land was worth $24,000, which was paid with $4,800 cash and a long-term note payable for $19,200.

c. Purchased a portable building with $21,000 cash and moved it onto the land.

d. Paid $6,600 cash for the premiums on two one-year insurance policies.

e. Provided services to a client and collected $3,200 cash.

f. Purchased additional computer equipment for $3,500. Paid $700 cash and signed a long-term note payable for the $2,800 balance.

g. Completed $3,750 of services for a client. This amount is to be paid within 30 days.

h. Purchased $750 of additional office equipment on credit.

i. Completed another software job for $9,200 on credit.

j. Received a bill for rent on a computer that was used on the completed job. The $320 rent must be paid within 30 days.

k. Collected $4,600 from the client described in transaction i.

l. Paid $1,600 wages to an assistant.

m. Paid the account payable created in transaction h.

n. Paid $425 cash for some repairs to an item of computer equipment.

o. Avery Wilson withdrew $3,875 in cash from the business for personal use.

p. Paid $1,600 wages to an assistant.

q. Paid $800 cash to advertise in the local newspaper.

Required

1. Open the following T-accounts: Cash; Accounts Receivable; Prepaid Insurance; Office Equipment; Computer Equipment; Building; Land; Accounts Payable; Long-Term Notes Payable; Avery Wilson, Capital; Avery Wilson, Withdrawals; Fees Earned; Wages Expense; Computer Rental Expense; Advertising Expense; and Repairs Expense.

2. Record the transactions by entering debits and credits directly in the accounts. Use the transaction letters to identify each debit and credit. Prepare a trial balance as of June 30.

3. Calculate the company's debt ratio. Use $107,350 as the ending total assets. Are the assets of the company financed more by debt or equity?

Leonard Management Services completed these transactions during November:

Problem 3-3A
Preparing and posting
general journal entries;
preparing a trial balance
LO 6, 7, 8

Nov. 1 Arthur Leonard, the owner, invested $28,000 cash and office equipment that had a
          fair value of $25,000 in the business.
       2 Prepaid $10,500 cash for three months' rent for an office.
       4 Made credit purchases of office equipment for $9,000 and office supplies for $1,200.
       8 Completed work for a client and immediately received $2,600 cash.
      12 Completed a $13,400 project for a client, who will pay within 30 days.
      13 Paid the account payable created on November 4.
      19 Paid $5,200 cash as the annual premium on an insurance policy.
      22 Received $7,800 as partial payment for the work completed on November 12.
      24 Completed work for another client for $1,900 on credit.
      28 Arthur Leonard withdrew $5,300 from the business for personal use.
      29 Purchased $1,700 of additional office supplies on credit.
      30 Paid $460 for the month's utility bill.

Required

1. Prepare general journal entries to record the transactions. Use General Journal, page 1.
2. Open the following accounts (use the balance column format): Cash (101); Accounts Receivable (106); Office Supplies (124); Prepaid Insurance (128); Prepaid Rent (131); Office Equipment (163); Accounts Payable (201); Arthur Leonard, Capital (301); Arthur Leonard, Withdrawals (302); Service Fees Earned (401); and Utilities Expense (690).
3. Post the entries to the accounts, and enter the balance after each posting.
4. Prepare a trial balance as of the end of the month.

Damon Oleson started a business called Knot Board on June 1 and completed several transactions during the month. His accounting and bookkeeping skills were not well polished and he needs some help gathering information at the end of the month. Presented below are the journal entries that he recorded during the month.

Problem 3-4A
Interpreting journals;
posting; correcting a trial
balance
LO 6, 7, 8

June 1	Cash	11,000	
	Store Equipment	9,000	
	Damon Oleson, Capital		20,000
2	Prepaid Insurance	400	
	Cash		400
6	Accounts Receivable	1,800	
	Fees Earned		1,800
9	Office Supplies	700	
	Office Equipment	4,200	
	Accounts Payable		4,900
11	Cash	2,100	
	Fees Earned		2,100
14	Accounts Payable	120	
	Office Supplies		120
20	Cash	1,500	
	Accounts Receivable		1,500
21	Accounts Payable	4,780	
	Cash		4,780
23	Automobile	8,000	
	Damon Oleson, Capital		8,000
28	Damon Oleson, Withdrawals	1,000	
	Cash		1,000
29	Salaries Expense	1,400	
	Cash		1,400
30	Office Supplies	390	
	Accounts Payable		390

Based on these entries, Oleson prepared the following trial balance:

KNOT BOARD Trial Balance For Month Ended June 30		
Cash	$ 7,200	
Accounts receivable	400	
Office supplies	790	
Prepaid insurance	4,000	
Automobiles	8,000	
Office equipment		$ 4,200
Store equipment		9,000
Accounts payable		930
Damon Oleson, capital		28,000
Damon Oleson, withdrawals		1,000
Fees earned		3,900
Salaries expense	1,500	
Total	$21,890	$47,030

Required

Preparation component:

Oleson remembers something about trial balances and realizes that the preceding one has at least one error. To help him find the mistakes, set up the following balance column accounts and post the entries to them: Cash (101); Accounts Receivable (106); Office Supplies (124); Prepaid Insurance (128); Automobiles (151); Office Equipment (163); Store Equipment (165); Accounts Payable (201); Damon Oleson, Capital (301); Damon Oleson, Withdrawals (302); Fees Earned (401); and Salaries Expense (622).

Analysis component:

Although Oleson's journal entries are correct, he forgot to provide explanations of the events. Analyze each entry and present a reasonable explanation of what happened. Then, prepare a correct trial balance and describe the errors that Oleson made.

Problem 3-5A
Analyzing account balances

 LO 6, 8

Cass Consulting's first seven transactions resulted in the following accounts, which have normal balances:

Cash	$12,485
Office supplies	560
Prepaid rent	1,500
Office equipment	11,450
Accounts payable	11,450
Stephanie Cass, capital	10,000
Stephanie Cass, withdrawals . .	6,200
Consulting fees earned	16,400
Operating expense	5,655

Required

Preparation component:

Prepare a trial balance for the business.

Analysis component:

Analyze the accounts and balances and prepare narratives that describe each of the seven most likely transactions that resulted in the previous account balances. Also, present a schedule that shows how the transactions resulted in the $12,485 Cash balance.

Problem 3-6A
Analyzing financial statements errors

LO 6

Rachel Rohr operates a computer programming company specializing in "html" programming and Web site construction. For the first few months of the company's life (through April), the accounting records were maintained by an outside bookkeeping service. According to those records, Rohr's owner's equity balance was $18,500 as of May 1. To save on expenses, Rohr decided to keep the records herself. She managed to record May's transactions properly, but was a bit rusty when the time came to prepare the financial statements. Her first versions of the balance sheet and income statement follow. Rohr is bothered that the company operated at a loss during the month, even though she had been very busy. Using the information contained in the original financial statements, prepare revised statements, including a statement of changes in owner's equity, for the month of May.

R² CONSULTING Income Statement For Month Ended May 31		
Revenue:		
Investments by owner		$ 4,000
Unearned programming fees ..		9,000
Total		$ 13,000
Operating expense:		
Rent expense	$4,100	
Telephone expense	700	
Office equipment	6,500	
Advertising expense	4,300	
Utilities expense	400	
Insurance expense	800	
Withdrawals by owner	7,000	
Total operating expense		23,800
Net income (loss)		$(10,800)

R² CONSULTING Balance Sheet May 31				
Assets			**Liabilities**	
Cash	$ 4,900		Accounts payable	$ 1,400
Accounts receivable ..	2,800		Programming fees earned ...	30,000
Prepaid insurance ...	1,900		Short-term notes payable....	18,000
Prepaid rent	4,100		Total liabilities	$49,400
Office supplies	400			
Computer equipment .	40,000		**Owner's Equity**	
Salaries expense	3,000		Rachel Rohr, capital........	7,700
			Total liabilities and	
Total assets	$57,100		owner's equity...........	$57,100

Lester Fenwick started a real estate agency and completed seven transactions, including Fenwick's initial investment of $11,900 cash. After these transactions, the ledger included the following accounts with their normal balances:

Cash	$15,820
Office supplies	462
Prepaid insurance	2,240
Office equipment	11,550
Accounts payable	11,550
Lester Fenwick, capital	11,900
Lester Fenwick, withdrawals ..	5,460
Commissions earned	16,800
Advertising expense	4,718

Analytical and Review Problems

A & R Problem 3-1

Required

Preparation component:

Prepare a trial balance for the business.

Analysis component:

Analyze the accounts and balances and prepare a list that describes each of the seven transactions and its amount. Also, present a schedule that shows how the transactions resulted in the $15,820 Cash balance.

A & R Problem 3-2

Sandra Castell started a computer consulting business called Aribas Computer Services. She invested $25,000 and her automobile which had a market value of $23,000. The business was an instant success; however she could not say the same about her bookkeeper who prepared the following trial balance:

ARIBAS COMPUTER SERVICES
Trial Balance
September 30, 1999

Cash	$26,200	
Accounts receivable	4,000	
Supplies	4,800	
Automobiles	26,000	
Accounts payable		$ -0-
Sandra Castell, capital		61,000
Total	$61,000	$61,000

The following information was obtained from the accounting records:

a. Consulting fees earned and billed during September amounted to $16,000 of which $9,000 was collected.

b. Office equipment purchased but not as yet paid for, $3,000.

c. Supplies purchased for cash, $1,800.

d. Paid $1,800 for two months' office rent.

e. Wages paid for September, $2,200.

f. Castell withdrew $3,000 for living expenses.

Required

1. List the errors the bookkeeper made.

2. Prepare a corrected trial balance.

3. Explain why the original trial balance balanced.

Serial Problem

Echo Systems

(This comprehensive problem starts in this chapter and continues in Chapters 4, 5, and 6. Because of its length, this problem is most easily solved if you use the Working Papers that accompany this text.)

On October 1, 19X1, Mary Graham organized a computer service company called **Echo Systems.** Echo is organized as a sole proprietorship and will provide consulting services, computer system installations, and custom program development. Graham has adopted the calendar year for reporting, and expects to prepare the company's first set of financial statements as of December 31, 19X1. The initial chart of accounts for the accounting system includes these items:

Account	No.	Account	No.
Cash	101	Mary Graham, Capital	301
Accounts Receivable	106	Mary Graham, Withdrawals	302
Computer Supplies	126	Computer Services Revenue	403
Prepaid Insurance	128	Wages Expense	623
Prepaid Rent	131	Advertising Expense	655
Office Equipment	163	Mileage Expense	676
Computer Equipment	167	Miscellaneous Expenses	677
Accounts Payable	201	Repairs Expense, Computer	684

Required

1. Prepare journal entries to record each of the following transactions for Echo Systems.

2. Open balance column accounts for the company and post the journal entries to them.

Oct. 1 Mary Graham invested $45,000 cash, an $18,000 computer system, and $9,000 of office equipment in the business.

   2 Paid rent in advance of $4,500.

   3 Purchased computer supplies on credit for $1,320 from Abbott Office Products.

   5 Paid $2,160 cash for one year's premium on a property and liability insurance policy.

   6 Billed Capital Leasing $3,300 for installing a new computer.

   8 Paid for the computer supplies purchased from Abbott Office Products.

   10 Hired Carly Smith as a part-time assistant for $100 per day, as needed.

   12 Billed Capital Leasing another $1,200 for computer services rendered.

   15 Received $3,300 from Capital Leasing on their account.

   17 Paid $705 to repair computer equipment damaged when moving into the new office.

   20 Paid $1,860 for an advertisement in the local newspaper.

Oct.	22	Received $1,200 from Capital Leasing on their account.
	28	Billed Decker Company $3,225 for services.
	31	Paid Carly Smith for seven days' work.
	31	Mary Graham withdrew $3,600 cash from the business for personal use.
Nov.	1	Reimbursed Mary Graham's business automobile expense for 1,000 kilometres at $0.25 per kilometre.
	2	Received $4,650 cash from Elite Corporation for computer services rendered.
	5	Purchased $960 of computer supplies from Abbott Office Products.
	8	Billed Fostek Co. $4,350 for computer services rendered.
	13	Notified by Alamo Engineering Co. that Echo's bid of $3,750 for an upcoming project was accepted.
	18	Received $1,875 from Decker Company against the bill dated October 28.
	22	Donated $750 to the United Way in the company's name.
	24	Completed work for Alamo Engineering Co. and sent them a bill for $3,750.
	25	Sent another bill to Decker Company for the past due amount of $1,350.
	28	Reimbursed Mary Graham's business automobile expense for 1,200 kilometres at $0.25 per kilometre.
	30	Paid Carly Smith for 14 days' work.
	30	Mary Graham withdrew $1,800 cash from the business for personal use.

BEYOND THE NUMBERS

Refer to the financial statements and related information for **Alliance Communications, Inc.** in Appendix I. Find the answers to the following questions by analyzing the information in the report:

1. How many revenue categories does Alliance report on the consolidated statement of income?

2. What three current assets are reported on the company's consolidated balance sheet?

3. What three current liabilities are reported on the balance sheet?

4. What dollar amounts of income taxes are reported on its income statements for the annual reporting periods ending in 1997 and 1996?

5. During the annual reporting period ended March 31, 1997, how much cash did Alliance pay in dividends?

6. What is the company's debt ratio at the end of 1997? (Remember that liabilities = assets − shareholders' equity.) How does this compare to the ratio at the end of 1996?

Reporting in Action

Both **Alliance** and **Atlantis** design, produce, market and sell movies and TV programs. Key comparative figures ($ millions) for these two organizations follow:

Comparative Analysis

Key Figure	Alliance	Atlantis
Total liabilities	$ 203.3	$ 236.5
Total shareholder's equity	$ 150.4	$ 97.1

* Alliance figures are from the annual report for the fiscal year ended March 31,1997.

Atlantis figures are from the annual report for the fiscal year ended December 31, 1997.

Required:

Use the information in the table above to answer the following questions:

1. What are the total assets for (a) Alliance and (b)Atlantis?

2. What is the debt ratio for (a) Alliance and (b) Atlantis?

3. Which of the two companies has the higher degree of financial leverage?

Ethics Challenge

LO 2

Review the "Judgment and Ethics" case on page 99. Join a class discussion of the nature of your dilemma in this case. The guidance answer suggests that you should not comply with the assistant manager's request. In the class discussion evaluate at least two other courses of action you might consider and why.

Communicating in Practice

LO 9

The classroom should be divided into teams. Teams are to select an industry, and each team member is to select a different company in that industry. Each team member is to acquire the annual report of the company selected. Annual reports can be obtained in many ways including accessing this book's Web page or **http://www.sedar.com**. Use the annual report to compute the debt ratio. Communicate with teammates via a meeting, e-mail or telphone to discuss the meaning of this ratio, how different companies compare to each other, and the industry norm. The team must prepare a single memo reporting the ratios for each company and identify the conclusions or consensus of opinion reached during the team's discussion. The memo is to be duplicated and distributed to the instructor and all classmates.

Taking It to the Net

Visit the **Alliance** annual report Web site at **http://www.alliance.ca.** Select the link to visit the financial highlights of Alliance. If you prefer you may access the highlights directly with **http://www.alliance.ca/Shareholderinfo/AnnualReport.html.**

Required

1. Of the financial highlights Alliance reports, which are terms you have already learned in Chapters 1 through 3? Which terms are unfamiliar to you?
2. Visit the Canada Stock Link Page at **http://phobos.seneac.on.ca/~spang1.** Use this quote service to locate Alliance's most recent share price. Alliance's ticker symbol that you will need to use in the quote lookup service is AAC.A. This can also be accessed via the Alliance Web site above.

Teamwork in Action

LO 6

The general ledger shown below reflects the transactions for Musician Makers, a business that provides music lessons for individuals, for the month of November. Your team has the task of determining and reporting certain information. For efficiency, you can divide responsibilities among team members. Your team must validate the accuracy of the information to be reported. When reporting this information, if asked (by instructor or classmates), each team member must be prepared to explain how to derive the information. As a means of validating the information, each team member should explain to the team how to determine the information.

MUSICIAN MAKERS
General Ledger

Cash

Bal.	3900		
(a)	5000	(b)	1,000
(c)	400	(g)	500
(d)	50	(h)	120
(j)	120	(i)	200

Accounts Payable

		(e)	125

Unearned Lesson Revenue

		(j)	120

A. Melody, Capital

		Bal.	3075
		(a)	5000

Notes Payable

(b)	1000	Bal.	1000
		(g)	1500

A. Melody, Withdrawals

(i)	200		

Wage Expense

(h)	120		

Accounts Receivable		
Bal.	75	(d)	50
(f)	80		

Lesson Revenue		
		(c)	400
		(f)	80

Supplies		
Bal.	100		
(e)	125		

Equipment		
(g)	2000		

Required

1. A brief description of each transaction.
2. Calculate Net Income or Loss
3. Determine the amount by which owner's equity changed, the ending owner's equity; explain why owner's equity changed and determine the return on equity.
4. Proof that the accounting equation is in balance and a determination of the debt ratio.
5. Provide a description of cash flows by categories and the net change in cash that these cash flows result in.
6. Proof that the information in 5 is in agreement with the change in the balance in the cash account.
7. An explanation of why cash flow from operating activities is not in agreement with the net income which is frequently referred to as the result of operations.

Obtain a recent copy of the most prominent newspaper distributed in your area. Research the classified section and prepare a report that identifies the following findings (attach relevant classified clippings to your report). Alternatively, you may want to search the World Wide Web for the required job information. For documentation purposes you should print copies of Web sites accessed.

1. The number of listings for accounting positions and the various accounting job titles identified in these listings.
2. The number of listings for other job titles, with examples, that require or prefer accounting knowledge/experience but are not specifically accounting positions. The ads for these other positions may or may not actually identify the accounting knowledge preference/requirement but you may be aware that this is commonly considered a qualification for the position.
3. The salary range for the accounting and accounting-related positions if provided.
4. The job that appealed to you the most, the reason for its appeal, and the requirements to qualify for this position.

Hitting the Road

Read the article "BCE to take $3B hit after writedown" in the January 14, 1998, issue of *The Financial Post*.

Required

1. Identify the reason for BCE's reduction in profit.
2. What effect will the writedown have on BCE's long-term profitability? Why?
3. What effect will the writedown have on BCE's current and future cash flow?
4. What effect will the writedown have on BCE's credit rating?
5. What reaction did investors have to the news of the writedown?

Business Break

LO 3, 6

4

Adjusting Accounts for Financial Statements

A Look Back

Chapter 3 explained the analysis and recording of transactions. We learned how to work with source documents, T-accounts, double-entry accounting, general journal, general ledger, postings, and trial balances. These are important parts of the accounting process leading to financial statements.

A Look at This Chapter

This chapter focuses on the timing of reports and the need to adjust accounts. Adjusting accounts is important for recognizing revenues and expenses in the proper period. We describe why adjustments are necessary, how to record them, and their effects on financial statements. We also explain the adjusted trial balance and how we use it to prepare financial statements.

A Look Forward

Chapter 5 highlights the completion of the accounting cycle. We explain the important final steps in obtaining reliable, relevant and comparable accounting information. These include closing procedures, post-closing trial balances, and reversing entries.

Chapter Outline

▶ **Timing and Reporting**
- The Accounting Period
- Purpose of Adjusting
- Recognizing Revenues and Expenses
- Accrual Basis Compared to Cash Basis

▶ **Adjusting Accounts**
- Framework for Adjustments
- Adjusting Prepaid Expenses
- Adjusting for Amortization
- Adjusting Unearned Revenues
- Adjusting Accrued Expenses
- Adjusting Accrued Revenues
- Adjustments and Financial Statements

▶ **Adjusted Trial Balance**

▶ **Preparing Financial Statements**

▶ **Accrual Adjustments in Later Periods**
- Paying Accrued Expenses
- Receiving Accrued Revenues

▶ **Using the Information—Profit Margin**

▶ **Appendix 4A—Alternatives in Accounting for Prepaids**

▶ **Appendix 4B—Work Sheet Format for Adjusted Trial Balance**

Tacklers Need Money

Toronto, ON—In Toronto, a mecca of professional and amateur sports teams, there is a new team on the block. It's the **Toronto Tacklers,** the "new look" of rugby. The Tacklers are organized and owned by Rob Burston, a 28-year-old player/coach.

Burston has always been driven. He took just three years to finish college. And he did it while working half-time as a salesperson. So its no surprise the Tacklers, a team Burston organized three years ago, are moving just as fast, topping their division and winning the playoffs. "To take the championship in only our third year is incredible," says Burston proudly. "We wanted it bad, and we believed in each other."

So far, that belief has been a hit on the field and in the stands. Attendance has skyrocketed. This year, between ticket sales, promotional advertising and other revenues, the Tacklers took in over $490,000 in revenues. Since then, Burston's team has signed an exclusive deal with an athletic shoe company to market rugby shoes and apparel. He won't reveal the figure, but the smile on his face is revealing enough.

Burston's next move? He wants to upgrade the facilities and field. "Rugby is a great spectator sport," insists Burston. "And if we do it right, the sky's the limit." Still, it's likely to be a battle. Burston needs money to fund his ideas, and bankers and investors are not accustomed to funding sports teams. A banker, who Burston has negotiated with, warns of hurdles. "How do you predict income and cash flows in rugby? When do you recognize season ticket sales, promotional revenues and exclusive contracts? Are facility and field costs expenses or assets? He must overcome these financial hurdles."

Such hurdles don't frighten Burston, who grew up poor with a "can't make it" label. Yet he is a realist who's now working with financial advisors in preparing pro forma statements to see his dream come true.

Learning Objectives

LO 1 Explain the importance of periodic reporting and the time period principle.

LO 2 Describe the purpose of adjusting accounts at the end of a period.

LO 3 Explain accrual accounting and how it adds to the usefulness of financial statements.

LO 4 Identify the types of adjustments and their purpose.

LO 5 Prepare and explain adjusting entries for prepaid expenses, amortization, and unearned revenues.

LO 6 Prepare and describe adjusting entries for accrued expenses and accrued revenues.

LO 7 Explain how accounting adjustments link to financial statements.

LO 8 Explain and prepare an adjusted trial balance.

LO 9 Prepare financial statements from an adjusted trial balance.

LO 10 Record and describe entries for later periods that result from accruals.

LO 11 Compute profit margin and describe its use in analyzing company performance.

CHAPTER PREVIEW

Financial statements reflect revenues when earned and expenses when incurred. This is known as accrual accounting. Accrual accounting requires several steps. We described many of these important steps in Chapter 3. We showed how companies use accounting systems to collect information about *external* transactions and events. We also explained how journals, ledgers, and other procedures are useful in preparing financial statements.

This chapter emphasizes the accounting process for producing useful information involving *internal* transactions and events. An important part of this process is adjusting the account balances. The adjusted account balances are what is reported in financial statements that are prepared according to accepted principles. Adjusting of accounts is necessary so that financial statements at the end of a reporting period reflect the effects of all transactions. We also identify and explain an important measure of company performance drawn from these statements (profit margin) and how users put it to work.

Timing and Reporting

Regular or periodic reporting is an important part of the accounting process. The point in time or the period of time over which a report refers impacts this process. This section describes the more important impacts of accounting time periods.

The Accounting Period

L01 Explain the importance of periodic reporting and the time period principle.

The value of information is often linked to its timeliness. Useful information must reach decision makers frequently and promptly. To provide timely information, accounting systems prepare periodic reports at regular intervals. This results in an accounting process impacted by the time period (or periodicity) principle. The **time period principle** assumes that an organization's activities can be divided into specific time periods such as a month, a three-month quarter, or a year.

Financial statements are prepared for time periods that are considered important for decision making and regulatory purposes. Time periods covered by statements are called **accounting** (or **reporting**) **periods.** Most organizations use a year as their primary accounting period. Reports covering a one-year period are known as *annual financial statements*. Many organizations also prepare **interim financial reports** covering one, three or six months of activity. In particular, most large companies provide quarterly reports. See Exhibit 4.1, which illustrates the various periods.

Exhibit 4.1

Accounting Periods

The annual reporting period is not always the same as a calendar year that ends on December 31. An organization can adopt a **fiscal year** consisting of any 12 consecutive months. It is also acceptable to adopt an annual reporting period of 52 weeks. Many companies, particularly in the food industry, use this method because it conforms more readily to their business cycle. For example, **The Second Cup's** 1997 fiscal year ended on June 28, and its 1996 year on June 29.

Companies not experiencing much seasonal variation in sales volume within the year often choose the calendar year as their fiscal year. For example, the financial statements of **Inco** reflect a fiscal year that ends on December 31. Companies experiencing seasonal variations in sales often choose a fiscal year corresponding to their **natural business year.** The natural business year ends when sales activities are at their lowest point during the year. The natural business year for retail stores ends around January 31, after the holiday seasons. An example of this includes **Mark's Work Warehouse** which starts its annual accounting period on or near February 1.

Purpose of Adjusting

The usual process during an accounting period is to record external transactions and events (with outside parties). After external transactions are recorded, several accounts in the ledger need adjusting for their balances to appear in financial statements. This need arises because internal transactions and events remain unrecorded.

An example is the costs of certain assets that expire or are consumed as time passes. The Prepaid Insurance account of **FastForward** is one of these. FastForward's trial balance shown in Exhibit 4.2 shows Prepaid Insurance with a balance of $2,400. This amount is the premium for two years of insurance protection beginning on December 1, 1997. By December 31, 1997, one month's coverage is used up, and the $2,400 is no longer the premium paid for the remaining 23 months of prepaid insurance. Because the coverage costs an average of $100 per month ($2,400/24 months), the Prepaid Insurance account balance must be reduced by one month's cost. The income statement must report this $100 cost as insurance expense for December.

LO 2 Describe the purpose of adjusting accounts at the end of a period.

Exhibit 4.2

Trial Balance

FastForward Trial Balance December 31, 1997		
	Debit	**Credit**
Cash	$ 7,950	
Accounts receivable	-0-	
Prepaid insurance	2,400	
Supplies	3,720	
Equipment	26,000	
Accounts payable		$ 1,100
Unearned consulting revenue		3,000
Note payable		5,100
C. Taylor, Capital		30,000
C. Taylor, Withdrawals	600	
Consulting revenue		3,800
Rental revenue		300
Rent expense	1,000	
Salaries expense	1,400	
Utilities expense	230	
Total	$43,300	$43,300

Another example is the $3,720 balance in Supplies. This account includes the cost of supplies that were used in December. The cost of these supplies must be reported as a December expense. The balances of both Prepaid Insurance and Supplies accounts must be *adjusted* before they are reported on the December 31 balance sheet.

Another adjustment necessary for FastForward relates to one month's usage of equipment. The balances of Unearned Consulting Revenue, Consulting Revenue, and Salaries Expense accounts also often need adjusting before appearing on the December statements. We explain how this adjusting process is carried out in the next section.

Recognizing Revenues and Expenses

LO 3 Explain accrual accounting and how it adds to the usefulness of financial statements.

Decision makers need timely financial information. We use the time period principle in dividing a company's activities into specific time periods. Yet because of the need for regular reporting of information, activities must be reported on before their completion. This means we must make some adjustments in reporting to not mislead decision makers

Two main principles we use in the adjusting process are *revenue recognition* and *matching.* Chapter 2 explains that the revenue recognition principle requires revenue be reported when earned, not before and not after. Revenue is earned for most companies when services and products are delivered to customers which is normally considered to be the point of sale. If FastForward provides consulting to a client in December, the revenue is earned in December. This means it must be reported on the December income statement, even if the client paid for the services in a month other than December. A major goal of the adjusting process is to have revenue recognized (reported) in the time period when it is earned.

Did You Know?

Is it Revenue, or Is It Not?
Centennial Technology, like many companies, recognizes revenue when products are shipped. What is not common is that the CEO of Centennial shipped products to the warehouses of friends and reported it as revenue (he's in jail now). **Informix,** a database software maker, also recorded revenue when products were passed to distributors. It admits now that there were "errors in the way revenues had been recorded." These and other risky revenue recognition practices are often revealed by a large increase in accounts receivable relative to sales.

The **matching principle** aims to report expenses in the same accounting period as the revenues that are earned as a result of these expenses. This matching of costs (expenses) with benefits (revenues) is a major part of the adjusting process. A common example is a business like FastForward that earns monthly revenues while operating out of rented store space. The earning of revenues required rented space. The matching principle tells us that rent must be reported on the income statement for December, even if rent is paid in a month either before or after December. This ensures the rent expense for December is matched with December's revenues.

Matching expenses with revenues often requires us to predict certain events. When we use financial statements we must understand that they use predictions. This means they include measures that are not precise. **Atlantis Communication's** annual report explains its film and television production costs from shows such as "Traders" and "The Adventures of Sinbad" are matched to revenues based on a ratio of current revenues from the show divided by its predicted total revenues.

Accrual Basis Compared to Cash Basis

Accrual basis accounting uses the adjusting process to recognize revenues when earned and to match expenses with revenues. This means the economic effects of revenues and expenses are recorded when earned or incurred, not when cash is received or paid.

Cash basis accounting means revenues are recognized when cash is received and that expenses are recorded when cash is paid. If a business earns revenue in December but cash is not received from clients until January, then cash basis accounting reports this revenue in January. Because revenues are reported when cash is received and expenses are deducted when cash is paid, the cash basis net income for a period is the difference between revenues received in cash (called *receipts*) and expenses paid in cash (called *expenditures* or *disbursements*).

Cash basis accounting for the income statement, balance sheet, and statement of changes in owner's equity is not consistent with accepted accounting principles. It is commonly held that accrual accounting provides a better indication of business performance than information about current cash receipts and payments.[1] Accrual accounting also increases the *comparability* of financial statements from one period to another. Yet many companies still find cash basis accounting useful for several internal reports and decisions.

To see the impact of these different accounting systems let's consider the Prepaid Insurance of FastForward. FastForward paid $2,400 for two years of insurance coverage beginning on December 1. Accrual accounting means that $100 of insurance expense is reported on December's income statement. Another $1,200 of expense is reported in 1998, and the remaining $1,100 is reported as expense in the first 11 months of 1999. This allocation of insurance cost across these three fiscal years is illustrated in Exhibit 4.3.

Exhibit 4.3

Accrual Basis Accounting for Prepaid Insurance

December Transaction: Purchase 24 months' insurance beginning December 1997

Insurance Expense 1997			
Jan $-0-	Feb $-0-	Mar $-0-	Apr $-0-
May $-0-	June $-0-	July $-0-	Aug $-0-
Sept $-0-	Oct $-0-	Nov $-0-	Dec $100

Insurance Expense 1998			
Jan $100	Feb $100	Mar $100	Apr $100
May $100	June $100	July $100	Aug $100
Sept $100	Oct $100	Nov $100	Dec $100

Insurance Expense 1999			
Jan $100	Feb $100	Mar $100	Apr $100
May $100	June $100	July $100	Aug $100
Sept $100	Oct $ 100	Nov $100	Dec $-0-

A cash basis income statement for December 1997 reports insurance expense of $2,400 as shown in Exhibit 4.4. The income statements for 1998 and 1999 report no insurance expense from this policy. This compares to the accrual basis accounting that shows each of the 24 months has $100 of insurance expense. The accrual basis balance sheet reports the remaining unexpired premium as a Prepaid Insurance asset. The cash basis never reports this asset. The cash basis information is less useful for most decisions because reported income for 1997–1999 fails to match the cost of insurance used for those years with the benefits received.

Exhibit 4.4

Cash Basis Accounting for Prepaid Insurance

December Transaction: Purchase 24 months' insurance beginning December 1997

Insurance Expense 1997			
Jan $-0-	Feb $-0-	Mar $-0-	Apr $-0-
May $-0-	June $-0-	July $-0-	Aug $-0-
Sept $-0-	Oct $-0-	Nov $-0-	Dec $2,400

Insurance Expense 1998			
Jan $-0-	Feb $-0-	Mar $-0-	Apr $-0-
May $-0-	June $-0-	July $-0-	Aug $-0-
Sept $-0-	Oct $-0-	Nov $-0-	Dec $-0-

Insurance Expense 1999			
Jan $-0-	Feb $-0-	Mar $-0-	Apr $-0-
May $-0-	June $-0-	July $-0-	Aug $-0-
Sept $-0-	Oct $-0-	Nov $-0-	Dec $-0-

[1] *Statement of Financial Accounting Concepts No. 1,* "Objectives of Financial Reporting by Business Enterprises" (Norwalk: The Financial Accounting Standards Board CT, 1978), par. 44.

The accrual basis is generally accepted for external reporting because it gives more useful information. The cash basis is not acceptable for a balance sheet, income statement, or statement of changes in owner's equity because it gives incomplete information about assets, liabilities, revenues and expenses. Yet information about cash flows is also useful. This is why companies reporting generally accepted financial statements include a statement of cash flows.

Flash back

1. Describe a company's annual reporting period.
2. Why do companies prepare interim financial statements?
3. What accounting principles most directly propel the adjusting process?
4. Is cash basis accounting consistent with the matching principle? Why?
5. If your company pays a $4,800 premium on April 1, 1998, for two years insurance coverage, how much insurance expense is reported in 1999 using cash basis accounting?

Answers—p. 175

Adjusting Accounts

The process of adjusting accounts is similar to our process of analyzing and recording transactions in the prior chapter. We must analyze each account balance and the transactions and events that affect it to determine any needed adjustments. An **adjusting entry** is recorded to bring an asset or liability account balance to its proper amount when an adjustment is needed. This entry also updates the related expense or revenue account and is necessary to prepare the financial statements. Adjusting entries are posted to accounts like any other entry. This section explains why adjusting entries are needed to provide useful information. We also show the mechanics of adjusting entries and their links to financial statements.

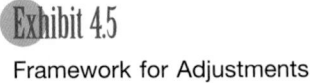
LO4   Identify the types of adjustments and their purpose.

Framework for Adjustments

Adjustments are necessary for transactions and events that extend over more than one period. It is helpful to group adjustments by their timing of cash receipt or payment in comparison to when they are recognized as revenues or expenses. Exhibit 4.5 identifies the five main adjustments. These involve both expenses and revenues.

Exhibit 4.5

Framework for Adjustments

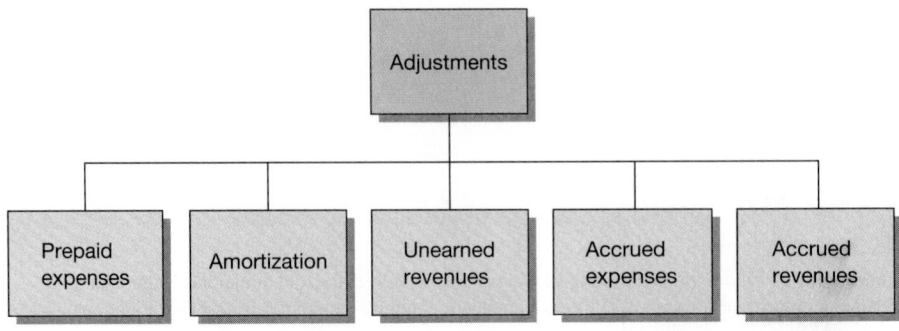

Prepaid expenses, amortization, and unearned revenues each reflect transactions where cash is paid or received *before* a related expense or revenue is recognized.[2] Accrued expenses and accrued revenues reflect transactions where cash is paid or received *after* a related expense or revenue is recognized. Adjusting entries are necessary for each of these so that revenues, expenses, assets and liabilities are correctly reported. It is helpful to remember that each adjusting entry affects one or more income statement accounts *and* one or more balance sheet accounts. Also note that an adjusting entry never includes the Cash account.

LO 5 Prepare and explain adjusting entries for prepaid expenses, amortization, and unearned revenues.

Adjusting Prepaid Expenses

Prepaid expenses refer to items *paid for* in advance of receiving their benefits. Prepaid expenses, also called *deferred expenses,* are assets. As these assets are used, their costs become expenses. Adjusting entries for prepaids involve increasing (debiting) expenses and decreasing (crediting) assets as shown in Exhibit 4.6.

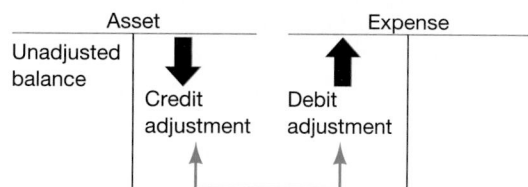

Exhibit 4.6

Adjusting for Prepaid Expenses

The adjustments are made to reflect economic events (including passage of time) impacting the amount of prepaid expenses. This section describes the accounting for three common prepaid expenses: insurance; supplies; and amortization.

Prepaid Insurance

We illustrate prepaid insurance using FastForward's payment of $2,400 for two years of insurance protection beginning on December 1, 1997. The cash payments were illustrated in Exhibit 4.4 for 1997–1999. The following entry records the purchase of the insurance:

Dec. 1	Prepaid Insurance	2,400	
	Cash		2,400
	To record purchase of insurance for 24 months.		

With the passage of time, the benefit of the insurance protection gradually expires and a portion of the Prepaid Insurance asset becomes an expense. One month's insurance coverage expires by December 31, 1997. This expense is $100 or 1/24 of $2,400. Our adjusting entry to record this expense and reduce the asset is:

Adjustment (a)			
Dec. 31	Insurance Expense	100	
	Prepaid Insurance		100
	To record expired insurance.		

Assets = Liabilities + Equity
+100   −100
−100

Posting this adjusting entry affects the accounts shown in Exhibit 4.7.

---

[2] Prepaids are also called *deferrals* because the recognition of an expense or revenue is *deferred.*

Exhibit 4.7

Insurance Accounts after
Adjusting for Prepaids

Prepaid Insurance				Insurance Expense		
Dec. 26	2,400	Dec. 31	100	Dec. 31	100	
Balance	2,300					

After posting, the $100 balance in Insurance Expense and the $2,300 balance in Prepaid Insurance are ready for reporting in the financial statements. If the adjustment is *not* made at December 31, then (a) expenses are understated by $100 and net income is overstated by $100 for the December income statement, and (b) both Prepaid Insurance and Owner's Equity are overstated by $100 in the December 31 balance sheet. It is also evident in Exhibit 4.3 that 1998 adjustments must transfer a total of $1,200 from Prepaid Insurance to Insurance Expense, and 1999 adjustments must transfer the remaining $1,100 to Insurance Expense.

Supplies

Store supplies are another prepaid expense often requiring adjusting. FastForward purchased $3,720 of supplies in December and used some of them during this month. Consuming these supplies creates expenses equal to their cost. Daily usage of supplies was not recorded in FastForward's accounts because this information was not needed. Also when we report account balances in financial statements only at the end of a month, recordkeeping costs can be reduced by making only one adjusting entry at that time. This entry needs to record the total cost of all supplies used in the month.

Because we prepare an income statement for December, the cost of supplies used during this month must be recognized as an expense. FastForward computes ("takes inventory of") the remaining unused supplies. The cost of the remaining supplies is then deducted from the cost of the purchased supplies to compute the amount used. FastForward has $2,670 of supplies remaining out of the $3,720 purchased in December. The $1,050 difference between these two amounts is the cost of the supplies consumed. This amount is December's Supplies Expense. Our adjusting entry to record this expense and reduce the Supplies asset account is:

Assets = Liabilities + Equity
−1,050   −1,050

	Adjustment (b)		
Dec. 31	Supplies Expense	1,050	
	Supplies		1,050
	To record supplies used.		

Posting this adjusting entry affects the accounts shown in Exhibit 4.8.

Exhibit 4.8

Supplies Accounts after
Adjusting for Prepaids

Supplies				Supplies Expense		
Dec. 2	2,500	Dec. 31	1,050	Dec. 31	1,050	
6	1,100					
26	120					
Total	3,720	Total	1,050			
Balance	2,670					

The balance of the supplies account is $2,670 after posting and equals the cost of remaining unused supplies. If the adjustment is *not* made at December 31, then (a) expenses are understated by $1,050 and net income overstated by $1,050 for the December income statement, and (b) both Supplies and owner's equity are overstated by $1,050 in the December 31 balance sheet.

Other Prepaid Expenses

There are other prepaid expenses. These include Prepaid Rent, and are accounted for exactly like Insurance and Supplies above. We should also note that some prepaid expenses are both paid for and fully used up within a single accounting period. One example is when a company pays monthly rent on the first day of each month. The payment creates a prepaid expense on the first day of each month that fully expires by the end of the month. In these special cases we can record the cash paid with a debit to the expense account instead of an asset account. This practice is described more completely later in the chapter.

Appraiser

You are hired as an appraiser to estimate the value of a small publishing company. This company recently signed a well-known athlete to write a book. The company agreed to pay the athlete (author) $500,000 upon signing, plus future royalties on the book. Your analysis of the company's financial statements finds the $500,000 is not reported as an expense. Instead, it is reported as part of Prepaid Expenses. A note to the statement says *"prepaid expenses include author signing fees that are matched against future expected sales."* Is this accounting for the $500,000 signing bonus acceptable? How does it affect your analysis?

You Make the Call

Answer—p. 174

Adjusting for Amortization

Capital assets include long-term tangible assets such as **plant and equipment** which are used to produce and sell products and services and **intangible assets** such as patents which convey the right to use a product or process. These assets are expected to provide benefits for more than one period. Examples of plant and equipment are land, buildings, machines, vehicles and fixtures. All plant and equipment assets, except for land, eventually wear out or decline in usefulness. The costs of these assets are deferred and steadily reported as expenses in the income statement over the assets' useful lives (benefit periods). **Amortization**[3] or **depreciation** is the process of computing expense from allocating the cost of capital assets, as the benefit is derived from their use, over their expected useful lives. Amortization expense is recorded with an adjusting entry similar to that for prepaid expenses. This entry is more involved because a special account is used to record the declining asset balance.

FastForward uses equipment in earning revenue. This equipment's cost must be amortized. Recall that FastForward made two purchases of equipment, one for $20,000 and the other for $6,000, in early December. Chuck Taylor expects the equipment to have a useful life (benefit period) of four years. Taylor expects to sell the equipment for about $8,000 at the end of four years. This means the net cost expected to expire over the useful life is $18,000 ($26,000 − $8,000).

There are several methods we can use to allocate this $18,000 net cost to expense. FastForward uses straight-line amortization.[4] The **straight-line amortization method** allocates equal amounts of an asset's cost to the periods bene-

---

[3] In 1990, the revised *CICA Handbook,* section 3600, recommended the use of the term *amortization* instead of *depreciation,* but the use of *depreciation* was not ruled out. Also, *fixed assets* was replaced by *capital assets.* Despite these recommendations the new terminology has not yet been adopted by all users. Thus, *depreciation* and *depletion* continue as common terms.

[4] We explain the details of amortization or depreciation methods later in this book (Chapter 12). We briefly describe the straight-line method here to help you understand the adjusting process.

fiting over its useful life. When the $18,000 net cost is divided by the 48 months in the asset's useful life, we get an average monthly cost of $375 ($18,000/48). Our adjusting entry to record monthly amortization expense is:

Adjustment (c)			
Dec. 31	Amortization Expense — Equipment	375	
	Accumulated Amortization — Equipment		375
	To record monthly amortization on equipment.		

Assets = Liabilities + Equity
−375   −375

Exhibit 4.9

Accounts after Amortization Adjustments

Posting this adjusting entry affects the accounts shown in Exhibit 4.9.

Equipment	
Dec. 3	20,000
6	6,000
Bal.	26,000

Accumulated Amortization — Equipment	
	Dec. 31 375

Amortization Expense — Equipment	
Dec. 31 375	

After posting the adjustment, the Equipment account less its Accumulated Amortization—Equipment account equal the December 31 balance sheet amount for this asset. The balance in the Amortization Expense—Equipment account is the expense reported in the December income statement. If the adjustment is *not* made at December 31, then (a) expenses are understated by $375 and net income overstated by $375 for the December income statement, and (b) both assets and owner's equity are overstated by $375 in the December 31 balance sheet.

It is common for decreases in an asset account to be recorded with a credit to the account. This procedure is *not* followed when recording amortization. Instead, amortization is recorded in a contra account. A **contra account** is an account linked with another account and having an opposite normal balance. It is reported as a subtraction from the other account's balance. For FastForward, the contra account is Accumulated Amortization—Equipment.

The use of contra accounts allow balance sheet readers to know both the cost of assets and the total amount of amortization charged to expense. By knowing both these amounts, decision makers can better assess a company's productive capacity and any need to replace assets. FastForward's balance sheet shows both the $26,000 original cost of equipment and the $375 balance in accumulated amortization contra account. This information reveals that the equipment is close to new. If FastForward only reported the net cost of $25,625, users cannot assess the equipment's age or its need for replacement.

Notice the title of the contra account is *accumulated amortization.* This means the account includes total amortization expense for all prior periods when the assets were being used. FastForward's Equipment and Accumulated Amortization accounts would appear as follows on February 28, 1998, after the three monthly adjusting entries shown in Exhibit 4.10.

Exhibit 4.10

Accounts after Three Months of Amortization Adjustments

Equipment	
Dec. 3	20,000
6	6,000
Total	26,000

Accumulated Amortization— Equipment	
	Dec. 31 375
	Jan. 31 375
	Feb. 28 375
	Total 1,125

These account balances are reported in the assets section on the February 28 balance sheet as shown in Exhibit 4.11.

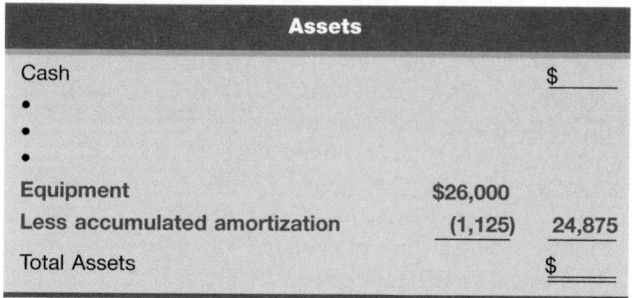

Assets		
Cash		$ ___
•		
•		
•		
Equipment	$26,000	
Less accumulated amortization	(1,125)	24,875
Total Assets		$ ___

Exhibit 4.11

Accumulated Amortization Contra Account in the Balance Sheet

Small Business Owner
You are preparing to make an offer to purchase a small family-run restaurant. The manager gives you a copy of her amortization schedule for the restaurant's building and equipment. It shows costs of $75,000 and accumulated amortization of $55,000. This leaves a net total for building and equipment of $20,000. Is this information valuable in deciding on a purchase offer for the restaurant?

You Make the Call

Answer—p. 174

Adjusting Unearned Revenues

Unearned revenues refer to cash *received* in advance of providing products and services. Unearned revenues, also known as Deferred Revenues, are a liability. When cash is accepted, an obligation to provide products and services is also accepted. As products and services are provided, the amount of unearned revenues becomes *earned* revenues. Adjusting entries for unearned revenues involve increasing (crediting) revenues and decreasing (debiting) unearned revenues as shown in Exhibit 4.12.

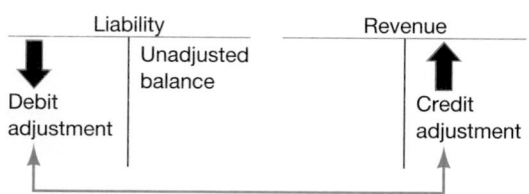

Exhibit 4.12

Adjusting for Unearned Revenues

These adjustments reflect economic events (including passage of time) that impact unearned revenues.

We see an example of unearned revenues in **Rogers Communication's** 1996 annual report. Rogers reports Unearned Revenue of $91.3 million on its balance sheet. Another example is **Air Canada,** which reports advance (unearned) ticket sales in 1996 of $270 million:

> The value of unused transportation is included in current liabilities.

Unearned revenues are over 10% of total current liabilities for both companies.

Bird Money
Game day for the Toronto Blue Jays includes adjusting accounts. When the Jays receive cash from season ticket sales and broadcast fees at the beginning of the season, it is recorded in an unearned revenue account called "Deferred Game Revenues." The Jays recognize this unearned revenue on a game-by-game basis. Because the regular baseball season begins in April and ends in September, revenue recognition is mainly limited to this period.

FastForward also has unearned revenues. FastForward agreed on December 26 to provide consulting services to a client for a fixed fee of $1,500 per month. On that same day, this client paid the first two months' fees in advance covering the period December 27 to February 24. The entry to record the cash received in advance is:

Dec. 26	Cash	3,000	
	Unearned Consulting Revenue		3,000
	Received advance payment for services over the next two months.		

Assets = Liabilities + Equity
+3,000   +3,000

This advance payment increases cash and creates an obligation to do consulting work over the next two months. As time passes and the consultation is provided, FastForward will earn this revenue. There are no external transactions linked with this earnings process. By December 31, FastForward provides five days' service and earns one-sixth of the $1,500 revenue for the first month. This amounts to $250 ($1,500 × 5/30). The *revenue recognition principle* implies that $250 of unearned revenue is reported as revenue on the December income statement. The adjusting entry to reduce the liability account and recognize earned revenue is:

	Adjustment (d)		
Dec. 31	Unearned Consulting Revenue	250	
	Consulting Revenue ($1,500 × 5/30) . .		250
	To record the earned portion of revenue received in advance.		

Assets = Liabilities + Equity
         −250   +250

The accounts look as shown in Exhibit 4.13 after posting the adjusting entry.

Exhibit 4.13

Revenue Accounts after Adjusting for Prepaids

Unearned Consulting Revenue			
Dec. 31	250	Dec. 26	3,000
		Balance	2,750

Consulting Revenue		
	Dec. 10	2,200
	12	1,600
	31	250
	Total	4,050

L0 6 Prepare and describe adjusting entries for accrued expenses and accrued revenues.

The adjusting entry transfers $250 out of unearned revenue (a liability account) to a revenue account. If the adjustment is *not* made, then (a) revenue and net income are understated by $250 in the December income statement, and (b) Unearned Revenue is overstated and owner's equity understated by $250 on the December 31 balance sheet.

Adjusting Accrued Expenses

Accrued expenses refer to costs incurred in a period that are both unpaid and unrecorded. Accrued expenses are part of expenses and reported on the income statement. When costs are incurred in acquiring products and services, there is an obligation to pay for them. The costs of products and services acquired but not yet paid are accrued expenses. Adjusting entries for recording accrued expenses involve increasing (debiting) expenses and increasing (crediting) liabilities as shown in Exhibit 4.14.

Exhibit 4.14

Adjusting for Accrued Expenses

This adjustment recognizes expenses that are incurred in a period but not yet paid for. Common examples of accrued expenses are salaries, interest, rent and taxes. We use salaries and interest to show how to adjust accounts for accrued expenses.

Accrued Salaries Expense

FastForward's employee earns $70 per day or $350 for a five-day workweek beginning on Monday and ending on Friday. This employee gets paid every two weeks on Friday. On the 12th and the 26th of December the wages are paid, recorded in the journal, and posted to the ledger. The *unadjusted* Salaries Expense and Cash paid for salaries appear as shown in Exhibit 4.15.

Cash		
Dec. 12	700	
26	700	

Salaries Expense		
Dec. 12	700	
26	700	

Exhibit 4.15

Salary and Cash Accounts before Adjusting

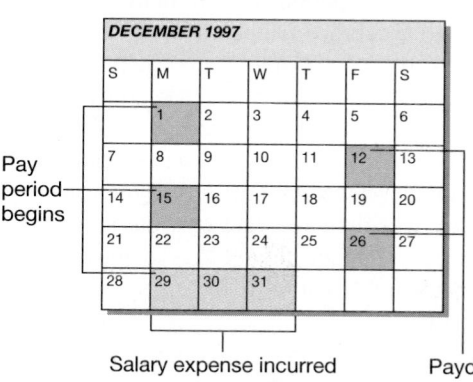

Exhibit 4.16

Salary Accrual Period and Paydays

The calendar in Exhibit 4.16 shows three working days after the December 26 payday (29, 30 and 31). This means the employee earns three days' salary by the close of business on Wednesday, December 31. While this salary cost is incurred, it is not yet paid or recorded. The period-end financial statements are incomplete if FastForward fails to report both the added expense and the liability to the employee for unpaid salary. The period-end adjusting entry to account for accrued salaries is:

	Adjustment (e)		
Dec. 31	Salaries Expense	210	
	Salaries Payable		210
	To record three days' accrued salary (3 × $70).		

Assets = Liabilities + Equity
+210   − 210

After the adjusting entry is posted, the expense and liability accounts appear as shown in Exhibit 4.17.

Exhibit 4.17

Salary Accounts after
Accrual Adjustments

Salaries Expense		
Dec. 12	700	
26	700	
31	210	
Total	1,610	

Salaries Payable		
	Dec. 31	210

This means that $1,610 of salaries expense is reported on the income statement and that a $210 salaries payable (liability) is reported in the balance sheet. If the adjustment is *not* made, then (a) Salaries Expense is understated and net income overstated by $210 in the December income statement, and (b) Salaries Payable is understated and owner's equity overstated by $210 on the December 31 balance sheet.

Accrued Interest Expense

It is common for companies to have accrued interest expense on notes payable and certain accounts payable at the end of a period. Interest expense is incurred with the passage of time. Unless interest is paid on the last day of an accounting period, we need to adjust accounts for interest expense incurred but not yet paid. This means we must accrue interest cost since the most recent payment date up to the end of the period.[5] We fully describe computation of interest expense later in the book. The adjusting entry is similar to the one for accruing unpaid salary, with a debit to Interest Expense and a credit to Interest Payable (liability).

Adjusting Accrued Revenues

Accrued revenues refer to revenues earned in a period that are both unrecorded and not yet received in cash (or other assets). Accrued revenues are part of revenues and must be reported on the income statement. An example is a house painter who bills customers when the job is done. If one-third of a house is painted by the end of a period, then one-third of the painter's billing is recorded as revenue in the period even though it is not yet billed or collected. When products and services are delivered, we expect to receive payment for them. Adjusting entries recognize accrued revenues for the value of products and services delivered that are both unrecorded and not yet collected in cash or other assets. The adjusting entries increase (debit) assets and increase (credit) revenues as shown in Exhibit 4.18.

Exhibit 4.18

Adjusting for Accrued
Revenues

This adjustment recognizes revenues earned in a period but not yet received in cash. Common examples of accrued revenues are fees for services and products, interest and rent. We use service fees and interest to show how to adjust accounts for accrued revenues.

---

[5] The formula for computing accrued interest is: *Payable amount* × *Annual interest rate* × *Fraction of year since last payment date.*

Accrued Services Revenue

Many revenues are recorded when cash is received from a customer or when products and services are sold on credit. Accrued revenues are not recorded until adjusting entries are made at the end of the accounting period. These accrued revenues are earned but unrecorded because either the customer has not yet paid for them or the seller has not yet billed the customer.

FastForward provides us one example. In the second week of December, FastForward agreed to provide consulting services to the athletic department of a junior college for a fixed fee of $2,700 per month. The terms of the initial agreement call for FastForward to provide services from the 12th of December, 1997, through the 10th of January 1998, or 30 days of service. The athletic department agrees to pay $2,700 cash to FastForward on January 10, 1998, when the service period is complete.

At December 31, 1997, 20 days of services are already provided to the college. Since the contracted services are not yet entirely provided, the college is not yet billed nor has FastForward recorded the services already provided. FastForward has earned two-thirds of the one month's fee, or $1,800 ($2,700 × 20/30). The *revenue recognition principle* implies we must report the $1,800 on the December income statement because it is earned in December. The balance sheet also must report that this junior college owes FastForward $1,800. The year-end adjusting entry to account for accrued consulting services revenue is:

	Adjustment (f)		
Dec. 31	Accounts Receivable	1,800	
	Consulting Revenue		1,800
	To record 20 days' accrued revenue.		

Assets = Liabilities + Equity
+1,800   +1,800

The debit to receivable reflects the amount owed to FastForward from the junior college for consulting services already provided. After the adjusting entry is posted, the affected accounts look as shown in Exhibit 4.19.

Accounts Receivable			
Dec. 12	1,900	Dec. 22	1,900
31	1,800		
Total	3,700	Total	1,900
Balance	1,800		

Consulting Revenue		
	Dec. 10	2,200
	12	1,600
	31	250
	31	1,800
	Total	5,850

Exhibit 4.19

Receivable and Revenue Accounts after Accrual Adjustments

Accounts receivable are reported on the balance sheet at $1,800, and $5,850 of revenues are reported on the income statement. If the adjustment is *not* made, then (a) both Consulting Revenue and net income are understated by $1,800 in the December income statement, and (b) both Accounts Receivable and owner's equity are understated by $1,800 on the December 31 balance sheet.

Loan Officer

You are a loan officer when an owner of a stereo components store applies for a business loan from your bank. Your analysis of the store's financial statements reveals a record increase in revenues and profits for the current year. Further analysis shows nearly all of this increase is due to a promotional sales campaign where the consumer bought now but pays nothing until January 1 of next year. The store owner recorded all of these sales as revenue. Do you see any concerns in approving a loan to this store?

You Make the Call

Answer—p. 174

Accrued Interest Revenue

In addition to the accrued interest expense we described earlier, interest can yield an accrued revenue when a company is owed money (or other assets) from a debtor. If a company is holding notes or accounts receivable that produce interest revenue, we must adjust the accounts to record any earned and yet uncollected interest revenue. The adjusting entry is similar to the one for accruing services revenue, with a debit to Interest Receivable (asset) and a credit to Interest Revenue.

Judgment and Ethics

Financial Officer
You are the financial officer for a retail outlet company. At the calendar year-end when you are reviewing adjusting entries to record accruals, you are called into the president's office. The president asks about accrued expenses and instructs you to not record these expenses until next year because they will not be paid until January or later. The president also asks how much current year's revenues increased by the recent purchase order from a new customer. You state there is no effect on sales until next year because the purchase order says merchandise is to be delivered after January 15 and that is when your company plans to make delivery. The president points out that the order is already received, that your company is ready to make delivery, and tells you to record this sale in the current year. Your company would report a net income instead of a net loss if you carried out the president's orders for adjusting accruals. What do you do?

Answer—p. 174

Mid-Chapter Demonstration Problem

The owner of a lawn service company prepares monthly financial statements. The following situations arise at the end of July. Prepare the appropriate adjusting entries as of July 31. Appropriate entries have been made to the end of June.

a. A customer paid for the entire summer's service in April. The journal entry credited the Unearned Service Fees account when the payment was received. The monthly fee is $500.

b. The weekly salary expense of $1,000 was paid to the employees on Friday, July 27th. The employees are paid weekly and work Monday to Friday.

c. The yearly insurance bill amounting to $1,200 was paid in March. The journal entry debited the Prepaid Insurance account when the payment was made.

Solution to Mid-Chapter Demonstration Problem

a. Unearned Service Fees   500
        Service Fees Earned   500
    To record service fees earned for July.

b. Salaries Expense   400
        Salaries Payable   400
    To record salaries for the last two days of July.

c. Insurance Expense   100
        Prepaid Insurance   100
    To record insurance for July.

Adjustments and Financial Statements

The process of adjusting accounts is intended to bring an asset or liability account balance to its correct amount. This process and its related adjusting entry also updates a related expense or revenue account. These adjustments are necessary for transactions and events that extend over more than one period. Adjusting entries are posted like any other entry.

Exhibit 4.20 lists the five major types of transactions requiring adjustment. Adjusting entries are necessary for each. Understanding this exhibit is important to understanding the adjusting process and its importance to financial statements. Remember each adjusting entry affects one or more income statement accounts *and* one or more balance sheet accounts. Note that an adjusting entry never affects cash.

LO7 Explain how accounting adjustments link to financial statements.

| Type | Before Adjusting | | Adjusting Entry |
	Balance Sheet Account	Income Statement Account	
Prepaid Expense	Asset Overstated	Expense Understated	Dr. Expense
	Equity Overstated		Cr. Asset
Amortization	Asset Overstated	Expense Understated	Dr. Expense
	Equity Overstated		Cr. Contra Asset
Unearned Revenues	Liability Overstated	Revenue Understated	Dr. Liability
	Equity Understated		Cr. Revenue
Accrued Expenses	Liability Understated	Expense Understated	Dr. Expense
	Equity Overstated		Cr. Liability
Accrued Revenues	Asset Understated	Revenue Understated	Dr. Asset
	Equity Understated		Cr. Revenue

Exhibit 4.20

Summary of Adjustments and Financial Statement Links

Exhibit 4.21 summarizes the adjusting entries of FastForward on December 31. The posting of adjusting entries to individual ledger accounts is shown when we described the transactions above and is not repeated here. Adjusting entries are often set apart from other journal entries with the caption Adjusting Entries.

Exhibit 4.21

Journalizing Adjusting Entries of FastForward

FASTForward

GENERAL JOURNAL			Page #	
Date	Account Titles and Explanation	PR	Debit	Credit
1997	Adjusting Entries			
Dec. 31	Insurance Expense		100	
	Prepaid Insurance			100
	To record expired insurance.			
Dec. 31	Supplies Expense		1,050	
	Supplies			1,050
	To record supplies used.			
Dec. 31	Amortization Expense		375	
	Accumulated Amortization—Equipment			375
	To record monthly amortization on equipment.			
Dec. 31	Unearned Consulting Revenue		250	
	Consulting Revenue ($1,500 × 5/30)			250
	To record earned revenue received in advance.			
Dec. 31	Salaries Expense		210	
	Salaries Payable			210
	To record three days' accrued salary (3 × $70).			
Dec. 31	Accounts Receivable		1,800	
	Consulting Revenue			1,800
	To record 20 days' accrued revenue.			

Answers—p. 175

Flash back

6. If you omit an adjusting entry for accrued service revenues of $200 at year-end, what is the effect of this error on the income statement and balance sheet?

7. Explain the term *contra account*.

8. What is an accrued expense? Give an example.

9. Describe how an unearned revenue arises. Give an example.

Adjusted Trial Balance

LO 8 Explain and prepare an adjusted trial balance.

Exhibit 4.22

Unadjusted and Adjusted Trial Balances for FastForward

An **unadjusted trial balance** is a listing of accounts and balances prepared *before* adjustments are recorded. An **adjusted trial balance** is a list of accounts and balances prepared *after* adjusting entries are recorded and posted to the ledger. Exhibit 4.22 shows the unadjusted and adjusted trial balances for FastForward at December 31, 1997. Notice several new accounts arising from the adjusting entries. The listing of accounts is also slightly changed to match the order in the chart of account numbers listed at the end of the book.

FASTFORWARD
Trial Balances
December 31, 1997

	Unadjusted Trial Balance Dr.	Unadjusted Trial Balance Cr.	Adjustments Dr.	Adjustments Cr.	Adjusted Trial Balance Dr.	Adjusted Trial Balance Cr.
Cash	$ 7,950				$ 7,950	
Accounts receivable			(f)1,800		1,800	
Supplies	3,720			(b)1,050	2,670	
Prepaid insurance	2,400			(a) 100	2,300	
Equipment	26,000				26,000	
Accumulated amortization—Equipment				(c) 375		$ 375
Accounts payable		$ 1,100				1,100
Salaries payable				(e) 210		210
Unearned consulting revenue		3,000	(d) 250			2,750
Note payable		5,100				5,100
Chuck Taylor, capital		30,000				30,000
Chuck Taylor, withdrawals	600				600	
Consulting revenue		3,800		(d) 250		5,850
				(f) 1,800		
Rental revenue		300				300
Amortization expense—Equipment			(c) 375		375	
Salaries expense	1,400		(e) 210		1,610	
Insurance expense			(a) 100		100	
Rent expense	1,000				1,000	
Supplies expense			(b)1,050		1,050	
Utilities expense	230				230	
Totals	$43,300	$43,300	$3,785	$3,785	$45,685	$45,685

We can prepare financial statements directly from information in the *adjusted* trial balance. An adjusted trial balance includes all balances appearing in financial statements. We know that a trial balance summarizes information in the ledger by listing accounts and their balances. This summary is easier to work from than the entire ledger when preparing financial statements.

Exhibit 4.23 shows how FastForward's revenue and expense balances are transferred from the adjusted trial balance to the (1) income statement, and (2) statement of changes in owner's equity. Note how we use the net income and withdrawals account to prepare the statement of changes in owner's equity.

Exhibit 4.24 shows how FastForward's asset and liability balances on the adjusted trial balance are transferred to the balance sheet. The ending owner's equity is determined on the statement of changes in owner's equity and transferred to the balance sheet. There are different formats for the balance sheet. The **account form** lists assets on the left and liabilities and owner's equity on the right side of the balance sheet. Its name comes from its link to the accounting equation, *assets = liabilities + equity*. The balance sheet in Exhibit 2.15 (on p. 64) is in account form. The **report form balance sheet** lists items vertically as shown in Exhibit 4.24. **Alliance Communications** uses a report form. Both forms are widely used and are considered equally helpful to users.

We usually prepare financial statements in the order shown: income statement, statement of changes in owner's equity, and balance sheet.[6] This order makes sense since the balance sheet uses information in the statement of changes in owner's equity, which in turn uses information from the income statement.

Preparing Financial Statements

LO 9 Prepare financial statements from an adjusted trial balance.

Exhibit 4.23

Preparing the Income Statement and Statement of Changes in Owner's Equity from the Adjusted Trial Balance

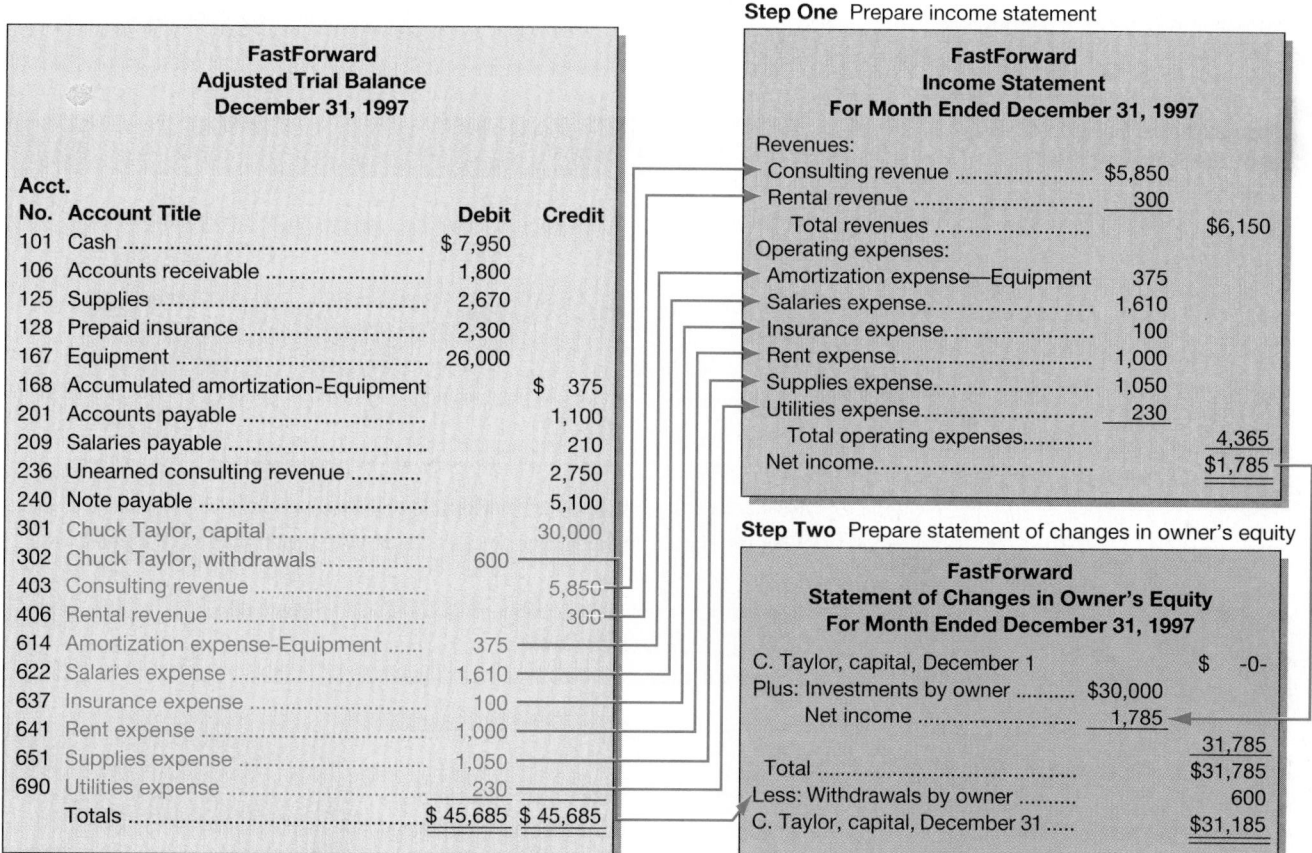

Step One Prepare income statement

FastForward
Adjusted Trial Balance
December 31, 1997

Acct. No.	Account Title	Debit	Credit
101	Cash	$ 7,950	
106	Accounts receivable	1,800	
125	Supplies	2,670	
128	Prepaid insurance	2,300	
167	Equipment	26,000	
168	Accumulated amortization-Equipment		$ 375
201	Accounts payable		1,100
209	Salaries payable		210
236	Unearned consulting revenue		2,750
240	Note payable		5,100
301	Chuck Taylor, capital		30,000
302	Chuck Taylor, withdrawals	600	
403	Consulting revenue		5,850
406	Rental revenue		300
614	Amortization expense-Equipment	375	
622	Salaries expense	1,610	
637	Insurance expense	100	
641	Rent expense	1,000	
651	Supplies expense	1,050	
690	Utilities expense	230	
	Totals	$ 45,685	$ 45,685

FastForward
Income Statement
For Month Ended December 31, 1997

Revenues:
Consulting revenue $5,850
Rental revenue 300
   Total revenues $6,150
Operating expenses:
Amortization expense—Equipment   375
Salaries expense 1,610
Insurance expense 100
Rent expense 1,000
Supplies expense 1,050
Utilities expense 230
   Total operating expenses 4,365
Net income $1,785

Step Two Prepare statement of changes in owner's equity

FastForward
Statement of Changes in Owner's Equity
For Month Ended December 31, 1997

C. Taylor, capital, December 1 $ -0-
Plus: Investments by owner $30,000
    Net income 1,785
                      31,785
Total $31,785
Less: Withdrawals by owner 600
C. Taylor, capital, December 31 ..... $31,185

---

[6] The statement of cash flows is often the final statement prepared. The cash ledger account is very helpful for this purpose. Its preparation is illustrated in the next chapter.

Step Three Prepare balance sheet

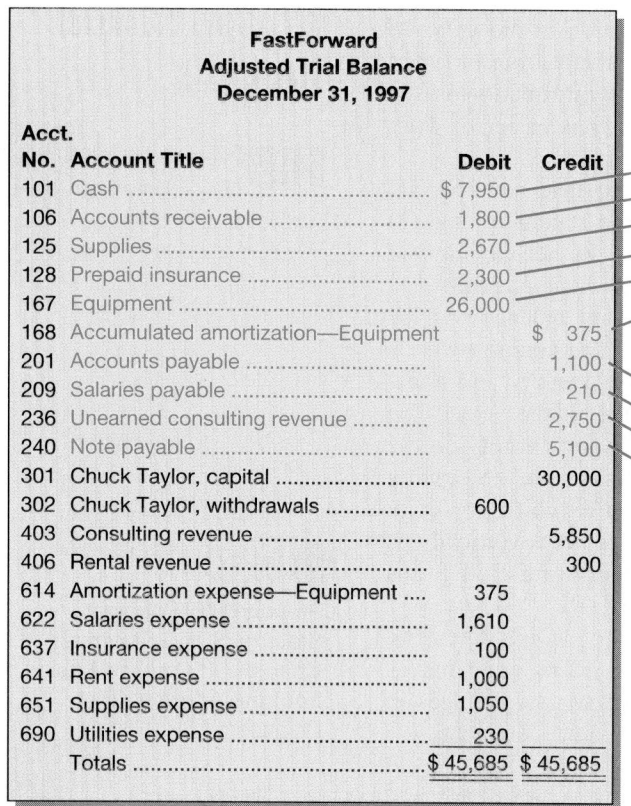

FastForward
Adjusted Trial Balance
December 31, 1997

Acct. No.	Account Title	Debit	Credit
101	Cash	$ 7,950	
106	Accounts receivable	1,800	
125	Supplies	2,670	
128	Prepaid insurance	2,300	
167	Equipment	26,000	
168	Accumulated amortization—Equipment		$ 375
201	Accounts payable		1,100
209	Salaries payable		210
236	Unearned consulting revenue		2,750
240	Note payable		5,100
301	Chuck Taylor, capital		30,000
302	Chuck Taylor, withdrawals	600	
403	Consulting revenue		5,850
406	Rental revenue		300
614	Amortization expense—Equipment	375	
622	Salaries expense	1,610	
637	Insurance expense	100	
641	Rent expense	1,000	
651	Supplies expense	1,050	
690	Utilities expense	230	
	Totals	$ 45,685	$ 45,685

FastForward
Balance Sheet
December 31, 1997

Assets

Cash		$ 7,950
Accounts receivable		1,800
Supplies		2,670
Prepaid insurance		2,300
Equipment	$ 26,000	
Less accumulated amortization	(375)	25,625
Total assets		$ 40,345

Liabilities

Accounts payable	$ 1,100	
Salaries payable	210	
Unearned consulting revenue	2,750	
Note payable	5,100	
Total liabilities		$ 9,160

Owner's Equity

C. Taylor, capital, December 31, 1997	$ 31,185
Total liabilities and owner's equity	$ 40,345

From statement of changes
in owner's equity in Exhibit 4.23

Exhibit 4.24

Preparing the Balance Sheet
from the Adjusted Trial
Balance

Flash back

10. Jordan Air Company has the following information in its unadjusted and adjusted trial balances:

	Unadjusted		Adjusted	
	Debit	**Credit**	**Debit**	**Credit**
Prepaid insurance	$6,200		$5,900	
Salaries payable				$1,400

What are the adjusting entries that Jordan Air likely recorded?

11. What types of accounts are taken from the adjusted trial balance to prepare an income statement?

12. In preparing financial statements from an adjusted trial balance, what statement is usually prepared second?

Answers—p. 175

Zurich Speeds Up Information

In 1996 Zurich Canada developed the Personal Financial Solutions to provide one complete picture of its broker affiliates across Canada. Now, the people managing the broker channel always have their fingers on the pulse of broker performance. This frees its accounting professionals to take a more active role managing and strategizing in the business. [Source: *Computing Canada,* September 29, 1997.]

Did You Know?

Accrued revenues at the end of one accounting period often result in cash *receipts* from customers in the next period. Also, accrued expenses at the end of one accounting period often result in cash *payments* in the next period. This section explains how we account for these cash receipts or payments in these later periods.

Accrual Adjustments in Later Periods

LO10 Record and describe entries for later periods that result from accruals.

Paying Accrued Expenses

FastForward recorded three days of accrued salaries for its employee with this adjusting entry:

Dec. 31	Salaries Expense	210	
	Salaries Payable		210
	To record three days' accrued salary		
	(3 × $70).		

Assets = Liabilities + Equity
      +210   −210

When the first payday of the next period occurs on Friday, January 9, the following entry settles the accrued liability (salaries payable) and records added salaries expense for work in January:

Jan. 9	Salaries Payable (3 days at $70)	210	
	Salaries Expense (7 days at $70)	490	
	Cash		700
	Paid two weeks salary including three days		
	accrued in December.		

Assets = Liabilities + Equity
 −700   −210   −490

The first debit in the January 9 entry records the payment of the liability for the three days' salary accrued on December 31. The second debit records the salary for January's first seven working days (including the New Year's Day holiday) as an expense of the new accounting period. The credit records the total amount of cash paid to the employee.

Receiving Accrued Revenues

FastForward made the following adjusting entry to record 20 days' accrued revenue earned from its consulting contract with a junior college:

Dec. 31	Accounts Receivable	1,800	
	Consulting Revenue		1,800
	To record 20 days' accrued revenue.		

Assets = Liabilities + Equity
 +1,800   +1,800

When the first month's fee is received on January 10, FastForward makes the following entry to remove the accrued asset (accounts receivable) and recognize the added revenue earned in January:

Jan. 10	Cash	2,700	
	Accounts Receivable		1,800
	Consulting Revenue		900
	Received cash for accrued asset, and		
	earned consulting revenue.		

Assets = Liabilities + Equity
 +2,700   +900
 −1,800

The debit reflects the cash received. The first credit reflects the removal of the receivable, and the second credit records the earned revenue.

Flash back

13. Music-Mart records $1,000 of accrued salaries on December 31. Five days later on January 5 (the next payday), salaries of $7,000 are paid. What is the January 5 entry?

14. Does it make any difference if cash receipts of unearned revenues and cash payments of prepaid expenses are recorded first in the income statement or balance sheet accounts?

Answers—p. 175

Profit Margin   USING THE INFORMATION

LO 11 Compute profit margin and describe its use in analyzing company performance.

Preparers of information want financial statements to reflect relevant information about a company's assets, liabilities, revenues and expenses. A primary goal of this effort is to provide information to help internal and external decision makers evaluate a company's performance during a reporting period. This includes evaluating management's success in producing profits. This type of information can suggest ways to improve operations and helps in predicting future results.

In using accounting information to evaluate operating results, one helpful measure is the ratio of a company's net income to sales. This ratio is called the **profit margin,** or **return on sales,** and is computed as shown in Exhibit 4.25.

Exhibit 4.25

Profit Margin

$$\text{Profit margin} = \frac{\text{Net income}}{\text{Revenues}}$$

This ratio can be interpreted as reflecting the portion of profit in each dollar of revenue.

To illustrate how we compute and use the profit margin, we look at the results of **Loblaw Companies Limited.** Profit margin as shown in Exhibit 4.26 is one measure we can use to evaluate Loblaw's performance during the past few years:

Exhibit 4.26

Loblaw's Profit Margin

Accounting measures	Year					
(in millions)	1996	1995	1994	1993	1992	1991
Net income	$ 174	$ 147	$ 126	$ 90	$ 76	$ 99
Sales	9,848	9,854	10,000	9,356	9,262	8,533
Profit margin................	1.76%	1.49%	1.26%	0.96%	0.82%	1.16%
Industry profit margin[1]	1.91%	2.53%	2.78%	2.71%	1.98%	1.96%

[1]All groceries – Dun & Bradstreet

Loblaw's average profit margin is 1.25% over this period. Note that 1994 stands out as the year with the highest sales. Profit margins in this industry are notoriously low because of very intense competition. It is only in 1996 that Loblaw approaches the industry average.

When we evaluate profit margin of a sole proprietorship, we should modify the above formula by subtracting from net income the value of the owner's efforts. To illustrate this for **FastForward,** let's assume that the efforts of Chuck Taylor, the owner, are worth $1,500 per month. FastForward's profit margin for December 1997 is then computed as shown in Exhibit 4.27.

$$\text{Modified Profit margin} = \frac{\$1,785 - \$1,500}{\$6,150} = 4.6\%$$

Exhibit 4.27

Modified Profit Margin

Flash back

15. Define and interpret the profit margin ratio.

16. If Fila's profit margin is 22.5% and its net income is $1,012,500, what is Fila's total revenue for the reporting period?

Answer—p. 175

Summary

LO1 Explain the importance of periodic reporting and the time period principle. The value of information is often linked to its timeliness. Useful information must reach decision makers frequently and promptly. To provide timely information, users of accounting systems prepare periodic reports at regular intervals. The time period principle assumes that an organization's activities can be divided into specific time periods such as a month, a three-month quarter, or a year for periodic reporting.

LO2 Describe the purpose of adjusting accounts at the end of a period. After external transactions are recorded, several accounts in the ledger often need adjusting for their balances to appear in financial statements. This need arises because internal transactions and events remain unrecorded. The purpose of adjusting accounts at the end of a period is to recognize revenues earned and expenses incurred during the period that are not yet recorded.

LO3 Explain accrual accounting and how it adds to the usefulness of financial statements. Accrual accounting recognizes revenue when earned and expenses when incurred. Accrual accounting reports the economic effects of events when they occur, not necessarily when cash inflows and outflows occur. This information is viewed as valuable in assessing a company's financial position and performance. Yet cash flow information is also useful.

LO4 Identify the types of adjustments and their purpose. Adjustments can be grouped according to their timing of cash receipts or payments relative to when they're recognized as revenues or expenses. There are two major groups, *prepaids* and *accruals*. Both of these can be subdivided into expenses and revenues. Adjusting entries are necessary for each of these groups so that revenues, expenses, assets and liabilities are correctly reported for each period.

LO5 Prepare and explain adjusting entries for prepaid expenses, amortization, and unearned revenues. Prepaid expenses refer to items paid for in advance of receiving their benefits. Prepaid expenses are assets. As this asset is used, its cost becomes an expense. Adjusting entries for prepaids involve increasing (debiting) expenses and decreasing (crediting) assets. Unearned revenues (or revenues received in advance) refer to cash received in advance of providing products and services. Unearned revenues are a liability. As products and services are provided, the amount of unearned revenues becomes earned revenues. Adjusting entries for unearned revenues involve increasing (crediting) revenues and decreasing (debiting) unearned revenues.

LO6 Prepare and describe adjusting entries for accrued expenses and accrued revenues. Accrued expenses refer to costs incurred in a period that are both unpaid and unrecorded. Accrued expenses are part of expenses and reported on the income statement. Adjusting entries for recording accrued expenses involve increasing (debiting) expenses and increasing (crediting) liabilities. Accrued revenues refer to revenues earned in a period that are both unrecorded and not yet received in cash. Accrued revenues are part of revenues and reported on the income statement. Adjusting entries for recording accrued revenues involve increasing (debiting) assets and increasing (crediting) revenues.

LO7 Explain how accounting adjustments link to financial statements. Accounting adjustments bring an asset or liability account balance to its correct amount. They also update related expense or revenue accounts. Every adjusting entry affects one or more income statement accounts *and* one or more balance sheet accounts. An adjusting entry never affects cash. Adjustments are necessary for transactions and events that extend over more than one period. Exhibit 4.20 summarizes financial statement links by type of adjustment.

Explain and prepare an adjusted trial balance. An adjusted trial balance is a list of accounts and balances prepared after adjusting entries are recorded and posted to the ledger. Financial statements are often prepared from the adjusted trial balance.

Prepare financial statements from an adjusted trial balance. We can prepare financial statements directly from the adjusted trial balance that includes all account balances. Revenue and expense balances are transferred to the income statement and statement of changes in owner's equity. Asset, liability and owner's equity balances are transferred to the balance sheet. We usually prepare statements in the following order: income statement, statement of changes in owner's equity, and balance sheet.

Record and describe entries for later periods that result from accruals. Accrued revenues at the end of one accounting period usually result in cash receipts from customers in later periods. Accrued expenses at the end of one accounting period usually result in cash payments in later periods. When cash is received or paid in these later periods, the entries must account for the accrued assets or liabilities initially recorded.

 Compute profit margin and describe its use in analyzing company performance. Profit margin is defined as the reporting period's net income divided by revenue for the same period. Profit margin reflects a company's earnings activities by showing how much profit is in each dollar of revenue. Analyzing company performance using this ratio is helped by computing similar ratios for competitors.

Guidance Answers to **You Make the Call**

Appraiser

We know prepaid expenses are items paid for in advance of receiving their benefits. Prepaid expenses are assets and are expensed as they are used up. The publishing company's treatment of the signing bonus is acceptable provided there are future book sales against which we can match the $500,000 expense. As an appraiser, you are concerned about the likelihood of future book sales and the risks involved. The most conservative appraiser would adjust the records used for analysis so that all $500,000 is treated as an expense for the period when the athlete (author) signs. The more risky the likelihood of future book sales are, the more likely your analysis treats the $500,000 as an expense, and not a prepaid expense (asset).

Small Business Owner

We know amortization is a process of cost allocation, not asset valuation. Knowing the amortization schedule of the restau-

rant is not especially useful in your estimation of what the restaurant's building and equipment are currently worth. Your assessment of the age, quality and usefulness of the building and equipment is much more important. Also, you would use the current market values of similar assets in estimating the value of this restaurant's building and equipment.

Loan Officer

Your concern in lending to this store owner is with the analysis of current year's sales. While increased revenues and profits are great, your concern is with the collectibility of these promotional sales. If the owner sold products to customers with poor records of paying bills, then collectibility of these sales is low. Your analysis must assess this possibility and recognize any expected losses. If the owner sold only to financially secure customers, then you can reliably count on receiving these accrued revenues.

Guidance Answer to **Judgment and Ethics**

Financial Officer

It appears you must make a choice between following the president's orders or not. The requirements of acceptable practice are clear. Omitting adjustments and early recognition of revenue can mislead users of financial statements (including managers, owners and lenders). One action is to request a second meeting with the president where you explain that accruing expenses and recognizing revenue when earned are required practices. You should

also mention the ethical implications of not complying with accepted practice. Point out that the president's orders involve intentional falsification of the statements. If the president persists, you might discuss the situation with legal counsel and any auditors involved. Your ethical action might cost you this job. But the potential pitfalls of falsification of statements, reputation loss, personal integrity, and other costs are too great.

Guidance Answers to Flashbacks

1. An annual reporting (or accounting) period covers one year and refers to the preparation of annual financial statements. The annual reporting period is not always the same as a calendar year that ends on December 31. An organization can adopt a fiscal year consisting of any 12 consecutive months. It is also acceptable to adopt an annual reporting period of 52 weeks.

2. Interim (less than one year) financial statements are prepared to provide decision makers information frequently and promptly.

3. The revenue recognition principle and the matching principle lead most directly to the adjusting process.

4. No. Cash basis accounting is not consistent with the matching principle because it does not always report expenses in the same period as the revenues earned as a result of those expenses.

5. No. expense is reported in 1999. Under cash basis accounting the entire $4,800 is reported as expense in 1998 when the premium is paid.

6. If the accrued services revenue adjustment of $200 is not made, then both revenue and net income are understated by $200 on the current year's income statement. Assets and equity are also understated.

7. A contra account is an account that is subtracted from the balance of a related account. Use of a contra account often provides more complete information than simply reporting a net amount.

8. An accrued expense refers to costs incurred in a period that are both unpaid and unrecorded prior to adjusting entries. One example is salaries earned by employees but not yet paid at the end of a period.

9. An unearned revenue arises when cash (or other assets) is received from a customer before the services and products are delivered to the customer. Magazine subscription receipts in advance are one example.

10. The probable adjusting entries of Jordan Air are:

Insurance Expense	300	
Prepaid Insurance		300
To record insurance expired.		
Salaries Expense	1,400	
Salaries Payable		1,400
To record accrued salaries.		

11. Revenue accounts and expense accounts.

12. Statement of changes in owner's equity is usually prepared second.

13. The January 5 entry to settle the accrued salaries and pay for added salaries is:

Jan. 5	Salaries Payable	1,000	
	Salaries Expense	6,000	
	Cash		7,000
	Paid salary including accrual from December.		

14. When adjusting entries are correctly prepared, it does not make any difference whether cash receipts of unearned revenues and cash payments of prepaid expenses are recorded in balance sheet accounts or in income statement accounts. The financial statements of these companies are identical.

15. Profit margin is defined as net income divided by revenue. It can be interpreted as the portion of profit in each dollar of revenue.

16. We know that Fila's profit margin of 22.5% equals $1,012,500 ÷ Revenues. Solving for revenues, we compute revenues as $4,500,000 ($1,012,500 ÷ 22.5%).

Demonstration Problem

The following information relates to Best Plumbing on December 31, 19X8. The company uses the calendar year as its annual reporting period. The company initially records prepaid and unearned items in balance sheet accounts.

a. The company's weekly payroll is $2,800, paid every Friday for a five-day workweek. December 31, 19X8, falls on a Wednesday, but the employees will not be paid until Friday, January 2, 19X9.

b. Eighteen months earlier, on July 1, 19X7, the company purchased equipment that cost $10,000 and had no salvage value. Its useful life is predicted to be five years.

c. On October 1, 19X8, the company agreed to work on a new housing project. For installing plumbing in 24 new homes, the company was paid $144,000 in advance. When the $144,000 cash was received on October 1, 19X8, that amount was credited to the Unearned Plumbing Revenue account. Between October 1 and December 31, 19X8, work on 18 homes was completed.

d. On September 1, 19X8, the company purchased a one-year insurance policy for $1,200. The transaction was recorded with a $1,200 debit to Prepaid Insurance.

e. On December 29, 19X8, the company renders a $5,000 service which has not been billed as of December 31, 19X8.

Required

1. Prepare the adjusting entries needed on December 31, 19X8, to record the previously unrecorded effects of the events.

2. Prepare T-accounts for accounts affected by the adjusting entries. Post the adjusting entries to the T-accounts. Determine the adjusted balances for the Unearned Plumbing Revenue account and the Prepaid Insurance account.

3. Complete the following table describing the effects of your adjusting entries on the 19X8 income statement and the December 31, 19X8, balance sheet. Use parentheses to indicate a decrease.

Entry	Amount in the Entry	Effect on Net Income	Effect on Total Assets	Effect on Total Liabilities	Effect on Owner's Equity
a					
b					
c					
d					
e					

Planning the Solution

- Analyze the information for each situation to determine which accounts need to be updated with an adjustment.

- Calculate the size of each adjustment and prepare the necessary journal entries.

- Show the amount entered by each adjustment in the designated accounts, determine the adjusted balance, and then determine the balance sheet classification that the account falls within.

- Determine each entry's effect on net income for the year and on total assets, total liabilities, and owner's equity at the end of the year.

Solution to Demonstration Problem

1. Adjusting journal entries.

a. Dec. 31	Wages Expense	1,680	
	Wages Payable		1,680
	To accrue wages for the last three days of the year ($2,800 × 3/5).		
b. Dec. 31	Amortization Expense, Equipment	2,000	
	Accumulated Amortization, Equipment		2,000
	To record amortization expense for the year ($10,000/5 = $2,000).		
c. Dec. 31	Unearned Plumbing Revenue	108,000	
	Plumbing Services Revenue		108,000
	To recognize plumbing revenues earned ($144,000 × 18/24).		
d. Dec. 31	Insurance Expense	400	
	Prepaid Insurance		400
	To adjust for the expired portion of insurance ($1,200 × 4/12),		
e. Dec. 31	Accounts Receivable	5,000	
	Plumbing Service Revenue		5,000
	To record plumbing revenues earned.		

2.

Wages Expense	
(a) 1,680	

Wages Payable	
	(a) 1,680

Amortization Expense, Equipment	
(b) 2,000	

Accumulated Amortization, Equipment	
	(b) 2,000

Unearned Plumbing Revenue	
	Balance 144,000
(c) 108,000	
	Balance 36,000

Plumbing Services Revenue	
	(c) 108,000
	(e) 5,000
	Balance 113,000

Insurance Expense	
(d) 400	

Prepaid Insurance	
Balance 1,200	(d) 400
Balance 800	

Accounts Receivable	
(e) 5,000	

3.

Entry	Amount in the Entry	Effect on Net Income	Effect on Total Assets	Effect on Total Liabilities	Effect on Owner's Equity
a	$1,680	$1,680 ↓	No effect	$1,680 ↑	$1,680 ↓
b	$2,000	$2,000 ↓	$2,000 ↓	No effect	$2,000 ↓
c	$108,000	$108,000 ↑	No effect	$108,000 ↓	$108,000 ↑
d	$400	$400 ↓	$400 ↓	No effect	$400 ↓
e	$5,000	$5,000 ↑	$5,000 ↑	No effect	$5,000 ↑

4A

APPENDIX

Alternatives in Accounting for Prepaids

Learning Objective

LO 12 Identify and explain two alternatives in accounting for prepaids.

This section explains two alternatives in accounting for prepaid expenses and unearned revenues. We show the accounting for both alternatives.

Recording Prepaid Expenses in Expense Accounts

We explained that prepaid expenses are assets when they are purchased and are recorded with debits to asset accounts. Adjusting entries transfer the costs that expire to expense accounts at the end of an accounting period. We noted that some prepaid expenses are purchased and fully expire before the end of an accounting period. In these cases we can avoid adjusting entries by charging the prepaid items to expense accounts when purchased.

There is an alternative practice of recording *all* prepaid expenses with debits to expense accounts. If any prepaids remain unused or unexpired at the end of an accounting period, then adjusting entries must transfer the cost of the unused portions from expense accounts to prepaid expense (asset) accounts. This alternative practice is acceptable. The financial statements are identical under either procedure, but the adjusting entries are different.

To illustrate the accounting differences between these two practices, let's look at FastForward's cash payment of December 26 for 24 months of insurance coverage beginning on December 1. FastForward recorded that payment with a debit to an asset account. But it could have recorded a debit to an expense account. These alternatives are shown in Exhibit 4A.1.

Exhibit 4A.1

Initial Entry for Prepaid Expenses for Two Alternatives

		Payment Recorded as Asset	Payment Recorded as Expense
Dec. 26	Prepaid Insurance	2,400	
	Cash	2,400	
26	Insurance Expense		2,400
	Cash		2,400

At the end of the accounting period on December 31, insurance protection for one month is expired. This means $100 ($2,400/24) of the asset expires and becomes an expense for December. The adjusting entry depends on how the original payment is recorded. See Exhibit 4A.2.

When these entries are posted to the accounts we can see that these two alternative practices give identical results. The December 31 adjusted account balances show prepaid insurance of $2,300 and insurance expense of $100 for both methods. See Exhibit 4A.3.

	Payment Recorded as Asset	Payment Recorded as Expense
Dec. 31 Insurance Expense	100	
Prepaid Insurance		100
31 Prepaid Insurance		2,300
Insurance Expense		2,300

Exhibit 4A.2

Adjusting Entry for Prepaid Expenses for Two Alternatives

Payment Recorded as Asset

Prepaid Insurance

Dec. 26	2,400	Dec. 31	100
	−100		
Balance	2,300		

Insurance Expense

Dec. 31	100		

Payment Recorded as Expense

Prepaid Insurance

Dec. 31	2,300		

Insurance Expense

Dec. 26	2,400	Dec. 31	2,300
	−2,300		
Balance	100		

Exhibit 4A.3

Account Balances under Two Alternatives for Recording Prepaid Expenses

Recording Unearned Revenues in Revenue Accounts

Unearned revenues are liabilities requiring delivery of products and services. We explained how unearned revenues are recorded as credits to liability accounts when cash and other assets are received. Adjusting entries at the end of an accounting period transfer to revenue accounts the earned portion of unearned revenues. We know that some unearned revenues are received and fully earned before the end of an accounting period. In these cases we can avoid adjusting entries by recording unearned revenues into revenue accounts when received.

As with prepaid expenses, there is an alternative practice of recording *all* unearned revenues with credits to revenue accounts. If any revenues are unearned at the end of an accounting period, then adjusting entries must transfer the unearned portions from revenue accounts to unearned revenue (liability) accounts. This alternative practice is acceptable. While the adjusting entries are different for these two alternatives, the financial statements are identical.

To illustrate the accounting differences between these two practices, let's look at FastForward's December 26 receipt of $3,000 for consulting services covering the period December 27 to February 24. FastForward recorded this transaction with a credit to a liability account. The alternative is to record it with a credit to a revenue account as shown in Exhibit 4A.4.

		Receipt Recorded as Liability	Receipt Recorded as Revenue
Dec. 26	Cash	3,000	
	Unearned Consulting Revenue	3,000	
26	Cash		3,000
	Consulting Revenue		3,000

Exhibit 4A.4

Initial Entry for Unearned Revenues for Two Alternatives

By the end of the accounting period (December 31), FastForward earns $250 of this revenue. This means $250 of the liability is satisfied. Depending on how the initial receipt is recorded, the adjusting entry is as shown in Exhibit 4A.5.

Exhibit 4A.5

Adjusting Entry for Unearned
Revenues for Two Alternatives

		Receipt Recorded as Liability	Receipt Recorded as Revenue
Dec. 31	Unearned Consulting Revenue	250	
	Consulting Revenue		250	
31	Consulting Revenue		2,750
	Unearned Consulting Revenue		2,750

After adjusting entries are posted, the two alternatives give identical results. The December 31 adjusted account balances in Exhibit 4A.6 show unearned consulting revenue of $2,750 and consulting revenue of $250 for both methods.

Exhibit 4A.6

Account Balances under Two
Alternatives for Recording
Unearned Revenues

Receipt Recorded as Liability

Unearned Consulting Revenue

Dec. 31	250	Dec. 26	3,000
			−250
		Balance	2,750

Consulting Revenue

		Dec. 31	250

Receipt Recorded as Revenue

Unearned Consulting Revenue

		Dec. 31	2,750

Consulting Revenue

Dec. 31	2,750	Dec. 26	3,000
			−2,750
		Balance	250

Flash back

17. Miller Company records cash receipts of unearned revenues and cash payments of prepaid expenses in balance sheet accounts. Bud Company records these items in income statement accounts. Explain any difference in the financial statements of these two companies from their alternative accounting for prepaids.

Summary of Appendix 4A

LO 12 **Identify and explain two alternatives in accounting for prepaids.** It is acceptable to charge all prepaid expenses to expense accounts when they are purchased. When this is done, adjusting entries must transfer any unexpired amounts from expense accounts to asset accounts. It is also acceptable to credit all unearned revenues to revenue accounts when cash is received. In this case the adjusting entries must transfer any unearned amounts from revenue accounts to unearned revenue accounts.

Guidance Answer to Flash backs

17. When adjusting entries are correctly prepared, the financial statements of these companies will be identical under both methods.

Work Sheet Format for Adjusted Trial Balance

We show in the next chapter how to prepare an adjusted trial balance and financial statements from a work sheet. To focus on the important aspects of the adjusting process in this chapter, we did not introduce the work sheet format. Yet some users prefer this format in introducing the adjusted trial balance, and we present it in Exhibit 4B.1.

	Unadjusted Trial Balance		Adjustments		Adjusted Trial Balance	
	Dr.	Cr.	Dr.	Cr.	Dr.	Cr.
Cash	$ 7,950				$ 7,950	
Accounts receivable			(f)1,800		1,800	
Supplies	3,720			(b)1,050	2,670	
Prepaid insurance	2,400			(a) 100	2,300	
Equipment	26,000				26,000	
Accumulated amortization—equipment				(c) 375		$ 375
Accounts payable		$ 1,100				1,100
Note payable		5,100				5,100
Salaries payable				(e) 210		210
Unearned consulting revenue		3,000	(d) 250			2,750
Chuck Taylor, capital		30,000				30,000
Chuck Taylor, withdrawals	600				600	
Consulting revenue		3,800		(d) 250		5,850
				(f) 1,800		
Rental revenue		300				300
Amortization expense—equipment			(c) 375		375	
Salaries expense	1,400		(e) 210		1,610	
Insurance expense			(a) 100		100	
Rent expense	1,000				1,000	
Supplies expense			(b)1,050		1,050	
Utilities expense	230				230	
Totals	$43,300	$43,300	$3,785	$3,785	$45,685	$45,685

Exhibit 4B.1

Work Sheet Format for Preparing the Adjusted Trial Balance

Glossary

Account form balance sheet A balance sheet that lists assets on the left and liabilities and owner's equity on the right side of balance sheet. (p. 169)

Accounting period The length of time covered by financial statements and other reports; also called *reporting periods*. (p. 152)

Accrual basis accounting The approach to preparing financial statements that uses the adjusting process to recognize revenues when earned and expenses when incurred, not when cash is paid or received; the basis for generally accepted accounting principles. (p. 155)

Accrued expenses Costs incurred in a period that are both unpaid and unrecorded; adjusting entries for recording accrued expenses involve increasing (debiting) expenses and increasing (crediting) liabilities. (p. 162)

Accrued revenues Revenues earned in a period that are both unrecorded and not yet received in cash (or other assets); adjusting entries for recording accrued revenues involve increasing (debiting) assets and increasing (crediting) revenues. (p. 164)

Adjusted trial balance A listing of accounts and balances prepared after adjustments are recorded and posted to the ledger. (p. 168)

Adjusting entry A journal entry at the end of an accounting period to bring an asset or liability account balance to its proper amount while also updating the related expense or revenue account. (p. 156)

Amortization The expense created by allocating the cost of capital assets to the periods in which they are used; represents the cost of using the assets. (p. 159)

Capital assets Include long-term tangible assets, such as plant and equipment, and intangible assets, such as patents. Capital assets are expected to provide benefits for more than one period. (p. 159)

Cash basis accounting Revenues are recognized when cash is received and expenses are recorded when cash is paid. (p. 155)

Contra account An account linked with another account and having an opposite normal balance; reported as a subtraction from the other account's balance so that more complete information than simply the net amount is provided. (p. 160)

Depreciation See *amortization*.

Fiscal year The 12 consecutive months (or 52 weeks) selected as an organization's annual accounting period. (p. 153)

Intangible assets Long-lived (capital) assets which have no physical substance but convey a right to use a product or process. (p. 159)

Interim financial reports Financial reports covering less than one year; usually based on one- or three- or six-month periods. (p. 152)

Matching principle The broad principle that requires expenses to be reported in the same period as the revenues that were earned as a result of the expenses. (p. 154)

Natural business year A 12-month period that ends when a company's sales activities are at their lowest point. (p. 153)

Plant and equipment Tangible long-lived assets used to produce goods or services. (p. 159)

Prepaid expenses Items paid for in advance of receiving their benefits; classified as assets. (p. 157)

Profit margin The ratio of a company's net income to its revenues; measures the portion of profit in each dollar of revenue. (p. 172)

Report form balance sheet A balance sheet that lists items vertically with assets above the liabilities and owner's equity. (p. 169)

Return on sales Another name for *profit margin*. (p. 172)

Straight-line amortization method Allocates equal amounts of an asset's cost to expense in each accounting period during its useful life. (p. 159)

Time period principle A broad principle that assumes that an organization's activities can be divided into specific time periods such as months, quarters, or years. (p. 152)

Unadjusted trial balance A listing of accounts and balances prepared before adjustments are recorded and posted to the ledger. (p. 168)

The superscript letter A identifies assignment material based on Appendix 4A; the superscript letter B identifies material based on Appendix 4B.

Questions

1. What type of business is most likely to select a fiscal year that corresponds to the natural business year instead of the calendar year?

2. What kind of assets require adjusting entries to record amortization?

3. What contra account is used when recording and reporting the effects of amortization? Why is it used?

4. Where is an unearned revenue reported in the financial statements?

5. What is an accrued revenue? Give an example.

6. What is the difference between the cash and accrual bases of accounting?

7. Where is a prepaid expense reported in the financial statements?

8. Why is the accrual basis of accounting preferred over the cash basis?

9A. If a company initially records prepaid expenses with debits to expense accounts, what type of account is debited in the adjusting entries for prepaid expenses?

10. Why does a sole proprietorship require special procedures in calculating the profit margin?

11. Review the consolidated balance sheet of **Alliance,** Inc. in Appendix I. Identify two asset accounts that require adjustment before annual financial statements can be prepared. What would the effect on the income statement be if these two asset accounts were not adjusted?

12. Review the Notes to the Financial Statements of **Atlantis** in Appendix I. As a simplification, assume that the company did not sell any capital assets (fixed assets) during 1997. How much amortization was recorded in the adjusting entry for amortization at the end of 1997?

13. Review the chapter's opening scenario, Toronto Tacklers Need Money. Identify two current sources of revenue for the **Toronto Tacklers.** Identify two additional sources of revenue that the Toronto Tacklers might be able to develop. What does it mean when the article states that Burston is currently preparing pro forma financial statements?

In its first year of operations, Harris Co. earned $39,000 in revenues and received $33,000 cash from customers. The company incurred expenses of $22,500, but had not paid for $2,250 of them at year-end. In addition, Harris prepaid $3,750 for expenses that would be incurred the next year. Calculate the first year's net income under a cash basis and calculate the first year's net income under an accrual basis.

Quick Study

QS 4-1
Accural and cash accounting

LO 3

In recording its transactions during the year, Stark Company records prepayments of expenses in asset accounts and receipts of unearned revenues in liability accounts. At the end of its annual accounting period, the company must make three adjusting entries. They are: (a) to accrue salaries expense, (b) to adjust the Unearned Services Revenue account to recognize earned revenue, and (c) to record the earning of services revenue for which cash will be received the following period. For each of these adjusting entries, use the numbers assigned to the following accounts to indicate the correct account to be debited and the correct account to be credited.

1. Prepaid Salaries Expense
2. Cash
3. Salaries Payable
4. Accounts Receivable
5. Salaries Expense
6. Services Revenue Earned
7. Unearned Services Revenue

QS 4-2
Preparing adjusting entries

LO 4

In making adjusting entries at the end of its accounting period, Carter Insurance Agency failed to record $1,400 of insurance premiums that had expired. This cost had been initially debited to the Prepaid Insurance account. The company also failed to record accrued salaries payable of $800. As a result of these oversights, the financial statements for the reporting period will: [choose the best alternative from the following] (a) understate assets by $1,400, (b) understate expenses by $2,200, (c) understate net income by $800, or (d) overstate liabilities by $800.

QS 4-3
Effects of adjusting entries

LO 4,7

The following information has been taken from Shank Company's unadjusted and adjusted trial balances:

	Unadjusted		Adjusted	
	Debit	**Credit**	**Debit**	**Credit**
Prepaid insurance	$3,100		$2,950	
Interest payable				$700

QS 4-4
Interpreting adjusting entries

LO 4

Given this trial balance information which of the following items must be included in the adjusting entries?

a. A $150 debit to Insurance Expense and a $700 debit to Interest Expense.
b. A $150 credit to Prepaid Insurance and a $700 debit to Interest Payable.
c. A $150 debit to Insurance Expense and a $700 debit to Interest Payable.

QS 4-5ᴬ
Preparing adjusting
entries

Foster Company initially records prepaid and unearned items in income statement accounts. Given Foster Company's practices which of the following choices applies to the preparation of adjusting entries at the end of the company's first accounting period?

a. Unpaid salaries will be recorded with a debit to Prepaid Salaries and a credit to Salaries Expense.

b. The cost of unused office supplies will be recorded with a debit to Supplies Expense and a credit to Office Supplies.

c. Unearned fees will be recorded with a debit to Consulting Fees Earned and a credit to Unearned Consulting Fees.

d. Earned but unbilled consulting fees will be recorded with a debit to Unearned Consulting Fees and a credit to Consulting Fees Earned.

e. None of the above is correct.

QS 4-6
Analyzing accounting
adjustments

LO 11

Revell Corporation had net income of $37,925 and revenue of $390,000 for the year ended December 31, 19X7. Calculate Revell's profit margin. Interpret the profit margin calculation.

QS 4-7
Identifying accounting
adjustments

LO 4

Classify the following adjusting entries as involving prepaid expenses (P), amortization (A), unearned revenues (U), accrued expenses (E), or accrued revenues (R).

_____ **a.** Entry to record annual amortization expense.

_____ **b.** Entry to show wages earned but not yet paid.

_____ **c.** Entry to show revenue earned but not yet billed.

_____ **d.** Entry to show expiration of prepaid insurance.

_____ **e.** Entry to show revenue earned that was previously received as cash in advance.

QS 4-8
Recording and analyzing
adjusting entries

LO 7

Adjusting entries affect one balance sheet account and one income statement account. For the entries listed below identify the account to be debited and the account to be credited. Indicate which of the two accounts is the income statement account and which is the balance sheet account.

a. Entry to record annual amortization expense.

b. Entry to show wages earned but not yet paid.

c. Entry to show revenue earned that was previously received as cash in advance.

d. Entry to show expiration of prepaid insurance.

e. Entry to show revenue earned but not yet billed.

Exercises

Exercise 4-1
Adjusting entries

Prepare adjusting journal entries for the financial statements for the year ended December 31, 19X7, for each of these independent situations. Assume that prepaid expenses are initially recorded in asset accounts. Assume that fees collected in advance of work are initially recorded as liabilities.

a. Amortization on the company's equipment for 19X7 was estimated to be $16,000.

b. The Prepaid Insurance account had a $7,000 debit balance at December 31, 19X7, before adjusting for the costs of any expired coverage. An analysis of the company's insurance policies showed that $1,040 of unexpired insurance remained in effect.

c. The Office Supplies account had a $300 debit balance on January 1, 19X7; $2,680 of office supplies were purchased during the year; and the December 31, 19X7, count showed that $354 of supplies are on hand.

d. One-half of the work for a $10,000 fee received in advance has now been performed.

e. The Prepaid Insurance account had a $5,600 debit balance at December 31, 19X7, before adjusting for the costs of any expired coverage. An analysis of the company's insurance policies showed that $4,600 of coverage had expired.

f. Wages of $4,000 have been earned by workers but not paid as of December 31, 19X7.

Resource Management has five part-time employees each of whom earns $100 per day. They are normally paid on Fridays for work completed on Monday through Friday of the same week. They were all paid in full on Friday, December 28, 19X7. The next week, all five of the employees worked only four days because New Year's Day was an unpaid holiday. Show the adjusting entry that would be recorded on Monday, December 31, 19X7, and the journal entry that would be made to record paying the employees' wages on Friday, January 4, 19X8.

Exercise 4-2
Adjusting and subsequent entries for accrued expenses
LO 6, 10

In the blank space beside each of these adjusting entries, enter the letter of the explanation that most closely describes the entry:

a. To record the year's amortization expense.

b. To record accrued salaries expense.

c. To record the year's consumption of a prepaid expense.

d. To record accrued income.

e. To record accrued interest expense.

f. To record the earning of previously unearned income.

Exercise 4-3
Identifying adjusting entries
LO 4

_____ **1.**	Unearned Professional Fees	18,450	
	Professional Fees Earned		18,450
_____ **2.**	Interest Receivable.	2,700	
	Interest Earned.		2,700
_____ **3.**	Amortization Expense.	49,500	
	Accumulated Amortization.		49,500
_____ **4.**	Salaries Expense	16,400	
	Salaries Payable.		16,400
_____ **5.**	Interest Expense	3,800	
	Interest Payable		3,800
_____ **6.**	Insurance Expense.	4,200	
	Prepaid Insurance.		4,200

Determine the missing amounts in each of these four independent situations:

Exercise 4-4
Missing data in supplies expense calculations
LO 5

	a	b	c	d
Supplies on hand—January 1	$ 300	$1,600	$1,360	?
Supplies purchased during the year	2,100	5,400	?	$6,000
Supplies on hand—December 31	750	?	1,840	800
Supplies expense for the year	?	1,300	9,600	6,575

The following three situations require adjusting journal entries to prepare financial statements as of April 30. For each situation, present the adjusting entry and the entry that would be made to record the payment of the accrued liability during May.

a. The company has a $780,000 note payable that requires 0.8% interest to be paid each month on the 20th of the month. The interest was last paid on April 20 and the next payment is due on May 20.

b. The total weekly salaries expense for all employees is $9,000. This amount is paid at the end of the day on Friday of each week with five working days. April 30 falls on Tuesday of this year, which means that the employees had worked two days since the last payday. The next payday is May 3.

c. On April 1, the company retained a lawyer at a flat monthly fee of $2,500. This amount is payable on the 12th of the following month.

Exercise 4-5
Adjustments and payments of accrued items
LO 6, 10

Exercise 4-6
Amounts of cash and
accrual basis expenses

LO 3

On March 1, 19X1, a company paid a $16,200 premium on a three-year insurance policy for protection beginning on that date. Fill in the blanks in the following table:

| | Balance Sheet Asset under the: | | | Insurance Expense under the: | |
	Accrual Basis	Cash Basis		Accrual Basis	Cash Basis
Dec. 31/X1 $ _____		$ _____	19X1 $ _____		$ _____
Dec. 31/X2 _____		_____	19X2 _____		_____
Dec. 31/X3 _____		_____	19X3 _____		_____
Dec. 31/X4 _____		_____	19X4 _____		_____
			Total $ _____		$ _____

Exercise 4-7
Unearned and accrued
revenues

LO 5, 6, 10

Landmark Properties owns and operates an apartment building and prepares annual financial statements based on a March 31 fiscal year.

a. The tenants of one of the apartments paid five months' rent in advance on November 1, 19X7. The monthly rental is $1,500 per month. The journal entry credited the Unearned Rent account when the payment was received. No other entry had been recorded prior to March 31, 19X8. Give the adjusting journal entry that should be recorded on March 31, 19X8.

b. On January 1, 19X8, the tenants of another apartment moved in and paid the first month's rent. The $1,350 payment was recorded with a credit to the Rent Earned account. However, the tenants have not paid the rent for February or March. They have agreed to pay it as soon as possible. Give the adjusting journal entry that should be recorded on March 31, 19X8.

c. On April 2, 19X8, the tenants described in part b paid $4,050 rent for February, March, and April. Give the journal entry to record the cash collection.

Exercise 4-8
Identifying the effects of
adjusting entries

LO 5, 6, 10

Following are two income statements for Pemberton Company for the year ended December 31. The left column was prepared before any adjusting entries were recorded and the right column includes the effects of adjusting entries. The company records cash receipts and disbursements related to unearned and prepaid items in balance sheet accounts. Analyze the statements and prepare the adjusting entries that must have been recorded. Thirty percent of the additional fees were earned but not billed and the other 70% were earned by performing services that the customers had paid for in advance.

PEMBERTON COMPANY Income Statements For Year Ended December 31	Before Adjustments	After Adjustments
Revenues:		
Fees earned	$24,000	$30,000
Commissions earned	42,500	42,500
Total revenues	$66,500	$72,500
Operating expenses:		
Amortization expense, computers		$ 1,500
Amortization expense, office furniture . . .		1,750
Salaries expense	$12,500	14,950
Insurance expense		1,300
Rent expense	4,500	4,500
Office supplies expense		480
Advertising expense	3,000	3,000
Utilities expense	1,250	1,320
Total operating expenses	$21,250	$28,800
Net income	$45,250	$43,700

Classic Customs began operations on December 1. In setting up the bookkeeping procedures, the company decided to debit expense accounts when the company prepays its
expenses and to credit revenue accounts when customers pay for services in advance. Prepare
journal entries for items *a* through *d* and adjusting entries as of December 31 for items *e*
through *g*:

a. Supplies were purchased on December 1 for $3,000.

b. The company prepaid insurance premiums of $1,440 on December 2.

c. On December 15, the company received an advance payment of $12,000 from one cus-
tomer for remodelling work.

d. On December 28, the company received $3,600 from a second customer for remodel-
ling work to be performed in January.

e. By counting them on December 31, Classic Customs determined that $1,920 of supplies
were on hand.

f. An analysis of the insurance policies in effect on December 31 showed that $240 of
insurance coverage had expired.

g. As of December 31, only one project had been completed. The $6,300 fee for this par-
ticular project had been received in advance.

Exercise 4-9A
Adjustments for prepaid
items recorded in
expense and revenue
accounts

LO 12

Pavillion Company experienced the following events and transactions during July:

July   1   Received $2,000 in advance of performing work for Andrew Renking.
         6   Received $8,400 in advance of performing work for Matt Swarbuck.
        12   Completed the job for Andrew Renking.
        18   Received $7,500 in advance of performing work for Drew Sayer.
        27   Completed the job for Matt Swarbuck.
        31   The job for Drew Sayer is still unfinished.

a. Give journal entries (including any adjusting entry as of the end of the month) to record
these events using the procedure of initially crediting the Unearned Fees account when
a payment is received from a customer in advance of performing services.

b. Give journal entries (including any adjusting entry as of the end of the month) to record
these events using the procedure of initially crediting the Fees Earned account when a
payment is received from a customer in advance of performing services.

c. Under each method, determine the amount of earned fees that should be reported on the
income statement for July and the amount of unearned fees that should appear on the
balance sheet as of July 31.

Exercise 4-10A
Alternative procedures for
revenues received in
advance

LO 12

Use the following information to calculate the profit margin for each case:

	Net Income	Revenue
a.	$ 3,490	$ 31,620
b.	96,744	394,953
c.	110,204	252,786
d.	55,026	1,350,798
e.	79,264	433,914

Which of the five companies is the most profitable according to the profit margin ratio?
Interpret the profit margin ratio of the most profitable company.

Exercise 4-11
Calculating the profit
margin

LO 11

Problems

Problem 4-1

Adjusting and subsequent journal entries

LO 5, 6, 7, 10

Garza Company's annual accounting period ends on December 31, 19X8. Garza follows the practice of recording prepaid expenses and unearned revenues in balance sheet accounts. The following information concerns the adjusting entries to be recorded as of that date:

a. The Office Supplies account started the year with a $3,000 balance. During 19X8, the company purchased supplies at a cost of $12,400, which was added to the Office Supplies account. The inventory of supplies on hand at December 31 had a cost of $2,640.

b. An analysis of the company's insurance policies provided these facts:

Policy	Date of Purchase	Years of Coverage	Total Cost
1	April 1, 19X7	2	$15,840
2	April 1, 19X8	3	13,068
3	August 1, 19X8	1	2,700

The total premium for each policy was paid in full at the purchase date, and the Prepaid Insurance account was debited for the full cost. Appropriate adjusting entries have been made to December 31, 19X7.

c. The company has 15 employees who earn a total of $2,100 in salaries for every working day. They are paid each Monday for their work in the five-day workweek ending on the preceding Friday. December 31, 19X8, falls on Tuesday, and all 15 employees worked the first two days of the week. Because New Year's Day is a paid holiday, they will be paid salaries for five full days on Monday, January 6, 19X9.

d. The company purchased a building on August 1, 19X8. The building cost $855,000 and is expected to have a $45,000 salvage value at the end of its predicted 30-year life.

e. Because the company is not large enough to occupy the entire building, it arranged to rent some space to a tenant at $2,400 per month, starting on November 1, 19X8. The rent was paid on time on November 1, and the amount received was credited to the Rent Earned account. However, the tenant has not paid the December rent. The company has worked out an agreement with the tenant, who has promised to pay both December's and January's rent in full on January 15. The tenant has agreed not to fall behind again.

f. On November 1, the company also rented space to another tenant for $2,175 per month. The tenant paid five months' rent in advance on that date. The payment was recorded with a credit to the Unearned Rent account.

Required

1. Use the information to prepare adjusting entries as of December 31, 19X8.

2. Prepare journal entries to record the subsequent cash transactions in January 19X8 described in parts *c* and *e*.

Check Figure Insurance expense, $12,312

Problem 4-2

Adjusting entries, financial statements, and profit margin

LO 5, 6, 7, 9, 11

Southwest Careers, a school owned by S. Carr, provides training to individuals who pay tuition directly to the business. The business also offers extension training to groups in off-site locations. The school's unadjusted trial balance as of December 31, 19X8, follows. Southwest Careers follows the practice of initially recording prepaid expenses and unearned revenues in balance sheet accounts. Facts that require eight adjusting entries on December 31, 19X8, are presented after the trial balance:

SOUTHWEST CAREERS Unadjusted Trial Balance December 31, 19X8		
Cash	$ 26,000	
Accounts receivable		
Teaching supplies	10,000	
Prepaid insurance	15,000	
Prepaid rent	2,000	
Professional library	30,000	
Accumulated amortization, professional library ..		$ 9,000
Equipment	70,000	
Accumulated amortization, equipment		16,000
Accounts payable		36,000
Salaries payable		
Unearned extension fees		11,000
S. Carr, capital		63,600
S. Carr, withdrawals	40,000	
Tuition fees earned		102,000
Extension fees earned		38,000
Amortization expense, equipment		
Amortization expense, professional library		
Salaries expense	48,000	
Insurance expense		
Rent expense	22,000	
Teaching supplies expense		
Advertising expense	7,000	
Utilities expense	5,600	
Totals	$275,600	$275,600

Additional facts:

a. An analysis of the company's policies shows that $3,000 of insurance coverage has expired.

b. An inventory shows that teaching supplies costing $2,600 are on hand at the end of the year.

c. The estimated annual amortization on the equipment is $12,000.

d. The estimated annual amortization on the professional library is $6,000.

e. The school offers off-campus services for specific employers. On November 1, the company agreed to do a special six-month course for a client. The contract calls for a monthly fee of $2,200, and the client paid the first five months' fees in advance. When the cash was received, the Unearned Extension Fees account was credited.

f. On October 15, the school agreed to teach a four-month class for an individual for $3,000 tuition per month payable at the end of the class. The services to date have been provided as agreed, but no payment has been received.

g. The school's two employees are paid weekly. As of the end of the year, two days' wages have accrued at the rate of $100 per day for each employee.

h. The balance in the Prepaid Rent account represents the rent for December.

Required

1. Prepare T-accounts with the balances listed in the unadjusted trial balance of Southwest.

2. Prepare the eight necessary adjusting journal entries and post them to the T-accounts.

3. Update the balances in the T-accounts for the effects of the adjusting entries and prepare an adjusted trial balance.

4. Prepare the school's income statement and statement of changes in owner's equity for 19X8, and prepare the balance sheet as of December 31, 19X8.

5. Calculate the company's profit margin for the year.

Check Figure Ending owner's equity, $62,100

Problem 4-3B
Comparing the
unadjusted and adjusted
trial balances, preparing
financial statements, and
calculating profit margin

LO 5, 6, 7, 9, 11

In the following six-column table for RPE Company, the first two columns contain the unadjusted trial balance for the company as of July 31, 19X8. The last two columns contain the adjusted trial balance as of the same date.

	Unadjusted Trial Balance		Adjustments		Adjusted Trial Balance	
Cash	$ 27,000				$ 27,000	
Accounts receivable	12,000				22,460	
Office supplies	18,000				3,000	
Prepaid insurance	7,320				4,880	
Office equipment	92,000				92,000	
Accum. amortization, office equipment		$ 12,000				$ 18,000
Accounts payable		9,300				10,200
Interest payable						800
Salaries payable						6,600
Unearned consulting fees		16,000				14,300
Long-term notes payable		44,000				44,000
R. P. Edds, capital		28,420				28,420
R. P. Edds, withdrawals	10,000				10,000	
Consulting fees earned		156,000				168,160
Amortization expense, office equipment					6,000	
Salaries expense	71,000				77,600	
Interest expense	1,400				2,200	
Insurance expense					2,440	
Rent expense	13,200				13,200	
Office supplies expense					15,000	
Advertising expense	13,800				14,700	
Totals	$265,720	$265,720			$290,480	$290,480

Required

Preparation component:

1. Prepare the company's income statement and the statement of changes in owner's equity for the year ended July 31, 19X8.
2. Prepare the company's balance sheet as of July 31, 19X8.
3. Calculate the company's profit margin for the year.

Analysis component:

4. Analyze the differences between the unadjusted and adjusted trial balances to determine the adjustments that must have been made. Show the results of your analysis by inserting the adjusting journal entries that must have been recorded by the company in the two middle columns. Label each entry with a letter, and provide a short description of the purpose for recording it. (Use the Working Papers that accompany the book or recreate the table.)

Check Figure Profit margin, 22%

The records for Urban Landscape Co. were kept on the cash basis instead of the accrual basis. However, the company is now applying for a loan and the bank wants to know what its net income for 19X8 was under generally accepted accounting principles. Here is the income statement for 19X8 under the cash basis:

Problem 4-4
Accrual basis income

LO 3

URBAN LANDSCAPE CO. Income Statement (Cash Basis) For Year Ended December 31, 19X8	
Revenues	$525,000
Expenses	330,000
Net income	$195,000

This additional information was gathered to help the accountant convert the income statement to the accrual basis:

	As of Dec. 31/X7	As of Dec. 31/X8
Accrued revenues	$12,000	$16,500
Unearned revenues	66,000	21,000
Accrued expenses	14,700	9,000
Prepaid expenses	27,000	20,700

All prepaid expenses from the beginning of the year were consumed or expired, all unearned revenues from the beginning of the year were earned, and all accrued expenses and revenues from the beginning of the year were paid or collected.

Required

Prepare an accrual basis income statement for this business for 19X8. Provide schedules that explain how you converted from cash revenues and expenses to accrual revenues and expenses.

Check Figure Net income, $243,900

For these adjusting and transaction entries, enter the letter of the explanation that most closely describes the adjustment or transaction in the blank space beside each entry. (You can use some letters more than once.)

a. To record collection of an unearned revenue.
b. To record the earning of previously unearned income.
c. To record payment of an accrued expense.
d. To record collection of an accrued revenue.
e. To record an accrued expense.
f. To record accrued income.
g. To record the year's consumption of a prepaid expense.
h. To record payment of a prepaid expense.
i. To record the year's amortization expense.

Problem 4-5
Identifying adjusting and subsequent entries

LO 4, 10

_____	**1.** Amortization Expense	3,000	
	Accumulated Amortization		3,000
_____	**2.** Unearned Professional Fees	2,000	
	Professional Fees Earned		2,000
_____	**3.** Rent Expense	1,000	
	Prepaid Rent		1,000
_____	**4.** Interest Expense	4,000	
	Interest Payable		4,000

		Debit	Credit
_____	5. Prepaid Rent	3,500	
	Cash		3,500
_____	6. Salaries Expense	5,000	
	Salaries Payable		5,000
_____	7. Insurance Expense	6,000	
	Prepaid Insurance		6,000
_____	8. Salaries Payable	1,500	
	Cash		1,500
_____	9. Cash	6,500	
	Unearned Professional Fees		6,500
_____	10. Cash	9,000	
	Interest Receivable		9,000
_____	11. Interest Receivable	7,000	
	Interest Earned		7,000
_____	12. Cash	8,000	
	Accounts Receivable		8,000

Problem 4-6
Preparing financial
statements from the
adjusted trial balance and
calculating profit margin

LO 7, 9, 11

This adjusted trial balance is for Conquest Company as of December 31, 19X8:

	Debit	Credit
Cash	$ 22,000	
Accounts receivable	44,000	
Interest receivable	10,000	
Notes receivable (due in 90 days)	160,000	
Office supplies	8,000	
Automobiles	160,000	
Accumulated amortization, automobiles		$ 42,000
Equipment	130,000	
Accumulated amortization, equipment		10,000
Land	70,000	
Accounts payable		88,000
Interest payable		12,000
Salaries payable		11,000
Unearned fees		22,000
Long-term notes payable		130,000
J. Conroe, capital		247,800
J. Conroe, withdrawals	38,000	
Fees earned		420,000
Interest earned		16,000
Amortization expense, automobiles	18,000	
Amortization expense, equipment	10,000	
Salaries expense	180,000	
Wages expense	32,000	
Interest expense	24,000	
Office supplies expense	26,000	
Advertising expense	50,000	
Repairs expense, automobiles	16,800	
Total	$998,800	$998,800

Required

1. Use the information in the trial balance to prepare (a) the income statement for the year ended December 31, 19X8; (b) the statement of changes in owner's equity for the year ended December 31, 19X8; and (c) the balance sheet as of December 31, 19X8.

2. Assume that the value of J. Conroe's management contributions as owner are valued at $30,000. Calculate the modified profit margin for 19X8.

Check Figure Total assets, $552,000

The following events occurred for a company during the last two months of its fiscal year ended December 31:

Nov. 1 Paid $1,500 for future newspaper advertising.
       1 Paid $2,160 for insurance through October 31 of the following year.
      30 Received $3,300 for future services to be provided to a customer.
Dec.   1 Paid $2,700 for the services of a consultant, to be received over the next three months.
      15 Received $7,650 for future services to be provided to a customer.
      31 Of the advertising paid for on November 1, $900 worth had not yet been published by the newspaper.
      31 Part of the insurance paid for on November 1 had expired.
      31 Services worth $1,200 had not yet been provided to the customer who paid on November 30.
      31 One-third of the consulting services paid for on December 1 had been received.
      31 The company had performed $3,000 of the services that the customer had paid for on December 15.

Problem 4-7A
Recording prepaid expenses and unearned revenues
LO 5, 6, 12

Required

Preparation component:

1. Prepare entries for the above events under the approach that records prepaid expenses as assets and records unearned revenues as liabilities. Also, prepare adjusting entries at the end of the year.

2. Prepare entries under the approach that records prepaid expenses as expenses and records unearned revenues as revenues. Also, prepare adjusting entries at the end of the year.

Analysis component:

3. Explain why the alternative sets of entries in requirements 1 and 2 do not result in different financial statement amounts.

The Perfecto Company's annual accounting period ends on October 31, 19X8. Perfecto follows the practice of recording prepaid expenses and unearned revenues in balance sheet accounts. The following information concerns the adjusting entries that need to be recorded as of that date:

a. The Office Supplies account started the fiscal year with a $500 balance. During the fiscal year, the company purchased supplies at a cost of $3,650, which was added to the Office Supplies account. The inventory of supplies on hand at October 31 had a cost of $700.

b. An analysis of the company's insurance policies provided these facts:

Alternate Problems

Problem 4-1A
Adjusting and subsequent journal entries
LO 5, 6, 7, 10

Policy	Date of Purchase	Years of Coverage	Total Cost
1	April 1, 19X7	2	$3,000
2	April 1, 19X8	3	3,600
3	August 1, 19X8	1	660

The total premium for each policy was paid in full at the purchase date, and the Prepaid Insurance account was debited for the full cost.

c. The company has 10 employees who earn a total of $800 for every working day. They are paid each Monday for their work in the five-day workweek ending on the preceding Friday. October 31, 19X8, falls on Monday, and all five employees worked the first day of the week. They will be paid salaries for five full days on Monday, November 7, 19X8.

d. The company purchased a building on August 1, 19X8. The building cost $155,000, and is expected to have a $20,000 salvage value at the end of its predicted 25-year life.

e. Because the company is not large enough to occupy the entire building, it arranged to rent some space to a tenant at $600 per month, starting on September 1, 19X8. The rent was paid on time on September 1, and the amount received was credited to the Rent Earned account. However, the tenant has not paid the October rent. The company has worked out an agreement with the tenant, who has promised to pay both October's and November's rent in full on November 15. The tenant has agreed not to fall behind again.

f. On September 1, the company also rented space to another tenant for $525 per month. The tenant paid five months' rent in advance on that date. The payment was recorded with a credit to the Unearned Rent account.

Required

1. Use the information to prepare adjusting entries as of October 31, 19X8.

2. Prepare journal entries to record the subsequent cash transactions described in items *c* and *e*.

Problem 4-2A
Adjusting entries; financial
statements; profit margin

LO 5, 6, 7, 9, 11

Presented below is the unadjusted trial balance for Design Institute as of December 31, 19X8. Design Institute follows the practice of initially recording prepaid expenses and unearned revenues in balance sheet accounts. The institute provides one-on-one training to individuals who pay tuition directly to the business and also offers extension training to groups in off-site locations. Presented after the trial balance are facts that will lead to eight adjusting entries as of December 31, 19X8.

DESIGN INSTITUTE Unadjusted Trial Balance December 31, 19X8		
Cash	$ 50,000	
Accounts receivable		
Teaching supplies	60,000	
Prepaid insurance	18,000	
Prepaid rent	2,600	
Professional library	10,000	
Accumulated amortization, professional library ..		$ 1,500
Equipment	30,000	
Accumulated amortization, equipment		16,000
Accounts payable		12,200
Salaries payable		
Unearned extension fees		27,600
Jay Stevens, capital		68,500
Jay Stevens, withdrawals	20,000	
Tuition fees earned		105,000
Extension fees earned		62,000
Amortization expense, equipment		
Amortization expense, professional library		
Salaries expense	43,200	
Insurance expense		
Rent expense	28,600	
Teaching supplies expense		
Advertising expense	18,000	
Utilities expense	12,400	
Totals	$292,800	$292,800

Additional facts:

a. An analysis of the company's policies shows that $6,400 of insurance coverage has expired.

b. An inventory shows that teaching supplies costing $2,500 are on hand at the end of the year.

c. The estimated annual amortization on the equipment is $4,000.

d. The estimated annual amortization on the professional library is $2,000.

e. The school offers off-campus services for specific operators. On November 1, the company agreed to do a special four-month course for a client. The contract calls for a $4,600 monthly fee, and the client paid the first two months' fees in advance. When the cash was received, the Unearned Extension Fees account was credited.

f. On October 15, the school agreed to teach a four-month class to an individual for $2,200 tuition per month payable at the end of the class. The services have been provided as agreed, and no payment has been received.

g. The school's only employee is paid weekly. As of the end of the year, three days' wages have accrued at the rate of $180 per day.

h. The balance in the Prepaid Rent account represents the rent for December.

Required

1. Prepare T-accounts with the balances listed in the unadjusted trial balance of Southwest Careers.

2. Prepare the eight necessary adjusting journal entries and post them to the T-accounts.

3. Update the balances in the T-accounts for the effects of the adjusting entries and prepare an adjusted trial balance.

4. Prepare the company's income statement and the statement of changes in owner's equity for 19X8, and prepare the balance sheet as of December 31, 19X8.

5. Calculate the company's profit margin for the year. The owner was not actively involved in managing the company.

Presented below is a six-column table for Personal Consulting Company. The first two columns contain the unadjusted trial balance for the company as of July 31, 19X8, and the last two columns contain the adjusted trial balance as of the same date. The two middle columns are left blank.

Problem 4-3A[B]
Comparing the unadjusted and adjusted trial balances; preparing financial statements; calculating profit margin

LO 5, 6, 7, 9, 11

	Unadjusted Trial Balance		Adjustments		Adjusted Trial Balance	
Cash	$ 48,000				$ 48,000	
Accounts receivable	70,000				76,660	
Office supplies	30,000				7,000	
Prepaid insurance	13,200				8,600	
Office equipment	150,000				150,000	
Accumulated amortization, office equipment		$ 30,000				$ 40,000
Accounts payable		36,000				42,000
Interest payable						1,600
Salaries payable						11,200
Unearned consulting fees		30,000				17,800
Long-term notes payable		80,000				80,000
Dick Persons, capital		70,200				70,200
Dick Persons, withdrawals	10,000				10,000	
Consulting fees earned		264,000				282,860
Amortization expense, office equipment					10,000	
Salaries expense	115,600				126,800	
Interest expense	6,400				8,000	
Insurance expense					4,600	
Rent expense	24,000				24,000	
Office supplies expense					23,000	
Advertising expense	43,000				49,000	
Totals	$510,200	$510,200			$545,660	$545,660

Required

Preparation component:

1. Prepare the company's income statement and the statement of changes in owner's equity for the year ended July 31, 19X8.
2. Prepare the company's balance sheet as of July 31, 19X8.
3. Calculate the company's modified profit margin for the year, assuming the value of the owner's services to the business during the year was $30,000.

Analysis component:

4. Analyze the differences between the unadjusted and adjusted trial balances to determine the adjustments that must have been made. Show the results of your analysis by inserting the adjusting journal entries that must have been recorded by the company in the two middle columns. Label each entry with a letter, and provide a short description of the purpose for recording it. (Use the Working Papers that accompany the book or recreate the table.)

Problem 4-4A
Accrual basis income

LO 3

The records for Craven Products were kept on the cash basis instead of the accrual basis. However, the company is now applying for a loan and the bank wants to know what its net income for 19X8 was under generally accepted accounting principles. Here is the income statement for 19X8 under the cash basis:

CRAVEN PRODUCTS Income Statement (Cash Basis) For Year Ended December 31, 19X8	
Revenues	$165,000
Expenses	66,000
Net income	$ 99,000

This additional information was gathered to help the accountant convert the income statement to the accrual basis:

	As of Dec. 31/X7	As of Dec. 31/X8
Accrued revenues	$11,100	$ 3,600
Unearned revenues	7,050	7,800
Accrued expenses	4,800	11,400
Prepaid expenses	6,300	3,300

All prepaid expenses from the beginning of the year were consumed or expired, all unearned revenues from the beginning of the year were earned, and all accrued expenses and revenues from the beginning of the year were paid or collected.

Required

Prepare an accrual basis income statement for this business for 19X8. Provide schedules that explain how you converted from cash revenues and expenses to accrual revenues and expenses.

Problem 4-5A
Identifying adjusting and
subsequent entries

LO 4,10

For these adjusting and transaction entries, enter the letter of the explanation that most closely describes the adjustment or transaction in the blank space beside each entry. (You can use some letters more than once.)

a. To record collection of an accrued revenue.

b. To record payment of an accrued expense.

c. To record payment of a prepaid expense.

d. To record the year's amortization expense.

e. To record the earning of previously unearned income.

f. To record the year's consumption of a prepaid expense.

g. To record accrued income.

h. To record collection of an unearned revenue.

i. To record an accrued expense.

____ **1.** Salaries Payable 8,000
     Cash 8,000

____ **2.** Amortization Expense 6,000
     Accumulated Amortization 6,000

____ **3.** Unearned Professional Fees 3,500
     Professional Fees Earned 3,500

____ **4.** Interest Receivable 1,500
     Interest Earned 1,500

____ **5.** Cash 5,000
     Accounts Receivable 5,000

____ **6.** Interest Expense 9,000
     Interest Payable 9,000

____ **7.** Cash 4,000
     Unearned Professional Fees 4,000

____ **8.** Insurance Expense 3,000
     Prepaid Insurance 3,000

____ **9.** Rent Expense 6,500
     Prepaid Rent 6,500

____ **10.** Prepaid Rent 7,000
     Cash 7,000

____ **11.** Salaries Expense 1,000
     Salaries Payable 1,000

____ **12.** Cash 2,000
     Interest Receivable 2,000

Problem 4-6A

Preparing financial statements from the adjusted trial balance; calculating profit margin

LO 7, 9, 11

This adjusted trial balance is for Horizon Courier as of December 31, 19X8:

	Debit	Credit
Cash	$ 48,000	
Accounts receivable	110,000	
Interest receivable	6,000	
Notes receivable (due in 90 days)	200,000	
Office supplies	12,000	
Trucks	124,000	
Accumulated amortization, trucks		$ 48,000
Equipment	260,000	
Accumulated amortization, equipment		190,000
Land	90,000	
Accounts payable		124,000
Interest payable		22,000
Salaries payable		30,000
Unearned delivery fees		110,000
Long-term notes payable		190,000
K. Ainesworth, capital		115,000
K. Ainesworth, withdrawals	40,000	
Delivery fees earned		580,000
Interest earned		24,000
Amortization expense, trucks	24,000	
Amortization expense, equipment	46,000	
Salaries expense	64,000	
Wages expense	290,000	
Interest expense	25,000	
Office supplies expense	33,000	
Advertising expense	26,400	
Repairs expense, trucks	34,600	
Total	$1,433,000	$1,433,000

Required

1. Use the information in the trial balance to prepare (a) the income statement for the year ended December 31, 19X8, (b) the statement of changes in owner's equity for the year ended December 31, 19X8, and (c) the balance sheet as of December 31, 19X8.

2. Calculate the profit margin for 19X8. Assume that the management contributions of the owner during 19X8 are valued at $30,000. Calculate the modified profit margin for 19X8.

Problem 4-7A[A]

Recording prepaid expenses and unearned revenues

LO 5, 6, 12

The following events occurred for a company during the last two months of its fiscal year ended May 31:

Apr.   1   Paid $3,450 for future consulting services.
      1   Paid $2,700 for insurance through March 31 of the following year.
    30   Received $7,500 for future services to be provided to a customer.
May   1   Paid $3,450 for future newspaper advertising.
    23   Received $9,450 for future services to be provided to a customer.
    31   Of the consulting services paid for on April 1, $1,500 worth had been received.
    31   Part of the insurance paid for on April 1 had expired.
    31   Services worth $3,600 had not yet been provided to the customer who paid on April 30.
    31   Of the advertising paid for on May 1, $1,050 worth had not been published yet.
    31   The company had performed $4,500 of the services that the customer had paid for on May 23.

Required

Preparation component:

1. Prepare entries for the above events under the approach that records prepaid expenses and unearned revenues in balance sheet accounts. Also, prepare adjusting entries at the end of the year.

2. Prepare journal entries under the approach that records prepaid expenses and unearned revenues in income statement accounts. Also, prepare adjusting entries at the end of the year.

Analysis component:

3. Explain why the alternative sets of entries in requirements 1 and 2 do not result in different financial statement amounts.

The Salaries Payable account of James Bay Company Limited appears below:

Salaries Payable			
Entries during 1999	389,120	Bal. Jan. 1, 1999	22,520
		Entries during 1999	388,400

Analytical and Review Problems

A & R Problem 4-1

The company records the salary expense and related liability at the end of each week and pays the employees on the last Friday of the month.

Required

Calculate:

1. Salary expense for 1999.

2. How much was paid to employees in 1999 for work done in 1998?

3. How much was paid to employees in 1999 for work done in 1999?

4. How much will be paid to employees in 2000 for work done in 1999?

The records for Jan Kauffman's home nursing business were kept on the cash basis instead of the accrual basis. However, the company is now applying for a loan and the bank wants to know what its net income for 1999 was under generally accepted accounting principles. Here is the income statement for 1999 under the cash basis:

A & R Problem 4-2

KAUFFMAN'S HOME NURSING Income Statement (Cash Basis) For Year Ended December 31, 1999	
Revenues	$245,000
Expenses	154,000
Net income	$91,000

This additional information was gathered to help the accountant convert the income statement to the accrual basis:

	As of Dec. 31/98	As of Dec. 31/99
Accrued revenues	$5,600	$7,700
Unearned revenues	30,800	9,800
Accrued expenses	6,860	4,200
Prepaid expenses	12,600	9,660

All prepaid expenses from the beginning of the year were consumed or expired, all unearned revenues from the beginning of the year were earned, and all accrued expenses and revenues from the beginning of the year were paid or collected.

Required

Prepare an accrual basis income statement for this business for 1999. Provide schedules that explain how you converted from cash revenues and expenses to accrual revenues and expenses.

Serial Problem

Echo Systems

(This comprehensive problem was introduced in Chapter 3 and continues in Chapters 5 and 6. If the Chapter 3 segment has not been completed, the assignment can begin at this point. You need to use the facts presented on pages 146–147 in Chapter 3. Because of its length, this problem is most easily solved if you use the Working Papers that accompany this book.)

After the success of its first two months, Mary Graham has decided to continue operating Echo Systems. (The transactions that occurred in these months are described in Chapter 3.) Before proceeding in December, Graham adds these new accounts to the chart of accounts for the ledger:

Account	No.
Accumulated Amortization, Office Equipment	164
Accumulated Amortization, Computer Equipment	168
Wages Payable	210
Unearned Computer Services Revenue	236
Amortization Expense, Office Equipment	612
Amortization Expense, Computer Equipment	613
Insurance Expense	637
Rent Expense	640
Computer Supplies Expense	652

Required

1. Prepare journal entries to record each of the following transactions for Echo Systems. Post the entries to the accounts in the ledger.
2. Prepare adjusting entries to record the events described on December 31. Post the entries to the accounts in the ledger.
3. Prepare an adjusted trial balance as of December 31, 19X1.
4. Prepare an income statement for the three months ended December 31, 19X1.
5. Prepare a statement of changes in owner's equity for the three months ended December 31, 19X1.
6. Prepare a balance sheet as of December 31, 19X1.

Transactions and other data:

Dec. 2 Paid $1,050 to the Lakeshore Mall for the company's share of mall advertising costs.
3 Paid $600 to repair the company's computer.
4 Received $3,750 from Alamo Engineering Co. for the receivable from the prior month.
10 Paid Carly Smith for six days' work at the rate of $100 per day.
14 Notified by Alamo Engineering Co. that Echo's bid of $6,000 on a proposed project was accepted. Alamo paid an advance of $1,500.
15 Purchased $1,155 of computer supplies on credit from Abbott Office Products.
16 Sent a reminder to Fostek Co. to pay the fee for services originally recorded on November 8.
20 Completed project for Elite Corporation and received $5,625 cash.

22–26 Took the week off for the holidays.

28 Received $2,850 from Fostek Co. on their receivable.

29 Reimbursed Mary Graham's business automobile expenses of 600 kilometres at $0.25 per kilometre.

31 Mary Graham withdrew $1,800 cash from the business..

31 The following information was collected to be used in adjusting entries prior to preparing financial statements for the company's first three months:

a. The December 31 inventory of computer supplies was $720.

b. Three months have passed since the annual insurance premium was paid.

c. As of the end of the year, Carly Smith has not been paid for four days of work at the rate of $100 per day.

d. The computer is expected to have a four-year life with no salvage value.

e. The office equipment is expected to have a three-year life with no salvage value.

f. Prepaid rent for three of the four months has expired.

BEYOND THE NUMBERS

Refer to the financial statements and related information for **Alliance, Inc.** in Appendix I. Find the answers to the following questions by analyzing the information in the report:

1. What is the nature of Alliance's other assets?

2. What is the total amount recorded as property and equipment and what is the amount of accumulated amortization as of March 31, 1997? How do these totals compare to March 31, 1996?

3. What is the company's profit margin for 1997 and 1996?

Both **Alliance** and **Atlantis** design, produce, and market television programs. Key comparative figures ($ millions) for these two organizations follow:

Key figures	Alliance		Atlantis	
	1997	**1996**	**1997**	**1996**
Net income	$ 18.2	$ 10.4	$ 5.6	$ 6.9
Net Sales	$282.6	$268.9	$178.0	$138.0

* Alliance figures are from the annual reports for the fiscal years ended March 31, 1997 and 1996. Atlantis figures are from the annual reports for the fiscal years ended December 31, 1997 and 1996.

Required

1. Calculate the profit margins for (a) Alliance and (b) Atlantis for the two years of data provided.

2. Which company is more successful earning profit on a dollar of revenue?

3. For each company write the following sentence: For every dollar of sales generated (insert Alliance or Atlantis) makes an average profit of _____ cents.

4. Would it be appropriate to calculate the modified profit margin for Alliance and Atlantis?

Reporting in Action

LO 4, 7, 11

Comparative Analysis

LO 11

Ethics Challenge
LO 7

Jackie Houston is a new accountant for Seitzer company. She is learning on the job from Bob Welch who has already worked several years for Seitzer. Jackie and Bob are working on preparing adjusting journal entries to post and record in anticipation of producing the annual financial statements. Jackie has calculated that amortization expense for the fiscal year should be recorded as:

Amortization Expense—Equipment	$123,546
Accumulated Amortization—Equipment	$123,546

Bob is rechecking the numbers and says that he agrees with her computation. However, he says that the credit entry should be directly to the equipment account. He argues that while accumulated amortization is taught in the classroom, "it is a lot less hassle to not use a contra account and just credit the equipment account directly for the annual allocation of amortization. And, besides, the balance sheet shows the same amount for total assets under both methods."

Required

1. How should amortization be recorded? Do you support Jackie or Bob?
2. Evaluate the strengths and weaknesses of Bob's reasons for preferring his method.
3. Indicate whether the situation faced by Jackie is an ethical problem.

Communicating in Practice
LO 1, 2, 7

Failure to use accounting principles properly can have significant influence on reported profits as well as the success or failure of a business. Obtain a copy of the article "Cendant chief won't quit over audit woes," by Bloomberg News, *The Globe and Mail,* July 15, 1998. Read the article and write a summary that includes the following:

1. Identification of the specific accounting principle that this article discusses and an explanation of what this principle requires and prohibits.
2. A description of the accounting practice for **Cendant** that is questioned in the article.
3. Identification of who has the authority to investigate the challenged practices.
4. Identification of the stakeholders in this case and possible consequences of the questioned accounting practice.
5. An explanation of how this relates to the material in this chapter.

Taking It to the Net
LO 1, 11

Access the **Cangene** promotional Web site at **http://www.cangene.ca.** Visit several hotlinks on the site to get a feel for the company's products.

1. What is the primary product that Cangene sells?
2. Review the Cangene Annual Report.
   a. What is the fiscal year-end of Cangene? Does it appear that Cangene uses a 12-month or 52-week annual reporting period?
   b. What are net sales for Cangene for the annual accounting period ended July 31, 1997?
   c. What is net income for Cangene for the annual accounting period ended July 31, 1997?
   d. Compute profit margin for Cangene for the annual accounting period ended July 31, 1997.
   e. Why do you think Cangene is employing a fiscal year-end in July? Does it relate to their natural business year?

Teamwork in Action
LO 4, 7

Adjusting Accounts

Each member of a team has the responsibility to become a resident expert on a specific type of adjustment. This expertise will be used to facilitate their teammates' understanding of the concepts relevant to the adjustments process and that specific adjustment. Follow the procedures outlined below:

1. Refer to Exhibit 4.20 on p. 167. Each team member is to select their area of expertise by choosing one type of adjustment listed in the exhibit. You have approximately two minutes to make your choices.

2. Learning teams are to disburse and expert teams are to be formed. Expert teams are made up of students who have selected the same area of expertise. The instructor will identify the location where each expert team will meet.

3. Expert teams will collaborate to develop a presentation of items A–E listed below. Each student must write up the presentation in a format that they can actually show to their learning teams in the next step in the activity.

   a. A specific example (with amounts and dates) of a situation that would require the adjustment selected.

   b. The adjusting journal entry for this situation with posting illustrated in T-accounts.

   c. An identification and description of the relevant accounting principle.

   d. A description of what the post-adjustment account balances reflect and identification of the statement(s) these balances are reported on.

   e. A statement of how failure to make these adjustments affects financial statements.

4. Regroup to original teams. In rotation each expert is to make the presentation developed in 3 to their own team members. Experts are to encourage and respond to questions.

Pair up with a classmate. Visit the business area of your community or a shopping mall. Identify 10 businesses that operate in the area that you visit. Try to construct your list so that it contains a mix of retail and service businesses. Hypothesize whether the companies operate on a 12-month fiscal period that coincides with the calendar year-end or whether they use a "natural business" fiscal year. Visit each shop in turn, introduce yourself to the employee you are visiting with, and try to confirm whether you made a correct determination of the fiscal year-end for the store. In some instances the personnel available for questioning may not know the answer to your question. If you cannot confirm the answer, thank the employee and note that you could not test your hypothesis of fiscal year-end. After the visits are complete, compute the percent of fiscal year-ends that you correctly anticipated.

Hitting the Road

LO 1

Read the article, "Car and Strive," in the September 1996 issue of *Canadian Business*.

Business Break

LO 11

Required

1. Contrast the profitability of **Magna** in the early 1990s to 1996.

2. What is the amount of revenue for Magna in the 1996 fiscal year?

3. What is the reason for Magna's success?

4. Despite its recent profitability what does the article identify as a possible problem for Magna?

5

CHAPTER

Completing the Accounting Cycle and Classifying Accounts

A Look Back

Chapter 4 explained the timing of reports. We described why adjusting accounts is important for recognizing revenues and expenses in the proper period. We explained how to prepare an adjusted trial balance and use it as an aid in preparing financial statements.

A Look at This Chapter

This chapter emphasizes the final steps in the accounting process and reviews the entire accounting cycle. We explain the closing process including accounting procedures and use of a post-closing trial balance. We describe a work sheet and other tools for helping us prepare financial statements. A classified balance sheet is explained along with showing how analysts use this information.

A Look Forward

Chapter 6 looks at accounting for merchandising activities. We describe the sale and purchase of merchandise and its implications for preparing and analyzing financial statements.

Accounting Edge

Montreal, PQ—Marie Nguyen wasn't trying to jump on the latest management bandwagon. But when she founded **Statistics Analysis** in 1991 to analyze marketing survey data, her son did her company's accounting. When demand for her services grew—and her son went off to become a correspondent—Nguyen knew she needed outside accounting help. She lacked the knowledge to prepare work sheets and financial reports and to use other tools needed for business decisions. "I realized how little I knew—like not even knowing how to bill clients or set salaries," said Nguyen.

For support, Nguyen turned her books over to a local firm called Accounting Assistance. The firm took care of her basic accounting needs, but it also told her something that shocked her. She was consistently underestimating—sometimes by as much as 75%—her expenses. Today, Accounting Assistance is not only keeping Nguyen's books, it is helping with strategic analyses. Nguyen says her profits have doubled since she started using accounting information.

Nguyen relies on outsourcing, contracting out services she once did in-house. More business owners are using outsourcing as a strategic tool. Instead of simply looking for cost savings, they seek services at a higher quality than they can do themselves. Providers review every part of the accounting cycle using worksheets and other tools such as what-if and ratio analyses. A recent survey of executives showed the top two reasons to outsource are improving company focus and reaching company potential. Effectively managing data and preparing classified financial reports are important steps in achieving these goals. A study by a large accounting firm found that companies who effectively used these services had 22% more revenues than those that didn't including greater profit margins and cash flows.

Accounting is the gold mine of outsourcers. They look for ways companies can better manage and analyze financial data. The surprise is they tackle tasks with tools readily available to us. The tasks include payroll, recordkeeping, statement preparation and computing. They now are experimenting with inventory, pensions and sales—even customer service. This creates enormous accounting-related opportunities in managing and analyzing data. As one consultant said, "I have data everywhere but not a drop of information." Work sheets and other analysis tools are one remedy.

[Source: Adapted from *Business Week*, May 13, 1996.]

Learning Objectives

LO 1 Explain why temporary accounts are closed each period.

LO 2 Describe and prepare closing entries.

LO 3 Explain and prepare a post-closing trial balance.

LO 4 Prepare a work sheet and explain its usefulness.

LO 5 Identify steps in the accounting cycle.

LO 6 Explain and prepare a classified balance sheet.

LO 7 Compute the current ratio and describe what it reveals about a company's financial condition.

CHAPTER PREVIEW

Financial statement preparation is a major purpose of accounting. Many of the important steps leading to financial statements are explained in earlier chapters. We described how transactions and events are analyzed, journalized, and posted. We also described important adjustments that are often necessary to properly reflect revenues when earned and expenses when incurred.

This chapter describes the final steps in the accounting process leading to financial statements. It includes the closing process that prepares revenue, expense, and withdrawals accounts for the next reporting period and updates the owner's capital account. A work sheet is described as a useful tool in preparing financial statements. We explain how accounts are classified on a balance sheet to give more useful information to decision makers. We also describe the current ratio and explain how it is used by decision makers to assess a company's ability to pay its liabilities in the near future. These tools for managing and analyzing data are the kind Marie Nguyen refers to in the opening article. Such tools improve decision making.

Closing Process

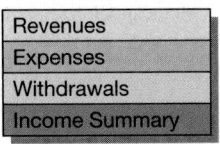

Explain why temporary accounts are closed each period.

The **closing process** is an important step at the end of an accounting period that prepares accounts for recording the transactions of the *next* period. In the closing process we must:

1. Identify accounts for closing.
2. Record and post the closing entries.
3. Prepare post-closing trial balance.

The purpose of the closing process is twofold. First, it resets revenue, expense, and withdrawal account balances to zero at the end of every period. This is done so that these accounts can measure revenue, expense, and withdrawal amounts for the next period. This is important if we wish to know how a company performs during a period of time. Second, it helps in summarizing a period's revenues and expenses. We use an Income Summary account for this purpose. This section explains the three steps in the closing process.

Temporary and Permanent Accounts

Temporary (or nominal) accounts accumulate data related to one accounting period. They include all income statement accounts, withdrawals accounts, and the Income Summary. They are temporary because the accounts are opened at the beginning of a period, used to record events for that period, and then closed at the end of the period. They are nominal because the accounts describe events or changes that have occurred rather than the financial position that exists at the end of the period. *The closing process applies only to temporary accounts.*

Permanent (or real) accounts report on activities related to one or more future accounting periods. They carry their ending balances into the next period, and include all balance sheet accounts. Asset, liability, and owner's equity accounts are not closed as long as a company continues to own the assets, owe the liabilities, and have owner's equity. These accounts are not closed. They are permanent because they describe the existing financial position.

Temporary Accounts

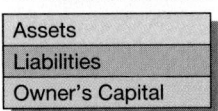

Revenues
Expenses
Withdrawals
Income Summary

Permanent Accounts

Assets
Liabilities
Owner's Capital

Recording and Posting Closing Entries

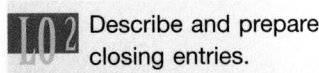

Describe and prepare closing entries.

Recording and posting **closing entries** transfer the end-of-period balances in revenue, expense, and withdrawals accounts to the permanent owner's capital account.

Closing entries are a necessary step at the end of the period after financial statements are prepared because we want:

- Revenue, expense and withdrawals accounts to (a) be reflected in owner's equity and (b) begin the next period with zero balances.
- Owner's capital account to reflect (a) increases from net income and (b) decreases from net losses and withdrawals from the period just ending.

An income statement aims to report revenues earned and expenses incurred during one accounting period. It is prepared from information recorded in revenue and expense accounts. The statement of changes in owner's equity aims to report changes in the owner's capital account during one period. It uses information accumulated in the withdrawals account. Because revenue, expense, and withdrawals accounts accumulate information for only one period, they must start each period with zero balances.

To close revenue and expense accounts, we transfer their balances first to an account called **Income Summary.** Income Summary is a temporary account that contains a credit for the sum of all revenues and a debit for the sum of all expenses. Its balance equals net income or net loss, and is transferred to the owner's capital account. Next, we transfer the withdrawals account balance to the owner's capital account. After these closing entries are posted, the revenue, expense, Income Summary, and withdrawals accounts have zero balances. These accounts are then said to be closed or cleared, as illustrated in Exhibit 5.1.

Four-Step Closing Process

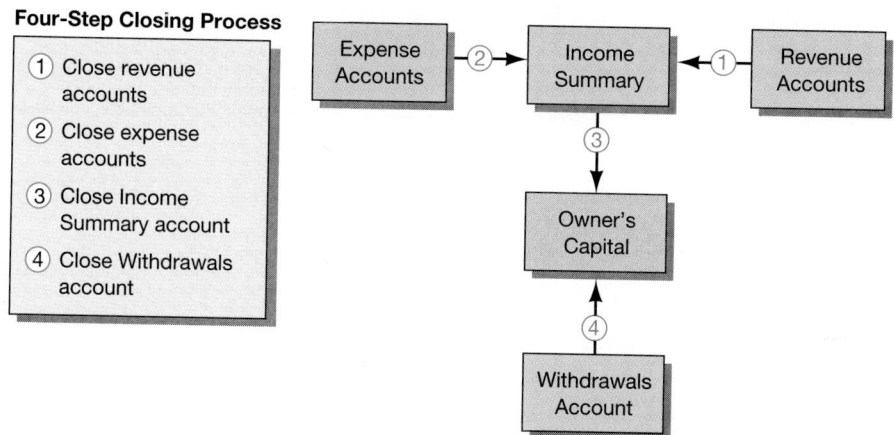

1. Close revenue accounts
2. Close expense accounts
3. Close Income Summary account
4. Close Withdrawals account

Exhibit 5.1

Closing Process for a Proprietorship

FastForward's adjusted trial balance on December 31, 1997, is repeated in Exhibit 5.2. Exhibit 5.3 uses the adjusted account balances from Exhibit 5.2 to show the four types of entries necessary to close FastForward's revenue, expense, Income Summary, and withdrawals accounts. We explain each of these four types.

Close Credit Balances in Revenue Accounts to Income Summary

The first closing entry transfers credit balances in revenue accounts to the Income Summary account. We get accounts with credit balances to zero by debiting them. For FastForward, this journal entry is:

Dec. 31	Consulting Revenue	5,850	
	Rental Revenue	300	
	Income Summary		6,150
	To close revenue accounts and create Income Summary account.		

This entry closes revenue accounts and leaves them with zero balances. This clearing of accounts allows them to record new revenues for the next period.

The Income Summary account is created and used only for the closing process. The $6,150 credit balance in Income Summary equals the total revenues for the year.

Exhibit 5.2

Adjusted Trial Balance

FASTForward

FastForward Adjusted Trial Balance December 31, 1997		
Cash	$ 7,950	
Accounts receivable	1,800	
Supplies	2,670	
Prepaid insurance	2,300	
Equipment	26,000	
Accumulated amortization—equipment		$ 375
Accounts payable		1,100
Note payable		5,100
Salaries payable		210
Unearned consulting revenue		2,750
Chuck Taylor, capital		30,000
Chuck Taylor, withdrawals	600	
Consulting revenue		5,850
Rental revenue		300
Amortization expense—equipment	375	
Salaries expense	1,610	
Insurance expense	100	
Rent expense	1,000	
Supplies expense	1,050	
Utilities expense	230	
Totals	$45,685	$45,685

Exhibit 5.3

Closing Entries of
FastForward

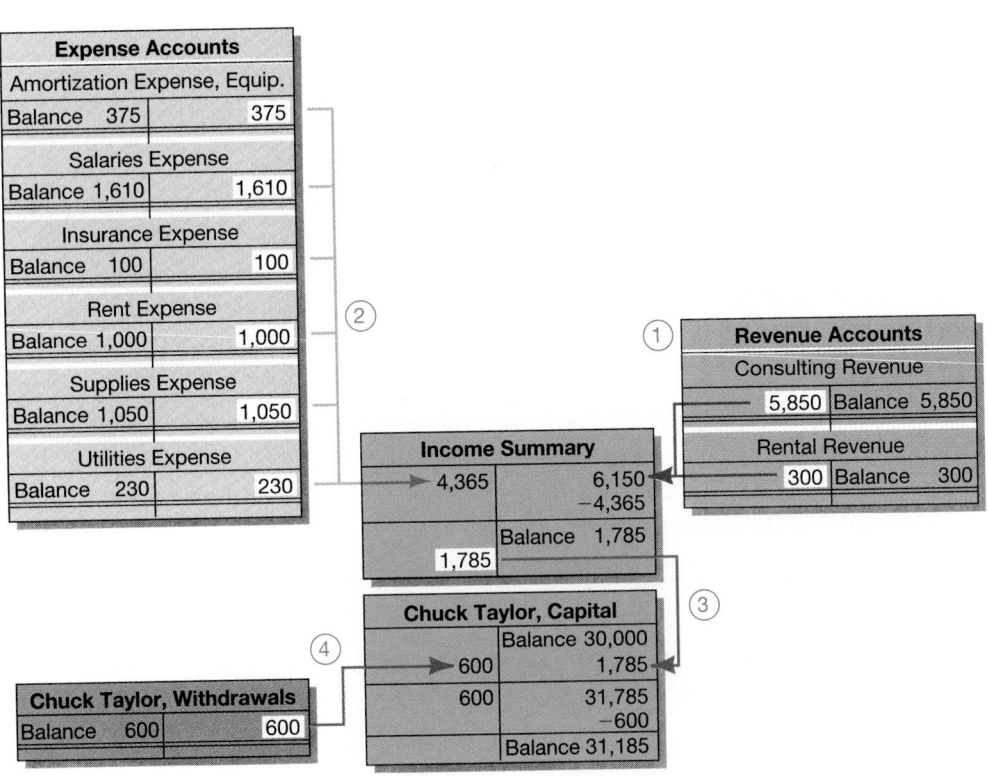

Close Debit Balances in Expense Accounts to Income Summary

The second closing entry transfers debit balances in expense accounts to the Income Summary account. This step gathers all the expense account debit balances in the Income Summary account. We get expense accounts' debit balances to zero by crediting them. This allows these accounts to accumulate a record of new expenses in the next period. This second closing entry for FastForward is:

Dec. 31	Income Summary	4,365	
	Amortization Expense—Equipment ...		375
	Salaries Expense		1,610
	Insurance Expense		100
	Rent Expense		1,000
	Supplies Expense		1,050
	Utilities Expense		230
	To close expense accounts.		

Exhibit 5.3 shows that posting this entry gives each expense account a zero balance. This prepares each account for expense entries for the next period. The entry makes the balance of Income Summary equal to December's net income of $1,785. All debit and credit balances related to expense and revenue accounts have now been collected in the Income Summary account as shown in Exhibit 5.4.

Income Summary	
4,365	6,150

Exhibit 5.4

Income Summary after Closing Revenue and Expense Accounts

Close Income Summary to Owner's Capital

The third closing entry transfers the balance of the Income Summary account to the owner's capital account. This entry closes the Income Summary account and adds the company's net income to the owner's capital account:

Dec. 31	Income Summary	1,785	
	Chuck Taylor, Withdrawals *Capital* ..		1,785
	To close the Income Summary account.		

The Income Summary account has a zero balance after posting this entry. It continues to have a zero balance until the closing process occurs at the end of the next period. The owner's capital account has now been increased by the amount of net income. Since we know the normal balance of owner's capital is a credit, increases to owner's capital from net income are credits.

Close Withdrawals Account to Owner's Capital

The fourth closing entry transfers any debit balance in the withdrawals account to the owner's capital account. This entry for FastForward is:

Dec. 31	Chuck Taylor, Capital	600	
	Chuck Taylor, Withdrawals		600
	To close the withdrawals account.		

This entry gives the withdrawals account a zero balance, and the account is ready to accumulate next period's payments to owner. This entry also reduces the capital account balance to the $31,185 amount reported on the balance sheet.

Sources of Closing Entry Information

We can identify the accounts needing to be closed and the amounts in the closing entries by looking to individual revenue, expense, and withdrawals accounts

Exhibit 5.5

Preparing Closing Entries from
an Adjusted Trial Balance

in the ledger. If we prepare an adjusted trial balance after the adjusting process, the information for closing entries is easily listed on the trial balance. This is illustrated in Exhibit 5.5 where we show how to prepare closing entries using only the adjusted trial balance.

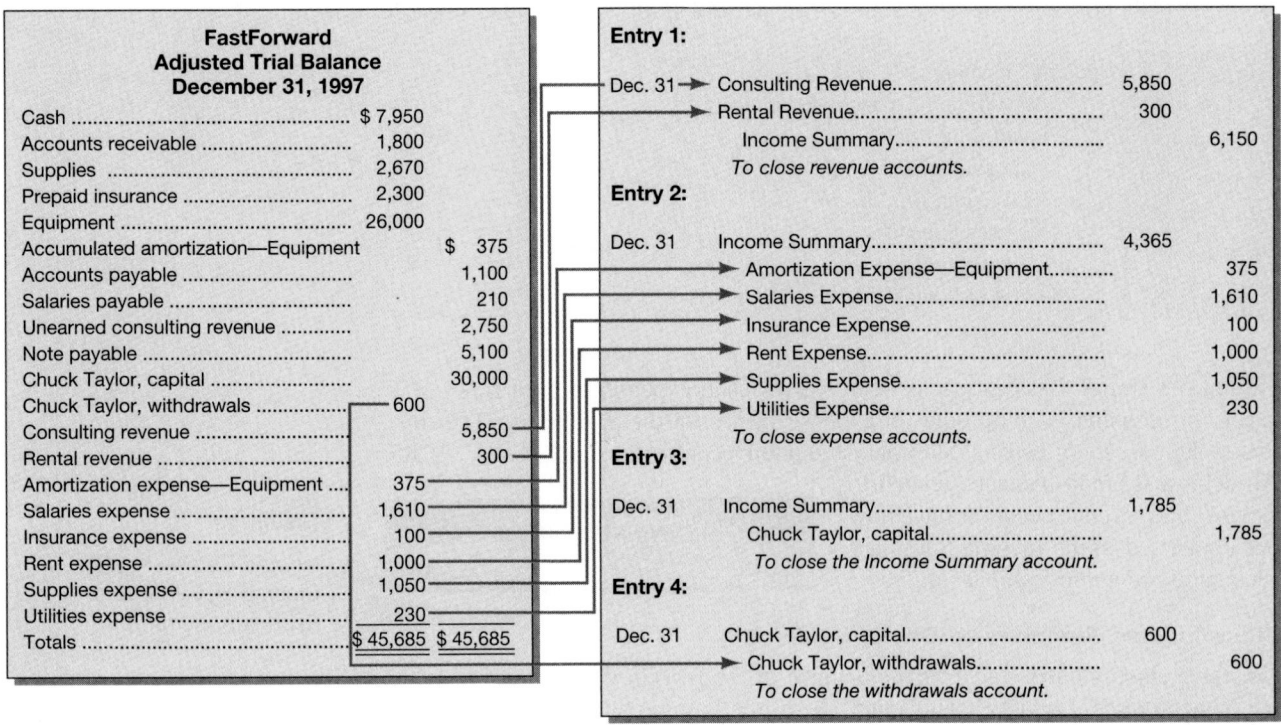

We are not usually able to make all adjusting and closing entries on the last day of each period. This is because information about certain transactions and events that require adjusting is not always available until several days or even weeks later. This means that some adjusting and closing entries are recorded later but dated as of the last day of the period. Financial statements therefore reflect what is known on the date they are prepared instead of what was known as of the last day of the period.

One example is a company that receives a utility bill on January 14 for costs incurred for the month of December. When the bill is received the company records the expense and the payable as of December 31. The income statement for December then reflects expenses incurred and the December 31 balance sheet includes the payable even though the amounts are not actually known on December 31.

Did You Know?

Virtual Financial Statements

Leading-edge companies venturing into the information age are seeing major changes in the accounting process. Quantum leaps in computing technology are increasing the importance of accounting analysis and interpretation. Companies are moving toward the "virtual financial statement." This means with a click of a mouse managers can get up-to-date financials and slash thousands of hours now required in the closing process. Those with knowledge of the accounting process have a competitive advantage in this information age.
[Source: *Computing Canada*, September 15, 1997.]

Post-Closing Trial Balance

A **post-closing trial balance** is a list of permanent accounts and their balances from the ledger after all closing entries are journalized and posted. It is a list of balances for accounts not closed. These accounts are a company's assets, liabilities, and owner's equity at the end of a period. They are identical to those in the balance sheet. The aim of a post-closing trial balance is to verify that (1) total debits equal total credits for permanent accounts, and (2) all temporary accounts have zero balances.

FastForward's post-closing trial balance is shown in Exhibit 5.6. The post-closing trial balance is the last step in the accounting process. Exhibit 5.7 shows the entire ledger of FastForward as of December 31, 1997. We should note that the temporary accounts (revenue, expense and withdrawals accounts) have balances equal to zero. Like with the trial balance, the post-closing trial balance does not prove all transactions are recorded or that the ledger is correct.

L0 3 Explain and prepare a post-closing trial balance.

Exhibit 5.6

Post-Closing Trial Balance

FASTForward

FastForward Post-Closing Trial Balance December 31, 1997		
Cash	$ 7,950	
Accounts receivable	1,800	
Supplies	2,670	
Prepaid insurance	2,300	
Equipment	26,000	
Accumulated amortization—Equipment		$ 375
Accounts payable		1,100
Note payable		5,100
Salaries payable		210
Unearned consulting revenue		2,750
Chuck Taylor, capital		31,185
Totals	$40,720	$40,720

Closing Entries for Corporations

Our discussion to this point regarding closing entries relates to activities and accounts of a proprietorship. Closing entries for a partnership are similar to a proprietorship, but they are different for a corporation. The first two closing entries for a corporation are exactly the same. That is, a corporation's revenue and expense accounts are closed to the Income Summary account. The last two closing entries for a corporation are different.

Recall that a corporation's balance sheet shows shareholders' equity as contributed capital and retained earnings. This means the third closing entry for a corporation closes the Income Summary account to the Retained Earnings account. As an example, **Canadian Pacific** reported net income of $829 million in 1996. This means the credit balance in the Income Summary account after the revenue and expense accounts are closed is $829 million. Canadian Pacific's third closing entry to update its Retained Earnings account is (in millions):

Dec. 31	Income Summary	829	
	Retained Earnings		829
	To close the Income Summary account to Retained Earnings.		

Exhibit 5.7

FASTForward

Ledger after the Closing
Process for FastForward

Ledger
Asset Accounts

Cash   #101

Date	Debit	Credit	Balance
1997 Dec. 1	30,000		30,000
2		2,500	27,500
3		20,000	7,500
10	2,200		9,700
12		1,000	8,700
12		700	8,000
22	1,900		9,900
24		900	9,000
24		600	8,400
26	3,000		11,400
26		2,400	9,000
26		120	8,880
26		230	8,650
26		700	7,950

Supplies   #125

Date	Debit	Credit	Balance
1997 Dec. 2	2,500		2,500
6	1,100		3,600
26	120		3,720
31		1,050	2,670

Prepaid Insurance   #128

Date	Debit	Credit	Balance
1997 Dec. 26	2,400		2,400
31		100	2,300

Equipment   #167

Date	Debit	Credit	Balance
1997 Dec. 3	20,000		20,000
6	6,000		26,000

Accumulated Amortization, Equipment   #168

Date	Debit	Credit	Balance
1997 Dec. 31		375	375

Accounts Receivable   #106

Date	Debit	Credit	Balance
1997 Dec. 12	1,900		1,900
22		1,900	-0-
31	1,800		1,800

Liability and Equity Accounts

Accounts Payable   #201

Date	Debit	Credit	Balance
1997 Dec. 6		1,100	1,100

Salaries Payable   #209

Date	Debit	Credit	Balance
1997 Dec. 31		210	210

Unearned Consulting Revenue   #236

Date	Debit	Credit	Balance
1997 Dec. 26		3,000	3,000
31	250		2,750

Note Payable   #240

Date	Debit	Credit	Balance
1997 Dec. 6		6,000	6,000
24	900		5,100

Chuck Taylor, Capital   #301

Date	Debit	Credit	Balance
1997 Dec. 1		30,000	30,000
31		1,785	31,785
31	600		31,185

Chuck Taylor, Withdrawals   #302

Date	Debit	Credit	Balance
1997 Dec. 24	600		600
31		600	-0-

Exhibit 5.7 *(continued)*

Revenue and Expense Accounts (including Income Summary)												

Consulting Revenue			#403
Date	Debit	Credit	Balance
1997 Dec. 10		2,200	2,200
12		1,600	3,800
31		250	4,050
31		1,800	5,850
31	5,850		-0-

Salaries Expense			#622
Date	Debit	Credit	Balance
1997 Dec. 12	700		700
26	700		1,400
31	210		1,610
31		1,610	-0-

Supplies Expense			#651
Date	Debit	Credit	Balance
1997 Dec. 31	1,050		1,050
31		1,050	-0-

Utilities Expense			#690
Date	Debit	Credit	Balance
1997 Dec. 26	230		230
31		230	-0-

Rental Revenue			#406
Date	Debit	Credit	Balance
1997 Dec. 12		300	300
31	300		-0-

Insurance Expense			#637
Date	Debit	Credit	Balance
1997 Dec. 31	100		100
31		100	-0-

Rent Expense			#641
Date	Debit	Credit	Balance
1997 Dec. 12	1,000		1,000
31		1,000	-0-

Income Summary			#901
Date	Debit	Credit	Balance
1997 Dec. 31		6,150	6,150
31	4,365		1,785
31	1,785		-0-

Amortization Expense, Equipment			#614
Date	Debit	Credit	Balance
1997 Dec. 31	375		375
31		375	-0-

The fourth closing entry uses a Dividends Declared account instead of a withdrawals account. Canadian Pacific declared $166 million in cash dividends. Its fourth closing entry to update Retained earnings is (in millions):

Dec. 31	Retained Earnings	166	
	Dividends Declared		166
	To close the Cash Dividends Declared account to Retained Earnings.		

Dividends are normally a return of earnings. They are then accounted for by reducing the earnings retained by the corporation. We explain and show detailed entries for paying dividends to shareholders in Chapter 16.

Flashback

1. What are the four major closing entries?
2. Why are revenue and expense accounts called temporary? Are there other temporary accounts?
3. What accounts are listed on the post-closing trial balance?

Answers—p. 227

Work Sheet as a Tool

LO 4 Prepare a work sheet and explain its usefulness.

Preparers use various analyses and internal documents when organizing information for reports to internal and external decision makers. **Working papers** are internal documents that are used to assist the preparers in doing the analyses and organizing the information for reports to be presented to internal and external decision makers. The **work sheet** is a useful tool for preparers in working with accounting information. It is not usually given to decision makers.

Silicon Accounting

An electronic work sheet is increasingly common in business. Popular spreadsheet software such as Excel, Lotus 1-2-3 and QuattroPro are putting electronic work sheets and their benefits within the reach of small business owners. This technology allows us to easily change numbers, assess the impact of alternative strategies, and ease the recordkeeping burden. It can also dramatically decrease the time devoted to the accounting process and other procedures required at the end of a period.

Benefits of a Work Sheet

A work sheet is *not* a required financial report. When a business has only a few accounts and adjustments, preparing a work sheet is unnecessary. Computerized accounting systems give financial statements without the need to generate a work sheet. Yet there are several potential benefits from using a manual or electronic work sheet:

1. It helps preparers avoid errors when working with a lot of information for accounting systems involving many accounts and adjustments.
2. It captures the entire accounting process, linking economic transactions and events to their effects in financial statements.
3. Auditors of financial statements often use a work sheet for planning and organizing the audit. It can also be used to reflect any additional adjustments necessary as a result of the audit.
4. It is useful in preparing interim (monthly or quarterly) financial statements when journalizing and posting of adjusting entries are postponed until the year-end.
5. It is helpful in showing the effects of proposed or "what-if" transactions.

Using a Work Sheet

The work sheet can simplify our efforts in preparing financial statements. It is prepared before making adjusting entries at the end of a reporting period. The work sheet stores information about accounts, their needed adjustments, and financial statements. A complete work sheet contains information recorded in the journal and shown in the statements. Exhibit 5.8 shows us the form of a work sheet and the five steps in preparing one.

The multicolumn work sheet provides two columns each for the unadjusted trial balance, the adjustments, the adjusted trial balance, the income statement, and the balance sheet and statement of changes in owner's equity. A work sheet can contain two separate columns for the statement of changes in owner's equity and two separate columns for the balance sheet. Because the statement of changes in owner's equity often includes only a few items, this usually is not done.

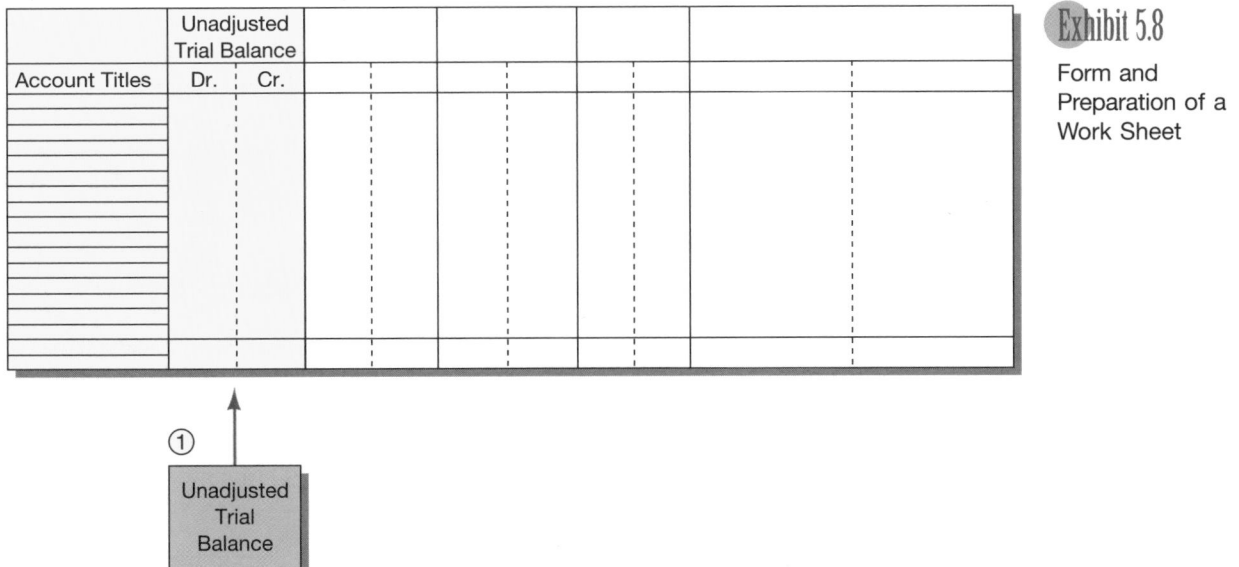

Exhibit 5.8

Form and
Preparation of a
Work Sheet

We use the information of **FastForward** to describe and interpret the work sheet. Important steps in preparing the work sheet are explained below. Each step is shown with reference to Exhibits 5.9a through 5.9e.

Exhibit 5.9

Worksheet for FastForward

5.9a Step 1: ☐ Prepare unadjusted trial balance;

	Unadjusted Trial Balance	
Account	Dr.	Cr.
Cash	7,950	
Supplies	3,720	
Prepaid insurance	2,400	
Equipment	26,000	
Accumulated amortization-Equipment		
Accounts payable		1,100
Note payable		5,100
Unearned consulting revenue		3,000
Chuck Taylor, capital		30,000
Chuck Taylor, withdrawals	600	
Consulting revenue		3,800
Rental revenue		300
Salaries expense	1,400	
Rent expense	1,000	
Utilities expense	230	
Totals	43,300	43,300

① Step 1. Prepare Unadjusted Trial Balance

Turn to Exhibit 5.9a. The first step in using a work sheet is to list the title of every account with a balance in a company's ledger.[1] The unadjusted debit or credit balances of accounts are taken from the ledger and recorded in the two columns of the unadjusted trial balance. The totals of these two columns must be equal. Exhibit 5.9a shows FastForward's work sheet after completing this first step.

FastForward completed a number of transactions during December 1997. The unadjusted trial balance in Exhibit 5.9a reflects the account balances after the December transactions are recorded but *before any adjusting entries are journalized or posted.* Sometimes blank lines are left on the work sheet based on past experience where more than one line is needed to enter adjustments for certain accounts. Exhibit 5.9a shows Consulting Revenue as an example. An alternative is to squeeze adjustments on one line or to combine the effects of two or more adjustments in one amount.

② Step 2. Enter Adjustment

Turn to the first transparency, Exhibit 5.9b. The next step in preparing a work sheet is to enter adjustments in the columns labelled Adjustments, as shown in Exhibit 5.9b. The adjustments shown are the same ones we discussed in Chapter 4. Notice that an identifying letter relates the debit and credit of each adjustment. This is called "keying" the adjustments. After preparing a work sheet, we still must enter adjusting entries in the journal and post them to the ledger. The identifying letters help match correctly the debit and credit of each adjusting entry. Exhibit 5.9b shows six adjustments for FastForward that we explained in Chapter 4:

a. Expiration of $100 of prepaid insurance.
b. Used $1,050 of supplies.
c. Amortization on equipment of $375.
d. Earned $250 of previously unearned revenue.
e. Accrued $210 of salaries owed to an employee.
f. Accrued $1,800 of revenue owed by a customer.

In entering adjustments, we sometimes find additional accounts that need to be inserted on the work sheet. The additional accounts can be inserted below the initial list.

③ Step 3. Prepare Adjusted Trial Balance

Turn to the second transparency, Exhibit 5.9c. The adjusted trial balance is prepared by combining the adjustments with the unadjusted balances for each account. As an example, in Exhibit 5.9c, the Prepaid Insurance account has a $2,400 debit balance in the Unadjusted Trial Balance columns. This $2,400 debit is combined with the $100 credit in the Adjustments columns to give Prepaid Insurance a $2,300 debit in the Adjusted Trial Balance columns. The totals of the Adjusted Trial Balance columns confirm the equality of debits and credits.

④ Step 4. Sort Adjusted Trial Balance Amounts to Financial Statements

Turn to the third transparency, Exhibit 5.9d. This step involves sorting adjusted amounts to their proper financial statement columns. Expense items go to the Income Statement Debit column and revenues to the Income Statement Credit column. Assets and withdrawals go to the Balance Sheet or Statement of Changes in Owner's Equity Debit column. Liabilities and owner's capital go to the Balance Sheet or Statement of Changes in Owner's Equity Credit column.

---

[1] In practice, accounts with a zero balance which are likely to require an adjusting entry would also be listed.

⑤ **Step 5. Total Statement Columns, Compute Income or Loss, and Balance Columns**

Turn to the fourth transparency, Exhibit 5.9e. Each statement column is totalled. The difference between totals of the Income Statement columns is net income or net loss. This is because revenues are entered in the Credit column and expenses in the Debit column. If the Credit total exceeds the Debit total, there is net income. If the Debit total exceeds the Credit total, there is a net loss. FastForward's work sheet shows the Credit total exceeds the Debit total, giving a $1,785 net income.

The net income in the Income Statement columns is added to the Balance Sheet or Statement of Changes in Owner's Equity Credit column. This is done because the last two columns include balance sheet accounts, but the amount shown for capital is not the ending capital. By adding net income to the last Credit column this implies it is to be added to owner's capital. If a loss occurs, it is added to the last Debit column. This implies it is to be subtracted from owner's capital. While the ending balance of owner's capital does not appear in the last two columns as a single amount, it is computed as the owner's capital account balance plus net income (or minus net loss) minus the withdrawals account balance.

When net income or net loss is added to the proper Balance Sheet or Statement of Changes in Owner's Equity column, the totals of the last two columns must balance. If they do not balance, one or more errors were made. The error or errors can be mathematical or involve error in sorting one or more amounts to columns. A balance in the last two columns is not proof of no errors. These columns can balance when certain types of errors exist. For example, if an asset amount is incorrectly carried into the Income Statement Debit column, the columns still balance. Also, if a liability amount is carried into the Income Statement Credit column, the columns still balance. Either error causes net income to be incorrect. But the columns still balance.

Entering adjustments in the Adjustments columns of a work sheet does not adjust the ledger accounts. Adjusting entries still must be entered in the General Journal and posted to ledger accounts. The work sheet helps because its Adjustments columns provide the information for these entries. Adjusting entries in Exhibit 5.9b are the same adjusting entries we described in Chapter 4 (page 167). In addition, all items in the Income Statement columns must be closed to Income Summary. The net income or net loss shown on the work sheet must be closed to owner's capital. The withdrawals account in the last Debit column also must be closed to owner's capital.

Auditor

You are auditing the financial statements of a food service client. This client owns and operates her own restaurant. You ask and receive a printout of her electronic work sheet used to prepare financial statements. There is no amortization adjustment, yet this client owns a large amount of food service equipment. Does the lack of an amortization adjustment concern you?

You Make the Call

Answer—p. 227

Work Sheet Application and Analysis

A work sheet does not substitute for financial statements. The work sheet is a tool we use at the end of an accounting period to help organize and manage data. Once we are satisfied that all the appropriate adjustments have been made, we use the information in the work sheet to prepare the financial statements. The financial statements of FastForward are shown in Exhibit 5.10. FastForward's statement of cash flows is discussed in the next section and is prepared from the Cash account and supporting documents. While we can prepare all the statements at this point, we must remember that adjusting entries must be journalized and posted before moving to the closing process.

Exhibit 5.10

Financial Statement from the
Work Sheet

FASTFORWARD Income Statement For Month Ended December 31, 1997		
Revenues:		
Consulting Revenue	$ 5,850	
Rental revenue	300	
Total revenues		$ 6,150
Expenses		
Amortization expense—Equipment:	$ 375	
Salaries expense	1,610	
Insurance expense	100	
Rent expense	1,000	
Supplies expense	1,050	
Utilities expense	230	
Total expenses		4,365
Net income		$ 1,785

FASTFORWARD Statement of Changes in Owner's Equity For Month Ended December 31, 1997		
C. Taylor, capital, December 1, 1997		$ -0-
Add: Investment by owner	$30,000	
Net income	1,785	31,785
Total		$31,785
Less: Withdrawal by owner		600
C. Taylor, capital, December 31, 1997		$31,185

FASTFORWARD Balance Sheet December 31, 1997		
Assets		
Cash		$ 7,950
Accounts receivable		1,800
Supplies		2,670
Prepaid insurance		2,300
Equipment	$26,000	
Accumulated amortization—Equipment	(375)	25,625
Total assets		$40,345
Liabilities		
Accounts payable		$ 1,100
Salaries payable		210
Unearned consulting revenue		2,750
Note payable		5,100
Total liabilities		$ 9,160
Owner's Equity		
Chuck Taylor, capital		31,185
Total liabilities and owner's equity		$40,345

Work sheets are also useful in analyzing the effects of proposed or what-if transactions. This is done by entering their adjusted financial statement amounts in the first two columns, arranging them in the form of financial statements. Proposed transactions are entered in the second two columns. Extended amounts in the last columns show the effects of these proposed transactions on financial statements. These final columns are called **pro forma statements** because they show the statements *as if* the proposed transactions occurred.

Flashback

4. Where do we get the amounts entered in the Unadjusted Trial Balance columns of a work sheet?

5. What are advantages of using a work sheet to prepare adjusting entries?

Answers—p. 227

Statement of Cash Flows

All of FastForward's cash receipts and cash payments are recorded in its Cash account in the Ledger. This Cash account holds information about cash flows from operating, investing, and financing activities. To see this, we show the Cash account for FastForward in Exhibit 5.11.

Exhibit 5.11

Cash Account of FastForward

Cash			
Investment by owner (1)	30,000	Purchase of supplies (2)	2,500
Consulting services revenue earned (5).	2,200	Purchase of equipment (3)......	20,000
		Payment of rent (6)	1,000
Collection of account receivable (9)	1,900	Payment of salary (7)	700
		Payment of note payable (10) ...	900
Receipts for future services (12)..	3,000	Withdrawal by owner (11)	600
		Payment of insurance (13)......	2,400
		Purchase of supplies (14)	120
		Payment of utilities (15)........	230
		Payment of salary (16).........	700
Total increases	37,100	Total decreases	29,150
Less decreases.	−29,150		
Balance	7,950		

The Cash account reports individual cash transactions by types of receipts and payments. Adjustments never affect the Cash account; they are not cash-related activities. To prepare the statement of cash flows we must determine whether a cash inflow or outflow is an operating, investing, or financing activity. We then report amounts in their proper category on the statement of cash flows. FastForward's statement of cash flows is shown in Exhibit 5.12.

Our analysis of the Cash account provided us a direct means to prepare the statement of cash flows. Yet there are two limitations with this method. First, companies often have so many individual cash receipts and disbursements that it is not practical to review them all. Second, the Cash account often does not contain a description of each cash transaction. Later in this book we show how we can prepare the statement of cash flows when facing these limitations.

Exhibit 5.12

Statement of Cash Flows

FastForward Statement of Cash Flows For Month Ended December 31, 1997		
Cash flows from operating activities:		
Cash received from clients	$ 7,100	
Cash paid for supplies	(2,620)	
Cash paid for rent	(1,000)	
Cash paid for insurance	(2,400)	
Cash paid for utilities	(230)	
Cash paid to employee	(1,400)	
Net cash used by operating activities		$ (550)
Cash flows from investing activities:		
Purchase of equipment	$(20,000)	
Net cash used by investing activities		(20,000)
Cash flows from financing activities:		
Investment by owner	$ 30,000	
Partial repayment of note payable	(900)	
Withdrawal by owner	(600)	
Net cash provided by financing activities		28,500
Net increase in cash		$ 7,950
Cash balance, December 1, 1997		-0-
Cash balance, December 31, 1997		$ 7,950

Reviewing the Accounting Cycle

 Identify steps in the accounting cycle.

The **accounting cycle** refers to the steps in preparing financial statements for users. It is called a cycle because the steps are repeated each reporting period. Exhibit 5.13 lists the 10 steps in the cycle. They are shown in order, beginning with analyzing transactions and ending with a post-closing trial balance or reversing entries. Steps 1 through 3 usually occur often as a company conducts transactions. Steps 4 through 9 are done at the end of the period. Reversing entries in step 10 are optional and are explained in the appendix to this chapter. Detailed descriptions for all of these steps are in Chapters 3, 4, and 5.

We briefly review these steps in Exhibit 5.14 to emphasize their importance in providing users information for decision making.

Exhibit 5.13

Steps in the Accounting Cycle

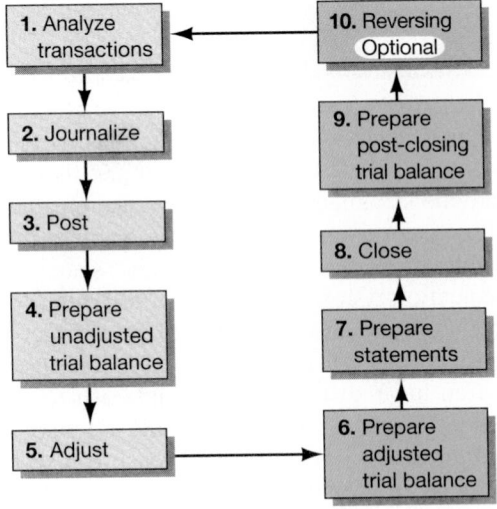

*Steps can be done on a work sheet. A work sheet is especially useful in planning adjustments and in projecting an adjusted trial balance. But adjustments must always be journalized and posted.

1. Analyze transaction	Analyze transactions in preparation for journalizing.
2. Journalize	Record debits and credits with explanations in a journal.
3. Posting	Transfer debits and credits from journal entries to the ledger accounts.
4. Unadjusted trial balance	Summarize ledger accounts and amounts.
5. Adjusting	Record adjustments to bring account balances up to date; journalize and post adjusting entries to the accounts.
6. Adjusted trial balance	Summarize adjusted ledger accounts and amounts.
7. Statement preparation	Use adjusted trial balance to prepare: income statement, statement of changes in owner's equity, balance sheet, and statement of cash flows (details in preparing the statement of cash flows are in Chapter 16).
8. Closing	Journalize and post entries to close temporary (revenue, expense and withdrawals) accounts and update the owner's capital account.
9. Post-closing trial balance	Tests clerical accuracy of adjusting and closing steps.
10. Reversing	Reverse certain adjustments in the next period—optional step, see Appendix 5A.

Exhibit 5.14

Summary of Steps in Accounting Cycle

Flash back

6. What are the benefits of a work sheet?

7. What steps in the accounting cycle are optional?

Answers—p. 227

Use the information from the completed work sheet in Exhibit 5.9 to prepare the closing entries for July 31.

Mid-Chapter Demonstration Problem

Solution to Mid-Chapter Demonstration Problem

Jul 31	Consulting Revenue	5,850	
	Rental revenue	300	
	Income Summary		6,150
	To close the revenue accounts and create the Income Summary account.		
Jul 31	Income Summary	4,365	
	Salaries Expense		1,610
	Rent Expense		1,000
	Utilities Expense		230
	Insurance Expense		100
	Supplies Expense		1,050
	Amortization Expense—Equipment		375
	To close the expense accounts and debit the Income Summary account.		
Jul 31	Income Summary	1,785	
	Chuck Taylor, Capital		1,785
	To close the Income Summary account.		
Jul 31	Chuck Taylor, Capital	600	
	Chuck Taylor, Withdrawals		600
	To close the Withdrawals account.		

Classified Balance Sheet

LO 6 Explain and prepare a classified balance sheet.

Our discussion to this point has been limited to unclassified financial statements. An **unclassified balance sheet** is one where its items are broadly grouped into assets, liabilities and owner's equity. One example is FastForward's balance sheet in Exhibit 5.10. A **classified balance sheet** organizes assets and liabilities into important subgroups. The information in a balance sheet is more useful to users in making decisions if assets and liabilities are classified into subgroups. One example is information to identify liabilities that are due shortly from those not due for several years. Information in this case helps us assess a company's ability to meet liabilities when they come due.

Classification Scheme

There is no required layout for a classified balance sheet. Yet a classified balance sheet often contains common groupings as shown in Exhibit 5.15.

Exhibit 5.15

Sections of a Classified Balance Sheet

Assets	Liabilities and Owner's Equity
Current Assets	Current Liabilities
Long-Term Investments	Long-Term Liabilities
Capital Assets: Plant and Equipment	Owner's Equity
Intangible Assets	

One of the more important classifications is the separation between current and noncurrent items for both assets and liabilities. Current items are those expected to come due (both collected and owed) within the longer of one year or the company's normal operating cycle. An **operating cycle** is the length of time between (1) paying employees who perform services and receiving cash from customers for a service company and (2) paying for merchandise and receiving cash from customers for a company that sells goods.

Exhibit 5.16 shows the steps of an operating cycle for both service and merchandising companies. For a company selling services, the operating cycle is the average time between (1) paying employees who do the services and (2) receiving cash from customers. For a company selling products, the operating cycle is the average time between (1) paying suppliers for merchandise and (2) receiving cash from customers.

Exhibit 5.16

Operating Cycles for a Service Company and a Merchandise Company

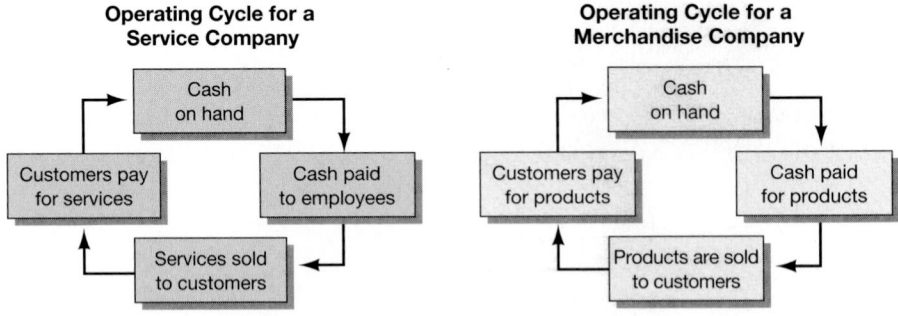

Most operating cycles are less than one year. This means most companies use a one-year period in deciding which assets and liabilities are current. Yet there are companies with an operating cycle longer than one year. One example is companies that routinely allow customers to take more than one year to pay for purchases, such as a land developer. Another example is producers of beverages and other products that require ageing for several years. These companies use their operating cycle in deciding which balance sheet items are current.[2]

---

[2] In these uncommon situations, companies provide supplemental information about their current assets and liabilities to allow users to compare them with other companies.

A balance sheet usually lists current assets before long-term assets, and current liabilities before long-term liabilities. This gives a marked position to assets that are most easily converted to cash, and liabilities that are shortly coming due. Items in the current group are usually listed in the order of how quickly they will be converted to or paid in cash.

Classification Example

The balance sheet for **Music Components** is shown in Exhibit 5.17. It shows the most commonly used groupings. Its assets are classified into (1) current assets, (2) long-term investments, (3) plant and equipment, and (4) intangible assets. Its liabilities are classified as either current or long-term. Not all companies use the same categories of assets and liabilities on their balance sheets. **Compaq's** 1996 balance sheet lists only three asset classes: current assets; property, plant and equipment; and other assets.

Music Components
Balance Sheet
January 31, 1998

Exhibit 5.17

A Classified Balance Sheet

Assets			
Current assets:			
Cash		$ 6,500	
Temporary investments		2,100	
Accounts receivable		4,400	
Notes receivable		1,500	
Merchandise inventory		27,500	
Prepaid expenses		2,400	
Total current assets			$ 44,400
Long-term investments:			
BCE common shares		18,000	
Land held for future expansion		48,000	
Total investments			66,000
Capital assets:			
Plant and equipment:			
Store equipment	$ 33,200		
Less accumulated amortization	8,000	25,200	
Buildings	170,000		
Less accumulated amortization	45,000	125,000	
Land		73,200	
Total plant and equipment			223,400
Intangible assets:			
Trademark			10,000
Total assets			$343,800
Liabilities			
Current liabilities:			
Accounts payable	$ 15,300		
Wages payable	3,200		
Notes payable	3,000		
Current portion of long-term liabilities	7,500		
Total current liabilities		$ 29,000	
Long-term liabilities:			
Notes payable (net of current portion)		150,000	
Total liabilities			$179,000
Owner's Equity			
D. Bowie, capital			164,800
Total liabilities and owner's equity			$343,800

Classification Groups

This section describes the most common groups in a classified balance sheet.

Current Assets

Current assets are cash and other resources that are expected to be sold, collected, or used within the longer of one year or the company's operating cycle.[3] Examples are cash, temporary investments in marketable securities, accounts receivable, notes receivable, goods for sale to customers (called *merchandise* or *inventory*), and prepaid expenses. **Loblaw's** 1996 current assets are reported as shown in Exhibit 5.18.

Exhibit 5.18

Current Assets Section

Loblaw	
Current Assets *(in millions):*	
Cash and short-term investments	$ 883
Accounts receivables	845
Inventories	15,897
Prepaid expenses and other assets	368
Total Current Assets	**$17,993**

A company's prepaid expenses are usually small compared to other assets and are often combined and shown as a single item. It is likely the Prepaid Expenses in Exhibit 5.17 and 5.18 include items such as prepaid insurance, prepaid rent, office supplies and store supplies. Prepaid expenses are usually listed last because they will not be converted to cash but will be consumed as an expense.

Long-Term Investments

A second balance sheet classification is **long-term investments.** Notes receivable and investments in shares and bonds are in many cases long-term assets. This is because they are held for more than one year or the operating cycle. Note the *temporary* investments in Exhibit 5.17 are current assets and not shown as long-term investments. We explain the differences between temporary and long-term investments later in this book. Long-term investments also often include land that is not being used in operations but is being held for future expansion.

Capital Assets

Plant and equipment

Plant and equipment, also called *plant assets,* are tangible long-lived assets used to produce or sell products and services. Examples are equipment, vehicles, buildings, and land. It is important that items in this group are both *long-lived* and *used to produce or sell products and services.* Land held for future expansion is *not* a plant and equipment asset because it is not used to produce or sell products and services. Plant and equipment assets are also called "*property, plant and equipment*" or "*land, buildings and equipment.*" The order of listing plant assets within this category varies.

Intangible assets

Intangible assets are long-term resources used to produce or sell products and services: they lack physical form. Examples are patents, trademarks, copyrights, franchises, and goodwill. Their value comes from the privileges or rights granted to or held by the owner. **McGraw-Hill Ryerson Limited** includes intangible assets for 1996 as shown in Exhibit 5.19.

Exhibit 5.19

Intangible Assets Section

McGraw-Hill Ryerson	
Intangible assets, net (in thousands)	$4,028

McGraw-Hill's's intangibles include prepublication costs, contracts, copyrights, trademarks and goodwill.

---

[3] *CICA Handbook,* "Current Assets and Current Liabilities," par. 1510.01.

Current Liabilities

Current liabilities are obligations due to be paid or settled within the longer of one year or the operating cycle. They are usually settled by paying out current assets. Current liabilities include accounts payable, notes payable, wages payable, taxes payable, interest payable, and unearned revenues. Any portion of a long-term liability due to be paid within the longer of one year or the operating cycle is a current liability. Exhibit 5.17 shows how the current portion of long-term liabilities is usually reported. Unearned revenues are current liabilities when they will be settled by delivering products or services within the longer of the year or the operating cycle. While practice varies, current liabilities are often reported in the order of those to be settled first.

Long-Term Liabilities

Long-term liabilities are obligations not due within the longer of one year or the operating cycle. Notes payable, mortgages payable, bonds payable, and lease obligations are often long-term liabilities. If a company has both short- and long-term items in one of these accounts, it is common to separate them in the ledger for reporting.

Owner's Equity

Owner's equity is the owner's claim on the assets of a company. It is reported in the equity section with an owner's capital account for a proprietorship. For a partnership the equity section reports a capital account for each partner. For a corporation the equity section is called Shareholders' Equity and is divided into two main subsections: Share Capital and Retained Earnings. Chapter 1 described these alternative organization forms in more detail.

⭐ Flashback

8. Identify which of the following assets are classified as (1) current assets or (2) capital assets: (a) land used in operations, (b) office supplies, (c) receivables from customers due in 10 months, (d) insurance protection for the next nine months, (e) trucks used to provide services to customers, (f) trademarks used in advertising the company's services.

9. Name two examples of assets classified as long-term investments on the balance sheet.

10. Explain an operating cycle for a service company.

Answers—p. 228

Current Ratio

An important use of a financial statement for decision makers is in helping them assess a company's ability to pay its debts in the near future. This analysis affects decisions by suppliers in allowing a company to buy on credit. It affects decisions by creditors about lending money to a company. It can also affect creditors' decision about loan terms, including the interest rate, due date, and any requirements for collateral for the loan. An assessment of the ability to pay debts can also affect an internal manager's decisions about using cash to pay existing debts when they come due.

LO7 Compute the current ratio and describe what it reveals about a company's financial condition.

The **current ratio** is one important measure used to evaluate a company's ability to pay its short-term obligations. It is computed by dividing current assets by current liabilities (see Exhibit 5.20):

Exhibit 5.20

Current Ratio

$$\text{Current ratio} = \frac{\text{Current assets}}{\text{Current liabilities}}$$

Using financial information for **Canadian Tire**, we compute its current ratios for 1993–1996. The results are shown in Exhibit 5.21.

Exhibit 5.21

Canadian Tire's Current Ratios

Canadian Tire (in millions)				
December 31	1996	1995	1994	1993
Total current assets	$1,339	$1,559	$1,655	$1,388
Total current liabilities	864	911	1,044	692
Current ratio.	1.55	1.71	1.59	2.01
Industry current ratio	1.75	1.70	1.65	1.70

Canadian Tire's current ratio dipped to 1.55 in 1996 compared to the prior three years. The current ratio for all of these years suggest that Canadian Tire's short-term obligations can be covered with short-term assets on hand. If the ratio moved closer to 1, Canadian Tire could expect to face more problems in covering liabilities. We often look to a company's sales to see if there is sufficient cash inflow to cover liabilities. If the ratio is less than 1, it means that Canadian Tire's current liabilities exceed its current assets. Canadian Tire would likely face serious problems in covering current liabilities with current assets when its ratio is under 1.

You Make the Call

Analyst
You are analyzing the financial condition of a sports and fitness club. Your main goal is to assess the club's ability to meet upcoming loan payments in the next period. You compute its current ratio and it is 1.2. You also find a major portion of Accounts Receivable is due from one client who has not made any payments in the past 12 months. Removing this accounts receivable from current assets drops the current ratio to 0.7. What do you conclude?

Answer—p. 227

Flashback

11. If a company misclassifies a portion of liabilities as long-term when they are short-term, how does this affect its current ratio?

Answers—p. 228

Summary

LO 1 Explain why temporary accounts are closed each period. Temporary accounts are closed at the end of each accounting period for two main reasons. First, the closing process updates the owner's capital account to include the effects of all transactions and events recorded for the period. Second, it prepares revenue, expense, and withdrawals accounts for the next reporting period by giving them zero balances.

LO 2 Describe and prepare closing entries. Recording and posting closing entries transfer the end-of-period balances in revenue, expense and withdrawals accounts to the owner's capital account. Closing entries involve four steps: (1) close credit balances in revenue accounts to income summary, (2) close debit balances in expense accounts to income summary, (3) close income summary to owner's capital, and (4) close withdrawals account to owner's capital.

LO 3 Explain and prepare a post-closing trial balance. A post-closing trial balance is a list of permanent accounts and their balances after all closing entries are journalized and posted. Permanent accounts are asset, liability and owner's equity accounts. The purpose of a post-closing trial balance is to verify that (1) total debits equal total credits for permanent accounts and (2) all temporary accounts have zero balances.

LO 4 Prepare a work sheet and explain its usefulness. A work sheet can be a useful tool in preparing and analyzing financial statements. It is helpful at the end of a period in preparing adjusting entries, an adjusted trial balance, and financial statements. A work sheet often contains five pairs of columns for an unadjusted trial balance, the adjustments, an adjusted trial balance, an income statement, and the balance sheet (including the statement of changes in owner's equity).

LO 5 Identify steps in the accounting cycle. The accounting cycle consists of ten steps: (1) analyze transactions, (2) journalize, (3) posting, (4) an unadjusted trial balance, (5) adjusting, (6) an adjusted trial balance, (7) statement preparation, (8) closing, (9) a post-closing trial balance, and (10) optional reversing entries. If a work sheet is prepared, it covers steps 4-6.

LO 6 Explain and prepare a classified balance sheet. Classified balance sheets usually report four groups of assets: current assets, long-term investments, plant and equipment, and intangible assets. Also, they include at least two groups of liabilities: current and long-term. Owner's equity for proprietorships and partners' equity for partnerships both report the capital account balances. A corporation reports shareholders' equity into contributed capital and retained earnings.

LO 7 Compute the current ratio and describe what it reveals about a company's financial condition. A company's current ratio is defined as current assets divided by current liabilities. We use it to evaluate a company's ability to pay its current liabilities out of current assets.

Guidance Answers to **You Make the Call**

Auditor

You are concerned about the absence of an amortization adjustment. Equipment does depreciate, and financial statements recognize this occurrence. Its absence suggests an error or a misrepresentation. You must follow up and require management to adjust the statements for amortization. Also, if fraud is suggested, then you must substantially expand audit tests, obtain legal advice, and prepare to withdraw from the audit engagement.

Analyst

A current ratio of 1.2 suggests sufficient current assets to cover upcoming current liabilities. But a ratio of 1.2 does not give you much buffer in case of error in measuring current assets or current liabilities. Removing tardy receivables further reduces the current ratio to 0.7. This suggests current assets cannot cover current liabilities. Your assessment is that the sports and fitness club is unlikely to meet upcoming loan payments.

Guidance Answers to Flash backs

1. The four major closing entries consist of closing: (1) credit balances in revenue accounts to Income Summary, (2) debit balances in expense accounts to Income Summary, (3) Income Summary to owner's capital, and (4) withdrawals account to owner's capital.
2. Revenue and expense accounts are called temporary because they are opened and closed every reporting period. The Income Summary and owner's withdrawals accounts are also temporary accounts.
3. Permanent accounts are listed on the post-closing trial balance. These accounts are the asset, liability and owner's equity accounts.
4. Amounts in the Unadjusted Trial Balance columns are taken from account balances in the ledger.
5. A work sheet offers the advantage of listing on one page all of the necessary information to record adjusting entries.
6. A work sheet can help in: (a) avoiding errors, (b) linking transaction and events to their effects in financial

statements, (c) showing adjustments for audit purposes, (d) preparing interim financial statements, and (e) showing effects from proposed or "what-if" transactions.

7. Reversing entries is an optional step in the accounting cycle. Also, a worksheet is an optional tool in completing steps 4-6.
8. Current assets: *b, c, d.* Capital assets: *a, e, f.*
9. Investment in common stock, investment in bonds, land held for future expansion.
10. An operating cycle for a company is the length of time between (1) purchases of services and products from sup-

pliers to carry out a company's plans and (2) the sale of services and products to customers. The length of a company's operating cycle depends on its activities. For a service company, the operating cycle is the average time between (1) paying employees who do the services and (2) receiving cash from customers.

11. Since the current ratio is defined as current assets divided by current liabilities, then ignoring a portion of current liabilities (1) decreases the reported amount of current liabilities and (2) increases the current ratio because current assets are now divided by a smaller number.

Demonstration Problem

This partial worksheet shows the December 31, 19X1, adjusted trial balance of Westside Appliance Repair Company:

	Adjusted Trial Balance		Income Statement		Statement of Owner's Equity and Balance Sheet	
Cash.	$ 83,300					
Notes receivable.	60,000					
Prepaid insurance.	19,000					
Prepaid rent	5,000					
Equipment	165,000					
Accumulated amortization, equipment		$52,000				
Accounts payable.		37,000				
Long-term notes payable		58,000				
B. Westside, capital		173,500				
B. Westside, withdrawals	25,000					
Repair services revenue		294,000				
Interest earned.		6,500				
Amortization expense, equipment	26,000					
Wages expense	179,000					
Rent expense.	47,000					
Insurance expense	7,000					
Interest expense.	4,700					
Totals	$621,000	$621,000				

Required

1. Complete the work sheet by extending the adjusted trial balance totals to the appropriate financial statement columns.
2. Prepare closing entries for Westside Appliance Repair Co.
3. Set up Income Summary and B. Westside, capital accounts and post the closing entries to these accounts.
4. Determine the balance of the B. Westside, capital account to be reported on the December 31, 19X1, balance sheet.

Planning the Solution

■ Extend the adjusted trial balance account balances to the appropriate financial statement columns.

■ Prepare entries to close the revenue accounts to Income Summary, to close the expense accounts to Income Summary, to close Income Summary to the capital account, and to close the withdrawals account to the capital account.

■ Post the first and second closing entries to the Income Summary account. Examine the balance of income summary and verify that it agrees with the net income shown on the worksheet.

■ Post the third and fourth closing entries to the capital account.

Solution to Demonstration Problem

1. Completing the worksheet:

	Adjusted Trial Balance		Income Statement		Balance Sheet and Statement of Changes in Owner's Equity	
Cash	83,300				83,300	
Notes receivable.	60,000				60,000	
Prepaid insurance.	19,000				19,000	
Prepaid rent	5,000				5,000	
Equipment	165,000				165,000	
Accumulated amortization, equipment		$52,000				52,000
Accounts payable.		37,000				37,000
Long-term notes payable		58,000				58,000
B. Westside, capital		173,500				173,500
B. Westside, withdrawals	25,000				25,000	
Repair services revenue		294,000		294,000		
Interest earned		6,500		6,500		
Amortization expense, equipment	26,000		26,000			
Wages expense	179,000		179,000			
Rent expense.	47,000		47,000			
Insurance expense	7,000		7,000			
Interest expense.	4,700		4,700			
Totals	621,000	621,000	263,700	300,500	357,300	320,500
Net Income			36,800			36,800
Totals			300,500	300,500	357,300	357,300

2. Closing Entries:

Dec. 31	Repair Services Revenue.	294,000	
	Interest Earned.	6,500	
	Income Summary		300,500
	To close the revenue accounts and credit the Income Summary account.		
31	Income Summary.	263,700	
	Amortization Expense, Equipment.		26,000
	Wages Expense.		179,000
	Rent Expense		47,000
	Insurance Expense		7,000
	Interest Expense.		4,700
	To close the expense accounts and debit the Income Summary account.		
31	Income Summary.	36,800	
	B. Westside, Capital		36,800
	To close the Income Summary account.		
31	B. Westside, Capital	25,000	
	B. Westside, Withdrawals.		25,000
	To close the withdrawals account.		

3.

Income Summary					Account No. 999
Date	**Explanation**	**PR**	**Debit**	**Credit**	**Balance**
19X1					
Jan. 1	Beginning balance				-0-
Dec. 31	Close Revenue Accounts			300,500	300,500
31	Close Expense Accounts		263,700		36,800
31	Close Income Summary		36,800		-0-

B. Westside, Capital					Account No. 301
Date	**Explanation**	**PR**	**Debit**	**Credit**	**Balance**
19X1					
Jan. 1	Beginning balance				173,500
Dec. 31	Close Income Summary			36,800	210,300
31	Close B. Westside, withdrawals		25,000		285,300

4. The final capital balance of $285,300 will be reported on the December 31, 19X1 balance sheet. Note that the final capital balance reflects the increase due to the net income earned during the year and the decrease for the owner's withdrawals during the year.

Reversing Entries and Account Numbering

Learning Objective

LO 8 Prepare reversing entries and explain their purpose.

This appendix describes both reversing entries and the account numbering system applied in companies.

Reversing Entries

Reversing entries are optional entries. They are linked to accrued assets and liabilities that were created by adjusting entries at the end of a reporting period. Reversing entries are used to simplify a company's recordkeeping.

Exhibit 5A.1 shows how reversing entries work for **FastForward.** The top of the exhibit shows the adjusting entry FastForward recorded on December 31, 1997, for the employee's earned but unpaid salary. The entry recorded three days' salary to increase December's total salary expense to $1,610. The entry also recognized a liability of $210. The expense is reported on December's income statement and the expense account is closed. As a result, the ledger on January 1, 1998, reflects a $210 liability and a zero balance in the Salaries Expense account. At this point, the choice is made between using or not using reversing entries.

Accounting without Reversing Entries

The path down the left side of Exhibit 5A.1 is described in Chapter 4. That is, when the next payday occurs on January 9, we record payment with a compound entry that debits both the expense and liability accounts. Posting that entry creates a $490 balance in the expense account and reduces the liability account balance to zero because the debt has been settled.

The disadvantage of this approach is the complex compound journal entry required on January 9. Paying the accrued liability means this entry differs from the routine entries made on all other paydays. To construct the proper entry on January 9, we must recall the effect of the adjusting entry. Reversing entries overcome this disadvantage.

Accounting with Reversing Entries

The right side of Exhibit 5A.1 shows how a reversing entry on January 1 overcomes the disadvantage of the complex January 9 entry. The reversing entry is the exact opposite of the adjusting entry recorded on December 31. The Salaries Payable lia-

Exhibit 5A.1

Reversing Entries for
Accrued Expenses

Accrue salaries expense on December 31, 1997

Salaries Expense 210
  Salaries Payable 210

Salaries Expense

Date	Expl.	Debit	Credit	Balance
1997				
Dec. 12	(7)	700		700
26	(16)	700		1,400
31	(e)	210		1,610

Salaries Payable

Date	Expl.	Debit	Credit	Balance
1997				
Dec. 31	(e)		210	210

*No reversing entry recorded on
January 1, 1998*

NO ENTRY

Salaries Expense

Date	Expl.	Debit	Credit	Balance
1998				

Salaries Payable

Date	Expl.	Debit	Credit	Balance
1997				
Dec. 31	(e)		210	210
1998				

*Reversing entry recorded on
January 1, 1998*

Salaries Payable 210
  Salaries Expense 210

Salaries Expense

Date	Expl.	Debit	Credit	Balance
1998				
Jan. 1			210	(210)

Salaries Payable

Date	Expl.	Debit	Credit	Balance
1997				
Dec. 31	(e)		210	210
1998				
Jan. 1		210		-0-

Pay the accrued and current salaries on January 9, the first payday in 1998.

Salaries Expense 490
Salaries Payable 210
  Cash 700

Salaries Expense

Date	Expl.	Debit	Credit	Balance
1998				
Jan. 9		490		490

Salaries Payable

Date	Expl.	Debit	Credit	Balance
1997				
Dec. 31	(e)		210	210
1998				
Jan. 9		210		-0-

Salaries Expense 700
  Cash 700

Salaries Expense

Date	Expl.	Debit	Credit	Balance
1998				
Jan. 1			210	(210)
Jan. 9		700		490

Salaries Payable

Date	Expl.	Debit	Credit	Balance
1997				
Dec. 31	(e)		210	210
1998				
Jan. 1		210		-0-

Under both approaches, the expense and liability accounts have
the same balances after the subsequent payment on January 9:

Salaries Expense _____ $490
Salaries Payable _____ $ 0

bility is debited for $210, meaning that this account now has a zero balance after the entry is posted. Technically, the Salaries Payable account now understates the liability, but this in not a problem since financial statements are not prepared before the liability is settled on January 9. The credit to the Salaries Expense account is unusual because it gives the account an *abnormal credit balance.*

Because of the reversing entry, the January 9 entry to record payment is simple. This entry debits the Salaries Expense account for the full $700 paid. It is the same as all other entries made to record 10 days' salary for the employee.

We should also look at the accounts on the lower right side of Exhibit 5A.1. After the payment entry is posted, Salaries Expense account has a $490 balance that reflects seven days' salary of $70 per day. The zero balance in the Salaries Payable account is now correct. The lower section of the exhibit shows that the

Answer—p. 234

Flashback

12. How are financial statements affected by a decision to make reversing entries?

expense and liability accounts have exactly the same balances whether reversing occurs or not.

As a general rule, adjusting entries that create new asset or new liability accounts are likely candidates for reversing.

Account Numbering System

We described a three-digit account numbering system in Chapter 3. In such a system, the code number assigned to an account both identifies the account and gives information about the account's financial statement category.

In this section we describe a more detailed system, although we see many different systems in practice. The first digit in an account's number identifies its primary balance sheet or income statement category. For example, account numbers beginning with a 1 are assigned to asset accounts and account numbers beginning with a 2 are assigned to liability accounts. Exhibit 5A.2 shows how numbers could be assigned to the accounts of a company that buys and sells merchandise:

101 – 199	Asset accounts
201 – 299	Liability accounts
301 – 399	Owner's equity (including withdrawals)
401 – 499	Sales or revenue accounts
501 – 599	Cost of goods sold accounts (These are discussed in Chapter 6.)
601 – 699	Operating expense accounts
701 – 799	Accounts that reflect unusual and/or infrequent gains
801 – 899	Accounts that reflect unusual and/or infrequent losses

Exhibit 5A.2

Account Numbering for a Merchandiser

The second digit of each account number identifies its classification within the primary category, as shown by Exhibit 5A.3.

101 – 199	**Assets**
101 – 139	Current assets (second digit is 0, 1, 2, or 3)
141 – 149	Long-term investments (second digit is 4)
151 – 179	Plant assets (second digit is 5, 6, or 7)
181 – 189	Natural resources (second digit is 8)
191 – 199	Intangible assets (second digit is 9)
201 – 299	**Liabilities**
201 – 249	Current liabilities (second digit is 0, 1, 2, 3, or 4)
251 – 299	Long-term liabilities (second digit is 5, 6, 7, 8, or 9)

Exhibit 5A.3

Second Digit Account Numbering

The third digit completes the unique code for each account. For example, specific current asset accounts might be assigned the numbers shown in Exhibit 5A.4.

An extensive list of accounts using this code is provided in an appendix to this book.

A three-digit account numbering system is often adequate for smaller businesses. A numbering system for more complex businesses might use four, five, or even more digits.

101 – 199	**Assets**
101 – 139	Current assets
101	Cash
106	Accounts Receivable
110	Rent Receivable
128	Prepaid Insurance

Exhibit 5A.4

Three Digit Account Numbering

Summary of Appendix 5A

LO 8 **Prepare reversing entries and explain their purpose.** Reversing entries are an optional step. They are applied to accrued assets and liabilities. The purpose of reversing entries is to simplify subsequent journal entries. Financial statements are unaffected by the choice to use or not use reversing entries.

Guidance Answer to Flashbacks

12. Financial statements are unchanged by the choice between using or not using reversing entries.

Glossary

Accounting cycle Recurring steps performed each accounting period, starting with recording transactions in the journal and continuing through the post-closing trial balance. (p. 220)

Classified balance sheet A balance sheet that presents the assets and liabilities in relevant subgroups. (p. 222)

Closing entries Journal entries recorded at the end of each accounting period that transfer the end-of-period balances in revenue, expense, and withdrawals accounts to the permanent owner's capital account in order to prepare for the upcoming period and update the owner's capital account for the events of the period just finished. (p. 206)

Closing process A step at the end of the accounting period that prepares accounts for recording the transactions of the next period. (p. 206)

Current assets Cash or other assets that are expected to be sold, collected, or used within the longer of one year or the company's operating cycle. (p. 224)

Current liabilities Obligations due to be paid or settled within the longer of one year or the operating cycle. (p. 225)

Current ratio A ratio that is used to evaluate a company's ability to pay its short-term obligations, calculated by dividing current assets by current liabilities. (p. 226)

Income Summary A temporary account used only in the closing process to where the balances of revenue and expense accounts are transferred; its balance equals net income or net loss and is transferred to the owner's capital account or the Retained Earnings account for a corporation. (p. 207)

Intangible assets Long-term assets (resources) used to produce or sell products or services; these assets lack physical form. (p. 224)

Long-term investments Assets such as notes receivable or investments in stocks and bonds which are held for more than one year or the operating cycle. (p. 224)

Long-term liabilities Obligations that are not due to be paid within the longer of one year or the operating cycle. (p. 225)

Nominal accounts Another name for *temporary accounts.* (p. 206)

Operating cycle of a business The average time between paying cash for employee salaries or merchandise and receiving cash from customers. (p. 222)

Owner's equity The owner's claim on the assets of a company. (p. 225)

Permanent accounts Accounts that are used to report on activities related to one or more future accounting periods; their balances are carried into the next period and include all balance sheet accounts; real account balances are not closed as long as the company continues to own the assets, owe the liabilities, and have owner's equity; also called *real accounts.* (p. 206)

Plant and equipment Tangible long-lived assets used to produce or sell products and services; also called *plant assets.* (p. 224)

Post-closing trial balance A list of permanent accounts and their balances from the ledger after all closing entries are journalized and posted; a list of balances for all accounts not closed. (p. 211)

Pro forma statements Statements that show the effects of the proposed transactions as if the transactions had already occurred. (p. 219)

Real accounts Another name for *permanent accounts.* (p. 206)

Reversing entries Optional entries recorded at the beginning of a new year that prepare the accounts for simplified journal entries subsequent to accrual adjusting entries. (p. 231)

Temporary accounts Accounts that are used to describe revenues, expenses, and owner's withdrawals for one accounting period; they are closed at the end of the reporting period; also called *nominal accounts.* (p. 206)

Unclassified balance sheet A balance sheet that broadly groups the assets, liabilities, and owner's equity. (p. 222)

Work sheet A 10-column spreadsheet used to draft a company's unadjusted trial balance, adjusting entries, adjusted trial balance, and financial statements; an optional step in the accounting process. (p. 214)

Working papers Internal documents that are used to assist the preparers in doing the analyses and organizing the information for reports to be presented to internal and external decision makers. (p. 214)

A superscipt letter^A identifies assignment material based on Appendix 5A.

Questions

1. What two purposes are accomplished by recording closing entries?
2. What are the four closing entries?
3. What accounts are affected by closing entries? What accounts are not affected?
4. Describe the similarities and differences between adjusting and closing entries.
5. What is the purpose of the Income Summary account?
6. Explain whether an error has occurred if a post-closing trial balance includes an Amortization Expense, Building account.
7. How is an unearned revenue classified on the balance sheet?
8. What classes of assets and liabilities are shown on a typical classified balance sheet?
9. What is a company's operating cycle?
10. What are the characteristics of plant and equipment?
11^A. What tasks are performed with the work sheet?
12^A. Why are the debit and credit entries in the Adjustments columns of the work sheet identified with letters?

13^A. How do reversing entries simplify a company's bookkeeping efforts?
14^A. If a company accrued unpaid salaries expense of $500 at the end of a fiscal year, what reversing entry could be made? When would it be made?
15. Refer to the **Alliance** Consolidated Statements of Earnings and Retained Earnings in Appendix I at the end of the book. What journal entry was recorded as of March 31, 1997, to close the Interest account?
16. Refer to the December 31, 1997, consolidated balance sheet for **Atlantis Communications** in Appendix I at the end of the book. What percent of Atlantis' long-term debt is coming due before December 31, 1998?

17. What are three reasons why a company might wish to outsource services previously performed by a business in-house? Identify five common services that businesses may outsource.

Jontil Co. began the current period with a $14,000 balance in the Peter Jontil, Capital account. At the end of the period, the company's adjusted account balances include the following temporary accounts with normal balances:

Service fees earned	$35,000
Salaries expense	19,000
Amortization expense	4,000
Interest earned	3,500
Peter Jontil, withdrawals	6,000
Utilities expense	2,300

After closing the revenue and expense accounts, what will be the balance of the Income Summary account?

After all of the closing entries are journalized and posted, what will be the balance of the Peter Jontil, Capital account?

Quick Study

QS 5-1
Effects of closing entries

LO 1

List the following steps of the accounting cycle in the proper order:

a. Preparing the unadjusted trial balance.
b. Preparing the post-closing trial balance.
c. Journalizing and posting adjusting entries.
d. Journalizing and posting closing entries.
e. Preparing the financial statements.
f. Journalizing transactions.
g. Posting the transaction entries.
h. Completing the work sheet.

QS 5-2
Explaining the accounting cycle

LO 5

QS 5-3

Classifying balance sheet items

 LO 6

The following are categories on a classified balance sheet:

A. Current assets

B. Investments

C. Property, plant, and equipment

D. Intangible assets

E. Current liabilities

F. Long-term liabilities

For each of the following items, select the letter that identifies the balance sheet category in which the item should appear.

_____ **1.** Store equipment

_____ **2.** Wages payable

_____ **3.** Cash

_____ **4.** Notes payable (due in three years)

_____ **5.** Land not currently used in business operations

_____ **6.** Accounts receivable

_____ **7.** Trademarks

QS 5-4

Computing current ratio

LO 7

Calculate Tucker Company's current ratio, given the following information about its assets and liabilities:

Accounts receivable	$15,000
Accounts payable	10,000
Buildings	42,000
Cash	6,000
Long-term notes payable . . .	20,000
Office supplies	1,800
Prepaid insurance	2,500
Unearned services revenue . .	4,000

QS 5-5

Applying a work sheet

LO 4

In preparing a work sheet, indicate the financial statement debit column to which a normal balance of each of the following accounts should be extended. Use IS for the Income Statement Debit column and BS for the Balance Sheet or Statement of Changes in Owner's Equity Debit column.

1. Equipment

2. Owner, withdrawals

3. Insurance expense

4. Prepaid insurance

5. Accounts receivable

6. Amortization expense, equipment

QS 5-6

Interpreting a work sheet

LO 4

The following information is from the work sheet for Hascal Company as of December 31, 19X1. Using this information, determine the amount for S. Hascal, capital that should be reported on the December 31, 19X1, balance sheet.

	Income Statement		Statement of Changes in Owner's Equity and Balance Sheet	
	Dr.	Cr.	Dr.	Cr.
S. Hascal, capital				65,000
S. Hascal, withdrawals			32,000	
Totals	115,000	174,000		

On December 31, 19X1, Yacht Management Co. prepared an adjusting entry for $6,700 of earned but unrecorded management fees earned. On January 16, 19X2, Ace received $15,500 of management fees which included the fees earned in 19X1. Assuming the company uses reversing entries, prepare the reversing entry and the January 16, 19X2, entry.

QS 5-7ᴬ
Reversing entries

LO 8

The following adjusted trial balance contains the accounts and balances of Painters Co. as of December 31, 19X1, the end of its fiscal year:

Exercises

Exercise 5-1
Closing entries

LO 1,2

No.	Title	Debit	Credit
101	Cash	$18,000	
126	Supplies	12,000	
128	Prepaid insurance	2,000	
167	Equipment	23,000	
168	Accumulated amortization, equipment		$ 6,500
301	R. Tanner, capital		46,600
302	R. Tanner, withdrawals	6,000	
404	Services revenue		36,000
612	Amortization expense, equipment	2,000	
622	Salaries expense	21,000	
637	Insurance expense	1,500	
640	Rent expense	2,400	
652	Supplies expense	1,200	
	Totals	$89,100	$89,100

Required

Journalize closing entries for the company.

The adjusted trial balance for West Plumbing Co. follows. Prepare a work sheet with debit and credit columns under each of the following headings: Adjusted Trial Balance, Closing Entries, and Post-Closing Trial Balance. Complete the work sheet by providing four closing entries and the post-closing trial balance.

Exercise 5-2
Preparing closing entries and the post-closing trial balance

LO 2,3

No.	Title	Adjusted Trial Balance	
101	Cash	$ 8,200	
106	Accounts receivable	24,000	
153	Trucks	41,000	
154	Accumulated amortization, trucks		$ 16,500
193	Franchise	30,000	
201	Accounts payable		14,000
209	Salaries payable		3,200
233	Unearned fees		2,600
301	F. West, capital		64,500
302	F. West, withdrawals	14,400	
401	Plumbing fees earned		79,000
611	Amortization expense, trucks	11,000	
622	Salaries expense	31,500	
640	Rent expense	12,000	
677	Miscellaneous expenses	7,700	
901	Income summary		
	Totals	$179,800	$179,800

Exercise 5-3
Closing entries

LO 2

The following balances of the Retained Earnings and temporary accounts are from High Rider's adjusted trial balance:

Account Title	Debit	Credit
Retained earnings		$42,100
Cash dividends declared	$7,500	
Services revenue		32,000
Interest earned		5,300
Salaries expense	25,400	
Insurance expense	3,800	
Rental expense	6,400	
Supplies expense	3,100	
Amortization expense, trucks	10,600	

Required

a. Prepare the closing entries.

b. Determine the amount of retained earnings to be reported on the company's balance sheet.

Exercise 5-4
Preparing and posting closing entries

LO 2

Open the following T-accounts with the provided balances. Prepare closing journal entries and post them to the accounts.

M. Jones, Capital		
	Dec. 31	41,000

Rent Expense		
Dec. 31	8,600	

M. Jones, Withdrawals		
Dec. 31	24,000	

Salaries Expense		
Dec. 31	20,000	

Income Summary		

Insurance Expense		
Dec. 31	3,500	

Services Revenue		
	Dec. 31	73,000

Amortization Expense		
Dec. 31	16,000	

Exercise 5-5
Preparing a classified balance sheet

LO 6

Use the following adjusted trial balance of Hanson Trucking Company to prepare a classified balance sheet as of December 31, 19X1.

Account Title	Debit	Credit
Cash	$ 7,000	
Accounts receivable	16,500	
Office supplies	2,000	
Trucks	170,000	
Accumulated amortization, trucks		$ 35,000
Land	75,000	
Accounts payable		11,000
Interest payable		3,000
Long-term notes payable		52,000
S. Hanson, capital		161,000
S. Hanson, withdrawals	19,000	
Trucking fees earned		128,000
Amortization expense, trucks	22,500	
Salaries expense	60,000	
Office supplies expense	7,000	
Repairs expense, trucks	11,000	
Total	$390,000	$390,000

Use the information provided in Exercise 5-5 to determine the value of the current ratio as of the balance sheet date.

Exercise 5-6
Calculating the current ratio

Calculate the current ratio in each of the following cases:

	Current Assets	Current Liabilities
Case 1	$ 78,000	$31,000
Case 2	104,000	75,000
Case 3	44,000	48,000
Case 4	84,500	80,600
Case 5	60,000	99,000

Exercise 5-7
Calculating the current ratio

These accounts are from the Adjusted Trial Balance columns in a company's 10-column work sheet. In the blank space beside each account, write the letter of the appropriate financial statement column to which a normal account balance should be extended.

A. Debit column for the income statement

B. Credit column for the income statement

C. Debit column for the balance sheet and statement of changes in owner's equity

D. Credit column for the balance sheet and statement of changes in owner's equity

Exercise 5-8
Extending adjusted account balances on a work sheet

_____ **1.** Service Fees Revenue

_____ **2.** Insurance Expense

_____ **3.** Accumulated Amortization, Machinery

_____ **4.** Interest Earned

_____ **5.** Accounts Receivable

_____ **6.** Rent Expense

_____ **7.** Amortization Expense, Machinery

_____ **8.** Cash

_____ **9.** Office Supplies

_____ **10.** Accounts Payable

_____ **11.** Owner, Capital

_____ **12.** Wages Payable

_____ **13.** Machinery

_____ **14.** Interest Receivable

_____ **15.** Interest Expense

_____ **16.** Owner, Withdrawals

Use the following information from the Adjustments columns of a 10-column work sheet to prepare adjusting journal entries:

Exercise 5-9
Preparing adjusting entries from work sheet information

		Adjustments	
No.	**Title**	**Debit**	**Credit**
109	Interest receivable	(d) 580	
124	Office supplies		(b) 1,650
128	Prepaid insurance		(a) 900
164	Accumulated amortization, office equipment		(c) 3,300
209	Salaries payable		(e) 660
409	Interest earned		(d) 580
612	Amortization expense, office equipment	(c) 3,300	
620	Office salaries expense	(e) 660	
636	Insurance expense, office equipment	(a) 432	
637	Insurance expense, store equipment	(a) 468	
650	Office supplies expense	(b) 1,650	
	Totals	7,090	7,090

Exercise 5-10^A

Completing the income
statement columns and
preparing closing entries

LO 4

These partially completed Income Statement columns from a 10-column work sheet are for WinSail Rental Co. Use the information to determine the amount that should be entered on the Net income line of the work sheet. In addition, draft closing entries for the company. The owner, Jack Cooper, did not make any withdrawals.

	Debit	Credit
Rent earned		102,000
Salaries expense	45,300	
Insurance expense	6,400	
Dock rental expense	15,000	
Boat supplies expense	3,200	
Amortization expense, boats	19,500	
Totals		
Net income		
Totals		

Exercise 5-11^A

Extending accounts in the
work sheet

LO 4

The Adjusted Trial Balance columns of a 10-column work sheet for Plummer Co. follow. Complete the work sheet by extending the account balances into the appropriate financial statement columns and by entering the amount of net income for the reporting period.

No.	Title	Adjusted Trial Balance	
101	Cash	$ 6,000	
106	Accounts receivable	26,200	
153	Trucks	82,000	
154	Accumulated amortization, trucks		$ 33,000
193	Franchise	30,000	
201	Accounts payable		14,000
209	Salaries payable		3,200
233	Unearned fees		2,600
301	F. Plummer, capital		75,500
302	F. Plummer, withdrawals	14,400	
401	Plumbing fees earned		98,000
611	Amortization expense, trucks	11,000	
622	Salaries expense	37,000	
640	Rent expense	12,000	
677	Miscellaneous expenses	7,700	
	Totals	$226,300	$226,300

Exercise 5-12^A

Reversing entries

LO 8

Breaker Corporation records the prepaid assets and unearned revenues in balance sheet accounts. The following information was used to prepare adjusting entries for Breaker Corporation as of August 31, the end of the company's fiscal year:

a. The company has earned $5,000 of unrecorded service fees.

b. The expired portion of prepaid insurance is $2,700.

c. The earned portion of the Unearned Fees account balance is $1,900.

d. Amortization expense for the office equipment is $2,300.

e. Employees have earned but have not been paid salaries of $2,400.

Required

Prepare the appropriate reversing entries that would simplify the bookkeeping effort for recording subsequent events related to these adjustments.

The following two conditions existed for Maxit Co. on October 31, 19X1, the end of its fiscal year:

a. Maxit rents a building from its owner for $3,200 per month. By a prearrangement, the company delayed paying October's rent until November 5. On this date, the company paid the rent for both October and November.

b. Maxit rents space in a building it owns to a tenant for $750 per month. By prearrangement, the tenant delayed paying the October rent until November 8. On this date, the tenant paid the rent for both October and November.

Required

1. Prepare the adjusting entries that Maxit should record for these situations as of October 31.

2. Assuming that Maxit does not use reversing entries, prepare journal entries to record Maxit's payment of rent on November 5 and the collection of rent on November 8 from Maxit's tenant.

3. Assuming that Maxit does use reversing entries, prepare those entries and the journal entries to record Maxit's payment of rent on November 5 and the collection of rent on November 8 from Maxit's tenant.

Exercise 5-13A
Reversing entries

LO 8

Bradshaw Repairs' adjusted trial balance on December 31, 19X2, appeared as follows:

Problems

Problem 5-1
Closing entries, financial statements, and current ratio

LO 6, 7, 2

No.	BRADSHAW REPAIRS Adjusted Trial Balance December 31, 19X2 Title	Debit	Credit
101	Cash	$ 13,000	
124	Office supplies	1,200	
128	Prepaid insurance	1,950	
167	Equipment	48,000	
168	Accumulated amortization, equipment		$ 4,000
201	Accounts payable		12,000
210	Wages payable		500
301	H. Bradshaw, capital		40,000
302	H. Bradshaw, withdrawals	15,000	
401	Repair fees earned		77,750
612	Amortization expense, equipment	4,000	
623	Wages expense	36,500	
637	Insurance expense	700	
640	Rent expense	9,600	
650	Office supplies expense	2,600	
690	Utilities expense	1,700	
	Totals	$134,250	$134,250

Required

Preparation component:

1. Prepare an income statement and a statement of changes in owner's equity for the 19X2 year and a classified balance sheet at the end of the year. There were no owner investments during the year.

2. Enter the adjusted trial balance in the first two columns of a six-column table that also has columns for closing entries and for a post-closing trial balance. Insert an Income Summary account in the trial balance.

3. Enter the closing entries in the table and prepare journal entries for them.

4. Determine the company's current ratio.

Check Figure Ending capital balance, $47,650

Analysis component:

5. Assume that the adjusted trial balance differs as follows:

a. None of the $700 insurance expense had expired during the year but instead was a prepayment of future insurance protection.

b. There were no earned but unpaid wages at the end of the year.

Describe the changes in the financial statements that would result from these assumptions.

Problem 5-2
Closing entries, financial statements, and ratios

LO 2, 6, 7

The adjusted trial balance for Graw Construction as of December 31, 19X2, follows:

No.	**GRAW CONSTRUCTION** **Adjusted Trial Balance** **December 31, 19X2** Title	Debit	Credit
101	Cash	$ 4,000	
104	Temporary investments	22,000	
126	Supplies	7,100	
128	Prepaid insurance	6,000	
167	Equipment	39,000	
168	Accumulated amortization, equipment		$ 20,000
173	Building	130,000	
174	Accumulated amortization, building		55,000
183	Land	45,000	
201	Accounts payable		15,500
203	Interest payable		1,500
208	Rent payable		2,500
210	Wages payable		1,500
213	Property taxes payable		800
233	Unearned professional fees		6,500
251	Long-term notes payable		66,000
301	T. Graw, capital		82,700
302	T. Graw, withdrawals	12,000	
401	Professional fees earned		96,000
406	Rent earned		13,000
407	Dividends earned		1,900
409	Interest earned		1,000
606	Amortization expense, building	10,000	
612	Amortization expense, equipment	5,000	
623	Wages expense	31,000	
633	Interest expense	4,100	
637	Insurance expense	9,000	
640	Rent expense	12,400	
652	Supplies expense	6,400	
682	Postage expense	3,200	
683	Property taxes expense	4,000	
684	Repairs expense	7,900	
688	Telephone expense	2,200	
690	Utilities expense	3,600	
	Totals	$363,900	$363,900

An analysis of other information reveals that Graw Construction is required to make a $6,600 payment on the long-term note payable during 19X3. Also, T. Graw invested $50,000 cash early in the year.

Required

1. Present the income statement, statement of changes in owner's equity, and classified balance sheet.

2. Present the closing entries made at the end of the year.

3. Use the information in the financial statements to calculate these ratios:

   a. Return on equity.

   b. Modified return on equity assuming the owner's efforts are valued at $12,000 for the year.

   c. Debt ratio.

   d. Profit margin (use total revenues as the denominator).

   e. Current ratio.

Check Figure Total assets, $178,100

On June 1, 19X1, Jennifer Farrow created a new travel agency called Worldwide Tours. The company records prepaid and unearned items in balance sheet accounts. These events occurred during the company's first month:

June 1   Farrow invested $20,000 cash and computer equipment worth $40,000.
     2   Rented furnished office space by paying $1,700 rent for the first month.
     3   Purchased $1,100 of office supplies for cash.
    10   Paid $3,600 for the premium on a one-year insurance policy. Insurance coverage began on June 10.
    14   Paid $1,800 for two weeks' salaries to employees.
    24   Collected $7,900 of commissions from airlines on tickets obtained for customers.
    28   Paid another $1,800 for two weeks' salaries.
    29   Paid the month's $650 telephone bill.
    30   Paid $250 cash to repair the company's computer.
    30   Farrow withdrew $1,500 cash from the business for personal use.

Problem 5-3
Performing the steps in the accounting cycle

LO 2, 3, 5

The company's chart of accounts included these accounts:

101	Cash	405	Commissions Earned
106	Accounts Receivable	612	Amortization Expense,
124	Office Supplies		Computer Equipment
128	Prepaid Insurance	622	Salaries Expense
167	Computer Equipment	637	Insurance Expense
168	Accumulated Amortization,	640	Rent Expense
	Computer Equipment	650	Office Supplies Expense
209	Salaries Payable	684	Repairs Expense
301	J. Farrow, Capital	688	Telephone Expense
302	J. Farrow, Withdrawals	901	Income Summary

Required

1. Use the balance-column format to create each of the listed accounts.

2. Prepare journal entries to record the transactions for June and post them to the accounts.

3. Prepare an unadjusted trial balance as of June 30.

4. Use the following information to journalize and post adjusting entries for the month:

   a. Two-thirds of one month's insurance coverage was consumed.

   b. There were $700 of office supplies on hand at the end of the month.

   c. Amortization on the computer equipment was estimated to be $600.

   d. The employees had earned $320 of unpaid and unrecorded salaries.

   e. The company had earned $1,650 of commissions that had not yet been billed.

5. Prepare an income statement, a statement of changes in owner's equity, and a balance sheet.

6. Prepare journal entries to close the temporary accounts and post them to the accounts.

7. Prepare a separate post-closing trial balance.

Check Figure Ending capital balance, $60,330

Problem 5-4
Balance sheet classifications

LO 6

In the blank space beside each numbered balance sheet item, enter the letter of its balance sheet classification. If the item should not appear on the balance sheet, enter a *z* in the blank.

a. Current assets
b. Investments
c. Plant and equipment
d. Intangible assets

e. Current liabilities
f. Long-term liabilities
g. Owner's equity
h. Shareholders' equity

_____ **1.** Amortization expense, trucks
_____ **2.** L. Hale, capital
_____ **3.** Interest receivable
_____ **4.** L. Hale, withdrawals
_____ **5.** Automobiles
_____ **6.** Notes payable—due in three years
_____ **7.** Accounts payable
_____ **8.** Prepaid insurance
_____ **9.** Common share capital
_____ **10.** Unearned services revenue
_____ **11.** Accumulated amortization, trucks

_____ **12.** Cash
_____ **13.** Building
_____ **14.** Retained earnings
_____ **15.** Office equipment
_____ **16.** Land (used in operations)
_____ **17.** Repairs expense
_____ **18.** Prepaid property taxes
_____ **19.** Current portion of long-term note payable
_____ **20.** Investment in Magna common shares (long-term holding)

Problem 5-5
Work sheet, journal entries, financial statements, and current ratio

LO 4, 6, 7

This unadjusted trial balance is for Whiten Construction Co. as of the end of its 19X2 fiscal year. The beginning balance of the owner's capital balance was $52,660 and the owner invested another $25,000 cash in the company during the year.

No.	**WHITEN CONSTRUCTION CO.** **Unadjusted Trial Balance** **April 30, 19X2** Title	Debit	Credit
101	Cash	$ 17,500	
126	Supplies	8,900	
128	Prepaid insurance	6,200	
167	Equipment	131,000	
168	Accumulated amortization, equipment		$ 25,250
201	Accounts payable		5,800
203	Interest payable		
208	Rent payable		
210	Wages payable		
213	Business tax payable		
251	Long-term notes payable		24,000
301	R. Whiten, capital		77,660
302	R. Whiten, withdrawals	30,000	
401	Construction fees earned		134,000
612	Amortization expense, equipment		
623	Wages expense	45,860	
633	Interest expense	2,640	
637	Insurance expense		
640	Rent expense	13,200	
652	Supplies expense		
683	Business tax expense	4,600	
684	Repairs expense	2,810	
690	Utilities expense	4,000	
	Totals	$266,710	$266,710

Required

Preparation component:

1. Prepare a 10-column work sheet for 19X2, starting with the unadjusted trial balance and including adjustments based on these additional facts:

a. The inventory of supplies at the end of the year had a cost of $3,200.

b. The cost of expired insurance for the year is $3,900.

c. Annual amortization on the equipment is $8,500.

d. The April utilities expense of $550 was not included in the trial balance because the bill arrived after it was prepared. The $550 amount owed needs to be recorded.

e. The company's employees have earned $1,600 of accrued wages.

f. The lease for the office requires the company to pay total rent for the year ended April 30 equal to 10% of the company's annual revenues. The rent is paid to the building owner with monthly payments of $1,100. If the annual rent exceeds the total monthly payments, the company must pay the excess before May 31. If the total is less than the amount previously paid, the building owner will refund the difference by May 31.

g. Additional business tax of $900 has been assessed but has not been paid or recorded in the accounts.

h. The long-term note payable bears interest at 1% per month, which the company is required to pay by the 10th of the following month. The balance of the Interest Expense account equals the amount paid during the past fiscal year. The interest for April has not yet been paid or recorded. In addition, the company is required to make a $5,000 payment on the note on June 30, 19X2.

2. Use the work sheet to journalize the adjusting and closing entries.

3. Prepare an income statement, a statement of changes in owner's equity, and a classified balance sheet. Calculate the company's current ratio.

Analysis component:

4. Analyze the following potential errors and describe how each would affect the 10-column work sheet. Explain whether the error is likely to be discovered in completing the work sheet and, if not, the effect of the error on the financial statements.

a. Assume the adjustment for supplies consumption credited Supplies for $3,200 and debited the same amount to Supplies Expense.

b. When completing the adjusted trial balance in the work sheet, the $17,500 cash balance was incorrectly entered in the Credit column.

The unadjusted trial balance for Shooting Ranges as of December 31, 19X1, follows:

Check Figure Total assets, $120,250

Problem 5-6A
Adjusting, reversing, and subsequent entries

LO 4, 8

SHOOTING RANGES
December 31, 19X1
Unadjusted Trial Balance

Cash	$ 13,000	
Accounts receivable		
Supplies	5,500	
Equipment	130,000	
Accumulated amortization, equipment		$ 25,000
Interest payable		
Salaries payable		
Unearned membership fees		14,000
Notes payable		50,000
S. Becker, capital		58,250
S. Becker, withdrawals	20,000	
Membership fees earned		53,000
Amortization expense, equipment		
Salaries expense	28,000	
Interest expense	3,750	
Supplies expense		
Totals	$200,250	$200,250

Required

1. Prepare a six-column table with two columns under each of the following headings: Unadjusted Trial Balance, Adjustments, and Adjusted Trial Balance. Complete the table by entering adjustments that reflect the following information:

   a. As of December 31, employees have earned $900 of unpaid and unrecorded salaries. The next payday is January 4, and the total amount of salaries to be paid is $1,600.

   b. The cost of supplies on hand at December 31 is $2,700.

   c. The note payable requires an interest payment to be made every three months. The amount of unrecorded accrued interest at December 31 is $1,250, and the next payment is due on January 15. This payment will be $1,500.

   d. An analysis of the unearned membership fees shows that $5,600 remains unearned at December 31.

   e. In addition to the membership fees included in the revenue account balance, the company has earned another $9,100 in fees that will be collected on January 21. The company is also expected to collect $8,000 on the same day for new fees earned during January.

   f. Amortization expense for the year is $12,500.

2. Prepare journal entries for the adjustments drafted in the six-column table.

3. Prepare journal entries to reverse the effects of the adjusting entries that involve accruals.

4. Prepare journal entries to record the cash payments and collections that are described for January.

Check Figure Total debits in adjusted trial balance, $224,000

Alternate Problems

Problem 5-1A
Closing entries, financial statements, and current ratio

LO 2, 6, 7

Western Shoe Shops' adjusted trial balance on December 31, 19X2, appeared as follows:

WESTERN SHOE SHOPS Adjusted Trial Balance December 31, 19X2		Debit	Credit
101	Cash	$ 13,450	
125	Store supplies	4,140	
128	Prepaid insurance	2,200	
167	Equipment	33,000	
168	Accumulated amortization, equipment		$ 9,000
201	Accounts payable		1,000
210	Wages payable		3,200
301	Pearl Jones, capital		31,650
302	Pearl Jones, withdrawals	16,000	
401	Repair fees earned		62,000
612	Amortization expense, equipment	3,000	
623	Wages expense	28,400	
637	Insurance expense	1,100	
640	Rent expense	2,400	
651	Store supplies expense	1,300	
690	Utilities expense	1,860	
	Totals	$106,850	$106,850

Required

Preparation component:

1. Prepare an income statement and a statement of changes in owner's equity for the 19X2 year, and a classified balance sheet at the end of the year. There were no owner investments during the year.

2. Enter the adjusted trial balance in the first two columns of a six-column table that also has columns for closing entries and for a post-closing trial balance. Insert an Income Summary account in the trial balance.

3. Enter the closing entries in the table and prepare journal entries for them.

4. Determine the company's current ratio.

Analysis component:

5. Assume that the adjusted trial balance differs as follows:
   a. None of the $1,100 insurance expense had expired during the year but instead was a prepayment of future insurance protection.
   b. There were no earned but unpaid wages at the end of the year.

   Describe the changes in the financial statements that would result from these assumptions.

Following is the adjusted trial balance for the Canner Co. as of December 31, 19X2:

Problem 5-2A
Closing entries, financial statements, and ratios
LO 2, 6, 7

	CANNER co. Adjusted Trial Balance December 31, 19X2	Debit	Credit
101	Cash	$ 6,400	
104	Temporary investments	10,200	
126	Supplies	3,600	
128	Prepaid insurance	800	
167	Equipment	18,000	
168	Accumulated amortization, equipment		$ 3,000
173	Building	90,000	
174	Accumulated amortization, building		9,000
183	Land	28,500	
201	Accounts payable		2,500
203	Interest payable		1,400
208	Rent payable		200
210	Wages payable		1,180
213	Property taxes payable		2,330
233	Unearned professional fees		650
251	Long-term notes payable		32,000
301	Joe Canner, capital		91,800
302	Joe Canner, withdrawals	6,000	
401	Professional fees earned		47,000
406	Rent earned		3,600
407	Dividends earned		500
409	Interest earned		1,120
606	Amortization expense, building	2,000	
612	Amortization expense, equipment	1,000	
623	Wages expense	17,500	
633	Interest expense	1,200	
637	Insurance expense	1,425	
640	Rent expense	1,800	
652	Supplies expense	900	
682	Postage expense	310	
683	Property taxes expense	3,825	
684	Repairs expense	579	
688	Telephone expense	421	
690	Utilities expense	1,820	
	Totals	$196,280	$196,280

An analysis of other information reveals that the company is required to make a $6,400 payment on the long-term note payable during 19X3. Also, Joe Canner invested $30,000 cash in the business early in the year.

Required

1. Present the income statement, statement of changes in owner's equity, and classified balance sheet.
2. Present the four closing entries that would be made at the end of the year.
3. Use the information in the financial statements to calculate the values of these ratios:
   a. Return on equity.
   b. Modified return on equity, assuming the owner's efforts are worth $15,000 per year.
   c. Debt ratio.
   d. Profit margin (use total revenues as the denominator).
   e. Current ratio.

Problem 5-3A
Performing the steps in
the accounting cycle
LO 2, 3, 5

On July 1, 19X1, Cindy Tucker created a new self-storage business called Lockit Co. These events occurred during the company's first month:

July	1	Tucker invested $20,000 cash and buildings worth $120,000.
	2	Rented equipment by paying $1,800 rent for the first month.
	5	Purchased $2,300 of office supplies for cash.
	10	Paid $5,400 for the premium on a one-year insurance policy.
	14	Paid an employee $900 for two weeks' salary.
	24	Collected $8,800 of storage fees from customers.
	28	Paid another $900 for two weeks' salary.
	29	Paid the month's $300 telephone bill.
	30	Paid $850 cash to repair a leaking roof.
	31	Tucker withdrew $1,600 cash from the business for personal use.

The company's chart of accounts included these accounts:

101	Cash	401	Storage Fees Earned
106	Accounts Receivable	606	Amortization Expense,
124	Office Supplies		Buildings
128	Prepaid Insurance	622	Salaries Expense
173	Buildings	637	Insurance Expense
174	Accumulated Amortization,	640	Rent Expense
	Buildings	650	Office Supplies Expense
209	Salaries Payable	684	Repairs Expense
301	Cindy Tucker, Capital	688	Telephone Expense
302	Cindy Tucker, Withdrawals	901	Income Summary

Required

1. Use the balance-column format to create each of the listed accounts.
2. Prepare journal entries to record the transactions for July and post them to the accounts. Record prepaid and unearned items in balance sheet accounts.
3. Prepare an unadjusted trial balance as of July 31.
4. Use the following information to journalize and post adjusting entries for the month:
   a. Two-thirds of one month's insurance coverage was consumed.
   b. There was $1,550 of office supplies on hand at the end of the month.
   c. Amortization on the buildings was estimated to be $1,200.
   d. The employee had earned $180 of unpaid and unrecorded salary.
   e. The company had earned $950 of storage fees that had not yet been billed.
5. Prepare an income statement, a statement of changes in owner's equity, and a balance sheet.
6. Prepare journal entries to close the temporary accounts and post them to the accounts.
7. Prepare a separate post-closing trial balance.

In the blank space beside each numbered item, enter the letter of its balance sheet classification. If the item should not appear on the balance sheet, enter a *z* in the blank.

a. Current assets
b. Investments
c. Plant and equipment
d. Intangible assets

e. Current liabilities
f. Long-term liabilities
g. Owner's equity
h. Shareholders' equity

_____ 1. Office supplies
_____ 2. Owner, capital
_____ 3. Common share capital
_____ 4. Notes receivable—due in 120 days
_____ 5. Accumulated amortization, trucks
_____ 6. Salaries payable
_____ 7. Commissions earned
_____ 8. Retained earnings
_____ 9. Office equipment
_____ 10. Notes payable—due in three years
_____ 11. Building

_____ 12. Prepaid insurance
_____ 13. Current portion of long-term note payable
_____ 14. Interest receivable
_____ 15. Short-term investments
_____ 16. Land (used in operations)
_____ 17. Copyrights
_____ 18. Owner, withdrawals
_____ 19. Cash dividends declared
_____ 20. Investment in Ford common shares (long-term holding)

Problem 5-4A
Balance sheet classifications
LO 6

Presented below is the unadjusted trial balance of Boomer Demolition Company as of the end of its June 30 fiscal year. The beginning balance of the owner's capital balance was $36,900 and the owner invested another $30,000 cash in the company during the year.

Problem 5-5A
Work sheet, journal entries, financial statements, and current ratio
LO 4, 6, 7

BOOMER Demolition Company Unadjusted Trial Balance June 30, 19X2		Debit	Credit
101	Cash	$ 9,000	
126	Supplies	18,000	
128	Prepaid insurance	14,600	
167	Equipment	140,000	
168	Accumulated amortization, equipment		$ 10,000
201	Accounts payable		16,000
203	Interest payable		
208	Rent payable		
210	Wages payable		
213	Business tax payable		
251	Long-term notes payable		20,000
301	R. Boomer, capital		66,900
302	R. Boomer, withdrawals	24,000	
401	Demolition fees earned		177,000
612	Amortization expense, equipment		
623	Wages expense	51,400	
633	Interest expense	2,200	
637	Insurance expense		
640	Rent expense	8,800	
652	Supplies expense		
683	Business tax expense	8,400	
684	Repairs expense	6,700	
690	Utilities expense	6,800	
	Totals	$289,900	$289,900

Required

Preparation component:

1. Prepare a 10-column work sheet for 19X2, starting with the unadjusted trial balance and including these additional facts:
   a. The inventory of supplies at the end of the year had a cost of $8,100.

b. The cost of expired insurance for the year is $11,500.

c. Annual amortization on the equipment is $18,000.

d. The June utilities expense of $700 was not included in the trial balance because the bill arrived after it was prepared. The $700 amount owed needs to be recorded.

e. The company's employees have earned $2,200 of accrued wages.

f. The lease for the office requires the company to pay total rent for each fiscal year equal to 8% of the company's annual revenues. The rent is paid to the building owner with monthly payments of $800. If the annual rent exceeds the total monthly payments, the company must pay the excess before July 31. If the total is less than the amount previously paid, the building owner will refund the difference by July 31.

g. Additional business tax of $450 has been assessed but has not been paid or recorded in the accounts.

h. The long-term note payable bears interest at 1% per month, which the company is required to pay by the tenth of the following month. The balance of the Interest Expense account equals the amount paid during the year. The interest for June has not yet been paid or recorded. In addition, the company is required to make a $4,000 payment on the note on August 30, 19X2.

2. Use the work sheet to journalize the adjusting and closing entries.

3. Prepare an income statement, a statement of changes in owner's equity and a classified balance sheet. Calculate the company's current ratio.

Analysis component:

4. Analyze the following independent errors and describe how each would affect the 10-column work sheet. Explain whether the error is likely to be discovered in completing the work sheet and, if not, the effect of the error on the financial statements.

a. The adjustment for consumption of the insurance coverage credited the Prepaid Insurance account for $3,100 and debited the same amount to the Insurance Expense account.

b. When completing the adjusted trial balance in the work sheet, the $6,700 Repairs Expense account balance was extended to the Debit column for the balance sheet.

Problem 5-6A[A]
Adjusting, reversing, and subsequent entries

This six-column table for Machine Rental Co. includes the unadjusted trial balance as of December 31, 19X2:

MACHINE RENTAL CO. December 31, 19X2					
	Unadjusted Trial Balance		Adjustments		Adjusted Trial Balance
Cash	$ 9,000				
Accounts receivable					
Supplies	6,600				
Machinery	40,100				
Accumulated amortization, machinery		$15,800			
Interest payable					
Salaries payable					
Unearned rental fees		5,200			
Notes payable		20,000			
Kara Smith, capital		13,200			
Kara Smith, withdrawals	10,500				
Rental fees earned		37,000			
Amortization expense, machinery					
Salaries expense	23,500				
Interest expense	1,500				
Supplies expense					
Totals	$91,200	$91,200			

Required

1. Complete the six-column table by entering adjustments that reflect the following information:

a. As of December 31, employees have earned $420 of unpaid and unrecorded wages. The next payday is January 4, and the total amount of wages to be paid is $1,250.

b. The cost of supplies on hand at December 31 is $2,450.

c. The note payable requires an interest payment to be made every three months. The amount of unrecorded accrued interest at December 31 is $500, and the next payment is due on January 15. This payment will be $600.

d. An analysis of the unearned rental fees shows that $3,100 remains unearned at December 31.

e. In addition to the machinery rental fees included in the revenue account balance, the company has earned another $2,350 in fees that will be collected on January 21. The company is also expected to collect $4,400 on the same day for new fees earned during that month.

f. Amortization expense for the year is $3,800.

2. Prepare journal entries for the adjustments drafted in the six-column table.

3. Prepare journal entries to reverse the effects of the adjusting entries that involve accruals.

4. Prepare journal entries to record the cash payments and collections that are described for January.

The owner of Dynamo Stores has come to you for assistance because his bookkeeper has just moved to another city. The following is the only information his bookkeeper left him.

(1) Balance sheets as of December 31, 1998 and 1999.

Analytical and Review Problems

A & R Problem 5-1

	1998	1999
Assets	$210,000	$168,000
Liabilities	$ 63,000	$42,000
Capital	147,000	126,000
	$210,000	$168,000

(2) The owner withdrew $105,000 in 1999 for his personal use.

(3) The business incurred total expenses of $168,000 for 1999, of which $126,000 was for wages and $42,000 was for advertising.

Required

1. Compute the total revenue and net income for 1999.

2. Prepare closing or clearing entries for 1999 (omit narratives).

A & R Problem 5-2

The partially completed work sheet for the current fiscal year of Sandy's Delivery Service appears below:

	SANDY'S DELIVERY SERVICE Work Sheet For the Year Ended December 31, 1999									
Account Titles	**Trial Balance**		**Adjustments**		**Adjusted Trial Balance**		**Income Statement**		**Balance Sheet**	
	Dr.	**Cr.**	**Dr.**	**Cr.**	**Dr.**	**Cr.**	**Dr.**	**Cr.**	**Dr.**	**Cr.**
Cash	10,650									
Accounts receivable	7,000				9,000					
Supplies on hand	4,200								1,600	
Prepaid insurance	2,400									
Prepaid rent	1,800									
Delivery trucks	40,000				40,000					
Accounts payable		3,130				3,130				
Unearned delivery fees		4,500								2,000
Sandra Berlasty, capital, Dec. 31, 1998		50,000								
Sandra Berlasty, drawing	3,000									
Delivery service revenue		18,500								
Advertising expense	600									
Gas and oil expense	680									
Salaries expense	5,600									
Utilities expense	200									
	76,130	76,130								
Insurance expense					800					
Rent expense					900					
Supplies expense										
Amortization expense—delivery trucks										
Accumulated amortization—delivery trucks										2,000
Accrued salaries payable										400
Net income										

Required

1. Complete the work sheet.
2. Journalize the adjusting and closing entries (omit narratives).

Serial Problem

Echo Systems

(The first two segments of this comprehensive problem were in Chapters 3 and 4, and the final segment is presented in Chapter 6. If the Chapter 3 and 4 segments have not been completed, the assignment can begin at this point. It is recommended that you use the Working Papers that accompany this book because they reflect the account balances that resulted from posting the entries required in Chapters 3 and 4.)

The transactions of Echo Systems for October through December 19X1 have been recorded in the problem segments in Chapters 3 and 4, as well as the year-end adjusting entries. Prior to closing the revenue and expense accounts for 19X1, the accounting system is modified to include the Income Summary account, which is given the number 901.

Required

1. Record and post the appropriate closing entries.
2. Prepare a post-closing trial balance.

BEYOND THE NUMBERS

Refer to the financial statements and related information for **Alliance Communications Corp.** in Appendix I. Find the answers to the following questions by analyzing the information in the report.

Reporting in Action

LO 2

Required

1. For the fiscal year ended March 31, 1997, what amount will be credited to Income Summary to summarize Alliance's revenues earned for the period?
2. For the fiscal year ended March 31, 1997, what amount will be debited to Income Summary to summarize the expenses for the period?
3. For the fiscal year ended March 31, 1997, what will the balance of the Income Summary account be before it is closed to Retained Earnings?

Both **Alliance** and **Atlantis** produce, market and sell television programs and movies. Key comparative figures ($ thousands) for these two organizations follow:

Comparative Analysis

LO 7

Key Figures	Alliance		Atlantis	
	1997	**1996**	**1997**	**1996**
Current Assets	$169,233	$123,119	$219,735	$117,134
Current Liabilities	$112,852	$ 79,295	$125,100	$ 66,283

* Alliance figures are from the annual reports for the fiscal years ended March 31,1997 and 1996. Atlantis figures are from the annual reports for the fiscal years ended December 31, 1997 and 1996.

Required

1. Compute the current ratios for both years for the two companies.
2. Which company has the better ability to pay its short-term obligations?
3. Comment on each company's current ratio behaviour for the two years.
4. How do Alliance's and Atlantis' current ratios compare to their industry average ratio of 1.6?

On January 20, 1998, Jennifer Nelson, the staff accountant, for Newby Enterprises is feeling pressure to complete the preparation of the annual financial statements. The president of the company has said he needs up-to-date financial statements to share with several bankers on January 21 at a dinner meeting that has been called to discuss the possibility of Newby obtaining loan financing for a special building project. Jennifer knows that she won't be able to gather all the needed information in the next 24 hours to prepare the entire set of adjusting entries that must be posted before the financial statements will accurately portray the company's performance and financial position for the fiscal period just ended December 31, 1997. Jennifer ultimately decides to estimate several expense accruals at the last minute. When deciding on estimates for the expenses Jennifer uses low estimates as she doesn't want to make the financial statements look worse than they possibly are in reality. Jennifer finishes the financial statements before the deadline and gives them to the president without mentioning that several accounts could only be estimated as to their balance on December 31, 1997.

Ethics Challenge

LO 5

Required

1. Note several courses of action that Jennifer could have taken instead of the one she ultimately decided on.
2. If you were in Jennifer's situation what would you have done? Briefly justify your response.

Communicating in Practice

LO 1

Assume one of your teammates said that the going or continuing-concern principle states that the books of a company should be ongoing and therefore not "closed" until that business is terminated. Obviously that teammate does not understand the objective of the closing process nor the meaning of the going-concern principle. Write a memo to this teammate that explains the concept of the closing process by drawing analogies between (a) a scoreboard for an athletic event and the revenue and expense accounts of a business, and (b) the team's record book and the capital account. (Hint: Think about what would happen if the scoreboard was not cleared before the start of a new game). Your memo should also clarify the real meaning of the going-concern principle.

Taking It to the Net

LO 7

Visit **The Gap's** homepage at **http://www.gap.com.** (It is possible that The Gap's web address might have changed since the publication of this text. If the address given does not lead you to The Gap's homepage use a web browser such as Yahoo or Alta Vista to locate The Gap's homepage.)

Required

1. Use the hotlink "Company History" to read the story of The Gap's creation and evolution.
2. To what does the name "The Gap" refer?
3. Chronicle the new types of stores that The Gap has opened throughout the 1980s and 1990s.
4. Access The Gap's annual financial report by using the hotlink provided. (Hint: If an Adobe reader is required and the computer you are using is not so equipped, you may alternatively read the annual report information at **http://www.sec.gov/cgi-bin/srch-edgar?gap**.)
5. Compute the current ratio for The Gap for the last three years. Comment on the company's trend in liquidity.

Teamwork in Action

LO 2

The unadjusted trial balance and adjustment data for Noseworthy Investigators are presented below. *Each team member* is to assume *one* of the responsibilities listed after the data. After completing each of these responsibilities, you are to work as a team to prove the accounting equation utilizing information from teammates (1 & 4). If your equation does not balance, you are to work as a team to resolve your error. As "time is money," therefore, the team's goal is to complete the task as quickly as possible.

Title	Debit	Credit
Cash	$ 15,000	
Supplies	11,000	
Prepaid Insurance	2,000	
Equipment	24,000	
Accumulated Amortization, equipment		$ 6,000
Accounts Payable		2,000
D. Noseworthy, capital		31,000
D. Noseworthy, withdrawals	5,000	
Investigation fees earned		32,000
Rent expense	14,000	
Totals	$71,000	$71,000

Additional year-end data:

a. Expired insurance was $1,200
b. Equipment amortized was $3,000
c. Unused supplies was $4,000
d. Services in the amount of $500 have been provided and have not been billed or collected.

Responsibilities for individual team member assignment:

1. Determine the accounts and adjusted balances to be extended to the Balance Sheet columns of the work sheet. Also determine the total assets and total liabilities.

2. Determine the adjusted revenue account balance and prepare the entry to close this account.

3. Determine the adjusted balances for expense accounts and prepare the entry to close these accounts.

4. Draw T-accounts for D. Noseworthy, capital that reflect the unadjusted trial balance amount and a T-account for income summary. Prepare the third closing entry without amounts and the fourth closing entry with amounts. Ask teammates (2 & 3) for the appropriate postings for income summary. Obtain amounts to complete the third closing entry and post both the third and fourth closing entry. Provide the team with final capital account balance to complete the activity by proving the accounting equation.

Select a company in your community which you may visit in person or interview on the telephone. Call ahead to the company to arrange a time when you can interview a member of the accounting department who helps in the preparation of the annual financial statements for the company. During the interview inquire about the following aspects of the company's accounting cycle:

a. Does the company prepare interim financial statements? What time period is used for the interim statements?

b. Does the company use the cash or accrual basis of accounting?

c. Does the company use a worksheet to aid in the preparation of the financial statements? Why or why not?

d. Does the company use a spreadsheet program to construct the worksheet? If so, which software program is used?

e. How long does it usually take after the end of the 12-month fiscal period to complete the finished annual financial statements?

Hitting the Road
LO 5

Read "An Enormous Temptation to Waste" in the February 10, 1997, issue of *Business Week*.

Required

1. What are possible advantages and disadvantages of stockpiling cash?

2. What are some of the reasons for the growth in cash for the companies highlighted in the article?

3. Under what asset subgroup does cash appear on a classified balance sheet?

4. What ratio does the article use to target the companies with the greatest relative amounts of cash?

5. How would the current ratio for the companies be affected by the stockpiling of cash?

Business Break
LO 6,7

6

Accounting for Merchandising Activities

▶ A Look Back

Chapter 5 focused on the final steps of the accounting process. We explained the importance of proper revenue and expense recognition, and described the closing process. We also showed how to prepare financial statements from accounting records.

▶ A Look at This Chapter

This chapter emphasizes merchandising activities. We explain how the reporting of merchandising activities differs from service activities. Both the perpetual and periodic inventory systems are described. We also analyze and record merchandise purchases and sales transactions, and explain adjustments and the closing process for merchandising companies.

▶ A Look Forward

Chapter 7 extends our analysis of merchandising activities. We focus on the valuation of inventory. Topics include the items in inventory, costs assigned, costing methods used, and inventory estimation techniques.

Chapter Outline

Fizzling Inventory

Toronto, ON—By June 1997, 27-year-old Rob Stavos was living his dreams. He'd just opened **Liquid Nectar,** a small retail outlet devoted to serving the quirky tastes of young and old alike. But within months, this young entrepreneur's dream had become a nightmare.

Liquid Nectar started out with a bang. Customers raved about its stock of exotic and unique beverage products. Profit margins on successful drinks far outweighed the costs of unsold products. "We were ready to take on the large producers," boasts Rob. Within two months, however, Rob lost control of inventory and margins were being squeezed. What happened? Was Liquid Nectar soon be to another flash-in-the pan?

Two problems emerged. One is Rob installed what's called a periodic inventory system. This system reports inventory levels at periodic intervals such as once a month. This means the inventory system couldn't give Rob up-to-date information on sales and inventory he'd need for stocking and ordering. "Our popular brands were being sold out and nothing was in inventory," says Rob. "We were turning away too many customers." Hardly a ticket for success. The second problem is Rob did not skillfully negotiate purchase contracts. Purchase discounts and returns left too much power and decisions with suppliers.

But Rob fought back. With the help of a consultant, Rob installed a perpetual inventory system and renegotiated purchase contracts. His new inventory system gives up-to-date details on sales and inventory. "We now know what's hot and what's not," says Rob, "and we don't turn away customers." Also, his new contracts allow Rob to return unsold inventories and to deeply discount others. "This time," claims Rob, "we'll not disappoint!" And the future of Liquid Nectar looks downright bubbly.

CHAPTER PREVIEW

Merchandising activities are a major part of modern business. Consumers expect a wealth of products, discount prices, inventory on demand, and high quality. This chapter introduces us to the business and accounting practices used by companies engaged in merchandising activities. These companies buy products and then resell them to customers. We show how financial statements capture these merchandising activities. The new financial statement elements created by merchandising activities are explained. We also analyze and record merchandise purchases and sales of these companies. Adjustments and the closing process for merchandising companies are explained. An understanding of these important topics is what Rob Stavos of **Liquid Nectar** needed to avoid the problems he encountered.

Merchandising Activities

LO1 Describe merchandising activities and identify business examples.

Our emphasis in previous chapters was on the accounting and reporting activities of companies providing services. Examples include **Sympatico, AOL Canada, Canadian Airlines, Tilden,** and **Four Seasons Hotels.** In return for services provided to its customers, a service company receives commissions, fares or fees as revenue. Its net income for a reporting period is the difference between its revenues and the operating expenses incurred in providing services.

A merchandising company's activities are different from those of a service company. A **merchandiser** earns net income by buying and selling merchandise. **Merchandise** consists of products, also called goods, that a company acquires for the purpose of reselling them to customers. Merchandisers are often identified as either wholesalers or retailers.

A **wholesaler** is a "go-between" that buys products from manufacturers or other wholesalers and sells them to retailers or other wholesalers. Wholesalers provide promotion, market information, and financial assistance to retailers. They also provide a sales force, reduced inventory costs, less risk, and market information to manufacturers. Wholesalers include companies such as **Provigo, Cassidy's, The Oshawa Group** and **Westfair Foods.** A **retailer** is a *middleman* that buys products from manufacturers or wholesalers and sells them to consumers. Examples of retailers include **The Bay, Loblaw, Zellers, The Gap,** and **Sam the Record Man.** Retailers, such as **Bell Canada,** often sell both products and services.

Reporting Financial Performance

LO2 Identify and explain the important components of income for a merchandising company.

Net income to a merchandiser means that revenue from selling merchandise exceeds both the cost of merchandise sold to customers and cost of other operating expenses for the period (see Exhibit 6.1). The usual accounting term for revenues from selling merchandise is sales and the term used for the cost of

Exhibit 6.1

Computing Income for Both a Merchandising Company and a Service Company

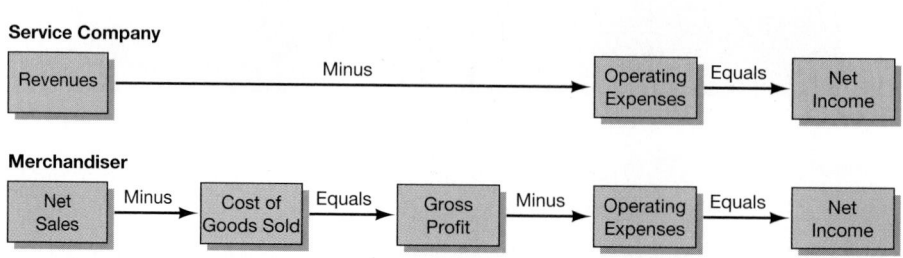

buying and preparing the merchandise is an expense called *cost of goods sold.*[1]
A merchandiser's other expenses are often called *operating expenses.*

The condensed income statement for Z-Mart in Exhibit 6.2 shows us how these
three elements of net income are related. This statement shows Z-Mart sold products to customers for $314,700. Z-Mart acquired these goods at a cost
of $230,400. This yields a $84,300 gross profit. **Gross profit,** also
called *gross margin,* equals net sales less cost of goods sold. Gross
profit is important to the profitability of merchandisers. Changes in
gross profit often greatly impact a merchandiser's operations since
gross profit must cover all other expenses plus yield a return for the
owner. Z-Mart, for instance, used gross profit to cover $71,400 of other
expenses. This left $12,900 in net income for the year 1999.

Exhibit 6.2

Condensed Income
Statement for a Merchandiser

Z-MART	
Condensed Income Statement	
For Year Ended December 31, 1999	
Net sales	$314,700
Cost of goods sold	(230,400)
Gross profit from sales	$ 84,300
Total other expenses	(71,400)
Net income	$ 12,900

Reporting Financial Condition

A merchandising company's balance sheet includes an item not on the balance
sheet of a service company. This item is a current asset called merchandise
inventory. **Merchandise inventory** refers to products a company owns for the
purpose of selling to customers. Exhibit 6.3 shows the classified balance sheet
for Z-Mart, including merchandise inventory of $21,000. The cost of this asset

LO3 Identify and explain
the inventory asset of
a merchandising company.

Exhibit 6.3

Classified Balance Sheet for
a Merchandiser

Z-Mart		
Balance Sheet		
December 31, 1999		
Assets		
Current assets:		
Cash		$ 8,200
Accounts receivable		11,200
Merchandise inventory		21,000
Prepaid expenses		1,100
Total current assets		$41,500
Capital assets:		
Office equipment	$ 4,200	
Less accumulated amortization	1,400	2,800
Store equipment	30,000	
Less accumulated amortization	6,000	24,000
Total capital assets		26,800
Total assets		$68,300
Liabilities		
Current liabilities:		
Accounts payable		$16,000
Salaries payable		800
Total liabilities		$16,800
Owner's Equity		
K. Marty, capital		51,500
Total liabilities and owner's equity		$68,300

---

[1] Cost of goods sold is often described as an operating expense. Also, many companies use the
term *sales* in their income statements to describe revenues. **Loblaw** is one example. Because the
CICA Handbook does not specifically require the separate disclosure of cost of goods sold, most
Canadian companies combine their cost of goods sold and operating expenses into one amount.

includes the cost incurred to buy the goods, ship them to the store, and other costs necessary to make them ready for sale. Although companies usually hold inventories of other items such as supplies, most companies simply refer to merchandise inventory as *inventory*.

Operating Cycle

A merchandising company's operating cycle begins with the purchase of merchandise and ends with the collection of cash from the sale of merchandise. An example is a merchandiser who buys products at wholesale and distributes and sells them to consumers at retail. The length of an operating cycle differs across the types of businesses. Department stores such as **The Bay** and **Eatons** commonly have operating cycles from three to five months. But operating cycles for grocery merchants such as **Loblaw** and **Safeway** usually range from one to two months.

Exhibit 6.4 graphically shows an operating cycle for a merchandiser with (1) cash sales and (2) credit sales. The cash sales cycle moves from (a) merchandise purchases to (b) inventory for sale to (c) cash collections. The credit sales cycle moves from (a) merchandise purchases to (b) inventory for sale to (c) accounts receivable to (d) cash collections. Credit sales delay the receipt of cash until the account receivable is paid by the customer. Companies try to shorten their operating cycles to increase income. Assets tied up in inventory or receivables are not productive assets since they do not earn a return such as interest.

Exhibit 6.4

Operating Cycle of a Merchandiser

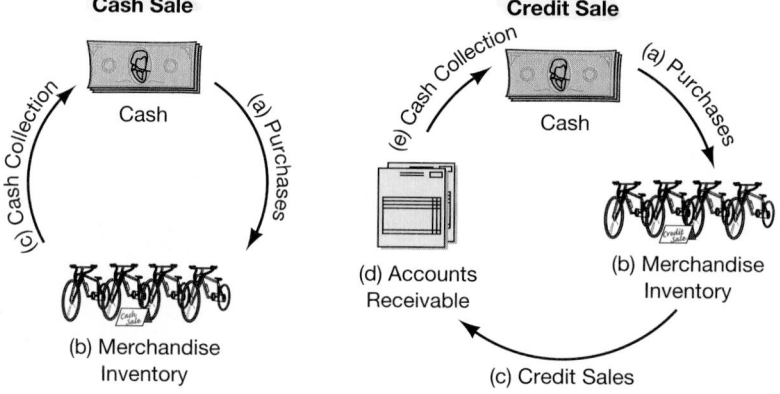

Inventory Systems

Exhibit 6.5

Merchandising Cost Flow

We explained that a merchandising company's income statement includes an item called *cost of goods sold* and its balance sheet includes a current asset called *inventory*. **Cost of goods sold** is the cost of merchandise sold to customers during a period. It is often the largest single deduction on the income statement of a merchandiser. **Inventory** represents the cost of merchandise on hand. These accounts are part of merchandising activities captured in Exhibit 6.5. This exhibit shows that a company's merchandise available for sale is a combination of what it begins with (beginning inventory) and what it purchases (net cost of purchases). The merchandise available is either sold (cost of goods sold) or kept for future sales (ending inventory).

There are two inventory accounting systems used to collect information about cost of goods sold and cost of inventory on hand. The two systems are called *periodic* and *perpetual*. We introduce these systems in this section.

Periodic Inventory System

A **periodic inventory system** requires updating the inventory account only at the *end of a period* to reflect the quantity and cost of both goods on hand and goods sold. It does not require continual updating of the inventory account. The company records the cost of new merchandise in a temporary Purchases account. When merchandise is sold, revenue is recorded but the cost of the merchandise sold is *not* yet recorded as a cost. When financial statements are prepared, the company takes a *physical count of inventory* by counting the quantities of merchandise on hand. Cost of merchandise on hand is determined by relating the quantities on hand to records showing each item's original cost. This cost of merchandise on hand is used to compute cost of goods sold. The inventory account is then adjusted to reflect the amount computed from the physical count of inventory.

Periodic systems were historically used by companies such as hardware, drug, and department stores that sold large quantities of low-value items. Without today's computers and scanners, it was not feasible for accounting systems to track such small items as pencils, toothpaste, paper clips, socks, and toothpicks through inventory and into customers' hands.

Perpetual Inventory System

A **perpetual inventory system** gives a continual record of the amount of inventory on hand. A perpetual system accumulates the net cost of merchandise purchases in the inventory account and subtracts the cost of each sale from the same inventory account. When an item is sold, its cost is recorded in a *Cost of Goods Sold* account. With a perpetual system we can find out the cost of merchandise on hand at any time by looking at the balance of the inventory account. We can also find out the cost of goods sold to date during a period by looking at the balance in the Cost of Goods Sold account.

Before advancements in computing technology, a perpetual system was often limited to businesses making a limited number of daily sales such as automobile dealers and major appliance stores. Because there were relatively few transactions, a perpetual system was feasible. In today's information age, with widespread use of computing technology, the use of a perpetual system has dramatically grown. The number of companies that use a perpetual system continues to increase.

Perpetual Information

Today's information technology is transforming merchandising activities. Computers and perpetual inventory systems are taking the guesswork out of wholesale buying, slashing inventory cycles, keeping popular items in stock, and cutting return rates. These advances have enabled **Maple Leaf Meats** to use a "centralized volume based purchasing..." system, says Maryanne Chantler the director of Purchasing. She identified savings of up to 30% in packaging material expenditures. [Source: *Food in Canada,* September 1997.]

Did You Know?

Because perpetual inventory systems give users more timely information and are widely used in practice, our discussion in this chapter emphasizes a perpetual system. Many companies provide their suppliers with point-of-sale data which allow the suppliers to know how quickly items are being sold so that replacement merchandise can be shipped on a timely basis. *We analyze and record merchandising transactions using both periodic and perpetual inventory systems in the appendix to this chapter.*

L04 Describe both periodic and perpetual inventory systems.

Answers—p. 286

Flashback

1. Describe a company's cost of goods sold.
2. What is gross profit for a merchandising company?
3. Explain why use of the perpetual inventory system has grown dramatically.

Accounting for Merchandise Purchases

We explained how with a perpetual inventory system, the cost of merchandise bought for resale is recorded in the Merchandise Inventory asset account. Z-Mart records a $1,200 cash purchase of merchandise on November 2 with this entry:

Assets = Liabilities + Equity
+1,200
−1,200

Nov. 2	Merchandise Inventory	1,200	
	Cash		1,200
	Purchased merchandise for cash.		

LO 5 Analyze and record transactions for merchandise purchases using a perpetual system.

The invoice for this merchandise in shown in Exhibit 6.6. The buyer usually receives the original, while the seller keeps a copy. Notice this single source document serves as the purchase invoice of Z-Mart (buyer) and the sales invoice for Trek (seller). The amount recorded for merchandise inventory includes its purchase cost, shipping fees, taxes, and any other costs necessary to make it ready for sale.

Exhibit 6.6

Invoice

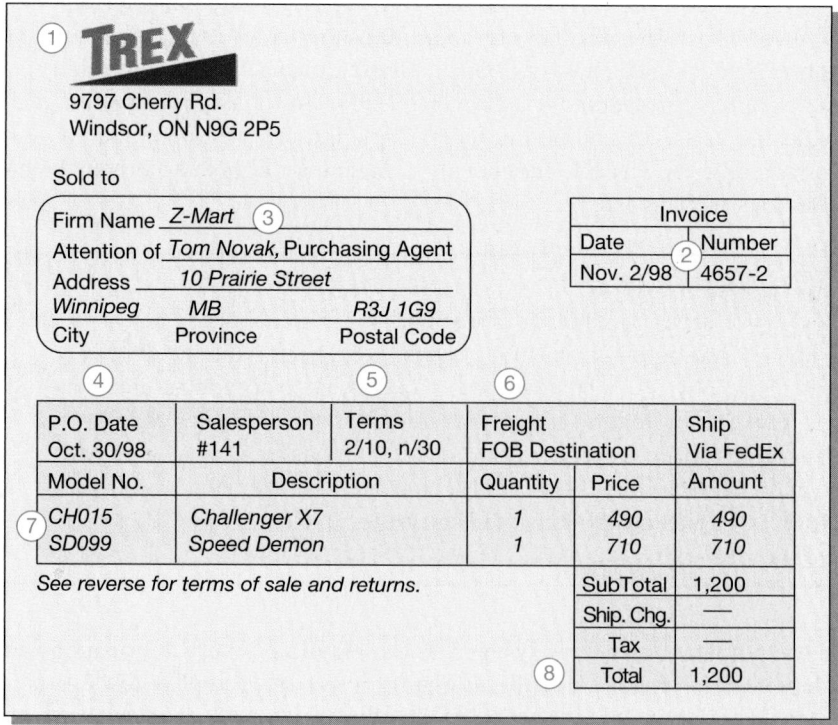

More generally, for us to compute the total cost of merchandise purchases, we must adjust the invoice cost for (1) any discounts given to a purchaser by a supplier, (2) any returns and allowances for unsatisfactory items received from a supplier, and (3) any required freight costs paid by a purchaser. This section explains how these items affect our recorded cost of merchandise purchases.

Trade Discounts

When a manufacturer or wholesaler prepares a catalogue of items it has for sale, each item is usually given a **list price,** also called a *catalogue price.* List price often is not the intended selling price of an item. Instead, the intended selling price equals list price minus a given percent called a **trade discount.**

The amount of trade discount usually depends on whether a buyer is a wholesaler, retailer, or final consumer. A wholesaler buying in large quantities is often granted a larger discount than a retailer buying in smaller quantities. A trade discount reduces a list price and is used to compute the actual selling price of the goods.

Trade discounts are commonly used by manufacturers and wholesalers to change selling prices without republishing their catalogues. When a seller wants to change selling prices, it can notify its customers merely by sending them a new table of trade discounts that they can apply to catalogue prices.

Because a list price is not intended to reflect actual selling price of merchandise, a buyer does not enter list prices and trade discounts in its accounts. Instead, a buyer records the net amount of list price minus trade discount. In the November 2 purchase of merchandise by Z-Mart, it received a 40% trade discount for the items that were listed in the seller's catalogue at $2,000. Z-Mart's purchase price is $1,200, computed as [$2,000 − (40% × $2,000)].

Purchase Discounts

The purchase of goods on credit requires a clear statement of expected amounts and dates of future payments to avoid misunderstandings. **Credit terms** for a purchase are a listing of the amounts and timing of payments between a buyer and seller. Credit terms usually reflect ordinary practices in an industry. In some industries, purchasers expect terms requiring payment within 10 days after the end of a month where purchases occur. These credit terms are entered on sales invoices or tickets as "n/10 EOM." The **EOM** refers to "end of month." In some other industries, invoices are often due and payable 30 calendar days after the invoice date. These credit terms are entered as "n/30." The 30-day period is called the **credit period.** Exhibit 6.7 portrays credit terms.

Sellers often grant a **cash discount** when the credit period is long and buyers pay promptly. A buyer views a cash discount as a **purchase discount.** A seller views a cash discount as a **sales discount.** If cash discounts for early payment exist, they are described in the credit terms on an invoice. As an example, credit terms of "2/10, n/60" mean there is a 60-day credit period before full payment is due. But the seller

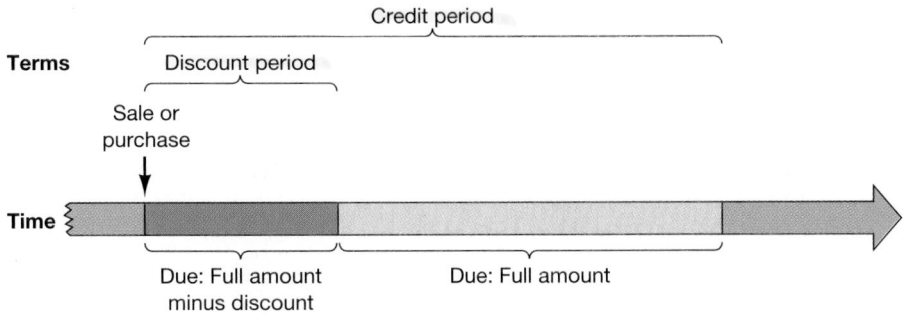

Exhibit 6.7

Credit Terms

allows a buyer to deduct 2% of the invoice amount from the payment if it is paid within 10 days of the invoice date. Sellers do this to encourage early payment. A **discount period** is the period where the reduced payment can be made.

To illustrate how a buyer accounts for a purchase discount, we assume that Z-Mart's purchase of merchandise for $1,200 was on credit with terms of 2/10, n/30. Z-Mart's entry to record this credit purchase is:

Assets = Liabilities + Equity
+1,200   +1,200

(a) Nov. 2	Merchandise Inventory	1,200	
	Accounts Payable		1,200
	Purchased merchandise on credit, invoice dated November 2, terms 2/10, n/30.		

If Z-Mart takes advantage of the discount and pays the amount due on November 12, the entry to record payment is:

Assets = Liabilities + Equity
−24   −1,200
−1,176

(b) Nov. 12	Accounts Payable	1,200	
	Merchandise Inventory (2%×$1,200) . .		24
	Cash		1,176
	Paid for the purchase of November 2 less the discount.		

Z-Mart's Merchandise Inventory account now reflects the net cost of merchandise purchased. Its Accounts Payable account also shows the debt is satisfied.

Merchandise Inventory				Accounts Payable			
Nov. 2	1,200	Nov. 12	24	Nov. 12	1,200	Nov. 2	1,200
Balance	1,176					Balance	-0-

Companies' buying practices can impact gross profit. **Home Depot,** for instance, reported an increase in gross profit for 1996 compared to 1995. It explained in its Management Discussion and Analysis section that:

> The improvement resulted primarily from more effective buying practices, which resulted in lowering the cost of merchandise.

Managing Discounts

A buyer's failure to pay within a discount period is often quite expensive. If Z-Mart does not pay within the 10-day discount period, it delays the payment by 20 more days. This delay costs Z-Mart an added 2%. Most buyers try to take advantage of purchase discounts. We can approximate Z-Mart's annual rate of interest attached to not paying within the discount period. For Z-Mart's terms of 2/10, n/30, missing the 2% discount for an additional 20 days is equal to an annual interest rate of 36.5%, computed as (365 days ÷ 20 days × 2%).

You Make the Call

Purchasing Agent
You're the purchasing agent for a merchandising company. You purchase a batch of CDs on terms of 3/10, n/90. But your company has limited cash and you would need to borrow funds at an 11% annual rate to pay within the discount period. Do you take advantage of the purchase discount?

Answer—p. 286

Most companies set up a system to pay invoices with favourable discounts within the discount period. Careful cash management means that no invoice is paid until the last day of a discount period. One technique to achieve these goals is to file each invoice so that it automatically comes up for payment on the last day of its discount period. A simple manual system uses 31 folders, one for each day in a month. After an invoice is recorded, it is placed in the folder matching the last day of its discount period. If the last day of an invoice's discount period is November 12, it is filed in folder number 12. This invoice and other invoices in the same folder are removed and paid on November 12. Computerized systems achieve the same result by using a code identifying the last date in the discount period. When that date occurs, the system automatically identifies accounts to be paid.

Credit Manager

You are the new credit manager for a merchandising company that purchases its merchandise on credit. You are trained for your new job by the outgoing employee. You are to oversee payment of payables to maintain the company's credit standing with suppliers and to take advantage of favourable cash discounts. The outgoing employee explains the computer system is programmed to prepare cheques for amounts net of favourable cash discounts, and cheques are dated the last day of the discount period. But you are told cheques are not mailed until five days later. "It's simple," this employee explains. "Our company gets free use of cash for an extra five days, and our department looks better. When a supplier complains, we blame the computer system and the mail room." Your first invoice arrives with a 10-day discount period for a $10,000 purchase. This transaction occurs on April 9 with credit terms of 2/10, n/30. Do you mail the $9,800 cheque on April 19 or April 24?

Judgment and Ethics

Answer—p. 286

Purchase Returns and Allowances

Purchase returns are merchandise received by a purchaser but returned to the supplier. A *purchase allowance* is a reduction in the cost of defective merchandise received by a purchaser from a supplier. Purchasers will often keep defective but still marketable merchandise if the supplier grants an acceptable allowance.

The purchaser usually informs the supplier in writing of any returns and allowances. This is often with a letter or a debit memorandum. A **debit memorandum** is a form issued by the purchaser to inform the supplier of a debit made to the supplier's account, including the reason for a return or allowance. The purchaser sends the debit memorandum to the supplier and also keeps a copy. Exhibit 6.8 shows a debit memorandum prepared by Z-Mart requesting an allowance from Trek for the defective *SpeedDemon* mountain bike. The purchaser's accounting for a debit memorandum requires updating the Merchandise Inventory account to reflect returns and allowances. The November 15 entry by Z-Mart for the purchase allowance requested in the debit memorandum is:

(c) Nov. 15	Accounts Payable	300	
	Merchandise Inventory		300
	Returned defective merchandise.		

Assets = Liabilities + Equity
−300   −300

If this had been a return, then the recorded cost[2] of the defective merchandise is entered. Z-Mart's agreement with this supplier says the cost of returned and defective merchandise is offset against Z-Mart's next purchase or its current

---

[2] Recorded cost is the cost reported in an inventory account minus any discounts.

Exhibit 6.8

Debit Memorandum

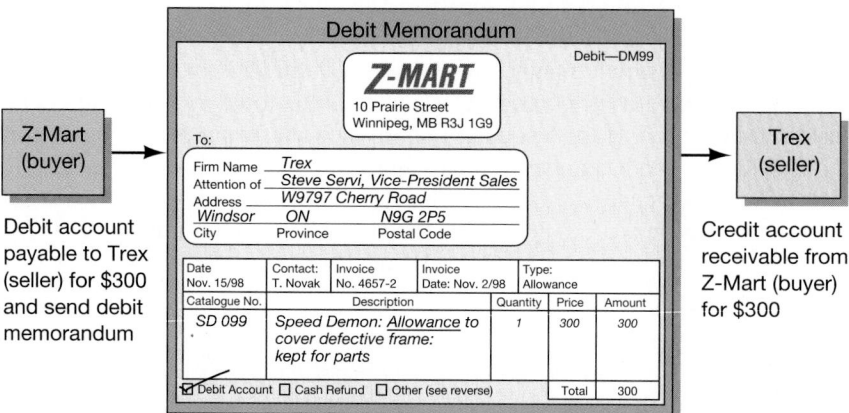

Case: Z-Mart (buyer) proposes $300 allowance for defective merchandise from Trex (seller)

account payable balance. Some agreements with suppliers involve refunding the cost to a buyer. If there is a refund of cash, then the Cash account is debited for $300 instead of Accounts Payable.

Discounts and Returns

When goods are returned within the discount period, a buyer will take the discount only on the remaining balance of the invoice. As an example, suppose Z-Mart purchases $1,000 of merchandise offered with a 2% cash discount. Two days later, Z-Mart returns $100 of goods before the invoice is paid. When Z-Mart later pays within the discount period, it can take the 2% discount only on the $900 balance. The discount is $18 (2% × $900) and the cash payment is $882 ($900 − $18).

Did You Know?

Clout!
Merchandising companies are unleashing a barrage of demands on suppliers. These include special discounts for new stores, payment of fines for shipping errors, and huge numbers of free samples. One merchandiser warned its supplier that it would impose fines of up to $30,000 for errors in bar-coding on products the supplier shipped. Merchandisers' goals are to slash inventories, shorten lead times, and eliminate error. [Source: *Materials Management & Distribution*, October 1997.]

Transportation Costs

Depending on terms negotiated with suppliers, a company is often responsible for paying shipping costs on purchases, often called *transportation-in* or *freight-in* costs. Z-Mart's $1,200 purchase on November 2 is on terms of FOB destination. This means Z-Mart is not responsible for paying transportation costs.

A different situation arises when a company is responsible for paying transportation costs. These transportation costs are often made to an independent carrier but are also sometimes made to the seller. Transportation costs are often included on the invoice when owed to the seller. Transportation costs owed to an independent carrier usually are not included on the invoice. The cost principle requires these transportation costs be included as part of the cost of purchased merchandise. This means a separate entry is necessary when they are not listed on the invoice. For example, Z-Mart's entry to record a $75 freight charge to an independent carrier for merchandise purchased FOB shipping point is:

(d) Nov. 24	Merchandise Inventory	75	
	Cash		75
	Paid freight charges on purchased merchandise.		

Assets = Liabilities + Equity
+ 75
− 75

Transportation-in costs are different from the costs of shipping goods to customers. Transportation-in costs are included in the cost of merchandise inventory whereas the costs of shipping goods to customers are not. The costs of shipping goods to customers are recorded in a Delivery Expense account when the seller is responsible for these costs. Delivery Expense, also called *freight-out* or *transportation-out,* is reported as a selling expense in the income statement.

Transfer of Ownership

The buyer and seller must reach agreement on who is responsible for paying any freight costs and who bears the risk of loss during transit for merchandising transactions. This is essentially the same as asking at what point does ownership transfer from the buyer to the seller. The point of transfer is called the **FOB** point, where FOB stands for *free on board.* The point when ownership transfers from the seller to the buyer determines who pays transportation costs (and other incidental costs of transit such as insurance).

Exhibit 6.9 identifies two alternative points of transfer. The first is FOB shipping point. *FOB shipping point,* also called *FOB factory,* means the buyer accepts ownership at the seller's place of business. The buyer is then responsible for paying shipping costs and bears the risk of damage or loss when goods are in transit. The goods are part of the buyer's inventory when they are in transit since ownership has transferred to the buyer.

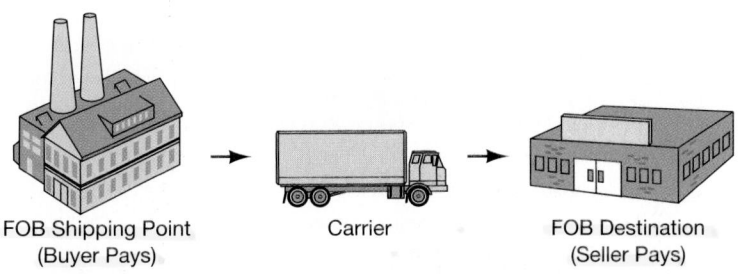

FOB Shipping Point
(Buyer Pays)   Carrier   FOB Destination
(Seller Pays)

	Ownership transfers when goods passed to	Transportation costs paid by
FOB Shipping Point	Carrier	Buyer
FOB Destination	Buyer	Seller

Exhibit 6.9

Identifying transfer of ownership

Midway Games is a leader in entertainment software and uses FOB shipping point. Midway has released many outstanding games including Mortal Kombat, Cruis'n USA, Cruis'n World, NBA Jam, Joust, Defender, Pacman, and Space Invaders. Its subsidiary, **Atari,** has had similar success. Midway is given the right by **Nintendo** and **Sega** to self-manufacture cartridges for their 16-bit platforms. Midway often uses manufacturers in Mexico where the platforms are purchased on an "as is" and "where is" basis. This means they "are delivered to the Company FOB place of manufacture and shipped at the Company's own expense and risk." Shipping usually takes 3 to 10 days, "depending on the mode of transport and location of manufacturer."[3]

---

[3] Source: Midway Games Inc., *Form 10-K405* (6-30-97).

The second point of transfer is *FOB destination.* FOB destination means ownership of the goods transfers to the buyer at the buyer's place of business. The seller is responsible for paying shipping charges and bears the risk of damage or loss in transit. The seller does not record revenue from this sale until the goods arrive at the destination because this transaction is not complete before that point.

Compaq Computer previously shipped its products by FOB shipping point. Compaq found customers' delivery firms to be undependable in picking up shipments at scheduled times and caused backups at the plant, missed deliveries, and unhappy consumers. Compaq then changed its agreements to FOB destination and its problems were eliminated.

There are situations when the party not responsible for shipping costs pays the carrier. In these cases, the party paying these costs either bills the party responsible or, more commonly, adjusts its account payable or receivable with the other party. For example, a buyer who pays a carrier when terms are FOB destination can decrease its account payable to the seller by the amount of shipping cost. Similarly, a seller who pays a carrier when terms are FOB shipping point can increase its account receivable from the buyer by the amount of shipping cost.

Recording Purchases Information

We explained how purchase discounts, purchase returns and allowances, and transportation-in are included in computing the total cost of merchandise inventory. Our initial recording of purchases (less trade discounts) is as debits to Merchandise Inventory. Any later purchase discounts, returns and allowances are credited to Merchandise Inventory. Transportation-in is debited to Merchandise Inventory. Z-Mart's 1999 total cost of merchandise purchases is made up of the items listed in Exhibit 6.10.

Exhibit 6.10

Total Cost of Merchandise Purchases Computation

Z-Mart Total Cost of Merchandise Purchases For Year Ended December 31, 1999	
Invoice cost of merchandise purchases	$235,800
Less: Purchase discounts received	(4,200)
Purchase returns and allowances received	(1,500)
Add cost of transportation-in	2,300
Total cost of merchandise purchases	$232,400

Combining these costs in the Merchandise Inventory account means this account reflects the net cost of purchased merchandise according to the *cost principle.* Recall that the Merchandise Inventory account is updated after each transaction affecting the cost of goods purchased. We later explain how this account is updated each time merchandise is sold. These timely updates of the Merchandise Inventory account reflect a perpetual inventory system.

The accounting system described here does not provide separate records for total purchases, total purchase discounts, total purchase returns and allowances, and total transportation-in. Yet managers usually need this information to evaluate and control each of these cost elements. Many companies collect this information in supplementary records. **Supplementary records,** also called *supplemental records,* are a register of information outside the usual accounting records and accounts. We explain in Chapter 8 a process where supplementary records can be maintained.

Answers—p. 286

Accounting for Merchandise Sales

We already explained how companies buying merchandise for resale account for purchases, purchase discounts, and purchase returns and allowances. Merchandising companies also must account for sales, sales discounts, sales returns and allowances, and cost of goods sold. A merchandising company such as Z-Mart reports these items in an income statement as shown in Exhibit 6.11. This section explains how information in this computation is derived from transactions involving sales, sales discounts, and sales returns and allowances.

Exhibit 6.11

Gross Profit Section of Income Statement

Z-Mart Computation of Gross Profit For Year Ended December 31, 1999		
Sales		$321,000
Less: Sales discounts	$4,300	
Sales returns and allowances	2,000	6,300
Net sales		$314,700
Cost of goods sold		(230,400)
Total cost of merchandise purchases		$ 84,300

Gross Profit

LO 6 Analyze and record transactions for sales of merchandise using a perpetual system.

This section explains how information in this computation is derived from transactions involving sales, sales discounts, and sales returns and allowances.

Sales Transactions

Each sales transaction for a seller of merchandise involves two related parts. One part is the revenue received in the form of an asset from a customer. The second part is recognizing the cost of merchandise sold to a customer. Accounting for a sales transaction means capturing information about both parts.

Sales transactions of merchandisers usually include both sales for cash and sales on credit. Whether a sale is for cash or on credit, a sales transaction requires two entries: one for revenue and one for cost. As an example, Z-Mart sold $2,400 of merchandise on credit on November 3. The revenue part of this transaction is recorded as:

(e) Nov. 3	Accounts Receivable	2,400	
	Sales		2,400
	Sold merchandise on credit.		

Assets = Liabilities + Equity
+2,400   +2,400

This entry reflects an increase in Z-Mart's assets in the form of an account receivable. It also shows the revenue from the credit sale.[4] If the sale is for cash, the debit is to Cash instead of Accounts Receivable.

---

[4] We describe in Chapter 8 how companies account for sales to customers who use third-party credit cards such as those issued by banks.

The cost of the merchandise Z-Mart sold on November 3 is $1,600. We explain in Chapter 7 how the cost of this merchandise is computed. The entry to record the cost part of this sales transaction (under a perpetual inventory system) is:

Assets = Liabilities + Equity
−1,600   −1,600

Nov. 3	Cost of Goods Sold	1,600	
	Merchandise Inventory		1,600
	To record the cost of Nov. 3 sale.		

Since the cost part is recorded each time a sale occurs, the Merchandise Inventory account reflects the cost of the remaining merchandise on hand.

Sales Discounts

Selling goods on credit demands that expected amounts and dates of future payments be made clear to avoid misunderstandings. We explained earlier in this chapter how credit terms often include a discount to encourage early payment. Companies granting cash discounts to customers refer to these as *sales discounts*. Sales discounts can benefit a seller by decreasing the delay in receiving cash. Prompt payments also reduce future efforts and costs of billing customers.

A seller does not know whether a customer will pay within the discount period and take advantage of a cash discount at the time of a credit sale. This means a sales discount is usually not recorded until a customer pays within the discount period. As an example, Z-Mart completed a credit sale for $1,000 on November 12, subject to terms of 2/10, n/60. The entry to record this sale is:

Assets = Liabilities + Equity
+1,000   +1,000

Nov. 12	Accounts Receivable	1,000	
	Sales		1,000
	Sold merchandise under terms		
	of 2/10, n/60.		

This entry records the receivable and the revenue as if the full amount will be paid by the customer.

But the customer has two options. One option is to wait 60 days until January 11 and pay the full $1,000. In this case, Z-Mart records the payment as:

Assets = Liabilities + Equity
+1,000
−1,000

Jan. 11	Cash	1,000	
	Accounts Receivable		1,000
	Received payment for November 12 sale.		

The customer's second option is to pay $980 within a 10-day period running through November 22. If the customer pays on or before November 22, Z-Mart records the payment as:

Assets = Liabilities + Equity
+980   −20
−1,000

Nov. 22	Cash	980	
	Sales Discounts	20	
	Accounts Receivable		1,000
	Received payment for November 12 sale		
	less the discount.		

Sales discounts are recorded in a *contra-revenue* account called Sales Discounts. This is so management can monitor sales discounts to assess their effectiveness and cost. The Sales Discounts account is deducted from the Sales account when computing a company's net sales. While information about sales discounts is useful, it is seldom reported on income statements distributed to external users.

Discount Miscount

Penguin Books reported unauthorized discounts were given to some of its merchandisers. This led to a $163 million charge against Penguin's 1996 income. [Source: *Business Week,* April 14, 1997.]

Did You Know?

Sales Returns and Allowances

Sales returns refer to merchandise that customers return to the seller after a sale. Many companies allow customers to return merchandise for a full refund. *Sales allowances* refer to reductions in the selling price of merchandise sold to customers. This can occur with damaged merchandise that a customer is willing to purchase with a decrease in selling price. Sales returns and allowances involve dissatisfied customers and the possibility of lost future sales. Managers need information about returns and allowances to monitor these problems. Many accounting systems record returns and allowances in a separate contra-revenue account for this purpose.

Recall Z-Mart's sale of merchandise on November 3. As already recorded, the merchandise is sold for $2,400 and cost $1,600. But what if the customer returns part of the merchandise on November 6, where returned items sell for $800 and cost $600? The revenue part of this transaction must reflect the decrease in sales from the customer's return:

(f) Nov. 6	Sales Returns and Allowances	800	
	Accounts Receivable		800
	Customer returned merchandise.		

Assets = Liabilities + Equity
− 800   −800

Z-Mart can record this return with a debit to the Sales account instead of Sales Returns and Allowances. This method provides the same net sales, but does not provide information managers need in monitoring returns and allowances. By using the Sales Returns and Allowances contra account, this information is available. Published income statements usually omit this detail and show only net sales.

MegaBooks and MegaHeadaches

Book Merchandisers such as **Barnes & Noble** and **Borders Books** can return unsold books to publishers at purchase price. Publishers say returns of new hardcover books are now running between 35% and 50%. This compares with 15% to 25% ten years ago. Also, competition for big hits is prompting huge author advances that together with returns are depressing publishers' earnings [Source: *Business Week,* April 14, 1997.]

Did You Know?

If the merchandise returned to Z-Mart is not defective and can be resold to another customer, then Z-Mart returns these goods to its inventory. The entry necessary to restore the cost of these goods to the Merchandise Inventory account is:

Nov. 6	Merchandise Inventory	600	
	Cost of Goods Sold		600
	Returned goods to inventory.		

Assets = Liabilities + Equity
+ 600   +600

But if the merchandise returned is defective, the seller may discard the returned items. In this case, the cost of returned merchandise is not restored to the Merchandise Inventory account. Instead, most companies leave the cost of defective merchandise in the Cost of Goods Sold account.[5]

Another possibility is that $800 of the merchandise Z-Mart sold on November 3 is defective but the customer decides to keep it because Z-Mart grants the customer a price reduction of $500. The only entry Z-Mart must make in this case is one to reflect the decrease in revenue:

Assets = Liabilities + Equity
−500   −500

Nov. 6	Sales Returns and Allowances	500	
	Accounts Receivable		500
	To record sales allowance.		

The seller usually prepares a **credit memorandum** to confirm a customer's return or allowance. A credit memorandum informs a customer of a credit to its Account Receivable account from a sales return or allowance. The information in a credit memorandum is similar to that of a debit memorandum. Z-Mart's credit memorandum issued to the customer for the return of $800 of merchandise on November 6 is shown in Exhibit 6.12.

Exhibit 6.12

Credit Memorandum

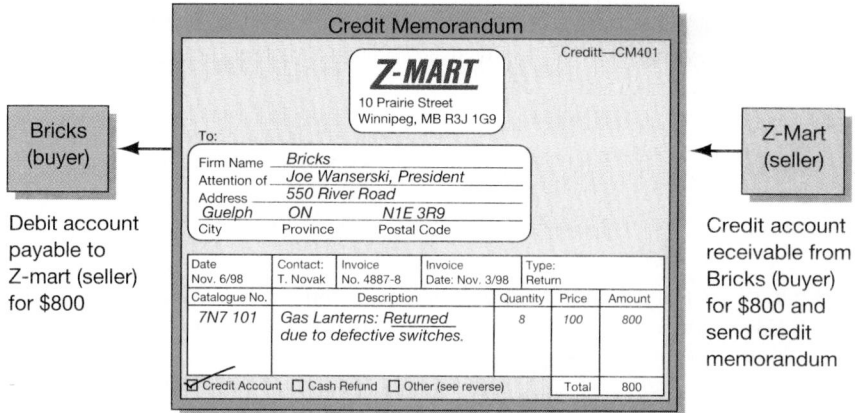

Case: Z-Mart (seller) accepts $800 of returned merchandise from Bricks (buyer)

Additional Merchandising Issues

This section identifies and explains how merchandising activities affect other accounting processes. We address cost and price adjustments, preparing adjusting and closing entries, and relations between important accounts.

Cost and Price Adjustments

Buyers and sellers often find they need to adjust the amount owed between them. Examples include a situation where purchased merchandise does not meet specifications, unordered goods are received, different quantities are received than were ordered and billed, and errors occur in billing. The original balance can sometimes be adjusted by the buyer without negotiation. An example would be

---

[5] When managers want to monitor the cost of defective merchandise, a better method is to remove their cost from Cost of Goods Sold and charge it to a *Loss from Defective Merchandise* account.

when a seller makes an error on an invoice. If the buyer discovers an error, the buyer can make an adjustment and notify the seller by sending a debit memorandum or a credit memorandum. Sometimes adjustments can be made only after negotiations between the buyer and seller. For example, a buyer claims some merchandise does not meet specifications. In these cases the amount of allowance given by the seller is usually arrived at only after discussion.

Flashback

7. Why are sales discounts and sales returns and allowances recorded in contra-revenue accounts instead of directly in the Sales account?

8. Under what conditions are two entries necessary to record a sales return?

9. When merchandise is sold on credit and the seller notifies the buyer of a price reduction, does the seller send a credit memorandum or a debit memorandum?

Answers-p. 286

Mid-Chapter Demonstration Problem

Beta Company, a retail store had the following transactions in March:

March 2   Purchased merchandise from Alfa Company under the following terms: $1,800 invoice price, 2/15, n/60, FOB factory.
3   Paid $125 for shipping charges on the purchase of March 2.
4   Returned to Alfa Company unacceptable merchandise that had an invoice price of $300.
17   Sent a cheque to Alfa Company for the March 2 purchase, net of the discount and the returned merchandise.

Required

a. Present the journal entries Beta Company should record for these transactions.
b. Present the journal entries Alfa Company should record for these transactions.

Solution to Mid-Chapter Demonstration Problem

a. Beta Company

March 2	Merchandise Inventory.	1,800	
	Accounts Payable (Alfa Company) . . .		1,800
	Purchased merchandise on credit.		
March 3	Merchandise Inventory.	125	
	Cash		125
	Paid shipping charges on purchased merchandise.		
March 4	Accounts Payable (Alfa Company)	300	
	Merchandise Inventory		300
	Returned unacceptable merchandise.		
March 17	Accounts Payable (Alfa Company)	1,500	
	Merchandise Inventory		30
	Cash		1,470
	Paid balance within the discount period and took a 2% discount.		

Solution to Mid-Chapter Demonstration Problem (continued)	b. Alfa Company			
	March 2	Acounts Receivable (Beta Company)	1,800	
		Sales		1,800
		Sold merchandise under terms of 2/15, n/60.		
	March 4	Sales Returns and Allowances	300	
		Accounts Receivable (Beta Company) . .		300
		Customer returned merchandise.		
	March 17	Cash	1,470	
		Sales discounts	30	
		Accounts Receivable (Beta Company) . .		1,500
		Received payment for March 2 sale less discount.		

Adjusting Entries

LO7 Prepare adjustments and close accounts for a merchandising company.

Most adjusting entries are the same for merchandising companies and service companies. The adjustments for both types of companies involve prepaid expenses, amortization, accrued expenses, unearned revenues, and accrued revenues.

A merchandising company using a perpetual inventory system is often required to make one additional adjustment. This adjustment updates the Merchandise Inventory account to reflect any losses of merchandise. Merchandising companies can lose merchandise in several ways, including theft and deterioration. **Shrinkage** refers to the loss of inventory for merchandising companies.

While a perpetual inventory system tracks all goods as they move in and out of the company, a perpetual system is unable to directly measure shrinkage. Yet we can compute shrinkage by comparing a physical count of the inventory with recorded quantities. A physical count is usually performed at least once annually to verify the Merchandise Inventory account. Most companies record any necessary adjustment due to shrinkage by charging it to Cost of Goods Sold, assuming shrinkage is not abnormally large.

As an example, Z-Mart's Merchandise Inventory account at the end of 1999 had a balance of $21,250. But a physical count of inventory revealed only $21,000 of inventory on hand. The adjusting entry to record this $250 shrinkage is:

Assets = Liabilities + Equity
−250   −250

Dec. 31	Cost of Goods Sold	250	
	Merchandise Inventory		250
	To adjust for $250 shrinkage disclosed by physical count of inventory.		

Did You Know?

Wanted for Shrinkage
According to the Retail Council of Canada, the shrinkage rate from hardware stores and lumberyards was just over 1% of sales last year. That represents $150-million worth of merchandise. [Source: *Hardware Merchandising*, January 1998.]

Closing Entries

Closing entries are similar for merchandising companies and service companies when using a perpetual system. The one difference is we must close temporary

Z-Mart Adjusted Trial Balance December 31, 1999		
Cash	$ 8,200	
Accounts receivable	11,200	
Merchandise inventory	21,000	
Office supplies	550	
Store supplies	250	
Prepaid insurance	300	
Office equipment	4,200	
Accumulated amortization, office equipment		$ 1,400
Store equipment	30,000	
Accumulated amortization, store equipment		6,000
Accounts payable		16,000
Salaries payable		800
K. Marty, capital		42,600
K. Marty, withdrawals	4,000	
Sales		321,000
Sales discounts	4,300	
Sales returns and allowances	2,000	
Cost of goods sold	230,400	
Amortization expense, store equipment	3,000	
Amortization expense, office equipment	700	
Office salaries expense	25,300	
Sales salaries expense	18,500	
Insurance expense	600	
Rent expense, office space	900	
Rent expense, selling space	8,100	
Office supplies expense	1,800	
Store supplies expense	1,200	
Advertising expense	11,300	
Totals	$387,800	$387,800

Exhibit 6.13

Adjusted Trial Balance

accounts related to merchandising activities. We show the closing process for Z-Mart using its 1999 adjusted trial balance in Exhibit 6.13.

Z-Mart's trial balance includes several accounts unique to merchandising companies. These include: Merchandise Inventory, Sales, Sales Discounts, Sales Returns and Allowances, and Cost of Goods Sold. Their existence in the ledger means the four closing entries for a merchandiser are slightly different from the ones described in Chapter 5 for a service company. These differences are bolded in the closing entries in Exhibit 6.14.

Merchandising Cost Flows

Exhibit 6.15 shows the relation between inventory, purchases, and cost of goods sold across periods. We already explained how the net cost of purchases captures trade discounts, purchase discounts granted, and purchase returns and allowances. These items comprising the cost of purchases are recorded in the Merchandise Inventory account when using a perpetual system. When each sale occurs the cost of items sold is transferred from Merchandise Inventory to the Cost of Goods Sold account. Cost of goods sold is reported on the income statement. The ending balance in Merchandise Inventory is reported on the balance sheet.

LO 8 Analyze and interpret cost flows and operating activities of a merchandising company.

Exhibit 6.14

Closing Entries for Z-Mart

Entry 1: Close Credit Balances in Temporary Accounts to Income Summary.

The first entry closes temporary accounts having credit balances. Z-Mart has one temporary account with a credit balance and it is closed with the entry:

Dec. 31	Sales	321,000	
	Income Summary		321,000
	To close temporary accounts having credit balances.		

Posting this entry to the ledger gives a zero balance to the Sales account and opens the Income Summary account.

Entry 2: Close Debit Balances in Temporary Accounts to Income Summary.

The second entry closes temporary accounts having debit balances. These include Cost of Goods Sold, Sales Discounts, and Sales Returns and Allowances. This entry also yields the amount of net income as the balance in the Income Summary account.
Z-Mart's second closing entry is:

Dec. 31	Income Summary	308,100	
	Sales Discounts		4,300
	Sales Returns and Allowances		2,000
	Cost of Goods Sold		230,400
	Amortization Expense, Store Equipment		3,000
	Amortization Expense, Office Equipment		700
	Office Salaries Expense		25,300
	Sales Salaries Expense		18,500
	Insurance Expense		600
	Rent Expense, Office Space		900
	Rent Expense, Selling Space		8,100
	Office Supplies Expense		1,800
	Store Supplies Expense		1,200
	Advertising Expense		11,300
	To close temporary accounts having debit balances.		

Entry 3: Close Income Summary to Owner's Capital.

The third closing entry is the same for a merchandising company and a service company. It closes the Income Summary account and updates the owner's capital account for income or loss. Z-Mart's third closing entry is:

Dec. 31	Income Summary	12,900	
	K. Marty, Capital		12,900
	To close the Income Summary account.		

Notice the $12,900 amount in the entry is net income reported on the income statement in Exhibit 6.2.

Entry 4: Close Withdrawals Account to Owner's Capital.

The fourth closing entry for a merchandising company is the same as the fourth closing entry for a service company. It closes the withdrawals account and reduces the owner's capital account balance to the amount shown on the balance sheet. The fourth closing entry for Z-Mart is:

Dec. 31	K. Marty, Capital	4,000	
	K. Marty, Withdrawals		4,000
	To close the withdrawals account.		

When this entry is posted, all temporary accounts are cleared and ready to record events for year 2000. The Owner's Capital account also is updated and reflects transactions of 1999.

Notice the Merchandise Inventory account balance at the end of period one is the amount of beginning inventory in period two. The sequence of events during period two (and every period) is the same as during period one. The cost of each purchase is added to the Merchandise Inventory account and the cost of each sale is transferred from Merchandise Inventory to Cost of Goods Sold. At the end of the period, the Merchandise Inventory balance is reported on the balance sheet.

Merchandising Cost Accounts

To explain how merchandising transactions affect the Merchandise Inventory and Cost of Goods Sold accounts, we list Z-Mart's merchandising activities during 1999 in Exhibit 6.16 and show the impact of these activities in ledger T-accounts of Exhibit 6.17. The amounts in these exhibits are linked by superscripts a–h.

We explained how the perpetual inventory accounting system does not include separate accounts for purchases, purchase discounts, purchase returns and allowances, and transportation-in. But Z-Mart, like many companies, keeps supplementary records about these items. These supplementary records are used to accumulate the information in Exhibit 6.16. Z-Mart also keeps a separate record for the cost of merchandise returned by customers and restored in inventory.

The Merchandise Inventory and Cost of Goods Sold T-accounts in Exhibit 6.17 reflect the effects of these merchandising activities for Z-Mart. Most amounts in these T-accounts are summary representations of several entries during the year 1999.

Exhibit 6.15

Merchandising Cost Flows Across Periods*

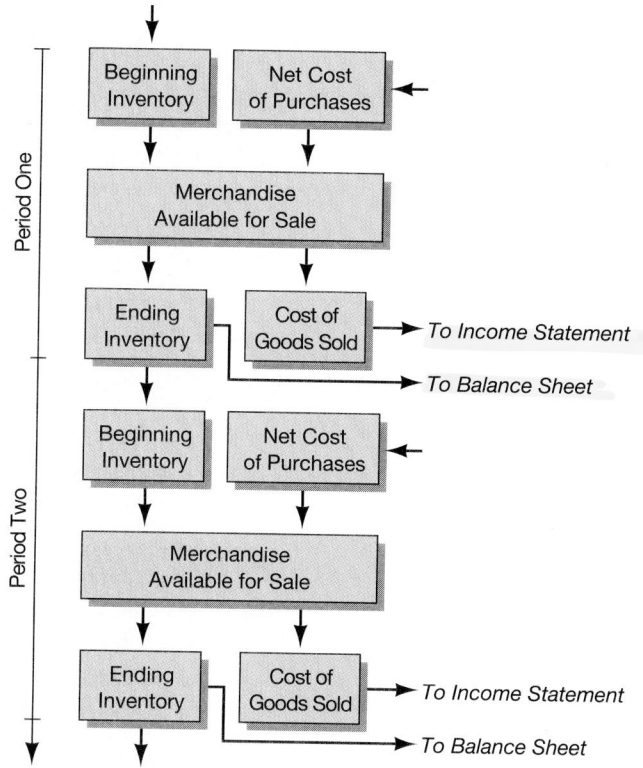

* Cost of goods sold is reported on the income statement. Ending Inventory is reported on the balance sheet. One period's ending inventory is the next period's beginning inventory.

Z-Mart's merchandising activities for 1999	
Z-Mart's beginning inventory on January 1, 1999	19,000 a
Invoice cost of merchandise purchases	$235,800 b
Cost of freight to bring merchandise to Z-Mart's store	2,300 c
Purchase discounts Z-Mart received from making payments within discount periods	4,200 d
Refunds and credit granted to Z-Mart from purchase returns and allowances	1,500 e
Cost of merchandise sold to customers	231,550 f
Cost of merchandise returned by customers and restored to Z-Mart's inventory	1,400 g
Cost of inventory shrinkage computed by physical count of inventory at year-end	250 h

Exhibit 6.16

Summary of Merchandising Activities

Flashback

10. When a merchandising company uses a perpetual inventory system, why is it often necessary to adjust the Merchandise Inventory balance with an adjusting entry?

11. What temporary accounts do you expect to find in a merchandising business but not in a service business?

12. Describe the closing entries normally made by a merchandising company.

Answers—p. 286

Exhibit 6.17

Merchandising Transactions
Reflected in T-Accounts

Merchandise Inventory			
Dec. 31, 1998, balance	19,000[a]		
Reflects entries to record		Reflects entries to record	
purchases of merchandise. . . .	235,800[b]	purchase discounts	
		during 1999	4,200[d]
Reflects entries to		Reflects entries to	
record merchandise returned		record purchase returns and	
by customers and restored to		allowances during 1999	1,500[e]
inventory during 1999	1,400[g]	Reflects cost of	
Reflects transportation-in		sales transactions	
costs incurred during 1999 . . .	2,300[c]	during 1999	231,550[f]
Total.	258,500	Total.	237,250
	−237,250		
Dec. 31, 1999, unadjusted balance	21,250		
		Dec. 31 Shrinkage	250[h]
Total.	21,250	Total.	250
	−250		
Dec. 31, 1999, adjusted balance	21,000		

Cost of Goods Sold			
Reflects entries to		Reflects entries to	
record the cost part		record merchandise returned	
of sales transactions	231,550[f]	by customers and restored to	
Inventory shrinkage recorded		inventory during 1999	1,400[g]
in December 31, 1999,			
adjusting entry	250[h]		
Total.	231,800	Total.	1,400
	−1,400		
Balance (before closing).	230,400		

Notice the Cost of Goods Sold balance of $230,400 is the amount reported on the income statement in Exhibit 6.2. The Merchandise Inventory balance of $21,000 is the amount reported as a current asset on the balance sheet in Exhibit 6.3. These amounts also appeared on Z-Mart's adjusted trial balance in Exhibit 6.13.

Income Statement Formats

LO 9 Define and prepare multiple-step and single-step income statements.

Generally accepted accounting principles do not require companies to use a specific format for financial statements. We see many different formats in practice. The first part of this section describes two common income statement formats using Z-Mart's data: multiple-step and single-step. The last part of this section compares accrual and cash flow measures of gross profit for merchandising activities.

Multiple-Step Income Statement

Multiple-step income statements often contain more detail than simply a listing of revenues and expenses. There are two general types of multiple-step income statement. The usual format we see in external reports is what people commonly call the *multiple-step* format. A more detailed format is also available, but usually seen only in internal documents. It is called the *classified, multiple-step* format. Both formats can be used in either a perpetual or periodic system.

Classified, Multiple-Step Format

Exhibit 6.18 shows a **classified, multiple-step income statement** for Z-Mart. This format shows detailed computations of net sales and cost of goods sold. Operating expenses are classified separately as selling expenses or general and administrative expenses. This format reports subtotals between sales and net income. This is why it is called a *classified* format.

Z-Mart Income Statement For Year Ended December 31, 1999			
Sales....................................			$321,000
Less: Sales discounts....................		$ 4,300	
Sales returns and allowances..............		2,000	6,300
Net sales.............................			$314,700
Cost of goods sold:			
Merchandise inventory, December 31, 1998 ...		$ 19,000	
Total cost of merchandise purchases*........		232,400	
Goods available for sale		$251,400	
Merchandise inventory, December 31, 1999 ...		21,000	
Cost of goods sold			230,400
Gross profit from sales			$ 84,300
Operating expenses:			
Selling expenses:			
Amortization expense, store equipment	$ 3,000		
Sales salaries expense	18,500		
Rent expense, selling space	8,100		
Store supplies expense.................	1,200		
Advertising expense	11,300		
Total selling expenses.................		$ 42,100	
General and administrative expenses:			
Amortization expense, office equipment	$ 700		
Office salaries expense.................	25,300		
Insurance expense	600		
Rent expense, office space	900		
Office supplies expense	1,800		
Total general and administrative expenses ...		29,300	
Total operating expenses.................			71,400
Net income			$ 12,900

*Using *supplementary records,* the Total Cost of Merchandise Purchases is comprised of: invoice cost of merchandise (235,800) − discounts (4,200) − returns and allowances (1,500) + freight (2,300). See Exhibit 6.10 and related discussion for further explanation.

Exhibit 6.18

Classified, Multiple-Step Income Statement

Z-Mart's sales section is the same as shown earlier in the chapter. The cost of goods sold section draws on supplementary records Z-Mart keeps for merchandise purchases, purchase discounts, purchase returns and allowances, and transportation-in. The difference between net sales and cost of goods sold is Z-Mart's gross profit. Its operating expenses are classified into two categories. **Selling expenses** include the expenses of promoting sales through displaying and advertising merchandise, making sales, and delivering goods to customers. **General and administrative expenses** support the overall operations of a company and include expenses related to accounting, human resource management, and financial management.

Expenses are often divided between categories when they contribute to more than one activity. Exhibit 6.18 shows Z-Mart allocates rent expense of $9,000 for its store building between two categories. Selling expense includes $8,100 of it while $900 is listed as general and administrative expense.[6] Any cost allocation should reflect an economic relation between the amounts assigned and the activities. Allocation of Z-Mart's rent is based on relative rental values.

Multiple-Step Format

Exhibit 6.19 shows a multiple-step income statement format common in external reports. In comparison to Exhibit 6.18, a multiple-step statement leaves out detailed computations of net sales and cost of goods sold. Selling expenses are also combined with general and administrative expenses.

We frequently see even more condensed formats in practice. For example, **Alliance's** income statement in Appendix I shows a single line item titled *Direct operating expenses*. Yet its annual report gives management's discussion and analysis of these expenses.

Exhibit 6.19

Multiple-Step Income Statement

Z-Mart Income Statement For Year Ended December 31, 1999		
Net sales		$314,700
Cost of goods sold		230,400
Gross profit from sales		$ 84,300
Operating expenses:		
Amortization expense	$ 3,700	
Salaries expense	43,800	
Rent expense	9,000	
Insurance expense	600	
Supplies expense	3,000	
Advertising expense	11,300	
Total operating expenses		71,400
Net income		$ 12,900

Single-Step Income Statement

A **single-step income statement** is another widely used format. This format is shown in Exhibit 6.20 for Z-Mart. This simple format includes cost of goods sold as an operating expense and shows only one subtotal for total expenses. Operating expenses are highly summarized.

Exhibit 6.20

Single-Step Income Statement

Z-Mart Income Statement For Year Ended December 31, 1999		
Net sales		$314,700
Cost of goods sold	$230,400	
Selling expenses	42,100	
General and administrative expenses	29,300	
Total expenses		301,800
Net income		$ 12,900

---

[6] These expenses can be recorded in a single ledger account or in two separate accounts. If they are recorded in one account, we allocate its balance between the two expenses when preparing statements.

Many companies use formats that combine features of both the single- and multiple-step statements. As long as income statement items are shown sensibly, management can choose the format it wants.[7] Similar options are available for the statement of changes in owner's equity and statement of cash flows for both merchandising companies and service companies.

Merchandising Cash Flows

Another aspect of effectively reporting on merchandising activities relates to their cash flow impacts. Merchandising sales and costs reported in the income statement usually differ from their cash receipts and payments for the period. This is because an income statement is prepared using accrual accounting, not cash flows. Recognition of sales is rarely equal to cash received from customers. Also, recognition of cost of goods sold is rarely equal to cash paid to suppliers.

LO 10 Analyze and interpret accruals and cash flows for merchandising activities.

Exhibit 6.21

Analysis of Merchandising Cash Flows

Z-Mart For Year Ended December 31, 1999			
Income Statement		**Statement of Cash Flows**	
Net Sales	$314,700	$309,200	Receipts from Customers
Cost of Goods Sold	230,400	240,900	Payments to Suppliers
Gross Profit	84,300	68,300	Net Cash Flows from Customers and Suppliers

We use Z-Mart's data in Exhibit 6.21 to illustrate this point. Z-Mart's net sales in the income statement total $314,700. Yet cash receipts from customers are only $309,200 (shown on the right half of Exhibit 6.21). This difference reflects a $5,500 *increase* in Accounts Receivable during 1999 for Z-Mart. An increase in Accounts Receivable means a delay in Z-Mart's receipt of cash from customers. It also means cash received from customers this period is less than net sales. To see this, recall that net sales and cash received are the same if all net sales are cash sales. But when some or all net sales are credit sales, then net sales and cash are likely different amounts. Since Accounts Receivable increased during the period, we know cash received is less than net sales. For Z-Mart, this relation is revealed as follows:

Net Sales	$314,700
Less increase in Accounts Receivable . .	5,500
Cash received from customers	$309,200

But if Accounts Receivable had decreased, then cash received would be greater than net sales.

We apply similar analysis to cost of goods sold. Z-Mart's cost of goods sold reported in its income statement totals $230,400. Yet cash paid to suppliers is $240,900. The difference between cost of goods sold and cash paid to suppliers reflects *two* items: (1) *change in inventory*, and (2) *change in accounts payable*. An increase in inventory implies more goods were purchased than sold this period. But a decrease in inventory implies less goods were purchased than sold this period. An increase in accounts payable suggests less cash is paid to suppliers than the cost of this period's purchases. But a decrease in accounts payable suggests more cash is paid to suppliers than the cost of this period's purchases. We know from Exhibit 6.21 the cash paid to suppliers is $10,500 more than cost of goods sold. This $10,500 difference reflects a $2,000 *increase* in inventory

---

[7] We describe certain items in later chapters, such as extraordinary gains and losses, that must be shown in certain locations on the income statement.

(purchased *more* than sold) and a $8,500 *decrease* in Accounts Payable (paid for *more* than current purchases) in 1999 for Z-Mart.

Recall that cost of goods sold and cash paid are the same if inventory and account payable levels don't change during the period. But when one or both account balance change, then cost of goods sold and cash paid are likely different amounts. For Z-Mart, this relation for 1999 is shown as follows:

Cost of Goods Sold	$230,400
Add increase in Inventory	2,000
Add decrease in Accounts Payable	8,500
Cash paid to suppliers	$240,900

Buying and selling merchandise is the most important activity for a merchandiser such as Z-Mart. We need to analyze both accrual and cash flows of this activity for signs of opportunity or problems. The increase in Accounts Receivable reflects an attempt by Z-Mart to meet competition and increase sales. It is trying to expand its sales by extending credit to more customers. But extending credit to customers who don't pay their bills can backfire. We must always analyze important differences in accrual and cash flow figures and identify their causes for effective decision making.

Acid-Test and Gross Margin   USING THE INFORMATION

Companies with merchandising activities have at least two major differences from service companies. First, merchandise inventory often makes up a large part of assets, especially current assets. Second, merchandising activities result in cost of goods sold. Cost of goods sold is often the largest cost for these companies. Companies with merchandising activities change the way we use ratio analysis. This is especially the case with the current ratio (see Chapter 5) and the profit margin ratio (see Chapter 4). This section describes adjustments to these ratios to help us analyze merchandising companies.

Acid-Test Ratio

LO 11 Compute the acid-test ratio and explain its use as an indicator of a company's liquidity.

Merchandise inventory is a current asset. For many merchandising companies, inventory makes up a large portion of current assets. This often means a large part of current assets is not readily available for paying liabilities. This is because inventory must be sold and any resulting accounts receivable need be collected before cash is available.

Information about current assets is important since we use it in assessing a company's ability to pay its current liabilities. We explained how the current ratio, defined as current assets divided by current liabilities, is useful in assessing a company's ability to pay current liabilities. Yet since it is sometimes unreasonable to assume inventories are a source of payment for current liabilities, we look to another measure.

One measure used to help us assess a company's ability to pay its current liabilities is the acid-test ratio. The acid-test ratio differs from the current ratio by excluding less liquid current assets such as inventory. Liquidity refers to how quickly an item is converted to cash. The less liquid assets are those that will take longer to convert to cash. The **acid-test ratio,** also called *quick ratio,* is defined as *quick assets* (cash, short-term investments, and receivables) divided by current liabilities. This is similar to the current ratio except that the numerator omits inventory and prepaid expenses. Exhibit 6.22 shows both the acid-test and current ratios of **Canadian Tire** for 1994-1996.

(in thousands)	1996	1995	1994
Canadian Tire:			
Total quick assets	$ 946	$1,106	$1,206
Total current assets	1,340	1,559	1,655
Total current liabilities	863	911	1,044
Acid-Test ratio	1.10	1.21	1.16
Current ratio	1.55	1.71	1.59
Industry:			
Industry acid-test ratio	1.1	1.3	1.3
Industry current ratio	3.6	3.9	3.9

Exhibit 6.22

Canadian Tire's Acid-Test and Current Ratios

The formula for the acid-test ratio is shown in Exhibit 6.23.

$$\text{Acid-test ratio} = \frac{\text{Quick assets}}{\text{Current liabilities}}$$

Exhibit 6.23

Acid-test ratio

We compute **Canadian Tire's** 1996 acid-test ratio by using information in Exhibit 6.22 as follows:

$$\frac{\$946}{\$863} = 1.10$$

Notice Canadian Tire's acid-test and current ratios drop in 1996 compared with prior years. While the industry ratios also dropped, neither declined to the extent of Canadian Tire's ratios. Canadian Tire's current ratios for 1994-1996 suggest its short-term obligations can be covered with short-term assets. An acid-test ratio less than 1 would mean that Canadian Tire's current liabilities exceed its quick assets. Although the acid-test ratio is lower in 1996, it does not appear that Canadian Tire is in any danger of not meeting its current liabilities.

A common rule of thumb is the acid-test ratio should have a value of at least 1.0 to conclude a company is unlikely to face liquidity[8] problems in the near future. A value less than 1.0 suggests a liquidity problem unless a company can generate enough cash from sales or if the accounts payable are not due until late in the next period. Similarly, a value greater than 1.0 can hide a liquidity problem if payables are due shortly and receivables won't be collected until late in the next period. Our analysis of Canadian Tire emphasizes that one ratio is seldom enough to reach a conclusion as to strength or weakness. The power of a ratio is often its ability to identify areas we need to analyze in more detail.

Supplier

You're a supplier of building materials. A retail store approaches you for credit on future purchases of materials. You don't have any prior experience with this store. You ask and receive the store's financial statements to assess its ability to make payment on purchases. The store's current ratio is 2.1 and its acid-test ratio is 0.5. You find inventory makes up most of current assets. Do you extend credit to this store?

Answer—p. 286

Gross Margin Ratio

A major cost of merchandising companies is its cost of goods sold. For many merchandising companies, cost of goods sold makes up the majority of its costs. This means success for merchandising companies often depends on the relation between sales and cost of goods sold.

LO 12 Compute the gross margin ratio and explain its use as an indicator of profitability.

---

[8] Liquidity is the ability to convert assets into ready cash.

We described the importance of the profit margin ratio in Chapter 4. Gross profit, also called gross margin, is a major part of a profit margin for merchandising companies. To help us focus on this important item, users often compute a gross margin ratio. Without sufficient gross profit, a merchandising company will likely fail. The gross margin ratio differs from the profit margin ratio by excluding all costs except cost of goods sold. The **gross margin ratio** is defined as gross margin (net sales minus cost of goods sold) divided by net sales. Exhibit 6.24 shows the gross margin ratios of **Mitel Corporation** for 1995-1997.

Exhibit 6.24

Mitel's Gross
Margin Ratio

(in millions)	1997	1996	1995
Gross Margin	$ 351.1	$ 284.1	$ 266.1
Net Sales	695.5	576.4	589.4
Gross margin ratio	**50.5%**	**49.3%**	**45.1%**

The formula for the gross margin ratio is shown in Exhibit 6.25.

Exhibit 6.25

Gross Margin Ratio

$$\text{Gross margin ratio} = \frac{\textbf{Gross Margin}}{\textbf{Net Sales}}$$

This ratio is interpreted as reflecting the gross margin in each dollar of sales. To illustrate how we compute and use the gross margin ratio, we look at the results of Mitel for the past few years as reported in Exhibit 6.24. From the information in this exhibit, we can compute Mitel's 1997 gross margin ratio as:

$$\frac{\$351}{\$696} = 0.505$$

This means that each $1 of sales for Mitel yields about 50¢ in gross margin to cover all other expenses and still produce a profit for the company.

Results in Exhibit 6.24 also show Mitel's gross margin ratio is increasing over 1995-1997. The 1997 gross margin ratio, for instance, increases to 50.5% from 45.1% in 1995. This increase is an important development. Success for companies such as Mitel depends on maintaining an adequate gross margin. Data in this exhibit also reveal that Mitel's sales are increasing over this period while its gross margin is increasing which might indicate that Mitel is enjoying some economies of scale.

You Make the Call

Chief Financial Officer
You're a chief financial officer of a merchandising company. You're analyzing profitability for your company and compute a 36% gross margin ratio and a 17% net profit margin ratio. Industry averages are 44% for gross margin and 16% for net profit margin. Do these ratios concern you?

Answer—p. 286

★ Flash back

13. What income statement format shows detailed computations for net sales and cost of goods sold? What format gives no subtotals except total expenses?

14. Which assets are "quick assets" in computing the acid-test ratio?

15. What ratio is a more strict test of a company's ability to meet its short-term obligations, the acid-test ratio or current ratio?

Answers—p. 286

Summary

LO1 **Describe merchandising activities and identify business examples.** Operations of merchandising companies involve buying products and reselling them. Examples of merchandisers include **The Bay, Home Hardware, Shoppers' Drug Mart, Radio Shack,** and **Coles Bookstores.**

LO2 **Identify and explain the important components of income for a merchandising company.** A merchandiser's costs on an income statement include an amount for cost of goods sold. Gross profit, or gross margin, equals net sales minus cost of goods sold.

LO3 **Identify and explain the inventory asset of a merchandising company.** The current asset section of a merchandising company's balance sheet includes merchandise inventory. Merchandise inventory refers to the products a merchandiser sells and are on hand at the balance sheet date.

LO4 **Describe both periodic and perpetual inventory systems.** A perpetual inventory system continuously tracks the cost of goods on hand and the cost of goods sold. A periodic system accumulates the cost of goods purchased during the period and does not compute the amount of inventory on hand or the cost of goods sold until the end of a period.

LO5 **Analyze and record transactions for merchandise purchases using a perpetual system.** For a perpetual inventory system, purchases net of trade discounts are added (debited) to the Merchandise Inventory account. Purchase discounts and purchase returns and allowances are subtracted (credited) to Merchandise Inventory, and transportation-in costs are added (debited) to Merchandise Inventory. Many companies keep supplementary records to accumulate information about the total amounts of purchases, purchase discounts, purchase returns and allowances, and transportation-in.

LO6 **Analyze and record transactions for sales of merchandise using a perpetual system.** A merchandiser records sales at list price less any trade discounts. The cost of items sold is transferred from Merchandise Inventory to Cost of Goods Sold. Refunds or credits given to customers for unsatisfactory merchandise are recorded (debited) in Sales Returns and Allowances, a contra account to Sales. If merchandise is returned and restored to inventory, the cost of this merchandise is removed from Cost of Goods Sold and transferred back to Merchandise Inventory. When cash discounts from the sales price are offered and customers pay within the discount period, the seller records (debits) discounts in Sales Discounts, a contra account to Sales. Debit and credit memoranda are documents sent between buyers and sellers to communicate that the sender is either debiting or crediting an account of the recipient.

LO7 **Prepare adjustments and close accounts for a merchandising company.** With a perpetual inventory system, it is often required to make an adjustment for inventory shrinkage. This is computed by comparing a physical count of inventory with the Merchandise Inventory account balance. Shrinkage is normally charged to Cost of Goods Sold. Temporary accounts of merchandising companies include Sales, Sales Discounts, Sales Returns and Allowances, and Cost of Goods Sold. Each is closed to Income Summary.

LO8 **Analyze and interpret cost flows and operating activities of a merchandising company.** Net costs of merchandise purchases flows into Merchandise Inventory and from there to Cost of Goods Sold on the income statement. Any remaining Merchandise Inventory balance is reported as a current asset on the balance sheet. This is the beginning inventory for the next period.

LO9 **Define and prepare multiple-step and single-step income statements.** Multiple-step income statements include greater detail for sales and expenses than do single-step income statements. Classified multiple-step income statements are usually limited to internal use. It shows more details, including computations of net sales and cost of goods sold, and reporting of expenses in categories reflecting different activities. Income statements published for external parties can be either multiple-step or single-step.

LO10 **Analyze and interpret accruals and cash flows for merchandising activities.** Merchandising sales and costs of sales reported in the income statement usually differ from their corresponding cash receipts and payments for the period. Cash received from customers equals net sales less the increase (or plus the decrease) in Accounts Receivable during the period. Cash paid to suppliers equals cost of goods sold less the increase (or plus the decrease) in Accounts Payable during the period and less the decrease (or plus the increase) in Merchandise Inventory during the period.

LO11 **Compute the acid-test ratio and explain its use as an indicator of a company's liquidity.** The acid-test ratio is computed as quick assets (cash, short-term investments, and receivables) divided by current liabilities. It is an indicator of a company's ability to pay its current liabilities with its existing quick assets. A ratio equal to or greater than one is often considered adequate.

LO12 **Compute the gross margin ratio and explain its use as an indicator of profitability.** The gross margin (or gross profit) ratio is computed as gross margin (net sales minus cost of goods sold) divided by net sales. It is an indicator of a company's profitability in merchandising absent operating expenses. A gross margin ratio must be large enough to cover operating expenses and give an adequate net profit margin.

Guidance Answers to **You Make the Call**

Purchasing Agent

Delaying payment for 90 days costs your company an additional 3%. You can approximate the annual rate of interest attached to not paying within the discount period. For terms of 3/10, n/90, missing the 3% discount for an additional 80 days is equal to an annual interest rate of 13.69%, computed as (365 days ÷ 80 days × 3%). Since you can borrow funds at 11% (assuming no other processing costs), it is better to borrow and pay within the discount period. You save 2.69% (13.69% − 11%) in interest costs by not delaying payment.

Supplier

A current ratio of 2.1 suggests there is sufficient current assets to cover current liabilities. But an acid-test ratio of 0.5 is low for most businesses. This says quick assets can only cover about one-half of current liabilities. This implies the store depends on profits from sales of inventory to pay current lia-

bilities. If sales of inventory stall or profit margins decrease, then the likelihood of this store defaulting on its payments increases. Your decision is probably not to extend credit to the store. If you do extend credit, then you are likely to closely monitor the store's financial condition.

Chief Financial Officer

Your company's net profit margin is about equal to the industry average and suggests a typical industry performance. However, gross profit margin reveals a markedly different picture. This ratio indicates your company is paying far more in cost of goods sold or receiving far less in sales than competitors. Your attention must be directed to finding the problem with costs of goods sold, sales or both. One positive note is your company's expenses make up 19% of sales (36% − 17%). This favourably compares with competitors' expenses making up 28% of sales (44% − 16%).

Guidance Answer to **Judgment and Ethics**

Credit Manager

Your decision is whether to comply with prior policy or create new policy to not abuse discounts offered by suppliers. Your first step should be to meet with your superior to find out if the automatic late payment policy is the actual policy and, if so, its rationale. It is possible the prior employee was reprimanded because of this behaviour. If it is the policy to pay late, then you must apply your own sense of right and wrong. One point of view is that the late payment policy is unethical. A deliberate plan to make late payments means the company lies when it pretends to make purchases within the credit terms.

There is the potential that your company can lose its ability to get future credit. Another view is the late payment policy is acceptable. There may exist markets where attempts to take discounts through late payments are accepted as a continued phase of price negotiation. Also, your company's suppliers can respond by billing your company for the discounts not accepted because of late payments. This is a dubious viewpoint, especially given the old employee proposes you cover up late payments as computer or mail problems, and given that some suppliers have previously complained.

Guidance Answers to **Flash backs**

1. Cost of goods sold is the cost of merchandise sold to customers during a period.
2. Gross profit is the difference between net sales and cost of goods sold.
3. Widespread use of computing and related technology in today's information age has dramatically increased use of the perpetual inventory system in practice.
4. Under credit terms of 2/10, n/60, the credit period is 60 days and the discount period is 10 days.
5. *b*
6. *FOB* means free on board. It is used in identifying the point where ownership transfers from seller to buyer. *FOB destination* means the seller does not transfer ownership of goods to the buyer until they arrive at the buyer's place of business. The seller is responsible for paying shipping charges and bears the risk of damage or loss during shipment.
7. Recording sales discounts and sales returns and allowances separate from sales gives useful information to managers for internal monitoring and decision making.

8. When a customer returns merchandise and the seller restores the merchandise to inventory, two entries are necessary. One entry records the decrease in revenue and credits the customer's account. The second entry debits inventory and reduces cost of goods sold.
9. A credit memorandum.
10. Merchandise Inventory balance may need adjusting to reflect shrinkage.
11. Sales, Sales Discounts, Sales Returns and Allowances, and Cost of Goods Sold.
12. Four closing entries: (1) close credit balances in temporary accounts to income summary, (2) close debit balances in temporary accounts to income summary, (3) close income summary to owner's capital, and (4) close withdrawals account to owner's capital.
13. Classified, multiple-step income statement. Single-step income statement.
14. Cash, short-term investments, and receivables.
15. Acid-test ratio.

Use the following adjusted trial balance and additional information to complete the requirements:

INGERSOLL ANTIQUES Adjusted Trial Balance December 31, 19X2		
Cash	$ 19,000	
Merchandise inventory	50,000	
Store supplies	1,000	
Equipment	44,600	
Accumulated amortization, equipment		$ 16,500
Accounts payable		8,000
Salaries payable		1,000
Dee Rizzo, capital		69,000
Dee Rizzo, withdrawals	8,000	
Sales		325,000
Sales discounts	6,000	
Sales returns and allowances	5,000	
Cost of goods sold	148,000	
Amortization expense, store equipment	4,000	
Amortization expense, office equipment	1,500	
Sales salaries expense	28,000	
Office salaries expense	32,000	
Insurance expense	12,000	
Rent expense (70% is store, 30% is office)	24,000	
Store supplies expense	6,000	
Advertising expense	30,400	
Totals	$419,500	$419,500

Ingersoll Antiques' *supplementary records* for 19X2 reveal the following merchandising activities:

Invoice cost of merchandise purchases	$140,000
Purchase discounts received	3,500
Purchase returns and allowances received	2,600
Cost of transportation-in	4,000

Required

1. Use the supplementary records to compute the total cost of merchandise purchases.
2. Prepare a 19X2 classified, multiple-step income statement for internal use. The beginning inventory at January 1, 19X2 is $60,100.
3. Present a single-step income statement for 19X2 similar to the one in Exhibit 6.20.
4. Prepare closing entries.
5. Compute the acid test ratio and the gross margin ratio. Explain the meaning of each ratio and interpret them for Ingersoll Antiques.

Planning the Solution

■ Compute the total cost of merchandise purchases.
■ Compute net sales. Then, to compute cost of goods sold, add the net cost of merchandise purchases for the year to the beginning inventory and subtract the cost of the ending inventory. Subtract cost of goods sold from net sales to get gross profit. Then, classify the operating expenses as selling expenses and general administrative expenses.

■ To prepare the single-step income statement, begin with the net sales. Then, list and subtract the cost of goods sold and operating expenses.

■ The first closing entry debits all temporary accounts with credit balances and opens the Income Summary account. The second closing entry credits all temporary accounts with debit balances. The third entry closes the Income Summary account to the owner's capital account, and the fourth closing entry closes the withdrawals account to the capital account.

■ Identify the current assets on the adjusted trial balance that qualify to be included in the numerator of the acid test ratio. Compute the acid test ratio by dividing the numerator of relevant account(s) by the total amount of current liabilities. Compute the gross margin ratio by dividing the gross profit found in Requirement 2 by net sales. Explain and interpret each ratio.

Solution to Demonstration Problem

1.

Invoice cost of merchandise purchases	$140,000
Less: Purchase discounts received	(3,500)
Purchase returns and allowances received	(2,600)
Add cost of transportation-in	4,000
Total cost of merchandise purchases	$137,900

2. Classified, multiple-step income statement

INGERSOLL ANTIQUES
Income Statement
For Year Ended December 31, 19X2

Sales.			$325,000
Less: Sales discounts		$ 6,000	
Sales returns and allowances		5,000	11,000
Net sales			$314,000
Cost of goods sold:			
Merchandise inventory, December 31, 19X1 . . .		$ 60,100	
Invoice cost of merchandise purchases	$140,000		
Less: Purchase discounts received	(3,500)		
Purchase returns and allowances received	(2,600)		
Add cost of transportation-in	4,000		
Total cost of merchandise purchases		137,900	
Goods available for sale		$198,000	
Less: Merchandise inventory, December 31, 19X2		50,000	
Cost of goods sold			148,000
Gross profit from sales			$166,000
Operating expenses:			
Selling expenses:			
Amortization expense, store equipment	$ 4,000		
Sales salaries expense	28,000		
Rent expense, selling space	16,800		
Store supplies expense.	6,000		
Advertising expense	30,400		
Total selling expenses.		$ 85,200	

(continued)

General and administrative expenses:

Amortization expense, office equipment	$ 1,500	
Office salaries expense	32,000	
Insurance expense	12,000	
Rent expense, office space	7,200	
Total general and administrative expenses . . .	52,700	
Total operating expenses		137,900
Net income		$ 28,100

3. Single-step income statement

INGERSOLL ANTIQUES
Income Statement
For Year Ended December 31, 19X2

Net sales		$314,000
Operating expenses:		
Cost of goods sold	$148,000	
Selling expenses	85,200	
General and administrative expenses	52,700	285,900
Net income		$ 28,100

4.

Dec. 31	Sales	325,000	
	Income Summary		325,000
	To close temporary accounts with credit balances.		
31	Income Summary	296,900	
	Sales Discounts		6,000
	Sales Returns and Allowances		5,000
	Cost of Goods Sold		148,000
	Amortization Expense, Store Equipment		4,000
	Amortization Expense, Office Equipment		1,500
	Sales Salaries Expense		28,000
	Office Salaries Expense		32,000
	Insurance Expense		12,000
	Rent Expense		24,000
	Store Supplies Expense		6,000
	Advertising Expense		30,400
	To close temporary accounts with debit balances.		
31	Income Summary	28,100	
	Dee Rizzo, Capital		28,100
	To close the Income Summary account.		
31	Dee Rizzo, Capital	8,000	
	Dee Rizzo, Withdrawals		8,000
	To close the withdrawals account.		

5. Acid test ratio = (Cash)/(Accounts payable + Salaries payable)

$$= \$19,000/(\$8,000 + \$1,000) = \$19,000/\$9,000 = \underline{\underline{2.11}}$$

Gross margin = Gross profit/ Net sales = \$166,000/\$314,000 = $\underline{\underline{0.53}}$

Ingersoll Antiques has a very healthy acid test ratio of 2.11. Ingersoll Antiques has over $2.00 in quick, liquid assets to satisfy each $1.00 in current liabilities. (Note that neither supplies nor inventory are considered liquid assets readily convertible into cash for use in satisfying short-term obligations.) The gross margin of 0.53 shows that Ingersoll Antiques spends 47 cents of every dollar in net sales on the costs of acquiring the merchandise it sells. This leaves 53 cents of every dollar in net sales to cover other expenses incurred in the business and to provide for a profit.

Periodic and Perpetual Inventory Systems: Accounting Comparisons

Learning Objective

LO 13   Record and compare merchandising transactions using both periodic and perpetual inventory systems.

Recall that under a perpetual system, the Merchandise Inventory account is updated after each purchase and each sale. The Cost of Goods Sold account also is updated after each sale so that during the period the account balance reflects the period's total cost of goods sold to date.

Under a periodic inventory system, the Merchandise Inventory account is updated only once each accounting period. This update occurs at the *end* of the period. During the next period, the Merchandise Inventory balance remains unchanged. It reflects the beginning inventory balance until it is updated again at the end of the period. Similarly, in a periodic inventory system, cost of goods sold is not recorded as each sale occurs. Instead, the total cost of goods sold during the period is computed at the end of the period.

Recording Merchandise Transactions

Under a perpetual system, each purchase, purchase return and allowance, purchase discount, and transportation-in transaction is recorded in the Merchandise Inventory account. Under a periodic system, a separate temporary account is set up for each of these items. At the end of a period, each of these temporary accounts is closed and the Merchandise Inventory account is updated. To illustrate the differences, we use parallel columns to show journal entries for the most common transactions using both periodic and perpetual inventory systems (we drop explanations for simplicity).

Purchases

Z-Mart purchases merchandise for $1,200 on credit with terms of 2/10, n/30. Z-Mart's entry to record this credit purchase is:

(a)

Periodic		Perpetual	
Purchases 1,200		Merchandise Inventory .. 1,200	
Accounts Payable . . .	1,200	Accounts Payable . . .	1,200

The periodic system uses a temporary *Purchases* account that accumulates the cost of all purchase transactions during the period.

Purchase Discount

When Z-Mart pays the supplier for the previous purchase within the discount period, the required payment is $1,176 ($1,200 × 98%) and is recorded as:

(b)   **Periodic**

Accounts Payable	1,200	
Purchase Discounts . .		24
Cash		1,176

Perpetual

Accounts Payable	1,200	
Merchandise Inventory		24
Cash		1,176

The periodic system uses a temporary *Purchase Discounts* account that accumulates discounts taken on purchase transactions during the period. If payment is delayed until after the discount period expires, the entry under both methods is to debit Accounts Payable and credit Cash for $1,200 each.

Purchase Returns and Allowances

Z-Mart returns merchandise purchased on November 2 because of defects. If the recorded cost[9] of the defective merchandise is $300, Z-Mart records the return with this entry:

(c)   **Periodic**

Accounts Payable	300	
Purchase Returns and		
Allowances		300

Perpetual

| Accounts Payable . . . . . . | 300 | |
| Merchandise Inventory | | 300 |

This entry is the same if Z-Mart is granted a price reduction (allowance) instead of returning the merchandise. In the periodic system, the temporary *Purchase Returns and Allowances* account accumulates the cost of all returns and allowances transactions during a period.

Transportation-In

Z-Mart paid a $75 freight charge to haul merchandise to its store. In the periodic system, this cost is charged to a temporary *Transportation-In* account.

(d)   **Periodic**

| Transportation-In . . . . . . | 75 | |
| Cash . . . . | | 75 |

Perpetual

| Merchandise Inventory . . | 75 | |
| Cash . . . . | | 75 |

Sales

Z-Mart sold $2,400 of merchandise on credit and Z-Mart's cost of this merchandise is $1,600:

(e)   **Periodic**

| Accounts Receivable . . . | 2,400 | |
| Sales . . . . | | 2,400 |

Perpetual

Accounts Receivable . . .	2,400	
Sales		2,400
Cost of Goods Sold	1,600	
Merchandise Inventory		1,600

Under the periodic system the cost of goods sold is not recorded at the time of sale. We later show how the periodic system computes total cost of goods sold at the end of a period.

Sales Returns

A customer returns part of the merchandise from the previous transaction, where returned items sell for $800 and cost $600

Z-Mart restores the merchandise to inventory and records the return as:

---

[9] Recorded cost is the cost recorded in the account after any discounts.

(f)

Periodic		
Sales Returns and		
Allowances	800	
Accounts Receivable .		800

Perpetual		
Sales Returns and		
Allowances	800	
Accounts Receivable .		800
Merchandise Inventory ..	600	
Cost of Goods Sold ..		600

The periodic system records only the revenue reduction.

The periodic and perpetual inventory systems show differences in the adjusting and closing entries. Z-Mart's unadjusted trial balances at the end of 1999 under each system are shown in Exhibit 6A.1.

Adjusting and Closing Entries

 Exhibit 6A.1

Comparison of Unadjusted Trial Balances—Periodic and Perpetual

Z-Mart Unadjusted Trial Balance December 31, 1999 Periodic		
Cash	$ 8,200	
Accounts Receivable	11,200	
Merchandise inventory	19,000	
Office Supplies	550	
Store Supplies	250	
Prepaid Insurance	300	
Office equipment	4,200	
Accumulated amortization—		
office equipment		1,400
Store equipment	30,000	
Accumulated amortization—		
store equipment		6,000
Accounts Payable		16,000
Salaries Payable		800
K. Marty, capital		42,600
K. Marty, withdrawals	4,000	
Sales		321,000
Sales discounts	4,300	
Sales returns and		
allowances	2,000	
Purchases	235,800	
Purchase discounts		4,200
Purchase returns and		
allowances		1,500
Transportation-in	2,300	
Amortization expense—		
store equipment	3,000	
Amortization expense—		
office equipment	700	
Office salaries expense	25,300	
Sales salaries expense	18,500	
Insurance expense	600	
Rent expense—office space	900	
Rent expense—selling space	8,100	
Office supplies expense	1,800	
Store supplies expense	1,200	
Advertising expense	11,300	
Totals	$393,500	$393,500

Z-Mart Unadjusted Trial Balance December 31, 1999 Perpetual		
Cash	$ 8,200	
Accounts receivable	11,200	
Merchandise inventory	21,250	
Office Supplies	550	
Store Supplies	250	
Prepaid Insurance	300	
Office equipment	4,200	
Accumulated amortization—		
office equipment		1,400
Store equipment	30,000	
Accumulated amortization—		
store equipment		6,000
Accounts payable		16,000
Salaries payable		800
K. Marty, capital		42,600
K. Marty, withdrawals	4,000	
Sales		321,000
Sales discounts	4,300	
Sales returns and		
allowances	2,000	
Cost of goods sold	230,150	
Amortization expense—		
store equipment	3,000	
Amortization expense—		
office equipment	700	
Office salaries expense	25,300	
Sales salaries expense	18,500	
Insurance expense	600	
Rent expense—office space	900	
Rent expense—selling space	8,100	
Office supplies expense	1,800	
Store supplies expense	1,200	
Advertising expense	11,300	
Totals	$387,800	$387,800

The Merchandise Inventory balance is $19,000 under the periodic system and $21,250 under the perpetual system. Because the periodic system does not revise the Merchandise Inventory balance during the period, the $19,000 amount is the beginning inventory. The $21,250 balance under the perpetual system is the recorded ending inventory before adjusting for any inventory shrinkage.

A physical count of inventory taken at the end of the period disclosed $21,000 of merchandise on hand. We then know inventory shrinkage is $21,250 − $21,000 = $250. The adjusting entry for shrinkage along with closing entries under the two systems is shown in Exhibit 6A.2.

Exhibit 6A.2

Comparison of Adjusting and Closing Entries—Periodic and Perpetual

Periodic		
Adjusting entries		
Closing entries		
(1)		
Sales	321,000	
Merchandise Inventory	21,000	
Purchase Discounts	4,200	
Purchase Returns and		
Allowances	1,500	
Income Summary		347,700
(2)		
Income Summary	334,800	
Sales discounts		4,300
Sales Returns and		
Allowances		2,000
Merchandise Inventory		19,000
Purchases		235,800
Transportation-In		2,300
Amortization Expense—		
store equipment		3,000
Amortization Expense—		
office equipment		700
Office Salaries Expense		25,300
Sales Salaries Expense		18,500
Insurance Expense		600
Rent Expense, Office Space .		900
Rent Expense, Selling Space .		8,100
Office Supplies Expense		1,800
Store Supplies Expense		1,200
Advertising Expense		11,300
(3)		
Income Summary	12,900	
K. Marty, Capital		12,900
(4)		
K. Marty, Capital	4,000	
K. Marty, Withdrawals		4,000

Perpetual		
Adjusting entries		
Cost of Goods Sold	250	
Merchandise Inventory		250
Closing entries		
(1)		
Sales	321,000	
Income Summary		321,000
(2)		
Income Summary	308,100	
Sales discounts		4,300
Sales Returns and		
Allowances		2,000
Cost of Goods Sold		230,400
Amortization Expense—		
store equipment		3,000
Amortization Expense—		
office equipment		700
Office Salaries Expense		25,300
Sales Salaries Expense		18,500
Insurance Expense		600
Rent Expense, Office Space .		900
Rent Expense, Selling Space .		8,100
Office Supplies Expense		1,800
Store Supplies Expense		1,200
Advertising Expense		11,300
(3)		
Income Summary	12,900	
K. Marty, Capital		12,900
(4)		
K. Marty, Capital	4,000	
K. Marty, Withdrawals		4,000

The periodic system does not require an adjusting entry to record inventory shrinkage. Instead, the periodic system puts the ending inventory of $21,000 in the Merchandise Inventory account in the first closing entry, and removes the $19,000 beginning inventory balance from the account in the second closing entry.

By updating Merchandise Inventory and closing Purchases, Purchase Discounts, Purchase Returns and Allowances, and Transportation-In, the periodic system transfers the cost of goods sold amount to Income Summary. Review the periodic side of Exhibit 6A.2 and notice that the boldface items affect Income Summary as follows:

Credited to Income Summary in the first closing entry:	
Merchandise inventory	$21,000
Purchase discounts	4,200
Purchase returns and allowances	1,500
Debited to Income Summary in the second closing entry:	
Merchandise inventory	(19,000)
Purchases	(235,800)
Transportation-in	(2,300)
Net effect on Income Summary	($230,400)

This $230,400 effect on Income Summary is the cost of goods sold amount. This figure is confirmed as follows:

Beginning inventory		$19,000
Purchases	$235,800	
Less purchase discounts	(4,200)	
Less purchase returns and allowances	(1,500)	
Plus transportation-in	2,300	
Net cost of goods purchased		232,400
Cost of goods available for sale		$251,400
Less ending inventory		(21,000)
Cost of goods sold		$230,400

The periodic system transfers cost of goods sold to the Income Summary account but does not use a Cost of Goods Sold account.

The periodic system does not measure shrinkage. Instead it computes cost of goods available for sale, subtracts the cost of ending inventory, and defines the difference as cost of goods sold. This difference, called the cost of goods sold, includes shrinkage.

Adjusting Entry Method to Record Changes in Merchandise Inventory

In our discussion of the periodic system, the change in the Merchandise Inventory account is recorded as part of the closing process. The closing entry method is common in practice. Yet an alternative method, called the adjusting entry method, also is commonly used.[10] The adjusting entry method records the change in the Merchandise Inventory account with adjusting entries. Under this method, the first two closing entries do not include changes in the Merchandise Inventory account.

Adjusting Entries

Under the adjusting entry method of the periodic system, Z-Mart removes the beginning balance from the Merchandise Inventory account by recording this adjusting entry at the end of 1999:

Dec. 31	Income Summary	19,000	
	Merchandise Inventory		19,000
	To remove beginning balance from the Merchandise Inventory account.		

---

[10] The adjusting entry method also is used by many computerized accounting systems that do not allow the Merchandise Inventory account (a permanent account) to be changed in the closing process.

A second adjusting entry gives the correct ending balance in the Merchandise Inventory account:

Dec. 31	Merchandise Inventory	21,000	
	Income Summary		21,000
	To insert correct ending balance in the		
	Merchandise Inventory account.		

Exhibit 6A.3

Merchandise Inventory
T-Account

Merchandise Inventory			
Beg. Bal.	19,000		
		19,000	Adj.
Adj.	21,000		
End.Bal.	21,000		

After these entries are posted, Exhibit 6A.3 shows the Merchandise Inventory account has a $21,000 debit balance:

These adjustments also leave the Income Summary account with a $2,000 credit balance.

Closing Entries

If the adjusting entry method for inventory is used, the closing entries differ only by not including the Merchandise Inventory account. In particular, entries (1) and (2) in Exhibit 6A.2 are the same except for removing the Merchandise Inventory account and its balance from both entries. Entry (3) to close Income Summary is the same as in this exhibit. The only difference is that the adjusting entry method took us four entries instead of two to get the net income of $12,900.

Flash back

16. What account is used in a perpetual inventory system but not in a periodic system?

17. Which of the following accounts are temporary accounts? (a) Merchandise Inventory, (b) Purchases, (c) Transportation-In.

18. How is cost of goods sold computed under a periodic inventory accounting system?

19. Do reported amounts of ending inventory and net income differ if the adjusting entry method to recording the change in inventory is used instead of the closing entry method?

Answers-p. 296

Summary of Appendix 6A

LO 13 **Record and compare merchandising transactions using both periodic and perpetual inventory systems.** Transactions involving the sale and purchase of merchandise are recorded and analyzed under both inventory systems. Adjusting and closing entries for both inventory systems are also illustrated and explained.

Guidance Answers to Flash backs

16. Cost of Goods Sold.

17. (b) Purchases and (c) Transportation-In.

18. Under a periodic inventory system, the cost of goods sold is determined at the end of an accounting period by adding the net cost of goods purchased to the beginning inventory and subtracting the ending inventory.

19. Both methods report the same ending inventory and net income.

Glossary

Acid-test ratio A ratio used to assess the company's ability to settle its current debts with its existing assets; it is the ratio between a company's quick assets (cash, short-term investments, and receivables) and its current liabilities. (p. 282)

Cash discount A reduction in the price of merchandise that is granted by a seller to a purchaser in exchange for the purchaser paying within a specified period of time called the *discount period.* (p. 263)

Classified, multiple-step income statement An income statement format that shows intermediate totals between sales and net income and detailed computations of net sales and costs of goods sold. (p. 279)

Cost of goods sold The cost of merchandise sold to customers during a period. (p. 260)

Credit memorandum A notification that the sender has entered a credit in the recipient's account maintained by the sender. (p. 272)

Credit period The time period that can pass before a customer's payment is due. (p. 263)

Credit terms The description of the amounts and timing of payments that a buyer agrees to make in the future. (p. 263)

Debit memorandum A notification that the sender has entered a debit in the recipient's account maintained by the sender. (p. 265)

Discount period The time period in which a cash discount is available and a reduced payment can be made by the buyer. (p. 264)

EOM The abbreviation for *end-of-month,* used to describe credit terms for some transactions. (p. 263)

FOB The abbreviation for *free on board,* the designated point at which ownership of goods passes to the buyer; FOB shipping point (or factory) means that the buyer pays the shipping costs and accepts ownership of the goods at the seller's place of business; FOB destination means that the seller pays the shipping costs and the ownership of the goods transfers to the buyer at the buyer's place of business. (p. 267)

General and administrative expenses Expenses that support the overall operations of a business and include the expenses of such activities as providing accounting services, human resource management, and financial management. (p. 279)

Gross margin The difference between net sales and the cost of goods sold; also called *gross profit.* (p. 259)

Gross margin ratio Gross margin (net sales minus cost of goods sold) divided by net sales; also called gross profit ratio. (p. 284)

Gross profit The difference between net sales and the cost of goods sold.; also called *gross margin.* (p. 259)

Inventory See *Merchandise inventory.*

List price The catalogue price of an item before any trade discount is deducted. (p. 263)

Merchandise Products, also called *goods,* that a company acquires for the purpose of reselling them to customers. (p. 258)

Merchandiser Earns net income by buying and selling merchandise. (p. 258)

Merchandise inventory Products that a company owns for the purpose of selling them to customers. (p. 259)

Periodic inventory system A method of accounting that records the cost of inventory purchased but does not track the quantity on hand or sold to customers; the records are updated at the end of each period to reflect the results of physical counts of the items on hand. (p. 261)

Perpetual inventory system A method of accounting that maintains continuous records of the cost of inventory on hand and the cost of goods sold. (p. 261)

Purchase discount A term used by a purchaser to describe a cash discount granted to the purchaser for paying within the discount period. (p. 263)

Retailer A middleman that buys products from manufacturers or wholesalers and sells them to consumers. (p. 258)

Sales discount A term used by a seller to describe a cash discount granted to customers for paying within the discount period. (p. 263)

Selling expenses The expenses of promoting sales by displaying and advertising the merchandise, making sales, and delivering goods to customers.(p. 279)

Shrinkage Inventory losses that occur as a result of shoplifting or deterioration. (p. 274)

Single-step income statement An income statement format that includes cost of goods sold as an operating expense and shows only one subtotal for total expenses. (p. 280)

Supplementary records A register of information outside the usual accounting records and accounts; also called *supplemental records.* (p. 268)

Trade discount A reduction below a list or catalogue price that may vary in amount for wholesalers, retailers, and final consumers. (p. 263)

Wholesaler A "middleman" that buys products from manufacturers or other wholesalers and sells them to retailers or other wholesalers. (p. 258)

Questions

1. What items appear in the financial statements of merchandising companies but not in the statements of service companies?
2. Explain how a business can earn a gross profit on its sales and still have a net loss.
3. Why would a company offer a cash discount?
4. What is the difference between a sales discount and a purchase discount?
5. Distinguish between cash discounts and trade discounts. Is the amount of a trade discount on purchased merchandise recorded in the accounts?
6. How does a company that uses a perpetual inventory system determine the amount of inventory shrinkage?
7. Why would a company's manager be concerned about the quantity of its purchase returns if its suppliers allow unlimited returns?
8. Does the sender of a debit memorandum record a debit or a credit in the account of the recipient? Which does the recipient record?

9. What is the difference between single-step and multiple-step income statement formats?
10. In comparing the accounts of a merchandising company with those of a service company, what additional accounts would the merchandising company be likely to use, assuming it employs a perpetual inventory system?
11. Refer to the income statement for **Alliance** in Appendix I at the end of the book. Does the company present a detailed calculation of the cost of goods sold?
12. Refer to the balance sheet for **Atlantis** in Appendix I. What would be the equivalent for inventory in Atlantis' balance sheet?
13. Rob Stavos talks about the need to be skillful in negotiating purchase contracts with suppliers. What type of shipping terms should Rob Stavos attempt to negotiate to minimize his freight-in costs?

The superscript letter ^{A} identifies assignment material based on Appendix 6A.

Quick Study

QS 6-1

Contrast periodic and perpetual systems

LO 4

For each description below identify whether the reference is to a periodic or perpetual inventory system.

a. Requires a physical count of inventory to determine the amount of inventory to report on the balance sheet.

b. Records the cost of goods sold each time a sales transaction occurs.

c. Provides more timely information to managers.

d. Was traditionally used by companies such as drug and department stores that sold large quantities of low-valued items.

e. Requires an adjusting entry to record inventory shrinkage.

QS 6-2

Journal entries—perpetual system

LO 5

Prepare journal entries to record each of the following transactions of a merchandising company. Show any supporting calculations. Assume a perpetual inventory system.

Mar. 5   Purchased 500 units of product with a list price of $5 per unit. The purchaser was granted a trade discount of 20% and the terms of the sale were 2/10, n/60.

Mar. 7   Returned 50 defective units from the March 5 purchase and received full credit.

Mar. 15   Paid the amount due resulting from the March 5 purchase, less the return and applicable discount, on March 7.

QS 6-3

Journal entries—perpetual system

LO 6

Prepare journal entries to record each of the following transactions of a merchandising company. Show any supporting calculations. Assume a perpetual inventory system.

Apr. 1   Sold merchandise for $2,000, granting the customer terms of 2/10, EOM. The cost of the merchandise was $1,400.

Apr. 4   The customer in the April 1 sale returned merchandise and received credit for $500. The merchandise, which had cost $350, was returned to inventory.

Apr. 11   Received payment for the amount due resulting from the April 1 sale, less the return and applicable discount, on April 4.

QS 6-4
Shrinkage
LO 7

Beamer Company's ledger on July 31, the end of the fiscal year, includes the following accounts which have normal balances:

Merchandise inventory	$ 34,800
J. Beamer, capital	115,300
J. Beamer, withdrawals	4,000
Sales	157,200
Sales discounts	1,700
Sales returns and allowances	3,500
Cost of goods sold	102,000
Amortization expense	7,300
Salaries expense	29,500
Miscellaneous expenses	2,000

A physical count of the inventory discloses that the cost of the merchandise on hand is $32,900. Prepare the entry to record this information.

QS 6-5
Closing entries
LO 7

Refer to QS 6-4 and prepare the entries to close the income statement accounts. Do not forget to take into consideration the entry that was made to solve QS 6-4.

QS 6-6
Profitability
LO 2, 12

Compute net sales and gross profit and gross profit ratio in each of the following situations:

	a	b	c	d
Sales	$130,000	$512,000	$35,700	$245,700
Sales discounts	4,200	16,500	400	3,500
Sales returns and allowances	17,000	5,000	5,000	700
Cost of goods sold	76,600	326,700	21,300	125,900

Interpret the gross profit ratio for situation *a*.

QS 6-7
Liquidity ratio
LO 11

Use the following information to compute the acid-test ratio. Explain what the acid test ratio of a company evaluates. Comment on the ratio you compute.

Cash	$1,200
Accounts receivable	2,700
Inventory	5,000
Prepaid expenses	600
Accounts payable	4,750
Other current liabilities	950

QS 6-8
Contrasting liquidity ratios
LO 11

Explain the similarities and differences between the acid test ratio and the current ratio.

Exercises

Exercise 6-1
Merchandising terms

LO 1, 2

Insert the letter for each term in the blank space beside the definition that it most closely matches:

A. Cash discount
B. Credit period
C. Discount period
D. FOB destination
E. FOB shipping point
F. Gross profit
G. Merchandise inventory
H. Purchase discount
I. Sales discount
J. Trade discount

_____ **1.** An agreement that ownership of goods is transferred at the buyer's place of business.

_____ **2.** The time period in which a cash discount is available.

_____ **3.** The difference between net sales and the cost of goods sold.

_____ **4.** A reduction in a receivable or payable that is granted if it is paid within the discount period.

_____ **5.** A purchaser's description of a cash discount received from a supplier of goods.

_____ **6.** An agreement that ownership of goods is transferred at the seller's place of business.

_____ **7.** A reduction below a list or catalogue price that is negotiated in setting the selling price of goods.

_____ **8.** A seller's description of a cash discount granted to customers in return for early payment.

_____ **9.** The time period that can pass before a customer's payment is due.

_____ **10.** The goods that a company owns and expects to sell to its customers.

Exercise 6-2
Recording journal entries for merchandise transactions

LO 5

Prepare journal entries to record the following transactions for a retail store. Assume a perpetual inventory system.

Mar. 2 Purchased merchandise from Blanton Company under the following terms: $3,600 invoice price, 2/15, n/60, FOB factory.
      3 Paid $200 for shipping charges on the purchase of March 2.
      4 Returned to Blanton Company unacceptable merchandise that had an invoice price of $600.
     17 Sent a cheque to Blanton Company for the March 2 purchase, net of the returned merchandise and applicable discount.
     18 Purchased merchandise from Fleming Corp. under the following terms: $7,500 invoice price, 2/10, n/30, FOB destination.
     21 After brief negotiations, received from Fleming Corp. a $2,100 allowance on the purchase of March 18.
     28 Sent a cheque to Fleming Corp. paying for the March 18 purchase, net of the discount and the allowance.

Exercise 6-3
Analyzing and recording merchandise transactions and returns

LO 5, 6

On May 11, Wilson Sales accepted delivery of $30,000 of merchandise it purchased for resale. With the merchandise was an invoice dated May 11, with terms of 3/10, n/90, FOB Hostel Corporation's factory. The cost of the goods to Hostel was $20,000. When the goods were delivered, Wilson paid $335 to Express Shipping Service for the delivery charges on the merchandise. The next day, Wilson returned $1,200 of goods to the seller, who received them one day later and restored them to inventory. The returned goods had cost Hostel $800. On May 20, Wilson mailed a cheque to Hostel Corporation for the amount owed on that date. It was received the following day.

Required

a. Present the journal entries that Wilson Sales should record for these transactions. Assume that Wilson Sales uses a perpetual inventory system.

b. Present the journal entries that Hostel Corporation should record for these transactions. Assume that Hostel uses a perpetual inventory system.

Sundown Company purchased merchandise for resale from Raintree with an invoice price of $22,000 and credit terms of 3/10, n/60. The merchandise had cost Raintree $15,000. Sundown paid within the discount period. Assume that both the buyer and seller use perpetual inventory systems.

Required

a. Prepare the entries that the purchaser should record for the purchase and payment.

b. Prepare the entries that the seller should record for the sale and collection.

c. Assume that the buyer borrowed enough cash to pay the balance on the last day of the discount period at an annual interest rate of 8% and paid it back on the last day of the credit period. Compute how much the buyer saved by following this strategy. (Use a 365-day year.)

Exercise 6-4
Analyzing and recording merchandise transactions and discounts
LO 5, 6

Using the data provided, from the general ledger and supplementary records, determine each of the missing numbers in the following situations:

	a	b	c
Invoice cost of merchandise purchases	$90,000	$40,000	$30,500
Purchase discounts received	4,000	?	650
Purchase returns and allowances received	3,000	1,500	1,100
Cost of transportation-in	?	3,500	4,000
Merchandise inventory (beginning of period) . . .	7,000	?	9,000
Total cost of merchandise purchases	89,400	39,500	?
Merchandise inventory (end of period)	4,400	7,500	?
Cost of goods sold	?	41,600	34,130

Exercise 6-5
Components of cost of goods sold
LO 8

Friar Company's ledger and supplementary records at the end of the period disclose the following information:

Sales	$340,000
Sales discounts	5,500
Sales returns	14,000
Merchandise inventory (beginning of period)	30,000
Invoice cost of merchandise purchases	175,000
Purchase discounts received	3,600
Purchase returns and allowances received	6,000
Cost of transportation-in	11,000
Gross profit from sales	145,000
Net income	65,000

Exercise 6-6
Calculating expenses and cost of goods sold
LO 8

Required

Compute the (a) total operating expenses, (b) cost of goods sold, and (c) merchandise inventory (end of period).

Exercise 6-7
Calculating expenses and income
LO 2, 8

Fill in the blanks in the following income statements. Identify any losses by putting the amount in parentheses.

	a	b	c	d	e
Sales	$60,000	$42,500	$36,000	$?	$23,600
Cost of goods sold:					
Merchandise inventory (beginning) ..	$ 6,000	$17,050	$ 7,500	$ 7,000	$ 2,560
Total cost of merchandise purchases	36,000	?	?	32,000	5,600
Merchandise inventory (ending)	?	(2,700)	(9,000)	(6,600)	?
Cost of goods sold	$34,050	$15,900	$?	$?	$ 5,600
Gross profit	$?	$?	$ 3,750	$45,600	$?
Expenses	9,000	10,650	12,150	2,600	6,000
Net income (loss)	$?	$15,950	$(8,400)	$43,000	$?

Exercise 6-8
Sales returns and allowances
LO 6

Travis Parts was organized on June 1, 19X1, and made its first purchase of merchandise on June 3. The purchase was for 1,000 units of Product X at a price of $10 per unit. On June 5, Travis sold 600 of the units for $14 per unit to Decker Co. Terms of the sale were 2/10, n/60. Prepare entries to record the sale and each of the following independent alternatives under a perpetual inventory system.

a. On June 7, Decker returned 100 units because they did not fit the customer's needs. Travis restored the units to its inventory.

b. Decker discovered that 100 units were damaged but of some use. Therefore, Decker kept the units. Travis sent Decker a credit memorandum for $600 to compensate for the damage.

c. Decker returned 100 defective units and Travis concluded that the units could not be resold. As a result, Travis discarded the units.

Exercise 6-9
Purchase returns and allowances
LO 5

Refer to Exercise 6-8 and prepare the appropriate journal entries on the books of Decker Co. to record the purchase and each of the three independent alternatives presented. Assume that Decker is a retailer that uses a perpetual inventory system and purchased the units for resale.

Exercise 6-10
Effects of merchandising activities on the accounts
LO 8

The following amounts taken from supplementary and accounting records summarize Transeer Company's merchandising activities during 19X2. Set up T-accounts for Merchandise Inventory and Cost of Goods Sold. Then record the summarized activities directly in the accounts and compute the account balances.

Cost of merchandise transferred to customers in sales transactions	$186,000
Merchandise inventory balance, Dec. 31, 19X1	27,000
Invoice cost of merchandise purchases	190,500
Shrinkage determined on December 31, 19X2	700
Cost of transportation-in	1,900
Cost of merchandise returned by customers and restored to inventory ...	2,200
Purchase discounts received	1,600
Purchase returns and allowances received	4,100

Exercise 6-11
Adjusting and closing entries
LO 7

The following list includes selected real accounts and all of the temporary accounts taken from the December 31, 19X1, unadjusted trial balance of Perry Sales, a business that is owned by Deborah Perry. Use the information in these columns to journalize adjusting and closing entries. Assume a perpetual inventory system.

	Debit	Credit
Merchandise inventory	$28,000	
Prepaid selling expenses	5,000	
Deborah Perry, withdrawals	1,800	
Sales		$429,000
Sales returns and allowances	16,500	
Sales discounts	4,000	
Cost of goods sold	211,000	
Sales salaries expense	47,000	
Utilities expense	14,000	
Selling expenses	35,000	
Administrative expenses	95,000	

Additional information: Accrued sales salaries amount to $1,600. Prepaid selling expenses of $2,000 have expired. A physical count of merchandise inventory discloses $27,450 of goods on hand.

Compute the current and acid-test ratios in each the following cases:

Exercise 6-12
Acid-test ratio

LO 11

	Case X	Case Y	Case Z
Cash	$ 800	$ 910	$1,100
Short-term investments			500
Receivables		990	800
Inventory	2,000	1,000	4,000
Prepaid expenses	1,200	600	900
Total current assets	$4,000	$3,500	$7,300
Current liabilities	$2,200	$1,100	$3,650

Which case is in the best position to most easily meet short-term obligations? Explain your choice.

Briefly explain why a company's manager would want the accounting system to record a customer's return of unsatisfactory goods in the Sales Returns and Allowances account instead of the Sales account. In addition, explain whether the information would be useful for external decision makers.

Exercise 6-13
Sales returns and allowances

LO 2, 6

A retail company recently completed taking a physical count of the ending merchandise inventory to use in preparing adjusting entries. In determining the cost of the counted inventory, company employees failed to consider that $2,000 of incoming goods had been shipped by a supplier on December 31 under an FOB factory agreement. These goods had been recorded in Merchandise Inventory as a purchase, but they were not included in the physical count because they were not on hand. Explain how this overlooked fact would affect the company's financial statements and these ratios: return on equity, debt ratio, current ratio, profit margin, and acid-test ratio.

Exercise 6-14
Physical count error interpreted as shrinkage

LO 7

Journalize the following merchandising transactions for Scout Systems assuming (a) a periodic system and (b) perpetual system.

1. On November 1 Scout Systems purchases merchandise for $1,400 on credit with terms of 2/10, n/30.

2. On November 5 Scout Systems pays for the previous purchase.

3. On November 7 Scout Systems received payment for returned defective merchandise of $100 that was purchased on November 1.

Exercise 6-15ᴬ
Journal entries to contrast the periodic and perpetual systems

LO 5, 6

4. On November 10 Scout Systems pays $80 to haul merchandise to its store.
5. On November 13 Scout Systems sells merchandise for $1,500 on account. The cost of the merchandise was $750.
6. On November 16 a customer returns merchandise from the November 13th transaction. The returned item sold for $200 and cost $100.

Exercise 6-16
Profitability and key merchandising cash flows

LO 10

A company reports the following balances and activity for the current period:

Net Sales	$1,005,000
Cost of Goods Sold	560,000
Increase in Accounts Receivable	40,000
Cash payments to suppliers	510,000

Required

1. Compute gross profit
2. Compute cash received from customers.
3. Compute net cash flows from customers and to suppliers.

Problems

Problem 6-1
Journal entries for merchandising activities (perpetual system)

LO 5, 6

Prepare general journal entries to record the following perpetual system merchandising transactions of Belton Company. (Use a separate account for each receivable and payable; for example, record the purchase on July 1 in Accounts Payable—Jones Company.)

July 1 Purchased merchandise from Jones Company for $6,000 under credit terms of 1/15, n/30, FOB factory.
2 Sold merchandise to Terra Co. for $800 under credit terms of 2/10, n/60, FOB shipping point. The merchandise had cost $500.
3 Paid $100 for freight charges on the purchase of July 1.
8 Sold merchandise that cost $1,200 for $1,600 cash.
9 Purchased merchandise from Keene Co. for $2,300 under credit terms of 2/15, n/60, FOB destination.
12 Received a $200 credit memorandum acknowledging the return of merchandise purchased on July 9.
12 Received the balance due from Terra Co. for the credit sale dated July 2, net of the discount.
16 Paid the balance due to Jones Company within the discount period.
19 Sold merchandise that cost $900 to Urban Co. for $1,250 under credit terms of 2/15, n/60, FOB shipping point.
21 Issued a $150 credit memorandum to Urban Co. for an allowance on goods sold on July 19.
22 Received a debit memorandum from Urban Co. for an error that overstated the total invoice by $50.
24 Paid Keene Co. the balance due after deducting the discount.
30 Received the balance due from Urban Co. for the credit sale dated July 19, net of the discount.
31 Sold merchandise that cost $3,200 to Terra Co. for $5,000 under credit terms of 2/10, n/60, FOB shipping point.

Problem 6-2
Journal entries for merchandising activities (perpetual system)

LO 5, 6

Prepare general journal entries to record the following perpetual system merchandising transactions of Hanifin Company. (Use a separate account for each receivable and payable; for example, record the purchase on August 1 in Accounts Payable—Dickson Company.)

Aug. 1 Purchased merchandise from Dickson Company for $6,000 under credit terms of 1/10, n/30, FOB destination.
4 At Dickson's request, paid $100 for freight charges on the August 1 purchase, reducing the amount owed to Dickson.
5 Sold merchandise to Griften Corp. for $4,200 under credit terms of 2/10, n/60, FOB destination. The merchandise had cost $3,000.

8 Purchased merchandise from Kendall Corporation for $5,300 under credit terms of 1/10, n/45, FOB shipping point, plus $240 shipping charges. The invoice showed that at Hanifin's request, Kendall had paid $240 shipping charges and added that amount to the bill.

9 Paid $120 shipping charges related to the August 5 sale to Griften Corp.

10 Griften returned merchandise from the August 5 sale that had cost $500 and been sold for $700. The merchandise was restored to inventory.

12 After negotiations with Kendall Corporation concerning problems with the merchandise purchased on August 8, received a credit memorandum from Kendall granting a price reduction of $800.

15 Received balance due from Griften Corp. for the August 5 sale less the return on August 10.

18 Paid the amount due Kendall Corporation for the August 8 purchase less the price reduction granted.

19 Sold merchandise to Farley for $3,600 under credit terms of 1/10, n/30, FOB shipping point. The merchandise had cost $2,500.

22 Farley requested a price reduction on the August 19 sale because the merchandise did not meet specifications. Sent Farley a credit memorandum for $600 to resolve the issue.

29 Received Farley's payment of the amount due from the August 19 purchase.

30 Paid Dickson Company the amount due from the August 1 purchase.

The following amounts appeared on Davison Company's adjusted trial balance as of October 31, 19X2, the end of its fiscal year:

Problem 6-3
Income statement computations and formats

LO 9, 10

	Debit	Credit
Merchandise inventory	$ 31,000	
Other assets	128,400	
Liabilities		$ 35,000
B. Davison, capital		117,650
B. Davison, withdrawals	16,000	
Sales		212,000
Sales discounts	3,250	
Sales returns and allowances	14,000	
Cost of goods sold	82,600	
Sales salaries expense	29,000	
Rent expense, selling space	10,000	
Store supplies expense	2,500	
Advertising expense	18,000	
Office salaries expense	26,500	
Rent expense, office space	2,600	
Office supplies expense	800	
Totals	$364,650	$364,650

On October 31, 19X1, the company's merchandise inventory amounted to $25,000. *Supplementary records* of merchandising activities during the 19X2 year disclosed the following:

Invoice cost of merchandise purchases	$91,000
Purchase discounts received	1,900
Purchase returns and allowances received	4,400
Cost of transportation-in	3,900

Required

1. Compute the company's net sales for the year.
2. Compute the company's total cost of merchandise purchased for the year.

3. Prepare a classified, multiple-step income statement for internal use (see Exhibit 6.18) that lists the company's net sales, cost of goods sold, and gross profit, as well as the components and amounts of selling expenses and general and administrative expenses.

4. Present a condensed single-step income statement that lists these costs: cost of goods sold, selling expenses, and general and administrative expenses.

5. Accounts receivable decreased during the period by $30,000. Compute cash received from customers.

Check Figure Part 4, total expenses, $172,000

Problem 6-4
Closing entries and interpreting information about discounts and returns

LO 7

Use the data for Davison Company in Problem 6-3 to complete the following requirements:

Required

Preparation component:

1. Prepare closing entries for the company as of October 31.

Analysis component:

2. All of the company's purchases were made on credit and the suppliers uniformly offer a 3% sales discount. Does it appear that the company's cash management system is accomplishing the goal of taking all available discounts? Explain.

3. In prior years, the company has experienced a 4% return rate on its sales, which means that approximately 4% of its gross sales were for items that were eventually returned outright or that caused the company to grant allowances to customers. How does this year's record compare with prior years' results?

Check Figure Second closing entry: debit to Income Summary, $189,250

Problem 6-5
Adjusting entries, income statements, and acid-test ratio

LO 11, 7, 9

The following unadjusted trial balance was prepared at the end of the fiscal year for Tinker Sales Company:

TINKER SALES COMPANY Unadjusted Trial Balance July 31, 19X2		
Cash	$ 4,200	
Merchandise inventory	11,500	
Store supplies	4,800	
Prepaid insurance	2,300	
Store equipment	41,900	
Accumulated amortization, store equipment		$ 15,000
Accounts payable		9,000
Betsey Tinker, capital		35,200
Betsey Tinker, withdrawals	3,200	
Sales		104,000
Sales discounts	1,000	
Sales returns and allowances	2,000	
Cost of goods sold	37,400	
Amortization expense, store equipment		
Salaries expense	31,000	
Insurance expense		
Rent expense	14,000	
Store supplies expense		
Advertising expense	9,900	
Totals	$163,200	$163,200

Rent and salaries expense are equally divided between the selling and general and administrative functions. Tinker Sales Company uses a perpetual inventory system.

Required

1. Prepare adjusting journal entries for the following:
   a. Store supplies on hand at year-end amount to $1,650.
   b. Expired insurance, an administrative expense, for the year is $1,500.
   c. Amortization expense, a selling expense, for the year is $1,400.
   d. A physical count of the ending merchandise inventory shows $11,100 of goods on hand.

2. Prepare a multiple-step income statement for external users (see Exhibit 6.19).

3. Prepare a single-step income statement that would be provided to external users (see Exhibit 6.20).

4. Compute the company's current and acid-test ratios as of July 31, 19X2.

Check Figure Part 3, total expenses, $98,750

Prepare general journal entries to record the following perpetual system merchandising transactions of Minchew Company. (Use a separate account for each receivable and payable; for example, record the purchase on May 2 in Accounts Payable—Mobley Co.). Minchew Company does not use supplemental records for inventory accounting.

Alternate Problems

Problem 6-1A
Journal entries for merchandising activities (perpetual system)

LO 5, 6

May 2 Purchased merchandise from Mobley Co. for $9,000 under credit terms of 1/15, n/30, FOB factory.

4 Sold merchandise to Cornerstone Co. for $1,200 under credit terms of 2/10, n/60, FOB shipping point. The merchandise had cost $750.

4 Paid $150 for freight charges on the purchase of May 2.

9 Sold merchandise that cost $1,800 for $2,400 cash.

10 Purchased merchandise from Richter Co. for $3,450 under credit terms of 2/15, n/60, FOB destination.

12 Received a $300 credit memorandum acknowledging the return of merchandise purchased on May 10.

14 Received the balance due from Cornerstone Co. for the credit sale dated May 4, net of the discount.

17 Paid the balance due to Mobley Co. within the discount period.

20 Sold merchandise that cost $1,350 to Harrill Co. for $1,875 under credit terms of 2/15, n/60, FOB shipping point.

22 Issued a $225 credit memorandum to Harrill Co. for an allowance on goods sold on May 20.

23 Received a debit memorandum from Harrill Co. for an error that overstated the total invoice by $75.

25 Paid Richter Co. the balance due after deducting the discount.

31 Received the balance due from Harrill Co. for the credit sale dated May 20, net of the discount.

31 Sold merchandise that cost $4,800 to Cornerstone Co. for $7,500 under credit terms of 2/10, n/60, FOB shipping point.

Prepare general journal entries to record the following perpetual system merchandising transactions of Treadwell Company. (Use a separate account for each receivable and payable; for example, record the purchase on July 3 in Accounts Payable—CMP Corp.) Treadwell Company does not use supplemental records for inventory accounting.

Problem 6-2A
Journal entries for merchandising activities (perpetual system)

LO 5, 6

July 3 Purchased merchandise from CMP Corp. for $15,000 under credit terms of 1/10, n/30, FOB destination.

4 At CMP's request, paid $250 for freight charges on the July 3 purchase, reducing the amount owed to CMP.

7 Sold merchandise to Harbison Co. for $10,500 under credit terms of 2/10, n/60, FOB destination. The merchandise had cost $7,500.

10 Purchased merchandise from Cimarron Corporation for $13,250 under credit terms of 1/10, n/45, FOB shipping point, plus $600 shipping charges. The invoice showed that at Treadwell's request, Cimarron had paid the $600 shipping charges and added that amount to the bill.

11 Paid $300 shipping charges related to the July 7 sale to Harbison Co.

12   Harbison returned merchandise from the July 7 sale that had cost $1,250 and been sold for $1,750. The merchandise was restored to inventory.

14   After negotiations with Cimarron Corporation concerning problems with the merchandise purchased on July 10, received a credit memorandum from Cimarron granting a price reduction of $2,000.

17   Received balance due from Harbison Co. for the July 7 sale less the return on July 12.

20   Paid the amount due Cimarron Corporation for the July 10 purchase less the price reduction granted.

21   Sold merchandise to Hess for $9,000 under credit terms of 1/10, n/30, FOB shipping point. The merchandise had cost $6,250.

24   Hess requested a price reduction on the July 21 sale because the merchandise did not meet specifications. Sent Hess a credit memorandum for $1,500 to resolve the issue.

31   Received Hess' payment of the amount due from the July 21 purchase.

31   Paid CMP Corp. the amount due from the July 3 purchase.

Problem 6-3A
Income statement calculations and formats

LO 9, 10

The following amounts appeared on Reyna Company's adjusted trial balance as of May 31, 19X2, the end of its fiscal year:

	Debit	Credit
Merchandise inventory	$ 46,500	
Other assets	192,600	
Liabilities		$ 52,500
Paul Reyna, capital		176,475
Paul Reyna, withdrawals	24,000	
Sales		318,000
Sales discounts	4,875	
Sales returns and allowances	21,000	
Cost of goods sold	123,900	
Sales salaries expense	43,500	
Rent expense, selling space	15,000	
Store supplies expense	3,750	
Advertising expense	27,000	
Office salaries expense	39,750	
Rent expense, office space	3,900	
Office supplies expense	1,200	
Totals	$546,975	$546,975

On May 31, 19X1, the company's merchandise inventory amounted to $37,500. *Supplementary records* of merchandising activities during the 19X2 year disclose the following:

Cost of merchandise purchases	$136,500
Purchase discounts received	2,850
Purchase returns and allowances received	6,600
Cost of transportation-in	5,850

Required

1. Compute the company's net sales for the year.

2. Compute the company's total cost of merchandise purchased for the year.

3. Present a classified, multiple-step income statement for internal users (see Exhibit 6.18) that lists the company's net sales, cost of goods sold, and gross profit, as well the components and amounts of selling expenses and general and administrative expenses.

4. Present a condensed single-step income statement that lists these costs: cost of goods sold, selling expenses, and general and administrative expenses.

5. Accounts receivable increased by $50,000 during the period. Compute cash received from customers.

Use the data for Reyna Company in Problem 6-3A to meet the following requirements:

Required

Preparation component:

1. Prepare closing entries for the company as of May 31.

Analysis component:

2. All of the company's purchases were made on credit and the suppliers uniformly offer a 3% sales discount. Does it appear that the company's cash management system is accomplishing the goal of taking all available discounts? Explain.

3. In prior years, the company has experienced a 4% return rate on its sales, which means that approximately 4% of its gross sales were for items that were eventually returned outright or that caused the company to grant allowances to customers. How does this year's record compare to prior years' results?

Problem 6-4A
Closing entries and interpreting information about discounts and returns

LO 7

The following unadjusted trial balance was prepared at the end of the fiscal year for Resource Products Company:

Problem 6-5A
Adjusting and closing entries, income statements, and acid-test ratio

LO 11, 7, 9

RESOURCE PRODUCTS COMPANY Unadjusted Trial Balance October 31, 19X2		
Cash	$6,400	
Merchandise inventory	23,000	
Store supplies	9,600	
Prepaid insurance	4,600	
Store equipment	83,800	
Accumulated amortization, store equipment		$30,000
Accounts payable		16,000
Jan Smithers, capital		70,400
Jan Smithers, withdrawals	6,400	
Sales		208,000
Sales discounts	2,000	
Sales returns and allowances	4,000	
Cost of goods sold	74,800	
Amortization expense, store equipment		
Salaries expense	62,000	
Insurance expense		
Rent expense	28,000	
Store supplies expense		
Advertising expense	19,800	
Totals	$324,400	$324,400

Rent and salaries expense are equally divided between the selling and administrative functions. Resource Products Company uses a perpetual inventory system.

Required

1. Prepare adjusting journal entries for the following:
   a. Store supplies on hand at year-end amount to $3,300.

b. Expired insurance, an administrative expense, for the year is $3,000.

c. Amortization expense, a selling expense, is $2,800 for the year.

d. A physical count of the ending merchandise inventory shows $22,200 of goods on hand.

2. Prepare a multiple-step income statement for external users (see Exhibit 6.19).

3. Prepare a single-step income statement that would be provided to external users (see Exhibit 6.20).

4. Compute the company's current and acid-test ratios as of October 31, 19X2.

Analytical and Review Problems

A & R Problem 6-1A

The partially completed work sheet of Incomplete Data Company appears below:

INCOMPLETE DATA COMPANY								
Work Sheet for the Year Ended December 31, 1999								
	Trial Balance		Adjustments		Income Statement		Balance Sheet	
Account Titles	Debit	Credit	Debit	Credit	Debit	Credit	Debit	Credit
Cash	36,780							
Accounts receivable							4,600	
Merchandise inventory.					31,400	26,400		
Prepaid fire insurance	720						480	
Prepaid rent	4,800							
Office equipment							12,000	
Accum. amortization—office equipment . . .		4,500						
Accounts payable		8,000						
Clay Camp, capital		24,000						
Clay Camp, drawing							20,000	
Sales		320,000						
Sales returns and allowances.					1,000			
Purchases	219,200							
Purchases returns and allowances						1,400		
Advertising expense	1,000							
Supplies expense	1,800							
Salaries expense.	23,200							
Utilities expense	1,400							
Fire insurance expense								
Rent expense					2,400			
Amortization expense—office equipment. . .					1,600			
Salaries payable								660

Required:

Complete the work sheet for the year ended December 31, 1999.

The following are the selected data for the Allen Sales Company for the year 1999.

1. Selected closing entries:

Income Summary	298,000	
Purchases Returns and Allowances	2,500	
Purchases		205,000
Freight-In		4,200
Sales Salaries Expense		40,000
Advertising Expense		10,000
Rent Expense, Office Space		8,000
Delivery Expense		4,800
Office Salaries Expense		26,000
Amortization, Office Equipment		2,000
Miscellaneous Expense		500
To close expense and other nominal accounts		
G. Allen, Capital	28,000	
G. Allen, Withdrawals		28,000
To close the withdrawals account.		

2. G. Allen follows the practice of withdrawing half of the annual net income from the business.

3. There were no sales returns and allowances for the year. However, sales discounts amounted to $2,000.

4. Inventories:
December 31, 1998—$35,000
December 31, 1999—$29,000

Required

1. Compute the amount of net income for 1999.

2. Compute the amount of sales for 1999.

3. Prepare a classified income statement for 1999.

(The first three segments of this comprehensive problem were presented in Chapters 3, 4, and 5. If those segments have not been completed, the assignment can begin at this point. However, you should use the Working Papers that accompany this text because they reflect the account balances that resulted from posting the entries required in Chapters 3, 4, and 5.)

Serial Problem
Echo Systems

Earlier segments of this problem have described how Mary Graham created Echo Systems on October 1, 19X1. The company has been successful, and its list of customers has started to grow. To accommodate the growth, the accounting system is ready to be modified to set up separate accounts for each customer. The following list of customers includes the account number used for each account and any balance as of the end of 19X1. Graham decided to add a fourth digit with a decimal point to the 106 account number that had been used for the single Accounts Receivable account. This modification allows the existing chart of accounts to continue being used. The list also shows the balances that two customers owed as of December 31, 19X1:

Customer Account	No.	Dec. 31 Balance
Alamo Engineering Co.	106.1	
Buckman Services	106.2	
Capital Leasing	106.3	
Decker Co.	106.4	$1,350
Elite Corporation	106.5	
Fostek Co.	106.6	$1,500
Grandview Co.	106.7	
Hacienda, Inc.	106.8	
Images, Inc.	106.9	

In response to frequent requests from customers, Graham has decided to begin selling computer software. The company will extend credit terms of 1/10, n/30 to customers who purchase merchandise. No cash discount will be available on consulting fees. The following additional accounts were added to the General Ledger to allow the system to account for the company's new merchandising activities:

Account	No.
Merchandise Inventory	119
Sales	413
Sales Discounts	414
Sales Returns and Allowances	415
Cost of Goods Sold	502

Because the accounting system does not use reversing entries, all revenue and expense accounts have zero balances as of January 1, 19X2.

Required

1. Prepare journal entries to record each of the following transactions for Echo Systems.
2. Post the journal entries to the accounts in the company's General Ledger. (Use asset, liability, and equity accounts that start with balances as of December 31, 19X1.)
3. Prepare a partial worksheet consisting of the first six columns similar to the one shown in Appendix 4B that shows the unadjusted trial balance, the March 31 adjustments, and the adjusted trial balance. Do not prepare closing entries and do not journalize the adjusting entries or post them to the ledger.
4. Prepare an interim income statement for the three months ended March 31, 19X2. Use a single-step format like the one in Exhibit 6.20. List all expenses without differentiating between selling expenses and general and administrative expenses.
5. Prepare an interim statement of changes in owner's equity for the three months ended March 31, 19X2.
6. Prepare an interim balance sheet as of March 31, 19X2.

Transactions:

Jan. 4 Paid Carly Smith for five days at the rate of $100 per day, including one day in addition to the four unpaid days from the prior year.

5 Mary Graham invested an additional $24,000 cash in the business.

7 Purchased $5,600 of merchandise from Shephard Corp. with terms of 1/10, n/30, FOB shipping point.

9 Received $1,500 from Fostek Co. as final payment on its account.

11 Completed five-day project for Alamo Engineering Co. and billed them $4,500, which is the total price of $6,000 less the advance payment of $1,500.

13 Sold merchandise with a retail value of $4,200 and a cost of $3,360 to Elite Corporation with terms of 1/10, n/30, FOB shipping point.

15 Paid $700 for freight charges on the merchandise purchased on January 7.

16 Received $3,000 cash from Grandview Co. for computer services.

17 Paid Shephard Corp. for the purchase on January 7, net of the discount.

20 Elite Corporation returned $400 of defective merchandise from its purchase on January 13. The returned merchandise, which had a cost of $320, was scrapped.

22 Received the balance due from Elite Corporation net of the discount and the credit for the returned merchandise.

24 Returned defective merchandise to Shephard Corp. and accepted credit against future purchases. Its cost, net of the discount, was $396.

26 Purchased $8,000 of merchandise from Shephard Corp. with terms of 1/10, n/30, FOB destination.

26 Sold merchandise with a cost of $4,640 for $5,800 on credit to Hacienda, Inc.

29 Received a $396 credit memo from Shephard Corp. concerning the merchandise returned on January 24.

31 Paid Carly Smith for 10 days' work at $100 per day.

Feb. 1   Paid $3,375 to the Lakeshore Mall for another three months' rent in advance.
   3   Paid Shephard Corp. for the balance due, net of the cash discount, less the $396 amount in the credit memo.
   5   Paid $800 to the local newspaper for advertising.
   11   Received the balance due from Alamo Engineering Co. for fees billed on January 11.
   15   May Graham withdrew $4,800 cash for personal use.
   23   Sold merchandise with a cost of $2,560 for $3,200 on credit to Grandview Co.
   26   Paid Carly Smith for eight days' work at $100 per day.
   27   Reimbursed Mary Graham's business automobile expenses for 600 kilometres at $0.25 per kilometre.

Mar. 8   Purchased $2,400 of computer supplies from Abbott Office Products on credit.
   9   Received the balance due from Grandview Co. for merchandise sold on February 23.
   11   Repaired the company's computer at the cost of $860.
   16   Received $4,260 cash from Images, Inc. for computing services.
   19   Paid the full amount due to Abbott Office Products, including amounts created on December 15 and March 8.
   24   Billed Capital Leasing for $5,900 of computing services.
   25   Sold merchandise with a cost of $1,002 for $1,800 on credit to Buckman Services.
   30   Sold merchandise with a cost of $1,100 for $2,220 on credit to Decker Company.
   31   Reimbursed Mary Graham's business automobile expenses for 400 kilometres at $0.25 per kilometre.

Information for the March 31 adjustments and financial statements:

a. The March 31 inventory of computer supplies is $2,115.

b. Three more months have passed since the company purchased the annual insurance policy at the cost of $2,160.

c. Carly Smith has not been paid for seven days of work.

d. Three months have passed since any prepaid rent cost has been transferred to expense. The monthly rent is $1,125.

e. Amortization on the computer for January through March is $1,125.

f. Amortization on the office equipment for January through March is $750.

g. The March 31 inventory of merchandise is $980.

BEYOND THE NUMBERS

Refer to the financial statements and related information for **Alliance** in Appendix I. Find the answers to the following questions by analyzing the information in the report.

1. Catagorize the assets on the Alliance balance sheet as to short-term, current and non-current for the fiscal year ended March 31, 1997 and 1996. See Note 1 in the Notes to the Financial Statements for assistance.

2. Compute the current and acid-test ratios as of the end of the fiscal years ended March 31, 1997, and March 31, 1996. Comment on what you find.

Reporting in Action

LO 11, 8

Dominion Textile produces and sells textiles. **Semi-Tech Corp.** manufactures and distributes consumer durables. Key comparative figures ($ millions) for these two organizations follow:

Comparative Analysis

LO 12

Key Figures	DomTex		Semi-Tech	
	1997	1996	1997	1996
Net Sales	$1,110	$1,146	$1,799	$1,692
Cost of Sales	$ 959	$ 991	$1,243	$1,116

*DomTex figures are from the annual reports for the fiscal years ended June 30,1997 and 1996.
Semi-Tech figures are from the annual reports for the fiscal years ended March 31, 1997 and 1996.

Required

1. Compute the dollar amount of the gross margin and the gross margin ratio for the two years shown for both companies.
2. Which company earns more in gross profit for each dollar of net sales?
3. Did the gross margin ratios improve or decline for the companies?

Ethics Challenge

LO 6

Claire Phelps is a popular high school student who attends approximately four dances a year at her high school. Each dance requires a new dress and accessories that necessitate a financial outlay of $100 to $200 per event. Claire's parents inform her that she is "on her own" with respect to financing the dresses. After incurring a major hit to her savings for the first dance in her second year, Claire developed a different approach. She buys the dress on credit the week before the dance, wears it to the dance, and returns the dress the next week to the store for a full refund on her charge card.

Required

1. Comment on the ethics exhibited by Claire and possible consequences of her actions.
2. How does the store account for the dresses that Claire returns?

Communicating in Practice

LO 4, 8, 7

Assume you are the accountant for Music, Videos and More, a retailer that sells goods for home entertainment needs. The owner of the business, Mr. Um Paah, recently reviewed the annual financial statements and sent you an e-mail stating that he is sure you overstated net income. He explains that he makes this claim because, although he has invested a great deal in security, he is sure shoplifting and other forms of inventory shrinkage have still taken place. He does not see any deduction for such loss on the income statement.

Required

Prepare a memo (or e-mail) that responds to the owner's concerns. If the response is to be made via e-mail you are to assume your instructor is the owner instead of Mr. Um Paah

Taking It to the Net

LO 1

In the last few years the amount of merchandising activity on the Web has grown dramatically. Use a Web search engine (such as Lycos, Yahoo, or Alta Vista) and search for the word "merchandising." Explore the Web addresses located by the search engine and make a list of at least 10 products that companies or individuals are trying to market and sell using the Web.

Teamwork in Action

LO 2, 8, 12

World Brands Company's ledger and supplementary records at the end of the period disclose the following information:

Sales	$430,000
Sales returns	18,000
Merchandise inventory (beginning of period)	49,000
Invoice cost of merchandise purchases	180,000
Purchase discounts received	4,500
Sales discounts	6,600
Purchase returns and allowances received	5,500
Cost of transportation-in	11,000
Operating Expenses	20,000
Merchandise inventory (end of period)	42,000

Required

1. *Each* member of the team is to assume the responsibility for computing *one* of the amounts listed below. You are not to duplicate your teammates' work. Get necessary amounts from a teammate. Each member is to explain their computation to the team in preparation for reporting to class.

a. Net sales

b. Total cost of merchandise purchases

c. Cost of goods sold

d. Gross profit

e. Net income

2. Check your net income with the instructor. If correct, proceed to 3.

3. Assume a physical inventory disclosed that the actual ending inventory was $38,000. Discuss how this would affect previously computed amounts.

Arrange an interview (in person or by phone) with the manager of a retail shop in a mall or in the downtown area of your community. Explain to the manager that you are an accounting student learning about merchandising operations and the accounting for sales returns and sales allowances. Ask the manager what the store policy is regarding returns. Also find out if sales allowances are ever negotiated with customers. Inquire whether management ever perceives that customers are abusing return policies and what actions management takes to counter the abuses. Be prepared to discuss your findings in class.

Hitting the Road

LO 1

Read the article "Bay Snaps up Kmart," in the February 7, 1998, issue of *The Financial Post*.

Business Break

LO 9

Required

1. According to the article, who is **Hudson's Bay Company's** strongest competitor?

2. What strategy is The Bay using to compete more effectively against its number one rival?

3. After reading the article do you think the new strategy of The Bay will be effective?

4. What problem has **Zellers** had and how does The Bay plan to solve it?

7

Merchandise Inventories and Cost of Sales

A Look Back

Chapter 6 focused on merchandising activities and how they're reported. Both the perpetual and periodic inventory systems were described. We also analyzed and recorded merchandise purchases and sales, and explained adjustments and the closing process for merchandising companies.

A Look at This Chapter

This chapter emphasizes accounting for inventory. We describe the methods available for assigning costs to inventory, and we explain the items and costs making up merchandise inventory. We also analyze the effects of inventory for financial reporting, and we discuss other methods of estimating and measuring inventory.

A Look Forward

Chapter 8 expands our study of accounting to information systems and special journals. We explain how computing technology is expanding accounting opportunities, and we explain the importance of knowing where information is located in special journals.

Chapter Outline

Wired in Calgary

Calgary, AB—Big is not better. Or so says Lenny Russo the 29-year-old owner of **Wired,** an electronics retailer and service provider. Russo built his modest store by taking jobs nobody wanted. "Big stores give a hard sell, take your cash, and maybe see you later," says Russo. "Don't get me wrong. They've got a place. It just isn't my place." What Russo's place *is* is selling, installing and servicing home entertainment systems to college students, young families, clubs, and other establishments. "I deal with small fry," says Russo. "I give people a great system fitting their needs, and they give me their business." He now has his own space downtown and business is good.

But it wasn't always that way. "The biggest hurdle," bemoans Russo "was getting the money to get going and to expand." Russo's hurdle was pushing the numbers and getting financial statements together. "The bank wanted to know things like gross margin, turnover and inventory on hand." Adds Russo, "'Til then I thought turnover was something you ate." The other hang-up Russo faced was measuring inventory. "I started by keeping track of each item sold and recording its cost." But business grew and Russo's system overloaded.

Needless to say, Russo has figured out a lot of things in his few years in business. Now he can talk the talk with the best of them. "I can tell you about turnover and liquidity ratios, and other financial jazz. But," laughs Russo "don't tell my family!" Somehow, one gets the feeling the Russo family would be proud.

Learning Objectives

LO 1   Compute inventory in a perpetual system using the methods of specific identification, weighted average, FIFO, and LIFO.

LO 2   Identify the items making up merchandise inventory.

LO 3   Identify the costs of merchandise inventory.

LO 4   Analyze the effects of inventory methods for financial reporting.

LO 5   Analyze the effects of inventory errors on current and future financial statements.

LO 6   Compute the lower of cost or market value of inventory.

LO 7   Apply both the retail inventory and gross profit methods to estimate inventory.

LO 8   Assess inventory management using both merchandise turnover and days' sales in inventory.

CHAPTER PREVIEW

Activities of merchandising companies involve the purchase and resale of products. We explained accounting for merchandisers in the last chapter and explained how perpetual and periodic inventory systems account for merchandise inventory. In this chapter we extend our study and analysis of inventory by identifying the items making up inventory and their computation. We also explain methods used to assign costs to merchandise inventory *and* to cost of goods sold. These methods include those that differ from historical cost. The principles and methods we describe are used in department stores, grocery stores, and many other merchandising companies who purchase products for resale. These principles and methods affect reported amounts of income, assets, and equity. Understanding these fundamental concepts of inventory accounting increases our ability to analyze and interpret financial statements. Like Lenny Russo in the opening article, an understanding of these topics also helps in running one's own business.

Assigning Costs to Inventory

LO1 Compute inventory in a perpetual system using the methods of specific identification, weighted average, FIFO, and LIFO.

Accounting for inventory affects both the balance sheet and income statement. A major goal in accounting for inventory is matching relevant costs against revenues. This is important to properly compute income.[1] We discussed the *matching principle* in Chapter 4. We use it when accounting for inventory to decide how much of the cost of the goods available for sale is deducted from sales and how much is carried forward as inventory and matched against future sales. Management must make this decision along with several others when accounting for inventory. These decisions include:

■ Costing method (specific identification, weighted-average, FIFO, or LIFO)
■ Inventory system (perpetual or periodic)
■ Items included and their costs.
■ Use of market or other estimates.

These decisions affect the reported amounts for inventory, cost of goods sold, gross profit, income, current assets, and other accounts. This chapter discusses all of these important issues and their reporting effects.

One of the most important decisions in accounting for inventory is determining the per unit costs assigned to inventory items. When all units are purchased at the same unit cost, this process is simple. But when identical items are purchased at different costs, a question arises as to what amounts are recorded in cost of goods sold when sales occur and what amounts remain in inventory. When using a perpetual inventory system, we must record cost of goods sold and reductions in inventory as sales occur. A periodic inventory system determines cost of goods sold and inventory amounts at the end of a period (see Appendix 7A). How we assign these costs to inventory and cost of goods sold affects the reported amounts for both systems.

There are four methods often used in assigning costs to inventory and cost of goods sold: (1) specific identification: (2) weighted-average: (3) first-in, first-out: and (4) last-in, first-out. Each method assumes a particular pattern for how costs flow through inventory. All four methods are accepted under GAAP and are described in this section. A method is acceptable whether or not the actual physical flow of goods follows the cost flow assumption.[2] Exhibit 7.1 shows the use of these methods among larger companies.

---

[1] *CICA Handbook,* section 3030, "Inventories," par. .09.

[2] Physical flow of goods depends on the type of product and the way it is stored. Perishable goods such as fresh fruit demand that a business attempts to sell them in a first-in, first-out pattern. Other products such as lanterns or grills can often be sold in a last-in, first-out pattern. But physical flow and cost flow need not be the same.

We use information from **Trekking,** a sporting goods store, to describe the four methods. Among its many products, Trekking carries one type of mountain bike. Its sales of mountain bikes are directed at biking clubs and purchases are usually in amounts of 10 or more bikes. We use data from Trekking's August 1998 transactions with mountain bikes. Its mountain bike ("unit") inventory at the beginning of August, and its purchases during August are shown in Exhibit 7.2.

Frequency in Use of Inventory Methods in Practice

FIFO 47%
Other* 5%
LIFO 4%
Weighted-Average 45%
*Includes specific identification.

Aug.	1	Beginning inventory	10 units @ $ 91 = $ 910
Aug.	3	Purchased	15 units @ $106 = 1,590
Aug.	17	Purchased	20 units @ $115 = 2,300
Aug.	28	Purchased	10 units @ $119 = 1,190
		Total	55 units $5,990

Exhibit 7.2

Cost of Goods Available for Sale

Trekking ends August with 12 bikes on hand in inventory. Trekking had two sales of mountain bikes to two different biking clubs in August as shown in Exhibit 7.3.

Aug.	14	Sales	20 units @ $130 = $2,600
Aug.	31	Sales	23 units @ $150 = 3,450
		Total	43 units $6,050

Exhibit 7.3

Retail Sales of Goods

We explained in the last chapter how use of perpetual inventory systems is increasing dramatically due to advances in information and computing technology. Widespread use of electronic scanners and product bar codes further encourage its use. Accordingly, we discuss the assigning of costs to inventory in a perpetual system. But we also describe the assigning of costs to inventory using a periodic system in Appendix 7A. Recall a periodic inventory system computes cost of goods available for sale and allocates it between cost of goods sold and ending inventory at the *end of the period.* When we assign an amount to ending inventory, this determines the amount of cost of goods sold.[3] This is because by subtracting ending inventory from cost of goods available for sale we get cost of goods sold.

We know the merchandise inventory account is perpetually updated to reflect purchases and sales. The important accounting aspects of a perpetual system were described in Chapter 6 and are:

■ Each purchase of merchandise for resale increases (debits) inventory.

■ Each sale of merchandise decreases (credits) inventory and increases (debits) costs of goods sold.

■ Necessary costs of merchandise such as transportation-in increase (debits) inventory and cost reductions such as purchase discounts and purchase returns and allowances decrease (credits) inventory.

Except for any inventory shrinkage, the balance in the merchandise inventory account reflects the amount of merchandise on hand at any time.

---

[3] Similarly, when we assign an amount to cost of goods sold, this determines the amount of ending inventory.

Specific Identification

When each item in inventory can be directly identified with a specific purchase and its invoice, we can use **specific identification** (also called **specific invoice inventory pricing**) to assign costs. Trekking's internal documents reveal 6 of the 12 unsold units are from the August 28 purchase and another 6 are from the August 17 purchase. Specifically, we use this information along with specific identification to assign costs to the goods sold and to ending inventory as shown in Exhibit 7.4.

Exhibit 7.4

Specific Identification Computations

Date	Purchases	Sales (at cost)	Inventory Balance
Aug. 1			10 @ $ 91 = $ 910
Aug. 3	15 @ $106 = $1,590		10 @ $ 91 } 15 @ $106 } = $2,500
Aug. 14		8 @ $91 = $ 728 } 12 @ $106 = $1,272 } = $2,000	2 @ $ 91 } 3 @ $106 } = $ 500
Aug. 17	20 @ $115 = $2,300		2 @ $ 91 } 3 @ $106 } 20 @ $115 } = $2,800
Aug. 28	10 @ $119 = $1,190		2 @ $ 91 } 3 @ $106 } 20 @ $115 } 10 @ $119 } = $3,990
Aug. 31		2 @ $91 = $ 182 } 3 @ $106 = $ 318 } 14 @ $115 = $1,610 } 4 @ $119 = $ 476 } = $2,586	6 @ $115 } 6 @ $119 } = $1,404

When using specific identification, Trekking's cost of goods sold reported on the income statement is **$4,586** and its ending inventory reported on the balance sheet is **$1,404**. *The assignment of costs to cost of goods sold and inventory using specific identification is the same for both the perpetual and periodic systems.*

Weighted Average

The **weighted-average** (also called **average cost**) **method** of assigning cost requires computing the average cost per unit of merchandise inventory at the time of each sale. Some systems are set up to compute this average after each purchase. The important point is we compute weighted-average cost at the time of each sale by dividing the cost of goods available for sale by the units on hand. Using weighted average for Trekking means the costs of mountain bikes are assigned to inventory and goods sold as shown in Exhibit 7.5.

Trekking's cost of goods sold reported on the income statement is **$4,622** ($2,000 + $2,622) and its ending inventory reported on the balance sheet is **$1,368.** *The assignment of costs to cost of goods sold and inventory using weighted average usually gives different results depending on whether a perpetual or periodic system is used.* This is because weighted average under a perpetual system recomputes the per unit cost at the time of each sale, whereas under the periodic system the per unit cost is only computed at the end of a period. The weighted-average perpetual system often raises a rounding problem in the computations because the currency figures are limited to two decimal places. The typical solution is to adjust or "plug" the cost of goods sold figure after calculating the closing inventory amount at the weighted-average cost. This adjustment is seldom more than a few dollars.

Date	Purchases	Sales (at cost)	Inventory Balance	
Aug. 1			10 @ $ 91	= $910
Aug. 3	15 @ $106 = $1,590		10 @ $ 91 ⎱ 15 @ $106 ⎰	= $2,500 (or $100 per unit)a
Aug.14		20 @ $100 = $2,000	5 @ $100	= $ 500 (or $100 per unit)b
Aug.17	20 @ $115 = $2,300		5 @ $100 ⎱ 20 @ $115 ⎰	= $2,800 (or $112 per unit)c
Aug.28	10 @ $119 = $1,190		5 @ $100 ⎱ 20 @ $115 ⎰ 10 @ $119	= $3,990 (or $114 per unit)d
Aug.31		23 @ $114 = $2,622	12 @ $114	= $1,368 (or $114 per unit)e

Exhibit 7.5

Weighted-Average
Computations—Perpetual
System

a $100 per unit = [$2,500 inventory balance ÷ 25 units in inventory]
b $100 per unit = [$500 inventory balance ÷ 5 units in inventory]
c $112 per unit = [$2,800 inventory balance ÷ 25 units in inventory]
d $114 per unit = [$3,990 inventory balance ÷ 35 units in inventory]
e $114 per unit = [$1,368 inventory balance ÷ 12 units in inventory]

First-In, First-Out

The **first-in, first-out (FIFO)** method of assigning cost to inventory and the goods sold assumes inventory items are sold in the order acquired. When sales occur, costs of the earliest units acquired are charged to cost of goods sold. This leaves the costs from the most recent purchases in inventory. Use of FIFO for Trekking means the costs of mountain bikes are assigned to inventory and goods sold as shown in Exhibit 7.6.

Date	Purchases	Sales (at cost)	Inventory Balance	
Aug. 1			10 @ $ 91	= $ 910
Aug. 3	15 @ $106 = $1,590		10 @ $ 91 ⎱ 15 @ $106 ⎰	= $2,500
Aug. 14		10 @ $ 91 = $ 910 ⎱ 10 @ $106 = $1,060 ⎰ = $1,970	5 @ $106	= $ 530
Aug. 17	20 @ $115 = $2,300		5 @ $106 ⎱ 20 @ $115 ⎰	= $2,830
Aug. 28	10 @ $119 = $1,190		5 @ $106 ⎱ 20 @ $115 ⎰ 10 @ $119	= $4,020
Aug. 31		5 @ $106 = $ 530 ⎱ 18 @ $115 = $2,070 ⎰ = $2,600	2 @ $115 ⎱ 10 @ $119 ⎰	= $1,420

Exhibit 7.6

FIFO Computations—
Perpetual System

Trekking's cost of goods sold reported on the income statement is **$4,570** ($1,970 + $2,600) and its ending inventory reported on the balance sheet is **$1,420.** *The assignment of costs to cost of goods sold and inventory using FIFO is the same for both the perpetual and periodic systems.*

Last-In, First-Out

The **last-in, first-out (LIFO)** method of assigning cost assumes that costs for the most recent purchased are sold first and charged to cost of goods sold. The earliest purchases are assigned to inventory. Like the other methods, LIFO is acceptable even when the physical flow of goods does not follow a last-in, first-out pattern.

One appeal of LIFO is that ongoing companies do replace inventory items they sell. When goods are sold, replacements are purchased. Sales cause replacement of goods. Then a proper matching of costs with revenues is to match replacement costs with sales causing the new replacements. While costs for the most recent purchases are not replacement costs, they often are close approximations (and sometimes equal) to replacement costs. Because LIFO assigns the most recent purchase costs to cost of goods sold, LIFO (compared to FIFO or weighted average) comes closest to matching replacement costs with revenues.

Use of LIFO for Trekking means costs of mountain bikes are assigned to inventory and goods sold as shown in Exhibit 7.7.

Exhibit 7.7

LIFO Computations—
Perpetual System

Date	Purchases	Sales (at cost)	Inventory Balance
Aug. 1			10 @ $ 91 = $ 910
Aug. 3	15 @ $106 = $1,590		10 @ $ 91 15 @ $106 } = $2,500
Aug. 14		15 @ $106 = $1,590 5 @ $ 91 = $ 455 } = $2,045	5 @ $ 91 = $ 455
Aug. 17	20 @ $115 = $2,300		5 @ $ 91 20 @ $115 } = $2,755
Aug. 28	10 @ $119 = $1,190		5 @ $ 91 20 @ $115 10 @ $119 } = $3,945
Aug. 31		10 @ $119 = $1,190 13 @ $115 = $1,495 } = $2,685	5 @ $ 91 7 @ $115 } = $1,260

Trekking's cost of goods sold reported on the income statement is **$4,730** ($2,045 + $2,685) and its ending inventory reported on the balance sheet is **$1,260.** *The assignment of costs to cost of goods sold and inventory using LIFO usually gives different results depending on whether a perpetual or periodic system is used.* This is because LIFO under a perpetual system assigns the most recent costs to goods sold at the time of each sale, whereas the periodic system waits to assign costs until the end of a period.

Inventory Costing and Technology

A perpetual inventory system can be kept in either electronic or manual form. A manual form is often too costly for most businesses, especially those with many purchases and sales or many units in inventory. But advances in information and computing technology have greatly reduced the cost of a perpetual inventory system. Instead, many companies are now asking whether they can afford not to have a perpetual inventory system. This is because timely access to information is being used strategically by companies to gain a competitive advantage. Scanned sales data, for instance, can reveal crucial information on buying patterns. It can also help companies target promotional and advertising activities. These and other applications have greatly increased use of the perpetual system.

Subsidiary Inventory Records

The Merchandise Inventory account is a controlling account to a subsidiary Merchandise Inventory Ledger. This subsidiary Ledger contains a separate record for each product and it can be in electronic or paper form. A typical ledger is

Whirlwind on the Web
In 1994 **MicroAge Toronto** rolled out a single inventory control and invoicing system replacing three existing systems. A client can call up the MicroAge Toronto Web site to place orders or check product pricing. Once an order is placed the system initiates all steps necessary to fulfill it, sets up a schedule, and tracks each step using a bar code scanning system. In each department, and at branch locations, staff use computer monitors to view work in progress. Each step in the transaction is date and time stamped and the next person handling the order is automatically notified. Since the new system was introduced the time to process orders has been reduced by 20 to 25% with annual savings of $200,000. [Source: *Canadian Business*, March 1998.]

Did You Know?

shown in Exhibit 7.8. This record shows both the units and costs for each purchase and sale, along with the balance after each purchase and sale. The record also gives the item, catalogue number, and its location. The subsidiary Merchandise Inventory Ledger is updated after each purchase and sale transaction. This ledger reveals a FIFO cost flow assumption is being used for sports bags.

Exhibit 7.8

Subsidiary Inventory Record

| Item | Leather Sports Bags | | Location code | W18C2 |
| Catalogue No. | LSB-117 | | Units: Maximum 25 Minimum 5 | |

| | Purchases | | | Sales | | | Balance | | |
Date	Units	Cost	Total	Units	Cost	Total	Units	Cost	Total
Aug. 1							10	$100	$1,000
12				4	$100	$400	6	100	600
18	20	$110	$2,200				6	100	2,800
							20	110	
30				6	100	600			
				2	110	220	18	110	1,980
Totals	20		$2,200	12		$1,220			

Subsidiary inventory records assist managers in planning and controlling inventory. Exhibit 7.8 reveals a policy of maintaining no more than 25 sports bags to avoid over-investment in this inventory, and no less than 5 sports bags on hand to avoid out-of-stock occurrences. These records also permit companies to compare a physical count of items on hand to the record. Differences are investigated to identify their cause.

Inventory Items and Costs

This section identifies the items and costs making up merchandise inventory. This is important given the major impact of inventory in financial statements. We also describe the importance and methods of taking a physical count of inventory.

Items in Merchandise Inventory

LO 2 Identify the items making up merchandise inventory.

Merchandise inventory includes all goods owned by a company and held for sale. This rule holds regardless of where goods are located at the time inventory is counted. Most inventory items are no problem when applying this rule. We often must simply see that all items are counted, nothing is omitted, and computations are correct. But certain items require special attention. These include goods in transit, goods on consignment, and goods damaged or obsolete.

Goods in Transit

Do we include in a purchaser's inventory the goods in transit from a supplier? Our answer depends on whether the rights and risks of ownership have passed from the supplier to the purchaser. If ownership has passed to the purchaser, they are included in the purchaser's inventory. We explained in Chapter 6 how we determine this by looking at the term FOB destination or shipping point. If the purchaser is responsible for paying freight charges, then ownership passes when goods are loaded on the means of transportation. If the supplier is to pay freight charges, ownership passes when goods arrive at their destination.

Goods on Consignment

Goods on consignment are goods shipped by their owner, called the **consignor,** to another party called the **consignee.** A consignee is to sell goods for the owner. Consigned goods are owned by the consignor and are reported in the consignor's inventory. **Slugger Sports Memorabilia** for instance, pays sports celebrities such as Wayne Gretzky to sign memorabilia. These autographed items (hockey sticks, baseballs, jerseys, photos, etc.) are offered to shopping networks on consignment as well as sold through catalogues and dealers.

Goods Damaged or Obsolete

Damaged goods and obsolete (or deteriorated) goods are not counted in inventory if they are unsalable. If these goods are salable at a reduced price, they are included in inventory at a conservative estimate of their **net realizable value.** Net realizable value is sales price minus the cost of making the sale. The period when damage or obsolescence (or deterioration) occurs is the period where the loss is reported.

Did You Know?

Inventory Online

Beamscope Canada Inc., a leading distributor of home office products, computer software, and video entertainment has developed software allowing customers to review the specifications of Beamscope products and place inventory orders via a computer system. In Beamscope's warehouses, new orders are picked, scanned, placed on a conveyer, boxed and readied for truck pickup for next day delivery to customers. The company generates 25,000 shipments a month. In 1993 shipments were six to seven shipping days behind and the sales force spent 25% of their time addressing shipping problems. Today, that number is negligible. Beamscope's improved supply chain is one of the reasons why company sales have rocketed. [Source: *Materials Management & Distribution,* November 1996.]

Costs of Merchandise Inventory

LO3 Identify the costs of merchandise inventory.

Costs included in merchandise inventory are those expenditures necessary, directly or indirectly, in bringing an item to a salable condition and location.[4] This means the cost of an inventory item includes its invoice price minus any discount, plus any added or incidental costs necessary to put it in a place and condition for sale. Added or incidental costs can include import duties, transportation-in, storage, insurance, and costs incurred in an aging process (for example, aging of wine and cheese).

---

[4] Ibid., par. 3030.02.

Accounting principles imply that incidental costs are assigned to every unit purchased. This is so that all inventory costs are properly matched against revenue in the period when inventory is sold. The *materiality principle* or the *cost-to-benefit constraint* is used by some companies to not assign incidental costs of acquiring merchandise to inventory. These companies argue that either incidental costs are immaterial or that the effort in assigning these costs to inventory outweighs the benefits. Such companies price inventory using invoice prices only. When this is done, the incidental costs are allocated to cost of goods sold in the period when they are incurred.

Barcoded Lobsters?

A few years ago, the world of barcoding was enthralled by a novel experiment in which honeybees were barcoded with tiny tags as part of a pollination research study. Now, scientists at the University of Prince Edward Island have developed bar codes applied to lobsters in a way to study diseases which occur when lobsters are kept in pounds for extended periods. The lobster industry is worth about $300 million in Nova Scotia. Post-harvest losses have been estimated to range from 10 to 15% in a given year's catch. [Source: *Bar Code Quarterly,* April, 1997.]

Did You Know?

Physical Count of Merchandise Inventory

The Inventory account under a perpetual system is always up to date. Yet events can occur where the Inventory account balance is different from inventory on hand. Such events include theft, loss, damage and errors. This means that nearly all companies take a *physical count* of inventory at least once each year, sometimes called *taking an inventory.* This often occurs at the end of its fiscal year or when inventory amounts are low. This physical count is used to adjust the Inventory account balance to the actual inventory on hand. There is also need for a physical count of inventory under a periodic system (see Appendix 7A).

We determine a dollar amount for the physical count of inventory on hand at the end of a period by: (1) counting the units of each product on hand, (2) multiplying the count for each product by its cost per unit, and (3) adding the costs for all products. When taking a count, items are less likely to be counted more than once or omitted if we use prenumbered *inventory tickets.* We show a typical inventory ticket in Exhibit 7.9.

The process of a physical count is fairly standard. Before beginning a physical count of inventory, we prepare at least one inventory ticket for each product on hand. These tickets are issued to employees doing the count. An employee will count the quantity of a product and obtain information on its purchase date, selling price, and cost. This information is sometimes included with the products, but must often be obtained from accounting records or invoices. Once the necessary information is collected, the employee records it on the inventory ticket and signs the form. The inventory ticket is then attached to the counted inventory. Another employee often recounts and re-checks information on the ticket, signs the ticket, and returns it to the manager. To ensure no ticket is lost or missed, internal control procedures verify that all prenumbered tickets are returned. The unit and cost data on inventory tickets are aggregated by multiplying the number of units for each product by its unit cost. This gives us the dollar amount for each product in inventory. The sum total of all products is the dollar amount reported for inventory on the balance sheet.

Exhibit 7.9

Inventory Ticket

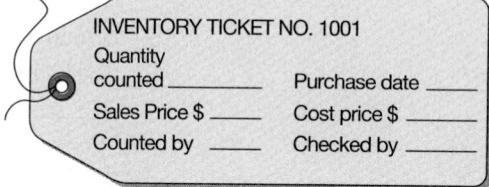

INVENTORY TICKET NO. 1001
Quantity
counted _____   Purchase date _____
Sales Price $ _____   Cost price $ _____
Counted by _____   Checked by _____

Flash back

1. What accounting principle most governs allocation of cost of goods available for sale between ending inventory and cost of goods sold?

2. If **Irwin Toys** sells goods to **The Bay** with terms FOB Irwin Toys' factory, does Irwin Toys or The Bay report these goods in its inventory when they are in transit?

3. An art gallery purchases a painting for $11,400. Additional costs in obtaining and offering the artwork for sale include $130 for transportation-in, $150 for import duties, $100 for insurance during shipment, $180 for advertising, $400 for framing, and $800 for sales salaries. For computing inventory cost, what is assigned to the painting?

Answers—p. 339

Inventory Analysis and Effects

This section analyzes and compares the effects of using alternative inventory costing methods. We also analyze the income effects of inventory methods, examine managers' preferences for an inventory method, and look at the effects of inventory errors.

Financial Reporting

LO4 Analyze the effects of inventory methods for financial reporting.

When purchase prices do not change, the choice of an inventory costing method is unimportant. All methods assign the same cost amounts when prices remain constant. But when purchase prices are rising or falling, the methods are likely to assign different cost amounts. We show these differences in Exhibit 7.10 using Trekking's segment income statement for its mountain bike operations.

Exhibit 7.10

Income Statement Effects of Inventory Costing Methods

TREKKING COMPANY Segment Income Statement—Mountain Bikes Month Ending August 31, 1998				
	Specific Identification	Weighted Average	FIFO	LIFO
Sales	$6,050	$6,050	$6,050	$6,050
Cost of goods sold	4,586	4,622	4,570	4,730
Gross profit	$1,464	$1,428	$1,480	$1,320
Operating expenses	450	450	450	450
Income before taxes	$1,014	$ 978	$1,030	$ 870

The different inventory costing methods show different results. Because Trekking's purchase prices rose in August, FIFO assigned the least amount to cost of goods sold. This led to the highest gross profit and the highest income. LIFO assigned the highest amount to cost of goods sold. This yields the lowest gross profit and the lowest net income. As expected, amounts from using the weighted-average method fall between FIFO and LIFO.[5] The amounts from using specific identification depend on what units are actually sold.

All four inventory costing methods are acceptable in practice. Each method offers certain advantages. One advantage of specific identification is it exactly matches costs and revenues. This is important when each unit has unique features affecting

---

[5] The weighted-average amount can be outside the FIFO or LIFO amounts if prices do not steadily increase or decrease but exhibit a cyclical pattern.

the cost of that unit. An advantage of weighted average is that it tends to smooth out price changes. The advantage of FIFO is that it assigns an amount to inventory on the balance sheet that closely approximates current replacement cost. The advantage of LIFO is that it assigns the most recent costs incurred to cost of goods sold, and likely better matches current costs with revenues on the income statement.

The choice of an inventory costing method often dramatically impact the amounts on financial statements. **New Brunswick Power Corporation,** for instance, recently changed its inventory method and reported this change in its annual report as follows:

> Note 2 Changes in Accounting Policies
> Commencing April 1, 1995, the Corporation changed the method of valuation of oil and coal inventory from the first-in, first-out method to the average cost method…The change has resulted in a decrease in the year end value of oil and coal inventory amounting to $1,283,000 and a corresponding increase in the cost of fuel consumed during the year.

Companies disclose the method used in their financial statements or notes. This is required reporting by the *full-disclosure principle.*[6] Because of its impact, it is important for us to know and understand inventory costing in our analysis of financial statements.

Financial Planner
You are the financial planner for several clients. Your clients periodically request your advice on analysis of financial statements of companies where they have investments. One of these clients asks you about any necessary adjustments to the merchandise inventory account of a company using FIFO in light of recent inflation. What is your advice? Does your advice depend on changes in the costs of these inventories for the company?

You Make the Call

Answer—p. 339

Flashback

4. Describe one advantage for each inventory costing method: specific identification, weighted average, FIFO, and LIFO.

5. When costs and prices are rising, does LIFO or FIFO report higher net income?

6. When costs and prices are rising, what effect does weighted average have on a balance sheet compared to FIFO?

Answers—p. 339

Consistency in Reporting

Because inventory costing methods can materially affect amounts on financial statements, some managers might be inclined to choose a method most consistent with their hoped for results each period. These managers' objective might be to pick the method giving the most favourable financial statement amounts. Managers might also be inclined to pick the method giving them the highest bonus since many management bonus plans are based on net income. If managers are allowed to pick the method each period, it would be more difficult for users of financial statements

---

[6] Ibid., par. 1506.16.

to compare a company's financial statements from one period to the next. If income increased, for instance, a user would need to decide whether it results from successful operations or from the accounting method change. The consistency principle is used to avoid this problem.

The **consistency principle** requires a company to use the same accounting methods period after period so the financial statements are comparable across periods.[7] The consistency principle applies to all accounting methods. Whenever a company must choose between alternative methods, consistency requires that the company continue to use the selected method period after period. Users of financial statements can then assume a company uses the same methods across years and they can make comparisons of a company's statements across periods.

The consistency principle *does not* require a company to use one method exclusively. It can use different methods to value different categories of inventory. Moore Corporation, for instance, includes the following note in its 1997 annual report:

> The cost of the principal raw material inventories and the raw material content of finished goods inventories in the United States is determined on the last-in, first-out basis. The cost of all other inventories is determined on the first-in, first-out basis.

Also, the consistency principle doesn't mean a company can never change from one accounting method to another. Instead it means a company must argue that the method it is changing to will improve its financial reporting. Under this circumstance, a change is acceptable. Yet when such a change is made, the full-disclosure principle requires that the notes to the statements report the type of change, its justification, and its effect on net income.[8]

Judgment and Ethics

Inventory Manager
You are the inventory manager for a merchandiser. Your compensation includes a bonus plan based on the amount of gross profit reported in the financial statements. Your superior comes to you and asks your opinion in changing the inventory costing method from weighted average to FIFO. Since costs have been rising and are expected to continue to rise, your superior predicts the company will be more attractive to investors because of the reported higher income. This is because weighted average dampens the effect of inventory price changes. You realize this proposed change will likely increase your bonus as well. What do you recommend?

Answer—p. 339

LO 5 Analyze the effects of inventory errors on current and future financial statements.

Errors in Reporting Inventory

Companies must take care in computing and taking a physical count of inventory. If inventory is reported in error, it causes misstatements in cost of goods sold, gross profit, net income, current assets, and owner's equity. It also means misstatements will exist in the next period's statements. This is because ending inventory of one period is the beginning inventory of the next. An error carried forward causes misstatements in the next period's cost of goods sold, gross profit, and net income. Since the inventory amount often is large, misstatements can reduce the usefulness of financial statements.

---

[7] Ibid., par. 1000.23.

[8] Ibid., par. 1506.16.

Income Statement Effects

The income statement effects of an inventory error are evident by looking at the components of cost of goods sold in Exhibit 7.11. The effect of an inventory error on cost of goods sold is determined by computing it with the incorrect amount and comparing it to when using the correct amount.

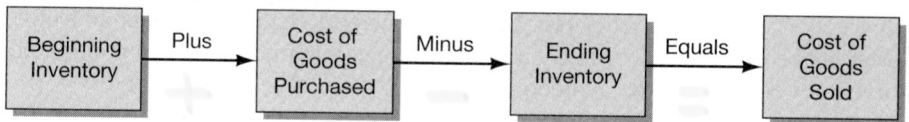

Exhibit 7.11

Cost of Goods Sold Components

We can see, for example, that understating ending inventory will overstate cost of goods sold. An overstatement in cost of goods sold yields an understatement in net income. We can do the same analysis with overstating ending inventory and for an error in beginning inventory. Exhibit 7.12 shows the effects of inventory errors on the current period's income statement amounts.

Inventory Error	Cost of Goods Sold	Net Income
Understate ending inventory	Overstated	Understated
Understate beginning inventory	Understated	Overstated
Overstate ending inventory	Understated	Overstated
Overstate beginning inventory	Overstated	Understated

Exhibit 7.12

Effects of Inventory Errors on This Period's Income Statement

Notice that inventory errors yield opposite effects in cost of goods sold and net income. Inventory errors also carry over to the next period, yielding a reverse effect.

To show these effects we look at an inventory error for a company with $100,000 in sales for years 1998, 1999 and 2000. If this company maintains a $20,000 inventory during this period and makes $60,000 in purchases in each of these years, then its cost of goods sold is $60,000 and its gross profit is $40,000 each year. Now what if this company errs in computing its 1998 ending inventory, and reports $16,000 instead of the correct amount of $20,000? The effects of this error are shown in Exhibit 7.13.

Income Statement					
	1998		**1999**		**2000**
Sales	$100,000		$100,000		$100,000
Cost of goods sold:					
Beginning inventory $20,000		$16,000*(d)		$20,000	
Cost of goods purchased 60,000		60,000		60,000	
Goods available for sale . $80,000		$76,000		$80,000	
Ending inventory 16,000*		20,000		20,000	
Cost of goods sold	64,000 (a)		56,000(e)		60,000
Gross profit	$ 36,000 (b)		$ 44,000 (f)		$ 40,000
Operating expenses	10,000		10,000		10,000
Net income	$ 26,000 (c)		$ 34,000 (g)		$ 30,000

* Correct amount is $20,000.

Exhibit 7.13

Effects of Inventory Errors on Three Periods' Income Statements

(a) overstated by 4000$
(b) understated by 4000$
(c) understated by 4000 $
(d) understatement of 4000$
(e)   "   "
(f) overstatement of 4000$.
(g)   "   "

The $4,000 understatement of the 1998 ending inventory causes a $4,000 overstatement in 1998 cost of goods sold and a $4,000 understatement in both 1998 gross profit and 1998 net income. Because 1998 ending inventory becomes the 1999 beginning inventory, this error also causes an understatement in 1999 cost of goods sold and a $4,000 overstatement in both 1999 gross profit and 1999 net income. An inventory error does not affect the third period, year 2000.

If 1998 ending inventory had been overstated, it would have yielded opposite results. In this case the 1998 net income would have been overstated and the 1999 income understated. Because an inventory error causes an offsetting error in the next period, it is sometimes said to be *self-correcting.* But do not think this makes inventory errors less serious. Managers, lenders, owners and other users make important decisions on changes in net income and cost of goods sold. Inventory errors must be avoided.

doesn't reflect on the 3rd period

Balance Sheet Effects

Balance sheet effects of an inventory error are evident by looking at the components of the accounting equation in Exhibit 7.14.

Exhibit 7.14

Accounting Equation

$$\textbf{Assets = Liabilities + Owner's Equity}$$

We can see, for example, that understating ending inventory will understate both current and total assets. An understatement in ending inventory also yields an understatement in owner's equity because of the understatement in net income. We can do the same analysis with overstating ending inventory. Exhibit 7.15 shows the effects of inventory errors on the current period's balance sheet amounts.

Exhibit 7.15

Effects of Inventory Errors on
This Period's Balance Sheet

Inventory Error	Assets	Owner's Equity
Understate ending inventory	Understated	Understated
Overstate ending inventory	Overstated	Overstated

Errors in beginning inventory do not yield misstatements in the balance sheet, but they do affect the income statement.

Flash back

7. A company takes a physical count of inventory at the end of 1999 and finds ending inventory is overstated by $10,000. Does this error cause cost of goods sold to be overstated or understated in 1999? In year 2000? By how much?

Answer—p. 339

Mid-Chapter Demonstration Problem

Coe Company had $435,000 of sales during each of three consecutive years, and it purchased merchandise costing $300,000 during each of the years. It also maintained a $105,000 inventory from the beginning to the end of the three-year period. However, in accounting under a periodic inventory system, it made an error at the end of year 1 that caused its ending year 1 inventory to appear on its statements at $90,000 rather than the correct $105,000.

Required

1. State the actual amount of the company's gross profit in each of the years.
2. Prepare a comparative income statement like Exhibit 7.13 to show the effect of this error on the company's cost of goods sold and gross profit in year 1, year 2, and year 3.

1. $\$435,000 - \$300,000 = \$135,000$
2.

Year	1	2	3
Sales	$435,000	$435,000	$435,000
Cost of goods sold:			
Beginning inventory . . . $105,000		$ 90,000	$105,000
Purchases 300,000		300,000	300,000
Goods available for sale . $405,000		$390,000	$405,000
Ending inventory 90,000		105,000	105,000
Cost of goods sold	315,000	285,000	300,000
Gross profit	$120,000	$150,000	$135,000

Solution to Mid-Chapter Demonstration Problem

This section describes other methods to value inventory. Knowledge of these methods is important for users in understanding and analyzing financial statements.

Other Inventory Valuations

LO 6 Compute the lower of cost or market amount of inventory.

Lower of Cost or Market

We explained how costs are assigned to ending inventory and cost of goods sold using one of four costing methods (specific identification, weighted-average, FIFO, or LIFO). Yet the cost of inventory is not necessarily the amount always reported on a balance sheet. Accounting principles require that inventory be reported at market value when market is lower than cost. Merchandise inventory is then said to be reported on the balance sheet at the *lower* **of cost or market (LCM).**

Computing the Lower of Cost or Market

In applying LCM, *market* can be defined as either net realizable value or current replacement cost. *Net realizable value (NRV)* is the amount the company expects to receive when it sells the merchandise less any costs of preparing the merchandise for sale, such as repairs, or selling costs, such as commissions. *Replacement cost (RC)* is the current cost of purchasing the same items in the usual manner. Motivation behind replacement cost as market is that when sales price declines, the replacement cost is likely to decline. The decline in replacement cost reflects a loss of value in inventory. This is because the cost of inventory is higher than the current replacement cost. It is also important we know what is meant when we use the term *market,* i.e., NRV or RC. The choice of either NRV or RC as the market value depends on which amount is more reliable. Most Canadian companies tend to use NRV as their definition of market value.[9]

When market is lower than cost, a loss is recognized. This is done by recording the decline in merchandise inventory from cost to market at the end of the period. LCM is applied in one of three ways: (1) separately to each individual item, (2) to major categories of items, and (3) to the whole of inventory. The less similar are the items making up inventory, the more likely companies apply LCM to individual items. Advances in technology further encourage the individual item application.

---

[9] C. Byrd and Ida Chen, *Financial Reporting in Canada 1997* (Toronto: CICA, 1997), p. 169.

We show how LCM is applied to the ending inventory of a motorsports retailer. Inventory data for this retailer along with LCM computations are shown in Exhibit 7.16.

Exhibit 7.16

Lower of Cost or Market Computations

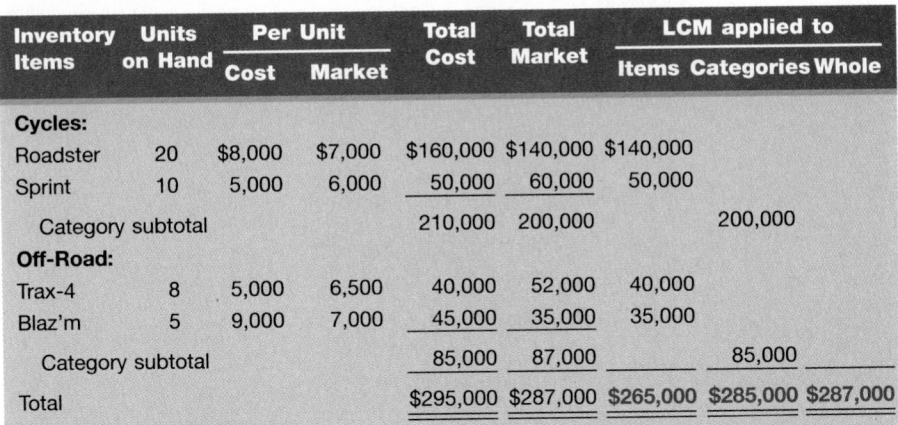

Inventory Items	Units on Hand	Per Unit Cost	Per Unit Market	Total Cost	Total Market	LCM applied to Items	LCM applied to Categories	LCM applied to Whole
Cycles:								
Roadster	20	$8,000	$7,000	$160,000	$140,000	$140,000		
Sprint	10	5,000	6,000	50,000	60,000	50,000		
Category subtotal				210,000	200,000		200,000	
Off-Road:								
Trax-4	8	5,000	6,500	40,000	52,000	40,000		
Blaz'm	5	9,000	7,000	45,000	35,000	35,000		
Category subtotal				85,000	87,000		85,000	
Total				$295,000	$287,000	$265,000	$285,000	$287,000

When LCM is applied to the *whole* of inventory, market is calculated as $287,000. Since this is $8,000 lower than the $295,000 cost, it is the amount reported for inventory on the balance sheet. When LCM is applied to individual *items* of inventory, market is $265,000. Since market is again less than the $295,000 cost, it is the amount reported for inventory. When LCM is applied to the major *categories* of inventory, market is $285,000. Anyone of these three applications of LCM is acceptable. **Canadian Tire** reports that its:

> Merchandise inventories are valued at the lower of cost and estimated net realizable value.

The *direct method* is a common way of recording inventory at market. The direct method substitutes market value for cost in the inventory account. Using LCM applied on the whole of inventory from Exhibit 7.16 we make the following entry to do this: Cost of Goods Sold Dr. $8,000; Merchandise Inventory Cr. $8,000. The Merchandise Inventory account balance is now $287,000, computed as $295,000 − $8,000.

Conservatism Principle

We explained how accounting rules require writing inventory down to market when market is less than cost. But inventory usually can't be written up to market when market exceeds cost. If writing inventory down to market is acceptable, why can't we write inventory up to market? One reason is a concern that the gain from a market increase is not realized until a sales transaction verifies the gain. But this problem also applies to when market is less than cost and that does not stop us from writing it down. The primary reason is the conservatism principle.

The **conservatism principle** says when more than one estimate of amounts to be received or paid in the future are about equally likely, then the less optimistic amount should be used.[10] This principle guides accounting professionals in uncertain situations where amounts must be estimated. LCM is often justified with reference to **conservatism.** Because the value of inventory is uncertain, writing inventory down when its market value falls is the less optimistic estimate of the amount of inventory.

---

[10] *CICA Handbook,* section 1000, "Financial Statement Concepts," par. 21(d).

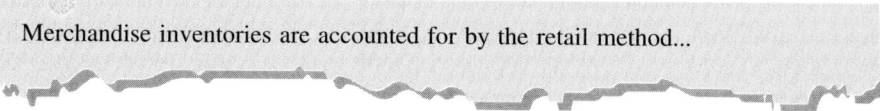

Flashback

8. A company's ending inventory includes the following items:

Product	Units on Hand	Unit Cost	Market Value per Unit
A	20	$6	$5
B	40	9	8
C	10	12	15

Using LCM applied separately to individual items, compute the reported amount for inventory.

Answer—p. 339

Retail Inventory Method

Many companies prepare financial statements on a quarterly or monthly basis. Monthly or quarterly statements are called **interim statements** because they are prepared between the traditional annual statements. The cost of goods sold information needed to prepare interim statements is readily available if a perpetual inventory system is used. But a periodic system requires a physical inventory to determine cost of goods sold. To avoid the time-consuming and expensive process of taking a physical inventory each month or quarter, some companies use the **retail inventory method** to estimate cost of goods sold and ending inventory. Some companies even use the retail inventory method to prepare the annual statements. **Mark's Work Warehouse,** for instance, reports in its 1997 annual report that:

LO7 Apply both the retail inventory and gross profit methods to estimate inventory.

> Merchandise inventories are accounted for by the retail method...

But all companies should take a physical inventory at least once each year to identify any errors or shortages.

Computing the Retail Inventory Estimate

When the retail inventory method is used to estimate inventory, we need to know the amount of inventory a company had at the beginning of the period in both *cost* and *retail* amounts. We already explained the cost of inventory. The retail amount of inventory refers to its dollar amount measured using selling prices of inventory items. We also need the net amount of goods purchased (minus returns, allowances and discounts) during the period, both at cost and at retail. The amount of net sales at retail is also needed.

A three-step process is used to estimate ending inventory after we compute the amount of goods available for sale during the period both at cost and at retail. This process is shown in Exhibit 7.17.

The reasoning behind the retail inventory method is if we can get a good estimate of the cost to retail ratio, then we can apply (multiply) this ratio to ending inventory at retail to estimate ending inventory at cost. We show in Exhibit 7.18 how these steps are applied to estimate ending inventory.

Exhibit 7.17

Inventory Estimation using Retail Inventory Method

Exhibit 7.18

Computing Ending Inventory
Using the Retail Inventory
Method

		At Cost	At Retail
Goods available for sale:			
Beginning inventory		$20,500	$ 34,500
Cost of goods purchased		39,500	65,500
Goods available for sale		$60,000	$100,000
Step 1:	Deduct net sales at retail		70,000
	Ending inventory at retail		$ 30,000
Step 2:	Cost to retail ratio: ($60,000 ÷ $100,000) = 60%		
Step 3:	Estimated ending inventory at cost ($30,000 × 60%)	$18,000	

Let's recap the steps in Exhibits 7.17 and 7.18 to make certain we understand them. First, there are $100,000 of goods (at retail selling prices) available for sale this period. Second, the cost of these goods is 60% of their $100,000 retail value. Third, we see that $70,000 of these goods are sold, leaving $30,000 (retail value) of unsold merchandise in ending inventory. Fourth, since cost for this store is 60% of retail, the estimated cost of ending inventory is $18,000.

Estimating Physical Inventory at Cost

Items for sale by retailers usually carry price tags listing selling prices. So when a retailer takes a physical inventory, it commonly totals inventory using selling prices of items on hand. It then reduces the dollar total of this inventory to a cost basis by applying the cost to retail ratio. This is done because selling prices are readily available and using the cost to retail ratio drops the need to look up invoice prices of items on hand.

Let's assume the company in Exhibit 7.18 estimates its inventory by the retail method and takes a physical inventory using selling prices. If the retail value of this physical inventory is $29,600, then we can compute the cost of this inventory by applying its cost to retail ratio as follows: **$29,600 × 60% = $17,760.** The $17,760 cost figure for ending physical inventory is an acceptable number for annual financial statements. It is also acceptable to Revenue Canada for tax reporting.

Estimating Inventory Shortage at Cost

The inventory estimate in Exhibit 7.18 is an estimate of the amount of goods on hand (at cost). Since it is computed by deducting sales from goods available for sale (at retail), it does not reveal any shrinkage due to breakage, loss, or theft. But we can estimate the amount of shrinkage by comparing the inventory computed in Exhibit 7.18 with the amount from taking a physical inventory. In Exhibit 7.18, for example, we estimated ending inventory at retail as $30,000. But a physical inventory revealed only $29,600 of inventory on hand (at retail). The company has an inventory shortage (at retail) of $400, computed as $30,000 − $29,600. The inventory shortage (at cost) is $240, computed as $400 × 60%.

Gross Profit Method

The **gross profit method** estimates the cost of ending inventory by applying the gross profit ratio to net sales (at retail). A need for this type of estimate can arise when inventory is destroyed, lost, or stolen. These cases need an estimate of inventory so a company can file a claim with its insurer. Users also apply this method to see if inventory amounts from either management or a physical count are reasonable. The gross profit method is useful in these cases. This method uses the historical relation between cost of goods sold and net sales to estimate the proportion of cost of goods sold making up current sales. This cost of goods sold estimate is then subtracted from cost of goods available for sale to give us an estimate of ending inventory at cost. These two steps are shown in Exhibit 7.19.

Sales	$31,500
Sales returns	1,500
Inventory, January 1, 1999	12,000
Net cost of goods purchased	20,500

Exhibit 7.19

Inventory Estimation Using Gross Profit Method

We need certain accounting data to use the gross profit method. This includes the gross profit ratio, beginning inventory (at cost), the net cost of goods purchased, and net sales (at retail). To illustrate, assume a company's inventory is destroyed by fire in March of 1999. This company's normal gross profit ratio is 30% of net sales. When the fire occurs, the company's accounts showed the balances as per Exhibit 7.19.

We can use the gross profit method to estimate this company's inventory loss. We first need to recognize that whatever portion of each dollar of net sales is gross profit, the remaining portion is cost of goods sold. If this company's gross profit ratio is 30%, then 30% of each net sales dollar is gross profit and 70% is cost of goods sold. We show in Exhibit 7.20 how this 70% is used to estimate lost inventory.

Goods available for sale:		
Inventory, January 1, 1999		$12,000
Net cost of goods purchased		$20,500
Goods available for sale		$32,500
Less estimated cost of goods sold:		
Sales	$31,500	
Less sales returns	(1,500)	
Net sales	$30,000	
Estimated cost of goods sold (70% × $30,000)		(21,000)
Estimated March inventory loss		$11,500

Exhibit 7.20

Computing Inventory Using the Gross Profit Method

To help understand Exhibit 7.20 think of subtracting ending inventory from goods available for sale to get the cost of goods sold. In Exhibit 7.20 we estimate ending inventory by subtracting cost of goods sold from the goods available for sale.

Merchandise Turnover and Days' Sales in Inventory

USING THE INFORMATION

This section describes how we use information about inventory to assess a company's short-term liquidity (ability to pay) and its management of inventory. Two measures useful for these assessments are defined and explained.

LO 8 Assess inventory management using both merchandise turnover and days' sales in inventory.

Merchandise Turnover

We described in prior chapters two important ratios useful in evaluating a company's short-term liquidity: current ratio and acid-test ratio. A company's ability to pay its short-term obligations also depends on how quickly it sells its merchandise inventory. **Merchandise turnover,** also called *inventory turnover,* is one ratio used to evaluate this and is computed as shown in Exhibit 7.21.

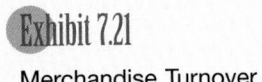

Exhibit 7.21

Merchandise Turnover

$$\text{Merchandise turnover} = \frac{\text{Cost of goods sold}}{\text{Average merchandise inventory}}$$

This ratio tells us how many *times* a company turns over its inventory during a period. Average merchandise inventory is usually computed by adding beginning and ending inventory amounts and dividing the total by two. If a company's sales vary within the year, it is often better to take an average of inventory amounts at the end of each quarter or month.

Users apply merchandise turnover to help analyze short-term liquidity. It is also used to assess whether management is doing a good job controlling the amount of inventory on hand. A ratio that is low compared to competitors suggests inefficient use of assets. The company may be holding more merchandise than is needed to support its sales volume. Similarly, a ratio that is high compared to those of competitors suggests the amount of inventory is too low. This can mean lost sales because customers must back-order merchandise. There is no simple rule with merchandise turnover except to say a high ratio is preferable provided inventory is adequate to meet demand.

We know how an inventory costing method such as weighted-average, FIFO, or LIFO affects reported amounts of inventory and cost of goods sold. But an inventory costing method also affects computation of merchandise turnover. To compare merchandise turnover ratios across companies that use different costing methods can be misleading.

Did You Know?

Eliminating Inventory Costs

Holding inventory costs money and reducing this aspect of supply-chain cost has led to the development of technologies and expertise in materials requirements planning and inventory management. The aim of inventory management is to balance the materials requirements of the buyer's company against the cost of acquiring the materials and possessing them. Where applied properly, there is no doubt that just-in-time delivery can provide big cost savings. Some companies figure that for every dollar saved on labour costs, they can also save 60 cents as a result of quality improvement, and at least another dollar on the remainder of JIT implementation. [Source: *Modern Purchasing*, March 1997.]

Days' Sales in Inventory

To better interpret merchandise turnover, many users look to measure the adequacy of inventory in meeting sales demand. **Days' sales in inventory,** also called *days' stock on hand,* is a ratio that tells us how much inventory we have on hand in terms of day's sales. It can also be interpreted as the number of days we can sell from inventory if no new items are purchased. This ratio is often viewed as a measure of the buffer against out of stock inventory and is useful in evaluating liquidity of inventory. Days' sales in inventory is computed as shown in Exhibit 7.22.

Exhibit 7.22

Days' Sales in Inventory

$$\text{Days' sales in inventory} = \frac{\text{Ending inventory}}{\text{Cost of goods sold} \times 365}$$

The focus of days' sales in inventory is on ending inventory. Days' sales in inventory estimates how many days it will take to convert inventory on hand at the end of the period into accounts receivable or cash. Notice the different focus of days' sales in inventory and merchandise turnover. Days' sales in inventory focuses on ending inventory whereas merchandise turnover focuses on *average* inventory.

Analysis of Inventory Management

Inventory management is a major emphasis of most merchandisers. Merchandisers must both plan and control inventory purchases and sales. **Toys "Я" Us** is one of those merchandisers. Its merchandise inventory at February 1, 1997, exceeded $2.2 billion. Toys "Я" Us' inventory comprised 70% of it current assets and nearly 30% of its total assets. We apply the analysis tools in this section to Toys "Я" Us using its February 1, 1997, financial statements. The relevant data and analysis are shown in Exhibit 7.23.

| | Year Ended | | |
	Feb. 1, 1997	Feb. 3, 1996	Jan. 28, 1995
Cost of goods sold	$6,892.5	$6,592.3	$6,008.0
Ending merchandise inventory . . .	2,214.6	1,999.5	1,999.1
Merchandise turnover	3.27 times	3.30 times	3.18 times
Industry Merchandise turnover . . .	3.9 times	3.9 times	3.8 times
Days' sales in inventory	117.3 days	110.7 days	121.5 days
Industry days' sales in inventory . .	93.9 days	101.4 days	95.6 days

Exhibit 7.23

Merchandise Turnover and Days' Sales in Inventory for Toys "Я" Us

The 1997 merchandise turnover of 3.27 for Toys "Я" Us is computed as: $6,892.5 ÷ ([$2,214.6 + $1,999.5] ÷ 2). This means Toys "Я" Us turns over its inventory about 3.27 times per year, or about once every 112 days (365 days ÷ 3.27). We like merchandise turnover to be high provided inventory is not out of stock and the company is not turning away customers. The 1997 days' sales in inventory of 117.3 for Toys "Я" Us helps us assess this likelihood and is computed as: ($2,214.6 ÷ $6,892.5) × 365. This tells us Toys "Я" Us is carrying about 117 days of sales in its inventory. This inventory buffer seems more than adequate. Toys "Я" Us might benefit from management efforts to increase merchandise turnover. Comparisons to 1996 for Toys "Я" Us are unfavourable as revealed by a decrease in merchandise turnover and an increase in days' sales in inventory.

Consultant

You are hired as a consultant to analyze inventory management for a retail store. Your preliminary analysis yields a merchandise turnover ratio of 5.0 and a days' sales in inventory measure of 73 days. The industry norm for merchandise turnover is about 4.4 and for days' sales in inventory it is about 74 days. Using this information, where do you direct your attention?

You Make the Call

Answer—p. 339

9. The following data pertains to a company's inventory during 1999:

	Cost	Retail
Beginning inventory	$324,000	$530,000
Cost of goods purchased	195,000	335,000
Net Sales		320,000

Using the retail method, estimate the cost of ending inventory.

10. Explain how merchandise turnover and days' sales in inventory are both useful in analyzing inventory.

Answers—p. 339

Summary

LO 1 Compute inventory in a perpetual system using the methods of specific identification, weighted-average, FIFO, and LIFO. Costs are assigned to the cost of goods sold account *each time* that a sale occurs in a perpetual system. Specific identification assigns a cost to each item sold by referring to its actual cost (for example, its net invoice cost). Weighted average assigns a cost to items sold by taking the current balance in the merchandise inventory account and dividing it by the total items available for sale to determine the weighted-average cost per unit. We then multiply the number of units sold by this cost per unit to get the cost of each sale. FIFO assigns cost to items sold assuming earliest units purchased are the first units sold. LIFO assigns cost to items sold assuming the most recent units purchased are the first units sold.

LO 2 Identify the items making up merchandise inventory. Merchandise inventory comprises goods owned by a company and held for resale. Three special cases merit our attention. Goods in transit are reported in inventory of the company that holds ownership rights. Goods out on consignment are reported in inventory of the consignor. Goods damaged or obsolete are reported in inventory at a conservative estimate of their net realizable value, computed as sales price minus the cost of making the sale.

LO 3 Identify the costs of merchandise inventory. Costs of merchandise inventory comprise expenditures necessary, directly or indirectly, in bringing an item to a salable condition and location. This means the cost of an inventory item includes its invoice price minus any discount, plus any added or incidental costs necessary to put it in a place and condition for sale.

LO 4 Analyze the effects of inventory methods for financial reporting. When purchase prices don't change, the choice of an inventory method is unimportant.

But when purchase prices are rising or falling, the methods are likely to assign different cost amounts. Specific identification exactly matches costs and revenues. Weighted average smoothes out price changes. FIFO assigns an amount to inventory closely approximating current replacement cost. LIFO assigns the most recent costs incurred to cost of goods sold, and likely better matches current costs with revenues.

LO 5 Analyze the effects of inventory errors on current and future financial statements. An error in the amount of ending inventory affects assets (inventory), net income (cost of goods sold), and owner's equity of that period. Since ending inventory is next period's beginning inventory, an error in ending inventory affects next period's cost of goods sold and net income. The financial statement effects of errors in one period are offset (reverse) in the next.

LO 6 Compute the lower of cost or market amount of inventory. Inventory is reported at market value when market is *lower* than cost. This is called the lower of cost or market amount of inventory. Market may be measured as net realizable value or replacement cost. Lower of cost or market can be applied separately to each item, to major categories of items, or to the whole of inventory.

LO 7 Apply both the retail inventory and gross profit methods to estimate inventory. The retail inventory method involves three computations: (1) goods available at retail minus net sales at retail gives ending inventory at retail, (2) goods available at cost divided by goods available at retail gives the cost to retail ratio, and (3) ending inventory at retail is multiplied by the cost to retail ratio to give estimated ending inventory at cost. The gross profit method involves two computations: (1) net sales at retail multiplied by the gross profit ratio gives estimated cost of goods sold, and (2) goods available at cost minus estimated cost of goods sold gives estimated ending inventory at cost.

LO 8 **Assess inventory management using both merchandise turnover and days' sales in inventory.** We prefer a high merchandise turnover provided inventory is not out of stock and customers are not being turned away. We use days' sales in inventory to assess the likelihood of inventory being out of stock. We prefer a small number of days' sales in inventory provided we can serve customer needs and provide a buffer for uncertainties. Together, each of these ratios helps us assess inventory management and evaluate a company's short-term liquidity.

Guidance Answers to **You Make the Call**

Financial Planner

The FIFO method means the oldest costs are the first ones recorded in cost of goods sold. This leaves the most recent costs in ending inventory. You report this to your client and note that in most cases the ending inventory of a company using FIFO is reported at or near its replacement cost. This means your client need not in most cases adjust inventory. If there are major increases in replacement cost compared to the cost of recent purchases reported in inventory, a better matching of costs to revenues may be achieved by using LIFO. However, this would reduce the balance sheet value of the inventory. (*Note:* Decreases in costs of purchases are recognized under the lower of cost or market adjustment.)

Consultant

Your client's merchandise turnover is markedly higher than the norm, whereas its days' sales in inventory is approximately at the norm. Since your client's turnover is already 14% better than average, you are probably best served by directing attention at days' sales in inventory. You should see if your client can reduce the level of inventory while maintaining its service to customers. Casual analysis suggests your client can reduce its level of inventory. This is suggested by recognizing the average company maintains the same level of days' sales in inventory with a much lower turnover. Given your client's higher turnover, it should be able to hold less inventory.

Guidance Answer to **Judgment and Ethics**

Inventory Manager

Your recommendation is a difficult one. Increased profits may attract investors but they will also increase your bonus. The question becomes one of motivation. That is, would the change really be better for the investors or, would the change take place only because your bonus would increase? This presents the classic conflict of interests. Another problem is that profits can be manipulated by changing accounting methods, and if this is the motivation the profession would frown on the change.

Guidance Answers to Flash backs

1. The matching principle.
2. The Bay.
3. Total cost is $12,180, computed as: $11,400 + $130 + $150 + $100 + $400.
4. Specific identification exactly matches costs and revenues. Weighted average tends to smooth out price changes. FIFO assigns an amount to inventory that closely approximates current replacement cost. LIFO assigns the most recent costs incurred to cost of goods sold, and likely better matches current costs with revenues.
5. FIFO. FIFO gives a lower cost of goods sold and a higher gross profit and higher net income.
6. Weighted average gives a lower inventory figure on the balance sheet as compared to FIFO. FIFO's inventory amount will approximate current replacement costs. Weighted-average costs increase but more slowly because of the effect of averaging.

7. Cost of goods sold is understated by $10,000 in 1999 and overstated by $10,000 in year 2000.
8. The reported inventory amount is $540, computed as (20 × $5) + (40 × $8) + (10 × $12).
9. The estimated ending inventory (at cost) is $327,000 and is computed as:
   Step 1: ($530,000 + $335,000) − $320,000 = $545,000
   Step 2: $\dfrac{\$324,000 + \$195,000}{\$530,000 + \$335,000} = 60\%$

   Step 3: $545,000 × 60% = $327,000
10. We like merchandise turnover to be high provided inventory is not out of stock and customers are not being turned away. We use days' sales in inventory to assess the likelihood of inventory being out of stock. We want days' sales in inventory to be as low as possible but adequate to serve customer needs and provide a buffer for uncertainties. Each of these ratios together allow us to assess these effects.

Demonstration Problem

Tale Company uses a perpetual inventory system and had the following beginning inventory and purchases during 19X1:

Date		Units	Unit Cost
		Item X	
Jan. 1	Inventory	400	$14
Mar. 10	Purchase	200	15
May 9	Purchase	300	16
Sept. 22	Purchase	250	20
Nov. 28	Purchase	100	21

At December 31, 19X1, there were 550 units of X on hand. Sales of units were as follows:

Jan. 15	200 units at $30
April 1	200 units at $30
Nov. 1	300 units at $35

Additional data for use in applying the specific identification method:

The specific units in inventory are from the May 9 and Sept. 22 purchases. The 400 units on hand on Jan. 1 are sold. The 200 units acquired on Mar. 10 are sold. The 100 units acquired on Nov. 28 are sold.

Required

1. Calculate the cost of goods available for sale.
2. Using the preceding information, apply the four different methods of inventory costing (FIFO, LIFO, weighted average, and specific identification) to calculate the ending inventory and the cost of goods sold under each different method.
3. In preparing the financial statements for 19X1, the bookkeeper was instructed to use FIFO but failed to do so and computed the cost of goods sold according to LIFO. Determine the size of the misstatement of 19X1's income from this error. Also determine the effect of the error on the 19X2 income. Assume no income taxes.
4. The management of the company would like a report showing how net income would change if the company changes from FIFO to another method. Prepare a schedule showing the costs of goods sold amount under each method. Calculate the amount by which each cost of goods sold total is different from the FIFO cost of goods to inform management how net income would change if another method were used.

Planning the Solution

- Make a schedule showing the calculation of the cost of goods available for sale. Multiply the units of beginning inventory and each purchase by the appropriate unit costs to determine the total cost of goods available for sale.
- Prepare a perpetual FIFO schedule showing the composition of beginning inventory and how the composition of inventory changes after each purchase of inventory and after each sale.
- Prepare a perpetual LIFO schedule showing the composition of beginning inventory and how the composition of inventory changes after each purchase of inventory and after each sale.
- Make a schedule of purchases and sales recalculating the average cost of inventory after each purchase to arrive at the weighted-average cost of ending inventory. Add up the average costs associated with each sale to determine the cost of goods sold using the weighted-average method.
- Prepare a schedule showing the computation of the cost of goods sold and ending inventory using the specific identification method. Use the information provided to determine which specific units were sold and which specific units remain in inventory.

- Compare the ending 19X1 inventory amounts under FIFO and LIFO to determine the misstatement of 19X1 income that resulted from using LIFO. The 19X2 and 19X1 errors are equal in amount but have opposite effects.
- Create a schedule showing the cost of goods sold under each method and how net income would differ from FIFO net income if an alternate method were to be adopted.

Solution to Demonstration Problem

1. Cost of goods available for sale:

Item X				
Date		Units	Unit Cost	Total Cost
Jan. 1	Inventory	400	$14	$ 5,600
Mar. 10	Purchase	200	15	3,000
May 9	Purchase	300	16	4,800
Sept. 22	Purchase	250	20	5,000
Nov. 28	Purchase	100	21	2,100
Total cost of goods available for sale				$20,500

2a. FIFO perpetual basis:

Date	Purchases	Sales (at cost)	Inventory Balance
Jan. 1			400 @ $14 = $5,600
Jan. 15		200 @ $14 = $2,800	200 @ $14 = $2,800 (400-200 sold)
Mar. 10	200 @ $15 = $3,000		200 @ $14 } 200 @ $15 } = $5,800
April 1		200 @ $14 = $2,800	200 @ $15 = $3,000 (400-200 sold)
May 9	300 @ $16 = $4,800		200 @ $15 } 300 @ $16 } = $7,800
Sept.22	250 @ $20 = $5,000		200 @ $15 } 300 @ $16 } = $12,800 250 @ $20 }
Nov. 1		200 @ $15 = $3,000 100 @ $16 = $1,600	200 @ $16 } 250 @ $20 } = $8,200 (750-300 sold)
Nov. 28	100 @ $21 = $2,100		200 @ $16 } 250 @ $20 } = $10,300 100 @ $21 }
Total cost of goods sold		$10,200	

Note to students: **In a classroom situation** once cost of goods available for sale is known we can compute the amount for either cost of goods sold or ending inventory; it is a matter of preference. **But in practice,** *the cost of items sold are identified as sales are made and immediately transferred from the inventory account to the cost of goods sold account. This transfer then makes it unnecessary to calculate either account balance at the end of a period. The first solution showing the line-by-line approach to the solution better illustrates actual application whereas the alternate solutions shown here illustrate that once the concepts are understood other solution approaches are available.* Some students feel that the alternate solutions are less time-consuming to prepare than the line-by-line method illustrated above.

Alternate FIFO Solution Presentation (cost of goods sold is calculated first)

Jan. 1 inventory (400 @ $14)		$ 5,600
Purchases:		
Mar. 10 purchase (200 @ $15)	$3,000	
May 9 purchase (300 @ $16)	4,800	
Sept. 22 purchase 250 @ $20)	5,000	
Nov. 28 purchase (100 @ $21)	2,100	14,900
Cost of goods available for sale		$20,500
Cost of goods sold:		
Jan. 15 sold (200 @ $14)	$2,800	
Apr. 1 sold (200 @ $14)	2,800	
Nov. 1 sold (200 @ $15)		
(100 @ $16)	4,600	10,200
Ending inventory		$10,300
Proof of ending inventory FIFO perpetual:		
Ending inventory at FIFO cost:		
Nov. 28 purchase (100 @ $21)	$2,100	
Sept. 22 purchase (250 @ $20)	5,000	
May 9 purchase 200 @ $16)	3,200	
FIFO cost of ending inventory		$10,300

The following schedule illustrates for the FIFO method how one can just as easily solve for ending inventory first once cost of goods sold is known.

FIFO perpetual method with Ending Inventory calculated first.

Jan. 1 inventory (400 @ $14)	$5,600	
Purchases:		
Mar. 10 purchase (200 @ $15)	$3,000	
May 9 purchase (300 @ $16)	4,800	
Sept. 22 purchase (250 @ $20)	5,000	
Nov. 28 purchase (100 @ $21)	2,100	14,900
Cost of goods available for sale		$20,500
Ending inventory at FIFO cost:		
(see note below)		
Nov. 28 purchase (100 @ $21)	$2,100	
Sept. 22 purchase (250 @ $20)	5,000	
May 9 purchase (200 @ $16)	3,200	
FIFO cost of ending inventory		$10,300
FIFO cost of goods sold		$10,200
Proof of cost of goods sold FIFO perpetual:		
Cost of goods sold:		
Jan. 15 sold (200 @ $14)	$ 2,800	
April 1 sold (200 @ $14)	2,800	
Nov. 1 sold (200 @ $15)		
(100 @ $16)	4,600	$10,200

Note: Since FIFO assumes earlier costs relate to items sold when determining ending inventory we must assign the most recent costs first.

2b. LIFO perpetual method:

Date	Purchases	Sales (at cost)	Inventory Balance
Jan. 1			400 @ $14 = $5,600
Jan. 15		200 @ $14 = $2,800	200 @ $14 = $2,800 (400-200 sold)
Mar. 10	200 @ $15 = $3,000		200 @ $14 200 @ $15 } = $5,800
April 1		200 @ $15 = $3,000 (last ones purchased are sold)	200 @ $14 = $2,800 (400-200 sold)
May 9	300 @ $16 = $4,800		200 @ $14 300 @ $16 } = $7,600
Sept.22	250 @ $20 = $5,000		200 @ $14 300 @ $16 } = $12,600 250 @ $20
Nov. 1		250 @ $20 = $5,000 50 @ $16 = $ 800	200 @ $14 250 @ $16 } = $6,800 (750-300 sold)
Nov. 28	100 @ $21 = $2,100		200 @ $14 250 @ $16 } = $8,900 100 @ $21
Total cost of goods sold		$11,600	

Alternate LIFO Solution Presentation

Cost of goods available for sale . . . . (from earlier calculation in 1 above)		$20,500
Cost of goods sold with LIFO perpetual		
Jan. 15 200 units @ $14	$2,800	
April 1 200 units @ $15	$3,000	
Nov. 1 250 units @ $20	$5,000	
50 units @ $16	$800	
Total cost of goods sold		11,600
Ending inventory at LIFO cost:		$8,900
Proof of ending inventory LIFO perpetual:		
Jan. 1 inventory (200 @ $14)	$2,800	
May 9 purchase (250 @ $16)	4,000	
Nov. 28 purchase (100 @ $21)	2,100	
LIFO cost of ending inventory		$8,900

2c. Weighted average cost method:

Date	Purchase	Sales at Average Cost	Inventory Balance
Jan. 1			400 @ $14 = $5,600
Jan. 15		200 @ $14 = $2,800	200 @ $14 = $2,800
March 10	200 @ $15 = $3,000		200 @ $14 200 @ $15 = $5,800 (avg. cost is $14.50)
April 1		200 @ $14.50 = $2,900	200 @ $14.50 = $2,900
May 9	300 @ $16 = $4,800		200 @ $14.50 300 @ $16 = $7,700 (avg. cost is $15.40)
Sept. 22	250 @ $20 = $5,000		200 @ $14.50 300 @ $16 250 @ $20 = $12,700 (avg. cost is $16.93)
Nov. 1		300 @ $16.93 = $5,079	450 @ $16.93 = $7,618.50
Nov. 28	100 @ $21 = $2,100		450 @ $16.93 100 @ $21 = $9,718.50
Cost of Goods Sold		$10,779	

Note: The cost of goods sold ($10,779) plus ending inventory ($9,718.50) is slightly less than the cost of goods available for sale ($20,500) due to rounding error.

2d. Specific identification method:

Cost of goods available for sale		$20,500
(from earlier calculation in 1 above)		
Cost of goods sold:		
Jan. 1 purchase (400 @ $14)	$5,600	
Mar. 10 purchase (200 @ $15)	3,000	
Nov. 28 purchase (100 @ $21)	2,100	
Total cost of goods sold		10,700
Ending inventory		9,800
Proof of ending inventory under specific identification:		
May 9 purchase (300 @ $16)	$4,800	
Sept. 22 purchase (250 @ $20)	5,000	
Total ending inventory under specific identification		$ 9,800

3. If LIFO was mistakenly used when FIFO should have been used, cost of goods sold in 19X1 would be overstated by $1,400, which is the difference between the FIFO and LIFO amounts of ending inventory. Income would be understated in 19X1 by $1,400. In 19X2, income would be overstated by $1,400 because of the understatement of the beginning inventory.

4. Analysis of the effects of alternative inventory methods:

	Cost of Goods Sold	Difference from FIFO Cost of Goods Sold	Effect on Net Income if adopted instead of FIFO
FIFO	$10,200	—	—
LIFO	$11,600	+ $1,400	Net income would be $1,400 lower
Weighted Average	$10,779	+ $ 579	Net income would be $579 lower
Specific Identification	$10,700	+ $ 500	Net income would be $500 lower

Assigning Costs to Inventory— Periodic System

Learning Objectives

LO 9 Compute inventory in a periodic system using the methods of specific identification, weighted average, FIFO, and LIFO.

The aim of the periodic system is the same as the perpetual system: to assign costs to the inventory and the goods sold. The same four methods are used in assigning costs: specific identification; weighted average; first-in, first-out; and last-in, first-out. We use information from **Trekking** to describe how we assign costs using these four methods with a periodic system. Data for sales and purchases are reported in the chapter and are not repeated here.

We explained the accounting under a periodic system in Appendix 6A. The important accounting aspects of a periodic system are:

■ Each purchase of merchandise for resale increases (debit) the purchases account.

■ Costs of merchandise sold is not recorded at the time of each sale. A physical count of inventory at the end of the period is used to compute cost of goods sold and inventory amounts.

■ Necessary costs of merchandise such as transportation-in, and cost reductions such as purchase discounts and purchase returns and allowances, are recorded in separate accounts.

Specific Identification

The amount of costs assigned to inventory and cost of goods sold is the same under the perpetual and periodic systems. This is because specific identification precisely define what units are in inventory and which are sold.

Weighted Average

The weighted-average method of assigning cost involves three important steps. (See Exhibits 7A.1 and 7A.2.) First, we multiply the per unit cost for beginning inventory and each particular purchase by their corresponding number of units. Second, we add these amounts and divide by the total number of units available for sale to find the *weighted-average cost per unit:*

Exhibit 7A.1

Weighted-Average Cost per Unit

Step 1:	10 units @ $ 91 =	$ 910	
	15 units @ $106 =	1,590	
	20 units @ $115 =	2,300	
	10 units @ $119 =	1,190	
	55	$5,990	
Step 2:	$5,990/55 = **$108.91** weighted-average cost per unit		

The third step is to use the weighted-average cost per unit to assign costs to inventory and to units sold:

Total cost of 55 units available for sale	$5,990
Less **ending inventory** priced on a weighted-average cost basis:	
12 units at $108.91 each	1,307
Cost of goods sold	$4,683

Exhibit 7A.2

Weighted-Average
Computations—Periodic

First-In, First-Out

The first-in, first-out (FIFO) method of assigning cost to inventory and goods sold using the periodic system is shown in Exhibit 7A.3.

Total cost of 55 units available for sale		$5,990
Less ending inventory priced using FIFO:		
10 units from August 28 purchase at $119 each	$1,190	
2 units from August 17 purchase at $115 each	230	
12 units in ending inventory		1,420
Cost of goods sold		$4,570

Exhibit 7A.3

FIFO Computations—
Periodic System

Trekking's ending inventory reported on the balance sheet is **$1,420** and its cost of goods sold reported on the income statement is **$4,570** [$910 + $1590 + (18@115)]. Notice these amounts are the same as computed using the perpetual system. This will always occur because the most recent purchases are in ending inventory under both systems.

Last-In, First-Out

The last-in, first-out (LIFO) method of assigning costs to the 12 remaining units in inventory and to cost of goods sold using the periodic system is shown in Exhibit 7A.4.

Total cost of 55 units available for sale		$5,990
Less ending inventory priced using LIFO:		
10 units in beginning inventory at $ 91 each	$910	
2 units from August 3 purchase at $106 each	212	
12 units in ending inventory		1,122
Cost of goods sold		$4,868

Exhibit 7A.4

LIFO Computations—
Periodic System

Trekking's ending inventory reported on the balance sheet is **$1,122** and its cost of goods sold reported on the income statement is **$4,868.** Notice when LIFO is used with the periodic system, cost of goods sold is assigned costs from the most recent purchases for the period. With a perpetual system, cost of goods sold is assigned costs from the most recent purchases *prior to each sale.*

Flash back

11. A company reports the following beginning inventory and purchases (and ends the period with 30 units on hand):

Units		Unit	Cost
Beginning Inventory	100	$10
Purchases #1	40	12
#2	20	14

a. Compute ending inventory using FIFO.

b. Compute cost of goods sold using LIFO.

Answer—p. 348

Summary of Appendix 7A

LO 9 **Compute inventory in a periodic system using the methods of specific identification, weighted average, FIFO, and LIFO.** Periodic systems allocate the cost of goods available for sale between cost of goods sold and ending inventory *at the end of a period.* Specific identification and FIFO give identical results whether the periodic or perpetual system is used. LIFO assigns cost to cost of goods sold assuming the last units purchased for the period are the first units sold. Weighted-average cost computes cost per unit by taking the total cost of both beginning inventory and net purchases and dividing by the total number of units available. It then multiplies cost per unit by the number of units sold to give cost of goods sold.

Guidance Answer to Flash back

11. a. Ending inventory = (20 × $14) + (10 × $12) = $400

b. Cost of goods sold = (20 × $14) + (40 × $12) + (70 × $10) = $1,460

Glossary

Average cost method Another name for *weighted average inventory pricing.* (p. 320)

Conservatism A shortened reference to the *conservatism principle.* (p. 332)

Conservatism principle The accounting principle that guides accountants to select the less optimistic estimate when two estimates of amounts to be received or paid are about equally likely. (p. 332)

Consignee One who receives and holds goods owned by another party for the purpose of selling the goods for the owner. (p. 324)

Consignor An owner of goods who ships them to another party who will then sell the goods for the owner. (p. 324)

Consistency principle The accounting requirement that a company use the same accounting methods period after period so that the financial statements of succeeding periods will be comparable. (p. 328)

Days' sales in inventory An estimate of how many days it will take to convert the inventory on hand at the end of the period into accounts receivable or cash; calculated by dividing the ending inventory by cost of goods sold and multiplying the result by 365; also called days' stock on hand. (p. 336)

First-in, first-out inventory pricing (FIFO) The pricing of an inventory under the assumption that inventory items are sold in the order acquired; the first items received were the first items sold. (p. 321)

Gross profit method A procedure for estimating an ending inventory in which the past gross profit rate is used to estimate cost of goods sold, which is then subtracted from the cost of goods available for sale to determine the estimated ending inventory. (p. 334)

Interim statements Monthly or quarterly financial statements prepared in between the traditional, annual statements. (p. 333)

Last-in, first-out inventory pricing (LIFO) The pricing of an inventory under the assumption that the most recent items purchased are sold first and their costs are charged to cost of goods sold. (p. 321)

Lower of cost or market (LCM) The required method of reporting merchandise inventory in the balance sheet where market value is reported when market is lower than cost; the market value may be defined as net realizable value or current replacement cost on the date of the balance sheet. (p. 331)

Merchandise turnover The number of times a company's average inventory was sold during an accounting period, calculated by dividing cost of goods sold by the average merchandise inventory balance; also called *inventory turnover.* (p. 335)

Net realizable value The expected sales price of an item minus the cost of making the sale. (p. 324)

Retail inventory method A method for estimating an ending inventory cost based on the ratio of the amount of goods for sale at cost to the amount of goods for sale at marked selling prices. (p. 333)

Specific identification method Another name for specific invoice inventory pricing. (p. 320)

Specific invoice inventory pricing The pricing of an inventory where the purchase invoice of each item in the ending inventory is identified and used to determine the cost assigned to the inventory. (p. 320)

Weighted-average inventory pricing An inventory pricing system in which the unit prices of the beginning inventory and of each purchase are weighted by the number of units in the beginning inventory and each purchase. The total of these amounts is then divided by the total number of units available for sale to find the unit cost of the ending inventory and of the units that were sold. (p. 320)

A superscript letter ^{A} *identifies assignment material based on Appendix 7A.*

Questions

1. What accounts are used in a periodic inventory system but not in a perpetual inventory system?
2. What is meant when it is said that inventory errors correct themselves?
3. If inventory errors correct themselves, why be concerned when such errors are made?
4. Where is merchandise inventory disclosed in the financial statements?
5. Why are incidental costs often ignored in pricing an inventory? Under what accounting principle is this permitted?
6. Give the meanings of the following when applied to inventory: (a) FIFO, (b) LIFO, and (c) cost.
7. If prices are falling, will the LIFO or the FIFO method of inventory valuation result in the lower cost of goods sold?
8. May a company change its inventory pricing method each accounting period?
9. Does the accounting principle of consistency preclude any changes from one accounting method to another?

10. What effect does the full-disclosure principle have if a company changes from one acceptable accounting method to another?
11. What guidance for accountants is provided by the principle of conservatism?
12. What is the usual meaning of the word *market* as it is used in determining the lower of cost or market for merchandise inventory?
13. Refer to **Alliance's** financial statements in Appendix I. On March 31, what percentage of Alliance's assets was represented by what would be Alliance's inventory?
14. Refer to **Atlantis'** financial statements in Appendix I. Is it possible to determine a cost of sales figure for Atlantis?
15. Refer to the **Wired** scenario at the beginning of the chapter. What does Russo need to know about Wired to be able to calculate gross margin and inventory turnover?

---

1. At year-end Carefree Company has shipped, FOB destination, $500 of merchandise which is still in transit to Stark Company. Which company should include the $500 as part of inventory at year-end?
2. Carefree Company has shipped goods to Stark and has an arrangement that Stark will sell the goods for Carefree. Identify the consignor and the consignee. Which company should include any unsold goods as part of inventory?

Quick Study

QS 7-1
Inventory ownership

LO 2

A car dealer acquires a used car for $3,000. Additional costs in obtaining and offering the car for sale include $150 for transportation-in, $200 for import duties, $50 for insurance during shipment, $25 for advertising, and $250 for sales staff salaries. For computing inventory, what cost is assigned to the used car acquired?

QS 7-2
Inventory costs

LO 3

QS 7-3

Calculating cost of goods available for sale

LO 1

A company has beginning inventory of 10 units at $50. Every week for four weeks an additional 10 units are purchased at respective costs of $51, $52, $55, and $60. Calculate the cost of goods available for sale and the units available for sale.

QS 7-4

Inventory ownership

LO 2

Crafts and More, a distributor of handmade gifts, operates out of owner Scott Arlen's home. At the end of the accounting period, Arlen tells us he has 1,500 units of products in his basement, 30 of which were damaged by water leaks and cannot be sold. He also has another 250 units in his van, ready to deliver to fill a customer order, terms FOB destination, and another 70 units out on consignment to a friend who owns a stationery store. How many units should be included in the end-of-period inventory?

QS 7-5

Inventory costs

LO 3

Rigby & Son, antique dealers, purchased the contents of an estate for a bulk bid price of $37,500. The terms of the purchase were FOB shipping point, and the cost of transporting the goods to Rigby & Son's warehouse was $1,200. Rigby & Son insured the shipment at a cost of $150. Prior to placing the goods in the store, they cleaned and refurbished some merchandise at a cost of $490 for labour and parts. Determine the cost of the inventory acquired in the purchase of the estate's contents.

QS 7-6

Inventory costing methods

LO 1

A company had the following beginning inventory and purchases during January for a particular item. On January 28, 345 units were sold. What is the cost of the 140 units that remain in the ending inventory, assuming (a) FIFO, (b) LIFO, and (c) weighted average? Assume the sale of 205 units was made on January 26. (Round numbers to the nearest cent.)

	Units	Unit Cost
Beginning inventory on January 1	310	$3.00
Purchase on January 9	75	3.20
Purchase on January 25	100	3.35

QS 7-7

Contrasting inventory costing methods

LO 4

Identify the inventory costing method most closely related to each of the following statements, assuming a period of rising costs:

a. Matches recent costs against revenue.

b. Understates current value of inventory on a balance sheet.

c. Results in a balance sheet inventory closest to replacement costs.

d. Is best when each unit of product has unique features that affect cost.

QS 7-8A

Inventory errors

LO 5

The Weston Company maintains its inventory records on a periodic basis. In taking a physical inventory at the end of 19X1, certain units were counted twice. Explain how this error affects the following: (a) 19X1 cost of goods sold, (b) 19X1 gross profit, (c) 19X1 net income, (d) 19X2 net income, (e) the combined two-year income, and (f) income in years after 19X2.

QS 7-9

Applying LCM to inventories

LO 6

Thrifty Trading Co. has the following products in its ending inventory:

Product	Quantity	Cost	Market
Aprons	9	$6.00	$5.50
Bottles	12	3.50	4.25
Candles	25	8.00	7.00

Calculate lower of cost or market (a) for the inventory as a whole and (b) applied separately to each product.

The inventory of Bell Department Store was destroyed by a fire on September 10, 19X1. The following 19X1 data were found in the accounting records:

Jan. 1 inventory	$180,000
Jan. 1 – Sept. 10 purchases (net) . . .	$342,000
Jan. 1 – Sept. 10 sales	$675,000
19X1 estimated gross profit rate	42%

Determine the cost of the inventory destroyed in the fire.

QS 7-10
Estimating inventories
LO 7

Parfour, Inc., made purchases of a particular product in the current year as follows:

Jan. 1	Beginning inventory	100 units @ $10.00 =	$ 1,000
Mar. 14	Purchased	250 units @ $15.00 =	3,750
July 30	Purchased	400 units @ $20.00 =	8,000
Oct. 26	Purchased	600 units @ $25.00 =	15,000
	Units available	1,350 units	
	Cost of goods available for Sale . . .		$27,750

Parfour, Inc., made sales on the following dates at a selling price of $40 a unit:

Jan. 10	90 units
Mar. 15	140 units
Oct. 5	300 units
Total	530 units

Required

The business uses a perpetual inventory system. Determine the costs that should be assigned to the ending inventory and to goods sold under each of the following: (a) costs are assigned on the basis of FIFO, and (b) costs are assigned on the basis of weighted average. Also calculate the gross margin under each of the methods.

Exercises

Exercise 7-1
Alternative cost flow assumptions, perpetual inventory system—FIFO and weighted average
LO 1

Refer to the data in Exercise 7-1. Assume that ending inventory is comprised of the entire March 14 purchase and 570 units of the October 26 purchase. Using the specific identification method calculate the costs of good sold and the gross margin.

Exercise 7-2
Specific identification inventory method
LO 1

Trout, Inc., made purchases of a particular product in the current year (19x1) as follows:

Jan. 1	Beginning inventory	120 units @ $6.00 =	$ 720
Mar. 7	Purchased	250 units @ $5.60 =	1,400
July 28	Purchased	500 units @ $5.00 =	2,500
Oct. 3	Purchased	450 units @ $4.60 =	2,070
Dec. 19	Purchased	100 units @ $4.10 =	410
	Total	1,420 units	$7,100

Trout, Inc., made sales on the following dates at selling price of $15 a unit:

Jan. 10	70 units
Mar. 15	125 units
Oct. 5	600 units
Total	795 units

Exercise 7-3
Alternative cost flow assumptions, perpetual inventory system.
LO 1

Required

The business uses a perpetual inventory system, and the ending inventory consists of 625 units, 500 from the July 28 purchase and 125 from the Oct. 3 purchase. Determine the share of the $7,100 cost of the units for sale that should be assigned to the ending inventory and to goods sold under each of the following: (a) costs are assigned on the basis of specific invoice prices, (b) costs are assigned on a weighted-average cost basis, (c) costs are assigned on the basis of FIFO, and (d) costs are assigned on the basis of LIFO.

Exercise 7-4

Income statement effects of alternative cost flow assumptions

 LO 4

Use the data in Exercise 7-3 to construct comparative income statements for Trout, Inc. (year end 19X1) similar to those shown in Exhibit 7.10 in the chapter. Assume that operating expenses are $1,250. The applicable income tax rate is 30%.

1. Which method results in the highest net income?

2. Does the weighted average net income fall between the FIFO and LIFO net incomes?

3. If costs were rising instead of falling which method would result in the highest net income?

Exercise 7-5A

Alternative cost flow assumptions, periodic inventory system

 LO 9

Paddington Gifts, Inc., made purchases of a particular product in the current year as follows:

Jan.	1	Beginning inventory	120 units @ $3.00 =	$ 360
Mar.	7	Purchased	250 units @ $2.80 =	700
July	28	Purchased	500 units @ $2.50 =	1,250
Oct.	3	Purchased	450 units @ $2.30 =	1,035
Dec.	19	Purchased	100 units @ $2.05 =	205
		Total	1,420 units	$3,550

Required

The business uses a periodic inventory system, and the ending inventory consists of 150 units, 50 from each of the last three purchases. Determine the share of the $3,550 cost of the units for sale that should be assigned to the ending inventory and to goods sold under each of the following: (a) costs are assigned on the basis of specific invoice prices, (b) costs are assigned on a weighted-average cost basis, (c) costs are assigned on the basis of FIFO, and (d) costs are assigned on the basis of LIFO. Which method provides the lowest net income?

Exercise 7-6A

Alternative cost flow assumptions, periodic inventory system

LO 9

Jasper & Williams, Inc., made purchases of a particular product in the current year as follows:

Jan.	1	Beginning inventory	120 units @ $2.00 =	$ 240
Mar.	7	Purchased	250 units @ $2.30 =	575
July	28	Purchased	500 units @ $2.50 =	1,250
Oct.	3	Purchased	450 units @ $2.80 =	1,260
Dec.	19	Purchased	100 units @ $2.96 =	296
		Total	1,420 units	$3,621

Required

The company uses a periodic inventory system, and the ending inventory consists of 150 units, 50 from each of the last three purchases. Determine the share of the $3,621 cost of the units for sale that should be assigned to the ending inventory and to goods sold under each of the following: (a) costs are assigned on the basis of specific invoice prices, (b) costs are assigned on a weighted-average cost basis, (c) costs are assigned on the basis of FIFO, and (d) costs are assigned on the basis of LIFO. Which method provides the lowest net income?

Assume that The John Henry Company had $900,000 of sales during each of three consecutive years, and it purchased merchandise costing $500,000 during each of the years. It also maintained a $200,000 inventory from the beginning to the end of the three-year period. However, in accounting under a periodic inventory system, it made an error at the end of year 1 that caused its ending year 1 inventory to appear on its statements at $180,000 rather than the correct $200,000.

Exercise 7-7
Analysis of inventory errors
LO 5

Required

1. State the actual amount of the company's gross profit in each of the years.
2. Prepare a comparative income statement like Exhibit 7.13 to show the effect of this error on the company's cost of goods sold and gross profit in year 1, year 2, and year 3.

Showtime Company's ending inventory includes the following items:

Exercise 7-8
Lower of cost or market
LO 6

Product	Units on Hand	Unit Cost	Net Realizable Value per Unit
BB	22	$50	$54
FM	15	78	72
MB	36	95	91
SL	40	36	36

Net realizable value is determined to be the best measure of market. Calculate lower of cost or market for the inventory (a) as a whole and (b) applied separately to each product.

During 19X1, Harmony Co. sold $130,000 of merchandise at marked retail prices. At the end of 19X1, the following information was available from its records:

Exercise 7-9
Estimating ending inventory—retail method
LO 7

	At Cost	At Retail
Beginning inventory	$31,900	$64,200
Net purchases	57,810	98,400

Use the retail method to estimate Harmony's 19X1 ending inventory at cost.

Assume that in addition to estimating its ending inventory by the retail method, Harmony Co. of Exercise 7-9 also took a physical inventory at the marked selling prices of the inventory items at the end of 19X1. Assume further that the total of this physical inventory at marked selling prices was $27,300. Then, (a) determine the amount of this inventory at cost and (b) determine Harmony's 19X1 inventory shrinkage from breakage, theft, or other causes at retail and at cost.

Exercise 7-10
Reducing physical inventory to cost—retail method
LO 7

On January 1, The Parts Store had a $450,000 inventory at cost. During the first quarter of the year, it purchased $1,590,000 of merchandise, returned $23,100, and paid freight charges on purchased merchandise totalling $37,600. During the past several years, the store's gross profit on sales has averaged 30%. Under the assumption the store had $2,000,000 of sales during the first quarter of the year, use the gross profit method to estimate its inventory at the end of the first quarter.

Exercise 7-11
Estimating ending inventory—gross profit method
LO 7

Exercise 7-12
Merchandise turnover and
days' stock on hand

 LO 8

From the following information for Russo Merchandising Co., calculate merchandise turnover for 19X3 and 19X2 and days' stock on hand at December 31, 19X3, and 19X2. (Round answers to one decimal place.)

	19X3	19X2	19X1
Cost of goods sold	$643,825	$426,650	$391,300
Inventory (December 31)	96,400	86,750	91,500

Comment on Russo's efficiency in using its assets to support increasing sales from 19X2 to 19X3.

Problems

Problem 7-1
Alternative cost flows—
perpetual system

LO 1

The Hall Company has the following inventory and purchases during the fiscal year ended December 31, 19X8.

Beginning	500 units	$45/unit
Feb. 10	250 units	42/unit
Mar. 13	100 units	29/unit
Aug. 21	130 units	50/unit
Sept. 5	245 units	48/unit

Hall Company has two sales during the period. The specific units sold are the entire beginning inventory plus 65 units of the 3/13 purchase. The units have a selling price of $75.00 per unit.

Mar. 15	330 units
Sept. 10	235 units

Hall Company employs a perpetual inventory system.

Required

1. Calculate cost of goods available for sale and units available for sale.
2. Calculate units remaining in ending inventory.
3. Calculate the dollar value of ending inventory using (a) FIFO method, (b) LIFO method, (c) specific identification, (d) weighted average method.
4. Calculate the gross profit earned by Hall Company under each of the costing methods in (3).

Analysis Component:

5. If the Hall Company's manager earns a bonus based on a percentage of gross profit which method of inventory costing will she prefer?

Check Figure Ending
inventory (FIFO), $28,930

Problem 7-2ᴬ
Alternative cost flows—
periodic system

LO 9

Mill House Company began 19X1 with 20,000 units of Product X in its inventory that cost $15 each, and it made successive purchases of the product as follows:

Mar. 7	28,000 units @ $18 each
May 25	30,000 units @ $22 each
Aug. 1	20,000 units @ $24 each
Nov. 10	33,000 units @ $27 each

The company uses a periodic inventory system. On December 31, 19X1, a physical count disclosed that 35,000 units of Product X remained in inventory.

Required

1. Prepare a calculation showing the number and total cost of the units available for sale during 19X1.
2. Prepare calculations showing the amounts that should be assigned to the 19X1 ending inventory and to cost of goods sold, assuming (a) a FIFO basis, (b) a LIFO basis, and (c) a weighted-average cost basis.

Check Figure Cost of
goods sold (FIFO):
$1,896,000

Green Jeans, Inc., sold 5,500 units of its product at $45 per unit during 19X1. Incurring operating expenses of $6 per unit in selling the units, it began the year with and made successive purchases of the product as follows:

January 1 beginning inventory	600 units @ $18 per unit
Purchases:	
February 20	1,500 units @ $19 per unit
May 16	700 units @ $20 per unit
October 3	400 units @ $21 per unit
December 11	3,300 units @ $22 per unit
	6,500 units

Problem 7-3A
Income statement comparisons and cost flow assumptions

LO 4, 9

Required

Preparation component:

1. Prepare a comparative income statement for the company, showing in adjacent columns the net incomes earned from the sale of the product, assuming the company uses a periodic inventory system and prices its ending inventory on the basis of: (a) FIFO, (b) LIFO, and (c) weighted-average cost.

Analysis component:

2. How would the results of the three alternatives change if Green Jeans had been experiencing declining prices in the acquisition of additional inventory?

Check Figure Net income (LIFO), $98,600

Shockley Co. keeps its inventory records on a periodic basis. The following amounts were reported in the company's financial statements:

Problem 7-4
Analysis of inventory errors

LO 5

	Financial Statements for Year Ended December 31		
	19X1	**19X2**	**19X3**
(a) Cost of goods sold	$ 715,000	$ 847,000	$ 770,000
(b) Net income	220,000	275,000	231,000
(c) Total current assets	1,155,000	1,265,000	1,100,000
(d) Owner's equity	1,287,000	1,430,000	1,232,000

In making the physical counts of inventory, the following errors were made:
Inventory on December 31, 19X1: Understated $66,000
Inventory on December 31, 19X2: Overstated $30,000

Required

Preparation component:

1. For each of the preceding financial statement items—(a), (b), (c), and (d)—prepare a schedule similar to the following and show the adjustments that would have been necessary to correct the reported amounts.

Check Figure Corrected net income (19X2), $179,000

	19X1	19X2	19X3
Cost of goods sold:			
Reported			
Adjustments: Dec. 31/X1 error			
Dec. 31/X2 error			
Corrected			

Analytical component:

2. What is the error in the aggregate net income for the three-year period that resulted from the inventory errors? Explain why this result occurs. Also explain why the understatement of inventory by $66,000 at the end of 19X1 resulted in an understatement of equity by the same amount that year.

Problem 7-5
Lower of cost or market

LO 6

The following information pertains to the physical inventory of Electronics Unlimited taken at December 31:

| | | Per Unit | |
Product	Units on Hand	Cost	Market Value
Audio equipment:			
Receivers	335	$90	$98
CD players	250	111	100
Cassette decks	316	86	95
Turntables	194	52	41
Video equipment:			
Televisions	470	150	125
VCRs	281	93	84
Video cameras	202	310	322
Car audio equipment:			
Cassette radios	175	70	84
CD radios	160	97	105

Required

Calculate the lower of cost or market (a) for the inventory as a whole, (b) for the inventory by major category, and (c) for the inventory, applied separately to each product.

Check Figure Lower of cost or market: (a) $274,702; (b) $270,332; (c) $263,024

Problem 7-6
Retail inventory method

LO 7

The records of Basics Company provided the following information for the year ended December 31:

	At Cost	At Retail
January 1 beginning inventory	$ 471,350	$ 927,150
Purchases	3,328,830	6,398,700
Purchase returns	52,800	119,350
Sales		5,495,700
Sales returns		44,600

Required

1. Prepare an estimate of the company's year-end inventory by the retail method.

2. Under the assumption the company took a year-end physical inventory at marked selling prices that totalled $1,675,800, prepare a schedule showing the store's loss from theft or other cause at cost and at retail.

Check Figure Inventory shortage at cost, $41,392

Problem 7-7
Gross profit method

LO 7

Walker Company wants to prepare interim financial statements for the first quarter of 19X1. The company uses a periodic inventory system but would like to avoid making a physical count of inventory. During the last five years, the company's gross profit rate has averaged 35%. The following information for the year's first quarter is available from its records:

January 1 beginning inventory	$	300,260
Purchases		945,200
Purchase returns		13,050
Transportation-in		6,900
Sales		1,191,150
Sales returns		9,450

Required

Use the gross profit method to prepare an estimate of the company's March 31 inventory.

Check Figure Estimated March 31 inventory, $471,205

The Clinton Company has the following inventory purchases during the fiscal year ended December 31, 19X8.

Beg.	600 units	$55/unit
Jan. 10	450 units	56/unit
Feb. 13	200 units	57/unit
July 21	230 units	58/unit
Aug. 5	345 units	59/unit

Clinton Company has two sales during the period. The specific units sold are the entire beginning inventory plus 165 units of the 2/13 purchase. The units have a selling price of $90 per unit.

Feb. 15	430 units
Aug. 10	335 units

Clinton Company employs a perpetual inventory system.

Required

1. Calculate cost of goods available for sale and units available for sale.
2. Calculate units remaining in ending inventory.
3. Calculate the dollar value of ending inventory using (a) FIFO method, (b) LIFO method, (c) specific identification, (d) weighted-average method.
4. Calculate the gross profit earned by Clinton Company under each of the cost methods in (3).

Analysis Component:

5. If the Clinton Company's manager earns a bonus based on a percentage of gross profit which method of inventory costing will he prefer?

Alternate Problems
Alternative cost flows—
perpetual system

Problem 7-1A

LO 1

Sea Blue Co. began 19X1 with 6,300 units of Product B in its inventory that cost $35 each, and it made successive purchases of the product as follows:

January 4	10,500 units @ $33 each
May 18	13,000 units @ $32 each
July 9	12,000 units @ $29 each
November 21 . .	15,500 units @ $26 each

The company uses a periodic inventory system. On December 31, 19X1, a physical count disclosed that 16,500 units of Product B remained in inventory.

Required

1. Prepare a calculation showing the number and total cost of the units available for sale during the year.
2. Prepare calculations showing the amounts that should be assigned to the ending inventory and to cost of goods sold assuming (a) a FIFO basis, (b) a LIFO basis, and (c) a weighted-average cost basis.

Problem 7-2AA
Alternative cost flows—
periodic system

LO 9

Problem 7-3A[A]
Income statement comparisons and cost flow assumptions

LO 4, 9

The Denney Company sold 2,500 units of its product at $98 per unit during 19X1. Incurring operating expenses of $14 per unit in selling the units, it began the year with, and made successive purchases of, units of the product as follows:

January 1 beginning inventory . .	740 units costing $58 per unit
Purchases:	
April 2	700 units @ $59 per unit
June 14	600 units @ $61 per unit
August 29	500 units @ $64 per unit
November 18	800 units @ $65 per unit
	3,340 units

Required

Preparation component:

1. Prepare a comparative income statement for the company, showing in adjacent columns the net incomes earned from the sale of the product, assuming the company uses a periodic inventory system and prices its ending inventory on the basis of (a) FIFO, (b) LIFO, and (c) weighted-average cost.

Analysis component:

2. How would the results of the three alternatives change if Denney had been experiencing decreasing prices in the acquisition of additional inventory?

Problem 7-4A
Analysis of inventory errors

LO 5

Matchstick Company keeps its inventory records on a periodic basis. The following amounts were reported in the company's financial statements:

	Financial Statements for Year Ended December 31		
	19X1	**19X2**	**19X3**
(a) Cost of goods sold	$205,200	$212,800	$196,030
(b) Net income	174,800	211,270	183,910
(c) Total current assets	266,000	276,500	262,950
(d) Owner's equity	304,000	316,000	336,000

In making the physical counts of inventory, the following errors were made:
Inventory on December 31, 19X1: Overstated $17,000
Inventory on December 31, 19X2: Understated $25,000

Required

Preparation component:

1. For each of the preceding financial statement items—(a), (b), (c), and (d)—prepare a schedule similar to the following and show the adjustments that would have been necessary to correct the reported amounts.

	19X1	19X2	19X3
Cost of goods sold:			
Reported			
Adjustments: Dec. 31/X1 error			
Dec. 31/X2 error			
Corrected			

Analysis component:

2. What is the error in the aggregate net income for the three-year period that resulted from the inventory errors?

The following information pertains to the physical inventory of Office Outfitters taken at December 31:

Problem 7-5A
Lower of cost or market

LO 6

		Per Unit	
Product	**Units on Hand**	**Cost**	**Market Value**
Office furniture:			
Desks	436	$261	$305
Credenzas	295	227	256
Chairs	587	49	43
Bookshelves	321	93	82
Filing cabinets:			
Two-drawer	214	81	70
Four-drawer	398	135	122
Lateral	175	104	118
Office equipment:			
Fax machines	430	168	200
Copiers	545	317	288
Typewriters	352	125	117

Required

Calculate the lower of cost or market (a) for the inventory as a whole, (b) for the inventory by major category, and (c) for the inventory, applied separately to each product.

The records of The R.E. McFadden Co. provided the following information for the year ended December 31:

Problem 7-6A
Retail inventory method

LO 7

	At Cost	**At Retail**
January 1 beginning inventory	$ 81,670	$114,610
Purchases	502,990	767,060
Purchase returns	10,740	15,330
Sales		786,120
Sales returns		4,480

Required

1. Prepare an estimate of the company's year-end inventory by the retail method.
2. Under the assumption the company took a year-end physical inventory at marked selling prices that totalled $78,550, prepare a schedule showing the store's loss from theft or other cause at cost and at retail.

Four Corners Equipment Co. wants to prepare interim financial statements for the first quarter of 19X1. The company uses a periodic inventory system but would like to avoid making a physical count of inventory. During the last five years, the company's gross profit rate has averaged 30%. The following information for the year's first quarter is available from its records:

Problem 7-7A
Gross profit method

LO 7

January 1 beginning inventory	$ 752,880
Purchases	2,132,100
Purchase returns	38,370
Transportation-in	65,900
Sales	3,710,250
Sales returns	74,200

Required

Use the gross profit method to prepare an estimate of the company's March 31, 19X1, inventory.

Analytical and Review Problems

A & R Problem 7-1

The following information is taken from the records of Bradford Company for four consecutive operating periods:

	Periods			
	1	**2**	**3**	**4**
Beginning inventory	$29,000	$41,000	$31,000	$37,000
Ending inventory	41,000	31,000	37,000	19,000
Net income	25,000	29,000	33,000	41,000

Assume that the company made the errors below:

Period	Error in Ending Inventory	
1	Overstated	$5,000
2	Understated	8,000
3	Overstated	6,000

Required

1. Compute the revised net income for each of the four periods.
2. Assuming that the company's ending inventory for period 4 is correct, how would these errors affect the total net income for the four periods combined? Explain.

A & R Problem 7-2

The records of Thomas Company as of December 31, 1999, show the following:

	Net Purchases	Net Income	Accounts Payable	Inventory
Balance per company's books	$329,000	$22,100	$29,200	$20,500
(a)				
(b)				
(c)				
(d)				
(e)				
Correct balances				

The accountant of Thomas Company discovers in the first week of January 2000 that the following errors were made by his staff.

a. Goods costing $4,500 were in transit (FOB shipping point) and were not included in the ending inventory. The invoice had been received and the purchase recorded.

b. Damaged goods (cost $4,100) that were being held for return to the supplier were included in inventory. The goods had been recorded as a purchase and the entry for the return of these goods had also been made.

c. Inventory items costing $3,900 were incorrectly excluded from the final inventory. These goods had not been recorded as a purchase and had not been paid for by the company.

d. Goods that were shipped FOB destination had not yet arrived and were not included in inventory. However, the invoice had arrived on December 30, 1996, and the purchase for $2,700 was recorded.

e. Goods that cost $2,400 were segregated and not included in inventory because a customer expressed an intention to buy the goods. The sale of the goods for $4,200 had been recorded in December 1999.

Required

Using the format provided above, show the correct amount for net purchases, net income, accounts payable, and inventory for Thomas Company as at December 31, 1999.

BEYOND THE NUMBERS

Reporting in Action

LO 3, 8

Refer to the financial statements and related information for **Alliance** in Appendix I. Answer the following questions by analyzing the information in Alliance's report:

1. What is the total amount of inventories held by Alliance on March 31, 1997? On March 31, 1996? (Assume that Alliance's inventories are equivalent to "Investment in...programs" and "...programs in progress.")

2. Inventories represent what percent of total assets on March 31, 1997? On March 31, 1996?

3. Comment on the relative size of inventories Alliance holds compared to other types of assets.

Comparative Analysis

LO 8

Both **NIKE** and **Reebok** design, produce, market, and sell sports footwear and apparel. Key comparative figures ($ millions) for these two companies follow:

	NIKE		Reebok	
Key figures	**1997**	**1996**	**1996**	**1995**
Inventory	$1,339	$ 931	$ 555	$ 635
Cost of Sales	$5,503	$3,907	$2,144	$2,114

* NIKE figures are from the annual reports for the fiscal years ended May 31,1997 and 1996.

Reebok figures are from the annual reports for the fiscal years ended December 31, 1996 and 1995.

Required

1. Calculate the merchandise turnover for NIKE (1997) and Reebok (1996).

2. Calculate the days' sales in inventory for both companies for the two years given.

3. Comment on your findings.

Ethics Challenge

LO 4

Diversion, Inc. is a retail sports store carrying primarily women's golf apparel and equipment. The store is at the end of its second year of operation and, as new businesses often do, is struggling a bit to be profitable. The cost of inventory items has increased just in the short time the store has been in business. In the first year of operation the store accounted for inventory costs using the LIFO method. A loan agreement the store has with Dollar Bank, its prime source of financing, requires that the store maintain a certain profit margin and current ratio. The store's owner, Cindy Foor, is looking over Diversion's annual financial statements after year-end inventory has been taken. The numbers are not very favourable and the only way the store can meet the required financial ratios agreed upon with the bank is to change from the LIFO to FIFO method of inventory. The store originally decided upon LIFO for inventory costing because they felt that LIFO yielded a better matching of costs to revenues. Cindy, recalculates the ending inventory using FIFO and submits her income statement and balance sheet to the loan officer at the bank for the required bank review of the loan. As Cindy mails the financial statements to the bank she thankfully reflects on the latitude she has as manager in choosing an inventory costing method.

Required

1. Why does Diversion's use of FIFO improve the profit margin and current ratio?

2. Is the action by Diversion's owner ethical?

Communicating in Practice
LO 4

Assume you are the accountant for a wholesale produce business that has just completed its first year of operations. Due to catastrophic weather conditions, resulting in the destruction of crops, the cost of acquiring produce to resell has dramatically escalated during the later part of this fiscal period. Your client, Mr. P. Greenhouse, mentioned that because the business sells perishable goods, he has striven to maintain a first-in, first-out flow of goods. Although sales have been good for a first year- business, the high cost of inventory towards the end of the year has caused the business to be in a tight cash position. Mr. Greenhouse has expressed a concern regarding the ability of the business to meet the income tax obligations.

Required

Prepare a memo that explains and justifies the inventory evaluation method you recommend that your client, Mr. Greenhouse, adopt. If the response is to be made via e-mail you are to assume your instructor is the owner instead of Mr. P. Greenhouse.

Taking It to the Net
LO 8

Visit the **Corel Corporation** Web site at **www.corel.com.** Navigate the financial statements and financial statement footnotes collecting the information you need to answer the following questions. If the Corel Corporation Web site is not found consult the Corel Corporation financial information at the SEDAR database.

1. What product does Corel Corporation sell that is very popular with college students?
2. What form of inventory costing does Corel Corporation use? (Hint: Consult the footnotes to the financial statements to read details about Corel Corporation's inventory practices.)
3. Calculate Corel Corporation's gross margin for the most current year's data found at the Web site.
4. Calculate inventory turnover and days' sales in inventory for the most current year's data found at the Web site.

Teamwork in Action
LO 1,4

Each member of the team has the responsibility to become a resident expert on a specific inventory method. This expertise will be used to facilitate their teammates understanding of the concepts relevant to the method they have chosen. Follow the procedure outlined below:

1. Each team member is to select their area for expertise development by choosing one of the following inventory methods: specific identification, weighted average, FIFO, LIFO. Allow one minute to choose.
2. Learning teams are to disburse and expert teams are to be formed. Expert teams will be made up of students who have all selected the same area of expertise. The instructor will identify the location of the room where each expert team will meet.
3. Using data below, expert teams will collaborate to develop a presentation that illustrates each of the relevant procedures and concepts listed below the data. Each student must write up the presentation in a format that they can actually show to their learning teams in the next step in the activity.

Data:
Sunmann, Inc. had the following beginning inventory and made purchases of a particular product in the current year as follows:

Jan. 1 Beginning inventory	50 units @ $10 =	$ 500
Jan. 14 Purchased	150 units @ $12 =	1,800
Apr. 30 Purchased	200 units @ $15 =	3,000
Sept.26 Purchased	300 units @ $20 =	6,000

Sunmann, Inc., made sales on the following dates at $35 a unit:

Jan. 10	30 units (actual cost $10)
Feb. 15	100 units (actual cost $12)
Oct. 5	350 units (actual cost 100 @ $15 and 250 @ $20)

Procedures and concepts to illustrate in expert presentation:

a. Identify the costs to be assigned to the units sold.

b. Identify the costs to be assigned to the units in the ending inventory.

c. How likely is it that this method will reflect the actual physical flow of goods and how relevant is that factor in determining if this is an acceptable method to use?

d. What is the impact of this method versus others in determining the net income of this business.

e. How closely does the valuation of the ending inventory reflect replacement costs for these units?

4. Re-form learning teams. In rotation each expert is to present to their teams that which they developed in 3. Experts are to encourage and respond to questions.

With another classmate visit your local mall or downtown retail area. Visit five or six stores. In each store note whether the store uses a barcoding system to help manage its inventory. Try to find at least one store that does not use barcoding. If a store does not use barcoding ask the store's manager or retail clerk whether they know which type of inventory costing method the store employs. Use a spreadsheet or word-processing program to build a table that shows columns for the name of store visited, type of merchandise sold, use of barcoding or not, and use of inventory costing method used if barcoding is not employed. If the manager is easy to talk to you might also inquire as to what the store's merchandise turnover is and how often physical inventory is taken.

Hitting the Road
LO 2, 3

Read the article "Michael Dell: Whirlwind on the Web" in the April 7, 1997, issue of *Business Week*.

Answer the following questions:

1. How many days of sales does Dell have in inventory?

2. How does Dell's days of sales in inventory compare with one of their chief competitors?

3. What are three techniques described in the article that Dell uses to improve inventory management?

Business Break
LO 8

8

CHAPTER

Accounting Information Systems

Chapter Outline

▶ **Fundamental System Principles**
  ■ Control Principle
  ■ Relevance Principle
  ■ Compatibility Principle
  ■ Flexibility Principle
  ■ Cost-Benefit Principle

▶ **Components of Accounting Systems**
  ■ Source Documents
  ■ Input Devices
  ■ Information Processor
  ■ Information Storage
  ■ Output Devices

▶ **Special Journals in Accounting**
  ■ Basics of Special Journals
  ■ Subsidiary Ledgers
  ■ Sales Journal
  ■ Cash Receipts Journal
  ■ Purchases Journal
  ■ Cash Disbursements Journal
  ■ General Journal Transactions

▶ **Technology-Based Accounting Information Systems**
  ■ Computer Technology in Accounting
  ■ Data Processing in Accounting
  ■ Computer Networks in Accounting
  ■ Enterprise-Application Software

▶ **Using the Information— Business Segments**

▶ **Appendix 8A—Special Journals under a Perpetual System**

What's the Score?

Moncton, NB—It was the worst event in Marie Lanctot's early career as owner of **Outdoors Unlimited.** She'd lobbied hard to carry **REV Sports** products in her sporting goods store. Her rejection letter was harsh, and to the point. "The financial condition and records of Outdoors Unlimited do not support a business relationship at this time...," the letter said.

Marie knew she'd pushed the limit in keeping her own records. "I purchased the best accounting software according to small business magazines. But," says Marie. "I didn't have any idea how to use it." Marie thought she knew how to enter her store's sales and purchases data. Yet it turned out some data were entered in ledgers and not in journals, and vice versa. "The software created lovely reports, but I didn't know if they were correct," admits Marie. "Ledgers, journals, footings, crossfootings—it was all a confusion to me!" Most frustrating was that Marie knew her store was doing well, and for unknown reasons her financials weren't reflecting it.

"I ended up taking an evening course," says Marie. "I learned how to set up an accounting system and how to keep special journals. I set up my records as I went through the course." Marie now regularly creates schedules of accounts payable and accounts receivable. "I use ledgers and aging schedules to identify late paying customers. I also keep payable records to help me better time payments to suppliers." Marie also points out that Outdoors Unlimited now carries REV's products.

And what about that accounting software? "It's great software," says Marie. "But it ought to carry the warning: *A lack of accounting knowledge can damage your company's health.*"

Learning Objectives

LO 1 Identify fundamental principles of accounting information systems.

LO 2 Identify components of accounting information systems.

LO 3 Explain the goals and uses of special journals.

LO 4 Describe the use of controlling accounts and subsidiary ledgers.

LO 5 Journalize and post transactions using special journals.

LO 6 Prepare and test the accuracy of subsidiary ledgers.

LO 7 Explain how technology-based information systems impact accounting.

LO 8 Analyze a company's performance and financial condition by business segments.

CHAPTER PREVIEW

Accounting for business activities requires we collect and process information. As the number or complexity of business activities rises, demands placed on accounting information systems increase. Accounting information systems must meet this challenge in an efficient and effective manner. In this chapter we learn about fundamental principles guiding information systems, and we study components making up these systems. We also explain procedures that use special journals and subsidiary ledgers to make accounting information systems more efficient. Our understanding of the details of accounting reports makes us better decision makers when using financial information and it improves our ability to analyze and interpret financial statements. Like Marie Lanctot in the opening article, knowledge of these topics helps in successfully running a company.

Fundamental System Principles

LO1 Identify fundamental principles of accounting information systems.

Accounting information systems collect and process data from transactions and events, organize them in useful forms, and communicate results to decision makers. These systems are crucial to effective decision making for both internal and external users of information. With increasing complexity of business operations, and the growing need for information, accounting information systems are more important than ever before.

All decision makers in practice today need to have a basic knowledge of how accounting information systems work. It gives them a better understanding of information constraints, measurement limitations, and potential applications. It allows them to make more informed decisions, and to better balance the risks and returns of various strategies by effectively using accounting information. This section explains the five fundamental principles of accounting information systems, which are shown in Exhibit 8.1.

Exhibit 8.1

System Principles

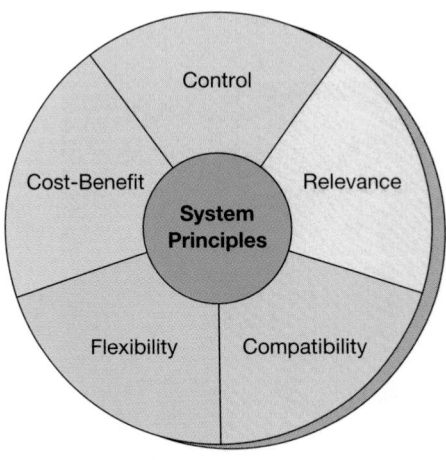

Control Principle

Managers need to control and monitor business activities. To this end, the **control principle** requires an accounting information system to have internal controls. *Internal controls* are methods and procedures allowing mangers to control and monitor activities. They include policies to direct operations toward common goals, procedures to ensure reliable financial reports, safeguards to protect company assets and methods to achieve compliance with laws and regulations.

Relevance Principle

Decision makers need relevant information to make informed decisions. The **relevance principle** requires that an accounting information system report useful, understandable, timely and pertinent information for effective decision making. This means an information system is designed to capture data that make a difference in decisions. To ensure this, it is important all decision makers, both internal and external, be consulted when identifying relevant information for disclosure.

Compatibility Principle

Accounting information systems must be consistent with the aims of a company. The **compatibility principle** requires that an accounting information system conform with a company's activities, personnel, and structure. It must also adapt to the unique characteristics of a company. The system must not be intrusive but, rather, in harmony with and driven by company goals. **Outdoors Unlimited** described in the opening article, for example, needs a simple retail information system. **Moore Corporation,** on the other hand, demands a manufacturing information system that is able to assemble data from its global operations. These two systems are not compatible, yet they are effective for the two different companies.

Flexibility Principle

Accounting information systems must be able to adjust to changes. The **flexibility principle** requires that an accounting information system adapt to changes in the company, business environment, and needs of decision makers. Technological advances, competitive pressures, consumer tastes, regulations, and company activities constantly change. A system must be designed to adapt to these changes.

Cost-Benefit Principle

Accounting information systems must balance costs and benefits. The **cost-benefit principle** requires the benefits from an activity in an accounting information system to outweigh the costs of that activity. The costs and benefits of an activity impact on the decisions of both external and internal information users. They also affect costs of computer systems, personnel and other direct and indirect costs. Decisions regarding other system's principles (control, relevance, compatibility and flexibility) are affected by the cost-benefit principle.

Accounting information systems consist of people, records, methods, and equipment. These systems are designed to capture information about a company's transactions and to provide output including financial, managerial, and tax reports. Because all accounting information systems have these same goals, they have some basic components. These components apply whether or not a system is heavily computerized. Yet the components of computerized systems usually provide more accuracy, speed, efficiency, and convenience.

There are five basic components of an accounting information system, source documents: input devices, information processors, information storage, and output devices. Exhibit 8.2 shows these components in a series of steps. Yet we know there is a lot of two-way communication between many of these components. We describe each of these components in this section.

Components of Accounting Systems

LO2 Identify components of accounting information systems.

Source Documents

We described source documents in Chapter 3 and explained their importance for both business transactions and information collection. Source documents provide the basic information processed by an accounting system. Most of us are familiar

Source Document → Input Devices → Information Processor → Information Storage → Output Devices

Exhibit 8.2

Accounting System Components

with source documents such as bank statements and cheques received from others. Other examples of source documents include invoices from suppliers, billings to customers, and employee earnings records.

Source documents are often paper-based. Yet, increasingly, source documents are taking other forms such as electronic files and Web communications. Also a growing number of companies are sending invoices directly from their systems to their customers' systems. The Web is playing a major role in this transformation from paper-based to "paperless" systems.

Accurate source documents are crucial to accounting information systems. Input of faulty or incomplete information seriously impairs the reliability and relevance of information systems. This is commonly referred to as "garbage in, garbage out." Information systems are set up with special attention on control procedures to limit the possibility of faulty data entering the system.

Input Devices

Input devices capture information from source documents and enable its transfer to the information processing component of the system. These devices often involve converting data on source documents from written or electronic form to a form useable for the system. Input devices are also used in directing the information processing component on how best to process information. Journal entries, both electronic and paper-based, are a type of input device. If we record transactions using the **SPATS** software accompanying this book, a computer keyboard serves as an input device. Keyboards, scanners, and modems are some of the most common input devices in practice today.

Another increasingly common input device is a *bar code reader.* They are commonly used by many merchandisers, but are growing in importance as input and control devices for military, law enforcement, and special business applications. Bar code readers capture code numbers and transfer these data to the organization's computer for processing. An *optical scanner* is another popular input device that is expanding in its applications. It can capture writing samples and other input directly from source documents.

Did You Know?

Self Check-Out

A system developed by **Optimal Robotics Corp.** of Montreal allows customers to check out and pay for groceries or other goods without having recourse to a human cashier. Optimal has the only system in North America that allows shoppers to scan, bag, and pay for their purchases on their own. They can use cash or debit or credit cards, in most cases with no need for help from store personnel. [Source: *Canadian Press,* April 1998.]

Accounting information systems encourage accuracy by using set methods for inputting data. Controls are also used to ensure only authorized individuals can input data to the system. Controls increase the reliability of the system. They also allow false information to be traced back to its source.

Information Processor

An **information processor** interprets, transforms, and summarizes information for use in analysis and reporting. An important part of an information processor in accounting systems will *always* be the use of professional judgment. Accounting principles are never so structured that they limit the need for professional judgment. Other parts of an information processor include journals, ledgers, working papers, and posting procedures. Each assists in transforming raw data to useful information.

Increasingly, computer technology is assisting manual information processors. This assistance is freeing accounting professionals to take on greater analysis, interpretative, and managerial roles. This assistance to information processors includes both computing *hardware* and *software*. Hardware is the computing equipment, and software is the directions for hardware. Software consists of computer programs that specify operations performed on data. Software often controls much of the accounting system including input, file management, processing and output. **Microsoft**, the world's largest software producer, is a major part of this evolution. It reported 1996 revenues of more than US$8.6 billion, with much of this from software sales.

Information Storage

Information storage is the component of an accounting system that keeps data in a form accessible to information processors. When data is input and processed, it is usually saved for use in future analysis or reports. This database must be accessible for preparing periodic financial reports and other analyses. Information storage is also set up to help in the creation of internal reports. Auditors focus on this database when auditing financial statements. Companies also maintain files of source documents to resolve errors or disputes.

Technology increasingly assists with information storage. While previous systems consisted almost exclusively of paper documents, there is growing use of CDs, hard drives, tapes and other electronic storage devices. Advances in information storage enable accounting systems to store more detailed data than ever before. This means managers have more data to access and work with in planning and controlling business activities. Information storage can be "on-line," meaning data can be accessed whenever it is needed, or it can be "off-line," meaning data cannot be accessed. Access often requires assistance and authorization. Information storage is also increasingly augmented by Web sources such as Toronto Stock Exchange databases, CICA standards, and financial and product markets.

Output Devices

Output devices are the means to take information out of an accounting system and make it available to users. Output devices provide users with a variety of items including graphics, analysis reports, bills to customers, cheques to suppliers, employee paycheques, financial statements, and internal reports. The most common output devices are printers and monitors; others include telephones or direct Web communication with the systems of suppliers or customers. When requests for output occur, an information processor takes the needed data from a database and prepares the necessary report. This report is then sent to an output device.

Information can be provided in many different ways. A bank customer, for instance, can telephone directly into his or her account to learn the balance. A touch-tone telephone can serve as an input/output device. In response to a recording, the customer presses buttons to provide information needed for authorization. The customer is then given information, which is sent back over the communication line. Another kind of output is an electronic fund transfer (ETF), a method of paying employees without writing paycheques. A company's accounting system can send payroll data directly to the accounting system of its bank. The output of this company's system is the electronic fund transfer from its bank account to its employees' bank accounts. The output device, in this instance, is an interface between both accounting systems. Still another output device involves a company recording payroll data on tape or CD and forwarding it to the bank. This tape or disk is then used by the bank to transfer wages earned to employees' accounts.

Flash back

1. Identify the five primary components of an accounting information system.
2. What is the aim of the information processor component of an accounting system?
3. What uses are made of data in the information storage component of an accounting system?

Answers—p. 394

Judgment and Ethics

Public Accountant
You are a public accountant consulting with a client. This client's business has grown to the point where its accounting system must be updated to handle both the volume of transactions and management's needs for information. Your client requests your advice in purchasing new software for its accounting system. You have been offered a 10% commission by a software company for each purchase of its system by one of your clients. Do you think your evaluation of alternative software is affected by this commission arrangement? Do you think this commission arrangement is appropriate? Do you tell your client about the commission arrangement before making a recommendation?

Answer—p. 393

Special Journals in Accounting

LO3 Explain the goals and uses of special journals.

This section describes the underlying operations of accounting information systems. These operations are set up to be efficient in processing transactions and events. They are part of all systems in various forms. They are also increasingly assisted by technology. But even in technologically advanced systems, an understanding of the operations we describe in this section will aid us in using, interpreting and applying accounting information. It also improves our understanding of the workings of computer-based systems. We must remember that all accounting systems have common purposes whether or not they heavily depend on technology.

This section focuses on special journals and subsidiary ledgers that underlie accounting systems. We describe how special journals are used to capture transactions, and we explain how subsidiary ledgers are set up to capture details of certain accounts. This section uses selected transactions of **Outdoors Unlimited** to illustrate these important points.

Since Outdoors Unlimited uses a *periodic* inventory system, the special journals are set up using this system. The increasing use of a perpetual system, as described in Chapters 6 and 7, leads us to show in Appendix 8A the slight change in special journals when using a *perpetual* system. We also include a note at the bottom of each of the major journals explaining the minor change required if a company uses a perpetual system. Another reason to focus on special journals in a periodic system is due to the greater use of special journals in this system as opposed to a perpetual system. This is because many perpetual systems use computer technology, and their "special journals" are often in electronic form and automate several recordkeeping duties such as posting and preparing accounts receivable and payable schedules.

Basics of Special Journals

A General Journal is a flexible journal where we can record any transaction. Yet using a General Journal means that each debit and each credit entered must be individually posted to its respective account. This requires time and effort in posting individual debits and credits, especially for less technologically advanced systems. The costs of posting accounts can be reduced by organizing transactions into common groups and providing a separate special journal. A **special journal** is used in recording and posting transactions of similar type. Most transactions of a merchandiser, for instance, fall into four groups: sales on credit, purchases on credit, cash receipts, and cash disbursements. Exhibit 8.3 shows the special journals for these groups. This section assumes the use of these special journals along with the General Journal.

Sales Journal	Cash Receipts Journal	Purchases Journal	Cash Disbursement Journal	General Journal
For recording credit sales	For recording cash receipts	For recording credit purchases	For recording cash payments	For transactions not in special journals

Exhibit 8.3

Using Special Journals with a General Journal

Notice the General Journal continues to be used for transactions not covered by special journals and for adjusting, closing, and correcting entries. We show in the discussion below how special journals are efficient tools in helping journalize and post transactions. This is done, for instance, by accumulating debits and credits of similar transactions, which allows us to post amounts entered in the columns as column *totals* rather than as individual amounts. The advantage of this system increases as the number of transactions increase. Special journals also allow an efficient division of labour. This can be an effective control procedure.

Subsidiary Ledgers

Accounting information systems must provide several detailed listings of amounts. One of the most important listings is the amounts due from customers, called *accounts receivable*, and amounts owed to creditors, called *accounts payable*. We can expand the General Ledger to collect this information, but this is uncommon. Instead we often create a separate ledger called a subsidiary ledger.

A **subsidiary ledger** is a listing of individual accounts with a common characteristic. Using subsidiary ledgers removes unnecessary details from the General Ledger. Two common subsidiary ledgers are:

■ Accounts Receivable Ledger for storing transaction data with individual customers.
■ Accounts Payable Ledger for storing transaction data with individual creditors.

Individual accounts are often arranged alphabetically in subsidiary ledgers. We further explain the use of accounts receivable and accounts payable ledgers below.

LO4 Describe the use of controlling accounts and subsidiary ledgers.

Accounts Receivable Ledger

When we recorded credit sales in prior transaction analysis we debited Accounts Receivable. Yet when a company has more than one credit customer, the accounts receivable records must show how much *each* customer purchased, paid, and still owes. This information is collected for companies with credit customers by keeping a separate Account Receivable for each customer.

A separate account for each customer can be kept in the General Ledger containing the other financial statement accounts. However, this is not common. Instead, the General Ledger continues to keep a single Accounts Receivable account and a *subsidiary ledger* is set up to keep a separate account for each customer. This subsidiary ledger is called the **Accounts Receivable Ledger** (also called *Accounts Receivable Subsidiary Ledger* or *Customers' Ledger*). Like a General Ledger, a subsidiary ledger can exist in electronic (tape or CD) or paper (book or tray) form. Customer accounts in a subsidiary ledger are kept separate from the Accounts Receivable account in the General Ledger.

Exhibit 8.4 shows the relation between the Accounts Receivable account and its related accounts in the subsidiary ledger. After all items are posted, the balance in the Accounts Receivable account must equal the sum of balances in the customers' accounts. The Accounts Receivable account is said to control the Accounts Receivable Ledger and is referred to as a **controlling account**. Since the Accounts Receivable Ledger is a supplementary record controlled by an Accounts Receivable account in the General Ledger, it is called a subsidiary ledger.

Accounts Payable Ledger

There are other controlling accounts and subsidiary ledgers. We know, for example, that many companies buy on credit from several suppliers. This means a company must keep a separate account for each creditor. It does this by keeping an Accounts Payable controlling account in the General Ledger and a separate account for each creditor in an **Accounts Payable Ledger** (also called *Accounts Payable Subsidiary Ledger* or *Creditors' Ledger*). The controlling account, subsidiary ledger, and columnar journal format described with accounts receivable also apply to Accounts Payable accounts.

Other Subsidiary Ledgers

Subsidiary ledgers are also common for several other accounts. A company with many items of equipment, for example, might keep only one Equipment account in its General Ledger. But this company's Equipment account would control a subsidiary ledger where each item of equipment is recorded in a separate account. Similar treatment is common with investments, inventory, payables, and other large accounts needing separate detailed records.

Moore Corporation, one of the largest manufacturers of business forms, reports detailed sales information by geographic area which includes Canada, the United States, Europe, Latin America, and Asia Pacific, in its 1997 annual report. Yet Moore's accounting system most certainly keeps more detailed sales records than reflected in its annual report. Moore, for instance, sells hundreds of different products and is likely able to analyze the sales performance of each one of them. This detail can be captured by many different general ledger sales accounts.

Exhibit 8.4

Accounts Receivable Controlling Account and Subsidiary Ledger

General Ledger
Used for preparing financial statements and other reports

Accounts Receivable Subsidiary Ledger
Used for preparing bills sent to customers and other reports

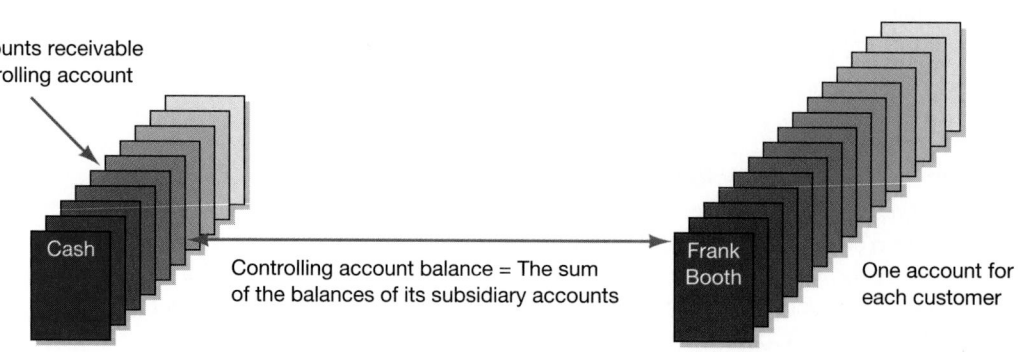

Accounts receivable controlling account

Cash

Controlling account balance = The sum of the balances of its subsidiary accounts

Frank Booth

One account for each customer

But it is likely captured by using supplementary records that function like subsidiary ledgers. The concept of a subsidiary ledger can be applied in many different ways to ensure that our accounting system captures sufficient details to support analyses that decision makers need.

Sales Journal

A **sales journal** is used to record sales of merchandise on credit. Sales of merchandise for cash are not recorded in a sales journal, but instead are recorded in a cash receipts journal. Sales of nonmerchandise assets on credit are recorded in the General Journal.

LO5 Journalize and post transactions using special journals.

Exhibit 8.5

Sales Journal with Posting

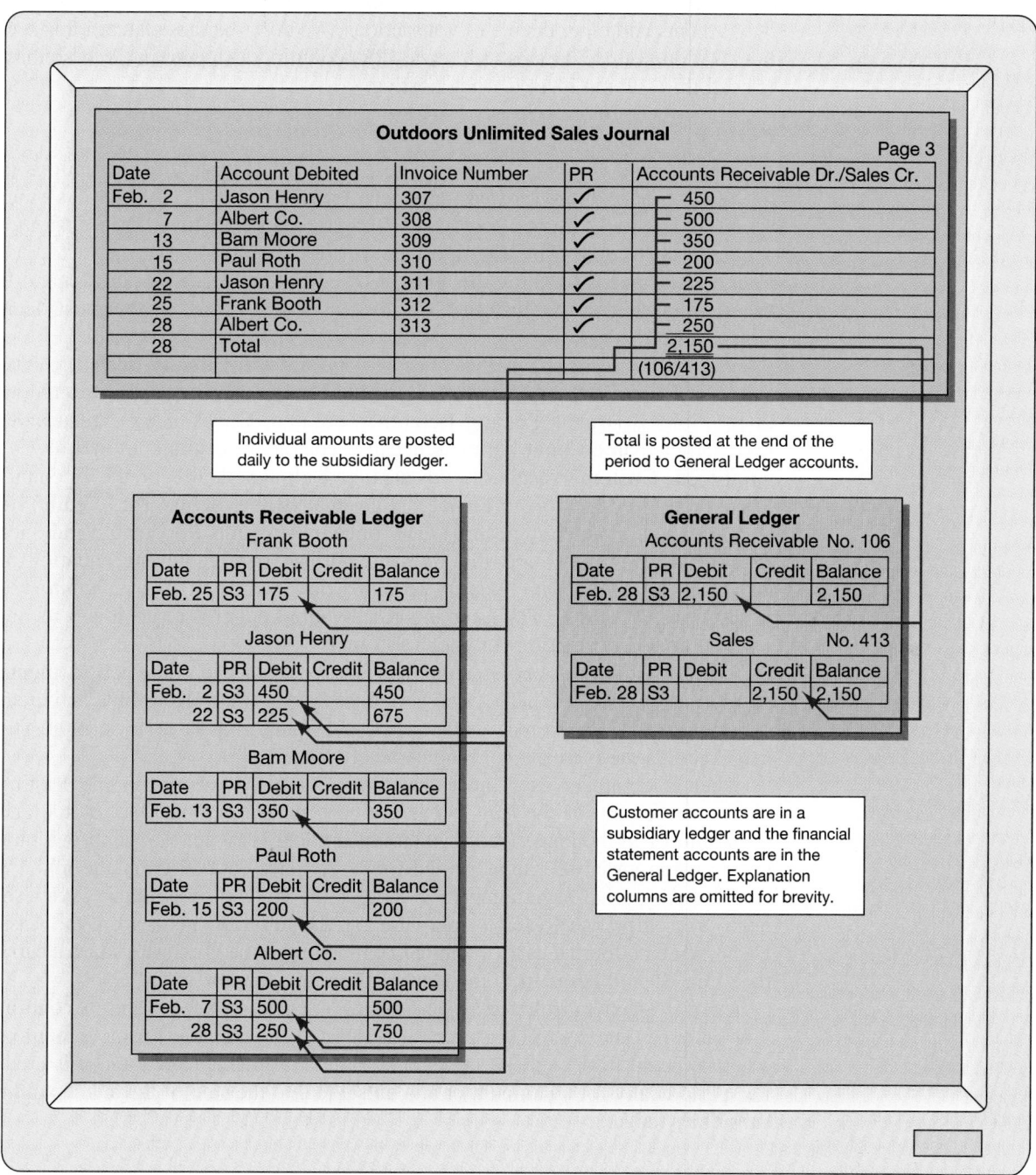

Note: Sales Journal in a perpetual system requires a new column on the far right titled "Cost of Goods Sold Dr., Inventory Cr." (see Exhibit 8.18).

Journalizing

Credit sale transactions are recorded with information about each sale entered separately in a Sales Journal. This information is often taken from a copy of the sales ticket or invoice prepared at the time of sale. The top of Exhibit 8.5 shows a Sales Journal from a sporting goods merchandiser, **Outdoors Unlimited**. The Sales Journal in this exhibit is called a columnar journal because it has columns for recording the date, customer's name, invoice number, and amount of each credit sale.[1] A **columnar journal** is a journal with more than one column.

Each transaction recorded in the Sales Journal yields a debit to Accounts Receivable and a credit to Sales. We only need one column for these two accounts. An exception is when managers need more information about taxes, returns, departments and other details of transactions. We describe these later in this section. We do not use the post reference (PR) column when entering transactions. Instead this column is used when posting.

Posting

A Sales Journal is posted as shown in Exhibit 8.5. Individual transactions in the Sales Journal are posted regularly (typically each day) to customer accounts in the Accounts Receivable Ledger. These postings keep customer accounts up to date. This is important for the person granting credit to customers, who needs to know the amount owed by credit-seeking customers. If this information in the customer's account is out of date, an incorrect decision can be made.

When sales recorded in the Sales Journal are individually posted to customer accounts in the Accounts Receivable Ledger, check marks are entered in the Sales Journal's Posting Reference column. Check marks are usually used rather than account numbers because customer accounts are not always numbered. Customer accounts are arranged alphabetically in the Accounts Receivable Ledger for reference. Note that when debits (or credits) to Accounts Receivable are posted twice (once to Accounts Receivable and once to the customer's account) this does not violate the accounting equation of debits equal credits. *The equality of debits and credits is always maintained in the General Ledger.* The Accounts Receivable Ledger is a subsidiary record with detailed information for each customer.

The Sales Journal's *Amount* column is totalled at the end of the period (month of February in this case). The total is debited to Accounts Receivable and credited to Sales. The credit records the period's revenue from sales on account. The debit records the increase in accounts receivable.

When a company uses more than one journal, it records in the Posting Reference column of the *ledgers* (before each posted amount) the journal and page number in the journal from where the amount is taken. We identify a journal by using an initial. Items posted from the Sales Journal carry the initial *S* before their journal page numbers in the Posting Reference columns. Likewise, items from the Cash Receipts Journal carry the initial *R*, items from the Cash Disbursements Journal carry the initial *D*, items from the Purchases Journal carry the initial *P*, and items from the General Journal carry the initial *G*.

There is a general rule for all postings to a subsidiary ledger and its controlling account: The controlling account is debited periodically for an amount or amounts equal to the sum of the debits to the subsidiary ledger, and it is credited periodically for an amount or amounts equal to the sum of the credits to the subsidiary ledger.

---

[1] We do not record explanations in any of our special journals for brevity purposes.

In the following table indicate in which journal each transaction should be recorded:

a. Purchase of office supplies for cash.
b. Sale of merchandise on account.
c. Entry to record amortization expense for the period.
d. Purchase of merchandise on account.
e. Sale of scrap material for cash.
f. Collection of the amount of the sale in *b*.

Mid-Chapter Demonstration Problem

a. Cash disbursements journal
b. Sales journal
c. General journal
d. Purchases journal
e. Cash receipts journal
f. Cash receipts journal

Solution to Mid-Chapter Demonstration Problem

Testing the Ledger

Account balances in the General Ledger and subsidiary ledgers are tested for accuracy after posting is complete. We do this by first preparing a trial balance of the General Ledger to confirm debits equal credits (see Chapter 4 for preparing a trial balance). If debits equal credits in the trial balance, the accounts in the General Ledger, including the controlling accounts, are assumed to be correct. Second, we test the subsidiary ledgers by preparing a schedule of accounts receivable.

A **schedule of accounts receivable** is a listing of accounts from the Accounts Receivable Ledger with their balances and the sum of all balances. If this total equals the balance of the Accounts Receivable controlling account, the accounts in the Accounts Receivable Ledger are assumed correct. Exhibit 8.6 shows a schedule of accounts receivable drawn from the Accounts Receivable Ledger of Exhibit 8.5.

LO 6 Prepare and test the accuracy of subsidiary ledgers.

Exhibit 8.6

Schedule of Accounts Receivable

Additional Issues

This section looks at three additional issues with the Sales Journal: (1) recording sales taxes, (2) recording sales returns and allowance, and (3) using sales invoices as a journal.

Sales Taxes

Most provinces and the federal government require retailers to collect sales taxes from customers and to periodically send these taxes to the appropriate agency. When using a columnar Sales Journal, we can have a record of taxes collected by adding columns to the journal as shown in Exhibit 8.7.

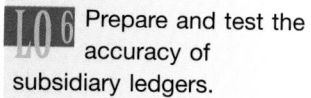

OUTDOORS UNLIMITED Schedule of Accounts Receivable February 28, 1998	
Frank Booth	$ 175
Jason Henry	675
Bam Moore	350
Paul Roth	200
Albert Co.	750
Total accounts receivable	$2,150

Exhibit 8.7

Sales Journal with Information on Sales Taxes

Outdoors Unlimited Sales Journal						Page 3
Date		Account Debited	Invoice Number	PR	Accounts Receivable Dr.	Sales Taxes Payable Cr.	Sales Cr.
Dec.	1	Favre Co.	7-1698		103	3	100

We described how column totals of a Sales Journal are commonly posted at the end of each period (month for Outdoors Unlimited). This now includes crediting the Sales Taxes Payable account for the total of the Sales Taxes Payable column. Individual amounts in the Accounts Receivable column are posted daily to customer accounts in the Accounts Receivable Ledger. Individual amounts in the Sales Taxes Payable and Sales columns are not posted. Companies that collect sales taxes on their cash sales can also use a special Sales Taxes Payable column in their Cash Receipts Journal.

Provincial Sales Tax

All provinces except Alberta require retailers to collect a **provincial sales tax (PST)** from their customers and to periodically remit this tax to the appropriate provincial authority. When special journals are used, a column is provided for PST in the Sales Journal and the Cash Receipts Journal. A record of PST is obtained by recording in the PST column the appropriate amount of PST on cash sales (Cash Receipts Journal) and sales on account (Sales Journal). It should be noted that not all sales are subject to PST.

PST may be paid on items that are not part of inventory for resale but will be consumed or are long-term assets. In these cases, the PST paid is not allocated to a separate account. Instead it is allocated as part of the expense or asset cost associated with the purchase.

Goods and Services Tax

The **goods and services tax (GST)** is a 7% tax on almost all goods and services provided in Canada. It is a federal tax on the consumer. However, unlike the PST, businesses pay GST up front but generally receive a full credit or refund for all GST paid. Ultimately, only the final consumer bears the burden of this tax. This is because businesses collect GST on sales, but since they receive full credit for GST paid on their purchases, they only remit the difference to the appropriate federal authority. To illustrate the collection and payment of GST consider the following example.

LM Company assembles riding mowers. It pays $200 for materials which are subject to GST of $14. LM pays the $14 to its suppliers who remit the $14 to Revenue Canada. LM now has a $14 GST debit, that is, a prepaid GST or input tax credit. The journal entry would be:

Date	Material	200.00	
	GST Payable	14.00	
	Accounts Payable		214.00
	To record purchase of material.		

LM sells the mower to KD Company, a dealer, for $500 and collects $35 in GST. LM remits the $35, minus the $14 input credit, that is, the GST paid to its suppliers. KD now has a $35 GST credit, that is, prepaid GST. The entry to record the sale by LM is:

Date	Accounts Receivable—KD	535.00	
	GST Payable		35.00
	Sales Revenue		500.00
	To record sale to LM.		

KD sells the mower to CC, the consumer, for $800 and collects $56 in GST. KD remits the $56, minus the $35 GST credit to Revenue Canada.

To summarize:

	GST Paid	GST Collected	GST Remitted
Materials supplier		$14	$14
LM Company	$14	35	21
KD Company	35	56	21
CC (the consumer)	56		$56

The total GST remitted is $56, the same amount that CC, the consumer, paid. The supplier, and LM and KD companies act as collection agents, collecting the tax along each stage of the process.

To facilitate the recording of GST, special GST (credit) columns must be provided not only in the Sales Journal and the Cash Receipts Journal, as in the case of PST, but also GST (debit) columns in the Purchases Journal and Cash Disbursements Journal. To illustrate, assume that Berlasty Company uses specialized journals shown in Exhibit 8-8. The following transactions were completed and recorded during December:

Dec. 01 Purchases on account, $1,000 from Jason Supply, terms n/30.
    03 Paid transportation on the Dec. 1 purchase, $30.
    09 Purchases for cash, $500.
    15 Cash sale, $1,200 (subject to 8% PST and 7% GST).
    28 Paid for the Dec. 1 purchase.
    30 Sales to S. Burns on account, $2,000 ($1,500 subject to 8% PST and $2,000 subject to 7% GST).

Purchases Journal

Date	Account Credited	Terms	PR	Accounts Payable Credit	Purchases Debit	Office Supplies Debit	GST Payable Debit
Dec. 1	Jason Supply	n/30		1,070.00	1,000.00		70.00
				1,070.00	1,000.00		70.00
							(225)

Cash Disbursements Journal

Date	Ch. No.	Account Debited	PR	Other Accounts Debit	GST Payable Debit	Accts. Payable Debit	Purch. Disc. Credit	Cash Credit
Dec. 3	256	Transportation-in		30.00	2.10			32.10
9	257	Purchases		500.00	35.00			535.00
28	258	Accts. Pay/						
		Jason Supply				1,070.00		1,070.00
				530.00	37.10	1,070.00		1,637.10
					(225)			

Sales Journal

Date	Account Debited	Invoice No.	PR	Acct. Rec. Debit	PST Payable Credit	GST Payable Credit	Sales Credit
Dec. 30	S. Burns	2734		2,260.00	120.00	140.00	2,000.00
					(224)	(225)	

Exhibit 8-8

Special Journals with PST and GST Columns as Applicable

Cash Receipts Journal								
Date	Account Credited	Explanation	PR	Other Accounts Credit	Accts. Rec. Credit	PST Payable Credit	GST Payable Credit	Sales Credit	Cash Debit
Dec. 15						96.00	84.00	1,200.00	1,380.00
						(224)	(225)		

After the posting is completed, as described earlier in the chapter, the PST and GST T-accounts would appear as follows:

PST (224)		
	SJ	120.00
	CRJ	96.00
Balance		216.00

GST (225)			
PJ	70.00	SJ	140.00
CDJ	37.10	CRS	84.00
Balance			116.90

On December 31, PST payable amounts to $216 and GST payable amounts to $116.90. The computation of GST is not uniform throughout the country. In some of the provinces, the computation is as illustrated above, that is, PST and GST are computed as a percentage of the selling price. In other provinces, PST is initially computed as a percentage of the selling price and GST is computed as a percentage of the total of the selling price plus the PST. It should also be noted that while GST is a 7% federal tax, thus uniform in each of the provinces, PST is a provincial tax and differs in percentage from province to province. Nova Scotia charges a **harmonized sales tax (HST)** of 15% which is comprised of the 7% GST and the PST of 8%. The preceding discussion is based on Ontario's PST of 8%.

In Exhibit 8-8, one account was used to record GST on purchases and on sales. Some accountants prefer to record GST on purchases in a Prepaid GST account and GST on sales in a GST Payable account. Thus, if two accounts are used in Exhibit 8-8, the GST Payable Debit column in the Purchases Journal and the Cash Disbursements Journal would be changed to Prepaid GST. The Sales Journal and the Cash Receipts Journal would remain as illustrated. The use of one or two accounts to account for GST is a matter of preference; the final result is the same.

Remittance of GST

The GST is administered by Revenue Canada Customs and Excise. Remittance is accompanied by a Goods and Services Tax Return.

Frequency of filing returns is dependent on the size of the business. Large businesses (annual sales in excess of $6 million) are required to file GST returns monthly. Medium-sized businesses (annual sales of $500,000 to $6 million) are required to file quarterly. Small businesses (annual sales up to $500,000) have the option of filing annually but paying quarterly installments. GST for a period must be remitted to Revenue Canada by the end of the month following the month (quarter) collected.

Sales Returns and Allowances

A company with only a few sales returns and allowances can record them in a General Journal with an entry like:

Assets = Liabilities + Equity
−175   −175

Mar. 17	Sales Returns and Allowances	414	17.50	
	Accounts Receivable—Ray Ball	106/✓		17.50
	Customer returned merchandise.			

The debit in this entry is posted to the Sales Returns and Allowances account. The credit is posted to both the Accounts Receivable controlling account and to the customer's account (posted daily). We also include the account number and the check mark, 106/, in the PR column on the credit line. This means both the Accounts Receivable controlling account in the General Ledger and the Ray Ball account in the Accounts Receivable Ledger are credited for $17.50. Both are credited because the balance of the controlling account in the General Ledger does not equal the sum of the customer account balances in the subsidiary ledger unless both are credited.

A company with a large number of sales returns and allowances can save costs by recording them in a special Sales Returns and Allowances Journal similar to Exhibit 8.9. A company can design and use a special journal for any group of similar transactions if there are enough transactions to warrant a journal. When using a Sales Returns and Allowances Journal to record returns, amounts in the journal are posted daily to customers' accounts. The journal total is posted as a debit to Sales Returns and Allowances and as a credit to Accounts Receivable at the end of the month.

Outdoors Unlimited Sales Returns and Allowances Journal

Page 1

Date	Account Credited	Credit Memo No.	PR	Sales Returns & Allowances Dr. Accounts Receivable Cr.
Mar. 7	Robert Moore	203	✓	10
14	James Warren	204	✓	12
18	T.M. Jones	205	✓	6
23	Sam Smith	206	✓	18
31	Total			46
				(414/106)

Exhibit 8.9

Sales Returns and Allowances Journal

Sales Invoices as a Sales Journal

Some merchandisers avoid using Sales Journals for credit sales to save costs. Instead they post each sales invoice total directly to the customer's account in the subsidiary Accounts Receivable Ledger. They then put copies of invoices in numerical order in a file. At the end of the month, they total all invoices for that month and make a general journal entry to debit Accounts Receivable and credit Sales for the total. The bound invoice copies essentially act as a Sales Journal. This procedure is called *direct posting of sales invoices*.

Flashback

4. When special journals are used, where are all cash payments by cheque recorded?

5. How does a columnar journal save posting time and effort?

6. How do debits and credits remain equal when credit sales to customers are posted twice (once to Accounts Receivable and once to the customer's account)?

7. How do we identify the journal from where an amount in a ledger account was posted?

Answers—p. 394

Cash Receipts Journal

A **Cash Receipts Journal** records all receipts of cash. A Cash Receipts Journal must be a columnar journal because different accounts are credited when cash is received from different sources.

Journalizing

Cash receipts usually fall into one of three groups: (1) cash from credit customers in payment of their accounts, (2) cash from cash sales, and (3) cash from other sources. The Cash Receipts Journal in Exhibit 8.10 has a special column for credits when cash is received from one or more of these three sources. We describe how to journalize transactions for each of these three sources in this section. The next section describes how to post these transactions.[2]

Cash from Credit Customers

To record cash received in payment of a customer's account, the customer's name is first entered in the Cash Receipts Journal's Account Credited column. Then the amounts debited to Cash and Sales Discounts (if any) are entered in their respective journal columns, and the amount credited to the customer's account is entered in the Accounts Receivable Credit column. Note the Accounts Receivable Credit column contains only credits to customer accounts.

The posting procedure is twofold. First, individual amounts are posted to subsidiary ledger accounts. Second, column totals are posted to general ledger accounts. Let's look at the Accounts Receivable Credit column as an example. First, individual credits are posted regularly (daily) to customer accounts in the subsidiary Accounts Receivable Ledger. Second, the column total is posted at the end of the period (month) as a credit to the Accounts Receivable controlling account.

Cash Sales

When cash sales are collected and totalled at the end of a day, the daily total is recorded with a debit to Cash and a credit to Sales. If we use a Cash Receipts Journal as in Exhibit 8.10, the debits to Cash are entered in the Cash Debit column, and the credits in a special column titled Sales Credit. By using a separate Sales Credit column, we can post the total cash sales for a month as a single amount, the column total. When recording daily cash sales in the Cash Receipts Journal, we place a check mark in the Posting Reference (PR) column to indicate that no amount is individually posted from that line of the journal. Sometimes companies also use a double check ($\sqrt{\sqrt{}}$) to identify amounts that are not posted to customer accounts from amounts that are posted. Although cash sales are usually journalized daily (or at point of sale) in practice, cash sales are journalized weekly in Exhibit 8.10 for brevity.

Cash from Other Sources

Most cash receipts are from collections of accounts receivable and from cash sales. But other sources of cash include borrowing money from a bank, interest on account, or selling unneeded assets. The Other Accounts Credit column is for receipts that do not occur often enough to warrant a separate column. This means items entered in this column are few and are posted to a variety of general ledger accounts. Postings are less apt to be omitted if these items are posted daily. The Cash Receipts Journal's Posting Reference column is used only for daily postings from the Other Accounts and Accounts Receivable columns. The account numbers in the Posting Reference column refer to items that are posted to general ledger accounts. Note that check marks indicate either that an item (like a day's cash sales) is either not posted or is posted to the subsidiary Accounts Receivable Ledger.

---

[2] We include explanations in the Cash Receipts Journal to avoid listing the cash receipt transactions for February.

Cash Receipts Journal
with Posting

Outdoors Unlimited Cash Receipts Journal

Page 2

Date	Accounts Credited	Explanation	PR	Cash Dr.	Sales Discount Dr.	Accounts Receivable Cr.	Sales Cr.	Other Accounts Cr.
Feb. 7	Sales	Cash sales	✓	4,450			4,450	
12	Jason Henry	Invoice, Feb 2	✓	441	9	450		
14	Sales	Cash sales	✓	3,925			3,925	
17	Albert Co.	Invoice, Feb 7	✓	490	10	500		
20	Notes Payable	Note to bank	245	750				750
21	Sales	Cash sales	✓	4,700			4,700	
22	Interest revenue	Bank account	409	250				250
23	Bam Moore	Invoice, Feb 13	✓	343	7	350		
25	Paul Roth	Invoice, Feb15	✓	196	4	200		
28	Sales	Cash sales	✓	4,225			4,225	
28	Totals			19,770	30	1,500	17,300	1,000
				(101)	(415)	(106)	(413)	(✓)

Individual amounts in the other Accounts Credit and Accounts Receivable Credit columns are posted daily.

Column totals, except for Other Accounts column, are posted at the end of the period.

Accounts Receivable Ledger
Frank Booth

Date	PR	Debit	Credit	Balance
Feb. 25	S3	175		175

Jason Henry

Date	PR	Debit	Credit	Balance
Feb. 2	S3	450		450
12	R2		450	-0-
22	S3	225		225

Bam Moore

Date	PR	Debit	Credit	Balance
Feb. 13	S3	350		350
23	R2		350	-0-

Paul Roth

Date	PR	Debit	Credit	Balance
Feb. 15	S3	200		200
25	R2		200	-0-

Albert Co.

Date	PR	Debit	Credit	Balance
Feb. 7	S3	500		500
17	R2		500	-0-
28	S3	250		250

General Ledger
Cash   No. 101

Date	PR	Debit	Credit	Balance
Feb. 28	R2	19,770		19,770

Accounts Receivable   No. 106

Date	PR	Debit	Credit	Balance
Feb. 28	S3	2,150		2,150
28	R2		1,500	650

Notes Payable   No. 245

Date	PR	Debit	Credit	Balance
Feb. 20	R2		750	750

Sales   No. 413

Date	PR	Debit	Credit	Balance
Feb. 28	S3		2,150	2,150
28	R2		17,300	19,450

Sales Discounts   No. 415

Date	PR	Debit	Credit	Balance
Feb. 28	R2	30		30

Interest Revenue   No. 409

Date	PR	Debit	Credit	Balance
Feb. 22	R2		250	250

Note: Cash Receipts Journal in a perpetual system requires a new column on the far right titled "Cost of Goods Sold Dr., Inventory Cr." (see Exhibit 8.18).

Posting

At the end of a period (month), the amounts in the Accounts Receivable, Sales, Sales Discounts, and Cash columns of the Cash Receipts Journal are posted as column totals. The transactions recorded in all journals must result in equal debits and credits to general ledger accounts. To be sure that total debits and credits in a columnar journal are equal, we often crossfoot column totals before posting them. To *foot* a column of numbers is to add it. To *crossfoot* we add the debit column totals and we add the credit column totals. We then compare the two sums for equality. Footing and crossfooting of the numbers in Exhibit 8.11 are as follows:

Exhibit 8.11

Footing and Crossfooting Journal Amounts

Debit Columns		Credit Columns	
Sales discounts debit	$ 30	Other accounts credit	$ 1,000
Cash debit.	19,770	Accounts receivable credit . .	1,500
		Sales credit	17,300
Total	$ 19,800	Total	$ 19,800

After crossfooting the journal to confirm debits equal credits, we post the totals of all but the Other Accounts column as indicated by their column headings. Because individual items in the Other Accounts column are posted daily, this column total is not posted. We place a check mark below the Other Accounts column to indicate that this column total is not posted. The account numbers of the accounts where the remaining column totals are posted are in parentheses below each column. Posting items daily from the Other Accounts column with a delayed posting of the offsetting items in the Cash column (total) causes the General Ledger to be out of balance during the month. But this doesn't matter because posting the Cash column total causes the offsetting amounts to reach the General Ledger before the trial balance or other financial statements are prepared.

You Make the Call

Retailer
You are a retailer in computer equipment and supplies. You want to know how promptly customers are paying their bills. This information can help you in deciding whether to extend credit, and in planning your own cash payments. Where might you look for this information?

Answer—p. 393

Purchases Journal

A **Purchases Journal** is used to record all purchases on credit. Purchases for cash are recorded in the cash disbursements journal.

Journalizing

A Purchases Journal with one column for dollar amounts can be used to record purchases of merchandise on credit. But a Purchases Journal usually is more useful if it is a multicolumn journal where all credit purchases, not only merchandise, are recorded. Exhibit 8.12 shows a multicolumn Purchases Journal.

Purchase invoices or other source documents are used in recording transactions in the Purchases Journal. Journalizing is similar to the Sales Journal. We use the invoice date and terms to compute the date when payment for each purchase is due. The Purchases Debit column is used for recording merchandise purchases. When a purchase involves an amount recorded in the Other Accounts Debit column we use the Account column to identify the general ledger account debited. Outdoors Unlimited also includes a separate column for credit purchases of office supplies. A separate column such as this is useful whenever several transactions involve debits

Outdoors Unlimited Purchases Journal

Page 1

Date	Account	Date of Invoice	Terms	PR	Accounts Payable Cr.	Purchases Dr.	Office Supplies Dr.	Other Accounts Dr.
Feb. 3	Horning Supply Co.	Feb. 2	n/30	✓	350	275	75	
5	Ace Mfg. Co.	5	2/10, n/30	✓	200	200		
13	Wynet & Co.	10	2/10, n/30	✓	150	150		
20	Smite Co.	18	2/10, n/30	✓	300	300		
25	Ace Mfg. Co.	24	2/10, n/30	✓	100	100		
28	Store Supplies/ITT Co.	28	n/30	125✓	225	125	25	75
28	Totals				1,325	1,150	100	75
					(201)	(505)	(124)	(✓)

Individual amounts in the Other Accounts Debit and Accounts Payable Credit columns are posted daily.

Column totals, except for Other Accounts column, are posted at the end of the period.

Accounts Payable Ledger
Ace Mfg. Company

Date	PR	Debit	Credit	Balance
Feb. 5	P1		200	200
25	P1		100	300

ITT Company

Date	PR	Debit	Credit	Balance
Feb. 28	P1		225	225

Hornung Supply Company

Date	PR	Debit	Credit	Balance
Feb. 3	P1		350	350

Smite Company

Date	PR	Debit	Credit	Balance
Feb. 20	P1		300	300

Wynet and Company

Date	PR	Debit	Credit	Balance
Feb. 13	P1		150	150

General Legder
Office Supplies No. 124

Date	PR	Debit	Credit	Balance
Feb. 28	P1	100		100

Store Supplies No. 125

Date	PR	Debit	Credit	Balance
Feb. 28	P1	75		75

Accounts Payable No. 201

Date	PR	Debit	Credit	Balance
Feb. 28	P1		1,325	1,325

Purchases No. 505

Date	PR	Debit	Credit	Balance
Feb. 28	P1	1,150		1,150

Note: Purchases Journal in a perpetual system replaces "Purchases Dr." with "Inventory Dr." (see Exhibit 8.19).

Exhibit 8.12

Schedule of Accounts Payable

to a specific account. Each company uses its own judgment in deciding on the number of separate columns necessary. The Other Accounts Debit column allows the Purchases Journal to be used for all purchase transactions involving credits to Accounts Payable. The Accounts Payable Credit column is used to record the amounts credited to each creditor's account.

Posting

The amounts in the Accounts Payable Credit column are posted regularly (daily) to individual creditor accounts in a subsidiary Accounts Payable Ledger. Each line of the Account column in Exhibit 8.12 shows the subsidiary ledger account that is posted for these amounts in the Accounts Payable Credit column. Individual amounts in the Other Accounts Debit column usually are posted daily to their general ledger accounts. At the end of the month, all column totals except the Other Accounts Debit column are posted to their general ledger accounts. The balance in the Accounts Payable controlling account must equal the sum of the account balances in the subsidiary Accounts Payable Ledger after posting.

Testing the Ledger

Account balances in the General Ledger and subsidiary ledgers are tested for accuracy after posting of the Purchases Journal is complete. Similar to the procedures followed for testing the ledger for the Sales Journal we perform two steps. First, we prepare a trial balance of the General Ledger to confirm debits equal credits. If debits equal credits in the trial balance, the accounts in the General Ledger, including the controlling accounts, are assumed to be correct. Second, we test the subsidiary ledgers by preparing a schedule of accounts payable. A **schedule of accounts payable** is a listing of accounts from the Accounts Payable Ledger with their balances and the sum of all balances. If this total equals the balance of the Accounts Payable controlling account, the accounts in the Accounts Payable Ledger are assumed correct.

Cash Disbursements Journal

A **Cash Disbursements Journal**, also called a *Cash Payments Journal*, is used to record all payments of cash. It is a multicolumn journal because cash payments are made for several different purposes.

Journalizing

A Cash Disbursements Journal is similar to a Cash Receipts Journal except with repetitive cash payments instead of receipts. Exhibit 8.13 shows the Cash Disbursements Journal for Outdoors Unlimited. We see repetitive credits to the Cash column of this journal. We also commonly see credits to Purchases Discounts and debits to the Accounts Payable account. Many companies purchase merchandise on credit and, therefore, a Purchases column is not often needed. Instead, the occasional cash purchase is recorded in the Other Accounts Debit column and Cash Credit column as shown on line 2 of Exhibit 8.13.

The Cash Disbursements Journal has a column titled Cheque Number (Ch. No.). For control over cash disbursements, all payments except for very small amounts are made by cheque.[3] Cheques should be prenumbered and entered in the journal in numerical order with each cheque's number in the column headed Ch. No. This makes it possible to scan the numbers in the column for omitted cheques. When a Cash Disbursements Journal has a column for cheque numbers, it is sometimes called a **Cheque Register**.

You Make the Call

Controller
You are a controller for a merchandising company. You want to analyze your company's cash payments to suppliers, including an analysis of purchases discounts. Where might you look for this information?

Answer—p. 393

---

[3] We describe a system for controlling small cash payments in Chapter 9.

Exhibit 8.13

Cash Disbursements Journal with Posting

Outdoors Unlimited Cash Disbursements Journal

Page 2

Date	Ch. No.	Payee	Account Debited	PR	Cash Cr.	Purchases Discounts Cr.	Other Accounts Dr.	Accounts Payable Dr.
Feb. 3	105	L & N Railroad	Transportation-In	508	15		15	
12	106	East Sales Co.	Purchases	505	25		25	
15	107	Ace Mfg. Co.	Ace Mfg. Co.	✓	196	4		200
15	108	Jerry Hale	Salaries Expense	622	250		250	
20	109	Wynet & Co.	Wynet & Co.	✓	147	3		150
28	110	Smite Co.	Smite Co.	✓	294	6		300
28		Totals			927	13	290	650
					(101)	(507)	(✓)	(201)

Column totals, except for Other Accounts column, are posted at the end of the period.

Individual amounts in the Other Accounts column and Accounts Payable column are posted daily.

General Ledger

Cash   No. 101

Date	PR	Debit	Credit	Balance
Feb. 28	R2	19,770		19,770
28	D2		927	18,843

Accounts Payable   No. 201

Date	PR	Debit	Credit	Balance
Feb. 28	P1		1,325	1,325
28	D2	650		675

Purchases   No. 505

Date	PR	Debit	Credit	Balance
Feb. 12	D2	25		25
28	P1	1,150		1,175

Purchases Discounts   No. 507

Date	PR	Debit	Credit	Balance
Feb. 28	D2		13	13

Transportation-In   No. 508

Date	PR	Debit	Credit	Balance
Feb. 3	D2	15		15

Salaries Expense   No. 622

Date	PR	Debit	Credit	Balance
Feb. 15	D2	250		250

Accounts Payable Ledger

Ace Mfg. Company

Date	PR	Debit	Credit	Balance
Feb. 5	P1		200	200
15	D2	200		-0-
25	P1		100	100

ITT Company

Date	PR	Debit	Credit	Balance
Feb. 28	P1		225	225

Hornung Supply Company

Date	PR	Debit	Credit	Balance
Feb. 3	P1		350	350

Smite Company

Date	PR	Debit	Credit	Balance
Feb. 20	P1		300	300
28	D2	300		-0-

Wynet & Company

Date	PR	Debit	Credit	Balance
Feb. 13	P1		150	150
20	D2	150		-0-

Note: Cash Disbursements Journal in a perpetual system replaces "Purchases Discounts Cr." with "Inventory Cr." (see Exhibit 8A.4).

Posting

Individual amounts in the Other Accounts Debit column of a Cash Disbursements Journal are usually posted to their general ledger accounts on a regular (daily) basis. Individual amounts in the Accounts Payable Debit column are also posted regularly (daily) to the specific creditors' accounts in the subsidiary Accounts Payable Ledger. At the end of the period (month), we crossfoot column totals and post the Accounts Payable Debit column total to the Accounts Payable controlling account. Also at the end of the period the Purchases Discounts Credit column total is posted to the Purchases Discounts account and the Cash Credit column total is posted to the Cash account. The Other Accounts column total is not posted at the end of the period.

Exhibit 8.14 shows a schedule of accounts payable drawn from the Accounts Payable Ledger of Exhibit 8.13.

Exhibit 8.14

Schedule of Accounts Payable

OUTDOORS UNLIMITED
Schedule of Accounts Payable
February 28, 1998

Ace Mfg. Company	$ 100
ITT Company	225
Hornung Supply Company	350
Total accounts payable	$ 675

Flash back

8. What is the normal recording and posting procedure when using special journals and controlling accounts with subsidiary ledgers?

9. What is the rule for posting to a subsidiary ledger and its controlling account?

10. How do we test the accuracy of account balances in the General Ledger and subsidiary ledgers after posting?

Answers—p. 394

General Journal Transactions

When special journals are used we still need a General Journal for adjusting, closing and correcting entries, and for special transactions not recorded in special journals. These special transactions include purchases returns and allowances, purchases of plant assets by issuing a note payable, sales returns if a Sales Returns and Allowances Journal is not used, and receiving a note receivable from a customer. We described transactions recorded in a General Journal in Chapter 3.

Flash back

11. How are sales taxes recorded in the context of special journals?

12. What is direct posting of sales invoices?

13. Why does a company need a General Journal when using special journals for sales, purchases, cash receipts, and cash disbursements?

Answers—p. 394

Technology-Based Accounting Information Systems

Accounting information systems are supported with technology. This technology can range from simple calculators to state-of-the-art advanced electronic systems. Because technology is increasingly important in accounting information systems we discuss in this section the impact of computer technology, how data processing works with accounting data, and the role of computer networks.

Middleware

The latest buzz in information systems is about "middleware." Middleware is software allowing different computer programs used in a company or across companies to work together. It allows transfer of purchase orders, invoices and other electronic documents between trading partners' accounting systems. It also helps each partner's bank handle the electronic payments. [Source: *Marketing News*, January 1998.]

Did You Know?

Computer Technology in Accounting

Computer technology can broadly be separated into hardware and software support. **Computer hardware** is the physical equipment in a computerized accounting information system. The physical equipment includes processing units, hard drives, RAM, modems, CD-ROM drives, speakers, monitors, workstations, servers, notebooks, printers, scanners, and jukeboxes. Computer hardware is increasingly assisting accounting and accounting-related professionals in their work. Computer hardware often provides more accuracy, speed, efficiency, and convenience in performing accounting tasks.

LO 6 Explain how technology-based information systems impact accounting.

Computer software is the programs that direct the operations of computer hardware. A program is a series of commands directing operations such as data access from input or storage, data processing, or data output. A program can be written, for instance, to process customer orders of merchandise. A typical program works as follows. It creates a shipping order identifying products to be sent to customers. If this shipment causes the quantity on hand to fall below some minimum level, the program creates a purchase order to be approved by a manager. If the quantity on hand is less than what a customer ordered, the program creates a partial shipping order and a report to the customer that the remainder is on back order. If replacements are not on order already, the program creates a purchase order. If no units of the ordered product are on hand, the program creates a notification for the customer of a back order and creates a purchase order if necessary. The program continually processes customer orders as they arrive. This program can also be linked with accounting records for sales and accounts receivable, and it can deal with cash and trade discounts that might be offered to customers.

Widespread use of computer technology has increased the type and power of off-the-shelf programs that are ready to use. **Off-the-shelf programs** are multipurpose software applications for a variety of computer operations. These include familiar word processing programs such as *Word®* and *WordPerfect®*, spreadsheet programs such as *Excel®* and *Lotus 1-2-3®*, and database management programs such as *dBase®*. Other off-the-shelf programs meet the needs of specialized users. These include accounting programs such as *ACCPAC Plus®*, and *Simply Accounting®*. Off-the-shelf programs are designed to be user-friendly and guide users through all steps.

Software Accountants

A new generation of Windows-based accounting software is available. With the touch of a key, users can shift from cash to accrual accounting, and create "real-time" inventory reports showing all payments, charges, and credit limits at any point in the accounting cycle. Many also include "alert signals" notifying the user, say, when a large order might exceed a customer's credit limit or when purchase orders are needed. They also support all four inventory costing methods and do perpetual updating of records as each transaction occurs. Peachtree Software is the market leader for small businesses, and most programs cost under $250, with some as low as $50. [Source: *Canadian Business*, September 1997.]

Did You Know?

Off-the-shelf accounting programs can operate more efficiently as *integrated* systems. In an integrated system, actions taken in one part of the system automatically affect related parts. When a credit sale is recorded in an integrated system, for instance, several parts of the system are automatically updated. First, the system stores transaction data (as in a journal) so that we can review the entire entry at a later time. Second, it automatically updates the Cash and Accounts Receivable accounts. Third, it updates the record of amounts owed by a customer. Fourth, it updates the record of products held for sale to show the number of units sold and the number remaining.

Computer hardware and software can dramatically reduce the time and effort devoted to recordkeeping tasks. Less directed effort at recordkeeping tasks enables accounting professionals to take on more analysis and managerial type decision making. These advances have created an even greater demand for accounting professionals who understand financial reports and can draw insights and information from mountains of processed data. We must remember the primary demand for accounting knowledge is created by the need for information and not by the need for recordkeeping. Accounting professionals are in increasing demand because of expertise in determining relevant and reliable information for decision making. They are also valuable in analyzing the effects of transactions and events on a company and how they are reflected in financial statements and management reports.

Knowledge of the accounting described in this book enables us to understand and use accounting output. It also enables us to understand the transactions and events driving the output. In this way, and in this way only, can we expect to reap the full benefits of accounting reports. All the reports available can't help the external or internal user who fails to understand the accounting principles and methods determining the information.

Data Processing in Accounting

Accounting systems differ in how input is entered and processed. **On-line processing** enters and processes data as soon as source documents are available. This means databases are immediately updated. **Batch processing** accumulates source documents for a period of time and then processes them all at once such as once a day, week, or month.

The advantage of on-line processing is up-to-date databases. This often requires additional costs related to both software and hardware requirements. Common on-line processing in practice includes airline reservations, credit card records, and rapid mail-order processing. The advantage of batch processing is it only requires periodic updating of databases. Records used in sending bills to customers, for instance, might require updating only once a month. The disadvantage of batch processing is when updated databases could be helpful to management when making business decisions.

Computer Networks in Accounting

Networking or linking computers with each other can create technology advances. **Computer networks** are links among computers giving different users and different computers access to a common database and programs. Many colleges' computer labs, for instance, are networked. A small computer network is called a *local area network (LAN)*. This type of network links machines with *hard-wire* hookups. Large computer networks extending over long distances often rely on *modem* communication.

Demand for information sometimes requires advanced networks. The system used by **Federal Express** for tracking packages and billing customers, and the

Bombardier's Segment Contribution Matrix for Sales					
	Sales Contribution ($mil.)		Sales Contribution (in %)		1-Year Growth Rate (%)
Segment	**1997**	**1996**	**1997**	**1996**	
Industry:					
Transportation	$1,597	$1,575	20	22	1
Motorized Consumer Products	1,866	1,554	23	22	20
Aerospace	3,985	3,508	50	49	14
Services	367	346	5	5	6
Bombardier Capital	161	140	2	2	15
Total Revenues	$7,976	$7,123	100	100	
Geographic Segments:					
Canada	$5,387	$4,504	68	63	20
United States & Mexico	949	840	12	12	13
Europe	1,640	1,779	20	25	−8
Total	$7,976	$7,123	100	100	

Exhibit 8.16

Segment Contribution Matrix

The second and third columns lists 1997 and 1996 sales data by segment. This data is drawn from Note 22 in Bombardier's 1997 annual report. We see Bombardier's total 1997 sales is $7,976 million and is divided into four product segments and three geographic segments. Yet several questions remain unanswered. What is the contribution of one segment versus another to total sales? Is there evidence of growth or decline by source? What is the highest growth segment? And which is the lowest? A segment contribution matrix provides us a starting point in answering such crucial questions.

Columns four and five of Exhibit 8.16 give us Bombardier's sales contribution in percent by segment. This number is computed by taking a segment's sales and dividing by total sales. For example, the 1997 sales contribution in percent for the Transportation segment is computed as: $1,597 ÷ $7,976 = 0.20 or 20%. These results tell us transportation equipment makes up 20% of total sales.

The far right column shows the one-year growth rate in segment sales. A one-year growth rate is computed as: [current period sales − prior period sales] ÷ prior period sales. For example, Bombardier's sales in its Transportation segment for 1996 was $1,575. This means the one-year growth rate in sales for its Transportation segment is computed as: [$1,597 − $1,575] ÷ $1,575 = 0.01 or 1%. These growth rates reveal several interesting findings. First, the Motorized Consumer Products segment is growing faster than any other segment. Second, Europe had a marked decline in sales. Third, Canada had a 20% increase in sales. We can also extend our analysis to segment contribution matrixes for other measures such as operating income and assets. We show pie charts of Bombardier's assets breakdown in Exhibit 8.17 as an example of other analyses available to us.

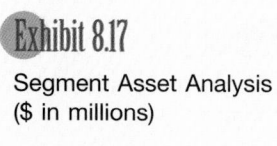

Exhibit 8.17

Segment Asset Analysis
($ in millions)

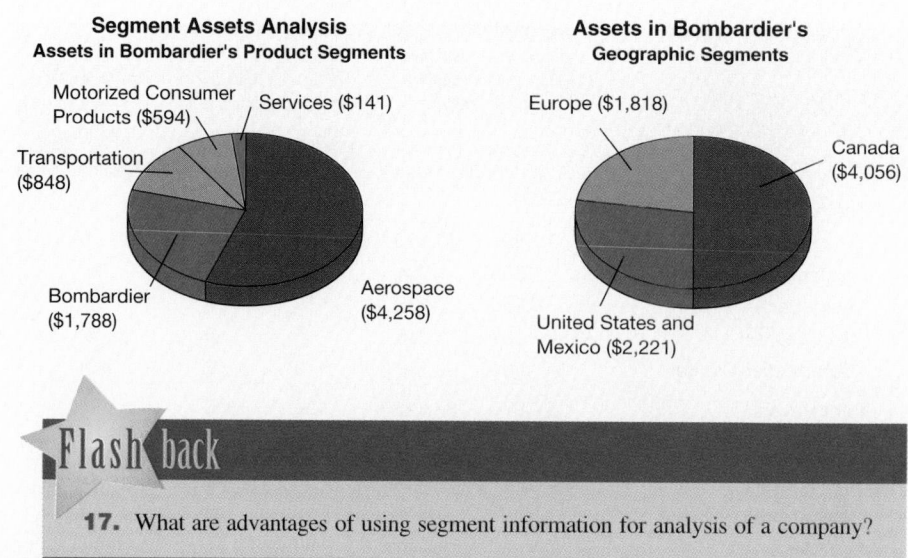

Segment Assets Analysis
Assets in Bombardier's Product Segments

Motorized Consumer Products ($594)   Services ($141)

Transportation ($848)

Bombardier ($1,788)

Aerospace ($4,258)

Assets in Bombardier's
Geographic Segments

Europe ($1,818)

Canada ($4,056)

United States and Mexico ($2,221)

Flash back

Answers—p. 394

17. What are advantages of using segment information for analysis of a company?

You Make the Call

Banker
You are the banker when an owner of a merchandising business in bicycles requests a loan to expand operations. This merchandiser shows you his financials. They reveal a solid net income of $220,000, reflecting a 10% increase over the prior year. You also ask about any segments or geographical focus. The owner tells you that $160,000 of net income is from Cuban sales, reflecting a 60% increase over the prior year, and Canadian net income was $60,000, reflecting a 40% decrease in sales. The owner is a Cuban immigrant and he tells of his relationships with family and friends in Cuba. Does this segment information impact your loan decision?

Answer—p. 393

Summary

LO 1 Identify fundamental principles of accounting information systems. Accounting information systems are guided by five fundamental principles in carrying out their tasks: control, relevance, compatibility, flexibility, and cost-benefit principles.

LO 2 Identify components of accounting information systems. There are five basic components of an accounting information system: source documents, input devices, information processors, information storage, and output devices.

LO 3 Explain the goals and uses of special journals. Special journals are used for recording and posting transactions of similar type, each meant to cover one kind of transaction. Four of the most common special journals are the Sales Journal, Cash Receipts Journal, Purchases Journal, and Cash Disbursements Journal. Special journals

are efficient and cost effective tools in helping journalize and post transactions. Special journals also allow an efficient division of labour that is also an effective control procedure.

LO 4 Describe the use of controlling accounts and subsidiary ledgers. A General Ledger keeps controlling accounts such as Accounts Receivable or Accounts Payable, but details on individual accounts making up the controlling account are kept in a subsidiary ledger (such as an Accounts Receivable Ledger). The balance in a controlling account must equal the sum of its subsidiary account balances after posting is complete.

LO 5 Journalize and post transactions using special journals. Special journals are devoted to similar kinds of transactions. Transactions are journalized on one line of a special journal, with columns devoted to specific accounts, dates, names, posting references, explanations and other necessary information. Posting is threefold: (1) individual amounts in the Other Accounts column are posted to their general ledger accounts on a regular (daily) basis, (2) individual amounts in a column that is posted in total to a controlling account at the end of a period (month) are posted regularly (daily) to its account in the subsidiary ledger, and (3) total amounts for all columns except the Other Accounts column are posted at the end of a period (month) to their column's account title.

LO 6   Prepare and test the accuracy of subsidiary ledgers. Account balances in the General Ledger and its subsidiary ledgers are tested for accuracy after posting is complete. This procedure is twofold: (1) prepare a trial balance of the General Ledger to confirm debits equal credits, and (2) prepare a schedule of a subsidiary ledger to confirm the controlling account's balance equals the subsidiary ledger's balance. A schedule is a listing of accounts from a ledger with their balances and the sum of all balances.

LO 7   Explain how technology-based information systems impact accounting. Technology-based information systems aim to increase the accuracy, speed, efficiency and convenience of accounting procedures. Developments in hardware and software, data processing, and networking all impact accounting in varying degrees.

LO 8   Analyze a company's performance and financial condition by business segments. A business segment is a part of a company that is separately identified by its products or services or by the geographic market it serves. Analysis of a company's segments is aided by a segment contribution matrix listing of one or more accounting measures such as sales by segments. This listing usually includes amounts contributed both in dollars and percents, and its growth rate.

Guidance Answers to **You Make the Call**

Retailer

The Accounts Receivable Ledger has much of the information you need. It lists detailed information for each customer's account, including the amounts, dates for transactions, and dates of payments. It can be reorganized into an "aging schedule" to show how long customers wait in paying their bills. We describe an aging schedule in Chapter 10.

Controller

Much of the information you need is in the Accounts Payable Ledger. It contains information for each supplier, the amounts due, and when payments are made. This ledger along with information on credit terms should enable you to conduct your analyses.

Banker

This merchandiser's segment information is likely to greatly impact your loan decision. The risks associated with this merchandiser's two sources of net income are quite different. While net income is up by 10%, Canadian operations are performing poorly and Cuban operations are subject to many uncertainties. These uncertainties depend on political events, friends and family relationships, Cuban economic conditions, and a host of other risks. While net income figures suggested a low-risk loan opportunity, the segment information reveals a high-risk potential.

Guidance Answer to **Judgment and Ethics**

Public Accountant

As a professional accountant you are guided by the Professional Codes of Conduct described in Chapter 1. You should recognize the main issue: whether commissions have an actual or perceived impact on the integrity and objectivity of your advice. The code says you should not accept a commission if you either perform an audit or review of the client's financial statements or if you review prospective financial information for the client. The code also precludes a commission if you compile the client's statements, unless the compilation report discloses a lack of independence. Even in situations where a commission is allowed, the code requires you tell the client of your commission arrangement. These suggested actions seem appropriate even if you are not bound by the code. Also, you need to seriously examine the merits of agreeing to a commission arrangement when you are in a position to exploit it.

Guidance Answers to Flashbacks

1. The five primary components are source documents, input devices, information processors, information storage, and output devices.

2. Information processor interprets, transforms, and summarizes the recorded information so that it can be used in analysis and reports.

3. Data saved in data storage are used to prepare periodic financial reports, special-purpose internal reports, and as source documentation for auditors and other users.

4. All cash payments by cheque are recorded in the Cash Disbursements Journal.

5. Columnar journals allow us to accumulate repetitive debits and credits and post them as column totals rather than as individual amounts.

6. The equality of debits and credits is kept within the General Ledger. The subsidiary ledger keeps the customer's individual account and is used only for supplementary information.

7. An initial and page number of the journal from where the amount was posted is entered in the Posting Reference column of the ledger account next to the amount.

8. The normal recording and posting procedures are threefold. First, transactions are entered in a special journal column if applicable. Second, individual amounts are posted to the subsidiary ledger accounts. Third, column totals are posted to general ledger accounts.

9. The controlling account must be debited periodically for an amount or amounts equal to the sum of the debits to the subsidiary ledger, and it must be credited periodically for an amount or amounts equal to the sum of the credits to the subsidiary ledger.

10. Tests for accuracy of account balances in the General Ledger and subsidiary ledgers are twofold. First, we prepare a trial balance of the General Ledger to confirm debits equal credits. Second, we test the subsidiary ledgers by preparing schedules of accounts receivable and accounts payable.

11. A separate column for Sales Taxes Payable is included in both the Cash Receipts Journal and the Sales Journal.

12. This refers to a procedure of using copies of sales invoices as a Sales Journal. Each invoice total is posted directly to the customer's account, and all invoices are totalled at month-end for posting to the General Ledger accounts.

13. The General Journal is still needed for adjusting, closing and correcting entries, and for special transactions such as sales returns, purchases returns, and plant asset purchases.

14. Integrated systems can save time and minimize errors. This is because actions taken in one part of the system automatically affect and update related parts.

15. Computer systems offer increased accuracy, speed, efficiency, and convenience.

16. Computer networks can create advantages by linking computers, giving different users and different computers access to a common database and programs.

17. Segment information helps us evaluate the risk and return attributes of a company. Companies operating in different business segments often have different rates of profitability, risk, and growth for these segments. This information helps us gain insight into the performance of segments and its importance for a company's future.

Demonstration Problem

The Pepper Company completed these transactions during March of the current year:

Mar. 4 Sold merchandise on credit to Jennifer Nelson, Invoice No. 954, $16,800. (Terms of all credit sales are 2/10, n/30.)

6 Purchased office supplies on credit from Mack Company, $1,220. Invoice dated March 3, terms n/30.

6 Sold merchandise on credit to Dennie Hoskins, Invoice No. 955, $10,200.

11 Received merchandise and an invoice dated March 11, terms 2/10, n/30, from Defore Industries, $52,600.

12 Borrowed $26,000 by giving Commerce Bank a long-term promissory note payable.

14 Received payment from Jennifer Nelson for the March 4 sale less the discount.

16 Received a credit memorandum from Defore Industries for unsatisfactory merchandise received on March 11 and returned for credit, $200.

16 Received payment from Dennie Hoskins for the March 6 sale less the discount.

18 Purchased store equipment on credit from Schmidt Supply, invoice dated March 15, terms n/30, $22,850.

20 Sold merchandise on credit to Marjorie Allen, Invoice No. 956, $5,600.

21 Sent Defore Industries Cheque No. 516 in payment of its March 11 invoice less the discount.

22   Received merchandise and an invoice dated March 18, terms 2/10, n/30, from the Welch Company, $41,625

26   Issued a credit memorandum to Marjorie Allen for defective merchandise sold on March 22 and returned for credit $600.

31   Issued Cheque No. 517, payable to Payroll, in payment of sales salaries for the month, $15,900. Cashed the cheque and paid the employees.

31   Cash sales for the month were $134,680. (Normally, cash sales are recorded daily; however, they are recorded only once in this problem to reduce the repetitive entries.)

31   Post to the customer and creditor accounts and post any amounts that should be posted as individual amounts to the general ledger accounts.

31   Foot and crossfoot the journals and make the month-end postings.

Required

1. Open the following general ledger accounts: Cash (101), Accounts Receivable (106), Office Supplies (124), Store Equipment (165), Accounts Payable (201), Long-Term Notes Payable (251), Sales (413), Sales Returns and Allowances (414), Sales Discounts (415), Purchases (505), Purchases Returns and Allowances (506), Purchase Discounts (507) and Sales Salaries Expense (621).

2. Open the following accounts receivable ledger accounts: Marjorie Allen, Dennie Hoskins, and Jennifer Nelson.

3. Open the following accounts payable ledger accounts: Defore Industries, Mack Company, Schmidt Supply, and Welch Company.

4. Enter the transactions in a Sales Journal, a Purchases Journal, a Cash Receipts Journal, a Cash Disbursements Journal, and a General Journal similar to the ones illustrated in the chapter. Post at the end of the month.

5. Prepare a trial balance and test the accuracy of the subsidiary ledgers by preparing schedules of accounts receivable and payable.

Planning the Solution

■ Set up the required general ledger and subsidiary ledger accounts and the five required journals as illustrated in the chapter

■ First read and analyze each transaction and decide in which special journal (or general journal) the transaction would be recorded.

■ Now record each transaction in the proper journal.

■ Once you have recorded all the transactions total the journal columns.

■ Now post from each journal to the appropriate ledger accounts.

■ After you have completed posting prepare a trial balance to prove the equality of the debit and credit balances in your general ledger.

■ Finally, prepare a schedule of accounts receivable and accounts payable. Compare the total of the schedules to the accounts receivable and accounts payable control account balances making sure that they agree.

Solution to Demonstration Problem

Sales Journal				Page 2
Date	Account Debited	Invoice Number	PR	A/R Dr. Sales Cr.
Mar. 4	Jennifer Nelson.	954	✓	16,800
6	Dennie Hoskins.	955	✓	10,200
20	Marjorie Allen	956	✓	5,600
31	Totals			32,600
				(106/413)

Purchases Journal — Page 3

Date		Account	Date of Invoice	Terms	PR	Accounts Payable Credit	Purchases Debit	Office Supplies Debit	Other Accounts Debit
Mar.	6	Office Supplies/ Mack Co.	Mar 3	n/30	✓	1,220		1,220	
	11	Defore Industries	Mar 11	2/10, n/30	✓	52,600	52,600		
	18	Store Equipment/ Schmidt Supp.	Mar 15	n/30	165/✓	22,850			22,850
	22	Welch Company	Mar 18	2/10, n/30	✓	41,625	41,625		
	30	Totals				118,295	94,225	1,220	22,850
						(201)	(505)	(124)	(✓)

Cash Receipts Journal — Page 3

Date		Account Credited	Explanation	PR	Cash Debit	Sales Discount Debit	Accounts Receivable Credit	Sales Credit	Other Accounts Credit
Mar.	12	L.T. Notes Pay	Note to bank	251	26,000				26,000
	14	Jennifer Nelson	Invoice, Mar 4	✓	16,464	336	16,800		
	16	Dennie Hoskins	Invoice, Mar 6	✓	9,996	204	10,200		
	31	Sales	Cash sales	✓	134,680			134,680	
	30	Totals			187,140	540	27,000	134,680	26,000
					(101)	(415)	(106)	(413)	(✓)

Cash Disbursements Journal — Page 4

Date		Ch. No.	Payee	Account Debited	PR	Cash Credit	Pur. Disc. Credit	Other Accounts Debit	Accounts Payable Debit
Mar.	21	516	Defore Industries	Defore Industries	✓	51,352	1,048		52,400
	31	517	Payroll	Sales Salaries Expense	621	15,900		15,900	
	30		Totals			67,252	1,048	15,900	52,400
						(101)	(507)	(✓)	(201)

General Journal — Page 2

Mar. 16	Accounts Payable—Defore Industries	201/✓	200	
	Purchases Returns and Allowances	506		200
26	Sales Returns and Allowances	414	600	
	Accounts Receivable—Marjorie Allen .	106/✓		600

Accounts Receivable Ledger

Marjorie Allen

Date	Explanation	PR	Debit	Credit	Balance
Mar. 20		S2	5,600		5,600
26		G2		600	5,000

Dennie Hoskins

Date	Explanation	PR	Debit	Credit	Balance
Mar. 6		S2	10,200		10,200
16		R3		10,200	-0-

Jennifer Nelson

Date	Explanation	PR	Debit	Credit	Balance
Mar. 4		S2	16,800		16,800
14		R3		16,800	-0-

Accounts Payable Ledger

Defore Industries

Date	Explanation	PR	Debit	Credit	Balance
Mar. 11		P3		52,600	52,600
Mar. 16		G2	200		52,400
Mar. 21		D4	52,400		-0-

Mack Company

Date	Explanation	PR	Debit	Credit	Balance
Mar. 6		P3		1,220	1,220

Schmidt Supply

Mar. 18		P3		22,850	22,850

Welch Company

Mar. 22		P3		41,625	41,625

General Ledger

Cash — Acct. No. 101

Date	Explanation	PR	Debit	Credit	Balance
Mar. 31		R3	187,140		187,140
31		D4		67,252	119,888

Accounts Receivable — Acct. No. 106

Date	Explanation	PR	Debit	Credit	Balance
Mar. 26		G2		600	(600)
31		S2	32,600		32,000
31		R3		27,000	5,000

Office Supplies — Acct. No. 124

Mar. 31		P3	1,220		1,220

Store Equipment — Acct. No. 165

Mar. 18		P3	22,850		22,850

Accounts Payable — Acct. No. 201

Mar. 6		G2	200		(200)
31		P2		118,295	118,095
31		D4	52,400		65,695

Long-Term Notes Payable — Acct. No. 251

Mar. 12				26,000	26,000

Sales — Acct. No. 413

Mar. 31		S2		32,600	32,600
31		R3		134,680	167,280

Sales Returns and Allowances — Acct. No. 414

Mar. 26		G2	600		600

Sales Discounts — Acct. No. 415

Mar. 31		R3	540		540

Purchases — Acct. No. 505

Mar. 31		P2	94,225		94,225

Purchases Returns and Allowances — Acct. No. 506

Mar. 6		G2		200	200

Purchases Discounts — Acct. No. 507

Mar. 31		D4		1,048	1,048

Sales Salaries Expense — Acct. No. 621

Mar. 31		D4	15,900		15,900

PEPPER COMPANY
Trial Balance
March 31, 19XX

Cash	$119,888	
Accounts receivable	5,000	
Office supplies	1,220	
Store equipment	22,850	
Accounts payable		$ 65,695
Long-term notes payable		26,000
Sales		167,280
Sales returns and allowances	600	
Sales discounts	540	
Purchases	94,225	
Purchases returns and allowances		200
Purchases discounts		1,048
Sales salaries expense	15,900	
Totals	$260,223	$260,223

PEPPER COMPANY
Schedule of Accounts Receivable
March 31, 19XX

Marjorie Allen	$5,000
Total accounts receivable	$5,000

PEPPER COMPANY
Schedule of Accounts Payable
March 31, 19XX

Mack Company	$ 1,220
Schmidt Supply	22,850
Welch Company	41,625
Total accounts payable	$65,695

Special Journals under a Perpetual System

This appendix shows the special journals under a perpetual inventory system. Each journal is slightly impacted. The Sales Journal and the Cash Receipts Journal each require one new column titled *Cost of Goods Sold Dr., Inventory Cr.* The Purchases Journal replaces the "Purchases Dr." column with an *Inventory Dr.* column in a perpetual system. The Cash Disbursements Journal replaces the "Purchases Discounts Cr." column with an *Inventory Cr.* column in a perpetual system. These changes are illustrated below.

Learning Objective

LO 9 Apply journalizing and posting of transactions using special journals in a perpetual inventory system.

Sales Journal

The Sales Journal for **Outdoors Unlimited** using the perpetual inventory system is show in Exhibit 8A.1. The difference in the Sales Journal between the perpetual and periodic system is the addition of a new column to record cost of goods sold and inventory amounts for each sale. The periodic system does not record the increase in cost of goods sold and decrease in inventory at the time of sale. The total of the cost of goods sold and inventory amount column is posted to both of their General Ledger accounts at the end of the period (month).

Outdoors Unlimited Sales Journal					Page 3
Date	Account Debited	Invoice Number	PR	Accounts Receivable Dr. Sales Cr.	Cost of Goods Sold Dr. Inventory Cr.
Feb. 2	Jason Henry	307	✓	450	315
7	Albert Co.	308	✓	500	355
13	Bam Moore	309	✓	350	260
15	Paul Roth	310	✓	200	150
22	Jason Henry	311	✓	225	155
25	Frank Booth	312	✓	175	95
28	Albert Co.	313	✓	250	170
28	Total			2,150	1,500
				(106/413)	(502/119)

Exhibit 8A.1

Sales Journal—Perpetual System

Cash Receipts Journal

The Cash Receipts Journal under the perpetual system is shown in Exhibit 8A.2. Note the addition of a new column on the far right side to record debits to Cost of Goods Sold and credits to Inventory for the cost of merchandise sold.

Consistent with the Cash Receipts Journal shown under the periodic system in the chapter, we only show the weekly cash sale entries. But remember that under a perpetual system these cash sales are recorded at the point of sale. To do that here would make this journal extremely lengthy since Outdoors Unlimited is a retailer with many cash sales every day. Note also that cash received from earlier credit sales does not result in amounts entered in the far right column. This is because the costs for these sales were recorded in the Sales Journal at the point of sale. The total of the cost of goods sold and inventory amount column is posted to both of their General Ledger accounts at the end of the period (month).

Exhibit 8A.2

Cash Receipts Journal—
Perpetual System

									Cost of
					Sales	Accounts		Other	Goods
	Account			Cash	Discount	Receivable	Sales	Accounts	Sold Dr.
Date	Credited	Explanation	PR	Dr.	Cr.	Cr.	Cr.	Cr.	Inventory Cr.
Feb. 7	Sales	Cash sales	✓	4,450			4,450		3,150
12	Jason Henry	Invoice, Feb. 2	✓	441	9	450			
14	Sales	Cash sales	✓	3,925			3,925		2,950
17	Albert Co.	Invoice, Feb. 7	✓	490	10	500			
20	Notes Payable	Note to bank	245	750				750	
21	Sales	Cash sales	✓	4,700			4,700		3,400
22	Interest revenue	Bank account	409	250				250	
23	Bam Moore	Invoice, Feb. 13	✓	343	7	350			
25	Paul Roth	Invoice, Feb. 15	✓	196	4	200			
28	Sales	Cash sales	✓	4,225			4,225		3,050
28	Totals			19,770	30	1,500	17,300	1,000	12,550
				(101)	(415)	(106)	(413)	(✓)	(502/119)

Outdoors Unlimited Cash Receipts Journal   *Page 2*

Purchases Journal

The Purchases Journal under the perpetual system is shown in Exhibit 8A.3. This journal in a perpetual system includes the Inventory column where the periodic system had the Purchases column. All else is identical under the two systems.

Exhibit 8A.3

Purchases Journal—
Perpetual System

					Accounts		Office	Other
		Date of			Payable	Inventory	Supplies	Accounts
Date	Account	Invoice	Terms	PR	Cr.	Dr.	Dr.	Dr.
Feb. 3	Homung Supply Co.	Feb. 2	n/30	✓	350	275	75	
5	Ace Mfg. Co.	Feb. 5	2/10, n/30	✓	200	200		
13	Wynet and Co.	Feb. 10	2/10, n/30	✓	150	150		
20	Smite Co.	Feb. 18	2/10, n/30	✓	300	300		
25	Ace Mfg. Co.	Feb. 24	2/10, n/30	✓	100	100		
28	Store Supplies/ITT Co.	Feb. 28	n/30	125/✓	225	125	25	75
28	Totals				1,325	1,150	100	75
					(201)	(505)	(124)	(✓)

Outdoors Unlimited Purchases Journal   *Page 1*

Cash Disbursements Journal

The Cash Disbursements Journal in a perpetual system is shown in Exhibit 8A.4. This journal includes the Inventory column where the periodic system had the Purchases Discounts column. All else is identical under the two systems. When a company has several cash purchases of inventory, it often adds a new column for Inventory Debit entries.

Outdoors Unlimited Cash Disbursements Journal							Page 2
Date	Ch. No.	Payee	Account Debited	PR	Cash Cr.	Inventory Cr.	Other Accounts Dr.	Accounts Payable Dr.
Feb. 3	105	L. and N. Railroad	Transportation-In	508	15		15	
12	106	East Sales Co.	Purchases	505	25		25	
15	107	Ace Mfg. Co.	Ace Mfg. Co.	✓	196	4		200
15	108	Jerry Hale	Salaries Expense	622	250		250	
20	109	Wynet and Co.	Wynet and Co.	✓	147	3		150
28	110	Smite Co.	Smite Co.	✓	294	6		300
28		Totals			927	13	290	650
					(101)	(507)	(✓)	(201)

Exhibit 8A.4

Cash Disbursements
Journal—Perpetual System

Summary of Appendix 8A

LO 9 **Journalize and post transactions using special journals in a perpetual inventory system.**
Transactions are journalized and posted using special journals in a perpetual system. The methods are similar to those in a periodic system. The primary difference is cost of goods sold and inventory need adjusting at the time of each sale. This normally results in the addition of one or more columns in each special journal devoted to these accounts.

Glossary

Accounting information system The people, records, methods, and equipment that collect and process data from transactions and events, organize them in useful forms, and communicate results to decision makers. (p. 366)

Accounts Payable Ledger. A subsidiary ledger listing individual credit supplier accounts. (p. 372)

Accounts Receivable Ledger. A subsidiary ledger listing individual credit customer accounts. (p. 372)

Batch processing An approach to inputting data that accumulates source documents for a period of time and then processes them all at once such as once a day, week or month. (p. 388)

Business segment A part of a company that can be separately identified by the products or services that it provides or a geographic market that it serves. (p. 390)

Cash disbursements journal The special journal that is used to record all payments of cash; also called cash payments journal. (p. 384)

Cash Receipts Journal The special journal that is used to record all receipts of cash. (p. 379)

Cheque Register Another name for a cash disbursements journal when the journal has a column for cheque numbers. (p. 384)

Columnar journal A journal with more than one column. (p. 374)

Compatibility principle An information system principle requiring that an accounting information system conform with a company's activities, personnel, and structure. (p. 367)

Computer hardware The physical equipment in a computerized accounting information system. (p. 387)

Computer network A link among computers giving different users and different computers access to a common database and programs. (p. 388)

Computer software The programs that direct the operations of computer hardware. (p. 387)

Controlling account A general ledger account the balance of which (after posting) equals the sum of the balances of the accounts in a related subsidiary ledger. (p. 372)

Control principle An information system principle requiring that an accounting information system aid managers in controlling and monitoring business activities. (p. 366)

Cost-benefit principle An information system principle requiring that the benefits from an activity in an accounting information system outweigh the costs of that activity. (p. 367)

Enterprise-application software Programs that manage a company's vital operations which range from order-taking programs to manufacturing to accounting. (p. 389)

Flexibility principle An information system principle requiring that an information system adapt to changes in the company, business environment, and needs of decisions makers. (p. 367)

GST (goods and services tax) A federal tax on the consumer on almost all goods and services. (p. 376)

HST (Harmonized Sales Tax) The sales tax in the Atlantic Provinces which is a combination of the GST and PST. (p. 378)

Information processor The component of an accounting system that interprets, transforms, and summarizes information for use in analysis and reporting. (p. 368)

Information storage The component of an accounting system that keeps data in a form accessible to information processors. (p. 369)

Input device A means of capturing information from source documents and enabling its transfer to the information processing component of an accounting system. (p. 368)

Off-the-shelf programs Multipurpose software applications for a variety of computer operations. (p. 387)

On-line processing An approach to inputting data whereby the data on each source document is input as soon as the document is available. (p. 388)

Output devices The means by which information is taken out of the accounting system and made available for use. (p. 369)

PST (provincial sales tax) A provincial tax collected by retailers on customer purchases. (p. 376)

Purchases Journal A journal that is used to record all purchases on credit. (p. 382)

Relevance principle An information system principle requiring that an accounting information system report useful, understandable, timely and pertinent information for effective decision-making. (p. 366)

Sales journal A journal used to records sales of merchandise on credit. (p. 373)

Schedule of accounts payable A list of the balances of all the accounts in the Accounts Payable Ledger that is summed to show the total amount of accounts payable outstanding. (p. 384)

Schedule of accounts receivable A list of the balances of all the accounts in the Accounts Receivable Ledger that is summed to show the total amount of accounts receivable outstanding. (p. 375)

Segment contribution matrix A table listing one or more important measures such as sales by segment and also usually includes amounts in dollars and percents along with a growth rate. (p. 391)

Special journal Any journal that is used for recording and posting transactions of a similar type. (p. 371)

Subsidiary ledger A listing of individual accounts with a common characteristic. (p. 371)

Questions

1. When special journals are used, separate special journals normally are used to record each of four different types of transactions. What are these four types of transactions?

2. Why should sales to and receipts of cash from credit customers be recorded and posted daily?

3. Both credits to customer accounts and credits to miscellaneous accounts are individually posted from a Cash Receipts Journal similar to the one in Exhibit 8.10. Why not put both kinds of credits in the same column and save journal space?

4. What procedures allow copies of a company's sales invoices to be used as a Sales Journal?

5. When a General Journal entry is used to record a returned credit sale, the credit of the entry must be posted twice. Does this cause the trial balance to be out of balance? Why or why not?

6. What notations are entered into the posting reference column of a ledger account?

7. What are the five basic components of an accounting system?

8. What are source documents? Give some examples.

9. What is the purpose of an input device? Give some examples of input devices for computer systems.

10. What is the difference between data that is stored off-line and data that is stored on-line?

11. What purpose is served by the output devices of an accounting system?

12. What is the difference between batch and on-line processing?

13. Look in Appendix I at **Alliance's** financial statements. Locate the footnote that discusses Alliance's segmented information. What industry segment does Alliance predominantly operate in? What proportion of Alliance's revenue came from foreign sources in 1997?

14. Look in Appendix I at **Atlantis'** financial statements. Locate the footnote that reports segmented information. What is the source of Atlantis' revenue?

15. Identify all of the special journals that Marie Lanctot is now likely keeping for **Outdoors Limited**. What does Marie mean when she says she now keeps an aging schedule on late paying customers.

Trenton Iron Works uses a Sales Journal, a Purchases Journal, a Cash Receipts Journal, a Cash Disbursements Journal, and a General Journal. Trenton recently completed the following transactions. List the transaction letters and next to each letter give the name of the journal in which the transaction should be recorded.

a. Sold merchandise on credit.

b. Purchased shop supplies on credit.

c. Paid an employee's salary.

d. Paid a creditor.

e. Purchased merchandise on credit.

f. Borrowed money from the bank.

g. Sold merchandise for cash.

The Nostalgic Book Shop uses a Sales Journal, a Purchases Journal, a Cash Receipts Journal, a Cash Disbursements Journal, and a General Journal. The following transactions occurred during the month of November. Journalize the November transactions that should be recorded in the General Journal.

Nov. 2 Purchased merchandise on credit for $2,900 from the Ringdol Co., terms 2/10, n/30.

12 The owner contributed an automobile worth $15,000 to the business.

16 Sold merchandise on credit to R. Wyder for $1,100, terms n/30.

19 R. Wyder returned $150 of merchandise originally purchased on November 16.

28 Returned $170 of defective merchandise to the Ringdol Co. from the November 2 purchase.

Identify the role in an accounting system played by each of the lettered items by assigning a number from the list on the left:

1. Source documents
2. Input devices
3. Information processor
4. Information storage
5. Output devices

_____ a. Bar code reader

_____ b. Filing cabinet

_____ c. Bank statement

_____ d. Calculator

_____ e. Computer keyboard

_____ f. Floppy diskette

_____ g. Computer monitor

_____ h. Invoice from a supplier

_____ i. Computer hardware and software

_____ j. Computer printer

Fill in the blanks:

a. A _____ is an input device that captures writing and other input directly from source documents.

b. _____ – _____ _____ are programs that help manage a company's vital operations, from manufacturing to accounting.

c. With _____ processing, source documents are accumulated for a period of time and then processed all at the same time, such as once a day, week, or month.

d. A computer _____ allows different computer users to share access to the same data and programs.

Quick Study

QS 8-1
Special journal identification

LO 3

QS 8-2
Entries belonging to the general journal

LO 3

QS 8-3
Accounting information system components

LO 2

QS 8-4
Accounting information system components

LO 2

QS 8-5
Required segment reporting

LO 8

A company with publicly traded securities operates in more than one industry. Which of the following items of information about each business segment must the company report?

a. Revenues
b. Net sales
c. Operating profits
d. Operating expenses
e. Capital expenditures
f. Amortization and depreciation
g. Cash flows
h. Identifiable assets

QS 8-6
Accounting information system principles

LO 1

Required

Match the system principles below with the statements which follow.

A. Control principle
B. Relevance principle
C. Compatibility principle
D. Flexibility principle
E. Cost-benefit principle

_____ 1. The principle requiring the information system to adapt to the unique characteristics of the company.

_____ 2. The principle that affects all other information system principles.

_____ 3. The principle requiring the accounting information system to change in response to technological advances and competitive pressures.

_____ 4. The principle requiring the accounting information system to help with monitoring activities.

_____ 5. The principle requiring the system to provide timely information for effective decision-making.

Exercises

Exercise 8-1
The Sales Journal

LO 5

Spindle Corporation uses a Sales Journal, a Purchases Journal, a Cash Receipts Journal, a Cash Disbursements Journal, and a General Journal. The following transactions occurred during the month of February:

Feb. 2 Sold merchandise to S. Mayer for $450 cash, Invoice No. 5703.
5 Purchased merchandise on credit from Camp Corp., $2,300.
7 Sold merchandise to J. Eason for $1,150, terms 2/10, n/30, Invoice No. 5704.
8 Borrowed $8,000 by giving a note to the bank.
12 Sold merchandise to P. Lathan for $320, terms n/30, Invoice No. 5705.
16 Received $1,127 from J. Eason to pay for the purchase of February 7.
19 Sold used store equipment to Whiten, Inc., for $900.
25 Sold merchandise to S. Summers for $550, terms n/30, Invoice No. 5706.

Required

On a sheet of notebook paper, draw a Sales Journal like the one that appears in Exhibit 8.5. Journalize the February transactions that should be recorded in the Sales Journal.

Exercise 8-2
The Cash Receipts Journal

LO 5

SeaMap Company uses a Sales Journal, a Purchases Journal, a Cash Receipts Journal, a Cash Disbursements Journal, and a General Journal. The following transactions occurred during the month of September:

Sept. 3 Purchased merchandise on credit for $3,100 from Pacer Co.
7 Sold merchandise on credit to J. Namal for $900, subject to an $18 sales discount if paid by the end of the month.
9 Borrowed $2,750 by giving a note to the bank.
13 Issued 350 common shares in exchange for $3,500 cash.
18 Sold merchandise to B. Baird for $230 cash.
22 Paid Pacer Co. $3,100 for the merchandise purchased on September 3.
27 Received $882 from J. Namal in payment of the September 7 purchase.
30 Paid salaries of $1,600.

Required

On a sheet of notebook paper, draw a multicolumn Cash Receipts Journal like the one that appears in Exhibit 8.10. Journalize the September transactions that should be recorded in the Cash Receipts Journal.

Chem Corp. uses a Sales Journal, a Purchases Journal, a Cash Receipts Journal, a Cash Disbursements Journal, and a General Journal. The following transactions occurred during the month of July:

July 1 Purchased merchandise on credit for $8,100 from Angler, Inc., terms n/30.
   8 Sold merchandise on credit to B. Harren for $1,500, subject to a $30 sales discount if paid by the end of the month.
  10 Issued 40 common shares in exchange for $2,000 cash.
  14 Purchased store supplies from Steck Company on credit for $240, terms n/30.
  17 Purchased office supplies on credit from Marten Company for $260, terms n/30.
  24 Sold merchandise to W. Winger for $630 cash.
  28 Purchased store supplies from Hadley's for $90 cash.
  29 Paid Angler, Inc., $8,100 for the merchandise purchased on July 1.

Required

On a sheet of notebook paper, draw a multicolumn Purchases Journal like the one that appears in Exhibit 8.12. Journalize the July transactions that should be recorded in the Purchases Journal.

Exercise 8-3
The Purchases Journal

LO 5

Aeron Supply uses a Sales Journal, a Purchases Journal, a Cash Receipts Journal, a Cash Disbursements Journal, and a General Journal. The following transactions occurred during the month of March:

Mar. 3 Purchased merchandise for $2,750 on credit from Pace, Inc., terms 2/10, n/30.
   9 Issued Cheque No. 210 to Narlin Corp. to buy store supplies for $450.
  12 Sold merchandise on credit to K. Camp for $670, terms n/30.
  17 Issued Cheque No. 211 for $1,500 to repay a note payable to City Bank.
  20 Purchased merchandise for $3,500 on credit from LeBaron, terms 2/10, n/30.
  29 Issued Cheque No. 212 to LeBaron to pay the amount due for the purchase of March 20, less the discount.
  31 Paid salary of $1,700 to E. Brandon by issuing Cheque No. 213.
  31 Issued Cheque No. 214 to Pace, Inc., to pay the amount due for the purchase of March 3.

Required

On a sheet of notebook paper, draw a multicolumn Cash Disbursements Journal like the one that appears in Exhibit 8.13. Journalize the March transactions that should be recorded in the Cash Disbursements Journal.

Exercise 8-4
The Cash Disbursements Journal

LO 5

Simon Pharmacy uses the following journals: Sales Journal, Purchases Journal, Cash Receipts Journal, Cash Disbursements Journal, and General Journal. On June 5, Simon purchased merchandise priced at $12,000, subject to credit terms of 2/10, n/30. On June 14, the pharmacy paid the net amount due. However, in journalizing the payment, the bookkeeper debited Accounts Payable for $12,000 and failed to record the cash discount. Cash was credited for the actual amount paid. In what journals would the June 5 and the June 14 transactions have been recorded? What procedure is likely to discover the error in journalizing the June 14 transaction?

Exercise 8-5
Special journal transactions

LO 5

Exercise 8-6

Posting to subsidiary
ledger accounts

LO 5, 6

At the end of May, the Sales Journal of Camper Goods appeared as follows:

			Sales Journal		
Date		Account Debited	Invoice Number	PR	A/R Dr. Sales Cr.
May	6	Brad Smithers.	190		2,880.00
	10	Dan Holland	191		1,940.00
	17	Sanders Farrell	192		850.00
	25	Dan Holland	193		340.00
	31	Total			6,010.00

Camper had also recorded the return of merchandise with the following General Journal entry:

May 20	Sales Returns and Allowances	250	
	Accounts Receivable—Sanders Farrell . . .		250
	Customer returned merchandise.		

Required

1. On a sheet of notebook paper, open a subsidiary Accounts Receivable Ledger that has a T-account for each customer listed in the Sales Journal. Post to the customer accounts the entries in the Sales Journal and any portion of the General Journal entry that affects a customer's account.

2. Open a General Ledger that has T-accounts for Accounts Receivable, Sales, and Sales Returns and Allowances. Post the Sales Journal and any portion of the general journal entry that affects these accounts.

3. Prepare a list or schedule of the accounts in the subsidiary Accounts Receivable Ledger and add their balances to show that the total equals the balance in the Accounts Receivable controlling account.

Exercise 8-7

Posting from special
journals and subsidiary
ledgers to T-accounts

LO 5, 6

Following are the condensed journals of Tipper Trophies. The journal column headings are incomplete in that they do not indicate whether the columns are debit or credit columns.

Sales Journal		Purchases Journal	
Account	Amount	Account	Amount
Jack Hertz	3,700	Grass Corp.	5,400
Trudy Stone	8,400	Sulter, Inc..	4,500
Dave Waylon.	1,000	McGrew Company.	1,700
Total.	13,100	Total	11,600

	General Journal		
	Sales Returns and Allowances	300.00	
	Accounts Receivable – Jack Hertz		300.00
	Accounts Payable – Grass Corp	750.00	
	Purchases Returns and Allowances		750.00

Cash Receipts Journal

Account	Other Accounts	Accounts Receivable	Sales	Sales Discounts	Cash
Jack Hertz		3,400		68	3,332
Sales			2,250		2,250
Notes Payable.	4,500				4,500
Sales			625		625
Trudy Stone		8,400		168	8,232
Store Equipment	500				500
Totals	5,000	11,800	2,875	236	19,439

Cash Disbursements Journal

Account	Other Accounts	Accounts Payable	Purchase Discounts	Cash
Prepaid Insurance	850			850
Sulter, Inc.		4,500	135	4,365
Grass Corp.		4,650	93	4,557
Store Equipment	1,750			1,750
Totals	2,600	9,150	228	11,522

Required

1. Prepare T-accounts on notebook paper for the following General Ledger and subsidiary ledger accounts. Separate the accounts of each ledger group as follows:

General Ledger Accounts	Accounts Receivable Ledger Accounts
Cash	Jack Hertz
Accounts Receivable	Trudy Stone
Prepaid Insurance	Dave Waylon
Store Equipment	
Accounts Payable	
Notes Payable	
Sales	Accounts Payable Ledger Accounts
Sales Discounts	Grass Corp.
Sales Returns and Allowances	McGrew Company
Purchases	Sulter, Inc.
Purchase Discounts	
Purchase Returns and Allowances	

2. Without referring to any of the illustrations in the chapter that show complete column headings for the journals, post the journals to the proper T-accounts.

Exercise 8-8
Accounts Receivable Ledger

LO 5, 6

Skillern Company posts its sales invoices directly and then binds the invoices to make them into a Sales Journal. Skillern had the following sales amounts, excluding sales taxes, during January. Sales are subject to a 10% Provincial Sales Tax and the 7% Goods and Services Tax.

Jan. 2	Jay Newton.........	$ 3,600
8	Adrian Carr..........	6,100
10	Kathy Olivas	13,400
14	Lisa Mack...........	20,500
20	Kathy Olivas	11,200
29	Jay Newton.........	7,300
	Total.............	$62,100

Required

1. On a sheet of notebook paper, open a subsidiary Accounts Receivable Ledger having a T-account for each customer. Post the invoices to the subsidiary ledger.
2. Give the General Journal entry to record the end-of-month total of the Sales Journal.
3. Open an Accounts Receivable controlling account and a Sales account and post the general journal entry.
4. Prepare a list or schedule of the accounts in the subsidiary Accounts Receivable Ledger and add their balances to show that the total equals the balance in the Accounts Receivable controlling account.

Exercise 8-9
Errors related to the Purchases Journal

LO 5

A company that records credit purchases in a Purchases Journal and records purchase returns in its General Journal made the following errors. List each error by letter and, opposite each letter, tell when the error should be discovered:

a. Made an addition error in determining the balance of a creditor's account.
b. Made an addition error in totalling the Office Supplies column of the Purchases Journal.
c. Posted a purchase return to the Accounts Payable account and to the creditor's account but did not post to the Purchases Returns and Allowances account.
d. Posted a purchases return to the Purchase Returns and Allowances account and to the Accounts Payable account but did not post to the creditor's account.
e. Correctly recorded a $4,000 purchase in the Purchase Journal but posted it to the creditor's account as a $400 purchase.

Exercise 8-10
Analyzing segment information

LO 8

Refer to Exhibit 8.16 in the chapter and complete the segment contribution matrix for Gen X Sports Company. Analyze and interpret the resulting matrix, including identification of segments with the highest and lowest growth rates.

Gen X Sports Company Segment Contribution Matrix for Sales					
Segment	Sales Contribution ($mil.)		Sales Contribution (in %)		1-Year Growth Rate %
	1999	1998	1999	1998	
Specialty:					
Skiing Group	$5,235	$3,585			
Skating Group	800	400			
Specialty Footwear	1,200	860			
Other Specialty	975	525			
Subtotal					
General Merchandise:					
Canada	$2,725	$1,839			
United States	4,988	2,788			
Europe	497	743			
Subtotal					
Total					

Newton Company completed these transactions during April of the current year. The terms of all credit sales are 2/10, n/30.

Problems

Problem 8-1
Special journals, subsidiary ledgers, schedule of accounts receivable

LO 5, 6

Apr. 2 Purchased merchandise on credit from Baskin Company, invoice dated April 2, terms 2/10, n/60, $13,300.

  3 Sold merchandise on credit to Linda Hobart, Invoice No. 760, $3,000.

  3 Purchased office supplies on credit from Eau Claire Inc., $1,380. Invoice dated April 2, terms n/10 EOM.

  4 Issued Cheque No. 587 to *The Record* for advertising expense, $999.

  5 Sold merchandise on credit to Paul Abrams, Invoice No. 761, $8,000.

  6 Received an $85 credit memorandum from Eau Claire Inc. for office supplies received on April 3 and returned for credit.

  9 Purchased store equipment on credit from Frank's Supply, invoice dated April 9, terms n/10 EOM, $11,125.

  11 Sold merchandise on credit to Kelly Schaefer, Invoice No. 762, $9,500.

  12 Issued Cheque No. 588 to Baskin Company in payment of its April 2 invoice, less the discount.

  13 Received payment from Linda Hobart for the April 3 sale, less the discount.

  13 Sold merchandise on credit to Linda Hobart, Invoice No. 763, $4,100.

  14 Received payment from Paul Abrams for the April 5 sale, less the discount.

  16 Issued Cheque No. 589, payable to Payroll, in payment of the sales salaries for the first half of the month, $9,750. Cashed the cheque and paid the employees.

  16 Cash sales for the first half of the month were $50,840. (Cash sales are usually recorded daily from the cash register readings. However, they are recorded only twice in this problem to reduce the repetitive transactions.)

  17 Purchased merchandise on credit from Spocket Company, invoice dated April 16, terms 2/10, n/30, $12,750.

  18 Borrowed $50,000 from First Bank by giving a long-term note payable.

  20 Received payment from Kelly Schaefer for the April 11 sale, less the discount.

  20 Purchased store supplies on credit from Frank's Supply, invoice dated April 19, terms n/10 EOM, $730.

  23 Received a $400 credit memorandum from Sprocket Company for defective merchandise received on April 17 and returned.

  23 Received payment from Linda Hobart for the April 13 sale, less the discount.

  25 Purchased merchandise on credit from Baskin Company, invoice dated April 24, terms 2/10, n/60, $10,375.

  26 Issued Cheque No. 590 to Sprocket Company in payment of its April 16 invoice, less the return and the discount.

  27 Sold merchandise on credit to Paul Abrams, Invoice No. 764, $3,070.

  27 Sold merchandise on credit to Kelly Schaefer, Invoice No. 765, $5,700.

  30 Issued Cheque No. 591, payable to Payroll, in payment of the sales salaries for the last half of the month, $9,750.

  30 Cash sales for the last half of the month were $70,975.

Required

Preparation component:

1. Open the following General Ledger accounts: Cash, Accounts Receivable, Long-Term Notes Payable, Sales, and Sales Discounts. Also open subsidiary accounts receivable ledger accounts for Paul Abrams, Linda Hobart, and Kelly Schaefer.

2. Prepare a Sales Journal and a Cash Receipts Journal like the ones illustrated in this chapter.

3. Review the transactions of Newton Company and enter those transactions that should be journalized in the Sales Journal and those that should be journalized in the Cash Receipts Journal. Ignore any transactions that should be journalized in a Purchases Journal, a Cash Disbursements Journal, or a General Journal.

4. Post the items that should be posted as individual amounts from the journals.

5. Foot and crossfoot the journals and make the month-end postings.

6. Prepare a trial balance of the General Ledger and test the accuracy of the subsidiary ledger by preparing a schedule of accounts receivable.

Check Figure Trial balance totals, $205,185

Analysis component:

7. Assume that the sum of the account balances on the schedule of accounts receivable does not equal the balance of the controlling account in the General Ledger. Describe the steps you would go through to discover the error(s).

Problem 8-2
Special journals, subsidiary ledgers, schedule of accounts payable

LO 5,6

On March 31, Newton Company had a cash balance of $167,000 and a Long-Term Notes Payable balance of $167,000. The April transactions of Newton Company included those listed in Problem 8-1.

Required

1. Open the following General Ledger accounts: Cash, Office Supplies, Store Supplies, Store Equipment, Accounts Payable, Long-Term Notes Payable, Purchases, Purchases Returns and Allowances, Purchases Discounts, Sales Salaries Expense, and Advertising Expense. Enter the March 31 balances of Cash and Long-Term Notes Payable ($167,000 each).

2. Open subsidiary Accounts Payable Ledger accounts for Frank's Supply, Baskin Company, Sprocket Company, and Eau Claire Inc.

3. Prepare a General Journal and a Cash Disbursements Journal like the ones illustrated in this chapter. Prepare a Purchases Journal with a debit column for purchases, a debit column for other accounts, and a credit column for accounts payable.

4. Review the April transactions of Newton Company and enter those transactions that should be journalized in the General Journal, the Purchases Journal, or the Cash Disbursements Journal. Ignore any transactions that should be journalized in a Sales Journal or Cash Receipts Journal.

5. Post the items that should be posted as individual amounts from the journals. (Normally, such items are posted daily, but since they are few in number in this problem you are asked to post them only once.)

6. Foot and crossfoot the journals and make the month-end postings.

7. Prepare a trial balance and a schedule of accounts payable.

Check Figure Trial balance totals, $191,438

Problem 8-3
Special journals, subsidiary ledgers, trial balance

LO 5,6

(If the Working Papers that accompany this text are not being used, omit this problem.)

It is December 16 and you have just taken over the accounting work of Saskan Enterprises, whose annual accounting period ends each December 31. The company's previous accountant journalized its transactions through December 15 and posted all items that required posting as individual amounts, as an examination of the journals and ledgers in the Working Papers will show.

The company completed these transactions beginning on December 16:

Dec. 16 Sold merchandise on credit to Vickie Foresman, Invoice No. 916, $7,700. (Terms of all credit sales are 2/10, n/30.)

17 Received a $1,040 credit memorandum from Shore Company for merchandise received on December 15 and returned for credit.

17 Purchased office supplies on credit from Brown Supply Company, $615. Invoice dated December 16, terms n/10 EOM.

18 Received a $40 credit memorandum from Brown Supply Company for office supplies received on December 17 and returned for credit.

20 Issued a credit memorandum to Amy Ihrig for defective merchandise sold on December 15 and returned for credit, $500.

21 Purchased store equipment on credit from Brown Supply Company, invoice dated December 21, terms n/10 EOM, $6,700.

22 Received payment from Vickie Foresman for the December 12 sale less the discount.

23 Issued Cheque No. 623 to Sunshine Company in payment of its December 15 invoice less the discount.

24 Sold merchandise on credit to Bill Grigsby, Invoice No. 917, $1,200.

24 Issued Cheque No. 624 to Shore Company in payment of its December 15 invoice less the return and the discount.

25 Received payment from Amy Ihrig for the December 15 sale less the return and the discount.

26 Received merchandise and an invoice dated December 25, terms 2/10, n/60, from Sunshine Company, $8,100.

29 Sold a neighbouring merchant five boxes of file folders (office supplies) for cash at cost, $50.

30 Ken Shaw, the owner of Saskan Enterprises, used Cheque No. 625 to withdraw $2,500 cash from the business for personal use.

31 Issued Cheque No. 626 to Jamie Green, the company's only sales employee, in payment of her salary for the last half of December, $2,020.

31 Issued Cheque No. 627 to Countywide Electric Company in payment of the December electric bill, $710.

31 Cash sales for the last half of the month were $29,600. (Cash sales are usually recorded daily but are recorded only twice in this problem to reduce the repetitive transactions.)

Required

1. Record the transactions in the journals provided.

2. Post to the customer and creditor accounts and also post any amounts that should be posted as individual amounts to the General Ledger accounts. (Normally, these amounts are posted daily, but they are posted only once by you in this problem because they are few in number.)

3. Foot and crossfoot the journals and make the month-end postings.

4. Prepare a December 31 trial balance and test the accuracy of the subsidiary ledgers by preparing schedules of accounts receivable and payable.

Check Figure Trial balance totals, $221,160

The Bledsoe Company completed these transactions during March of the current year. Sales are subject to a 10% PST and the 7% GST.

Mar. 2 Sold merchandise on credit to Leroy Hackett, Invoice No. 854, $15,800. (Terms of all credit sales are 2/10, n/30.)

3 Purchased office supplies on credit from Arndt Company, $1,120. Invoice dated March 3, terms n/10 EOM.

3 Sold merchandise on credit to Sam Snickers Invoice No. 855, $9,200.

5 Received merchandise and an invoice dated March 3, terms 2/10, n/30, from Defore Industries, $42,600.

6 Borrowed $72,000 by giving Commerce Bank a long-term promissory note payable.

9 Purchased office equipment on credit from Jett Supply, invoice dated March 9, terms n/10 EOM, $20,850.

10 Sold merchandise on credit to Marjorie Coble, Invoice No. 856, $4,600.

12 Received payment from Leroy Hackett for the March 2 sale less the discount.

13 Sent Defore Industries Cheque No. 416 in payment of its March 3 invoice less the discount.

13 Received payment from Sam Snickers for the March 3 sale less the discount.

14 Received merchandise and an invoice dated March 13, terms 2/10, n/30, from the Welch Company, $31,625.

15 Issued Cheque No. 417, payable to Payroll, in payment of sales salaries for the first half of the month, $15,900. Cashed the cheque and paid the employees.

15 Cash sales for the first half of the month were $164,680. (Normally, cash sales are recorded daily; however, they are recorded only twice in this problem to reduce the repetitive entries.)

15 Post to the customer and creditor accounts and also post any amounts that should be posted as individual amounts to the General Ledger accounts. (Normally, such items are posted daily, but you are asked to post them on only two occasions in this problem because they are few in number.)

16 Purchased store supplies on credit from Arndt Company, $1,670. Invoice dated March 16, terms n/10 EOM.

17 Received a credit memorandum from the Welch Company for unsatisfactory merchandise received on March 14 and returned for credit, $2,425.

19 Received a credit memorandum from Jett Supply for office equipment received on March 9 and returned for credit, $630.

Problem 8-4
Special journals, subsidiary ledgers, trial balance

LO 5, 6

20   Received payment from Marjorie Coble for the sale of March 10 less the discount.
23   Issued Cheque No. 418 to the Welch Company in payment of its invoice of March 13 less the return and the discount.
27   Sold merchandise on credit to Marjorie Coble, Invoice No. 857, $13,910.
28   Sold merchandise on credit to SamSnickers, Invoice No. 858, $5,315.
31   Issued Cheque No. 419, payable to Payroll, in payment of sales salaries for the last half of the month, $15,900. Cashed the cheque and paid the employees.
31   Cash sales for the last half of the month were $174,590.
31   Post to the customer and creditor accounts and post any amounts that should be posted as individual amounts to the General Ledger accounts.
31   Foot and crossfoot the journals and make the month-end postings.

Required

1. Open the following General Ledger accounts: Cash, Accounts Receivable, Office Supplies, Store Supplies, Office Equipment, Accounts Payable, PST Payable, GST Payable, Long-Term Notes Payable, Sales, Sales Discounts, Purchases, Purchases Returns and Allowances, Purchases Discounts, and Sales Salaries Expense.

2. Open the following Accounts Receivable Ledger accounts: Marjorie Coble, Leroy Hackett, and Sam Snickers.

3. Open the following Accounts Ppayable Ledger accounts: Arndt Company, Defore Industries, Jett Supply, and the Welch Company.

4. Enter the transactions in a Sales Journal, a Purchases Journal, a Cash Receipts Journal, a Cash Disbursements Journal, and a General Journal similar to the ones illustrated in this chapter. Post when instructed to do so.

5. Prepare a trial balance and test the accuracy of the subsidiary ledgers by preparing schedules of accounts receivable and payable.

Check Figure Trial balance totals, $552,942.15

Alternate Problems

Problem 8-1A
Special journals, subsidiary ledgers, schedule of accounts receivable

LO 5, 6

Eldridge Industries completed these transactions during July of the current year:

July 1   Purchased merchandise on credit from Beech Company, invoice dated June 30, terms 2/10, n/30, $6,300.
3   Issued Cheque No. 300 to *The Weekly Journal* for advertising expense, $575.
5   Sold merchandise on credit to Karen Harden, Invoice No. 918, $18,400. (The terms of all credit sales are 2/10, n/30.)
6   Sold merchandise on credit to Paul Kane, Invoice No. 919, $7,500.
7   Purchased store supplies on credit from Blackwater Inc., $1,050. Invoice dated July 7, terms n/10 EOM.
8   Received a $150 credit memorandum from Blackwater Inc. for store supplies received on July 7 and returned for credit.
9   Purchased store equipment on credit from Poppe's Supply, invoice dated July 8, terms n/10 EOM, $37,710.
10   Issued Cheque No. 301 to Beech Company in payment of its June 30 invoice, less the discount.
13   Sold merchandise on credit to Kelly Grody, Invoice No. 920, $8,350.
14   Sold merchandise on credit to Karen Harden, Invoice No. 921, $4,100.
15   Received payment from Karen Harden for the July 5 sale, less the discount.
15   Issued Cheque No. 302, payable to Payroll, in payment of the sales salaries for the first half of the month, $30,620. Cashed the cheque and paid the employees.
15   Cash sales for the first half of the month were $121,370. (Cash sales are usually recorded daily from the cash register readings. However, they are recorded only twice in this problem to reduce the repetitive transactions.)
16   Received payment from Paul Kane for the July 6 sale, less the discount.
17   Purchased merchandise on credit from Sprague Company, invoice dated July 17, terms 2/10, n/30, $8,200.
20   Purchased office supplies on credit from Poppe's Supply, $750. Invoice dated July 19, terms n/10 EOM.
21   Borrowed $20,000 from College Bank by giving a long-term note payable.
23   Received payment from Kelly Grody for the July 13 sale, less the discount.
24   Received payment from Karen Harden for the July 14 sale, less the discount.

24 Received a $2,400 credit memorandum from Sprague Company for defective merchandise received on July 17 and returned.

26 Purchased merchandise on credit from Beech Company, invoice dated July 26, terms 2/10, n/30, $9,770.

27 Issued Cheque No. 303 to Sprague Company in payment of its July 17 invoice, less the return and the discount.

29 Sold merchandise on credit to Paul Kane, Invoice No. 922, $28,090.

30 Sold merchandise on credit to Kelly Grody, Invoice No. 923, $15,750.

31 Issued Cheque No. 304, payable to Payroll, in payment of the sales salaries for the last half of the month, $30,620.

31 Cash sales for the last half of the month were $79,020.

Required

Preparation component:

1. Open the following General Ledger accounts: Cash, Accounts Receivable, Long-Term Notes Payable, Sales, and Sales Discounts. Also open subsidiary Accounts Receivable Ledger accounts for Karen Harden, and Kelly Grody, and Paul Kane.

2. Prepare a Sales Journal and a Cash Receipts Journal similar to the ones illustrated in this chapter.

3. Review the transactions of Eldridge Industries and enter those transactions that should be journalized in the Sales Journal and those that should be journalized in the Cash Receipts Journal. Ignore any transactions that should be journalized in a Purchases Journal, a Cash Disbursements Journal, or a General Journal.

4. Post the items that should be posted as individual amounts from the journals. (Normally, such items are posted daily; but since they are few in number in this problem you are asked to post them only once.)

5. Foot and crossfoot the journals and make the month-end postings.

6. Prepare a trial balance of the General Ledger and test the accuracy of the subsidiary ledger by preparing a schedule of accounts receivable.

Analysis component:

7. Assume that the sum of the account balances on the schedule of accounts receivable does not equal the balance of the controlling account in the General Ledger. Describe the steps you would go through to discover the error(s).

On June 30, Eldridge Industries had a cash balance of $165,600 and a Long-Term Notes Payable balance of $165,600. The July transactions of Eldridge Industries included those listed in Problem 8-1A.

Required

1. Open the following general ledger accounts: Cash, Office Supplies, Store Supplies, Store Equipment, Accounts Payable, Long-Term Notes Payable, Purchases, Purchases Returns and Allowances, Purchases Discounts, Sales Salaries Expense, and Advertising Expense. Enter the June 30 balances of Cash and Long-Term Notes Payable ($165,600 each).

2. Open subsidiary Accounts Payable Ledger accounts for Poppe's Supply, Beech Company, Sprague Company, and Blackwater Inc.

3. Prepare a General Journal and a Cash Disbursements Journal like the ones illustrated in this chapter. Prepare a Purchases Journal with a debit column for purchases, a debit column for other accounts, and a credit column for accounts payable.

4. Review the July transactions of Eldridge Industries and enter those transactions that should be journalized in the General Journal, the Purchases Journal, or the Cash Disbursements Journal. Ignore any transactions that should be journalized in a Sales Journal or Cash Receipts Journal.

5. Post the items that should be posted as individual amounts from the journals. (Normally, such items are posted daily, but since they are few in number in this problem you are asked to post them only once.)

6. Foot and crossfoot the journals and make the month-end postings.

7. Prepare a trial balance and a schedule of accounts payable.

Problem 8-2A
Special journals, subsidiary ledgers, schedule of accounts payable

LO 5, 6

Problem 8-3A
Special journals,
subsidiary ledgers, trial
balance
LO 5, 6

(If the Working Papers that accompany this text are not being used, omit this problem.)

It is December 16 and you have just taken over the accounting work of Starshine Products, whose annual accounting period ends December 31. The company's previous accountant journalized its transactions through December 15 and posted all items that required posting as individual amounts, as an examination of the journals and ledgers in the booklet of working papers will show.

The company completed these transactions beginning on December 16:

Dec. 16 Purchased office supplies on credit from Green Supply Company, $765. Invoice dated December 16, terms n/10 EOM.

16 Sold merchandise on credit to Heather Flatt, Invoice No. 916, $4,290. (Terms of all credit sales are 2/10, n/30.)

18 Issued a credit memorandum to Amy Izon for defective merchandise sold on December 15 and returned for credit, $200.

19 Received a $640 credit memorandum from Walters Company for merchandise received on December 15 and returned for credit.

20 Received a $143 credit memorandum from Green Supply Company for office supplies received on December 16 and returned for credit.

20 Purchased store equipment on credit from Green Supply Company, invoice dated December 19, terms n/10 EOM, $7,475.

21 Sold merchandise on credit to Jan Wildman, Invoice No. 917, $5,520.

22 Received payment from Heather Flatt for the December 12 sale less the discount.

25 Received payment from Amy Izon for the December 15 sale less the return and the discount.

25 Issued Cheque No. 623 to Walters Company in payment of its December 15 invoice less the return and the discount.

25 Issued Cheque No. 624 to Sunshine Company in payment of its December 15 invoice less a 2% discount.

28 Received merchandise with an invoice dated December 28, terms 2/10, n/60, from Sunshine Company, $6,030.

28 Sold a neighbouring merchant a carton of calculator tape (store supplies) for cash at cost, $58.

29 Marlee Levin, the owner of Starshine Products, used Cheque No. 625 to withdraw $4,000 cash from the business for personal use.

30 Issued Cheque No. 626 to Midwest Electric Company in payment of the December electric bill, $990.

30 Issued Cheque No. 627 to Jamie Ford, the company's only sales employee, in payment of her salary for the last half of December, $2,620.

31 Cash sales for the last half of the month were $66,128. (Cash sales are usually recorded daily but are recorded only twice in this problem to reduce the repetitive transactions.)

Required

1. Record the transactions in the journals provided.

2. Post to the customer and creditor accounts and also post any amounts that should be posted as individual amounts to the General Ledger accounts. (Normally, these amounts are posted daily, but they are posted only once by you in this problem because they are few in number.)

3. Foot and crossfoot the journals and make the month-end postings.

4. Prepare a December 31 trial balance and test the accuracy of the subsidiary ledgers by preparing schedules of accounts receivable and payable.

Crystal Company completed these transactions during November of the current year. Sales are subject to a 10% PST and the 7% GST.

Problem 8-4A
Special journals,
subsidiary ledgers, trial
balance
LO 5, 6

Nov. 1   Purchased office equipment on credit from Jett Supply, invoice dated November 1, terms n/10 EOM, $5,062.

   2   Borrowed $86,250 by giving Jefferson Bank a long-term promissory note payable.

   4   Received merchandise and an invoice dated November 3, terms 2/10, n/30, from Defore Industries, $11,400.

   5   Purchased store supplies on credit from Atlas Company, $1,020. Invoice dated November 5, terms n/10 EOM.

   8   Sold merchandise on credit to Leroy Holmes, Invoice No. 439, $6,350. (Terms of all credit sales are 2/10, n/30.)

  10   Sold merchandise on credit to Sam Spear, Invoice No. 440, $12,500.

  11   Received merchandise and an invoice dated November 10, terms 2/10, n/30, from The Welch Company, $2,887.

  12   Sent Defore Industries Cheque No. 633 in payment of its November 3 invoice less the discount.

  15   Issued Cheque No. 634, payable to Payroll, in payment of sales salaries for the first half of the month, $8,435. Cashed the cheque and paid the employees.

  15   Cash sales for the first half of the month were $27,170. (Normally, cash sales are recorded daily; however, they are recorded only twice in this problem to reduce the number of repetitive entries.)

  15   Post to the customer and creditor accounts and also post any amounts that should be posted as individual amounts to the General Ledger accounts. (Normally, such items are posted daily, but you are asked to post them on only two occasions in this problem because they are few in number.)

  15   Sold merchandise on credit to Marjorie Cook, Invoice No. 441, $4,250.

  16   Purchased office supplies on credit from Atlas Company, $559. Invoice dated November 16, terms n/10 EOM.

  17   Received a credit memorandum from The Welch Company for unsatisfactory merchandise received on November 10 and returned for credit, $487.

  18   Received payment from Leroy Holmes for the November 8 sale less the discount.

  19   Received payment from Sam Spear for the November 10 sale less the discount.

  19   Issued Cheque No. 635 to The Welch Company in payment of its invoice of November 10 less the return and the discount.

  22   Sold merchandise on credit to Sam Spear, Invoice No. 442, $2,595.

  24   Sold merchandise on credit to Marjorie Cook, Invoice No. 443, $3,240.

  25   Received payment from Marjorie Cook for the sale of November 15 less the discount.

  26   Received a credit memorandum from Jett Supply for office equipment received on November 1 and returned for credit, $922.

  30   Issued Cheque No. 636, payable to Payroll, in payment of sales salaries for the last half of the month, $8,435. Cashed the cheque and paid the employees.

  30   Cash sales for the last half of the month were $35,703.

  30   Post to the customer and creditor accounts and post any amounts that should be posted as individual amounts to the General Ledger accounts.

  30   Foot and crossfoot the journals and make the month-end postings.

Required

1. Open the following General Ledger accounts: Cash, Accounts Receivable, Office Supplies, Store Supplies, Office Equipment, Accounts Payable, PST Payable, GST Payable, Long-Term Notes Payable, Sales, Sales Discounts, Purchases, Purchases Returns and Allowances, Purchases Discounts, and Sales Salaries Expense.

2. Open the following Accounts Receivable Ledger accounts: Marjorie Cook, Leroy Holmes, and Sam Spear.

3. Open the following accounts payable ledger accounts: Atlas Company, Defore Industries, Jett Supply, and The Welch Company. Enter the transactions in a Sales Journal, a Purchases Journal, a Cash Receipts Journal, a Cash Disbursements Journal, and a General Journal similar to the ones illustrated in this chapter. Post when instructed to do so.

4. Prepare a trial balance and test the accuracy of the subsidiary ledgers by preparing schedules of accounts receivable and payable.

Analytical and Review Problem

A & R Problem 8-1

The following problem is designed to test your ability in the use of special journals and subsidiary ledgers. The special journals of James Bay Department Store are reproduced below, followed by a number of representative transactions that occurred during the period. The money columns in the journals are numbered to minimize clerical work in recording each transaction.

Accounts Receivable Debit	Sales Credit						PST Credit	GST Credit
	Men's Clothing	Women's Clothing	Appliances	Furniture	Bargain Basement	Other Departments		
1	2	3	4	5	6	7	8	9

Cash Debit	Sales Discounts Debit	Sales Credit						Accounts Receivable Credit	Other Accounts Credit	PST Credit	GST Credit
		Men's Clothing	Women's Clothing	Appliances	Furniture	Bargain Basement	Other Departments				
10	11	12	13	14	15	16	17	18	19	20	21

Purchases Debit						Prepaid GST Debit	Accounts Payable Credit
Men's Clothing	Women's Clothing	Appliances	Furniture	Bargain Basement	Other Departments		
22	23	24	25	26	27	28	29

Accounts Payable Debit	Supplies Expense Debit	Other Accounts Debit	Prepaid GST Debit	Cash Credit		Debit	Credit
30	31	32	33	34		35	36

2. Transactions (Note: All sales are subject to a provincial sales tax (PST) of 8% and the federal goods and services tax (GST) of 7%.) (Note: All purchases are subject to 7% GST.)

a. Borrowed $52,500 from Great Northern Bank on note payable.

b. Sale on account $450 to J.C. Snead—Men's Clothing.

c. Sale for cash of baked goods—$15.

d. Purchases of $15,750 on account of goods—Bargain Basement from Lonbec Co.

e. Purchases of $12,300 on account of Appliances from Canlec Inc.

f. Sale on account $2,100 of Furniture to Gates Brown.

g. Sale for cash $1,500 less 5% discount— Appliances.

h. Collection of account receivable from Cec Oak, $900.

i. Payment of account payable to J.T. Ingis, $8,800.

j. J.C. Snead returned for credit a shirt that had a flaw—$60.

Debit	Credit

Required

1. Identify each of the journals.

2. Journalize by indicating the column number in the spaces provided after each transaction. For example: Purchase for cash of supplies (immediately expense).

Debit	Credit
31, 33	34

3. Indicate how the data in the special journals are posted to various accounts by filling in the spaces provided with the following posting possibilities.

a. Posted as a debit to some General Ledger account.

b. Posted as a debit to some subsidiary ledger account.

c. Posted as a credit to some General Ledger account.

d. Posted as a credit to some subsidiary ledger account.

e. Not posted.

Note: The numbers in parentheses are the identification numbers for the money columns of the special journals. For example: (31) money column.

	Posted
3. (00) Total of column (34) Example	c
a. Total of column 1.	
b. Detail item of column 3.	
c. Detail item of column 8.	
d. Total of column 9.	
e. Detail items of column 17.	
f. Total of column 20.	
g. Total of column 26.	
h. Detail items of column 27.	
i. Detail items of column 32.	
j. Detail items of column 1.	
k. Total of column 19.	
l. Detail items of column 18.	
m. Total of column 29.	
n. Total of column 5.	
o. Detail items of column 10.	
p. Detail items of column 21.	

Comprehensive Problem
Alpine Company
LO 1

(If the Working Papers that accompany this text are not available, omit this comprehensive problem.)

Assume it is Monday, May 1, the first business day of the month, and you have just been hired as the accountant for Alpine Company, which operates with monthly accounting periods. All of the company's accounting work has been completed through the end of April and its ledgers show April 30 balances. During your first month on the job, you record the following transactions:

May 1   Issued Cheque No. 3410 to S&M Management Co. in payment of the May rent, $3,710. (Use two lines to record the transaction. Charge 80% of the rent to Rent Expense, Selling Space and the balance to Rent Expense, Office Space.)

2   Sold merchandise on credit to Essex Company, Invoice No. 8785, $6,100. (The terms of all credit sales are 2/10, n/30.)

2   Issued a $175 credit memorandum to Nabors, Inc., for defective merchandise sold on April 28 and returned for credit. The total selling price (gross) was $4,725.

3   Received a $798 credit memorandum from Parkay Products for merchandise received on April 29 and returned for credit.

4   Purchased on credit from Thompson Supply Co.: merchandise, $37,072; store supplies, $574; and office supplies, $83. Invoice dated May 4, terms n/10 EOM.

5   Received payment from Nabors, Inc., for the remaining balance from the sale of April 28 less the May 2 return and the discount.

8   Issued Cheque No. 3411 to Parkay Products to pay for the $7,098 of merchandise received on April 29 less the May 3 return and a 2% discount.

9   Sold store supplies to the merchant next door at cost for cash, $350.

10   Purchased office equipment on credit from Thompson Supply Co., invoice dated May 10, terms n/10 EOM, $4,074.

11   Received payment from Essex Company for the May 2 sale less the discount.

11 Received merchandise and an invoice dated May 10, terms 2/10, n/30, from Gale, Inc., $8,800.

12 Received an $854 credit memorandum from Thompson Supply Co. for defective office equipment received on May 10 and returned for credit.

15 Issued Cheque No. 3412, payable to Payroll, in payment of sales salaries, $5,320, and office salaries, $3,150. Cashed the cheque and paid the employees.

15 Cash sales for the first half of the month, $59,220. (Such sales are normally recorded daily. They are recorded only twice in this problem to reduce the repetitive entries.)

15 Post to the customer and creditor accounts. Also, post individual items that are not included in column totals at the end of the month to the General Ledger accounts. (Such items are normally posted daily, but you are asked to post them only twice each month because they are few in number.)

16 Sold merchandise on credit to Essex Company, Invoice No. 8786, $3,990.

17 Received merchandise and an invoice dated May 14, terms 2/10, n/60, from Chandler Corp., $13,650.

19 Issued Cheque No. 3413 to Gale, Inc. in payment of its May 10 invoice less the discount.

22 Sold merchandise to Oscar Services, Invoice No. 8787, $6,850, terms 2/10, n/60.

23 Issued Cheque No. 3414 to Chandler Corp. in payment of its May 14 invoice less the discount.

24 Purchased on credit from Thompson Supply Co.: merchandise, $8,120; store supplies, $630; and office supplies, $280. Invoice dated May 24, terms n/10 EOM.

25 Received merchandise and an invoice dated May 23, terms 2/10, n/30, from Parkay Products, $3,080.

26 Sold merchandise on credit to Deaver Corp., Invoice No. 8788, $14,210.

26 Issued Cheque No. 3415 to Trinity Power in payment of the April electric bill, $1,283.

29 The owner, Clint Barry, withdrew $7,000 from the business for personal use, using Cheque No. 3416.

30 Received payment from Oscar Services for the May 22 sale less the discount.

30 Issued Cheque No. 3417, payable to Payroll, in payment of sales salaries, $5,320, and office salaries, $3,150. Cashed the cheque and paid the employees.

31 Cash sales for the last half of the month were $66,052.

31 Post to the customer and creditor accounts. Also, post individual items that are not included in column totals at the end of the month to the General Ledger accounts.

31 Foot and crossfoot the journals and make the month-end postings.

Required

1. Enter the transactions in the appropriate journals and post when instructed to do so. Use a periodic inventory system.

2. Prepare a trial balance in the Trial Balance columns of the provided work sheet form and complete the work sheet using the following information. (Assume Alpine uses the closing entry approach to record the change in the Merchandise Inventory account.)

   a. Expired insurance, $553.

   b. Ending store supplies inventory, $2,632.

   c. Ending office supplies inventory, $504.

   d. Estimated amortization of store equipment, $567.

   e. Estimated amortization of office equipment, $329.

   f. Ending merchandise inventory, $176,400.

3. Prepare a May multiple-step classified income statement, a May statement of owner's equity, and a May 31 classified balance sheet.

4. Prepare and post adjusting and closing entries.

5. Prepare a post-closing trial balance. Also prepare a list of the Accounts Receivable Ledger accounts and a list of the Accounts Payable Ledger accounts. Total the balances of each to confirm that the totals equal the balances in the controlling accounts.

BEYOND THE NUMBERS

Refer to the financial statements and related information for **Alliance** in Appendix I. Record answers to the following questions by analyzing information in the report:

1. Identify the note disclosing Alliance's segment information.

2. For fiscal year ended March 31, 1997, compute the percent of total revenue Alliance earned from foreign sources.

3. Compute the percent change in revenue from foreign sources for the fiscal years ending in 1996 and 1997. Comment on your findings.

Inco is the world's largest nickel producer and **Alcan** is the largest producer of flat-rolled aluminum products. Key comparative figures ($ millions) for these two organizations follow:

INCO Net Sales by Segment	Fiscal Year Ended Dec. 31, 1997	Fiscal Year Ended Dec. 31, 1996
Canada..........................	$ 268	$ 267
United States	685	715
Europe	495	569
Indonesia	40	53
Japan and other	879	856
Total............................	$2,367	$2,460

Figures are from the annual reports for the fiscal years ended December 31, 1997 and 1996.

Alcan Total Revenue by Segment	Fiscal year ended Dec. 31, 1997	Fiscal year ended Dec. 31, 1996
Canada..........................	$1,169	$1,210
United States	3,063	2,871
South America..................	395	579
Europe	2,609	2,633
Asia and Pacific.................	515	290
All other	26	31
Total............................	$7,777	$7,614

Figures are from the annual reports for the fiscal years ended December 31, 1997 and 1996.

Required

1. Compute the percent change in total net sales (Inco) and total revenue (Alcan) for the years given. Comment on your findings.

2. Compute the percent change in revenue by each geographic segment for each company. Comment on your findings.

3. Identify the geographic segment experiencing the largest growth in revenue for each company.

John Harris is a public accountant and a sole practitioner. He has been practising as an auditor for 10 years. Recently a long-standing audit client asked John to design and implement an integrated computer accounting information system. The fees associated with this additional engagement with the client are very attractive. However, John wonders if he can remain objective in his evaluation of the client's accounting system and records on subsequent annual audits if he puts himself in the position of auditing a system he was responsible for installing. John knows that the professional auditing standards require him to remain independent in fact and appearance of all of his auditing clients.

Reporting in Action

LO 8

Comparative Analysis

LO 8

Ethics Challenge

LO 7

Required

1. What do you think auditing standards mean when they require independence in fact? In appearance?

2. Why is it important that auditors remain independent of their clients?

3. Do you think John can accept this engagement and remain independent? Justify your response.

Communicating in Practice
LO 3, 4

Your friend, Ivanna B. Sweeter, has a small retail operation called "Goodies" that sells candies and nuts. Ivanna acquires her goods from a few select vendors. Purchase orders are generally made by phone and on credit. Sales are primarily for cash. Ivanna keeps her own manual accounting system using a general journal and a general ledger. At the end of each business day she records one summary entry for cash sales.

Recently, Ivanna began offering goodies packaged in creative and interesting gift packages. This has increased sales substantially and she is now receiving orders from corporate clients and others who order quantities and prefer to buy on credit. Increased sales translates to increased purchases. To expand her gift package selection, Ivanna is considering purchasing packaging supplies from other vendors. As a result of increased credit transactions, both purchases and sales, keeping the accounting records has become extremely time consuming. Ivanna would like to continue to maintain her own manual system. Ivanna calls you for advice. Write a memo to Ivanna advising her as to how she might modify her current manual accounting system to accommodate the expanded business activities described. She is accustomed to checking her ledger using a trial balance. Your memo should explain the advantages of what you propose and of any other verification techniques you recommend.

Taking It to the Net
LO 8

This chapter describes the impact of the accounting standard for reporting of segment information. Companies have criticized current regulatory discussions that seek to expand the information companies must report on their business segments. To learn more about current CICA deliberations on this topic and others you should visit the CICA's Web site at **http://www.cica.ca**.

Required

1. How is the Table of Contents for the CICA Web site organized? Identify the topical areas one can visit at this Web site.

2. Visit the Accounting Standards Project page of the Web site. What standards projects has the CICA undertaken most recently?

Teamwork in Action
LO 5, 6

Let's divide the labour! Each member of the team is to assume responsibility for *one* of the six tasks below.

1. Journalizing in the Purchases Journal.
2. Journalizing in the Cash Disbursement Journal
3. Maintaining and verifying the Accounts Payable Ledger
4. Journalizing in the Sales and General Journal
5. Journalizing in the Cash Receipts Journal
6. Maintaining and verifying the Accounts Receivable Ledger

The team should follow the procedures described below in carrying out responsibilities.

Work Procedures

1. After responsibilities 1–6 are assigned, each member of the team is to quickly read through the list of transactions in Problem 8-4, p. 411 identifying with initials the journal each transaction is to be recorded in. Upon completion, the team leader is to read transaction dates and the appropriate team member is to vocalize responsibility. Any disagreement from teammates must be resolved within the team.

2. Arrange seating to make it easier to access the necessary data for tasks assigned.

3. Journalize and continually update subsidiary ledgers. Journal recorders may want to alert subsidiary ledger maintainers when they have an entry to be posted to their subsidiary.

4. Students 1,2, 4 and 5 are to summarize and prove journals while students 3 and 6 are to prepare schedules.

5. The team leader is to take charge of the General Ledger, rotating team members to obtain amounts to be posted. The person responsible for a journal must complete appropriate post references in the journal. Other team members should verify accuracy of account balance computations. To avoid any abnormal account balances, post in the following order: P, S, G, CR, CD. *Note: Posting of any necessary individual General Ledger amounts are done at this time as well.*

6. The team leader is to read out general ledger account balances while one other team member fills in the trial balance form. Concurrently one member should keep a running balance of debit account balance totals and another credit account balance totals. Verify the final total of the trial balance and the schedules. If necessary, the team is to resolve any errors. Turn in the trial balance and schedules to instructor.

Join with a classmate and arrange a time when you can perform a brief accounting information systems survey by phone. Select five companies at random from the *Yellow Pages* of your community. This survey is probably most easily administered to small service companies in your area. Call each company and ask to speak to a person who is knowledgeable about the accounting system of the company. Explain that you are completing a brief phone survey for your introductory accounting class and that it will only take a few minutes to answer your questions. Your survey should ask the following questions:

1. Is the company's accounting system computerized?

2. If computerized what brand of software is used? Is this software a customized program written specifically for the company or is it a standardized program available to many companies? (Note: Some companies use a combination.)

3. What input device(s) is used to enter transactions into the system?

4. Does the company use on-line or batch processing?

5. Does the company use a network or stand-alone computer workstations?

Hitting the Road
LO 2

Both the CICA's Accounting Standards Board (AcSB) and the AICPA's Financial Accounting Standards Board (FASB) have been criticized for the way in which accounting standards are set. Read the article "Corporate America Is Fed Up with FASB" in the April 21, 1997, edition of *Business Week*.

1. What key reasons are identified in the article's table as criticisms by companies of the FASB?

2. Why are companies critical of FASB's proposal on segment reporting?

3. In addition to the reasons cited in the article, are there other reasons you can think of why companies do not wish to expand segment reporting beyond what is currently required?

Business Break
LO 8

9

Internal Control and Cash

▶ A Look Back

Chapter 8 focused on accounting information systems. We explained the fundamental principles and components of information systems, the use of special journals and subsidiary ledgers, and technology-based systems. We also discussed segment reporting and how to analyze these data.

▶ A Look at This Chapter

This chapter extends our study of accounting information systems to the area of internal control and accounting for cash. We describe procedures that are good for internal control. We also explain the control of and accounting for cash.

▶ A Look Forward

Chapter 10 focuses on temporary investments and receivables. These items are the most liquid assets other than cash. We explain how to account and report for these assets.

Chapter Outline

▶ **Internal Control**
- Purpose of Internal Control
- Principles of Internal Control
- Technology and Internal Control
- Limitations of Internal Control

▶ **Control of Cash**
- Cash, Cash Equivalents, and Liquidity
- Control of Cash Receipts
- Control of Cash Disbursements

▶ **Banking Activities as Controls**
- Basic Bank Services
- Electronic Funds Transfer
- Bank Statement
- Bank Reconciliation

▶ **Using the Information—Days' Sales Uncollected**

Losing Control

Toronto, ON—Jason Barron is a 23-year-old entrepreneur and owner of **Barron Sports.** He's one of the people we see toting a cart full of souvenirs, pennants, and various fan-crazed items on our way to baseball games and other sporting events. "I started doing Argonaut football games when I was 15," says Barron. "I sell at all of Toronto's big sporting events. And I now hire people to sell items at sporting events in other Canadian cities." But Barron is a victim of employee theft and fraud.

"I had no idea what types of controls I needed when I hired people to sell for me," says Barron. "I was learning on the run, and it nearly cost me everything." Barron's problems grew from his success. Profit margins on items he sold were enormous, and sales were brisk. He quickly hired additional people to sell for him and began covering more events. But he had no real system of control, either for cash or the salable items.

"I didn't know the first thing about recordkeeping, internal control, or cash accounting," admits Barron. "It really hit home when I sent one shipment of items to a person working for me in Calgary. It was for the Flames' games. The items I sent cost me about $2,500, but they sell for about $12,000." But Barron got back only a little more than $6,800, yet everything was supposedly sold. What happened? "The person selling for me had lots of excuses—shoplifting, damage, not delivered—you name it. It was clear to me he had ripped me off to a tune of more than $5,000 in one month! That's when I knew I couldn't continue like this."

Barron responded with several new control procedures. They included making all employees accountable for sale items, and making them pay for items lost or stolen. In return, he substantially increased sales commissions. These changes and others greatly cut into profit margins, but nearly eliminated the cost of employee theft and fraud. "Things are back on track," says Barron. "I want to do the playoff games this year, and hopefully be at the Grey Cup." Like a good coach, Barron has cut distractions and is now focused on the sales game.

CHAPTER PREVIEW

We all are aware of reports and experiences involving theft and fraud. These activities affect us and produce various actions. These actions include locking doors, chaining bikes, reviewing sales receipts, and acquiring alarm systems. A company also takes actions to safeguard, control, and manage what it owns. Experience tells us small companies are most vulnerable. This is usually due to weak internal controls. It is management's responsibility to set up policies and procedures to safeguard a company's assets, especially cash. To do so, management and employees must understand and apply principles of internal control. This chapter describes these principles and how we apply them. We learn about important internal control policies and procedures. We focus special attention on cash. This is because cash is easily transferable and often at high risk of loss. Several controls for cash are explained including a voucher system, petty cash funds, and reconciling bank accounts. This chapter also describes a method of accounting for purchases that helps us decide whether cash discounts on purchases are being lost and, if so, how much is lost. Our understanding of these controls and procedures makes us more secure in carrying out business activities and in assessing those activities of companies. Like Jason Barron in the opening article, knowledge of these topics is crucial in successfully running a company.

Internal Control

This section describes internal control and its fundamental principles. We also discuss the impact of computing technology for internal control and the limitations of control procedures.

Purpose of Internal Control

LO1 Define internal control and its purpose.

Managers of small businesses often control the entire operation. They supervise workers, participate in all activities, and make major decisions. These managers, for instance, usually buy all the assets and services used in the business. They also hire and manage employees, negotiate all contracts, and sign all cheques. These managers know from personal contact and observation whether the business is actually receiving the assets and services paid for. Larger companies find it increasingly difficult to maintain this close personal contact. At some point, managers must delegate responsibilities and rely on formal procedures rather than personal contact in controlling and knowing all operations of the business.

These managers use an internal control system to monitor and control its operations. An **internal control system** is all policies and procedures managers use to:

- Protect assets
- Ensure reliable accounting
- Promote efficient operations
- Urge adherence to company policies

A properly designed internal control system is a key part of systems design, analysis, and performance. Managers place a high priority on internal control systems. This is because these systems can prevent avoidable losses, help managers plan operations, and monitor company and human performance. While internal controls can't guarantee anything, the risks associated with these activities decline.

Did You Know?

Principles of Internal Control

Internal control policies and procedures vary from company to company. They depend on factors such as the nature of the business and its size. Yet certain fundamental internal control principles apply to all companies. The **principles of internal control** are to:

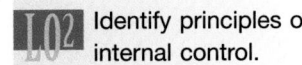

Identify principles of internal control.

1. Establish responsibilities.
2. Maintain adequate records.
3. Insure assets and bond key employees.
4. Separate recordkeeping from custody of assets.
5. Divide responsibility for related transactions.
6. Apply technological controls.
7. Perform regular and independent reviews.

We explain these seven principles in the next section. We also describe how internal control procedures minimize the risk of fraud and theft. These procedures ensure that the accounting records are reliable and accurate.

Establish Responsibilities

Proper internal control means responsibility for each task is clearly established and assigned to one person. When responsibility is not identified, it is difficult to determine who is at fault when a problem occurs. When two salesclerks share access to the same cash register, for instance, it is difficult to identify which clerk is at fault if there is a cash shortage. Neither clerk can prove or disprove the alleged shortage. To prevent this problem, one clerk might be given responsibility for handling all cash sales. Alternately, a company can use a register with separate cash drawers for each clerk. Most of us have experienced waiting in line at a retail counter during a change of shift for employees and seeing them swap cash drawers for this purpose.

Maintain Adequate Records

Good recordkeeping is part of an internal control system. It helps protect assets and ensures that employees use prescribed procedures. Reliable records are also a source of information that management uses to monitor company operations. When detailed records of manufacturing equipment and tools are kept, for instance, items are unlikely to be lost or stolen without the discrepancy being noticed. Similarly, transactions are less likely to be entered to incorrect accounts if a chart of accounts is set up and used carefully. If this chart is not set up or used incorrectly, managers might never discover excessive expenses or inflated sales.

   Many preprinted forms and internal business papers are also designed and properly used in a good internal control system. When sales slips are properly designed, for instance, sales personnel can record needed information efficiently without errors or delays to customers. And when sales slips are prenumbered and accounted for, each sales slip issued is the responsibility of one salesperson. This means a salesperson is not able to pocket cash by making a sale and destroying the sales slip. Computerized point-of-sale systems achieve the same control results.

Insure Assets and Bond Key Employees

Good internal control means that assets are adequately insured against casualty, and employees handling cash and negotiable assets are bonded. An employee is *bonded* when a company purchases an insurance policy, or a bond, against losses from theft by that employee. Bonding reduces the risk of loss suffered from theft. It also discourages theft because bonded employees know that an independent bonding company is involved when theft is uncovered.

Did You Know?

High-Tech Threads

Theft and counterfeiting is a concern of most companies. But **Intermec Systems Corporation** has developed a technique for permanently marking paper, currency, and all physical assets. Its new technique involves embedding a square-inch tag made of nylon fibres with different light-absorbing properties. Each pattern of fibres creates a unique optical signature. They hope to embed tags in everything from compact disks and credit cards to designer clothes and accessories to help fight theft and counterfeiting. Retailers will be able to verify products by running scanners over the fibre tag. [Source: *Materials Management & Distribution*, October 1997.]

Separate Recordkeeping from Custody of Assets

An important principle of internal control is that a person who controls or has access to an asset must not keep that asset's accounting records. This principle reduces the risk of theft or waste of an asset because the person with control over the asset knows that records of the asset are kept by another person. Also the recordkeeper doesn't have access to the asset and has no reason to falsify records. This means that two people must both agree to commit a fraud, called *collusion*, if the asset is stolen and the theft is hidden from the records. Because collusion in this case is necessary to commit the fraud, it is less likely to occur.

Divide Responsibility for Related Transactions

Good internal control divides responsibility for a transaction or a series of related transactions between two or more individuals or departments. This is to ensure the work of one acts as a check on the other. But this principle, often called *separation of duties,* is not a call for duplication of work. Each employee or department should perform unduplicated effort.

Examples of transactions for divided responsibility are placing purchase orders, receiving merchandise, and paying vendors. These tasks shouldn't be given to one individual or department. Assigning responsibility for any of these tasks to one party creates a case where mistakes and perhaps fraud are more likely to occur. Having an independent person, for example, check incoming goods for quality and quantity, encourages more care and attention to detail than when checked by the person placing the order. Added protection can result from identifying a third person to approve payment of the invoice. Again the risk of both error and fraud is reduced. We can even designate a fourth person with authority to write cheques as another measure of protection.

Apply Technological Controls

Cash registers, cheque protectors, time clocks, mechanical counters, and personal identification scanners are examples of control devices that can improve internal control. They should be used effectively. A cash register with a locked-in tape or electronic file makes a record of each cash sale. A cheque protector perforates the amount of a cheque into its face and makes it difficult to alter the amount. A time clock registers the exact time an employee both arrives on and departs from the job. Mechanical change and currency counters can quickly and accurately count amounts. And personal scanners can limit access to only those individuals authorized. Each of these and other technological controls are effective parts of many internal control systems.

Face Codes

We're all familiar with bar codes, but how about "face codes"? **Viisage Technology** has licensed a powerful face-recognition program from MIT. It snaps a digital picture of the face and converts key facial features—say, the distance between the eyes—into a series of numerical values. These can be stored on an ID or ATM card as a simple bar code. Searching through tens of thousands of faces is a snap. Welfare agencies in Massachusetts are already using the system to identify fraudulent welfare cases. [Source: *Business Week,* May 5, 1997.]

Did You Know?

Perform Regular and Independent Reviews

No internal control system is entirely effective. Changes in personnel and technological advances present opportunities for shortcuts and other lapses. So does the stress of time pressures. To counter these changes, regular reviews of internal control systems are needed to ensure that procedures are followed. These reviews are preferably done by internal auditors who are employees not directly involved in operations. Their independent perspective encourages an evaluation of the efficiency as well as the effectiveness of the internal control system.

Many companies also pay for audits by independent auditors who are professional accountants. These external auditors test the company's financial records and then give an opinion as to whether the company's financial statements are presented fairly in accordance with generally accepted accounting principles. Before external auditors decide on how much testing is needed, they evaluate the risk of errors occurring in the internal control system. In the process of their evaluation, they often identify internal controls needing improvement. This information is often helpful to a client.

Campaign Manager

You are leading a campaign to influence the government to improve the health care system. Your funding is limited and you try hiring people committed to your cause and who will work for less. A systems analyst recently volunteered her services and put together a Web strategy to attract supporters. She also strongly encouraged you to force all employees to take at least one week of vacation per year. Why does she feel so strongly about a "forced vacation" policy?

You Make the Call

Answer—p. 454

Technology and Internal Control

The fundamental principles of internal control are relevant no matter what the technological state of the accounting system. This includes purely manual systems to those fully automated with only electronic documentation. Yet the technology impacts an internal control system in several important ways. Perhaps the most obvious is that technology is allowing us quicker access to ever-increasing information databases. Used effectively, managers' ability to monitor and control business operations is greatly improved. This section describes some technological impacts we must be alert to.

Reduced Processing Errors

Technologically advanced systems reduce the number of errors in processing information. Provided the software and data entries are correct, the risk of mechanical and mathematical errors is nearly eliminated. Yet erroneous data entry does occur and one must be alert to that possibility. The decreasing human involvement in later data processing can cause data entry errors to go undiscovered. Similarly, errors in software can produce consistent erroneous processing of transactions. It is important to continually check and monitor all types of systems.

More Extensive Testing of Records

A company's regular review and audit of electronic records can include more extensive testing when information is easily and rapidly accessed. When accounting records are kept manually, auditors and others likely select only small samples of data to test. But when data is accessible with computer technology, then large samples or even complete data files can be quickly reviewed and analyzed.

Limited Evidence of Processing

Because many data processing steps are increasingly done by computer, fewer "hard copy" items of documentary evidence are available for review. Yet technologically advanced systems can store additional evidence. They can, for instance, record information such as who made the entries, the date and time, and the source of their entry. Technology can also be designed to require use of passwords or other identification before access to the system is granted. This means that internal control depends more on the design and operation of the information system and less on analysis of the documents left behind by the system.

Crucial Separation of Duties

Technological advances in accounting information systems are so efficient that they often require fewer employees. This reduction in workforce carries a risk that separation of crucial responsibilities is lost. Companies that use advanced technology also need employees with special skills to operate programs and equipment. The duties of these employees must be controlled and monitored to minimize risk of error and fraud. Better control is maintained if, for instance, the person designing and programming the system does not serve as the operator. Also the control over programs and files related to cash receipts and disbursements must be separated. Cheque-writing activities should not be controlled by a computer operator in order to avoid risk of fraud. Yet achieving acceptable separation of duties can be especially difficult in small companies with few employees.

Did You Know?

Calling All Techies
Most internal control systems today demand input from information technology workers. The shortage of high-tech workers is so pronounced that the federal government has temporarily relaxed immigration requirements to allow foreign workers easier and faster entry into Canada. Demand far outstrips supply, producing a bidding war for digital talent. Giants such as **IBM Canada Ltd.** and **Northern Telecom Ltd.** are planning to take on hundreds of new programmers and other skilled staffers this year, while smaller firms will hire hundreds more. As the competition for talent grows, so do salaries. According to **Ward Associates,** a Toronto-based recruiter, salaries of network administrators and architects have increased to $75,000 in 1997 from a high of $50,000 in 1995.
[Source: *Canadian Business,* November 14, 1997.]

Limitations of Internal Control

All internal control policies and procedures have limitations. Probably the most serious source of these limitations is the human element. Internal control policies and procedures are applied by people and often impact other people. This human element creates several potential limitations that we can categorize as either (1) human error, or (2) human fraud.

Human error is a factor whenever internal control policies and procedures are carried out by people. *Human error* can occur from negligence, fatigue, misjudgment or confusion. *Human fraud* involves intent by people to defeat internal controls for personal gain. Fraudulent behaviour can defeat many internal controls. This includes collusion to thwart the separation of duties principle as explained above. This human element highlights the importance of establishing an *internal control environment*. This environment conveys management's attitude and commitment to internal control policies and procedures.

Another important limitation of internal control is the *cost-benefit principle.* This means the costs of internal controls must not exceed their benefits. Analysis of costs and benefits must consider all factors, including the impact on morale. Most companies, for instance, have a legal right to read employees' e-mail. Yet companies seldom exercise that right unless confronted with evidence of potential harm to the company. The same holds for drug testing, phone tapping and hidden cameras. The bottom line is that no internal control system is perfect and that managers must establish internal control policies and procedures with a net benefit to the company.

Flashback

1. Fundamental principles of internal control state that (choose the correct statement):

   a. Responsibility for a series of related transactions (such as placing orders for, receiving, and paying for merchandise) should be assigned to one person.

   b. Responsibility for specific tasks should be shared by more than one employee so that one serves as a check on the other.

   c. Employees who handle cash and negotiable assets are bonded.

2. What are some impacts of computing technology for internal control?

Answers—p. 455

Control of Cash

Cash is a necessary asset and part of every company. Most companies also include *cash equivalents,* which are similar to cash, as part of cash. We define cash equivalents later in this section. It is important we apply principles of good internal control to cash. Cash is the most liquid of all assets and is easily hidden and moved. A good system of internal control for cash provides adequate procedures for protecting both cash receipts and cash disbursements. These procedures should meet three basic guidelines:

1. Separate handling of cash from recordkeeping of cash.
2. Cash receipts are promptly (daily) deposited in a bank.
3. Cash disbursements are made by cheque.

The first guideline aims to minimize errors and fraud by a division of duties. When duties are separated, it requires two or more people to collude for cash to be stolen and the theft to be concealed in the accounting records. The second guideline aims to use immediate (daily) deposits of all cash receipts to produce a timely independent test of the accuracy of the count of cash received. It also reduces cash theft or loss, and it reduces the risk of an employee personally using the money before depositing it. The third guideline aims to use payments by cheque to develop a bank record of cash disbursements. This guideline also reduces the risk of cash theft.

One exception to the third guideline is to allow small disbursements of currency and coins from a *petty cash fund*. We describe a petty cash fund later in this section. Another important point is that the deposit of cash receipts and the use of cheques for cash disbursements allows a company to use bank records as a separate external record of cash transactions. We explain how to use bank records to confirm the accuracy of a company's own records later in this section.

The exact procedures used to achieve control over cash vary across companies. They depend on such factors as company size, number of employees, volume of cash transactions, and sources of cash. We must therefore view the procedures described in this section as illustrative of those in practice today.

Cash, Cash Equivalents, and Liquidity

LO3 Define cash and cash equivalents and how they are reported.

Cash is an important asset for every company and must be managed. Companies also need to carefully control access to cash by employees and others who are inclined to take it for personal use. Good accounting systems support both goals by managing how much cash is on hand and controlling who has access to it. The importance of accounting for cash is highlighted by the inclusion of a statement of cash flows in a complete set of financial statements. That statement identifies activities affecting cash.[1] The purpose of this section is to define cash and cash equivalents. It also explains liquidity and its relation to cash and cash equivalents.

Cash Defined

Cash includes currency, coins, and amounts on deposit in bank accounts, chequing accounts (also called *demand deposits*) and some savings accounts (also called *time deposits*). Cash also includes items that are acceptable for deposit in these accounts such as customers' cheques, cashier's cheques, certified cheques, and money orders.

Cash Equivalents Defined

To increase their return on investment, many companies invest idle cash in assets called cash equivalents. **Cash equivalents** are short-term, highly liquid investment assets meeting two criteria:

1. Readily convertible to a known cash amount.
2. Are subject to an insignificant risk of changes in value.

Investments purchased within three months of their maturity dates usually satisfy these criteria.[2] Examples of cash equivalents are short-term investments in treasury bills, commercial paper such as short-term corporate notes payable, and money market funds.

---

[1] We described the statement of cash flows in earlier chapters and discussed cash flow relative to various topics. Chapter 16 explains the statement of cash flows in detail.

[2] *CICA Handbook,* section 1540, "Cash Flow Statements," par. .08.

Reporting Cash and Cash Equivalents

Because cash equivalents are similar to cash, many companies combine them with cash as a single item on the balance sheet. **Dominion Textile Inc.,** for instance, reports the following on its June 30, 1997, balance sheet:

Cash and cash equivalents .... $ 66.9 (million)

Another case is that of **Semi-Tech Corporation** where its March 31, 1997, balance sheet reports a Cash and cash equivalent balance of over $332 (million). The Notes to the Consolidated Financial Statements report:

Cash equivalents consist of highly liquid investments with maturities of three months or less when purchased. **STC** places its temporary cash investments with high credit quality financial institutions. At March 31, 1997, the balance of cash and cash equivalents include time deposits and short-term investments...

Liquidity

Cash is the usual means of payment when paying for other assets, services, or liabilities. **Liquidity** refers to how easily an asset can be converted into another asset or be used in paying for services or obligations. All assets can be judged on their liquidity. Cash and similar assets are called **liquid assets** because they are converted easily into other assets or used in paying for services or liabilities. A company needs more than valuable assets to operate. A company must own some liquid assets, for example, so that bills are paid on time and purchases are made for cash when necessary.

Flashback

3. Why must a company own liquid assets?
4. Why does a company own cash equivalent assets in addition to cash?
5. Identify at least two assets that are classified as a cash equivalent.

Answers—p. 455

Control of Cash Receipts

Internal control of cash receipts ensures all cash received is properly recorded and deposited. Cash receipts arise from many transactions including cash sales, collections of customers' accounts, receipts of interest and rent, bank loans, sale of assets, and owners' investments. The principles of internal control apply to all types of cash receipts. This section explains internal control over two important types of cash receipts: over-the-counter and mail.

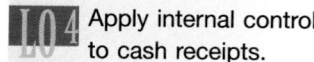

Apply internal control to cash receipts.

Over-the-Counter Cash Receipts

Over-the-counter cash sales should be recorded on a cash register at the time of each sale for internal control. To help ensure that correct amounts are entered, each register should be located so customers can read the amounts entered. Clerks also should be required both to enter each sale before wrapping merchandise and to give the customer a receipt for each sale. The design of each cash register should provide a permanent, locked-in record of each transaction. In many systems, the register is directly linked with computing and accounting services. Many software programs accept cash register transactions and enter them in accounting records. Less technology-dependent registers simply print a record of each transaction on a paper tape or electronic file locked inside the register.

One principle of internal control states that custody over cash should be separate from its recordkeeping. For over-the-counter cash sales, this separation begins with the cash register. The clerk who has access to cash in the register should not have access to its locked-in record. At the end of the clerk's work period, the clerk should count the cash in the register, record the amount, and turn over the cash and a record of its amount to an employee in the cashier's office. The employee in the cashier's office, like the clerk, has access to the cash and should not have access to accounting records (or the register tape or file). A third employee compares the record of total register transactions (or the register tape or file) with the cash receipts reported by the cashier's office. This record (or register tape or file) is the basis for a journal entry recording over-the-counter cash sales. Note the third employee has access to the records for cash but not to the actual cash. The clerk and the employee from the cashier's office have access to cash but not to the accounting records. This means the accuracy of cash records and amounts are automatically checked. None of them can make a mistake or divert cash without the difference being revealed.

Did You Know?

Register Mammoth

Wal-Mart uses an enormous network of information links with its point-of-sale cash registers. With annual sales of more than $100 billion, it uses efficient information systems to coordinate sales, purchases, and distribution. Three Buenos Aires supercentres, for instance, ring up some 15,000 sales on heavy days. Wal-Mart is now the dominant discounter in Canada, the U.S., and Mexico. Yet even it makes mistakes, from a glut of ice-fishing huts in tropical Puerto Rico to a dearth of snowshoes in wintertime Ontario. But using cash register information, it is quick to fix mistakes and to capitalize on sales trends. [Source: *Business Week*, June 23, 1997.]

Cash Over and Short

Sometimes errors in making change are discovered when there are differences between the cash in a cash register and the record of the amount of cash sales. Even though a cashier is careful, one or more customers can be given too much or too little change. This means at the end of a work period, the cash in a cash register might not equal the cash sales entered. This difference is reported in the **Cash Over and Short** account. This account is an income statement account recording the income effects of cash overages and cash shortages from errors in making change and missing petty cash receipts. As an example, if a cash register shows cash sales of $550 but the count of cash in the register is $555, the entry to record cash sales and its overage is:

Assets = Liabilities + Equity
+555   + 5
                +550

Cash	555	
Cash Over and Short		5
Sales		550
To record day's cash sales and overage.		

If a cash register shows cash sales of $625 but the count of cash in the register is $621, the entry to record cash sales and its shortage is:

Cash	621	
Cash Over and Short	4	
Sales		625
To record day's cash sales and shortage.		

Assets = Liabilities + Equity
+621   − 4
                +625

Because customers are more likely to dispute being shortchanged, the Cash Over and Short account usually has a debit balance at the end of an accounting period. This debit balance reflects an expense. It can be shown on the income statement as an item in general and administrative expenses. But since the amount is usually small, it is often combined with other small expenses and reported as part of *miscellaneous expenses*. If Cash Over and Short has a credit balance at the end of the period, it usually is shown on the income statement as part of *miscellaneous revenues*.

Cash Receipts by Mail

Control of cash receipts that arrive through the mail starts with the person who opens the mail. Preferably, two people are assigned the task and are present when opening the mail. The person opening the mail makes a list (in triplicate) of money received. This list should contain a record of each sender's name, the amount, and an explanation for what purpose the money is sent. The first copy is sent with the money to the cashier. A second copy is sent to the accounting area. A third copy is kept by the clerk who opened the mail. The cashier deposits the money in the bank, and the recordkeeper records amounts received in the accounting records.

This process reflects excellent internal control. First, when the bank balance is reconciled by another person (explained later in the chapter), errors or fraud by the clerk, the cashier, or the recordkeeper are revealed. They are revealed because the bank's record of cash deposited must agree with the records from each of three people. Note how this arrangement virtually eliminates the possibility of errors and fraud. The exception is when employees collude. If the clerk does not report all receipts correctly, for instance, customers will question their account balances. If the cashier does not deposit all receipts, for instance, the bank balance does not agree with the recordkeeper's cash balance. The recordkeeper and the person who reconciles the bank balance do not have access to cash and, therefore, have no opportunity to divert cash to themselves. This system makes errors and fraud highly unlikely.

Control of Cash Disbursements

Control of cash disbursements is especially important for companies. Most large thefts occur from payments of fictitious invoices. The key to controlling cash disbursements is to require that all expenditures be made by cheque. The only exception is for small payments from petty cash. Another key is when the authority to sign cheques is assigned to a person other than the owner, then that person must not have access to the accounting records. This separation of duties helps prevent an employee from hiding fraudulent disbursements in the accounting records.

The manager of a small business often signs cheques and knows from personal contact that the items being paid for are actually received. This arrangement is impossible in large businesses. Instead, internal control procedures must be substituted for personal contact. These procedures are designed to assure the cheque signer that the obligations recorded were properly incurred and should be paid. These controls are achieved through a voucher system. This section describes the voucher system, explains the petty cash system, and describes the management of cash disbursements for purchases.

Paper Chase

Paper documents are still common in business today. Yet companies are increasingly converting to electronic documents. The purposes and features of most documents remain basically the same in either system. But the internal control system must change to reflect different risks and concerns. These include issues of confidentiality and competitive sensitive information that are placed at risk in electronic-based systems.

Voucher System of Control

LO 5 Apply the voucher system to control cash disbursements.

A **voucher system** is a set of procedures and approvals designed to control cash disbursements and acceptance of obligations. The voucher system of control establishes procedures for:

- Accepting obligations resulting in cash disbursements.
- Verifying, approving, and recording obligations.
- Issuing cheques for payment of verified, approved, and recorded obligations.
- Requiring obligations be recorded when incurred.
- Treating each purchase as an independent transaction.

A good voucher system produces these results for every transaction. This applies even when many purchases are made from the same company during a period.

A voucher system's control over cash disbursements begins when a company incurs an obligation that will result in a payment of cash. A key factor in this system is that only approved departments and individuals are authorized to incur such obligations. The system also often limits the kind of obligations that a department or individual can incur. In a large retail store, for instance, only a purchasing department should be authorized to incur obligations from merchandise purchases. Another key factor is that procedures for purchasing, receiving, and paying for merchandise are often divided among several departments. These departments include the one requesting the purchase, the purchasing department, the receiving department, and the accounting department. To coordinate and control the responsibilities of these departments, several different business papers are used. Exhibit 9.1 shows how these papers are accumulated in a **voucher.** A voucher is an internal business paper (or "folder") that is used to accumulate other papers and information needed to control cash disbursements and to ensure a transaction is properly recorded. We next discuss each document entering a voucher. This is to show how a company uses this system in controlling cash disbursements for merchandise purchases.

Exhibit 9.1

Voucher and Business Documents

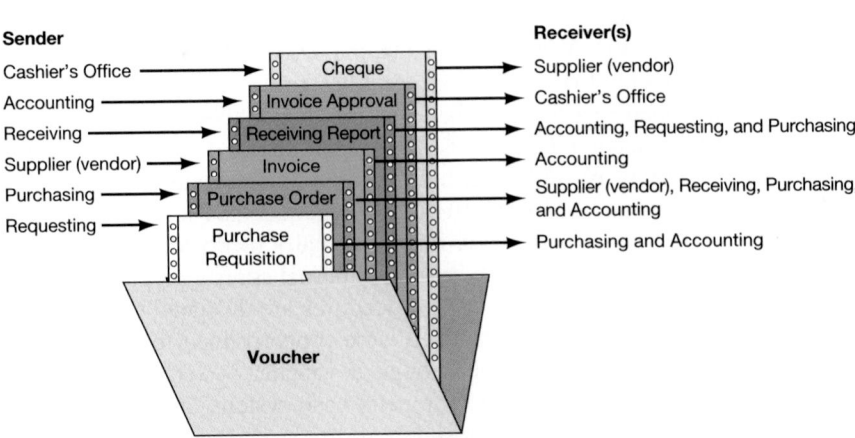

Purchase Requisition

Department managers in larger stores are usually not allowed to place orders directly with suppliers. If each manager deals directly with suppliers, the merchandise purchased and the resulting liabilities are not well controlled. To gain control over purchases and the resulting liabilities, department managers are often required to place all orders through a purchasing department. When merchandise is needed, a department manager must inform the purchasing department of its needs by preparing and signing a purchase requisition. A **purchase requisition** lists the merchandise needed by a department and requests that it be purchased—see Exhibit 9.2. Two copies of the purchase requisition are sent to the purchasing department. The purchasing department sends one copy to the accounting department. When the accounting department receives a purchase requisition, it creates and maintains a voucher for this transaction. A third copy of the requisition is kept by the requesting department as back up.

Purchase Requisition		No. 917
Z-Mart		

From ___ Sporting Goods Department ___   **Date** _____ October 28, 1998 _____

To ____ Purchasing Department _____   **Preferred Vendor** ___ Trex _____

Request purchase of the following item(s):

Model No.	Description	Quantity
CH 015	Challenger X7	1
SD 099	SpeedDemon	1

Reason for Request _____ Replenish inventory _____

Approval for Request _____ *J.Z.* _____

For Purchasing Department use only: Order Date Oct. 30/98   P.O. No. ____ P98 ___

Exhibit 9.2

Purchase Requisition

Purchase Order

A **purchase order** is a business paper used by the purchasing department to place an order with a seller, also called a **vendor.** A vendor usually is a manufacturer or wholesaler. A purchase order authorizes a vendor to ship ordered merchandise at the stated price and terms—see Exhibit 9.3. When the purchasing department receives a purchase requisition, it prepares at least four copies of a purchase order. The copies are distributed as follows: *Copy 1* is sent to the vendor as a purchase request and as authority to ship merchandise; *Copy 2* is sent, along with a copy of the purchase requisition, to the accounting department where it is entered in the voucher and used in approving payment of the invoice; *Copy 3* is sent to the requesting department to inform its manager that action is being taken; *Copy 4* is sent to the receiving department; and *Copy 5* is retained on file by the purchasing department.

Year 2000

Year 2000 has a special meaning to systems experts. Generations of computer systems are designed to work on dates beginning with 19. This means new software is necessary to make them usable in the year 2000 and beyond. Cost estimates at the national level are significant. Companies in the financial services area are especially hard hit. The CICA has a guideline for companies on disclosure of the uncertainty caused by the year 2000 issue. [Source: *Canadian Business,* November 14, 1997.]

Did You Know?

Exhibit 9.3

Purchase Order

Purchase Order				No. P98
Z-Mart				
10 Prairie Street				
Winnipeg, MB R3J 1G9				

To: Trex
9797 Cherry Road
Windsor, ON N9G 2P5

Date _____ Oct. 30/98 _____
FOB _____ Destination _____
Ship by _ As soon as possible _____
Terms _____ 2/15, n/30 _____

Request shipment of the following item(s):

Model No.	Description	Quantity	Price	Amount
CH 015	Challenger X7	1	490	490
SD 099	SpeedDemon	1	710	710

All shipments and invoices must
include purchase order number

Ordered by

J.W.

Invoice

An **invoice** is an itemized statement of goods prepared by the vendor (seller) listing the customer's name, the items sold, the sales prices, and the terms of sale. An invoice is also a bill sent to the buyer by the seller. From the vendor's point of view, it is a *sales invoice*. The vendor sends the invoice to a buyer, or **vendee,** who treats it as a *purchase invoice*. When receiving a purchase order, the vendor ships the ordered merchandise to the buyer and includes or mails a copy of the invoice covering the shipment to the buyer. The invoice is sent to the buyer's accounting department where it is placed in the voucher. Exhibit 6.6 on page 262 shows Z-Mart's purchase invoice.

Receiving Report

Many companies maintain a special department to receive all merchandise or other purchased assets. When each shipment arrives, this receiving department counts the goods and checks them for damage and agreement with the purchase order. It then prepares four or more copies of a receiving report. A **receiving report** is used within the company to notify the appropriate persons that ordered goods are received and to describe the quantities and condition of the goods. One copy is placed in the voucher. Copies are also sent to the requesting department and the purchasing department to notify them that goods arrived. The receiving department retains a copy in its files.

Invoice Approval

When a receiving report arrives, the accounting department should have copies of these papers on file in the voucher: purchase requisition, purchase order, invoice, and receiving report. With the information on these papers, the accounting department can record the purchase and approve its payment before the end of the discount period. In approving an invoice for payment, this department checks and compares information across all papers. To facilitate this checking and to ensure that no step is omitted, the department often uses an **invoice approval form,** also called *cheque authorization*. Exhibit 9.4 shows an invoice approval form. An invoice approval is a checklist of steps necessary for approving an invoice for recording and payment. It is a separate business paper either filed in the voucher or preprinted on the voucher. It is sometimes stamped on the invoice. Exhibit 9.4 shows the invoice approval as a separate document.

Invoice Approval			
	No.	By	Date
Purchase requisition	917	*TL*	Oct. 28/98
Purchase order	P98	*JW*	Oct. 30/98
Receiving report	R85	*JK*	Nov. 3/98
Invoice:	1915		
Price		*QK*	Nov. 12/98
Calculations		*QK*	Nov. 12/98
Terms		*QK*	Nov. 12/98
Approved for payment		*BC*	Nov. 12/98

Exhibit 9.4

Invoice Approval

As each step in the checklist is approved, the clerk initials the invoice approval and records the current date. Approval implies the following actions have been taken for each step:

1. *Requisition check* Items on invoice are requested, as shown on purchase requisition.
2. *Purchase order check* Items on invoice are ordered, as shown on purchase order.
3. *Receiving report check* Items on invoice are received, as shown on receiving report.
4. *Invoice check:*   *Price* Invoice prices are as agreed with the vendor (on purchase order).
        Calculations Invoice has no mathematical errors.
        Terms Terms are as agreed with the vendor (on purchase order).

The Voucher

Once an invoice is checked and approved, the voucher is complete. A complete voucher is a record summarizing a transaction. The voucher shows a transaction is certified as correct and it authorizes recording an obligation for the buyer. A voucher also contains approval for paying the obligation on an appropriate date. The physical form of vouchers varies across companies. Many are designed so that the invoice and other related source documents are placed inside the voucher, which is often a folder.

Completion of a voucher usually requires a person to enter certain information required on the inside and outside of the voucher. Typical information required on the inside of a voucher is shown in Exhibit 9.5, and that for the out-

Exhibit 9.5

Inside of a Voucher

Z-Mart
Winnipeg, MB
Voucher No. 4657

Date ____ Oct. 28, 1998 ____

Pay to ____ Trex ____

City ____ Windsor ____ Province ____ Ontario ____

For the following: (attach all invoices and supporting papers)

Date of Invoice	Terms	Invoice Number and Other Details	Terms
Nov. 2, 1998	2/15, n/30	Invoice No. 1915	1,200
		Less discount	24
		Net amount payable	1,176

Payment approved

N. O. Neal

Auditor

Exhibit 9.6

Outside of a Voucher

Accounting Distribution		Voucher No. <u>4657</u>	

Account Debited	Amount
Merch. Inventory	1,200
Store Supplies	
Office Supplies	
Sales Salaries	
Other	
Total Vouch. Pay. Cr.	1,200

Due Date _____ November 12, 1998
Pay to _____ Trex
City _____ Windsor
Province _____ ON

Summary of charges:
    Total charges _____ 1,200
    Discount _____ 24
    Net payment _____ 1,176

Record of payment:
    Paid _____
    Cheque No. _____

side is shown in Exhibit 9.6. The information is taken from the invoice and the supporting documents filed in the voucher. A complete voucher is sent to an authorized individual (often called an *auditor*). This person performs a final review, approves the accounts and amounts for debiting (called the *accounting distribution*), and authorizes recording of the voucher.

When a voucher is approved and recorded, it is filed until its due date, when it is sent to the cashier's office for payment. The person issuing cheques relies on the approved voucher and its signed supporting documents as proof that an obligation is incurred and must be paid. The purchase requisition and purchase order confirm the purchase is authorized. The receiving report shows items are received, and the invoice approval form verifies the invoice is checked for errors. There is little chance for error. There is even less chance for fraud without collusion, unless all the documents and signatures are forged.

Did You Know?

Anyone Smell a Rat?
Weak internal control contributed to a debacle at **Centennial Technologies**, once a high-tech dynamo. Fictitious sales receipts, altered inventory tags, and recording sales that were never shipped are some of the actions carried out by Centennial's management to deceive users. CEO Emanuel Pinez was eventually indicted on five counts of fraud. Yet many of these accounting shenanigans could have been avoided with better internal control and oversight. [Source: *Business Week,* March 24, 1997.]

Expenses in a Voucher System

Obligations should be approved for payment and recorded as liabilities as soon as possible after they are incurred. This practice should be applied to all purchases. It should also be applied to all expenses. When a company receives a monthly telephone bill, for instance, the charges (especially long-distance and costly calls) should be examined for accuracy. A voucher is prepared and the telephone bill is filed inside the voucher. This voucher is then recorded with a journal entry. If the amount is due at once, a cheque is issued. If not, the voucher is filed for payment on its due date.

Requiring vouchers be prepared for expenses when they are incurred helps ensure that every expense payment is valid. Yet invoices or bills for such items as repairs are often not received until weeks after work is done. If no records of repairs exist, it can be difficult to determine whether the invoice amount is correct. Also, if no records exist, it is possible for a dishonest employee to collude with a dishonest seller to get more than one payment for an obligation, or for payment of excessive amounts, or for payment for goods and services not received. An effective voucher system helps prevent each of these frauds.

Flash back

6. Good internal control procedures for cash receipts imply (choose one):
   a. All cash disbursements, other than those for very small amounts, are made by cheque.
   b. An accounting employee should count cash received from sales and promptly deposit receipts.
   c. Cash receipts by mail should be opened by an accounting employee who is responsible for recording and depositing receipts.
7. Do all companies require a voucher system? At what point in a company's growth do you recommend a voucher system?

Answers—p. 455

Petty Cash System of Control

A basic principle for controlling cash disbursements is that all payments are made by cheque. An exception to this rule is made for *petty cash disbursements.* Petty cash disbursements are the small amount payments required in most companies for items such as postage, courier fees, repairs, and supplies. Any amounts other than small payments are excluded. If firms made all small payments by cheque, it would require numerous cheques for small amounts. This system would be both time-consuming and expensive. To avoid writing cheques for small amounts, a company usually sets up a petty cash fund and uses the money in this fund to make small payments.

LO 6 Explain and record petty cash fund transactions.

Operating a Petty Cash Fund

Establishing a petty cash fund requires estimating the total amount of small payments likely to be made during a short period such as a week or month. A cheque is then drawn by the company cashier's office for an amount slightly in excess of this estimate. This cheque is recorded with a debit to the Petty Cash account (an asset) and a credit to Cash. The cheque is cashed, and the currency is given to an employee designated as the *petty cashier,* also called *petty cash custodian.* The petty cashier is responsible for safekeeping of the cash, for making payments from this fund, and for keeping accurate records.

The petty cashier should keep petty cash in a locked box in a safe place. As each disbursement is made, the person receiving payment signs a *petty cash receipt,* also called *petty cash ticket*—see Exhibit 9.7. The petty cash receipt is then placed in the petty cashbox with the remaining money. Under this system

Petty Cash Receipt	No. 9
Z-Mart	

For	Delivery charges	Date	Dec. 15/98
Charge to	Transportation-in	Amount	$29.00
Approved by	*Jim Gibbs*	Received by	*Dick Fitch*

Exhibit 9.7

Petty Cash Receipt

the sum of all receipts plus the remaining cash equals the total fund amount. A $100 petty cash fund, for instance, contains any combination of cash and petty cash receipts that total $100 (examples are $100 cash, or $80 cash plus $20 in receipts, or $10 cash plus $90 in receipts). Each disbursement reduces cash and increases the amount for receipts in the petty cashbox. When the cash is nearly gone, the fund should be reimbursed.

When it is time to reimburse the petty cash fund, the petty cashier should sort the paid receipts by the type of expense or other accounts to be debited in recording payments from the fund. The accounts are then totalled, and the totals are used in making the entry to record the reimbursement. The petty cashier presents all *paid* receipts to the company's cashier. The company's cashier stamps all receipts paid so they can't be reused, files them for recordkeeping, and gives the petty cashier a cheque for their sum. When this cheque is cashed and the money returned to the cashbox, the total money in the box is restored to its original amount. The fund is now ready to begin a new cycle of operations.

Illustration of a Petty Cash Fund

Z-Mart uses a petty cash fund to avoid writing an excessive number of cheques for small amounts. Z-Mart initially established a petty cash fund on November 1, 1998. It designated one of its office employees, Jim Gibbs, as petty cashier. A $75 cheque was drawn, cashed, and the proceeds turned over to Gibbs. The entry to recorded the set up of this petty cash fund is:

Assets = Liabilities + Equity
+75
−75

Nov. 1	Petty Cash	75	
	Cash		75
	To establish a petty cash fund.		

This entry transfers $75 from the regular Cash account to the Petty Cash account. After the petty cash fund is established, the Petty Cash account is not debited or credited again unless the size of the total fund is changed. A fund probably should be increased if it is being used up and reimbursed too frequently. If the fund is too large, some of its money should be redeposited in the cash account.

Exhibit 9.8

Petty Cash Payments Report

Z-MART		
Petty Cash Payments Report		
Miscellaneous expenses		
Nov. 2 Washing windows	$10.00	
Nov. 17 Washing windows	10.00	
Nov. 27 Computer repairs	26.50	$46.50
Transportation-in		
Nov. 5 Delivery of merchandise purchased	$ 6.75	
Nov. 20 Delivery of merchandise purchased	8.30	15.05
Delivery expense		
Nov. 18 Customer's package delivered		5.00
Office supplies		
Nov. 15 Purchased office supplies		4.75
Total		$ 71.30

During November, Jim Gibbs, the petty cashier, made several payments from petty cash. He asked each person who received payment to sign a receipt. On November 27, after making a $26.50 payment for repairs to an office computer, only $3.70 cash remained in the fund. Gibbs then summarized and totalled the petty cash receipts as shown in Exhibit 9.8. He gave this summary and all petty cash receipts to the company's cashier in exchange for a $71.30 cheque to reimburse the fund. Gibbs cashed the cheque and put the $71.30 cash in the petty cashbox. The reimbursement cheque is recorded as follows:

Nov. 27	Miscellaneous Expenses	46.50	
	Transportation-In	15.05	
	Delivery Expense	5.00	
	Office Supplies	4.75	
	Cash		71.30
	To reimburse petty cash.		

Assets = Liabilities + Equity
−71.30   −46.50
                        −15.05
                        − 5.00
                        − 4.75

Information for this entry is from the petty cashier's summary of payments. The debits in this entry record the petty cash payments.

A petty cash fund is often reimbursed at the end of an accounting period even if the petty cash fund is not low on money. This is done to record expenses in the proper period. If the fund is not reimbursed at the end of a period, the financial statements show both an overstated petty cash asset and understated expenses or assets that were paid out of petty cash. Yet the amounts involved are rarely significant to most users of financial statements.

Increasing or Decreasing Petty Cash Fund

A decision to increase or decrease a petty cash fund is often made when reimbursing the fund. To illustrate, let's assume Z-Mart decides to *increase* the petty cash fund of Jim Gibbs to $100 on November 27 when it reimburses the fund. This entry is identical to the one above except for two changes: (1) include a debit to Petty Cash for $25 (this increases the fund from $75 to $100), and (2) credit Cash for $96.30 ($71.30 reimbursement of expenses plus $25 increase in the fund).

Alternatively, if Z-Mart *decreases* the petty cash fund from $75 to $55 on November 27, there are two changes required for the entry on this date: (1) include a credit to Petty Cash for $20 (this decreases the fund from $75 to $55), and (2) credit Cash for $51.30 ($71.30 reimbursement of expense minus $20 decrease in the fund).

Internal Auditor

You are an internal auditor for a company. You are currently making surprise counts of three $200 petty cash funds. You arrive at the office of one of the petty cashiers while she is on the telephone. You explain the purpose of your visit, and the petty cashier asks politely that you come back after lunch so that she can finish the business she's conducting by long distance. You agree and return after lunch. The petty cashier opens the petty cashbox and shows you nine new $20 bills with consecutive serial numbers plus receipts totalling $20. Do you take further action or comment on these events in your report to management?

Judgment and Ethics

Answer—p. 454

Cash Over and Short

Sometimes a petty cashier fails to get a receipt for a payment. When this occurs and the fund is later reimbursed, the petty cashier often won't recall the purpose of the payment. This mistake causes the fund to be *short.* If the petty cash fund is short, this shortage is recorded as an expense in the reimbursing entry with a debit to the Cash Over and Short account. An overage in the petty cash fund is recorded with a credit to Cash Over and Short in the reimbursing entry.

Answers—p. 455

Flash back

8. Why are some cash payments made from a petty cash fund?

9. Why should a petty cash fund be reimbursed at the end of an accounting period?

10. What are three results of reimbursing the petty cash fund?

Mid-Chapter Demonstration Problem

Castillo Company established a $75 petty cash fund on February 10. On February 28, the fund had $3.64 in cash and receipts for these expenditures: postage due, $15.25; office supplies, $45.26; and miscellaneous expenses, $10.50. The petty cashier could not account for the $0.35 shortage in the fund. Prepare (a) the February 10 entry to establish the fund and (b) the February 28 entry to reimburse the fund and increase it to $100.

Solution to Mid-Chapter Demonstration Problem

(a) Petty cash fund	75.00	
Cash		75.00
To establish petty cash fund.		
(b) Petty cash fund	25.00	
Postage expense	15.25	
Office expense	45.26	
Miscellaneous expense	10.50	
Cash over and short	0.35	
Cash		96.36
To reimburse petty cash fund and increase fund by $25.00.		

LO7 Apply the net method to control purchase discounts.

Control of Purchase Discounts

This section explains how a company can gain more control over purchase discounts. Chapter 6 described entries to record the receipt and payment of an invoice for a purchase of merchandise under the perpetual inventory system. When Z-Mart purchased merchandise with a $1,200 invoice price with terms of 2/10, n/30, it made the entries:

Assets = Liabilities + Equity
+1,200   +1,200

Nov. 2	Merchandise Inventory	1,200	
	Accounts Payable		1,200
	Purchased merchandise on credit, invoice dated November 2, terms 2/10, n/30.		

Purchased merchandise on credit, invoice dated November 2, terms 2/10, n/30. When Z-Mart takes advantage of the discount and pays the amount due on November 12, the entry is:

Assets = Liabilities + Equity
−   24   −1,200
−1,176

Nov. 12	Accounts Payable	1,200	
	Merchandise Inventory (2% × $1,200)		24
	Cash		1,176
	Paid for the purchase of November 2 less the discount.		

These entries reflect the **gross method** of recording purchases. The *gross* method records the invoice at its gross amount of $1,200 *before* recognizing the cash discount. Many companies record invoices in this way.

Another method of recording purchases is the **net method.** The net method records the invoice at its net amount *after* recognizing the cash discount. This method is viewed as providing more useful information to management. If Z-Mart uses the net method of recording purchases, it deducts the potential $24 cash discount from the gross amount and records the initial purchase at the $1,176 net amount:

Nov. 2	Merchandise Inventory	1,176	
	Accounts Payable		1,176
	Purchased merchandise on credit, invoice dated November 2, terms 2/10, n/30.		

Assets = Liabilities + Equity
+1,176   +1,176

If the invoice for this purchase is paid within the discount period, the entry to record the payment debits Accounts Payable and credits Cash for $1,176. But if payment is not made within the discount period and the discount is *lost,* the following entry must be made when the invoice is paid: *(with the net method)*

Dec. 2	Accounts Payable	1,176	
	Discounts Lost	24	
	Accounts Payable		1,200
	To record the discount lost.		

Assets = Liabilities + Equity
−1,200   −1,176   −24

A cheque for the full $1,200 invoice amount is thus sent to the creditor.

The net method gives management an advantage in controlling and monitoring purchase discounts. When invoices are recorded at *gross* amounts, the amount of discounts taken is deducted from the balance of the Merchandise Inventory account. This means the amount of any discounts lost is not reported in any separate account or on the income statement. Discounts lost are unlikely to be noticed by management. But when purchases are recorded at *net* amounts, a **discounts lost** expense is brought to management's attention as an operating expense on the income statement. Management can then seek to identify the reason for discounts lost such as oversight, carelessness, or unfavourable terms. This practice gives management better control over persons responsible for paying bills on time to ensure they take advantage of favourable discounts. This mean it's less likely that favourable discounts are lost.

Banking Activities as Controls

Banks are used by most companies for many different services. One of their most important services is helping companies control cash and cash transactions. Banks safeguard cash, provide detailed and independent records of cash transactions, and are a source of cash financing. This section describes services and documents provided by banking activities that increase managers control over cash.

Basic Bank Services

This first section explains basic bank services. We include the bank account, bank deposits, and cheques. Each of these services contribute to either or both the control or safeguarding of cash.

L0 8 Identify control features of banking activities.

Bank Account

A bank account is a record set up by a bank for a customer permitting this customer to deposit money for safeguarding and cheque withdrawals. To control access to a bank account, all persons authorized to use a bank account must sign a signature card. A **signature card** includes the signatures of each person authorized to sign cheques from the account. Bank employees use signature cards to verify signatures on cheques. This lowers the risk of loss from forgery for both banks and customers. Many companies have more than one bank account. This is for various reasons including serving local needs and for special transactions such as payroll.

Bank Deposit

Each bank deposit is supported by a deposit slip. A **deposit slip** lists the items such as currency, coins, and cheques deposited along with each of their dollar amounts. The bank gives the customer a copy of the deposit slip or a deposit receipt as proof of the deposit. Exhibit 9.9 shows a deposit slip.

Exhibit 9.9

Deposit Slip

Did You Know?

Booting Up Your Banker

Many companies are now balancing chequebooks and paying bills via PC. The convenience and low cost of wire transfers or chequing account balances anytime, anywhere, are attracting thousands of small businesses to banking by PC. The user dials into a private line at the bank or its vendor to access information that is encrypted before it is transferred. Programs offer features such as the ability to stop payment on a cheque and move money between accounts. Users can also get account balances and identify cheques and deposits that have cleared. Even taxes, suppliers, creditors and employees can be paid electronically using a PC. [Source: *Marketing,* September 30, 1996.]

Bank Cheque

To withdraw money from an account a customer uses a cheque. A **cheque** is a document signed by the depositor instructing the bank to pay a specified amount of money to a designated recipient. A cheque involves three parties: a *maker* who signs the cheque, a *payee* who is the recipient, and a *bank* on which the cheque is drawn. The bank provides a depositor with cheques that are serially numbered and imprinted with the name and address of both the depositor and bank. Both cheques and deposit slips are imprinted with identification codes in magnetic ink for computer processing. Exhibit 9.10 shows a cheque. This cheque is accompanied with an optional *remittance advice* giving an explanation for the payment. When a remittance advice is unavailable, the memo line is often used for a brief explanation.

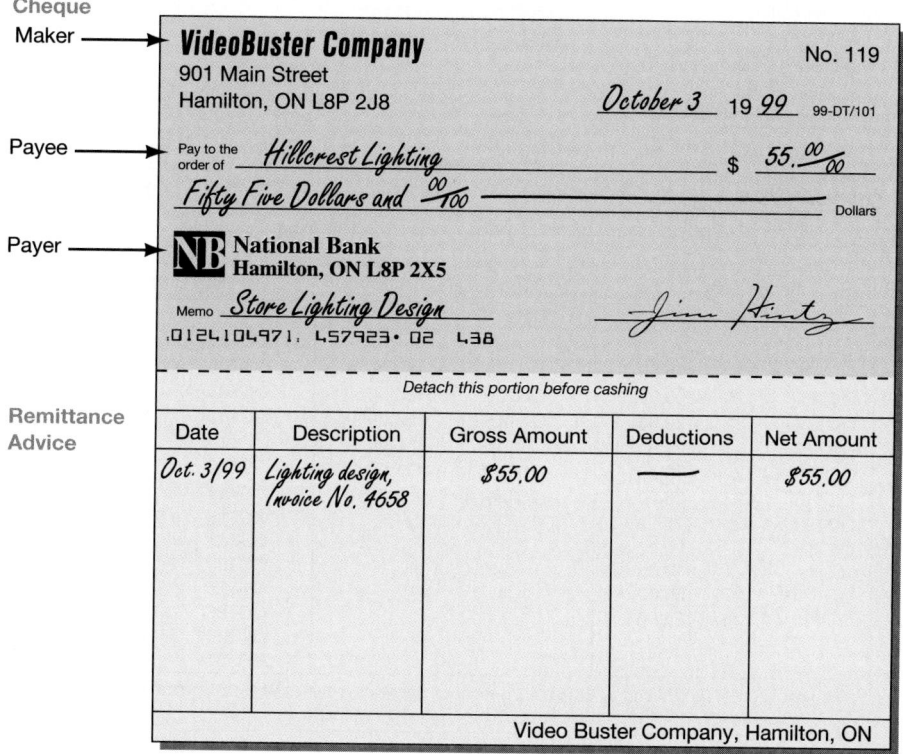

Exhibit 9.10

Cheque with Remittance Advice

Electronic Funds Transfer

Electronic funds transfer (EFT) is the use of electronic communication to transfer cash from one party to another. No paper documents are necessary. Banks simply transfer cash from one account to another with a journal entry. Companies are increasingly using EFT because of its convenience and low cost. It can cost, for instance, up to a dollar to process a cheque through the banking system, whereas EFT cost is near zero. We see items such as payroll, rent, utilities, insurance and interest payments being handled by EFT. The bank statement lists cash withdrawals by EFT with cheques and other deductions. Cash receipts by EFT are listed with deposits and other additions. A bank statement is sometimes a depositor's only notice of an EFT.

Bank Statement

At least once a month, the bank sends the depositor a bank statement showing the activity in the accounts during the month. Different banks use a variety of formats for their bank statements. Yet all of them include the following items of information:

1. Beginning of month balance of the depositor's account.
2. Cheques and other debits decreasing the account during the month.
3. Deposits and other credits increasing the account during the month.
4. End of month balance of the depositor's account.

This information reflects the bank's records. Exhibit 9.11 shows a bank statement. Identify each of the four items listed above.

Part A of Exhibit 9.11 summarizes changes in the account. Part B lists paid cheques in numerical order along with other debits. Part C lists deposits and credits to the account, and part D shows the daily account balances.

Exhibit 9.11

Bank Statement

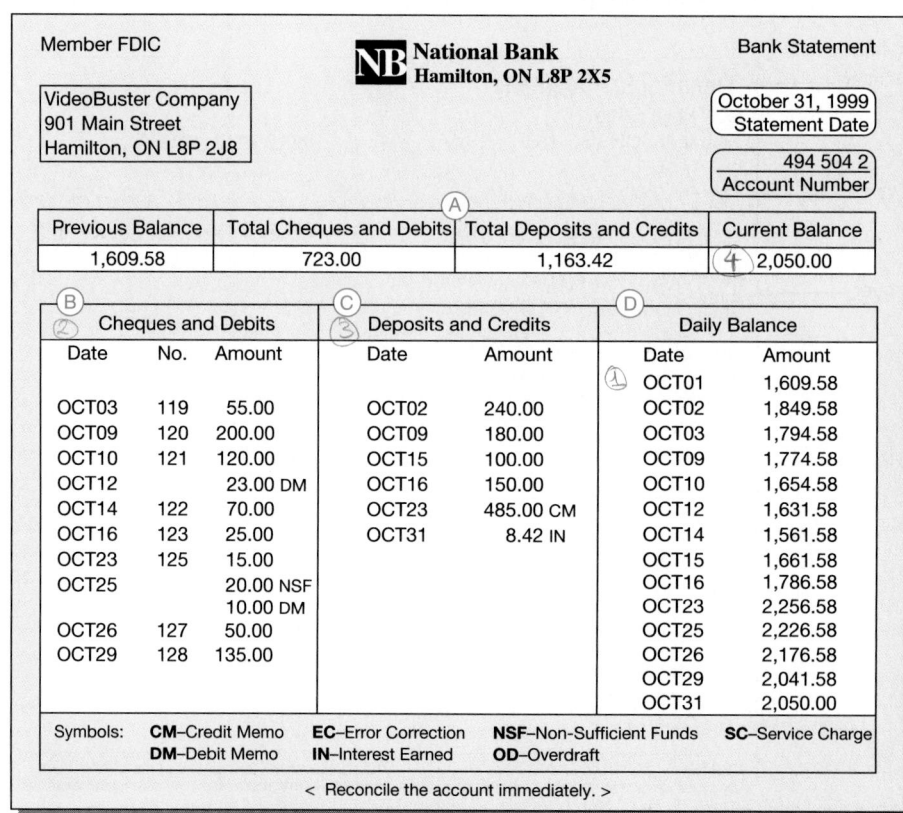

Previous Balance	Total Cheques and Debits	Total Deposits and Credits	Current Balance
1,609.58	723.00	1,163.42	2,050.00

B Cheques and Debits				**C Deposits and Credits**			**D Daily Balance**	
Date	No.	Amount		Date	Amount		Date	Amount
							OCT01	1,609.58
OCT03	119	55.00		OCT02	240.00		OCT02	1,849.58
OCT09	120	200.00		OCT09	180.00		OCT03	1,794.58
OCT10	121	120.00		OCT15	100.00		OCT09	1,774.58
OCT12		23.00 DM		OCT16	150.00		OCT10	1,654.58
OCT14	122	70.00		OCT23	485.00 CM		OCT12	1,631.58
OCT16	123	25.00		OCT31	8.42 IN		OCT14	1,561.58
OCT23	125	15.00					OCT15	1,661.58
OCT25		20.00 NSF					OCT16	1,786.58
		10.00 DM					OCT23	2,256.58
OCT26	127	50.00					OCT25	2,226.58
OCT29	128	135.00					OCT26	2,176.58
							OCT29	2,041.58
							OCT31	2,050.00

Symbols:	**CM**–Credit Memo	**EC**–Error Correction	**NSF**–Non-Sufficient Funds	**SC**–Service Charge
	DM–Debit Memo	**IN**–Interest Earned	**OD**–Overdraft	

< Reconcile the account immediately. >

Enclosed with a bank statement are the depositor's cancelled cheques along with any debit or credit memoranda affecting the account. **Cancelled cheques** are cheques the bank has paid and deducted from the customer's account during the month. Other deductions also often appear on a bank statement and include: (1) service charges and fees assessed by the bank, (2) customers' cheques deposited that are uncollectible, (3) corrections of previous errors, (4) withdrawals through automatic teller machines (ATM)[3], and (5) periodic payments arranged in advance by a depositor. Except for service charges, the bank notifies the depositor of each deduction with a debit memorandum when the bank reduces the balance. A copy of each debit memorandum is usually sent with the monthly statement.[4]

---

[3] Because of a desire to make all disbursements by cheque, most business chequing accounts do not allow ATM withdrawals.

[4] A depositor's account is a liability on the bank's records. This is because the money belongs to the depositor and not the bank. When a depositor increases the account balance, the bank records it with a *credit* to the account. Also, debit memos from the bank produce *credits* on the depositor's books, and credit memos produce *debits*.

While deposits increase a depositor's bank balance, there are other transactions which increase the depositor's account. Examples are amounts the bank collects on behalf of the depositor and corrections of previous errors. Credit memoranda notify the depositor of all increases when they are recorded. A copy of each credit memorandum is often sent with the bank statement. Another item added to the bank balance is interest earned by the depositor. Many chequing accounts pay the depositor interest based on the average cash balance maintained in the account. The bank computes the amount of interest earned and credits it to the depositor's account each month. In Exhibit 9.11, the bank credits $8.42 of interest to the account of **VideoBuster.** We describe the methods used to compute interest in the next chapter.

Bank Reconciliation

When a company deposits all receipts intact and when all payments except petty cash payments are by cheque, the bank statement serves as a device for proving the accuracy of the depositor's cash records. We test the accuracy by preparing a bank reconciliation. A **bank reconciliation** explains the difference between the balance of a chequing account according to the depositor's records and the balance reported on the bank statement.

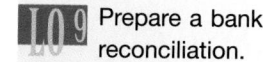 Prepare a bank reconciliation.

Purpose of Bank Reconciliation

The balance of a chequing account reported on the bank statement is rarely equal to the balance in the depositor's accounting records. This is usually due to information that one party has that the other does not. We must therefore prove the accuracy of both the depositor's records and those of the bank. This means we must *reconcile* the two balances and explain or account for the differences in these two balances.

Among the factors causing the bank statement balance to differ from the depositor's book balance are:

1. *Outstanding cheques.* These are cheques written (or drawn) by the depositor, deducted on the depositor's records, and sent to the payees. But they have not yet reached the bank for payment and deduction at the time of the bank statement.

2. *Deposits in transit (outstanding deposits).* These are deposits made and recorded by the depositor but not recorded on the bank statement. For example, companies often make deposits at the end of a business day, after the bank is closed. A deposit in the bank's night depository on the last day of the month is not recorded by the bank until the next business day and does not appear on the bank statement for that month. Also, deposits mailed to the bank near the end of a month may be in transit and unrecorded when the statement is prepared.

3. *Deductions for uncollectible items and for services.* A company sometimes deposits a customer's cheque that is uncollectible. This usually is because the balance in the customer's account is not large enough to cover the cheque. This cheque is called a *nonsufficient funds (NSF)* cheque. The bank initially credited the depositor's account for the amount of the deposited cheque. When the bank learns the cheque is uncollectible, it debits (reduces) the depositor's account for the amount of that cheque. The bank may also charge the depositor a fee for processing an uncollectible cheque and notify the depositor of the deduction by sending a debit memorandum. While each deduction should be recorded by the depositor when a debit memorandum is received, an entry is sometimes not made until the bank reconciliation is prepared.

   Other possible bank charges to a depositor's account reported on a bank statement include the printing of new cheques and a service charge for maintaining the account. Notification of these charges is *not* provided until the statement is mailed.

4. *Additions for collections and for interest.* Banks sometimes act as collection agents for their depositors by collecting notes and other items. Banks can also receive electronic fund transfers to the depositor's account. When a bank collects an item it adds it to the depositor's account, less any service fee. It also sends a credit memorandum to notify the depositor of the transaction. When the memorandum is received, it should be recorded by the depositor. Yet they sometimes remain unrecorded until the time of the bank reconciliation.

Many bank accounts earn interest on the average cash balance in the account during the month. If an account earns interest, the bank statement includes a credit for the amount earned during the past month. Notification of earned interest is provided by the bank statement.

5. *Errors.* Both banks and depositors can make errors. Errors by the bank might not be discovered until the depositor prepares the bank reconciliation. Also, the depositor's errors sometimes are not discovered until the bank balance is reconciled.

Steps in Reconciling a Bank Balance

The employee who prepares the bank reconciliation should not be responsible for cash receipts, processing cheques, or maintaining cash records. This employee needs to gather information from the bank statement and from other records. A reconciliation requires this person to:

■ Compare deposits on the bank statement with deposits in the accounting records. Identify any discrepancies and determine which is correct. List any errors or unrecorded deposits.

■ Inspect all additions (credits) on the bank statement and determine whether each is recorded in the books. These items include collections by the bank, correction of previous bank statement errors, and interest earned by the depositor. List any unrecorded items.

■ Compare cancelled cheques on the bank statement with actual cheques returned with the statement. For each cheque, make sure the correct amount is deducted by the bank and the returned cheque is properly charged to the account. List any discrepancies or errors.

■ Compare cancelled cheques on the bank statement with cheques recorded in the books. (The bank statement often lists cancelled cheques in numerical order to help in this step.) List any outstanding cheques. Also, while companies with good internal controls would rarely write a cheque without recording it, we should inspect and list any cancelled cheques unrecorded in the books.

■ Identify any outstanding cheques listed on the previous month's bank reconciliation that are not included in the cancelled cheques on this month's bank statement. List these cheques that remain outstanding at the end of the current month. Send the list to the cashier's office for follow-up with the payees to see if the cheques were actually received.

■ Inspect all deductions (debits) to the account on the bank statement and determine whether each is recorded in the books. These include bank charges for newly printed cheques, NSF cheques, and monthly service charges. List items not yet recorded.

When this information is gathered, the employee can complete the reconciliation.

We use the guidelines listed above and follow nine specific steps in preparing the bank reconciliation. It is helpful to refer to the bank reconciliation for VideoBuster shown in Exhibit 9.12 as we describe these steps. The nine steps are:

1. Identify the bank balance of the cash account (*balance per bank*).
2. Identify and list any unrecorded deposits and any bank errors understating the bank balance. Add them to the bank balance.

3. Identify and list any outstanding cheques and any bank errors overstating the bank balance. Deduct them from the bank balance.

4. Compute the *adjusted bank balance,* also called *corrected* or *reconciled balance.*

5. Identify the company's balance of the cash account (*balance per book*).

6. Identify and list any unrecorded credit memoranda from the bank, interest earned, and errors understating the book balance. Add them to the book balance.

7. Identify and list any unrecorded debit memoranda from the bank, service charges, and errors overstating the book balance. Deduct them from the book balance.

8. Compute the *adjusted book balance,* also called *corrected* or *reconciled balance.*

9. Verify the two adjusted balances from steps 4 and 8 are equal. If yes, they are reconciled. If not, check for mathematical accuracy and missing data.

Illustrating a Bank Reconciliation

We illustrate a bank reconciliation by preparing one for VideoBuster as of October 31. In preparing to reconcile the bank account, the VideoBuster employee gathers the following data:

■ Bank balance shown on the bank statement is $2,050.

■ Cash balance shown in the accounting records is $1,404.58.

■ A $145 deposit was placed in the bank's night depository on October 31 and is not recorded on the bank statement.

■ Enclosed with the bank statement is a credit memorandum showing the bank collected a note receivable for the company on October 23. The note's proceeds of $500 (minus a $15 collection fee) were credited to the company's account. This credit memorandum is not yet recorded by the company.

■ The bank statement shows a credit of $8.42 for interest earned on the average cash balance in the account. There was no prior notification of this item and it is not yet recorded on the company's books.

■ A comparison of cancelled cheques with the company's books showed two cheques are outstanding—No. 124 for $150 and No. 126 for $200.

■ Other debits on the bank statement that are not recorded on the books include (a) a $23 charge for cheques printed by the bank, and (b) an NSF cheque for $20 plus a related $10 processing fee. The NSF cheque is from a customer, Frank Heflin, on October 16 and was included in that day's deposit.

Exhibit 9.12

Bank Reconciliation

VIDEOBUSTER					
Bank Reconciliation					
October 31, 1999					
① Bank statement balance.......		$2,050.00	⑤ Book balance		$1,404.58
② Add:			⑥ Add:		
Deposit of Oct 31 in transit...		145.00	Collection of $500 note less		
			$15 collection fee......	$485.00	
			Interest earned.........	8.42	$ 493.42
		$2,195.00			$1,898.00
③ Deduct:			⑦ Deduct:		
Outstanding cheques:			NSF cheque plus service		
No. 124..............	$150.00		fee................	$ 30.00	
No. 126..............	200.00	$ 350.00	Cheque printing charge....	23.00	$ 53.00
④ Adjusted bank balance		$1,845.00	⑧ Adjusted book balance......		$1,845.00

⑨ Balances are equal (reconciled)

Exhibit 9.12 is the bank reconciliation reflecting these items. The circled numbers in this reconciliation correspond to the nine steps listed earlier.

When the reconciliation is complete, the employee sends a copy to the accounting department so that any needed journal entries are recorded. For instance, entries are needed to record any unrecorded debit and credit memoranda and any company mistakes. Another copy goes to the cashier's office. This is especially important if the bank has made an error needing correction.

High-Tech Recs

High-tech reconciliations are today available on your PC and via the Web. With little or no fee, one can link into financial information that is updated continuously throughout the day—called real-time reconciliations. These programs do automatic bank reconciliations, and the software highlights such mistakes as transposed numbers or cheques not previously recorded. Data can be easily downloaded and used in other applications. But one must still be able to analyze and interpret the accounting data. [Source: *Business Week*, June 20, 1997.]

Recording Adjusting Entries from Bank Reconciliation

A bank reconciliation helps locate errors by either the bank or the depositor. It also identifies unrecorded items that need recording on the company's books. In VideoBuster's reconciliation, for instance, the adjusted balance of $1,845.00 is the correct balance as of October 31. But the company's accounting records show a $1,404.58 balance. We must prepare journal entries to adjust the book balance to the correct balance. It is important to remember only the items reconciling the book balance side require adjustment. This means four entries are required for VideoBuster:

Collection of Note

The first entry is to record the net proceeds of VideoBuster's note receivable collected by the bank, the expense of having the bank perform that service, and the reduction in the Notes Receivable account:

Assets = Liabilities + Equity
+485   −15
−500

Oct. 31	Cash	485.00	
	Collection Expense	15.00	
	Notes Receivable		500.00
	To record collection fee and proceeds of a note collected by the bank.		

Interest Earned

The second entry records the interest credited to VideoBuster's account by the bank:

Assets = Liabilities + Equity
+8.42   +8.42

Oct. 31	Cash	8.42	
	Interest Earned		8.42
	To record interest earned on the average cash balance in the chequing account.		

Interest earned is a revenue, and the entry recognizes both the revenue and the related increase in Cash.

NSF Cheque

The third entry records the NSF cheque that is returned as uncollectible. The $20 cheque was received from Heflin in payment of his account and deposited. When the cheque cleared the banking system, Heflin's bank account was found to have insufficient funds to cover the cheque. The bank charged $10 for handling the NSF cheque and deducted $30 total from VideoBuster's account. The company must reverse the entry made when the cheque was received and also record the $10 fee:

Oct. 31	Accounts Receivable—Frank Heflin	30.00	
	Cash		30.00
	To charge Frank Heflin's account for his NSF cheque and for the bank's fee.		

Assets = Liabilities + Equity
+30
−30

This entry reflects business practice by adding the NSF $10 fee to Heflin's account. The company will try to collect the entire $30 from Heflin.

Cheque Printing

The fourth entry debits Miscellaneous Expenses for the cheque printing charge:

Oct. 31	Miscellaneous Expenses	23.00	
	Cash		23.00
	Cheque printing charge.		

Assets = Liabilities + Equity
−23   −23

After these four entries are recorded, the balance of cash is increased to the correct amount of $1,845 ($1,404.58 + $485 + $8.42 − $30 − $23).

Flash back

11. What is a bank statement?
12. What is the meaning of the phrase *to reconcile a bank balance?*
13. Why do we reconcile the bank statement balance of cash and the depositor's book balance of cash?
14. List items affecting the bank side of a reconciliation and indicate if the items are added or subtracted.
15. List items affecting the book side of a reconciliation and indicate if the items are added or subtracted.

Answers—p. 455

Days' Sales Uncollected

USING THE INFORMATION

Many companies attract customers by selling to them on credit. This means that cash flows from customers are delayed until accounts receivable are collected. Users of accounting information often want to know how quickly a company can convert its accounts receivable into cash. This is important for evaluating a company's liquidity.

One way users evaluate the liquidity of receivables is looking at the **days' sales uncollected,** also called *days' sales in receivables.* This measure is computed by taking the current balance of receivables and dividing by net credit sales over the year just completed, and then multiplying by 365 (number of days in a year). But for external decision makers, the amount of net credit sales usually is not reported. In this case, net sales is commonly used in the computation. This formula for days' sales uncollected is shown in Exhibit 9.13.

LO 10 Compute days' sales uncollected ratio and use it to analyze liquidity.

Exhibit 9.13

Days' Sales Uncollected
Formula

$$\text{Days' sales uncollected} = \frac{\text{Accounts receivable}}{\text{Net sales}} \times 365$$

Z-Mart, for instance, reports accounts receivable of $11,200 at the end of 1999 (see p. 275) and net sales of $314,700 (see p. 279) for the year. By dividing $11,200 by $314,700, we find the receivables balance is 3.56% of that year's sales. Because there are 365 days in a year, the $11,200 balance is 3.56% of 365 days of sales, or 13 days of sales.

We use the number of days' sales uncollected to estimate how much time is likely to pass before we receive cash receipts from credit sales equal to the current amount of accounts receivable. For evaluation, we need to compare this estimate to the days' sales uncollected figures for other companies in the same industry. We also make comparisons between current and prior periods.

To illustrate an analysis of the number of days' sales uncollected, we select data from the annual reports of two grocery companies, **Oshawa Group Limited** and **George Weston Limited**. The days' sales uncollected figures, and their component figures, for Oshawa and Weston are shown in Exhibit 9.14. Days' sales uncollected for Oshawa at their January 1997 year-end is computed as ($ in millions):

$$\frac{\$313}{\$6,384} \times 365 = 18 \text{ days}$$

This means it will take about 18 days to collect cash on ending accounts receivable. This number reflects on one or more of the following factors: a company's ability in collecting receivables, the financial health of its customers, customer payment strategies, or sales discount terms.

Exhibit 9.14

Analysis Using Days'
Sales Uncollected[5]

Company	Figure ($ millions)	1997	1996	1995
Oshawa	Accounts Receivable	$ 313	$ 264	$ 249
	Net Sales	$ 6,384	$ 6,161	$ 6,070
	Days' Sales Uncollected	18 days	16 days	15 days
		1996	**1995**	**1994**
Weston	Accounts Receivable	$ 348	$ 370	$ 385
	Net Sales	$12,709	$12,966	$13,002
	Days' Sales Uncollected	10 days	10 days	11 days

To better assess this figure for Oshawa we compare it to the two prior years' numbers and with those of Weston. We see that Weston's days' sales uncollected is steady, varying from 10 to 11 days for the past three years. But in comparison to Weston, the Oshawa figure is somewhat larger. While Weston has reduced its days' sales uncollected from 11 days in 1994 to 10 days in 1996, Oshawa has not. This means improved liquidity in receivables for Weston. Improved liquidity often translates into increased profitability. While we don't show the analysis here, the profitability of Weston exceeds that of Oshawa over 1994–1996. Running a financially successful company requires continuous monitoring of the liquidity of its assets.

---

[5] Oshawa's year-end is the 52 weeks ending at the end of January while Weston's year-end is December 31. Therefore, Weston's 1996 figures are comparable to Oshawa's 1997 figures.

Flashback

16. Why is the days' sales uncollected computation usually based on net sales instead of credit sales?

Answers—p. 455

Salesperson
You are a salesperson for a retailer who markets direct to consumers. You and the entire sales staff are told by your accounting division to take action to reduce days' sales uncollected. What can you do to reduce days' sales uncollected?

You Make the Call

Answer—p. 454

Summary

LO1 Define internal control and its purpose. An internal control system consists of the policies and procedures that managers use to protect assets, ensure reliable accounting, promote efficient operations, and urge adherence to company policies. It is a key part of systems design, analysis and performance. It can prevent avoidable losses and help managers both plan operations and monitor company and human performance.

LO2 Identify principles of internal control. Principles of good internal control include establishing responsibilities, maintaining adequate records, insuring assets and bonding employees, separating recordkeeping from custody of assets, dividing responsibilities for related transactions, applying technological controls, and performing regular independent reviews.

LO3 Define cash and cash equivalents and how they are reported. Cash includes currency and coins, and amounts on deposit in bank, chequing and some savings accounts. It also includes items that are acceptable for deposit in these accounts. Cash equivalents are short-term, highly liquid investment assets meeting two criteria: readily convertible to a known cash amount, and are subject to an insignificant risk of changes in value. Examples of cash equivalents are short-term investments in treasury bills, commercial paper, and money market funds. Because cash equivalents are similar to cash, most companies combine them with cash as a single item on the balance sheet. Cash and cash equivalents are liquid assets because they are converted easily into other assets or used in paying for services or liabilities.

LO4 Apply internal control to cash receipts. Internal control of cash receipts ensures all cash received is properly recorded and deposited. Cash receipts arise from many transactions including cash sales, collections of customers' accounts, receipts of interest and rent, bank loans, sale of assets, and owner investments. Attention is focused on two important types of cash receipts: over-the-counter and mail. The principles of internal control are applied in both cases. Good internal control for over-the-counter cash receipts includes use of a cash register, customer review, receipts, a permanent transaction record, and the separation of the custody of cash from its recordkeeping. Good internal control for cash receipts by mail includes at least two people assigned to open the mail and prepare a list when money is received with each sender's name, amount, and explanation. These systems allow managers to monitor and control cash receipts.

LO5 Apply the voucher system to control cash disbursements. A voucher system is a set of procedures and approvals designed to control cash disbursements and acceptance of obligations. The voucher system of control relies on several important documents including the voucher and many supporting files. A voucher system's control over cash disbursements begins when a company incurs an obligation that will result in payment of cash. A key factor in this system is that only approved departments and individuals are authorized to incur certain obligations. To coordinate and control responsibilities of these departments, several different business documents are used.

LO 6 **Explain and record petty cash fund transactions.**
Petty cash disbursements are payments of small amounts for items such as postage, courier fees, repairs and supplies. To avoid writing cheques for small amounts, a company usually sets up one or more petty cash funds and uses the money to make small payments. A petty fund cashier is responsible for safekeeping of the cash, for making payments from this fund, and for keeping receipts and records. A Petty Cash account is debited when the fund is established or increased in size. The cashier presents all paid receipts to the company's cashier for reimbursement. Petty cash disbursements are recorded whenever the fund is replenished with debits to expense accounts reflecting receipts and a credit to cash. The petty cash fund is now restored to its full amount and is ready to cover more small expenditures.

LO 7 **Apply the net method to control purchase discounts.** The net method gives management an advantage in controlling and monitoring purchase discounts. When invoices are recorded at gross amounts, the amount of discounts taken is deducted from the balance of the Merchandise Inventory account. This means the amount of any discounts lost is not reported in any account or on the income statement. Discounts lost are unlikely to come to the attention of management. But when purchases are recorded at net amounts, a discounts lost expense is brought to management's attention as an operating expense on the income statement. Management can then seek to identify the reason for discounts lost such as oversight, carelessness or unfavourable terms.

LO 8 **Identify control features of banking activities.**
Banks offer several basic services that promote either or both the control or safeguarding of cash. These involve the bank account, the bank deposit, and chequing. A bank account is set up by a bank and permits a customer to deposit money for safeguarding and cheque withdrawals. A bank deposit is money contributed to the account with a deposit slip as proof. A cheque is a document signed by the depositor instructing the bank to pay a specified amount of money to a designated recipient. Electronic funds transfer uses electronic communication to transfer cash from one party to another, and it decreases certain risks while exposing others. Companies increasingly use it because of its convenience and low cost.

LO 9 **Prepare a bank reconciliation.** A bank reconciliation is prepared to prove the accuracy of the depositor's and the bank's records. In completing a reconciliation, the bank statement balance is adjusted for such items as outstanding cheques and unrecorded deposits made on or before the bank statement date but not reflected on the statement. The depositor's cash account balance also often requires adjustment. These adjustments include items such as service charges, bank collections for the depositor, and interest earned on the account balance.

LO 10 **Compute days' sales uncollected ratio and use it to analyze liquidity.** Many companies attract customers by selling to them on credit. This means that cash flows from customers are delayed until accounts receivable are collected. Users of accounting information often want to know how quickly a company can convert its accounts receivable into cash. This is important for evaluating a company's liquidity. The days' sales uncollected ratio is one measure reflecting on liquidity. It is computed by dividing the current balance of receivables by net sales over the year just completed, and then multiplying by 365. The number of days' sales uncollected is used to estimate how much time is likely to pass before cash receipts from net sales are received equal to the current amount of accounts receivable. Our analysis needs to compare this estimate to those for other companies in the same industry, and with prior years' estimates.

Guidance Answers to **You Make the Call**

Campaign Manager

A forced vacation policy is part of a system of good internal controls. When employees are forced to take vacations, their ability to hide any fraudulent behaviour decreases. This is because someone must take on the responsibilities of the person on vacation, and the replacement employee potentially can uncover fraudulent behaviour or records. A forced vacation policy is especially important for employees in more sensitive positions of handling money or other easily transferable assets.

Salesperson

There are several steps a salesperson can take to reduce days' sales uncollected. These include: (1) decreasing the proportion of sales on account to total sales by encouraging more cash sales, (2) identifying customers most delayed in their payments and encouraging earlier payments or cash sales, and (3) implementing more strict credit policies to eliminate credit sales to customers who never pay.

Guidance Answer to **Judgment and Ethics**

Internal Auditor

Your problem is whether to accept the situation or to dig further to see if the petty cashier is abusing petty cash. Since you were asked to postpone your count and the fund consists of new $20 bills, you have legitimate concerns on whether money is being borrowed for personal use. You should conduct a further investigation. One result might show the most recent reimbursement of the fund was for $180 (9 × $20) or more. In that case, this reimbursement can leave the fund with sequentially numbered $20 bills. But if the most recent reimbursement was for less than $180, the presence of nine sequentially numbered $20 bills suggests the $180 of new $20 bills were obtained from a bank as replacement for bills that had been removed. Neither situation shows the cashier is stealing money. Yet the second case indicates the cashier "borrowed" the cash and later replaced it after the auditor showed up. In writing your report you must not conclude the cashier is unethical unless evidence along with your knowledge of company policies supports it. Your report must present facts according to the evidence.

Guidance Answers to Flash backs

1. *c*

2. Technology reduces processing errors, allows more extensive testing of records, limits the amount of hard evidence of processing steps, and highlights the importance of maintaining separation of duties.

3. A company owns liquid assets so that it can purchase other assets, buy services, and pay obligations.

4. A company owns cash equivalents because they yield a return greater than what is earned by cash.

5. Examples of cash equivalents are: 90-day treasury bills issued by the government, money market funds, and commercial paper.

6. *a*

7. Not necessarily. A voucher system is used when a manager can no longer control the purchasing procedures through personal supervision and direct participation in business activities.

8. If all cash payments are made by cheque, numerous cheques for small amounts must be written. Because this practice is expensive and time consuming, a petty cash fund is established to make small cash payments.

9. If the petty cash fund is not reimbursed at the end of an accounting period, the transactions in petty cash are not yet recorded in the accounts and the petty cash asset is overstated. But these amounts are rarely large enough to affect users' decisions based on financial statements.

10. First, when the petty cash fund is reimbursed, the petty cash transactions are recorded in their proper accounts. Second, reimbursement also gives money allowing the fund to continue being used. Third, reimbursement identifies any cash shortage or overage in the fund.

11. A bank statement is a report prepared by the bank describing the activities in a depositor's account.

12. To reconcile a bank balance means to explain the difference between the cash balance in the depositor's accounting records and the balance on the bank statement.

13. The purpose of the bank reconciliation is to determine if any errors have been made by the bank or by the depositor and to determine if the bank has completed any transactions affecting the depositor's account that the depositor has not recorded. It is also an internal control mechanism to ensure that the company's cash system is operating properly.

14. Outstanding cheques—subtracted
Unrecorded deposits—added

15. Bank service charges—subtracted
Debit memos—subtracted
NSF cheques—subtracted
Interest earned—added
Credit memos—added

16. The calculation is based on net sales because the amount of credit sales normally is not known by statement readers.

Demonstration Problem

Consider the following facts and prepare a bank reconciliation for Jamboree Enterprises for the month ended November 30, 19X1.

The following information was available to reconcile Jamboree Enterprise's book balance of cash with its bank statement balance as of November 30, 19X1:

a. After all posting was completed on November 30, the company's Cash account had a $16,380 debit balance, but its bank statement showed a $38,520 balance.

b. Cheques No. 2024 for $4,810 and No. 2036 for $5,000 were outstanding.

c. In comparing the cancelled cheques returned by the bank with the entries in the accounting records, it was found that Cheque No. 2025 was correctly drawn for $1,000 but was erroneously entered in the accounting records as $880 for rent expense.

d. The November 30 deposit of $17,150 was placed in the night depository after banking hours on that date and this amount did not appear on the bank statement.

e. In reviewing the bank statement a cheque belonging to Jumbo Enterprises in the amount of $160 was erroneously drawn against Jamboree's account.

f. A credit memorandum enclosed with the bank statement indicated that the bank had collected a $30,000 note and $900 of related interest on Jamboree's behalf. This event was not recorded by Jamboree before receiving the statement.

g. A debit memorandum for $1,100 listed a $1,100 NSF cheque. The cheque had been received from a customer, Marilyn Welch. Jamboree had not recorded this bounced cheque before receiving the statement.

h. Bank service charges for November totalled $40. This event was not recorded by Jamboree before receiving the statement.

Planning the Solution

■ Set up a schedule like the following with a bank side and a book side for the reconciliation. Leave room on both sides to add several items and to deduct several items. Each column will result in a reconciled balance.

JAMBOREE ENTERPRISES Bank Reconciliation November 30, 19X1	
Bank statement balance	Book balance of cash . . . .
Add:	Add: . . . .
Deduct:	Deduct: . . . .
Reconciled balance	Reconciled balance . . . .

■ Examine each item given about Jamboree to determine whether it affects the book balance or the bank balance. Also for each item decide whether it should be added or deducted from the bank or book balance.

■ After all items have been analyzed complete the form and arrive at a reconciled balance agreeing the bank side of the reconciliation to the book side.

■ Now for every reconciling item on the book side prepare an appropriate adjusting entry. Any additions to the book side require an adjusting entry that debits cash. Conversely any deduction on the book side will require an adjusting entry that credits cash.

Solution to Demonstration Problem

JAMBOREE ENTERPRISES Bank Reconciliation November 30, 19X1					
Bank statement balance		$38,520	Book balance of cash		$16,380
Add:			Add:		
Deposit of November 30		$17,150	Collection of note		$30,000
Bank error		160	Interest earned		900
Total		$17,310	Total		$30,900
Total		$55,830	Total		$47,280
Deduct:			Deduct:		
Outstanding cheques			NSF cheque		$ 1,100
# 2024	$4,810		Recording error		120
# 2036	5,000	9,810	Service charge		40
			Total		$ 1,260
Reconciled balance		$46,020	Reconciled balance		$46,020

Required Adjusting Entries

Cash	30,900	
Notes Receivable		30,000
Interest Earned		900
To record collection of note principal and interest.		
Accounts Receivable—Marilyn Welch	1,100	
Cash		1,100
To reinstate account due to NSF cheque.		
Rent Expense	120	
Cash		120
To correct recording error on Cheque no. 2025.		
Bank Service Charges	40	
Cash		40
To record bank service charges.		

Glossary

Bank reconciliation An analysis that explains the difference between the balance of a chequing account shown in the depositor's records and the balance reported on the bank statement. (p. 447)

Cancelled cheques Cheques that the bank has paid and deducted from the customer's account during the month. (p. 446)

Cash Includes currency, coins, and amounts on deposit in bank chequing or savings accounts. (p. 430)

Cash equivalents Short-term, highly liquid investment assets that are readily convertible to a known cash amount and are subject to an insignificant risk of changes in value. (p. 430)

Cash Over and Short account An income statement account used to record cash shortages and cash overages arising from omitted petty cash receipts and from errors in making change. (p. 432)

Cheque A document signed by the depositor instructing the bank to pay a specified amount of money to a designated recipient. (p. 445)

Days' sales uncollected A measure of the liquidity of receivables computed by taking the current balance of receivables and dividing by the credit (or net) sales over the year just completed, and then multiplying by 365 (the number of days in a year); also called *days' sales in receivables.* (p. 451)

Deposit slip Lists the items such as currency, coins, and cheques deposited along with each of their dollar amounts. (p. 444)

Discounts lost An expense resulting from failing to take advantage of cash discounts on purchases. (p. 443)

Electronic funds transfer The use of electronic communication to transfer cash from one party to another. (p. 445)

Gross method A method of recording purchases at the full invoice price without deducting any cash discounts. (p. 443)

Internal control system All the policies and procedures managers use to protect assets, ensure reliable accounting, promote efficient operations, and urge adherence to company policies. (p. 424)

Invoice An itemized statement of goods prepared by the vendor that lists the customer's name, the items sold, the sales prices, and the terms of sale. (p. 436)

Invoice approval form A document containing a checklist of steps necessary for approving an invoice for recording and payment; also called cheque authorization form. (p. 436)

Liquid asset An asset such as cash that is easily converted into other types of assets or used to buy services or to pay liabilities. (p. 431)

Liquidity A characteristic of an asset that refers to how easily the asset can be converted into cash or another type of asset or used in paying for services or obligations. (p. 431)

Net method A method of recording purchases at the full invoice price less any cash discounts. (p. 443)

Principles of internal control Fundamental principles of internal control that apply to all companies requiring management to establish responsibility, maintain adequate records, insure assets and bond key employees, separate recordkeeping from custody of assets, divide responsibility for related transactions, apply technological controls, and perform regular and independent reviews. (p. 425)

Purchase order A business paper used by the purchasing department to place an order with the seller (vendor); authorizes the vendor to ship the ordered merchandise at the stated price and terms. (p. 435)

Purchase requisition A business paper listing the merchandise needed by a department and requests that it be purchased. (p. 435)

Receiving report A form used within a company to notify the appropriate persons that ordered goods are received and to describe the quantities and condition of the goods. (p. 436)

Signature card Includes the signatures of each person authorized to sign cheques from the account. (p. 444)

Vendee The buyer or purchaser of goods or services. (p. 436)

Vendor The seller of goods or services, usually a manufacturer or wholesaler. (p. 435)

Voucher An internal business paper (or "folder") used to accumulate other papers and information needed to control cash disbursements and to ensure that the transaction is properly recorded. (p. 434)

Voucher system A set of procedures and approvals designed to control cash disbursements and acceptance of obligations. (p. 434)

Questions

1. Which of the following assets is most liquid and which is least liquid: merchandise inventory, building, accounts receivable, cash?

2. List the seven broad principles of internal control.

3. Why should the person who keeps the record of an asset not be the person responsible for custody of the asset?

4. Internal control procedures are important in every business, but at what stage in the development of a business do they become critical?

5. Why should responsibility for a sequence of related transactions be divided among different departments or individuals?

6. Why should all receipts be deposited intact on the day of receipt?

7. When merchandise is purchased for a large store, why are department managers not permitted to deal directly with suppliers?

8. What is a petty cash receipt? Who signs a petty cash receipt?

9. Alliance's consolidated statement of cash flows (changes in financial position) (see Appendix I) describes the changes in Cash and short-term investments that occurred during the year ended March 31, 1997. What amount was provided by (or used in) investing activities and what amount was provided by (or used in) financing activities?

10. Alliance's balance sheet (see Appendix I) depicts the cash and short-term investments of Alliance as of March 31, 1997, and March 31, 1996. Contrast the magnitude of Cash and short-term investments with the other current assets as of March 31, 1997. Compare the cash and marketable securities on hand as of March 31, 1997, with March 31, 1996.

11. Identify the internal controls that Jason Barron implemented to help manage the employee theft he was experiencing. Do you think that increasing the sales commission to employees is a type of internal control? Explain.

Quick Study

QS 9-1
Terminology

What is the difference between the terms *liquidity* and *cash equivalent?*

QS 9-2
Internal control objectives

LO 1,2

a. What is the main objective of internal control and how is it accomplished?

b. Why should recordkeeping for assets be separated from custody over the assets?

QS 9-3
Internal controls for cash

LO 4

In a good system of internal control for cash that provides adequate procedures for protecting both cash receipts and cash disbursements, three basic guidelines should always be observed. What are these guidelines?

a. The petty cash fund of the Wee Ones Agency was established at $75. At the end of the month, the fund contained $12.74 and had the following receipts: film rentals, $19.40; refreshments for meetings, $22.81 (both expenditures to be classified as Entertainment Expense); postage, $6.95; and printing, $13.10. Prepare the journal entries to record (a) the establishment of the fund and (b) the reimbursement at the end of the month.

b. Explain when the Petty Cash account would be credited in a journal entry.

QS 9-4
Petty cash accounting
LO 6

a. Identify whether each of the following items affects the bank or book side of the reconciliation and indicate if the amount represents an addition or a subtraction:
(1) Deposits in transit.
(2) Interest on average monthly balance.
(3) Credit memos.
(4) Bank service charges.
(5) Outstanding cheques.
(6) Debit memos.
(7) NSF cheques.

b. Which of the previous items require a journal entry?

QS 9-5
Bank reconciliations
LO 9

Which accounting method uses a Discounts Lost account and what is the advantage of this method?

QS 9-6
Accounting for purchases
LO 7

A company had the following balances:

QS 9-7
Days' sales uncollected
LO 10

	1997	1996
Accounts receivable	$ 75,692,000	$ 70,484,000
Net Sales	$2,591,933,000	$2,296,673,000

What is the difference in the number of days' sales uncollected in 1997 and 1996? According to this ratio analysis, is the company's collection of receivables improving? Explain your answer.

Exercises

Exercise 9-1
Analyzing internal control
LO 2

Lombard Company is a young business that has grown rapidly. The company's bookkeeper, who was hired two years ago, left town suddenly after the company's manager discovered that a great deal of money had disappeared over the past 18 months. An audit disclosed that the bookkeeper had written and signed several cheques made payable to the bookkeeper's brother and then recorded the cheques as salaries expense. The brother, who cashed the cheques but had never worked for the company, left town with the bookkeeper. As a result, the company incurred an uninsured loss of $84,000.

Evaluate Lombard Company's internal control system and indicate which principles of internal control appear to have been ignored in this situation.

What internal control procedures would you recommend in each of the following situations?

a. A concession company has one employee who sells T-shirts and sunglasses at the beach. Each day, the employee is given enough shirts and sunglasses to last through the day and enough cash to make change. The money is kept in a box at the stand.

b. An antique store has one employee who is given cash and sent to garage sales each weekend. The employee pays cash for merchandise to be resold at the antique store.

Exercise 9-2
Recommending internal control procedures
LO 2

Exercise 9-3
Internal control over cash receipts

LO 4

Some of Fannin Co.'s cash receipts from customers are sent to the company in the mail. Fannin's bookkeeper opens the letters and deposits the cash received each day. What internal control problem is inherent in this arrangement? What changes would you recommend?

Exercise 9-4
Petty cash fund

LO 6

Eanes Co. established a $200 petty cash fund on January 1. One week later, on January 8, the fund contained $27.50 in cash and receipts for these expenditures: postage, $64.00; transportation-in, $19.00; store supplies, $36.50; and miscellaneous expenses, $53.00. Eanes uses the perpetual method to account for merchandise inventory.

Prepare the journal entries to (a) establish the fund on January 1 and (b) reimburse it on January 8. Now assume that the fund was not only reimbursed on January 8 but also increased to $500 because it was exhausted so quickly. (c) Give the entry to reimburse the fund and increase it to $500.

Exercise 9-5
Petty cash fund

LO 6

Brady Company established a $400 petty cash fund on September 9. On September 30, the fund had $164.25 in cash and receipts for these expenditures: transportation-in, $32.45; office supplies, $113.55; and miscellaneous expenses, $87.60. Brady uses the periodic method to account for merchandise inventory. The petty cashier could not account for the $2.15 shortage in the fund. Prepare (a) the September 9 entry to establish the fund and (b) the September 30 entry to reimburse the fund and reduce it to $300.

Exercise 9-6
Bank reconciliation

LO 9

Medline Service Co. deposits all receipts intact on the day received and makes all payments by cheque. On July 31, 19X1, after all posting was completed, its Cash account showed an $11,352 debit balance. However, Medline's July 31 bank statement showed only $10,332 on deposit in the bank on that day. Prepare a bank reconciliation for Medline, using the following information:

a. Outstanding cheques, $1,713.
b. Included with the July cancelled cheques returned by the bank was an $18 debit memorandum for bank services.
c. Cheque No. 919, returned with the cancelled cheques, was correctly drawn for $489 in payment of the utility bill and was paid by the bank on July 15. However, it had been recorded with a debit to Utilities Expense and a credit to Cash as though it were for $498.
d. The July 31 cash receipts, $2,724, were placed in the bank's night depository after banking hours on that date and were unrecorded by the bank at the time the July bank statement was prepared.

Exercise 9-7
Adjusting entries resulting from bank reconciliation

LO 9

Give the journal entries that Medline Service Co. should make as a result of having prepared the bank reconciliation in the previous exercise.

Exercise 9-8
Bank reconciling items and required entries

LO 9

Set up a table with the following headings for a bank reconciliation as of September 30:

Bank Balance		Book Balance			Not Shown on the
Add	Deduct	Add	Deduct	Must Adjust	Reconciliation

For each item that follows, place an X in the appropriate columns to indicate whether the item should be added to or deducted from the book or bank balance, or whether it should not appear on the reconciliation. If the book balance is to be adjusted, place a Dr. or Cr. in the Must Adjust column to indicate whether the Cash balance should be debited or credited.

1. Interest earned on the account.
2. Deposit made on September 30 after the bank was closed.
3. Cheques outstanding on August 31 that cleared the bank in September.
4. NSF cheque from customer returned on September 15 but not recorded by the company.
5. Cheques written and mailed to payees on September 30.
6. Deposit made on September 5 that was processed on September 8.
7. Bank service charge.
8. Cheques written and mailed to payees on October 5.
9. Cheques written by another depositor but charged against the company's account.
10. Principal and interest collected by the bank but not recorded by the company.
11. Special charge for collection of note in No. 10 on company's behalf.
12. Cheque written against the account and cleared by the bank; erroneously omitted by the bookkeeper.

Peltier's Imports uses the perpetual method to account for merchandise inventory and had the following transactions during the month of May. Prepare entries to record the transactions assuming Peltier's records invoices (a) at gross amounts and (b) at net amounts.

May 2 Received merchandise purchased at a $2,016 invoice price, invoice dated April 29, terms 2/10, n/30.

   10 Received a $416 credit memorandum (invoice price) for merchandise received on May 2 and returned for credit.

   17 Received merchandise purchased at a $4,480 invoice price, invoice dated May 16, terms 2/10, n/30.

   26 Paid for the merchandise received on May 17, less the discount.

   28 Paid for the merchandise received on May 2. Payment was delayed because the invoice was mistakenly filed for payment today. This error caused the discount to be lost. The filing error occurred after the credit memorandum received on May 10 was attached to the invoice dated April 29.

Exercise 9-9
Recording invoices at gross or net amounts

LO 7

Federated Merchandise Co. reported net sales for 19X1 and 19X2 of $565,000 and $647,000. The end-of-year balances of accounts receivable were December 31, 19X1, $51,000; and December 31, 19X2, $83,000. Calculate the days' sales uncollected at the end of each year and describe any changes in the apparent liquidity of the company's receivables.

Exercise 9-10
Liquidity of accounts receivable

LO 10

Palladium Art Gallery completed the following petty cash transactions during February of the current year:

Feb. 2 Drew a $300 cheque, cashed it, and gave the proceeds and the petty cash box to Nick Reed, the petty cashier.

   5 Purchased paper for the copier, $10.13.

   9 Paid $22.50 COD charges on merchandise purchased for resale. Assume Palladium uses the perpetual method to account for merchandise inventory.

   12 Paid $9.95 postage to express mail a contract to a client.

   14 Reimbursed Gina Barton, the manager of the business, $58.00 for business auto expenses.

   20 Purchased stationery, $77.76.

   23 Paid a courier $18.00 to deliver merchandise sold to a customer.

   25 Paid $15.10 COD charges on merchandise purchased for resale.

   28 Paid $64.00 for stamps.

   28 Reed sorted the petty cash receipts by accounts affected and exchanged them for a cheque to reimburse the fund for expenditures. However, there was only $21.23 in cash in the fund, and he could not account for the shortage. In addition, the size of the petty cash fund was increased to $400.

Problems

Problem 9-1
Establishing, reimbursing, and increasing the petty cash fund

LO 6

Required

1. Prepare a journal entry to record establishing the petty cash fund.

2. Prepare a summary of petty cash payments that has these categories: delivery expense, mileage expense, postage expense, transportation-in (merchandise inventory), and office supplies. Sort the payments into the appropriate categories and total the expenditures in each category.

3. Prepare the journal entry to record the reimbursement and the increase of the fund.

Check Figure Feb. 28, Cash $378.77 Cr.

Problem 9-2
Petty cash fund reimbursement and analysis of errors

 6

El Gatto Co., has only a General Journal in its accounting system and uses it to record all transactions. However, the company recently set up a petty cash fund to facilitate payments of small items. The following petty cash transactions were noted by the petty cashier as occurring during April (the last month of the company's fiscal year):

Apr. 1 Received a company cheque for $250 to establish the petty cash fund.

15 Received a company cheque to replenish the fund for the following expenditures made since April 1 and to increase the fund to $450.
    a. Paid $78 for janitorial service.
    b. Purchased office supplies for $63.68.
    c. Purchased postage stamps for $43.50.
    d. Paid $57.15 to *The County Crier* for an advertisement in the newspaper.
    e. Discovered that $11.15 remained in the petty cash box.

30 The petty cashier noted that $293.39 remained in the fund and decided that the April 15 increase in the fund was too large. Therefore, a company cheque was drawn to replenish the fund for the following expenditures made since April 15 and to reduce the fund to $400.
    f. Purchased office supplies for $48.36.
    g. Reimbursed office manager for business auto, $28.50.
    h. Paid $39.75 courier charges to deliver merchandise to a customer.

Required

Preparation component:

1. Prepare journal entries to record the establishment of the fund on April 1 and its replenishments on April 15 and on April 30.

Analysis component:

2. Explain how the company's financial statements would be affected if the petty cash fund is not replenished and no entry is made on April 30. (Hint: The amount of office supplies that appears on a balance sheet is determined by a physical count of the supplies on hand.)

Check Figure Cash credits: April 15, $438.85; April 30, $66.61

Problem 9-3
Preparation of bank reconciliation and recording adjustments

LO 9

The following information was available to reconcile Archdale Company's book balance of cash with its bank statement balance as of October 31, 19X1:

a. After all posting was completed on October 31, the company's Cash account had a $26,193 debit balance, but its bank statement showed a $28,020 balance.

b. Cheques No. 3031 for $1,380 and No. 3040 for $552 were outstanding on the September 30 bank reconciliation. Cheque No. 3040 was returned with the October cancelled cheques, but Cheque No. 3031 was not. It was also found that Cheque No. 3065 for $336 and Cheque No. 3069 for $2,148, both drawn in October, were not among the cancelled cheques returned with the statement.

c. In comparing the cancelled cheques returned by the bank with the entries in the accounting records, it was found that Cheque No. 3056 for the October rent was correctly drawn for $1,250 but was erroneously entered in the accounting records as $1,230.

d. A credit memorandum enclosed with the bank statement indicated that the bank had collected a $9,000 non-interest-bearing note for Archdale, deducted a $45 collection fee, and credited the remainder to the account. This event was not recorded by Archdale before receiving the statement.

e. A debit memorandum for $805 listed a $795 NSF cheque plus a $10 NSF charge. The cheque had been received from a customer, Jefferson Tyler. Archdale had not recorded this bounced cheque before receiving the statement.

f. Also enclosed with the statement was a $15 debit memorandum for bank services. It had not been recorded because no previous notification had been received.

g. The October 31 cash receipts, $10,152, were placed in the bank's night depository after banking hours on that date and this amount did not appear on the bank statement.

Required

Preparation component:

1. Prepare a bank reconciliation for the company as of October 31, 19X1.

2. Prepare the general journal entries necessary to bring the company's book balance of cash into conformity with the reconciled balance.

Analysis component:

3. Assume that an October 31, 19X1, bank reconciliation for the company has already been prepared and some of the items were treated incorrectly in preparing the reconciliation. For each of the following errors, explain the effect of the error on: (1) the final balance that was calculated by adjusting the bank statement balance, and (2) the final balance that was calculated by adjusting the Cash account balance.

a. The company's Cash account balance of $26,193 was listed on the reconciliation as $26,139.

b. The bank's collection of a $9,000 note less the $45 collection fee was added to the bank statement balance.

Check Figure Reconciled balance, $34,308

Walburg Company reconciled its bank and book statement balances of cash on August 31 and showed two cheques outstanding at that time, No. 5888 for $1,038.05 and No. 5893 for $484.25. The following information was available for the September 30, 19X1, reconciliation:

Problem 9-4
Preparation of bank reconciliation and recording adjustments

 LO 9

From the September 30 bank statement

BALANCE OF PREVIOUS STATEMENT ON AUG. 31/X1 . . .	16,800.75
6 DEPOSITS AND OTHER CREDITS TOTALLING	11,182.85
9 CHEQUES AND OTHER DEBITS TOTALLING	9,620.05
CURRENT BALANCE AS OF SEPT. 30/X1	18,363.55

=== CHEQUING ACCOUNT TRANSACTIONS ===

DATE	AMOUNT	TRANSACTION DESCRIPTION	DATE	AMOUNT	TRANSACTION DESCRIPTION
Sept. 05	1,103.75	+Deposit	Sept. 25	2,351.70	+Deposit
Sept. 12	2,226.90	+Deposit	Sept. 30	22.50	+Interest
Sept. 17	588.25	−NSF cheque	Sept. 30	1,385.00	+Credit memo
Sept. 21	4,093.00	+Deposit			

DATE	CHEQUE NO.	AMOUNT	DATE	CHEQUE NO.	AMOUNT
Aug. 03	5888	1,038.05	Sept. 22	5904	2,080.00
Sept. 07	5901*	1,824.25	Sept. 20	5905	937.00
Sept. 04	5902	731.90	Sept. 28	5907*	213.85
Sept. 22	5903	399.10	Sept. 29	5909*	1,807.65

*Indicates a skip in cheque sequence.

From Walburg Company's accounting records:

Cash Receipts Deposited

Date			Cash Debit
Sept.	5		1,103.75
	12		2,226.90
	21		4,093.00
	25		2,351.70
	30		1,582.75
			11,358.10

Cash Disbursements

Cheque No.		Cash Credit
5901		1,824.25
5902		731.90
5903		399.10
5904		2,050.00
5905		937.00
5906		859.30
5907		213.85
5908		276.00
5909		1,807.65
		9,099.05

Cash   **Acct. No. 101**

Date		Explanation	PR	Debit	Credit	Balance
Aug.	31	Balance				15,278.45
Sept	30	Total receipts	R12	11,358.10		26,636.55
	30	Total disbursements	D23		9,099.05	17,537.50

Cheque No. 5904 was correctly drawn for $2,080 to pay for computer equipment; however, the bookkeeper misread the amount and entered it in the accounting records with a debit to Computer Equipment and a credit to Cash as though it were for $2,050.

The NSF cheque was originally received from a customer, Delia Hahn, in payment of her account. Its return was not recorded when the bank first notified the company. The credit memorandum resulted from the collection of a $1,400 note for Walburg Company by the bank. The bank had deducted a $15 collection fee. The collection has not been recorded.

Required

Preparation component:

1. Prepare a September 30 bank reconciliation for the company.

2. Prepare the general journal entries needed to adjust the book balance of cash to the reconciled balance.

Analysis component:

3. The preceding bank statement discloses three places where the cancelled cheques returned with the bank statement are not numbered sequentially. In other words, some of the prenumbered cheques in the sequence are missing. Several possible situations would explain why the cancelled cheques returned with a bank statement might not be numbered sequentially. Describe three situations, each of which is a possible explanation of why the cancelled cheques returned with a bank statement are not numbered sequentially.

Check Figure Reconciled balance, $18,326.75

Problem 9-5
Principles of internal control

LO 2

For the following five scenarios identify the principle of internal control that is violated. Next make a recommendation of what the business should do to ensure adherence to principles of internal control.

1. At Stratford Iron Company, Jill and Joan alternate lunch hours. Normally Jill is the petty cash custodian but if someone needs petty cash when Jill is at lunch Joan fills in as custodian.

2. Nadine McDonald does all the posting of patient charges and payments at the Northampton Medical Clinic. Every night Nadine backs up the computerized accounting system to a tape and stores the tape in a locked file at her desk.

3. Jack Mawben prides himself on hiring quality workers who require little supervision. As office manager, Jack gives his employees full discretion over their tasks and has seen no reason to perform independent reviews of their work for years.

4. Bill Clark's manager has told him to "reduce overhead" no matter what! Bill decides to raise the deductible on the plant's property insurance from $5,000 to $10,000. This cuts the property insurance premium in half. In a related move, he decides that bonding of the plant's employees is really a waste of money since the company has not experienced any losses due to employee theft. Bill saves the entire amount of the bonding insurance premium by dropping the bonding insurance.

5. Catherine Young records all incoming customer cash receipts for her employer and also posts the customer payments to their accounts.

Dodge & Sons completed the following petty cash transactions during July of the current year:

Alternate Problems

Problem 9-1A
Establishing, reimbursing, and increasing the petty cash fund

LO 6

July 5   Drew a $200 cheque, cashed it, and turned the proceeds and the petty cash box over to Jackie Boone, the petty cashier.

6   Paid $14.50 COD charges on merchandise purchased for resale. Dodge & Sons uses the perpetual inventory method to account for merchandise inventory.

11   Paid $8.75 delivery charges on merchandise sold to a customer.

12   Purchased file folders, $12.13.

14   Reimbursed Collin Dodge, the manager of the business, $9.65 for office supplies purchased.

18   Purchased paper for printer, $22.54.

27   Paid $47.10 COD charges on merchandise purchased for resale.

28   Purchased stamps, $16.

30   Reimbursed Collin Dodge $58.80 for business car expenses.

31   Jackie Boone sorted the petty cash receipts by accounts affected and exchanged them for a cheque to reimburse the fund for expenditures. However, there was $11.53 in cash in the fund, and she could not account for the overage. In addition, the size of the petty cash fund was increased to $250.

Required

1. Prepare a general journal entry to record establishing the petty cash fund.

2. Prepare a summary of petty cash payments that has these categories: delivery expense, mileage expense, postage expense, transportation-in, and office supplies. Sort the payments into the appropriate categories and total the expenses in each category.

3. Prepare the general journal entry to record the reimbursement and the increase of the fund.

The accounting system used by The Thrifty Company requires that all entries be journalized in a General Journal. To facilitate payments for small items, Thrifty established a petty cash fund. The following transactions involving the petty cash fund occurred during February (the last month of the company's fiscal year).

Problem 9-2A
Petty cash fund; reimbursement and analysis of errors

LO 6

Feb. 3   A company cheque for $150 was drawn and made payable to the petty cashier to establish the petty cash fund.

14   A company cheque was drawn to replenish the fund for the following expenditures made since February 3 and to increase the fund to $175.
   a.   Purchased office supplies, $16.29.
   b   Paid $17.60 COD charges on merchandise purchased for resale. Thrifty uses the perpetual method to account for merchandise inventory.
   c.   Paid $36.57 to Data Services for minor repairs to computer.
   d.   Paid $14.82 for items classified as miscellaneous expenses.
   e.   Discovered that only $62.28 remained in the petty cash box.

28   The petty cashier noted that $48.81 remained in the fund, and decided that the February 14 increase in the fund was not large enough. A company cheque was

drawn to replenish the fund for the following expenditures made since February 14, and to increase it to $250.

f. Paid $40 to *The Smart Saver* for an advertisement in a monthly newsletter.
g. Paid $28.19 for office supplies.
h. Paid $58 to Best Movers for delivery of merchandise to a customer.

Required

Preparation component:

1. Prepare general journal entries to record the establishment of the fund on February 3 and its replenishment on February 14 and on February 28.

Analysis component:

2. Explain how the company's financial statements would be affected if the petty cash fund is not replenished and no entry is made on February 28. (Hint: The amount of Office Supplies that appears on a balance sheet is determined by a physical count of the supplies on hand.)

Problem 9-3A
Preparation of bank reconciliation and recording adjustments

 LO 9

The following information was available to reconcile Bohannon Co.'s book cash balance with its bank statement balance as of December 31, 19X1:

a. The December 31 cash balance according to the accounting records was $31,743.70, and the bank statement balance for that date was $45,091.80.

b. Cheque No. 1273 for $1,084.20 and Cheque No. 1282 for $390, both written and entered in the accounting records in December, were not among the cancelled cheques returned. Two cheques, No. 1231 for $2,289 and No. 1242 for $370.50, were outstanding on November 30 when the bank and book statement balances were last reconciled. Cheque No. 1231 was returned with the December cancelled cheques, but Cheque No. 1242 was not.

c. When the December cheques were compared with entries in the accounting records, it was found that Cheque No. 1267 had been correctly drawn for $2,435 to pay for office supplies, but was erroneously entered in the accounting records as though it were drawn for $2,453.

d. Two debit memoranda were included with the returned cheques and were unrecorded at the time of the reconciliation. One of the debit memoranda was for $749.50 and dealt with an NSF cheque for $732 that had been received from a customer, Tork Industries, in payment of their account. It also assessed a $17.50 fee for processing. The second debit memorandum covered cheque printing and was for $79. These transactions had not been recorded by Bohannon before receiving the statement.

e. A credit memorandum indicated that the bank had collected a $20,000 note receivable for the company, deducted a $20 collection fee, and credited the balance to the company's account. This transaction was not recorded by Bohannon before receiving the statement.

f. The December 31 cash receipts, $7,666.10, had been placed in the bank's night depository after banking hours on that date and did not appear on the bank statement.

Required

Preparation component:

1. Prepare a bank reconciliation for the company as of December 31.

2. Prepare the general journal entries necessary to bring the company's book balance of cash into conformity with the reconciled balance.

Analysis component:

3. Explain the nature of the messages conveyed by a bank to one of its depositors when the bank sends a debit memo and a credit memo to the depositor.

Safety Systems reconciled its bank balance on April 30 and showed two cheques outstanding at that time, No. 1771 for $781 and No. 1780 for $1,325.90. The following information is available for the May 31, 19X1, reconciliation:

Problem 9-4A
Preparation of bank reconciliation and recording adjustments

LO 9

From the May 31 bank statement:

BALANCE OF PREVIOUS STATEMENT ON APR. 30/X1 . . .	$18,290.70	
5 DEPOSITS AND OTHER CREDITS TOTALLING	16,416.80	
9 CHEQUES AND OTHER DEBITS TOTALLING	12,898.90	
CURRENT BALANCE AS OF THIS STATEMENT	21,808.60	

============ CHEQUING ACCOUNT TRANSACTIONS ============

DATE	AMOUNT	TRANSACTION DESCRIPTION	DATE	AMOUNT	TRANSACTION DESCRIPTION
May 4	2,438.00	+Deposit	May 25	7,200.00	+Credit memo
May 14	2,898.00	+Deposit	May 26	2,079.00	+Deposit
May 18	431.80	−NSF cheque	May 31	12.00	−Service charge
May 22	1,801.80	+Deposit			

DATE	CHEQUE NO.	AMOUNT	DATE	CHEQUE NO.	AMOUNT
Apr 01	1771*	781.00	May 26	1785	157.20
May 04	1782	1,285.50	May 25	1787*	8,032.50
May 02	1783	195.30	May 29	1788	554.00
May 11	1784	1,449.60			

*Indicates a skip in cheque sequence.

From Safety Systems' accounting records:

Cash Receipts Deposited

Date		Cash Debit
May	4	2,438.00
	14	2,898.00
	22	1,801.80
	26	2,079.00
	31	2,526.30
		11,743.10

Cash Disbursements

Cheque No.		Cash Credit
1782		1,285.50
1783		195.30
1784		1,449.60
1785		157.20
1786		353.10
1787		8,032.50
1788		544.00
1789		639.50
		12,656.70

Cash   **Acct. No. 101**

Date		Explanation	PR	Debit	Credit	Balance
Apr.	30	Balance				16,183.80
May	31	Total receipts	R7	11,743.10		27,926.90
	31	Total disbursements	D8		12,656.70	15,270.20

Cheque No. 1788 was correctly drawn for $554 to pay for May utilities; however, the bookkeeper misread the amount and entered it in the accounting records with a debit to Utilities Expense and a credit to Cash as though it were for $544. The bank paid and deducted the correct amount.

The NSF cheque was originally received from a customer, Gertie Mayer, in payment of her account. Its return was unrecorded. The credit memorandum resulted from a $7,300 note that the bank had collected for the company. The bank had deducted a $100 collection fee and deposited the remainder in the company's account. The collection has not been recorded.

Required

Preparation component:

1. Prepare a bank reconciliation for Safety Systems.
2. Prepare the general journal entries needed to adjust the book balance of cash to the reconciled balance.

Analysis component:

3. The preceding bank statement discloses two places where the cancelled cheques returned with the bank statement are not numbered sequentially. In other words, some of the prenumbered cheques in the sequence are missing. Several possible situations would explain why the cancelled cheques returned with a bank statement might not be numbered sequentially. Describe three possible situations why this might occur.

Problem 9-5A
Principles of internal control

LO 2

For the following five scenarios identify the principle of internal control that is violated. Next make a recommendation of what the business should do to insure adherence to principles of internal control.

1. Tamerick Company is a fairly small organization but has segregated the duties of cash receipts and cash disbursements. However, the employee responsible for cash disbursements also reconciles the monthly bank account.
2. Stan Spencer is the most computer literate employee in his company. His boss has recently asked him to put password protection on all the office computers. Stan's main job at the company is to process payroll. Stan has put a password in place that now only allows his boss access to the file where pay rates are changed and personnel are added/or deleted from the company payroll.
3. Starlight Theatre has a computerized order taking system for its tickets. The system is active all week and backed up every Friday night.
4. Trek There Company has two employees handling acquisitions of inventory. One employee places purchase orders and pays vendors. The second employee receives the merchandise.
5. The owner of Holiday Helper uses a cheque protector to perforate cheques making it difficult for anyone to alter the amount of the cheque. The cheque protector sits on the owner's desk in an office that houses company cheques and is often unlocked.

Analytical and Review Problems

A & R Problem 9-1

The bank statement for October arrived in Friday's mail. You were especially anxious to receive the statement as one of your assignments was to prepare a bank reconciliation for the Saturday meeting. You got around to preparing the reconciliation rather late in the afternoon and found all the necessary data with the exception of the bank balance. The bottom portion of the bank statement was smudged, and several figures, including the balance, were obliterated. A telephone call to the bank was answered by a recording with the information that the bank was closed until 10 a.m. Monday. Since the reconciliation had to be prepared, you decided to plug in the bank balance.

In preparation, you assembled the necessary material as follows:

a. Cash balance per books was $6,800.
b. From the cancelled cheques returned by the bank you determined that six cheques remained outstanding. The total of these cheques was $3,700.
c. In checking the cancelled cheques you noted that Cheque No. 274 was properly made for $416 but was recorded in the cash disbursement journal as $461. The cheque was in payment of an account.
d. Included with the bank statement were two memoranda; the credit memorandum was for collection of a note for $1,500 and $90 of interest thereon and the debit memorandum was for $12 of bank charges.

e. While you were sorting the cancelled cheques, one of the cheques caught your attention. You were astounded by the similarity of name with that of your company and the similarity of the cheques. The cheque was for $620 and was obviously in error charged to your company's account.

f. From the deposit book you determined that a $2,500 deposit was made after hours on October 31.

Required

1. Prepare a bank reconciliation statement as of October 31 (plug in the indicated bank balance).
2. Prepare the necessary journal entries.

Your assistant prepared the following bank reconciliation statement. It appears that the statement is unacceptable and the task of preparing a proper reconciliation falls upon you.

A & R Problem 9-2

BRANDON COMPANY
Bank Reconciliation
May 31, 1999

Balance per books May 31		$9,500
Add:		
Note collected	$1,000	
Interest on note	60	
Deposit in transit	2,455	3,515
		13,015
Deduct:		
Bank charges	10	
NSF cheque	500	
Outstanding cheques	1,800	
Error in Cheque No. 78 issued for $762 and		
recorded in the books as $726	36	2,346
Indicated bank balance		10,669
Balance per bank statement		9,359
Discrepancy		$1,310

Required

1. Prepare a proper bank reconciliation showing the true cash balance.
2. Prepare the necessary journal entries.

Wanda White acquired a sports equipment distribution business with a staff of six salespersons and two clerks. Because of the trust that Wanda had in her employees—after all, they were all her friends and just like members of the family—she believed that an honour system in regard to the operation of the petty cash fund was adequate. Consequently, Wanda placed $300 in a coffee jar, which, for convenience, was kept in a cupboard in the common room. All employees had access to the petty cash fund and withdrew amounts as required. No vouchers were required for withdrawals. As required, additional funds were placed in the coffee jar and the amount of the replenishment was charged to "miscellaneous selling expense."

A & R Problem 9-3

Required

1. From the internal control point of view, discuss the weaknesses of the petty cash fund operation and suggest steps necessary for improvement.
2. Does the petty cash fund operation as described above violate any of the generally accepted accounting principles? If yes, which and how is the principle(s) violated?

BEYOND THE NUMBERS

Reporting in Action

LO 3, 10

Refer to the financial statements and related information for **Alliance** in Appendix I. Record answers to the following questions by analyzing information from its statements:

1. For both fiscal year-ends 1997 and 1996, determine the total amount of cash and cash equivalents that Alliance held at the end of the accounting year. Determine the percent this amount represents of total assets, total liabilities, and total shareholders' equity. Comment on any trends.
2. For 1997, use the information in the consolidated statement of changes in financial position to determine the percent change between the beginning of the year and end of the year amounts of cash and cash equivalents.
3. What is the number of days' sales uncollected as of March 31, 1997, and March 31, 1996? Has the collection of receivables improved?

Comparative Analysis

LO 10

Both **Alliance** and **Atlantis** produce, and market movies and television programs. Key comparative figures ($thousands) for these two organizations follow:

| | Alliance | | Atlantis | |
Key figures	1997	1996	1997	1996
Accounts Receivable	$ 82,184	$ 53,081	$145,611	$ 75,645
Revenues	$282,599	$268,945	$177,960	$137,984

* Alliance figures are from the annual reports for the fiscal years ended March 31,1997 and 1996.
Atlantis figures are from the annual reports for the fiscal years ended December 31, 1997 and 1996.

Required

Compute the days' sales uncollected for both companies for the two years of data provided. Comment on the days' uncollected trend for both companies. Which company has had the larger percent change in days' sales uncollected?

Ethics Challenge

LO 2

Marge Page, Dot Night, and Colleen Walker work for a family physician, Dr. Linda Thomen, who is in a private practice. Dr. Thomen is fairly knowledgeable about sound office management practices and has segregated the cash receipt duties as follows. Marge opens the mail and prepares a triplicate list of money received. She sends the one copy of the list to Dot, the cashier, who deposits the receipts daily in the bank. Colleen, the recordkeeper, also receives a copy of the list and posts payments to patients' accounts. About once a month the office clerks decide to have an expensive lunch compliments of Dr. Thomen. Dot endorses a patient's cheque in Dr. Thomen's name and cashes it at the bank. Marge destroys the remittance advice accompanying the cheque. Colleen posts the payment to the customer's account as a miscellaneous credit. The clerks justify their actions given their relatively low pay and knowing that Dr. Thomen will likely never miss the payment.

Required

1. Who would be the best person in Dr. Thomen's office to reconcile the bank statement?
2. Would a bank reconciliation detect the office fraud scheme?
3. What are some ways that would uncover this type of scheme?
4. Suggest additional internal controls that Dr. Thomen may want to implement.

Communicating in Practice

LO 7

The owner of a company sends you an e-mail expressing concern that the company is losing money by not taking advantage of discounts offered by vendors. The company currently uses the gross method of recording purchases. The owner is considering requiring a review of all invoices and payment dates from the previous period. But due to the volume of purchases the owner recognizes this is time consuming and costly. The owner seeks your advice as to how the business might monitor purchase discounts in the future. Provide a response.

Visit the internal control Web site at **http://www.duc.auburn.edu/~auaudit/icwhat.html**. Explore this Web site and record answers to the following questions.

1. How does this Web site define internal control?
2. What are some controls this Web site suggests should be part of your "personal internal control system"?
3. What purposes do internal controls serve in a university environment?
4. Contrast preventative and detective controls.
5. Who is responsible for implementing and maintaining a system of internal controls?

Taking It to the Net
LO 1, 2

Let's bring a voucher system alive! One team will be called upon to personify the operation of a voucher system. Yet all teams must prepare for the potential to be selected by doing the following:

1. Each team is to identify the documents in a voucher system. The team leader will play the voucher, and each team member is to assume "the role" of one or more documents.
2. To prepare for your individual role you are to:
   a. Find an illustration for the document within the chapter.
   b. Write down your function as this document, where you originate and how you flow through the voucher system.
3. Rehearse the role play of operating the system. You may use text illustrations as props and for visual effect you may wear nametags identifying the part you play.

Teamwork in Action
LO 5

Browse around a store in your town or at a mall. Using your observation skills try to note between 5 and 10 internal controls this store is implementing.

Hitting the Road
LO 1

Read the article "The Heavy Burden of Light Fingers" in the December 16, 1996, issue of *Business Week*.

1. What schemes do employees use to defraud companies?
2. What is the average amount of loss experienced by companies due to employee fraud?
3. According to the article, how are employee frauds uncovered?

Business Break
LO 1

10

CHAPTER

Receivables and Temporary Investments

Chapter Outline

Debt into Gold—or—Finlay!

Winnipeg, MN—Today's economy runs on credit sales. These credit sales produce accounts receivable that are often the largest current asset a company owns. But not all accounts receivable are paid. Some end up as "bad debts"—accounts that a company cannot collect.

Enter George and Lucille Finlay. The Finlay's first started collecting on other companies' bad debt accounts in 1986 from their kitchen table in Brandon, Manitoba. They used something more powerful than technology and pressure tactics to collect money debtors owed; they used a philosophy of "respect for people." The Finlay's personally know the psychology of debtors. They found themselves in a huge hole in 1986 after their business went belly up. "You've got to be sympathetic, you've got to listen with your heart as well as your head," say George Finlay.

The Finlay's "polite persistence" has paid off. Their entrepreneurial spirit led them to create **Manitoba Collections Corp. (MCC),** a Winnipeg-based company that is now one of the largest purchasers of bad credit card debts. Last year, their company earned $6 million. And their net profit margin is a cool 67%.

Through all of their success, MCC has maintained its reputation for ethical dealings in an industry still plagued by abusive and questionable tactics. They also keep a down-to-earth management style. One example is if revenue targets are met, MCC will fly all employees and guests to a baseball game in Toronto. It's vintage Finlay: bold and flamboyant. Interestingly, Finlay recently turned down a huge cash offer for the company. Why? "It wasn't enough. We're going places," he says. It might be the World Series of profits. [Source: Adapted from *Business Week*, August 11, 1997.]

MCC Net Income

CHAPTER PREVIEW

This chapter focuses on accounts receivable, short-term notes receivable, and temporary investments. We describe each of these assets, their use in practice, and how they are accounted for and reported on in financial statements. This knowledge helps us use accounting information to make better decisions. It can also help in predicting bad debts as shown in the opening article.

Accounts Receivable

A *receivable* refers to an amount due from another party. Receivables along with cash, cash equivalents, and temporary investments make up the most liquid assets of a company. The two most common receivables are accounts receivable and notes receivable. Other receivables include interest receivable, rent receivable, tax refund receivable, and amounts due from other parties such as officers and employees.

Accounts receivable refers to amounts due from customers for credit sales. This section begins by describing how accounts receivable arise and their different sources. These sources include sales when customers use credit cards issued by third parties, and when a company gives credit directly to customers. When a company extends credit directly to customers it must (1) maintain a separate account receivable for each customer and (2) account for bad debts from credit sales.

Recognizing Accounts Receivable

 Describe accounts receivable and how they occur and are recorded.

Accounts receivable arise from credit sales to customers by both retailers and wholesalers. The amount of credit sales has increased in recent years, reflecting several factors including an efficient banking system and a sound economy. Retailers such as the **The Bay, Eatons** and **Sears Canada** hold millions of dollars in accounts receivable. Similar amounts are held by wholesalers such as **Irwin Toy Limited, George Weston Limited, The Oshawa Group** and **Canadian Tire Corporation**. Exhibit 10.1 shows the dollar amount of accounts receivable and its percent of total assets for four companies.

Exhibit 10.1

Accounts Receivable for Selected Companies

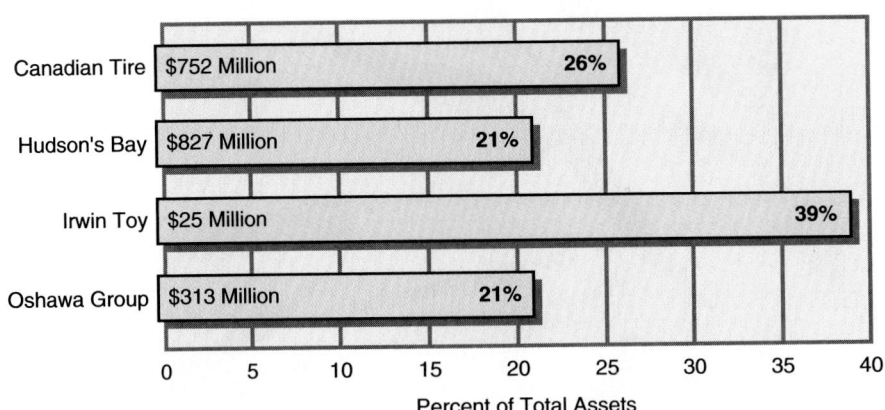

Sales on Credit

We explained in Chapter 8 how credit sales are recorded by debiting an Accounts Receivable account for a specific customer. This is important for showing us how much each customer purchases, how much each customer has paid, and how much each customer still owes. This information provides the basis for sending bills to customers, and gives important data for other managerial analyses. To maintain this information, companies that extend credit directly to their customers must maintain a separate account receivable for each of them. The General Ledger continues to report a single Accounts Receivable amount along with the other financial statement accounts, but a supplementary record is created where a separate account is maintained for each customer. This supplementary record is the *Accounts Receivable Ledger.*

Exhibit 10.2 shows the relation between the Accounts Receivable account in the General Ledger and the individual customer accounts in the Accounts Receivable Ledger for **TechCom,** a small electronics wholesaler. This exhibit reports the effects of two transactions impacting TechCom's accounts receivable for July 15. While TechCom's transactions are mainly in cash, it does deal almost daily with two major credit customers: CompStore and RDA Electronics. Exhibit 10.2 shows the $3,000 total of these two customers' balances in the Accounts Receivable Ledger is equal to the balance of the Accounts Receivable control account in the General Ledger.

Beginning-of-day, July 15

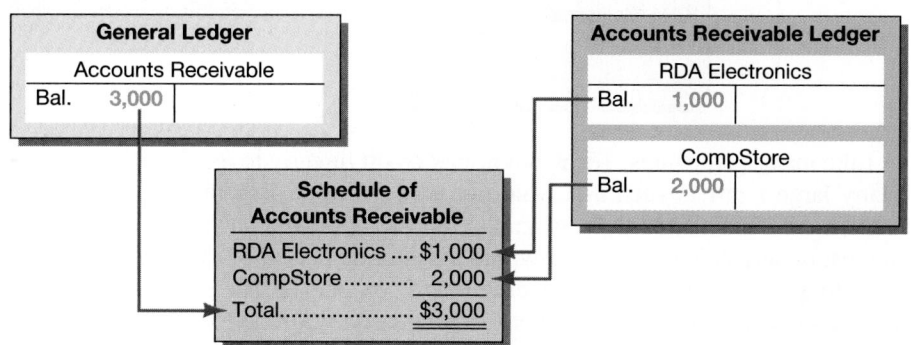

Exhibit 10.2

Accounts Receivable Account and the Accounts Receivable Ledger

To see how accounts receivable from credit sales are recognized in the accounting records, we look at two transactions on July 15 with TechCom's two major credit customers. The first is a credit sale of $950 to CompStore. A credit sale is posted with both a debit to the Accounts Receivable account in the General Ledger and with a debit to the appropriate customer account in the Accounts Receivable Ledger. The second transaction is a collection of $720 from RDA Electronics from prior credit sales. Cash receipts from a credit customer are posted with a credit to both the Accounts Receivable account in the General Ledger and the appropriate customer account.[1] Both transactions are reflected in Exhibit 10.3. Note that these transactions would typically be recorded in the appropriate Sales and Cash Receipts Journals. We use the General Journal format here for simplicity.

July 15	Accounts Receivable—CompStore	950	
	Sales		950
	To record credit sales.		
15	Cash	720	
	Accounts Receivable—RDA Electronics		720
	To record collection of credit sales.		

Exhibit 10.3

Accounts Receivable Transactions

Exhibit 10.4 shows the General Ledger account and the Accounts Receivable Ledger at the end of the day for July 15. The General Ledger account shows the

---

[1] Posting debits or credits to Accounts Receivable twice does not violate the requirement that debits equal credits. The equality of debits and credits is maintained in the General Ledger. The Accounts Receivable Ledger is a supplementary record providing detailed information on each customer.

effects of the sale, the collection, and the resulting balance of $3,230. These events are reflected in the customers' accounts: RDA Electronics has an ending balance of $280 and CompStore owes $2,950. The $3,230 sum of their accounts equals the debit balance of the General Ledger account.

Exhibit 10.4

Accounts Receivable Account and the Accounts Receivable Ledger

Part C: End-of-day, July 15

Like many companies, TechCom grants credit directly to qualified customers. Many large retailers such as **Canadian Tire** and **The Bay** maintain their own credit card. This allows them to grant credit to approved customers and to earn interest on any balance not paid within a specified period of time. It also allows them to avoid the fee charged by credit card companies. The entries in this case are the same as those above except for the possibility of added interest revenue. If a customer owes interest on the bill, then we debit Accounts Receivable and credit Interest Revenue for this amount.

Did You Know?

Cyber Receivables

Cyber receivables are the result of new cyber-merchants. Setting up shop in cyberspace is easier than ever. New programs help merchants build Web storefronts quickly and easily. Merchants simply enter product details such as names and prices, and out comes a respectable-looking site complete with order forms. These storefront programs can be listed as part of a cybermall, and they offer secure credit card orders and track sales and site visits.
[Source: Canadian Internet Mall.]

Credit Card Sales

Many companies allow customers to use credit cards such as Visa, MasterCard, or American Express to charge purchases. This practice gives the customers the ability to make purchases without cash or cheques. It also allows them to defer their payments to the credit card company. Once credit is established with the credit card company, the customer does not have to open an account with each store. Customers using credit cards can make single monthly payments instead of several to different creditors.

There are good reasons why companies allow customers to use credit cards instead of granting credit directly. First, the company does not have to evaluate the credit standing of each customer or make decisions about who gets credit and how much. Second, the company avoids the risk of extending credit to customers who cannot or do not pay. This risk is transferred to the credit card company. Third, the company typically receives cash from the credit card company sooner than if it granted credit directly to customers. Fourth, a variety of credit options for customers offers a potential increase in sales volume. **Sears Canada** historically offered credit only to customers using a SearsCharge card, but changed its policy to permit customers to charge purchases to third-party companies. It reported this as follows:

> **SearsCharge** increased its share of Sears retail sales even as the company expanded the payment options available to its customers with the acceptance in 1993 of VISA, MasterCard, and American Express in addition to the Discover Card.

In dealing with some credit cards, usually those issued by banks, the company deposits a copy of each credit card sales receipt in its bank account just like it deposits a customer's cheque. The company receives a credit to its chequing account without delay. Other credit cards require the company to send a copy of each receipt to the credit card company. Until payment is received, the company has an account receivable from the credit card company. In return for the services provided by the credit card company, the selling company pays a fee often ranging from 2% to 5% of credit card sales. This charge is deducted from the credit to the chequing account or the cash payment to the company.

Debit Card Sales

The use of debit cards is becoming more common and popular with consumers. Payment for a purchase is electronically transferred from the customer's bank account to the vendor's bank account when authorized by the customer at the point of sale. In essence, it is similar to a sale for cash.

Entrepreneur
You are the owner of a small retail store. You are considering allowing customers to purchase merchandise using credit cards. Until now, your store only accepted cash and cheques. What form of analysis do you use to make this decision?

Answer—p. 503

The procedures used in accounting for credit card sales depend on whether cash is received immediately on deposit or is delayed until paid by the credit card company. For instance, if TechCom has $100 of credit card sales with a 4% fee and cash is received immediately, the entry is

July 15	Cash	96	
	Credit Card Expense	4	
	Sales		100
	To record credit card sales less a 4% credit card expense.		

Assets = Liabilities + Equity
+96   −4
                            +100

If TechCom must send a copy of the credit card sales receipts to a credit card company and wait for payment, the entry on the date of sale is:

July 15	Accounts Receivable—Credit Card Company	100	
	Sales		100
	To record credit card sales.		

Assets = Liabilities + Equity
+100   +100

When cash is received from the credit card company, the entry to record the receipt and the deduction of the fee is:

Assets = Liabilities + Equity
+96   −4
−100

July 30	Cash	96	
	Credit Card Expense	4	
	Accounts Receivable—Credit Card		
	Company		100
	To record cash receipt less 4% credit card		
	expense.		

Note the credit card expense is not recorded until cash is received from the credit card company. This practice is a matter of convenience. By following this practice, the selling company avoids having to compute and record the credit card expense each time sales are recorded. Instead, the expense related to many sales can be computed once and recorded when cash is received. But the *matching principle* requires reporting credit card expense in the same period as the sale. Therefore, if the sale and cash receipt occur in different periods, we must accrue and report the credit card expense in the period of the sale by using an adjusting entry at the end of the year. If TechCom requires a year-end adjustment of $24 of accrued credit card expense on a $600 receivable that the credit card company has not yet paid, we must make the following entry:

Assets = Liabilities + Equity
−24   −24

Dec. 31	Credit Card Expense	24	
	Accounts Receivable—Credit Card		
	Company		24
	To accrue credit card expense that is		
	unrecorded at the end of the year.		

The following entry records the cash collection in January:

Assets = Liabilities + Equity
+576
−576

Jan. 5	Cash	576	
	Accounts Receivable—Credit Card		
	Company		576
	To record collection of amount due from		
	Credit Card Company.		

Some firms report credit card expense in the income statement as a type of discount deducted from sales to get net sales. Other companies classify it as a selling expense or even as an administrative expense. Arguments can be made for all three alternatives.

Flash back

1. In recording credit card sales, when do you debit Accounts Receivable and when do you debit Cash?
2. When are credit card expenses recorded in cases where sales receipts must be accumulated before they can be sent to the credit card company? When are these expenses incurred?
3. If payment for a credit card sale is not received by the end of the accounting period, how do you account for the credit card expense from that sale?

Answers—p. 503

Valuing Accounts Receivable

When a company grants credit to its customers, there usually are a few customers who do not pay what they promised. The accounts of these customers are **uncollectible accounts**, commonly called **bad debts**. The total amount of uncollectible accounts is an expense of selling on credit. Why do companies sell on credit if it is likely some accounts will prove uncollectible? The answer is companies believe granting credit will increase revenues and profits to offset bad debts. They are willing to incur bad debt losses if the net effect is to increase sales and profits.

Two methods are used by companies to account for uncollectible accounts: (1) direct write-off method, and (2) allowance method. We describe both of these methods below.

Credit Woes

The days of easy money are ending for credit card issuers. Costs of financing credit card operations are rising for all issuers, owing to record default rates. Much of this is the fault of issuers who have flooded the market with offers of credit cards with low "teaser" rates. In response, credit card users have greatly increased their debts, and many are unable to pay them. The table here shows the sources of credit card fraud activity.

Credit Card Fraud Activity
January 1997–September 1997
Total cases: 82,090

- ■ Counterfeit
- ■ Stolen
- ■ Lost
- ■ Fraudulent Use of Account
- □ Miscellaneous
- ■ Non receipt
- □ Fraudulent Applications

40.3%   1%   5.7%   6.6%   6.8%   18.9%   20.8%

Source: Canadian Bankers Association

Did You Know?

Direct Write-Off Method

The **direct write-off method** of accounting for bad debts records the loss from an uncollectible account receivable at the time it is determined to be uncollectible. No attempt is made to estimate uncollectible accounts or bad debt expense. Bad debt expense is recorded when specific accounts are written off as uncollectible. If TechCom determines on January 23 it cannot collect $520 owed by an individual named Jack Kent, this loss is recognized using the direct write-off method in the following entry:

LO 2 Apply the direct write-off and allowance methods to account for accounts receivable.

Jan. 23	Bad Debt Expense	520	
	Accounts Receivable—Jack Kent		520
	To write off uncollectible account under the direct write-off method.		

Assets = Liabilities + Equity
−520   −520

The debit in this entry charges the uncollectible amount directly to the current year's Bad Debt Expense account. The credit removes the balance of the account from the subsidiary ledger and from the controlling account.

Sometimes an account written off is later collected. This can be due to factors such as continual collection efforts or the good fortune of a customer. If the account of Jack Kent that was written off directly to Bad Debt Expense is later collected in full, the following two entries record this recovery:

Assets = Liabilities + Equity
+520   +520

Mar. 11	Accounts Receivable—Jack Kent	520	
	Bad Debt Expense		520
	To reinstate account of Jack Kent previously written off.		

Assets = Liabilities + Equity
+520
−520

Mar. 11	Cash	520	
	Accounts Receivable—Jack Kent		520
	In full payment of account.		

Sometimes an amount previously written off directly to Bad Debt Expense is recovered in the year following the write-off. If there is no balance in the Bad Debt Expense account from previous write-offs and no other write-offs are expected, the credit portion of the entry recording the recovery can be made to a Bad Debt Recoveries revenue account.

Companies must weigh at least two principles when considering use of the direct write-off method: (1) matching principle, and (2) materiality principle.

Matching Principle Applied to Bad Debts

The **matching principle** requires expenses be reported in the same accounting period as the sales they helped produce. This means that if extending credit to customers helped produce sales, the bad debt expense linked to those sales is matched and reported in the same period as sales. The direct write-off method usually doesn't match revenues and expenses. This mismatch occurs because bad debt expense is not recorded until an account becomes uncollectible, which often does not occur during the same accounting period.

Materiality Principle Applied to Bad Debts

The **materiality principle** states that an amount can be ignored if its effect on the financial statements is unimportant to users. The materiality principle permits the matching principle to be ignored and use of the direct write-off method in accounting for expenses from bad debts when bad debt expenses are very small in relation to a company's other financial statement items such as sales and net income. This requires that bad debt expense be unimportant for decisions made by users of the company's financial statements.

Allowance Method

The **allowance method** of accounting for bad debts matches the *expected* loss from uncollectible accounts receivable against the sales they helped produce in that period. We must use expected losses since management cannot exactly identify at the time of sale the customers who will not pay their bills. This means that at the end of each period the allowance method requires us to estimate the total bad debts expected to result from that period's sales. An allowance is then recorded for this expected loss. This method has two advantages over the direct write-off method: (1) bad debt expense is charged to the period when the related sales are recognized, and (2) accounts receivable are reported on the balance sheet at the estimated amount of cash to be collected.

Recording Estimated Bad Debt Expense

The allowance method estimates bad debt expense at the end of each accounting period and records it with an adjusting entry. TechCom, for instance, had credit sales of approximately $300,000 during its first year of operations. At the end of the first year, $20,000 of credit sales remained uncollected. Based on the experience of similar businesses, TechCom estimated $1,500 of accounts receivable are uncollectible. This estimated expense is recorded with the following adjusting entry:

Dec. 31	Bad Debt Expense	1,500	
	Allowance for Doubtful Accounts		1,500
	To record estimated bad debts.		

Assets = Liabilities + Equity
−1,500   −1,500

The debit in this entry means the estimated bad debts expense of $1,500 from selling on credit is matched on the income statement with the $300,000 sales it helped produce. The credit in this entry is to a contra account called **Allowance for Doubtful Accounts**. A contra account is used because at the time of the adjusting entry, we do not know which customers will not pay. Because specific bad accounts are not identifiable at the time of the adjusting entry, they cannot be removed from the subsidiary Accounts Receivable Ledger. Because the customer accounts are left in the subsidiary ledger, the controlling account for Accounts Receivable cannot be reduced. Instead, the Allowance for Doubtful Accounts account *must* be credited.

Bad Debts and Related Accounts in Financial Statements

The process of evaluating customers and approving them for credit usually is not assigned to the selling department of a company. Given its goal of increasing sales, the selling department might have different motives in approving customers for credit. Because the selling department is not responsible for granting credit, it should not be held responsible for bad debt expense. This means bad debt expense often appears on the income statement as an administrative expense rather than a selling expense.

Recall TechCom has $20,000 of outstanding accounts receivable at the end of its first year of operations. After the bad debts adjusting entry is posted, TechCom's Accounts Receivable and Allowance for Doubtful Accounts have balances as shown in Exhibit 10.5.

Accounts Receivable		Allowance for Doubtful Accounts	
Dec. 31 20,000			Dec. 31 1,500

Exhibit 10.5

General Ledger Balances after Bad Debts Adjusting Entry

The Allowance for Doubtful Accounts credit balance of $1,500 has the effect of reducing accounts receivable (net of the allowance) to their estimated realizable value. **Realizable value** is the expected proceeds from converting this asset into cash. Although $20,000 is legally owed to TechCom by its credit customers, only $18,500 is expected to be realized in cash collections from customers.

In the balance sheet, the Allowance for Doubtful Accounts is subtracted from Accounts Receivable to show the amount expected to be realized. This information is often reported as shown in Exhibit 10.6.

Current assets:		
Accounts receivable	$20,000	
Less allowance for doubtful accounts	(1,500)	18,500

Exhibit 10.6

Balance Sheet Presentation of Allowance for Doubtful Accounts

Sometimes the contra account to Accounts Receivable is not reported separately. This alternative presentation is shown in Exhibit 10.7.

Exhibit 10.7

Alternative Presentation of Allowance for Doubtful Accounts

| Accounts receivable (net of $1,500 estimated uncollectible accounts) . . . | $18,500 |

Writing Off a Bad Debt

When specific accounts are identified as uncollectible, they are written off against the Allowance for Doubtful Accounts. After spending a year trying to collect from Jack Kent, for instance, TechCom finally decides his $520 account is uncollectible and makes the following entry to write it off:

Assets = Liabilities + Equity
+520
−520

Jan. 23	Allowance for Doubtful Accounts	520	
	Accounts Receivable—Jack Kent		520
	To write off an uncollectible account.		

Posting the credit of this write-off entry to the Accounts Receivable account removes the amount of the bad debt from the controlling account. Posting it to Jack Kent's account removes the amount of the bad debt from the subsidiary ledger. By removing it from the subsidiary ledger, TechCom avoids the cost of additional collection efforts. After this entry is posted, the General Ledger accounts appear as shown in Exhibit 10.8.

Exhibit 10.8

General Ledger Balances after Write-Off

Accounts Receivable				Allowance for Doubtful Accounts			
Dec. 31	20,000					Dec. 31	1,500
		Jan. 23	520	Jan. 23	520		

Note two aspects of this entry and related accounts. First, while bad debts are an expense of selling on credit, the allowance account is debited in the write-off. The expense account is not debited. The expense account is not debited because bad debt expense is previously estimated and recorded with an adjusting entry at the end of the period in which the sale occurred. Second, while the write-off removes the amount of the account receivable from the ledgers, it doesn't affect the estimated realizable value of TechCom's net accounts receivable as shown here in Exhibit 10.9.

Exhibit 10.9

Realizable Value before and after Write-Off

	Before Write-Off	After Write-Off
Accounts receivable	$20,000	$19,480
Less allowance for doubtful accounts	1,500	980
Estimated realizable accounts receivable . . .	$18,500	$18,500

Neither total assets nor net income are affected by the write-off of a specific account. But both total assets and net income are affected from recognizing the year's bad debts expense in the adjusting entry.

Recovery of a Bad Debt

When a customer fails to pay and the account is written off, his or her credit standing is jeopardized. The customer sometimes chooses to voluntarily pay all or part of the amount owed after the account is written off as uncollectible. This payment helps restore credit standing. When a recovery of a bad debt occurs, it is recorded in the customer's subsidiary account where this information is retained for use in future credit evaluation.

A company makes two entries when collecting an account previously written off. The first is to reverse the original write-off and reinstate the customer's account. The second entry records the collection of the reinstated account. If on March 11 Jack Kent pays in full his account that TechCom previously wrote off, the entries to record this bad debt recovery are:

Mar. 11	Accounts Receivable—Jack Kent	520		Assets = Liabilities + Equity
	Allowance for Doubtful Accounts		520	+520
	To reinstate the account of Jack Kent previously written off.			−520
Mar. 11	Cash	520		Assets = Liabilities + Equity
	Accounts Receivable—Jack Kent		520	+520
	In full payment of account.			−520

Jack Kent paid the entire amount previously written off, but in some cases a customer may pay only a portion of the amount owed. A question then arises of whether the entire balance of the account is returned to accounts receivable or just the amount paid. The answer is a matter of judgment. If we believe this customer will later pay in full, the entire amount owed is returned to accounts receivable. But only the amount paid is returned if we expect no further collection.

Flash back

4. Using the matching principle, why must bad debts expenses be estimated?

5. What term describes the balance sheet valuation of accounts receivable less the allowance for doubtful accounts?

6. Why is estimated bad debts expense credited to a contra account rather than to the Accounts Receivable controlling account?

Answers—p. 503

Estimating Bad Debt Expense

Companies with credit sales estimate bad debt expense. They do this to help them manage their receivables and to set credit policies. The allowance method of accounting for bad debts also requires an estimate of bad debt expense to prepare the adjusting entry at the end of each accounting period. How does a company estimate bad debt expense? There are two general methods. One is based on the income statement relation between bad debt expense and sales. The second is based on the balance sheet relation between accounts receivable and allowance for doubtful accounts. Both methods require an analysis of past experience.

LO3 Estimate uncollectibles using methods based on sales and accounts receivable.

Percent of Sales Method

The percent of sales method uses income statement relations to estimate bad debts. It is based on the idea that a percentage of a company's credit sales for the period are uncollectible.[2] The income statement would then report that percentage as the amount of bad debt expense. Assume MusicLand, for instance, has credit sales of $400,000 in 1999. Based on past experience and the experience of similar companies, MusicLand estimates 0.6% of credit sales are uncollectible. Using this prediction, MusicLand expects $2,400 of bad debt expense from 1999's sales ($400,000 × 0.006 = $2,400). The adjusting entry to record this estimated expense is:

Dec. 31	Bad Debt Expense	2,400		Assets = Liabilities + Equity
	Allowance for Doubtful Accounts		2,400	−2,400 −2,400
	To record estimated bad debts.			

---

[2] Note the focus is on *credit* sales. Cash sales do not produce bad debts, and they are generally not used in this estimation. But if cash sales are relatively small compared to credit sales, there is no major impact from including them.

This entry does not mean the December 31, 1999, balance in Allowance for Doubtful Accounts is $2,400. A $2,400 balance occurs only if the account had a zero balance immediately prior to posting the adjusting entry. For several reasons the unadjusted balance of Allowance for Doubtful Accounts is not likely to be zero.

One reason is unless MusicLand is in its first period of operations, the Allowance for Doubtful Accounts usually has a credit balance at the beginning of the period. This is because after the first period of applying the allowance method the beginning of the second period carries a credit balance in the allowance account from the adjusting entry made at the end of the first period to reflect estimated bad debt expense. In the second period, entries are made to write off uncollectible accounts and the allowance account is reduced (debited). The cumulative effect of these entries is reflected in the ending balance of the allowance account. This balance, *prior to adjustment*, can be a debit or a credit balance. This unadjusted ending balance reflects the beginning credit balance and the write-offs during the period.

A second reason is since bad debt expense is estimated each period, the total amount of expense recorded in past periods is not likely to equal the amounts written off as uncollectible. Although expense estimates are based on past experience, some differences between recorded expenses and amounts written off are expected to show up in the unadjusted Allowance for Doubtful Accounts balance.

A third reason is some of the amounts written off as uncollectible during the current period probably relate to credit sales made during this current period. These debits impact the unadjusted Allowance for Doubtful Accounts balance. They may even cause the account to have a debit balance prior to posting the adjusting entry for bad debt expense.

These reasons mean we do not expect the Allowance for Doubtful Accounts to have an unadjusted balance of zero at the end of the period. This also means the adjusted balance reported on the balance sheet normally does not equal the amount of expense reported on the income statement. Expressing bad debt expense as a percent of sales is an estimate based on past experience. As new experience is obtained, we can find that the percent used is too high or too low. When this happens, a different rate is used in future periods.

Accounts Receivable Methods

The *accounts receivable* method uses balance sheet relations to estimate bad debts. It is based on the idea some portion of the end-of-period accounts receivable balance is not collectible. Its objective for the bad debts adjusting entry is to make the Allowance for Doubtful Accounts balance equal to the portion of outstanding accounts receivable estimated to be uncollectible. To obtain this required balance for the Allowance for Doubtful Accounts account, we compare its balance before the adjustment with the required balance. The difference between the two is debited to Bad Debt Expense and credited to Allowance for Doubtful Accounts. Estimating this required balance for the allowance account is done in one of two ways: (1) by using a simple percent estimate of uncollectibles from the total outstanding accounts receivable, and (2) by aging accounts receivable.

Percent of Accounts Receivable Method

The *percent of accounts receivable* approach assumes a percent of a company's outstanding receivables is uncollectible. This estimated percent is based on past experience and the experience of similar companies. It also is impacted by current conditions such as recent economic conditions and difficulties faced by customers. The total dollar amount of all outstanding receivables is multiplied by an estimated percent to get the estimated dollar amount of uncollectible accounts. This amount is reported in the balance sheet as the balance for Allowance for Doubtful Accounts. To put the balance in this account, we prepare an adjusting entry debiting Bad Debt Expense and crediting Allowance for Doubtful Accounts. The amount of the adjustment is the amount necessary to give us the required balance in Allowance for Doubtful Accounts.

Assume **MusicLand** has $50,000 of outstanding accounts receivable on December 31, 1999. Past experience suggests 5% of outstanding receivables are uncollectible. After the adjusting entry is posted, we want the Allowance for Doubtful Accounts to show a $2,500 credit balance (5% of $50,000). Also assume before the adjustment the account appears as:

Allowance for Doubtful Accounts			
		Dec. 31, 1998, balance	2,000
Feb. 6	800		
July 10	600		
Nov. 20	400		
		Unadjusted balance	200

The $2,000 beginning balance is from the December 31, 1998, balance sheet. During 1999, accounts of specific customers are written off on February 6, July 10, and November 20. This means the account has a $200 credit balance prior to the December 31, 1999, adjustment. The adjusting entry to give the allowance the required $2,500 balance is:

Dec. 31	Bad Debt Expense	2,300	
	Allowance for Doubtful Accounts		2,300
	To record estimated bad debts.		

Assets = Liabilities + Equity
−2,300   −2,300

After this entry is posted the allowance has a $2,500 credit balance as shown in Exhibit 10.10.

Allowance for Doubtful Accounts			
		Dec. 31, 1998, balance	2,000
Feb. 6	800		
July 10	600		
Nov. 20	400		
		Unadjusted balance	200
		Dec. 31 adjustment	**2,300**
		Dec. 31, 1999, balance	2,500

Exhibit 10.10

Allowance for Doubtful Accounts after Bad Debts Adjusting Entry

High-Tech Estimates

Technology can assist users in estimating bad debts. Both the sales-based and receivables-based methods of estimating bad debts are easily included in computerized information systems. Using current and past data in the system, estimates of bad debts are obtained with adjustments for different assumptions. Spreadsheet programs can also be used for estimating bad debts.

Did You Know?

Aging of Accounts Receivable Method

Both the percent of sales (income statement) method and the percent of accounts receivable (balance sheet) method use information from *past* experience to estimate the amount of bad debts expense. Another balance sheet method using receivables information produces a more precise estimate and uses both past experience and current information. The **aging of accounts receivable** method examines each account receivable to estimate the amount uncollectible. Receivables are classified by how long they have been outstanding. Then, estimates of uncollectible amounts are made assuming the longer an amount is outstanding, the more likely it is uncollectible.

Did You Know?

Mining Data and Fool's Gold
Michael Drosnin's best-selling book, *The Bible Code,* claims to find hidden messages in the Bible about dinosaurs, Bill Clinton, and the Land of Magog. The pitfall Drosnin stumbled into reminds us of the dangers of modern technology and "data mining." Done right, data mining can help discover trends, weed out credit card fraud, identify bad credit risks, and estimate uncollectibles. Done wrong, it produces bogus correlations. For instance, historically the single best predictor of the Standard & Poor's 500 stock index was butter production in Bangladesh. The lesson: Use common sense in mining data and beware of fool's gold. [Source: *Business Week,* June 16, 1997.]

In aging accounts receivable outstanding at the end of a period, we examine each account and classify them by how much time has passed since they were created. Classifications depend on the judgment of a company's management. But classes are often based on 30-day (or one-month) periods. After the outstanding amounts are classified (or aged), past experience is used to estimate the percent of each class that is uncollectible. These percents are applied to the amounts in each class to get the required balance of the Allowance for Doubtful Accounts. This computation is performed by setting up a schedule like Exhibit 10.11 for MusicLand.

Exhibit 10.11

Aging of Accounts
Receivable

		MUSICLAND Schedule of Accounts Receivable by Age December 31, 1999				
Customer's Name	**Total**	**Not Yet Due**	**1 to 30 Days Past Due**	**31 to 60 Days Past Due**	**61 to 90 Days Past Due**	**Over 90 Days Past Due**
Charles Abbot	$ 450	$ 450				
Frank Allen	710			$ 710		
George Arden	500	300	$ 200			
Paul Baum	740				$ 100	$ 640
ZZ Services	1,000	810	190			
Totals	$49,900	$37,000	$6,500	$3,500	$1,900	$1,000
Percent Uncollectible..		× 2%	× 5%	× 10%	× 25%	× 40%
Estimated uncollectible accounts.....	$ 2,290	$ 740	$ 325	$ 350	$ 475	$ 400

Exhibit 10.11 lists each customer's account with its total balance. Then, each individual balance is assigned to one of five classes based on the age of its balance. In computerized systems, the task of aging accounts receivable is readily accomplished by the use of a spreadsheet or specialized computer programs.

When all accounts are aged, the amounts in each class are totalled and multiplied by the estimated percent of uncollectible accounts for each class. The reasonableness of the percents used are reviewed regularly to reflect changes in the company and economy. The following excerpt from the 1996 annual report of **Sears** shows such a review:

Provision for uncollectible accounts increased 58.6% and net charge-offs increased 51.1% from 1995. These increases reflect the 12.6% growth in domestic credit card receivables from 1995 levels and the continuing industry-wide trend of increased delinquencies and bankruptcies. The Company has responded to the aforementioned trend by implementing an aggressive action plan which includes enhanced collection efforts and increased investment in technology designed to improve collection staff productivity.

For MusicLand we see from Exhibit 10.11 it is owed $3,500 that is 31 to 60 days past due. MusicLand's management estimates 10% of the amounts in this age class are not collectible. The dollar amount of uncollectibles in this class is $350 ($3,500 × 10%). The total in the first column tells us the adjusted balance in MusicLand's Allowance for Doubtful Accounts should be $2,290 ($740 + $325 + $350 + $475 + $400). Because the allowance account has an unadjusted credit balance of $200, the required adjustment to the Allowance for Doubtful Accounts is $2,090. This computation is shown in Exhibit 10.12.

Unadjusted balance	$ 200 credit
Required balance	2,290 credit
Required adjustment	$2,090 credit

Exhibit 10.12

Computing Required Adjustment for Accounts Receivable Method

MusicLand records the following adjusting entry:

Dec. 31	Bad Debt Expense	2,090	
	Allowance for Doubtful Accounts		2,090
	To record estimated bad debts.		

Assets = Liabilities + Equity
−2,090   −2,090

Alternatively, if MusicLand's allowance had an unadjusted *debit* balance of $500, then the required adjustment and its related entry would be:

Unadjusted balance	$ 500 debit
Required balance	2,290 credit
Required adjustment	$2,790 credit

Dec. 31	Bad Debt Expense	2,790	
	Allowance for Doubtful Accounts		2,790
	To record estimated bad debts.		

Assets = Liabilities + Equity
−2,790   −2,790

When the percent of sales (income statement) method is used, MusicLand's bad debt expense for 1999 is estimated at $2,400. When the percent of accounts receivable (balance sheet) method is used, the estimate is $2,300. And when the aging of accounts receivable method is used, the estimate is $2,090. We usually expect these amounts to be different since each method gives only an estimate of future payments. But the aging of accounts receivable method is a more detailed examination of specific accounts and is usually the most reliable.[3] Exhibit 10.13 summarizes the principles guiding all three estimation methods and their focus of analysis.

Exhibit 10.13

Methods to Estimate Bad
Debts

Income Statement Focus	Balance Sheet Focus	Balance Sheet Focus
Percent of Sales Emphasis on Matching Sales ←—→ Bad Debt Expense	**Percent of Receivables** Emphasis on Realizable Value Accounts ←—→ Allowance Receivable for Doubtful (total) Accounts	**Aging of Receivables** Emphasis on Realizable Value Accounts ←—→ Allowance Receivable for Doubtful (individual) Accounts

Flash back

7. SnoBoard Company's end of period Dec. 31, 1999, balance in the allowance for doubtful accounts is a credit of $440. It estimates from an aging of accounts receivable that $6,142 is uncollectible. Prepare SnoBoard's year-end adjusting entry for bad debts.

8. Record entries for the following transactions:

January 10, 1999   The $300 account of customer Cool Jam is determined uncollectible.

April 12, 1999   Cool Jam pays in full its account that was deemed uncollectible on January 10, 1999.

Answers—p. 503

Installment Accounts Receivable

Many companies allow their credit customers to make periodic payments over several months. When this is done, the selling company's assets may be in the form of installment accounts receivable. *Installment accounts receivable* are amounts owed by customers from credit sales where payment is required in periodic amounts over an extended time period. Source documents for installment accounts receivable includes sales slips or invoices describing the sales transactions. When payments are made over several months or if the credit period is long, the customer is usually charged interest. Although installment accounts receivable may have credit periods of more than one year, they should be classified as current assets if the company regularly offers customers such terms.

Companies sometime allow customers to sign a note receivable for sales. Also, companies sometime ask for a note to replace an account receivable when a customer requests additional time to pay its past-due account. A note receivable is a written document that promises payment and is signed by the customer. If the credit period is long, the customer is usually charged interest. As with installment receivables, these types of notes receivable are classified as current assets even when their credit period is longer than one year if this is a regular part of the company's business. Sellers generally prefer to receive notes receivable over any type of accounts receivable when the credit period is long and the receivable relates to a single sale for a fairly large amount. This is because of legal reasons. If a lawsuit is needed to collect from a customer, a note is a written acknowledgment by the buyer of the debt, its amount, and its terms. We explain the details of notes receivable next.

---

[3] In many cases, the aging analysis is supplemented with information about specific customers allowing management to decide whether those accounts should be classified as uncollectible. This information often is supplied by the sales and credit department managers.

Labour Union Chief
You are representing your employee union in contract negotiations with management. One week prior to contract discussions, management released financial statements showing zero growth in earnings. This is far below the 10% growth predicted earlier. In your review of the financial statements you find the company increased its "allowance for uncollectible accounts" from 1.5% to 4.5% of accounts receivable. Apart from this change, earnings would show a 9% growth. Does this information impact your negotiations?

Answer—p. 503

Notes Receivable

LO 4 Describe a note receivable and the computation of its maturity date and interest.

A **promissory note** is a written promise to pay a specified amount of money either on demand or at a definite future date. Promissory notes are used in many transactions including paying for products and services, in the lending and borrowing of money, and to cover accounts receivable.

Exhibit 10.14 shows a promissory note dated July 10, 1999. For this note, Julia Browne promises to pay TechCom or to its order (according to TechCom's instructions) a specified amount of money ($1,000), called the **principal** of the note at a definite future date (October 8, 1999). As the one who signed the note and promised to pay it at maturity, Julia Browne is the **maker** of the note. As the person to whom the note is payable, TechCom is the **payee** of the note. To Julia Browne, the illustrated note is a liability called a *note payable*. To TechCom, the same note is an asset called a *note receivable*.

Interest rates on notes are typically expressed as an annual rate. The promissory note in Exhibit 10.14 bears interest at 12% per annum. The rate of interest this note bears is written on the note. Interest is the charge for using (not paying) the money until a later date. To a borrower, interest is an expense. To a lender, it is a revenue.

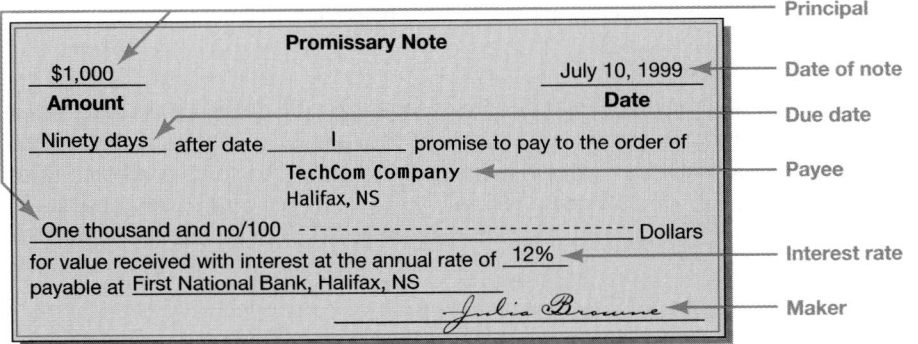

Exhibit 10.14

A Promissory Note

Computations for Notes

We need knowledge of certain computations for notes to understand them. This section describes these computations including determining maturity date, the period covered, and interest computation.

Maturity Date

The **maturity date** of a note is the day the note (principal and interest) must be repaid. The *period* of a note is the time from the note's date to its maturity date. Many notes mature in less than a full year, and the period covered by them is often expressed in days. When the time of a note is expressed in days, the maturity date is the specified number of days after the note's date. As an example, a one-day note dated June 15 matures and is due on June 16. Also, a 90-day note dated July 10 matures on October 8. This October 8 due date is computed as shown in Exhibit 10.15.

Exhibit 10.15

Maturity Date Computation

Days in July	31
Minus the date of the note	10
Days remaining in July	21
Add days in August	31
Add days in September	30
Days to equal 90 days or **Maturity Date, October 8**	8
Period of the note in days	90

The period of a note is sometimes expressed in months or years. When months are used, the note matures and is payable in the month of its maturity on the *same day of the month* as its original date. A three-month note dated July 10, for instance, is payable on October 10. The same analysis applies when years are used.

Interest Computation

Interest is the cost of borrowing money for the borrower or the profit from lending money for the lender. Unless otherwise stated, the rate of interest on a note is the rate charged for the use of the principal for one year. The formula for computing interest on a note is as shown in Exhibit 10.16.

Exhibit 10.16

Formula for Computing Interest

$$\begin{array}{cccc}
\textbf{Principal} & \textbf{Annual} & \textbf{Time} & \\
\textbf{of the} \times & \textbf{interest} \times & \textbf{expressed} = & \textbf{Interest} \\
\textbf{note} & \textbf{rate} & \textbf{in years} &
\end{array}$$

As an example, interest on a $1,000, 12%, six-month note is computed as:

$$\$1,000 \times 12\% \times \frac{6}{12} = \$60$$

It is also common practice that notes are due and payable on a specific date. When the term of the note is expressed in days, we use the exact number of days to calculate the interest. Unless otherwise instructed, you are to solve problems using the specific number of days and a 365-day year. Using the promissory note above where we have a 90-day, 12%, $1,000 note, interest is computed as follows:

$$\text{Interest} = \text{Principal} \times \text{Rate} \times \frac{\text{Exact days}}{365}$$

or

$$\$1,000 \times 12\% \times \frac{90}{365} = \$29.59$$

Alternative Method of Interest Calculation

In calculating interest in the foregoing example, the "exact," or proper, method was used. For classroom purposes, however, instructors may prefer to use a less accurate simplified method of interest calculation in order to focus on comprehension rather than on lengthy procedural calculation. Students must be aware that this method is for instructional purposes only and *is not an acceptable method in practice*. To simplify interest calculations, the following assumptions are made:

1. Treat a year as having 360 days divided into 12 months of 30 days each.
2. Use the exact days of the note.

Thus, interest on a 90-day, 12%, $1,500 note is calculated as:

$$\$1,500 \times 12\% \times \frac{90}{360} = \$45$$

To facilitate the use of the alternative method of interest calculation, certain exercises and problems may be designated by your instructor for use of this method.

LO 5   Record the receipt of a note receivable.

Receipt of a Note

Notes receivable are usually recorded in a single Notes Receivable account to simplify recordkeeping. We need only one account because the original notes are kept on file. This means the maker, rate of interest, due date, and other information can be learned by examining each note.[4]

   To illustrate recording for the receipt of a note, we use the $1,000, 90-day, 12% promissory note in Exhibit 10.14. TechCom receives this note at the time of a product sale to Julia Browne. This transaction is recorded as:

July 10	Notes Receivable	1,000	
	Sales		1,000
	Sold merchandise in exchange for a 90-day, 12% note.		

Assets = Liabilities + Equity
+1,000   +1,000

Another common transaction is when a company accepts a note from an overdue customer as a way of granting a time extension on a past-due account receivable. When this occurs, a company may collect part of the past-due balance in cash. This partial payment forces a concession from the customer, reduces the customer's debt (and the seller's risk), and produces a note for a smaller amount. TechCom, for instance, agreed to accept $232 in cash and a $600, 60-day, 15% note from Jo Cook to settle her $832 past-due account. TechCom made the following entry to record receipt of this cash and note:

Oct. 5	Cash	232	
	Notes Receivable	600	
	Accounts Receivable—Jo Cook		832
	Received cash and note in settlement of account.		

Assets = Liabilities + Equity
+232
+600
−832

On February 3, management decided that the $1,450 account of Jack Thomas was uncollectible and should be written off as a bad debt. Three months later, Jack Thomas negotiated that he would pay $450 immediately and sign an 8%, six-month note dated May 1, for $1,000.

Required

Provide journal entries for the write off of Thomas' account on February 3 and its settlement on May 1.

Mid-Chapter Demonstration Problem

---

[4] When a company does hold a large number of notes, it sometimes sets up a controlling account and a subsidiary ledger for notes.

Solution to Mid-Chapter Demonstration Problem

Feb. 3	Allowance for doubtful accounts	1,450	
	Accounts receivable—J. Thomas		1,450
	Write off of J. Thomas account.		

May 1	Accounts receivable—J. Thomas	1,450	
	Allowance for doubtful accounts		1,450
	To reestablish J. Thomas account.		
	Cash	450	
	Notes receivable—J. Thomas	1,000	
	Accounts receivable—J. Thomas		1,450
	To record partial payment and acceptance of a six-month, 8% note from J. Thomas.		

LO6 Record the payment and dishonouring of a note, and adjustments for interest on a note.

Paying and Dishonouring a Note

The principal and interest of a note are due on its maturity date. The maker of the note usually *honours* or pays the note and pays it in full. But sometimes a maker *dishonours* the note and does not pay it at maturity.

Recording a Honoured Note

We use the TechCom note transaction above (page 491) to illustrate the honouring of a note. When Jo Cook pays the note on its due date, TechCom records its receipt as:

Assets = Liabilities + Equity
+614.79   +14.79
−600.00

Dec. 4	Cash	614.79	
	Notes Receivable		600.00
	Interest Earned		14.79
	Collected Jo Cook note with interest of $600 × 15% × 60/365.		

Interest Earned, also called Interest Revenue, is reported on the current period's income statement.

Recording a Dishonoured Note

When a note's maker is unable or refuses to pay at maturity, the note is dishonoured. The act of **dishonouring** a note does not relieve the maker of the obligation to pay. The payee should use every legitimate means to collect. But how do companies report this event? We first note the balance of the Notes Receivable account normally includes only those notes that have not matured. When a note is dishonoured, we therefore remove the amount of this note from the Notes Receivable account and charge it back to an account receivable from its maker. TechCom, for instance, holds an $800, 12%, 60-day note of Greg Hart. At maturity, Hart dishonoured the note. TechCom records this dishonouring of its Notes Receivable as follows:

Assets = Liabilities + Equity
+815.78   +15.78
−800.00

Oct. 14	Accounts Receivable—Greg Hart	815.78	
	Interest Earned		15.78
	Notes Receivable		800.00
	To charge the account of Greg Hart for a dishonoured note including interest of $800 × 12% × 60/365.		

Charging a dishonoured note back to the account of its maker serves two purposes. First, it removes the amount of the note from the Notes Receivable account, leaving in the account only notes that have not matured. It also records the dishonoured note in the maker's account. Second, and most important, if the maker of the dishonoured note applies for credit in the future, his or her account will show all past dealings, including the dishonoured note. Restoring the account also reminds the company to continue collection efforts. Also, note that Hart owes both principal and interest. This entry records the full amount owed in Hart's account and credits the interest to Interest Earned. This assures that interest is included in efforts to collect from Hart.

End-of-Period Interest Adjustment

When notes receivable are outstanding at the end of an accounting period, accrued interest is computed and recorded. This recognizes both the interest revenue when it is earned and the added asset (interest) owned by the note's holder. For instance, on December 16, TechCom accepted a $3,000, 60-day, 12% note from a customer in granting an extension on a past-due account. When TechCom's accounting period ends on December 31, $14.79 of interest accrues on this note ($3,000 × 12% × 15/365). The following adjusting entry records this revenue:

Dec. 31	Interest Receivable	14.79	
	Interest Earned		14.79
	To record accrued interest.		

Assets = Liabilities + Equity
+14.79   +14.79

This adjusting entry means interest earned appears on the income statement of the period when it is earned. It also means interest receivable appears on the balance sheet as a current asset.

Receiving Interest Previously Accrued

When the December 16 note above is collected on February 14, TechCom's entry to record the cash receipt is:

Feb. 14	Cash	3,059.18	
	Interest Earned		44.39
	Interest Receivable		14.79
	Notes Receivable		3,000.00
	Received payment of a note and its interest.		

Assets = Liabilities + Equity
+3,059.18   +44.39
−14.79
−3,000.00

Total interest earned on this note is $59.18. This entry's credit to Interest Receivable records collection of the interest of $14.79 accrued in the December 31 adjusting entry. The interest earned in this period is $44.39 and reflects TechCom's revenue from holding the note from January 1 to February 14.

Flash back

9. Wiley purchases $7,000 of merchandise from Stamford Company on December 16, 1999. Stamford accepts Wiley's $7,000, 90-day, 12% note as payment. Stamford's annual accounting period ends on December 31 and it doesn't make reversing entries. Prepare entries for Stamford Company on December 16, 1999, and December 31, 1999.

10. Using the information in 9, prepare Stamford's March 16, 2000, entry if Wiley dishonours the note.

Answers—pp. 503–504

Converting Receivables to Cash before Maturity

LO7 Explain how receivables can be converted to cash before maturity.

Sometimes companies convert receivables to cash before they are due. Reasons for this include the need for cash or a desire to not be involved in collection activities. Converting receivables is usually done either (1) by selling them or (2) by using them as security for a loan. A recent survey showed about 20% of large companies obtain cash from either the sale of receivables or the pledging of receivables as security. In some industries such as textiles and furniture, this is common practice. Recently, this practice has grown to other industries, especially the apparel industry. Also, many small companies use sale of receivables as an immediate source of cash. This is especially the case for those selling to companies and government agencies that often delay payment.

Selling Accounts Receivable

A company can sell its accounts receivable to a finance company or bank. The buyer, called a *factor*, charges the seller a *factoring fee* and then collects the receivables as they come due. By incurring a factoring fee, the seller receives cash earlier and passes the risk of bad debts to the factor. The seller also avoids costs of billing and accounting for the receivables.

If TechCom, for instance, sells $20,000 of its accounts receivable and is charged a 2% factoring fee, it records this sale as:

Assets = Liabilities + Equity
+19,600   −400
−20,000

Aug. 15	Cash	19,600	
	Factoring Fee Expense	400	
	Accounts Receivable		20,000
	Sold accounts receivable for cash, less a 2% factoring fee.		

Factoring is a major business today. **Household Financial Services** is a large factoring firm with volume of about $280 million in recent years. Interestingly, much of the factoring industry's business comes from textile and apparel businesses.

Pledging Accounts Receivable as Loan Security

A company can also raise cash by borrowing money and then *pledging* its accounts receivable as security for the loan. Pledging receivables does not transfer the risk of bad debts to the lender. The borrower retains ownership of the receivables. But if the borrower defaults on the loan, the lender has a right to be paid from cash receipts as the accounts receivable are collected. When TechCom borrowed $35,000 and pledged its receivables as security, it recorded this transaction as:

Assets = Liabilities + Equity
+35,000   +35,000

Aug. 20	Cash	35,000	
	Notes Payable		35,000
	Borrowed money with a note secured by pledging accounts receivable.		

Because pledged receivables are committed as security for a specific loan, the borrower's financial statements should disclose the pledging of accounts receivable. TechCom, for instance, includes the following note with its financial statements regarding its pledged receivables: "Accounts receivable in the amount of $40,000 are pledged as security for a $35,000 note payable to First National Bank." Another example is from the notes of **Mark's Work Warehouse Ltd.**:

Credit Facilities—Security provided includes a...general assignment of accounts receivable...

Cash Poor?

Both **Zenith** and **Packard Bell** used its receivables to get much needed cash. Zenith obtained a three-year, $60 million credit agreement by pledging its accounts receivable as collateral. **Intel** converted accounts receivable to a note receivable for a major customer—widely assumed to be Packard Bell. [Source: *Business Week*, December 11, 1995.]

Did You Know?

Discounting Notes Receivable

Notes receivable can be converted to cash before they mature. Companies who may need cash sooner to meet their obligations can discount notes receivable at a financial institution or bank. TechCom, for instance, discounted a $3,000, 90-day, 10% note receivable at First National Bank. TechCom held the note for 50 of the 90 days before discounting it. The bank applied a 12% rate in discounting the note. TechCom received proceeds of $3,033.55 from the bank.[5] It recorded the discounting of this note as:

Aug. 25	Cash	3,033.55	
	Interest Revenue		33.55
	Notes Receivable		3,000.00
	Discounted a note receivable.		

Assets = Liabilities + Equity
+3,033.55   +33.55
−3,000.00

Notes receivable are discounted without recourse or with recourse. When a note is discounted *without recourse*, the bank assumes the risk of a bad debt loss and the original payee does not have a contingent liability. A **contingent liability** is an obligation to make a future payment if, and only if, an uncertain future event occurs. A note discounted without recourse is like an outright sale of an asset. If a note is discounted *with recourse* and the original maker of the note fails to pay the bank when it matures, the original payee of the note must pay for it. This means a company discounting a note with recourse has a contingent liability until the bank is paid. A company should disclose contingent liabilities in notes to its financial statements. TechCom included the following note: "The Company is contingently liable for a $3,000 note receivable discounted with recourse." A similar example of a receivables sale with recourse is from the notes of Bombardier:

The total recourse against the Corporation relating to the finance receivables amounts to 7% as at January 31, 1997 under the United States agreements and 7.6%...under the Canadian agreements...

Full-Disclosure

The disclosure of contingent liabilities in notes is consistent with the **full-disclosure principle.** This principle requires financial statements (including notes) to report all relevant information about the operations and financial position of

---

[5] Computer programs are used in practice to easily compute bank proceeds. TechCom's proceeds from the bank are computed as:

Principal of Note	$3,000.00
+ Interest from Note ($3,000 × 10% × 90/365) . . .	73.97
= Maturity Value	3,073.97
− Bank Discount ($3,073.97 × 12% × 40/365) . . .	(40.42)
= Proceeds	$3,033.55

a company. Relevance is judged by whether its disclosure impacts users' evaluation of a company. Besides contingent liabilities, other items often reported to satisfy the full-disclosure principle are long-term commitments under contracts and accounting methods used.

Contingent Liabilities

In addition to discounted notes, a company should disclose any items where it is contingently liable. Examples are potential tax assessments, debts of others guaranteed by the company, and outstanding lawsuits against the company. Information about these helps users predict events that might affect the company.

Long-Term Commitments under Contracts

A company should disclose any long-term commitments under contract. The most common example is signing a long-term lease requiring annual payments, even when the obligation doesn't appear in the accounts. Another case is when a company pledges part of its assets as security for loans or has commitments to complete capital projects. These commitments restrict the flexibility of a company. For example, Onex Corporation stated in its annual report that "The estimated total cost to complete approved capital projects…at December 31, 1997 was approximately $11 million."

Accounting Methods Used

When more than one accounting method can be used, a company must describe the one it uses. This is especially important when the choice can materially impact net income.[6] A company, for instance, must report the method it uses in accounting for revenues and receivables and in accounting for inventory. This information helps users in their analysis of a company.

Temporary Investments

LO 8 Describe temporary investments in debt and equity securities.

Recall from Chapter 9 that cash equivalents are investments that are easily converted to known amounts of cash and are subject to insignificant risk of changes in value. Many investments mature within twelve months (or the operating cycle if longer). These investments are **temporary investments**, also called **short-term investments** or (*marketable securities*). Management expects to convert them to cash within one year or the current operating cycle of the business, whichever is longer.[7] Temporary investments are current assets and serve a similar purpose to cash equivalents.

Temporary investments can include both debt and equity securities. *Debt securities* reflect a creditor relationship and include investments in notes, bonds, and certificates of deposit. Debt securities are issued by governments, companies and individuals. *Equity securities* reflect an ownership relationship and include shares of stock issued by companies. In notes to their financial statements, companies usually give a description of their temporary investments.

Accounting for Temporary Investments

This section explains the basics of accounting for temporary investments in both debt and equity securities.

Debt Securities

Temporary investments are recorded at cost when purchased. TechCom, for instance, purchased short-term notes payable of **Transalta Corporation** for $4,000 on January 10. TechCom's entry to record this purchase is:

Assets = Liabilities + Equity
+4,000
−4,000

Jan. 10	Temporary investments	4,000	
	Cash		4,000
	Bought $4,000 of Transalta notes due May 10.		

---

[6] *CICA Handbook*, section 1505, "Disclosure of Accounting Policies," par. .09.

[7] *CICA Handbook*, section 1510, "Current Assets and Current Liabilities," par. .01

These notes mature on May 10 and the cash proceeds are $4,000 plus $120 interest. When the proceeds are received, TechCom records this as:

May 10	Cash	4,120	
	Temporary investments		4,000
	Interest Earned		120
	Received cash proceeds from matured notes.		

Assets = Liabilities + Equity
+4,120   +120
−4,000

Equity Securities

The cost of an investment includes all necessary costs to acquire it, including commissions paid. TechCom, for instance, purchased 200 common shares of **Bell Canada** as a temporary investment. It paid $75 per share plus $300 in commissions. The entry to record this purchase is

June 2	Temporary investments	15,300	
	Cash		15,300
	Bought 200 common shares of Bell at		
	$75 plus $300 commission.		

Assets = Liabilities + Equity
+15,300
−15,300

Note the commission is not recorded in a separate account.

TechCom received $0.40 a share cash dividend on its Bell shares during the current period. This dividend is credited to a revenue account as follows:

Dec. 12	Cash	80	
	Dividends Earned		80
	Received dividend of $0.40 per share on		
	200 shares of Bell.		

Assets = Liabilities + Equity
+80   +80

Presentation of Temporary Investments

Companies must report most temporary investments at their cost or carrying value and also disclose their market values.[8] This last section describes the financial statement presentation for temporary investments.

LO 9 Record LCM adjustment and sale of temporary investments.

Lower of Cost or Market (LCM)

Temporary investments in marketable securities should be reported on the balance sheet at the lower of cost or market (LCM). To calculate the lower of cost or market, the total cost of all marketable securities held as temporary investments (called the portfolio) is compared with the total market value of the portfolio. Comparison on an item-by-item basis is normally not done.

For example, assume that TechCom did not have any temporary investments prior to its purchase of the Bell shares on June 2, 1999. Later during 1999, TechCom purchased two other temporary investments in marketable securities. On December 31, 1999, the lower of cost or market is determined by comparing the total cost and total market value of the entire portfolio, as follows:

Temporary Investments	Cost	Market	LCM
Alcan Aluminium common shares	$42,600	$43,500	
Imperial Oil common shares	30,500	28,200	
Bell Canada common shares	15,300	14,500	
Total	$88,400	$86,200	$86,200

---

[8] *CICA Handbook*, section 3010, "Temporary Investments," par. .05

The difference between the $88,400 cost and the $86,200 market value amounts to a $2,200 loss of market value.

Since all of the temporary investments were purchased during 1999, this $2,200 market value decline occurred entirely during 1999. The following adjusting entry on December 31, 1999, records the loss:

Assets = Liabilities + Equity
−2,200   −2,200

Dec. 31	Loss on Temporary Investments	2,200	
	Allowance to Reduce Temporary Investments to Market		2,200
	To record the decline in the value of temporary investments.		

The Loss on Temporary Investments account is closed to Income Summary and is reported on the income statement. The Allowance to Reduce Temporary Investments to Market account is a contra asset account. Its balance is subtracted from the total cost of the temporary investments so that on the balance sheet they are reported at the lower of cost or market. For example, TechCom would report its temporary investments as follows:

Current assets:	
Cash and cash equivalents	$xx,xxx
Temporary investments, at lower of cost or market (cost, $ 88,400)	86,200

In this example, notice that the $2,200 loss recorded during 1999 is equal to the December 31, 1999, balance in the Allowance account. This occurs because we have assumed that no investments were owned prior to 1999. Therefore, the allowance Account had a zero balance on December 31, 1998.

If an additional loss occurs in a future year, the allowance Account balance after recording that loss probably will not equal the amount of that loss. To see why this is true, assume that on December 31, 2000, the total cost of TechCom's temporary investments portfolio is $108,475 and the total market value is $104,700 (assume additions to the investment portfolio during 2000). In other words, market value is $3,775 less than cost. Because the Allowance account already has a credit balance of $2,200 as a result of the adjusting entry made on December 31, 2000, the adusting entry to record the 2000 loss is:

Assets = Liabilities + Equity
−1,575   −1,575

Dec. 31	Loss on Temporary Investments	1,575	
	Allowance to Reduce Temporary Investments to Market		1,575
	To record the decline in the value of temporary investments.		

Thus, the loss recorded in 2000 is $1,575 and the December 31, 2000, balance in the Allowance Account is $3,775.

Because temporary investments in marketable equity securities must be reported at the lower of cost or market, market value increases above cost are not recorded as gains until the investments are sold. However, if a portfolio of temporary investments has been written down to a market value below cost, later increases in market value up to the original cost are reported on the income statement.[9]

For example, assume that on December 31, 2001, the market value of TechCom's temporary investments is $500 less than cost. Since the Allowance account had a credit balance of $3,775 at the end of 2000, the December 31, 2001, adjusting entry is:

---

[9] Canadian GAAP is unclear about reversing previous losses when the allowance method is used. Generally, practice appears to accept these recoveries on the basis that they reverse previous increases to the Allowance account. Generally, if the direct method is used, any recoveries would not be included.

Dec. 31	Allowance to Reduce Temporary Investments		
	to Market	3,275	
	Gain on Temporary Investments		3,275
	To adjust the Allowance account to $500.		

Assets = Liabilities + Equity
+3,275   +3,275

Notice that the only entries that change the Allowance (contra asset) account balance are the end-of-period adjusting entries. The entries to record purchases and sales of investments during a period do not affect the Allowance account.

The balance sheet presentation of temporary investments usually reports the fair market value for the *total* of the temporary investment portfolio instead of each individual investment. The cost is also usually reported. A typical presentation of temporary investments is shown in Exhibit 10.17.

Current assets:	
Temporary investments, at market value (cost is $108,475)	**107,975**

Exhibit 10.17

Statement Presentation of
Temporary Investments

Even though the contra account to Temporary Investments is not shown, we can determine its balance is $500 by comparing the $108,475 cost with the $107,975 net amount.

If cost and market are about the same, a company can just report the investments at cost. For example, the 1997 balance sheet for **Lafarge Canada Inc.** shows this information:

Current assets:	
Short-term investments, at cost which approximates	
market value	**$222,208,000**

Some people criticize the lower of cost or market method because it is a departure from the cost principle. In recent years, however, an increasing number of people have criticized LCM because it does not record all changes in value, including increases above the original cost. In fact, the CICA's Accounting Standards Board has issued a new *CICA Handbook* section for financial instruments which indicates that some financial assets may be reported at a value which is higher than market value.[10] However, as of 1998, no new provisions for temporary investments have been issued. Thus, for the time being, at least, we will continue to use LCM.

Selling Temporary Investments

When individual securities are sold, the difference between the net proceeds from the sale (sales price less brokerage fees) and the *cost* of the individual securities sold is recognized as a gain or a loss. When TechCom sells its $15,300 temporary investment in Bell Canada shares on January 15 for net proceeds of $16,400, it recognizes a gain of $1,100. The entry to record this sale is:

Jan. 15	Cash	16,400	
	Gain on Sale of Temporary Investments . .		1,100
	Temporary Investments		15,300
	To record sale of 300 shares of Bell Canada.		

This gain is reported in Other Revenues and Gains on the income statement. If a loss is recorded, it is shown in Other Expenses and Losses.

---

[10] *CICA Handbook*, section 3860, par. .89

Flash back

11. How are temporary investments reported on the balance sheet—at cost or market values?
12. Normally, how often would an adjusting entry to record LCM be entered?
13. What happens when a previously written down portfolio increases in value?
14. Where are unrealized losses on temporary investments reported?

Answers—p. 504

Accounts Receivable Turnover   USING THE INFORMATION

LO 10 Compute accounts receivable turnover and use it to analyze liquidity.

In Chapter 8 we discussed *days' sales uncollected* and how it helps us assess a company's short-term liquidity or nearness to cash of its receivables. For companies selling on credit, we want to assess both the quality and liquidity of its accounts receivable. *Quality* of its receivables refers to the likelihood of collection without loss. Experience shows the longer receivables are outstanding beyond their due date, the lower the likelihood of collection. *Liquidity* of its receivables refers to the speed of collection.

The **accounts receivable turnover** is a measure of both the quality and liquidity of accounts receivable. It indicates how often, on average, receivables are received and collected during the period. The formula for this ratio is shown in Exhibit 10.18.

Exhibit 10.18

Accounts Receivable Turnover Formula

$$\text{Accounts receivable turnover} = \frac{\text{Net sales}}{\text{Average accounts receivable}}$$

We actually want *credit* net sales in the numerator because cash sales do not create receivables. Since financial statements rarely report credit net sales, our analysis uses total net sales. The denominator in this turnover formula is the *average* accounts receivable balance during the period. The average is often computed as: (beginning balance + ending balance) ÷ 2. This method of estimating the average balance provides a useful result if seasonal changes in the accounts receivable balances during the year are not extreme.

Accounts receivable turnover shows us how often a company converts its average accounts receivable balance into cash during the period. TechCom, for instance, has an accounts receivable turnover of 5.1. This shows its average accounts receivable balance is converted into cash 5.1 times during the year. Exhibit 10.19 shows graphically this turnover activity for TechCom.

Exhibit 10.19

Rate of Accounts Receivable Turnover for TechCom

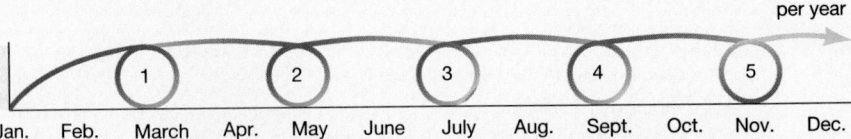

Accounts receivable turnover also helps us evaluate how well management is doing in granting credit to customers in a desire to increase sales revenues. A high turnover in comparison with competitors suggests management should consider using more liberal credit terms to increase sales. A low turnover suggests management should consider more strict credit terms and more aggressive collection efforts to avoid having its resources tied up in accounts receivable.

To illustrate, we use data from the annual reports of two competing companies: **Imperial Oil** and **Ocelot Energy**. Exhibit 10.20 shows results from our computation of accounts receivable turnover for these two companies.

Company	Figure ($ millions)	1997	1996	1995
Imperial	Net sales	$10,669	$10,377	$9,428
	Average accounts receivable	$ 1,110	$ 1,068	$1,026
	Accounts receivable turnover	9.6	9.7	9.2
Ocelot	Net Sales	$ 119	$ 154	$ 123
	Average accounts receivable	$ 20	$ 25	$ 21
	Accounts receivable turnover	6.0	6.2	5.9

Exhibit 10.20

Analysis using accounts receivable turnover

To illustrate how we compute and use accounts receivable turnover, look at the numbers of Imperial for 1995–1997 as reported in Exhibit 10.21. First, note that we compute Imperial's 1997 turnover as ($ in millions):

$$\frac{\$10,669}{\$1,110} = 9.6$$

This means Imperial's average accounts receivable balance is converted into cash 9.6 times during 1997. Also, Imperial's turnover improved from 1995 to 1997, and it is superior to Ocelot. Is Imperial's turnover too high? Because sales are growing dramatically over this same period it doesn't appear Imperial's turnover is too high. Instead, Imperial's management seems to be doing an excellent job at managing its receivables. This is especially apparent when compared to Ocelot and most of its other competitors. Turnover for Imperial's competitors is generally in the range of 6 to 7 over this same period.

Pet Care

You are a veterinarian operating a small animal hospital. Your practice has turned less profitable and you hire a financial analyst to examine your financials and to recommend solutions. The analyst's report highlights several problems including accounts receivable. It states "...accounts receivable turnover is far too low. Tighter credit policies are recommended along with discontinuing service to those most delayed in payments." How do you interpret these recommendations? What actions do you take?

Judgment and Ethics

Answer—p. 503

Flash back

15. A company needs cash and has substantial accounts receivable. What alternatives are available for getting cash from its accounts receivable prior to receiving payments from credit customers? Show the entry made for each alternative.

16. Compute Mytel's accounts receivable turnover for 1999 using the following information:

(In thousands)	1999	1998
Accounts receivable	762,024	580,313
Total current assets	1,543,523	1,470,750
Net sales	3,205,025	2,704,448
Net income	255,832	117,208

Answers—p. 504

Summary

LO1 **Describe accounts receivable and how they occur and are recorded.** Accounts receivable refer to amounts due from customers for credit sales. The subsidiary ledger lists the amounts owed by individual customers. Credit sales arise from at least two sources: (1) sales on credit and (2) credit card sales. Sales on credit refers to a company granting credit directly to customers. Credit card sales involve use of a third party issuing a credit card.

LO2 **Apply the direct write-off and allowance methods to account for accounts receivable.** The direct write-off method charges Bad Debt Expense when accounts are written off as uncollectible. This method is acceptable only when the amount of bad debt expense is immaterial. Under the allowance method, bad debt expense is recorded with an adjustment at the end of each accounting period debiting the expense and crediting the Allowance for Doubtful Accounts. The uncollectible accounts are later written off with a debit to the Allowance for Doubtful Accounts.

LO3 **Estimate uncollectibles using methods based on sales and accounts receivable.** Uncollectibles are estimated by focusing on either (a) the income statement relation between bad debt expense and credit sales or (b) the balance sheet relation between accounts receivable and the Allowance for Doubtful Accounts. The first approach emphasizes the matching principle for the income statement. The second approach can include either a simple percent relation with accounts receivable or the aging of accounts receivable. It emphasizes realizable value of accounts receivable for the balance sheet.

LO4 **Describe a note receivable and the computation of its maturity date and interest.** A note receivable is a written promise to pay a specified amount of money either on demand or at a definite future date. The maturity date of a note is the day the note (principal and interest) must be repaid. Interest rates are typically stated in annual terms. When a note's time to maturity is more or less than one year, the amount of interest on a note is computed by expressing time as a fraction of one year and multiplying the note's principal by this fraction and the annual interest rate.

LO5 **Record the receipt of a note receivable.** A note is recorded at its principal amount by debiting the Notes Receivable account. The credit amount is to the asset or service provided in return for the note.

LO6 **Record the payment and dishonouring of a note, and adjustments for interest on a note.** When a note is honoured, the payee debits the money received and credits both Notes Receivable and the interest earned.

Dishonoured notes are credited to Notes Receivable and debited to Accounts Receivable (and to the account of the maker in attempts to collect). Interest is earned from holding a note. This interest is recorded for the time period it is held in the accounting period reported on.

LO7 **Explain how receivables can be converted to cash before maturity.** There are three usual means to convert receivables to cash before maturity. First, a company can sell accounts receivable to a factor, who charges a factoring fee. Second, a company can borrow money by signing a note payable that is secured by pledging the accounts receivable. Third, notes receivable can be discounted at a bank, with or without recourse. The full-disclosure principle requires companies to disclose the amount of receivables pledged and the contingent liability for notes discounted with recourse.

LO8 **Describe temporary investments in debt and equity securities.** Temporary investments can include both debt and equity securities. *Debt securities* reflect a creditor relationship and include investments in notes, bonds, and certificates of deposit. Debt securities are issued by governments, companies and individuals. Equity securities reflect an ownership relationship and include shares issued by companies.

LO9 **Record LCM adjustment and sale of temporary investments.** Temporary investments are recorded at cost, and any dividends or interest from these investments are recorded in their income statement accounts. Temporary investments are reported on the balance sheet at the lower of cost or market. Writedowns to market are credited to an allowance account and the loss is reported on the income statement. When temporary investments are sold, the difference between the net proceeds from the sale (sales price less brokerage fees) and the cost of the temporary investment is recognized as a gain or a loss.

LO10 **Compute accounts receivable turnover and use it to analyze liquidity.** Accounts receivable turnover is a measure of both the quality and liquidity of accounts receivable. Quality of receivables refers to its likelihood of collection without loss. Experience shows the longer receivables are outstanding beyond their due date, the lower the likelihood of collection. Liquidity of receivables refers to its speed of collection. The accounts receivable turnover measure indicates how often, on average, receivables are received and collected during the period. Accounts receivable turnover is computed as sales divided by average accounts receivable for the period.

Guidance Answers to **You Make the Call**

Entrepreneur

Your analysis of allowing credit card sales should estimate the benefits against the costs. The primary benefit is the potential to increase sales by attracting customers who prefer the convenience of credit cards. The primary cost is the fee charged by the credit card company for providing this service to your store. Your analysis should therefore estimate the expected increase in sales dollars from allowing credit card sales and then subtract (1) the normal costs and expenses, and (2) the credit card fees, associated with this expected increase in sales dollars. If your analysis shows an increase in profit from allowing credit card sales, your store should probably allow them.

Labour Union Chief

Yes, this information is likely to impact your negotiations. The obvious question is why the company increased the allowance to such a large extent. This major increase in allowance means a substantial increase in bad debts expense *and* a decrease in earnings. Also, this change coming immediately prior to labour contract discussions raises concerns since it reduces the union's bargaining power for increased compensation. You want to ask management for supporting documentation justifying this increase. Also, you want data for two or three prior years, and similar data from competitors. These data should give you some sense of whether the change in the allowance for uncollectibles is justified or not.

Guidance Answer to **Judgment and Ethics**

Pet Care

The analyst's recommendations are twofold. First, the analyst is suggesting a more stringent screening of clients according to their credit standing. Second, the analyst suggests dropping those clients who are most overdue or delinquent in their payments. You are likely bothered by these suggestions. While they are probably financially wise recommendations, you are troubled about eliminating services to those pet owners who are less able to pay. One possible alternative is to follow the analyst's recommendations while at the same time implementing a care program directed at those clients less able to pay for services. This allows you to continue services to clients less able to pay, and lets you discontinue services to clients able but unwilling to pay for services.

Guidance Answers to **Flash backs**

1. If cash is received as soon as copies of credit card sales receipts are deposited in the bank, the business debits Cash at the time of the sale. If the business does not receive payment until after it submits the receipts to the credit card company, it debits Accounts Receivable at the time of the sale.

2. The credit card expenses are *recorded* when the cash is received from the credit card company; however, they are *incurred* at the time of the related sales.

3. An adjusting entry must be made to satisfy the matching principle. The credit card expense must be reported in the same period as the sale.

4. Bad debts expense must be matched with the sales that gave rise to the accounts receivable. This requires that companies estimate bad debts before they learn which accounts are uncollectible.

5. Realizable value.

6. The estimated amount of bad debts expense cannot be credited to the Accounts Receivable account because the specific customer accounts that will prove uncollectible cannot be identified and removed from the subsidiary Accounts Receivable Ledger. If the controlling account were credited directly, its balance would not equal the sum of the subsidiary account balances.

7.
1999			
Dec. 31	Bad Debts Expense	5,702	
	Allowance for Doubtful Accounts		5,702

8.
1999			
Jan. 10	Allowance for Doubtful Accounts	300	
	Accounts Receivable— Cool Jam		300
Apr. 12	Accounts Receivable— Cool Jam	300	
	Allowance for Doubtful Accounts		300
12	Cash	300	
	Accounts Receivable— Cool Jam		300

9.
1999			
Dec. 16	Notes Receivable	7,000	
	Sales		7,000
	(90 day, 12% note).		
31	Interest Receivable	35	
	Interest Earned		35
	($7,000 × 12% × 15/365)		

10.

2000			
Mar. 16	Accounts Receivable—Wiley .	7,207	
	Interest Earned		172
	Interest Receivable		35
	Notes Receivable		7,000

11. At lower of cost or market.

12. Usually, only once per year; at the year-end.

13. The allowance is reduced and the offsetting credit is recorded in the income statement as a gain.

14. The income statement.

15. Alternatives are (1) selling their accounts receivable to a factor, and (2) pledging accounts receivable as loan

security. The entries to record these transactions take the following form:

(1) Cash	#	
Factoring Fee Expense	#	
Accounts Receivable		#
(2) Cash	#	
Notes Payable		#

16. Accounts receivable turnover =

$$\frac{3,205,025}{(762,024 + 580,313)/\,2} = 4.78 \text{ times}$$

Demonstration Problem

Garden Company had the following transactions during 19X2:

May 8   Purchased 300 of Cangene Corporation common shares as a temporary investment. The cost of $40 per share plus $975 in broker's commissions was paid in cash.

July 14   Wrote off a $750 account receivable arising from a sale to Briggs Company several months ago. (Garden Company uses the allowance method.)

July 30   Garden Company receives a $1,000, three-month, 10% promissory note for a product sale to Sumrell Company.

Aug. 15   Accepted a $2,000 down payment and a $10,000 note receivable from a customer in exchange for an inventory item that normally sells for $12,000. The note was dated August 15, bears 12% interest, and matures in six months.

Sept. 2   Sold 100 shares of Cangene Corporation at $47 per share, and continued to hold the other 200 shares. The broker's commission on the sale was $225.

Sept. 15   Received $9,850 in return for discounting without recourse the $10,000 note (dated August 15) at the local bank.

Oct. 2   Purchased 400 shares of Moore Corp. for $60 per share plus $1,600 in commissions. The shares are to be held as a temporary investment.

Nov. 1   Garden Company makes a $200 credit card sale with a 4% fee. The cash is received immediately from the credit card company.

Nov. 5   Garden Company makes a $500 credit card sale with a 5% fee. The payment from the credit card company is received on Nov. 7.

Nov. 15   Briggs Company pays the full amount of $750 previously written off on July 14. Record the bad debt recovery.

Nov. 20   Sumrell Company refuses to pay the note that was due to Garden Company on Oct. 30. Make the journal entry to charge the dishonoured note plus accrued interest to Sumrell Company's accounts receivable.

Required

1. Prepare journal entries to record these transactions on the books of Garden Company.

2. Prepare an adjusting journal entry as of December 31, 19X2, for the following item.

a. Bad debts expense is estimated by an aging of accounts receivable. The unadjusted balance of the Allowance for Doubtful Accounts account is a $1,000 debit, while the required balance is estimated to be a $20,400 credit.

b. Alternatively, assume that bad debts expense is estimated at year-end using a percentage of sales approach. As in part *a* assume that the Allowance for Doubtful Accounts account has a $1,000 debit balance before adjustment. The company estimates bad debts to be 1% of credit sales of $2,000,000.

Planning the Solution

■ Examine each item to determine which accounts are affected and produce the needed journal entries.

■ With respect to the year-end adjustment, record the bad debts expense.

Solution to Demonstration Problem

1.

May 8	Temporary investments	12,975	
	Cash		12,975
	Purchased 300 shares of Cangene Corporation. Cost is (300 × $40) + $975.		
July 14	Allowance for Doubtful Accounts	750	
	Accounts Receivable—Briggs Company		750
	Wrote off an uncollectible account.		
July 30	Notes Receivable—Sumrell Company	1,000	
	Sales		1,000
	Sold merchandise in exchange for a three-month, 10% note.		
Aug. 15	Cash	2,000	
	Notes Receivable	10,000	
	Sales		12,000
	Sold merchandise to customer for $2,000 cash and $10,000 note receivable.		
Sept. 2	Cash	4,475	
	Gain on Sale of Investment		150
	Temporary investments		4,325
	Sold 100 shares of Cangene Corporation for $47 per share less a $225 commission. The original cost is ($12,975 × 100/300).		
Sept. 15	Cash	9,850	
	Interest Expense	150	
	Notes Receivable		10,000
	Discounted note receivable dated August 15.		
Oct. 2	Temporary investments	25,600	
	Cash		25,600
	Purchased 400 shares of Moore Corp. for $60 per share plus $1,600 in commissions.		
Nov. 1	Cash	192	
	Credit Card Expense	8	
	Sales		200
	To record credit card sale less a 4% credit card expense.		
Nov. 2	Accounts Receivable—Credit Card Company	500	
	Sales		500
	To record credit card sale.		
Nov. 7	Cash	475	
	Credit Card Expense	25	
	Accounts Receivable—Credit Card Company		500
	To record cash receipt less a 5% credit card expense.		
Nov. 15	Accounts Receivable—Briggs Company . . .	750	
	Allowance for Doubtful Accounts		750
	To reinstate the account of Briggs Company previously written off.		
Nov. 15	Cash	750	
	Accounts Receivable—Briggs Company		750
	In full payment of account.		

Nov. 20	Accounts Receivable—Sumrell Company . .	1,025	
	Interest Earned		25
	Notes Receivable—Sumrell Company .		1,000
	To charge the account of Sumrell Company for a dishonoured note including interest of $1,000 × 10% × 3/12.		
Dec. 31	Bad Debt Expense	21,400	
	Allowance for Doubtful Accounts		21,400
	To adjust the allowance account from $1,000 debit balance to $20,400 credit balance.		
Alternate Approach			
	Bad Debt Expense	20,000	
	Allowance for Doubtful Accounts		20,000
	To provide for bad debts as 1% × $2,000,000 in credit sales. (Note: Disregard any existing balance in the Allowance Account when making the entry using the income statement approach.)		

(Note to Students: When using the income statement approach which requires estimating bad debts as a percent of sales or net credit sales the Allowance Account balance is not considered when making the adjusting entry. While this might seem arbitrary it is not. The income statement approach estimates bad debt expense using the relation between bad debt expense and sales. These are both income statement accounts. The Allowance Account is a balance sheet account. It is therefore logical that its balance must be considered only when using the balance sheet approach.)

Glossary

Accounts Receivable Amounts due from customers for credit sales. (p. 474)

Accounts receivable turnover A measure of both the quality and liquidity of accounts receivable; it indicates how often, on average, receivables are received and collected during the period; computed by dividing credit sales (or net sales) by the average accounts receivable balance. (p. 500)

Aging of accounts receivable A process of classifying accounts receivable in terms of how long they have been outstanding for the purpose of estimating the amount of uncollectible accounts. (p. 486)

Allowance for Doubtful Accounts A contra asset account with a balance equal to the estimated amount of accounts receivable that will be uncollectible; also called the Allowance for Uncollectible Accounts. (p. 481)

Allowance method of accounting for bad debts An accounting procedure that (1) estimates and reports bad debt expense from credit sales during the period of the sales, and (2) reports accounts receivable as the amount of cash proceeds that is expected from their collection (their estimated realizable value). (p. 480)

Bad debts The accounts of customers who do not pay what they have promised to pay; the amount is an expense of selling on credit; also called *uncollectible accounts*. (p. 479)

Contingent liability An obligation to make a future payment if, and only if, an uncertain future event actually occurs. (p. 495)

Direct write-off method of accounting for bad debts A method of accounting for bad debts that records the loss from an uncollectible account receivable at the time it is determined to be uncollectible; no attempt is made to estimate uncollectible accounts or bad debt expense. (p. 479)

Dishonouring a note When a note's maker is unable or refuses to pay at maturity. (p. 492)

Full-disclosure principle The accounting principle that requires financial statements (including the footnotes) to report all relevant information about the operations and financial position of the entity. (p. 496)

Interest The charge for using (not paying) money until a later date. (p. 490)

Maker of a note One who signs a note and promises to pay it at maturity. (p. 489)

Matching principle Requires expenses to be reported in the same accounting period as the sales they helped produce. (p. 480)

Materiality principle States that an amount may be ignored if its effect on the financial statements is unimportant to their users. (p. 480)

Maturity date of a note The date on which a note and any interest are due and payable. (p. 489)

Payee of a note The one to whom a promissory note is made payable. (p. 489)

Principal of a note The amount that the signer of a promissory note agrees to pay back when it matures, not including the interest. (p. 489)

Promissory note A written promise to pay a specified amount of money either on demand or at a definite future date. (p. 489)

Realizable value The expected proceeds from converting assets into cash. (p. 481)

Short-term investments Another name for *temporary investments*. (p. 496)

Temporary investments Current assets that serve a similar purpose to cash equivalents; generally management expects to convert them into cash within 12 months (or the operating cycle if longer); can be either debt or equity securities. (p. 496)

Uncollectible accounts See *bad debts*. (p. 479)

Questions

1. How do businesses benefit from allowing their customers to use credit cards?

2. Explain why writing off a bad debt against the Allowance Account does not reduce the estimated realizable value of a company's accounts receivable.

3. Why does the Bad Debt Expense account usually not have the same adjusted balance as the Allowance for Doubtful Accounts?

4. Why does the direct write-off method of accounting for bad debts commonly fail to match revenues and expenses?

5. What is the essence of the accounting principle of materiality?

6. Why might a business prefer a note receivable to an account receivable?

7. What does it mean to sell a receivable without recourse?

8. Under what conditions should investments be classified as current assets?

9. If a temporary investment in securities cost $6,780 and was sold for $7,500, how should the difference between the two amounts be recorded?

10. On a balance sheet, what valuation must be reported for temporary investments?

11. Review the consolidated balance sheet for **Alliance, Inc.** in Appendix I. What is the company's policy with respect to losses on its Loans Receivable?

12. Review the consolidated balance sheet for **Atlantis** in Appendix I. When are the accounts receivable due?

13. Who would be the major customers of **CFS**?

On April 18, Kimmell Industries, Inc., made a temporary investment in 200 common shares of Computer Links. The purchase price was $42.50 and the broker's fee was $350. On June 30, Kimmell received $2 per share in dividends. Prepare the April 18 and June 30 journal entries.

Quick Study

QS 10-1
Temporary equity investments
LO 8

Journalize the following transactions:

a. Sold $10,000 in merchandise on MasterCard credit cards. The sales receipts were deposited in our business account. MasterCard charges us a 5% fee.

b. Sold $3,000 on miscellaneous credit cards. Cash will be received within 10 days and a 4% fee will be charged.

QS 10-2
Credit card transactions
LO 1

Foster Corporation uses the allowance method to account for uncollectibles. On October 31, they wrote off a $1,000 account of a customer, Gwen Rowe. On December 9, they received a $200 payment from Rowe.

a. Make the appropriate entry or entries for October 31.

b. Make the appropriate entry or entries for December 9.

QS 10-3
Allowance method of accounting for bad debts
LO 2

QS 10-4
Accounts receivable
allowance method of
accounting for bad debts

LO 2

Duncan Company's year-end trial balance shows accounts receivable of $89,000, allowance for doubtful accounts of $500 (credit), and sales of $270,000. Uncollectibles are estimated to be 1.5% of outstanding accounts receivable.

a. Prepare the December 31 year-end adjustment.

b. What amount would have been used in the year-end adjustment if the allowance account had a year-end debit balance of $200?

c. Assume the same facts, except that Duncan estimates uncollectibles as 1% of sales. What amount would be used in the adjustment?

QS 10-5
Note receivables

LO 5, 6

On August 2, 19X1, SLM, Inc., received a $5,500, 90-day, 12% note from customer Will Carr as payment on his account. Prepare the August 2 and maturity date entries, assuming the note is honoured by Carr.

QS 10-6
Note receivables

LO 5, 6

Seaver Company's December 31 year-end trial balance shows an $8,000 balance in Notes Receivable. This balance is from one note dated December 1, with a period of 45 days and 9% interest. Prepare the December 31 and maturity date entries, assuming the note is honoured.

QS 10-7
Accounts receivable
turnover

LO 10

The following facts were extracted from the comparative balance sheets of Ernest Blue, P.C.:

	19X2	19X1
Accounts receivable	$152,900	$133,700
Sales (net)	754,200	810,600

Compute the accounts receivable turnover for 19X2.

Exercises

Exercise 10-1
Transactions involving
temporary investments

LO 9

Prepare general journal entries to record the following transactions involving the temporary investments of Morton Financial Corp., all of which occurred during 19X1:

a. On February 15, paid $150,000 to purchase $150,000 of Canadian General's 90-day short-term notes payable, which are dated February 15 and pay 10% interest.

b. On March 22, bought 700 common shares of Royal Industries at $25.50 plus a $250 brokerage fee.

c. On May 16, received a cheque from Canadian General in payment of the principal and 90 days' interest on the notes purchased in transaction *a*.

d. On July 30, paid $50,000 to purchase $50,000 of OMB Electronics' 8% notes payable, dated July 30, 19X1, and due January 30, 19X2.

e. On September 1, received a $0.50 per common share cash dividend on the Royal Industries shares purchased in transaction *b*.

f. On October 8, sold 350 shares of Royal Industries common shares for $32 per share, less a $175 brokerage fee.

g. On October 30, received a cheque from OMB Electronics for three months' interest on the notes purchased in transaction *d*.

Exercise 10-2
Credit card transactions

LO 1

Aston Corporation allows customers to use two credit cards in charging purchases. With the OmniCard, Aston receives an immediate credit when it deposits sales receipts in its chequing account. OmniCard assesses a 4% service charge for credit card sales. The second credit card that Aston accepts is Colonial Bank Card. Aston sends its accumulated receipts to Colonial Bank on a weekly basis and is paid by Colonial approximately 10 days later. Colonial Bank charges 2% of sales for using its card. Prepare entries in journal form to record the following credit card transactions of Aston Corporation:

Apr. 6   Sold merchandise for $9,200, accepting the customers' OmniCards. At the end of the day, the OmniCard receipts were deposited in Aston's account at the bank.

10   Sold merchandise to a customer for $310 and accepted the customer's Colonial Bank Card.

17   Mailed $5,480 of credit card receipts to Colonial Bank, requesting payment.

28   Received Colonial Bank's cheque for the April 17 billing, less the normal service charge.

Jenkins Inc. recorded the following transactions during November 19X1:

Exercise 10-3
Subsidiary ledger accounts
LO 1

Nov. 3	Accounts Receivable—ABC Shop	4,417	
	Sales		4,417
8	Accounts Receivable—Colt Enterprises	1,250	
	Sales		1,250
11	Accounts Receivable—Red McKenzie	733	
	Sales		733
19	Sales Returns and Allowances	189	
	Accounts Receivable—Red McKenzie		189
28	Accounts Receivable—ABC Shop	2,606	
	Sales		2,606

Required

1. Open a General Ledger having T-accounts for Accounts Receivable, Sales, and Sales Returns and Allowances. Also, open a subsidiary Accounts Receivable Ledger having a T-account for each customer. Post the preceding entries to the General Ledger accounts and the customer accounts.

2. List the balances of the accounts in the subsidiary ledger, total the balances, and compare the total with the balance of the Accounts Receivable controlling account.

At the end of its annual accounting period, Bali Company estimated its bad debts as one-half of 1% of its $875,000 of credit sales made during the year. On December 31, Bali made an addition to its Allowance for Doubtful Accounts equal to that amount. On the following February 1, management decided the $420 account of Catherine Hicks was uncollectible and wrote it off as a bad debt. Four months later, on June 5, Hicks unexpectedly paid the amount previously written off. Give the journal entries required to record these events.

Exercise 10-4
Allowance for doubtful accounts
LO 2,3

At the end of each year, Deutch Supply Co. uses the simplified balance sheet approach to estimate bad debts. On December 31, 19X1, it has outstanding accounts receivable of $53,000 and estimates that 4% will be uncollectible. Give the entry to record bad debt expense for 19X1 (a) under the assumption that the Allowance for Doubtful Accounts has a $915 credit balance before the adjustment and (b) give the entry under the assumption that the Allowance for Doubtful Accounts has a $1,332 debit balance before the adjustment.

Exercise 10-5
Bad debt expense
LO 2,3

Prepare journal entries to record these transactions:

Mar. 21   Accepted a $3,100, six-month, 10% note dated today from Bradley Brooks in granting a time extension on his past-due account.

Sept. 21   Brooks dishonoured his note when presented for payment.

Dec. 31   After exhausting all legal means of collection, wrote off Brooks' account against the Allowance for Doubtful Accounts.

Exercise 10-6
Dishonour of a note
LO 6

Exercise 10-7
Honouring of a note
receivable

LO 6

Prepare journal entries to record these transactions:

Oct. 31   Accepted a $5,000, six-month, 8% note dated today from Leann Grimes in grant-
           ing a time extension on her past-due account.
Dec. 31   Adjust the books for the interest due on the Grimes note.
Apr. 30   Grimes honoured her note when presented for payment.

Exercise 10-8
Selling and pledging
accounts receivable

LO 7

On July 31, Konrad International had $125,900 of accounts receivable. Prepare journal entries
to record the following August transactions. Also, prepare any footnotes to the August 31
financial statements that should be reported as a result of these transactions.

Aug. 2   Sold merchandise to customers on credit, $6,295.
       7   Sold $18,770 of accounts receivable to Fidelity Bank. Fidelity charges a 1.5% fee.
      15   Received payments from customers, $3,436.
      25   Borrowed $10,000 from Fidelity Bank, pledging $14,000 of accounts receivable
           as security for the loan.

Exercise 10-9
Accounts receivable
turnover

LO 10

The following information is from the financial statements of Whimsy, Inc.:

	19X3	19X2	19X1
Net sales	$305,000	$236,000	$288,000
Accounts receivable (December 31)	22,900	20,700	17,400

Compute Whimsy's accounts receivable turnover for 19X2 and 19X3. Compare the two
results and give a possible explanation for any significant change.

Exercise 10-10
Accounting for notes
receivable transactions

LO 5, 6

Following are transactions of The Barnett Company:

19X1

Dec. 16   Accepted a $8,600, 60-day, 7% note dated this day in granting Carmel Karuthers
           a time extension on her past-due account.
      31   Made an adjusting entry to record the accrued interest on the Karuthers note.
      31   Closed the Interest Earned account.

19X2

Feb. 14   Received Karuthers' payment for the principal and interest on the note dated
           December 16.
Mar. 2   Accepted a $4,000, 8%, 90-day note dated this day in granting a time extension
           on the past-due account of ATW Company.
      17   Accepted a $1,600, 30-day, 9% note dated this day in granting Leroy Johnson a
           time extension on his past-due account.
Apr. 16   Johnson dishonoured his note when presented for payment.
May   1   Wrote off the Johnson account against Allowance for Doubtful Accounts.
June 10   Received ATW's payment for the principal and interest on the note dated March 2.

Required

Preparation component:

Prepare journal entries to record The Barnett Company's transactions.

Problems

Problem 10-1
Accounting for temporary
investments

LO 8, 9

Checkers, Inc., had no temporary investments prior to 19X1 but had the following transactions involving temporary investments in securities during 19X1:

Mar. 16   Purchased 3,000 common shares of **Dofasco Ltd.**, at $22.25 plus a $1,948 bro-
           kerage fee.
Apr. 1   Paid $100,000 to buy 90-day Treasury bills, $100,000 principal amount, 5%, dated
           April 1.
June 7   Purchased 1,800 common shares of Power Corp., at $49.50 plus a $1,235 bro-
           kerage fee.

20   Purchased 700 common shares of Westburne Ltd. at $15.75 plus a $466 brokerage fee.

July   3   Received a cheque for the principal and accrued interest on the Treasury bills that matured on June 30.

15   Received a $0.95 per share cash dividend on the Dofasco common shares.

28   Sold 1,500 of the Dofasco common shares at 26 less a $912 brokerage fee.

Sept.   1   Received a $2.10 per share cash dividend on the Power Corp. common shares.

Dec.   15   Received a $1.35 per share cash dividend on the remaining Dofasco common shares owned.

31   Received a $1.60 per share cash dividend on the Power Corp. common shares.

Required

Prepare journal entries to record the preceding transactions.

Accessories Unlimited allows a few customers to make purchases on credit. Other customers may use either of two credit cards. Express Bank deducts a 3% service charge for sales on its credit card but credits the chequing accounts of its commercial customers immediately when credit card receipts are deposited. Accessories Unlimited deposits the Express Bank credit card receipts at the close of each business day.

When customers use UniCharge credit cards, Accessories Unlimited accumulates the receipts for several days before submitting them to UniCharge for payment. UniCharge deducts a 2% service charge and usually pays within one week of being billed. Accessories Unlimited completed the following transactions during the month of May:

May   4   Sold merchandise on credit to Anne Bismarck for $565. (The terms of all credit sales are 2/15, n/30, and all sales are recorded at the gross price.)

5   Sold merchandise for $5,934 to customers who used their Express Bank credit cards. Sold merchandise for $4,876 to customers who used their UniCharge cards.

8   Sold merchandise for $3,213 to customers who used their UniCharge credit cards.

10   The UniCharge card receipts accumulated since May 5 were submitted to the credit card company for payment.

13   Wrote off the account of Mandy Duke against Allowance for Doubtful Accounts. The $329 balance in Duke's account stemmed from a credit sale in October of last year.

17   Received the amount due from UniCharge.

18   Received Bismarck's cheque paying for the purchase of May 4.

Required

Prepare journal entries to record the preceding transactions and events.

On December 31, 19X1, SysComm Corporation's records showed the following results for the year:

Cash sales	$1,803,750
Credit sales	3,534,000

In addition, the unadjusted trial balance included the following items:

Accounts receivable	$1,070,100 debit
Allowance for doubtful accounts	15,750 debit

Required

1. Prepare the adjusting entry needed in SysComm's books to recognize bad debts under each of the following independent assumptions:
   a. Bad debts are estimated to be 2% of credit sales.
   b. Bad debts are estimated to be 1% of total sales.
   c. An analysis suggests that 5% of outstanding accounts receivable on December 31, 19X1, will become uncollectible.

Problem 10-2
Credit sales and credit card sales

LO 1

Problem 10-3
Estimating bad debt expense

LO 2, 3

Check Figure: Bad Debt Expense (1a), $70,680 Dr.

2. Show how Accounts Receivable and the Allowance for Doubtful Accounts would appear on the December 31, 19X1, balance sheet given the facts in requirement 1a.
3. Show how Accounts Receivable and the Allowance for Doubtful Accounts would appear on the December 31, 19X1, balance sheet given the facts in requirement 1c.

Problem 10-4
Aging accounts receivable
LO 2, 3

Jewell, Inc., had credit sales of $2.6 million in 19X1. On December 31, 19X1, the company's Allowance for Doubtful Accounts had a credit balance of $13,400. The accountant for Jewell has prepared a schedule of the December 31, 19X1, accounts receivable by age and, on the basis of past experience, has estimated the percentage of the receivables in each age category that will become uncollectible. This information is summarized as follows:

December 31, 19X1 Accounts Receivable	Age of Accounts Receivable	Expected Percentage Uncollectible
$730,000	Not due (under 30 days)	1.25%
354,000	1 to 30 days past due	2.00
76,000	31 to 60 days past due	6.50
48,000	61 to 90 days past due	32.75
12,000	Over 90 days past due	68.00

Required

Preparation component:

1. Compute the amount that should appear in the December 31, 19X1, balance sheet as the allowance for doubtful accounts.
2. Prepare the journal entry to record bad debt expense for 19X1.

Analysis component:

3. On June 30, 19X2, Jewell, Inc. concluded that a customer's $3,750 receivable (created in 19X1) was uncollectible and that the account should be written off. What effect will this action have on Jewell's 19X2 net income? Explain your answer.

Check Figure Bad Debt Expense, $31,625 Dr.

Problem 10-5
Recording accounts receivable transactions and bad debt adjustments
LO 2, 3

Harrell Industries began operations on January 1, 19X1. During the next two years, the company completed a number of transactions involving credit sales, accounts receivable collections, and bad debts. These transactions are summarized as follows:

19X1

a. Sold merchandise on credit for $1,144,500, terms n/30.
b. Wrote off uncollectible accounts receivable in the amount of $17,270.
c. Received cash of $667,100 in payment of outstanding accounts receivable.
d. In adjusting the accounts on December 31, concluded that 1.5% of the outstanding accounts receivable would become uncollectible.

19X2

e. Sold merchandise on credit for $1,423,800, terms n/30.
f. Wrote off uncollectible accounts receivable in the amount of $26,880.
g. Received cash of $1,103,900 in payment of outstanding accounts receivable.
h. In adjusting the accounts on December 31, concluded that 1.5% of the outstanding accounts receivable would become uncollectible.

Required

Prepare journal entries to record Harrell's 19X1 and 19X2 summarized transactions and the adjusting entries to record bad debt expense at the end of each year.

Check Figure 19X2 Bad Debt Expense, $31,275.30 Dr.

Following are transactions of The Perry-Finch Company:

19X1

Dec. 16   Accepted a $9,600, 60-day, 9% note dated this day in granting Hal Krueger a time extension on his past-due account.

   31   Made an adjusting entry to record the accrued interest on the Krueger note.

   31   Closed the Interest Earned account.

19X2

Feb. 14   Received Krueger's payment for the principal and interest on the note dated December 16.

Mar.   2   Accepted a $5,120, 10%, 90-day note dated this day in granting a time extension on the past-due account of ARC Company.

   17   Accepted a $1,600, 30-day, 9% note dated this day in granting Penny Bobek a time extension on her past-due account.

Apr. 16   Bobek dishonoured her note when presented for payment.

   21   Discounted, with recourse, the ARC Company note at BancFirst at a cost of $50.

June   2   Received notice from BancFirst that ARC Company defaulted on the note due May 31. Paid the bank the principal plus interest due on the note. (Hint: Create an account receivable for the maturity value of the note.)

July 16   Received payment from ARC Company for the maturity value of its dishonoured note plus interest for 45 days beyond maturity at 10%.

Aug.   7   Accepted a $5,440, 90-day, 12% note dated this day in granting a time extension on the past-due account of Mertz & Ivy.

Sept.   3   Accepted a $2,080, 60-day, 10% note dated this day in granting Cecile Duval a time extension on her past-due account.

   18   Discounted, without recourse, the Duval note at BancFirst at a cost of $25.

Nov.   5   Received payment of principal plus interest from Mertz & Ivy for the note of August 7.

Dec.   1   Wrote off the Penny Bobek account against Allowance for Doubtful Accounts.

Required

Preparation component:

Prepare journal entries to record Perry-Finch's transactions.

Analysis component:

What reporting is necessary when a business discounts notes receivable with recourse and these notes have not reached maturity by the end of the fiscal period? Explain the reason for this requirement and what accounting principle is being satisfied.

Problem 10-6
Analysis and journalizing of notes receivable transactions
LO 5, 6

Franklin Security, Inc. has relatively large idle cash balances and invests them in common shares that it holds as temporary investments. Following is a series of events and other facts relevant to the temporary investment activity of the company:

19X1

Jan. 20   Purchased 900 shares of Jannock Limited at $18.75 plus a $590 commission.

Feb.   9   Purchased 2,200 shares of Shell Canada at $46.85 plus a $2,633 commission.

Oct. 12   Purchased 500 shares of Magna, Inc., at $55.50 plus an $832 commission.

19X2

Apr. 15   Sold 900 shares of Jannock Limited at $21.75 less a $685 commission.

July   5   Sold 500 shares of Magna at $49.10 less a $478 commission.

   22   Purchased 1,600 shares of Silcorp at $36.25 plus a $1,740 commission.

Aug. 19   Purchased 1,800 shares of Emco Limited at $28 plus a $1,260 commission.

19X3

Feb. 27   Purchased 3,400 shares of Mitel Ltd. at $23.65 plus a $1,521 commission.

Mar.   3   Sold 1,600 shares of Silcorp at $31.25 less a $1,750 commission.

June 21   Sold 2,200 shares of Shell at $40 less a $2,640 commission.

   30   Purchased 1,200 shares of Bombardier at $47.50 plus a $1,995 commission.

Nov.   1   Sold 1,800 shares of Emco at $42.75 less a $2,309 commission.

Required

Prepare journal entries to record the temporary investment activity across the years.

Problem 10-7
Entries for temporary investments

LO 8, 9

Alternate Problems

Problem 10-1A
Accounting for temporary investments

LO 8, 9

McLean Systems, Inc., had no temporary investments on December 31, 19X1, but had the following transactions involving temporary investments in securities during 19X2:

Feb. 6 Purchased 3,400 common shares of Westburne Inc. at $29.50 plus a $2,507 brokerage fee.
     15 Paid $20,000 to buy six-month Treasury bills with a principal amount of $20,000, paying 5%, dated February 15.
Apr. 7 Purchased 1,200 common shares of Gentra Inc. at $13.25 plus a $477 brokerage fee.
June 2 Purchased 2,500 common shares of Zycom Corp. at $32.75 plus a $2,865 brokerage fee.
     30 Received a $1.75 per share cash dividend on the Westburne common shares.
Aug. 11 Sold 850 shares of the Westburne common shares at 25 less a $531 brokerage fee.
     16 Received a cheque for the principal and accrued interest on the Treasury bills purchased February 15.
     24 Received a $0.20 per share cash dividend on the Gentra common shares.
Nov. 9 Received a $1.00 per share cash dividend on the remaining Westburne common shares.
Dec. 18 Received a $0.45 per share cash dividend on the Gentra common shares.

Required

Prepare general journal entries to record the preceding transactions.

Problem 10-2A
Credit sales and credit card sales

LO 1

Ace Office Supply Co. allows a few customers to make purchases on credit. Other customers may use either of two credit cards. Commerce Bank deducts a 3% service charge for sales on its credit card, but immediately credits the chequing account of its commercial customers when credit card receipts are deposited. Ace deposits the Commerce Bank credit card receipts at the close of each business day.

When customers use the Fortune card, Ace accumulates the receipts for several days and then submits them to the Fortune Credit Company for payment. Fortune deducts a 2% service charge and usually pays within one week of being billed.

Ace completed the following transactions in July:

July 2 Sold merchandise on credit to J.R. Lacey for $2,780. (Terms of all credit sales are 2/10, n/30; all sales are recorded at the gross price.)
      8 Sold merchandise for $3,248 to customers who used their Commerce Bank credit cards. Sold merchandise for $1,114 to customers who used their Fortune cards.
     12 Received Lacey's cheque paying for the purchase of July 2.
     13 Sold merchandise for $2,960 to customers who used their Fortune cards.
     16 The Fortune card receipts accumulated since July 8 were submitted to the credit card company for payment.
     20 Wrote off the account of River City Rentals against Allowance for Doubtful Accounts. The $398 balance in River City's account stemmed from a credit sale in November of last year.
     23 Received the amount due from Fortune Credit Company.

Required

Prepare journal entries to record the preceding transactions.

Problem 10-3A
Estimating bad debt expense

LO 2, 3

On December 31, 19X1, Genie Service Corp.'s records showed the following results for the year:

Cash sales	$1,015,000
Credit sales	1,241,000

In addition, the unadjusted trial balance included the following items:

Accounts receivable	$475,000 debit
Allowance for doubtful accounts	5,200 credit

Required

1. Prepare the adjusting entry on the books of Genie Service Corp. to estimate bad debts under each of the following independent assumptions:

   a. Bad debts are estimated to be 2.5% of credit sales.

   b. Bad debts are estimated to be 1.5% of total sales.

   c. An analysis suggests that 6% of outstanding accounts receivable on December 31, 19X1, will become uncollectible.

2. Show how Accounts Receivable and the Allowance for Doubtful Accounts would appear on the December 31, 19X1, balance sheet given the facts in requirement *1a*.

3. Show how Accounts Receivable and the Allowance for Doubtful Accounts would appear on the December 31, 19X1, balance sheet given the facts in requirement *1c*.

NutraMade Corporation had credit sales of $3.5 million in 19X1. On December 31, 19X1, the company's Allowance for Doubtful Accounts had a debit balance of $4,100. The accountant for NutraMade has prepared a schedule of the December 31, 19X1, accounts receivable by age and, on the basis of past experience, has estimated the percentage of the receivables in each age category that will become uncollectible. This information is summarized as follows:

Problem 10-4A
Aging accounts receivable

LO 2, 3

December 31, 19X1 Accounts Receivable	Age of Accounts Receivable	Expected Percentage Uncollectible
$296,400	Not due (under 30 days)	2.0%
177,800	1 to 30 days past due	4.0
58,000	31 to 60 days past due	8.5
7,600	61 to 90 days past due	39.0
3,700	Over 90 days past due	82.5

Required

Preparation component:

1. Compute the amount that should appear in the December 31, 19X1, balance sheet as the Allowance for Doubtful Accounts.

2. Prepare the journal entry to record bad debts expense for 19X1.

Analysis component:

3. On July 31, 19X2, NutraMade concluded that a customer's $2,345 receivable (created in 19X1) was uncollectible and that the account should be written off. What effect will this action have on NutraMade's 19X2 net income? Explain your answer.

Spring Products Co. began operations on January 1, 19X1, and completed a number of transactions during 19X1 and 19X2 that involved credit sales, accounts receivable collections, and bad debts. These transactions are summarized as follows:

Problem 10-5A
Recording accounts receivable transactions and bad debt adjustments

LO 2, 3

19X1

a. Sold merchandise on credit for $673,490, terms n/30.

b. Received cash of $437,250 in payment of outstanding accounts receivable.

c. Wrote off uncollectible accounts receivable in the amount of $8,330.

d. In adjusting the accounts on December 31, concluded that 1% of the outstanding accounts receivable would become uncollectible.

19X2

e. Sold merchandise on credit for $930,100, terms n/30.

f. Received cash of $890,220 in payment of outstanding accounts receivable.

g. Wrote off uncollectible accounts receivable in the amount of $10,090.

h. In adjusting the accounts on December 31, concluded that 1% of the outstanding accounts receivable would become uncollectible.

Required

Prepare general journal entries to record the 19X1 and 19X2 summarized transactions of Spring Products Co., and the adjusting entries to record bad debt expense at the end of each year.

Problem 10-6A
Analyzing and journalizing notes receivable transactions

LO 5, 6

Following are transactions of Metro, Inc.:

19X1

Nov. 16 Accepted a $3,700, 90-day, 12% note dated this day in granting Bess Parker a time extension on her past-due account.

Dec. 31 Made an adjusting entry to record the accrued interest on the Parker note.

    31 Closed the Interest Earned account.

19X2

Feb. 14 Received Parker's payment for the principal and interest on the note dated November 16.

    28 Accepted a $12,400, 9%, 30-day note dated this day in granting a time extension on the past-due account of The Simms Co.

Mar. 1 Accepted a $5,100, 60-day, 10% note dated this day in granting Bedford Holmes a time extension on his past-due account.

    23 Discounted, without recourse, the Holmes note at Security Bank at a cost of $50.

    30 The Simms Co. dishonoured its note when presented for payment.

June 15 Accepted a $1,900, 60-day, 9% note dated this day in granting a time extension on the past-due account of Sarah Mayfield.

    21 Accepted a $9,300, 90-day, 12% note dated this day in granting Vince Soto a time extension on his past-due account.

July 5 Discounted, with recourse, the Soto note at Security Bank at a cost of $200.

Aug. 14 Received payment of principal plus interest from Mayfield for the note of June 15.

Sept. 25 Received notice from Security Bank that the Soto note had been paid.

Nov. 30 Wrote off The Simms Co.'s account against Allowance for Doubtful Accounts.

Required

Preparation component:

Prepare journal entries to record Metro's transactions.

Analysis component:

What reporting is necessary when a business discounts notes receivable with recourse and these notes have not reached maturity by the end of the fiscal period? Explain the reason for this requirement and what accounting principle is being satisfied.

Problem 10-7A
Entries for temporary investments

LO 8, 9

Dayton Enterprises has idle cash balances and invests them in common shares that it holds as temporary investments. Following is a series of events and other facts relevant to the temporary investment activity of the company:

19X1

Mar. 10 Purchased 2,400 shares of Agrium Inc. at $33.25 plus $1,995 commission.

May 7 Purchased 5,000 shares of Fonorola, Inc., at $17.50 plus $2,625 commission.

Sept. 1 Purchased 1,200 shares of Placer Dome Inc. at $49 plus $1,176 commission

19X2

Apr. 26 Sold 5,000 shares of Fonorola at $16.40 less $2,362 commission.

    27 Sold 1,200 shares of Placer Dome at $52 less $1,672 commission.

June 2 Purchased 3,600 shares of Domtar, Inc., at $18.85 plus $2,222 commission.

    14 Purchased 900 shares of Sears Canada Inc. at $24.50 plus $541 commission.

19X3

Jan. 28 Purchased 2,000 shares of The Cott Corp. at $41 plus $3,280 commission.
      31 Sold 3,600 shares of Domtar at $16.65 less $1,586 commission.
Aug. 22 Sold 2,400 shares of Agrium at $29.75 less $2,339 commission.
Sept. 3 Purchased 1,500 shares of Malette, Inc., at $29 plus $870 commission.
Oct. 9 Sold 900 shares of Sears at $27.50 less $619 commission.

Required

Prepare journal entries to record the temporary investment activity across the years.

Shortcash Company required a loan of $15,000 and was offered two alternatives by the Security Bank. The alternatives are:

a. Shortcash would give the bank a one-year $15,000 note payable, dated November 1, 1998, with interest at 9%.

b. Shortcash would give the bank a one-year $16,350 non-interest-bearing note payable dated November 1, 1998. The bank would precalculate and deduct $1,350 of interest from the face amount of the note.

Required

1. Prepare all the necessary entries (including repayment on October 31, 1999) with regard to alternative *a*. Assume that Shortcash Company's fiscal year ends December 31.

2. Repeat the journal entries for alternative *b*.

The Tor-Mont Company has been in business three years and has applied for a significant bank loan. Prior to considering the applications, the bank asks you to conduct an audit for the last three years. Concerning accounts receivable, you find that the company has been charging off receivables as they finally proved uncollectible and treating them as expenses at the time of write-off.

Your investigation indicates that receivable losses have approximated (and can be expected to approximate) 2% of net sales. Until this first audit, the company's sales and direct receivable write-off experience was:

		Accounts Written Off In		
Year of Sales	**Amount of Sales**	**1997**	**1998**	**1999**
1997	$450,000	$1,500	$6,000	$1,800
1998	600,000	—	3,000	7,200
1999	750,000	—	—	4,500

Required

1. Indicate the amount by which net income was understated or overstated each year because the company used the direct write-off method rather than the generally acceptable allowance method.

2. Prepare all the entries for each of the three years that would have been made if Tor-Mont had used the allowance method from the start of the business.

3. Which of the entries in (2) are year-end adjusting entries?

Analytical and Review Problems

A & R Problem 10-1*

A & R Problem 10-2

---

*Interest to be calculated on a monthly basis.

BEYOND THE NUMBERS

Reporting in Action

LO 10

Refer to the financial statements and related information for **Alliance** in Appendix I. Answer the following questions by analyzing information in its statements:

1. Alliance 's most liquid assets include "cash and short-term investments" and "accounts receivable." What is Alliance 's total amount of cash and cash equivalents on March 31, 1997?

2. Express Alliance's total liquid assets as of March 31, 1997 (include Distribution contracts receivable), as a percent of current liabilities. Do the same for March 31, 1996. Comment on the company's ability to satisfy current liabilities at the end of the fiscal year 1997 as compared to the end of fiscal year 1996.

3. What criteria did Alliance use to classify items as cash equivalents?

4. Compute Alliance 's accounts receivable turnover as of March 31, 1997.

Comparative Analysis

LO 10

Both **Alliance** and **Atlantis** produce and market movies and television programs. Key comparative figures ($ thousands) for these two organizations follow:

Key Figures	Alliance		Atlantis	
	1997	1996	1997	1996
Accounts Receivable, Net	$ 82,184	$ 53,081	$145,611	$ 75,645
Net Sales	$282,599	$268,945	$177,960	$137,984

* Alliance figures are from the annual reports for the fiscal years ended March 31,1997 and 1996.
Atlantis figures are from the annual reports for the fiscal years ended December 31, 1997 and 1996.

Required

1. Compute the accounts receivable turnover for Alliance as of March 31, 1997, and Atlantis as of December 31, 1996.

2. How many days does it take each company, on average, to collect its receivables?

3. Which company is more efficient in collecting the accounts receivable?

Ethics Challenge

LO 2, 3

Randy Meyer is the chief executive officer of a medium-sized company in Regina, Saskatchewan. Several years ago Randy persuaded the board of directors of his company to base a percent of his compensation on the net income the company earns each year. Each December Randy estimates year-end financial figures in anticipation of the bonus he will receive. If the bonus is not as high as he would like he offers several accounting recommendations to his controller for year-end adjustments. One of his favourite recommendations is for the controller to reduce the estimate of doubtful accounts. Randy has used this technique with success for several years.

1. What effect does lowering the estimate for doubtful accounts have on the income statement and balance sheet of Randy's company?

2. Do you think Randy's recommendations to adjust the allowance for doubtful accounts is within his right as CEO or do you think this action is an ethics violation? Justify your response.

3. What type of internal control might be useful for this company in overseeing the CEO's recommendations for accounting changes?

Communicating in Practice

LO 2, 3

As the accountant for Stephenson Distributing, you recently attended a sales managers' meeting devoted to a discussion of the company's credit policies. At the meeting, you reported that bad debt expense for the past year was estimated to be $59,000 and accounts receivable at the end of the year amounted to $1,750,000 less a $43,000 allowance for doubtful accounts. Sylvia Greco, one of the sales managers, expressed confusion over the fact that bad debt expense and the allowance for doubtful accounts were different amounts. To save time at the meeting, you agreed to discuss the matter with Greco after the meeting.

Because the meeting lasted longer than expected, Greco had to leave early to catch a plane back to her sales district. As a result, you need to write a memorandum to her explaining why a difference in bad debt expense and the allowance for doubtful accounts is not unusual. (Assume that the company estimates bad debt expense to be 2% of sales.)

Visit the Web site entitled "How to Collect Debts" at **http://www.insiderreports.com/BIZR PRTS/B2524.htm**. If you are unable to connect to the Web site listed here, then as an alternate exercise search the Web for five good business tips on effective management of credit customers.

Required

1. Identify four procedures that should routinely be included in dealing with credit customers.
2. What are the author's view in the report ("How to Collect Debts") about phone calls, use of collection agencies, and use of humour in collection letters?
3. Identify the recommended content for a collection letter.

Each member of a team is to participate in estimating uncollectibles based on the aging schedule and estimated percents shown in Problem 10-4A. The division of labour is up to the team. Time is money and your goal is to complete this task as soon as possible. After estimating uncollectibles, check your estimate with the instructor. If the team's estimate is correct, the team should proceed, using the other information in the problem, to prepare the adjusting entry and the presentation of net realizable accounts receivable as it should be shown on the December 31, 19X1 Balance Sheet. Your team is to discuss these requirements and ensure all team members concur with and understand the team's solution.

Most of us have seen television commercials that advertise with a quote similar to the following: "Be sure to bring your VISA because we do not accept American Express." Conduct your own research via interviews, phone calls, or the Internet to determine the reason why companies discriminate in their use of major credit cards.

Read the article "The Sherlock Holmes of Accounting" in the September 5, 1994, issue of *Business Week*.

Required

1. Who is the "Sherlock Holmes of Accounting"?
2. How does "Sherlock" decide which companies are investigated?
3. Do companies suffer any consequences if investigated by "Sherlock"?
4. What is a forensic accountant?
5. What criticisms does "Sherlock" make of **Seitel** company with respect to their accounting?

Taking It to the Net
LO 2

Teamwork in Action
LO 3

Hitting the Road
LO 1

Business Break
LO 2

11

Payroll Liabilities

Chapter Outline

Overpaid Taxes

Regina, SK—As part of its annual audit **Canstruck Construction's** external auditor was reviewing payroll related taxes and found that a number of assumptions were made based on tax rates at the beginning of the project.

Although some of the tax rates had decreased from one year to the next, Canstruck Construction continued to charge the original, higher rate, For example, the employment insurance rate had dropped during the second year of the contract. However Canstruck Construction did not adjust the rate, which resulted in a significant employment insurance overcharge.

The external auditor reported his findings to management. Canstruck Construction was not able to recover its portion of the employment insurance. However, employees were able to recover their overpayment when they filed their annual income tax forms.

"I almost lost that contract," said Vladimir Canstruck, owner of the company. "If I'd known that the employment insurance rates had been lowered, I could have put in a lower bid and not lost any sleep." On the suggestion of the external auditor, Canstruck purchased a computerized accounting package suitable for small business. Payroll withholdings amounts are calculated automatically and for a small annual fee Canstruck Construction receives updates when rates change. [Source: The Institute of Internal Auditors, "Overpaid Taxes," *Internal Auditor,* April 1998.]

Learning Objectives

LO 1 List the taxes and other items frequently withheld from employee's wages.

LO 2 Make the calculations necessary to prepare a Payroll Register and prepare the entry to record payroll liabilities.

LO 3 Prepare journal entries to record the payments to employees and explain the operation of a payroll bank account.

LO 4 Calculate the payroll costs levied on employers and prepare the entries to record the accrual and payment of these amounts.

LO 5 Calculate and record employee fringe benefit costs and show the effect of these items on the total cost of employing labour.

HAPTER PREVIEW

Wages or salaries generally amount to one of the largest expenses incurred by a business. Accounting for employees' wages and salaries is one task that is shared by almost all business entities. Payroll accounting:

■ Records cash payments to employees.

■ Provides valuable information regarding labour costs.

■ Accounts for amounts withheld from employees' pay.

■ Accounts for employee (fringe) benefits and payroll costs paid by the employer.

■ Provides the means to comply with governmental regulations on employee compensation.

As you study this chapter, you will learn the general processes all businesses follow to account for these items.

Items Withheld from Employees' Wages

LO1 List the taxes and other items frequently withheld from employees' wages.

An understanding of payroll accounting and the design and use of payroll records requires some knowledge of the laws and programs that affect payrolls. Many of these require **payroll deductions**, amounts withheld from the wages of employees. Consequently, the more pertinent of these are discussed in the first portion of this chapter before the subject of payroll records is introduced.

Withholding Employees' Income Tax

With few exceptions, employers are required to calculate, collect, and remit to the Receiver General of Canada the income taxes of their employees. Historically, when the first federal income tax law became effective in 1917, it applied to only a few individuals having high earnings. It was not until World War II that income taxes were levied on substantially all wage earners. At that time Parliament recognized that many individual wage earners could not be expected to save sufficient money with which to pay their income taxes once each year. Consequently, Parliament instituted a system of pay-as-you-go withholding of taxes at their source each payday. This pay-as-you-go withholding of employee income taxes requires an employer to act as a tax collecting agent of the federal government.

The amount of income taxes to be withheld from an employee's wages is determined by his or her wages and the amount of **personal tax credits.** Each individual is entitled, in 1998, to some or all of the following annual amounts which are subject to tax credits (as applicable):

1.	Basic personal amount	$6,456
2.	Married or equivalent	5,380
	(with maximum earnings stipulated)	

The total of each taxpayer's personal tax credits is deducted from income to determine the level of income tax deductions from the individual's gross pay. For example, an individual with a gross weekly salary of $500 and personal tax credits of $6,456 (1998 net claim code 1 on the TD1 form) would have $83.90 of income taxes withheld. Another individual with the same gross salary but with personal tax credits of $11,783 (claim code 5) would have $58.50 withheld.

Employers are responsible for determining the amount of income tax owed by each employee every payday and withholding it from his or her pay for that period. However, to do this an employer must know the credits claimed by each employee. Consequently, every employee is required to file with the employer an employee's Personal Tax Credit Return, Form TD1, on which he or she claims the applicable credit. The taxpayer must file a revised Form TD1 each time the exemptions change during a year. The TD1 form is shown in Exhibit 11.1.

In determining the amounts of income taxes to be withheld from the wages of employees, employers normally use payroll deductions tables provided by Revenue Canada, Taxation. The tables indicate the tax to be withheld from any amount of wages and with any number of credits. The to-be-withheld amounts include both federal and provincial income taxes except for the province of Quebec. The province of Quebec levies and collects its own income tax and its own pension plan contributions. Employers in that province remit separately, to the respective authority, federal and provincial tax deductions. Calculation of deductions is simplified for computer users if they request "tables on diskette" from Revenue Canada. In addition to determining and withholding income taxes from each employee's wages every payday, employers are required to remit the withheld taxes to the Receiver General of Canada each month.

Pay or Else
Delay or failure to pay withholding taxes to government agencies has severe consequences. Fines, for instance, can be imposed at a rate of 10% of taxes owed for each month they are not paid. In repeated cases, a 20% penalty can be levied, with interest, on the unpaid balance. If a corporation fails to remit deductions, the directors may be held personally responsible for the payments due plus penalties and interest.

Did You Know?

Canada Pension Plan (CPP)

The **Canada Pension Plan** applies, with few exceptions, to everyone who is working. Every employee and self-employed person between the ages of 18 and 70 must make contributions in required amounts to the Canada Pension Plan (CPP). Self-employed individuals are required to periodically remit appropriate amounts to the Receiver General of Canada. Employee contributions are deducted by the employer from salary, wages, or other remuneration paid to the employee. Furthermore, each employer is required to contribute an amount equal to that deducted from the employees' earnings.

Contributions are based on earnings, with the first $3,500 of each employee's annual income being exempt. On earnings above that amount and up to the 1998 ceiling of $36,900 a year, the employee contributes at a rate of 3.2%. The total contribution from both employee and employer is 6.4% on the $33,400 of annual earnings between $3,500 and $36,900. Thus, the maximum contribution to the Canada Pension Plan is $1,068.80 each from the employee and the employer. The $3,500 exemption is adjusted for weekly or monthly pay periods by dividing by the appropriate number; that is, 52, 12, and so on.

Employers are responsible for making the proper deductions from their employees' earnings. They remit these deductions each month, together with their own contributions, to the Receiver General of Canada.

Self-employed individuals pay the combined rate for employees and employers, or 6.4% on annual earnings between $3,500 and the exempt ceiling of $36,900.

Exhibit 11.1

TD1 Form

Revenue   Revenu
Canada   Canada

PERSONAL TAX CREDITS RETURN
Instructions

Complete this return if you have a new employer or payer, and you will receive one or more of the following types of income:
- salary, wages, commissions, pensions, or any other remuneration; or
- Employment Insurance benefits.

You **do not** have to file a new return every year unless your marital status changes or you expect a change in your personal credits for that year. Complete a new return no later than seven days after the change. It is an offence to file a false return.

If you make regular spousal support payments, or if you regularly contribute to a registered retirement savings plan (RRSP) during the year, you can reduce the amount of tax to be withheld from your income. To make this request, you have to write to your tax services office for a letter of authority.

You do not need a letter of authority if your employer deducts RRSP contributions from your salary.

If you receive non-employment income, such as a pension or Old Age Security, and you want to have extra tax deducted at source, you can complete Form TD3, *Request for Income Tax Deduction on Non-Employment Income.*

If you need help, ask your employer or payer, or call your tax services office or tax centre. You can find the telephone numbers listed under "Revenue Canada" in the Government of Canada section of your telephone book.

TD1 E (98)   Confidential calculation on back — Employee's copy

- -

Employer's or payer's copy

Revenue   Revenu
Canada   Canada

PERSONAL TAX CREDITS RETURN
After you complete this return, give it to your employer or payer.

Last name (capital letters)	Usual first name and initials	Employee number
Address	For non-residents only – country of permanent residence	Social insurance number
Postal code		Date of birth Year Month Day

1. Basic personal amount
Everyone can claim **$6,456** as the basic personal amount.
- If you choose to claim this amount, enter **$6,456.**
- If you choose not to claim this amount (e.g., when you have more than one employer or payer and you have already claimed the basic personal amount), enter 0 in box ◾A◾ on the other side of this return. Do not complete sections 2 to 8. You may want to complete sections 10 to 12.
- If you are a non-resident, and you are including 90% or more of your annual world income when determining your taxable income in Canada, you can claim certain personal amounts. If you are including less than 90% of your annual world income, enter 0 in box ◾A◾ on the other side of this return. If you are not sure about your non-resident status, or need more information, call your tax services office or tax centre.

Credit claimed $

2. Spousal amount
You can claim an amount for supporting your spouse if you are **married or have a common-law spouse.**

Generally, a common-law spouse is a person of the opposite sex with whom you live in a common-law relationship for any continuous period of at least 12 months, including any period of separation (due to a breakdown in the relationship) of less than 90 days. It can also be a person of the opposite sex with whom you live in a common-law relationship and who is the natural or adoptive parent of your child. If you are not sure about your status, or need more information, call your tax services office or tax centre.

Equivalent-to-spouse amount
You can claim an equivalent-to-spouse amount if you are **single, divorced, separated, or widowed,** and you support a dependant who is:
- under 18, your parent or grandparent, or mentally or physically infirm;
- related to you by blood, marriage, or adoption; and
- living with you, in Canada, in a home that you maintain; (a dependant may live away from home while attending school.)

Calculating the amount
If you marry during the year, your spouse's net income includes the income earned before and during the marriage.
If the net income for the year of your spouse or dependant will be:
- more than $5,918, enter 0;
- $538 or less, enter **$5,380;** or
- more than $538, complete calculation 2 on the back of this return and enter the result as credit claimed.

If your equivalent-to-spouse claim is for an infirm dependant age 18 or older, you may be able to claim an amount in section 3. Otherwise, any person you claim here cannot be claimed again in section 3.

Credit claimed $

3. Amount for infirm dependants age 18 or older
You can claim an amount for each infirm dependant age 18 or older who is your or your spouse's:
- child or grandchild, and has a physical or mental infirmity; or
- parent, grandparent, brother, sister, aunt, uncle, niece, or nephew, who resides in Canada, and has a physical or mental infirmity.

Calculating the amount
If your dependant's net income for the year will be:
- $4,103 or less, enter **$2,353;** or
- more than $4,103, complete calculation 3 on the back of this return and **enter** the result as credit claimed.
You can claim an amount for each infirm dependant you have.

Credit claimed $

4. Amount for eligible pension income
Eligible pension income includes pension payments received from a pension plan or fund as a life annuity, and foreign pension payments. It does not include payments from the Canada Pension Plan or Quebec Pension Plan, Old Age Security, guaranteed supplements, or lump-sum withdrawals from a pension fund.

If you receive an eligible pension income, you can claim your eligible pension income or $1,000, whichever amount is **less.**

Credit claimed $

5. Age amount
If you will be 65 or older at the end of the year and your estimated net income from all sources for the year will be:
- $25,921 or less, enter **$3,482;**
- more than $25,921, but less than $49,134.33, complete calculation 5 on the back of this return and **enter** the result as credit claimed; or
- more than $49,134.33, enter **$0.**

Credit claimed $

TD1 E (98)   (Ce formulaire existe aussi en français.)   0500   Canada

Exhibit 11.1

TD1 Form
(continued)

Calculation 2: net income more than $538, calculate: .... **$ 5,918**

    Minus: net income of spouse or dependant .... _____

    Total .... _____

Report the total in section 2 as a credit claimed.

Calculation 3: net income more than $4,103, calculate: **$ 6,456**

    Minus: dependant's net income .... _____

If more than $2,353, enter $2,353 .... _____

Minus: equivalent-to-spouse amount claimed in section 2 ...... _____

Total: If negative, **enter 0** .... _____

Report the total in section 3 as a credit claimed.

Calculation 5: net income over $25,921, but less than

  Reduced by: $49,134.33, calculate basic age amount :...... **$ 3,482** **A**

1. Annual estimated net income $ _____

2. Less base amount .... $ = 25.921

3. Line 1 minus line 2 .... $ _____

4. Multiply line 3 _____ by 15% .... $ _____ **B**

Total: A minus B. If negative, enter 0 .... $ _____

Report the total in section 5 as a credit claimed.

Claim Codes	
Total claim amount	Claim codes
No claim amount	0
Minimum $ 6,456	1
$ 6,456.01 - 8,037	2
8,037.01 - 9,619	3
9,619.01 - 11,202	4
11,202.01 - 12,783	5
12,783.01 - 14,364	6
14,364.01 - 15,946	7
15,946.01 - 17,527	8
17,527.01 - 19,109	9
19,109.01 - 20,693	10
$ 20,693.01 - and over Manual calculation required by employer	X
No tax withholding required	E

✂

6. Tuition fees and education amount

Enter your tuition fees, for courses you will take in the year, to attend a university, college, or an institution that the Minister of Human Resources Development has certified .... _____

Add $200 for each month in the year that you will be enrolled full-time in a qualifying educational program at a university, college, or a school offering job retraining courses or correspondence courses .... _____

Subtotal .... _____

Subtract any scholarships, fellowships, or bursaries you will receive in the year (do not report the first $500) .... _____

Enter the total amount claimed. If the amount is negative, **enter 0.** .... **Credit claimed** $ _____

7. Disability amount

You can claim $4,233 if you are severely impaired, mentally or physically, and are claiming the disability amount by using Form T2201, *Disability Tax Credit Certificate.*
Such an impairment has to markedly restrict your daily living activities. The impairment has to last, or be expected to last, for a continuous period of at least 12 months.
Enter the total amount claimed .... **Credit claimed** $ _____

8. Amounts transferred from your spouse, or dependants

You can transfer any of the following amounts that your spouse, or dependants do not need to reduce their federal income tax to zero.

Age amount – If your spouse will be 65 or older this year, you can claim any unused balance of the age amount to a maximum of **$3,482** .... _____

Pension income amount – If your spouse receives eligible pension income, you can claim any unused balance of the eligible pension amount to a maximum of **$1,000** .... _____

Disability amount – If your spouse or dependant is disabled, you can claim the unused balance of their disability amount, to a maximum of **$4,233** for each person .... _____

Tuition fees and education amount – If you are supporting a spouse, child or grandchild attending a university, college, or a certified educational institution, you can claim the unused balance of their tuition fees and education amounts to a maximum of **$5,000** for each person .... _____

Enter the total amount calculated .... **Credit claimed** $ _____

9. Total all your personal tax credit amounts from sections 1 to 8 .... **Total of credits** $ _____

See the claim codes at the top of this page to determine which claim code applies to you. Enter this code in box **A** .
If the total of your tax credits is more than your total employment income from all sources for the year, your claim code is "E."   _____ **A**

Additional information

10. Additional tax to be deducted

If you receive other income, you may want to have more tax deducted from each pay. By doing this, you may not have to pay as much tax when you file your income tax return. To choose this option, state the amount of additional tax you want to have deducted from each pay. To change this deduction later, you have to complete a new TD1 return. $ _____

11. Deduction for living in a prescribed zone (e.g., Yukon Territory, or Northwest Territories)

If you live in the Yukon Territory, Northwest Territories, or another prescribed zone for more than six months in a row, beginning or ending this year, you can claim:

- $7.50 for each day that you live in the prescribed zone; or
- $15 for each day that you live in the prescribed zone, if during that time you live in a dwelling that you maintain, and you are the only person living in that dwelling who is claiming this deduction.
  For more information, get Form T2222 and the publication, *Northern Residents Deductions – Places in Prescribed Zones,* which you can get from any tax services office or tax centre. $ _____

12. If you live in **Ontario, Manitoba, Saskatchewan,** or **British Columbia** enter the number of your dependants under 18 years old at the end of the year.   _____

For **Ontario, Manitoba,** and **Saskatchewan** residents, only the spouse with the higher net income can enter an amount.
If you live in **Ontario, Manitoba,** or **British Columbia,** do not include a child claimed for the equivalent-to-spouse amount in section 2.

I certify that the information given in this return is, to the best of my knowledge, correct and complete.

Signature _____   Date _____

Printed in Canada

Employment Insurance (EI)

To alleviate hardships caused by interruptions in earnings through unemployment, the federal government, with the concurrence of all provincial governments, implemented an employee/employer-financed unemployment insurance plan. Under the Employment Insurance Act, 1996, compulsory **employment insurance** coverage was extended to all Canadian workers who are not self-employed. As of January 1, 1998, over 12 million employees, including teachers, hospital workers, and top-level executives, were covered by the insurance plan.

Employment Insurance consists of a two-part re-employment system:

1. Income benefits provide temporary income support for claimants while they look for work.

2. Active Re-Employment Benefits and Support Measures: Unemployed workers will get help from a set of re-employment benefits and support measures that will be tailored to meet the needs of individuals and local circumstances. The emphasis is on flexibility and employment results.

The employment insurance fund from which benefits are paid is jointly financed by employees and their employers. Under the current act, in 1998 employers are required to deduct from their employees' wages 2.7% of insured earnings, to add a contribution of 1.4 times the amount deducted from employees' wages, and to remit both amounts to the Receiver General of Canada. Insured earnings, in most instances, refer to gross earnings. Although an employee may receive taxable benefits or allowances that would be included in gross earnings but would not be considered insurable earnings. However, in this text, gross earnings will be insurable earnings. The maximum amount deductible per year is $1,053.00 (in 1998). The maximum insurable earnings for 1998 are $39,000.

The Employment Insurance Act, in addition to setting rates, requires that an employer

1. Withhold from the wages of each employee each payday an amount of employment insurance tax calculated at the current rate.

2. Pay an employment insurance tax equal to 1.4 times the amount withheld from the wages of all employees.

3. Periodically remit both the amounts withheld from employees' wages and the employer's tax to the Receiver General of Canada. (Remittance is discussed later in this chapter.)

4. Complete a "Record of Employment" because of termination of employment, illness, injury, or pregnancy.

5. Keep a record for each employee that shows among other things wages subject to employment insurance and taxes withheld. (The law does not specify the exact form of the record, but most employers keep individual employees earnings records similar to the one shown later in this chapter.)

Weekly Employment Benefits

Under EI, a claimant who simply works the entrance requirements will receive an EI income benefit but not their maximum benefits; that is, their weekly cheque will be less than 55% of their weekly earnings.

To obtain their maximum benefit, a claimant must work at least two weeks more than the regional minimum requirement expressed in weeks. The benefit level will be calculated by taking a claimant's total earnings within the preceding 26-week period and dividing by the number of weeks worked, or the minimum divisor, whichever is higher.

Use of Withholding Tables

Employers may use **wage bracket withholding tables** in determining Canada Pension Plan and employment insurance to be withheld from employees' gross earnings. These tables are also available on computer disks from Revenue Canada for computer applications.

Determining the amount of withholdings from an employee's gross wages is quite easy when tables on disk are used. Exhibit 11.2 shows the screens used to determine withholding amounts. First the gross pay is entered in the "Gross income for the pay period" area. Then the "View Deductions" button is clicked. The "Payroll Deductions for Regular Salary" automatically appears.

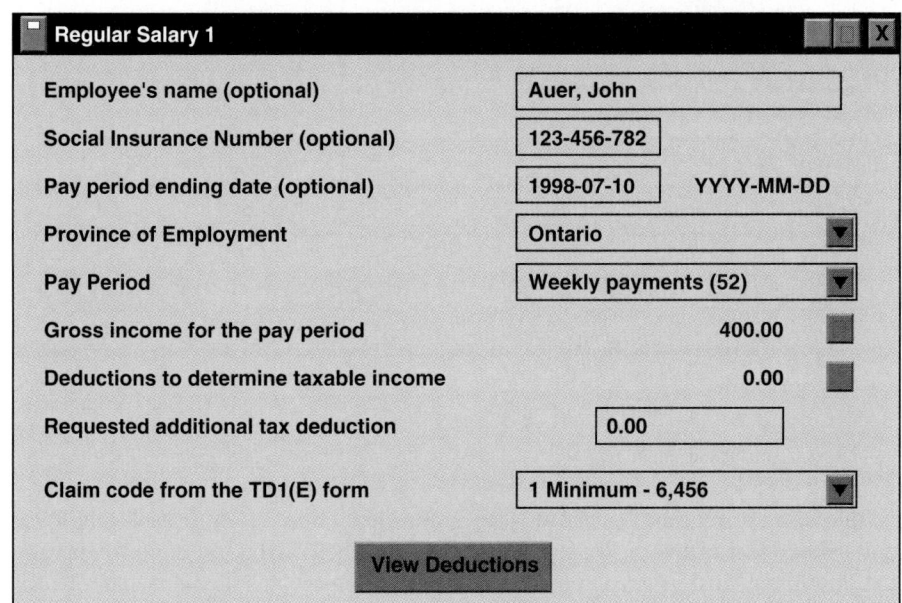

Exhibit 11.2

1998 Tables on Diskette Screens

Exhibit 11.2

1998 Tables on Diskette
Screens (continued)

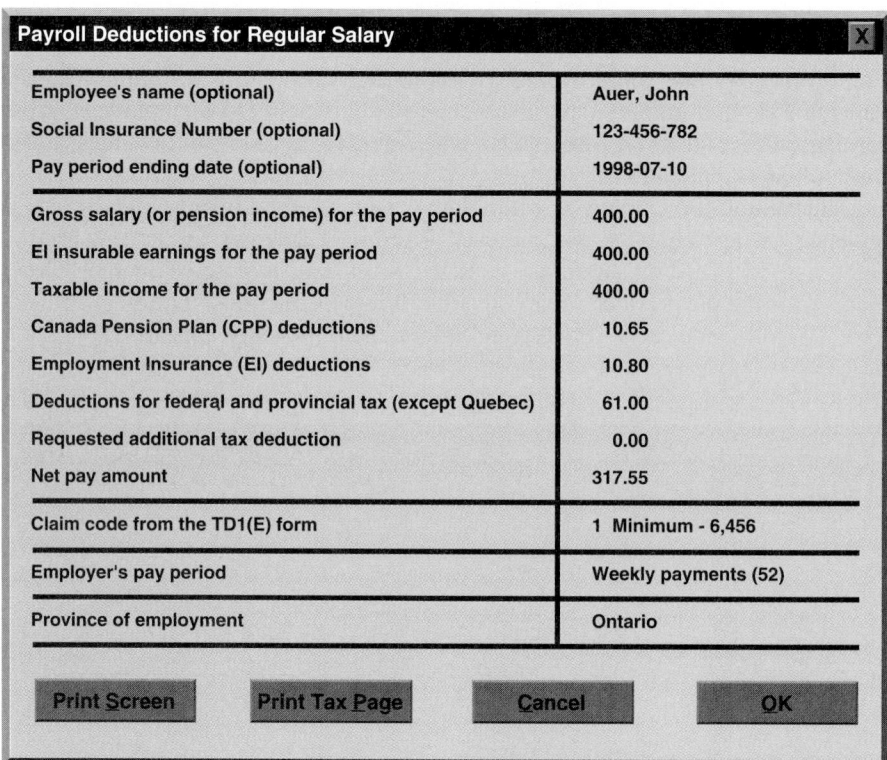

The T-4 Form

Employers are required to report wages and deductions both to each employee and to the local office of Revenue Canada. On or before the last day of February, the employer must give each employee a T-4 summary, a statement that tells the employee:

- Total wages for the preceding year.
- Taxable benefits received from the employer.
- Income taxes withheld.
- Deductions for registered pension plan.
- Canada Pension Plan contributions.
- Employment insurance deductions.

On or before the last day of February the employer must forward to the district taxation office copies of the employee's T-4 statements plus a T-4 that summarizes the information contained on the employee's T-4 statements. The T-4 form is shown in Exhibit 11.3.

Wages, Hours, and Union Contracts

All provinces have laws establishing maximum hours of work and minimum pay rates. And, while the details vary with each province, generally employers are required to pay an employee for hours worked in excess of 40 in any one week at the employee's regular pay rate plus an overtime premium of at least one-half of his or her regular rate. This gives an employee an overtime rate of at least $1\frac{1}{2}$ times his or her regular hourly rate for hours in excess of 40 in any one week. In addition, employers commonly operate under contracts with their employees' union that provide even better terms. For example, union contracts often provide for time-and-a-half for work on Saturdays, and double time for Sundays and hol-

A T4 form is shown containing the following:

Revenue Canada / Revenu Canada	T4 – 1997 Supplementary Supplémentaire	STATEMENT OF REMUNERATION PAID ÉTAT DE LA RÉMUNÉRATION PAYÉE	08-083-926 R

14 Employment income before deductions	16 Employee's CPP contributions	17 Employee's QPP contributions	18 Employee's EI premiums	20 Registered pension plan contributions	22 Income tax deducted	24 EI insurable earnings	26 CPP/QPP pensionable earnings	28 Exempt CPP/QPP EI
65,150:97	969:00		1,131:00	3,969:00	14,774:70	39000:00		RPC/RRQ AE
Revenus d'emploi avant retenues	Cotisations de l'employé au RPC	Cotisations de l'employé au RRQ	Cotisations de l'employé à l'AE	Cotisations à un régime de pension agréé	Impôt sur le revenu retenu	Gains assurables d'AE	Gains donnant droit à pension – RPC/RRQ	Exemption

Box 14 includes these amounts / La case 14 comprend tous ces montants	30 Housing, board, and lodging / Logement, pension et repas	32 Travel in a prescribed zone / Voyage dans une zone visée par règlement	34 Personal use of employer's auto / Usage personnel de l'auto de l'employeur	36 Interest-free and low-interest loan / Prêts sans intérêt ou à faible intérêt	38 Stock option benefits / Avantages tirés d'une option d'achat d'actions	40 Other taxable allowances and benefits / Autres allocations et avantages imposables	42 Employment commissions / Commissions d'emploi
						1065:50	

44 Union dues	46 Charitable donations		50 Pension plan or DPSP registration number	52 Pension adjustment	10 Province of employment	12 Social insurance number	If your SIN is not in box 12, see the back of this slip.
865:07	500:00		0345702		B.C.		Si votre NAS ne figure pas à la case 12, lisez le verso de ce feuillet.
Cotisations syndicales	Dons de bienfaisance		Numéro d'agrément d'un RPDB ou d'un régime de pension	Facteur d'équivalence	Province d'emploi	Numéro d'assurance sociale	

Employee's name and address – Nom et adresse de l'employé

Surname (in capital letters) / Nom de famille (en lettres majuscules)   First name / Prénom   Initials / Initiales

→   MACHLACHLAN, SHANNON K.

Employer's name – Nom de l'employeur
B.C. SOLOR ENERGY INC.

58 Employee no. – N° de l'employé	54 Business No. – N° d'entreprise
16752	

Footnotes – Notes :

T4 Supplementary - Supplémentaire (97)   0762   Return with T4 Summary return / À retourner avec la déclaration T4 *Sommaire*   **1**

Exhibit 11.3

T-4 Form

idays. When an employer is under a union contract in which the terms are better than those provided for by law, the contract terms take precedence over the law.

In addition to specifying working hours and wage rates, union contracts often provide for the collection of employees' union dues by the employer. Such a requirement commonly provides that the employer shall deduct dues from the wages of each employee and remit the amounts deducted to the union. The employer is usually required to remit once each month reporting each employee's name and the amount deducted from his or her pay.

Other Payroll Deductions

In addition to the payroll deductions discussed thus far, employees may individually authorize additional deductions. Some examples of these might be:

1. Deductions to accumulate funds for the purchase of Canada Savings Bonds.
2. Deductions to pay health, accident, hospital, or life insurance premiums.
3. Deductions to repay loans from the employer or the employees' credit union.
4. Deductions to pay for merchandise purchased from the company.
5. Deductions for donations to charitable organizations such as the United Way.

Pay Stats

Comparing pay is tricky business. Mexico, for example, has long been regarded as poor on the hourly base pay scale. But we must recognize that base pay makes up only 30% of a Mexican worker's total compensation. Mexican workers typically receive full pay 365 days a year—even though they take vacations and holidays, and usually work only 40 to 48 hours a week. They often receive profit-sharing plans, punctuality bonuses, saving plans, and 30 days' extra pay as a Christmas bonus. Even with these benefits, Mexican workers are still estimated to make about $10 less per hour than their North American counterparts. [Source: *Business Week*, October 31, 1994.]

Did You Know?

Timekeeping

Compiling a record of the time worked by each employee is called **timekeeping.** The method used to compile such a record depends on the nature of the company's business and the number of its employees. In a very small business, timekeeping may consist of no more than notations of each employee's working time made in a memorandum book by the manager or owner. In many companies, however, time clocks are used to record on clock cards each employee's time of arrival and departure. The time clocks are usually placed near entrances to the office, store, or factory. At the beginning of each payroll period, a **clock card** for each employee (see Exhibit 11.4) is placed in a rack for use by the employee. Upon arriving at work, each employee takes his or her card from the rack and places it in a slot in the time clock. This actuates the clock to stamp the date and arrival time on the card. The employee then returns the card to the rack. Upon leaving the plant, store, or office for lunch or at the end of the day, the procedure is repeated. The employee takes the card from the rack, places it in the clock, and the time of departure is automatically stamped, As a result, at the end of each period, the card shows the hours the employee was at work.

Exhibit 11.4

An Employee's Clock Card

Flash back

1. What is the purpose of the federal Employment Insurance scheme?
2. When must T-4 statements be given to employees?
3. What are other typical nonmandatory payroll deductions?

Answers—p. 540

The Payroll Register

LO 2 Make the calculations necessary to prepare a Payroll Register and prepare the entry to record payroll liabilities.

Each pay period the total hours worked as compiled on clock cards or by other means is summarized in a Payroll Register, an example of which is shown in Exhibit 11.5. The illustrated register is for a weekly pay period and shows the payroll data for each employee on a separate line.

In Exhibit 11.5, the columns under the heading Daily Time show the hours worked each day by each employee. The total of each employee's hours is entered in the column headed Total Hours. If hours include overtime hours, these are entered in the column headed O.T. Hours.

The Regular Pay Rate column shows the hourly pay rate of each employee. Total hours worked multiplied by the regular pay rate equals regular pay. Overtime hours multiplied by the overtime premium rate (50% in this case) equals overtime premium pay. And regular pay plus overtime premium pay is the **employee's gross pay**.

The amounts withheld from each employee's gross pay are recorded in the Deductions columns of the payroll register. For example, you determine the income tax deductions by matching the gross pay of each employee to the tax deduction tables and then enter the results in the tax deduction column. Income tax deductions are based on the gross pay less the amounts deducted for employment insurance and Canada Pension Plan. The tax tables allow for these adjustments and separate books are available for each province. However, for simplicity, assume that income tax deductions are 20% of the employee's gross pay.

Exhibit 11.5

Payroll Register

| Employees | Clock Card No. | Daily Time | | | | | | | Total Hours | O.T. Hours | Earnings | | | |
		M	T	W	T	F	S	S			Reg. Pay Rate	Regular Pay	O.T. Premium Pay	Gross Pay
Auer, John	118	8	8	8	8	8			40		10.00	400.00		400.00
Cheung, Joen	109	0	8	8	8	8	8		40		12.00	480.00		480.00
Daljit, Moe	121	8	8	8	8	8	8	4	52	12	15.00	780.00	90.00	870.00
Lee, Shannon	104	8	8		8	8	8	4	44	4	14.00	616.00	28.00	644.00
Prasad, Sunil	108		8	8	8	8	4	8	44	4	15.00	660.00	30.00	690.00
Rupert, Allan	105	8	8	8	8	8			40		12.00	480.00		480.00
Totals												3,416.00	148.00	3,564.00

Register July 10, 1998

| | Deductions | | | | | Payment | | Distribution | |
	EI Premium	Income Taxes	Hosp. Ins.	CPP	Total Deductions	Net Pay	Cheque No.	Sales Salaries	Office Salaries
1	10.80	80.00	18.00	10.65	119.45	280.55	754	400.00	
2	12.96	96.00	18.00	13.21	140.17	339.83	755	480.00	
3	23.49	174.00	24.00	25.69	247.18	622.82	756		870.00
4	17.39	128.80	18.00	18.45	182.64	461.36	757		644.00
5	18.63	138.00	24.00	19.93	200.56	489.44	758	690.00	
6	12.96	96.00	18.00	13.21	140.17	339.83	759	480.00	
	96.23	712.80	120.00	101.14	1,030.17	2,533.83		2,050.00	1,514.00

As previously stated, the income tax withheld depends on each employee's gross pay and personal tax credits. You can determine these amounts by first referring to the personal tax credits and then to the appropriate wage bracket withholding tables. You enter them in the column headed Income Taxes.

The column headed Hosp. Ins. shows the amounts withheld to pay for hospital Insurance for the employees and their families. The total withheld from all employees is a current liability of the employer until paid to the insurance company. Likewise, the total withheld for employees' union dues is a current liability until paid to the union.

Additional columns may be added to the Payroll register for any other deductions that occur sufficiently often to warrant special columns. For example, a company that regularly deducts amounts from its employees' pay for Canada Savings bonds may add a special column for this deduction.

An employee's gross pay less total deductions is the **employee's net pay** and is entered in the Net Pay column. The total of this column is the amount the employees are to be paid. The numbers of the cheques used to pay the employees are entered in the column headed Cheque No.

The Distribution columns are used to classify the various salaries in terms of different kinds of expense. Here you enter each employee's gross salary in the proper column according to the type of work performed. The column totals then indicate the amounts to be debited to the salary expense accounts.

Recording the Payroll

Generally, a Payroll Register such as the one shown is a supplementary memorandum record. As such, you do not post its information directly to the accounts. Instead, you must first record the payroll with a General Journal entry, which is then posted to the accounts. The entry to record the payroll shown in Exhibit 11.5 is:

July 10	Sales Salaries Expense	2,050.00	
	Office Salaries Expense	1,514.00	
	Employment Insurance Payable		96.23
	Employees' Income Taxes Payable . . .		712.80
	Employees' Hospital Insurance Payable		120.00
	Canada Pension Plan Payable		101.14
	Payroll Payable		2,533.83
	To record the July 10 payroll.		

The debits of the entry were taken from the Payroll Register's distribution column totals. They charge the employees' gross earnings to the proper salary expense accounts. The credits to EI Payable, Employees' Income Taxes Payable, Employees' Hospital Insurance Payable, and CPP Payable record these amounts as current liabilities. The credit to Payroll Payable (also called Salaries Payable, Wages Payable, or Accrued Salaries Payable, etc.) records as a liability the net amount to be paid to the employees.

Flash back

4. What constitutes the employee's gross pay?

5. What is the employee's net pay?

Answers—p. 540

Paying the Employees

LO3 Prepare journal entries to record the payments to employees and explain the operation of a payroll bank account.

Almost every business pays its employees by cheques. In a company that has few employees, these cheques often are drawn on the regular bank account and entered in a Cash Disbursements Journal (or Cheque Register) like the one described in Chapter 4. Since each cheque is debited to the Payroll Payable account, posting labour can be saved by adding a Salaries Payable column in the journal. If such a column is added, entries to pay the employees shown in the Exhibit 11.5 payroll will appear as in Exhibit 11.6. Most employers furnish each employee an earnings statement each payday. The statement gives the employee a record of hours worked, gross pay, deductions, and net pay. The statements often takes the form of a detachable paycheque portion that is removed before the cheque is cashed. A paycheque earnings statement is reproduced in Exhibit 11.7.

Lawn Worker

You take a summer job working for a family friend who runs a small lawn mowing service. When the time arrives for your first paycheque, the owner slaps you on the back, gives you full payment in cash, winks, and adds: "No need to pay those high taxes, eh." What are your responsibilities in this case? Do you take any action?

Judgment and Ethics

Answer—p. 539

Payroll Bank Account

A business with many employees will often use a special **payroll bank account** to pay its employees. When such an account is used, one cheque for the total payroll is drawn on the regular bank account and deposited in the special payroll bank account.

 Exhibit 11.6

Cash Disbursements Journal

					Cash Disbursements Journal					
Date	Cheque No.	Payee	Account Debited	PR	Other Accts. Debit	Accts. Pay. Debit	Payroll Payable Debit	Pur. Dis. Credit	Cash Credit
July 10	754	John Auer	Payroll Pay				280.55		280.55
	755	Joan Cheung	"				339.83		339.83
	756	Moe Daljit	"				622.82		622.82
	757	Shannon Lee	"				461.36		461.36
	758	Sunil Prasad	"				489.44		489.44
	759	Allan Rupert	"				339.83		339.83

Then individual payroll cheques are drawn on this special account. Because only one cheque for the payroll total is drawn on the regular bank account each payday, use of a special payroll bank account simplifies internal control, especially the reconciliation of the regular bank account. It may be reconciled without considering the payroll cheques outstanding, and there may be many of these. Many financial institutions offer a payroll service whereby the employees' net pay is transferred electronically into their accounts. The employer simply transfers the net amount of the payroll to the institution along with the employees' names and the accounts to be credited.

 Exhibit 11.7

A Payroll Cheque

John Auer	40		10.00	400.00		400.00	10.80	80.00	10.65	18.00	119.45	280.55
Employee	Total Hours	O.T. Hours	Reg. Pay Rate	Regular Pay	O.T. Prem. Pay	Gross Pay	EI Premium	Income Taxes	CP Plan	Hosp. Ins.	Total Deductions	Net Pay

STATEMENT OF EARNINGS AND DEDUCTIONS FOR EMPLOYEE'S RECORDS—DETACH BEFORE CASHING CHEQUE

VALLEY SALES COMPANY
2590 Dixon Road • Cambridge, Ontario

No. 1517

PAY TO THE
ORDER OF ___John Auer_____ Date _July 10, 1998_ $ __280.55__

___Two Hundred eighty - fifty - five cents__ - - - - - - - - - - - - - -

Merchants National Bank
Cambridge, Ontario

VALLEY SALES COMPANY

Jane R. Morris

When a company uses a special payroll account, it must complete the following steps to pay the employees:

1. Record the information shown on the payroll Register in the usual manner with a General Journal entry similar to the one previously illustrated. This entry causes the sum of the employees' net pay to be credited to the liability account (Salaries Payable).

2. Have a single cheque written that is payable to Payroll Bank account for the total amount of the payroll and enter the payment in the Cheque Register. This requires a debit to Salaries Payable and a credit to Cash.

3. Have the cheque deposited in the payroll bank account. This transfers an amount of money equal to the payroll total from the regular bank account to the special payroll bank account.

4. Have individual payroll cheques drawn on the special payroll bank account and delivered to the employees. As soon as all employees cash their cheques, the funds in the special account will be exhausted. Typically, companies will arrange for the bank to charge all service costs to the regular bank account.

A special Payroll Cheque Register may be used in connection with a payroll bank account. However, most companies do not use such a register. Instead, the payroll cheque numbers are entered in the Payroll Register so that it serves as a Cheque Register.

Employee's Individual Earnings Record

An **Employee's Individual Earnings Record**, as shown in Exhibit 11.8, provides for each employee, in one record, a full year's summary of the employee's working time, gross earnings, deductions, and net pay. In addition, it accumulates information that

1. Serves as a basis for the employer's payroll tax returns.
2. Indicates when an employee's earnings have reached the maximum amounts for CPP and EI deductions.
3. Supplies data for the T4 slip, which must be given to the employee at the end of the year.

The payroll information on an Employee's Individual Earnings Record is taken from the Payroll Register. The information as to earnings, deductions, and net pay is first recorded on a single line in the Payroll Register. Then, each pay period the information is posted from the Payroll Register to the earnings record. Note the last column of the record. It shows an employee's cumulative earnings and is used to determine when the earnings reach the maximum amounts taxed and are no longer subject to the various payroll taxes.

Flash back

6. Why would a company use a special payroll bank account?

7. What is the purpose of the employee's earnings record?

Answers—p. 540

Employee's Name John Auer   SIN No. 123-456-789   Employee No. 114

Home
Address 111 South Greenwood   Notify in Case
of Emergency Margaret Auer   Phone
No. 964-9834

Employed May 15, 1993   Date of
Termination   Reason

Date of
Birth June 6, 1972   Date
Becomes 65 June 6, 2037   Male (**X**)
Female ( )   Married ( )
Single (**X**)   Number of
Exemptions 0   Pay
Rate $10.00

Occupation Clerk   Place Warehouse

				Time Lost	Time Worked											
Date																
Per. Ends	**Paid**	**Hrs.**	**Rea-son**	**Total**	**O.T. Hours**	**Reg. Pay**	**O.T. Pay**	**Gross Pay**	**EI Prem**	**Income Taxes**	**Hosp. Ins.**	**CPP**	**Total Deduc-tions**	**Net Pay**	**Cheque No.**	**Cumu-lative Earnings**
2-Jan	2-Jan			40		400.00		400.00	10.80	80.00	18.00	10.65	119.45	280.55	673	400.00
9-Jan	9-Jan			40		400.00		400.00	10.80	80.00	18.00	10.65	119.45	280.55	701	800.00
16-Jan	16-Jan			40		400.00		400.00	10.80	80.00	18.00	10.65	119.45	280.55	743	1,200.00
23-Jan	23-Jan	4	Sick	36		360.00		360.00	9.72	72.00	18.00	9.37	109.09	250.91	795	1,560.00
30-Jan	30-Jan			40		400.00		400.00	10.80	80.00	18.00	10.65	119.45	280.55	839	1,960.00
6-Feb	6-Feb			40		400.00		400.00	10.80	80.00	18.00	10.65	119.45	280.55	854	2,360.00
13-Feb	13-Feb			40		400.00		400.00	10.80	80.00	18.00	10.65	119.45	280.55	893	2,760.00
20-Feb	20-Feb			40		400.00		400.00	10.80	80.00	18.00	10.65	119.45	280.55	932	3,160.00
10-Jul	10-Jul			40		400.00		400.00	10.80	80.00	18.00	10.65	119.45	280.55	1517	9.560.00

Exhibit 11.8

Employee's Individual Earnings Record

Mid-Chapter Demonstration Problem

At the end of its first weekly pay period in the year, Saskat Company's payroll record showed that its sales employees had earned $5,580 and its office employees had earned $3,450. The employees were to have $315 of EI and $225 of CPP withheld plus $1,545 of income taxes, $270 of union dues, and $855 of hospital insurance premiums. Give the General Journal entry to record the payroll.

Solution to Mid-Chapter Demonstration Problem

Jan. 5	Sales Salaries Expense	5,580	
	Office Salaries Expense	3,450	
	EI Payable		315
	CPP Payable		225
	Employees' Income Taxes Payable		1,545
	Employees' Union Dues Payable		270
	Employees' Hospital Insurance Payable . .		855
	Payroll Payable		5,820

Payroll Deductions Required of the Employer

LO4 Calculate the payroll costs levied on employers and prepare the entries to record the accrual and payments of these amounts.

Under the previous discussion of the Canada Pension Plan, it was pointed out that pension deductions are required in like amounts on both employed workers and their employers. A covered employer is required by law to deduct from the employees' pay the amounts of their Canada Pension Plan, but in addition, the employer must pay an amount equal to the sum of the employees' Canada pension. Commonly, the amount deducted by the employer is recorded at the same time the payroll to which it relates is recorded. Also, since both the employees' and employer's shares are reported on the same form and are paid in one amount, the liability for both is normally recorded in the same liability account, the Canada Pension Plan Payable account.

In addition to the Canada Pension Plan, an employer is required to pay employment insurance that is 1.4 times the sum of the employees' employment insurance deductions. Most employers record both of these payroll deductions with a General Journal entry that is made at the time the payroll to which they relate is recorded. For example, the entry to record the employer's amounts on the payroll in Exhibit 11.5 (p. 531) is:

July 10	Benefits Expense	235.86	
	Employment Insurance Payable		134.72
	Canada Pension Plan Payable		101.14
	To record the employer's payroll taxes.		

The debit of the entry records as an expense the payroll taxes levied on the employer, and the credits record the liabilities for the taxes. The $134.72 credit to Employment Insurance Payable is 1.4 times the sum of the amounts deducted from the pay of the employees whose wages are recorded in the Payroll Register of Exhibit 11.5, and the credit to Canada Pension Plan Payable is equal to the total of the employees' pension plan deductions.

Paying the Payroll Deductions

Income tax, Employment Insurance, and Canada Pension Plan amounts withheld each payday from the employees' pay plus the employer's portion of employment insurance and Canada Pension Plan are current liabilities until paid to the Receiver General of Canada. The normal method of payment is to pay the amounts due at any chartered bank or remit directly to the Receiver General of Canada. Payment of these amounts is usually required to be made before the 15th of the month following the month that deductions were made from the earnings of the employees. Large employers are required to remit on the 10th and 25th of each month. Payment of these liabilities is recorded in the same manner as payment of any other liabilities.

Did You Know?

Tax Aid
Computer technology has reduced errors and increased speed in computing taxes as compared with manual use of tax tables. Tax tables can be stored on computer or downloaded off the Web and then used to accurately compute payroll deductions.

Accruing Payroll Deductions on Wages

Mandatory payroll deductions are levied on wages actually paid. In other words, accrued wages are not subject to payroll deductions until they are paid. Nevertheless, if the requirements of the matching principle are to be met, both accrued wages and the accrued deductions on the wages should be recorded at the end of an accounting period. However, since the amounts of such deductions vary little from one accounting period to the next and often are small in amount, many employers apply the materiality principle and do not accrue payroll deductions.

Flashback

8. If Marita Company deducted $1,750 for Employment Insurance and $1,275 for CPP from its employees in April, what would the benefits expense be for the month?

9. When are the payments for employee deductions due to the Receiver General?

Answers—p. 540

In addition to the wages earned by employees and the related amounts paid by the employer, many companies provide their employees a variety of benefits. Since the costs of these benefits are paid by the employer and the benefits are in addition to the amount of wages earned, they are often called **employee fringe benefits**. For example, an employer may pay for part (or all) of the employees' medical insurance, life insurance, and disability insurance. Another typical employee benefit involves employer contributions to a retirement income plan. Workers' compensation is required to be paid by employers according to the legislation in each province. Perhaps the most typical employee benefit is vacation pay.

Employee (Fringe) Benefit Costs

LO5 Calculate and record employee fringe benefit costs and show the effect of these items on the total cost of employing labour.

Workers' Compensation

Legislation is in effect in all provinces for payments to employees for an injury or disability arising out of or in the course of their employment. Under the provincial workers' compensation acts, employers are, in effect, required to insure their employees against injury disability that may arise as a result of employment. Premiums are normally based on (1) accident experience of the industrial classification to which each business is assigned and (2) the total payroll.

Procedures for payment are as follows:

1. At the beginning of each year, every covered employer is required to submit to the Workers' Compensation Board[1] an estimate of his or her expected payroll for the ensuing year.

2. Provisional premiums are then established by the board relating estimated requirements for disability payments to estimated payroll. Provisional premium notices are then sent to all employers.

3. Provisional premiums are normally payable in from three to six installments during the year.

4. At the end of each year, actual payrolls are submitted to the board, and final assessments are made based on actual payrolls and actual payments. Premiums are normally between 1% and 3% of gross payroll and are borne by the employer.

Employer Contributions to Employee Insurance and Retirement Plans

The entries to record employee benefits costs depend on the nature of the benefit. Some employee retirement plans are quite complicated and involve accounting procedures that are too complex for discussion in this introductory course. In other cases, however, the employer simply makes periodic cash contributions to a retirement fund for each employee and records the amounts contributed as expense. Other employee benefits that require periodic cash payments by the employer include employer payments of insurance premiums for employees.

---

[1] In Ontario, the Worker's Compensation Board has been renamed as the Workplace Safety and Insurance Board (WSIB).

In the case of employee benefits that simply require the employer to make periodic cash payments, the entries to record the employer's obligations are similar to those used for payroll deductions.[2] For example, assume an employer with five employees has agreed to pay medical insurance premiums of $40 per month for each employee. The employer also will contribute 10% of each employee's salary to a retirement program. If each employee earns $2,500 per month, the entry to record these employee benefits for the month of July is

Jul. 31	Benefits Expense	1,450	
	Employees' Medical Insurance Payable		200
	Employees' Retirement Program Payable [($2,500 × 5) × 10%]		1,250

Vacation Pay

Employers are required to allow their employees paid vacation time (at a minimum rate of 4% of gross earnings) as a benefit of employment. For example, many employees receive two weeks' vacation in return for working 50 weeks each year. The effect of a two-week vacation is to increase the employer's payroll expenses by 4% (2/50 = .04). After five years of service most employees are entitled to three-week vacation (i.e., 3/49 = 6.12%). However, new employees often do not begin to accrue vacation time until after they have worked for a period of time, perhaps as much as a year. The employment contract may say that no vacation is granted until the employee works one year, but if the first year is completed, the employee receives the full two weeks. Contracts between the employer and employee may allow for vacation pay in excess of the 4% minimum.

To account for vacation pay, an employer should estimate and record the additional expense during the weeks the employees are working and earning the vacation time. For example, assume that a company with a weekly payroll of $20,000 grants two weeks' vacation after one year's employment. The entry to record the estimated vacation pay is

| Date | Benefits Expense . . . . | 800 | |
| | Estimated Vacation Pay Liability ($20,000 × .04) . . . . | | 800 |

As employees take their vacations and receive their vacation pay, the entries to record the vacation payroll take the following general form:

Date	Estimated Vacation Pay Liability	xxx	
	Employees' EI and CPP Payable		xxx
	Employees' Income Taxes Payable . . .		xxx
	Other withholding liability accounts such as Employees' Hospital Insurance Payable		xxx
	Payroll Payable		xxx

Mandatory payroll deductions and employee benefits costs are often a major category of expense incurred by a company. They may amount to well over 25% of the salaries earned by employees.

---

[2] Some payments of employee benefits must be added to the gross salary of the employee for the purpose of calculating income tax, CPP, and EI payroll deductions. However, in this chapter and in the problems at the end of the chapter, the possible effect of employee benefit costs on payroll taxes is ignored to avoid undue complexity in the introductory course.

10. How is the cost of Workers' Compensation determined?

11. Assume a company with an annual payroll of $160,000 grants three weeks' vacation to its employees. Record the estimated vacation pay for the year.

Answers—p. 540

Computerized Payroll Systems

Manually prepared records like the ones described in this chapter are used in many small companies. However, an increasing number of companies use computers to process their payroll. The computer programs are designed to take advantage of the fact that the same calculations are performed each pay period. Also, much of the same information must be entered for each employee in the Payroll Register, on the employee's earnings record, and on the employee's paycheque. The computers simultaneously store or print the information in all three places.

Summary

LO1 List the taxes and other items frequently withheld from employees' wages. Amounts withheld from employees' wages include federal income taxes, employment insurance, and Canada Pension Plan. Payroll costs levied on employers include employment insurance, Canada Pension, and workers' compensation. An employee's gross pay may be the employee's specified wage rate multiplied by the total hours worked plus an overtime premium rate multiplied by the number of overtime hours worked. Alternatively, it may be the given periodic salary of the employee. Taxes withheld and other deductions for items such as union dues, insurance premiums, and charitable contributions are subtracted from gross pay to determine the net pay.

LO2 Make the calculations necessary to prepare a Payroll Register and prepare the entry to record payroll liabilities. A Payroll Register is used to summarize all employees' hours worked, regular and overtime pay, payroll deductions, net pay, and distribution of gross pay to expense accounts during each pay period. It provides the necessary information for journal entries to record the accrued payroll and to pay the employees.

LO3 Prepare journal entries to record the payments to employees and explain the operation of a payroll bank account. A payroll bank account is a separate account

that is used solely for the purpose of paying employees. Each pay period, an amount equal to the total net pay of all employees is transferred from the regular bank account to the payroll bank account. Then cheques are drawn against the payroll bank account for the net pay of the employees.

LO4 Calculate the payroll costs levied on employers and prepare the entries to record the accrual and payment of these amounts. When a payroll is accrued at the end of each pay period, payroll deductions and levies also should be accrued with a debit to Benefits Expense and credits to appropriate liability accounts.

LO5 Calculate and record employee fringe benefit costs and show the effect of these items on the total cost of employing labour. Fringe benefit costs that involve simple cash payments by the employer should be accrued with an entry similar to the one used to accrue payroll levies. To account for the expense associated with vacation pay, you should estimate the expense and allocate the estimated amounts to the pay periods during the year. These allocations are recorded with a debit to Employees' Benefits Expense and a credit to Estimated Vacation Pay Liabilities. Then payments to employees on vacation are charged to the estimated liability.

Guidance Answer to **Judgment and Ethics**

Lawn Worker

You need to be concerned about being an accomplice to unlawful payroll activities. Not paying federal and provincial taxes on wages earned is unlawful and unethical. Such payments won't provide CPP and EI contributions. The best course of action is to request payment by cheque. If this fails to change the owner's payment practices, you must consider quitting this job.

Guidance Answers to Flash backs

1. Employment insurance is designed to alleviate hardships caused by interruptions in earnings through unemployment.
2. On or before the last day in February.
3. Deductions for Canada Savings Bonds, health or life insurance premiums, loan repayments, and donations to charitable organizations.
4. Regular pay plus overtime pay.
5. Gross pay less all the deductions.
6. A payroll bank account simplifies the payments to the employees and the internal control.

7. An employee's earnings record serves as a basis for the employer's tax returns, indicates when the maximum CPP and EI deductions have been reached and supplies the data for the employees' T-4 slips.
8. $3,725 = ($1,750 × 1.4) + $1,275
9. Normally by the 15th of the following month; large employers must remit on the 10th and 25th of each month.
10. Premiums are based on the accident experience in the specific industry and on the size of the employer's payroll.
11. $9,600 = ($160,000 × .06)

Demonstration Problem

Presented below are various items of information about three employees of the Deluth Company for the week ending November 27, 1998.

	Billings	Dephir	Singe
Wage rate (per hour)	$ 15	$ 30	$ 18
Overtime premium	50%	50%	50%
Annual vacation	2 weeks	4 weeks	3 weeks
Cumulative wages as of			
November 20, 1998	$28,500	$52,600	$14,800
For the week (pay period) ended			
November 27, 1998:			
Hours worked	40	44	48
Medical insurance:			
Deluth's contribution	$ 25	$ 25	$ 25
Withheld from employee	18	18	18
Union dues withheld	50	70	50
Income tax withheld	120	276	187
Employment insurance withheld	16	—	25
Canada Pension withheld	17	—	28
Payroll deduction rates:			
Income taxes		assume 20% of gross wages	
Employment insurance		2.7% to an annual maximum of $1,053 per week	
Canada Pension Plan		3.2% less annual exemption of $3,500; maximum per year is $1,068.80	

Required

In solving the following requirements, round all amounts to the nearest whole dollar. Prepare schedules that determine, for each employee and for all employees combined, the following information:

1. Wages earned for the regular 40-hour week, total overtime pay, and gross wages.
2. Vacation pay accrued for the week.
3. Deductions withheld from the employees' wages.
4. Costs imposed on the employer.
5. Employees' net pay for the week.
6. Employer's total payroll-related cost (wages, mandatory deductions, and fringe benefits).

Present journal entries to record the following:

7. Payroll expense.

8. Payroll deductions and employees' benefits expense.

Planning the Solution

■ Calculate the gross pay for each employee.

■ Compute the amounts deducted for each employee and their net pay.

■ Compute the employer's share of payroll deductions.

■ Prepare the necessary journal entries.

Solution to Demonstration Problem

1. The gross wages (including overtime) for the week:

	Billings	Dephir	Singe	Total
Regular wage rate	$ 15	$ 30	$ 18	
Regular hours	× 40	× 44	× 48	
Regular pay	$600	$1,320	$864	$2,784
Overtime premium	$ 7.5	$ 15	$ 9	
Overtime hours	-0-	× 4	× 8	
Total overtime pay	$ -0-	$ 60	$ 72	$ 132
Gross wages	$600	$1,380	$936	$2,916

2. The vacation pay accrued for the week:

	Billings	Dephir	Singe	Total
Annual vacation	2 weeks	4 weeks	3 weeks	
Weeks worked in year	50 weeks	48 weeks	49 weeks	
Vacation pay as a percentage of regular pay	4.00%	8.33%	6.12%	
Regular pay this week	× $600	× $1,380	× $936	
Vacation pay this week	$ 24	$ 115	$ 57	$196

The information in the following table is needed for parts 3 and 4:

			Earnings Subject to	
Employees	Earnings through November 20	Earnings This Week	CPP	Employment Ins.
Billings	$28,500	$ 600	$ 533	$ 600
Dephir[1]	52,600	1,380	—	—
Singe[2]	14,800	936	869	936
Totals		$2,916	1,402	$1,536

---

[1] Dephir's earnings have exceeded the CPP maximum of $39,600 and EI maximum of $39,000 and the maximum deductions of $1,068.80 (CPP) and $1,053.00 (EI). Therefore, neither CPP nor EI is deducted.

[2] EI deduction calculations from the diskette ignore the maximum weekly earnings of $750. Deductions would cease when the yearly maximum deduction of $1,053 is reached.

3. Amounts withheld from the employees:

	Billings	Dephir	Singe	Total
Income tax withheld	$120	$276	$187	$583
CPP withheld	17	—	28	45
EI withheld	16	—	25	41
Totals	$153	$276	$240	$669

4. The costs imposed on the employer.

	Billings	Dephir	Singe	Total
CPP (1.0)	$17	—	$28	$45
Employment Insurance (1.4)	22	—	35	57
Totals	39	—	63	102

5. The net amount paid to the employees:

	Billings	Dephir	Singe	Total
Regular pay	$600	$1.320	$864	$2,784
Overtime pay	-0-	60	72	132
Gross pay	$600	$1.380	$936	$2,916
Withholdings:				
Income tax withholding	$120	$ 276	$187	$ 583
CPP withholding	17	—	28	45
EI withholding	16	—	25	41
Medical insurance	18	18	18	54
Union dues	50	70	50	170
Total withholdings	$221	$ 364	$308	$ 893
Net pay to employees	$379	$1,016	$628	$2,023

6. The total payroll-related cost to the employer.

	Billings	Dephir	Singe	Total
Regular pay	$600	$1,320	$ 864	$2,784
Overtime pay	-0-	60	72	132
Gross pay	$600	$1,380	$ 936	$2,916
Deductions and fringe benefits:				
CPP	$ 17	$ —	$ 28	$ 45
EI	22	—	35	57
Vacation	24	115	57	196
Medical insurance	25	25	25	75
Total deductions and fringe benefits .	$ 88	$ 140	$ 145	$ 373
Total payroll-related cost	$688	$1,520	$1,081	$3,289

7. Journal entry for payroll expense:

1998			
Nov. 27	Salary Expense	2,916	
	Employees' Income Taxes Payable . . .		583
	Employees' CPP Payable		45
	Employees' EI Payable		41
	Employees' Medical Insurance Payable		54
	Employees' Union Dues Payable		170
	Payroll Payable		2,023
	To record payroll expense.		

8. Journal entry for payroll deductions and employees' benefit expense:

1998			
Nov. 27	Benefits Expense	373	
	Employees' CPP Payable		45
	Employees' EI Payable		57
	Accrued Vacation Pay Payable		196
	Employees' Medical Insurance Payable		75
	To record employer's share of payroll deductions and benefits expense.		

Glossary

Canada Pension Plan A national contributory retirement pension scheme. (p. 523)

Clock card A card issued to each employee that the employee inserts in a time clock to record the time of arrival and departure to and from work. (p. 530)

Employee fringe benefits Payments by an employer, in addition to wages and salaries, that are made to acquire employee benefits such as insurance coverage and retirement income. (p. 537)

Employment insurance An employment/employer-financed unemployment insurance plan. (p. 526)

Employee's gross pay The amount an employee earns before any deductions for taxes or other items such as union dues or insurance premiums. (p. 530)

Employee's Individual Earnings Record A record of an employee's hours worked, gross pay, deductions, net pay, and certain personal information about the employee. (p. 534)

Employee's net pay The amount an employee is paid, determined by subtracting from gross pay all deductions

for taxes and other items that are withheld from the employee's earnings. (p. 531)

Payroll bank account A special bank account a company uses solely for the purpose of paying employees by depositing in the account each pay period an amount equal to the total employees' net pay and drawing the employees' payroll cheques on the account. (p. 533)

Payroll deduction An amount deducted from an employee's pay, usually based on the amount of an employee's gross pay. (p. 522)

Personal tax credit Amounts that may be deducted from an individual's income taxes and that determine the amount of income taxes to be withheld. (p. 522)

Timekeeping The process of recording the time worked by each employee. (p. 530)

Wage bracket withholding table A table showing the amounts to be withheld from employees' wages at various levels of earnings. (p. 527)

Questions

1. Who pays the contributions to the Canada Pension Plan?

2. Who pays premiums under the workers' compensation laws?

3. What benefits are paid to unemployed workers for funds raised by the Federal Employment Insurance Act?

4. Who pays federal employment insurance? What is the rate?

5. What are the objectives of employment insurance laws?

6. To whom and when are payroll deductions remitted?

7. What determines the amount that must be deducted from an employee's wages for income taxes?

8. What is a tax withholding table?

9. What is the Canada Pension Plan deduction rate for self-employed individuals?

10. How is a clock card used in recording the time an employee is on the job?

11. How is a special payroll bank account used in paying the wages of employees?

12. At the end of an accounting period a firm's special payroll bank account has a $562.35 balance because the payroll cheques of two employees have not cleared the bank. Should this $562.35 appear on the firm's balance sheet? If so, where?

13. What information is accumulated on an employee's individual earnings record? Why must this information be accumulated? For what purposes is the information used?

14. What payroll charges are levied on the employer? What amounts are deducted from the wages of an employee?

15. What are employee fringe benefits? Name some examples.

Quick Study

QS 11-1
Payroll expenses

A company deducts $260 in employment insurance and $205 in Canada pension from the weekly payroll of its employees. How much is the company's expense for these items for the week?

QS 11-2
Preparing payroll journal entries

Tracon Co. has six employees, each of whom earns $3,000 per month. Income taxes are 20% of gross pay and the company deducts EI and CPP. Prepare the March 31 journal entry to record payroll for the month.

QS 11-3
Paying employers

Use the information in QS 11-2 to record the payment of the wages to the employees for March assuming that Tracon uses a payroll bank account.

QS 11-4
Payroll journal entry

Racon Co. has eight employees, each of whom earns $3,500 per month. Income taxes are 20% of gross pay and the company deducts EI and CPP. Prepare the April 30 journal entry to record Racon's payroll expenses for the month.

QS 11-5
Recording fringe benefits costs

Racon Co. (see QS 11-4) contributes 8% of an employee's salary to a retirement program, medical insurance premiums of $60 per employee, and vacation allowance equivalent to 5% of the employee's salary. Prepare a journal entry to record the fringe benefit costs for April.

Exercises

Exercise 11-1
Calculating gross and net pay

Julie Leung, an employee of the Import Company Limited, worked 48 hours during the week ended January 5. Her pay rate is $20 per hour, and her wages are subject to no deductions other than income taxes, employment insurance, and Canada Pension Plan. The overtime premium is 50% and is applicable to any time greater than 40 hours per week. Calculate her regular pay, overtime premium pay, gross pay, EI, CPP, income tax deductions (assume a tax deduction rate of 20%), total deductions, and net pay.

The following information as to earnings and deductions for the pay period ended May 17 was taken from a company's payroll records:

Exercise 11-2
Calculating payroll deductions and recording the payroll

LO 1

Employees' Names	Weekly Gross Pay	Earnings to End of Previous Week	Income Taxes	Health Insurance Deductions
Hellena Chea	$ 720	$ 12,510	$144.00	$ 24.00
Joseph Lim	610	10,320	91.00	24.00
Dino Patelli	830	15,500	142.00	36.00
Shari Quinata	1,700	29,500	395.00	24.00
	$3,860		$772.00	$108.00

Calculate the employees' EI and CPP withholdings, the amounts paid to each employee, and prepare a General Journal entry to record the payroll. Assume all employees work in the office.

Use the information provided in Exercise 11-2 to complete the following requirements:

1. Prepare a General Journal entry to record the employer's payroll costs resulting from the payroll.
2. Prepare a General Journal entry to record the following employee benefits incurred by the company: (a) health insurance costs equal to the amounts contributed by each employee and (b) contributions equal to 10% of gross pay for each employee's retirement income program.

Exercise 11-3
Calculating and recording payroll deductions

LO 4

Manchuran Company's employees earn a gross pay of $20 per hour and work 40 hours each week. Machuran Company contributes 8% of gross pay to a retirement program for employees and pays medical insurance premium of $50 per week per employee. What is Manchuran Company's total cost of employing a person for one week? (Assume that individual wages are less than the $36,900 Canada Pension Plan limit).

Exercise 11-4
Analyzing total labour costs

LO 5

Bellward Corporation grants vacation time of two weeks to those employees who have worked for the company one complete year. After 10 years of service employees receive four weeks of vacation. The monthly payroll for January totals $320,000 of which 70% is payable to employees with 10 or more years of service. On January 31, record the January expense arising from the vacation policy of the company.

Exercise 11-5
Calculating fringe benefits costs

LO 5

O'Riley Company's payroll costs and fringe benefit expenses include the normal CPP and EI contributions, retirement fund contributions of 10% of total earnings, and health insurance premiums of $120 per employee per month. Given the following list of employee annual salaries, payroll costs and fringe benefits constitute what percentage of salaries?

Exercise 11-6
Analyzing the cost of payroll deductions and fringe benefits

LO 4, 5

Doherty	$36,000
Fane	61,000
Kahan	59,000
Martin	37,000
Poon	48,000

Sharon Von Hatton is single and earns a weekly salary of $940. In response to a citywide effort to obtain charitable contributions to the local United Way programs, Von Hatton has requested that her employer withhold 2% of her salary (net of CPP, EI, and income taxes— assume a tax deduction rate of 20%). Under the program, what will be Von Hatton's annual contribution to the United Way?

Exercise 11-7
Other payroll deductions

LO 1

Problems

Problem 11-1
The Payroll Register and the payroll bank account

LO 1, 3

On January 6, at the end of the first weekly pay period of the year, a company's Payroll Register showed that its employees had earned $19,570 of sales salaries and $6,230 of office salaries. Withholdings from the employers' salaries were to include $740 of EI, $660 of CPP, $5,310 of income taxes, $930 of hospital insurance, and $420 of union dues.

Required

1. Prepare the General Journal entry to record the January 6 payroll.
2. Prepare a General Journal entry to record the employer's payroll expenses resulting from the January 6 payroll.
3. Under the assumption the company uses a payroll bank account and special payroll cheques in paying its employees, give the Cheque Register entry (Cheque No. 542) to transfer funds equal to the payroll from the regular bank account to the payroll bank account.
4. After the Cheque Register entry is made and posted, are additional debit and credit entries required to record the payroll cheques for the employees?

Problem 11-2
The Payroll Register, the payroll bank account, and payroll deductions

LO 1, 3, 4

The payroll records of Brownlee Corporation provided the following information for the weekly pay period ended December 21:

| Employees | Clock Card No. | Daily Time | | | | | | | Pay Rate | Hospital Insurance | Union Dues | Earnings to End of Previous Week |
		M	T	W	T	F	S	S				
Ray Loran	11	8	8	8	8	8	4	0	20.00	40.00	16.00	42,000
Kathy Sousa	12	7	8	6	7	8	4	0	18.00	40.00	15.00	46,000
Gary Smith	13	8	8	0	8	8	4	4	16.00	40.00	14.00	21,000
Nicole Parton	14	8	8	8	8	8	0	0	20.00	40.00	16.00	32,000
Diana Wood	15	0	6	6	6	6	8	8	18.00	40.00	15.00	36,000
										200.00	76.00	

Required

1. Enter the relevant information in the proper columns of a Payroll Register and complete the register for CPP and EI deductions. Charge the wages of Kathy Sousa to Office Salaries Expense and the wages of the remaining employees to Service Wages Expense. Calculate income tax deductions at 20% of gross pay. Employees are paid an overtime premium of 50% for all hours in excess of 40 per week.
2. Prepare a General Journal entry to record the Payroll Register information.
3. Make the Cheque Register entry (Cheque No. 399) to transfer funds equal to the payroll from the regular bank account to the payroll bank account under the assumption the company uses special payroll cheques and a payroll bank account in paying its employees. Assume the first payroll cheque is numbered 530 and enter the payroll cheque numbers in the Payroll Register.
4. Prepare a General Journal entry to record the employer's payroll costs resulting from the payroll.

A company accumulated the following information for the weekly pay period ended December 22:

Problem 11-3
The Payroll Register, payroll taxes, and employee fringe benefits
LO 1, 4, 5

Employees	Clock Card No.	M	T	W	T	F	S	S	Pay Rate	Medical Insurance	Union Dues	Earnings to End of Previous Week
Shannon Fong	21	8	8	8	8	8	4	0	18.00	30.00	20.00	41,000
Karen Horta	22	7	8	6	7	8	4	0	16.00	28.00	18.00	44,000
Garth Koran	23	8	8	0	8	8	4	4	14.00	25.00	16.00	19,000
Nicha Daljit	24	8	8	8	8	8	0	0	18.00	30.00	20.00	34,000
										113.00	74.00	

Required

1. Enter the relevant information in the proper columns of a Payroll Register and complete the register for CPP and EI deductions. Assume the first employee is a salesperson, the second two work in the shop, and the last one works in the office. Calculate income tax deductions at 20% of gross pay. Employees are paid an overtime premium of 50% for all hours in excess of 40 per week.

2. Prepare a General Journal entry to record the Payroll Register information.

3. Make the Cheque Register entry to transfer funds equal to the payroll from the regular bank account (Cheque No. 522) under the assumption the company uses special payroll cheques and a payroll bank account in paying its employees. Assume the first payroll cheque is numbered 230 and enter the payroll cheque numbers in the Payroll Register.

4. Prepare a General Journal entry to record the employer's payroll deductions resulting from the payroll.

5. Prepare General Journal entries to accrue employee fringe benefit costs for the week. Assume the company matches the employees' payments for medical insurance and contributes an amount equal to 8% of each employees' gross pay to a retirement program. Also, each employee accrues vacation pay at the rate of 6% of the wages and salaries earned. The company estimates that all employees eventually will be paid their vacation pay.

Problem 11-4
General Journal entries for payroll transactions
LO 3

A company has three employees, each of whom has been employed since January 1, earns $2,600 per month, and is paid on the last day of each month. On March 1, the following accounts and balances appeared in its ledger.

a. Employees Income Taxes Payable, $1,480 (liability for February only).
b. Employment Insurance Payable, $475 (liability for February).
c. Canada Pension Plan Payable, $390 (liability for February).
d. Employees' Medical Insurance Payable, $908 (liability for January and February).

During March and April, the company completed the following related to payroll.
Mar. 11   Issued Cheque No. 320 payable to Receiver General of Canada. The cheque was in payment of the February employee income taxes, EI and CPP amounts due.
     31   Prepared a General Journal entry to record the March Payroll Record which had the following column totals:

Income Taxes	EI	CPP	Medical Insurance	Total Deductions	Net Pay	Office Salaries	Shop Wages
$1,460	$230	$190	$260	$2,280	$5,660	$2,600	$5,200

31 Recorded the employer's $260 liability for its 50% contribution to the medical insurance plan of employees and 4% vacation pay accrued to the employees.

31 Issued Cheque No. 351 payable to Payroll Bank Account in payment of the March payroll. Endorsed the cheque, deposited it in payroll bank account, and issued payroll cheques to the employees.

31 Prepared a General Journal entry to record the employer's costs resulting from the March payroll.

Apr. 15 Issued Cheque No. 375 payable to the Receiver General in payment of the March mandatory deductions.

15 Issued Cheque No. 376 payable to All Canadian Insurance Company in payment of the employee medical insurance premiums for the first quarter.

Required

Prepare the necessary Cheque Register and General Journal entries to record the transactions.

Problem 11-5

The Payroll Register, the payroll bank account, and payroll deductions

LO 1, 3, 4

The following information was taken from the payroll records of Radical Software Company for the weekly pay period ending December 20:

Employees	Clock Card No.	Daily Time							Pay Rate	Hospital Insurance	Union Dues	Earnings to End of Previous Week
		M	T	W	T	F	S	S				
Pam Loella	41	0	8	8	8	8	4	4	18.00	40.00	20.00	40,000
Martan Mann	42	6	7	8	7	8	4	0	16.00	30.00	18.00	31,000
George Singe	43	8	4	0	8	8	4	4	18.00	40.00	20.00	26,000
Nathan Tang	44	8	8	8	8	8	0	4	16.00	30.00	18.00	35,000
Terry Vaughan	45	0	6	6	6	0	0	4	14.00	20.00	10.00	18,000
										160.00	86.00	

Required

1. Enter the relevant information in the proper columns of a Payroll Register and complete the register for CPP and EI deductions. The company pays time-and-a-half for hours in excess of 40 each week. Also, work on Saturdays is paid at time-and-a-half whether the total for the week is over 40 or not. Charge the wages of George Singe to Office Salaries Expense and the wages of the remaining employees to Plant Salaries Expense. Calculate income tax deductions at 20% of gross pay.

2. Prepare a General Journal entry to record the Payroll Register information.

3. Assume the company uses special payroll cheques drawn on a payroll bank account in paying its employees and make the Cheque Register entry (Cheque No. 848) to transfer funds equal to the payroll from the regular bank account to the payroll bank account. Also, assume the first payroll cheque is No. 632 and enter the payroll cheque numbers in the Payroll Register.

4. Prepare a General Journal entry to record the employer's payroll deductions resulting from the payroll.

On January 6, at the end of the first weekly pay period of the year, a company's Payroll Register showed that its employees had earned $23,400 of sales salaries and $5,820 of office salaries. Withholdings from the employees' salaries were to include $860 of EI, $710 of CPP, $6,180 of income taxes, $920 of hospital insurance, and $490 of union dues.

Required

1. Prepare the General Journal entry to record the January 6 payroll.
2. Prepare a General Journal entry to record the employer's payroll expenses resulting from the January 6 payroll.
3. Under the assumption the company uses a payroll bank account and special payroll cheques in paying its employees, give the Cheque Register entry (Cheque No. 874) to transfer funds equal to the payroll from the bank account to the payroll bank account.
4. After the Cheque Register entry is made and posted, are additional debit and credit entries required to record the payroll cheques and pay the employees?

Alternate Problems
Problem 11-1A
The Payroll Register and the payroll bank account
LO 1, 3

The payroll records of Wailee Corporation provided the following information for the weekly pay period ended December 21:

Problem 11-2A
The Payroll Register, the payroll bank account, and payroll deductions
LO 1, 3, 4

Employees	Clock Card No.	Daily Time							Pay Rate	Hospital Insurance	Union Dues	Earnings to End of Previous Week
		M	T	W	T	F	S	S				
Ben Amoko	31	8	8	8	8	8	0	0	17.00	30.00	12.00	28,000
Auleen Carson	32	7	8	8	7	8	4	0	18.00	30.00	12.00	36,000
Mitali De	33	8	8	0	8	8	4	4	18.00	30.00	12.00	28,000
Gene Deszca	34	8	8	8	8	8	0	0	15.00	30.00	12.00	32,000
Ysong Tan	35	0	6	6	6	6	8	8	15.00	30.00	12.00	26,000
										150.00	60.00	

Required

1. Enter the relevant information in the proper columns of a Payroll Register and complete the register for CPP and EI deductions. Charge the wages of Auleen Carson to Office Salaries Expense and the wages of the remaining employees to Service Wages Expense. Calculate income tax deductions at 20% of gross pay.
2. Prepare a General Journal entry to record the Payroll Register information.
3. Make the Cheque Register entry (Cheque No. 753) to transfer funds equal to the payroll from the regular bank account to the payroll bank account under the assumption the company uses special payroll cheques and a payroll bank account in paying its employees. Assume the first cheque is numbered 530 and enter the payroll cheque numbers in the Payroll Register.
4. Prepare a General Journal entry to record the employer's payroll costs resulting from the payroll.

Problem 11-3A
The Payroll Register,
payroll taxes, and
employee fringe benefits

LO 1, 4, 5

A company accumulated the following payroll information for the weekly pay period ended December 22:

Employees	Clock Card No.	Daily Time							Pay Rate	Medical Insurance	Union Dues	Earnings to End of Previous Week
		M	T	W	T	F	S	S				
Maria Gallego	51	8	8	8	8	8	0	0	20.00	30.00	20.00	46,000
Paul Iyogun	52	7	8	6	7	5	4	0	16.00	25.00	18.00	40,000
Shelly Jha	53	8	8	4	8	8	0	4	19.00	25.00	18.00	22,000
Ping Zhang	54	8	8	8	8	8	0	0	18.00	30.00	20.00	31,000
										110.00	76.00	

Required

1. Enter the relevant information in the proper columns of a Payroll Register and complete the register for CPP and EI deductions. Assume the first employee is a salesperson, the second two work in the shop, and the last one works in the office. Calculate income tax deductions at 20% of gross pay.

2. Prepare a General Journal entry to record the Payroll register information.

3. Make the Cheque Register entry to transfer funds equal to the payroll from the regular bank account to the payroll bank account (Cheque No. 412) under the assumption the company uses special payroll cheques and a payroll bank account in paying its employees. Assume the first payroll cheque is numbered 630 and enter the payroll cheque numbers in the Payroll Register.

4. Prepare a General Journal entry to record the employer's payroll deductions resulting from the payroll.

5. Prepare General Journal entries to accrue employee fringe benefits costs for the week. Assume the company matches the employees' payments for medical insurance and contributes an amount equal to 8% of each employees' gross pay to a retirement program. Also, each employee accrues vacation pay at the rate of 6% of the wages and salaries earned. The company estimates that all employees eventually will be paid their vacation pay.

Problem 11-4A
General Journal entries
for payroll transactions

LO 3

A company has three employees, each of whom has been employed since January 1, earns $2,300 per month, and is paid on the last day of each month. On March 1, the following accounts and balances appeared in its ledger:

a. Employees Income Taxes Payable, $1,290 (liability for February only).
b. Unemployment Insurance Payable, $460 (liability for February).
c. Canada Pension Plan Payable, $340 (liability for February).
d. Employees' Medical Insurance Payable, $935 (liability for January and February).

During March and April, the company completed the following transactions related to payroll:

Mar. 11   Issued Cheque No. 635 payable to Receiver General of Canada. The cheque was in payment of the February employee income taxes, EI and CPP amounts due.

31   Prepared a General Journal entry to record the March Payroll Record which had the following column totals:

Income Taxes	EI	CPP	Medical Insurance	Total Deductions	Net Pay	Office Salaries	Shop Wages
$1,190	$195	$160	$225	$1,770	$5,130	$2,300	$4,600

31 Recorded the employer's $225 liability for its 50% contribution to the medical insurance plan of employees and 4% vacation pay accrued to the employees.

31 Issued Cheque No. 718 payable to Payroll Bank Account in payment of the March payroll. Endorsed the cheque, deposited it in the payroll bank account, and issued payroll cheques to the employees.

Mar. 31 Prepared a General Journal entry to record the employer's payroll costs resulting from the March payroll.

Apr. 15 Issued Cheque No. 764 payable to the Receiver General in payment of the March mandatory deductions.

15 Issued Cheque No. 765 payable to National Insurance Company in payment of the employee medical insurance premiums for the first quarter.

Required

Prepare the necessary Cheque Register and General Journal entries to record the transactions.

The following information for the weekly pay period ended December 10 was taken from the records of a company:

Problem 11-5A
The Payroll Register, payroll taxes, and employee fringe benefits

LO 1, 3, 5

Employees	Clock Card No.	Daily Time							Pay Rate	Medical Insurance	Union Dues	Earnings to End of Previous Week
		M	T	W	T	F	S	S				
Raplh Abdoul	61	8	8	8	8	8	4	0	25.00	60.00	22.00	52,000
Ali Johnston	62	7	8	6	7	8	4	0	20.00	60.00	20.00	56,000
Sarah Bigalow	63	8	8	0	8	8	4	4	18.00	60.00	18.00	23,000
Leslie Worbetts	64	8	8	8	8	8	0	0	25.00	60.00	22.00	35,000
Ainsley Vangough	65	0	6	6	6	6	8	8	20.00	60.00	20.00	41,000
										300.00	102.00	

Required

1. Enter the relevant information in the proper columns of a Payroll Register and complete the register for CPP and EI deductions. Assume that the first employee works in the office, the second is a salesperson, and the last two work in the shop. Calculate tax deductions at 20% of gross pay. Employees are paid an overtime premium of 50% for all hours in excess of 40 per week.

2. Prepare a General Journal entry to record the Payroll Register information.

3. Make the Cheque Register entry (Cheque No. 389) to transfer funds equal to the payroll from the regular bank account to the payroll bank account. Assume the first payroll cheque is numbered 632 and enter the payroll cheque numbers in the Payroll Register.

4. Prepare a General Journal entry to record the employer's payroll deductions resulting from the payroll.

5. Prepare a General Journal entry to accrue employee fringe benefit costs for the week. Assume the company matches the employees' for medical insurance and contributes an amount equal to 8% of each employees' gross pay to a retirement program. Also, each employee accrues vacation pay at the rate of 6% of the wages and salaries earned. The company estimates that all employees eventually will be paid their vacation pay.

Analytical and Review Problems

A & R Problem 11-1

Using current year's withholding tables for Canada Pension Plan, employment insurance and income tax, update the Payroll Register of Exhibit 11.5. In computing income tax withholdings, state your assumption as to each employee's personal deductions. Assume that hospital insurance deductions continue at the same amounts as in Exhibit 11.5.

A & R Problem 11-2

The following data were taken from the Payroll Register of Eastcoastal Company:

Gross salary	xxx
Employee's income tax deductions	xxx
EI deductions	xxx
CPP deductions	xxx
Hospital insurance deductions	xxx
Union dues deductions	xxx

Eastcoastal contributes an equal amount to the hospital insurance plan, in addition to the statutory payroll taxes, and 6% of the gross salaries to a pension program.

Required

Record in General Journal form the payroll, payment of the employees, and remittance to the appropriate authority amounts owing in connection with the payroll. (Note: All amounts are to be indicated as xxx.)

BEYOND THE NUMBERS

Reporting in Action

LO 4, 5

Alliance Communications Corporation is a fully integrated supplier of entertainment products with interests in television, motion pictures, broadcasting, computer-generated animation facilities, music publishing and financing services. The financial statements and other information from Alliance's March 31, 1997, annual report are included in Appendix I at the end of the book.

According to Canadian generally accepted accounting principles, specific information relating to payroll expenses and liabilities is generally not required. Review the financial statements of Alliance Communications Corporation for the fiscal year ended March 31, 1997, and answer the following questions:

1. Where do you think payroll liabilities (income tax withheld from employees, CPP due, EI due, etc.) are reported? (Hint: Look at the consolidated balance sheet).
2. Where do you think wages and salaries are reported? (Hint: Look at the consolidated income statement. You may want to consider the balance sheet, too).
3. Where do you think that payroll benefits expense is reported? (Hint: Look at the consolidated income statement. You may want to consider the balance sheet, too).
4. The financial statements shown in Appendix I are meant for the shareholders of Alliance Communications Corporations. Do you think that the GAAP requirements related to payroll liabilities and expenses are adequate for published financial statements? Support your answers.
5. What additional payroll information (expenses, liabilities, etc.) do you think that management requires to adequately direct the company. Explain.

In view of the minimal GAAP requirements related to the reporting of payroll liabilities and expenses, comparison of payroll data for public companies such as **Alliance Communications Corporation** is difficult, if not impossible. Imagine that you were considering investing in Alliance Communications Corporation or **Imax Corporation**. Imax designs and manufactures projection and sound systems for giant-screen theatres based on proprietary and patented technology and is a producer and distributor of giant-screen theatres. Answer the following questions.

Comparative Analysis

LO 1

Required

1. Does the lack of public disclosure of specific payroll liabilities and expenses present a major problem for investors? Explain your answer

2. Assume that you were able to obtain additional information about payroll liabilities and expenses. What information would you request? How would the information help you in your investment decision?

Moe Daljit is the accountant for Valley Sales Company. Valley Sales Company is currently experiencing a cash shortage because its Pacific Rim customers have not been paying their accounts on a timely basis. The owner has been unable to arrange adequate bank financing to cover the cash shortage and has approached Moe suggesting that Moe delay sending the amounts withheld from employees to the Receiver General of Canada for a few months, "until things clear up." Then he adds, "After all, we will be sending the money to the Receiver General eventually."

Ethics Challenge

LO 4

Required

1. What are the company's responsibilities with respect to amounts withheld from employees' wages and salaries?

2. What are the ethical factors in this situation?

3. Would you recommend that Moe follow the owner's "suggestion"?

4. What alternatives might be available to the owner if Moe does not delay sending the amounts to the Receiver General of Canada?

Financial information is important to owners, employees, and parties outside the business. Listed below are items discussed in this chapter.

Communicating in Practice

LO 1, 2, 3, 4, 5

a. Personal Tax Credits Return Form TDI

b. Tables on Diskette (Wage Bracket Withholding Tables)

c. T-4 Form

d. Employee Clock Card

e. Payroll Register

f. Employee's Individual Earnings Record

g. Cash Disbursements Journal

h. Payroll Cheque

Required

For each form

1. Identify the user(s). Some forms may be used by more than one user. In these cases, identify all the users.

2. State what form is used *by each user*.

3. If you are working at present, ask your employer for a sample of each of the forms. Bring the forms to class, and compare the different forms used by different employers. Discuss why different employers use different forms.

Taking It to the Net

LO 2

Access the Web site of Revenue Canada at **http.//www.rc.gc.ca**. After you arrive at Revenue Canada's home page select either English or French.

Required

1. What are the two latest items on the What's New section on the Revenue Canada Web site?

2. List three job opportunities on the Job Opportunities section of the Revenue Canada Web site.

3. Describe two ways of obtaining the "Tables on Diskette."

Teamwork in Action

LO 2, 3, 4, 5

This activity is aimed at generating a team discussion of payroll transactions.

Required

1. Each team member is to select and investigate a computerized accounting package and answer the following questions:

   a. What is the name of the computerized accounting package?

   b. Does the computerized accounting package include a payroll module?

   c. How much does the computerized accounting package cost?

   d. To what size company is the computerized accounting package directed (e.g. small, medium, large)?

   e. Does the computerized accounting package include employee detail, list, and year-to-date summary?

   f. Does the computerized accounting package include employee hours work sheets?

   g. Can the computerized accounting package produce paycheques and payment cheques?

   h. Can the computerized accounting package produce individual payroll transactions and summaries?

   i. Can the computerized accounting package handle customized T4s?

   j. What special payroll features are included in the computerized accounting package?

2. Team members prepare a written summary of their findings in part 1 and report the results to their group.

3. Team members discuss the merits of the different computerized accounting packages from the viewpoint of payroll. After discussion, the group is to select the computerized accounting package that best addresses the needs of the business area they are interested in (e.g., small sales company, large manufacturing company, etc.) Prepare a presentation on the selected package demonstrating why it was selected. Include capabilities of the other packages for comparison purposes.

4. Group presents their findings to the whole class.

Using the Revenue Canada Web site (see Taking it to the Net, above) check the "What's New" area on a regular basis. If there are changes that affect payroll or withholdings, think about how it affects the material as presented in this chapter.

As a student interested in business, you should be reading the *The Globe and Mail Report on Business* or a similar Canadian financial newspaper on a regular basis. There are often reports on the effects of payroll-oriented subjects such as minimum wage rates, cost of employers' matching CPP and EI deductions, etc.

Required

For the rest of this semester read a financial paper on a regular basis and answer the following:

1. Was there an article related to payroll or payroll deductions?
2. How will the subject of the article affect business (e.g., increase costs, decrease costs, increase unemployment, etc.)?
3. Is the charge good or bad? Why?

12

Capital Assets: Plant and Equipment, Natural Resources, and Intangible Assets

A Look Back

Chapters 9 and 10 focused on short-term assets: cash, cash equivalents, receivables and temporary investments. We explained why they are known as liquid assets and described how companies account and report for them. Chapter 11 dealt with accounting for payroll and the payroll liability.

A Look at This Chapter

This chapter introduces us to capital (long-term) assets including property, plant and equipment, natural resources, and intangible assets. We explain how to record a capital asset's cost, the allocation of an asset's cost to periods benefiting from it, the recording of additional asset costs after an asset is purchased, and the disposing of an asset.

A Look Forward

Chapter 13 emphasizes both current and long-term liabilities. We explain how they are computed, recorded, and reported in financial statements. We also describe and apply present value concepts.

Chapter Outline

Section 1—Capital Assets: Property, Plant and Equipment

▶ **Cost of Capital Assets**
- Land
- Land Improvements
- Buildings
- Machinery and Equipment
- Lump-Sum Asset Purchase

▶ **Amortization**
- Factors in Computing Amortization
- Amortization Methods
- Partial Year Amortization
- Revising Amortization Rates
- Reporting Amortization on Assets

▶ **Revenue and Capital Expenditures**
- Repairs
- Betterments
- Low-Cost Asset Purchases

▶ **Disposals of Capital Assets**
- Discarding Capital Assets
- Selling Capital Assets
- Exchanging Capital Assets

Section 2—Natural Resources

▶ **Natural Resources**
- Acquisition Cost and Depletion
- Capital Assets Used in Extracting Resources

Section 3—Intangible Assets

▶ **Intangible Assets**
- Accounting for Intangible Assets
- Patents
- Copyrights
- Leaseholds
- Leasehold Improvements
- Goodwill
- Trademarks and Trade Names

▶ **Cash Flow Impacts of capital Assets**

▶ **Using the Information—Total Asset Turnover**

Bug Killer

Calgary, AB—Jenna Lee doesn't fancy herself a consumer crusader. "I'm no Ralph Nader," she says bluntly. But when the 19-year-old Calgary student stumbled upon a serious glitch in the amortization calculation in *PCaccount*, an accounting package for PCs, she complained to the program' s developer, **Intech.** When the company rudely brushed her off, she got angry enough to take her story to the *Alberta Chronicle*—a phone call that helped ignite a national firestorm of controversy.

Shortly after the *Chronicle's* August 1 exposé, a "deeply distressed" Samuel Carter, Intech's president, confessed that his company's line of accounting software contained a "few bugs" in its amortization schedules producing inaccurate calculations. With customers already surly over problems with Intech's customer-service lines, Carter moved quickly. He offered to replace disks on request for Intech' s one million customers.

The errors are no small problem—particularly to consumers who already used these amortization programs to prepare their financial or tax reports. Management experts say Intech's aggressive response to the problems helped defuse a potential disaster. "The public loves a confessed sinner," notes Sherry Williams of **Consumer Research.** Along with the replacement offer, Carter penned an apology in a letter to the product's

registered users: "We really let our customers down," he wrote. So far, Carter's willingness to publicly swallow a serving of humble pie appears to be working.

Not everyone is content, though. Even an apologetic telephone call from Intech's president and the offer of a replacement disk haven't managed to mollify Ms. Lee. "It shakes my faith in the whole industry," she says. "Next time, I'm doing my own amortization calculations!"

Learning Objectives

LO 1 Describe capital assets and issues in accounting for them.

LO 2 Apply the cost principle to compute the cost of capital assets.

LO 3 Explain amortization and the factors affecting its computation.

LO 4 Compute and record amortization using the methods of straight-line, units-of-production, and declining-balance.

LO 5 Compare and analyze amortization for different methods.

LO 6 Explain amortization for partial years and when estimates change.

LO 7 Distinguish between revenue and capital expenditures, and account for these expenditures.

LO 8 Account for asset disposal through discarding, selling, or exchanging an asset.

LO 9 Account for natural resources and their depletion.

LO 10 Account for intangible assets and their amortization.

LO 11 Identify cash flow impacts of capital asset transactions.

LO 12 Compute total asset turnover and apply it to analyze a company's use of assets.

CHAPTER PREVIEW

This chapter focuses on capital (long-term) assets used in the operation of a company. These assets can be grouped into property, plant and equipment, natural resources, and intangible assets. Capital assets are a major investment for most companies. They make up a major part of assets on the balance sheet and often represent one of the largest expenses on the income statement. They also affect the statement of cash flows when cash is spent to acquire capital assets or received from the sale of them. When companies acquire or build capital assets, it is often referred to as a "capital expenditure." Capital expenditures are important news because they impact both the short- and long-term success of a company. Both natural resources and intangible assets have similar impacts. Because of this and other reasons it is important we understand accounting for long-term assets. This chapter will describe the financial impact of these asset purchases. We also explain what distinguishes these assets from other types of assets, how to determine their cost, how to allocate their costs to periods benefiting from their use, and how we dispose of long-term assets. This knowledge can help us avoid blind reliance on software that might yield errors as evidenced in the opening article.

SECTION 1—CAPITAL ASSETS: PROPERTY, PLANT, AND EQUIPMENT

Capital assets are tangible assets used in the operations of a company and have a useful life of more than one accounting period. Capital assets, or *fixed assets*, include *plant and equipment*, or *property, plant and equipment*, *natural resources*, and *intangible assets*. For many companies, capital assets make up the single largest asset it owns. Exhibit 12.1 shows capital assets as a percent of total assets for several companies. Not only do they make up a large percent of these companies' assets but their dollar values are huge. **Imperial Oil's** capital assets, for instance, are reported at more than $8 billion. Also, **Bombardier** and **Alcan Aluminium** report capital assets of more than $1 billion and $5 billion, respectively.

Capital assets are set apart from other assets by two important features. First, they are used in operations. This makes them different, for instance, from *inventory* that is held for sale and not used in operations. The distinctive feature here is use and not type of asset. A company that purchases a computer for the purpose of selling it, reports it on the balance sheet as inventory. But if the same company purchases the same computer for use in operations, it is a capital asset. Another case

Exhibit 12.1

Capital Assets as Percent of Total Assets

is that of *long-term investments* such as land held for future expansion. If this same land holds a factory used in operations, the land is part of capital assets. Still another case is *equipment* held for use in event of a breakdown or for use in peak periods of production. This equipment is reported in capital assets. But if this same equipment is removed from use and held for sale it is not reported in capital assets.

A second important feature is that capital assets have useful lives extending over more than one accounting period. This makes capital assets different from *current assets* such as *supplies* that are usually consumed in a short time after they are placed in use. The cost of current assets is assigned to the single period when they are used. Many *prepaid expenses* are distinguished from capital assets based on the length of their useful lives.

The accounting for capital assets reflects these two important features. Since capital assets are used in operations, we try to match their costs against the revenue they generate. Also, since capital assets' useful lives extend over more than one period, our matching of costs and revenues must extend over several periods. We must measure capital assets (balance sheet focus) and allocate their cost to periods benefiting from their use (income statement focus).

Exhibit 12.2 shows the four main accounting issues with capital assets. They are:
1. Compute the costs of capital assets.
2. Allocate costs of capital assets against revenues for the periods they benefit.
3. Account for expenditures such as repairs and improvements to capital assets.
4. Record the disposal of capital assets.

LO1 Describe capital assets and issues in accounting for them.

Exhibit 12.2

Issues in Accounting for Capital Assets

This chapter focuses on the decisions and factors surrounding these four important issues.

Cost of Capital Assets

Capital assets are recorded at cost when purchased. This is consistent with the *cost principle*. **Cost** includes all normal and reasonable expenditures necessary to get the asset in place and ready for its intended use. The cost of a factory machine, for instance, includes its invoice price, less any cash discount for early payment, plus freight, unpacking, and assembling costs. The cost of a capital asset also includes the necessary costs of installing and testing a machine before placing it in use. Examples are the costs of building a base or foundation for a machine, of providing electrical hook-ups, and of adjusting the machine before using it in operations.

An expenditure must be normal, reasonable, and necessary in preparing an asset for its intended use to be charged to and reported as part of the cost of a capital asset. If a machine is damaged during unpacking, the repairs are not added to its cost. Instead, they are charged to an expense account. Also, a traffic fine paid for moving heavy machinery on city streets without a proper permit is not part of the machinery's cost. But payment for a proper permit is included in the

LO2 Apply the cost principle to compute the cost of capital assets.

cost of machinery. Charges in addition to the purchase price are sometimes incurred to modify or customize a new capital asset or to bring a used asset up to specifications. These charges are added to the asset's cost. We explain how to determine the cost of capital assets in the remainder of this section for each of the four major classes of capital assets.

Land

When land is purchased for a building site, its cost includes the total amount paid for the land, including any real estate commissions. Its cost also includes fees for insuring the title, legal fees, and any accrued property taxes paid by the purchaser. Payments for surveying, clearing, grading, draining and landscaping also are included in the cost of land. Other costs of land include assessments by the local government, whether incurred at the time of purchase or later, for items such as roadways, sewers and sidewalks. These assessments are included because they "permanently" add to the land's value.

Land purchased as a building site sometimes includes a building that must be removed. In such cases, the total purchase price is charged to the Land account. But the cost of removing the building, less any amounts recovered through sale of salvaged materials, is also added to the Land account. To illustrate, assume a company bought land for a retail store for cash of $167,000. This land contains an old service garage that is removed at a net cost of $13,000 ($15,000 in costs less $2,000 proceeds from salvaged materials). Additional closing costs totalled $10,000, consisting of brokerage fees ($8,000), legal fees ($1,500), and title costs ($500). The cost of this land is $190,000 and is computed as shown in Exhibit 12.3.

Exhibit 12.3

Computing Cost of Land

Net cash price of land	$167,000
Net cost of garage removal	13,000
Closing costs	10,000
Cost of Land	$190,000

Land Improvements

Because land has an unlimited life and is not consumed when it is used, it is not subject to amortization. But **land improvements** such as parking lot surfaces, driveways, fences, and lighting systems have limited useful lives. While these costs increase the usefulness of the land, they are charged to a separate Land Improvement account so their costs can be allocated to the periods they benefit.

Buildings

A Building account is charged for the costs of purchasing or constructing a building when it is used in operations. When purchased, the costs of a building usually include its purchase price, brokerage fees, taxes, title fees, and attorney costs. Its costs also include all expenditures to make it ready for its intended use. This includes any necessary repairs or renovations to prepare the building for use such as wiring, lighting, flooring and wall coverings.

When a building, or any capital asset, is constructed by a company for its own use, its cost includes materials and labour plus a reasonable amount of indirect overhead cost. Overhead includes the costs of heat, lighting, power, and amortization on machinery used to construct the asset. Cost of construction also includes design fees, building permits, and insurance during construction. But insurance costs for coverage after the asset is placed in use are an operating expense. **Alcan Aluminium,** for instance, recently reported plans in its 1997 annual report to construct capital assets for its own use.

...the Company announced it was proceeding with the construction of a 375,000-tonne smelter at Alma, Quebec. Total cost is estimated at $1,600 [million], most of which will be incurred over the next three years. Approximately $220 [million] is expected to be spent in 1998.

Machinery and Equipment

The cost of machinery and equipment consists of all costs normal and necessary to purchase them and prepare them for their intended use. It includes the purchase price, less discounts, and plus taxes, transportation charges, insurance while in transit, and the installing, assembling and testing of machinery and equipment. **Sony**, for instance, disclosed in a recent annual report that:

capital expenditures [much of this machinery and equipment] during the year under review increased 27.9% to ... $2,817 million ... Sony intends to further increase its capital expenditures.

Lump-Sum Asset Purchase

Capital assets often are purchased in a group with a single transaction for a lump-sum price. This transaction is called a *lump-sum purchase*, also called group or basket purchase. When this occurs, we allocate the cost of the purchase among the different types of assets acquired based on their *relative market values*. Their market values can be estimated by appraisal or by using the tax-assessed valuations of the assets. To illustrate, Cola Company, paid $90,000 cash to acquire land appraised at $30,000, land improvements appraised at $10,000, and a building appraised at $60,000. The $90,000 cost was allocated on the basis of appraised values as shown in Exhibit 12.4.

	Appraised Value	Percent of Total		Apportioned Cost	
Land	$ 30,000	30%	($30,000/$100,000)	$27,000	($90,000×30%)
Land improvements . .	10,000	10	($10,000/$100,000)	9,000	($90,000×10%)
Building	60,000	60	($60,000/$100,000)	54,000	($90,000×60%)
Totals	$100,000	100%		$90,000	

Exhibit 12.4

Computing Costs in a Lump-Sum Purchase

Flashback

1. Identify the asset category for each of the following: (a) office supplies, (b) office equipment, (c) merchandise, (d) land held for future expansion, (e) trucks used in operations.

2. Identify the account charged for each of the following expenditures: (a) purchase price of a vacant lot, (b) cost of paving that vacant lot.

3. What amount is recorded as the cost of a new machine given the following items related to its purchase: gross purchase price, $700,000; sales tax, $49,000; purchase discount taken, $21,000; freight to move machine to plant, $3,500; assembly costs, $3,000; cost of foundation for machine, $2,500; cost of spare parts used in maintaining the machine, $4,200?

Answers—p. 592

Amortization

LO3 Explain amortization and the factors affecting its computation.

We explained in the prior section how capital assets are purchased for use in operations for more than one period. It is helpful to think of a capital asset as an amount of "usefulness" contributing to the operations of a company throughout the asset's useful life. Because the lives of all capital assets other than land are limited, the amount of usefulness expires as an asset is used. This expiration of a capital asset's amount of usefulness is called amortization. **Amortization** is the process of allocating the cost of a capital asset to expense in the accounting period benefiting from its use, which is required by the matching principle. That is, a portion of the cost of the asset is matched against the revenue it helps to generate.

The term *amortization* is the general term used for many situations where amounts are allocated to different accounts over varying lengths of time. When the Accounting Standards Board revised and reissued the standard on capital assets (Section 3060),[1] they said that the cost of capital assets should be amortized over their useful lives in a rational and systematic manner. In practice, the term **depreciation** still tends to be used for plant assets such as machinery and buildings, and the term *depletion* still tends to be used for natural resources. Amortization continues to be used for intangible assets and other items such as premium or discount on long-term debt. *We will continue to use the terms depreciation and depletion from time to time. Remember that they are terms that are specialized names for amortization.*

When a company buys a delivery truck for use as a capital asset, for instance, it acquires an amount of usefulness in the sense that it obtains a quantity of transportation. The total cost of this transportation is the cost of the truck less the expected proceeds to be received when the truck is sold or traded in at the end of its useful life. This net cost is allocated to the accounting periods that benefit from the truck's use. This allocation of the truck's cost is amortization.

Note that amortization does not measure the decline in the truck's market value each period. Nor does it measure the physical deterioration of the truck each period. Amortization is a process of allocating a capital asset's cost to expense over its useful life, nothing more. Because amortization reflects the cost of using a capital asset, we do not begin recording amortization charges until the asset is actually put into use providing services or producing products. This section describes the factors we need in computing amortization, the amortization methods used, revisions in amortization, and amortization for partial periods.

Factors in Computing Amortization

Three factors are relevant in determining amortization. They are (1) cost, (2) salvage value, and (3) useful life.

Cost

The cost of a capital asset consists of all necessary and reasonable expenditures to acquire it and to prepare the asset for its intended use. We described the computation of cost earlier in this chapter.

Salvage Value

The total amount of amortization charged off over an asset's benefit period equals the asset's cost minus its estimated salvage value. **Salvage value**, also called *residual value* or *scrap value*, is an estimate of the asset's value at the end of its benefit period. This is often viewed as the amount we expect to receive from selling the asset at the end of its benefit period. If we expect an asset to be traded in on a new asset, its salvage value is the expected trade-in value.

---

[1] *CICA Handbook*, section 3060, "Capital Assets," par. .31.

Useful (Service) Life

The **useful life** of a capital asset is the length of time it is productively used in a company's operations. Useful life, also called *service life*, is not necessarily as long as the asset's total productive life. As an example, the productive life of a computer is often four to eight years or more. Yet some companies trade in old computers for new ones every two years. In this case, these computers have a two-year useful life. This means the cost of these computers (less their expected trade-in value) is charged to amortization expense over a two-year period.

Several variables often make the useful life of a capital asset hard to predict. A major variable is the wear and tear from use in operations. But two other variables, inadequacy and obsolescence, also demand consideration. When a company grows more rapidly than expected, its assets sometimes do not meet the company's productive demands. **Inadequacy** refers to the condition where the capacity of a company's capital assets is too small to meet the company's productive demands. Obsolescence, like inadequacy, is hard to predict because the timing of new inventions and improvements normally can't be predicted. **Obsolescence** refers to a condition where, because of new inventions and improvements, a capital asset is no longer useful in producing goods or services. A company usually disposes of an obsolete asset before it wears out.

A company is often able to better predict the useful life of a new asset based on its past experience with a similar asset. When it has no experience with a type of asset, a company relies on the experience of others or on engineering studies and judgment. In note 1 of its 1996 annual report, **Call-Net Enterprises** reported the following useful lives:

Depreciation and amortization are being provided based on the estimated useful lives of the assets on a straight-line basis as follows:

Buildings	40 years
Fibre optic cable and equipment	20 years
Multiplex and telephone switch equipment . . .	10 years
Computer equipment and software	3 to 5 years
Furniture and fixtures	5 years
Leasehold improvements	term of the lease
Equipment under capital lease	term of lease, not exceeding estimated useful life

Life Expectancy

The life expectancy of capital assets is often in the eye of the beholder. Take **Imperial Oil** and **Suncor Energy,** for instance. Both compete in the oil industry, yet their refineries' life expectancies are quite different. Imperial amortizes its refineries over 25 years, but Suncor amortizes its refineries over an average of 32 years. Such differences can dramatically impact their financial statement numbers. [Source: *Imperial Oil Annual Report,* 1997; *Suncor Energy Annual Report,* 1997.]

Did You Know?

Amortization Methods

There are many *amortization methods* for allocating a capital asset's cost over the accounting periods in its useful life. The most frequently used method of amortization is the straight-line method. Another common amortization method is the units-of-production method. We explain these two methods in this section.

LO4 Compute and record amortization using the methods of straight-line, units-of-production, and declining-balance.

We also describe accelerated amortization methods, with an emphasis on the declining-balance method.

The computations in this section use information from an athletic shoe manufacturer. In particular, we look at a machine used for inspecting athletic shoes before packaging. This machine is used by manufacturers such as **Converse, Reebok, Adidas** and **L.A.Gear,** and its data for amortization are shown in Exhibit 12.5.

Exhibit 12.5

Data for Athletic Shoe Testing Machine

Cost	$10,000
Salvage value	1,000
Amortizable cost	$ 9,000
Useful life:	
Accounting periods . .	5 years
Units inspected	36,000 shoes

Straight-Line Method

Straight-line amortization (or depreciation) charges the same amount to expense for each period of the asset's useful life. A two-step process is used to compute expense. We first compute the *amortizable cost* over the asset's life; this amount is also called the *cost to be amortized (or depreciated).* It is computed by subtracting the asset's salvage value from its total cost. Second, amortizable cost is divided by the number of accounting periods in the asset's useful life.

The formula and computation for straight-line amortization of the inspection equipment described above is shown in Exhibit 12.6.

Exhibit 12.6

Straight-Line Amortization Formula

$$\frac{\text{Cost} - \text{Salvage value}}{\text{Useful life in years}} = \frac{\$10,000 - \$1,000}{5 \text{ years}} = \$1,800 \text{ per year}$$

If this equipment is purchased on December 31, 1998, and used throughout its predicted useful life of five years, the straight-line method allocates an equal amount of amortization to each of the years 1999 through 2003. We make the following adjusting entry at the end of each of these five years to record straight-line amortization of this equipment:

Assets = Liabilities + Equity
− 1,800   − 1,800

Dec. 31	Amortization Expense	1,800	
	Accumulated Amortization, Equipment		1,800
	To record annual amortization over its five-year useful life.		

The $1,800 Amortization Expense appears on the income statement in operating expenses. This entry uses the common practice of crediting Accumulated Amortization, a contra account, to the Equipment account in the balance sheet.

The graph on the left in Exhibit 12.7 shows the $1,800 per year expense amount reported each of these five years. The graph on the right shows the amounts reported on each of the six December 31 balance sheets while the company owns the asset. The net balance sheet amount is the asset's **book value** for each of those years and is computed as the asset's original cost less its accumulated amortization. At the end of year two, its book value is $6,400 and is reported in the balance sheet as:

Equipment	$10,000	
Less accumulated amortization . . .	3,600	$6,400

Note the book value declines by $1,800 of amortization each year. From these graphs we can see why this method is called straight-line.

We can also compute a straight-line amortization rate, computed as 100% divided by the number of periods in the asset's useful life. In the case of our machine, this rate is 20% (100% ÷ 5 years). We use this rate and other information on this machine to compute its *straight-line amortization schedule* shown in Exhibit 12.8.

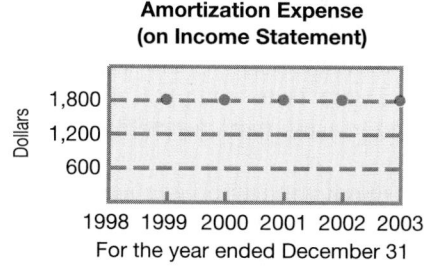

Amortization Expense
(on Income Statement)

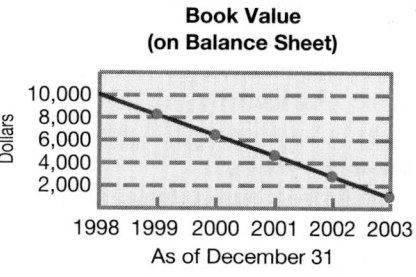

Book Value
(on Balance Sheet)

Exhibit 12.7

Financial Statement Effects
of Straight-Line Amortization

| Period | Amortization for the Period | | | End of Period | |
	Amortizable Cost	Amortization Rate	Amortization Expense	Accumulated Amortization	Book Value
1998	—	—	—	—	$10,000
1999	$9,000*	20%	$1,800	$1,800	8,200
2000	9,000	20	1,800	3,600	6,400
2001	9,000	20	1,800	5,400	4,600
2002	9,000	20	1,800	7,200	2,800
2003	9,000	20	1,800	9,000	1,000

Exhibit 12.8

Straight-Line Amortization
Schedule

*$10,000 − $1,000.

Note three items in this schedule. First, amortization expense is the same each period. Second, accumulated amortization is the sum of current and prior periods' amortization expense. Third, book value declines each period until it equals salvage value at the end of its useful life.

Straight-line is by far the most frequently applied amortization method in financial reporting. **Bombardier,** for instance, discloses its amortization method in its 1997 annual report as follows:

> Depreciation is computed under the straight-line method over the...estimated useful lives.

Units-of-Production Method

While many companies use straight-line amortization, other methods are common in certain industries. The main purpose of recording amortization is to provide relevant information about the cost of consuming an asset's usefulness. This means that in each accounting period an asset is used it is charged with a share of its cost. The straight-line method charges an equal share to each period. If capital assets are used about the same amount in each accounting period, this method produces a reasonable matching of expenses with revenues. Yet the use of some capital assets varies greatly from one accounting period to the next. A builder, for instance, may use a piece of construction equipment for a month and then not use it again for several months.

When use of equipment varies from period to period, the units-of-production amortization method can provide a better matching of expenses with revenues than straight-line amortization. **Units-of-production amortization** charges a varying amount to expense for each period of an asset's useful life depending on its usage.

A two-step process is used to compute units-of-production amortization. We first compute the *amortization per unit*. It is computed by subtracting the asset's salvage value from its total cost, and dividing by the total number of units expected to be produced during its useful life. Units of production can be expressed in units of product or in any other unit of measure such as hours used or distance driven. This gives us the amount of amortization per unit of service provided by the asset. The second step is to compute amortization expense for the period by multiplying the units used in the period by the amortization per unit.

The formula and computation for units-of-production amortization for the testing machine described above (note, we expect 7,000 shoes inspected in its first year) are shown in Exhibit 12.9.

Exhibit 12.9

Units-of-Production
Amortization Formula

Step 1:

$$\text{Amortization per unit} = \frac{\text{Cost} - \text{Salvage value}}{\text{Total units of production}} = \frac{\$10,000 - \$1,000}{36,000 \text{ units}} = \$0.25 \text{ per shoe}$$

Step 2:

$$\text{Amortization expense} = \text{Amortization per unit} \times \text{Units used in period}$$
$$0.25 \text{ per shoe} \quad \times \quad 7,000 \text{ shoes} \quad = \$1,750$$

Using the production estimates for the machine we compute the *units-of-production amortization schedule* shown in Exhibit 12.10. If the machine inspects 7,000 shoes in its first year, amortization for that first year is $1,750 (7,000 shoes at $0.25 per shoe). If the machine inspects 8,000 shoes in the second year, amortization for the second year is 8,000 shoes times $0.25 per shoe, or $2,000.

Exhibit 12.10

Units-of-Production
Amortization Schedule

| Period | Amortization for the Period | | | End of Period | |
	Number of Units	Amortization per Unit	Amortization Expense	Accumulated Amortization	Book Value
1998	—	—	—	—	$10,000
1999	7,000	$0.25	$1,750	$1,750	8,250
2000	8,000	0.25	2,000	3,750	6,250
2001	9,000	0.25	2,250	6,000	4,000
2002	7,000	0.25	1,750	7,750	2,250
2003	5,000	0.25	1,250	9,000	1,000

Note that amortization expense depends on unit output, accumulated amortization is the sum of current and prior periods' amortization expense, and book value declines each period until it equals salvage value at the end of its useful life.

Units-of-production amortization method is not as frequently applied as straight-line. **Imperial Oil,** for instance, is one company using it and reports the following in its 1996 annual report:

Depreciation and depletion are calculated using the unit-of-production method for producing properties.

Declining-Balance Method

This section describes an accelerated amortization method. An **accelerated amortization method** yields larger amortization expenses in the early years of an asset's life and smaller charges in later years. While there are several accelerated methods used in financial reporting, the most common is the declining-balance method. The **declining-balance** method of amortization uses an amortization rate of up to twice the straight-line rate and applies it to the asset's beginning-of-period book value. Because book value *declines* each period, the amount of amortization also declines each period.

A common amortization rate is twice the straight-line rate. This method is called *double-declining-balance* method. The double-declining-balance method is applied as follows: (1) compute the asset's straight-line amortization rate; (2) double it; and (3) compute amortization expense by applying this rate to the asset's beginning-of-period book value. Note salvage value is *not* used in these computations.

Let's return to the athletic shoe testing machine and apply the double-declining-balance method to compute its amortization expense. Exhibit 12.11 shows this formula and its first year computation for the testing machine. The three-step process is: (1) divide 100% by five years to determine the straight-line annual amortization rate of 20% per year, (2) double this 20% rate to get a declining-balance rate of 40% per year, and (3) compute annual amortization expense as shown in Exhibit 12.11.

 Exhibit 12.11

Double-Declining-Balance Amortization Formula

Step 1:

$$\text{Straight-line amortization rate} = 100\% \div \text{Useful life in periods} = 100\% \div 5 \text{ years} = 20\%$$

Step 2:

$$\text{Double-declining-balance rate} = 2 \times \text{Straight-line rate} = 2 \times 20\% = 40\%$$

Step 3:

$$\text{Amortization expense} = \text{Double-declining-balance rate} \times \text{Beginning period book value}$$

$$40\% \times \$10,000 = \$4,000$$

The *double-declining-balance amortization schedule* is shown in Exhibit 12.12. Note in year 2003, amortization expense is $296. This is not equal to 40% × $1,296, or $518.40. Instead, the $296 is computed by subtracting the $1,000 salvage value from the $1,296 book value at the beginning of the fifth year. This is done because an asset should not be amortized below its salvage value. If we had used the $518.40 for amortization expense in 2003, then ending book value would equal $777.60, which is less than the $1,000 salvage value.

Exhibit 12.12

Double-Declining-Balance Amortization Schedule

| | Amortization for the Period | | | End of Period | |
Period	Beginning-of-Period Book Value	Amortization Rate	Amortization Expense	Accumulated Amortization	Book Value
1998	—	—	—	—	$10,000
1999	$10,000*	40%	$4,000	$4,000	6,000
2000	6,000	40	2,400	6,400	3,600
2001	3,600	40	1,440	7,840	2,160
2002	2,160	40	864	8,704	1,296
2003	1,296	40	296*	9,000	1,000

*Year 2003 amortization is $1,296 − $1,000 = $296. This is because book value can't be less than salvage value.

Comparing Amortization Methods

Exhibit 12.13 shows the amortization expense for the athletic shoe testing machine under each of the three amortization methods.

LO 5 Compare and analyze amortization for different methods.

Exhibit 12.13

Amortization Methods
Compared

Period	Straight-Line	Units-of-Production	Double-Declining Balance
1999	$1,800	$1,750	$4,000
2000	1,800	2,000	2,400
2001	1,800	2,250	1,440
2002	1,800	1,750	864
2003	1,800	1,250	296
	$9,000	$9,000	$9,000

Note that while the amount of amortization expense per period is different for different methods, total amortization expense is the same for the machine's useful life. This is to say each method starts with a total cost of $10,000 and ends with a salvage value of $1,000. The difference is the pattern in amortization expense over the useful life. In this regard, note the book value of the asset when using straight-line is always greater than when using double-declining-balance, except at the beginning and end of an asset's useful life. Also, note the straight-line method yields a steady pattern of amortization expense, while the units-of-production does not because it depends on the number of units produced. But each of these methods is acceptable as they allocate cost in a rational and systematic manner.[2] The method chosen should be the one which provides the best matching of expenses to revenue.

Did You Know?

What's Hot in Amortization
A recent survey suggests 90% of companies use straight-line amortization for their capital assets, 7% use declining-balance, and 2% use units-of-production. [Source: *Financial Reporting in Canada*, 1997.]

Amortization for Income Tax Reporting

The rules a company follows for financial accounting purposes are usually different from the rules it follows for tax accounting purposes. Remember that financial accounting aims to report useful information on financial performance and position. Tax accounting reflects government objectives in raising revenues. Differences between these two accounting systems are normal and expected. Amortization is a common example.

The Income Tax Act requires that companies use a declining-balance method for calculating the maximum **capital cost allowance** (amortization or depreciation for tax purposes) that may be claimed in any period. This is because it reduces taxable income with higher amortization expense in the early years of an asset's life. But taxable income is higher in the later years. The government's goal here is to decrease taxes in the early years to encourage capital investment. This means a company can use these resources now to earn additional profit through lower taxes. The act specifies the rates for various classes of assets. For example, a rate of 20% would be used for general machinery and equipment, and a rate of 4% for most buildings. Further discussion of the details of tax accounting for capital assets is deferred to a more advanced course.

---

[2] Ibid.

AmortizationTech

Computer technology greatly simplifies amortization computations and revisions. There are many inexpensive, off-the-shelf software packages and business calculators that allow a user to choose from a variety of amortization methods for each asset entered. Detailed amortization schedules for both financial reporting and income tax reporting are quickly and accurately generated.

Partial Year Amortization

Capital assets are purchased and disposed of at various times during a period. When an asset is purchased (or disposed of) at a time other than the beginning or end of an accounting period, amortization is recorded for part of a year. This is so the year of purchase or the year of disposal is charged with its share of the asset's amortization.

LO 6 Explain amortization for partial years and when estimates change.

To illustrate let's return to the athletic shoe testing machine. *Assume this machine is purchased and placed in service on October 8, 1999*, and the annual accounting period ends on December 31. Recall this machine costs $10,000, has a useful life of five years, and a salvage value of $1,000. Because this machine is purchased and used for nearly three months in 1999, the annual income statement should report amortization expense on the machine for that part of the year. The amount of amortization reported usually is based on the assumption that an asset is purchased on the first of the month nearest the actual date of purchase. In this case, since the purchase occurred on October 8, we assume an October 1 purchase date. This means three months' amortization is recorded in 1999. If the purchase occurred anytime between October 16 through November 15, amortization is computed as if the purchase is on November 1. Using straight-line amortization, we compute three months' amortization of $450 as follows:

$$\frac{\$10,000 - \$1,000}{5 \text{ years}} = \$1,800 \times \frac{3}{12} = \$450$$

A similar computation is necessary when disposal of an asset occurs during a year. As an example, let's suppose the machine described above is sold on June 24, 2004. Amortization is recorded for the period January 1 through June 24 when it is disposed of. This partial year's amortization, computed to the nearest whole month, is:

$$\frac{\$10,000 - \$1,000}{5 \text{ years}} = \$1,800 \times \frac{6}{12} = \$900$$

Revising Amortization Rates

Because amortization is based on predictions of salvage value and useful life, amortization expense is an estimate. During the useful life of an asset, new information may indicate the original predictions are inaccurate. If our estimate of an asset's useful life and/or salvage value changes, what should we do? The answer is to use the new estimate of the remaining useful life to compute amortization for current and future periods. This means we revise amortization expense computation by spreading the remaining cost to be amortized over the revised useful life remaining. This approach is used for all amortization methods.

Let's return to our athletic shoe testing machine using straight-line amortization. At the beginning of this asset's third year, its book value is $6,400, computed as:

Cost	$10,000
Less two year's accumulated amortization . .	3,600
Book value	$ 6,400

At the beginning of its third year, we suppose the predicted number of years remaining in its useful life changes from three to four years *and* its estimate of salvage value changes to $400. Amortization for each of the machine's four remaining years is computed as shown in Exhibit 12.14.

Exhibit 12.14

Computing Revised Amortization Rates

$$\frac{\textbf{Book value} - \textbf{Revised salvage value}}{\textbf{Revised remaining useful life}} = \frac{\$6,400 - \$400}{4 \text{ years}} = \$1,500 \text{ per year}$$

This means $1,500 of amortization expense is recorded for the machine at the end of the third through sixth years of its remaining useful life.

Note this asset was amortized at the rate of $1,800 per year for the first two years. It is tempting to conclude that amortization expense is overstated in these first two years. But these expenses reflected the best information available at that time. Therefore we do not go back and restate past years' financial statements in light of this new information. Instead we adjust the current and future periods' statements to reflect this new information.

Revising estimates of the useful life or salvage value of a capital asset is referred to as a **change in an accounting estimate**. A change in an accounting estimate results from "the exercise of judgement and reappraisal as new events occur, as more experience is acquired, or as additional information is obtained."[3] Such a change in an accounting estimate is reflected in future financial statements, and does not result in changes in past statements.[4]

Flash back

4. On January 1, 1999, a company pays $77,000 to purchase office furniture with a zero salvage value. The furniture's useful life is somewhere between 7 to 10 years. What is the 1999 straight-line amortization on the furniture using a (a) 7-year useful life and (b) 10-year useful life?

Answer—p. 592

Reporting Amortization on Assets

Both the cost and accumulated amortization of capital assets are reported on the balance sheet. **Semi-Tech Corporation,** for instance, reports the following in its balance sheet:

($ in millions)	1997	1996
Property, plant and equipment:		
Land	$217	$172
Buildings	208	200
Machinery	333	309
Construction in Progress	6	9
	$764	$690
Less accumulated amortization	(280)	(251)
Total	$484	$439

---

[3] *CICA Handbook*, section 1506, "Accounting Changes," par. .22

[4] Ibid. par. .25

Many companies show capital assets on one line with the net amount of cost less accumulated amortization. When this is done the amount of accumulated amortization is disclosed in a note. Note that Alliance reports only the net amount of its property and equipment in its balance sheet in Appendix I. To satisfy the *full-disclosure principle*,[5] Alliance also describes its amortization methods in note 1 and the individual amounts comprising capital assets in note 3.

Reporting both the cost and accumulated amortization of capital assets helps balance sheet readers compare the assets of different companies. For example, a company holding assets costing $50,000 and accumulated amortization of $40,000 is likely in a different situation from a company with new assets costing $10,000. While the net unamortized cost is the same in both cases, the first company may have more productive capacity available but likely is facing the need to replace older assets. These insights are not provided if the two balance sheets report only the $10,000 book values.

We emphasize that amortization is a process of cost allocation. Capital assets are reported on a balance sheet at their remaining unamortized costs (book value), not at market values. This emphasis on costs rather than market values is based on the *going-concern principle* described in Chapter 2. This principle states that, unless there is evidence to the contrary, we assume a company continues in business. This implies that capital assets are held and used long enough to recover their cost through the sale of products and services. Since capital assets are not intended to be sold until they are no longer useful, their market values are not reported in the financial statements. Instead, assets are reported on a balance sheet at cost less accumulated amortization. This is the remaining portion of the cost that is expected to be recovered in future periods.

Accumulated amortization on a balance sheet does not reflect funds accumulated to buy new assets when the assets currently owned are replaced. Accumulated amortization is a contra account with a credit balance that can not buy anything. If a company has funds available to buy assets, the funds are shown on the balance sheet in liquid assets such as *Cash*.

Flashback

5. What is the meaning of the term *amortization* in accounting?

6. A company purchases a new machine for $96,000 on January 1, 1999. Its predicted useful life is five years or 100,000 units of product, and its salvage value is $8,000. During 1999, 10,000 units of product are produced. Compute the book value of this machine on December 31, 1999, assuming (a) straight-line amortization and (b) units-of-production amortization.

7. In early January 1999, a company acquires equipment at a cost of $3,800. The company estimates this equipment to have a useful life of three years and a salvage value of $200. Early in 2001, the company changes its estimate to a total four-year useful life and zero salvage value. Using straight-line amortization, what is amortization expense on this equipment for the year ended 2001?

Answers—p. 592

---

[5] *CICA Handbook*, section 3060, "Capital Assets," par. .58.

Judgment and Ethics

Controller
You are the controller for Fascar Company. Fascar has struggled financially for more than two years, and there are no signs of improvement. Fascar's operations require major investments in equipment, and amortization is a large item in computing income. Fascar's industry normally requires frequent replacements of equipment, and equipment is typically amortized over three years. Your company's president recently instructed you to revise estimated useful lives of equipment from three to six years and to use a six-year life on all new equipment. You suspect this instruction is motivated by a desire to improve reported income. What actions do you take?

Answer—p. 591

Mid-Chapter Demonstration Problem

Gemini Fitness Club used straight-line amortization for a machine that cost $43,500, under the assumption it would have a four-year life and a $4,500 trade-in value. After two years, Gemini determined that the machine still had three more years of remaining useful life, after which it would have an estimated $3,600 trade-in value. (a) Calculate the machine's book value at the end of its second year. (b) Calculate the amount of amortization to be charged during each of the remaining years in the machine's revised useful life.

Solution to Mid-Chapter Demonstration Problem

a.	Original cost of machine	$ 43,500
	Less two years' accumulated amortization	
	[($43,500 − $4,500)/4] × 2	(19,500)
	Book value at end of second year	$ 24,000

b.	Book value at end of second year	$ 24,000
	Less revised salvage value	(3,600)
	Remaining amortizable cost	$ 20,400
	Revised annual amortization to be charged = $20,400/3 =	$6,800

Revenue and Capital Expenditures

LO7 Distinguish between revenue and capital expenditures, and account for these expenditures.

When a capital asset is acquired and put into service, additional expenditures often are incurred after the acquisition to operate, maintain, repair and improve it. In recording these added expenditures, we must decide whether they are capitalized or expensed. To capitalize an expenditure is to debit the asset account. A main issue is whether more useful information is provided by reporting these expenditures as current expenses or by adding them to the capital asset's cost and amortizing them over its remaining useful life.

Revenue expenditures are additional costs of capital assets that do not materially increase the asset's life or productive capabilities. They are recorded as expenses and deducted from revenues in the current period's income statement. Examples of revenue expenditures, also called *income statement expenditures*, are supplies, fuel, lubricants and electric power. **Capital expenditures**, also called *balance sheet expenditures*, are additional costs of capital assets that provide material benefits extending beyond the current period. They are debited to asset accounts and reported on the balance sheet. Capital expenditures increase or improve the type or amount of service an asset provides. Examples are roofing replacement, plant expansion, and major overhauls of machinery and equipment.

Financial statements are affected for several years by the choice between recording costs as revenue expenditures or as capital expenditures. Managers must be careful in classifying them. This classification decision is helped by identifying costs as repairs, betterments, or low-cost asset purchases.

Repairs

Repairs are expenditures to keep the asset in normal, good operating condition. They are necessary if an asset is to perform to expectations over its useful life. Repairs do not extend an asset's useful life beyond its original estimate and do not increase its productivity beyond original expectations. Examples are costs of cleaning, lubricating, adjusting, and replacing (small) parts of a machine. Repairs are treated as *revenue expenditures*. This means their costs are reported as expenses on the current income statements. Consistent with this rule, **Air Canada** reports:

> Maintenance and repair costs are charged to operating expenses as incurred. Significant modification costs are capitalized and amortized over the remaining service lives of the assets.

Betterments

Betterments, also called *improvements*, are expenditures making a capital asset more efficient or productive. A betterment might increase the physical output or service capacity, lower operating costs, extend the useful life, or improve the quality of output. A betterment often involves adding a component to an asset or replacing one of its old components with a better component. However, a betterment does not always increase an asset's useful life. An example is replacing manual controls on a machine with automatic controls to reduce labour costs. This machine will still wear out just as fast as it would with manual controls.[6]

Because a betterment benefits future periods it is debited to the asset account as a capital expenditure. The new book value (less salvage) is amortized over the asset's remaining useful life. As an example, suppose a company pays $8,000 for a machine with an eight-year useful life and no salvage value. On January 2, after three years and $3,000 of amortization, it adds an automated system to the machine at a cost of $1,800. This results in reduced labour cost in operating the machine in future periods. The cost of this betterment is added to the Machinery account with this entry:

Jan. 2	Machinery	1,800	
	Cash		1,800
	To record installation of automated		
	control system.		

Assets = Liabilities + Equity
+ 1,800
− 1,800

After the betterment is added, the remaining cost to be amortized is $6,800, computed as $8,000 + $1,800 − $3,000. Amortization expense for the remaining five years is $1,360 per year, computed as $6,800/5 years as shown in Exhibit 12.15.

---

[6] One special type of betterment is an *addition*. Examples include a new wing to a factory or a new dock to a warehouse. All additions are capitalized.

Exhibit 12.15

Revised Amortization
Schedule from Betterments

	Before	Betterment	After
Original cost	$8,000	$1,800	$9,800
Accumulated amortization	(3,000)		(3,000)
Book value	$5,000		$6,800
Amortization in remaining years ($6,800/5 years) . .			$1,360

You Make the Call

Mechanic

You are a mechanic who recently opened your own auto service centre. Because of a cash shortage, you are preparing financial statements in the hope of getting a short-term loan from the bank. A friend of yours suggests you treat as many expenses as possible like capital expenditures. What are the impacts on financial statements of treating expenses as capital expenditures? What do you think is the aim of your friend's proposal?

Answer—p. 591

Low-Cost Asset Purchases

Maintaining individual capital asset records can be expensive, even in the most advanced system. For that reason many companies do not keep detailed records for assets costing less than some minimum amount such as $100. Instead, these low-cost capital assets are treated as a revenue expenditure. This means their costs are directly charged to an expense account at the time of purchase. This practice is acceptable under the *materiality principle*. Treating immaterial capital expenditures as revenue expenditures is unlikely to mislead users of financial statements. As an example, in its 1996 annual report **Coca-Cola** discloses that it only capitalizes *major* or material betterments:

> Additions and major replacements or betterments are added to the assets at cost. Maintenance and repair costs and minor replacements are charged to expense when incurred.

Flashback

8. At the beginning of the fifth year of a machine's estimated six-year useful life, the machine is overhauled and its estimated useful life is extended to nine years in total. This machine originally cost $108,000 and the overhaul cost is $12,000. Prepare the entry recording the cost of this overhaul.

9. Explain the difference between revenue expenditures and capital expenditures and how they are recorded.

10. What is a betterment? How is a betterment recorded?

Answers—p. 592

Disposals of Capital Assets

Capital assets are disposed of for several reasons. Many assets eventually wear out or become obsolete. Other assets are sold because of changing business plans. Sometimes an asset is discarded or sold because it is damaged by fire or accident. Regardless of the cause, disposals of capital assets occur in one of three ways: discarding, sale, or exchange. The accounting for each of these three types of disposals of capital assets is described in Exhibit 12.16.

 Account for asset disposal through discarding, selling, or exchanging an asset.

1. Record amortization expense up to the date of disposal. This updates the accumulated amortization account.
2. Remove the balances of the disposed asset and related accumulated amortization accounts.
3. Record any cash (and other assets) received or paid in the disposal.
4. Record any gain or loss resulting from comparing the asset's book value with the net amount received or paid at disposal.*

Exhibit 12.16

Accounting for Disposals of Capital Assets

*There is one exception to step 4 in the case of asset exchanges that we will describe later in this section.

Discarding Capital Assets

A capital asset is *discarded* when it is no longer useful to the company and it has no market value. To illustrate, assume a machine costing $9,000 with accumulated amortization of $9,000 is discarded on June 5. When accumulated amortization equals the asset's cost it is said to be fully amortized (zero book value). A *fully amortized* (or depreciated) asset does not usually yield a gain or loss on disposal. The entry to record the discarding of this asset is:

June 5	Accumulated Amortization, Machinery	9,000	
	Machinery		9,000
	To record the discarding of fully amortized machinery.		

Assets = Liabilities + Equity
+9,000
−9,000

Note this entry reflects all four steps of Exhibit 12.16. Step 1 is not needed since the machine is fully amortized. Step 2 is shown in the debit to Accumulated Amortization and credit to Machinery. Since no cash is involved, step 3 is irrelevant. Also, since book value is zero and no cash is involved, no gain or loss is recorded in step 4.

How do we account for discarding an asset that is not fully amortized? Or one whose amortization is not up to date? To answer this, consider equipment costing $8,000 with accumulated amortization of $6,000 on December 31 of the prior fiscal year-end. This equipment is being amortized using the straight-line method over eight years with zero salvage value. On July 1 it is discarded. Step 1 is to bring amortization expense up to date:

July 1	Amortization Expense	500	
	Accumulated Amortization, Equipment		500
	To record the first six months amortization ($1,000 × 6/12).		

Assets = Liabilities + Equity
−500   −500

The second and final entry reflects steps 2–4 of Exhibit 12.16.

July 1	Accumulated Amortization, Equipment	6,500	
	Loss on Disposal of Equipment	1,500	
	Equipment		8,000
	To record the discarding of machinery having a $1,500 book value.		

Assets = Liabilities + Equity
+6,500   −1,500
−8,000

The loss is computed by comparing the equipment's $1,500 ($8,000 − $6,000 − $500) book value with the zero net cash proceeds. The loss on disposal is reported in the Other Expenses and Losses section of the income statement. In some circumstances, an asset disposal might also yield a cash payment, such as a removal cost, instead of a receipt. Entries like those shown above are made in this case so that the income statement shows any gain or loss from disposal and the balance sheet reflects changes in the asset and accumulated amortization accounts.

Selling Capital Assets

To illustrate the accounting for selling capital assets we consider SportsWorld's April 1 sale of its delivery equipment costing $16,000 with accumulated amortization of $12,000 on December 31 of the prior fiscal year-end. Annual amortization on this equipment is $4,000 computed using straight-line amortization. The entry (step 1) to record amortization expense and update accumulated amortization to April 1 is:

Assets = Liabilities + Equity
−1,000   −1,000

April 1	Amortization Expense	1,000	
	Accumulated Amortization, Equipment		1,000
	To record the first three months amortization ($4,000 × 3/12).		

The second entry to reflect steps 2–4 of Exhibit 12.16 depends on the amount received in the sale. We consider three different possibilities.

Sale at Book Value

If SportsWorld receives $3,000 cash, an amount equal to the equipment's book value, there is no gain or loss on disposal. The entry is:

Assets = Liabilities + Equity
+3,000
+13,000
−16,000

April 1	Cash	3,000	
	Accumulated Amortization, Equipment	13,000	
	Equipment		16,000
	To record the sale of equipment for no gain or loss.		

Sale above Book Value

If SportsWorld receives $7,000 cash, an amount $4,000 above the equipment's book value, there is a gain on disposal. The entry is:

Assets = Liabilities + Equity
+7,000   +4,000
+13,000
−16,000

April 1	Cash	7,000	
	Accumulated Amortization, Equipment	13,000	
	Gain on Disposal of Equipment		4,000
	Equipment		16,000
	To record the sale of equipment for a $4,000 gain.		

Sale below Book Value

If SportsWorld receives $2,500 cash, an amount $500 below the equipment's book value, there is a loss on disposal. The entry is:

Assets = Liabilities + Equity
+2,500   −500
+13,000
−16,000

April 1	Cash	2,500	
	Loss on Disposal of Equipment	500	
	Accumulated Amortization, Equipment	13,000	
	Equipment		16,000
	To record the sale of equipment for a $500 loss.		

Companies at times restructure or downsize operations, which often involves selling capital assets. As part of its restructuring, **Woolworth** sold approximately 120 of its Woolco discount stores to Wal-Mart. Sale of its Woolco stores yielded a $168 million loss charged against revenues.

Exchanging Capital Assets

Many capital assets such as machinery, automobiles and office equipment are disposed of by exchanging them for new assets. In a typical exchange of capital assets, a trade-in allowance is received on the old asset and the balance is paid in cash. Accounting for the exchange of assets is similar to any other disposal with one exception depending on whether the old and the new assets are similar in the functions they perform. Trading an old truck for a new truck is an exchange of similar assets, whereas trading a truck for a machine is an exchange of dissimilar assets. The recognition of gains and losses on exchanging capital assets is shown in Exhibit 12.17.

Assets Exchanged	Losses Recognized	Gains Recognized
Dissimilar	Yes	Yes
Similar—Monetary	Yes	Yes
Similar—Nonmonetary	No	No

Exhibit 12.17

Gains and Losses on Capital Asset Exchanges

Note that gains and losses on dissimilar and monetary asset exchanges are recognized, but gains and losses are not generally recognized for similar, nonmonetary asset exchanges. The reason gains and losses from a similar asset exchange is not recognized is because the exchanged asset's earnings process is not considered complete. The decision to recognize a loss from a similar asset exchange is an application of *accounting conservatism*. This section explains the accounting for these cases.

Exchanging Dissimilar Assets

If a company exchanges a capital asset for another asset that is dissimilar in use or purpose, any gain or loss on the exchange is recorded. Any gain or loss is computed by comparing the book value of the asset given up with the fair market value of the asset received.

Receiving More in Exchange: A Gain

Let's assume a company exchanges both an old machine and $16,500 in cash for land. The old machine originally cost $18,000 and has accumulated amortization of $15,000 at the time of exchange. The land received has a fair market value of $21,000. Using the four steps outlined in Exhibit 12.16, the entry to record this exchange is:

Jan. 2	Land	21,000	
	Accumulated Amortization, Machinery	15,000	
	Machinery		18,000
	Cash		16,500
	Gain on Exchange of Assets		1,500
	To record exchange of old machine and cash for land.		

Assets = Liabilities + Equity
+21,000   +1,500
+15,000
−18,000
−16,500

We compute the gain on this transaction in the second column of Exhibit 12.18. Note the book value of the assets given totals $19,500. This includes the $16,500 cash and the $3,000 ($18,000 − $15,000) book value of the machine. This $19,500 book value of assets given is compared to the fair market value of the land received ($21,000). This yields a gain of $1,500 ($21,000 − $19,500).[7]

Exhibit 12.18

Computing Gain or Loss on Dissimilar Asset Exchanges

Dissimilar Plant Asset Exchange		Gain		Loss
Fair Market Value of Asset(s) Received			$21,000	$16,000
Book Value of Asset(s) Given:				
Machine	$ 3,000		$ 3,000	
Cash	16,500		16,500	
			19,500	19,500
Gain (Loss) on Exchange			$ 1,500	($ 3,500)

Receiving Less in Exchange: A Loss

Let's assume the same facts as in the exchange above except the land received has a fair market value of $16,000, not the $21,000 noted previously. The entry to record this exchange is:

Assets = Liabilities + Equity
+16,000   −3,500
+15,000
−18,000
−16,500

Jan. 2	Land	16,000	
	Loss on Exchange of Assets	3,500	
	Accumulated Amortization, Machinery	15,000	
	Machinery		18,000
	Cash		16,500
	To record exchange of old machine and cash for land.		

We compute the loss on this transaction in the third column of Exhibit 12.18. The $19,500 book value of assets given is compared to the fair market value of the land received ($16,000). This yields a loss of $3,500 ($16,000 − $19,500).

Exchanging Similar Assets—Monetary

In general, accounting for exchanges of similar assets depends on whether the amount of cash involved is more or less than 10% of the total consideration given up or received. If the amount of cash is more than 10%, the transaction is a monetary transaction and a gain or loss on the exchange is recorded in the same manner as for exchanges of dissimilar assets.

Receiving Less in Exchange: A Loss

Let's assume a company exchanges both old equipment and $33,000 in cash for new equipment. The old equipment originally cost $36,000 and has accumulated amortization of $20,000 at the time of exchange. The new equipment received has a fair market value of $42,000. This would be considered a monetary exchange because the cash involved is more than 10% of the value of the total consideration. These details are reflected in the middle column of Exhibit 12.19.

---

[7] We can also compute a gain or loss by comparing the machine's book value with the trade-in allowance for the machine. Since the fair market value of the land is $21,000 and the cash paid is $16,500, the trade-in allowance for the machine is $4,500. The difference between the machine's $3,000 book value and its $4,500 trade-in allowance gives us the $1,500 gain on exchange.

Similar Capital Asset Exchange		Loss		Gain
Fair Market Value of Asset(s) Received			$42,000	$52,000
Book Value of Asset(s) Given:				
Equipment	$16,000		$16,000	
Cash	33,000		33,000	
			49,000	49,000
Gain (Loss) on Exchange			($ 7,000)	$ 3,000

 Exhibit 12.19

Computing Gain or Loss on
Similar Asset Exchanges

The entry to record this similar, monetary, asset exchange is:

Jan. 3	Equipment (**new**)	42,000	
	Loss on Exchange of Similar Assets	7,000	
	Accumulated Amortization, Equipment	20,000	
	Equipment (**old**)		36,000
	Cash		33,000
	To record exchange of old equipment		
	and cash for new equipment.		

Assets = Liabilities + Equity
+42,000   −7,000
+20,000
−36,000
−33,000

Note the book value of the assets given totals $49,000. This includes the $33,000 cash and the $16,000 ($36,000 − $20,000) book value of the old equipment. This $49,000 book value of assets given is compared to the fair market value of the new equipment received ($42,000). This yields a loss of $7,000 ($42,000 − $49,000).

Receiving More in Exchange: A Gain

Let's assume the same facts as in the similar asset exchange above *except* the new equipment received has a fair market value of $52,000, not the $42,000 noted previously. The entry to record this exchange is:

Jan. 3	Equipment (**new**)	52,000	
	Accumulated Amortization, Equipment	20,000	
	Equipment (**old**)		36,000
	Cash		33,000
	Gain on Exchange of Similar Assets . .		3,000
	To record exchange of old equipment		
	and cash for new equipment.		

Assets = Liabilities + Equity
+52,000   +3,000
+20,000
−36,000
−33,000

We compute a gain on this transaction shown in the third column of Exhibit 12.19.

Exchanging Similar Assets—Nonmonetary

There are three possibilities when similar assets are exchanged and the amount of cash involved is less than 10% of the total consideration. First, no cash is paid or received and the assets are simply traded for each other. Second, a small amount of cash is paid. And third, a small amount of cash is received. In all three cases the asset received may not be recorded at an amount which is greater than its fair market value.

Case 1: No Cash Paid or Received

Let's assume a company exchanges its old equipment for new equipment and no cash is paid or received. This would be considered a nonmonetary exchange because the cash involved is less than 10% of the value of the total consideration. The old equipment originally cost $36,000 and has accumulated amortization of $20,000 at the time of exchange. The new equipment received has a fair market value of $19,000. In this case the new equipment is recorded at the net book value of the old equipment which is $16,000 ($36,000 − $20,000). These details are reflected in the second column of Exhibit 12.20.

The entry to record this exchange is:

Assets = Liabilities + Equity
+16,000
+20,000
−36,000

Jan. 3	Equipment (**new**)	16,000	
	Accumulated Amortization, Equipment	20,000	
	Equipment (**old**)		36,000
	To record exchange of old equipment for new equipment.		

Exhibit 12.20

Computing Gain or Loss on Similar Nonmonetary Asset Exchanges

Similar Capital Asset Exchange		Case 1	Case 2	Case 3
Cash Paid/Received		None	Cash Received	Cash Paid
Fair Market Value of				
Asset(s) Received		$19,000	$19,000	$19,000
Book Value of Asset(s) Given:				
Equipment	$16,000		$16,000	$16,000
Cash	Nil		(1,000)	1,000
		16,000	15,000	17,000
Gain (Loss) on Exchange		$ 3,000	$ 4,000	$ 2,000
Gain (Loss) Recorded		Nil	Nil	Nil

Case 2: $1,000 Cash Received

Let's assume the same company exchanges its same old equipment for new equipment and receives $1,000 in cash. This would be considered a nonmonetary exchange because the cash involved is less than 10% of the value of the total consideration. In this case the new equipment is recorded at the net book value of the old equipment less the cash received or $15,000 ($36,000 − $20,000 − $1,000). These details are reflected in the third column of Exhibit 12.20.

The entry to record this exchange is:

Assets = Liabilities + Equity
+1,000
+15,000
+20,000
−36,000

Jan. 3	Cash	1,000	
	Equipment (**new**)	15,000	
	Accumulated Amortization, Equipment	20,000	
	Equipment (**old**)		36,000
	To record exchange of old equipment for new equipment plus cash.		

Case 3: $1,000 Cash Paid

In this case the company exchanges its old equipment for new equipment and pays $1,000 in cash. This would still be considered a nonmonetary exchange because the cash involved is less than 10% of the value of the total consideration. The new equipment is recorded at the net book value of the old equipment plus the cash paid or $17,000 ($36,000 − $20,000 + $1,000). These details are reflected in the fourth column of Exhibit 12.20.

The entry to record this exchange is:

Assets = Liabilities + Equity
+17,000
+20,000
−36,000
−1,000

Jan. 3	Equipment (**new**)	17,000	
	Accumulated Amortization, Equipment	20,000	
	Equipment (**old**)		36,000
	Cash		1,000
	To record exchange of old equipment for new equipment and payment of cash.		

	Case 1	Case 2	Case 3
Cost of old equipment	$36,000	$36,000	$36,000
Less accumulated amortization	20,000	20,000	20,000
Book value of old equipment	16,000	16,000	16,000
Cash (received) paid	Nil	(1,000)	1,000
Cost recorded for new equipment	**$16,000**	**$15,000**	**$17,000**

Exhibit 12.21

Cost Basis of New Asset
When Gain Is Not
Recognized

The historical cost principle requires an asset be recorded at the cash or cash equivalent amount given in exchange. Referring to Exhibit 12.21, we see that the amounts recorded for the new equipment equal the historical cost book value of the old equipment ($16,000) plus the cash paid or less the cash received in the exchange. We carry over the old equipment's book value because its earnings process is not considered complete in these cases.

Although the general rule is that no gains or losses should be recorded on nonmonetary exchanges of similar assets, the maximum amount at which we may record the new asset is its market value. In Case 3 the value of the assets delivered is $17,000 ($1,000 cash plus equipment with a $16,000 book value). However, assume instead that the market value of the equipment received is only $14,000. The cost of the equipment received must not be recorded at more than $14,000. Therefore, we must record a $3,000 loss as follows:

Jan. 3	Equipment (**new**)	14,000	
	Accumulated Amortization, Equipment	20,000	
	Loss on exchange of equipment	3,000	
	Equipment (**old**)		36,000
	Cash		1,000
	To record exchange of old equipment		
	for new equipment and payment of cash.		

Assets = Liabilities + Equity
+14,000   −3,000
+20,000
−36,000
−1,000

In nonmonetary exchanges of similar assets, the cost of the asset received is recorded at the book value of the asset given up, minus any cash received or plus any cash paid, as long as this amount is not greater than the market value of the asset being received.[8] A loss might need to be recorded but it is unlikely that a gain would arise.

Flash back

11. A company acquires equipment on January 10, 1999, at a cost of $42,000. Straight-line amortization is used assuming a five-year life and $7,000 salvage value. On June 27, 2000, the company sells this equipment for $32,000. Prepare the entry or entries for June 27, 2000.

12. A company trades an old truck for a new truck. The original cost of the old truck is $30,000, and its accumulated amortization at the time of the trade is $23,400. The new truck has a cash price of $45,000. Prepare entries to record the trade under two different assumptions where the company receives (a) a $3,000 trade-in allowance or (b) a $7,000 trade-in allowance.

Answers—p. 592

---

[8] *CICA Handbook*, section 3830, "Non-Monetary Transactions," par. .10

Natural Resources

LO 9 Account for natural resources and their depletion.

SECTION 2—NATURAL RESOURCES

Natural resources are assets that include standing timber, mineral deposits, and oil and gas fields. Because they are physically consumed when used, they are often called *wasting assets*. The natural state of these assets represent "inventories" of raw materials that will be converted into a product by cutting, mining, or pumping. But until that conversion takes place, they are non-current assets and reported in a balance sheet using titles such as Timberlands, Mineral deposits, or Oil reserves. These natural resources are reported under either capital assets or a separate category. **Barrick Gold Corporation,** for instance, reports its natural resources under the balance sheet title *Property, plant and equipment.* In a note to the financial statements, **Barrick** reports separate amounts for *Property acquisition* and *Deferred mine costs and mineral properties in development.* **Abitibi Consolidated** reports its timber holdings as part of its Fixed assets.

Acquisition Cost and Depletion

Natural resources are initially recorded at cost. Cost includes all expenditures necessary to acquire the resource and prepare it for its intended use. **Depletion** (or amortization) is the process of allocating the cost of natural resources to periods when they are consumed, known as the resource's useful life. Natural resources are reported on the balance sheet at cost less *accumulated depletion.* The amount these assets are depleted each year by cutting, mining or pumping is usually based on units extracted or depleted. This is similar to units-of-production amortization. **Imperial Oil** uses this approach to amortize the costs of discovering and operating its oil wells.

To illustrate depletion of natural resources, let's consider a mineral deposit with an estimated 500,000 tonnes of available ore. It is purchased for $500,000 and we expect zero salvage value. The depletion charge per tonne of ore mined is $1, computed as $500,000 ÷ 500,000 tonnes. If 85,000 tonnes are mined and sold in the first year, the depletion charge for that year is $85,000. These computations are detailed in Exhibit 12.22.

Exhibit 12.22

Depletion Formula and Computations

Step 1:

$$\text{Depletion per unit} = \frac{\text{Cost} - \text{Salvage value}}{\text{Total units of capacity}} = \frac{\$500,000 - \$0}{500,000 \text{ tonnes}} = \$1 \text{ per tonne}$$

Step 2:

$$\text{Depletion expense} = \text{Depletion per unit} \times \text{Units extracted in period}$$
$$= \$1 \times 85,000 = \$85,000$$

Depletion expense is recorded as:

Assets = Liabilities + Equity
−85,000   −85,000

Dec. 31	Depletion Expense, Mineral Deposit	85,000	
	Accumulated Depletion, Mineral Deposit		85,000
	To record depletion of the mineral deposit.		

The balance sheet at the end of this first year reports the deposit as shown in Exhibit 12.23.

Mineral Deposit	$500,000	
Less Accumulated Depletion .	85,000	$415,000

Exhibit 12.23

Balance Sheet Presentation
of Natural Resources

Because the 85,000 tonnes of mined ore are sold in the year, the entire $85,000 depletion charge is reported on the income statement. But if some of the ore remains unsold at year-end, the depletion cost related to the unsold ore is carried forward on the balance sheet and reported as Unsold Ore Inventory, which is a current asset.

Capital Assets Used in Extracting Resources

The conversion of natural resources by mining, cutting, or pumping usually requires machinery, equipment and buildings. When the usefulness of these assets is directly related to the depletion of the natural resource, their costs are amortized over the life of the natural resource in proportion to the depletion charges. This means amortization is computed using the units-of-production method. For example, if a machine is permanently installed in a mine and one-eighth of the mine's ore is mined and sold in the year, then one-eighth of the machine's cost (less salvage value) is charged to amortization expense. If the machine is abandoned because the resources are fully extracted, any unamortized balance is written off. But if this machine will be moved to another site when extraction is complete, then it is amortized over its useful life.

SECTION 3—INTANGIBLE ASSETS

Intangible assets are rights, privileges, and competitive advantages to the owner of capital assets used in operations that have no physical substance. Examples are patents, copyrights, leaseholds, leasehold improvements, goodwill, and trademarks. Lack of physical substance is not sufficient for an asset to be an intangible. Notes and accounts receivable, for instance, lack physical substance but are not used in operations to produce products or services. Assets without physical substance that are not used in operations are reported as either current assets or investments. This section explains accounting for intangible assets and describes the more common types of intangible assets.

Intangible Assets

LO 10 Account for intangible assets and their amortization.

Accounting for Intangible Assets

Accounting for intangible assets is similar to that for all other capital assets. An intangible asset is recorded at cost when purchased. Its cost must be systematically allocated to expense over its estimated useful life through the process of amortization. The amortization period for an intangible asset must be 40 years or less.[9] Disposal of an intangible asset involves removing its book value, recording any asset received, and recognizing any gain or loss for the difference.

Amortization of intangible assets is similar to amortization of capital assets and depletion of natural resources in that it is a process of cost allocation. But only the straight-line method is used for amortizing intangibles *unless* the company can show another method is preferred. Another difference is the effects of

---

[9] *CICA Handbook*, section 3060, "Capital Assets," par. .32

amortization and depletion are recorded in a contra account (Accumulated Amortization or Accumulated Depletion), but amortization of intangible assets is usually credited directly to the intangible asset account. This means the original cost of intangible assets is rarely reported on the balance sheet. Instead, only the net amount of unamortized cost is reported.

Some intangibles have limited useful lives due to laws, contracts, or other characteristics of the asset. Examples are patents, copyrights and leaseholds. Other intangibles such as goodwill, trademarks and trade names have useful lives that can not be easily determined. The cost of intangible assets is amortized over the periods expected to benefit by their use (economic life). But in no case can this be longer than their legal existence. Also, the amortization period of intangible assets must never be longer than 40 years even when the life of an asset (for example, goodwill) can continue indefinitely into the future.

Intangible assets are often shown in a separate section of the balance sheet immediately after capital assets. **Bombardier,** for instance, follows this approach in reporting $229.6 million of *Other assets* in its January 31, 1997, balance sheet. Companies also usually disclose the amortization periods they apply to intangibles. **Rogers Communications'** 1997 annual report, for instance, says it amortizes the cost of subscribers and licences on an increasing charge basis over a 40-year period. Goodwill is amortized over periods of from 5 to 40 years on a straight-line basis.

Patents

The federal government grants patents to encourage the invention of new machines, mechanical devices, and production processes. A **patent** is an exclusive right granted to its owner to manufacture and sell a patented machine or device, or to use a process, for 17 years. When patent rights are purchased, the cost of acquiring the rights is debited to an account called *Patents*. If the owner engages in lawsuits to effectively defend a patent, the cost of lawsuits is debited to the Patents account. The costs of research and development leading to a new patent are expensed when incurred.[10]

Did You Know?

Drug War
Mention "drug war" and most people think of fighting cocaine or heroin use. But there's another drug war under way: Brand-name drugmakers' fight to stop generic copies of their products from hitting the market once their patents expire. Successfully delaying a generic rival means hundreds of millions of dollars in extra sales. [Source: *Canadian Business*, April 24, 1998.]

While a patent gives its owner exclusive rights to it for 17 years, the cost of the patent is amortized over its estimated useful life but not to exceed 17 years. If we purchase a patent costing $25,000 with a useful life of 10 years, we make the following adjusting entry at the end of each of the 10 years to amortize one-tenth of its cost:

Assets = Liabilities + Equity
−2,500   −2,500

Dec. 31	Amortization Expense, Patents	2,500	
	Patents		2,500
	To write off patent costs over its		
	10-year useful life.		

---

[10] *CICA Handbook*, section 3450, "Research and Development," par. .16 and .18

The debit of $2,500 to Amortization Expense appears on the income statement as a cost of the product or service provided under the protection of the patent. This entry uses the common practice of crediting the Patents account rather than using a contra account.

Copyrights

A copyright is granted by the federal government or by international agreement. A **copyright** gives its owner the exclusive right to publish and sell a musical, literary, or artistic work during the life of the creator plus 50 years. Yet the useful life of most copyrights is much shorter. The costs of a copyright are amortized over its useful life. The only identifiable cost of many copyrights is the fee paid to the Copyright Office. If this fee is immaterial, it is charged directly to an expense account. But if the identifiable costs of a copyright are material, they are capitalized (recorded in an asset account) and periodically amortized by debiting an account called *Amortization Expense, Copyrights.*

Go PHISH

PHISH, a popular band, refused to give up copyrights to their first two independently produced CDs when signing with a recording company. This was unique for the recording industry. These two CDs generate more money for PHISH than some of their more recent recordings that sold more copies.

Did You Know?

Leaseholds

Property is rented under a contract called a **lease.** The property's owner grants the lease and is called the **lessor.** The one who secures the right to possess and use the property is called the **lessee.** A **leasehold** refers to the rights granted to the lessee by the lessor in the lease. A leasehold is an intangible asset for the lessee.

Certain leases require no advance payment from the lessee but do require monthly rent payments. In this case we do not need a Leasehold account. Instead, the monthly payments are debited to a Rent Expense account. But if a long-term lease requires the lessee to pay the final period's rent in advance when the lease is signed, the lessee records this advance payment with a debit to a Leasehold account. Because the usefulness of the advance payment is not used until the final period, the Leasehold account balance remains intact until that time. Then, its balance is transferred to Rent Expense.[11]

A long-term lease can increase in value when current rental rates for similar property increase while the required payments under the lease remain constant. This increase in the value of a lease is not reported on the lessee's balance sheet since no extra cost is incurred to acquire it. But if the property is subleased and the new tenant makes a cash payment to the original lessee for the rights under the old lease, the new tenant debits this payment to a Leasehold account. The balance of this Leasehold account is amortized to Rent Expense over the remaining life of the lease.

---

[11] Some long-term leases give the lessee essentially the same rights as a purchaser and result in tangible assets and liabilities reported by the lessee. Chapter 13 describes these leases.

Leasehold Improvements

Long-term leases sometimes require the lessee to pay for alterations or improvements to the leased property, such as partitions, painting and storefronts. These alterations and improvements are called **leasehold improvements,** and their costs are debited to a *Leasehold Improvements* account. Since leasehold improvements become part of the property and revert to the lessor at the end of the lease, the lessee amortizes these costs over the life of the lease or the life of the improvements, whichever is shorter. The amortization entry debits Rent Expense and credits Leasehold Improvements.

Goodwill

Goodwill has a special meaning in accounting. **Goodwill** is the amount by which the value of a company exceeds the fair market value of this company's net assets if purchased separately. This usually implies the company has certain valuable attributes not measured among its net assets. These can include superior management, skilled workforce, good supplier and customer relations, quality products or services, good location, or other competitive advantages.

Goodwill Illustration

Conceptually, a company has goodwill when its rate of expected future earnings is greater than the rate of normal earnings for its industry. To illustrate this concept, consider the information in Exhibit 12.24 for two competing companies (Winter Gear and Wild Sports) of roughly equal size in the snowboard industry.

Exhibit 12.24

Data for Goodwill Illustration

	Wild Sports	Winter Gear
Net assets (excluding goodwill)	$190,000	$190,000
Normal rate of return in this industry . .	10%	10%
Normal return on net assets	$ 19,000	$ 19,000
Expected net income	24,000	19,000
Expected net income above normal . .	$ 5,000	$ -0-

The expected income for Wild Sports is $24,000. This is $5,000 higher than the norm (10%) for this industry. This implies Wild Sports has goodwill that yields above normal net income. But Winter Gear's net income of $19,000 is the norm for this industry. This suggests zero goodwill for Winter Gear. What this means is we are willing to pay more for Wild Sports than for Winter Gear because goodwill is a valued asset.

Goodwill is usually recorded only when an entire company or a business segment is purchased. In determining the purchase price of a company, the buyer and seller can estimate the amount of goodwill in more than one way. For instance, how do we value Wild Sports' $5,000 per year above normal net income? One way is to value goodwill at some *multiple* of above normal net income. If we choose a multiple of four, our goodwill estimate for Wild Sports is four times $5,000 (or $20,000). Another method is to assume the $5,000 above normal net income continues indefinitely. This is like an *annuity.* If we assume a 16% discount rate, our estimate of goodwill is $5,000/16%, or $31,250. We describe this computation in a later chapter. But whatever method we choose, the value of goodwill is confirmed only by the price the seller is willing to accept and the buyer is willing to pay.

Accounting for Goodwill

To keep financial statement information from being too subjective, goodwill is not recorded unless it is purchased. Goodwill is measured by subtracting the fair

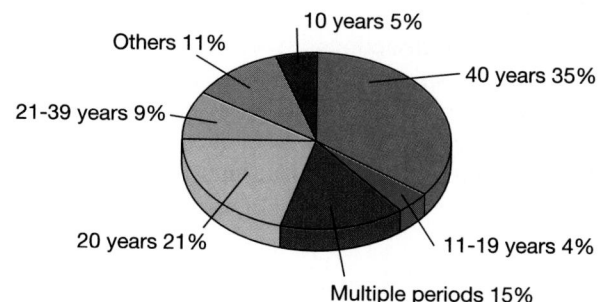

Exhibit 12.25

Goodwill Amortization Period

market value of the purchased company's net assets (excluding goodwill) from the purchase price. Goodwill is a major part of many company purchases. For instance, **Bombardier's** purchase of all the shares of **Waggonfabrik,** a German manufacturer of transportation equipment, included goodwill of $40.1 million.

Goodwill is amortized on a straight-line basis over its estimated useful life just like other intangible assets. Since estimating the useful life of goodwill is difficult, there is a wide range of estimates. Exhibit 12.25 shows us results from a recent survey on the goodwill amortization period. Note the most common amortization period is 40 years. This is not surprising because it allows companies to spread goodwill costs over more years.

Trademarks and Trade Names

Companies often adopt unique symbols or select unique names and brands in marketing their products. A **trademark** or **trade name** is a symbol, name, phrase, or jingle identified with a company, product or service. Examples are **Speedy Muffler, NIKE's** swoosh, **Tim Hortons, Second Cup, Coca-Cola** and **Honda.** Ownership and exclusive right to use a trademark or trade name is often established by showing that one company used it before another. But ownership is best established by registering a trademark or trade name with the government's Patent Office. The cost of developing, maintaining or enhancing the value of a trademark or trade name by means such as advertising is charged to expense when incurred. But if a trademark or trade name is purchased, its cost is debited to an asset account and amortized.

What's in a Name?

When it comes to brand building, nobody does it better than NIKE. Its swoosh is one of the best-known trademarks on the globe. It has helped **NIKE** pump out sales and earnings growth of nearly 40% for three years straight. Equally impressive in brand identity is the **"Intel Inside"** campaign created with a product consumers never see and few understand. [Source: *Business Week*, March 24, 1997.]

Did You Know?

Flashback

13. Give an example of both a natural resource and an intangible asset.

14. A mining company pays $650,000 for an ore deposit. The deposit is estimated to have 325,000 tonnes of ore that will be fully mined over the next 10 years. During the current year, 91,000 tonnes are mined, processed and sold. What is current year's depletion expense?

15. On January 6, 1999, a company pays $120,000 for a patent with a 17-year legal life to produce a toy that is expected to be marketable for about three years. Prepare entries to record its acquisition and the December 31, 1999, adjustment.

Answers—p. 592

Cash Flow Impacts of Capital Assets

LO 11 Identify cash flow impacts of capital asset transactions.

Acquisition and disposal transactions involving capital assets impact the statement of cash flows. Acquisitions of long-term assets are investing activities and are reported in the investing section of the statement of cash flows. Most acquisitions are an immediate *use* of cash and the amount paid at acquisition is deducted in the statement. **Alliance,** for instance, reports these as follows in its statement of cash flows:

> Cash provided (used) by investing activities ($ thousands):
> 1997 Net additions to property and equipment .... ($5,237)

Disposals of long-term assets usually create an immediate receipt of cash. When they do yield cash they are reported as a *source* of cash (an addition) in the investing section of the statement of cash flows or, as the case of Alliance, as a net figure. Gain or loss from disposal is the difference between an asset's book value and the value received. A gain or loss does not reflect any cash flow from investing activities (we explain this in Chapter 17).[12]

Total Asset Turnover   USING THE INFORMATION

LO 12 Compute total asset turnover and apply it to analyze a company's use of assets.

A company's assets are important in determining its ability to generate sales and earn profits. Managers devote a lot of attention to deciding what assets a company acquires, how much is invested in assets, and how assets can be used most efficiently and effectively. Decision makers and other users of financial statements are especially interested in evaluating a company's ability to use its assets in generating sales.

One measure of a company's ability in using its assets is **total asset turnover.** The formula for computing total asset turnover is shown in Exhibit 12.26.

Exhibit 12.26

Total Asset Turnover Formula

$$\text{Total asset turnover} = \frac{\text{Net sales}}{\text{Average total assets}}$$

Total asset turnover can be computed regardless of the type of company being evaluated. It can be applied to manufacturing and merchandising companies, and even to service companies. The numerator, net sales, reflects all operating revenues generated by the company. The denominator, average total assets, is usually measured by averaging total assets at the beginning of the period with total assets at the end of the period.

To illustrate, let's look at a company with total assets of $96,500 at the beginning of the year and $108,500 at the end of the year. Net sales for this company is $440,000 for the year. The company's total asset turnover for the current year is computed as:

$$\text{Total asset turnover} = \frac{\$440,000}{(\$96,500 + \$108,500)/2} = 4.3$$

We describe this company's use of assets in generating net sales by saying "it turned its assets over 4.3 times during the year." This means each $1.00 of assets produced $4.30 of net sales for the year.

---

[12] Also, amortization of capital assets do *not* impact cash (see Chapter 17).

Is a total asset turnover of 4.3 good or bad? It is safe to say all companies desire a high total asset turnover. But like many ratio analyses, a company's total asset turnover must be interpreted in comparison with prior years and with similar companies. Interpreting the total asset turnover also requires we understand the company's operations. Some operations are capital intensive, meaning a relatively large amount is invested in assets to generate sales. This suggests a relatively lower total asset turnover. Some other companies' operations are labour intensive, meaning sales are generated more by the efforts of people than the use of assets. In this case we expect a higher total asset turnover.[13]

To show how we analyze companies using total asset turnover, we use data from the annual reports of two competing companies: **George Weston** and the **Oshawa Group.** Exhibit 12.27 shows results from computing total asset turnover for these two companies.

Company	Figure ($ millions)	1996	1995
Weston	Net sales	$12,709	$12,966
	Average total assets	$5,282	$4,955
	Total asset turnover	2.41	2.62
Oshawa	Net sales	$6,384	$6,161
	Average total assets	$1,428	$1,344
	Total asset turnover	4.47	4.58

Exhibit 12.27

Analysis using total asset turnover

To show how we compute and use total asset turnover, let's look at the numbers for Weston in 1995–1996 as reported in Exhibit 12.27. We compute Weston's 1996 turnover as:

$$\text{Total asset turnover} = \frac{\$12,709}{\$5,282} = 2.41$$

This means Weston's average total asset balance is converted into sales 2.41 times in 1996. Another way to say this is that Weston generated $2.41 of net sales for each $1 of assets. We also see Weston's turnover is steady over the period 1995–1996, and is less than Oshawa's turnover. Is Weston's turnover high enough? Total asset turnover for Weston's other competitors, available in industry publications such as Dun & Bradstreet, is generally in the range of 2.0 to 2.5 over this same period. It appears Weston is competitive and possibly doing slightly better than its competitors on total asset turnover.

Environmentalist
You are an environmentalist battling a paper manufacturer on environmental concerns. The company claims it cannot afford any additional controls. It points to its low total asset turnover of 1.9 and argues it cannot compete with other companies where total asset turnover is much higher. Examples mentioned are food stores (5.5), wholesalers (4.0) and builders (3.5). The company suggests it might need to lay off workers to pay for any added costs. How do you respond?

You Make the Call

Answer—p. 591

---

[13] There is a relation between total asset turnover and net profit margin. Companies with low total asset turnover require higher profit margins (examples are hotels and real estate), whereas companies with high total asset turnover can succeed with lower profit margins (examples are food stores and merchandisers).

Summary

LO1 Describe capital assets and issues in accounting for them. Capital assets are tangible assets used in the operations of a company and have a useful life of more than one accounting period. Capital assets are set apart from other assets by two important features: use in operations and useful lives longer than one period. There are four main accounting issues with capital assets: (1) computing their costs, (2) allocating their costs to the periods they benefit, (3) accounting for their subsequent expenditures, and (4) recording their disposal.

LO2 Apply the cost principle to compute the cost of capital assets. Capital assets are recorded at cost when purchased. Cost includes all normal and reasonable expenditures necessary to get the asset in place and ready for its intended use. The cost of a lump-sum purchase is allocated among its individual assets based on their relative market values.

LO3 Explain amortization and the factors affecting its computation. Amortization is the process of allocating to expense the cost of a capital asset over the accounting periods benefiting from use of the capital asset. Amortization does not measure the decline in a capital asset's market value, nor does it measure the asset's physical deterioration. Amortization occurs when an asset is being used to produce products or services. Three factors determine amortization: cost, salvage value, and useful life. Salvage value is an estimate of the asset's value at the end of its benefit period. Useful (service) life is the length of time an asset is productively used in operations.

LO4 Compute and record amortization using the methods of straight-line, units-of-production, and declining-balance. The straight-line method of amortization divides the cost less salvage value by the number of periods in the asset's useful life to determine amortization expense for each period. The units-of-production method divides the cost less salvage value by the estimated number of units the asset will produce to determine the amortization per unit. The declining-balance method multiplies the asset's book value by a rate that is usually double the straight-line rate.

LO5 Compare and analyze amortization for different methods. The amount of amortization expense per period is usually different for different methods. Yet total amortization expense is the same for all methods. Each method starts with the same total cost and ends with the same salvage value. The difference is in the pattern in amortization expense over the asset's useful life. The book value of an asset when using straight-line is always

greater than when using double-declining-balance, except at the beginning and end. The straight-line method yields a steady pattern of amortization expense, while the units-of-production does not because it depends on the number of units produced. Amortization methods are acceptable if they allocate cost in a rational and systematic manner.

LO6 Explain amortization for partial years and when estimates change. Partial years' amortization is often required because assets are bought and sold throughout the year. Amortization is revised when changes in estimates such as salvage value and useful life occur. If the useful life of a capital asset changes, for instance, the remaining cost to be amortized is spread over the remaining (revised) useful life of the asset.

LO7 Distinguish between revenue and capital expenditures, and account for these expenditures. Revenue expenditures expire in the current period. They are debited to expense accounts and matched with current revenues. Repairs are an example of revenue expenditures. Capital expenditures benefit future periods and are debited to asset accounts. Betterments are a capital expenditure. Immaterial expenditures on capital assets are treated as revenue expenditures.

LO8 Account for asset disposal through discarding, selling, or exchanging an asset. When a capital asset is discarded, sold or exchanged, its cost and accumulated amortization are removed from the accounts. Any cash proceeds from discarding or selling an asset are recorded and compared to the asset's book value to determine gain or loss. When dissimilar assets are exchanged, the new asset is recorded at its fair value, and any gain or loss on disposal is recognized. When similar assets are exchanged, neither gains nor losses are normally recognized. The new asset account is debited for the book value of the old asset plus any cash paid and less any cash received.

LO9 Account for natural resources and their depletion. The cost of a natural resource is recorded in an asset account. Depletion of a natural resource is recorded by allocating its cost to expense normally using the units-of-production method. Depletion is credited to an Accumulated Depletion account.

LO10 Account for intangible assets and their amortization. An intangible asset is recorded at the cost incurred to purchase the asset. Allocation of the cost of an intangible asset to expense is normally done using the straight-line method and is called amortization. Amortization is recorded with a credit made directly to the asset account instead of a contra account. Intangible assets include patents, copyrights, leaseholds, goodwill, and trademarks.

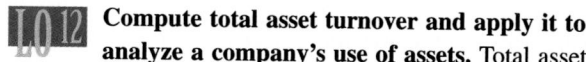 **Identify cash flow impacts of capital asset transactions.** Acquisition and disposal of capital assets impact the investing section of the statement of cash flows. Acquisitions are a use of cash, while disposals are a source of cash.

 Compute total asset turnover and apply it to analyze a company's use of assets. Total asset turnover measures a company's ability to use its assets to generate sales. Total asset turnover is defined as net sales divided by average total assets. The turnover measure is interpreted as the dollars of net sales generated for each dollar of assets. While all companies desire a high total asset turnover, it must be interpreted in comparison with prior years and with similar companies.

Guidance Answers to You Make the Call

Mechanic

Treating an expense as a capital expenditure means expenses will be lower and income higher. This is because unlike an expense, a capital expenditure is not expensed immediately. Instead, the cost of a capital expenditure is spread out over the asset's useful life. Treating an expense as a capital expenditure also means asset and equity totals are reported at a larger amount. This continues until the asset is fully amortized. Your friend is probably trying to help, but the suggestion hints at unethical behaviour. You must remember that only an expenditure benefiting future periods is a capital expenditure. If an item is truly an "expense" not benefiting future periods, then it must not be treated as a capital expenditure.

Environmentalist

You need to point out the company's comparison of its total asset turnover with food stores, wholesalers and builders is misdirected. You must explain these other industries' turnovers are higher because their profit margins are lower (about 2%). Profit margins for the paper industry are usually 3% to 3.5%. You also need to collect data from competitors in the paper industry to show that a 1.9 total asset turnover is about right for this industry. You might even go further and collect data on this company's revenues and expenses, along with compensation data for this company's high-ranking officers and employees.

Guidance Answer to Judgment and Ethics

Controller

Before you conclude this instruction is unethical, you might tell the president of your concern that the longer estimate does not seem realistic in light of past experience with three-year replacements. You might ask if the change implies a new replacement plan. Depending on the president's response, such a conversation might eliminate your concern. It is possible the president's decision to change estimated useful life reflects an honest and reasonable prediction of the future. Since the company is struggling financially, the president may have concluded the normal pattern of replacing assets every three years cannot continue. Perhaps the strategy is to avoid costs of frequent replacements and stretch use of the equipment a few years longer until financial conditions improve. Even if you

doubt the company will be able to use the equipment six years, you should consider the possibility the president has a more complete understanding of the situation and honestly believes a six-year life is a good estimate.

On the downside, you may be correct in suspecting the president is acting unethically. If you conclude the president's decision is unethical, you might confront the president with your opinion that it is unethical to change the prediction just to increase income. This is a personally risky course of action and you may want to remind the president of her own ethical responsibility. Another possibility is to wait and see if the auditor will insist on not changing the estimate. You should always insist the statements be based on reasonable estimates.

Guidance Answers to Flashbacks

1. (a) Office supplies—current assets
    (b) Office equipment—capital assets
    (c) Merchandise—current assets
    (d) Land held for future expansion—long-term investments
    (e) Trucks used in operations—capital assets

2. (a) Land
    (b) Land Improvements

3. $700,000 + $49,000 − $21,000 + $3,500 + $3,000 + $2,500 = $737,000

4. Straight-line with 7-year life: ($77,000/7) = $11,000
    Straight-line with 10-year life: ($77,000/10) = $7,700

5. Amortization is a process of allocating and charging the cost of capital assets to the accounting periods that benefit from the assets' use.

6. (a) Book value using straight-line amortization:
        $96,000 − [($96,000 - $8,000)/5] = $78,400

    (b) Book value using units of production:
        $96,000 − [($96,000 − $8,000) × (10,000/100,000)]
        = $87,200

7. ($3,800 − $200)/3 = $1,200
    $1,200 × 2 = $2,400
    ($3,800 − $2,400)/2 = $700

8.
Machinery	12,000	
Cash		12,000

9. A revenue expenditure benefits only the current period and should be charged to expense of the current period. A capital expenditure has a benefit that extends beyond the end of the current period and should be charged to an asset.

10. A betterment involves modifying an existing capital asset to make it more efficient, usually by replacing part of the asset with an improved or superior part. A betterment should be debited to the improved machine's account.

11.
Amortization Expense	3,500	
Accumulated Amortization		3,500
Cash	32,000	
Accumulated Amortization	10,500	
Gain on Sale of Equipment		500
Equipment		42,000

12.
(a)
Truck	45,000	
Loss on Trade-In	3,600	
Accumulated Amortization	23,400	
Truck		30,000
Cash		42,000

(b)
Truck	45,000	
Accumulated Amortization	23,400	
Truck		30,000
Cash		38,000
Gain on Trade-In		400

13. Examples of intangible assets are: Patents; Copyrights; Leaseholds; Leasehold improvements; Goodwill; Trademarks; Exclusive licences.

    Examples of natural resources are: Timberlands; Mineral deposits; Oil reserves.

14. $650,000 × (91,000/325,000) = $182,000

15.
Jan. 6	Patents	120,000	
	Cash		120,000
Dec. 31	Amortization Expense	40,000*	
	Patents		40,000

*Amortization computation:
$120,000/3 = $40,000

Demonstration Problem

On July 14, 19X1, Truro Company paid $600,000 to acquire a fully equipped factory. The purchase included the following:

Asset	Appraised Value	Estimated Salvage Value	Estimated Useful Life	Amortization Method
Land	$160,000			Not amortized
Land improvements	80,000	$ -0-	10 years	Straight line
Building	320,000	100,000	10 years	Double-declining balance
Machinery	240,000	20,000	10,000 units	Units of production*
Total	$800,000			

*The machinery is used to produce 700 units in 19X1 and 1,800 units in 19X2.

Required

1. Allocate the total $600,000 cost among the separate assets.

2. Compute the 19X1 (six months) and 19X2 amortization expense for each type of asset and compute the total amortization expense each year for all assets.

3. On the first day of 19X3 the machinery and $5,000 cash is exchanged for similar equipment with a fair value of $210,000. Journalize the exchange of assets.

4. Assume the exchange in part 3 was for dissimilar, not similar, equipment. Journalize the dissimilar exchange.

Additional company transactions to account for dealing with long-term assets:

5. On the last day of the fiscal year the company discards equipment that has been on the books for five years. The original cost of the equipment was $12,000 (estimated life of five years) and the salvage value is $2,000. No amortization has been recorded for the fifth year before the disposal occurs. Journalize the fifth year of amortization (straight-line method) and the asset disposal.

6. At the beginning of the year the company purchases with cash a patent right for $100,000. The company estimates the useful life of the patent to be 10 years. Journalize the patent acquisition and amortization for the year.

7. Late in the year the company makes its final addition to property and equipment with the acquisition for cash of an ore deposit for $600,000. Access roads and shafts are added for an additional cost of $80,000. Salvage value of the mine is estimated to be $20,000. The company estimates 330,000 tonnes of available ore. Only 10,000 tonnes of ore are mined and sold before the end of the year. Journalize the mine's acquisition and first year's depletion.

Planning the Solution

■ Complete a three-column worksheet showing these amounts for each asset: appraised value, percentage of total value, and allocated cost.

■ Using the allocated costs, compute the amount of amortization for 19X1 (only one-half year) and 19X2 for each asset. Then, summarize those computations in a table showing the total amortization for each year.

■ Remember that gains on nonmonetary exchanges of similar assets are not recognized. Make a journal entry to add the acquired machinery to the books, remove the machinery given in the Exchange along with its accumulated amortization, and the cash given in the exchange.

■ Remember that gains on exchanges of dissimilar assets are recognized. Make a journal entry to add the acquired machinery to the books, remove the machinery given in the exchange along with its accumulated amortization, and the cash given in the exchange. Also record the gain on the exchange in a separate account titled "Gain on Exchange of Dissimilar Assets."

■ Remember that all amortization must be recorded before removing a disposed asset from the books. Calculate and record the amortization expense for the fifth year using the straight-line method. Since salvage value has not been received at the end of the asset's life the amount of the salvage value becomes a loss on disposal. Record the loss on the disposal as well as the removal of the asset and its related accumulated amortization from the books.

■ Record the patent as an intangible asset for its purchase price. Use straight-line amortization over the years of useful life to calculate amortization expense. Remember that no accumulated amortization account is used in recording amortization expense. Rather the intangible asset account is credited directly.

■ Record the ore deposit as a natural resource asset including all additional costs to ready the mine for use. Calculate depletion per tonne using the depletion formula. Multiply the depletion amount per tonne by the amount of tonnes mined since the acquisition to calculate the appropriate depletion expense for the current year.

Solution to Demonstration Problem

1. Allocation of total cost among the assets:

Asset	Appraised Value	Percentage of Total Value	Allocated Cost
Land	$160,000	20%	$120,000
Land improvements	80,000	10	60,000
Building	320,000	40	240,000
Machinery	240,000	30	180,000
Total	$800,000	100%	$600,000

2. Amortization for each asset:

Land Improvements:

Cost	$ 60,000
Salvage value	-0-
Net cost	$ 60,000
Useful life	10 years
Annual expense ($60,000/10)	$ 6,000
19X1 amortization ($6,000 × 6/12)	$ 3,000
19X2 amortization	$ 6,000

Building:

Straight-line rate = 100%/10 = 10%
Double-declining-balance rate = 10% × 2 = 20%

19X1 amortization ($240,000 × 20% × 6/12)	$ 24,000
19X2 amortization [($240,000 − $24,000) × 20%]	$ 43,200

Machinery:

Cost	$180,000
Salvage value	20,000
Net cost	$160,000
Total expected units	10,000
Expected cost per unit ($160,000/10,000)	$ 16

Year	Units	×	Unit Cost	Amortization
19X1	700	×	$16	$11,200
19X2	1,800	×	$16	28,800

Total amortization expense:

	19X2	19X1
Land improvements	$ 6,000	$ 3,000
Building	43,200	24,000
Machinery	28,800	11,200
Total	$78,000	$38,200

3. Recording the exchange of similar assets with a gain on the exchange:

The book value on the date of exchange is $180,000 (allocated cost) − $40,000 (accumulated amortization). The cash involved is less than 10% of the value of the assets involved; therefore, this is a nonmonetary exchange of similar assets. The book value of the machinery given in the exchange of $140,000 plus the $5,000 cash paid thus becomes the recorded cost of the new asset.

Machinery (new) [$140,000 + $5,000]	145,000	
Accumulated Amortization, Old Machinery	40,000	
Old Machinery		180,000
Cash		5,000

4. Recording the exchange of dissimilar assets with a gain on the exchange:

Machinery (new)	210,000	
Accumulated Amortization, Old Machinery	40,000	
Old Machinery		180,000
Cash		5,000
Gain on exchange of dissimilar assets		65,000

5. Recording the amortization on the discarded asset:

Amortization Expense, Equipment	2,000	
Accumulated Amortization, Equipment		2,000
To record amortization to date of disposal:		
($12,000 − $2,000/5 = $2,000)		

Recording the loss on disposal and asset removal:

Accumulated Amortization, Equipment	10,000	
Loss on Disposal of Equipment	2,000	
Equipment		12,000
To record the discarding of machinery with a		
$2,000 book value.		

6.

Patent	100,000	
Cash		100,000
To record patent acquisition.		

Amortization Expense, Patent	10,000	
Patent		10,000
To record amortization expense:		
($100,000/10 years = $10,000)		

7.

Ore Deposit	680,000	
Cash		680,000
To record ore deposit acquisition and related costs.		

Depletion Expense, Ore Deposit	20,000	
Accumulated Depletion		20,000
To record depletion expense:		
[($680,000 − $20,000)/330,000 tonnes available] = $2.00 per tonne		
10,000 tonnes mined and sold × $2.00 = $20,000 depletion		

Glossary

Accelerated amortization method Amortization methods that produce larger amortization charges during the early years of an asset's life and smaller charges in the later years. (p. 566)

Amortization A process of systematically allocating the cost of a capital asset to expense over its estimated useful life. (p. 562)

Betterment An expenditure to make a capital asset more efficient or productive and/or extend the useful life of a capital asset beyond original expectations; also called *improvements*. (p. 573)

Book value The original cost of a capital asset less its accumulated amortization. (p. 564)

Capital assets Assets used in the operations of a company that have a useful life of more than one accounting period; also known as *fixed assets*, or *property, plant and equipment*. (p. 558)

Capital Cost Allowance (CCA) The system of amortization required by federal income tax law. (p. 568)

Capital expenditures Additional costs of capital assets that provide material benefits extending beyond the current period. (p. 572)

Change in an accounting estimate A change in a computed amount used in the financial statements that results from new information or subsequent developments and from better insight or improved judgment. (p. 570)

Copyright A right granted by the federal government or by international agreement giving the owner the exclusive privilege to publish and sell musical, literary, or artistic work during the life of the creator plus 50 years. (p. 585)

Cost Includes all normal and reasonable expenditures necessary to get a capital asset in place and ready for its intended use. (p. 559)

Declining-balance amortization An amortization method in which a capital asset's amortization charge for the period is determined by applying a constant amortization rate (up to twice the straight-line rate) each year to the asset's book value at the beginning of the year. (p. 567)

Depletion The process of allocating the cost of natural resources to the periods in which they are consumed. Another term for *amortization*. (p. 582)

Depreciation The process of allocating to expense the cost of a capital asset to the accounting periods benefiting from its use. Another term for *amortization*. (p. 562)

Goodwill The amount by which the value of a company exceeds the fair market value of the company's net assets if purchased separately. (p. 586)

Inadequacy A condition in which the capacity of the company's capital assets is too small to meet the company's productive demands. (p. 563)

Intangible assets Rights, privileges, and competitive advantages to the owner of capital assets used in operations that have no physical substance; examples include patents, copyrights, leaseholds, leasehold improvements, goodwill, and trademarks. (p. 583)

Land improvements Assets that increase the usefulness of land but that have a limited useful life and are subject to amortization. (p. 560)

Lease A contract allowing property rental. (p. 585)

Lessee The party to a lease that secures the right to possess and use the property. (p. 585)

Leasehold A name for the rights granted to the lessee by the lessor by a lease. (p. 585)

Leasehold improvements Alterations or improvements to leased property, such as partitions, painting, and store fronts. (p. 586)

Lessor The party to a lease that grants the right to possess and use property to another. (p. 585)

Natural resources Assets that are physically consumed when used; examples include timber, mineral deposits, and oil and gas fields; also called *wasting assets*. (p. 582)

Obsolescence A condition in which, because of new inventions and improvements, a capital asset can no longer be used to produce goods or services with a competitive advantage. (p. 563)

Patent An exclusive right granted to its owner by the federal government to manufacture and sell a machine or device, or to use a process, for 17 years. (p. 584)

Repairs Expenditures made to keep a capital asset in normal, good operating condition; treated as a revenue expenditure. (p. 573)

Revenue expenditure An expenditure that should appear on the current income statement as an expense and be deducted from the period's revenues because it does not provide a material benefit in future periods. (p. 572)

Salvage value Management's estimate of the amount that will be recovered at the end of a capital asset's useful life through a sale or as a trade-in allowance on the purchase of a new asset; also called *residual or scrap value*. (p. 562)

Straight-line amortization A method that allocates an equal portion of the total amortization for a capital asset (cost minus salvage) to each accounting period in its useful life. (p. 564)

Total asset turnover A measure of the ability of a company to use its assets to generate sales; computed by dividing net sales by average total assets. (p. 588)

Trademark or **trade name** Symbol, name, phrase, or jingle identified with a company or service. (p. 587)

Units-of-production amortization A method that charges a varying amount to expense for each period of an asset's useful life depending on its usage; expense is computed by taking the cost of the asset less its salvage value and dividing by the total number of units expected to be produced during its useful life. (p. 565)

Useful life The length of time in which a capital asset will be productively used in the operations of the business; also called *service life*. (p. 563)

Questions

1. What characteristics of a capital asset make it different from other assets?

2. What is the balance sheet classification of land held for future expansion? Why is the land not classified as a capital asset?

3. In general, what is included in the cost of a capital asset?

4. What is the difference between land and land improvements?

5. Does the balance of the account, Accumulated Amortization, Machinery, represent funds accumulated to replace the machinery when it wears out? What does the balance of Accumulated Amortization represent?

6. Why is capital cost allowance not generally accepted for financial accounting purposes?

7. What is the difference between repairs and betterments and how should they be recorded?

8. What accounting principle justifies charging the $75 cost of a capital asset immediately to an expense account?

9. What are some of the events that might lead to the disposal of a capital asset?

10. Should a gain on an exchange of capital assets be recorded?

11. How does accounting for long-term property and equipment impact the statement of cash flows?

12. How is total asset turnover computed? Why would a financial statement user be interested in computing total asset turnover?

13. What is the name for the process of allocating the cost of natural resources to expense as the natural resources are used?

14. What are the characteristics of an intangible asset?

15. Is the declining-balance method an acceptable means of computing depletion of natural resources?

16. What general procedures are followed in accounting for intangible assets?

17. When does a business have goodwill? Under what conditions can goodwill appear in a company's balance sheet?

18. X Company bought an established business and paid for goodwill. If X Company plans to incur substantial advertising and promotional costs each year to maintain the value of the goodwill, must the company also amortize the goodwill?

19. Refer to the consolidated balance sheets for **Alliance** in Appendix I. What phrase does Alliance use to describe its capital assets? What is the book value of capital assets as of March 31, 1997, and March 31, 1996?

20. Refer to the consolidated balance sheet of **Atlantis** in Appendix I. How are the property and equipment and intangibles of Atlantis presented on the balance sheet?

Explain the difference between (a) capital assets and current assets; (b) capital assets and inventory; and (c) capital assets and temporary investments.

Quick Study

QS 12-1
Defining capital assets

LO 1

Starbuck Lanes installed automatic score-keeping equipment. The electrical work required to prepare for the installation was $18,000. The invoice price of the equipment was $180,000. Additional costs were $3,000 for delivery and $12,600, sales tax. During the installation, a component of the equipment was damaged because it was carelessly left on a lane and hit by the automatic lane cleaning machine during a daily maintenance run. The cost of repairing the component was $2,250. What is the cost of the automatic score-keeping equipment?

QS 12-2
Cost of capital assets

LO 2

On January 2, 19X1, Crossfire acquired sound equipment for concert performances at a cost of $55,900. The rock band estimated they would use this equipment for four years, during which time they anticipated performing about 12 concerts. They estimated that at that point they could sell the equipment for $1,900. During 19X1, the band performed four concerts. Compute the 19X1 amortization using (a) the straight-line method and (b) the units-of-production method.

QS 12-3
Alternate amortization methods

LO 4

QS 12-4

Computing revised amortization

LO 6

Refer to the facts in QS 12-3. Assume that Crossfire chose straight-line amortization but recognized during the second year that due to concert bookings beyond expectations, this equipment would only last a total of three years. The salvage value would remain unchanged. Compute the revised amortization for the second year and the third year.

QS 12-5

Double-declining balance method

LO 4

A fleet of refrigerated delivery trucks acquired on January 5, 19X1, at a cost of $930,000 had an estimated useful life of eight years and an estimated salvage value of $150,000. Compute the amortization expense for the first three years under the double-declining-balance method for financial accounting purposes.

QS 12-6

Revenue and capital expenditures

LO 7

a. Classify the following expenditures as revenue or capital expenditures:
   (1) The cost of annual tune-ups for delivery trucks.
   (2) The cost of replacing a compressor for a meat-packing firm's refrigeration system that extends the estimated life of the system four years, $30,000.
   (3) The cost of $220,000 for an addition of a new wing on an office building.
   (4) The monthly replacement cost of filters on an air-conditioning system, $175.
b. Prepare the journal entry to record each of the above.

QS 12-7

Dissimilar asset exchanges

LO 8

Spectrum Flooring owned an automobile with a $15,000 cost and $13,500 accumulated amortization. In a transaction with a neighbouring computer retailer, Spectrum exchanged this auto for a computer with a fair market value of $4,500. Spectrum was required to pay an additional $3,750 cash. Prepare the entry to record this transaction for Spectrum.

QS 12-8

Similar asset exchange

LO 8

Mayes Co. owns an industrial machine that cost $38,400 and has been amortized $20,400. Mayes exchanged the machine for a newer model that has a fair market value of $17,000. Record the exchange assuming that Mayes (a) paid $1,500 and (b) received $1,000.

QS 12-9

Cash impacts from acquisitions and disposals

LO 11

Identify the section in the cash flow statement where the following transactions are reported along with whether it is a source or use of cash.
Key: **A.** Source of cash from investing activities
       B. Use of cash for investing activities

_____ **1.** Cash purchase of machinery
_____ **2.** Sale of patents for cash
_____ **3.** Purchase of productive timberland for cash
_____ **4.** Cash sale of factory warehouse

QS 12-10

Computing total asset turnover

LO 12

Photo Film Company reported the following facts in its 19X2 annual report: net sales of $13,557 million for 19X2 and $12,670 million for 19X1; total end-of-year assets of $14,968 million for 19X2 and $18,810 million for 19X1. Compute the total asset turnover for 19X2.

QS 12-11

Natural resources and depletion

LO 9

Sudbury Industries acquired an ore mine at a cost of $1,300,000. It was necessary to incur $200,000 to access the mine. The mine is estimated to hold 500,000 tonnes of ore and the estimated value of the land after the ore is removed is $150,000.

a. Prepare the entry to record the acquisition.
b. Prepare the year-end adjusting entry assuming that 90,000 tonnes of ore were removed from the mine this year.

Which of the following assets should be reported on the balance sheet as intangible assets? Which should be reported as natural resources? (a) leasehold, (b) salt mine, (c) building, (d) oil well, (e) trademark.

QS 12-12
Intangible assets and natural resources
LO 9, 10

On January 4 of the current year, Amber's Boutique incurred a $95,000 cost to modernize its store. The improvements included new floors, lighting, and shelving for the merchandise. It was estimated that these improvements would last for 10 years. Amber's leases its retail space and has eight years remaining on the lease. Prepare the entry to record the modernization and the adjusting entry at the end of the current year.

QS 12-13
Intangible assets and amortization
LO 10

Santiago Co. purchased a machine for $11,500, terms 2/10, n/60, FOB shipping point. The seller prepaid the freight charges, $260, adding the amount to the invoice and bringing its total to $11,760. The machine required a special steel mounting and power connections costing $795, and another $375 was paid to assemble the machine and get it into operation. In moving the machine onto its steel mounting, it was dropped and damaged. The repairs cost $190. Later, $30 of raw materials were consumed in adjusting the machine so that it would produce a satisfactory product. The adjustments were normal for this type of machine and were not the result of the damage. However, the items produced while the adjustments were being made were not saleable. Prepare a computation to show the cost of this machine for accounting purposes. (Assume Santiago pays for the purchase within the discount period.)

Exercises
Exercise 12-1
Cost of a capital asset
LO 2

Horizon Company paid $368,250 for real estate plus $19,600 in closing costs. The real estate included land appraised at $166,320; land improvements appraised at $55,440; and a building appraised at $174,240. Prepare a computation showing the allocation of the total cost among the three purchased assets and present the journal entry to record the purchase.

Exercise 12-2
Lump-sum purchase of capital assets
LO 2

After planning to build a new plant, Monarch Manufacturing purchased a large lot on which a small building was located. The negotiated purchase price for this real estate was $225,000 for the lot plus $120,000 for the building. The company paid $34,500 to have the old building torn down and $51,000 for landscaping the lot. Finally, it paid $1,440,000 in construction costs, which included the cost of a new building plus $85,500 for lighting and paving a parking lot next to the building. Present a single journal entry to record the costs incurred by Monarch, all of which were paid in cash.

Exercise 12-3
Recording costs of real estate
LO 2

On the first day of the year Barrow Company installed a computerized machine in its factory at a cost of $42,300. The machine's useful life was estimated at 10 years, or 363,000 units of product, with a $6,000 trade-in value. During its second year, the machine produced 35,000 units of product. Determine the machine's second-year amortization under the (a) straight-line, (b) units-of-production, and (c) double-declining-balance methods.

Exercise 12-4
Alternative amortization methods
LO 4

On April 1, 19X1, Rodgers Backhoe Co. purchased a trencher for $250,000. The machine was expected to last five years and have a salvage value of $25,000. Compute amortization expense for 19X2, using (a) the straight-line method and (b) the double-declining-balance method. Rodgers Backhoe has a December 31 year-end.

Exercise 12-5
Alternative amortization methods; partial year's amortization
LO 6

Exercise 12-6
Revising amortization rates
LO 6

BodySmart Fitness Club used straight-line amortization for a machine that cost $21,750, under the assumption it would have a four-year life and a $2,250 trade-in value. After two years, BodySmart determined that the machine still had three more years of remaining useful life, after which it would have an estimated $1,800 trade-in value. (a) Compute the machine's book value at the end of its second year. (b) Compute the amount of amortization to be charged during each of the remaining years in the machine's revised useful life.

Exercise 12-7
Income statement effects of alternative amortization methods
LO 5

Shamrock Enterprises recently paid $235,200 for equipment that will last five years and have a salvage value of $52,500. By using the machine in its operations for five years, the company expects to earn $85,500 annually, after deducting all expenses except amortization. Present a schedule showing income before amortization, amortization expense, and net income for each year and the total amounts for the five-year period, assuming (a) straight-line amortization and (b) double-declining-balance amortization.

Exercise 12-8
Alternate amortization methods
LO 5

In January 19X1, Labtech purchased computer equipment for $147,000. The equipment will be used in research and development activities for four years and then sold at an estimated salvage value of $30,000. Prepare schedules showing the amortization and book values for the four years assuming (a) straight-line amortization and (b) double-declining balance.

Exercise 12-9
Repairs and betterments
LO 7

Archer Company paid $262,500 for equipment that was expected to last four years and have a salvage value of $30,000. Prepare journal entries to record the following costs related to the equipment:

a. During the second year of the equipment's life, $21,000 cash was paid for a new component that was expected to increase the equipment's productivity by 10% each year.

b. During the third year, $5,250 cash was paid for repairs necessary to keep the equipment in good working order.

c. During the fourth year, $13,950 was paid for repairs that were expected to increase the useful life of the equipment from four to six years.

Exercise 12-10
Betterments
LO 7

Flemming Company owns a building that appeared on its balance sheet at the end of last year at its original $561,000 cost less $420,750 accumulated amortization. The building has been amortized on a straight-line basis under the assumption that it would have a 20-year life and no salvage value. During the first week in January of the current year, major structural repairs were completed on the building at a cost of $67,200. The repairs did not increase the building's capacity, but they did extend its expected life for 7 years beyond the 20 years originally estimated.

a. Determine the building's age as of the end of last year.

b. Give the entry to record the repairs, which were paid with cash.

c. Determine the book value of the building after the repairs were recorded.

d. Give the entry to record the current year's amortization.

Exercise 12-11
Partial year's amortization; disposal of capital asset
LO 8

Levy Co. purchased and installed a machine on January 1, 19X1, at a total cost of $92,750. Straight-line amortization was taken each year for four years, based on the assumption of a seven-year life and no salvage value. The machine was disposed of on July 1, 19X5, during its fifth year of service. Present the entries to record the partial year's amortization on July 1, 19X5, and to record the disposal under each of the following unrelated assumptions: (a) the machine was sold for $35,000 cash; and (b) Levy received an insurance settlement of $30,000 resulting from the total destruction of the machine in a fire.

Greenbelt Construction traded in an old tractor for a new tractor, receiving a $28,000 trade-in allowance and paying the remaining $82,000 in cash. The old tractor cost $95,000, and straight-line amortization of $52,500 had been recorded under the assumption that it would last eight years and have an $11,000 salvage value. Answer the following questions:

a. What was the book value of the old tractor?

b. What is the loss on the exchange?

c. What amount should be debited to the new Tractor account?

Exercise 12-12
Exchanging capital assets

LO 8

On January 2, 19X1, Hammond Service Co. disposed of a machine that cost $42,000 and had been amortized $22,625. Present the journal entries to record the disposal under each of the following unrelated assumptions:

a. The machine was sold for $16,250 cash.

b. The machine was traded in on a new machine of like purpose having a $58,500 cash price. A $20,000 trade-in allowance was received, and the balance was paid in cash.

c. The machine plus $1,500 was exchanged for a new machine of like purpose having a fair value $9,000.

d. The machine was traded for vacant land adjacent to the shop to be used as a parking lot. The land had a fair value of $37,500, and Hammond paid $12,500 cash in addition to giving the seller the machine.

Exercise 12-13
Recording capital asset disposal or exchange

LO 8

Refer to the statement of cash flows for **Atlantis** in Appendix I for the year-ended December 31, 1997, to answer the following:

a. What amount of cash is used to purchase fixed assets?

b. What amount of cash is received from sales of fixed assets?

c. How much amortization and depreciation is recorded?

d. What is the total amount of net cash used in investing activities?

e. Are there any gains or losses from sale of fixed assets?

Exercise 12-14
Cash flows related to capital assets

LO 11

Atherton Co. reported net sales of $4,862,000 for 19X2 and $7,542,000 for 19X3. End-of-year balances for total assets were: 19X1, $1,586,000; 19X2, $1,700,000; and 19X3, $1,882,000. Compute Atherton's total asset turnover for 19X2 and 19X3 and comment on the corporation's efficiency in the use of its assets.

Exercise 12-15
Evaluating efficient use of assets

LO 12

On April 2, 19X1, Cascade Mining Co. paid $3,633,750 for an ore deposit containing 1,425,000 tonnes. The company also installed machinery in the mine that cost $171,000, had an estimated seven-year life with no salvage value, and was capable of removing all the ore in six years. The machine will be abandoned when the ore is completely mined. Cascade began operations on May 1, 19X1, and mined and sold 156,200 tonnes of ore during the remaining eight months of the year. Give the December 31, 19X1, entries to record the depletion of the ore deposit and the amortization of the mining machinery.

Exercise 12-16
Depletion of natural resources

LO 9

The Falstaff Gallery purchased the copyright on an oil painting for $236,700 on January 1, 19X1. The copyright legally protects its owner for 19 more years. However, the company plans to market and sell prints of the original for only 12 years. Prepare journal entries to record the purchase of the copyright and the annual amortization of the copyright on December 31, 19X1.

Exercise 12-17
Amortization of intangible assets

LO 10

Exercise 12-18
Estimating goodwill

LO 10

Corey Boyd has devoted years to developing a profitable business that earns an attractive return. Boyd is now considering the possibility of selling the business and is attempting to estimate the value of the goodwill in the business. The fair value of the net assets of the business (excluding goodwill) is $437,000, and in a typical year net income is about $85,000. Most businesses of this type are expected to earn a return of about 10% on net assets. Estimate the value of the goodwill assuming (a) the value is equal to 10 times the excess earnings above average, and (b) the value can be found by capitalizing the excess earnings above average at a rate of 8%.

Problems

Problem 12-1
Real estate costs; partial year's amortization

LO 2, 3, 6

In 19X1, Lightscapes paid $2,800,000 for a tract of land and two buildings on it. The plan was to demolish Building One and build a new store in its place. Building Two was to be used as a company office and was appraised at a value of $641,300, with a useful life of 20 years and an $80,000 salvage value. A lighted parking lot near Building One had improvements (Land Improvements One) valued at $408,100 that were expected to last another 14 years and have no salvage value. Without considering the buildings or improvements, the tract of land was estimated to have a value of $1,865,600. Lightscapes incurred the following additional costs:

Cost to demolish Building One	$422,600
Cost of additional landscaping	167,200
Cost to construct new building (Building Three), having a useful life of 25 years and a $390,100 salvage value	2,019,000
Cost of new land improvements near Building Two (Land Improvements Two) which have a 20-year useful life and no salvage value	158,000

Required

1. Prepare a schedule having the following column headings: Land, Building Two, Building Three, Land Improvements One, and Land Improvements Two. Allocate the costs incurred by Lightscapes to the appropriate columns and total each column.
2. Prepare a single journal entry dated March 31 to record all the incurred costs, assuming they were paid in cash on that date.
3. Using the straight-line method, prepare December 31 adjusting entries to record amortization for the nine months of 19X1 during which the assets were in use.

Check Figure Accumulated Amortization, Land Improvements Two, $5,925

Problem 12-2
Capital asset costs; partial year's amortization; alternative methods

LO 2, 3, 6

Gunner Construction recently negotiated a lump-sum purchase of several assets from a company that was going out of business. The purchase was completed on March 1, 19X1, at a total cash price of $787,500 and included a building, land, certain land improvements, and 12 vehicles. The estimated market values of the assets were: building, $408,000; land, $289,000; land improvements, $42,500; and vehicles, $110,500. The company's fiscal year ends on December 31.

Required

Preparation component:

1. Prepare a schedule to allocate the lump-sum purchase price to the separate assets that were purchased. Also present the journal entry to record the purchase.
2. Compute the 19X1 amortization expense on the building using the straight-line method, assuming a 15-year life and a $25,650 salvage value.
3. Compute the 19X1 amortization expense on the land improvements assuming a five-year life and double-declining-balance amortization.

Check Figure 19X1, amortization expense on land improvements, $13,125

Analysis component:

4. Defend or refute this statement: Accelerated amortization results in lower taxes over the life of the asset.

Part 1. A machine that cost $210,000, with a four-year life and an estimated $20,000 salvage value, was installed in Casablanca Company's factory on January 1. The factory manager estimated that the machine would produce 475,000 units of product during its life. It actually produced the following units: year 1, 121,400; year 2, 122,400; year 3, 119,600; and year 4, 118,200. Note the total number of units produced by the end of year 4 exceeded the original estimate. Nevertheless, the machine should not be amortized below the estimated salvage value.

Required

Prepare a form with the following column headings:

Year	Straight-Line	Units-of-Production	Double-Declining-Balance

Then show the amortization for each year and the total amortization for the machine under each amortization method.

Part 2. Casablanca purchased a used machine for $167,000 on January 2. It was repaired the next day at a cost of $3,420 and installed on a new platform that cost $1,080. The company predicted that the machine would be used for six years and would then have a $14,600 salvage value. Amortization was to be charged on a straight-line basis. A full year's amortization was charged on December 31, the end of the first year of the machine's use. On September 30 of its sixth year in service, it was retired.

Required

1. Prepare journal entries to record the purchase of the machine, the cost of repairing it, and the installation. Assume that cash was paid.
2. Prepare entries to record amortization on the machine on December 31 of its first year and on September 30 in the year of its disposal.
3. Prepare entries to record the retirement of the machine under each of the following unrelated assumptions: (a) it was sold for $13,500; (b) it was sold for $36,000; and (c) it was destroyed in a fire and the insurance company paid $24,000 in full settlement of the loss claim.

Crenshaw Contractors completed these transactions involving the purchase and operation of heavy equipment:

19X1

July 1 Paid $255,440 cash for a new front-end loader, plus $15,200 in sales tax and $2,500 for transportation charges. The loader was estimated to have a four-year life and a $34,740 salvage value.

Oct. 2 Paid $3,660 to enclose the cab and install air conditioning in the loader. This increased the estimated salvage value of the loader by $1,110.

Dec. 31 Recorded straight-line amortization on the loader.

19X2

Feb. 17 Paid $920 to repair the loader after the operator backed it into a tree.

June 30 Paid $4,500 to overhaul the loader's engine. As a result, the estimated useful life of the loader was increased by two years.

Dec. 31 Recorded straight-line amortization on the loader.

Required

Prepare journal entries to record the transactions.

Problem 12-3
Alternative amortization methods; partial year's amortization; disposal of capital asset

LO 4, 6, 8

Check Figure Year 4, units-of-production amortization expense, $44,640

Problem 12-4
Partial year's amortization; revising amortization rates; revenue and capital expenditures

LO 6, 7

Check Figure Dec 31, 19X2, Accumulated Amortization, Heavy Equipment, $48,674

Problem 12-5
Partial year's amortization; revising amortization rates; exchanging capital assets

LO 6, 8

ACT, Inc., completed the following transactions involving delivery trucks:

19X1

Mar. 26   Paid cash for a new delivery truck, $19,415 plus $1,165 sales tax. The truck was estimated to have a five-year life and a $3,000 trade-in value.

Dec. 31   Recorded straight-line amortization on the truck.

19X2

Dec. 31   Recorded straight-line amortization on the truck. However, due to new information obtained earlier in the year, the original estimated useful life of the truck was changed from five years to four years, and the original estimated trade-in value was increased to $3,500.

19X3

July 7   Traded in the old truck and paid $13,565 in cash for a new truck. The new truck was estimated to have a six-year life and a $3,125 trade-in value. The invoice for the exchange showed these items:

Price of the new truck	$22,550
Trade-in allowance granted on the old truck	(9,750)
Balance of purchase price	$12,800
Sales tax	765
Total paid in cash	$13,565

Dec. 31   Recorded straight-line amortization on the new truck.

Check Figure July 7, 19X3, Loss on Exchange of Delivery Trucks, $1,527

Required

Prepare journal entries to record the transactions.

Problem 12-6
Partial year's amortization; alternative methods; disposal of capital assets

LO 6, 4, 8

Wallingford Co. completed the following transactions involving machinery:

Machine No. 15-50 was purchased for cash on May 4, 19X1, at an installed cost of $158,700. Its useful life was estimated to be six years with a $12,900 trade-in value. Straight-line amortization was recorded for the machine at the end of 19X1, 19X2, and 19X3. On April 27, 19X4, it was traded for Machine No. 17-95, a similar asset with an installed cash price of $185,700. A trade-in allowance of $90,330 was received for Machine No. 15-50, and the balance was paid in cash.

Machine No. 17-95's life was predicted to be four years with a $24,600 trade-in value. Double-declining-balance amortization on this machine was recorded each December 31. On November 5, 19X5, it was traded for Machine No. BT-311, which was a dissimilar asset with an installed cash price of $537,000. A trade-in allowance of $81,000 was received for Machine No. 17-95, and the balance was paid in cash.

It was estimated that Machine No. BT-311 would produce 600,000 units of product during its five-year useful life, after which it would have a $105,000 trade-in value. Units-of-production amortization was recorded for the machine for 19X5, a period in which it produced 93,000 units of product. Between January 1, 19X6, and August 24, 19X8, the machine produced 324,000 more units. On the latter date, it was sold for $243,600.

Check Figure Nov 5/X5 Gain on Sale of Machinery, $8,783.

Required

Prepare journal entries to record: (a) the purchase of each machine, (b) the amortization expense recorded on the first December 31 of each machine's life, and (c) the disposal of each machine. (Only one entry is needed to record the exchange of one machine for another.)

Part 1. In 19X1, The Pullman Company leased space in a building for 15 years. The lease contract calls for annual rental payments of $70,000 to be made on each July 1 throughout the life of the lease and also provides that the lessee must pay for all additions and improvements to the leased property. In 19X6, Pullman decided to sublease the space to Kidman & Associates for the remaining 10 years of the lease. On June 20, 19X6, Kidman paid $185,000 to Pullman for the right to sublease the space and agreed to assume the obligation to pay the $70,000 annual rent to the building owner beginning July 1, 19X6. After taking possession of the leased space, Kidman paid for improving the office portion of the leased space at a cost of $129,840. The improvements were paid for on July 5, 19X6, and are estimated to have a life equal to the 16 years remaining in the life of the building.

Problem 12-7
Intangible assets and
natural resources
LO 9, 10

Required

Prepare entries for Kidman to record (a) its payment to Pullman for the right to sublease the building space, (b) its payment of the 19X6 annual rent to the building owner, and (c) its payment for the office improvements. Also, prepare the adjusting entries required at the end of 19X6 to amortize (d) a proper share of the $185,000 cost of the sublease, (e) a proper share of the office improvements and (f) a proper share of the rent expense applicable to 19X6.

Part 2. On July 3 of the current year, Jackson Mining Co. paid $4,836,000 for land estimated to contain 7.8 million tonnes of recoverable ore of a valuable mineral. It installed machinery costing $390,000, which had a 10-year life and no salvage value, and was capable of exhausting the ore deposit in eight years. The machinery was paid for on July 25, nine days before mining operations began. The company removed 400,000 tonnes of ore during the first five months of operations.

Required

Preparation component:

Prepare entries to record (a) the purchase of the land, (b) the installation of the machinery, (c) the first five months' depletion under the assumption that the land will be valueless after the ore is mined, and (d) the first five months' amortization on the machinery, which will be abandoned after the ore is fully mined.

Check Figure Depletion
Expense, $248,000

Analysis component:

Describe the similarities and differences in depletion, and amortization.

Canadian Rental Co. an equipment rental business, has the following balance sheet on December 31, 19X1:

Problem 12-8
Goodwill
LO 10

Cash	$ 93,930
Equipment	678,800
Accumulated amortization, equipment	(271,500)
Buildings	340,000
Accumulated amortization, buildings	(182,400)
Land	93,000
Total assets	$751,830
Accounts payable	$ 18,650
Long-term note payable	337,250
J. Reynolds, capital	395,930
Total liabilities and owner's equity	$751,830

In this industry, earnings average 20% of owner's equity. Canadian Rental, however, is expected to earn $100,000 annually. The balance sheet amounts are reasonable estimates of fair market values for all assets except goodwill, which does not appear on the financial statement. In negotiations to sell the business, Canadian Rental has proposed that goodwill should be measured by capitalizing the amount of above-average earnings at a rate of 15%. On the other hand, the potential buyer thinks that goodwill should be valued at five times the amount of earnings above the average for the industry.

Required

1. Compute the amount of goodwill proposed by Canadian Rental.
2. Compute the amount of goodwill according to the potential buyer.
3. Suppose that the buyer purchases the business for the amount of the net assets reported on the December 31, 19X1, balance sheet plus the amount proposed by Canadian Rental for the goodwill. If the amount of expected earnings (before amortization of goodwill) is obtained the first year, and the goodwill is amortized over the longest permissible time period, what amount of net income will be reported for the first year after the business is purchased?
4. What rate of return on the buyer's investment does the first year's net income represent?

Check Figure Goodwill, $138,760 or $104,070

Alternate Problems

Problem 12-1A
Real estate costs; partial year's amortization

LO 2, 3, 6

In 19X1, Spicewood Technologies paid $1,350,000 for a tract of land on which two buildings were located. The plan was to demolish Building A and build a new shop in its place. Building B was to be used as a company office and was appraised at a value of $472,770, with a useful life of 15 years and a $90,000 salvage value. A lighted parking lot near Building B had improvements valued at $125,145 that were expected to last another six years and have no salvage value. Without considering the buildings or improvements, the tract of land was estimated to have a value of $792,585.

Spicewood incurred the following additional costs:

Cost to demolish Building A	$ 117,000
Cost of additional landscaping	172,500
Cost to construct new building (Building C), having a useful life of 20 years and a $295,500 salvage value	1,356,000
Cost of new land improvements near Building C, which have a 10-year useful life and no salvage value	101,250

Required

1. Prepare a schedule having the following column headings: Land, Building B, Building C, Land Improvements B, and Land Improvements C. Allocate the costs incurred by Spicewood to the appropriate columns and total each column.
2. Prepare a single journal entry dated October 1 to record all the incurred costs, assuming they were paid in cash on that date.
3. Using the straight-line method, prepare December 31 adjusting entries to record amortization for the three months of 19X1 during which the assets were in use.

The Timberline Company recently negotiated a lump-sum purchase of several assets from a contractor who was planning to change locations. The purchase was completed on September 30, 19X1, at a total cash price of $1,610,000, and included a building, land, certain land improvements, and six trucks. The estimated market values of the assets were: building, $784,800; land, $540,640; land improvements, $226,720; and trucks, $191,840. The company's fiscal year ends on December 31.

Required

Preparation component:

1. Prepare a schedule to allocate the lump-sum purchase price to the separate assets that were purchased. Also present the journal entry to record the purchase.

2. Compute the 19X1 amortization expense on the building using the straight-line method, assuming a 12-year life and a $100,500 trade-in value.

3. Compute the 19X1 amortization expense on the land improvements assuming a 10-year life and double-declining-balance amortization.

Analysis component:

4. Defend or refute this statement: Accelerated amortization results in higher taxes over the life of the asset.

Problem 12-2A
Capital asset costs; partial year's amortization; alternative methods
LO 2, 3, 6

Part 1. On January 2, Brodie Co. purchased and installed a new machine that cost $312,000, with a five-year life and an estimated $28,000 salvage value. Management estimated that the machine would produce 1,136,000 units of product during its life. Actual production of units was as follows: Year 1, 245,600; Year 2, 230,400; Year 3, 227,000; Year 4, 232,600; and Year 5, 211,200. Note that the total number of units produced by the end of Year 5 exceeded the original estimate. Nevertheless, the machine should not be amortized below the estimated salvage value.

Required
Prepare a schedule with the following column headings:

Year	Straight-Line	Units-of-Production	Double-Declining-Balance

Then show the amortization for each year and the total amortization for the machine under each amortization method.

Part 2. On January 1, Brodie purchased a used machine for $130,000. The next day, it was repaired at a cost of $3,390 and was mounted on a new platform that cost $4,800. Management estimated that the machine would be used for seven years and would then have a $18,000 salvage value. Amortization was to be charged on a straight-line basis. A full year's amortization was charged on December 31 of the first through the fifth years of the machine's use; and on April 1 of its sixth year of use, the machine was retired from service.

Required

1. Prepare journal entries to record the purchase of the machine, the cost of repairing it, and the installation. Assume that cash was paid.

2. Prepare entries to record amortization on the machine on December 31 of its first year and on April 1 in the year of its disposal.

3. Prepare entries to record the retirement of the machine under each of the following unrelated assumptions: (a) it was sold for $30,000; (b) it was sold for $50,000; and (c) it was destroyed in a fire and the insurance company paid $20,000 in full settlement of the loss claim.

Problem 12-3A
Alternative amortization methods; partial year's amortization; disposal of capital assets
LO 4, 6, 8

Problem 12-4A
Partial year's amortization; revising amortization rates; revenue and capital expenditures

LO 6, 7

Rush Delivery Service completed these transactions involving the purchase and operation of delivery equipment:

19X1

Mar. 25 Paid cash for a new delivery van, $24,950 plus $1,950 sales tax. The van was estimated to have a five-year life and a $3,400 salvage value.

Sept. 30 Paid $1,550 to replace the manual transmission in the van with an automatic transmission. This increased the estimated salvage value of the van by $200.

Dec. 31 Recorded straight-line amortization on the van.

19X2

May 10 Paid $600 to repair the van after the driver backed it into a loading dock.

Oct. 1 Paid $1,970 to overhaul the van's engine. As a result, the estimated useful life of the van was increased by two years.

Dec. 31 Recorded straight-line amortization on the van.

Required

Prepare journal entries to record the transactions.

Problem 12-5A
Partial year's amortization; revising amortization rates; exchanging capital assets

LO 6, 8

Precision Machine Shop completed the following transactions involving machinery:

19X1

June 24 Paid cash for a new machine, $106,600 plus $6,400 sales tax. The machine was estimated to have a six-year life and a $9,800 trade-in value.

Dec. 31 Recorded straight-line amortization on the machine.

19X2

Dec. 31 Recorded straight-line amortization on the machine. However, due to new information obtained earlier in the year, the original estimated useful life of the lathe was changed from six years to four years, and the original estimated trade-in value was increased to $13,050.

19X3

Nov. 4 Traded in the old machine and paid $89,500 in cash for a new, similar machine. The new machine was estimated to have an eight-year life and a $10,380 trade-in value. The invoice for the exchange showed these items:

Price of the new machine	$123,000
Trade-in allowance granted on the old machine	(38,000)
Balance of purchase price	$ 85,000
Sales tax	4,500
Total paid in cash	$ 89,500

Dec. 31 Recorded straight-line amortization on the new machine.

Required

Prepare journal entries to record the transactions.

Problem 12-6A
Partial year's amortization; alternative methods; disposal of capital assets

LO 6, 4, 8

Central Printing Co. completed the following transactions involving printing equipment:

Printing press A was purchased for cash on April 3, 19X1, at an installed cost of $169,400. Its useful life was estimated to be seven years with a $25,200 trade-in value. Straight-line amortization was recorded for the press at the end of 19X1, 19X2, and 19X3, and on July 2, 19X4, it was traded for printing press B, a similar asset with an installed cash price of $206,400. A trade-in allowance of $112,000 was received for printing press A, and the balance was paid in cash.

Printing press B's life was predicted to be ten years with an $22,000 trade-in value. Double-declining-balance amortization was recorded on each December 31 of its life. On March 31, 19X6, it was traded for a colour laser copier, which was a dissimilar asset with an installed cash price of $153,000. A trade-in allowance of $138,000 was received for printing press B, and the balance was paid in cash.

It was estimated that the copier would produce 1,000,000 copies during its four-year useful life, after which it would have a $13,000 trade-in value. Units-of-production amortization was recorded for the copier for 19X6, a period in which it produced 190,000 copies. Between January 1, 19X7, and February 10, 19X9, the copier produced 640,000 more copies. On the latter date, it was sold for $40,000.

Required

For each piece of equipment, prepare journal entries to record: (a) its purchase, (b) the amortization expense recorded on the first December 31 of its life, and (c) its disposal. (Only one entry is needed to record the exchange of one piece of equipment for another.)

Part 1. In 19X1, Granite Co. leased space in a building for 12 years. The lease contract requires: (1) $26,400 annual rental payments to be made each May 1 throughout the life of the lease, and (2) the lessee to pay for all additions and improvements to the leased property. In 19X8, Granite decided to sublease the space to Magnolia Service Co. for the remaining five years of the lease. On April 25, 19X8, Magnolia paid $30,000 to Granite for the right to sublease the space, and agreed to assume the obligation to pay the $26,400 annual rent to the building owner beginning May 1, 19X8. After taking possession of the leased space, Magnolia paid for improving the office portion of the leased space at a cost of $18,000. The improvements were paid for on May 6, 19X8, and are estimated to have a life equal to the 13 years remaining in the life of the building.

Problem 12-7A
Intangible assets and natural resources

LO 9, 10

Required

Prepare entries for Magnolia to record (a) its payment to Granite for the right to sublease the building space, (b) its payment of the 19X8 annual rent to the building owner, and (c) its payment for the office improvements. Also, prepare the adjusting entries required on December 31, 19X8, to amortize (d) a proper share of the $30,000 cost of the sublease, (e) a proper share of the office improvements and (f) a proper share of the rent expense applicable to 19X8.

Part 2. On February 19 of the current year, Wayman Industries paid $4,450,000 for land estimated to contain five million tonnes of recoverable ore of a valuable mineral. It installed machinery costing $200,000, which had a 16-year life and no salvage value, and was capable of exhausting the ore deposit in 12 years. The machinery was paid for on March 21, eleven days before mining operations began. The company removed 352,000 tonnes of ore during the first nine months of operations.

Required

Preparation component:

Prepare entries to record (a) the purchase of the land, (b) the installation of the machinery, (c) the first nine months' depletion under the assumption that the land will be valueless after the ore is mined, and (d) the first nine months' amortization on the machinery, which will be abandoned after the ore is fully mined.

Analysis component:

Describe the similarities and differences in depletion and amortization.

Kudos Casual Wear has the following balance sheet on December 31, 19X1:

Cash	$ 138,700
Merchandise inventory	607,950
Buildings	451,500
Accumulated amortization	(210,800)
Land	192,400
Total assets	$1,179,750
Accounts payable	$ 98,325
Long-term note payable	414,050
N. Pursley, capital	667,375
Total liabilities and owner's equity	$1,179,750

In this industry, earnings average 32% of owner's equity. Kudos, however, is expected to earn $230,000 annually. The balance sheet amounts are reasonable estimates of fair market values for all assets except goodwill, which does not appear on the financial statements. In negotiations to sell the business, Kudos has proposed that goodwill should be measured by capitalizing the amount of above-average earnings at a rate of 10%. On the other hand, the potential buyer thinks that goodwill should be valued at eight times the amount of earnings above the average for the industry.

Required

1. Compute the amount of goodwill proposed by Kudos.
2. Compute the amount of goodwill according to the potential buyer.
3. Suppose that the buyer purchases the business for the amount of the net assets reported on the December 31, 19X1, balance sheet, plus the amount proposed by Kudos for the goodwill. If the amount of expected earnings (before amortization of goodwill) is obtained the first year, and the goodwill is amortized over the longest permissible time period, what amount of net income will be reported for the first year after the business is purchased?
4. What rate of return on the buyer's investment does the first year's net income represent?

At the last meeting of the executive committee of Kearins, Ltd., Milton Vacon, controller, was severely criticized by both President Kearins and Kate Ryan, vice president of production. The subject of criticism was the recognition of periodic amortization. President Kearins was unhappy with the fact that what he referred to as "a fictitious item" was deducted, resulting in depressed net income. In his words, "Depreciation is a fiction when the assets being depreciated are worth far more than we paid for them. What the controller is doing is unduly understating our net income. This in turn is detrimental to our shareholders because it results in the undervaluation of our shares on the market."

Vice President Ryan was equally adamant about the periodic amortization charges; however, she came on from another side. She said, "Our maintenance people tell me that the level of maintenance is such that our plant and equipment will last virtually forever." She further stated that charging amortization on top of maintenance expenses is double-counting—it seems reasonable to charge either maintenance or amortization but not both.

The time taken by other pressing matters did not permit Vacon to answer; instead, the controller was asked to prepare a report to the executive committee to deal with the issues raised by the president and vice president.

Required

The controller asks you, his assistant, to prepare the required report.

The Shape Company purchased a large earth-mover four years ago at a cost of $750,000. At that time it was estimated that the economic life of the equipment would be 12 years and that its ultimate salvage value would be $140,000.

Assuming the company uses straight-line amortization, state whether each of the following events requires a revision of the original amortization rate, with reasons for your answer:

a. Due to persistent inflation, the present replacement cost of the same type of equipment is $975,000.

b. Because of the higher replacement cost, as described in (a) above, the ultimate salvage value is now estimated at $95,000.

c. The company, in connection with having its line of credit increased, was required by the bank to have the assets appraised. The earth-mover was estimated to have a current value of $450,000.

d. At the time the appraisal was made in (c) above, it was determined that technological change was progressing more slowly than originally estimated and that the earth-mover would probably remain in service for 15 years with the ultimate salvage value as originally estimated at the end of 12 years.

A & R Problem 12-2

BEYOND THE NUMBERS

Refer to the financial statements and related information for **Alliance** in Appendix I. Answer the following questions by analyzing the information in its annual report:

1. What percent of the original cost of Alliance's property and equipment remains to be amortized as of March 31, 1997 and 1996? Assume these assets have no salvage value.

2. Over what periods of time is Alliance amortizing intangible assets and goodwill?

3. What is the net change in total property and equipment (before amortization) for the year ended March 31, 1997? What is the amount of cash generated by (or used for) investment in property and equipment during the year ended March 31, 1997? What is one possible explanation for the difference between these two amounts?

4. Compute Alliance's total asset turnover for the year ended March 31, 1997.

Reporting in Action

Both **Alliance** and **Atlantis** produce and distribute movies and television programs. Key comparative figures ($thousands) for these two companies follow:

Key Figures	Alliance		Atlantis	
	1997	**1996**	**1997**	**1996**
Total Assets	$353,722	$238,898	$333,547	$334,826
Net Sales	$282,599	$268,945	$177,960	$137,984

* Alliance figures are from the annual reports for the fiscal years ended March 31, 1997 and 1996.

Atlantis figures are from the annual reports for the fiscal years ended December 31, 1997 and 1996.

Comparative Analysis

Required

1. Compute Alliance's total asset turnover as of March 31, 1997. Compute Atlantis' total asset turnover as of December 31, 1997.

Analysis Component:

2. Which company is more efficient in generating net sales given the total assets employed?

**Ethics
Challenge**

LO 3

Marcia Diamond is a small business owner and handles all the books for her business. Her company just finished a year when a large amount of borrowed funds were invested into a new building addition as well as numerous equipment and fixture additions. Marcia's banker requires that she submit semiannual financial statements for his file so he can monitor the financial health of her business. He has warned her that if profit margins erode he might raise the interest rate on the borrowed funds since this means the loan is riskier from the bank's point of view. Marcia knows profit margin is likely to decline in this current year. As she posts year-end adjusting entries she decides to apply the following amortization rule: All capital additions for the current year are considered put into service the first day of the following month.

Required

1. Identify the decisions managers like Ms. Diamond must make in applying amortization methods.
2. Is Marcia's decision an ethical violation or is it a legitimate decision that managers make in computing amortization?
3. How will Marcia's amortization rule affect the profit margin of her business?

**Communicating
in Practice**

LO 12

The classroom should be divided into teams. Teams are to select an industry, and each team member is to select a different company in that industry. Each team member is to acquire the annual report of the company selected. Annual reports can be obtained in many ways including accessing this book's Web page or **http://www.sedar.com**. Use the annual report to compute total asset turnover. Communicate with teammates via a meeting, e-mail or telephone to discuss the meaning of this ratio, how different companies compare to each other, and the industry norm. The team must prepare a single memo reporting the ratios for each company and identify the conclusions or consensus of opinion reached during the team's discussion. The memo is to be duplicated and distributed to the instructor and all classmates.

**Taking It to
the Net**

LO 1

Visit the Web site of the Canadian Intellectual Property Office at **http://strategis.ic.gc.ca**. Use the search function to look for any existing patents protecting some of your favourite products. For example, if you search "hockey skates" you will find a patent protecting a Blade for Ice Hockey Skates. Search three different products and note the range of patents protecting the product. (Note: If you have an idea for a new product you might also want to search the database to see if there are any preexisting patents on your idea.)

**Teamwork in
Action**

LO 3, 5, 4

Each member of the team has a responsibility to become a resident expert on a specific amortization method. This expertise is used to facilitate their teammates understanding of the concepts relevant to the method they have chosen. Follow the procedure outlined below:

1. Each team member is to select their area for expertise by choosing one of the following amortization methods: straight-line, units-of-production, and declining-balance. You have one minute to make your choice.
2. Learning teams are to disburse and expert teams are to be formed. Expert teams are made up of students who have all selected the same area of expertise. The instructor will identify the location where each expert team meets.
3. Using data below, the expert teams are to collaborate and develop a presentation illustrating each of the relevant procedures and concepts required below. Each expert team member must write-up the presentation in a format they can show to their learning teams in the next step in the activity.
4. **Data:**
   On January 8, 1998, Whitewater Riders purchased a van to transport rafters back to the point of departure at the conclusion of the rafting adventure tours they run. The cost of the van is $44,000. It has an estimated salvage value of $2,000 and is expected to be used for four years and to be driven 100,000 kilometres. The van is expected to be driven 20,000 kilometres in 1998, 30,000 kilometres in 1999, 34,000 in 2000, and 16,000 in 2001.

Procedures and concepts to illustrate in expert presentation:

a. Compute annual amortization expense for each year of the asset's estimated useful life.

b. Explain when and how annual amortization is recorded.

c. Explain the impact of this method versus other methods on net income over the life of the asset.

d. Identify the book value of the asset over each year of the asset's life and illustrate the reporting of this amount for any one year.

4. Re-form learning teams. In rotation, each expert is to present to their teams the results from part 3. Experts are to encourage and respond to questions.

Team up with one or more classmates for this activity. You are to brainstorm and do any necessary research to identify companies in your community or your area of the country that have and must account for the following assets: natural resource; patent; lease; leasehold improvement; copyright; trademark; and goodwill.

You might need to identify seven different companies given there are seven assets or you might find a company having more than one type of asset. Once you have matched a company with the asset, then identify the accounting this company must use for that asset to allocate its cost to the periods benefited from its use.

Read the article "Guardian of the Famous and the Dead" in the May 8, 1995, issue of *Business Week*.

1. What is the purpose of the **Curtis Management Group** run by CEO Mark A. Roesler?

2. What is the difference between a "trademark" and "rights of publicity"?

3. Identify one famous person in each of the following categories represented by the Curtis Management Group: movies, music, sports and historical.

Hitting the Road
LO 1

Business Break
LO 1

13

CHAPTER

Current and Long-Term Liabilities

Chapter Outline

Tax Cop

Ottawa, ON—Carmen Benish and her two comrades jump out of their battered Zhiguli and walk briskly to the door of a bicycle sales and services shop in the Moscow suburb of Podolsk. Ducking under bicycle frames and wheels hanging from the ceiling, they approach a salesclerk and flash their badges. A few days earlier, an undercover colleague made a purchase that wasn't rung up on the register. Now, Benish, Mikail Nikolas and Val Yaroslav are investigating whether the business is underreporting sales to avoid paying taxes. Two burly policemen in bulletproof vests stand guard as Benish and her fellow investigators confiscate Vladimir Zolov's records. "We pay our taxes on time. We are law-abiding citizens," he protests.

Benish is unique. She grew up in a tough Halifax environment. But Benish was determined to stay out of trouble. "I went to community college and took accounting and criminal justice," says Benish. "I also joined an international group. Loved the cultural differences." When she graduated with her degree this past June, she faced a dilemma. "I really liked both accounting and criminal justice," says Benish. "I didn't know which way to go."

Fortunately for Benish, her counsellor heard that sometimes people with exactly the type of background Benish has are hired by a unique program for international tax investigators. "It is a match made in heaven! I get to use my accounting and criminal justice background to help track down people who are underreporting international income to avoid taxes." Given the huge growth in international sales, this is a high priority.

Benish is presently assigned to a one-month internship in Moscow. "Russia's environment is a nightmare for us," says Peter Eastwood, Benish's supervisor. "But our job is to ensure that companies and their affiliates doing business here, pay their required taxes." These investigators also have considerable power. They can levy fines up to three times taxes owed, and can seize taxpayers' property and freeze bank accounts during investigations.

But the job is dangerous. Last year in Russia alone, 26 tax officials were killed and 74 wounded, while 18 tax offices were bombed or sprayed with gunfire. "Sure I'm scared sometimes." says Benish. "But I'm really having fun, and the odds of something bad happening are pretty low." Adds Benish, "No green eyeshades and cushy desk job for me!"

CHAPTER PREVIEW

Previous chapters introduced us to liabilities for accounts payable, notes payable, wages, and unearned revenues. In this chapter, we learn more about these liabilities and additional ones such as warranties, taxes, vacation pay, and leases. We also describe contingent liabilities and look at some long-term liabilities. This includes how we define, classify, and measure liabilities for the purpose of reporting useful information about them to decision makers. Understanding tax liabilities is especially important for Carmen Benish and people like her as described in the opening article.

Characteristics of Liabilities

This section discusses important characteristics of liabilities, how they are classified, and how they are reported when there are questions about them.

LO1 Describe current and long-term liabilities and their characteristics.

Defining Liabilities

A liability is a probable future payment of assets or services that a company is presently obligated to make as a result of past transactions or events.[1] This definition includes three crucial factors:

■ Due to past transaction or event
■ Present obligation
■ Future payment of assets or services

These elements are portrayed visually in Exhibit 13.1.

Exhibit 13.1

Characteristics of a Liability

Because of a past event ...

The company has a present obligation

... For future sacrifices

Past   Present   Future

Liabilities do not include all expected future payments. For example, most companies expect to pay wages to their employees in upcoming months and years. But these future payments are not liabilities because the company is not presently obligated to pay them until employees earn their future wages. In this case, there is no past event such as employee work resulting in a present obligation. Future liabilities will arise when employees perform their work.

Classifying Liabilities as Current or Long-Term

Information about liabilities is more useful when the balance sheet identifies them as either current or long-term. Decision makers need to know when obligations are due so they can plan for them and take appropriate action. Others use financial statements to predict future cash flows and knowing when obligations are due aids this process.

Current Liabilities

Current liabilities, also called *short-term liabilities*, are obligations expected to be paid using current assets or by creating other current liabilities (e.g., replacing an account payable with a note payable).[2] Current liabilities are due within one year or the company's operating cycle, whichever is longer. Examples of current liabilities are accounts payable, short-term notes payable, wages payable, warranty liabilities, lease liabilities, payroll and other taxes payable, and unearned revenues.

---

[1] *CICA Handbook*, section 1000, "Financial Statement Concepts," par. 32.
[2] *CICA Handbook*, section 1510, "Current Assets and Current Liabilities," par. .03

Long-Term Liabilities

A company's obligations not expected to be paid within one year (or a longer operating cycle) are reported as **long-term liabilities.** Long-term liabilities include long-term notes payable, warranty liabilities, lease liabilities, and bonds payable. They are sometimes reported on the balance sheet in a single long-term liabilities total. But many companies show them as two or more items such as *long-term debt* and *other liabilities.* **Barrick Gold Corporation,** for instance, reports long-term liabilities in its fiscal 1997 balance sheet of ($ millions): long-term debt, $500; reclamation and closure liabilities, $144; deferred income taxes, $145. These are reported after current liabilities.

Liabilities can be either current or long-term depending on their characteristics. A single liability also can be divided between these two sections if a company expects to make payments toward it in both the short- and long-term. **Alcan Aluminium,** for instance, reports in its 1997 balance sheet ($ millions): debt not maturing within one year, $1,241; debt maturing within one year, $36. The second item is reported in current liabilities. We sometimes see liabilities not having a fixed due date, but payable on the creditor's demand. They are reported as current liabilities because of the possibility of payment within the year or its longer operating cycle. Exhibit 13.2 shows amounts of current and long-term liabilities for selected companies.

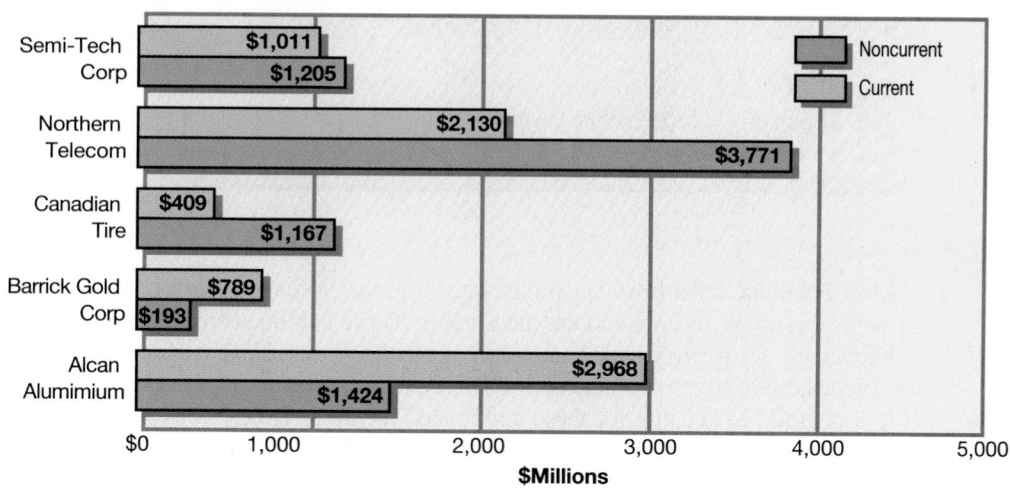

Exhibit 13.2

Current and Long-Term Liabilities

Uncertainty in Liabilities

Liabilities involve three important questions: Whom to pay? When to pay? How much to pay? Answers to these questions often are decided when a liability is incurred. For example, if a company has an account payable to a specific individual for $100, payable on August 15, 1999, there is no uncertainty about the answers. The company knows whom to pay, when to pay, and how much to pay. But we do see liabilities with uncertainty in one or more of the answers to these three questions.

Uncertainty in Whom to Pay

Certain liabilities involve uncertainty as to whom is to be paid. For instance, a company creates a liability with a known amount when issuing a note that is payable to its holder. This type of note is negotiable and can be sold by the holder to another party. Although a specific amount is payable to the note's holder at a specified date, the company does not know who the holder is until that date. Despite this uncertainty, the corporation reports this liability on its balance sheet.

Uncertainty in When to Pay

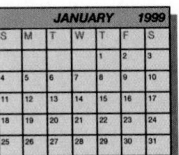

A company can have an obligation of a known amount to a known creditor but not know when it must be paid. For example, a legal services firm can accept fees in advance from a client who expects to use its services in the future. This means the legal services firm has a liability that is settled by providing services at an unknown future date. Even though this uncertainty exists, the firm's balance sheet must report this liability. These types of obligations are reported as current liabilities because they may be settled in the short term.

Uncertainty in How Much to Pay

A company can know it has an obligation but not know how much will be required to settle it. For example, a company using electrical power is billed only after the meter is read. This cost is incurred and the liability created before a bill is received. A liability to the electric company is reported as an estimated amount if the balance sheet is prepared before a bill arrives.

★Flash back

1. What is a liability?
2. Is every expected future payment a liability?
3. If a liability is payable in 15 months, is it classified as current or long-term?

Answers—p. 642

Known (Determinable) Liabilities

 Identify and describe known current liabilities.

Most liabilities arise from situations with little uncertainty. They are set by agreements, contracts, or laws and are measurable. These liabilities are called **known liabilities**, or sometimes called *definitely determinable liabilities*. Known liabilities include accounts payable, notes payable, payroll, sales taxes, unearned revenues, and leases. How we account for these and related liabilities is described in this section.

Accounts Payable

Accounts payable, or trade accounts payable, are amounts owed to suppliers for products or services purchased on credit. Accounting for accounts payable is explained and illustrated in several prior chapters. Much of our discussion of merchandising activities in Chapters 6 and 7, for instance, dealt with accounts payable.

Goods and Services Tax and Sales Taxes Payable

Sales tax liabilities arise because the federal government and most provincial governments require businesses to act as collection agencies for the Goods and Services Tax (GST) and provincial sales taxes (PSTs). When a business makes a sale, the customer is charged for the sales tax on top of the selling price, in most cases, and the tax is later paid to the government(s).

Chapter 6 illustrated how the sales taxes would be accumulated in the sales journal. Assume that Superior Clothing Store collected $8,750 of GST and $7,500 of PST[3] during September. At the end of September these amounts would appear

---

[3] In some jurisdictions the GST and PST are combined into the harmonized sales tax (HST).

on the balance sheet as current liabilities. The entry to pay these taxes during October would be as follows:

Oct. 25	GST Payable	8,750	
	Cash		8,750
	To pay GST for September.		

Assets = Liabilities + Equity
−8,750   −8,750

Oct. 25	PST Payable	7,500	
	Cash		7,500
	To pay PST for September.		

Assets = Liabilities + Equity
−7,500   −7,500

Note that the sales taxes are neither a revenue nor an expense for the enterprise. However, when a business purchases goods and services for its own use, the sales taxes (GST and PST) paid become part of the cost of these items. In the case of goods purchased for resale, either the business would be exempt from paying the sales taxes on the purchase or the sales taxes paid could be deducted from the sales taxes collected when determining the amount to be remitted to the government(s).

Unearned Revenues

Unearned revenues (also called deferred revenues, collections in advance, and pre-payments) are amounts received in advance from customers for future products or services. Advance ticket sales for sporting events or music concerts are examples of unearned revenues. **Orca Bay Hockey Holdings Inc.,** owners of the Vancouver Canucks, reported "Deferred revenue on advance sale of tickets" of nearly $6 million at June 30, 1997. When Orca sells $6 million of advanced tickets, its entry is:

July 30	Cash	6,000,000	
	Deferred Revenue		6,000,000
	To record sale of Canuck season tickets		

Assets   =   Liabilities + Equity
+6,000,000   +6,000,000

As the hockey season progresses Orca records the portion of revenue earned:

Oct. 30	Deferred Revenue	40,000	
	Season Ticket Revenue		40,000
	To record season ticket revenues earned.		

Assets   =   Liabilities + Equity
           −40,000   +40,000

Deferred Revenue is an unearned revenue account and is reported as a current liability. Beyond sporting and music events, unearned revenues arise with airline ticket sales, magazine publishers, construction projects, hotel reservations, and custom orders.

Short-Term Notes Payable

A **short-term note payable** is a written promise to pay a specified amount on a specified future date within one year or the company's operating cycle, whichever is longer. These promissory notes are negotiable (as are cheques). This means they can be transferred from party to party by endorsement. Written documentation is helpful in resolving disputes and for pursuing legal actions involving liabilities. Most notes payable are interest bearing to compensate for the time until payment is made. Short-term notes payable arise from many transactions. A company purchases merchandise on credit and sometimes extends the credit period by signing a note to replace an account payable. They also arise when money is borrowed from a bank. We describe both these cases in this section.

LO3 Prepare entries to account for short-term notes payable.

Note Given to Extend Credit Period

A company can create a note payable to replace an account payable. Most often, the creditor asks that an interest-bearing note be substituted for an overdue account payable that does not bear interest. A less common situation is where a debtor's weak financial condition encourages the creditor to obtain a note, sometimes for a lesser amount, and then close the account to ensure no additional credit sales are made to this customer.

Illustration of Note to Extend Credit Period

To illustrate, let's assume on August 23 that Wiley asks to extend its past-due $600 account payable to McGraw. After some negotiations, McGraw agrees to accept $100 cash and a 60-day, 12%, $500 note payable to replace the account payable. Wiley records this transaction with this entry:

Assets = Liabilities + Equity
−100   −600
        +500

Aug. 23	Accounts Payable—McGraw Company	600	
	Cash		100
	Notes Payable		500
	Gave $100 cash and a 60-day, 12% note to extend due date on account.		

Signing the note does not pay off Wiley's debt. Instead, the form of debt is changed from an account to a note payable. McGraw prefers the note over the account payable because it earns interest and also because it is documentation of the debt's existence, term and amount.

When the note comes due, Wiley pays the note and interest by giving McGraw a cheque for $509.86. This payment is recorded with this entry:

Assets = Liabilities + Equity
−509.86   −500   −9.86

Oct. 22	Notes Payable	500.00	
	Interest Expense	9.86	
	Cash		509.86
	Paid note with interest ($500 × 12% × 60/365).		

The interest expense is computed by multiplying the principal of the note ($500) by the annual interest rate (12%) for the fraction of the year the note is outstanding (60 days/365 days).

Note Given to Borrow from Bank

A bank nearly always requires a borrower to sign a promissory note when making a loan. The borrower then repays the note with a larger amount than received when the note matures. The difference between the amount received and the amount repaid is *interest*. A note often states the signer of the note promises to pay *principal* (the amount borrowed) plus interest. In this case the *face value* of the note equals principal. Face value is the value shown on the face of the note.

A bank sometimes has a borrower sign a note with a face value that includes both principal and interest. In this case the signer of the note receives *less* than the note's face value. The difference between the borrowed amount and the note's face value is interest. Since the borrowed amount is less than the note's face value, the difference is sometimes called **discount on note payable.**

To illustrate these two different loans, let's assume a company needs $2,000 for a specific project and borrows this money from a bank at 12% annual interest. The loan is made on September 30, 1999, and is due in 60 days.

Face Value Equals Amount Borrowed

The bank in this case requires the company to sign a note with a face value equal to the $2,000 borrowed. The note includes a statement similar to: "I promise to pay $2,000 plus interest at 12% within 60 days after September 30." This note is shown in Exhibit 13.3. The borrowing company records its receipt of cash and the new liability with this entry:

Sept.30	Cash	2,000.00	
	Notes Payable		2,000.00
	Borrowed $2,000 cash with a 60-day,		
	12%, $2,000 note.		

Assets = Liabilities + Equity
+2,000   +2,000

When the note and interest are paid 60 days later, the company records payment with this entry:

Nov. 29	Notes Payable	2,000.00	
	Interest Expense	39.45	
	Cash		2,039.45
	Paid note with interest		
	($2,000 × 12% × 60/365).		

Assets = Liabilities + Equity
−2,039.45 −2,000 −39.45

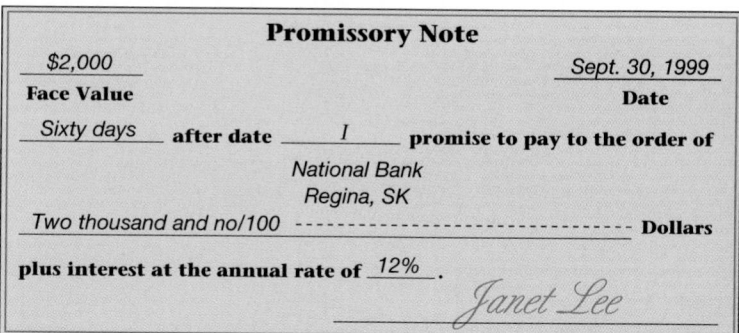

Promissory Note

$2,000   Sept. 30, 1999
Face Value   **Date**

Sixty days   after date ____*I*____ promise to pay to the order of

National Bank
Regina, SK

Two thousand and no/100 ----------------------------- **Dollars**

plus interest at the annual rate of _12%_ .

Janet Lee

Exhibit 13.3

Note Where Face Value Equals Amount Borrowed

Face Value Equals Amount Borrowed Plus Interest

The bank in this case writes a note with the 12% interest in its face value. This type of note includes a promise similar to: "I promise to pay $2,039.45 within 60 days after September 30." This note is shown in Exhibit 13.4. The note does not refer to the rate used to compute the $39.45 of interest included in the $2,039.45 face value. In other respects, this note is identical to the one above. Because this note lacks a stated interest rate it is sometimes called a **non-interest-bearing note.** This term can be misleading since the note does bear interest, but interest is included in the face value.

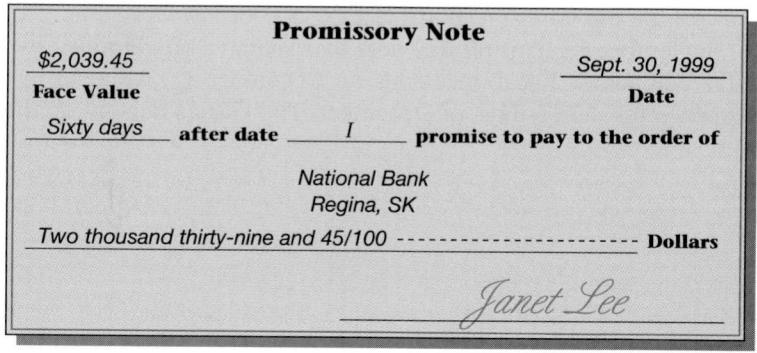

Promissory Note

$2,039.45   Sept. 30, 1999
Face Value   **Date**

Sixty days   after date ____*I*____ promise to pay to the order of

National Bank
Regina, SK

Two thousand thirty-nine and 45/100 -------------------- **Dollars**

Janet Lee

Exhibit 13.4

Note Where Face Value Equals Amount Borrowed plus Interest

When the face value of the note includes principal and interest, the borrowing company can record this note with an entry exactly like the previous September 30 entry. But it is more common to credit Notes Payable for the face value of the note and record the discount in a *contra-liability* account. This more common entry is:[4]

Assets = Liabilities + Equity
+2,000   +2,039.45
         −39.45

Sept.30	Cash	2,000.00	
	Discount on Notes Payable	39.45	
	Notes Payable		2,039.45
	Borrowed $2,000 cash with a 60-day,		
	12%, $2,039.45 note.		

Discount on Notes Payable is a contra-liability account to the Notes Payable account. If a balance sheet is prepared on September 30, the $39.45 discount is subtracted from the $2,039.45 balance in the Notes Payable account to reflect the $2,000 net amount borrowed as follows:[5]

Note payable	$2,039.45	
Less discount on note payable ...	39.45	$2,000

When this note matures 60 days later on November 29, the entry to record the company's $2,039.45 payment to the bank is:

Assets = Liabilities + Equity
−2,039.45 −2,039.45   −39.45
           +39.45

Nov. 29	Notes Payable	2,039.45	
	Interest Expense	39.45	
	Cash		2,039.45
	Discount on Notes Payable		39.45
	Paid note with interest.		

Rock Band

You are a member of a rock band. Your band needs $15,000 to upgrade equipment. You receive loan approvals for $15,000 at two banks. One bank's proposed loan contract reads: "Band promises to pay $15,000 plus interest at 14% in six months." The competing bank's contract reads: "Band promises to pay $16,000 in six months." Which loan do you prefer?

Answer—p. 641

End-of-Period Adjustments to Notes

When the end of an accounting period falls between the signing of a note payable and its maturity date, the *matching principle* requires us to record the accrued but unpaid interest on the note.

To illustrate these end-of-period adjustments, let's return to the short-term note above and assume the company borrowed the $2,000 on December 16, 1999, instead of September 30. This 60-day note then matures on February 14, 2000. Because the company's fiscal year ends on December 31, we need to record interest expense for the 15 days in December. The entries depend on the form of the note.

---

[4] The discount is computed as $2,000 \times 12\% \times 60/365$.

[5] We approximate the annual interest rate on a short-term loan as: ($interest paid ÷ $amount received) × (365 days ÷ loan period in days).

Face Value Equals Amount Borrowed

When the note's face value equals the amount borrowed, the accrued interest is charged to expense and credited to an Interest Payable account. To illustrate, we know 15 out of the 60-day loan period for the $2,000, 12% note have elapsed by December 31. This means one-fourth (15 days/60 days) of the $39.45 total interest is an expense of 1999. The borrowing company records this expense with the following adjusting entry at the end of 1999:

1999			
Dec. 31	Interest Expense	9.86	
	Interest Payable		9.86
	To record accrued interest on note ($2,000 × 12% × 15/365).		

Assets = Liabilities + Equity
       +9.86   −9.86

When this note matures on February 14, the company records this entry:

2000			
Feb. 14	Interest Expense ($2,000 × 12% × 45/365)	29.59	
	Interest Payable	9.86	
	Notes Payable	2,000.00	
	Cash		2,039.45
	Paid note with interest.		

Assets = Liabilities + Equity
−2039.45   −9.86   −29.59
             −2,000

This entry recognizes 45 days of interest expense for year 2000 and removes the balances of the two liability accounts.

Face Value Equals Amount Borrowed plus Interest

We now assume the face value of the note *includes* interest. To illustrate, we assume the borrowing company signs a $2,039.45 non-interest-bearing note on December 15. When recording this note on December 15, the company credits the $2,039.45 face value to Notes Payable and debits the $39.45 discount to a contra-liability account. At year-end, an adjusting entry is needed to record the accrual of 15 days of interest for 1999:

Dec. 31	Interest Expense	9.86	
	Discount on Notes Payable		9.86
	To record accrued interest on note ($2,000 × 12% × 15/365).		

Assets = Liabilities + Equity
       +9.86   −9.86

Note accrued interest is not credited to Interest Payable. Instead, this entry reduces the balance of the contra-liability account from $39.45 to $29.59. This increases the net note liability to $2,009.86 ($2,039.45 note less $29.59 discount).

When the note matures, we need an entry both to accrue interest expense for the last 45 days of the note and to record its payment:

2000			
Feb. 14	Interest Expense	29.59	
	Notes Payable	2,039.45	
	Discount on Notes Payable		29.59
	Cash		2,039.45
	Paid note with interest ($2,000 × 12% × 45/365).		

Assets = Liabilities + Equity
−2039.45   −2,039.45   −29.59
             +29.59

Did You Know?

IHOP notes
Many franchisers use notes to help entrepreneurs acquire one of its franchises. **International House of Pancakes (IHOP)** often allows about 80% of the franchise fee to be covered with a note payable. Payments on these notes are usually collected weekly.

Flashback

4. Why does a creditor want a past-due account replaced by a note?

5. A company borrows money by signing a note payable promising to pay $1,050 in six months. In recording the transaction, the company correctly debits $50 to Discount on Notes Payable. How much is borrowed? What annual rate of interest is charged?

Answers—p.642

Estimated Liabilities

LO4 Account for estimated liabilities including warranties and income taxes.

An **estimated liability** is a known obligation of an uncertain amount, but one that can be reasonably estimated. Three common examples are warranties offered by a seller, income taxes, and employee benefits such as vacation pay, pensions, and health care. We discuss each of these in this section. Other examples of estimated liabilities include property taxes and certain contracts to provide future services.

Warranty Liabilities

A warranty is an estimated liability of the seller. A **warranty** obligates a seller to pay for replacing or repairing the product (or service) when it fails to perform as expected within a specified period. Most cars, for instance, are sold with a warranty covering parts for a specified period of time. Ford reported nearly $6 billion in "dealer and customer allowances and claims" in 1996.

To comply with the *full disclosure* and *matching principles*, the seller reports the expected expense of providing the warranty in the period when revenue from the sale of the product is reported. The seller reports this warranty obligation as a liability, even though there is uncertainty about existence, amount, payee, and date of future sacrifices. The seller's warranty obligation does not require payments unless products fail and are returned for repairs. But future payments are probable and the amount of this liability can be estimated using, for instance, past experience with warranties.

Illustration of Warranty Liabilities

To illustrate, let's consider a dealer who sells a used car for $8,000 on December 1, 1999, with a one-year or 15,000-kilometre warranty covering parts. This dealer's experience shows warranty expense averages about 4% of a car's selling price. This means expense is expected to be $320 ($8,000 × 4%). The dealer records this estimated expense and liability with this entry:

Assets = Liabilities + Equity
     +320   −320

1999			
Dec. 1	Warranty Expense	320	
	Estimated Warranty Liability		320
	To record warranty expense and liability at 4% of selling price.		

This entry alternatively could have been made as part of end-of-period adjustments. Either way, it causes the estimated warranty expense to be reported on the 1999 income statement. Also, it results in a warranty liability on the balance sheet for December 31, 1999.

Suppose the customer returns the car for warranty repairs on January 9, 2000. The dealer performs this work by replacing parts costing $200. The entry to record partial settlement of the estimated warranty liability is:

2000			
Jan. 9	Estimated Warranty Liability	200	
	Auto Parts Inventory		200
	To record costs of warranty repairs.		

Assets = Liabilities + Equity
−200   −200

This entry does not record any additional expense in year 2000. Instead, this entry reduces the balance of the estimated warranty liability. Warranty expense was already recorded in 1999, the year the car was sold with the warranty and reported in the income statement.

What happens if total warranty costs turn out to be more or less than the estimated 4% or $320? The answer is that management should monitor actual warranty costs to see whether the 4% rate is accurate. If experience reveals a large difference from estimates, the rate should be changed for future sales. This means while differences are expected, they should be small.

Income Tax Liabilities for Corporations

Financial statements of both proprietorships and partnerships do not include income taxes because these organizations do not directly pay income taxes. Instead, taxable income for these organizations is carried to the owners' personal tax return and taxed at that level. But corporations are subject to income taxes and must estimate their income tax liability when preparing financial statements. We explain this process in this section. Then, in the next section, we discuss deferred (future) income tax liabilities arising from temporary differences[6] between GAAP and income tax rules.

Income tax expense for a corporation creates a liability until payment is made to the government. Because this tax is created through earning income, a liability is incurred when income is earned. This tax must usually be paid monthly under federal regulations. The monthly installment is equal to one-twelfth of the corporation's estimated income tax liability for the year.

Illustration of Income Tax Liabilities

To illustrate, let's consider a corporation who prepares monthly financial statements. Based on its income earned in 1998, this corporation estimates it will owe income taxes of $145,200 for 1999 or $12,100 per month. The following adjusting entry records this estimate:

Jan. 31	Income Tax Expense	12,100	
	Income Tax Payable		12,100
	Accrued income tax expense and liability		
	based on income for January.		

Assets = Liabilities + Equity
+12,100   −12,100

---

[6] Section 3465 "Income Taxes" of the *CICA Handbook* was released in December 1997. As of January 2000, the tax effect of temporary differences will be referred to as "Future income tax assets" or "Future income tax liabilities."

The tax installment is paid in the next month and the entry to record its payment is:

Assets = Liabilities + Equity
−12,100 −12,100

Feb. 10	Income Tax Payable	12,100	
	Cash		12,100
	Paid income tax installment for January 1999.		

This process of accruing and then paying taxes continues through the year. By the time annual financial statements are prepared at year-end, the corporation knows its total earned income and the actual amount of income taxes it must pay. This information allows it to update the expense and liability accounts.

Suppose this corporation determines that its income tax liability for 1999 is $156,700. The entry to record the additional income tax for 1999 is as follows:

Assets = Liabilities + Equity
+11,500 −11,500

Dec. 31	Income Tax Expense	11,500	
	Income Tax Payable		11,500
	To record additional tax expense and liability.		

This liability is settled when the corporation makes its final payment early in year 2000.

Deferred (Future) Income Tax Liabilities for Corporations

An income tax liability also can arise when the amount of income before taxes that is reported on a corporation's income statement is not the same as the amount of income reported on its income tax return. This difference occurs because income tax laws measure income differently than GAAP.[7]

Some differences between tax laws and GAAP are temporary. *Temporary differences* arise when the tax return and the income statement report a revenue or expense in different years. As an example, companies are often able to deduct higher amounts of amortization in the early years of an asset's life and smaller amounts in the later years for tax reporting. But for their income statements, they often report an equal amount of amortization expense each year. This means in the early years, amortization expense for tax reporting is more than amortization expense on the income statement. But in later years, amortization for tax reporting is less than amortization on the income statement.

When there are temporary differences between taxable income on the tax return and income before taxes on the income statement, corporations are required to compute income tax expense based on the income reported on the income statement. In the above example involving amortization, the result is income tax expense reported in the early years is more than the amount of income tax payable. This difference is called a **(deferred) future income tax liability.**

Illustration of Deferred Income Tax Liabilities

To illustrate, let's assume that after making and recording its monthly income tax payments, a corporation finds at the end of the year that an additional $25,000 of income tax expense should be recorded. But it also determines only $21,000

---

[7] Differences between tax laws and GAAP arise because Revenue Canada uses tax laws to generate receipts, stimulate the economy, and influence behaviour, whereas GAAP are intended to provide financial information useful for decision making.

is currently due and $4,000 is deferred to future years (a timing difference). The entry to record the required end-of-year adjustment is:

Dec. 31	Income Tax Expense	25,000	
	Income Tax Payable		21,000
	Future Income Tax Liability		4,000
	To record tax expense and deferred tax liability.		

Assets = Liabilities + Equity
+21,000   −25,000
+4,000

The credit to Income Taxes Payable reflects the amount currently due to be paid. The credit to Future Income Tax Liability reflects tax payments deferred until future years when the timing difference reverses.

Many corporations have deferred income tax liabilities. **Imperial Oil Limited,** for instance, reports deferred income taxes of $1 billion in its December 29, 1997, balance sheet.

Timing differences also can cause a company to pay income taxes before they are reported on the income statement as expense. If so, the company often reports a *future (deferred) income tax asset* on its balance sheet. This is similar to a prepaid expense. **Bombardier Inc.,** for instance, reports a deferred income tax balance of $13.8 million as part of other assets in its 1998 balance sheet.

Flashback

6. Estimated liabilities include an obligation to pay:
    a. An uncertain but reasonably estimated amount to a specific entity on a specific date.
    b. A known amount to a specific entity on an uncertain due date.
    c. A known amount to an uncertain entity on a known due date.
    d. All of the above.

7. A car is sold for $15,000 on June 1, 1999, with a one-year warranty covering parts and labour. Warranty expense is estimated at 1.5% of selling price. On March 1, 2000, the car is returned for warranty repairs for parts costing $75 and labour costing $60. The amount recorded as warranty expense at the time of the March 1 repairs is (a) $0, (b) $60, (c) $75, (d) $135, or (e) $225.

8. Why does a corporation accrue an income tax liability for quarterly reports?

Answers—p. 642

Contingent Liabilities

A **contingent liability** is a potential obligation that depends on a future event arising out of a past transaction or event. A typical example is a lawsuit pending in the court. Here a past transaction or event leads to a lawsuit whose result depends on the court's decision. More generally, any future payment for a contingent liability depends on whether an uncertain future event occurs.

LO 5 Explain how to account for contingent liabilities.

Accounting for Contingent Liabilities

Accounting for contingent liabilities depends on the likelihood of a future event occurring along with our ability to estimate the amount owed in the future if it occurs. Three categories are identified. (1) First, if the future event is *likely* (probable) and the amount owed can be *reasonably estimated*, we record this amount as a liability.[8] Examples are the estimated liabilities described earlier in the chapter

---

[8] *CICA Handbook*, section 3290, "Contingencies," par. .06

such as warranties and income taxes. (2) Second, if the future event is *unlikely* (remote), then we do not record or disclose any information regarding the contingent liability. (3) The third category covers contingent liabilities where the chance of the occurrence of the future event cannot be determined. If the future event could occur, then we disclose information about the contingent liability in the notes to the financial statements. Similarly, if the future event is likely but the amount cannot be reasonably estimated, then information about the contingent liability is disclosed in the notes to the financial statements.

Disclosing information about contingencies is motivated by the *full-disclosure principle*. This principle requires the reporting of information relevant to decision makers. The next section gives examples of contingent liabilities that require note disclosure.

Examples of Contingent Liability Disclosures

This section discusses examples of contingent liabilities that require note disclosure.

Potential Legal Claims

Many companies are sued or at risk for being sued for many reasons. The accounting question is: Should the defendant recognize a liability on its balance sheet or disclose a contingent liability in its notes while a lawsuit is outstanding and not yet settled? The answer is that a potential claim is recorded in the accounts only if payment for damages is likely and the amount can be reasonably estimated. If the potential claim cannot be reasonably estimated or it is less than likely but reasonably possible, then it is disclosed. **Canadian Tire,** for example, includes the following note in its recent annual report:

> The Corporation and certain of its subsidiaries are party to a number of legal proceedings. The Corporation believes that each such proceeding constitutes routine litigation incident to the business conducted by the Corporation and that the ultimate disposition of these matters will not have material adverse effect on its consolidated earnings, cash flow or financial position.

Debt Guarantees

Sometimes a company guarantees the payment of a debt owed by a supplier, customer, or another company. The guarantee means that if the debtor is not able to pay the debt when due, the guarantor will pay the debt on their behalf. The guarantor usually discloses the guarantee in its financial statement notes as a contingent liability. But if it is likely that the original debtor will default, the guarantor needs to record and report the guarantee in its financial statements as a liability. **Vengold Inc.** has an interesting guarantee with its officers as disclosed in their 1997 annual report:

> The Corporation has entered into employment agreements with four senior officers pursuant to which the Corporation has guaranteed housing loans in the amount of Cdn. $1,450,000.

Other Contingencies

Other examples of contingencies include environmental damages, possible tax assessments, insurance losses, and government investigations. **Suncor Inc.,** for instance, reports:

> The company is subject to various regulatory and statutory requirements relating to the protection of the environment. These requirements, in addition to contractual agreements and management decisions, result in the accrual of estimated reclamation and environmental remediation costs.

Like Suncor, many of these contingencies require both accrual and disclosure in notes to financial statements since they are likely to occur.

Eco Cops

What is it worth to be able to ski at Lake Louise? What is the cost when beaches are closed due to pollution? What is the life of a seal worth? These questions are part of measuring environmental liabilities of polluters. One method of measuring these liabilities is called contingent valuation where people are surveyed and asked to answer questions like these. Their answers are used by regulators to levy hefty fines, assess punitive damages, measure costs of clean up, and to assign penalties for damage to "environmental intangibles."

Did You Know?

Uncertainties

All organizations face uncertainties from future events such as natural disasters and the development of new competing products. If these events occur, they can damage a company's assets or drive it out of business. But these uncertainties are not contingent liabilities because they are future events not arising out of past transactions. Financial statements are not useful if they unduly speculate about the effects of possible future events such as these.

Flashback

9. A future payment is reported as a liability on the balance sheet if payment is contingent on a future event that:
   a. Is not likely but is reasonably possible and the payment cannot be reasonably estimated.
   b. Is likely and the payment can be reasonably estimated.
   c. Is not likely but the payment is known.

10. Under what circumstances is a future payment reported in financial statements as a contingent liability?

Answers—p. 642

Mid-Chapter Demonstration Problem

Lippitt Company is preparing adjusting entries at December 31. An analysis reveals the following:

1. The company is being sued by a dissatisfied customer. Legal advisors believe that it is likely that the company will have to pay damages in the amount of $7,500 which seems to be a reasonable estimate.
2. The Lippitt Company has guaranteed the $5,000 debt of a supplier. It is not likely that the supplier will default on the debt.
3. The company recognizes that $50,000 of $100,000 received in advance for products have now been earned.
4. The company provides a warranty for all of its products. However, its latest product has never been produced and sold so that it is impossible to determine the return rate for defective units.

Required

Indicate whether an adjusting entry is required for each of the above situations and why (not) at December 31.

Solution to Mid-Chapter Demonstration Problem

1. Because it is likely that the company will have to pay and the amount can be estimated an entry to record the liability and expense will be necessary.
2. No entry is necessary because the default is not likely. However, the contingent liability must be disclosed in the note to the financial statements.
3. An entry will be necessary to record the revenue and reduce the liabilty.
4. The company should record a liability for the warranty. It may be possible to determine the return rate by examining that for other, similar products. If an estimate is truly impossible, there must still be disclosure of the possible liability in the notes to the financial statements.

Long-Term Liabilities

LO 6 Describe accounting for long-term liabilities.

Long-term liabilities are obligations of a company not requiring payment within one year or a longer operating cycle. Long-term liabilities are often identical to current liabilities with the only exception being the greater time interval until an obligation comes due.

Long-term liabilities arise from many different transactions and events. Probably their most common source is when money is borrowed from a bank or when a note is issued to buy an asset. They also commonly arise when a company enters into a multiyear lease agreement that is similar to buying the asset. We explain each of these long-term liabilities in the context of discussing known, estimated, and contingent long-term liabilities. Another common source of long-term liabilities is the borrowing of money by issuing bonds to a number of creditors. Bonds are often outstanding for 30 years or more. Accounting for bonds is described in Chapter 17.

Because of the extended lives of long-term liabilities, accounting for them is often more complicated than accounting for short-term liabilities. In particular, the accountant may need to apply present value techniques to measure a long-term liability when it is created and to assign interest expense to each of the years in the liability's life.

Present Value Concepts

Information based on the concept of present value enters into many financing and investing decisions. It also enters into accounting for liabilities resulting from those decisions. Therefore, an understanding of present value is important for all business students.

Because this chapter focuses on liabilities, we explain present value concepts by referring to future cash outflows, payables, and interest expense. However, the same concepts also apply to future cash inflows, receivables, and interest income. The most fundamental **present value** concept is based on the idea that an amount of cash to be paid (or received) in the future has less value now than the same amount of cash to be paid (or received) today.

For example, $1 to be paid one year from now has a present value that is less than $1. To see why this is true, assume that $0.9259 is borrowed for one year at 8% interest. The amount of interest that will be incurred is $0.9259 $\times$ 8% =$0.0741. When the $0.0741 interest is added to the $0.9259, the sum equals the $1 payment that is necessary to repay the debt with interest, as shown here:

Amount borrowed	$0.9259
Interest for one year at 8%	$0.0741
Total debt after one year	$1.0000

In this example, the $0.9259 borrowed amount is the present value of the $1 future payment. To state the concept more generally, a borrowed amount is the present value of a future payment if the borrowed amount generates interest at a given rate and the future payment will repay the debt with interest.[9]

To carry this example of present value further, assume that the $1 payment is to be made after two years and the 8% interest is to be compounded annually. Compounding means that interest during the second period is based on the sum of the amount borrowed plus the interest accrued during the first period. In other words, the second period's interest is 8% multiplied by the sum of the original amount borrowed plus the interest earned during the first period.

In this example, where $1 is to be paid back after two years, the amount that can be borrowed (the present value) is $0.8573. The following calculation shows why $0.8573 is the present value:

Amount borrowed during first year	$0.8573
Interest during first year ($0.8573 $\times$ 8%)	0.0686
Amount borrowed during second year	$0.9259
Interest during second year ($0.9259 $\times$ 8%)	0.0741
Total debt after two years	$1.0000

Notice that the first year's interest is added to the principal amount borrowed so that the second year's interest is based on $0.9259.

Unless otherwise noted, the interest rates used in this text are annual rates and interest is compounded annually.

Present Value Tables

The present value of $1 to be paid after a number of periods in the future can be calculated by using this formula: $1/(1 + i)^n$. The symbol i in the equation is the interest rate per period and n is the number of periods until the future payment must be made. For example, the present value of $1 to be paid after two periods at 8% is $\$1/(1.08)^2$, which equals $0.8573.

---

[9] Exactly the same analysis applies to an investment. If $0.9259 is invested at 8%, it will generate $0.0741 interest revenue in one year, thereby amounting to a $1 receipt of principal and interest.

Although you can use this formula to find present values, other techniques are available. For example, many electronic calculators are preprogrammed to find present values. You can also use a **present value table** that shows present values computed with the formula at various interest rates for different time periods. In fact, many students find it helpful to learn how to make the calculations with the tables and then move on to use a calculator when they become comfortable with present value concepts.

Exhibit 13.5 shows present values of a future payment of $1 for up to 10 periods at five different interest rates. The present values in the table have been rounded to four decimal places.[10] (This table is taken from a larger and more complete table in Appendix II at the end of the book.)

To use this table, notice that the first value in the 8% column in Exhibit 13.5 is 0.9259. We used this value in the previous section as the present value of $1 at 8%. Go down one row in the same 8% column to find the present value of $1 discounted at 8% for two years. You should find the value of 0.8573 that we used in the second example. This value means that $0.8573 is the present value of the obligation to pay $1 after two periods, discounted at 8% per period.

Exhibit 13.5

Present Value of $1

| | Rate | | | | |
Periods	2%	4%	6%	8%	10%
1	0.9804	0.9615	0.9434	0.9259	0.9091
2	0.9612	0.9246	0.8900	0.8573	0.8264
3	0.9423	0.8890	0.8396	0.7938	0.7513
4	0.9238	0.8548	0.7921	0.7350	0.6830
5	0.9057	0.8219	0.7473	0.6806	0.6209
6	0.8880	0.7903	0.7050	0.6302	0.5645
7	0.8706	0.7599	0.6651	0.5835	0.5132
8	0.8535	0.7307	0.6274	0.5403	0.4665
9	0.8368	0.7026	0.5919	0.5002	0.4241
10	0.8203	0.6756	0.5584	0.4632	0.3855

Using a Present Value Table

To demonstrate how an accountant can measure a liability by using a present value table like Exhibit 13.5, assume that a company plans to borrow cash and then repay it as follows:

To be paid back after one year	$ 2,000
To be paid back after two years	3,000
To be paid back after three years	5,000
Total to be paid back	$10,000

If the company will have to pay 10% interest on this loan, how much will it be able to borrow? The answer is that it can borrow the present value of the three future payments, discounted at 10%. This is calculated in Exhibit 13.6 with values from Exhibit 13.5. The illustration shows that the company can borrow $8,054 at 10% in exchange for its promise to make the three payments at the scheduled dates.

---

[10] Four decimal places are sufficient for the applications in this book. Other situations may require more precision.

Years from Now	Expected Payments	Present Value of $1 at 10%	Present Value of Expected Payments
1	$2,000	0.9091	$1,818
2	3,000	0.8264	2,479
3	5,000	0.7513	3,757
Total present value of the payments			$8,054

Exhibit 13.6

Finding the Present Value of a Series of Unequal Payments

Present Values of Annuities

The $8,054 present value of the loan in Exhibit 13.6 is the sum of the present values of the three different payments. If the expected cash flows for a liability are not equal, their combined present value must be found by calculating each of their individual present values. In other cases, a loan may create an **annuity;** this is a series of equal payments occurring at equal time intervals. The present value of an annuity can be found with fewer calculations.

For example, suppose that a company can repay a 6% loan by making a $5,000 payment at the end of each year for the next four years. The amount to be borrowed under this loan equals the present value of the four payments discounted at 6%. The present value is calculated in Exhibit 13.7 by multiplying each payment by the appropriate value from Exhibit 13.5. The exhibit shows that the company can borrow $17,326 under these terms.

Because the series of $5,000 payments is an annuity, the accountant can determine the present value with either of two shortcuts. As shown in the third column of Exhibit 13.7, the total of the present values of $1 at 6% for periods one through four equals 3.4651. One shortcut multiplies this total of 3.4651 by the $5,000 annual payment to get the combined present value of $17,326. This shortcut requires only one multiplication instead of four.

Years from Now	Expected Payments	Present Value of $1 at 6%	Present Value of Expected Payments
1	$5,000	0.9434	$ 4,717
2	5,000	0.8900	4,450
3	5,000	0.8396	4,198
4	5,000	0.7921	3,961
Total		3.4651	$17,326

Exhibit 13.7

Finding the Present Value of a Series of Equal Payments (an Annuity) by Discounting Each Payment

The second shortcut uses an annuity table such as Exhibit 13.8.[11] (Exhibit 13.8 is taken from a more complete table in Appendix II at the end of the book.) Instead of having to take the sum of the individual present values from Exhibit 13.5, you can go directly to the annuity table to find the present (table) value that relates to a specific number of payments and a specific interest rate. Then, you multiply this table value by the amount of the payment to find the present value of all the payments in the annuity.

To continue the example, the second shortcut proceeds as follows: Enter Exhibit 13.8 on the row for four payments and go across until you reach the column for 6%; you will find the value 3.4651. This amount equals the present value of an annuity with four payments of $1, discounted at 6%. Then, multiply 3.4651 times $5,000 to get the $17,326 present value of the annuity.

---

[11] The present values in Exhibit 13.8 can be found by adding the individual payments in Exhibit 13.7.

Exhibit 13.8

Present Value of an Annuity
of $1

Payments	Rate				
	2%	4%	6%	8%	10%
1	0.9804	0.9615	0.9434	0.9259	0.9091
2	1.9416	1.8861	1.8334	1.7833	1.7355
3	2.8839	2.7751	2.6730	2.5771	2.4869
4	3.8077	3.6299	3.4651	3.3121	3.1699
5	4.7135	4.4518	4.2124	3.9927	3.7908
6	5.6014	5.2421	4.9173	4.6229	4.3553
7	6.4720	6.0021	5.5824	5.2064	4.8684
8	7.3255	6.7327	6.2098	5.7466	5.3349
9	8.1622	7.4353	6.8017	6.2469	5.7590
10	8.9826	8.1109	7.3601	6.7101	6.1446

Compounding Periods Shorter Than a Year

In the previous examples, the interest rates were applied to periods of one year. However, in many situations, interest is compounded over shorter periods. For example, the interest rate on bonds is usually described as an annual rate but the interest is actually paid every six months. As a result, the present value of the interest payments to be received from these bonds must be based on interest periods that are six months long.

To illustrate a calculation based on six-month interest periods, suppose that a borrower wants to know the present value of a series of ten $4,000 semiannual payments to be made over five years. These payments are to be discounted with an annual interest rate of 8%. Although the interest rate is described as an annual rate of 8%, it is actually a rate of 4% per six-month interest period. To find the present value of the series of $4,000 payments, enter Exhibit 13.8 on row 10 and go across to the 4% column. The table value is 8.1109, and the present value of the annuity is $32,444 (8.1109 × $4,000).

Study Appendix II at the end of the book to learn more about present value concepts. The appendix includes more complete present value tables and provides future value tables. It also includes exercises that will help you understand discounting.

Flash back

11. A company enters into an agreement to make four annual payments of $1,000 each, starting one year from now. The annual interest rate is 8%. The present value of these four payments is (a) $2,923, (b) $2,940, (c) $3,312, (d) $4,000, or (e) $6,733.

12. Suppose that a company has an option to pay either $10,000 after one year or $5,000 after six months and another $5,000 after one year. Which choice always has the smaller present value?

Answers—p. 642

Applying Present Value Concepts to Long-Term Notes

LO 8 Describe how present value concepts are used in accounting for long-term notes.

Earlier in the chapter, we stated that accountants use present value concepts to measure liabilities and to assign or allocate interest expense to each reporting period in a liability's life. In doing this, the liability is initially measured as the present value of the future payments. Over the life of the note, the amount of interest allocated to each period equals the product of multiplying the original interest rate by the balance of the liability at the beginning of the period. The balance at any point in time equals the original balance plus any allocated interest less any payments.[12]

Interest-Bearing Notes That Require a Single Payment

Suppose that a company buys equipment on January 2 with a fair market value of $45,000 by issuing an 8%, three-year note, with all of the interest paid at maturity. If the 8% interest is at the prevailing market rate, the face value of the note should be $45,000. The buyer records the purchase with this entry:

1999			
Jan. 2	Store Equipment	45,000.00	
	Notes Payable		45,000.00
	Issued a $45,000, three-year, 8% note payable for store equipment.		

Over the life of the note, the issuer reports annual interest expense equal to the original interest rate times each year's beginning balance for the liability. Exhibit 13.9 shows the interest allocation. Note that the interest is allocated by multiplying each year's beginning balance by the original 8% interest rate. Then, the interest is added to the beginning balance to find the ending balance, which then becomes the next year's beginning balance. Because the balance grows through compounding, the amount of interest allocated to each year increases over the life of the note. The final ending balance of $56,687 equals the original $45,000 borrowed plus the total interest of $11,687.

Beginning balance	$45,000	$48,600	$52,488
Interest rate	× 8%	× 8%	× 8%
Inertest expense	$ 3,600	$ 3,888	$ 4,199
Ending balance	$48,600	$52,488	$56,687

Allocation of Interest on a Note with All Interest Paid at Maturity

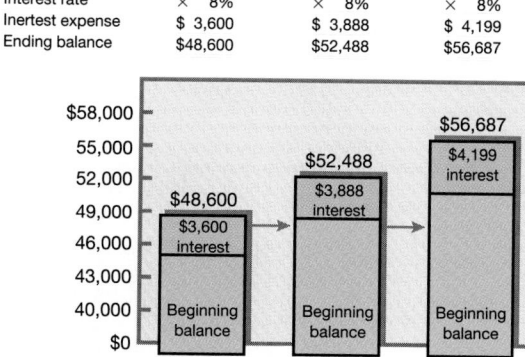

Non-Interest-Bearing Notes

Earlier in the chapter, we described so-called non-interest-bearing notes, which include the interest in their initial face values. When a non-interest-bearing note is used to purchase an asset, the note's face value is greater than the asset's fair value. As a result, the asset and the note should be recorded at the asset's fair value or at the note's fair value, whichever is more clearly determinable. The note's fair value can be estimated by finding the present value of its payments discounted at the market interest rate when it was issued.

---

[12] The liability's balance at any date is the present value of all the remaining future payments, discounted at the original interest rate.

For example, suppose that Harborg Company buys machinery on January 2, 1999, by issuing a non-interest-bearing, five-year, $10,000 note payable. The company's managers conclude that their estimate of the asset's fair value is less reliable than is the current 10% interest rate available to the company.

When the note is issued, its fair value equals the present value of the $10,000 payment due after five years discounted at 10%. Exhibit 13.5 shows us that the present value of 1 discounted at 10% for five years is 0.6209. Thus, the present (fair) value of the note is calculated as $10,000 × 0.6209 = $6,209. This is also the implied fair value of the asset. The following entry records the purchase:

1999			
Jan. 2	Machinery	6,209.00	
	Discount on Notes Payable	3,791.00	
	Long-Term Notes Payable		10,000.00
	Exchanged a five-year non-interest-bearing note for a machine.		

By recording the maturity value in one account and the discount in a contra account, the entry follows the typical approach of recording a non-interest-bearing note. In the entry, the $3,791 debit to Discount on Notes Payable equals the total amount of interest that must be allocated to the five years in the note's life.

In Exhibit 13.10, we calculate each year's interest and show the effect of the allocation on the discount and the net liability. The net liability balance grows over the five years until it reaches the maturity amount of $10,000. Note also that the discount balance decreases to $0 after five years. Because the discount is gradually reduced to zero, this process is often referred to as amortizing the discount.

Exhibit 13.10

Allocating Interest Expense over the Life of a Non-Interest-Bearing Loan

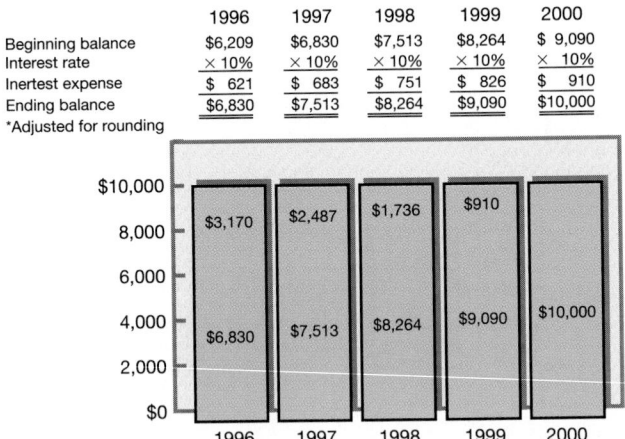

	1996	1997	1998	1999	2000
Beginning balance	$6,209	$6,830	$7,513	$8,264	$ 9,090
Interest rate	× 10%	× 10%	× 10%	× 10%	× 10%
Inertest expense	$ 621	$ 683	$ 751	$ 826	$ 910
Ending balance	$6,830	$7,513	$8,264	$9,090	$10,000

*Adjusted for rounding

Notice that the process of calculating each year's interest is the same as it was in the previous discussion of interest-bearing notes that require a single payment. The net liability balance at the beginning of each year is multiplied by the 10% interest rate to determine the interest for the year.

The first year's interest and reduction of the discount are recorded when the accountant makes this year-end adjusting entry:

1999			
Dec. 31	Interest Expense	621.00	
	Discount on Notes Payable		621.00
	To record interest expense accrued on a non-interest-bearing note.		

Similar entries are recorded at the end of each year until the balance of the discount account equals $0, and the net liability balance equals $10,000.

When the note matures on January 2, 2005, the issuer records the payment with this entry:

2005			
Jan. 2	Long-Term Notes Payable	10,000.00	
	Cash		10,000.00
	Paid non-interest-bearing note.		

Known (Determinable) *Long-Term* Liabilities

Many known or determinable liabilities are long-term. These include certain unearned revenues and notes payable. To illustrate, if *Maclean's* sells a special five-year magazine subscription, then it records amounts received for this subscription in an Unearned Subscription Revenues account. We know amounts in this account are liabilities, but are they current or long-term liabilities? The answer is both. The portion of *Maclean's* Unearned Subscription Revenues account that will be fulfilled in the next year is reported as a current liability. But the remaining portion is reported as a long-term liability.

The same analysis applies to notes payable. The borrower, for instance, reports a two-year note payable as a long-term liability in the first year it is outstanding. But in the second year, the borrower reclassifies this note as a current liability since it is due within one year or the longer operating cycle. Certain other known liabilities are rarely, if ever, reported in long-term liabilities. These include accounts payable, sales taxes, and wages and salaries.

The remainder of this section discusses two additional known liabilities: leases and the current portion of long-term debt.

Lease Liabilities

Leasing is one alternative to purchasing an asset and, in certain situations, is reported like a known liability. A company can lease an asset by agreeing to make a series of rental payments to the property owner, called the *lessor.* Because a lease gives the asset's user (called the lessee) exclusive control over the asset's usefulness, the lessee can use it to earn revenues. A lease creates a liability if it has essentially the same characteristics as a purchase of an asset on credit.

According to GAAP, the lessee must report a leased asset and a lease liability if the lease qualifies as a capital lease. A **capital lease** is a lease agreement transferring the risks and benefits associated with ownership to the lessee. This type of lease spans a number of years and creates a long-term liability that is paid off in a series of equal payments. **Loblaw Companies Limited,** for instance, reports "capital leases—building and equipment" with a book value of $56.4 million at December 31, 1996. The net present value of these long-term capital lease liabilities is $38 million.

When a capital lease is entered into, the lessee records a leased asset and amortizes it over its useful life. The lessee also records a lease liability and allocates interest expense to the years of the lease. This interest allocation process is the same as that for notes payable.

Leases that are not capital leases are called **operating leases.** The lessee does not record an operating lease as an asset nor as a liability. Instead, the lessee's income statement reports rent expense. It also does not report either interest or amortization expense related to an operating lease. Loblaw's rent expense on its operating leases totalled more than $125 million for the year ended December 31, 1996. Advanced courses provide details about the characteristics of both capital and operating leases, and accounting for them by both the lessor and lessee.

Flash back

13. Which one of the following requires a lessee to record a liability? (a) operating lease, (b) lessor, (c) contingent liability, (d) capital lease.

Answer—p. 642

Current Portion of Long-Term Debt

The **current portion of long-term debt** refers to a part of long-term debt that is due within one year. While long-term debt is *reported under long-term liabilities*, the portion due within the year is reported under current liabilities. To illustrate, let's assume a $7,500 debt is paid in installments of $1,500 per year for five years. The $1,500 due within the year is reported as a current liability. No journal entry is necessary. Instead, we properly classify the amounts for debt as either current or long-term when the balance sheet is prepared.

Estimated *Long-Term* Liabilities

Estimated liabilities are both current and long-term. These include employee benefits and future income taxes. Pension liabilities to employees are long-term to those workers who will not retire within one year or the longer operating cycle. But for employees who are retired or will retire within the year, a portion of pension liabilities is current in nature. The same analysis applies to employee health benefits, deferred income taxes payable, and warranties. For example, many warranties are for 30 or 60 days in length. Estimated costs under these warranties are properly reported in current liabilities. Yet many automobile warranties are for three years or 80,000 kilometres. A portion of these warranties is reported as long-term.

Contingent *Long-Term* Liabilities

Contingent liabilities are both current and long-term in nature. This extends to nearly every contingent liability including litigation, debt guarantees, environmental costs, government investigation, and tax assessments.

Times Interest Earned   USING THE INFORMATION

LO 9 Compute times interest earned ratio and use it to analyze liabilities.

A company incurs interest expense on many of its current and long-term liabilities. Examples extend from its short-term notes and current portion of long-term liabilities to its long-term notes, bonds, and capital leases. Many of these liabilities are likely to remain obligations in one form or another for a substantial period of time even if a company experiences a decline in operations. Because of this, interest expense is often viewed as a "fixed cost." This means the amount of interest is unlikely to fluctuate much from changes in sales.

While fixed costs can be advantageous when a company is growing, they create risk. This risk stems from the possibility a company might be unable to pay them if sales decline. Let's consider **X-Caliber's** results for 1999 and two possible outcomes for the year 2000 shown in Exhibit 13.11 ($ millions). X-Caliber is a manufacturer of water sports equipment and remains a family-owned operation.

	Year 1999	Year 2000	
		If Sales Increase	If Sales Decrease
Sales	$600	$900	$300
Expenses (75% of sales)	450	675	225
Income before interest	$150	$225	$ 75
Interest expense (fixed)	60	60	60
Net income	$ 90	$165	$ 15

Exhibit 13.11

X-Caliber's Actual and Possible Results for 1999–2000

Exhibit 13.11 shows expenses other than interest are projected to remain at 75% of sales. Expenses changing with sales volume are called *variable expenses*. But interest is expected to remain at $60,000 per year due to its fixed nature.

The second column of Exhibit 13.11 shows X-Caliber's income nearly doubles (100%) if sales increase by 50%. But also see that X-Caliber's profits fall sharply if sales decline by 50%. These numbers show a company's risk is affected by the amount of fixed interest charges it incurs each period.

The risk created by these fixed expenses is captured numerically with the **times interest earned** ratio. We use the formula in Exhibit 13.12 to compute this ratio.

$$\text{Times interest earned} = \frac{\text{Income before interest and taxes}}{\text{Interest expense}}$$

Exhibit 13.12

Times Interest Earned Formula

For 1999, X-Caliber's income before interest is $150,000. This means its ratio is computed as $150,000/$60,000, or 2.5 times. This ratio suggests X-Caliber faces relatively low risk. Its sales must decline sharply before it would be unable to cover its interest expenses. This result is comforting to the company's owners and creditors.

We must use care when computing the times interest earned ratio for a corporation. Since interest is deducted in determining taxable income for a corporation, this ratio is adjusted for a *corporation* and expressed as:

$$\begin{array}{c}\text{Times interest} \\ \text{earned} \\ \text{(corporation)}\end{array} = \frac{\text{Net income + Interest expense + Income tax expense}}{\text{Interest expense}}$$

Best Buy's times interest earned ratio for 1995–1997 is shown in Exhibit 13.13. Best Buy's ratio has fallen sharply from 4.37 in 1995 to 1.06 in 1997. This is a combination of several factors including reduced operating income and increased interest charges. Experience shows when this ratio falls below 1.5 for companies and remains at that level or lower for several periods, the default rate on liabilities increases sharply. This implies

Exhibit 13.13

Best Buy's Times
Interest Earned Ratio

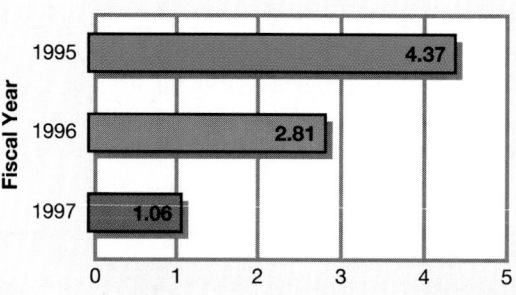

increased risk for those decision makers involved with
these types of companies and
their liabilities.

We must also interpret the
times interest earned ratio in
light of information about the
variability of a company's net
income before interest. If this
amount is stable from year to
year or is growing, the company can afford to take on added risk by borrowing. But if a company's income before interest varies greatly from year to
year, fixed interest charges can increase the risk that an owner will not earn
a positive return and be unable to pay interest charges.

You Make the Call

Entrepreneur
You are an entrepreneur looking to invest in and operate a local franchise
of a national chain. You narrow your alternatives to two. Each has an
expected annual net income *after* interest of $100,000. Net income for
the first franchise included an expected fixed interest charge of $200,000.
But expected fixed interest charge for the second franchise is $40,000.
Which franchise is more risky to you if sales forecasts are not met? Does
your decision change if the first franchise likely has more variability in its
income before interest?

Answer—p. 641

Flashback

14. Times interest earned ratio:
   a. Equals interest expense divided by net income.
   b. Is larger as the amount of fixed interest charges gets larger.
   c. Is best interpreted in light of information about the variability of a com-
      pany's net income before interest.

Answers—p. 642

Summary

LO1 **Describe current and long-term liabilities and
their characteristics.** Liabilities are probable future
payments of assets or services an entity is presently
obligated to make as a result of past events. Current
liabilities are due within one year or one operating cycle,
whichever is longer. All other liabilities are long-term
liabilities. One distinguishing characteristic among liabilities
is uncertainly about the identity of the creditor, due date,
and amount to be paid.

LO2 **Identify and describe known current liabilities.**
Known (or determinable) current liabilities are set by
agreements or laws and are measurable with little
uncertainly. The key is to identify known current liabilities.
They include accounts payable, sales taxes payable,
unearned revenues, notes payable, payroll liabilities, and the
current portion of long-term debt.

Prepare entries to account for short-term notes payable. Short-term notes payable are current liabilities and most bear interest. When a short-term note is interest-bearing, its face value equals the amount borrowed. This type of note also identifies a rate of interest to be paid at maturity. When a short-term note in non-interest-bearing, its face value equals the amount to be paid at maturity. This is because its face value includes interest.

Account for estimated liabilities including warranties and income taxes. Liabilities for warranties and income taxes are recorded with estimated amounts. Both warranties and income taxes are recognized as expenses when incurred. Deferred income tax liabilities are recognized if temporary differences between GAAP and tax rules result in recording more income tax expense than the amount to be currently paid.

Explain how to account for contingent liabilities. If an uncertain future payment depends on a probable future event and the amount is reasonably estimated, the payment is reported as a liability. But the future payment is reported as a contingent liability if (a) the future event is reasonably possible but not probable, or (b) the event is probable but the amount of the payment cannot be reasonably estimated.

Describe accounting for long-term liabilities. Long-term liabilities are obligations not requiring payment within one year or the longer operating cycle. Long-term liabilities are similar to current liabilities with the exception being the length of time until payment and the likely use of present value concepts. Lease liabilities are one type of long-term liability often used as an alternative to asset purchases. Capital leases are recorded as assets and liabilities. Other leases, called operating leases, are recorded as rent expense when the asset is used.

Explain and calculate the present value of an amount to be paid at a future date. The primary present value concept is that today's value of an amount of cash to be paid or received in the future is less than today's value of the same amount of cash to be paid or received today. Another present value concept is that interest is compounded, which means that the interest is added to the balance and used to determine interest for succeeding periods. An annuity is a series of equal payments occurring at equal time intervals.

Describe how present value concepts are used in accounting for long-term notes. Accountants may use present value concepts to measure liabilities and to determine the fair value of assets purchased in return for issuing debt. They also use present value concepts to allocate interest expense among the periods in a note's life by multiplying the note's beginning-of-period balance by the original interest rate. Non-interest-bearing notes are normally recorded with a discount account that is contra to the liability account. The balance in the account is amortized in the process of recognizing interest expense over the note's life.

Compute times interest earned ratio and use it to analyze liabilities. Times interest earned is computed by dividing a company's net income before interest by the amount of fixed interest charges incurred. If this company is a corporation, the numerator is net income before interest and taxes. This ratio reflects the company's ability to pay interest and earn a profit for its owners against declines in sales.

Guidance Answers to **You Make the Call**

Rock Band

Both banks have agreed to give the band $15,000, and both loans require repayment in six months. Provided terms in these contracts are similar, the only potential difference is in the amount of interest the band must pay. The second bank's contract makes this clear—since $15,000 is borrowed and the band must pay $16,000, the interest charged is $1,000. We must compute interest on the first bank's contract—it is $1,050, computed as $15,000 × 14% × 6/12. The band prefers the contract requiring less interest, which is the one reading: "Band promises to pay $16,000 within six months."

Entrepreneur

The risk is reflected by the ratio showing the number of times fixed interest charges are covered by net income *before* interest, known as the times interest earned ratio. This ratio for the first franchise is 1.5 [($100,000 + $200,000)/$200,000]. Whereas the ratio for the second franchise is 3.5 [($100,000 + $40,000)/$40,000]. This analysis shows the first franchise is more susceptible to the risk of incurring a loss if its sales decline and, therefore, is more risky. The second question asks about variability of income before interest. If income before interest varies greatly from year to year, this increases the risk an owner will not earn income. Since the first franchise has the greater variability, it makes it look an even worse investment.

Guidance Answers to Flashbacks

1. Liabilities are probable future payments of assets or services that an entity is presently obligated to make as a result of past transactions or events.

2. No, an expected future payment is not a liability unless an existing obligation was created by a past event or transaction.

3. In most cases, a liability due in 15 months is classified as long term. But it is classified as a current liability if the company's operating cycle is 15 months or longer.

4. A creditor might want to have a note payable instead of an account payable in order to (a) start charging interest and/or (b) have positive evidence of the debt and its terms.

5. The amount borrowed was $1,000 ($1,050 − $50). The rate of interest was 5% ($50/$1,000) for six months, which is an annual rate of 10%.

6. *a*

7. *a*

8. A corporation accrues an income tax liability for its interim financial statements because income tax expense is incurred when income is earned, not just at the end of the year.

9. *b*

10. A future payment is reported as a contingent liability if (a) the uncertain future event is likely but the amount of payment cannot be reasonably estimated, and (b) the uncertain future event is not likely but has a reasonable possibility of occurring.

11. *c*

12. The delayed payments would always have the lower present value.

13. *d*

14. *c*

Demonstration Problem

The following series of transactions and other events took place at the Kern Company during its calendar reporting year. Describe their effects on the financial statements by presenting the journal entries described in each situation.

a. Throughout September 19X1, Kern sold $140,000 of merchandise that was covered by a 180-day warranty. Prior experience shows that the costs of fulfilling the warranty will equal 5% of the sales revenue. Compute September's warranty expense and the increase in the warranty liability and show how it would be recorded with a September 30 adjusting entry. Also show the journal entry that would be made on October 8 to record an expenditure of $300 cash to provide warranty service on an item sold in September.

b. On October 12, Kern arranged with a supplier to replace an overdue $10,000 account payable by paying $2,500 cash and signing a note for the remainder. The note matured in 90 days and had a 12% interest rate. Show the entries that would be recorded on October 12, December 31, and January 10, 19X2 (when the note matures).

c. In late December the company learns that it is facing a product liability suit filed by an unhappy customer. The company's lawyer is of the opinion that although the company will likely suffer a loss from the lawsuit it is not possible to estimate the amount of the damages at the present time.

d. Kern Company has made and recorded its quarterly income tax payments. After final tax return preparation for the year the company discovers an additional $50,000 of income tax expense that should be recorded. A portion of this additional expense, $10,000 is deferrable to future years. Record the year-end income tax expense adjustment entry for the company.

e. Kern Company's net income for the year is $1,000,000. The interest expense and income tax expense for the years are $275,000 and $225,000 respectively. Calculate the number of times that fixed interest charges are earned.

f. On November 1 Kern Company borrows $5,000.00 from the bank on a 60-day, 14% note. Record the issuance of the note on November 1. Also record the repayment of the note with interest on December 30.

g. Kern Company signs a non-interest-bearing note promising to pay $2,050 within 60 days after December 16. Record the signing of the note, the interest accrual on December 31, and the repayment of the note on February 14 ($50 of interest is included in the note's face value of $2,050).

Planning the Solution

- For (a), compute the warranty expense for September and record it with an estimated liability. Record the October expenditure as a decrease in the liability.
- For (b), eliminate the liability for the account payable and create the liability for the note payable. Compute the interest expense for the 80 days that the note is outstanding in 19X1 and record it as an additional liability. Record the payment of the note, being sure to include the interest for the 10 days in 19X2.
- For (c) decide if the contingent liability for the company needs to be disclosed or accrued according to the two necessary criteria—probable loss and reasonably estimable.
- For (d) determine how much of the income tax expense is payable in the current year and how much needs to be deferred.
- For (e) calculate number of times interest charges are earned according to the formula given in the chapter. Remember that the numerator reflects income before interest and tax expense.
- For (f) record the issuance of the note. Calculate 60 days interest due and the payment of the note plus interest.
- For (g) record the note as a non-interesting-bearing note. Use the contra account Discount on Notes Payable for the interest portion of the proceeds upon issuance. Make the year-end adjustment for 15 days interest owed to Interest Expense and Discount on Notes Payable. Record the repayment of the note being sure to include the interest for the 45 days in 19X2.

Solution to Demonstration Problem

a. Warranty expense = 5% × $140,000 = $7,000

Sept.30	Warranty Expense	7,000.00	
	Estimated Warranty Liability		7,000.00
	To record warranty expense and liability at 5% of sales for the month.		

Oct. 8	Estimated Warranty Liability	300.00	
	Cash		300.00
	To record the cost of the warranty service.		

b. Interest expense for 19X1 = 12% × $7,500 × 80/365 = $197.26
Interest expense for 19X2 = 12% × $7,500 × 10/365 = $24.66

Oct. 12	Accounts Payable	10,000.00	
	Notes Payable		7,500.00
	Cash		2,500.00
	Paid $2,500 cash and gave a 90-day, 12% note to extend the due date on the account.		

Dec. 31	Interest Expense	197.26	
	Interest Payable		197.26
	To accrue interest on note payable.		

Jan. 10	Interest Expense	24.66	
	Interest Payable	197.26	
	Notes Payable	7,500.00	
	Cash		7,721.92
	Paid note with interest, including accrued interest payable.		

c. The pending lawsuit should be disclosed only in the financial statement notes. Although the loss is likely, no liability can be accrued since the loss cannot be reasonably estimated.

d.

Dec. 31	Income Taxes Expense	50,000.00	
	Income Taxes Payable		40,000.00
	Deferred Income Tax Liability		10,000.00
	To record income tax expense and the deferred tax liability		

e. Times interest earned $= \dfrac{\text{Income before interest and taxes}}{\text{Interest expense}}$

Income before interest $=$ Net income $+$ Interest expense $+$ Income taxes expense

Times interest earned $= \dfrac{\$1,000,000 + \$275,000 + \$225,000}{\$275,000} = 5.45$ times

f.

Nov. 1	Cash	5,000.00	
	Notes Payable		5,000.00
	Borrowed cash with a 60-day, 14% note.		

When the note and interest are paid 60 days later, Kern Company records the event with this entry:

Dec. 30	Notes Payable	5,000.00	
	Interest Expense	115.07	
	Cash		5,115.07
	Paid note with interest ($5,000 × 14% × 60/365).		

g.

Dec. 16	Cash	2,000.00	
	Discount on Notes Payable	50.00	
	Notes Payable		2,050.00
	Borrowed cash with a 60-day, non-interest-bearing note.		

Dec. 31	Interest Expense	12.50	
	Discount on Notes Payable		12.50
	To record accrued interest on note payable (15/60 days × $50).		

When the note matures on February 14, 19X2, Kern Company records this entry:

19X2			
Feb. 14	Interest Expense (45/60 days × $50)	37.50	
	Interest Payable	12.50	
	Notes Payable	2,000.00	
	Cash		2,050.00
	Paid note with interest.		

Glossary

Annuity A series of equal payments occurring at equal time intervals. (p. 633)

Capital lease A lease that gives the lessee the risks and benefits normally associated with ownership. (p. 637)

Contingent liability A potential liability that depends on a future event arising out of a past transaction; is not an existing liability. (p. 627)

Current liability Obligations due within a year or the company's operating cycle whichever is longer; paid using current assets or by creating other current liabilities. (p. 616)

Current portion of long-term debt The portion of long-term debt that is due within one year; reported under current liabilities on the balance sheet. (p. 638)

Deferred (future) income tax liability Payments of income taxes that are deferred until future years because of temporary differences between GAAP and tax rules. (p. 626)

Discount on note payable The difference between the face value of a non-interest-bearing note payable and the amount borrowed; represents interest that will be paid on the note over its life. (p. 620)

Estimated liability Obligation of an uncertain amount that can be reasonably estimated. (p. 624)

Known liability Obligations of a company with little uncertainty; set by agreements, contracts or laws; also called definitely determinable liabilities. (p. 618)

Long-term liability Obligations of a company not requiring payment within one year or a longer operating cycle. (p. 617)

Non-interest-bearing note A note that does not have a stated rate of interest; the interest is included in the face value of the note. (p. 621)

Operating lease A lease that is not a capital lease. (p. 637)

Present value The amount that can be invested (borrowed) at a given interest rate to generate a total future investment (debt) that will equal the amount of a specified future receipt (payment). (p. 631)

Present value table A table that shows the present value of an amount to be received when discounted at various interest rates for various periods of time, or the present value of a series of equal payments to be received for a varying number of periods when discounted at various interest rates. (p. 632)

Short-term note payable Current obligation in the form of a written promissory note. (p. 619)

Times interest earned The ratio of a company's income before interest divided by the amount of interest charges; used to evaluate the risk of being committed to make interest payments when income varies. (p. 639)

Warranty An agreement that obligates the seller or manufacturer to repair or replace a product when it breaks or otherwise fails to perform properly within a specified period. (p. 624)

Questions

1. What is the difference between a current and a long-term liability?

2. What is an estimated liability?

3. What are the three important questions concerning the certainty of liabilities?

4. Suppose that a company has a facility located in an area where disastrous weather conditions often occur. Should it report a probable loss from a future disaster as a liability on its balance sheet? Why?

5. Why are warranty liabilities usually recognized on the balance sheet as liabilities even when they are uncertain?

6. What factors affect the present value of a future $2,000 payment?

7. How would a lease create an asset and a liability for the lessee?

8. Find the note on commitments and contingencies following the financial statements of **Alliance** in Appendix I. What is the total minimum amount of operating lease payments in future years?

9. Refer to **Atlantis'** balance sheet in Appendix I. What accounts related to income taxes are on the balance sheet? Identify the meaning of each income tax account you identify.

Quick Study

QS 13-1

Distinguishing between current and long-term liabilities

Which of the following items would normally be classified as a current liability for a company that has a 15-month operating cycle?

a. Salaries payable.

b. A note payable due in 18 months.

c. Bonds payable that mature in two years.

d. A note payable due in 11 months.

e. The portion of a long-term note that is due to be paid in 15 months.

QS 13-2

Estimating warranty liabilities

On September 11, Valentine's Department Store sold a lawn mower for $400 with a one-year warranty that covers parts and labour. Warranty expense was estimated at 5% of sales. On July 24, the mower was brought in for repairs covered under the warranty requiring $15 in parts and $20 of labour. Prepare the July 24 journal entry to record the warranty repairs.

QS 13-3

Interest-bearing note transactions

On November 7, 19X1, the Eggemeyer Company borrowed $150,000 and signed a 90-day, 8% note payable with a face value of $150,000. Compute the accrued interest payable on December 31, and present the journal entry to record the paying of the note at maturity.

QS13-4

Non-interest-bearing note transactions

The Katie Company signs a non-interest-bearing note promising to pay $4,100 within 60 days after December 16. Record the signing of the note, the interest accrual on December 31, and the repayment of the note on February 14 ($100 of interest is included in the note's face value of $4,100).

QS 13-5

Recording an income tax liability.

Longfellow Company has made and recorded its monthly income tax payments. After final tax return preparation for the year the company discovers an additional $30,000 of income tax expense that should be recorded. A portion of this additional expense, $8,000 can be deferred to future years. Record the year-end income tax expense adjustment entry for Longfellow Company.

QS 13-6

Accounting for contingent liabilities

The following legal claims exist for the CT Company. Classify the required accounting treatment for each legal situation as (a) a liability that should be recorded or (b) an item that need only be described in the notes of the financial statement.

1. CT company estimates that one lawsuit could result in a damages award of $1,000,000; however, it is only reasonably possible that the plaintiff will win the case.

2. CT faces a probable loss on a pending lawsuit; however, the amount of the judgment cannot be reasonably estimated.

3. CT company estimates damages of another case at $2,500,000 with a high probability of losing the case.

QS 13-7

Accounting for sales tax payable

LO 2

Palm Computing sells $5,000 of merchandise for cash on September 30. The sales tax law requires Palm Computing to collect 4% sales tax on every dollar of merchandise sold. Record the entry for the $5,000 sale and applicable sales tax. Also record the entry that shows the remittance of the 4% tax on this sale to the government on October 15.

QS 13-8

Unearned revenue

LO 2

Ticketmaster receives $4,000,000 in advance cash ticket sales for a four date tour for the Rolling Stones. Record the advance ticket sales as a lump sum as of October 31. Record the revenue earned for the first concert date played on November 5.

On January 1, 19X1, a company borrowed $40,000 in exchange for an interest-bearing note. The note plus compounded interest at an annual rate of 12% is due on January 1, 19X3. Determine the amount that the company will pay on the due date.

QS 13-9
Note transaction
LO 6

Compute the times interest earned for a company that has income after interest expense and before taxes of $1,575,500 and interest expense of $137,000.

QS 13-10
Times interest earned
LO 9

The following list of items might appear as liabilities on the balance sheet of a company that has a two-month operating cycle. Identify the proper classification of each item. In the space beside each item write a *C* if it is a current liability, an *L* if it is a long-term liability, or an *N* if it is not a liability.

_____ **a.** Income taxes payable.
_____ **b.** Notes receivable in 30 days.
_____ **c.** Mortgage payable (payments due in the next 12 months).
_____ **d.** Notes payable in 6 to 12 months.
_____ **e.** Bonds payable (mature in 5 years).
_____ **f.** Notes payable in 13 to 24 months.
_____ **g.** Wages payable.
_____ **h.** Accounts receivable.
_____ **i.** Notes payable in 120 days.
_____ **j.** Mortgage payable (payments due after the next 12 months).

Exercises
Exercise 13-1
Classifying liabilities
LO 1

Mikado Co. sold a copier with a cost of $3,800 and a two-year parts and labour warranty to a customer on August 16, 19X1, for $5,500 cash. Mikado uses the perpetual system to account for inventories. Based on prior experience, Mikado expects to eventually incur warranty costs equal to 4% of this selling price. The liability expense is recorded with an adjusting entry at the end of the year. On November 22, 19X2, the copier required on-site repairs that were completed the same day. The cost of the repairs consisted of $69 for the materials taken from the parts inventory and $130 of labour that was fully paid with cash. These were the only repairs required in 19X2 for this copier.

a. How much warranty expense should the company report in 19X1 for this copier?
b. How much is the warranty liability for this copier as of December 31, 19X1?
c. How much warranty expense should the company report in 19X2 for this copier?
d. How much is the warranty liability for this copier as of December 31, 19X2?
e. Show the journal entries that would be made to record (1) the sale; (2) the adjustment on December 31, 19X1, to record the warranty expense; and (3) the repairs that occurred in November 19X2. Mikado uses the perpetual method system to account for merchandise inventories.

Exercise 13-2
Warranty expense and liability
LO 4

Constructo Company prepares interim financial statements each month. As part of the process, estimated income taxes are accrued each month for 30% of the current month's net income. The estimated income taxes are paid on the 15th of the following month for the amount accrued. These facts are known about the last quarter of 19X1:

a. October net income $27,900
  November net income 18,200
  December net income 32,700

b. After the tax return was completed in early January, the accountant determined that the Income Tax Payable for the last quarter should have been $29,100.

Exercise 13-3
Accounting for income taxes
LO 4

Required
1. Determine the amount of the adjustment needed on December 31 to produce the proper ending balance in the Income Tax Payable account.

2. Present the journal entries to record the adjustment to the Income Tax Payable account and to record the January 15 payment of the December taxes.

Portable Systems borrowed $94,000 on May 15, 19X1, for 60 days at 12% interest by signing a note.

a. On what date will this note mature?

b. How much interest expense is created by this note?

c. Suppose that the face value of the note equals the principal of the loan. Show the general journal entries to record issuing the note and paying it at maturity.

d. Suppose that the face value of the note is $95,880 which includes both the principal of the loan ($94,000) and the interest to be paid at maturity. Show the general journal entries to record issuing the note and paying it at maturity.

Accura Co. borrowed $150,000 on November 1, 19X1, for 90 days at 9% interest by signing a note.

a. On what date will this note mature?

b. How much interest expense is created by this note in 19X1? (Assume a 365-day year.)

c. How much interest expense is created by this note in 19X2? (Assume a 365-day year.)

d. Suppose that the face value of the note equals the principal of the loan. Show the general journal entries to record issuing the note, to accrue interest at the end of 19X1, and to record paying the note at maturity.

e. Suppose that the face value of the note ($153,375) includes both the principal of the loan ($150,000) and the interest to be paid at maturity. Show the general journal entries to record issuing the note, to accrue interest at the end of 19X1, and to record paying the note at maturity.

Lawrence Company is preparing adjusting entries at December 31. An analysis reveals the following:

1. During December, Lawrence Company sold 3,000 units of a product that carries a 60-day warranty. The sales for this product totalled $120,000. The company expects 8% of the units to need repair under warranty and it estimates that the average repair cost per unit will be $15.

2. The company is being sued by a disgruntled employee. Legal advisors believe that it is probable that the company will have to pay damages the amount of which cannot be reasonably estimated.

3. The Lawrence company has guaranteed the $5,000 debt of a supplier. It is not probable that the supplier will default on the debt.

4. The company records previously unrecorded cash sales of $2,000,000 and sales taxes payable at a rate of 5%.

5. The company recognizes that $50,000 of $100,000 received in advance for products has now been earned.

Required

Prepare any required adjusting entries at December 31 and indicate which items require financial statement disclosure.

The Rashad Company has the following selected accounts after posting adjusting entries:

Accounts Payable	$50,000
Notes Payable, six month	10,000
Accumulated Amortization, Equipment	20,000
Accrued Payroll Payable	5,000
Estimated Warranty Liability	12,000
Discount on Notes Payable, six month	1,000
Mortgage Payable	100,000

Prepare the current liability section of The Rashad Company's balance sheet, assuming $10,000 of the mortgage payable is due within the next year.

The Carson Company purchased some machinery on March 10 that had a cost of $56,000. Show the journal entry that would record this purchase under these three separate situations:

a. The company paid cash for the full purchase price.

b. The company gave an interest-bearing note for the full purchase price.

c. The company gave a non-interest-bearing one-year note for $61,600.

Exercise 13-8
Asset purchased with a note
LO 6

On January 2, 1996, the Brewster Co. acquired land by issuing a non-interest-bearing note for $20,000. The fair market value of the land was not reliably known, but the company knew that the market interest rate for the note was 6%. The note matures in three years on January 1, 1999.

a. What is the present value of the note at the time of the purchase?

b. What is the initial balance of the discount on the note payable?

c. Prepare a table that shows the amount of interest that will be allocated to each of the three years in the note's life and the ending balance of the net liability for each year.

d. Prepare a table that determines the ending balance of the discount on the note for each of the three years.

Exercise 13-9
Calculations for a non-interest-bearing note
LO 6

Use the data in Exercise 13-9 to prepare journal entries for these dates:

a. January 2, 1996 (land purchase).

b. December 31, 1996 (accrual entry).

c. December 31, 1997 (accrual entry).

d. December 31, 1998 (accrual entry).

e. January 1, 1999 (the payment of the note).

Exercise 13-10
Journal entries for non-interest-bearing note
LO 6

Use the following information to compute times interest earned:

	Net Income or (Loss)	Interest Expense
a.	$140,000	$48,000
b.	140,000	15,000
c.	140,000	8,000
d.	265,000	12,000
e.	79,000	12,000
f.	(4,000)	12,000

Exercise 13-11
Times interest earned
LO 9

Analysis component:

Which of the situations above demonstrates the strongest ability to pay fixed interest charges as they come due?

On October 29, 19X1, Sharp Products began to buy and resell electric razors for $80 each. Sharp uses the perpetual method to account for inventories. The razors are covered under a warranty that requires the company to replace any nonworking razor within 90 days. When a razor is returned, the company simply throws it away and mails a new one from inventory to the customer. The company's cost for a new razor is $18. The manufacturer has advised the company to expect warranty costs to equal 7% of the total sales. These events occurred in 19X1 and 19X2:

19X1

Nov. 11   Sold 75 razors for $6,000 cash.

7% x 6,000$

   30   Recognized warranty expense for November with an adjusting entry.

Dec. 9   Replaced 15 razors that were returned under the warranty.

   16   Sold 210 razors for $16,800 cash.

Problems
Problem 13-1
Estimated product warranty liabilities
LO 4

> 29   Replaced 30 razors that were returned under the warranty.
>
> 31   Recognized warranty expense for December with an adjusting entry.

19X2

> Jan. 5   Sold 130 razors for $10,400 cash.
>
> 17   Replaced 50 razors that were returned under the warranty.
>
> 31   Recognized warranty expense for January with an adjusting entry.

Required

1. How much warranty expense should be reported for November and December 19X1?

2. How much warranty expense should be reported for January 19X2?

3. What is the balance of the estimated warranty liability as of December 31, 19X1?

4. What is the balance of the estimated warranty liability as of January 31, 19X2?

5. Prepare journal entries to record the transactions and adjustments.

Problem 13-2
Transactions with short-
term notes payable

LO 3

The Langley Company entered into the following transactions involving short-term liabilities during 19X1 and 19X2:

19X1

Apr. 20   Purchased merchandise on credit from Franken, Inc., for $38,500. The terms were 1/10, n/30. Assume Franken uses a perpetual inventory system.

May 19   Replaced the account payable to Franken with a 90-day note bearing 9% annual interest. Langley paid $8,500 cash, with the result that the balance of the note was $30,000.

July 8   Borrowed $60,000 from Bank of the North by signing an interest-bearing note for $60,000. The annual interest rate was 10%, and the note has a 120-day term.

? Paid the note to Franken, Inc., at maturity.

? Paid the note to Bank of the North at maturity.

Nov. 28   Signed a non-interest-bearing note with a face value of $21,280 from Western Bank that matures in 60 days. The face value includes a principal amount of $21,000.

Dec. 31   Recorded an adjusting entry for the accrual of interest on the note to Western Bank.

19X2

? Paid the note to Western Bank at maturity.

Required

1. Determine the maturity dates of the three notes just described.

2. Determine the interest due at maturity for the three notes.

3. Determine the interest to be recorded in the adjusting entry at the end of 19X1.

4. Determine the interest to be recorded in 19X2.

5. Present journal entries for all the preceding events and adjustments.

Problem 13-3
Present value of possible
liabilities

LO 6

Sherlock Enterprises is negotiating the purchase of a new building. The seller has offered Sherlock the following three payment plans:

Plan A: $100,000 cash would be paid at once.

Plan B: $114,000 cash would be paid after two years.

Plan C: $58,000 cash would be paid at the end of each of the next two years.

The company's owner knows that the market interest rate is 8%.

Required

1. Use the market interest rate to determine present value of each of the three possible payment plans.

2. Show the journal entry that would be made to record the acquisition under each of the three plans. (Assume that the note's face value would include all interest to be paid.)

3. Identify the plan that creates the lowest cost for the company.

4. Assume that Plan B is adopted and the present value of the cash flows is used as the building's cost. Determine the amount of interest expense that will be reported in each of the two years in the note's life.

_____

face value = principal + interest

On January 2, 19X1, Watts Company acquired an item of equipment by issuing a $55,000 non-interest-bearing five-year note payable on December 31, 19X5. A reliable cash price for the equipment was not readily available. The market annual rate of interest for similar notes was 4% on the day of the exchange.

Required

(Round all amounts in your answers to the nearest whole dollar.)

1. Determine the initial net liability created by issuing this note.

2. Present a table showing the calculation of the amount of interest expense allocated to each year the note is outstanding and the carrying amount of the net liability at the end of each of those years.

3. Present a table that shows the balance of the discount at the end of each year the note is outstanding.

4. Prepare general journal entries to record the purchase of the equipment, the accrual of interest expense at the end of 19X1 and 19X2, and the accrual of interest expense and the payment of the note on December 31, 19X5.

5. Show how the note should be presented on the balance sheet as of December 31, 19X3.

_____

Here are condensed income statements for two unrelated companies:

Foxtrot Co.		Tango Co.	
Sales	$500,000	Sales	$500,000
Variable expenses (80%)	400,000	Variable expenses (60%)	300,000
Net income before interest	$100,000	Net income before interest	$200,000
Interest (fixed)	30,000	Interest (fixed)	130,000
Net income	$ 70,000	Net income	$ 70,000

Required

Preparation component:

1. What is the times interest earned for Foxtrot Co.?
2. What is the times interest earned for Tango Co.?
3. What happens to each company's net income if sales increase by 30%?
4. What happens to each company's net income if sales increase by 50%?
5. What happens to each company's net income if sales increase by 80%?
6. What happens to each company's net income if sales decrease by 10%?
7. What happens to each company's net income if sales decrease by 20%?
8. What happens to each company's net income if sales decrease by 40%?

Analysis component:

9. Comment on what you observe in relation to the fixed cost strategies of the two companies and the ratio values you computed in Parts 1 and 2.

Problem 13-4
Exchanging a note for a capital asset
LO 6, 7, 8

Check Figure 19X3 ending discount, $4,150

Problem 13-5
Times interest earned
LO 9

Check Figure Part 3, net income for Foxtrot Co., $100,000

On November 10, 19X1, Gourmet Co. began to buy and resell electric coffee grinders for $35 each. Gourmet uses the perpetual method to account for inventories. The coffee grinders are covered under a warranty that requires the company to replace any nonworking coffee grinder within 60 days. When a grinder is returned, the company simply throws it away and mails a new one from inventory to the customer. The company's cost for a new grinder is only $14. The manufacturer has advised the company to expect warranty costs to equal 10% of the total sales. These events occurred in 19X1 and 19X2:

19X1

Nov. 16 Sold 50 coffee grinders for $1,750 cash.
    30 Recognized warranty expense for November with an adjusting entry.
Dec. 12 Replaced six grinders that were returned under the warranty.
    18 Sold 150 coffee grinders for $5,250 cash.
    28 Replaced 17 grinders that were returned under the warranty.
    31 Recognized warranty expense for December with an adjusting entry.

19X2

Jan. 7 Sold 60 coffee grinders for $2,100 cash.
    21 Replaced 38 grinders that were returned under the warranty.
    31 Recognized warranty expense for January with an adjusting entry.

Required

1. How much warranty expense should be reported for November and December 19X1?
2. How much warranty expense should be reported for January 19X2?
3. What is the balance of the estimated warranty liability as of December 31, 19X1?
4. What is the balance of the estimated warranty liability as of January 31, 19X2?
5. Prepare journal entries to record the transactions and adjustments.

Problem 13-2A
Transactions with short-
term notes payable

LO 3

Palermo Company entered into the following transactions involving short-term liabilities during 19X1 and 19X2:

19X1

Apr. 22 Purchased merchandise on credit from Omni Products for $4,000. The terms were 1/10, n/30. Assume Omni uses a perpetual inventory system.
May 23 Replaced the account payable to Omni Products with a 60-day note bearing 15% annual interest. Palermo paid $400 cash, with the result that the balance of the note was $3,600.
July 15 Borrowed $9,000 from the Liberty Bank by signing an interest-bearing note for $9,000. The annual interest rate was 10%, and the note has a 120-day term.
   ? Paid the note to Omni Products at maturity.
   ? Paid the note to Liberty Bank at maturity.
Dec. 6 Signed a non-interest-bearing note with a face value of $16,180 from Metro Bank that matures in 45 days. The principal amount on the note is $16,000.
   31 Recorded an adjusting entry for the accrual of interest on the note to the Metro Bank.

19X2

   ? Paid the note to Metro Bank at maturity.

Required

1. Determine the maturity dates of the three notes just described.
2. Determine the interest due at maturity for the three notes.
3. Determine the interest to be recorded in the adjusting entry at the end of 19X1.
4. Determine the interest to be recorded in 19X2.
5. Present journal entries for all the preceding events and adjustments.

Holmes Enterprises is negotiating the purchase of a new building. The seller has offered Holmes the following three payment plans:

Plan A: $122,000 cash would be paid at once.
Plan B: $136,000 cash would be paid after two years.
Plan C: $70,000 cash would be paid at the end of each of the next two years.

The company's owner knows that the market interest rate is 6%.

Required

1. Use the market interest rate to determine present value of each of the three possible payment plans.
2. Show the journal entry that would be made to record the acquisition under each of the three plans. (Assume that the note's face value would include all interest to be paid.)
3. Identify the plan that creates the lowest cost for the company.
4. Assume that Plan B is adopted and the present value of the cash flows is used as the building's cost. Determine the amount of interest expense that will be reported in each of the two years in the note's life.

Problem 13-3A
Present value of possible liabilities
LO 6

On January 2, 20X1, Watts Company acquired an item of equipment by issuing a $77,000 non-interest-bearing five-year note payable on December 31, 20X5. A reliable cash price for the equipment was not readily available. The market annual rate of interest for similar notes was 6% on the day of the exchange.

Required

(Round all amounts in your answers to the nearest whole dollar.)

1. Determine the initial net liability created by issuing this note.
2. Present a table showing the calculation of the amount of interest expense allocated to each year the note is outstanding and the carrying amount of the net liability at the end of each of those years.
3. Present a table that shows the balance of the discount at the end of each year the note is outstanding.
4. Prepare general journal entries to record the purchase of the equipment, the accrual of interest expense at the end of 20X1 and 20X2, and the accrual of interest expense and the payment of the note on December 31, 20X5.
5. Show how the note should be presented on the balance sheet as of December 31, 20X3.

Problem 13-4A
Exchanging a note for a plant asset
LO 6, 7, 8

Here are condensed income statements for two unrelated companies:

Problem 13-5A
Times interest earned
LO 9

Solstice Co.	
Sales	$120,000
Variable expenses (50%) . . .	60,000
Net income before interest .	$ 60,000
Interest (fixed)	45,000
Net income	$ 15,000

Equinox Co.	
Sales	$120,000
Variable expenses (75%) . . .	90,000
Net income before interest .	$ 30,000
Interest (fixed)	15,000
Net income	$ 15,000

Required

Preparation component:

1. What is the times interest earned for Solstice?
2. What is the times interest earned for Equinox?
3. What happens to each company's net income if sales increase by 10%?
4. What happens to each company's net income if sales increase by 40%?

5. What happens to each company's net income if sales increase by 90%?
6. What happens to each company's net income if sales decrease by 20%?
7. What happens to each company's net income if sales decrease by 50%?
8. What happens to each company's net income if sales decrease by 80%?

Analysis component:

9. Comment on what you observe in relation to the fixed cost strategies of the two companies and the ratio values you computed in Parts 1 and 2.

Analytical and Review Problems

A & R Problem 13-1

Roger Rocket, ace righthander with the York Bluebirds, is negotiating for renewal of his contract. Prior to making an offer to Rocket, George Megabucks—owner of the team—asks you to check out three alternatives he intends to present to the pitcher. George is only willing to offer a three-year contract but is offering three different payment schemes as follows:

a. $300,000 payable at the end of each year for 10 years.
b. $750,000 payable at the end of each year for 3 years.
c. $1,800,000 payable on signing the three-year contract.

Required

Prepare journal entries for each of the alternatives as of the date of signing the contract and at the end of the first year. Also indicate balance sheet presentation as of the end of the first year. Assume:

1. The going rate of interest is 8%.
2. The company amortizes assets on a straight-line basis.

A & R Problem 13-2

On September 1, 20X1, Chang Company acquired a machine by paying $15,000 cash and signing a two-year note that carried a face amount of $90,000 due at the end of the two-year period; the note did not specify interest. Assume the going rate of interest for this company for this type of loan is 6%. The accounting period ends December 31.

Required

Give the entry to record the purchase of the machine and complete a tabulation as follows (round amounts to nearest dollar):

	Straight-Line Method	Interest Method
1. Cash to be paid at maturity	$_____	$_____
2. Total interest expense	$_____	$_____
3. Interest expense on income statement for 20X1	$_____	$_____
4. Amount of the liability reported on balance sheet at end of 20X1	$_____	$_____
5. Amortization expense for 20X1 (assume straight-line, partial year, no residual value, and useful life of five years)	$_____	$_____

Aardvark Exterminators provides pest control services and sells pool extermination products manufactured by other companies. The following six-column table contains the company's unadjusted trial balance as of December 31, 19X4.

AARDVARK EXTERMINATORS Six-Column Table December 31, 19X4					
	Unadjusted Trial Balance		Adjustments		Adjusted Trial Balance
Cash	$ 17,000				
Accounts receivable	4,000				
Allowance for doubtful accounts		$ 828			
Merchandise inventory	13,000				
Trucks	32,000				
Accum. amortization, trucks		-0-			
Equipment	45,000				
Accum. amort., equipment		12,200			
Accounts payable.		5,000			
Estimated warranty liability		1,500			
Unearned extermination services revenue. . .		-0-			
Long-term notes payable		15,000			
Discount on notes payable	3,974				
K. Jones, capital.		59,600			
K. Jones, withdrawals.	10,000				
Extermination services revenue		60,000			
Interest earned.		872			
Sales.		75,000			
Purchases	45,000				
Amort. expense, trucks.	-0-				
Amort. expense, equip.	-0-				
Wages expense	35,000				
Interest expense.	-0-				
Rent expense.	9,000				
Bad debt expense	-0-				
Miscellaneous expenses	1,226				
Repairs expense.	8,000				
Utilities expense.	6,800				
Warranty expense.	-0-				
Totals	$230,000	$230,000			

The following information applies to the company and its situation at the end of the year:

a. The bank reconciliation as of December 31, 19X4, includes these facts:

Balance per bank	$15,100
Balance per books	17,000
Outstanding cheques	1,800
Deposit in transit	2,450
Interest earned	52
Service charges (miscellaneous expense) . .	15

Included with the bank statement was a cancelled cheque that the company had failed to record. (This information allows you to determine the amount of the cheque, which was a payment of an account payable.)

b. An examination of customers' accounts shows that accounts totalling $679 should be written off as uncollectible. In addition, it has been determined that the ending balance of the Allowance for Doubtful Accounts account should be $700.

c. A truck was purchased and placed in service on July 1, 19X4. Its cost is being amortized with the straight-line method using these facts and predictions:

Original cost	$32,000
Expected salvage value	8,000
Useful life (years)	4

d. Two items of equipment (a sprayer and an injector) were purchased and put into service early in January 19X2. Their costs are being amortized with the straight-line method using these facts and predictions:

	Sprayer	Injector
Original cost	$27,000	$18,000
Expected salvage value	3,000	2,500
Useful life (years)	8	5

e. On August 1, 19X4, the company was paid $3,840 in advance to provide monthly service on an apartment complex for one year. The company began providing the services in August. When the cash was received, the full amount was credited to the Extermination Services Revenue account.

f. The company offers a warranty for all of the products it sells. The expected cost of providing warranty service is 2.5% of sales. No warranty expense has been recorded for 19X4. All costs of servicing products under the warranties in 19X4 were properly debited to the liability account.

g. The $15,000 long-term note is a five-year, non-interest-bearing note that was given to First National Bank on December 31, 19X2. The market interest rate on the date of the loan was 8%.

h. The ending inventory of merchandise was counted and determined to have a cost of $11,700. (Note that Aardvark's unadjusted trial balance includes a Purchases account. Thus, you know that Aardvark uses a periodic inventory system.)

Required

1. Use the preceding information to determine the amounts of the following items:
  a. The correct ending balance of Cash and the amount of the omitted cheque.
  b. The adjustment needed to obtain the correct ending balance of the Allowance for Doubtful Accounts.
  c. The annual amortization expense for the truck that was acquired during the year (computed to the nearest month).
  d. The annual amortization expense for the two items of equipment that were used during the year.
  e. The correct ending balances of the Extermination Services Revenue and Unearned Extermination Services Revenue accounts.
  f. The correct ending balances of the accounts for Warranty Expense and Estimated Warranty Liability.
  g. The correct ending balances of the accounts for Interest Expense and Discount on Notes Payable. (Round amounts to nearest whole dollar.)
  h. The cost of goods sold for the year.

2. Use the results of requirement 1 to complete the six-column table by first entering the appropriate adjustments for items *a* through *g* and then completing the adjusted trial balance columns. (Hint: Item *b* requires two entries.)

3. Present general journal entries to record the adjustments entered on the six-column table. Assume that Aarkvark uses the closing entry approach to account for changes in Merchandise Inventory.

4. Present a single-step income statement, a statement of changes in owner's equity, and a classified balance sheet.

BEYOND THE NUMBERS

Refer to the financial statements and related information for **Alliance** in Appendix I. Answer the following questions by analyzing the information in Appendix I:

1. Compute times interest earned for the years ended March 31, 1997 and 1996 and comment on Alliance's ability to cover its interest expense.

2. Does Alliance's note on commitments provide information allowing one to determine whether the company has entered into any operating or capital leases?

3. What evidence would you look for as an indication that Alliance has any temporary differences between the income reported on the income statement and the income reported on its tax return? Can you find any evidence of these differences for Alliance?

Reporting in Action

LO 5, 7

Both **Alliance** and **Atlantis** develop, produce and market movies and TV programs. Key comparative figures ($thousands) for these two organizations follow:

Key Figures	Alliance		Atlantis	
	1997	**1996**	**1997**	**1997**
Net Income	$18,188	$10,365	$5,565	$6,866
Income Tax Expense	9,788	1,935	4,262	3,547
Interest Expense	$ 1,296	$ 893	$ 947	$1,339

* Alliance figures are from the annual reports for the fiscal years ended March 31, 1997 and 1996.

Atlantis figures are from the annual reports for the fiscal years ended December 31, 1997 and 1996.

Comparative Analysis

LO 7

Required

1. Compute times interest earned for the two years presented for each company.

2. Comment on which company appears stronger in its ability to commit to interest payments if income should vary.

Mike Thatcher is a sales manager for an automobile dealership in Alberta. Mike earns a bonus each year based on revenue generated by the number of autos sold in the year less related warranty expenses. The quality of automobiles sold each year seems to vary since the warranty experience related to autos sold is highly variable. The actual warranty expenses have varied over the past 10 years from a low of 3% of an automobile's selling price to a high of 10%. In the past Mike has tended toward estimating warranty expenses on the high end just to be conservative. It is the end of the year and once again he must work with the dealership's accountant in arriving at the warranty expense accrual for the cars sold this year.

1. Does the warranty accrual decision present any kind of ethical dilemma for Mike Thatcher?

2. Since the warranty experience is not constant what percent do you think Mike should choose for this year? Justify your response.

Ethics Challenge

LO 4

Communicating in Practice
LO⁵

Norma Yagerhofer is the new manager of accounting and finance for a manufacturing company. Now that the end of the year is approaching, her problem is determining whether and how to describe the company's contingencies in financial statements. The general manager, Jonas Perlman, raised an objection to a specific contingency in Yagerhofer's proposal. Perlman objects to Yagerhofer's proposal to recognize an expense and a liability for warranty service on units of a new product that was just introduced in the company's fourth quarter. His scribbled comment on this point was, "There is no way that we can estimate this warranty cost. Besides, we don't owe anybody anything until the products break down and are returned for service. Let's just report an expense if and when we do the repairs."

Required

Develop a short written response for Yagerhofer to send to Perlman addressing his objection in a one-page memorandum dated December 21.

Taking It to the Net
LO¹

Visit the Canadian Bankers' Association Web site at **http://www.cbc.ca**. Find the link on the homepage to the Managing Money page. Once you have located the page find the section on "Checking Your Credit Rating." How can you correct any errors that might exist in your file?

Teamwork in Action
LO²,³

Your team is to assume you are in business and need to borrow $6,000 for short-term working capital. You have been shopping banks for a loan. To obtain the funds you have the following options:

1. Sign a $6,000, 90-day, 11% interest-bearing note, or
2. Sign a $6,172.50, 90-day, non-interest-bearing note.

Required

1. Discuss these options. Determine the best choice. Ensure all teammates concur with the decision and understand the rationale. Explain your decision to your instructor.
2. Each member of the team is to prepare one of the following entries:
   a. Option 1—date of borrowing
   b. Option 2—date of borrowing
   c. Option 1—maturity date
   d. Option 2—maturity date
3. In rotation, each member is to explain the entry prepared in (2) to the team. Ensure all team members concur with and understand the entries.
4. Assume the funds were borrowed on December 1 and your business has a fiscal year that coincides with a calendar year. Each member of the team is to prepare one of the following entries:
   a. Option 1—the year-end adjustment
   b. Option 2—the year-end adjustment
   c. Option 1—maturity date
   d. Option 2—maturity date
5. In rotation, each member is to explain the entry prepared in (4) to the team. Ensure all team members concur with and understand the entries.

Obtain a recent copy of *The Globe and Mail's Report on Business* or *The Financial Post.* Find three notices of offerings of long-term debt instruments and determine the interest rates charged.

a. Are the interest rates the same?

b. What seems to determine the interest rate? For example, is it the size of the offering, the size of the company, or some other factor(s)?

Hitting the Road

LO 6

Extended warranties of up to five years on automobiles and other long-lived consumer products have raised issues in connection with the recognition of income. Up to now, when an extended warranty was sold, all the revenue was recognized in the year of sale. Some accountants, however, have advocated that the revenue from the sale of the warranty should be recognized as the warranty period expires.

Business Break

LO 4

Required

1. Why should the revenue from the sale of extended warranties be deferred and recognized over the life of the warranty?

2. Contrast the rules now in effect with the proposed rules with respect to the effect on the income statements of companies selling extended warranties.

3. What accounting principle likely governed those who proposed to change the accounting rules for recognizing warranty revenue?

4. Is the rule for accounting for revenue from warranties consistent with the rules for accounting for expenses related to warranties?

14

Partnerships

A Look Back

Chapter 13 focused on current and long-term liabilities. We explained how liabilities are identified, computed, recorded, and reported in financial statements.

A Look at This Chapter

This chapter explains both the partnership and corporate forms of organization. Important characteristics of both forms of organization are described along with the accounting for important transactions.

A Look Forward

Chapter 15 extends our discussion of corporate accounting to dividends and other equity transactions. We also explain how income, earnings per share, and retained earnings are reported.

Chapter Outline

Go for It

Toronto, ON—What do we say to an 18-year-old who wants some extra spending money? Maybe, check the "help wanted" at **Zellers, Eatons, McDonald's** or **The Bay.** But do we ever say, "What do *you* want to do?" Well, Jennifer Wong did what she wanted to do. Wong decided to block print cotton T-shirts and dresses in her parent's garage to be sold at craft shows and festivals. One would not normally expect much success from such a venture.

But Wong's efforts paid off. In her first full year of business, at the ripe age of 19, her sales climbed to $110,000. In her second year, with a loan co-signed by her parents, she set up a small factory in a leased building in Scarborough. Jennifer formed a partnership with her friend, Malu Balizar, who invested $10,000 into the business. A partnership agreement was drawn up specifying how profits and losses would be divided between Jennifer and Malu and how the assets would be allocated if they decided to end the partnership. Wong has never looked back. Wong's clothing is funky, flowing and artsy. Each product is individually hand block printed with evocative designs and symbols, and signed by the artist. Jennifer's clothing isn't cheap—a T-shirt can cost $60 and a dress, $200 to $300—but the style holds up from year to year. Wong says her clothing "is customer driven and says something meaningful about our times." All clothing is made with natural dyes and uses only organic cotton.

Learning Objectives

LO 1 Identify characteristics of partnerships and similar organizations and explain the concepts of mutual agency and unlimited liability in a partnership.

LO 2 Prepare entries when forming a partnership.

LO 3 Allocate and record income and loss among partners.

LO 4 Account for the admission and withdrawal of a partner.

LO 5 Prepare entries for partnership liquidation.

CHAPTER PREVIEW

There are three common types of business organizations: corporations, partnerships and proprietorships. Partnerships are similar to proprietorships, except with more than one owner. This chapter explains partnerships. While corporations are fewest in number, they transact more business than all others combined. They are very important players in our global economy, with dollar sales at least 10 times the combined sales of unincorporated companies. Understanding the advantages and disadvantages of these forms of business organization was important for Jennifer Wong in her T-shirt venture. The opening article revealed her choice to form a partnership with her friend Malu, but this is not always best. This chapter focuses on partnerships.

Partnership Form of Organization

A **partnership** is an unincorporated association of two or more people to pursue a business for profit as co-owners. General partnerships are governed by provincial law and registration requirements. Many businesses are organized as partnerships. They are especially common in small retail and service businesses. Many professional practitioners also organize their practices as partnerships, including physicians, lawyers, and accountants. Two forms of partnerships are recognized by Canadian law: general partnerships and limited partnerships.

Characteristics of General Partnerships

LO1 Identify characteristics of partnerships and similar organizations and explain the concepts of mutual agency and unlimited liability in a partnership.

Partnerships are an important type of organization because of certain advantages they offer with their unique characteristics. We describe these characteristics in this section.

Voluntary Association

A partnership is a voluntary association between partners. Since joining a partnership involves increased risk to your personal financial position, your participation is voluntary.[1]

Partnership Agreement

Forming a partnership requires that two or more legally competent people (who are of age and of sound mental capacity) agree to be partners. Their agreement becomes a **partnership contract.** While it should be in writing to protect partners in the event of disagreement or dissolution of the business, the contract is binding even if it is only expressed verbally.[2] Lawyers prepare partnership contracts but it is common for public accountants to review these contracts and advise partners on tax matters relating to their share of partnership income.

Limited Life

The life of a partnership is limited. Death, bankruptcy, or any event taking away the ability of a partner to enter into or fulfill a contract ends a partnership. A partnership also can be terminated at will by any one of the partners. Conditions of termination may also be specified in the partnership contract.

---

[1] Some courts have ruled that partnerships are created by the actions of partners even when there is no expressed agreement to form one.

[2] Partnership agreements normally include the partners': (a) names and contributions, (b) rights and duties, (c) sharing of income and losses, (d) withdrawal arrangement, (e) dispute procedures, (f) admission and withdrawal of new partners, and (g) rights and duties in event a partner dies.

Strategic Alliances

A more recent form of partnership is the strategic alliance. A strategic alliance is formed when a firm combines with one or more firms for a specific period of time to accomplish a common goal. A recent survey by Ernst & Young of 822 Canadian high-tech firms found that 41% were involved in such alliances. Pharmaceutical companies, such as Glaxo Canada Inc., have formed alliances with other companies to combat particular diseases. Although businesses forming alliances are frequently corporations, the alliances they have formed are a type of partnership.

Did You Know?

Taxation

A partnership is not subject to taxes on its income. It has the same tax status as a proprietorship. The income or loss of a partnership is allocated to the partners according to the partnership agreement, and is included for determining the taxable income of each partner's tax return.[3] Allocation of partnership income or loss is done each year whether or not cash is distributed to partners.

Getting Along

An important advantage of a partnership form of organization over a proprietorship form is that a partner usually brings in extra resources with which to run the business. Partnership agreements can help avoid potential disputes about issues such as: Who invested what amounts of money in the partnership? Who performs what activities, and who reports to whom? Who will receive what share of partnership profits? How will assets be distributed in the event of liquidation? Not all potential disputes, however, can be anticipated in advance. It is important when selecting a partner to give serious thought about the character and personality of those with whom we are forming long-term relationships and not be blinded by the economic resources that a potential partner may be offering. Disputes are common in partnerships and can lead to disastrous consequences for the business and for the well-being of all involved.

Did You Know?

Mutual Agency

The relationship between partners in a general partnership involves **mutual agency.** This means each partner is a fully authorized agent of the partnership. As its agent a partner can commit or bind the partnership to any contract within the scope of the partnership's business. For instance, a partner in a merchandising business can sign contracts binding the partnership to buy merchandise, lease a store building, borrow money, or hire employees. These activities are all within the scope of business of a merchandising firm. But a partner in a law firm, acting alone, cannot bind the other partners to a contract to buy snowboards for resale or rent an apartment for parties. These actions are outside the normal scope of a law firm's business.

Partners can agree to limit the power of any one or more of the partners to negotiate contracts for the partnership. This agreement is binding on the partners and on outsiders who know it exists. But it is not binding on outsiders who don't know it exists. Outsiders unaware of the agreement have the right to assume each partner has normal agency powers for the partnership. Because mutual agency exposes all partners to the risk of unwise actions by any one partner, people should evaluate each potential partner before agreeing to join a partnership.

---

[3] The Income Tax Act requires that proper records be maintained by partnerships and all other forms of business ownership that fall under its provisions.

Unlimited Liability

When a general partnership can't pay its debts, the creditors usually can apply their claims to personal assets of partners. If a partner does not have enough assets to meet his or her share of the partnership debt, the creditors can apply their claims to the assets of the other partners. Because partners can be called on to pay the debts of a partnership, each partner is said to have **unlimited liability** for the partnership's debts. Mutual agency and unlimited liability are two main reasons why most partnerships have only a few members.

Co-Ownership of Property

Partnership assets are owned jointly by all partners. Any investment by a partner becomes the joint property of all partners. Partners have a claim on partnership assets based on their capital account.

Limited Partnerships

Some individuals who want to invest in a partnership are unwilling to accept the risk of unlimited liability. Their needs may be met with a **limited partnership.** Limited partnerships are established under provincial statutes that require registration. One or more partners in a limited partnership may be designated as a **general partner** who assumes management duties and unlimited liability for the debts and obligations of the partnership. The **limited partners** have no personal liability beyond the investment they invest in the partnership. A limited partnership is managed by the general partner(s). Limited partners have no active role except as specified in the partnership agreement. A limited partnership agreement must be drawn up for a limited partnership. This legal document often specifies unique procedures for allocating incomes and losses between general and limited partners. The same basic accounting procedures are used for both limited and **general partnerships.**

You Make the Call

Advisor

Your roommate has hair-dressing skills and is thinking of opening a barbershop that would cater to university students. He has a financially well off aunt with whom he would like to enter into partnership. His aunt is interested in the venture and would like a stake in the operation. However, she is heavily involved in other ventures and simply has no time to devote to another business activity. She is concerned about the extent of her liability should the business not succeed. What type of business organization might you recommend to your roommate?

Answers—p. 676

Basic Partnership Accounting

Accounting for a partnership is the same as accounting for a proprietorship except for transactions directly affecting partners' equity. Because ownership rights in a partnership are divided among partners, partnership accounting:

■ Uses a capital account for each partner.

■ Uses a withdrawals account for each partner.

■ Allocates net income or loss to partners according to the partnership agreement.

This section describes partnership accounting for organizing a partnership, distributing income and losses, and preparing financial statements.

Organizing a Partnership

When partners invest in a partnership, their capital accounts are credited for the invested amounts. Partners can invest both assets and liabilities. Each partner's investment is recorded at an agreed upon value, normally the fair market value of the assets and liabilities at their date of contribution.

> **L02** Prepare entries when forming a partnership.

To illustrate, Olivia Tsang and David Breck organize a partnership in 1999 called **BOARDS**. Their business offers year-round facilities for skateboarding and snowboarding. Tsang's initial net investment in BOARDS is $30,000, made up of cash ($7,000), boarding facilities ($33,000), and a note payable reflecting a bank loan for the business of ($10,000). Breck's initial investment is cash of $10,000. These amounts are the values agreed upon by both partners. The entries to record these investments are:

Tsang's Investment

Jan. 11	Cash	7,000	
	Boarding facilities	33,000	
	Note payable		10,000
	O. Tsang, Capital		30,000
	To record investment of Tsang.		

Assets = Liabilities + Equity
+7,000   +10,000   +30,000
+33,000

Breck's Investment

Jan. 11	Cash	10,000	
	D. Breck, Capital		10,000
	To record investment of Breck.		

Assets = Liabilities + Equity
+10,000   +10,000

The accounting for partnership transactions after it is formed is similar to a proprietorship. Chapters 2–5 described the basic accounting procedures for a proprietorship, and they apply here as well. The minor differences include (1) Partners' withdrawals of assets are debited to their withdrawals accounts. (2) In closing the accounts at the end of a period, the partners' capital accounts are credited or debited for their shares of net income or loss. (3) The withdrawals account of each partner is closed to that partner's capital account. These procedures are similar to those used for a single proprietorship, except that separate capital and withdrawals accounts are kept for each partner.

Dividing Income or Loss

Partners are not employees of the partnership; they are its owners. If partners devote their time and services to their partnership, they are understood to do so for profit, not for salary. This means that when partners compute the net income of a partnership, salaries to partners are not expenses on the income statement. But when net income or loss of a partnership is allocated among partners, the partners can agree to base part of their allocation on salary allowances reflecting the relative values of services they provide. Partners also can agree that division of partnership earnings includes a return based on the amount invested. For instance, since Tsang contributes three times the investment of Breck, it is only fair that this fact be considered when earnings are allocated between them. Their partnership agreement can provide for interest allowances based on their capital balances. Like salary allowances, these interest allowances are not expenses on the income statement.

Partners can agree to any method of dividing income or loss. But in the absence of an agreement, the law says that income or loss of a partnership is shared equally by the partners. If partners agree on how they share income but say nothing about losses, then losses are shared in the same way as income. Several methods of sharing partnership income or loss are used. Three frequently used methods divide income or loss using: (1) a stated fractional basis, (2) the ratio of capital investments, or (3) salary and interest allowances and any remainder in a fixed ratio.

Allocated on a Stated Fractional Basis

One way to divide partnership income or loss is to give each partner a fraction of the total. Partners must agree on the fractional share each receives. A fractional basis can be expressed as a ratio or percentage. A 2:1 basis is the same as 2/3 and 1/3. A 3:2 ratio can be expressed as 3/5 and 2/5 or as 60% and 40%. The partnership agreement of O. Tsang and D. Breck says Tsang receives two-thirds and Breck one-third of partnership income and loss. If their partnership's net income is $60,000, it is allocated to the partners, and the Income Summary account is closed, with the following entry:

Assets = Liabilities + Equity
−60,000
+40,000
+20,000

Dec. 31	Income Summary	60,000	
	O. Tsang, Capital		40,000
	D. Breck, Capital		20,000
	To allocate income and close the Income Summary account.		

Allocated on the Ratio of Capital Investments

Partners can also allocate income or loss on the ratio of the relative capital investments of each partner. Tsang and Breck agreed to share earnings on the ratio of their capital investments. Since Tsang invested $30,000 and Breck invested $10,000, this means Tsang receives three-fourths of any income or loss ($30,000/$40,000) and Breck receives one-fourth ($10,000/$40,000).

Allocated Using Salaries, Interest Allowance, and a Fixed Ratio

Service contributions and capital contributions of partners often are not equal. Salary allowances can make up for differences in service contributions. Also, interest allowances can make up for unequal capital contributions. When both service and capital contributions are unequal, the allocation of income and loss can include both salary and interest allowances.

In Olivia Tsang and David Breck's new partnership, both agree that Tsang's services are worth an annual salary of $36,000. Since Breck is less experienced in the business, his services are valued at $24,000 annually. To compensate Tsang and Breck fairly, given these differences in service and capital contributions, they agree to share income or loss as follows:

1. Annual salary allowances of $36,000 to Tsang and $24,000 to Breck.

2. Interest allowances equal to 10% of each partner's beginning-of-year capital balance.

3. Any remaining balance of income or loss to be shared equally.

The provisions for salaries and interest in this partnership agreement are called *allowances*. Allowances are *not* reported as salaries and interest expense on the income statement. They are a means of dividing the income or loss of a partnership.

Illustration When Income Exceeds Allowance

If BOARDS has first year income of $70,000 and Tsang and Breck apply the partnership agreement above, they allocate income or loss as shown in Exhibit 14.1. Tsang gets $42,000 and Breck gets $28,000 of the $70,000 total.

	Tsang	Breck	Total
Net income			$70,000
Salary allowances:			
Tsang	$36,000		
Breck		$24,000	
Interest allowances:			
Tsang (10% on $30,000)	3,000		
Breck (10% on $10,000)		1,000	
Total salaries and interest	39,000	25,000	64,000
Balance of net income			$ 6,000
Balance allocated equally:			
Tsang	3,000		
Breck		3,000	
Total allocated equally			6,000
Balance of net income			$ -0-
Shares of each partner	$42,000	$28,000	$70,000

Exhibit 14.1

Dividing Income When Income Exceeds Allowances

Illustration When Allowances Exceed Income

The method of sharing agreed to by Tsang and Breck must be followed even if net income is less than the total of the allowances. If BOARDS first year net income is $50,000 instead of $70,000, it is allocated to the partners as shown in Exhibit 14.2. Computations for salaries and interest are identical to those in Exhibit 14.1. When we apply the total allowances against net income, the balance of income is negative. This negative ($14,000) is allocated in the same manner as a positive balance. The equal sharing agreement means a negative ($7,000) is allocated to each partner to determine the final allocation. In this case, Tsang ends up with $32,000 and Breck gets $18,000.

	Tsang	Breck	Total
Net income			$50,000
Salary allowances:			
Tsang	$36,000		
Breck		$24,000	
Interest allowances:			
Tsang (10% on $30,000)	3,000		
Breck (10% on $10,000)		1,000	
Total salaries and interest	39,000	25,000	64,000
Balance of net income over allocated .			(14,000)
Balance allocated equally:			
Tsang	(7,000)		
Breck		(7,000)	
Total allocated equally			14,000
Balance of net income			$ -0-
Shares of each partner	$32,000	$18,000	$50,000

Exhibit 14.2

Dividing Income When Allowances Exceed Income

If BOARDS had experienced a loss, then Tsang and Breck share it in the same manner as the $50,000 income. The only difference is we would begin with a negative amount because of the loss. Specifically, partners are still allocated their salary and interest allowances, which further adds to the negative balance of the loss. This *total* negative balance *after* salary and interest allowances, or ($14,000) in our case, is allocated equally between the partners. These allocations are applied against the positive numbers from any allowances to determine each partner's share of the loss.

Flashback

3. Ben and Jerry form a partnership by contributing $70,000 and $35,000, respectively. They agree to an interest allowance equal to 10% of each partner's capital balance at the beginning of the year with the remaining income shared equally. Allocate first-year income of $40,000 to each partner.

4. What fraction does each partner receive if three partners share on a 1:2:3 basis?

Answers—p. 676

Partnership Financial Statements

Partnership financial statements are similar to those of a proprietorship. The **statement of changes in partners' equity** shows the capital balances at the beginning of the period, any additional investments made by the partners, the income or loss of the partnership, withdrawals by partners, and the ending capital balances. This statement, also called *statement of partners' capital,* usually shows these changes for each partner's capital account and includes the allocation of income among partners. To illustrate, Exhibit 14.3 shows the statement of changes in partners' equity for BOARDS prepared for the sharing agreement of Exhibit 14.1. Recall that BOARDS' first year income was $70,000. Also, Tsang withdrew $20,000 and Breck $12,000 at the end of the first year.

Exhibit 14.3

Statement of Changes in Partners' Equity

BOARDS Statement of Changes in Partners' Equity For Year Ended December 31, 1999				
		Tsang	Breck	Total
Beginning capital balances . . .		$ -0-	$ -0-	$ -0-
Plus:				
Investments by owners		30,000	10,000	40,000
Net income:				
Salary allowances	$36,000		$24,000	
Interest allowances	3,000		1,000	
Balance	3,000		3,000	
Total net income		42,000	28,000	70,000
Total		$72,000	$38,000	$110,000
Less partners' withdrawals . . .		(20,000)	(12,000)	(32,000)
Ending capital balances		$52,000	$26,000	$ 78,000

The owner's equity section of the balance sheet of a partnership usually shows the separate capital account balance of each partner. In the case of BOARDS, both O. Tsang, Capital and D. Breck, Capital are listed in the owners' equity section along with their balances of $52,000 and $26,000, respectively.

Parker and Poon began a partnership by investing $52,000 and $78,000, respectively. During the first year, the partnership earned $180,000. Prepare calculations that show how the income should be allocated to the partners under each of the following plans for sharing net incomes and losses:

a. The partners failed to agree on a method of sharing income.
b. The partners agreed to share incomes and losses in their investment ratio.
c. The partners agreed to share income by allowing an $85,000 per year salary allowance to Parker, a $65,000 per year salary allowance to Poon, 10% interest on beginning capital balances, and the remainder equally.

Planning the Solution

1. Set up a column for each partner as well as a column to keep track of allocated income.
2. Allocate income to each partner according to the terms of the partnership agreement.

	Share to Parker	Share to Poon	Income Allocated
Plan (a) $180,000 × (1/2)	$90,000	$ 90,000	$180,000
Plan (b) ($52,000/$130,000) × $180,000 .	$72,000		$ 72,000
($78,000/$130,000) × $180,000 .		$108,000	$108,000
	$72,000	$108,000	$180,000
Plan (c) Salary allowances	$85,000	$ 65,000	$150,000
Interest allowances:			
($52,000 × .1)	5,200		5,200
($78,000 × .1)		7,800	7,800
			$163,000
Remainder equally:			
($180,000 − $163,000)/2	8,500	8,500	17,000
	$98,700	$ 81,300	$180,000

A partnership is based on a contract between individuals. When a partner is added or a partner withdraws, the old partnership ends. Still, the business can continue to operate as a new partnership among the remaining partners. This section looks at how we account for the addition and withdrawal of a partner.

Admission of a Partner

There are two ways a new partner is admitted to a partnership. First, a new partner can purchase an interest from one or more current partners. Second, a new partner can invest cash or other assets.

Purchase of Partnership Interest

The purchase of partnership interest is *a personal transaction between one or more current partners and the new partner*. The purchaser does not become a partner until accepted by the current partners. Accounting for the purchase of partnership interest involves a reallocation of current partners' capital to reflect the transaction.

To illustrate, at the end of BOARDS first year, David Breck sells *one-half* of his partnership interest to Cris Davis for $18,000. Breck is selling a $13,000 recorded interest ($26,000 × 1/2) in the partnership (see Exhibit 14.3). The partnership records this as:

Assets = Liabilities + Equity
−13,000
+13,000

Jan. 4	D. Breck, Capital	13,000	
	C. Davis, Capital		13,000
	To record admission of Davis by purchase.		

After this entry is posted, BOARDS' owners' equity list O. Tsang, Capital, D. Breck, Capital, and C. Davis, Capital along with their balances of $52,000, $13,000 and $13,000, respectively.

Two aspects of this transaction are important. First, the $18,000 Davis paid to Breck is not recorded by the partnership. This is regardless of the amount paid by Davis to Breck. The partnership's assets, liabilities, and total equity are unaffected by this transaction. Second, Tsang and Breck must agree if Davis is to become a partner. If they agree to accept Davis, a new partnership is formed and a new contract with a new income-and-loss-sharing agreement is prepared. If Tsang or Breck refuses to accept Davis as a partner, then (under the Uniform Partnership Act) Davis gets Breck's sold share of partnership income and loss. If the partnership is liquidated, Davis gets Breck's sold share of partnership assets. But Davis gets no voice in managing the company until being admitted as a partner.

Investing Assets in a Partnership

Admitting a partner by accepting assets is a *transaction between the new partner and the partnership.* The invested assets become partnership property. To illustrate, if Tsang (with a $52,000 interest) and Breck (with a $26,000 interest) agree to accept Davis as a partner in BOARDS with her investment of $22,000, the entry to record Davis' investment is:

Assets = Liabilities + Equity
+22,000   +22,000

Jan. 4	Cash	22,000	
	C. Davis, Capital		22,000
	To record admission of Davis by investment.		

After this entry is posted, both assets (cash) and owners' equity (C. Davis, Capital) increase by $22,000. Davis now has 22% equity in the assets of the business, computed as $22,000 divided by the entire partnership equity ($52,000 + $26,000 + $22,000). But she doesn't necessarily have a right to 22% of income. Dividing income and loss is a separate matter on which partners must agree.

Bonus to Old Partners

When the current value of a partnership is greater than the recorded amounts of equity, the partners usually require a new partner to pay a bonus for the privilege of joining. To illustrate, let's say Tsang and Breck agree to accept Davis as a partner with a 25% interest in BOARDS. But they require Davis to invest $42,000. Recall, the partnership's accounting records show Tsang's recorded equity in the business is $52,000 and Breck's recorded equity is $26,000 (see Exhibit 14.3). They agree to accept Davis' $42,000 investment in return for a 25% share in both partnership's earnings and equity. Davis' equity is determined as follows:

Equities of existing partners ($52,000 + $26,000)	$ 78,000
Investment of new partner	42,000
Total partnership equity	$120,000
Equity of Davis (25% × $120,000)	$ 30,000

Although Davis invests $42,000, her equity in the recorded net assets of the partnership is only $30,000. The $12,000 difference usually is called a bonus and allocated to existing partners (Tsang and Breck) according to their net income/loss share ratio. Assume this to be 50:50. The entry to record this is:

Jan. 4	Cash	42,000	
	Davis, Capital		30,000
	Tsang, Capital ($12,000 × 1/2)		6,000
	Breck, Capital ($12,000 × 1/2)		6,000
	To record admission of Davis and bonus to old partners.		

Assets = Liabilities + Equity
+42,000   +30,000
                              +6,000
                              +6,000

Tsang and Breck share the $12,000 bonus according to their income-and-loss-sharing agreement. This bonus is always shared in this way because it is viewed as an increase in the value of the partnership that is not yet reflected in the accounts of the previous partners.

Bonus to New Partner

Existing partners can pay a bonus to a new partner. This usually occurs when they need additional cash or the new partner has exceptional talents. The new partner gets a larger equity than the amount invested. To illustrate, let's say Tsang and Breck agree to accept Davis as a partner with a 25% interest in both the partnership's earnings and equity, but they require Davis to only invest $18,000. Davis' equity is determined as:

Equities of existing partners ($52,000 + $26,000)	$78,000
Investment of new partner	18,000
Total partnership equity	$96,000
Equity of Davis (25% × $96,000)	$24,000

The entry to record Davis' investment is:

Jan. 4	Cash	18,000	
	Tsang, Capital ($6,000 × 1/2)	3,000	
	Breck, Capital ($6,000 × 1/2)	3,000	
	Davis, Capital		24,000
	To record Davis' admission and bonus.		

Assets = Liabilities + Equity
+18,000   −3,000
                              −3,000
                              +24,000

The old partners in accordance with their income-and-loss-sharing ratios contribute the $6,000 bonus to Davis. Davis' 25% equity doesn't necessarily entitle her to 25% of any income or loss. This is a separate matter for agreement by the partners.

Withdrawal of a Partner

There are generally two ways a partner withdraws from a partnership. First, the withdrawing partner can sell his or her interest to another person who pays cash or other assets to the withdrawing partner. For this we need only debit the withdrawing partner's capital account and credit the new partner's capital account. The second case is when cash or other assets of the partnership are distributed to the withdrawing partner in settlement of his or her equity interest. This section explains the accounting for this case.

To illustrate, let's assume in a future period that Breck withdraws from the partnership of BOARDS. The partners (Tsang, Breck, and Davis) share income and loss equally. Their partnership shows the following capital balances: Tsang, $84,000; Breck $38,000; and Davis $38,000. Accounting for the withdrawal depends on whether a bonus is paid or not. We describe three possibilities.

No Bonus

If Breck withdraws and takes cash equal to his equity, the entry is:

Assets = Liabilities + Equity
−38,000   −38,000

Oct. 31	Breck, Capital	38,000	
	Cash		38,000
	To record withdrawal of Breck and no bonus.		

Breck can take any combination of assets to which the partners agree to settle his equity. The withdrawal of Breck creates a new partnership between remaining partners. A new partnership contract and a new income-and-loss-sharing agreement are sometimes required.

Bonus to Remaining Partners

A withdrawing partner is sometimes willing to take less than the recorded value of his or her equity just to get out of the partnership or because the recorded value of some assets are overstated. Whatever the reason, when this occurs the withdrawing partner in effect gives a bonus to remaining partners equal to the equity left behind. The remaining partners share this un-withdrawn equity in their income-and-loss-sharing ratio. To illustrate, if Breck withdraws and agrees to take $34,000 cash in settlement of his equity, the entry is:

Assets = Liabilities + Equity
−34,000   −38,000
                       +2,000
                       +2,000

Oct. 31	Breck, Capital	38,000	
	Cash		34,000
	Tsang, Capital		2,000
	Davis, Capital		2,000
	To record withdrawal of Breck and bonus to remaining partners.		

Breck withdrew $4,000 less than his recorded equity. The amount not withdrawn is divided between Tsang and Davis in their income-and-loss-sharing ratio, which in this case is shared equally among partners.

Bonus to Withdrawing Partner

There are at least two reasons why a withdrawing partner may be able to receive more than his or her recorded equity. First, the recorded equity may be understated because asset values are understated. Second, the remaining partners may want to remove this partner by giving assets of greater value than this partner's recorded equity. When either case occurs, the withdrawing partner in effect receives a bonus. The remaining partners reduce their equity for this bonus using their income-and-loss-sharing ratio. To illustrate, if Breck withdraws and receives $40,000 cash in settlement of his equity, the entry is:

Assets = Liabilities + Equity
−40,000   −38,000
                       −1,000
                       −1,000

Oct. 31	Breck, Capital	38,000	
	Tsang, Capital	1,000	
	Davis, Capital	1,000	
	Cash		40,000
	To record withdrawal of and bonus to Breck.		

Death of a Partner

A partner's death dissolves a partnership. A deceased partner's estate is entitled to receive his or her equity. The partnership contract should contain provisions for settlement in this case. These usually include provisions for (a) a closing of the books to determine income or loss since the end of the previous period and (b) a method for determining and recording current values for assets and liabilities. The remaining partners and the deceased partner's estate then must agree to a settlement of the deceased partner's equity. This can involve selling the equity to remaining partners or to an outsider, or it can involve withdrawing assets.

Judgment and Ethics

Lawyer

You are a lawyer hired by the two remaining partners of a three-member partnership. The third partner recently died. The three partners shared income and loss in the ratio of their capital balances, which were equal. The partnership agreement says a deceased partner's estate is entitled to the "partner's percent share of partnership assets." The estate argues it is entitled to one-third of the current value of the partnership's total assets. The remaining partners say the distribution should use the asset's book values, which are only 75% of current value. They also point to partnership liabilities, which equal 40% of the assets' book value, and 30% of current value. What do you suggest?

Answer—p. 676

Liquidation of a Partnership

When a partnership is liquidated, its business is ended. Four steps are involved: (1) Noncash assets are sold for cash and a gain or loss on liquidation is recorded, (2) Gain or loss on liquidation is allocated to partners' using their income-and-loss ratio, (3) Liabilities are paid, and (4) Remaining cash is distributed to partners based on their capital balances. **Partnership liquidation** often follows one of two different cases described below.

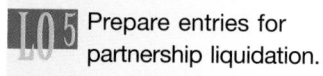

LO 5 Prepare entries for partnership liquidation.

No Capital Deficiency

The case of *no capital deficiency* is where all partners have a credit balance in their capital accounts before final distribution of cash. To illustrate, let's assume Tsang, Breck, and Davis operate their partnership in BOARDS for several years, sharing income and losses equally. The partners then decide to liquidate. On that date, the books are closed, and income from operations is transferred to partners' capital accounts. The partners' recorded equity balances immediately prior to liquidation are: Tsang $70,000; Breck $66,000; and Davis $62,000.

In a liquidation, some gains or losses commonly result from the sale of noncash assets. These *losses and gains are called losses and gains from liquidation*. Just like net incomes or losses, partners generally share the losses and gains from liquidation in their income-and-loss-sharing ratio. Assume BOARDS sells its noncash assets for a net gain on realization of $6,000. This is shared by the partners using their income-and-loss-sharing agreement (that is equal for these partners) yielding the partners' revised equity balances of: Tsang $72,000; Breck $68,000; and Davis $64,000.[4]

---

[4] The concepts behind these entries are not new. For example, assume BOARDS has two non-cash assets recorded as: boarding facilities, $15,000 and land, $25,000. The entry to sell these assets for $46,000 is:

Jan. 15	Cash	46,000	
	Boarding facilities		15,000
	Land		25,000
	Loss or Gain from Liquidation		6,000
	Sold noncash assets for a gain.		

We then record the allocation of any loss or gain (a gain in this case) from liquidation according to the partners' income-and-loss sharing agreement as:

Jan. 15	Loss or Gain from Liquidation	6,000	
	Tsang, Capital		2,000
	Breck, Capital		2,000
	Davis, Capital		2,000
	To allocate liquidation gain to partners.		

After partnership assets are sold and the gain or loss shared, any liabilities must be paid. Because creditors have first claim, they are paid first. After creditors are paid, the remaining cash is divided among the partners according to his or her capital account balance. BOARDS only liability at liquidation is $20,000 in accounts payable. The entries to record the creditor's payment and final distribution of cash to partners is:

Assets = Liabilities + Equity
−20,000 −20,000

Jan. 15	Accounts Payable	20,000	
	Cash		20,000
	To pay claims of creditors.		

Assets = Liabilities + Equity
−204,000   −72,000
          −68,000
          −64,000

15	Tsang, Capital	72,000	
	Breck, Capital	68,000	
	Davis, Capital	64,000	
	Cash		204,000
	To distribute remaining cash to partners.		

Remember the final cash payment is distributed to partners according to their capital account balances, whereas gains and losses from liquidation are allocated according to the income-and-loss-sharing ratio.

Capital Deficiency

The case of *capital deficiency* is where at least one partner has a debit balance in his or her capital account before the final distribution of cash. This can arise from liquidation losses, excessive withdrawals before liquidation, or recurring losses in prior periods. Partners with a capital deficiency must, if possible, cover the deficit by paying cash into the partnership.

To illustrate, let's assume Tsang, Breck, and Davis operate their partnership in BOARDS for several years, sharing income and losses equally. The partners then decide to liquidate. But contrary to the case above, and immediately prior to the final distribution of cash, the partners' recorded capital balances are: Tsang $19,000; Breck $8,000; and Davis ($3,000). Davis' capital deficiency means she owes the partnership $3,000. Both Tsang and Breck have a legal claim against Davis' personal assets. The final distribution of cash in this case depends on how this capital deficiency is handled.

Partner Pays Deficiency

Davis is obligated to pay $3,000 into the partnership to cover the deficiency. If Davis is willing and able to pay, the entry to record its receipt is:

Assets = Liabilities + Equity
+3,000   +3,000

Jan. 15	Cash	3,000	
	Davis, Capital		3,000
	To record payment of deficiency by Davis.		

After the $3,000 payment, the partners' capital balances are: Tsang $19,000; Breck $8,000; and Davis ($0). The entry to record the final cash distributions to partners is:

Assets = Liabilities + Equity
−27,000   −19,000
          −8,000

Jan. 15	Tsang, Capital	19,000	
	Breck, Capital	8,000	
	Cash		27,000
	To distribute remaining cash to partners.		

Partner Can't Pay Deficiency

When a partner is unable to pay the deficiency, it is absorbed by the remaining partners with credit balances. This is because of unlimited liability in a partnership. To illustrate, if Davis is unable to pay the $3,000 deficiency, Tsang and Breck share it based usually on their income-and-loss-sharing ratio. Since they share equally, both Tsang and Breck absorb $1,500 each of the deficiency. This is recorded as:

Jan. 15	Tsang, Capital	1,500	
	Breck, Capital	1,500	
	Davis, Capital		3,000
	To transfer Davis' deficiency to Tsang and Breck.		

Assets = Liabilities + Equity
−1,500
−1,500
+3,000

After Davis' deficiency is absorbed by Tsang and Breck, the capital accounts of the partners are: Tsang $17,500; Breck $6,500; and Davis ($0). The entry to record the final cash distributions to the partners is:

Jan. 15	Tsang, Capital	17,500	
	Breck, Capital	6,500	
	Cash		24,000
	To distribute remaining cash to partners.		

Assets = Liabilities + Equity
−24,000
−17,500
−6,500

The inability of Davis to cover her deficiency does not relieve her of liability. If she becomes able to pay at some future date, Tsang and Breck can each collect $1,500 from her.

The sharing of an insolvent partner's deficit by the remaining partners in their original income-and-loss-sharing ratio is generally regarded as equitable. In England, however, in 1904 in the case of *Garner v. Murray*, Judge Joyce ruled that the debit balance of the insolvent partner's capital account is a personal debt due to the other partners and to be borne by them in the ratio of their capital account balances immediately prior to liquidation.

While *Garner v. Murray* still appears to be good law, it is considered by most to be inequitable. The decision applies only when the partnership agreement does not cover the situation. It is therefore important to provide agreement for the sharing of a partner's debit balance by the remaining partners according to their income-and-loss-sharing ratio.

Summary

LO1 Identify characteristics of partnerships and similar organizations and explain the concepts of mutual agency and unlimited liability in a partnership.
A partnership is a voluntary association between the partners that is based on a contract. The life of a partnership is limited by agreement or by death or incapacity of a partner. Normally, each partner can act as an agent of the other partners and commit the partnership to any contract within the apparent scope of its business. All partners in a general partnership are personally liable for all the debts of the partnership. Limited partnerships include one or more general partners plus one or more limited partners whose liabilities are limited to the amount of their investments in the partnership. The risk of becoming a partner results in part from the fact that partnership characteristics include a mutual agency and unlimited liability.

LO2 Prepare entries when forming a partnership.
When partners invest in a partnership, their capital accounts are credited for the invested amounts. Partners can invest both assets and liabilities. Each partner's investment is recorded at an agreed upon value, normally the fair market value of the assets and liabilities at their date of contribution.

LO3 Allocate and record income and loss among partners. A partnership's net incomes or losses are allocated to the partners according to the terms of the partnership agreement. The agreement may specify that each partner will receive a given fraction, or that the allocation of incomes and losses will reflect salary allowances and/or interest allowances. When salary and/or interest allowances are granted, the residual net income or loss usually is allocated equally or on a stated fractional basis.

 Account for the admission and withdrawal of a partner. When a new partner buys a partnership interest directly from one or more of the existing partners, the amount of cash paid from one partner to another does not affect the total recorded equity of the partnership. The recorded equity of the selling partner(s) is simply transferred to the capital account of the new partner. Alternatively, a new partner may purchase an equity by investing additional assets in the partnership. When this occurs, part of the new partner's investment may be credited as a bonus to the capital accounts of the existing partners. Also, to gain the participation of the new partner, the existing partners may give the new partner a bonus whereby portions of the existing partners' capital balances are transferred to the new partner's capital account. Occasionally, goodwill is recorded when a partner invests in a partnership.

 Prepare entries for partnership liquidation. When a partnership is liquidated, losses and gains from selling the partnership assets are allocated to the partners according to their income-and-loss sharing ratio. If a partner's capital account has a balance that the partner cannot pay, the other partners generally must share the deficit in their relative income-and-loss sharing ratio.

Guidance Answers to **You Make the Call**

Advisor

One possibility is to recommend to your roommate that he consider a limited partnership. His aunt may be interested in becoming a limited partner so that her liability would be limited to her investment in the enterprise. A partnership agreement could be drawn up to reflect this arrangement as well as other matters such as how to share potential profits and losses.

Guidance Answers to **Judgment and Ethics**

Lawyer

The partnership agreement fails to mention liabilities or use the term "net assets." Still, to give the estate one-third of total assets is not fair to the remaining partners. This is because if the partner had lived and the partners had decided to liquidate, the liabilities must be paid first. Also, a settlement based on the recorded equity of the deceased partner would fail to recognize excess of current value over book value. These value increases would be realized if the partnership is liquidated. A fair settlement would seem to be a payment to the estate for the balance of the deceased partner's equity based on the *current value of net assets.*

Guidance Answers to

1. *b*

2. Unlimited liability means that the creditors of a partnership have the right to require each partner to be personally responsible for all partnership debts.

3.

	Ben	Jerry	Total
Net income			$40,000
Interest allowance	$ 7,000	$ 3,500	10,500
Remaining balance			$29,500
Balance allocated equally	14,750	14,750	29,500
Remaining balance			$ -0-
Shares of partners	$21,750	$18,250	

4. 1/6, 2/6, and 3/6

The following events affect the partner's capital accounts in several successive partnerships. On a work sheet with six money columns, one for each of five partners and a totals column, show the effects of the following events on the partners' capital accounts.

Part 1

Apr. 14/99   Ries and Bax create R&B Co. Each invests $10,000, and they agree to share profits equally.

Dec. 31/99   R&B Co. earns $15,000 in the year. Ries withdraws $4,000 from the partnership, and Bax withdraws $7,000.

Jan. 1/00   Royce is made a partner in RB&R Co. after contributing $12,000 cash. The partners agree that each will get a 10% interest allowance on their beginning capital balances. In addition, Bax and Royce are to receive $5,000 salary allowances. The remainder of the income is to be divided evenly.

Dec. 31/00   The partnership's income for the year is $40,000, and these withdrawals occur: Ries, $5,000; Bax, $12,500; and Royce, $11,000.

Jan. 1/01   For $20,000, Ries sells her interest to Murdock, who is accepted by Bax and Royce as a partner in the new BR&M Co. The profits are to be shared equally after Bax and Royce each receive $25,000 salaries.

Dec. 31/01   The partnership's income for the year is $35,000, and these withdrawals occur: Bax, $2,500, and Royce, $2,000.

Jan. 1/02   Elway is admitted as a partner after investing $60,000 cash in the new Elway & Associates partnership. Elway is given a 50% interest in capital after the other partners transfer $3,000 to his account from each of theirs. A 20% interest allowance (on the beginning-of-year capital balances) will be used in sharing profits, but there will be no salaries. Elway will get 40% of the remainder, and the other three partners will each get 20%.

Dec. 31/02   Elway & Associates earns $127,600 for the year, and these withdrawals occur: Bax, $25,000; Royce, $27,000; Murdock, $15,000; and Elway, $40,000.

Jan. 1/03   Elway buys out Bax and Royce for the balances of their capital accounts, after a revaluation[5] of the partnership assets. The revaluation gain is $50,000, which is divided in the previous 1:1:1:2 ratio. Elway pays the others from personal funds. Murdock and Elway will share profits on a 1:9 ratio.

Feb. 29/03   The partnership had $10,000 of income since the beginning of the year. Murdock retires and receives partnership cash equal to her capital balance. Elway takes possession of the partnership assets in his own name, and the business is dissolved.

Part 2

Journalize the events affecting the partnership for the year ended December 31, 2000.

Planning the Solution

■ Evaluate each transaction's effects on the capital accounts of the partners.

■ Each time a new partner is admitted or a partner withdraws, allocate any bonus based on the income or loss sharing agreement.

■ Each time a new partner is admitted or a partner withdraws, allocate subsequent net incomes or losses in accordance with the new partnership agreement.

■ Make an entry to record Royce's initial investment. Make an entry to record the allocation of interest, salaries, and remainders for December 31/00. Make an entry to show the cash withdrawals from the partnership on December 31/00. Make an entry to close the withdrawal accounts on December 31/00.

---

[5] A revaluation is a determination of the fair value of the partnership assets.

Solution to Problem

Part 1

Event	Ries	Bax	Royce	Murdock	Elway	Total
Apr. 14/99						
Initial investment	$10,000	$10,000				$ 20,000
Dec. 31/99						
Income (equal)	7,500	7,500				15,000
Withdrawals	(4,000)	(7,000)				(11,000)
Ending balance	$13,500	$10,500				$ 24,000
Jan. 1/00						
New investment			$12,000			12,000
Dec. 31/00						
10% interest	1,350	1,050	1,200			3,600
Salaries		5,000	5,000			10,000
Remainder (equal)	8,800	8,800	8,800			26,400
Withdrawals	(5,000)	(12,500)	(11,000)			(28,500)
Ending balance	$18,650	$12,850	$16,000			$ 47,500
Jan. 1/01						
Transfer interest	(18,650)			$18,650		-0-
Dec. 31/01						
Salaries		25,000	25,000			50,000
Remainder (equal)		(5,000)	(5,000)	(5,000)		(15,000)
Withdrawals		(2,500)	(2,000)			(4,500)
Ending balance	$ -0-	$30,350	$34,000	$13,650		$ 78,000
Jan. 1/02						
New investment					$ 60,000	60,000
Bonuses to Elway		(3,000)	(3,000)	(3,000)	9,000	-0-
Adjusted balance		$27,350	$31,000	$10,650	$ 69,000	$138,000
Dec. 31/02						
20% interest		5,470	6,200	2,130	13,800	27,600
Remain. (1:1:1:2)		20,000	20,000	20,000	40,000	100,000
Withdrawals		(25,000)	(27,000)	(15,000)	(40,000)	(107,000)
Ending balance		$27,820	$30,200	$17,780	$ 82,800	$158,600
Jan. 1/03						
Gain (1:1:1:2)		10,000	10,000	10,000	20,000	50,000
Adjusted balance		$37,820	$40,200	$27,780	$102,800	$208,600
Transfer interests		(37,820)	(40,200)		78,020	-0-
Adjusted balance		$ -0-	$ -0-	$27,780	$180,820	$208,600
Feb. 29/03						
Income (1:9)				1,000	9,000	10,000
Adjusted balance				$28,780	$189,820	$218,600
Settlements				(28,780)	(189,820)	(218,600)
Final balance				$ -0-	$ -0-	$ -0-

Part 2

2000			
Jan. 1	Cash	12,000	
	Royce, Capital		12,000
	To record investment of Royce.		
Dec. 31	Income Summary	40,000	
	Ries, Capital		10,150
	Bax, Capital		14,850
	Royce, Capital		15,000
	To allocate interest, salaries, and		
	remainders.		
Dec. 31	Ries, Withdrawals	5,000	
	Bax, Withdrawals	12,500	
	Royce, Withdrawals	11,000	
	Cash		28,500
	To record the cash withdrawals		
	by the partners.		
Dec. 31	Ries, Capital	5,000	
	Bax, Capital	12,500	
	Royce, Capital	11,000	
	Ries, Withdrawals		5,000
	Bax, Withdrawals		12,500
	Royce, Withdrawals		11,000
	To close the withdrawal accounts.		

Glossary

General partner A partner who assumes unlimited liability for the debts of the partnership; also, the general partner in a limited partnership is responsible for its management. (p. 664)

General partnership A partnership in which all partners have mutual agency and unlimited liability for partnership debts. (p. 664)

Limited partners Partners who have no personal liability for debts of the partnership beyond the amounts they have invested in the partnership. (p. 664)

Limited partnership A partnership that has two classes of partners, limited partners and general partners. (p. 664)

Mutual agency The legal relationship among the partners whereby each partner is an agent of the partnership and is able to bind the partnership to contracts within the apparent scope of the partnership's business. (p. 663)

Partnership An unincorporated association of two or more persons to pursue a business for profit as co-owners. (p. 662)

Partnership contract The agreement between partners that sets forth the terms under which the affairs of the partnership will be conducted. (p. 662)

Partnership liquidation The dissolution of a business partnership by (1) selling noncash assets for cash and allocating the gain or loss according to partners' income-and-loss ratio, (2) paying liabilities, and (3) distributing remaining cash to partners based on capital balances. (p. 673)

Statement of changes in partners' equity Shows the capital balances at the beginning of the period, any additional investments made by partners, the income or loss of the partnership, withdrawals by partners, and the capital balances. (p. 668)

Unlimited liability of partners The legal relationship among general partners that makes each of them responsible for paying all the debts of the partnership if the other partners are unable to pay their shares. (p. 664)

Questions

1. Amey and Lacey are partners. Lacey dies, and her son claims the right to take his mother's place in the partnership. Does he have this right? Why?
2. If a partnership contract does not state the period of time the partnership is to exist, when does the partnership end?
3. As applied to a partnership, what does the term mutual agency mean?
4. Can partners limit the right of a partner to commit their partnership to contracts? Would the agreement be binding (a) on the partners and (b) on outsiders?
5. What does the term unlimited liability mean when it is applied to members of a partnership?
6. How does a general partnership differ from a limited partnership?
7. George, Burton, and Dillman have been partners for three years. The partnership is being dissolved. George is leaving the firm, but Burton and Dillman plan to carry on the business. In the final settlement, George places a $75,000 salary claim against the partnership. He contends that he has a claim for a salary of $25,000 for each year because he devoted all of his time for three years to the affairs of the partnership. Is his claim valid? Why?
8. The partnership agreement of Jenny Nelmida and Fei Abella provides for a two-thirds, one-third sharing of income but says nothing about losses. The first year of partnership operations resulted in a loss and Nelmida argues that the loss should be shared equally because the partnership agreement said nothing about sharing losses. What do you think?
9. If the partners in Blume Partnership want the financial statements to show the procedures used to allocate the partnership income among the partners, on what financial statement should the allocation appear?
10. After all partnership assets are converted to cash and all liabilities have been paid, the remaining cash should equal the sum of the balances of the partners' capital accounts. Why?
11. Kay, Kat, and Kim are partners. In a liquidation, Kay's share of partnership losses exceeds her capital account balance. She is unable to meet the deficit from her personal assets, and the excess losses are shared by her partners. Does this relieve Kay of liability?
12. A partner withdraws from a partnership and receives assets of greater value than the book value of his equity. Should the remaining partners share the resulting reduction in their equities in the ratio of their relative capital balances or in their income-and-loss-sharing ratio?

Quick Study

QS 14-1
Partnership liability
LO 1

Kurt and Ellen are partners in operating a store. Without consulting Kurt, Ellen enters into a contract for the purchase of merchandise for the store. Kurt contends that he did not authorize the order and refuses to take delivery. The vendor sues the partners for the contract price of the merchandise. Will the partnership have to pay? Why? Does your answer differ if Kurt and Ellen are partners in a public accounting firm?

QS 14-2
Liability in limited partnerships
LO 1

Furst organized a limited partnership and is the only general partner. Nexx invested $20,000 in the partnership and was admitted as a limited partner with the understanding that he would receive 10% of the profits. After two unprofitable years, the partnership ceased doing business. At that point, partnership liabilities were $85,000 larger than partnership assets. How much money can the creditors of the partnership obtain from the personal assets of Nexx in satisfaction of the unpaid partnership debts?

QS 14-3
Partnership income allocation
LO 2

Ace and Bud are partners who agree that Ace will receive a $50,000 salary allowance after which remaining incomes or losses will be shared equally. If Bud's capital account is credited $1,000 as his share of the remaining net income in a given period, how much net income did the partnership earn?

QS 14-4
Partnership income allocation
LO 2

Roger Bussey and Art Beery are partners in a business they started two years ago. The partnership agreement states that Bussey should receive a salary allowance of $30,000 and that Beery should receive $40,000. Any remaining income or loss is to be shared equally. Determine each partner's share of the current year's net income of $104,000.

Logan and Smythe are partners, each with $30,000 in their partnership capital accounts. Fontaine is admitted to the partnership by an investment of $30,000. Make the entry to show Fontaine's admission to the partnership.

QS 14-5
Admission of a partner
LO 4

Fontaine agrees to pay Logan and Smythe $10,000 each for a one-third ($33\frac{1}{3}$%) interest in the Logan-Smythe partnership. At the time Fontaine is admitted each partner has a $30,000 capital balance. Make the journal entry to record Fontaine's purchase of the partners' interest.

QS 14-6
Partner admission through purchase of interest
LO 4

For each scenario below recommend a form of business organization. Along with each recommendation explain how business profits would be taxed if the form of organization recommended is adopted by the owners. Also list several advantages that the owners will enjoy from the form of business organization that you recommend.

1. Keith, Scott, and Brian are new college graduates in computer science. They are thinking of starting a Web-page creation company. They all have quite a few college debts and currently do not own any of the computer equipment that they will need to get the company started.

2. Dr. Marble and Dr. Sampson are new graduates from medical residency programs. They are both family practice physicians and would like to open a clinic in an underserved rural area. Although neither has any funds to bring to the new venture a banker has expressed interest in making a loan to provide start-up funds for the practice.

3. Matthew has been out of school for about five years and has become quite knowledgeable about the commercial real estate market. Matthew would like to organize a company that buys and sells real estate. Matthew feels like he has the expertise to manage the company but needs funds to invest in the commercial property.

Exercises

Exercise 14-1
Forms of organization
LO 1, 6

On March 1, 1998, Reed and Vaughn formed a partnership in the province of Ontario. Reed contributed $88,000 cash and Vaughn contributed land valued at $70,000 and a building valued at $120,000. Also, the partnership assumed responsibility for Vaughn's $80,000 long-term note payable associated with the land and building. The partners agreed to share profits as follows: Reed is to receive an annual salary allowance of $30,000, both are to receive an annual interest allowance of 10% of their original capital investment, and any remaining profit or loss is to be shared equally. On October 20, 1998, Reed withdrew cash of $32,000 and Vaughn withdrew $25,000. After the adjusting entries and the closing entries to the revenue and expense accounts, the Income Summary account had a credit balance of $79,000. Present general journal entries to record the initial capital investments of the partners, their cash withdrawals, and the December 31 closing of the income summary and withdrawals accounts. Finally, determine the balances of the partners' capital accounts as of the end of 1998.

Exercise 14-2
Journalizing partnership entries
LO 2, 3

Newton and Berry began a partnership by investing $50,000 and $75,000, respectively. During its first year, the partnership earned $165,000.

Required

Prepare calculations showing how the income should be allocated to the partners under each of the following plans for sharing net incomes and losses:

a. The partners failed to agree on a method of sharing income.

b. The partners agreed to share incomes and losses in proportion to their initial investments.

c. The partners agreed to share income by allowing a $55,000 per year salary allowance to Newton, a $45,000 per year salary allowance to Berry, 10% interest on their initial investments, and the balance equally.

Exercise 14-3
Income allocation in a partnership
LO 3

Exercise 14-4
Income allocation in a partnership
LO 3

Assume that the partners of Exercise 14-3 agreed to share net incomes and losses by allowing yearly salary allowances of $55,000 to Newton and $45,000 to Berry, 10% interest allowances on their investments, and the balance equally. (a) Determine the shares of Newton and Berry in a first-year net income of $94,400. (b) Determine the partners' shares in a first-year net loss of $15,700.

Exercise 14-5
Sale of a partnership interest
LO 4

The partners in the Royal Partnership have agreed that partner Prince may sell his $90,000 equity in the partnership to Duke, for which Duke will pay Prince $75,000. Present the partnership's journal entry to record the sale on September 30.

Exercise 14-6
Admission of a new partner
LO 4

The E-O Partnership has total partners' equity of $510,000, which is made up of Elm, Capital, $400,000, and Oak, Capital, $110,000. The partners share net incomes and losses in a ratio of 80% to Elm and 20% to Oak. On November 1, Ash is admitted to the partnership and given a 15% interest in equity and incomes and losses. Prepare the journal entry to record the entry of Ash under each of the following unrelated assumptions: Ash invests cash of (a) $90,000, (b) $125,000, and (c) $60,000.

Exercise 14-7
Retirement of a partner
LO 4

Holland, Flowers, and Wood have been partners sharing net incomes and losses in a 5:3:2 ratio. On January 31, the date Wood retires from the partnership, the equities of the partners are Holland, $350,000; Flowers, $240,000; and Wood, $180,000. Present general journal entries to record Wood's retirement under each of the following unrelated assumptions:
a. Wood is paid $180,000 in partnership cash for his equity.
b. Wood is paid $200,000 in partnership cash for his equity.
c. Wood is paid $150,000 in partnership cash for his equity.

Exercise 14-8
Liquidation of a partnership
LO 5

The Red, White & Blue partnership was begun with investments by the partners as follows: Red, $175,000; White, $220,000; and Blue, $205,000. The first year of operations did not go well, and the partners finally decided to liquidate the partnership, sharing all losses equally. On August 31, after all assets were converted to cash and all creditors were paid, only $60,000 in partnership cash remained.

Required

1. Calculate the capital account balances of the partners after the liquidation of assets and payment of creditors.
2. Assume that any partner with a deficit pays cash to the partnership to cover the deficit. Then, present the general journal entries on August 31 to record the cash receipt from the deficient partner(s) and the final disbursement of cash to the partners.
3. Now make the contrary assumption that any partner with a deficit is not able to reimburse the partnership. Present journal entries (a) to transfer the deficit of any deficient partners to the other partners and (b) to record the final disbursement of cash to the partners.

Exercise 14-9
Liquidation of a partnership
LO 5

Sandburg, McArthur, and Cox are partners who share incomes and losses in a 1:4:5 ratio. After lengthy disagreements among the partners and several unprofitable periods, the partners decided to liquidate the partnership. Before the liquidation, the partnership balance sheet showed total assets, $116,000; total liabilities, $88,000; Sandburg, Capital, $1,200; McArthur, Capital, $11,700; and Cox, Capital, $15,100. The cash proceeds from selling the assets were sufficient to repay all but $24,000 to the creditors. Calculate the loss from selling the assets, allocate the loss to the partners, and determine how much of the remaining liability should be paid by each partner.

Exercise 14-10
Liquidation of a limited partnership
LO 5

Assume that the Sandburg, McArthur, and Cox partnership of Exercise 14-9 is a limited partnership. Sandburg and McArthur are general partners and Cox is a limited partner. How much of the remaining $24,000 liability should be paid by each partner?

Tom Katz, Kaye Reeves, and Alice Troy invested $40,000, $56,000, and $64,000, respectively, in a partnership. During its first year, the firm earned $124,500.

Required

Prepare entries to close the firm's Income Summary account as of December 31 and to allocate the net income to the partners under each of the following assumptions:

a. The partners did not produce any special agreement on the method of sharing incomes.

b. The partners agreed to share net incomes and losses in the ratio of their beginning investments.

c. The partners agreed to share income by providing annual salary allowances of $33,000 to Katz, $28,000 to Reeves, and $40,000 to Troy; allowing 10% interest on the partners' beginning investments; and sharing the remainder equally.

Linda Nuñez and Ray Parker are in the process of forming a partnership to which Nuñez will devote one-half time and Parker will devote full time. They have discussed the following alternative plans for sharing net incomes and losses.

a. In the ratio of their initial investments, which they have agreed will be $21,000 for Nuñez and $31,500 for Parker.

b. In proportion to the time devoted to the business.

c. A salary allowance of $3,000 per month to Parker and the balance in accordance with their investment ratio.

d. A $3,000 per month salary allowance to Parker, 10% interest on their initial investments, and the balance equally.

The partners expect the business to generate income as follows: Year 1, $18,000 net loss; Year 2, $45,000 net income; and Year 3, $75,000 net income.

Required

1. Prepare three schedules with the following column headings:

Income/ Loss Sharing Plan	Year _____ .		
	Calculations	Nuñez	Parker

2. Complete a schedule for each of the first three years by showing how the partnership net income or loss for each year would be allocated to the partners under each of the four plans being considered. Round your answers to the nearest whole dollar

Brad Marshall, Jon Spiller, and Leigh Rand formed the MSR Partnership by making capital contributions of $183,750, $131,250, and $210,000, respectively. They anticipate annual net incomes of $225,000 and are considering the following alternative plans of sharing net incomes and losses: (a) equally; (b) in the ratio of their initial investments; or (c) salary allowances of $40,000 to Marshall, $30,000 to Spiller, and $45,000 to Rand; interest allowances of 10% on initial investments, with any remaining balance shared equally.

Required

1. Prepare a schedule with the following column headings:

Income/Loss Sharing Plan Totals	Calculations	Share to Marshall	Share to Spiller	Share to Rand

Use the schedule to show how a net income of $225,000 would be distributed under each of the alternative plans being considered. Round your answers to the nearest whole dollar.

Problems

Problem 14-1
Methods of allocating partnership income
LO 3

Problem 14-2
Allocating partnership incomes and losses; sequential years
LO 3

Problem 14-3
Partnership income allocation, statement of changes in partners' equity, and closing entries
LO 2,3

2. Prepare a statement of changes in partners' equity showing the allocation of income to the partners, assuming they agree to use alternative (c) and the net income earned is $105,000. During the year, Marshall, Spiller, and Rand withdraw $17,000, $24,000, and $32,000, respectively.

3. Prepare the December 31 journal entry to close Income Summary assuming they agree to use alternative (c) and the net income is $105,000. Also, close the withdrawals accounts.

Problem 14-4
Withdrawal of a partner

 4

Part 1. Godfrey, Gully, and Speck are partners with capital balances as follows: Godfrey, $84,000; Gully, $69,000; and Speck, $147,000. The partners share incomes and losses in a 3:2:5 ratio. Gully decides to withdraw from the partnership, and the partners agree to not have the assets revalued upon his retirement. Prepare general journal entries to record the February 1 withdrawal of Gully from the partnership under each of the following unrelated assumptions:

a. Gully sells his interest to Goldman for $80,000 after Godfrey and Speck approve the entry of Goldman as a partner.

b. Gully gives his interest to a son-in-law, Spain. Godfrey and Speck accept Spain as a partner.

c. Gully is paid $69,000 in partnership cash for his equity.

d. Gully is paid $107,000 in partnership cash for his equity.

e. Gully is paid $15,000 in partnership cash plus computer equipment that is recorded on the partnership books at $35,000 less accumulated amortization of $11,600.

Part 2. Assume that Gully does not retire from the partnership described in Part 1. Instead, Hatch is admitted to the partnership on February 1 with a 25% equity. Prepare general journal entries to record the entry of Hatch into the partnership under each of the following unrelated assumptions:

a. Hatch invests $100,000.

b. Hatch invests $72,500.

c. Hatch invests $131,000.

Problem 14-5
Liquidation of a partnership

LO 5

Swanson, Chapel, and Page plan to liquidate their partnership. They have always shared losses and gains in a 3:2:1 ratio, and on the day of the liquidation their balance sheet appeared as follows:

SWANSON, CHAPEL, AND PAGE			
Balance Sheet			
May 31, 19XX			
Assets		**Liabilities and Owners' Equity**	
Cash	$ 90,400	Accounts payable	$122,750
Inventory	268,600	David Swanson, capital	46,500
		Annie Chapel, capital	106,250
		Maria Page, capital	83,500
		Total liabilities and	
Total assets	$359,000	owners' equity	$359,000

Required

Under the assumption the inventory is sold and the cash is distributed to the proper parties on May 31, prepare the general journal entries for the sale, the gain or loss allocation, and the distribution of the cash in each of the following unrelated cases:

a. The inventory is sold for $300,000.

b. The inventory is sold for $250,000.

c. The inventory is sold for $160,000, and any partners with resulting deficits can and do pay in the amount of their deficits.

d. The inventory is sold for $125,000, and the partners have no assets other than those invested in the business.

Until November 16, 1999, Rohan, Kovak, and Keene were partners that shared incomes and losses in the ratio of their beginning-of-year capital account balances. On November 16, Rohan suffered a heart attack and died. Kovak and Keene immediately ended the business operations and prepared the following adjusted trail balance:

Problem 14-6
Withdrawal of a partner
LO 3

ROHAN, KOVAK, AND KEENE Adjusted Trial Balance November 16, 1999		
Cash	$ 10,625	
Accounts receivable	30,415	
Allowance for doubtful accounts		$ 1,115
Supplies inventory	46,875	
Equipment	148,860	
Accumulated amortization, equipment		14,842
Building	227,325	
Accumulated amortization, building		56,850
Land	14,800	
Accounts payable		22,688
Note payable (secured by mortgage)		37,005
Tracy Rohan, capital		141,040
Tracy Rohan, withdrawals	5,700	
Jackie Kovak, capital		141,040
Jackie Kovak, withdrawals	5,700	
Kerry Keene, capital		70,520
Kerry Keene, withdrawals	16,200	
Services revenue		75,150
Operating expense	53,750	
Totals	$560,250	$560,250

Required

1. Prepare the November 16 general journal entries to close the revenue, expense, income summary, and withdrawals accounts of the partnership.
2. Assume the estate of Rohan agreed to accept the land and building and to assume the mortgage note thereon on settlement of its claim against the partnership assets, and that Kovak and Keene planned to continue the business and rent the building from the estate. Prepare the partnership's December 1 general journal entry to transfer the land, building, and mortgage note in settlement with the estate.
3. Assume that, instead of the foregoing, the estate of Rohan demanded a cash settlement and the business had to be sold to a competitor, who gave $298,000 for the noncash assets and assumed the mortgage note but not the accounts payable. Prepare the December 1 general journal entry to transfer the noncash assets and mortgage note to the competitor, and the entries to allocate the gain or loss to the partners and to distribute the partnership cash.

Problem 14-7
Analytical essay
LO 2

Janet Koppen and Beverly Spikes want to form a partnership and are considering two methods of sharing incomes and losses. Method *a* splits all incomes and losses in a 2:3 ratio, or 40% to Koppen and 60% to Spikes. Method *b* depends on the income or loss of the partnership. If the partnership incurs a loss, the partners share it equally. If the income is in the range of $0 to $45,000, it is allocated based on an annual salary allowance of $15,000 to Koppen and $30,000 to Spikes. If the net income exceeds $45,000, the residual after the salary allowances is shared equally.

Koppen has retained you to write an evaluation of the two methods, indicating which is more favourable to her. Your discussion should include a comparison of the two methods at each of the three possible net income levels. Also discuss the importance of asking Koppen to estimate the partnership's future earnings.

Problem 14-8
Analytical essay

LO 3

Guido, DeVito, and Vanelli have been operating a successful partnership for several years. Even though business is good, DeVito and Vanelli have disagreed with Guido on several occasions regarding the business, and Guido is now withdrawing from the partnership. The partners agree that the book values of the assets are less than their market values. However, they do not want to change the recorded values at this time. As a result, the partners have agreed that Guido should withdraw cash in an amount greater than his capital account balance.

DeVito and Vanelli are not sure how to calculate the adjustments to their capital accounts (brought about by the difference between Guido's equity and the cash he is withdrawing). DeVito thinks they should split the difference in the ratio of their capital account balances. Vanelli thinks the adjustments should be calculated using their original income-and-loss-sharing ratio. Which partner do you think is correct? Explain the reasons for your answers.

Alternate Problems

Problem 14-1A
Methods of allocating
partnership income

LO 2

Paul Jones, Will Rogers, and Anne Thompson invested $82,000, $49,200, and $32,800, respectively, in a partnership. During its first year, the firm earned $135,000.

Required

Prepare entries to close the firm's Income Summary account as of December 31 and to allocate the net income to the partners under each of the following assumptions. (Round your answers to the nearest whole dollar.)
a. The partners did not specify any special method of sharing incomes.
b. The partners agreed to share net incomes and losses in the ratio of their beginning investments.
c. The partners agreed to share income by providing annual salary allowances of $48,000 to Jones, $36,000 to Rogers, and $25,000 to Thompson, allowing 10% interest on the partners' beginning investments and sharing the remainder equally.

Problem 14-2A
Allocating partnership
incomes and losses,
sequential years

LO 3

Jacob Jackson and K. D. Fletcher are in the process of forming a partnership to which Jackson will devote one-third time and Fletcher will devote full time. They have discussed the following alternative plans for sharing net incomes and losses.
a. In the ratio of their initial investments, which they have agreed will be $52,000 for Jackson and $78,000 for Fletcher.
b. In proportion to the time devoted to the business.
c. A salary allowance of $2,000 per month to Fletcher and the balance in accordance with their initial investment ratio.
d. A $2,000 per month salary allowance to Fletcher, 10% interest on their initial investments, and the balance equally.

The partners expect the business to generate income as follows: Year 1, $18,000 net loss; Year 2, $38,000 net income; and Year 3, $94,000 net income.

Required

1. Prepare three schedules with the following column headings:

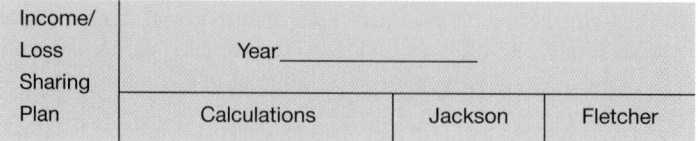

Income/ Loss Sharing Plan	Year_____		
	Calculations	Jackson	Fletcher

2. Complete a schedule for each of the first three years by showing how the partnership income or loss for each year would be allocated to the partners under each of the four plans being considered. Round your answers to the nearest whole dollar.

Problem 14-3A
Partnership income
allocation, statement of
changes in partners'
equity, and closing entries

LO 2

Ella Phillips, Chet Fong, and Lou Campos formed the PFC Partnership by making capital contributions of $72,000, $108,000, and $60,000, respectively. They anticipate annual net incomes of $120,000 and are considering the following alternative plans of sharing net incomes and losses: (a) equally, (b) in the ratio of their initial investments, or (c) salary allowances of $20,000 to Phillips, $15,000 to Fong, and $40,000 to Campos; interest allowances of 12% on initial investments, with any remaining balance shared equally.

Required

1. Prepare a schedule with the following column headings:

Inc./Loss Sharing Plan	Calculations	Share to Phillips	Share to Fong	Share to Campos	Totals

Use the schedule to show how a net income of $120,000 would be distributed under each of the alternative plans being considered. Round your answers to the nearest whole dollar.

2. Prepare a statement of changes in partners' equity showing the allocation of income to the partners, assuming they agree to use alternative (c) and the net income actually earned is $55,000. During the year, Phillips, Fong, and Campos withdrew $9,000, $19,000, and $12,000, respectively.

3. Prepare the December 31 journal entry to close Income Summary assuming they agree to use alternative (c) and the net income is $55,000. Also, close the withdrawals accounts.

Part 1. Soltani, Sugimoto and Suza are partners with capital balances as follows: Soltani, $303,000; Sugimoto, $74,000; and Suza, $223,000. The partners share incomes and losses in a 5:1:4 ratio. Soltani decides to withdraw from the partnership, and the partners agree to not have the assets revalued upon her retirement. Prepare general journal entries to record the April 30 withdrawal of Soltani from the partnership under each of the following unrelated assumptions:

a. Soltani sells her interest to Samba for $250,000 after Sugimoto and Suza approve the entry of Samba as a partner.

b. Soltani gives her interest to a daughter-in-law, Shulak. Sugimoto and Suza accept Shulak as a partner.

c. Soltani is paid $303,000 in partnership cash for her equity.

d. Soltani is paid $175,000 in partnership cash for her equity.

e. Soltani is paid $100,000 in partnership cash plus manufacturing equipment recorded on the partnership books at $269,000 less accumulated amortization of $168,000.

Part 2. Assume that Soltani does not retire from the partnership described in Part 1. Instead, Sung is admitted to the partnership on April 30 with a 20% equity. Prepare general journal entries to record the entry of Sung under each of the following unrelated assumptions:

a. Sung invests $150,000.

b. Sung invests $98,000.

c. Sung invests $213,000.

Huggins, Hart, and Love, who have always shared incomes and losses in a 2:1:2 ratio, plan to liquidate their partnership. Just prior to the liquidation their balance sheet appeared as follows:

Problem 14-4A
Withdrawal of a partner
LO 4

Problem 14-5A
Liquidation of a partnership
LO 5

HUGGINS, HART, AND LOVE
Balance Sheet
January 18, 19XX

Assets		Liabilities and Owner's Equity	
Cash	$174,300	Accounts payable	$171,300
Equipment	308,600	C. J. Huggins, capital.	150,200
		D. C. Hart, capital	97,900
		J. D. Love, capital	63,500
		Total liabilities and	
Total assets	$482,900	owners' equity.	$482,900

Required

Under the assumption the equipment is sold and the cash is distributed to the proper parties on January 18, prepare general journal entries for the sale, the gain or loss allocation, and the distribution of cash in each of the following unrelated cases:

a. The equipment is sold for $325,000.

b. The equipment is sold for $265,000.

c. The equipment is sold for $100,000, and any partners with resulting deficits can and do pay in the amount of their deficits.

d. The equipment is sold for $75,000, and the partners have no assets other than those invested in the business.

Problem 14-6A
Withdrawal of a partner

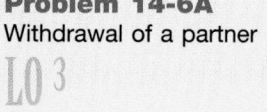

Until July 3, 1999, Daily, Murray, and Dryer were partners that shared incomes and losses in the ratio of their beginning-of-year capital account balances. On July 3, Murray suffered a heart attack and died. Daily and Dryer immediately terminated the partnership and prepared the following adjusted trail balance.

DAILY, MURRAY, AND DRYER Adjusted Trial Balance July, 3 1999		
Cash	$31,418	
Accounts receivable	18,322	
Allowance for doubtful accounts		$725
Supplies inventory	54,910	
Equipment	110,660	
Accumulated amortization, equipment		15,808
Building	303,300	
Accumulated amortization, building		68,390
Land	27,400	
Accounts payable		25,975
Note payable (secured by mortgage)		64,012
Jess Daily, capital		164,800
Jess Daily, withdrawals	21,700	
Mel Murray, capital		206,000
Mel Murray, withdrawals	38,200	
Pat Dryer, capital		41,200
Pat Dryer, withdrawals	10,500	
Services revenue		195,600
Operating expense	166,100	
Totals	$782,510	$782,510

Required

1. Prepare the July 3 general journal entries to close the revenue, expense, income summary, and withdrawals accounts of the partnership.

2. Assume the estate of Murray agreed to accept the land and building and to assume the mortgage note thereon in settlement of its claim against the partnership assets, and that Daily and Dryer planned to continue the business and rent the building from the estate. Prepare the partnership's July 16 general journal entry to transfer the land, building, and mortgage note in settlement with the estate.

3. Assume that, instead of the foregoing, the estate of Murray demanded a cash settlement and the business had to be sold to a competitor, who gave $350,000 for the noncash assets and assumed the mortgage note but not the accounts payable. Prepare the July 16 general journal entry to transfer the noncash assets and mortgage note to the competitor, and the entries to allocate the gain or loss to the partners and to distribute the partnership cash.

Janet Koppen and Beverly Spikes want to form a partnership and are considering two methods of sharing incomes and losses in a 2:3 ratio, or 40% to Koppen and 60% to Spikes. Method *b* depends on the income or loss of the partnership. If the partnership incurs a loss, the partners share it equally. If the income is in the range of $0 to $45,000, it is allocated based on an annual salary allowance of $15,000 to Koppen and $30,000 to Spikes. If the net income exceeds $45,000, the residual after the salary allowances is shared equally.

Spikes has retained you to write an evaluation of the two methods indicating which is most favourable to her. Your discussion should include a comparison of the two methods at each of the three possible net income levels. Also, discuss the importance of asking Spikes to estimate the partnership's future earnings.

Problem 14-7A
Analytical essay
LO 2

Kay Doobie, Ed Foley, and Brian McKenzie have been operating a partnership for several years. Business has not been good recently, and Doobie is withdrawing from the partnership. The partners agree that the market values of the assets are less than their recorded book values. However, they do not want to change the recorded values at this time. As a result, the partners have agreed that Doobie should withdraw cash in an amount that is less than her capital account balance.

Foley and McKenzie are not sure how to calculate the adjustments to their capital accounts (brought about by the difference between Doobie's equity and the cash she is withdrawing). Foley thinks they should split the difference in the ratio of their capital account balances. McKenzie thinks the adjustments should be calculated using their income-and-loss-sharing ratio. Which partner do you think is correct? Explain why.

Problem 14-8A
Analytical essay
LO 3

Jay and Mar entered into a partnership to carry on a business under the firm name of Jay-Mar Sportsland. Prior to the final signing of the agreement Jay asks you to evaluate the "income/loss distribution clause" contained in the agreement.

Your examination revealed that the agreement called for the following: equal sharing of net income and losses after an initial allocation of $40,000 to Jay and $10,000 to Mar in order to reflect the difference in time and expertise devoted to the business by each partner. The initial allocation would be made regardless of the level of net income/loss.

Analytical and Review Problems
A & R 14-1

Required

Prepare a report to Jay on the particular clause of the agreement. Your report should show the consequence of each partner of operating results as follows: (a) net income of $80,000, (b) net income of $20,000, (c) operation at break-even, that is, no net income or loss, (d) loss of $20,000, and (e) loss of $80,000.

The summarized balance sheet of Bell, Trunk, and Field showed:

A & R 14-2

Assets		Liabilities and Owners' Equity	
Cash	$ 20,000	Accounts payable	$60,000
Other assets	280,000	Bell, capital	80,000
		Trunk, capital	120,000
		Field, capital	40,000
Total assets	$300,000	Total equities	$300,000

The partnership has operated successfully for nearly 25 years, and Field, because of his age and health, is pushing for sale of the business. In fact, he has found Arn, a buyer who is willing to pay $320,000 cash and take over the liabilities. Both Bell and Thunk are not anxious to sell what they refer to as "our little gold mine." Field is adamant about getting out and has proposed the following:

1. Either sell to Arn, or Bell and Trunk (a new partnership) should buy out Field at an amount Field would receive if the business were sold to Arn.

2. Admit Arn to the partnership upon the purchase of Field's share for an amount Field and Arn will negotiate.

The present partnership calls for a distribution of net income/loss on a 3:5:2 basis. If Arn is admitted to partnership the ratio would not change; he would be entitled to Field's 20% share of net income/loss. If Bell and Trunk buy out for an amount based on the Arn offer, Bell and Trunk would continue to share net income/loss on the same relative basis. They would (the new partnership of Bell and Trunk) have to borrow sufficient funds from the bank to retain a minimum cash balance of $10,000.

Required

1. Prepare the general journal entry for admission of Arn to the partnership upon his purchase of Field's interest for an undisclosed amount.
2. Prepare the necessary entries to record Field's withdrawal from the partnership. The amount paid to Field is equal to the amount he would have received if the partnership were sold to Arn.

A & R 14-3
The Med Mart

LO 3

Martha Emerson and Florence Knight are partners who own and operate The Med Mart, a medical supply store. Emerson's recorded equity in the business is $129,000 and Knight's recorded equity is $69,000. They share incomes and losses by allowing annual salary allowances of $55,000 to Emerson and $30,000 to Knight, with any remaining balance being shared 70% to Emerson and 30% to Knight.

Gail Emerson, Martha Emerson's daughter, has been working in the store on a salary basis. In addition to working in the store, Gail is a registered nurse and works part-time at a nearby hospital. Because Gail is well known and liked by many of the doctors, nurses, and other employees at the hospital, she attracts a great deal of business to the store. The partners believe that at least one-third of the three years' sales can be traced directly to Gail's association with the store, and it is reasonable to assume she was instrumental in attracting even more.

Gail is paid $2,000 per month, but feels this is not sufficient to induce her to remain with the store as an employee. However, she likes the work and plans to continue in the medical field. What she really wants is to become a partner in the business.

Her mother is anxious for her to remain in the business and proposes the following.

a. That Gail Emerson be admitted to the partnership with a 20% equity in the net assets.
b. That she, Martha Emerson, transfer from her capital account to Gail's capital account one-half of the 20% interest; that Martha contribute cash to the firm for the other half of Gail's interest; and that Gail sign a note to Martha for the amount of cash paid by Martha.
c. That incomes and losses be shared by continuing the $55,000 and $30,000 salary allowance to the original partners and that Gail be given a $24,000 salary allowance, after which any remaining income or loss will be shared 50% to Martha Emerson, 30% to Florence Knight, and 20% to Gail Emerson.

Required

1. Prepare a schedule showing the partners' capital balances both before and immediately after Gail's admission to the partnership.
2. Assume the net incomes for the past three years were $87,600, $91,200, and $95,400, respectively. Prepare one schedule showing how net income was allocated during the past three years, and a second schedule showing how net income would have been allocated if Martha's proposal had been in effect all three years.
3. Describe how the admission of Gail would effect Florence's equity and share in future profits, and how the partnership might benefit from Gail's admission.

BEYOND THE NUMBERS

Ethics Challenge

LO 2

Paul, Frank and Basil formed a partnership 10 years ago and Paul is about to retire. Paul is not financially minded but he knows that he is entitled to one-third of partnership assets upon his retirement. Total assets have a book value of $900,000 and Paul feels that he is entitled to his share. Frank and Basil are aware that the market value of the firm's net assets approximates $1,500,000. Frank and Basil plan to form a new partnership.

Required

What are the financial and ethical implications of distributing $300,000 to Paul upon his retirement?

Your friend, Oliver Lung, recently completed his second year in his own business. Oliver's business is growing rapidly and he needs an infusion of funds to help finance the expansion. Oliver tells you about his friend Mary who has access to funds and is a creative individual with whom Oliver gets along very well. Oliver is considering offering Mary a piece of the business and forming a business partnership. Oliver says, "Mary and I go way back and are close friends so I don't think we need any formal written partnership agreement."

Required

Write a memo to your friend Oliver to explain the purpose of a partnership. Comment on why a written agreement is essential and what matters should be included in the agreement.

Communicating in Practice
LO 1, 3, 4

Visit the Edgar Web site (**http://www.sec.gov**). Search the Web site using the search word "Celtics." View the 1997 10K report filed by the Boston Celtic's partnership with the SEC. Answer the following questions:

1. What were the primary sources of revenue for the Celtics for the fiscal year ended June 30, 1997?

2. What was the net income for the limited partnership for the fiscal year ended June 30, 1997.

3. Trace the net income earned to the Statement of Partners' Capital.

4. Trace the ending capital shown on the Statement of Partners' Capital to the Balance Sheet as of June 30, 1997.

Taking It to the Net
LO 3

This activity is designed to reinforce team member's understanding of the partnership form of business.

A. A partnership is a form of multiple ownership. For legal and tax purposes no entity is recognized. Each group should consider how the entity concept relates to partnerships.

B. Creditors of a partnership may sue the partnership *jointly* or *severally*. Each group should discuss what is meant by these terms and be prepared to explain their understanding to the class.

C. Can a partner avoid paying income taxes by not withdrawing income the partnership? Each group should discuss this issue and be prepared to present their conclusion to the class.

Teamwork in Action
LO 4

Identify three partnership enterprises operating in your province or territory. Contact these businesses and ask how many partners comprise the partnership. Did any partners withdraw from the partnerships during the past year and did any new partners enter the partnership?

Hitting the Road
LO 1, 5

The effort involved in identifying the right partner is effort well spent. It can mean avoiding delays, misunderstanding, and the break-up of your relationship because of inability to get along. In the end, there is no substitute for the intensive screening of partners. Unless you are successful in finding a partner who is compatible and trustworthy, and someone with whom you can get along, you are likely better off looking for an alternative form of business ownership.

Business Break
LO 1

Required

The Canadian Management Network Internet site known as Strategis contain an interesting article about business partnership. The article is called *Business Turning Points: Finding A Partner*. The strategis Web site can be found at **http://strategis.ic.gc.ca**. The publication date of this article is September 22, 1997. Search for this article and answer the following questions:

a. According to this article what qualities should you look for in a good partner?

b. What qualities should you keep in mind that are indicative of poor partners?

15

CHAPTER

Corporations

A Look Back

Chapter 14 focused on partnerships. We explained the basic characteristics of partnerships and showed how to account for the division of partnership income, the admission and withdrawal of partners, and partnership liquidation.

A Look at This Chapter

This chapter explains the corporate form of organization. Important characteristics of the corporate form of organization are described along with the accounting for important transactions.

A Look Forward

Chapter 16 extends our discussion of corporate accounting to dividends and other equity transactions. We also explain how income, earnings per share, and retained earnings are reported.

Chapter Outline

Go for It

Toronto, ON—Jennifer Wong's business venture into block print cotton T-shirts is a model success story. Each product is individually hand block printed with evocative designs and symbols, and signed by the artist. After a successful first year Jennifer obtained funding from her parents and formed a partnership with her friend Malu Baltazar. Sales took off and additional funds were needed to meet the growing market demand. To complicate matters Malu had to leave the partnership for personal reasons. Malu's departure stripped the business of badly needed funds.

To finance growth of her company, Wong decided to incorporate and sold common shares to the public. The idea she says is to "sell it to people who had been supporting us so far as customers." The shares were priced at $5 per share. The issuance of shares has raised more than $5 million for working capital and expansion of her business. Wong already has plans for setting up a franchise in Vancouver. If all goes well, the biggest challenge will be "staying in tune with our customers as we grow," says Wong.

Learning Objectives

LO 1 Identify characteristics of corporations and their organization.

LO 2 Describe the components of shareholders' equity.

LO 3 Record the issuance of corporate shares.

LO 4 Explain the characteristics of common and preferred shares.

LO 5 Distribute dividends between common shares and preferred shares.

LO 6 Compute book value and explain its use in analysis.

CHAPTER PREVIEW

There are three common types of business organizations: corporations, partnerships and proprietorships. This chapter explains corporations. While corporations are fewest in number, they transact more business than all others combined. They are very important players in our global economy, with dollar sales at least ten times the combined sales of unincorporated companies. Understanding the advantages and disadvantages of these forms of business organization was important for Jennifer Wong in her T-shirt venture. The opening article revealed her choice to incorporate, but this is not always best. This chapter gives us information to make such a decision.

Corporate Form of Organization

A corporation is an entity that is created by law and is separate from its owners. It has most of the rights and privileges granted to individuals. Owners of corporations are called *shareholders* or *stockholders*. Corporations can be separated into privately held and publicly held corporations. A *privately held* corporation, also called closely held, does not offer its shares for public sale and usually has few shareholders. Most corporations formed in Canada are private corporations. Provincial securities acts generally limit the number of shareholders of private corporations to 50. A *publicly held* corporation offers its shares for public sale and can have thousands of shareholders. Public sale usually refers to trading in an organized stock market such as the Montreal, Toronto, Winnipeg, Alberta or Vancouver stock exchanges.

Characteristics of Corporations

LO1 Identify characteristics of corporations and their organization.

Corporations are important because of advantages created by the unique characteristics of the corporate structure of ownership. We describe these characteristics in this section.

Separate Legal Entity

A corporation is a separate legal entity. As a separate entity, a corporation conducts its affairs with the same rights, duties and responsibilities as a person. A corporation takes actions through its agents, who are its officers and managers.

Limited Liability of Shareholders

Because a corporation is a separate legal entity, it is responsible for its own acts and its own debt. Its shareholders are not liable for either. From the viewpoint of a shareholder, this lack of liability is one of the most important advantages of the corporate form of business. Shareholders invest in the business by contributing cash or other assets in return for ownership rights in the corporation. If the business fails the amount contributed by shareholders is the maximum loss to the shareholders. If there are insufficient assets to pay business creditor claims, creditors have no claim on the shareholders' personal assets. Because shareholder liability is limited to the amount of their investments, corporations are often referred to as limited companies.

Ownership Rights Are Transferable

Ownership of a corporation is by shares of its share capital that are usually easily bought or sold. The transfer of shares from one shareholder to another usually has no effect on the corporation or its operations.[1] Many corporations have

---

[1] But a transfer of ownership can create significant effects if it brings about a change in who controls the company's activities.

thousands or even millions of their shares bought and sold daily in major stock exchanges throughout the world. For example, it is not uncommon for **NIKE** to trade over 2,000,000 shares in one day.

Continuous Life

A corporation's life can continue indefinitely because it is not tied to the physical lives of its owners. The laws of the legal jurisdiction of its incorporation can sometimes initially limit a corporation's life. But a corporation's charter can be renewed and its life extended when the stated time expires. This means a corporation can have a perpetual life as long as it continues to be successful.

Shareholders Are Not Corporate Agents

A corporation acts through its agents, who are the officers or managers of the corporation. Shareholders who are not officers or managers of the corporation do not have the power to bind the corporation to contracts. This is also referred to as *lack of mutual agency*. Instead, shareholders participate in the affairs of the corporation only by voting in the shareholders' meetings.

Ease of Capital Accumulation

Buying shares in a corporation often is attractive to investors because: (1) shareholders are not liable for the corporation's actions and debts, (2) shares usually are transferred easily, (3) life of the corporation is unlimited, and (4) shareholders are not agents of the corporation. These advantages make it possible for some corporations to accumulate large amounts of capital from the combined investments of many shareholders. A corporation's capacity for raising capital is limited only by its ability to convince investors it can use their funds profitably. **Alcan Aluminum Limited**, for example, a Canadian-based company involved in ventures such bauxite mining, alumina refining, and power generation had by 1996 accumulated roughly $1,235 million from 21,500 shareholders who own 226,620,000 shares.[2]

Governmental Regulation

Corporations must meet requirements of provincial or federal incorporation laws. These laws subject a corporation to governmental regulation and control. Single proprietorships and partnerships escape some of these regulations, and often avoid having to file some governmental reports required of corporations. Private corporations or closely held corporations that restrict the transfer of shares to existing shareholders and refrain from distributing shares to the public, however, are exempt from most of the security and corporate legislation reporting requirements. According to the Canada Business Corporations Act, any company with gross revenues of $10 million or assets exceeding $5 million must make its financial statements public. This applies to both public and private corporations and their financial statements must be prepared according to Canadian generally accepted accounting principles. All public corporations that are registered with one of the provincial securities bodies, depending on which province, must file annual audited financial statements within 140–170 days of their fiscal year-end.

Many Canadian companies are also listed on U.S. stock exchanges. Those companies are required to file their annual reports with U.S. regulators. These corporations prepare forms 10-K and 10-Q which are very detailed documents of company descriptions. Some companies such as **Seagrams** actually issue their annual reports in U.S. dollars.

---

[2] *Annual Report*, Alcan Aluminum Limited, 1996.

Corporate Taxation

Corporations are subject to the same property and payroll taxes as proprietorships and partnerships. But corporations are subject to *additional* taxes not levied on either of these two forms. The combined top marginal rate for corporations is between 35% to 46% of a corporation's pretax income. For some corporations these rates are reduced by several percentage points due to various incentive provisions such as manufacturing and processing credits. According to the Micro-Economic Policy Analysis Branch of Strategis Canada, total corporate income taxes as a percent of Gross Domestic Product is about average among the G-7 countries. In comparison with our NAFTA partners, however, Canada ranks the best. When employer-paid social security contributions are factored into the corporate analysis Canada ties with the United Kingdom for the best ranking among G-7 countries.

The income of a corporation is taxed twice, first as income of the corporation and again as personal income to shareholders when cash is distributed to them as dividends. This is called *double taxation*. It differs from proprietorships and partnerships, which are not subject to income taxes as business units. Their income is taxed only as the personal income of their owners. For proprietorships and partnerships the income is taxable to the owners whether or not assets are actually withdrawn from the business.

The tax situation of a corporation is usually a disadvantage. But in some cases it can be an advantage to shareholders because corporation and individual tax rates are progressive. A progressive tax means higher levels of income are taxed at higher rates and lower levels of income are taxed at lower rates. This suggests taxes can be saved or at least delayed if a large amount of income is divided among two or more tax-paying entities. A person who has a large personal income and pays taxes at a high rate can benefit if some of the income is earned by a corporation the person owns, as long as the corporation avoids paying dividends or pays at a lower rate than the individual's rate. By not paying dividends, the corporation's income is taxed only once at the lower corporate rate, at least temporarily until dividends are paid.

Did You Know?

Choosing a Business Form

Choosing the proper form of entity for a business is crucial. Many factors should be considered including taxes, liability, tax and fiscal year-end, ownership structure, estate planning, business risks, and earnings and property distributions. The chart below gives a summary of several important characteristics of business organizations:

	Proprietorship	Partnership	Corporation
Business entity	yes	yes	yes
Legal entity	no	no	yes
Limited liability	no	no	yes
Business taxed	no	no	yes
One owner allowed	yes	no	yes

Organizing a Corporation

This section describes incorporation and treatment of the costs of organization.

Incorporation

A corporation may be created under either provincial law or federal laws. Those incorporated federally must comply with the Canada Business Corporations Act

(CBCA). Most of the provincial laws are modelled after the federal statute. Requirements vary across provinces and from the CBCA but essentially a legal document known as a charter, articles of incorporation, letters patent or memorandum of association is completed and signed by the prospective shareholders. They are called *incorporates* or *promoters*. The application should include the proposed name and address of the corporation, the name and address of the first directors, the classes and number of authorized shares and the name of the person incorporating the company. The application is then filed with the proper legal jurisdiction. Companies incorporating under the CBCA must file their applications with the Corporations Directorate of Industry Canada. When completed and all fees are paid, the charter is issued and the corporation is formed. Investors then purchase the corporation's shares, meet as shareholders, and elect a board of directors. Directors are responsible for guiding a corporation's affairs. To conduct business in a province in which the business is not incorporated, a corporation must obtain a licence from the province involved. A federally incorporated corporation may conduct business in every province but it must satisfy certain provincial registration requirements.

Netting Gold

Marc Andreessen co-founded Netscape at the age of 22, only four months after earning his degree in computer science. One year later at the age of 23, Andreessen and friends issued Netscape shares to the public. Netscape's shares, offered at $28 each, soared to nearly $75 before ending its first trading day at a less stratospheric $58. This made Andreessen a multimillionaire at 23.

[Source: *Business Week,* October 23, 1995, and *Netscape 10K Report.*]

Did You Know?

Organization Costs

Organization costs are the costs of organizing a corporation. They include legal fees, promoters' fees, and amounts paid to get a charter. The corporation records (debits) these costs to an asset account called Organization Costs. This intangible asset benefits the corporation throughout its life and its cost is amortized over a period no longer than 40 years. Canadian standards for intangible assets are consistent with U.S. standards but vary from international Standards. For example, IAS 22 requires amortization of intangible assets over a period of five years or less unless a longer term up to a maximum of 20 years can be justified.

Although not related to the benefit period, income tax rules currently permit a corporation to record 75% of organization costs as a tax deduction at an annual rate of 7% on a diminishing balance basis. This means many corporations use the same method for financial reporting to ease recordkeeping. Because organization costs usually are small in amount, the *materiality principle* supports this arbitrary short amortization period.

Startup Money

An important concern to many potential entrepreneurs is how to raise money to get the business started. Here are a few suggestions: (1) Seek help from family and friends, (2) Search out reputable venture capitalists, investors or small business development corporations, (3) Consider paying employees, investors and even suppliers with shares, and (4) Make good use of supplier credit and leasing sources.

Did You Know?

Management of a Corporation

Corporations have different organizational structures. Yet ultimate control of a corporation rests with its shareholders. They control a corporation through election of the *board of directors*, or simply directors. Individual shareholders' rights to affect management are limited to a vote in shareholders' meetings, where each of them has one vote for each common share owned. This relation is shown in Exhibit 15.1. A corporation's board of directors is responsible for and has final authority for managing the corporation's activities. It can act only as a collective body. An individual director has no power to transact corporate business. Although the board has final authority, it usually limits its actions to establishing broad policy.

Exhibit 15.1

Corporation Authority
Structure

A corporation usually holds a shareholders' meeting once each year to elect directors and transact other business as required by its bylaws. The CBCA requires public corporations to have at least three directors, two of whom must not be employees or officers of the corporation. Directors are not required to be shareholders but most jurisdictions require that directors be at least 18 years of age, not bankrupt and must be residents of Canada. A group of shareholders owning or controlling votes of more than a 50% share of a corporation's shares can elect the board and control the corporation. But in many corporations few shareholders attend the annual meeting or even care about getting involved in the voting process. This means a much smaller percent is often able to dominate the election of board members.

Shareholders who don't attend shareholders' meetings must be given an opportunity to delegate their voting rights to an agent. A shareholder does this by signing a document called a proxy. A **proxy** gives a designated agent the right to vote the shares. Prior to a shareholders' meeting, a corporation's board of directors usually mails to each shareholder an announcement of the meeting and a proxy listing the existing board chairperson as the voting agent of the shareholder. The announcement asks the shareholder to sign and return the proxy.

Day-to-day direction of corporate business is delegated to executive officers appointed by the board. The chief executive officer (CEO) of a corporation is often its president. Several vice presidents who report to the president, are commonly assigned specific areas of management responsibility such as finance, production and marketing. The corporation secretary keeps minutes for meetings of shareholders and directors, and ensures that all legal responsibilities are met. In a small corporation the secretary is also responsible for keeping a record of current shareholders and amounts of their investment.

Another common corporate structure is where the chairperson of the board of directors is the CEO. In this case, the president is usually designated the chief operating officer (COO). The rest of the structure is similar.

Rights of Shareholders

When investors buy a corporation's shares they acquire all *specific* rights granted by the corporation's charter to those shareholders; they also acquire *general* rights granted shareholders by the laws of the legal jurisdiction in which the company is incorporated. When a corporation has only one class of shares, those shares are identified as **common shares.** The rights of the common shareholders are equal in all respects under the CBCA and most provincial statutes. Common shares represent *residual equity*, meaning that creditors and other shareholders (if any) rank ahead of common shareholders if a corporation is liquidated. Common shareholders usually have the general right to:

1. Vote at shareholders' meetings.
2. Share equally with other common shareholders in any dividends. This means each common share receives the same dividend per share.
3. Share equally in any assets remaining after creditors are paid when the corporation is liquidated. This means each common share receives the same amount of remaining liquidated assets.
4. Sell or otherwise dispose of their shares.
5. Purchase additional shares of common shares issued by the corporation in the future, if specifically provided for in the articles of incorporation or charter. This right is called the **preemptive right.** It protects shareholders proportionate interest in the corporation. For example, a shareholder who owns 25% of a corporation's common shares has the first opportunity to buy 25% of any new common shares issued. This enables the shareholder to maintain a 25% interest if desired.

According to the Canada Business Corporations Act the right to vote, to receive dividends that have been declared, and the right to receive property of the corporation after its dissolution are three inherent rights. The CBCA permits a company to distribute these three rights among more than one class of shares. These rights can be distributed in any combination, so long as all three rights are being assigned. In summary, viewing all of the share classes together, each of these three basic rights is assigned to at least one class but not necessarily to all. Shareholders also have the right to receive timely reports on the corporation's financial position and results of operations.

Shares of a Corporation

This section explains share certificates, their transfer, and use of registrar and transfer agents.

Share Certificates and Transfer

When investors buy a corporation's shares, they sometimes receive a *share certificate* as proof they purchased shares.[3] In many corporations, only one certificate is issued for each block of shares purchased. A certificate can be for any number of shares. Exhibit 15.2 shows an actual share certificate of 50 shares of **Westfield Publishing Company, Ltd.** A certificate shows the company name, shareholder name, number of shares, and other important items.

Exhibit 15.2

Share Certificate

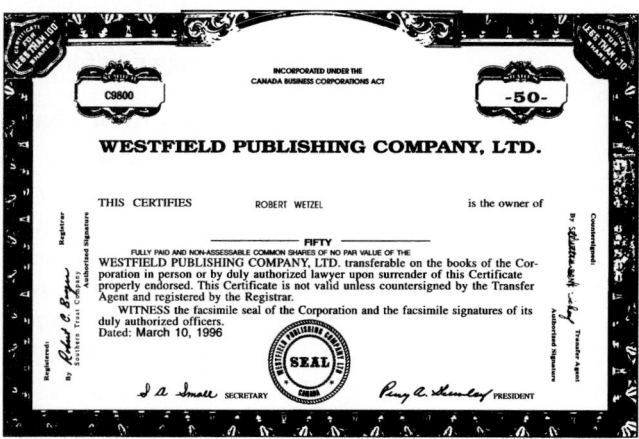

---

[3] Issuance of certificates is becoming less common. Instead, many shareholders maintain accounts with the corporation or their stockbrokers and never receive certificates.

When selling shares, a shareholder completes and signs a transfer endorsement on the back of the certificate and sends it to the corporation's secretary or transfer agent. The secretary or agent cancels and files the old certificate, and issues a new certificate to the new shareholder. If the old certificate represents more shares than were sold, the corporation issues two new certificates. One certificate goes to the new shareholder for the shares purchased and the other to the selling shareholder for the remaining unsold shares. Many shareholders have their shares held in the name of their brokerage firm. When this is done, the corporation's secretary or registrar keeps a record of who owns the shares and the shareholders do not receive share certificates.

Registrar and Transfer Agents

If a corporation's shares are traded on a major stock exchange, the corporation must have a *registrar* and a *transfer agent*. A registrar keeps shareholder records and prepares official lists of shareholders for shareholders' meetings and dividend payments. A transfer agent assists purchases and sales of shares by receiving and issuing certificates as necessary. Registrars and transfer agents usually are large banks or trust companies having computer facilities and staff to do this work.

Did You Know?

Online Trading

Financial institutions such as Scotia MacLeod, the Royal Bank, the Bank of Montreal and the National Bank of Canada are taking advantage of computer technology to offer their clients discount brokerage services. Providers of brokerage services over the Internet can pass along savings in labour and order-entry to clients. Not only can clients save on brokerage fees but also they can access the Net 24 hours a day from their home computers and receive service in both English and French. Users can obtain real time share quotes and current order status as well as closing prices on hundreds of company shares that allow them to manage their own investments.

Basics of Capital Stock

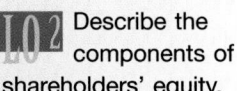 Describe the components of shareholders' equity.

Capital stock, also referred to as **share capital,** is a general term referring to all classes of a corporation's shares. The issuance of capital stock results in an increase in assets and a corresponding increase in shareholders' equity. The issuance of shares to obtain capital is often referred to as equity financing. This section introduces us to capital stock terminology and some of the basics in accounting for capital stock.

Authorized Shares

Authorized shares are the total amount of shares that a corporation's charter authorizes it to sell. Corporations formed under the Canada Business Corporations Act are permitted to issue an unlimited number of shares. Corporations disclose the number of shares authorized in the equity section of the balance sheet or its notes. **Alliance Communications Corporation** balance sheet in Appendix I reports in note 8 that the authorized capital stock of the company consists of an unlimited number of common shares comprised of Class A Voting Shares and Class B Non-Voting Shares.

Shareholders' Equity	1997	1996
Capital stock (note 8)	$88,836,000	$52,295,000

No formal journal entry is required for authorization of shares.

Selling Shares

Corporations can issue shares in at least two ways. They can either sell directly or indirectly to shareholders. *To sell directly*, a corporation advertises its shares issuance directly to potential buyers. This type of issuance is most common with privately held corporations. To *sell indirectly,* a corporation pays a brokerage house (investment banker) to issue its shares. Some brokerage houses *underwrite* an indirect issuance of shares, meaning they buy the shares from the corporation and take all gains or losses from its resale to shareholders.

IPO Growth in Information Technology

Information technology is becoming increasingly important to the Canadian economy. Since 1993, 132 Canadian Information and Technology firms went public in Canada raising $3.08 billion. The largest IPO in that sector in the first six months of 1997 was the privatization of **Manitoba Telecom Services Inc.,** which raised $910 million. [Source: Strategis Canada Web Site, October 10, 1997.]

Did You Know?

Market Value of Shares

Market value per share is the price at which a share is bought or sold. Market value is influenced by a variety of factors including expected future earnings, dividends, growth, and other company and economic events. Market values of frequently traded shares are reported daily in newspapers such as *The Globe and Mail* or are available immediately off the Web. Market values of shares not actively traded are more difficult to determine. Several techniques are used to estimate the value of these and other shares. Most all of these techniques use accounting information as an important input to this valuation process. We must remember the current market value of issued shares of a corporation (for example, buying and selling shares between investors) does not impact that corporation's shareholders' equity accounts.

Classes of Shares

A corporation's articles of incorporation authorize it to issue shares. Companies incorporated under the Canada Business Corporation Act are authorized to issue an unlimited number of shares. If all authorized shares have the same rights and characteristics, the shares are called common shares. There is no limit on the number of classes of shares set out in the articles of incorporation. Shares may be alphabetized by class such as Class A and Class B or may be assigned names such as common shares and preferred shares. We discuss preferred shares later in this chapter. **Alliance Communications Corporation**, for instance, has two types of common shares outstanding. Class A voting shares and Class B Non-Voting shares.

Stock Quotes

The **Imperial Oil** stock quote below is interpreted as (left to right): **Hi,** highest price in the past 52 weeks; **Lo,** lowest price in the past 52 weeks; **Stock,** company name; **Sym,** exchange symbol; **Div,** dividends paid per share in the past year; **Yld %,** dividend divided by closing price; **PE,** ratio of share price divided by earnings; **Vol 100s,** number of shares traded in 100s; **Hi,** highest price for the day; **Lo,** lowest price for the day; **Close,** closing price for the day; **Net Chg,** change in closing price from the prior day.

Did You Know?

52 Weeks

Hi	Lo	Stock Sym	Div	Yld %	PE	Vol 100s	Hi	Lo	Close	Net Chg
30.77	20.80	IMO	.74	2.8	17.3	31930	27.25	26.80	26.85	−.50

Shareholders' Equity

The equity of a corporation is known as **shareholders' equity** also called *stockholders' equity* or *corporate capital*. Shareholders' equity consists of (1) contributed (or paid-in) capital and (2) retained earnings. **Contributed capital** is the total amount of cash and other assets received by the corporation from its shareholders in exchange for all classes of shares issued. **Retained earnings** is the cumulative net income retained in a corporation. Retained earnings is increased by net income and decreased by dividends and net loss.

Exhibit 15.3 compares the equity accounts of a balance sheet for the three major forms of organizations: proprietorship, partnership and corporation. Exhibits 2.4, 2.7 and 2.8 in Chapter 2 show actual equity sections for each of these three forms when applied to **FastForward**. Further details regarding the equity section of a corporation are described in this and the next chapter.

Exhibit 15.3

Equity Accounts by Organizational Form

Flashback

1. Which of the following is not a characteristic of the corporate form of business? (a) ease of capital accumulation, (b) shareholders are liable for corporate debts, (c) ownership rights are easily transferred.

2. Why is income of a corporation said to be taxed twice?

3. What is a proxy?

Answers—p. 712

Common Shares

Accounting for the issuance of common shares involves (1) identifying the contributed capital and (2) keeping contributed capital separate from retained earnings. Issuance of shares affects only contributed capital accounts, no retained earnings accounts are affected.

Issuing Shares

Issuing Shares for Cash

LO3 Record the issuance of corporate shares.

The Canada Business Corporatons Act (CBCA), 1975, as well as the more recently passed provincial counterparts, require that all shares be of **no-par** or nominal value. These acts also require the total consideration received by the corporation for each share issued to be added to the stated capital account maintained for shares of that class. Some jurisdictions permit the issuance of par value shares. **Par value** is an arbitrary value a corporation places on each share of its share capital. Because of the rarity of par value shares in Canada this text will restrict itself to the accounting treatment of no-par shares only.

Shares are most commonly issued in exchange for cash. For example, the entry to record Dillon Snowboards' immediate issuance of 30,000 shares for $300,000 on June 5, 1999 is:

June 5	Cash	300,000	
	Common Shares		300,000
	Sold and issued 30,000 common shares at $10 per share.		

Assets = Liabilities + Equity
+300,000   +300,000

Exhibit 15.4 shows the shareholders' equity of Dillon Snowboards at the end of 1999 after earnings of $65,000 and no dividend payments.

Shareholders' Equity		
Contributed capital:		
Common Shares, no-par, unlimited shares authorized;		
30,000 shares issued and outstanding	$300,000	
Retained earnings	65,000	
Total shareholders' equity		$365,000

Exhibit 15.4

Shareholders' Equity

The retained earnings balance can also be negative, reflecting accumulated losses.

Issuing Shares for Noncash Assets

A corporation can receive assets other than cash in exchange for its shares.[4] The corporation records the assets acquired at the assets' fair market values as of the date of the transaction.

To illustrate, the entry to record receipt of land valued at $105,000 in return for immediate issuance of 4,000 common shares is:

June 10	Land	105,000	
	Common Shares		105,000
	Exchanged 4,000 common shares for land.		

Assets = Liabilities + Equity
+105,000   +105,000

If reliable fair values for the assets received cannot be determined, the fair market value of the shares given up is used to estimate the assets' values.

Issuing Shares for Organization Costs

A corporation sometimes gives shares to promoters in exchange for their services in organizing the corporation. In this case the corporation receives the intangible asset of Organization Costs in exchange for its shares. The entry to record receipt of services valued at $12,000 in organizing the corporation in return for immediate issuance of 600 common shares is:

June 5	Organization Costs	12,000	
	Common Shares		12,000
	Gave promoters 600 common shares in exchange for services in organizing the corporation.		

Assets = Liabilities + Equity
+12,000   +12,000

---

[4] It can also assume liabilities on assets received such as a mortgage on property.

Mid-Chapter Demonstration Problem

Roberto Ltd. issued 8,000 of its common shares on January 2, 1999. Present the journal entries that the company's accountant would use to record this event under each of the following independent situations:

a. The shares were sold for $1.50 per share.
b. The shares were issued for lawyer services valued at $6,000.
c. The shares were issued to a creditor who was owed $10,000.

Solution to Mid-Chapter Demonstration Problem

a.

Jan. 2	Cash	12,000	
	Common shares		12,000
	Issued common shares for Cash.		

b.

Jan. 2	Organization Cost	6,000	
	Common shares, ...		6,000
	Issued common shares for incorporation fees.		

c.

Jan 2	Accounts payable	10,000	
	Common shares		10,000
	Issued common shares in payment of debt.		

Issuing Shares through Subscriptions

Shares are usually sold for cash and immediately issued. But corporations sometimes issue shares through a subscription basis. A **shares subscription** involves selling shares where the investor agrees to buy a certain number of the shares at specified future dates and prices. The typical case is when a new corporation is formed and the organizers recognize both an immediate and future need for capital. The organizers can sell shares to investors who agree to contribute some cash now and to make additional contributions in the future.

Flashback

4. A company issues 7,000 common shares and a $40,000 note payable in exchange for equipment valued at $105,000. The entry to record this transaction includes a credit to (a) Retained earnings for $65,000, (b) Common shares for $65,000, (c) Common shares for $105,000.

Answers—p. 712

Preferred Shares

As mentioned earlier there is no limit on the number of classes of shares that a corporation can issue. **Preferred shares** have special rights that give it priority (or senior status) over common shares in one or more areas. Special rights typically include a preference for receiving dividends and for the distribution of assets if the corporation is liquidated. Preferred shares carry all the rights of common shares unless they are nullified in the corporate charter. Most preferred shares, for instance, do not have the right to vote. **Alliance**, for instance, has preferred shares outstanding without general voting rights.[5] See Exhibit 15.5.

Issuing Preferred Shares

A separate contributed capital account is used to record preferred shares. To illustrate, if Dillon Snowboards also had issued 50 preferred shares for $6,000 cash on July 1, 1999, the entry is:

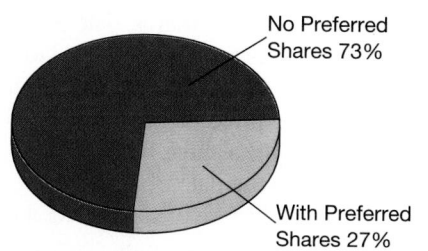

No Preferred Shares 73%

With Preferred Shares 27%

Exhibit 15.5

Corporations and Preferred Shares

July 1	Cash	6,000	
	Preferred shares		6,000
	Issued preferred shares for cash at $120 per share.		

Assets = Liabilities + Equity
+6,000   +6,000

The preferred shares account or accounts if there are more than one class of preferred shares, are included as part of contributed capital. The equity section of the year-end balance sheet for Dillon's Snowboards, including preferred shares, would appear as shown in Exhibit 15.6.

Exhibit 15.6

Shareholders' Equity with Common and Preferred shares

Shareholders' Equity		
Contributed capital:		
Preferred shares—no-par value; unlimited shares		
authorized; 50 shares issued and outstanding	$ 6,000	
Common Shares—no-par value; unlimited shares		
authorized; 30,000 shares issued and outstanding	300,000	
Total contributed capital		$306,000
Retained earnings		65,000
Total shareholders' equity		$371,000

Issuing no-par preferred shares is treated similar to no-par common shares. Also, issuing preferred shares for noncash assets is treated like similar entries for common shares.

Dividend Preference

Preferred shares usually carry a preference for dividends. This means preferred shareholders are allocated their dividends before any dividends are allocated to common shareholders. Simply put, a dividend cannot be paid to common shareholders unless preferred shareholders are paid first. The dividends allocated to preferred shareholders are usually expressed as a dollar amount per share or as a percent applied to the total stated value. Dividends could be expressed as $5.00 per share or as 5% of preferred shares with a total stated value of $100,000.

---

[5] A corporation can also issue more than one class of shares. If two classes of common shares are issued, the primary difference between them usually involves voting rights. Refer to question 9 at the end of this chapter regarding Alliance.

The reporting of preferred shares can appear complicated in practice. As an example, the December 31, 1996, annual report of **Noranda Inc.** showed among its various classes of shares that it had issued 12,000,000 cumulative, redeemable preferred shares Series F at a price of $25.00 per share that pay a fixed dividend at a rate of 5.8% per annum. A more complicated disclosure of preferred shares is found in the 1996 annual report of **Novicourt.** Novicourt was authorized to issue an unlimited number of preferred shares. The amount issued as of December 31,1996, totalled $4,984,000. These shares require Novicourt to pay dividends equal to the greater of (a) 8.50% annual rate and (b) the rate obtained by multiplying 8.5% by the ratio of the average price of gold at the second fixing on the London Metal Exchange each day during a three-month period ending on the fifteenth day of the second month prior to the date of payment of the dividend to the base price of gold established for the purpose of such dividend at U.S. $3.75 per ounce. Preferred dividends must be paid before common shareholders can receive a dividend. A preference for dividends does *not* ensure dividends. If the directors do not declare a dividend, neither the preferred nor the common shareholders receive one.

Cumulative or Noncumulative Dividend

LO5 Distribute dividends between common shares and preferred shares.

Most preferred shares carry a cumulative dividend right. **Cumulative preferred shareholders** have a right to be paid both current and all prior periods' unpaid dividends before any dividend is paid to common shareholders. When preferred shares are cumulative and the directors either do not declare a dividend to preferred shareholders or declare a dividend that does not satisfy the cumulative dividend, then the unpaid dividend amount is called **dividend in arrears.** Accumulation of dividends in arrears on cumulative preferred shares does not guarantee they will be paid. Some preferred shares are noncumulative. **Noncumulative preferred shares** have no right to prior periods' unpaid dividends if they were not declared.

To illustrate and show the difference between cumulative and noncumulative preferred shares, let's assume a corporation's outstanding shares includes (a) 1,000 shares of 9% preferred shares amounting to $100,000 and (b) 4,000 shares common shares amounting to $200,000. During 1999, the first year of the corporation's operations, the directors declare cash dividends of $5,000. In year 2000, it declares $42,000. Allocations of total dividends are shown in Exhibit 15.7.

Exhibit 15.7

Allocation of Dividends

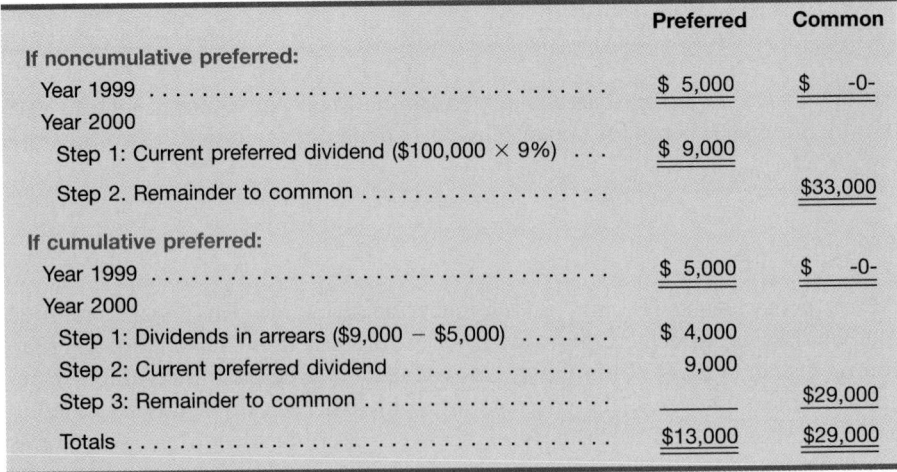

	Preferred	Common
If noncumulative preferred:		
Year 1999	$ 5,000	$ -0-
Year 2000		
Step 1: Current preferred dividend ($100,000 × 9%) . . .	$ 9,000	
Step 2. Remainder to common		$33,000
If cumulative preferred:		
Year 1999	$ 5,000	$ -0-
Year 2000		
Step 1: Dividends in arrears ($9,000 − $5,000)	$ 4,000	
Step 2: Current preferred dividend	9,000	
Step 3: Remainder to common		$29,000
Totals	$13,000	$29,000

Allocation of year 2000 dividends depends on whether the preferred shares are noncumulative or cumulative. With noncumulative preferred, the preferred shareholders never receive the $4,000 skipped in 1999. But if the preferred shares are cumulative, the $4,000 in arrears is paid in 2000 before the common shareholders receive a dividend.

Participating or Nonparticipating Dividend

Nonparticipating preferred shares have dividends limited to a maximum amount each year. This maximum is often stated as a percent of the share's issuance price or as a specific dollar amount per share. Once preferred shareholders receive this amount, the common shareholders receive any and all additional dividends.

Participating preferred shares have a feature where preferred shareholders share with common shareholders in any dividends paid in excess of the percent stated on the preferred shares. This participating feature does not apply until common shareholders receive dividends equal to the preferred share's dividend percent. While many corporations are authorized to issue participating preferred shares, they are rarely issued and most managers never expect to issue them. However they do exist. **Power Corporation of Canada**, for example, recently reported participating preferred shares of $1,875,974,000. These shares were entitled to a non-cumulative dividend of $0.0375 per share per annum before dividends on the subordinate voting shares, having the right to participate, share and share alike, with the holders of the subordinate voting shares in any dividends in any year after payment of a dividend of $0.0375 per share to the subordinate shares.

What then is the purpose of participating preferred shares? They are usually authorized as a defence against a possible *takeover* of the corporation by an "unfriendly" investor (or a group of investors) who intends to buy enough voting common shares to gain control. Taking a term from spy novels, the financial world refers to this kind of plan as a *poison pill* that a company swallows if it is threatened with capture by enemy investors.

A poison pill usually works as follows: A corporation's common shareholders on a given date are granted the right to purchase a large amount of participating preferred shares at a very low price. This right to purchase preferred shares is *not* transferable. This means if these shareholders sell their common shares, the buyers do *not* gain the right to purchase preferred shares. The right to purchase preferred shares can only be exercised if the directors identify an investor of a large block of common shares as an unfriendly investor.

If an unfriendly investor buys a large block of common shares (whose right to purchase participating preferred shares did *not* transfer to this buyer), the board can issue preferred shares at a low price to the remaining common shareholders who retained the right to purchase. Future dividends must now be divided between the newly issued participating preferred shares and the common shares. This usually transfers a large value of the common shares to preferred shares. This means the common shares owned by the unfriendly investor lose much of their value, and this reduces the potential benefit of a hostile takeover.

Financial Statement Disclosure of Dividends

Dividends are not incurred as time passes. A liability for a dividend does not exist until the directors declare a dividend. This means that if a preferred dividend date passes and the corporation's board fails to declare the dividend on its cumulative preferred shares, the dividend in arrears is not a liability. But when preparing financial statements, the *full-disclosure principle* requires the corporation to report the amount of preferred dividends in arrears as of the balance sheet date. This information is usually in a note.

Convertible Preferred Shares

Preferred shares are more attractive to investors if they carry a right to be exchanged for a fixed number of common shares. **Convertible preferred shares** give holders the option of exchanging their preferred shares into common shares at a specified rate. **Laidlaw,** for example, showed in its August 31, 1997, annual report 5% cumulative, convertible first preference preferred shares of $8.7 million. This feature offers holders of convertible preferred shares a higher potential return. When a company prospers and its common shares increase in value, convertible preferred shareholders can share in this success by converting their preferred shares into more valuable common shares. Also, these holders benefit from increases in the value of common shares without converting their preferred shares because the preferred share's market value is impacted by changes in the value of common shares.

Callable Preferred Shares

Callable preferred shares gives the issuing corporation the right to purchase (retire) their shares from its holders at specified future prices and dates. Many issues of preferred shares are callable. The amount paid to call and retire a preferred share is its **call price**, or *redemption value*. This amount is set at the time the shares are issued. The call price normally includes the issue price of the shares plus a premium giving holders additional return on their investment. When the issuing corporation calls and retires preferred shares, it must pay the call price and any dividends in arrears.

Motivation for Preferred Shares

There are several reasons for a corporation to issue preferred shares. One reason is to raise capital without sacrificing control of the corporation. For example, let's suppose the organizers of a company have $100,000 cash to invest and wish to organize a corporation needing $200,000 of capital to get off to a good start. If they sold $200,000 worth of common shares, they would have only 50% control and would need to negotiate extensively with other shareholders in making policy. But if they issue $100,000 worth of common shares to themselves and sell outsiders $100,000 of 8%, cumulative preferred shares with no voting rights, they retain control of the corporation.

A second reason for issuing preferred shares is to boost the return earned by common shareholders. To illustrate, let's suppose a corporation's organizers expect their new company to earn an annual after-tax income of $24,000 on an investment of $200,000. If they sell and issue $200,000 worth of common shares, this income produces a 12% return on the $200,000 of common shareholders' equity. But if they issue $100,000 of 8% preferred shares to outsiders and $100,000 of common shares to themselves, their own return increases to 16% per year as shown in Exhibit 15.8.

Exhibit 15.8

Return to Common
Shareholders

Net after-tax income	$24,000
Less preferred dividends at 8% ($100,000 × 8%)	(8,000)
Balance to common shareholders	$16,000
Return to common shareholders ($16,000/$100,000) . .	16%

Common shareholders earn 16% instead of 12% because assets contributed by preferred shareholders are invested to earn $12,000 while the preferred dividend payments amount to only $8,000.

Use of preferred shares to increase return to common shareholders is an example of **financial leverage.** Whenever the dividend rate on preferred shares is less than the rate the corporation earns on its assets, the effect of issuing preferred shares is to increase (or *lever*) the rate earned by common shareholders. Financial leverage also occurs when debt is issued and the interest rate paid on it is less than the rate earned from using the assets the creditors loaned to the corporation.

There are other reasons for issuing preferred shares. For example, a corporation's preferred shares may appeal to some investors who believe its common shares are too risky or that the dividend rate on common shares is too low. Also, if a corporation's management wants to issue common shares but believes the current market price for common shares is too low, the corporation may issue preferred shares that are convertible into common shares. If and when the price of common shares increases, the preferred shareholders can convert their shares into common shares.

Concert Organizer

You organize music concerts for profit. You've recently decided to move away from concerts targeted at under 5,000 people to those targeted at between 10,000 to 50,000 people. This demands funding. You decide to incorporate because of the increased risk of lawsuits and your desire to issue shares to meet funding demands. It is important to you that you keep control of the company for decisions on who to schedule and when. What type of shares issuance do you offer?

You Make the Call

Answer—p. 712

Flash back

5. In what ways do preferred shares often have priority over common shares?

6. Increasing the return to common shareholders by issuing preferred shares is an example of (a) financial leverage, (b) cumulative earnings, or (c) dividends in arrears.

7. A corporation has (a) $450,000 of preferred shares consisting of 9,000 shares of 10% cumulative and nonparticipating preferred shares and (b) $270,000 of common shares consisting of 27,000 shares issued and outstanding. No dividends have been declared for the past two years. During the current year, the corporation declares a $288,000 dividend. The amount paid to common shareholders is (a) $243,000, (b) $153,000, or (c) $135,000.

Answers—p. 712

Preferred Shares as Debt

According to section 3800 of the *CICA Handbook* the issuer of a financial instrument should classify it as a liability or as equity in accordance with the substance of the financial instrument. Prior to release of section 3800 debt and equity were required under GAAP to be classified according to their legal form. Now if an instrument requires the issuer to deliver cash or another financial asset under conditions that are potentially unfavourable the instrument should be classifed as a liability. Preferred shares may provide for mandatory redemption or contain a provision providing an accelerating dividend such that the dividend yield is scheduled to be so high that the issuer will be economically compelled to redeem the preferred shares. These preferred shares must be classified as liabilities for fiscal years on or after January 1,1996. Dividends relating to these preferred shares are to be shown in the income statement as a reduction similar to interest expense on long-term debt. Cumulative preferred dividends would be accrued whether or not the dividends were declared. This is a major change from previous GAAP which required that all preferred dividends be shown in the statement of retained earnings and only recorded when declared. This topic is treated in depth in more advanced accounting courses.

Did You Know?

Book Value per Share   USING THE INFORMATION

L0 6 Compute book value and explain its use in analysis.

This section explains how we compute book value and use it for analysis. We first focus on book value per share for corporations with only common shares outstanding, and then look at book value per share when both common and preferred shares are outstanding.

Book Value per Share When Only Common Shares are Outstanding

Book value per common share is the recorded amount of shareholders' equity applicable to common shares divided by the number of common shares outstanding. This ratio is defined in Exhibit 15.9.

Exhibit 15.9

Book Value per Common Share Formula

$$\text{Book Value per Common Share} = \frac{\text{Shareholders' Equity Applicable to Common Shares}}{\text{Number of Common Shares Outstanding}}$$

For instance, we can compute the book value per common share for Dillon Snowboards at the end of 1999 using data in Exhibit 15.7. Dillon has 30,000 outstanding common shares and the shareholders' equity applicable to common shares is $365,000. Common shares are entitled to total shareholders' equity when there are no preferred shares outstanding. Dillon's book value per common share is $12.17, computed as $365,000 divided by 30,000 shares.

Book Value per Share When Both Common and Preferred shares are Outstanding

To compute book value when *both common and preferred shares are outstanding*, we must first allocate total shareholders' equity between these two kinds of shares. The **book value per preferred share** is computed first, and its computation is shown in Exhibit 15.10.

Exhibit 15.10

Book Value per Preferred Share Formula

$$\text{Book Value per Preferred Share} = \frac{\text{Shareholders' Equity Applicable to Preferred Shares}}{\text{Number of Preferred Shares Outstanding}}$$

The shareholders' equity applicable to preferred shares equals the preferred share's call price (or average paid-in amount if the preferred is not callable) plus any cumulative dividends in arrears. The remaining shareholders' equity is the portion applicable to common shares.

To illustrate, let us look at the shareholders' equity section of **Music Live!** as shown in Exhibit 15.11. The preferred shares of Music Live! are callable at $108 per share, and two years of cumulative preferred dividends are in arrears.

Exhibit 15.11

Shareholders' Equity with Preferred and Common Shares

Shareholders' Equity	
Preferred shares, no-par value, $7 cumulative, 2,000 shares authorized, 1,000 shares issued and outstanding	$105,000
Common shares, no-par value, 12,000 shares authorized, 10,000 shares issued and outstanding	$260,000
Total contributed capital	$365,000
Retained Earnings	82,000
Total shareholders' equity	$447,000

The book values of Music Live! preferred and common shares are computed in Exhibit 15.12. Note the need to first allocate equity to preferred shares before we compute the book value of common shares.

Total shareholders' equity		$447,000
Less equity applicable to preferred shares:		
Call price (1,000 × $108)	$108,000	
Cumulative dividends in arrears ($100,000 × $7 × 2) ..	14,000	(122,000)
Equity applicable to common shares		$325,000
Book value per preferred share ($122,000/1,000)		**$ 122.00**
Book value per common share ($325,000/10,000)		**$ 32.50**

Exhibit 15.12

Computing Book Value Per Share

Book value per share is often used in analysis of a company. It reflects the amount each share is worth if a company is liquidated at amounts reported on the balance sheet. Book value is also the starting point in many share valuation methods. Other uses include merger negotiations, price setting for public utilities, and loan contracts. The main limitation in using book values is likely differences between book values and market values for both assets and liabilities. Professionals often adjust their analyses and the accounting numbers to reflect these differences.

Annual reports to shareholders sometimes disclose the book value per share. **Royal Bank's** common shares at the end of the first quarter of 1998 carried a book value of $28.66, while its market (share) value on the date of the release of the interim report was $76.35, over 266% of book value. Book value and liquidation value per share can also be different. This is because if a company is liquidated, the selling prices are often different from amounts reported on the balance sheet.

Investor

You are considering investing in **Ride**, a leading manufacturer of snowboards. Ride's current book value per common share is about $4, yet its common shares are priced at about $7 per share on the stock exchange. From this information, can you say whether Ride's net assets are priced higher or lower than their recorded values?

You Make the Call

Answer—p. 712

⭐ Flashback

8. A corporation's outstanding shares includes (a) $90,000 of cumulative preferred shares consisting of 1,000 shares and (b) 12,000 common shares. Preferred shares have a call price of $90 and dividends of $18,000 are in arrears. Total shareholders' equity is $630,000. What is the book value per common share?

9. The price at which a share is bought or sold is the (a) call price, (b) redemption value, or (c) market value.

Answers—p. 713

Summary

LO 1 **Identify characteristics of corporations and their organization.** Corporations are separate legal entities and their shareholders are not liable for corporate debts. Shares issued by corporations are easily transferred between shareholders, and the life of a corporation does not end with the incapacity or death of a shareholder. A corporation acts through its agents, who are its officers and managers, not its shareholders. Corporations are regulated by the government and are subject to income taxes.

LO 2 **Describe the components of shareholders' equity.** Authorized shares are the total amount of shares that a corporation's charter authorizes it to sell. Issued shares is the portion of authorized shares sold to shareholders. Shareholders' equity is made up of (a) contributed capital and (b) retained earnings. Contributed capital consists of funds raised by shares issuances—both common and preferred. Retained earnings consists of current and prior periods' earnings not distributed to shareholders.

LO 3 **Record the issuance of corporate shares.** When shares are issued, the proceeds are credited to the share capital account. This amount is contributed capital.

LO 4 **Explain the characteristics of common and preferred shares.** Preferred shares have a priority (or senior status) relative to common shares in one or more areas. The usual areas include preference as to (a) dividends and (b) assets in case of liquidation. But they usually do not have voting rights. Preferred shares can also be convertible or callable. Convertibility permits the holder to convert preferred shares to common shares. Callability permits the issuer to buy preferred shares under specified conditions.

LO 5 **Distribute dividends between common shares and preferred shares.** Preferred shareholders usually hold the right to receive dividend distributions before common shareholders. This right is known as dividend preference. When preferred shares are cumulative and in arrears, the amount in arrears must be distributed to preferred shareholders before any dividends are distributed to common shareholders.

LO 6 **Compute book value and explain its use in analysis.** Book value per common share is shareholders' equity applicable to common shares divided by the number of outstanding common shares. Book value per preferred share is shareholders' equity applicable to preferred shares divided by the number of outstanding preferred shares.

Guidance Answers to **You Make the Call**

Concert Organizer

Because you wish to maintain control of the company, you want to issue shares in a way that does not interfere with your ability to run the company in the way you desire. You have two basic options: (1) different classes of common shares, or (2) common and preferred shares. Your objective in this case is to issue shares to yourself that have all or a majority of the voting power. The other class of shares you issue would carry limited or no voting rights. In this way you maintain complete control and are able to raise your necessary funds.

Investor

Book value reflects recorded values. Ride's book value is about $4 per common share. The share price reflects the market's expectation of current values. Ride's market value is about $7 per common share. Comparing these figures suggests the current values of Ride's net assets is much higher than their recorded values ($7 vs. $4 per share, respectively).

Guidance Answers to

1. *b*
2. A corporation must pay taxes on its income and its shareholders must pay personal income taxes on dividends received from the corporation.
3. A proxy is a legal document used to transfer a shareholder's right to vote to another person.
4. *b*
5. Typically, preferred shares have a preference in receiving dividends and in the distribution of assets in the case of a company's liquidation.

6. *a*

7. *b*

Total dividend	$288,000
To preferred shareholders	135,000*
Remainder to common shareholders ..	$153,000

*$450,000 × .10 × 3 = $135,000

8.

Total shareholders' equity		$630,000
Less equity applicable to preferred shares:		
Call price (1,000 × $90)	$90,000	
Dividends in arrears	18,000	108,000
Equity applicable to common shares		$522,000
Book value of common shares ($522,000/12,000)		$43.50

9. *c*

Demonstration Problem

Barton Corporation was created on January 1, 1998. Barton is authorized by its articles of incorporation to issue 100,000 shares of $10 cumulative preferred shares and an unlimited number of no-par common shares. The following transactions relating to shareholders' equity occurred during the first two years of the company's operations.

1. Prepare the journal entries to record these transactions.

2. Prepare the balance sheet presentation of the organization costs, liabilities, and shareholders' equity as at December 31, 1998, and December 31, 1999. Include appropriate notes to the financial statements.

1998

Jan. 2 Issued 200,000 common shares at $12 per share.

2 Issued 100,000 common shares in exchange for a building valued at $820,000 and merchandise inventory valued at $380,000.

2 Acceped subscriptions for 150,000 common shares at $12 per share. The subscribers made no down payments, and the full purchase price was due on April 1, 1998.

3 Paid a cash reimbursement to the company's founders for $100,000 of organization costs; these costs are to be amortized over 10 years.

3 Issued 12,000 preferred shares for cash at $110 per share.

Apr. 1 Collected the full subscription price for the January 1 common shares and issued the shares.

Dec. 31 The income summary account for 1998 had a $125,000 credit balance before being closed to Retained Earnings; no dividends were declared on either common or preferred shares.

1999

June 4 Issued 100,000 common shares for cash at $15 per share.

Dec. 10 Declared dividends payable on January 10, 2,000 as follows:

To preferred shareholders for 1998	$120,000
To preferred shareholders for 1999	120,000
To common shareholders for 1999	300,000

Dec. 31 The income summary account for 1999 had a $1 million credit balance before being closed to Retained Earnings.

Planning the Solution

■ Record journal entries for the events in 1998 and 1999.

■ Close the accounts related to retained earnings at the end of each year.

■ Determine the balance sheet amount for 1998 and 1999 for unamortized organization costs.

■ Determine the balances for the 1998 and 1999 capital equity accounts for the balance sheet including information about the number of shares issued and a note regarding dividends in arrears.

■ Prepare the specified portions of the 1998 and 1999 balance sheets.

Solution to Demonstration Problem

1.

1998			
Jan. 2	Cash	2,400,000	
	Common Shares		2,400,000
	Issued 200,000 common shares.		
2	Building	820,000	
	Merchandise Inventory	380,000	
	Common Shares		1,200,000
	Issued 100,000 common shares.		
3	Subscriptions receivable	1,800,000	
	Common shares subscribed		1,800,000
	Recognize subscription contract for *150,000 common shares at $12 per share.*		
3	Organization Costs	100,000	
	Cash		100,000
	Reimbursed the founders for *organization costs.*		
3	Cash	1,320,000	
	Preferred shares		1,320,000
	Issued 12,000 preferred shares.		
Apr. 1	Cash	1,800,000	
	Subscriptions receivable		1,800,000
	Collected balance due on subscribed *common shares.*		
1	Common shares subscribed	1,800,000	
	Commons shares		1,800,000
	Issued 150,000 subscribed common shares.		
Dec. 31	Income Summary	125,000	
	Retained Earnings		125,000
	Close income summary and update *Retained Earnings.*		

1999			
June 4	Cash	1,500,000	
	Common Shares		1,500,000
	Issued 100,000 common shares.		
Dec. 10	Cash dividends declared	540,000	
	Dividends Payable, Common Shares .		300,000
	Dividends Payable, Preferred Shares .		240,000
	Declared current dividends and dividends *in arrears to common and preferred* *shareholders, payable on January 10, 2000.*		
Dec. 31	Income Summary	1,000,000	
	Retained Earnings		1,000,000
	To close the income summary account *and update retained earnings.*		
Dec. 31	Retained Earnings	540,000	
	Cash Dividends Declared		540,000
	To close to Retained Earnings the Cash *Dividends Declared.*		

2. Balance sheet presentations:

	As of December 31	
	1998	**1999**
Assets		
Organization Costs	$ 90,000	$ 80,000
Liabilities		
Dividends payable, common shares		$ 300,000
Dividends payable, preferred shares		240,000
Total liabilities		$ 540,000
Shareholders' Equity		
Contributed capital:		
Preferred shares, no-par value, $10 cumulative, 100,000 shares authorized, 12,000 shares issued and outstanding	$1,320,000	$1,320,000
Common shares, no-par value, unlimited shares authorized, 450,000 shares issued and outstanding in 1998, and 550,000 shares in 1999	$5,400,000	$6,900,000
Total contributed capital	$6,720,000	$8,220,000
Retained Earnings (see Note 1)	125,000	585,000
Total Shareholders' Equity	$6,845,000	$8,805,000

Note 1: As of December 31, 1998, there were $120,000 of Dividends in arrears on the preferred shares.

Glossary

Authorized shares The total amount of shares that a corporation's charter authorizes it to sell. Federally incoporated companies are authorized to issue an unlimited number. (p. 700)

Book value per common share The recorded amount of shareholder's equity applicable to common shares divided by the number of common shares outstanding. (p. 710)

Book value per preferred share The shareholder's equity applicable to preferred shares (equals the preferred share's call price—or issue price if the preferred is not callable—plus any cumulative dividends in arrears) divided by the number of preferred shares outstanding. (p. 710)

Call price The amount that must be paid to call and retire a preferred share. (p. 708)

Callable preferred shares Preferred shares that the issuing corporation, at its option, may retire by paying a specified amount (the call price) to the preferred shareholders plus any dividends in arrears. (p. 708)

Capital stock The general term referring to a corporation's stock used in obtaining its capital (owner financing); also called *share capital*. (p. 700)

Common shares Shares of a corporation that has only one class of shares. (p. 699)

Contributed capital The total amount of cash and other assets received by the corporation from its shareholders in exchange for all classes of shares issued. (p. 702)

Convertible preferred shares Preferred shares that give holders the option of exchanging their preferred shares into common shares at a specified rate. (p. 707)

Cumulative preferred shares Preferred shares on which undeclared dividends accumulate until they are paid; common shareholders cannot receive a dividend until all cumulative dividends have been paid. (p. 706)

Dividend in arrears An unpaid dividend on cumulative preferred shares; it must be paid before any regular dividends on the preferred shares and before any dividends on the common shares. (p. 706)

Financial leverage The achievement of an increased return on common shares by paying dividends on preferred shares or interest on debt at a rate that is less than the rate of return earned with the assets invested in the corporation by the preferred shareholders or creditors. (p. 708)

Market value per share The price at which stock is bought or sold. (p. 701)

Noncumulative preferred shares Preferred shares on which the right to receive dividends is lost for any year that the dividends are not declared. (p. 706)

No-par value shares A class of shares that has not been assigned a par value by the corporate charter. (p. 702)

Nonparticipating preferred shares Preferred shares on which dividends are limited to a maximum amount each year. (p. 707)

Organization costs The costs of bringing a corporation into existence, including legal fees, promoters' fees, and amounts paid to the incorporating legal jurisdiction. (p. 697)

Participating preferred shares Preferred shares with a feature that allows preferred shareholders to share with common shareholders in any dividends paid in excess of the percent stated on the preferred shares. (p. 707)

Par value An arbitrary value a corporation places on each share of its capital stock. (p. 703)

Preemptive right The right of common shareholders to protect their proportionate ownership in a corporation by having the first opportunity to buy additional common shares issued by the corporation. (p. 699)

Preferred shares Stock that gives its owners a priority status over common shareholders in one or more ways, such

as the payment of dividends or the distribution of assets on liquidation. (p. 704)

Proxy A legal document that gives an agent of a shareholder the power to exercise the voting rights of that shareholder's shares. (p. 698)

Retained earnings The cumulative net income retained by a corporation. (p. 702)

Share capital Another name for capital stock. (p. 700)

Shareholders' equity The equity of a corporation; also called *stockholders' equity* or *corporate capital*. (p. 702)

Share subscription A contractual commitment by an investor to purchase unissued shares at specific future dates and prices. (p. 704)

Questions

1. Who is responsible for directing the affairs of a corporation?
2. What are organization costs? List several examples of these costs.
3. How are organization costs classified on the balance sheet?
4. List the general rights of common shareholders.
5. What is the preemptive right of common shareholders?
6. What is the meaning of the call price of a share?
7. Why would an investor find convertible preferred shares attractive?
8. Examine the balance sheet for **Atlantis** in Appendix I at the end of the book and determine the classes of shares that the company has issued.
9. Refer to the balance sheet for **Alliance** in Appendix I at the end of the book. How many classes of shares is Alliance authorized to issue?
10. What steps did Jennifer Wong have to follow in order to incorporate her business?

Quick Study

QS 15-1
Characteristics of corporations

Of the following statements, which are true for the corporation form of business?

a. Capital often is more easily accumulated than with other forms of organization.
b. It has a limited life.
c. Owners have unlimited liability for corporate debts.
d. Distributed income is taxed twice in normal circumstances.
e. It is a separate legal entity.
f. Ownership rights cannot be easily transferred.
g. Owners are not agents of the corporation.

QS 15-2
Issuance of common shares

LO 3

On February 1, Excel Corporation issued 37,500 common shares for $252,000 cash. Present the entry to record this transaction.

Each of these entries was recently recorded by a different corporation. Provide an explanation for the event or transaction described by each entry.

QS 15-3
Interpreting journal entries
for share issuances
LO 3

a.
| Apr. 1 | Cash | 60,000 | |
| | Common Shares | | 60,000 |

b.
| Apr. 3 | Organization Costs | 90,000 | |
| | Common Shares | | 90,000 |

c.
Apr. 4	Subscriptions receivable	20,000	
	Cash	60,000	
	Common shares subscribed		80,000

d.
Apr. 5	Merchandise Inventory	90,000	
	Machinery	130,000	
	Notes Payable		144,000
	Common Shares		76,000

Holden Company's shareholders' equity includes 75,000 shares of 8% cumulative preferred shares that had been issued for $375,000 and 200,000 common shares. Holden did not declare any dividends during the prior year and now declares and pays a $108,000 cash dividend. Determine the amount distributed to each class of shareholders.

QS 15-4
Dividend allocation
between classes of
shareholders
LO 5

The shareholders' equity section of Courtland Company's balance sheet follows:

QS 15-5
Book value per common
share
LO 6

Shareholders' Equity	
Preferred shares, $5 cumulative, 10,000 shares authorized, issued and outstanding	$100,000
Common shares, 100,000 shares authorized, 75,000 shares issued and outstanding	375,000
Retained earnings	445,000
Total shareholders' equity	$920,000

The call price of the preferred shares is $30. Determine the book value per common share under the assumption that there are no dividends in arrears.

Present the general journal entries that an accountant would prepare to record the following issuances of shares in three different situations:

a. Two thousand shares of common shares are issued to the corporation's promoters in exchange for their efforts in creating it. Their efforts are estimated to be worth $30,000.

b. Four thousand common shares are issued for $70,000 cash.

c. One thousand preferred shares are issued for $120,000 cash.

Exercises

Exercise 15-1
Recording share
issuances
LO 3

Hanson, Inc. issued 6,000 of its common shares on February 2. Present the journal entries that the company's accountant would use to record this event under each of the following independent situations:

a. The shares were issued for lawyers services valued at $4,000 in establishing the corporation.

b. The shares have a $2 value.

c. The shares were issued to a creditor who was owed $12,000.

Exercise 15-2
Accounting for share
issuances
LO 3

Exercise 15-3
Dividends on common and noncumulative preferred shares

LO 5

The outstanding shares of Lipscomb includes 40,000 shares of 7.5% noncumulative preferred shares that had been issued for $400,000, as well as 100,000 common shares that had been issued at $1 per share. During its first four years of operation, the corporation declared and paid the following total amounts of dividends:

1999	$ 10,000
2000	24,000
2001	100,000
2002	196,000

Determine the amount of dividends paid in each year to each class of shareholders. Also determine the total dividends paid to each class in the four years combined.

Exercise 15-4
Dividends on common and cumulative preferred shares

LO 5

Use the data in Exercise 15-3 to determine the amount of dividends paid in each year to each class of shareholders, assuming that the preferred shares are cumulative. Also determine the total dividends paid to each class in the four years combined.

Exercise 15-5
Using preferred shares to create leverage

LO 2, 4

An individual entrepreneur is planning to start a new business and needs $312,500 of start-up capital. This person has $250,000 in personal assets that can be invested and thus needs to raise another $62,500 in cash. The founder will buy 5,000 common shares for $250,000 and has two alternative plans for raising the additional cash. One plan is to sell 1,250 common shares to one or more other investors for $62,500 cash. The second is to sell 625 shares of cumulative preferred shares to one or more investors for $62,500 cash (these shares have an annual 8% dividend rate).

1. If the business is expected to earn $45,000 of after-tax net income in the first year, what rate of return on beginning equity will the founder earn under each alternative? Which of the two plans will provide the higher return to the founder?

2. If the business is expected to earn $10,500 of after-tax net income in the first year, what rate of return on beginning equity will the founder earn under each alternative? Which of the two plans will provide the higher return to the founder?

Exercise 15-6
Identifying characteristics of preferred shares

LO 2, 4

Match each of the numbered descriptions with the characteristic of preferred shares that it best describes. Indicate your answer by writing the letter for the correct characteristic in the blank space next to each description.

A. Callable   **D.** Noncumulative
B. Convertible   **E.** Nonparticipating
C. Cumulative   **F.** Participating

_____ **1.** The holders of the shares can exchange it for common shares.

_____ **2.** The issuing corporation can retire the shares by paying a prearranged price.

_____ **3.** The holders of the shares are entitled to receive dividends in excess of the stated rate under some conditions.

_____ **4.** The holders of the shares are not entitled to receive dividends in excess of the stated rate.

_____ **5.** The holders of the shares lose any dividends that are not declared.

_____ **6.** The holders of the shares are entitled to receive current and all past dividends before common shareholders receive any dividends.

Next to the following list of eight general characteristics of business organizations, write a brief description of how each characteristic applies to corporations and general partnerships.

		Corporations	General Partnerships
1.	Life		
2.	Owners' liability		
3.	Legal status		
4.	Tax status of income		
5.	Owners' authority		
6.	Ease of formation		
7.	Transferability of ownership		
8.	Ability to raise large amounts of capital		

The balance sheet for Kuhn Corp. includes the following information:

Shareholders' Equity	
Preferred shares, 6% cumulative, $30 call price,	
5,000 shares issued and outstanding	$125,000
Common shares, 40,000 shares issued and outstanding	400,000
Retained earnings	267,500
Total shareholders' equity	$792,500

Determine the book value per share of the preferred and common shares under these two situations:

a. No preferred dividends are in arrears.

b. Three years of preferred dividends are in arrears.

Precision Products, Inc., was incorporated at the beginning of the year and engaged in a number of transactions. The following journal entries affected its shareholders' equity during its first year of operations:

a.	Cash	150,000	
	Common Shares (5,000 shares)		150,000
b.	Organization Costs	75,000	
	Common Shares (2,500 shares)		75,000
c.	Cash	21,500	
	Accounts Receivable	7,500	
	Office Equipment	10,750	
	Building	30,000	
	Accounts Payable		11,000
	Notes Payable		18,750
	Common Shares (1,000 shares)		40,000

d.	Cash	60,000	
	Accounts payable	20,000	
	Common Shares (2,000 shares)		80,000

Required

1. Provide explanations for the journal entries.
2. Prepare answers for the following questions:
   a. What is the total contributed capital?
   b. What is the book value per common share at the end of the year if contributed capital plus retained earnings equals $347,500?

Problem 15-2
Share subscriptions
LO 2, 3, 4

Micron Corporation is authorized to issue 60,000 shares of $4 cumulative and nonparticipating preferred and an unlimited number of no-par-value common shares. Micron Corporation then completed these transactions:

July 6   Accepted subscriptions to 80,000 common shares at $18 per share. Down payments equal to 25% of the subscription price accompanied each subscription. The balance is due on August 10.

July 20   Gave the corporation's promoters 2,000 common shares for their services in getting the corporation organized. The board valued the services at $35,000.

Aug. 4   Accepted subscription to 6,000 shares of preferred at $65 per share. The subscriptions were accompanied by 50% down payment. The balance is due on September 5.

10   Collected the balance due on the July 6 common subscriptions and issued the shares.

30   Accepted subscriptions to 1,000 shares of preferred at $62 per share. The subscriptions were accompanied by 50% down payments. The balance is due on October 30.

Sept. 5   Collected the balance due on the August 4 preferred subscriptions and issued the shares.

Required

1. Prepare general journal entries to record the transactions.
2. Prepare the shareholders' equity section of the corporation's balance sheet as of the close of business on September 30. Assume that retained earnings are $60,000.

Problem 15-3
Shareholders' equity
transactions
LO 2, 3, 4, 5

Solar Energy Company is authorized to issue an unlimited number of common shares and 100,000 shares of $10, noncumulative and nonparticipating, convertible preferred. The company completed the following transactions:

1997

Feb. 5   Issued 70,000 common shares at $10 for cash.

28   Gave the corporation's promoters 3,750 common shares for their services in organizing the corporation. The directors valued the services at $40,000.

Mar. 3   Issued 44,000 common shares in exchange for the following assets with the indicated reliable market values: land, $80,000; buildings, $210,000; and machinery, $155,000.

Dec. 31   Closed the Income Summary account. A $27,000 loss was incurred.

1998

Jan. 28   Issued 4,000 preferred shares at $100 for cash.

Dec. 15   Solar Energy Company's preferred shareholders submitted 2,500 of their convertible shares for conversion into common shares on this date. The convertible shareholders accepted nine common shares for each preferred share.

31   Closed the Income Summary account. A $98,000 net income was earned.

1999

Jan. 1   The board of directors declared a $10 cash dividend to preferred shares and $0.20 per share cash dividend to outstanding common shares, payable on February 5 to the January 24 shareholders of record.

Feb. 5   Paid the previously declared dividends.

Oct. 20 Accepted subscriptions to 4,000 common shares at $14.90 per share. Down payment of 40% accompanied the subscription contracts. The balance is due on January 20, 1995.

Dec. 31 Closed the Cash Dividends Declared and Income Summary accounts. A $159,000 net income was earned.

Required

1. Prepare general journal entries to record the transactions.

2. Prepare the shareholders' equity section of the balance sheet as of the close of business on December 31, 1999.

Segura Corporation's common shares are currently selling on a stock exchange at $170 per share, and a recent balance sheet shows the following information:

Problem 15-4
Computing book values
and dividend allocations

LO 5, 6

Shareholders' Equity	
Preferred shares, 5%, cumulative, 1,000 shares authorized,	
issued, and outstanding	$100,000
Common shares, 4,000 shares authorized, issued,	
and outstanding	160,000
Retained earnings	300,000
Total shareholders' equity	$560,000

Required

Preparation component:

1. What is the market value of the corporation's common shares?

2. How much capital was contributed by the residual owners of the company?

3. If no dividends are in arrears, what are the book values per share of the preferred shares and the common shares?

4. If two years' preferred dividends are in arrears, what are the book values per share of the preferred shares and the common shares?

5. If two years' preferred dividends are in arrears and the preferred shares are callable at $110 per share, what are the book values per share of the preferred shares and the common shares?

6. If two years' preferred dividends are in arrears and the board of directors declares dividends of $20,000 what total amount will be paid to preferred and common shareholders? What is the amount of dividends per share for the common shares?

Analysis component:

7. What are some factors that may contribute to the difference between the book value of common shares and its market value?

Problem 15-5
Calculating book values;
allocating dividends
between preferred and
common shares

 5,6

Part 1. The balance sheet of Desktop Services Corporation includes the following information:

Shareholders' Equity	
Preferred shares, cumulative, 8%, 2,500 shares authorized, issued and outstanding	$250,000
Common shares, unlimited number authorized, 40,000 shares issued and outstanding	400,000
Retained earnings	192,500
Total shareholders' equity	$842,500

Required

Assume that the preferred has a call price of $105 plus any dividends in arrears. Calculate the book value per share of the preferred and common under each of the following assumptions:

a. There are no dividends in arrears on the preferred.

b. One year's dividends are in arrears on the preferred.

c. Three years' dividends are in arrears on the preferred.

Part 2. Since its organization. TVP Corporation had 14,000 outstanding shares of $11 preferred and 235,000 shares of no-par-value common. No dividends have been paid this year, and none were paid during either of the past two years. However, the company has recently prospered, and the board of directors wants to know how much cash would be required to provide a $1.50 per share dividend on the common. Preferred was issued at $100 per share and the common at $10 per share.

Required

Prepare a schedule that shows the amounts of cash required for dividends to each class of shareholders to provide the desired $1.50 per share dividend to the common shareholders under each of the following assumptions:

a. The preferred is noncumulative and nonparticipating.

b. The preferred is cumulative and nonparticipating.

c. The preferred is cumulative and fully participating based on stated value.

d. The preferred is cumulative and participating to 14% based on stated value.

Problem 15-6
Allocating dividends in
sequential years between
preferred and common
shares

 5

Alphalon Cookware Company has 4,0000 outstanding shares of $8 preferred and 56,000 shares of no-par-value common. During a seven-year period, the company paid out the following amounts in dividends:

1993	$ -0-
1994	46,000
1995	-0-
1996	60,000
1997	74,000
1998	68,400
1999	144,000

No dividends were in arrears for the years prior to 1993.

Required

1. Prepare three schedules with column headings as follows:

Year	Calculations	Preferred Dividend per Share	Common Dividend per Share

2. Complete schedules under each of the following assumptions. (Round your answers to the nearest cent.) Preferred was issued at $100 per share and common at $10 per share.

   a. The preferred is noncumulative and nonparticipating.

   b. The preferred is cumulative and nonparticipating.

   c. The preferred is cumulative and fully participating based on percentage of stated value.

Daphne Thomas and Elizabeth White want to go into business as special event promoters. Both can contribute fairly large amounts of capital, but they will need to acquire additional equity capital from other investors in about a year. Thomas has the expertise to run the business, and White will handle the administrative details. They plan to hire about three employees initially and will distribute all profits annually. White wants to operate as a general partnership, but Thomas thinks they should form a corporation. Thomas asks you to write a brief supporting her view in favour of the corporate form. What would you include in your essay to convince White that a corporation would be preferable to a partnership in their situation?

Problem 15-7
Analytical essay
LO 1

Refer to the shareholders' equity section of the balance sheet in Problem 15-5. Assume, however, that an unlimited number of common shares are authorized instead of 40,000. Also, assume that the preferred is convertible into common at a rate of eight common shares for each share of preferred. If 1,000 shares of the preferred are converted into common, describe how this affects the shareholders' equity section of the balance sheet (immediately after the conversion). If you are a common shareholder in this company, and the company plans to pay total cash dividends of $300,000, does it make any difference to you whether or not the conversion takes place before the dividend declaration? Why?

Problem 15-8
Analytical essay
LO 5, 6

Livingston Company, Inc., was incorporated at the beginning of the year and engaged in a number of transactions. Presented below are all the journal entries that affected its shareholders' equity during its first year of operations:

Alternate Problems

Problem 15-1A
Shareholders' equity transactions
LO 2, 3, 6

a.	Cash	60,000	
	Common Shares (1,500 shares)		60,000
b.	Organization Costs	20,000	
	Common Shares (500 shares)		20,000
c.	Cash	6,650	
	Accounts Receivable	4,000	
	Office Equipment	6,000	
	Building	12,500	
	Accounts Payable		2,000
	Notes Payable		7,150
	Common shares (300 shares)		20,000
d.	Cash	30,000	
	Accounts payable	10,000	
	Common shares (700 shares)		40,000

Required

1. Provide explanations for the journal entries.
2. Prepare answers for the following questions:
   a. What is the total contributed capital?
   b. What is the book value per share of the common shares at the end of the year if contributed capital plus retained earnings equals $141,500?

Problem 15-2A
Share subscriptions
LO 2, 3, 4

Conran Corporation is authorized to issue 50,000 shares of $9 cumulative and nonpartici-pating preferred and an unlimited number of no-par-value common shares. Conran Corporation then completed these transactions:

Apr. 4 Accepted subscriptions to 65,000 common shares at $17 per share. Downpayments equal to 25% of the subscription price accompanied each subscription. The bal-ance is due on June 3.

11 Gave the corporation's promoters 1,300 common shares for their services in orga-nizing the corporation. The board valued the services at $26,000.

May 1 Accepted subscriptions to 5,000 preferred shares at $120 per share. The sub-scriptions were accompanied by 40% down payments. The balance is due on July 31.

June 3 Collected the balance due on the April 4 common subscriptions and issued the shares.

July 1 Accepted subscriptions to 2,000 preferred shares at $122 per share. The sub-scriptions were accompanied by 40% down payments. The balance is due on August 15.

31 Collected the balance due on the May 1 preferred subscriptions and issued the shares.

Required

1. Prepare general journal entries to record the transactions.
2. Prepare the shareholders' equity section of the corporation's balance sheet as of the close of business on July 31. Assume that retained earnings are $23,000.

Problem 15-3A
Shareholders' equity transactions
LO 2, 3, 4, 5

Coach Motor Company is authorized by its articles of incorporation to issue an unlimited number of common shares and 50,000 shares of $10, noncumulative and nonparticipating, convertible preferred. The company completed the following transactions:

1997

Feb. 2 Issued for cash 110,000 common shares at $1 per share.

28 Gave the corporation's promoters 65,000 common shares for their services in orga-nizing the corporation. The director's valued the services at $80,000.

Mar. 10 Issued 150,000 common shares in exchange for the following assets with the indi-cated reliable market values: land, $70,000; buildings, $130,000; and machinery, $89,000.

Dec. 31 Closed the Income Summary account. A $61,000 loss was incurred.

1998

Jan. 1 Issued for cash 6,000 preferred shares at $100 per share.

Dec. 1 Coach Motor Company's shareholders submitted 750 shares of their convertible preferred for conversion into common shares on this date. The convertible pre-ferred shareholders accepted 70 common shares for each share of preferred.

31 Closed the Income Summary account. A $196,000 net income was earned.

1999

Jan. 1 The board of directors declared a $10 cash dividend to preferred shares and $0.20 per share cash dividend to outstanding common shares, payable on January 25 to the January 15 shareholders of record.

25 Paid the previously declared dividends.

Nov. 15 Accepted subscriptions to 30,000 common shares at $3.20 per share. Down pay-ments of 25% accompanied the subscription contracts. The balance is due on February 15, 1995.

Dec. 31 Closed the Cash Dividends and Income Summary accounts. A $262,000 net income was earned.

Required

1. Prepare general journal entries to record the transactions.
2. Prepare the shareholders' equity section of the balance sheet as of the close of business on December 31, 1999.

Longhorn Products, Inc.'s common shares are currently selling on a stock exchange at $45 per share, and a recent balance sheet shows the following information:

Problem 15-4A
Computing book values
and dividend allocations
LO 5, 6

Shareholders' Equity	
Preferred shares, Cumulative, 8%, 1,500 shares authorized, issued and outstanding	$ 187,500
Common shares, 18,000 shares authorized, issued, and outstanding	450,000
Retained earnings	562,500
Total shareholders' equity	$1,200,000

Required

Preparation component:

1. What is the market value of the corporation's common shares?
2. If no dividends are in arrears, what are the book values per share of the preferred shares and the common shares?
3. If two years' preferred dividends are in arrears, what are the book values per share of the preferred shares and the common shares?
4. If two years' preferred dividends are in arrears and the preferred shares are callable at $140 per share, what are the book values per share of the preferred shares and the common shares?
5. If two years' preferred dividends are in arrears and the board of directors declares dividends of $50,000 what total amount will be paid to preferred and common shareholders? What is the amount of dividends per share for the common shares?

Analysis component:

1. Discuss why the book value of common shares may not be a good estimate of its market value.

Part 1. The balance sheet of Global Filter Company includes the following information:

Problem 15-5A
Calculating book values:
allocating dividends
between preferred and
common shares
LO 4, 5

Shareholders' Equity	
Share capital:	
Preferred, $11, cumulative and nonparticipating, 2,000 shares authorized and issued	$200,000
Common, no-par value, 60,000 shares authorized and issued	600,000
Retained earnings	120,000
Total shareholder's equity	$920,000

Required

Assume that the preferred shares have a call price of $106 plus any dividends in arrears. Calculate the book value per share of the preferred and common under each of the following assumptions:

a. No dividends are in arrears on the preferred shares.
b. One year's dividends are in arrears on the preferred shares.
c. Three years' dividends are in arrears on the preferred shares.

Part 2. Since its organization, Newhouse Corporation has had 3,200 outstanding shares of $11 preferred and 64,000 shares of no-par-value common. No dividends have been paid this year, and none were paid during either of the past two years. However, the company has recently prospered and the board of directors wants to know how much cash would be required to provide a $1.50 per share dividend on the common. The preferred was issued at $100 per share and the common at $10 per share.

Required

Prepare a schedule that shows the amounts of cash required for dividends to each class of shareholders to provide the desired $1.50 per share dividend under each of the following assumptions:

a. The preferred is noncumulative and nonparticipating.

b. The preferred is cumulative and nonparticipating.

c. The preferred is cumulative and fully participating based on stated value.

d. The preferred is cumulative and participating to 13% of stated value.

Problem 15-6A
Allocating dividends in sequential years between preferred and common shares.

LO 4

Oxford Bros. Company has 2,000 outstanding shares of $12 preferred and 30,000 shares of no-par-value common. During a seven-year period, the company paid out the following amounts in dividends:

1993	$ -0-
1994	54,000
1995	-0-
1996	30,000
1997	39,000
1998	48,000
1999	90,000

No dividends were in arrears for the years prior to 1993.

Required

1. Prepare three schedules with column headings as follows:

Year	Calculations	Preferred Dividend per Share	Common Dividend per Share

2. Complete a schedule under each of the following assumptions. (Round your calculations of dividends per share to the nearest cent.) The preferred was issued at $100 per share and common at $10 per share.

a. The preferred is noncumulative and nonparticipating.

b. The preferred is cumulative and nonparticipating.

c. The preferred is cumulative and fully participating based on a percentage of stated value.

Problem 15-7A
Analytical essay

LO 1

Daphne Thomas and Elizabeth White want to go into business as special-event promoters. Both can contribute fairly large amounts of capital, but they will need to acquire additional cash in about a year. Thomas has the expertise to run the business, and White will handle the administrative details. They plan to hire about three employees initially and will distribute all profits annually. White wants to operate as a partnership, but Thomas thinks they should form a corporation. White asks you to write a brief essay supporting her view in favour of the partnership form. What would you include in your essay to convince Thomas that a partnership might be preferable to a corporation in their situation?

Problem 15-8A
Analytical essay

LO 5, 6

Refer to the shareholders' equity section of the balance sheet in Problem 15-5A. Assume, however, that the common has 100,000 shares authorized instead of 60,000. Also, assume that the preferred shares are convertible into common at a rate of eight common shares for each of preferred. If 1,000 shares of the preferred are converted into common shares, describe how this affects the shareholders' equity section of the balance sheet (immediately after the conversion). If you are a common shareholder in this company, and cash dividends of $487,000 are to be paid out, does it make any difference to you whether or not the conversion takes place? Why?

Until March 2 of the current year, Knox, Lacy, and Mann were partners sharing losses and gains in a 4:4:2 ratio. On that date they received their certificate of incorporation of KLM Company, Limited. All the assets and liabilities of the partnership were taken over by the new corporation.

The trial balance of the partnership just before the transfer and the opening trail balance of the corporation appear below:

KNOX, LACY AND MANN
Post-Closing Trial Balance
March 2, 19XX

Cash	$ 4,500	
Accounts receivable	20,500	
Allowance for doubtful accounts		$ 500
Merchandise inventory	33,000	
Store equipment	13,500	
Accumulated amortization, store equipment		3,500
Land	8,500	
Building	65,000	
Accumulated amortization, building		9,500
Accounts payable		15,500
Mortgage payable		12,000
John Knox, capital		45,000
Robert Lacy, capital		40,000
George Mann, capital		19,000
	$145,000	$145,000

KLM COMPANY, LIMITED
Trial Balance
March 2. 19XX

Cash	$ 4,500	
Accounts receivable	20,500	
Allowance for doubtful accounts		$ 1,500
Merchandise inventory	25,000	
Store equipment	8,000	
Land	22,000	
Building	52,000	
Accounts payable		15,500
Mortgage payable		12,000
Share capital, common, no par value, 10,300 shares		103,000
	$132,000	$132,000

Required

Determine the number of shares of the new corporation owned by each of the three shareholders.

BEYOND THE NUMBERS

Reporting in Action

LO 2, 6

Refer to the financial statements and related information for **Atlantis** in Appendix I. Answer the following questions by analyzing the information in the report:

1. How many classes of shares is Atlantis authorized to issue?
2. Has Atlantis issued any preferred shares?
3. How many voting shares are outstanding as of December. 31, 1997, and what was their composition?
4. What is the book value of the common shares at December 31, 1997? Show calculations.
5. Obtain access to Atlantis' annual report for fiscal years ending after December 31, 1997. You may gain access to annual report information at following website: **http://www. sedar.com/dynamic_pages/issuerprofiles_e/i00002259.htm**. Have there been any issuances of preferred shares yet? Has the number of Atlantis common shares outstanding increased since December 31, 1997?

Comparative Analysis

LO 6

Both **NIKE** and **Reebok** design, produce, market, and sell sports footwear and apparel. Key comparative figures ($ thousands) for these two organizations follow:

Key Figures	NIKE		Reebok	
	1997	1996	1996	1995
Total shareholders' equity	$3,155,838	$2,431,400	$381,234	$895,289
Equity applicable to preferred	$ 300,000	$ 300,000		
Common Shares Issued	Class A&B	Class A&B	92,557	111,015
	289,270	287,258		
Treasury Shares Repurchased			36,716	36,211

* NIKE figures are from the annual reports for the fiscal years ended May 31, 1997 and 1996.
  Reebok figures are from the annual reports for the fiscal years ended December 31, 1996 and 1995.

Required

1. Compute the book value per common share for both Reebok and NIKE using the two years' data shown above.

Analysis component:

2. Identify causes of any changes in book value per share between the two years for each company.

Ethics Challenge

Jack and Bill are partners in a computer software company. They developed a word processing program that is remarkably similar to a **Corel** product. Jack telephones Bill at home one evening and says, "We should convert our partnership into a corporation before we launch this new word processing software. Let's withdraw most of our assets from the business before forming a corporate entity. If we are sued by Corel our liability will be to our business assets." Bill feels a little uneasy and replies, "Lets meet at 9 a.m. sharp to discuss this matter."

Required

Discuss the ethical issues in this case.

Communicating in Practice

LO 6

Investors use book value as a yardstick for investment in varying ways. Warren E. Buffett, one of the world's wealthiest individuals and a highly recognized investment expert, relies heavily on book value for investment decisions. But Buffet uses a slightly different computation for book value. Obtain a copy of the article "Buffet Takes Stock," by L. J. Davis, *The*

New York Times, April 1, 1990. Read the article and write a brief report that includes the following:

1. Traditional definition of the term "book value" and formulas for computation as found in this chapter.

2. Buffet's redefinition of the term "book value" and its formula for computation. Who is the source of this alternative definition and what is the person's relationship to Buffett?

3. Compute book value per share of common shares for a corporation of your choosing using (a) the traditional computation and (b) Buffet's computation. You will need an annual report which can be obtained in many ways including the following site: **http://www.sedar.com/dynamic_pages/new_docs/new.**

4. The market value of your chosen company's common shares on the date of the balance sheet in the annual report. (Research in financial press or online sites.)

5. An explanation of whether or not Buffett would have considered shares in the company you selected as a "sleeping beauty." (Hint: Answer is in article and with a comparison of two numbers.)

This activity in designed to reinforce team members' understanding of dividend allocation concepts.

1. Using the facts below, *each* team member is to determine the dividend allocation on a per share and per class basis for *one* of the assumptions that follow. Determine if this assumption results in arrears for future years. After determinations are complete, rotate around the team allowing each member to present their solution to the team. Do not proceed to the next team member until all team members express agreement with and understanding of the presentation. Be prepared to present to the class if you are called on to do so.

Facts:

Outstanding shares: 50,000 shares of 8% preferred shares (nonparticipating): $5,000,000
                                100,000 common shares: $5,000,000

Assumptions:

a. Preferred shares are noncumulative and a $200,000 dividend is declared.

b. Preferred shares are cumulative, no dividend arrears, and a $600,000 dividend is declared.

c. Preferred shares are cumulative, dividend arrears of $5 per share, and a dividend of $500,000 is declared.

d. Preferred shares are cumulative, two full years of dividend arrears, and a dividend of $1,800,000 is declared.

2. After completing a team discussion of each member's solution for the above assumptions, the team is to collaborate and determine how much of a dividend would need to be declared to ensure that a common shareholder receives $3 per share if the preferred shares are cumulative and have two full years of dividend arrears.

Review the different possible forms of business organization from the chapter. Identify a business in your area that is organized as (a) a sole proprietorship, (b) a general partnership, (c) a limited liability partnership, and (d) a corporation. You may need to confirm your identifications by placing a phone call to the various businesses.

Visit the *Canadian Business Magazine* Web site at **http://www.canbus.com**. Explore the Web site by clicking on the following links.

1. View the Table of Contents of the latest issue of *Canadian Business Magazine*. Scan it and read an article from the issue that interests you.

2. Visit Archives and read an article that interests you.

Teamwork in Action
LO 4

Hitting the Road
LO 1,5

Business Break

16

Corporate Reporting: Dividends, Shares, and Income

▶ **A Look Back**

Chapter 15 focused on the corporate forms of organization. We described important characteristics of corporations along with accounting for many of their important transactions.

▶ **A Look at This Chapter**

This chapter extends our discussion of corporate accounting to dividends, treasury shares, income reporting, and retained earnings. We also explain earnings per share, dividend yield, and the price-earnings ratio.

▶ **A Look Forward**

Chapter 17 focuses on accounting for notes and bonds. This includes the characteristics of these liabilities and their implications to users of financial statements.

Chapter Outline

▶ **Dividends**
- Cash Dividends
- Stock Dividends
- Stock Splits

▶ **Reacquisition of Shares**
- Purchasing Treasury Shares
- Reissuing Treasury Shares

▶ **Reporting Income Information**
- Continuing Operations
- Discontinued Segments
- Extraordinary Items
- Changes in Accounting Principles
- Earnings per Share
- Stock Options

▶ **Retained Earnings**
- Restricted Retained Earnings
- Appropriated Retained Earnings
- Prior Period Adjustments
- Changes in Accounting Estimates
- Statement of Changes in Shareholders' Equity

▶ **Using the Information — Dividend Yield and Price-Earnings Ratio**
- Dividend Yield
- Price-Earnings

Let's Have a Ceilidh

Cape Breton, NS—Cape Breton is the heart of Scottish music. On this fun-loving island is a pub called the Bonnie Piper in the city of Sydney. It is the brainchild of Charlie "Buck" MacPherson, a farm boy from nearby Inverness.

"I always wanted to see Scotland, and so my buddy and I took a $295 charter flight and our mountain bikes to Scotland after we finished our first year in college," says MacPherson. During their tour, they dropped into a pub called "The Bonnie Piper," recalls MacPherson. "While we drank our ale, I kept thinking a pub like this would be a hit back home."

Within two years, MacPherson was running an Scottish-style pub in the hub of Cape Breton. But after three years, with a debt of $78,000, his dream was fading. "The first two years were great, and I was turning a hefty profit," boasted MacPherson. So what happened? "The next year the city took four months putting in a new sewer system on our street. At times, I was the only person in the pub. And then to top it off, we had an electrical fire closing us down for another two months."

To stay afloat, MacPherson needed cash. But who would lend him money after such a disastrous year? "I thought I was finished," says MacPherson. But, never the quitter, MacPherson took the pub's records to the local bank officer. "He really understood the situation and explained things like continuing operations, unusual losses, and extraordinary items."

The bank officer decided poor performance was tied to the sewer work and the electrical fire. The pub's normal operations were highly profitable. "In the end, I got my loan and I'm back turning a nice profit." So the next time you're in Cape Breton, enjoy a touch of Scotland at the Bonnie Piper.

Learning Objectives

LO 1 Record transactions involving cash dividends.

LO 2 Describe stock dividends and stock splits.

LO 3 Account for stock dividends and stock splits.

LO 4 Record purchases and sales of treasury shares and the retirement of shares.

LO 5 Explain the form and content of a corporate income statement.

LO 6 Compute earnings per share and describe its use.

LO 7 Explain the items reported in retained earnings.

LO 8 Compute dividend yield and explain its use in analysis.

LO 9 Compute price-earnings ratio and describe its use in analysis.

CHAPTER PREVIEW

Corporations often enter into financing transactions involving changes in shareholders' equity. The first two major sections of this chapter focus on several of these transactions including cash and stock dividends, stock splits, and a company's transactions in its own shares. The third section of this chapter describes the reporting of income information, with emphasis on the form and content of the income statement including earnings per share. The final section looks at accounting for retained earnings including prior period adjustments, retained earnings restrictions, and reporting guidelines. Understanding these topics helps us read, interpret, and use financial statements for decision making. It also assists people like Charlie MacPherson, as described in the opening article, to properly report income.

Dividends

A corporation's retained earnings is that part of shareholders' equity created by a company's income and loss activities. Retained earnings equals the total cumulative amount of reported net income less net losses and dividends declared since the beginning of operations or the shareholders' residual interest in the corporation not created by their investments. Information about retained earnings is useful in predicting the future cash flows connected with dividends and other events. This section describes how dividends affect retained eanrings and discusses dividend transactions that involve both cash and shares.

Cash Dividends

Generally a corporation is permitted to pay cash dividends if retained earnings exist. To pay a cash dividend a corporation must also have cash *in addition to* retained earnings. The decision to pay cash dividends rests with the board of directors. The directors, for instance, may decide to keep the cash to invest in corporation growth. Or they may feel the cash is needed for unforeseen emergencies, unexpected opportunities, or for paying off debt.

Many corporations, on the other hand, pay cash dividends to their shareholders in regular amounts at regular dates. These cash flows provide a return to investors and almost always affect the stock's market value.

LO1 Record transactions involving cash dividends.

Entries for Cash Dividends

We sometimes assume for simplicity that dividends are declared and paid at the same time. But in practice the payment of dividends involves three important dates: declaration, record, and payment.

Date of declaration is the date on which the directors vote to pay a dividend. Shareholders receive a dividend only if the directors vote to declare one. Declaring a dividend creates a legal liability of the corporation to its shareholders. **Date of record** is the future date specified by directors for shareholders to receive dividends. The date of record usually follows the date of declaration by at least two weeks. Shareholders listed in the corporation's records on the date of record receive dividends. **Date of payment** is the date when shareholders receive payment. This date follows the date of record by enough time to allow the corporation to arrange cheques or other means to pay dividends. If a balance sheet is prepared between the date of declaration and the date of payment, a liability for the dividend is reported as a current liability.

We must record the legal liability created by declaring a dividend. To illustrate, the entry to record a January 9 declaration of a $1 per share dividend by the directors of Z-Tech with 5,000 outstanding common shares is:

Date of Declaration

Jan. 9	Cash Dividends Declared	5,000	
	Common Dividend Payable		5,000
	Declared a $1 per share cash dividend on common shares.		

Assets = Liabilities + Equity
    +5,000   −5,000

Cash Dividends Declared is a temporary (contra equity) account that accumulates information about the total dividends declared during the reporting period. It is *not* an expense account. Common Dividend Payable reflects the corporation's current liability to its shareholders.

The date of record is January 22 and is the date on which identification is made of shareholders who will receive dividends. No journal entry is needed at the date of record:

Date of Record

Jan. 22	No entry required

The date of payment requires an entry to record distribution of the cash dividend. The entry to record both the settlement of the liability and reduction of the cash balance on the date of payment is:

Date of Payment

Feb. 1	Common Dividend Payable	5,000	
	Cash		5,000
	Paid $1 per share cash dividend to common shareholders.		

Assets = Liabilities + Equity
    −5,000   −5,000

At the end of the reporting period, the balance of the Cash Dividends Declared account is closed to Retained Earnings. For instance, if Z-Tech declared four quarterly dividends of $5,000, the account would have a $20,000 balance at the end of the year. The required year-end closing entry is:

Dec. 31	Retained Earnings	20,000	
	Cash Dividends Declared		20,000
	To close Cash Dividends Declared account.		

Assets = Liabilities + Equity
          −20,000
          +20,000

If one of the declared dividends remains unpaid on December 31, this closing entry is still recorded because the act of declaration reduces retained earnings. The Common Dividend Payable liability account continues to carry a balance until dividends are paid. Its balance is reported on the December 31 balance sheet.

Dividend Decline

There has been a major decline in cash dividends as a percent of share prices. Cash dividends are increasingly viewed as an inefficient way to reward shareholders. Dividend tax rates can be very high, and these taxes are inescapable. Companies are instead buying back shares, paying down debt, or expanding the business.

[Source: *"Are Stocks Overpriced—Or the Yardsticks Flawed?" Business Week,* July 15, 1996.]

Did You Know?

Deficits and Cash Dividends

A corporation with a debit (abnormal) balance for retained earnings is said to have a deficit. A **deficit** arises when a company incurs cumulative losses or pays dividends greater than total profits earned in other years. A deficit is deducted on a corporation's balance sheet as shown in Exhibit 16.1.

Exhibit 16.1

Shareholders' Equity
with a Deficit

Common shares, no-par, 5,000 shares authorized and outstanding	$50,000
Retained earnings deficit	(6,000)
Total shareholders' equity	$44,000

In most jurisdictions, a corporation with a deficit is not allowed to pay a cash dividend to its shareholders. This legal restriction is designed to protect creditors of the corporation by preventing distribution of assets to shareholders at a time when the company is in financial difficulty. For example, the Canada Business Corporations Act of 1975 provides the following in section 40:

> A corporation shall not declare or pay a dividend if there are responsible grounds for believing that
> (a) the corporation is, or would after payment, be unable to pay its liabilities as they become due; or
> (b) the realizable value of the corporation's assets would thereby be less than the aggregate of its liabilities and stated capital of all classes.

The size of a company's deficit may differ depending on what GAAP the company is following. For example, the following information was extracted from the annual report of **Microcell Telecommunications Inc.,** a personal communications services operator based in Montreal:

	Dec. 31, 1996	Dec. 31, 1995
Accumulated deficit under Canadian GAAP	$ (7,767)	$ (36,623)
Accumulated deficit under U.S. GAAP	$(124,026)	$(367,479)

Liquidating Cash Dividends

The Cash Dividends Declared account is normally closed to the Retained Earnings account. But sometimes cash dividends are paid as a return of the capital contributed by shareholders. This means the Cash Dividends Declared account is closed with a debit entry to one of the contributed capital accounts instead of Retained Earnings. This kind of dividend is called a **liquidating cash dividend**, or simply *liquidating dividend*, because it returns a part of the original investment to the shareholders.

A liquidating dividend usually occurs when a company is completing a major downsizing, perhaps in preparation for a merger or closing. The equity from the outstanding shares cannot usually be used for a liquidating dividend unless all creditors are paid. This latter situation is typically limited to when a corporation is actually going out of business.

Flashback

1. The Cash Dividends Declared account is normally (a) reported on the balance sheet as a liability, (b) closed to Income Summary, (c) closed to Retained Earnings.
2. What three dates are involved in the process of paying a cash dividend?
3. When does a dividend become a legal obligation of the company?

Answers—p. 758

Stock Dividends

A corporation's directors can declare a stock dividend. A **stock dividend** occurs when a company distributes additional shares of its own stock to its shareholders without receiving any payment in return. Stock dividends and cash dividends are different. A stock dividend does not reduce a corporation's assets and shareholders' equity, while a cash dividend does both. A stock dividend simply transfers a portion of equity from retained earnings to contributed capital.

Reasons for Stock Dividends

If stock dividends do not affect assets or total shareholders' equity, then why declare and distribute them? There are several reasons. First, directors use stock dividends to keep the market price of the stock affordable. For example, if a profitable corporation grows but doesn't pay cash dividends, the price of its common shares continues to increase. The price of such a share may become so high that it discourages some investors from buying the stock. When a corporation declares a stock dividend, it increases the number of outstanding shares and lowers the per share price of its stock. Another reason for declaring a stock dividend is to provide evidence of management's confidence that the company is doing well. Finally, stock dividends conserve cash for business expansion that will hopefully lead to positive returns on shareholder investment.

LO 2 Describe stock dividends and stock splits.

Entries for Stock Dividends

A stock dividend does not affect a corporation's assets or total shareholders' equity, but it does affect the components of shareholders' equity. It does this by transferring part of retained earnings to contributed capital accounts. This is sometimes described as *capitalizing* retained earnings because it increases a company's contributed capital.

Accounting for a stock dividend depends on whether it is a small or large stock dividend. A **small stock dividend** is a distribution of less than or equal to 25% of the previously outstanding shares. It is unlikely to have a large effect on the share's market price and is, therefore, sometimes viewed as similar to a cash dividend. A small stock dividend is recorded by capitalizing retained earnings for an amount equal to the market value of the shares to be distributed.

A **large stock dividend** is a distribution of more than 25% of the previously outstanding shares. A large stock dividend is likely to have a noticeable effect on the stock's market price, and is unlikely viewed as a substitute for a cash dividend. A large stock dividend can be accounted for by a memo entry only. The main purpose of distributing it is to reduce the market price per share. Investors will own more shares but the shares are worth proportionally less.

To illustrate accounting for stock dividends, we use the shareholders' equity section of **X-Quest** shown in Exhibit 16.2 just *before* its declaration of a stock dividend.

X-QUEST Shareholders' Equity December 31, 2000	
Common shares—no-par value, 15,000 shares authorized,	
10,000 shares issued and outstanding	$108,000
Retained earnings	35,000
Total shareholders' equity	$143,000

Exhibit 16.2

Shareholders' Equity before the Stock Dividend

Recording a Stock Dividend

Let's assume the directors of X-Quest declare a 10% stock dividend on December 31, 2000. This stock dividend of 1,000 shares, computed as 10% of its 10,000 outstanding shares, is to be distributed on January 20 to the shareholders of record on January 15. Since the market price of X-Quest's stock on December 31 is $15 per share, the dividend declaration is recorded as:

LO 3 Account for stock dividends and stock splits.

Date of Declaration

Assets = Liabilities + Equity
−15,000
+15,000

Dec. 31	Stock Dividends Declared	15,000	
	Common Shares Dividend Distributable		15,000
	To record declaration of a stock dividend		
	of 1,000 common shares.		

The debit is recorded in the temporary (contra equity) account called Stock Dividends Declared. This account serves the same purpose as the Cash Dividends Declared account. A complete chart of accounts includes separate accounts for cash and stock dividends because the financial statements must report stock and cash dividends as separate events. If stock dividends are not frequently declared, a company might not keep a separate account for Stock Dividends Declared. Instead, it can record the debit directly to Retained Earnings. This approach is acceptable as long as the information is reported correctly in financial statements.

In the stock dividend declaration entry, the $15,000 credit is an increase to a contributed capital account called Common Shares Dividend Distributable. This account balance exists only until the shares are actually issued.

A stock dividend is never a liability on a balance sheet because it will never reduce assets. Instead, any declared but undistributed stock dividend appears on the balance sheet as a part of contributed capital in shareholders' equity. In particular, a balance sheet changes in three ways when declaring a stock dividend. First, the amount of equity attributed to common shares increases from $108,000 to $123,000 because 1,000 additional shares are declared for issuance. Second, retained earnings decreases by $15,000 (from $35,000 to $20,000) reflecting the transfer of amounts to contributed capital.

As part of the year-end closing process, X-Quest closes the Stock Dividends Declared account to Retained Earnings with the entry:

Assets = Liabilities + Equity
−15,000
+15,000

Dec. 31	Retained Earnings	15,000	
	Stock Dividends Declared		15,000
	To close the Stock Dividends		
	Declared account.		

The shareholders' equity of X-Quest is shown in Exhibit 16.3 after the 10% stock dividend is declared on December 31.

Exhibit 16.3

Shareholders' Equity after
Declaring a Stock Dividend

X-QUEST Shareholders' Equity December 31, 2000	
Common shares—no-par value, 15,000 shares authorized,	
10,000 shares issued and outstanding	$108,000
Common shares dividend distributable, 1,000 shares	15,000
Total contributed capital	$123,000
Retained earnings	20,000
Total shareholders' equity	$143,000

No entry is made on the date of record for a stock dividend. On January 20, the date of distribution, X-Quest distributes the new shares to shareholders and records this with the entry:

Date of Payment

Assets = Liabilities + Equity
−15,000
+15,000

Jan. 20	Common Shares Dividend Distributable . . .	15,000	
	Common Shares		15,000
	To record distribution of a 1,000-share		
	common shares dividend.		

The combined effect of these two stock dividend entries is to transfer (or capitalize) $15,000 of retained earnings to contributed capital. The amount of capitalized retained earnings equals the market value of the 1,000 issued shares ($15 × 1,000 shares). This stock dividend has no effect on X-Quest's assets or total shareholders' equity. Nor does it affect the ownership percent of the company by individual shareholders.

To show this, assume we own 200 shares of X-Quest prior to the 10% stock dividend. When X-Quest sends each shareholder one new share for each 10 shares held, we receive 20 new shares (10% × 200 shares). Exhibit 16.4 shows the effects of this 10% stock dividend for both X-Quest and our shares. There is no change in the book value of either X-Quest or our shares. Before the stock dividend, we owned 2% of X-Quest's shares, computed as 200 divided by 10,000 outstanding shares. After the dividend we hold 220 shares, but our holding still equals 2%, computed as 220 divided by 11,000 shares now outstanding. Total book value of our holding does not change and still equals $2,860. Before the stock dividend we owned 200 shares with a book value of $14.30 per share. After this dividend we hold 220 shares with a book value of $13.00 per share. The only change in our 2% investment is that it is now divided among 220 shares instead of 200 shares. Total shareholder's equity does not change. The only effect on shareholders' equity is a transfer of $15,000 from retained earnings to contributed capital.

Before 10% stock dividend	
Shareholders' equity:	
Common shares (10,000 shares)	$108,000
Retained earnings	35,000
Total shareholders' equity	**$143,000**
Book value per share = $143,000/10,000 shares = $14.30	
Book value of 200 shares = $14.30 × 200 = **$2,860**	
After 10% stock dividend is distributed	
Shareholders' equity:	
Common shares (11,000 shares)	$123,000
Retained earnings	20,000
Total shareholders' equity	**$143,000**
Book value per share = $143,000/11,000 shares = $13	
Book value of 220 shares = $13 × 220 = **$2,860**	

Exhibit 16.4

Effects of X-Quest's 10% Stock Dividend

Amount of Retained Earnings Capitalized

The Canada Business Corporations Act requires that if a corporation declares a stock dividend, it must capitalize an amount of retained earnings that equals the market value of the shares to be distributed. On the other hand the Ontario Corporations Act allows the board of directors to determine the amount of retained earnings to be capitalized. Since there is no consistency in corporate laws regarding the amount of retained earnings to be capitalized, corporations must observe the requirements of their jurdiction of incorporation.

Engineer
You are an engineer with some savings invested in shares. One of your share investments announces a 50% stock dividend. Has the value of your share investment increased?

You Make the Call

Answer—p. 757

Stock Splits

We explained that a stock dividend can reduce a stock's market price and make it more marketable to investors. A stock dividend does this by dividing a company's outstanding shares into smaller pieces. The total value of the company is unchanged, but the price of each new share is smaller. We can accomplish the same thing with a **stock split.** A stock split is the distribution of additional shares to shareholders according to their percent ownership. When a stock split occurs, the corporation calls in its outstanding shares and issues more than one new share in exchange for each old share.[1] Splits can be done in any ratio including two-for-one, three-for-one, or higher. It does this by reducing the issued value per share. For example, in May 1998 **Shaw Industries Ltd.** announced a three-for-one stock split of its Class A Subordinate Voting Shares and its Class B Multiple Voting Shares to shareholders of record as of the close of business on June 1, 1998. Final approval of such announcements is subject to shareholder approval.

To illustrate, CompTec has 100,000 no-par value common shares outstanding with a current market value of $88 per share. A two-for-one stock split replaces 100,000 shares with 200,000 common shares. Also, market value is reduced from $88 per share to about $44 per share.

A stock split does not affect shareholders' equity reported on CompTec's balance sheet. It also does not affect individual shareholder's percent ownership of CompTec. The Contributed Capital and Retained Earnings accounts are unchanged by a split, and *no journal entry is made.* The only effect on the accounts is a change in the account description for common shares. CompTec's two-for-one split on its shares means that after the split it changes the description about these shares to reflect the additional outstanding.

The difference between stock splits and large stock dividends is often blurred in practice. Many companies report stock splits in their financial statements without calling in the original shares. The "split" results in additional shares issued to shareholders by capitalizing retained earnings or transferring other contributed capital to Common Shares. This approach avoids administrative costs of splitting the stock. **Harley-Davidson** recently declared a 2-for-1 stock split in the form of a 100% stock dividend by transferring additional paid-in capital to common shares.

A **reverse stock split** is the opposite of a stock split. It increases both the market value per share and the issued value per share. It does this by specifying the ratio to be less than one-to-one such as one-for-two. This means shareholders end up with fewer shares after a reverse stock split.

Flashback

4. Which of the following statements is correct?

   a. A large stock dividend is recorded by capitalizing retained earnings equal to the market value of the distributable shares.

   b. Stock dividends and stock splits have the same effect on the total assets and retained earnings of the issuing corporation.

   c. A stock dividend does not transfer corporate assets to the shareholders but does require retained earnings be capitalized.

5. What distinguishes a large stock dividend from a small stock dividend?

6. What amount of retained earnings is capitalized for a small stock dividend?

Answers—p. 758

---

[1] To reduce administrative cost, most splits are done by issuing new certificates to shareholders for the additional shares they are entitled to receive. The shareholders keep the old certificates.

Under the Canada Business Corporations Act, as well as under the more recently passed provincial acts, such as the one in Ontario, a Corporation may purchase and retire shares of its own outstanding share capital if it can satisfy a solvency test applicable to cash dividends cited earlier in the chapter. Retiring shares reduces the number of issued shares. Purchases and retirements of shares are permissible under the CBCA only if they do not jeopardize the interests of creditors and shareholders. For instance, **Royal Bank** recently reported that "to enhance shareholder value Royal Bank repurchased 4.1 million common shares in the first half of 1997." Corporations acquire their own shares for several reasons. They can repurchase shares to avoid a hostile takeover by an investor. They can buy shares to maintain a strong or stable market. This is often done when a corporation's shares quickly and markedly decline in price. By buying shares, management shows its confidence in the price of its shares.

When shares are purchased for retirement, the stated capital account is debited at the product of the number of shares acquired multiplied by the weighted average per share invested by its shareholders. If the shares are purchased for less than the weighted average per share invested by the shareholderes, the difference is credited to a shareholders' equity account such as Contributed Capital from Retirement of Shares. On the other hand if the shares are purchased at more than the weighted average per share invested by the shareholders, the difference is debited to contributed capital from previous credit balances of share retirement transactions. Any difference remaining is debited to Retained Earnings.

For example, assume a corporation originally issued its no-par common shares at an average price of $12 per share. If the corporation later purchased and retired 1,000 of these shares at the same price for which they were issued, the entry to record the retirement is:

Reacquisition of Shares

May 1	Common Shares	12,000	
	Cash		12,000
	Purchased and retired 1,000 common shares at $12 per share.		

Assets = Liabilities + Equity
−12,000   −12,000

If the corporation paid $11 per share, the entry would be:

May 1	Common Shares	12,000	
	Cash		11,000
	Contributed Capital, from retirement of common shares		1,000
	Purchased and retired 1,000 common shares at $11 per share.		

Assets = Liabilities + Equity
−11,000   −12,000
　　　　　　　　　+1,000

If the corporation had paid $15 per share, the entry for the purchase and retirement is:

May 1	Cash	12,000	
	Retained Earnings	3,000	
	Cash		15,000
	Purchased and retired 1,000 common shares at $15 per share.		

Assets = Liabilities + Equity
+12,000   −3,000
−15,000

In addition to the reasons mentioned earlier as to why a corporation may purchase its own shares in the market there is another reason that applies to certain provincially incorporated corporations. In some provincial jurisdictions a corporation may buy these shares without having to retire them. The corporation can reissue these shares to employees as compensation. These reacquired shares are called **treasury shares.** Treasury shares are similar to unissued shares in several ways.

Neither treasury shares nor unissued shares is an asset. Neither receives cash dividends nor stock dividends. Neither allows the exercise of voting rights.

Treasury shares purchases require management to exercise ethical sensitivity. This is because corporate funds are being paid to specific shareholders instead of all shareholders. As a result, managers must be sure the purchase is in the best interest of all shareholders. These concerns cause most companies to fully disclose treasury shares transactions.

Judgment and Ethics

Director
You are a manager at Intex and a new member of its board of directors. The board is currently planning the agenda for its annual shareholders' meeting. The first item is whether to disclose a government contract Intex just signed. This contract will increase income and cash flows for current and future years. One officer said "the meeting should describe last year's activities, not future plans." After agreeing not to disclose the contract, the board moved to the next topic. It was a motion for shareholders to approve a compensation plan awarding managers options to acquire shares over the next two years. This plan gives managers a two-year option to buy shares at a fixed price equal to the stock price 30 days after the shareholders' meeting. If the share price increases in the next two years, managers can earn considerable money. Can you describe a potential problem here? What action do you take?

Answer—p. 758

LO 4 Record purchases and sales of treasury shares and the retirement of stock.

Purchasing Treasury Shares

Purchasing treasury shares reduces the corporation's assets and shareholders' equity by equal amounts.[2] We illustrate these effects on the balance sheet of **Cyber Corporation.** Exhibit 16.5 shows Cyber's account balances before any treasury shares purchase.

Exhibit 16.5

Balance Sheet before Purchasing Treasury Shares

CYBER CORP. Balance Sheet May 1, 1999			
Assets		**Shareholders' Equity**	
Cash	$ 30,000	Contributed capital:	
Other assets	95,000	Common shares, no-par, authorized and issued 10,000 shares	$100,000
		Retained earnings	25,000
Total assets	$125,000	Total shareholders' equity. . . .	$125,000

On May 1, 1999, Cyber purchased 1,000 of its own shares for $11,500. The entry to record this purchase is:

Assets = Liabilities + Equity
−11,500   −11,500

May 1	Treasury Shares, Common	11,500	
	Cash		11,500
	Purchased 1,000 treasury shares at $11.50 per share.		

This entry reduces its shareholders' equity by debiting the Treasury shares account, which is a *contra* to equity. Exhibit 16.6 shows the effects of this transaction on Cyber's balance sheet.

---
[2] We describe the *cost method* of accounting for treasury shares. It is the method most widely used. The *par value* method is another method explained in advanced courses.

CYBER CORP.			
Balance Sheet			
May 1, 1999			
Assets		**Shareholders' Equity**	
Cash	$ 18,500	Contributed capital:	
Other assets	95,000	Common shares, no-par, authorized and issued 10,000 shares, of which 1,000 are in treasury	$100,000
		Retained earnings, of which $11,500 is restricted by treasury shares purchase.	25,000
		Total	$125,000
		Less cost of treasury shares.	(11,500)
Total assets	$113,500	Total shareholders' equity	$113,500

Exhibit 16.6

Balance Sheet after Purchasing Treasury Shares

The treasury shares purchase reduces Cyber's cash, total assets, and total equity by $11,500. The equity reduction is reflected on the balance sheet by deducting the cost of treasury shares in the equity section. This purchase does not reduce the balance of either the Common Shares account or the Retained Earnings account. But two disclosures in this section describe the effects of the transaction. First, the shares description tells us 1,000 issued shares are in treasury, leaving only 9,000 shares outstanding. Second, the retained earnings description tells us it is partly restricted. We explain retained earnings' restrictions late in this chapter.

> **Buybacks Explode**
> As a consequence of corporations buying back their own shares, share prices often rise because there are now fewer on the market. Higher prices mean higher capital gains to investors. Many investors perfer capital gains to dividends because only 3/4 of the capital gains is taxable.

Reissuing Treasury Shares

Treasury shares can be reissued by selling them at cost, above cost, or below cost. This section explains the accounting for reissuing treasury shares.

Selling Treasury Shares at Cost

If the treasury shares are reissued at cost, the entry is the opposite of the entry made to record the purchase. For instance, if on May 20 Cyber reissues 100 of the treasury shares purchased on May 1 at the same $11.50 per share cost, the entry to record this sale is:

May 21	Cash	1,150	
	Treasury Shares, Common		1,150
	Received $11.50 per share for 100 treasury shares costing $11.50 per share.		

Assets = Liabilities + Equity
+1,150   +1,150

Selling Treasury Shares above Cost

If treasury shares are sold for more than cost, the amount received in excess of cost is credited to an account called Contributed Capital, Treasury shares Transactions. For instance, if Cyber receives $12 cash per share for 400 treasury shares costing $11.50 per share, the entry to record this sale is:

June 3	Cash	4,800	
	Treasury Shares, Common		4,600
	Contributed Capital, Treasury Shares Transactions		200
	Received $12 per share for 400 treasury shares costing $11.50 per share.		

Assets = Liabilities + Equity
+4,800   +4,600
                          +200

The Contributed Capital, Treasury Shares Transactions account is reported as a separate item in the contributed capital section of shareholders' equity. No gain is ever reported from the sale of treasury shares.

Selling Treasury Shares below Cost

When treasury shares are sold below cost, the entry to record the sale depends on whether there is a credit balance in the Contributed Capital, Treasury Shares Transactions account. If there is no balance, the excess of cost over the sales price is debited to Retained Earnings. But if the contributed capital account has a credit balance, the excess of the cost over the sales price is debited for an amount up to the balance in this account. When the credit balance in the contributed capital account is eliminated, any remaining difference between the cost and the selling price is debited to Retained Earnings.

To illustrate, if Cyber sells its remaining 500 treasury shares at $10 per share, the company's equity is reduced by $750 (500 shares × $1.50 per share excess of cost over selling price). This reissuance is recorded with the entry:

Assets = Liabilities + Equity
+5,000   −200
                −550
                +5,750

July 10	Cash	5,000	
	Contributed Capital, Treasury Shares Transactions	200	
	Retained Earnings	550	
	Treasury Shares, Common		5,750
	Received $10 per share for 500 treasury shares costing $11.50 per share.		

This entry eliminates the $200 credit balance in the contributed capital account created on June 3 and then reduces the Retained Earnings balance by the remaining $550 excess of cost over selling price. This means the purchase and reissuance of treasury shares caused Cyber to incur a net $550 decrease in retained earnings and total shareholders' equity. A company never reports a loss from the sale of treasury shares.

Did You Know?

Online Stock Trading
The volume of online stock trading has skyrocketed. **Charles Schwab**, for instance, reported nearly $100 billion in online customer assets in January 1998. It also reported more than a million active online trading accounts, and over a million daily online customer visits to its Web site. The trend in Canada is catching on as well. For example, the **Bank of Montreal's** InvestorLine discount brokerage service trades over 700 mutual funds daily through its Web site that is available at **http://www.bmo.com/investorline**.

Flash back

7. Purchase of treasury shares (a) has no effect on total assets, (b) reduces total assets and total shareholders' equity by equal amounts, or (c) is recorded with a debit to Retained Earnings.

8. Southern Inc. purchases shares of Northern Corp. Should these shares be classified as treasury shares by either company?

9. How do treasury shares affect the number of authorized, issued, and outstanding shares of stock?

Answers—p. 758

The Precision Company began 1999 with the following balances in its shareholders' equity accounts:

Common shares, no-par, 500,000 shares authorized,

200,000 shares issued and outstanding	$3,000,000
Retained earnings...	5,000,000
Total..	$8,000,000

All of the outstanding shares were issued for $15 when the company was created. Prepare journal entries to account for the following transactions during 1999:

Jan. 10   The board declared a $0.10 cash dividend per share to shareholders of record Jan. 28.
Feb. 15   Paid the cash dividend declared on January 10.
Mar. 31   Declared a 20% stock dividend. The market value of the stock was $18 per share.
Apr. 15   Distributed the stock dividend declared on March 31.
June 30   Purchased 30,000 treasury shares at $20 per share.
Aug. 31   Sold 20,000 treasury shares at $26 per share.
Nov. 30   Sold the remaining 10,000 treasury shares at $7 per share.

Mid-Chapter Demonstration Problem

Solution to Mid-Chapter Demonstration Problem

Jan. 10	Cash Dividends Declared	20,000	
	Common Dividend Payable		20,000
	Declared a $0.10 per share cash dividend on common shares.		
Feb. 15	Common Dividend Payable	20,000	
	Cash		20,000
	Paid $0.10 per share cash dividend to common shareholders.		
Mar. 31	Stock Dividends Declared	720,000	
	Common Shares Dividend Distributable		720,000
	Declared a small stock dividend of 20% or 40,000 shares; market value is $18 per share.		
Apr. 15	Common shares Dividend Distributable	720,000	
	Common Shares		720,000
	Distributed 40,000 common shares.		
June 30	Treasury Shares, Common	600,000	
	Cash		600,000
	Purchased 30,000 common shares at $20 per share.		
Aug. 31	Cash	520,000	
	Treasury Shares, Common		400,000
	Contributed Capital, Treasury Shares Transactions		120,000
	Sold 20,000 treasury shares at $26 per share.		
Nov. 30	Cash	70,000	
	Contributed Capital, Treasury Shares Transactions	120,000	
	Retained Earnings	10,000	
	Treasury shares, Common		200,000
	Sold 10,000 treasury shares at $7 per share.		

Reporting Income Information

LO5 Explain the form and content of a corporate income statement.

When a company's revenue and expense transactions are from routine, continuing operations, a single-step income statement is adequate for describing its performance. This format shows revenues followed by a list of operating expenses and then net income. But a company's activities often include many income-related events that are not part of a company's continuing, normal operations. Company's need to provide useful information in a format that helps users understand both current and past events and to predict future performance.

To meet this objective, companies often separate the income statement into different sections. The most important of these sections include: continuing operations, discontinued segments, extraordinary items, changes in accounting principles, and earnings per share. Exhibit 16.7 shows the entire 1999 income statement of **CompCAN.**

Continuing Operations

The first section of an income statement shows the revenues, expenses, and income generated by the company's continuing operations. This portion looks like the single-step income statement we first described in Chapter 6. Users especially rely on information in this section for predicting the results of future operations. This section is often viewed by users as the most important. Prior chapters have explained the nature of the items and measures included in income from continuing operations.

Discontinued Segments

Many companies have several different lines of business and deal with different groups of customers. **IBM Canada**, for instance, not only produces and sells computer hardware and software but also delivers systems design and repair services. Information about the segments of a company are of interest to users. A **segment of a business** is a part of a company's operations that serves a particular line of business or class of customers. A segment has assets, liabilities, and financial results of operations that can be distinguished from other parts of the company. Companies with operations in different segments are required to provide supplemental information about each of their major segments. As examples, **Shaw Communications** reports on the following five segments: cable television, radio, programming, telecommunications, and paging, and **Canadian Tire** reports its operations in three industry segments: Canadian Tire Retail, Financial Services, and Petroleum.

Reporting on Discontinued Segments

When a company incurs a gain or loss from selling or closing down a segment, this gain or loss is reported in a separate section of the income statement.[3] Section 2 of the income statement in Exhibit 16.7 includes this information. The purpose of reporting gains or losses from discontinued operations separately is to more clearly separate the results of discontinued segments from those of continuing operations. Income from operating the discontinued segment prior to its disposal also is reported in section 2. When the income statement includes results of prior years side by side, we must go back and restate prior years' results to separate out the revenues and expenses of the discontinued segment.

Separating Operating Results from Gain or Loss on Disposal

Section 2 of Exhibit 16.7 reports both (1) income from operating the discontinued segment during the year and (2) the loss from disposing of the segment's net assets. The income tax effects of each are also reported. This means the tax effects from the discontinued segment are separate from the reporting of continuing operations in section 1. If this was not so, the information would be less useful.

---

[3] *CICA Handbook*, section 1700.

Exhibit 16.7

Income Statement for a
Corporation

COMPCAN
Income Statement
For Year Ended December 31, 1999

Net sales		$8,440,000
Gain on sale of equipment		38,000
Total revenues		$8,478,000
Expenses:		
Cost of goods sold	$5,950,000	
Amortization expense	35,000	
Other selling, general, and administrative expenses	515,000	
Interest expense	20,000	
Income taxes expense	595,500	
Total expenses		(7,115,500)
Unusual loss on relocating a plant		(45,000)
Infrequent gain on sale of surplus land		72,000
Income from continuing operations		$1,389,500
Discontinued segment:		
Income from operating Division A (net of $180,000 income taxes)	$ 420,000	
Loss on disposal of Division A (net of $66,000 tax benefit)	(154,000)	266,000
Income before extraordinary items and cumulative effect of change in accounting principle		$1,655,500
Extraordinary items:		
Gain on sale of land taken by government (net of $61,200 income taxes)	$ 142,800	
Loss from earthquake damage (net of $270,000 income tax benefit)	(630,000)	(487,200)
Net income		$1,168,300
Earnings per common share (200,000 outstanding shares):		
Income from continuing operations		$ 6.95
Discontinued operations		1.33
Income before extraordinary items		$ 8.28
Extraordinary items		(2.44)
Net income (basic earnings per share)		$ 5.84

Circled markers: ① (first expense/continuing operations section), ② (discontinued segment), ③ (extraordinary items), ④ (earnings per common share).

Extraordinary Items

Section 3 of the income statement in Exhibit 16.7 reports **extraordinary gains
and losses.** The *CICA Handbook* identifies extraordinary gains and losses as items
that have all of the following characteristics: (a) they are not expected to occur frequently over several years, (b) they do not typify the normal business activities of
the entity, and (c) they do not depend primarily on decisions or determinations by
management or owners.[4] Reporting extraordinary items in a separate category helps
users predict future performance, absent the effects of extraordinary items.

Few items qualify as extraordinary items because they must meet both criteria of **unusual** and **infrequent.** For instance, the following items are *not* considered extraordinary:

---

[4] *CICA Handbook*, section 3480.

■ Write-downs of inventories.

■ Write-offs of receivables.

■ Gains or losses from exchanging foreign currencies.

■ Gains and losses from disposing segments.

■ Effects of labour strikes.

■ Accrual adjustments on long-term contracts.

■ Sale of equipment

The list of items usually considered extraordinary include:

■ Expropriation (take away) of property by a foreign government.

■ Condemning of property by a domestic government body.

■ Prohibition against using an asset by a newly enacted law.

■ Losses or gains from an unusual and infrequent calamity ("act of God").

Gains or losses that result from the inherent risks of normal business activities are not extraordinary and are reported in the continuing operations *but* below the normal revenues, expenses, gains, and losses. For instance **Magna International Inc.,** a full systems supplier to the global automotive market, reported gains of $189.6 million on the sale of some of its ownership interests. This item is separated from Magna's "income from operations," but is still part of its $603.4 million 1997 net income from continuing operations. Magna has no extraordinary items.

Section 1 of Exhibit 16.7 includes a "Gain on sale of equipment" that is neither unusual nor infrequent with total revenues. Also note both an unusual loss and an infrequent gain are reported at the *end* of section 1 below the normal revenues, gains, expenses, and losses. Proper classification of items demands examining the facts. Accounting principles require a few special items to be reported as extraordinary gains or losses to highlight their occurrence even when they don't meet the criteria.

You Make the Call

Farmer
You are a farmer with an orchard in Kentville, Nova Scotia. This winter a bad frost wiped out about half your trees. You are currently preparing an income statement for a bank loan. Can you claim the loss of apple trees as extraordinary and separate from continuing operations?

Answer—p. 758

Changes in Accounting Principles

The *consistency principle* requires a company to continue applying the same *accounting principles* once they are chosen. The phrase accounting principles in this context refers to accounting methods such as FIFO, LIFO, and straight-line amortization. But a company can change from one acceptable accounting principle to another as long as the change improves the usefulness of information in its financial statements. A company will also have a change in accounting principles when they adopt new standards issued by the CICA or IASC.

Changes in accounting principles usually affect a company's reported income in more than one way. Let's look at CompCAN's change in accounting principle reported in its income statement of Exhibit 16.7. CompCAN purchased its only amortizable asset early in **1996** for $320,000. This asset has a $40,000 salvage value and is being amortized using the double-declining balance method for the past three years. During **1999,** CompCAN decides its income statement would be more useful if amortization is computed using the straight-line method instead of by double-declining balance.

Exhibit 16.8 compares the results of applying these two amortization methods to the initial three years of this asset's useful life. The accelerated method yielded $185,000 of amortization from **1996** through **1998.** But if the straight-line method had been used from 1996–1998, only $105,000 of amortization would have been reported. To adjust accounts to the balances they would be using the straight-line method, CompCAN needs to decrease accumulated amortization of this asset by $80,000 gross. Also, since CompCAN is subject to a 30% income tax rate, we offset this gross debit with a credit of $24,000 (30% × $80,000) for deferred income taxes to be paid in the future. The $56,000 net is the resulting credit to equity. Because this credit increases equity, CompCAN adds it to 1999's income, the year the change is made.

	Double-Declining Amortization	Straight-Line Amortization	Pre-Tax Difference	After-Tax Cumulative Effect
Prior to change:				
1996	$ 80,000	$ 35,000		
1997	60,000	35,000		
1998	45,000	35,000		
Subtotal	$185,000	$105,000	$80,000	$56,000*
Year of change:				
1999	33,750	35,000**		
After change:				
2000–2003		35,000		

* Reported as an adjustment to the 1999 beginning balance of retained earnings as the cumulative adjustment for differences in the three years prior to the change in 1999, net of $24,000 additional taxes to be paid (30% × $80,000).

** Reported on the 1999 income statement as amortization expense.

Exhibit 16.8

Computing Cumulative Effect of a Change in Accounting Principle

Reporting on Changes in Accounting Principles

CompCAN's income statement in Exhibit 16.7 shows how we report a change in an accounting principle. First, section 1 of the income statement reports $35,000 of amortization using the straight-line method for 1999. This amount is taken from the straight-line method column in Exhibit 16.8. This means income for 1999 is computed using the new accounting principle. Straight-line amortization also will be used in **2000–2003.** The second effect of the change in accounting principle is the $56,000 catch-up adjustment reported as an adjustment to the beginning balance of retained earnings. This item is the cumulative effect of the change in accounting principle.

Two additional points are important. First, a note should describe the change and why it is an improvement over the old principle. Second, the note should describe what 1999's income would have been under the old method if the change had not occurred. For CompCAN, the note states 1999 amortization of $33,750 would be reported using double-declining balance instead of $35,000 under straight-line. This amount is in Exhibit 16.8 under the declining balance column for 1999.

Flash back

10. Which of the following is an extraordinary item? (a) a settlement paid to a customer injured while using a company's product, (b) a loss from damages to a plant caused by a meteorite, or (c) a loss from selling old equipment.

11. Identify the four major sections of the income statement that are potentially reported.

12. A company using FIFO for the past 15 years decides to switch to LIFO. The effect of this event on past years' net income is (a) reported as a prior period adjustment to retained earnings, (b) ignored, as it is a change in an accounting estimate, or (c) reported on the current year's income statement.

Answers—p. 758

Earnings per Share

LO 6 Compute earnings per share and describe its use.

Exhibit 16.9

Basic Earnings per Share Formula

The final section of the income statement in Exhibit 16.7 reports earnings per share results. This information is included on the face of the income statement in accordance with accounting standards. The presentation in Exhibit 16.7 for CompCAN is more complete than the minimum reporting requirements and shows the possible categories companies can and often do report.

Earnings per share is one of the most widely cited items of accounting information. **Earnings per share**, also called *net income per share*, is the amount of income earned by each share of a company's outstanding common shares. Investors find this ratio useful because it reports a company's earnings number in terms of a single common share. This aids investors in their valuation of common shares. This is especially helpful when compared with the stock market price per share discussed later in this chapter. Because of the importance and widespread use of earnings per share numbers, there are guidelines for computing it. The **basic earnings per share** formula is shown in Exhibit 16.9.

$$\text{Basic earnings per share} = \frac{\text{Net income} - \text{Preferred dividends}}{\text{Weighted-average common shares outstanding}}$$

This formula shows us the basic earnings per share computation depends on (1) preferred dividends and (2) weighted-average common shares outstanding. Our explanation begins by considering the simple case where there are no changes in shares outstanding during the period. We then look at what happens when the number of common shares outstanding changes.

No Changes in Common Shares Outstanding

Basic earnings per share is simple if (1) a company has only common shares and nonconvertible preferred shares outstanding and (2) the number of outstanding common shares does not change during the period. In this case, we take the amount of net income available to common shareholders and divide it by the number of common shares. The amount of income available to common shareholders depends on whether the preferred shares are cumulative or not. If preferred shares are *noncumulative*, the income available is the year's net income less any preferred dividends declared in that same year. If preferred shares are cumulative, the income available is the year's net income less the preferred dividends whether declared or not.

To illustrate, assume Quantum Co. earns $40,000 net income in 1999 and declares dividends of $7,500 on its noncumulative preferred shares. Quantum also had 5,000 common shares outstanding throughout 1999. This information allows us to compute Quantum's basic earnings per share as:

$$\text{Basic earnings per share} = \frac{\$40,000 - \$7,500}{5,000 \text{ shares}} = \$6.50$$

Changes in Common Shares Outstanding

This computation is more complex if the number of outstanding shares changes during the year. The number of shares outstanding may change for several reasons such as sales of additional shares, purchases of treasury shares, and stock dividends or splits. We consider each of these in this section.

Share Sales or Purchases in the Period

When a company sells additional shares or purchases treasury shares during the year, the denominator of the basic earnings per share formula is adjusted to equal the weighted-average number of outstanding shares. The idea behind this computation is to measure the average amount of earnings earned to the average number of shares outstanding during the year.

To illustrate, let's assume Quantum again earned $40,000 in year 2000, and it again declared preferred dividends of $7,500. But let's also assume Quantum sells 4,000 additional common shares on July 1, 2000, and purchases 3,000 shares for retirement on November 1, 2000. This means there were 5,000 shares outstanding for the first six months, and 9,000 shares outstanding for July through October (four months), but only 6,000 shares outstanding for the final two months. Exhibit 16.10 shows us how we compute Quantum's weighted-average number of shares outstanding for year 2000.

Time Period	Outstanding Shares	Fraction of Year	Weighted Average
January – June	5,000	6/12	2,500
July – October	9,000	4/12	3,000
November – December	6,000	2/12	1,000
Weighted average outstanding shares			6,500

Exhibit 16.10

Computing Weighted-Average Number of Shares

We can then compute Quantum's basic earnings per share computation using the weighted-average number of common shares outstanding as:

$$\text{Basic earnings per share} = \frac{\$40,000 - \$7,500}{6,500 \text{ shares}} = \$5.00$$

Quantum reports the $5 basic earnings per share number on the face of its December 31, 2000, income statement.

Stock Splits or Dividends in the Period

The number of outstanding shares is also affected by a stock split or stock dividend. These events do not produce additional assets and do not affect the amount of earnings. This means the numerator of basic earnings per share is unaffected. But earnings for the year are now spread out over a larger number of shares. This affects our computation of the weighted-average number of shares outstanding. We handle a stock split or stock dividend by restating the number of shares outstanding during the year to reflect the stock split or dividend *as if it occurred at the beginning of the year.*

To illustrate, let's assume Quantum executed a two-for-one stock split on December 1, 2000. This split causes the percent ownership of each share to be cut in half while doubling the number of shares outstanding prior to December 1. The only change in computing weighted-average shares outstanding is the inclusion of an additional multiplication reflecting the split. This effect of the split is seen with the inclusion of an additional column in Exhibit 16.11. The December outstanding shares already reflect the split and do not require any adjustment.

Time Period	Outstanding Shares	Effect of Split	Fraction of Year	Weighted Average
January – June	5,000	2	6/12	5,000
July – October	9,000	2	4/12	6,000
November	6,000	2	1/12	1,000
December	12,000	1	1/12	1,000
Weighted-average outstanding shares				13,000

Exhibit 16.11

Weighted-Average Number of Post-Split Shares

Our final step is to compute Quantum's basic earnings per share for year 2000 under the assumption of the two-for-one stock split:

$$\text{Basic earnings per share} = \frac{\$40,000 - \$7,500}{13,000 \text{ shares}} = \$2.50$$

We use the same sort of computations when stock dividends occur. For instance, if the two-for-one stock split had been a 10% stock dividend, the numbers of old outstanding shares are multiplied by 1.1 instead of 2.0. This is because 110% (or 1.1) of the original number of shares are now outstanding, computed as 100% +10%.

Did You Know?

Great Expectations

A company's earnings per share is a major factor in determining its share price. Even changes in earnings per share estimates can greatly affect a company's share price. For instance, an analyst recently lowered Citicorp's earnings per share forecast by 5%. Citicorp's shares fell 7 points, to 123, on this news. [Source: "Asian Flu," *Business Week*, January 19, 1998.]

Complex Capital Structure

A company can be classified as having either a simple or complex capital structure. A **simple capital structure** refers to a company with only common shares and non-convertible preferred shares outstanding. A simple capital structure excludes dilutive securities. *Dilutive securities* include options, rights to purchase common shares, and bonds or preferred shares convertible into common shares. These securities have the potential to increase the number of common shares outstanding. A company with a simple capital structure need only report basic earnings per share as described above.

A **complex capital structure** refers to companies with dilutive securities. A company with a complex capital structure must often report two earnings per share figures: basic earnings per share and diluted earnings per share. **Diluted earnings per share** is computed by adding all dilutive securities to the denominator of the basic earnings per share computation shown in Exhibit 16.9. Diluted earnings per share reflects the decrease in basic earnings per share if all dilutive securities were converted into common shares. Fully diluted earnings per share is an assumed figure that reports what earnings per share would have been if the assumed conversions had taken place. The net result may be to reduce earnings per share or to increase earnings per share. If earnings per share after the assumed conversions exceed basic earnings per share they are said to be *anti-dilutive* and need not be reported. **Gulfstream Resources,** for example, in its 1997 annual report noted that the fully diluted earnings per share calculation for the year was anti-dilutive.

To illustrate, we show the prior two years' earnings per share figures in Exhibit 16.12 taken from the income statement of **Polyair,** the maker of high-tech outdoor gear.

For Polyair Pack Inc., basic earnings per share is nearly identical to diluted earnings per share for the second quarters of 1997–1998. This means Polyair has almost no highly dilutive securities. But this is not always the case. **Provigo,** for instance, a leader in the retail and wholesale distribution of food and general merchandise located in Montreal, announced first quarter basic earnings per share of $0.20 per share in early 1998, while its diluted earnings per share was $0.18. This is a dilution of 10%. The effects of dilutive securities on EPS is a complex topic that is given much greater coverage in intermediate accounting courses.

Corporations must report earnings per share figures on the face of their income statements. They also usually report the amount of earnings per share for net income and each of the

Exhibit 16.12

Basic and Diluted Earnings per Share Disclosure

POLYAIR INTER PACK INC.		
	Quarter Ending April 30	
	1998	1997
Earnings per share		
Basic	$ 0.12	$ 0.08
Diluted	$ 0.12	$ 0.07
Weighted-average number of shares outstanding:		
Basic	6,820,000	6,820,000
Fully diluted	7,645,000	7,790,200

three subcategories of income (continuing operations, discontinued segments, and extraordinary items). Exhibit 16.7 shows CompCan's earnings per share in section 4. Since CompCan has a simple capital structure, it reports only basic earnings per share.

Flashback

13. During 1999, FDI reports net income of $250,000 and pays preferred dividends of $70,000. On January 1, 1999, the company had 25,000 outstanding common shares and purchased 5,000 treasury shares on July 1. The 1999 basic earnings per share is (a) $8, (b) $9, or (c) $10.

14. How are stock splits and stock dividends treated in computing the weighted-average number of outstanding common shares?

15. What two earnings per share figures are reported for a company with a complex capital structure?

Answers—p. 758

Stock Options

The vast majority of corporations whose shares are publicly traded offer stock options. A **stock option** is a right to purchase common shares at a fixed price over a specified period of time. As the share's price rises above the fixed price, the value of the option increases. Use of stock options is growing in popularity as a way to pay both managers and employees for performance. **Magna,** for instance, may grant options to purchase Class A Subordinate Voting Shares to full-time employees and **Canadian Tire** has granted stock options to certain employees for the purchase of Class A Non-Voting shares. **Starbucks** and **Home Depot** are leaders in offering stock options to both full and part-time employees. Stock options are said to motivate managers and employees to (1) focus on company performance, (2) take a long-run perspective, and (3) remain with the company. A stock option is like having an investment with no risk (or "a carrot with no stick").

To illustrate, let's say Quantum grants each of its employees the option to purchase 100 of its common shares at its current market price of $50 per share any time within the next 10 years. This means if Quantum's share price exceeds $50 per share, employees can exercise the option at a profit. For instance, if the share price rises to $70 per share, an employee can exercise the option at a gain of $20 per share ($70 share price less $50 option price). With 100 shares, a single employee has a total gain of $2,000, computed as $20 × 100 shares.

When options are granted, the difference between their estimated value and their exercise price is considered compensation expense. This expense is either recorded as compensation expense or is reported in notes to the financial statements. Most companies report this stock option compensation expense in their notes. **Alcan** in its 1996 annual report, for example, reported that 549,000 share options were excerized but not included in compensation expense. According to the notes, if Alcan had elected to recognize compensation for these shares in accordance with the methodlogy prescribed by the U.S. Financial Accounting Standards Board (FASB) net income would have been lower by $8,000,000 or $0.04 per share.

Retained Earnings

Retained earnings are made up of a company's profits and losses retained in the business. Specifically, it is the total cumulative amount of reported net income less any net losses and dividends declared since the company started operating. Retained earnings are part of the shareholders' claim on the company's net assets. Retained earnings do not imply there is a certain amount of cash available to pay shareholders, nor any other asset. This is highlighted in Exhibit 16.13 where we

LO7 Explain the items reported in retained earnings.

list the retained earnings, cash, and total assets from recent financial statements of **Imasco, Magna,** and **Corel.**

Exhibit 16.13

Retained Earnings, Cash, and Asset Balances

Company	Retained Earnings	Cash	Total Assets
Imasco	$ 2,502	$ 15	$ 59,749
Magna	1,302.3	878.8	5,328.7
Corel	(86.9)	6.9	398.5

This section describes important events and transactions affecting retained earnings. It also explains how we report retained earnings.

Restricted Retained Earnings

Most retained earnings are usually available for dividends. But there are sometimes restrictions placed on retained earnings. These include both legal and contractual restrictions. For instance, jurisdictions that permit treasury shares restrict the amount of treasury shares purchased to the amount of retained earnings. This is called a *statutory restriction.* Purchasing treasury shares transfers cash to shareholders and reduces assets and equity. But a treasury shares purchase does not directly reduce the balance of the Retained Earnings account. Instead, the corporation discloses this type of restriction on its retained earnings. The balance sheet in Exhibit 16.6 identifies the amount of **restricted retained earnings** created by treasury shares purchases.

Certain contracts such as loan agreements can also restrict retained earnings. These are called *contractual restrictions* and can include restrictions on paying dividends below a certain amount or percent of retained earnings. Restrictions are often described in a note to financial statements.

Appropriated Retained Earnings

In contrast to statutory or contractual retained earnings restrictions, a corporation's directors can voluntarily limit dividends because of a special need for cash such as the purchase of new facilities. When directors do this, management usually explains in a letter to shareholders or other means why dividends are being limited. They can also disclose this to users by setting up an amount of **appropriated retained earnings.** This appropriation is voluntary. It serves only to notify users of the directors' decision to not pay out cash dividends.

Prior Period Adjustments

Prior period adjustments refer to corrections of material errors in past years' financial statements. These errors may have resulted "from a mistake in computation affecting financial statements, from a misinterpretation or misrepresentation of information, from an oversight of information available at the time the financial statements were prepared that ought to have been taken into account, or from misappropriation of assets."[5] Examples include mistakenly omitting amortization, applying an unacceptable amortization method, and overlooking important facts in predicting an asset's useful life. Prior period adjustments are reported in the statement of retained earnings (or the statement of changes in shareholders' equity), net of any income tax effects. Prior period adjustments result in changing the beginning balance of retained earnings for events occurring prior to the earliest year reported on in the current set of financial statements. They do not affect the current income statement.

To illustrate, let's assume **CompCAN** makes an error in a 1997 journal entry for the purchase of land by incorrectly debiting an expense account. When this is discovered in 1999, the statement of retained earnings includes a prior period adjustment to correct this error as shown in Exhibit 16.14.

COMPCAN Statement of Retained Earnings For Year Ended December 31, 1999	
Retained earnings, December 31, 1998, as previously stated	$4,745,000
Prior period adjustment:	
Cost of land incorrectly expensed (net of $63,000 income taxes) . . .	147,000
Retained earnings, December 31, 1998, as adjusted	$4,892,000
Plus net income	1,162,500
Less cash dividends declared	(240,000)
Retained earnings, December 31, 1999	$5,814,500

Exhibit 16.14

Prior Period Adjustment in Statement of Retained Earnings

IAS 7 permits an alternative treatment of accounting errors. International accounting standards permit the amount of the correction to be included in the current period's results and comparative information presented as previously reported. Canadian GAAP does not allow this alternative treatment.

Changes in Accounting Estimates

Many items reported in financial statements are based on estimates. Future events are certain to reveal that some of these estimates were inaccurate even when based on the best data available at the time. Because these inaccuracies are not the result of mistakes, they are *not* considered accounting errors. This means any corrections due to these estimates are not reported as prior period adjustments. Instead, they are identified as **changes in accounting estimates,** and are accounted for in the current and future periods.

To illustrate, we know amortization is based on estimated useful lives and salvage values. As time passes and new information becomes available, we may need to change these estimates and the amounts reported as amortization expense. These types of changes in accounting estimates are not accounted for with a cumulative catch-up adjustment like a prior period adjustment. Instead, changes in accounting estimates are applied in determining revenues and expenses for the current and future periods. In Chapter 12, we explained one common change in an accounting estimate when we discussed revising amortization rates.

Statement of Changes in Shareholders' Equity

Many companies do not report a separate statement of retained earnings. Instead, they provide a statement of changes in shareholders' equity. A **statement of changes in shareholders' equity** lists the beginning and ending balances of each equity account and describes the changes that occurred during the year. The usual

---

[5] *CICA Handbook*, section 1506, par. 26.

format is to provide a column for each component of equity and use the rows to describe events occurring in the year. Exhibit 16.15 shows a condensed 1996 statement for **Z Company.**

Exhibit 16.15

Statement of Changes in Shareholders' Equity

	Common Shares and Capital			
(In millions)	Number of Shares	Amount	Retained earnings	Total
Balance at December 30, 1996	821	$2,583	$9,557	$12,140
Share sales	17	513	—	513
Share repurchase and retirement	(17)	(269)	(925)	(1,194)
Cash dividends declared	—	—	(156)	(156)
Other, net	—	70	342	412
Net income	—	—	5,157	5,157
Balance at December 28, 1997	821	$2,897	$13,975	$16,872

Z COMPANY — Statement of Changes in Shareholders' Equity — December 28, 1997

USING THE INFORMATION   Dividend Yield and the Price-Earnings Ratio

This section looks at two important ratios in investment analysis of common shares: dividend yield and the price-earnings ratio.

Dividend Yield

LO 8 Compute dividend yield and explain its use in analysis.

Investors buy a company's shares in anticipation of receiving a return from either or both cash dividends and stock price increases. Shares that pay large dividends on a regular basis are often called *income shares*. They are attractive to investors who want dependable cash flows from their investments. In contrast, some shares pay little or no dividends but are still attractive to investors because of their expected share price increases. The shares of companies that do not distribute cash but use their cash to finance expansion are often called *growth shares*.

One way to evaluate whether shares should be viewed as income shares or growth shares is to compute and analyze their dividend yield. **Dividend yield** tells us the annual amount of cash dividends distributed to common shareholders relative to the share's market value (price). More generally, it tells us the amount of cash distributed from a company relative to its total market value. The dividend yield formula in Exhibit 16.16 shows it is a rate of return based on annual cash dividends and the share's market value.

Exhibit 16.16

Dividend Yield Formula

$$\text{Dividend yield} = \frac{\text{Annual cash dividends per share}}{\text{Market value per share}}$$

Dividend yield can be computed for both current and prior periods using data on actual dividends and share prices. It can also be computed for future periods using expected values. Exhibit 16.17 shows recent dividend and share price

Exhibit 16.17

Dividend and Share Price Information

	1997		
	Common Dividend Per Share	Share Price	Dividend Yield
Viceroy Homes	$ 0.15	$ 2.15	7.0%
Nova Scotia Power	0.81	17.40	4.7%
Noranda	1.00	24.60	4.1%
CIBC	1.00	39.65	2.5%

data for **Viceroy Home, Nova Scotia Power, Noranda,** and **CIBC.** Dividend yields are also reported.

For the current low inflationery times these dividend yeilds would be considered high. Shares with high dividend yields can be classified as income shares. These shares' dividend yeilds are less than we might expect from investments in bonds but still high enough to conclude that dividends are a very important factor in assessing share values. While dividend yield is important to individuals in planning their personal cash flows (dividends now or share sales later), it is only one of many factors that we look at in analyzing companies for investment.

Flash back

16. When a corporation purchases treasury shares: (a) Retained Earnings is restricted by the amount paid, (b) it is recorded with a credit to Appropriated Retained Earnings, or (c) it is always retired.

17. Which of the following produces an expected dividend yield of 10% on common shares?
    a. Dividends of $100,000 are expected to be paid next year and expected net income is $1,000,000.
    b. Dividends of $50,000 were paid during the prior year and net income was $500,000.
    c. Dividends of $2 per share are expected to be paid next year and the current market value of the shares is $20 per share.

Answers—p. 758

Price-Earnings

We explained in prior chapters how a share's market value is affected by the stream of dividends expected to be paid out to shareholders. A share's market value is also affected by expected growth in earnings, dividends, and other items. A comparison of a company's earnings per share and its market price per share reveals information about the stock market's expectations for a company's future growth in earnings, dividends, and opportunities.

It is possible to make this comparison as a rate of return by dividing earnings per share by the market price per share. However, the comparison is traditionally done the other way and computed as a **price-earnings (or PE) ratio,** pronounced "*price earnings*" or "*price-to-earnings*" or "*PE*." Some analysts interpret this ratio as what price the market is willing to pay for a company's current earnings. For example, **CIBC,** in January 1997 was selling at 9.7 times earnings but in January 1998 the PE ratio was 11.6. It is interesting to note that during this period the bank's dividend yield decreased from 3.4 to 2.9. Price-earnings ratios differ across companies with the same earnings because of either higher or lower expectations of future earnings for individual companies.

The price-earnings ratio is defined as the market value (price) of a company's share divided by its earnings per share as shown in Exhibit 16.18.

LO 9 Compute price-earnings ratio and describe its use in analysis.

$$\text{Price-earnings} = \frac{\text{Market value per share}}{\text{Earnings per share}}$$

Exhibit 16.18

Price-Earnings Formula

The ratio is often computed using earnings per share reported in the most recent period. But many users compute this ratio using the expected earnings per share for the next period. To illustrate, let's assume a company's current market price is $100 per share and its next year's earnings are expected to be $8 per share. Its price-earnings ratio is 12.5, computed as $100 divided by $8.

Some analysts apply the price-earnings ratio to search for over- or underpriced shares. As a general rule, such analysts view shares with high PE ratios (say greater than 20 to 25) as more likely to be overpriced, while shares with low PE ratios (say less than 5 to 8) are more likely to be underpriced. These investors prefer to sell or avoid buying shares with high PE ratios, while they prefer to buy or hold shares with low PE ratios. The average PE ratio for the 1950–1995 period is about 14. But the PE ratio averages more than 16 when inflation is below 3.5%.

Yet investment decision making is rarely so simple as to rely on a single ratio. For instance, a company with a high PE ratio may prove to be a good investment if its earnings continue to increase beyond current expectations. Similarly, a company with a low PE ratio may prove to be a poor investment if its earnings decline below expectations. As with dividend yield, the price-earnings ratio is important in users' decisions, but it is only one piece of information. This information along with analysis of other accounting and market data must be interpreted as part of a complete analysis and not viewed in isolation.

Flashback

18. Compute the price-earnings ratio when earnings per share is $4.25 and the share price per share is $34.

19. Two companies in the same industry face similar levels of risk, have nearly the same level of earnings, and are expected to continue their historical record of paying $1.50 annual dividends per share. Yet one company has a PE ratio of 6 while the other has a PE ratio of 10. Which company has the more optimistic market expectation for future growth in earnings?

Answers—p. 758

You Make the Call

Teacher
You are a teacher and receive regular payments to a pension fund as part of your compensation. You can't withdraw these funds until age 65, but you can and do choose where to invest them. You plan to invest in one of two companies that you've concluded have identical future prospects. One has a PE of 19 and the other a PE of 25. Which do you invest in? Does it matter if your personal estimate of PE for these two companies is 29?

Answer—p. 757

Summary

LO1 Record transactions involving cash dividends. There are three important events involving cash dividends. The date of declaration is when the board of directors binds the company to pay the dividend. A dividend declaration reduces retained earnings and creates a current liability to the shareholders. The date of record is when recipients of the dividend are identified. No entry is necessary on the date of record. The date of payment is when cash is paid to shareholders of record and the current liability is removed from the books.

LO2 Describe stock dividends and stock splits. Both a stock dividend and a stock split divide a company's outstanding shares into smaller pieces. The total value of the company is unchanged, but the price of each new share is smaller. The additional shares of stock distributed to shareholders is done according to individual shareholders' percent ownership. Stock dividends and stock splits do not transfer any of the corporation's assets to shareholders. Stock dividends and stock splits do not affect assets, total shareholders' equity, or the equity attributed to each shareholder.

LO3 Account for stock dividends and stock splits. Small stock dividends (25%) are recorded by capitalizing retained earnings equal to the market value of the distributed shares. Large stock dividends (25%) are frequently given note disclosure. Stock splits are also not recorded with journal entries but require note disclosure.

LO4 Record purchases and sales of treasury shares and the retirement of shares. When a corporation purchases its own previously issued outstanding shares, the cost of these shares is debited to Treasury Shares. The balance of Treasury Shares is subtracted from total shareholders' equity in the balance sheet. If treasury shares are later reissued, the amount of any proceeds in excess of cost is credited to Contributed Capital, Treasury Shares Transactions. If the proceeds are less than cost, the difference is debited to Contributed Capital, Treasury Shares Transactions to the extent a credit balance exists in that account. Any remaining amount is debited to Retained Earnings. When shares are purchased for retirement, we remove all the contributed capital amounts related to the retired shares.

LO5 Explain the form and content of a corporate income statement. Corporate income statements are similar to those for proprietorships and partnerships except for the inclusion of income taxes. The income statement consists of four potential sections: (1) continuing operations, (2) discontinued segments, (3) extraordinary items, and (4) earnings per share. Many companies need only report income from continuing operations and earnings per share because the other three items are uncommon. The cumulative effect of a change in accounting principles is reported in the statement of retained earnings as an adjustment to the beginning retained earnings balance.

LO6 Compute earnings per share and describe its use. A company with a simple capital structure is one with no outstanding securities convertible into common shares. These companies compute basic earnings per share by dividing net income less any preferred dividends by the weighted-average number of outstanding common shares. A company with a complex capital structure has outstanding securities convertible into common shares. This company must often report both basis earnings per share and diluted earnings per share.

LO7 Explain the items reported in retained earnings. Legal jurisdictions limit dividends and reacquisition of shares purchases to the amount of retained earnings. Companies also enter into contracts that may limit the amount of dividends, even though the companies have both the cash and the retained earnings to pay them. Corporations may voluntarily appropriate retained earnings to inform shareholders why dividends are not larger. Prior period adjustments are corrections of material errors in past years' financial statements. They result in adjustments to retained earnings.

LO8 Compute dividend yield and explain its use in analysis. Dividend yield is the ratio of a share's annual cash dividends per share divided by its market value (price) per share. It gives the rate of return to shareholders from the company's cash dividends. Dividend yield can be compared with those of other companies and kinds of investments to determine whether the shares are income or growth shares.

LO9 Compute price-earnings ratio and describe its use in analysis. The price-earnings ratio of a common share is computed by dividing the share's market value (price) per share by its earnings per share. Some analysts view a high ratio as suggesting the shares are overvalued while a low ratio suggests the shares are undervalued. But a stock's market value is based on expectations that may prove to be better or worse than later performance. While the price-earnings ratio is important to many users of financial statements, it is must be applied as part of a complete analysis and not viewed in isolation.

Guidance Answers to You Make the Call

Engineer

The 50% stock dividend provides no direct income to you. But a stock dividend often reveals management's optimistic expectations about the future. It also can improve a share's marketability by making it affordable to more investors. Accordingly, a stock dividend is usually good news.

Farmer

The frost loss is probably not extraordinary. Nova Scotia experiences enough frost damage that it would be difficult to argue this event is both unusual and infrequent. Nevertheless, you would want to highlight the frost loss, and hope the bank would view this uncommon event separately from your continuing operations.

Teacher

If you've decided to invest in one of two investments, and your analysis suggests they have identical future prospects, then you should pick the better deal. Since one requires a payment of $19 for each $1 of earnings, while the other requires $25, then you would purchase the shares with the PE of 19 since it is a better deal. You would also make sure these companies earnings computations are roughly the same—for example, no extraordinary items, unusual events, and so forth. Also, it does matter what your estimate of PE is for these companies.

If you are willing to pay $29 for each $1 of earnings for these companies, then both are solid investments because you obviously expect both to exceed current market expectations.

Guidance Answers to **Judgment and Ethics**

Director

This case deals with insider trading in a company's shares. The ethical conflict is between your responsibility to Intex's shareholders (and the public) and your own interest in increasing your personal wealth with the options. If information about the new contract is kept private until after the option plan is approved and the options are priced, then you are likely to

make a lot of money. (Note, insider trading laws may make nondisclosure in this case a crime.) You should try to explain the ethical and legal concerns to the board. You might also consider whether staying on the board and working for this company is appropriate since it appears there was some intent to deceive outsiders even if not eventually implemented.

Guidance Answers to Flash backs

1. *c*
2. The three dates are the date of declaration, the date of record, and the date of payment.
3. A dividend is a legal liability at the date of declaration. It is also recorded on the date of declaration.
4. *c*
5. A small stock dividend is 25% or less of the previous outstanding shares. A large stock dividend is greater than 25%.
6. Retained earnings equal to the market value of the distributable shares should be capitalized.
7. *b*
8. No. The shares are an investment for Southern Co. and issued outstanding shares for Northern Corp.
9. Treasury shares do not affect the number of both authorized and issued shares. Treasury shares reduces the amount of outstanding shares.
10. *b*

11. The four major sections are income from continuing operations, discontinued segments, extraordinary items, and earnings per share.
12. *a*
13. *a* Weighted-average shares: $(25,000 \times 6/12) + (20,000 \times 6/12) = 22,500$
   Earnings per share: $(\$250,000 - \$70,000)/22,500 = \$8$
14. The number of shares previously outstanding are retroactively restated to reflect the stock split or stock dividend as if it occurred at the beginning of the year.
15. The two types are basic earnings per share and diluted earnings per share.
16. *a*
17. *c*
18. $\$34/\$4.25 = \$8$
19. The company with the higher PE ratio of 10.

Demonstration Problem

Refer back to the Mid-Chapter Demonstration Problem on page 743 and calculate the weighted average number of shares outstanding. Use the following information to prepare an income statement for 1999, including earnings per share results for each category of income.

Cumulative effect of a change in amortization method (net of tax benefit)	$ (136,500)
Expenses related to continuing operations	(2,072,500)
Extraordinary gain on expropriated land (net of tax)	182,000
Gain on disposal of discontinued segment's assets (net of tax)	29,000
Gain on sale of investment in shares	400,000
Loss from operating discontinued segment (net of tax benefit)	(120,000)
Income taxes on income from continuing operations	(225,000)
Prior period adjustment for error (net of tax benefit)	(75,000)
Sales	4,140,000
Infrequent loss	(650,000)

Planning the Solution

- Calculate the total cash dividend to be recorded by multiplying the cash dividend declared by the number of shareholders as of the date of record.
- Decide whether the stock dividend is a small or large dividend. Then, analyze each event to determine the accounts affected and the appropriate amounts to be recorded.
- Based on the shares of outstanding stock at the beginning of the year and the transactions during the year, compute the weighted-average number of outstanding shares for the year.
- Assign each of the listed items to an appropriate income statement category.
- Prepare an income statement similar to Exhibit 16.7, including appropriate earnings per share results.

Solution to Demonstration Problem

Computing the weighted-average of outstanding shares:

Time Period	Original Shares	Effect of Dividend	Post-Dividend Shares
January – April 15	200,000	1.2	240,000

Time Period	Post-Dividend Shares	Fraction of Year	Weighted Average
January – June	240,000	6/12	120,000
July – August	210,000	2/12	35,000
September – November	230,000	3/12	57,500
December	240,000	1/12	20,000
Weighted-average outstanding shares			232,500

THE PRECISION COMPANY Income Statement For Year Ended December 31, 1999		
Sales		$4,140,000
Expenses		(2,072,500)
Income taxes		(225,000)
Gain on sale of investment in shares		400,000
Infrequent loss		(650,000)
Income from continuing operations		$1,592,500
Discontinued operations:		
Loss from operating discontinued segment (net of tax benefit)	$(120,000)	
Gain on disposal of discontinued segment's assets (net of tax)	29,000	
Loss from discontinued segment		(91,000)
Income before extraordinary items and cumulative effect of a change in accounting principle		$1,501,500
Extraordinary items:		
Extraordinary gain on expropriated land (net of tax)		182,000
Net income		$1,683,500
Earnings per share (232,500 average shares outstanding):		
Income from continuing operations		$ 6.85
Loss from discontinued segment		(0.39)
Income before extraordinary gain		$ 6.46
Extraordinary gain		0.78
Net income		$ 7.24

Glossary

Appropriated retained earnings Retained earnings that are voluntarily restricted as a way of informing shareholders that dividends will be limited or not paid. (p. 752)

Basic earnings per share Calculated with the formula: (Net income − Preferred dividends)/Weighted-Average Common Shares Outstanding. (p. 748)

Changes in accounting estimates Corrections to previous estimates or predictions about future events and outcomes, such as salvage values and the useful lives of operating assets; the changes are accounted for in the current and future periods. (p. 753)

Complex capital structure A capital structure that includes outstanding rights or options to purchase common shares or securities that are convertible into common shares. (p. 750)

Date of declaration The date the directors vote to pay for a dividend. (p. 732)

Date of payment The date when shareholders receive the dividend payment. (p. 732)

Date of record The future date specified by the directors for identifying those shareholders listed in the corporation's records to receive dividends. (p. 732)

Deficit Arises when a corporation has a debit (abnormal) balance for retained earnings. (p. 733)

Diluted earnings per share An earnings per share calculation that requires that the effect of dilutive securities be added to the denominator of the basic earnings per share calculation. (p. 750)

Dividend yield A ratio that informs shareholders of the annual amount of cash dividends distributed to common shareholders relative to the share's market value (price). (p. 754)

Earnings per share The amount of income earned by each share of a company's outstanding common shares; also called net income per share. (p. 748)

Extraordinary gain or loss A gain or loss that is reported separate from continuing operations because it is not expected to occur frequently over several years, does not typify the normal business activities of the entity and does not depend primarily on decisions or determinations by management or owners. (p. 745)

Infrequent gain or loss A gain or loss that is not expected to occur again, given the operating environment of the business. (p. 745)

Large stock dividend A stock dividend that is more than 25% of the corporation's previously outstanding shares. (p. 735)

Liquidating cash dividend A distribution of corporate assets as a dividend that returns part of the original investment to the shareholders; these distributions are charged to contributed capital accounts. (p. 734)

Price-earnings ratio The ratio between a company's current market value per share and its earnings per share; used to gain understanding of the market's expectations for the stock. (p. 755)

Prior period adjustment A correction of a material error in a previous year that is reported in the statement of retained earnings (or statement of changes in shareholders' equity) net of any income tax effects. (p. 753)

Restricted retained earnings Retained earnings that are not available for dividends because of legal or contractual limitations. (p. 752)

Reverse stock split An act by a corporation to call in its stock and replace each share with less than one new share; reverse splits are opposite of stock splits as they increase both the market value per share and the issued value per share. (p. 738)

Segment of a business A component of a company's operations that serves a particular line of business or class of customers and that has assets, activities, and financial results of operations that can be distinguished from other parts of the business. (p. 744)

Simple capital structure A capital structure that consists of only common shares and nonconvertible preferred shares; it cannot include any options or rights to purchase common shares or any convertible preferred shares or bonds (dilutive securities). (p. 750)

Small stock dividend A stock dividend that is 25% or less of the corporation's previously outstanding shares. (p. 735)

Statement of changes in shareholders' equity A financial statement that lists the beginning and ending balances of each equity account and describes all the changes that occurred during the year. (p. 754)

Stock dividend A corporation's distribution of its own shares to its shareholders without receiving any payment in return. (p. 734)

Stock option A right to purchase common shares at a fixed price over a specified period of time. (p. 751)

Stock split An act by a corporation to call in its shares and replace each share with more than one new share; a stock split will decrease the market value per share and also the book per share. (p. 738)

Treasury shares Shares that were reacquired and are still held by the issuing corporation. (p. 739)

Unusual gain or loss A gain or loss that is abnormal or otherwise unrelated to the ordinary activities and environment of the business. (p. 745)

Questions

1. Identify and explain the importance of the three dates relevant to corporate dividends.

2. Why is the term *liquidating* dividend used to describe cash dividends that are debited against contributed capital accounts?

3. What effects does declaring a stock dividend have on the corporation's assets, liabilities, and total shareholders' equity? What effects does the distribution of the shares have?

4. What is the difference between a stock dividend and a stock split?

5. Courts in some countries have determined that a stock dividend is not taxable income to shareholders. What concept justifies this decision?

6. How does the purchase of treasury shares affect the purchaser's assets and total shareholders' equity?

7. Why do legal jurisdictions place limits on purchases of treasury shares?

8. Where on the income statement would a company report an abnormal gain that is not expected to occur more often than once every two years?

9. After taking five years' straight-line amortization expense for an asset that was expected to have an eight-year useful life, a company decided that the asset would last another six years. Is this decision a change in accounting principle? How would the financial statements describe this change?

10. How are earnings per share results computed for a corporation with a simple capital structure?

11. Refer to the financial statements for **Atlantis** in Appendix I at the end of the book. What is the balance of retained earnings as of December 31, 1997? What amount was paid out in dividends during 1997?

12. Refer to the financial statements for **Alliance** in Appendix I. How many voting shares were outstanding at the end of 1997?

13. Refer to the chapter's opening scenario. If you were helping MacPherson prepare documents to apply for a loan would you recommend a format such as Exhibit 16.7 in the chapter? Explain.

Prepare journal entries to record the following transactions for Desmond Corporation:

Apr. 15	Declared a $48,000 cash dividend payable to common shareholders.
June 30	Paid the dividend declared on April 15.
Dec. 31	Closed the Cash Dividends Declared account.

Quick Study

QS 16-1
Accounting for cash dividends

LO 1

The shareholders' equity section of Jamestown Co.'s balance sheet as of April 1 follows:

Common shares, no-par value, 375,000 shares authorized, 150,000 shares issued and outstanding	$1,102,500
Retained earnings	633,000
Total shareholders' equity	$1,735,500

On April 1, Jamestown declares and distributes a 10% stock dividend. The market value of the shares on this date is $25. Prepare the shareholders' equity section for Jamestown immediately following the stock dividend.

QS 16-2
Accounting for a small stock dividend

LO 3

On May 3, Nicholson Corp. purchased 3,000 of its own shares for $27,000. On November 4, Nicholson reissued 750 treasury shares for $7,080. Prepare the November 4 journal entry Nicholson should make to record the sale of the treasury shares.

QS 16-3
Purchase and sale of treasury shares

LO 4

Answer the questions about each of the following items related to a company's activities for the year:

a. After using an expected useful life of seven years and no salvage value to amortize its office equipment over the preceding three years, the company decided early this year that the equipment will last only two more years. How should the effects of this decision be reported in the current financial statements?

b. In reviewing the notes payable files, it was discovered that last year the company reported the entire amount of a payment on an installment note payable as interest expense. The mistake had a material effect on the amount of income in the prior year. How should the correction be reported in the current year financial statements?

QS 16-4
Accounting for estimate changes and error adjustments

LO 5,7

QS 16-5
Basic earnings per share
LO 6

The Nelson company earned a net income of $450,000. The number of common shares outstanding all year long was 200,000 and preferred shareholders received dividends totalling $10,000. Compute Nelson Company's basic earnings per share.

QS 16-6
Weighted-average shares outstanding
LO 6

On January 1, Harmon Company had 100,000 common shares outstanding. On February 1, Harmon company issued 20,000 additional common shares. On June 1, another 40,000 common shares were issued. Compute Harmon Company's weighted-average shares outstanding.

QS 16-7
Weighted-average common shares outstanding
LO 6,3

On January 1, Harrell Company had 150,000 common shares issued and outstanding. On April 1, it purchased 12,000 treasury shares and on June 2, declared a 20% stock dividend. Compute Harrell's weighted-average outstanding shares for the year.

QS 16-8
Dividend yield
LO 8

Cornerstone Company expects to pay out a $2.10 per share cash dividend next year on its common shares. The current market price per share is $28.50. Compute the expected dividend yield on the Cornerstone shares. Would you classify the Cornerstone shares as growth shares or income shares?

QS 16-9
Price-earnings ratio
LO 9

Compute a company's price-earnings ratio if its common shares have a market value of $30.75 per share and if its earnings per share are $4.10. Would an analyst viewing this stock consider that it might be over- or underpriced?

Exercises

Exercise 16-1
Stock dividends and per share values
LO 3

The shareholders' equity of Brinkman Motors, Inc., on February 5 consisted of the following:

Common shares, no-par value, 150,000 shares authorized, 60,000 shares issued and outstanding	$2,025,000
Retained earnings	675,000
Total shareholders' equity	$2,700,000

On February 5, the stock's market value was $40. On that date, the directors declared a 20% stock dividend distributable on February 28 to the February 15 shareholders of record. The stock's market value was $37 on March 2.

Required

1. Prepare entries to record the dividend declaration and distribution.
2. One shareholder owned 750 shares on February 5. Compute the per share and total book values of the investor's shares immediately before and after the dividend on February 5.
3. Compute the total market values of the investor's shares as of February 5 and March 2.

Exercise 16-2
Stock dividends and splits
LO 3

On June 30, 1999, Woodward Corporation's common shares were selling for $31 per share and the following information appeared in the shareholders' equity section of its balance sheet as of that date:

Common shares, no-par value, 60,000 shares authorized, 25,000 shares issued and outstanding	$350,000
Retained earnings	330,000
Total shareholders' equity	$680,000

Required

1. Assume that the company declares and immediately distributes a 100% stock dividend. The event is recorded by capitalizing the required minimum amount of retained earnings. Answer these questions about the shareholders' equity as it exists after issuing the new shares:
   a. What is the retained earnings balance?
   b. What is the total amount of shareholders' equity?
   c. How many shares are outstanding?
2. Assume that the company implements a two-for-one stock split instead of the stock dividend. Answer these questions about the shareholders' equity as it exists after issuing the new shares:
   a. What is the retained earnings balance?
   b. What is the total amount of shareholders' equity?
   c. How many shares are outstanding?
3. Briefly explain the difference, if any, that an investor would experience if new shares are distributed under a large dividend or a stock split.

On October 10, the shareholders' equity section of the balance sheet for Valley Systems, Inc., included this information:

Common shares, no-par value, unlimited number of shares authorized, 36,000 shares issued, and outstanding	$468,000
Retained earnings	432,000
Total shareholders' equity	$900,000

On the next day, the corporation purchased and retired 4,500 common shares at $30 per share. Explain how the equity section of Valley Systems will change after the purchase.

Exercise 16-3
Reporting a purchase and retirement of common shares.
LO 4

On October 10, the shareholders' equity section of the balance sheet for Affiliated Systems, Inc., included this information:

Common shares, no-par value, unlimited number of shares authorized, 36,000 shares issued, and outstanding	$468,000
Retained earnings	432,000
Total shareholders' equity	$900,000

On the next day, the corporation purchased and retired 4,500 common shares at $30 per share. Explain how the equity section of Affliated Systems will change after the purchase.

Exercise 16-4
Reporting a treasury shares purchase
LO 4

Use the information in Exercise 16-4 to develop the accountant's journal entries to record these events for Affiliated Systems, Inc.:
1. The purchase of the treasury shares on October 11.
2. The sale of 1,200 treasury shares on November 1 for cash at $36 per share.
3. The sale of all the remaining treasury shares on November 25 for cash at $25 per share.

Exercise 16-5
Journal entries for treasury shares transactions
LO 4

During 1999, Burks Merchandise, Inc. sold its interest in a chain of wholesale outlets. This sale took the company out of the wholesaling business completely. The company still operates its retail outlets. Following is a lettered list of sections of an income statement:
A. Income from continuing operations
B. Income from operating a discontinued segment
C. Gain or loss from disposing of a discontinued segment
D. Extraordinary gain or loss

Exercise 16-6
Income statement categories
LO 5

Indicate where each of the nine income-related items for the company would appear on the 1999 income statement by writing the letter of the appropriate section in the blank beside each item.

		Debit	Credit
____	1. Amortization expense	$ 262,500	
____	2. Gain on sale of wholesale segment (net of tax)		$ 675,000
____	3. Loss from operating wholesale segment (net of tax)	555,000	
____	4. Salaries expense	540,000	
____	5. Sales		2,700,000
____	6. Gain on condemnation of company property (net of tax)		330,000
____	7. Cost of goods sold	1,380,000	
____	8. Income taxes expense	207,000	

Exercise 16-7
Income statement presentation

LO 5

Use the data for Burks Merchandise, Inc., in Exercise 16-6 to present the income statement for 1999.

Exercise 16-8
Accounting for a change in accounting principle

LO 7

Canadian Home Company put an asset in service on January 1, 1999. Its cost was $225,000, its predicted service life was six years, and its expected salvage value was $22,500. The company decided to use double-declining-balance amortization and recorded these amounts of amortization expense in the first two years of the asset's life:

| 1999 . . . .$75,000 |
| 2000 . . . . 50,000 |

The scheduled amortization expense for 2001 was $33,333. After consulting with the company's auditors, management decided to change to straight-line amortization in 2001, without changing either the predicted service life or salvage value. Under this system, the annual amortization expense for all years in the asset's life would be $33,750. The company faces a 35% income tax rate.

1. Prepare a table like Exhibit 16.8 that deals with this situation.
2. How much amortization expense will be reported on the company's income statement for this asset in 2001 and in each of the remaining years of the asset's life?
3. What amount will be reported on the company's 2001 income statement as the after-tax cumulative effect of the change?

Exercise 16-9
Weighted-average shares outstanding and earnings per share

LO 6

A company reported $1,350,000 of net income for 1999. It also declared $195,000 of dividends on preferred shares for the same year. At the beginning of 1999, the company had 270,000 outstanding common shares. These two events changed the number of outstanding shares during the year:

Apr. 30   Sold 180,000 common shares for cash.
Oct. 31   Purchased 108,000 common shares for the treasury.

a. What is the amount of net income available to the common shareholders?
b. What is the weighted-average number of common shares for the year?
c. What is the basic earnings per share for the year?

Exercise 16-10
Weighted-average shares outstanding and earnings per share

LO 6

A company reported $480,000 of net income for 1999. It also declared $65,000 of dividends on preferred shares for the same year. At the beginning of 1999, the company had 50,000 outstanding common shares. These three events changed the number of outstanding shares during the year:

June   1   Sold 30,000 common shares for cash.
Aug. 31   Purchased and retired 13,000 common shares.
Oct.   1   Completed a three-for-one stock split.

a. What is the amount of net income available to the common shareholders?
b. What is the weighted-average number of common shares for the year?
c. What is the basic earnings per share for the year?

_____

Compute the dividend yield for each of these situations:

Exercise 16-11
Computing dividend yield

LO 8

	Annual Dividend per Share	Share's Market Price per Share
a.	$15.00	$216.00
b.	12.00	128.00
c.	6.00	61.00
d.	1.20	86.00
e.	11.00	130.00
f.	2.00	50.00

Which shares above would probably not be classified as income shares?

_____

Use the following information to compute the price-earnings ratio for each case:

Exercise 16-12
Computing the price-earnings ratio

LO 9

	Earnings per Share	Market Value per Share
a.	$10.00	$166.00
b.	9.00	86.00
c.	6.50	90.00
d.	1.50	36.00
e.	36.00	240.00

Which of the above stocks might an analyst investigate as being undervalued by the market?

The balance sheet for the Trevor Corporation reported the following components of shareholders' equity on December 31, 1999:

Problems

Problem 16-1
Cash dividends and retirement of shares transactions

LO 1,4

Common shares, no-par value, unlimited shares authorized, 20,000 shares issued and outstanding	$230,000
Retained earnings	135,000
Total shareholders' equity	$365,000

In 2000 Trevor Company had the following transactions affecting shareholders and the shareholder equity accounts:

Jan.   1   Purchased and retired 2,000 common shares at $20 per share.
Jan.   5   The directors declared a $2.00 per share cash dividend payable on Feb. 28 to the Feb. 5 shareholders of record.
Feb. 28   Paid the dividend declared on January 5.
July   6   Sold 750 common shares at $24 per share.
Aug. 22   Sold 1,250 common shares at $17 per share.
Sept. 5   The directors declared a $2.00 per share cash dividend payable on Oct. 28 to the Oct. 5 shareholders of record.

Oct. 28   Paid the dividend declared on September 5.
Dec. 31   Closed the $194,000 credit balance in the Income Summary account to Retained Earnings.
      31   Closed the Cash Dividends Declared account.

1. Prepare journal entries to record the transactions and closings for 2000.

2. Prepare a statement of retained earnings for the year-ended December 31, 2000.

3. Prepare the shareholders' equity section of the company's balance sheet as of December 31, 2000.

Check Figure

Retained earnings,
Dec. 31, 2000, $236,000

Problem 16-2
Cash dividends and
retirement of shares
transactions

LO 1, 4

The balance sheet for the Oppong Corporation, a provincially incorporated corporation, reported the following components of shareholders' equity on December 31, 1999:

Common shares, no-par value, unlimited shares authorized, 20,000 shares issued and outstanding	$230,000
Retained earnings	135,000
Total shareholders' equity	$365,000

In 2000 Oppong Company had the following transactions affecting shareholders and the shareholder equity accounts:

Jan.   1   Purchased 2,000 treasury shares at $20 per share.
Jan.   5   The directors declared a $2.00 per share cash dividend payable on Feb. 28 to the Feb. 5 shareholders of record.
Feb. 28   Paid the dividend declared on January 5.
July   6   Sold 750 of the treasury shares at $24 per share.
Aug. 22   Sold 1,250 of the treasury shares at $17 per share.
Sept. 5   The directors declared a $2.00 per share cash dividend payable on Oct. 28 to the Oct.. 5 shareholders of record.
Oct. 28   Paid the dividend declared on September 5.
Dec. 31   Closed the $194,000 credit balance in the Income Summary account to Retained Earnings.
      31   Closed the Cash Dividends Declared account.

1. Prepare journal entries to record the transactions and closings for 2000.

2. Prepare a statement of retained earnings for the year ended December 31, 2000.

3. Prepare the shareholders' equity section of the company's balance sheet as of December 31, 2000.

Check Figure

Retained earnings,
Dec. 31, 2000, $252,250

Problem 16-3
Describing equity changes
with journal entries and
account balances

LO 1, 3

At September 30, the end of the third quarter for Granger Co., Inc., these balances existed in its shareholders' equity accounts:

Common shares, unlimited authorized, 60,000 issued	$900,000
Retained earnings	640,000

Over the next three months, the following journal entries were recorded in the company's equity accounts:

Oct. 2	Cash Dividends Declared	120,000	
	Common Dividend Payable		120,000
25	Common Dividend Payable	120,000	
	Cash		120,000
31	Stock Dividends Declared (6,000 shares) . . .	150,000	
	Common Shares Dividend Distributable		150,000
Nov. 5	Common Shares Dividend Distributable . . .	150,000	
	Common Shares		150,000

Dec. 1	Memo—change the title of the common shares account to reflect the new number of shares outstanding of 198,000.		
31	Income Summary	420,000	
	Retained Earnings		420,000
31	Retained Earnings	270,000	
	Cash Dividends Declared		120,000
	Stock Dividends Declared		150,000

Required

1. Provide explanations for each of the journal entries.
2. Complete the following table showing the balances of the company's equity accounts (including the dividends declared accounts) at each of the indicated dates:

	Oct. 2	Oct. 25	Oct. 31	Nov. 5	Dec. 1	Dec. 31
Common shares	$_____	$_____	$_____	$_____	$_____	$_____
Stock dividend distributable . .	_____	_____	_____	_____	_____	_____
Retained earnings	_____	_____	_____	_____	_____	_____
Less:						
Cash dividends declared	_____	_____	_____	_____	_____	_____
Stock dividends declared	_____	_____	_____	_____	_____	_____
Combined balances of equity accounts	$_____	$_____	$_____	$_____	$_____	$_____

Check Figure
Total equity,
Dec. 31, $1,840,000

The equity sections from the 1999 and 2000 balance sheets of TRP Corporation appeared as follows:

Problem 16-4
Changes in retained earnings
LO 7

Shareholders' Equity (As of December 31, 1999)	
Common shares, no-par value, 50,000 shares authorized, 20,000 shares issued and outstanding	$140,000
Retained earnings	160,000
Total shareholders' equity	$300,000

Shareholders' Equity (As of December 31, 2000)	
Common shares, no-par value, 50,000 shares authorized, 23,700 shares issued	$169,400
Retained earnings ($15,000 restricted)	200,000
Total shareholders' equity	$369,400

The following events occurred during 2000:

Jan.   5   A $0.50 per share cash dividend was declared, and the date of record was five days later.
Mar. 20   1,500 common shares were purchased and retired.
Apr.   5   A $0.50 per share cash dividend was declared, and the date of record was five days later.
July   5   A $0.50 per share cash dividend was declared, and the date of record was five days later.
        31   A 20% stock dividend was declared when the market value was $12 per share.
Aug. 14   The dividend shares were issued.
Oct.   5   A $0.50 per share cash dividend was declared, and the date of record was five days later.

Required

1. How many shares were outstanding on each of the cash dividend dates?
2. How large were each of the four cash dividends?
3. How large was the capitalization of retained earnings for the stock dividend?
4. What was the price per share paid for the shares to be retired?
5. How much income did the company achieve during 2000?

Problem 16-5
Presenting items in an income statement

LO 5

The following table shows the balances from various accounts in the adjusted trial balance for Depew Corp. as of December 31, 1999:

	Debit	Credit
a. Interest earned		$ 12,000
b. Amortization expense, equipment	$ 36,000	
c. Loss on sale of office equipment	24,750	
d. Accounts payable		42,000
e. Other operating expenses	97,500	
f. Accumulated amortization, equipment		73,500
g. Gain from settling a lawsuit		42,000
h. Cumulative effect of change in accounting principle (pre-tax)	63,000	
i. Accumulated amortization, buildings		163,500
j. Loss from operating a discontinued segment (pre-tax)	19,500	
k. Gain on court ordered early settlement of debt (pre-tax)		28,500
l. Sales		970,500
m. Amortization expense, buildings	54,000	
n. Correction of overstatement of prior year's sales (pre-tax)	15,000	
o. Gain on sale of discontinued segment's assets (pre-tax)		33,000
p. Loss from settling a lawsuit	24,000	
q. Income taxes expense	?	
r. Cost of goods sold	487,500	

Required

Answer each of these questions by providing detailed schedules:

1. Assuming that the company's income tax rate is 30%, what are the tax effects and after-tax measures of the items labelled as pre-tax?
2. What is the amount of the company's income from continuing operations before income taxes? What is the amount of the company's income taxes expense? What is the amount of the company's income from continuing operations?
3. What is the amount of after-tax income associated with the discontinued segment?
4. What is the amount of income before extraordinary items and the cumulative effect of the change in principle?
5. What is the amount of net income for the year?

Problem 16-6
Changes in accounting principles

LO 5

On January 1, 1999, Pohl, Inc., purchased some equipment. Its cost was $600,000 and it was expected to have a salvage value of $30,000 at the end of its five-year useful life. Amortization was allocated to 1999, 2000, and 2001 with the declining-balance method at twice the straight-line rate. Early in 2002, the company concluded that changing to the straight-line method would produce more useful financial statements because it would be consistent with the practices of other firms in the industry.

Required

Preparation component:

1. Do generally accepted accounting principles allow Pohl, Inc., to change amortization methods in 2002?

2. Prepare a schedule that shows the amount of amortization expense allocated to 1999 through 2001 under the declining-balance method.

3. Prepare a schedule that shows the amount of amortization expense that would have been allocated to 1999 through 2001 under the straight-line method.

4. Combine the information from your answers to requirements 2 and 3 in a table like Exhibit 16.8 that computes the before- and after-tax cumulative effects of the change. The company's income tax rate is 30%. (For simplicity, round your answers to the nearest dollar.)

5. How should the cumulative effect be reported by the company? Does the cumulative effect increase or decrease net income?

6. How much amortization expense will be reported on the income statement for 2002?

Analysis component:

7. Assume that Pohl, Inc., makes the mistake of treating the change in amortization methods as a change in an accounting estimate. Using your answers from requirements 2, 3, and 4, describe the effect this error would have on the 2002 financial statements.

Check Figure
After-tax cumulative effect, $89,880

The income statements for Tennison, Inc., presented the following information when they were first published in 2000, 2001, and 2002:

Problem 16-7
Earnings per share calculations and presentation

LO 6

	2000	2001	2002
Sales	$370,000	$425,000	$412,500
Expenses	232,500	260,000	245,500
Income from continuing operations	$137,500	$165,000	$167,000
Loss on discontinued segment	(52,500)		
Income before extraordinary items	$ 85,000	$165,000	$167,000
Extraordinary gain (loss)		33,000	(70,000)
Net income	$ 85,000	$198,000	$ 97,000

The company also experienced some changes in the number of outstanding shares through the following events:

Outstanding shares on December 31, 1999	40,000
2000	
Purchase and retirement of shares on April 1	−4,000
Issuance of new shares on June 30	+12,000
10% stock dividend on October 1	+4,800
Outstanding shares on December 31, 2000	52,800
2001	
Issuance of new shares on July 1	+16,000
Purchase and retirement of shares on November 1	−4,800
Outstanding shares on December 31, 2001	64,000
2002	
Issuance of new shares on August 1	+20,000
Purchase and retirement of shares on September 1	−4,000
Three-for-one split on October 1	+160,000
Outstanding shares on December 31, 2002	240,000

Required

Preparation component:

1. Compute the weighted average of the outstanding common shares as of the end of 2000.
2. Compute the 2000 earnings per share amounts to report on the 2000 income statement for income from continuing operations, loss on discontinued segment, and net income.
3. Compute the weighted average of the outstanding common shares as of the end of 2001.
4. Compute the 2001 earnings per share amounts to report on the 2001 income statement for income from continuing operations, the extraordinary gain, and net income.
5. Compute the weighted average of the outstanding common shares as of the end of 2002.
6. Compute the 2002 earnings per share amounts to report on the 2002 income statement for income from continuing operations, the extraordinary loss, and net income.

Analysis component:

7. Write a brief explanation of how you would use the earnings per share statistics from requirement 6 to estimate earnings per share for 2003.

Check Figure
2001 earnings per share for
net income, $3.30

Alternate Problems

Problem 16-1A
Retirement of shares and cash dividends

LO 1, 4

The balance sheet for Caldwell Corp. reported the following components of shareholders' equity on December 31, 1999:

Common shares, no-par value, unlimited shares authorized, 100,000 shares issued and outstanding	$ 800,000
Retained earnings	1,080,000
Total shareholders' equity	$1,880,000

The company completed these transactions during 2000:

Jan. 10 Purchased and retired 20,000 common shares at $12 cash per share.

Mar. 2 The directors declared a $1.50 per share cash dividend payable on March 31 to the March 15 shareholders of record.

31 Paid the dividend declared on March 2.

Nov. 11 Issued 12,000 common shares at $13 per share.

25 Issued 8,000 common shares at $9.50 per share.

Dec. 1 The directors declared a $2.50 per share cash dividend payable on January 2, 2001, to the December 10 shareholders of record.

31 Closed the $536,000 credit balance in the Income Summary account to Retained Earnings.

31 Closed the Cash Dividends Declared account.

Required

1. Prepare general journal entries to record the transactions and closings for 2000.
2. Prepare a statement of retained earnings for 2000.
3. Prepare the shareholders' equity section of the company's balance sheet as of December 31, 2000.

Problem 16-2A
Treasury shares transactions and cash dividends

LO 1, 4

The balance sheet for Francois Corp. reported the following components of shareholders' equity on December 31, 1999:

Common shares, no-par value, unlimited shares authorized, 100,000 shares issued and outstanding	$ 800,000
Retained earnings	1,080,000
Total shareholders' equity	$1,880,000

The company completed these transactions during 2000:

Jan. 10 Purchased 20,000 treasury shares at $12 cash per share.

Mar. 2 The directors declared a $1.50 per share cash dividend payable on March 31 to the March 15 shareholders of record.

31 Paid the dividend declared on March 2.

Nov. 11 Sold 12,000 of the treasury shares at $13 per share.

25 Sold 8,000 of the treasury shares at $9.50 per share.

Dec. 1 The directors declared a $2.50 per share cash dividend payable on January 2, 2001, to the December 10 shareholders of record.

31 Closed the $536,000 credit balance in the Income Summary account to Retained Earnings.

31 Closed the Cash Dividends Declared account.

Required

1. Prepare general journal entries to record the transactions and closings for 2000.

2. Prepare a statement of retained earnings for 2000.

3. Prepare the shareholders' equity section of the company's balance sheet as of December 31, 2000.

At December 31, the end of the third quarter for Hixton Co., Inc., these balances existed in its shareholders' equity accounts:

Problem 16-3A
Describing equity changes with journal entries and account balances

LO 1,3

Common shares, no-par value, 48,000 shares issued	$672,000
Retained earnings	800,000

Over the next three months, the following journal entries were recorded in the company's equity accounts:

Jan. 17	Cash Dividends Declared	48,000	
	Common Dividend Payable		48,000
Feb. 5	Common Dividend Payable	48,000	
	Cash		48,000
28	Stock Dividends Declared (6,000 shares) . . .	126,000	
	Common Shares Dividend Distributable		126,000
Mar. 14	Common Shares Dividend Distributable . . .	126,000	
	Common shares		126,000
25	Memo—change the title of the common shares account to reflect the new number of Common Shares outstanding of 108,000.		
31	Income Summary	360,000	
	Retained Earnings		360,000
31	Retained Earnings	174,000	
	Cash Dividends Declared		48,000
	Stock Dividends Declared		126,000

Required

1. Provide explanations for each of the journal entries.

2. Complete the following table showing the balances of the company's equity accounts (including the dividend accounts) at each of the indicated dates:

	Jan. 17	Feb. 5	Feb. 28	Mar. 14	Mar. 25	Mar. 31
Common shares	$_____	$_____	$_____	$_____	$_____	$_____
Stock dividend distributable . .	_____	_____	_____	_____	_____	_____
Contr. capital in excess of par .	_____	_____	_____	_____	_____	_____
Retained earnings	_____	_____	_____	_____	_____	_____
Less:						
Cash dividends declared	_____	_____	_____	_____	_____	_____
Stock dividends declared	_____	_____	_____	_____	_____	_____
Combined balances of equity accounts	$_____	$_____	$_____	$_____	$_____	$_____

Problem 16-4A
Changes in retained earnings

LO 7

The equity sections from the 1999 and 2000 balance sheets of Thornhill Corporation appeared as follows:

Shareholders' Equity (As of December 31, 1999)	
Common shares, no-par value, 15,000 shares authorized, 8,500 shares issued and outstanding	$200,000
Retained earnings	135,000
Total shareholders' equity	$335,000

Shareholders' Equity (As of December 31, 2000)	
Common shares, no-par value, 15,000 shares authorized	222,000
Retained earnings ($20,000 restricted for retirement)	147,600
Total shareholders' equity	$369,600

The following events occurred during 2000:

Feb. 15 A $0.40 per share cash dividend was declared, and the date of record was five days later.

Mar. 2 500 common shares were purchased for retirement.

May 15 A $0.40 per share cash dividend was declared, and the date of record was five days later.

Aug. 15 A $0.40 per share cash dividend was declared, and the date of record was five days later.

Oct. 4 A 12.5% stock dividend was declared when the market value was $42 per share.
    20 The dividend shares were issued.

Nov. 15 A $0.40 per share cash dividend was declared, and the date of record was five days later.

Required

1. How many shares were outstanding on each of the cash dividend dates?
2. How large were each of the four cash dividends?
3. How large was the capitalization of retained earnings for the stock dividend?
4. What was the price per share paid for the retired shares?
5. How much income did the company achieve during 2000?

Problem 16-5A
Presenting items in an income statement

LO 5

The following table shows the balances from various accounts in the adjusted trial balance for Barbour Corp. as of December 31, 1999:

	Debit	Credit
a. Accumulated amortization, buildings		$ 200,000
b. Interest earned		10,000
c. Cumulative effect of change in accounting principle (pre-tax) ..		46,000
d. Sales		1,320,000
e. Income taxes expense	$?	
f. Loss on condemnation of property (pre-tax)	32,000	
g. Accumulated amortization, equipment		110,000
h. Other operating expenses	164,000	
i. Amortization expense, equipment	50,000	
j. Loss from settling a lawsuit	18,000	
k. Gain from settling a lawsuit		34,000
l. Loss on sale of office equipment	12,000	
m. Loss from operating a discontinued segment (pre-tax)	60,000	
n. Amortization expense, buildings	78,000	
o. Correction of overstatement of prior year's expense (pre-tax) ..		24,000
p. Cost of goods sold	520,000	
q. Loss on sale of discontinued segment's assets (pre-tax)	90,000	
r. Accounts payable		66,000

Required

Answer each of these questions by providing detailed schedules:

1. Assuming that the company's income tax rate is 25%, what are the tax effects and after-tax measures of the items labelled as "pre-tax"?

2. What is the amount of the company's income from continuing operations before income taxes? What is the amount of the company's income taxes expense? What is the amount of the company's income from continuing operations?

3. What is the amount of after-tax income associated with the discontinued segment?

4. What is the amount of income before extraordinary items and the cumulative effect of the change in principle?

5. What is the amount of net income for the year?

On January 1, 1999, Fricke Co., Inc., purchased some equipment. Its cost was $200,000 and it was expected to have no salvage value at the end of its five-year useful life. Amortization was allocated to 1999 through 2001 with the declining-balance method at twice the straight-line rate. Early in 2002, the company concluded that changing to the straight-line method would produce more useful financial statements because it would be consistent with the practices of other firms in the industry.

Problem 16-6A
Changes in accounting principles

LO 5

Required

Preparation component:

1. Do generally accepted accounting principles allow Fricke Co., Inc., to change amortization methods in 2002?

2. Prepare a schedule that shows the amount of amortization expense that was allocated to 1999 through 2001 under the declining-balance method.

3. Prepare a schedule that shows the amount of amortization expense that would have been allocated to 1999 through 2001 under the straight-line method.

4. Combine the information from your answers to parts 2 and 3 in a table like Exhibit 16.8 that computes the before- and after-tax cumulative effect of the change. The company's income tax rate is 25%.

5. How should the cumulative effect be reported by the company? Does the cumulative effect increase or decrease net income?

6. How much amortization expense will be reported on the income statement for 2002?

Analysis component:

7. Assume that, in error, Fricke Co., Inc., treats the change in amortization methods as a change in an accounting estimate. Using your answers from Parts 2, 3 and 4, describe the effect this error would have on the 2002 financial statements.

Problem 16-7A
Earnings per share calculations and presentation

The original income statements for Titus, Inc., presented the following information when they were first published in 2000, 2001, and 2002:

	2000	2001	2002
Sales	$250,000	$300,000	$400,000
Expenses	160,000	215,000	270,000
Income from continuing operations	$90,000	$85,000	$130,000
Loss on discontinued segment	(26,145)		
Income before extraordinary items	$63,855	$85,000	$130,000
Extraordinary gain (loss)		14,100	(37,125)
Net income	$63,855	$99,100	$92,875

The company also experienced some changes in the number of outstanding shares over the three years through the following events:

Outstanding shares on December 31, 1999	10,000
2000	
Treasury shares purchase on July 1	−1,000
Issuance of new shares on September 30	+3,500
20% stock dividend on December 1	+2,500
Outstanding shares on December 31, 2000	15,000
2001	
Issuance of new shares on March 31	+4,000
Treasury shares purchase on October 1	−1,500
Outstanding shares on December 31, 2001	17,500
2002	
Issuance of new shares on July 1	+3,000
Treasury shares purchase on October 1	−1,750
2-for-1 split on November 1	+18,750
Outstanding shares on December 31, 2002	37,500

Required

Preparation component:

1. Compute the weighted average of the outstanding common shares as of the end of 2000.

2. Use the results of part 1 to present the original earnings per share amounts for 2000 for income from continuing operations, loss on discontinued segment, and net income.

3. Compute the weighted average of the outstanding common shares as of the end of 2001.

4. Use the results of part 3 to present the original earnings per share amounts for 2001 for income from continuing operations, the extraordinary gain, and net income.

5. Compute the weighted average of the outstanding common shares as of the end of 2002.

6. Use the results of part 5 to present the earnings per share amounts for 2002 for income from continuing operations, the extraordinary loss, and net income.

Analysis component:

7. Write a brief explanation of how you would use the earnings per share statistics from part 6 to estimate earnings per share for 2003.

Part 1. The more recent business corporations acts restrict the directors by the "solvency" test in the matter of declaration and payment of dividends in money or property. A similar restriction is not, however, imposed in the case of a stock dividends.

Required

Discuss why a restriction is deemed necessary in the former but not in the latter situation.

Part 2. In the case of stock dividends, the Canada Business Corporations Act prescribes that the amount of retained earnings to be capitalized is the product of the number of shares issued as a stock dividends multiplied by the market value of each share. The revised Ontario Business Corporations Act does not stipulate the amount to be capitalized, simply stating that the amount to be added to the stated capital account is the amount declared by the directors.

Required

Can a case be made for either of the positions? Support your answer.

Over the last three years, Commonwealth Enterprises Ltd. has experienced the following income results (all numbers are rounded to the nearest thousand dollars):

	1996	1997	1998
Revenues	$11,000	$11,900	$14,600
Expenses	(7,000)	(7,900)	(7,700)
Gains	3,200	2,400	-0-
Losses	(1,200)	(1,900)	(3,900)
Net income	$ 6,000	$4,500	$ 3,000

Part 1. Use the information to develop a general prediction of the company's net income for 1999.

Part 2. A closer analysis of the information shows that the company discontinued a segment of its operations in 1998. The company's accountant has determined that the discounted segment produced the following amounts of income:

	1996	1997	1998
Revenues	$7,000	$2,600	$1,600
Expenses	(5,000)	(5,000)	(4,000)
Gains		400	
Losses	(1,200)	(1,500)	(900)
Loss on disposal of segment assets			(1,200)

Use the information to calculate the company's income without the discontinued segment and then develop a general prediction of the company's net income for 1999.

Part 3. A more in-depth analysis of the company's activity reveals that the company experienced these extraordinary items during the three years when it retired some of its debts before their scheduled maturity dates.

	1996	1997	1998
Extraordinary gain	$2,200	$2,000	
Extraordinary loss			$(1,700)

Use the information to calculate the company's income from continuing operations and develop a general prediction of the company's net income for 1999.

Analytical and Review Problems

A & R Problem 16-1

A & R Problem 16-2

BEYOND THE NUMBERS

Reporting in Action

LO 5, 6, 8, 9

Refer to the financial statements and related information for **Atlantis** in Appendix I. Answer the following questions by analyzing the information in the report:

1. What is the per share amount of cash dividends paid on common shares during fiscal year 1997?
2. How many common shares are outstanding at the end of fiscal year 1997? How does this number compare with the weighted average number of common shares outstanding at the end of fiscal year 1997?
3. Compare Atlantis's December 31, 1997, net income per common share to the net income per common share as of December 31, 1996.
4. Does Atlantis hold any treasury shares as of December 31, 1997?
5. Does Atlantis show any changes in accounting principles or extraordinary items for fiscal years ended December 31, 1997, and December 31, 1996?
6. Did Atlantis have any gains or losses on the disposal of a business segment during 1997?
7. Obtain access to Atlantis's annual report for fiscal years ending after December 31, 1997. This access may be through a shrink-wrapped annual report included with your text or you may gain access to annual report information at Atlantis's Web site: **http://sedar.com/dynamic_assoc_docs_e/doooo2259.htm.** Has Atlantis paid out any cash dividends paid since the fiscal year-end December 31, 1997?

Comparative Analysis

LO 6, 8, 9

Both **Atlantis** and **Alliance** are in the communications business. Key comparative figures ($ thousands except for per share data) for these two organizations follow:

Key Figures	Atlantis 1997	Alliance 1997
Net income	$795,822	$18,188
Dividends paid per share of common shares	$0.00	$0.00
Common shares outstanding	10,067,074	11,919,000
Market price per share (assumed)	$11.00	$28.00

* Atlantis figures are from the annual report for the fiscal year ended December 31,1997.
  Alliance figures are from the annual report for the fiscal year ended March 31, 1997.

Required

1. Compute the earnings per share for each company.
2. Compute the dividend yield for each company. Does the dividend yield of the companies characterize them as income or growth stocks?
3. Compute, compare, and interpret the price-earnings ratios for Atlantis and Alliance.

Ethics Challenge

LO 5

Recall the facts outlined in the chapter regarding **CompCAN's** change in accounting principle from the double-declining balance method of amortization to the straight-line method. Recall that CompCAN decides that its income statement would be more useful if amortization is computed using the straight-line method instead of the double-declining balance method. This change in accounting principle adds $56,000 to net income in the current year. As the auditor of the company you are reviewing the decision to make the change in accounting principle. You review the equipment in question and realize that it is a piece of high-tech equipment and the risk of obsolescence in the near future is relatively high. You are also aware that all members of top management receive year-end bonuses based on net income.

Required

As an auditor in this situation, would you support the change in principle or ask management to continue using the straight-line method? Justify your response.

The classroom should be divided into teams. Teams are to select an industry, and each team member is to select a different company in that industry. Each team member is to acquire the annual report of the company selected. Annual reports can be obtained in many ways including accessing this book's Web page or **http://www.sedar.com/**. Use the annual report to determine the earnings per share of common shares. Use the financial press to determine the market price of this stock. Use this data to determine the price-earnings ratio. Communicate with teammates via a meeting, e-mail or telephone to discuss the meaning of this ratio, how different companies compare to each other, and the industry norm. The team must prepare a single memo reporting the ratios for each company and identify the conclusions or consensus of opinion reached during the team's discussion. The memo is to be duplicated and distributed to the instructor and all classmates.

Communicating in Practice
LO 9

Visit the Canadian Stock Market Reporter Inc. Web site at **http://www.canstock.com/**. This site puts key financial data about companies at your fingertips. Using the stock symbols for **Atlantis** (AAC.A or AAC.B) and **Alliance** (ATV) search for the following information: (Hint: You may want to print out the various links you visit for easy reference later.)

1. Under the sidebar category "Quote" select the Yahoo detailed quote link. Record the market price per share, earnings per share, price-earnings ratio, and dividend per share for both companies.
2. Compute the dividend yield for each company using the data you collected in requirement 1.
3. Visit the sidebar category "Earnings." View at least three of the earnings consensus links. How much difference do you find among the experts regarding the companies' future earnings prospects?
4. Under the sidebar category "Fundamentals" select the dividends and splits link. Has either company's stock split recently?

Taking It to the Net
LO 6, 8, 9

Let's work as a team to reinforce understanding of accounting for treasury shares.

1. After a team discussion, write a brief team statement (a) generalizing what happens to a corporation's financial position when the entity engages in a stock "buyback" and (b) identifying reasons why a corporation would engage in this activity.
2. Assume an entity reacquired 100 shares of its $100 par value common shares at a cost of $134 per share. Discuss this entry to record the acquisition. After each member understands this entry, assign each team member the preparation of *one* of the following entries (assume each entry applies to all shares):
   a. Reissue at cost
   b. Reissue at $150 per share
   c. Reissue at $120 per share—assume the related contributed capital account has a $1,500 balance.
   d. Reissue at $120 per share—assume the related contributed capital account has a $1,000 balance.
   e. Reissue at $120 per share—assume the related contributed capital account does not have a balance.
3. In sequence, each member is to present his or her entry to the team and explain the similarities and differences between that entry and the previous entry. Encourage team members to ask questions and be sure concepts are understood before proceeding.

Teamwork In Action
LO 4

Watch a Canadian financial news television program. While watching, take notes on company happenings that are catching the attention of analysts following stocks. You might hear reference to over- and undervaluation of firms. You might also hear reporters talking about PE ratios, dividend yields, and earnings per share. Be prepared to give a brief description in class of your experience listening to the television financial news.

Hitting the Road
LO 6, 8, 9

In recent year firms have become very innovative in developing and offering to the public new types of financial securities. Obtain a copy of the May 29, 1998, edition of *Canadian Business Magazine*. Read the article on pages 25–25 entitled, "A Stock Dividend" under the risk and reward section of the magazine. Answer the following questions.

1. What is the meaning of split shares according to this article?
2. How does this conception of split shares differ from stock splits as discussed in your text?
3. Why aren't split shares all they are cracked up to be?

Business Break
LO 6

17

CHAPTER

Bonds and Long-Term Notes Payable

Chapter Outline

Get Real!

Montreal, PQ—Yvette Bourque has overcome odds before. Three years ago she had a plan to open a natural foods store near Montreal. But she needed money. She took plans for her store to the local bank. "The banker criticized my business plan and told me to get real," says Bourque. "That really got to me."

Bourque turned to her family and friends for start-up money. Motivated by the banker's remark, Bourque is now the proud owner of **Get Real!** "I sell *real* food like farm-raised seafood and natural and organic produce. It's successful beyond my wildest expectations. It's like a dream." Get Real! now offers a line of more than 2,000 products.

But Bourque faced another obstacle. "I wanted to open two more stores, one in Quebec City and one in Ottawa." Again, Bourque met with several bankers to get a loan. "Every bank wanted me to come to four meetings and prepare five sets of forecasts. Only then would they make a loan proposal, and none of them were acceptable to me. They viewed my plans as risky and I had little collateral."

Then Bourque got an idea. "I remembered when Ben & Jerry's was a tiny ice-cream parlor and advertised its shares on its ice-cream cartons. But I didn't want the headache of shareholders." Bourque decided to issue bonds on her own and got a lawyer to draw up papers. "I put up posters in the store and printed notices on my grocery bags offering bonds for sale. I also added the notice to my regular newspaper ads." For just the $25 par value, people could buy one of my 8% bonds.

"I was flooded with requests. Some people viewed the bonds as an investment, others as a novelty. In the backroom, I typed in names and addresses and printed up bond certificates. When people sent me a cheque, I sent the bonds." Bourque ended up raising over $200,000. "I'm really fired up! I've already rented a location in Ottawa, and I'm close to a deal in Quebec City." Thanks to one banker, Get Real! is a *real* success.

CHAPTER PREVIEW

Bonds are issued by companies and governments for financing their activities. In return for money, bonds promise to repay the lender with interest. This chapter explains the basics of bonds and the accounting for their issuance and retirement. The chapter also describes long-term notes including interest-bearing, non-interest-bearing, and installment notes. We explain how present value concepts impact both the accounting and reporting of bonds and notes. An appendix to this chapter discusses important present value concepts in accounting for liabilities. Understanding how bonds and notes are used to the advantage of a company, as shown in the opening article, is an important goal of this chapter.

Basics of Bonds

Corporations often finance operations and borrow money by issuing bonds.[1] A **bond** is a written promise to pay an amount identified as the par value of the bond along with interest at a stated annual rate. The **par value** of the bond, also called the *face amount* or *face value*, is paid at a specified future date known as the *maturity date of the bond*. Most bonds require the borrower to make semiannual interest payments. The amount of interest paid each year is determined by multiplying the par value of the bond by the stated rate of interest determined when the bonds are issued. This section explains the motivation and basics of bonds.

Bond Financing

LO1 Compare bond financing versus share financing.

Companies can finance their business activities in several ways including issuing notes, leasing assets, and selling shares. But projects demanding large amounts of money usually require funding from either bond or shares issuances. Bond financing offers both advantages and disadvantages.

Advantages of Bonds

There are three main advantages of bond financing.

1. *Bonds do not affect shareholder control.* Shares reflect an ownership right in the corporation, whereas a bond does not. A person who owns 1,000 of a corporation's 10,000 outstanding shares controls one-tenth of all shareholders' votes. But a person who owns a $1,000, 11%, 20-year bond has no ownership right. This person, or bondholder, has a receivable from the bond issuer. The right of the bondholder is to receive (1) 11% interest, or $110, each year the bond is outstanding and (2) $1,000 when the bond matures in 20 years.

2. *Interest on bonds is tax deductible.* But dividends to shareholders are not. For instance, a company with $10,000 available to pay interest on bonds, would only have $6,000 available to pay dividends (assuming a 40% tax rate).

3. *Bonds can increase return on equity.* When a company earns a higher return with the borrowed funds than it is paying in interest, it increases its return on equity. This process is called *financial leverage* or *trading on the equity*.

To illustrate, let's look at **Magnum Skates.** Magnum has $1 million in equity, and is planning a $500,000 expansion to meet increasing sales. Magnum predicts the $500,000 expansion will yield $125,000 in additional income before paying any interest. Magnum currently earns $100,000 per year and has no interest expense.

---

[1] Bonds are also issued by nonprofit corporations, as well as the federal government and other governmental units, such as cities and provinces. Although the examples in this chapter deal with business situations, all issuers use the same practices to account for their bonds.

Magnum is considering three plans. Plan A is to not expand. Plan B is to expand, and raise $500,000 from issuing shares. Plan C is to sell $500,000 worth of bonds paying 10% annual interest, or $50,000. Exhibit 17.1 shows us how these three plans affect Magnum's net income, equity, and return on equity.

	Plan A Don't Expand	Plan B Increase Equity	Plan C Issue Bonds
Income before interest	$ 100,000	$ 225,000	$ 225,000
Interest	—	—	(50,000)
Net income	**$ 100,000**	**$ 225,000**	**$ 175,000**
Equity	$1,000,000	$1,500,000	$1,000,000
Return on equity	**10.0%**	**15.0%**	**17.5%**

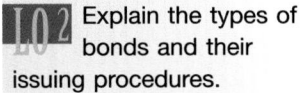

Exhibit 17.1

Financing with Bonds or Shares

Analysis of these plans shows the owners will earn a higher return on equity if expansion occurs. The preferred plan of expansion is by issuing bonds. Even though projected net income under Plan C ($175,000) is smaller than under Plan B ($225,000), the return on equity is larger because of less equity investment. This is an important result and yields a general rule: *return on equity increases when the expected rate of return from the new assets is greater than the rate of interest on the bonds.* Also, issuing bonds allows the current owners to remain in control.

Disadvantages of Bonds

There are two main disadvantages of bond financing.

1. *Bonds require payment of both periodic interest and par value at maturity.* Bond payments can be especially burdensome when a company's income is low and when it is struggling to survive. Shares, on the other hand, do not require payment of dividends. Cash dividends on shares are paid at the discretion of the issuer.

2. *Bonds can decrease return on equity.* When a company earns a lower return with the borrowed funds than it is paying in interest, it decreases its return on equity. This is the downside risk of financial leverage. It is more likely to arise when a company has periods of low income.

A company must weigh the risks of these disadvantages against the advantages on bond financing when deciding on whether to issue bonds to finance operations.

Types of Bonds

There exist many different kinds of bonds with various characteristics. We describe the more common kinds of bonds in this section.

LO2 Explain the types of bonds and their issuing procedures.

Secured and Unsecured Bonds

Secured bonds have specific assets of the issuing company pledged (or *mortgaged*) as collateral. This arrangement gives bondholders added protection against default by the issuer. If the issuing company fails to pay interest or par value, the secured bondholders can demand the collateral be sold and the proceeds used to pay the bond obligation.

Unsecured bonds, also called *debentures,* are backed by the issuer's general credit standing. Unsecured bonds are almost always more risky than secured bonds. Because of this added risk, a company generally must be financially strong to successfully issue debentures at a favourable rate of interest. It is common to see debentures on the balance sheets of companies such as **Air Canada, Bell Canada Enterprises, Bombardier, Canadian Tire,** and **Magna International.**

Companies can issue debentures whose claims on a company's assets are second to those of other unsecured liabilities. These debentures are called *subordinated debentures*, meaning these creditors' claims are subordinated to the claims of some others. **Magna** has issued subordinated debentures. In a liquidation, Magna's subordinated debentures would not be repaid until the claims of the more senior, unsecured liabilities are first settled.

Term and Serial Bonds

Term Bond

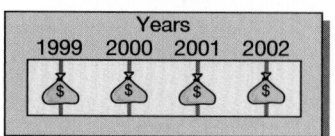

Serial Bond

Term bonds are scheduled for payment (maturity) at a single specified date. **Serial bonds** mature at several different dates (in series). This means serial bonds are repaid over a number of periods. For instance, $1 million of serial bonds might mature at the rate of $100,000 each year from 6 to 15 years after the bonds are issued. This involves 10 groups (or series) of bonds of $100,000 each where one series matures after six years, another after seven years, and another each successive year until the final series is repaid.

Many term bonds are also **sinking fund bonds.** To reduce the holder's risk, these bonds require the issuer to create a *sinking fund*, which is a group of assets used to retire the bonds at maturity. The issuer must start to set aside the assets to pay off these bonds before they mature.

Registered Bonds and Bearer Bonds

Registered Bond

Bearer Bond

Bonds issued in the names and addresses of their owners are **registered bonds.** The issuing company makes bond payments by sending cheques to these registered owners. When one investor sells a bond to another investor, the issuer must be notified of the change. Registered bonds offer the issuer the practical advantage of not having to actually issue bond certificates to investors. This arrangement protects investors against loss or theft of bonds.

Bonds payable to whoever holds them (the *bearer*) are called **bearer bonds,** or *unregistered bonds.* Since there may be no record of sales or exchanges, the holder of a bearer bond is presumed to be its rightful owner. As a result, lost or stolen bearer bonds are difficult to replace.

Many bearer bonds are also **coupon bonds.** This term reflects interest coupons that are attached to these bonds. Each coupon matures on a specific interest payment date. The owner detaches each coupon when it matures and presents it to a bank or broker for collection. At maturity, the owner follows the same process and presents the bond certificate for collection. Because there is no readily available record of who actually receives the interest, the income tax law discourages companies from issuing new coupon bonds.

Convertible and Callable Bonds

Convertible bonds can be exchanged by bondholders for a fixed number of shares of the issuing company's common shares. **Magna Corporation** for example had among its 1997 liabilities 7.25% convertible debentures with a par value of $150 million that had been issued for a net proceeds of $145.3 million net of issue costs. These debentures could be converted at any time at the option of holders into Class A Subordinate Voting Shares at a conversion price of $60.25 per share and mature on July 5, 2005. Convertible bonds offer bondholders the potential to participate in future increases in the share's market value. But if the shares do not appreciate, bondholders continue to receive periodic interest and will receive the par value when the bond matures. In most cases, the bondholders decide whether and when to convert the bonds to shares. **Callable bonds** have an option exerciseable by the issuer to retire them at a stated dollar amount prior to maturity. Callable bonds are often referred to as **redeemable bonds.**

Bond Trading

Bonds are securities and can be readily bought and sold. A large number of corporate bonds trade on major stock exchanges. A bond issue consists of a large number of bonds, usually in denominations of $1,000 or $5,000, and are sold to many different lenders. A *baby bond* is a bond with less than a $1,000 par value such as $100. Companies such as **Air Canada** and **St. Laurent Paperboard Inc.** have issued bonds in $100 denominations but such issues are rare. After bonds are issued, they often are bought and sold by investors, meaning any particular bond is probably owned by a number of people before it matures.

Because bonds are exchanged in the market, they have a market value (price). For convenience, bond market values are expressed as a percent of their par (face) value. For example, a company's bonds might be trading at $103\frac{1}{2}$, which means they can be bought or sold for 103.5% of their par value. Bonds can also trade below par value. For instance, if a company's bonds are trading at 95, they can be bought or sold at 95% of their par value.

Bond Quotes

The bond quote below is interpreted as (left to right): **Bonds,** company name; **Rate,** contract interest rate ($9\frac{1}{2}$%) for this bond; **Maturity,** year (2000) in which bond's principal is paid; **Cur Yld,** yield rate (9.2%) of bond at current price; **Vol,** dollars worth ($145,000) of bonds traded in 1000s; **Close,** closing price ($1,035) for the day as % of par value; **Net Chg,** change ($1.25) in closing price as a fraction of par from the prior day.

Bonds	Rate	Maturity	Cur.Yld	Vol	Close	Net Chg
Co. Name	$9\frac{1}{2}$%	2000	9.2%	$145,000	103.5	$1.25

Did You Know?

Bond Issuing Procedures

Bond issuances are governed by provincial and federal laws. Issuing company bonds usually requires approval by both the board of directors and shareholders. Authorization of bond issuances include the number of bonds authorized, their par value, and the contract interest rate.

The legal document identifying the rights and obligations of both the bondholders and the issuer is called the **bond indenture.** The bond indenture acts as the legal contract between the issuer and the bondholders. A bondholder may also receive a bond certificate as evidence of the company's debt. A **bond certificate,** such as shown in Exhibit 17.2, includes specifics such as the issuer's name, the bond's par value, the contract interest rate, and the maturity date. Many companies reduce costs by not issuing certificates to registered bondholders.

The issuing company normally sells the bonds to an investment firm called an *underwriter*. The underwriter then resells them to the public. An issuing company can also sell bonds directly to investors. When an underwriter sells bonds to a large number of investors, the bondholders' interests are represented and protected by a *trustee*. The trustee monitors the issuer to ensure it complies with the obligations in the bond indenture. Most trustees are large banks or trust companies.

Terms of a bond indenture are drawn up and accepted by the trustee before bonds are issued. When bonds are

Exhibit 17.2

Bond Certificate

offered to the public, called *floating an issue*, they must be registered with a securities commission. Registration requires the issuer to file extensive financial information in special reports.

Bond Issuances

This section explains accounting for bond issuances at par, below par (discount), and above par (premium). We also describe the amortization of a discount or premium, and how to record bonds issued between interest payment dates.

Issuing Bonds at Par

LO 3 Prepare entries to record bond issuance and bond interest expense.

To illustrate an issuance of bonds at par value, let's suppose Barnes Company receives authorization to issue $800,000 of 9%, 20-year bonds. The bonds are dated January 1, 2000, and are due on December 31, 2019. They pay interest semiannually on each June 30 and December 31. After the bond indenture is accepted by the trustee on behalf of the bondholders, all or a portion of the bonds can be sold to an underwriter. If all bonds are sold at their par value, Barnes Company makes this entry to record the sale:

Assets = Liabilities + Equity
+800,000 +800,000

2000			
Jan. 1	Cash	800,000	
	Bonds Payable		800,000
	Sold bonds at par.		

This entry reflects increases in the company's cash and long-term liabilities.

Six months later, the first semiannual interest payment is made, and Barnes records its payment with this entry:

Assets = Liabilities + Equity
−36,000 −36,000

2000			
June 30	Bond Interest Expense	36,000	
	Cash		36,000
	Paid semiannual interest on bonds.		
	(9% × $800,000 × 1/2)		

This entry is made every six months as Barnes pays its semiannual interest obligations until the bonds mature.

When the bonds mature 20 years later, Barnes Company records its payment of the maturity value with this entry:

Assets = Liabilities + Equity
−800,000 −800,000

2019			
Dec. 31	Bonds Payable	800,000	
	Cash		800,000
	Paid bonds at maturity.		

Did You Know?

Ratings Game

Many bond buyers look to rating services such as the Dominion Bond Rating Service for assessing the risk of bonds.. These services focus on the financial strength of the issuer rather than the market attractiveness of the bond. Financial statements are a crucial part of the information these services rely on in setting ratings. Dominion's ratings, from best quality to default, are: AAA (near perfection), AA (well above average), A (up to high average, upper-medium grade), BBB (up to low average, medium grade), BB (mildly speculative), B (middle speculative),CCC (highly speculative), CC (in default), C (second tier of debt of a company in default).

Determining Bond Discount or Premium

The interest rate paid by the issuer of bonds is specified in the indenture and on the bond certificates. Because it is stated in the indenture, this rate is called the **contract rate** of the bonds. The contract rate is also called the *coupon rate*, the *stated rate*, or the *nominal rate*. The amount of interest paid each year is determined by multiplying the par value of the bonds by the contract rate.

The contract rate is usually stated on an annual basis, even if the interest is paid semiannually. For example, let's suppose a company issues a $1,000, 8% bond paying interest semiannually. The annual interest of $80 (8% × $1,000) is paid in two semiannual payments of $40 each.

The contract rate sets the amount of interest the issuer pays in *cash*. But the contract rate is not necessarily the rate of *bond interest expense* actually incurred by the issuer. Bond interest expense depends on the market value of the issuer's bonds, which is determined by market expectations on the risk of lending to this issuer. This expected risk, along with the supply of and demand for bonds, is reflected in the market rate of interest for the bond. The **market rate** is the rate that borrowers are willing to pay and that lenders are willing to earn for a particular bond and its risk level. A market rate changes in response to changes in both a bond's risk level and the supply of and demand for bonds.

Because factors that determine market rate vary across companies, different companies face different market rates for their bonds. The market rate for a specific set of bonds depends on the level of risk investors assign to them. As the level of risk increases, the rate increases. The increased market rate compensates purchasers for the increased risk of bonds. Market rates also are affected by the length of the bonds' life. Long-term bonds generally have higher rates because they are more risky. This is because of the many things that can happen to a company over a long period of time.

Many bond issuers try to set a contract rate of interest equal to the market rate they expect as of the bonds' issuance date. When the contract rate and market rate are equal, the bonds sell at their par value. But when the contract does not equal the market rate, the bonds do not sell at their par value. Instead, they are sold at a *premium* above their par value or at a *discount* below their par value.

Exhibit 17.3 shows the relation between the contract rate, market rate, and a bond's issue price.

Some companies issue *zero-coupon bonds* that do not pay any periodic interest. This means the contract rate for zero-coupon bonds is

Contract rate is:		Bond sells:
Above market rate	⇒	At a premium
Equal to market rate	⇒	At par value
Below market rate	⇒	At a discount

Exhibit 17.3

Relation between Bond Issue Price, Contract Rate, and Market Rate

zero. Because this 0% contract rate is always below the market rate, these bonds are always issued at a discount, meaning their prices are always less than their par values.

Flashback

1. Unsecured bonds backed only by the issuer's general credit standing are called (a) serial bonds, (b) debentures, (c) registered bonds, (d) convertible bonds, or (e) bearer bonds.
2. How do you compute the amount of interest a bond issuer pays each year?
3. When the contract rate is above the market rate, do bonds sell at a premium or a discount? Do purchasers pay more or less than the par value of the bonds?

Answers—p. 809

LO 4 Compute and record amortization of bond discount.

Issuing Bonds at a Discount

We described how a **discount on bonds payable** occurs when a company issues bonds with a contract rate less than the market rate. This means the issue price is less than the bonds' par value.

To illustrate, **Fila** announces an offer to issue bonds with a $100,000 par value, an 8% annual contract rate, and a five-year life. The market rate for Fila's bonds is 10% meaning the bonds will sell at a discount since the contract rate is less than the market rate.[2] The issue price for these bonds is 97.277 (97.277% of par value).

These bonds obligate the issuer to pay out two different future cash flows:

1. $100,000 at the end of the bonds' five-year life.
2. $4,000 (4% × $100,000) at the end of each six-month interest period of the bonds' five-year life.

The pattern of cash flows for Fila's bonds is shown in Exhibit 17.4.

Exhibit 17.4

Cash Flows of Fila's Bonds

								$100,000
	$4,000	$4,000	$4,000	$4,000		$4,000	$4,000	$4,000
0	6 mo.	12 mo.	18 mo.	24 mo.	. . .	48 mo.	54 mo.	60 mo.

If Fila accepts $92,277 cash for its bonds on the issue date of December 31, 2000, it records the sale with this entry:

Assets   =   Liabilities + Equity
+92,277   +100,000
             − 7,723

2000			
Dec. 31	Cash	92,277	
	Discount on Bonds Payable	7,723	
	Bonds Payable		100,000
	Sold bonds at a discount on the original issue date.		

These bonds are reported in the long-term liability section of the issuer's balance sheet as shown in Exhibit 17.5.

Exhibit 17.5

Balance Sheet Presentation of Bond Discount

Long-term liabilities:		
Bonds payable, 8%, due December 31, 2005	$100,000	
Less discount on bonds payable	7,723	$92,277

The discount is deducted from the par value of the bonds to produce the **carrying (or book) value** of the bonds payable. The Discount on Bonds Payable is a contra liability account.

Bond Rater
You are a bond rater. It is your job to assign a rating to a bond issue that reflects its riskiness to bondholders. Identify factors you look at in assigning risk to bonds. For the factors you identify, indicate their likely levels for a bond issue sold at a discount.

Answer—p. 809

---

[2] The difference between the contract rate and the market rate of interest on a new bond issue is usually a fraction of a percent. But we use a difference of 2% here to emphasize the effects.

Amortizing a Bond Discount

The issuer (Fila) received $92,277 for its bonds and will pay bondholders $100,000 after five years have passed (plus interest payments). Because the $7,723 discount is eventually paid to bondholders at maturity, it is part of the cost of using the $92,277 for five years. The upper portion of Exhibit 17.6 shows that total interest cost of $47,723 is the difference between the total amount repaid to bondholders ($140,000) and the amount borrowed from bondholders ($92,277).

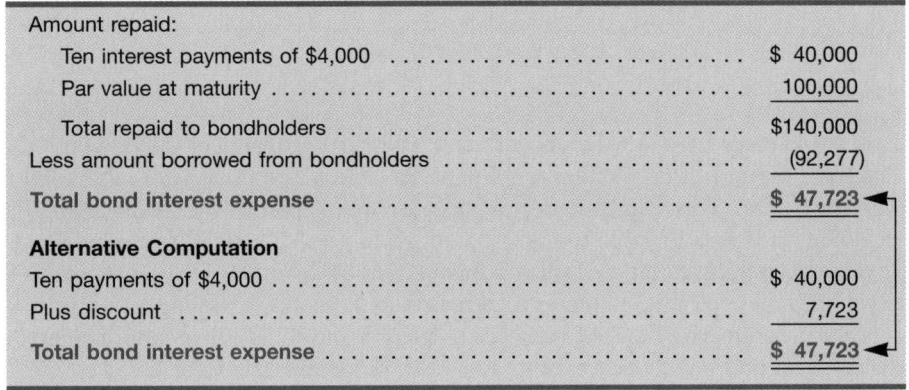

Amount repaid:	
Ten interest payments of $4,000	$ 40,000
Par value at maturity	100,000
Total repaid to bondholders	$140,000
Less amount borrowed from bondholders	(92,277)
Total bond interest expense	$ 47,723
Alternative Computation	
Ten payments of $4,000	$ 40,000
Plus discount	7,723
Total bond interest expense	$ 47,723

Exhibit 17.6

Total Bond Interest Expense for Bonds Issued at a Discount

Alternatively, we can compute total bond interest expense as the sum of the interest payments and the bond discount. This alternative computation is shown in the lower portion of Exhibit 17.6.

Accounting for Fila's bonds must include two procedures. First, total bond interest expense of $47,723 must be allocated across the 10 six-month periods in the bonds' life. Second, the carrying value of the bonds must be updated at each balance sheet date. Two alternative methods accomplish these objectives. They are the straight-line and the effective interest methods of allocating interest. Both methods reduce the discount on the bonds over the life of the bonds, and is often called *amortizing the bond discount*.

> **Junk Bond**
> Junk bonds are company bonds with low credit ratings. Issuers of junk bonds are more likely than average to default on repayment. On the other hand, the high risk of junk bonds can yield high returns to its bondholders if the issuer survives and repays its debt. Junk bond issuances are running at over $100 billion a year. Also, the percent of junk bond issuances in default has fallen from 33% in 1984-90 to only 9% in 1991-97. [Source: *Business Week*, March 2, 1998.]
>
> **Did You Know?**

Straight-Line Method

The **straight-line method** of allocating interest is the simpler of the two methods. It allocates an equal portion of the total bond interest expense to each of the six-month interest periods.

To apply the straight-line method to Fila's bonds, we divide the five years' total expense of $47,723 by 10 (the number of semiannual periods in the bonds' life). This gives us a total bond interest expense of $4,772 per period.[3] Alternatively, we can find this number by dividing the $7,723 original discount

---

[3] For simplicity, all computations are rounded to the nearest whole dollar. Do the same when solving the exercises and problems at the end of the chapter.

by 10. The resulting $772 is the amount of discount to be amortized in each interest period. When the $772 of amortized discount is added to the $4,000 cash payment, the total bond interest expense for each six-month period is $4,772.

The issuer records bond interest expense and updates the balance of the bond liability for each semiannual cash payment with this entry:

Assets = Liabilities + Equity
−4,000   +772   −4,772

2001			
June 30	Bond interest expense	4,772	
	Discount on Bonds Payable		772
	Cash		4,000
	To record six months' interest and discount amortization.		

This is the entry made at the end of each of the 10 semiannual interest periods. The $772 credit to the Discount on Bonds Payable account *increases* the bonds' carrying value. This increase occurs because we *decrease* the balance of the Discount on Bonds Payable (contra) account which is subtracted from the Bonds Payable account. Exhibit 17.7 shows this pattern of decreases in the Discount on Bonds Payable account, along with increases in the bonds' carrying value.

We can summarize the following points in applying straight-line amortization to the discount on Fila's bonds over its life of 10 semiannual periods:

Exhibit 17.7

Bond Discount and Carrying Value under Straight-Line

Date	Discount Balance	Carrying Value
Dec. 31/2000	$7,723	$ 92,277
Jun. 30/2001	6,951	93,049
Dec. 31/2001	6,179	93,821
Jun. 30/2002	5,407	94,593
Dec. 31/2002	4,635	95,365
Jun. 30/2003	3,863	96,137
Dec. 31/2003	3,091	96,909
Jun. 30/2004	2,319	97,681
Dec. 31/2004	1,547	98,453
Jun. 30/2005	775*	99,225
Dec 31/2005	-0-	100,000
*Adjusted for rounding.		

1. The $92,277 cash received from selling bonds equals the $100,000 par value of the bonds less the initial $7,723 discount from selling the bonds for less than par.

2. Semiannual bond interest expense of $4,772 equals total bond interest expense of $47,723 divided by 10 semiannual periods (alternatively computed as the cash paid of $4,000 plus the periodic discount amortization of $772).

3. Semiannual credit to the Discount on Bonds Payable account equals the total discount of $7,723 divided by 10 semiannual periods.

4. Semiannual $4,000 interest payment equals the bonds' $100,000 par value multiplied by the 4% semiannual contract rate.

5. Carrying (or book) value of bonds continues to grow each period by the $772 discount amortization until it equals the par value of the bonds when they mature.

Fila incurs a $4,772 bond interest expense each period but pays only $4,000. The $772 unpaid portion of expense is added to the balance of the liability by decreasing the discount contra account balance.

Effective Interest Method

The straight-line method yields changes in the bonds' carrying value (see Exhibit 17.7) while the amount for bond interest expense does not change (always equal to $4,772 for Fila bonds). This gives the impression of a changing interest rate when users divide a constant bond interest expense over a changing carrying value. As a result, the straight-line method should only be used when its results do not differ materially from those obtained by using the effective interest method.

The **effective interest method,** or simply *interest method*, allocates bond interest expense over the life of the bonds in a way that yields a constant rate of interest. This constant rate of interest is the market rate at the issue date. The effect of selling bonds at a premium or discount is the issuer incurs the prevailing market rate of interest at issuance and not the contract rate. Bond interest expense for a period is found by multiplying the balance of the liability at the beginning of that period by the bonds' original market rate. An *amortization table* can be constructed to help us keep track of interest allocation and the balances of bond-related accounts.

Exhibit 17.8 shows an amortization table for the Fila bonds. The key difference between the effective interest and straight-line methods lies in computation of bond interest expense. Instead of assigning an equal amount of interest to each interest period, the effective interest method assigns an increasing amount of interest over the Fila bonds' life because the balance of the liability increases over these five years. But both methods allocate the *same* $47,723 of total expense across the five years, but with different patterns.

Exhibit 17.8

Effective Interest
Amortization of Bond
Discount

Semiannual Interest Period	(A) Cash Interest Paid $100,000 × 4%	(B) Interest Expense E × 5%	(C) Discount Amortization (B-C)	(D) Unamortized Discount (D-C)	(E) Carrying Value 100,000-D
Dec. 31/2000				$7,723	$ 92,277
Jun. 30/2001	$ 4,000	$ 4,614	$ 614	$7,109	92,891
Dec. 31/2001	4,000	4,645	645	6,464	93,536
Jun. 30/2002	4,000	4,677	677	5,787	94,213
Dec. 31/2002	4,000	4,711	711	5,076	94,924
Jun. 30/2003	4,000	4,746	746	4,330	95,670
Dec. 31/2003	4,000	4,784	784	3,546	96,454
Jun. 30/2004	4,000	4,823	823	2,723	97,277
Dec. 31/2004	4,000	4,864	864	1,859	98,141
Jun. 30/2005	4,000	4,907	907	952	99,048
Dec. 31/2005	4,000	4,952	952	-0-	100,000
	$40,000	$47,723	$7,723		

Column A is the bonds' par value ($100,000) multiplied by the semiannual contract rate (4%).
Column B is the bonds' prior period carrying value multiplied by the semiannual market rate (5%).
Column C is the difference between interest paid and bond interest expense, or [(B)-(A)].
Column D is the prior period's unamortized discount less the current period's discount amortization.
Column E is the bonds' par value less unamortized discount, or [$100,000-(D)].

The amortization table shows how the balance of the discount (column D) is amortized by the effective interest method until it reaches zero. The bonds' carrying value changes each period until it equals par value at maturity. Total bond interest expense is $47,723, comprised of $40,000 of semiannual cash payments and $7,723 of the original discount below par value.

Except for differences in amounts, journal entries recording the expense and updating the liability balance are the same under the effective interest method and the straight-line method. For instance, the entry to record the interest payment at the end of the first interest period is:

2001			
June 30	Bond Interest Expense	4,614	
	Discount on Bonds Payable		614
	Cash		4,000
	To record six months' interest and discount amortization.		

Assets = Liabilities + Equity
−4000   +614   −4,614

We use the numbers in Exhibit 17.8 to make similar entries throughout the five-year life of the bonds.

Answers—p. 809

Flash back

Five-year, 6% bonds with a $100,000 par value are issued at a price of $91,893. Interest is paid semiannually, and the market rate is 8% on the issue date. Use this information to answer the following questions:

4. Are these bonds issued at a discount or premium? Explain why.

5. What is the issuer's journal entry to record the sale?

6. What is the amount of bond interest expense recorded at the first semiannual cash payment using the (a) straight-line method and (b) effective interest method?

Issuing Bonds at a Premium

LO 5 Compute and record amortization of bond premium.

When bonds carry a contract rate greater than the market rate, the bonds sell at a price greater than par value. The difference between par and market value is the **premium on bonds.** Buyers bid up the price of bonds above the bonds' par value until it reaches a level yielding the market rate.

To illustrate, assume that **Hydro Quebec** issues bonds with a $100,000 par value, a 12% annual contract rate, and a five-year life. The market rate for Hydro Quebec bonds is 10% on the issue date meaning the bonds will sell at a premium because the contract rate is greater than the market rate. This means buyers of these bonds will bid up the market price until the yield equals the market rate. The issue price for these bonds is 107.72 (107.72% of par value).

The Hydro Quebec's bonds obligate Hydro Quebec to pay out two different future cash flows:

1. $100,000 at the end of the bonds' five-year life.
2. $6,000 (6% × $100,000) at the end of each six-month interest period of the bonds' five-year life.

The pattern of cash flows for Hydro Quebec bonds is shown in Exhibit 17.9.

Exhibit 17.9

Cash Flows of Hydro Quebec Bonds

If Hydro Quebec accepts $107,720 cash for its bonds on the issue date of December 31, 2000, it records this sale with the entry:

Assets = Liabilities + Equity
+107,720   +100,000
           +7,720

2000			
Dec. 31	Cash	107,720	
	Premium on Bonds Payable		7,720
	Bonds Payable		100,000
	Sold bonds at a premium on the original issue date.		

These bonds are reported in the long-term liability section of the issuer's balance sheet as shown in Exhibit 17.10.

Exhibit 17.10

Balance Sheet Presentation of Bond Premium

Long-term liabilities:		
Bonds payable, 12%, due December 31, 2005	$100,000	
Plus premium on bonds payable	7,720	$107,720

The premium is added to the par value of the bonds to produce the carrying value of the bonds payable. The Premium on Bonds Payable is an adjunct (also called accretion) liability account.

Amortizing a Bond Premium

The issuer (Hydro Quebec) receives $107,720 for its bonds and will pay bondholders $100,000 after five years have passed (plus interest payments). Because the $7,720 premium is not repaid to bondholders at maturity, it reduces the expense of using the $107,720 for five years. The upper portion of Exhibit 17.11 shows that total bond interest expense of $52,280 is the difference between the total amount repaid to bondholders ($160,000) and the amount borrowed from bondholders ($107,720).

Amount repaid:	
Ten interest payments of $6,000	$ 60,000
Par value at Maturity	100,000
Total repaid to bondholders	$160,000
Less amount borrowed from bondholders	(107,720)
Total bond interest expense	$ 52,280
Alternative Computation	
Ten payments of $6,000	$ 60,000
Less premium	(7,720)
Total bond interest expense	$ 52,280

Exhibit 17.11

Total Bond Interest Expense for Bonds Issued at a Premium

Alternatively, we can compute total bond interest expense as the sum of the interest payments less the bond premium. The premium is subtracted because it will not be paid to the bondholders when the bonds mature. This alternative computation is shown in the lower portion of Exhibit 17.11. Total bond interest expense is allocated over the 10 semiannual periods with either the straight-line or the effective interest method.

Straight-Line Method

We explained how the straight-line method allocates an equal portion of total bond interest expense to each of the bonds' interest periods. To apply the straight-line method to Hydro Quebec bonds, we divide the five years' total bond interest expense of $52,280 by 10 (the number of semiannual periods in the bonds' life). This gives us a total bond interest expense of $5,228 per period.

The issuer records bond interest expense and updates the balance of the bond liability for each semiannual cash payment with this entry:

2001			
June 30	Bond interest expense	5,228	
	Premium on Bonds Payable	772	
	Cash		6,000
	To record six months' interest and premium amortization.		

Assets = Liabilities + Equity
−6,000   −772   −5,228

This is the entry made at the end of each of the 10 semiannual interest periods. The $772 debit to the Premium on Bonds Payable account *decreases* the bonds' carrying value.

Effective Interest Method

Exhibit 17.12 shows an amortization table using the effective interest method for the Hydro Quebec' bonds.

Exhibit 17.12

Effective
Interest
Amortization
of Bond
Premium

Semiannual Interest Period	(A) Cash Interest Paid $100,000 × 6%	(B) Interest Expense E × 5%	(C) Premium Amortization (A − B)	(D) Unamortized Premium (D − C)	(E) Carrying Value 100,000 + D
Dec. 31/2000				$7,720	$107,720
Jun. 30/2001	$ 6,000	$ 5,386	$ 614	7,106	107,106
Dec. 31/2001	6,000	5,355	645	6,461	106,461
Jun. 30/2002	6,000	5,323	677	5,784	105,784
Dec. 31/2002	6,000	5,289	711	5,073	105,073
Jun. 30/2003	6,000	5,254	746	4,327	104,327
Dec. 31/2003	6,000	5,216	784	3,543	103,543
Jun. 30/2004	6,000	5,177	823	2,720	102,720
Dec. 31/2004	6,000	5,136	864	1,856	101,856
Jun. 30/2005	6,000	5,093	907	949	100,949
Dec. 31/2005	6,000	5,051*	949	-0-	100,000
	$60,000	$52,280	$7,720		

Column A is the bonds' par value ($100,000) multiplied by the semiannual contract rate (6%).
Column B is the bonds' prior period carrying value multiplied by the semiannual market rate (5%).
Column C is the difference between interest paid and bond interest expense, or [(A)-(B)].
Column D is the prior period's unamortized premium less the current period's premium amortization.
Column E is the bonds' par value plus unamortized premium, or [$100,000+(D)].

Column B shows the amount of expense computed as the 5% market rate multiplied by the beginning carrying value. The amount of cash paid out in column A is larger than bond interest expense because the cash payment is based on the higher 6% contract rate. The excess cash payment over the expense reduces the principal. These amounts are shown in column C. Column E shows the new carrying value after the amortized premium in column C is deducted from the prior period's carrying value. Column D shows how the premium is reduced by the amortization process over the life of the bonds.

The effect of premium amortization on the bond interest expense and the bond liability is seen in the journal entry on June 30, 2001, when the issuer makes the first semiannual interest payment:

Assets = Liabilities + Equity
−6,000   −614   −5,386

2001			
June 30	Bond interest expense	5,386	
	Premium on Bonds Payable	614	
	Cash		6,000
	To record six months' interest and premium amortization.		

Similar entries are recorded at each payment date until the bonds mature at the end of 2005. The effective interest method yields decreasing amounts of bond interest expense and increasing amounts of premium amortization over the bonds' life.

Did You Know?

Amortization Magic
Amortization tables are made easy by spreadsheet software such as Excel and Lotus. We need only enter the bonds' par value, selling price, contract rate, market rate, and life to get a complete amortization table. All accounting entries and adjustments can be taken directly from this output.

Randall Computer Company issued 10-year, 10% bonds with a par value of $100,000 to Chance Company for $95,083 on March 1, 1999. The bonds are dated January 1, 1999.

Required

Prepare journal entries for Randall Computer Company for 1999 of January 1, July 1, and December 31. Assume that any discount or premium is amortized only at year-end.

1999			
Jan. 1	Cash	95,083	
	Discount on Bonds Payable	4,917	
	Bonds Payable		100,000
	Sold bonds at a discount.		
July 1	Interest Expense	5,000	
	Cash		5,000
	To record payment of six months' interest.		
Dec. 31	Interest Expense	5,000	
	Interest Payable		5,000
	To record payment of six months' interest.		
Dec. 31	Interest Expense	1,410	
	Discount on Bonds Payable		1,410
	To record amortization of the discount ($100,000 × .10 × 12/12 minus $95,083 × .12 × 12/12).		

Issuing Bonds between Interest Dates

Many bonds are sold on an interest payment date. But a company can sell its bonds at a date other than an interest payment date. When this occurs, the purchasers normally pay the issuer the purchase price plus any interest accrued since the prior interest payment date. This accrued interest is then repaid to purchasers on the next interest date.

To illustrate, let's suppose **Canadian Tire** sells $100,000 of its 9% bonds at par on March 1, 1999, which is two months after the original issue date. The interest on Canadian Tire's bonds is payable semiannually on each June 30 and December 31. Because two months have passed, the issuer collects two months' interest from the buyer at the time of the sale. This amount is $1,500 ($100,000 × 9% × 2/12). This case is reflected in Exhibit 17.13.

Stated issue
date January 1

Date of sale
March 1

First interest
date June 30

$1,500 accrued ← $3,000 earned →

Bondholder pays
$1,500 to issuer

Issuer pays
$4,500 to bondholder

Exhibit 17.13

Accruing Interest between Interest Dates

Canadian Tire's entry to record the sale of its bonds is:

Assets = Liabilities + Equity
+101,500   +100,000
             +1,500

Mar. 1	Cash	101,500	
	Interest Payable		1,500
	Bonds Payable		100,000
	Sold $100,000 of bonds with two months' accrued interest.		

The liabilities for interest payable and the bonds are recorded in separate accounts.

When the June 30 semiannual interest date arrives, Canadian Tire pays a full six months' interest of $4,500 ($100,000 × 9% × 1/2) to the bondholder. This payment includes the four months' interest of $3,000 earned by the bondholder from March 1 to June 30 *plus* the repayment of two months' accrued interest collected by Canadian Tire when the bonds were sold. Canadian Tire's entry to record this first interest payment is:

Assets = Liabilities + Equity
−4,500   − 1,500   −3,000

June 30	Interest Payable	1,500	
	Bond interest expense	3,000	
	Cash		4,500
	Paid semiannual interest on the bonds.		

The practice of collecting and then repaying accrued interest with the first interest payment is done to simplify the bond issuer's administrative efforts. To understand this, suppose a company sells bonds on 15 or 20 different dates between the original issue date and the first interest payment date. If the issuer did not collect accrued interest from buyers, it would need to pay different amounts of cash to each of them according to the time passed since they purchased the bonds. This means the issuer would need to keep detailed records of purchasers and the dates they bought their bonds. Issuers avoid this extra recordkeeping by having each buyer pay accrued interest at the time of purchase. Issuers then pay a full six months' interest to all purchasers, regardless of when they bought the bonds.

Accruing Bond Interest Expense

If a bond's interest period does not coincide with the issuing company's accounting period, an adjusting entry is necessary to recognize bond interest expense accruing since the most recent interest payment.

To illustrate, let's assume the Hydro Quebec bonds described in Exhibit 17.12 are issued on September 1, 2000, instead of December 31, 2000. As a result, four months' interest (and premium amortization) accrue before the end of the 2000 calendar year. Because the reporting period of Hydro Quebec ends on that date, an adjusting entry is needed to capture this information about the bonds.

Interest for the four months ended December 31, 2000, equals $3,591, which is 4/6 of the first six months' interest of $5,386. The premium amortization is $409, which is 4/6 of the first six months' amortization of $614. The sum of the bond interest expense and the amortization is $4,000 ($3,591 + $409), which equals 4/6 of the $6,000 cash payment due on March 1, 2001. We record these effects with this adjusting entry:

Assets = Liabilities + Equity
           −409   −3,591
+4,000

2000			
Dec. 31	Bond interest expense	3,591	
	Premium on Bonds Payable	409	
	Interest Payable		4,000
	To record four months' accrued interest and premium amortization.		

Similar entries are made on each December 31 throughout the five-year life of the bonds.

When the $6,000 cash payment occurs on the next interest date, the journal entry recognizes the bond interest expense and amortization for January and February of 2001. It must also eliminate the interest payable liability created by the December 31 adjusting entry. In this case we make the following entry to record payment on March 1, 2001:

2001			
Mar. 1	Interest Payable	4,000	
	Bond Interest Expense ($5,386 × 2/6)	1,795	
	Premium on Bonds Payable ($614 × 2/6) ..	205	
	Cash		6,000
	To record two months' interest and amortization and eliminate the accrued interest liability.		

Assets = Liabilities + Equity
−6,000   −4,000   −1,795
           −205

The interest payments made each September are recorded as normal because the entire six-month interest period is included within a single fiscal year.

Bond Pricing

Prices for bonds that are traded on an organized exchange are published in newspapers and available through online services. This information includes the bond price (called *quote*), its contract rate, and its market (called *yield*) rate. But only a fraction of bonds outstanding are actually traded on an organized exchange. Many others are rarely traded. To compute the price of a bond, we need to apply present value concepts. This can be done using special bond pricing tables or through computing the present value of a bond's cash flows. This section explains how we use *present value concepts* to price the Fila discount bond and the Hydro Quebec premium bond.

Present Value of a Discount Bond

The issue price of bonds is found by computing the present value of the bond's cash payments, discounted at the market rate of interest. When computing the present value of the Fila bond, we work with *semiannual* compounding periods because this is the time between interest payments. This means the annual market rate of 10% is changed to a semiannual rate of 5%. Also, the five-year life of the bonds is changed to 10 semiannual periods.

Our computation is twofold: (1) find the present value of the $100,000 maturity payment and (2) find the present value of the series of 10 payments of $4,000 each; see Exhibit 17.1. These present values can be found by using present value tables.[4] Appendix II lists some present value tables and explains how to use them. Table II.1 in Appendix II is used to compute the single $100,000 maturity payment, and Table II.3 in Appendix II is used to compute the $4,000 series of interest payments.

We first go to Table II.1 on row 10 and go across to the 5% column. The table value is 0.6139. Second, we go to Table II.3 on row 10 and go across to the 5% column, where the table value is 7.7217. The bond price is computed by multiplying the cash flow amounts by their corresponding table values and adding them together. Exhibit 17.14 shows this result.

Cash Flow	Table	Table Value	Amount	Present Value
$100,000 par value	II.1	0.6139	$100,000	$61,390
$4,000 interest payments	II.3	7.7217	4,000	30,887
Price of Bond				$92,277

Exhibit 17.14

Computing Fila's Bond Price

---

[4] Many inexpensive calculators provide present value functions for easy computation of bonds prices.

This means if 5% is semiannual market rate for Fila bonds, the maximum price that buyers will pay is $92,277. This amount is also the minimum price the issuer will accept.

Present Value of a Premium Bond

We estimate the issue price of Hydro Quebec' bonds by using the market rate to compute the present value of its future cash flows. When computing the present value of this bond, we work with *semiannual* compounding periods because this is the time between interest payments. This means the annual market rate of 10% is changed to a semiannual rate of 5%. Also, the five-year life of the bonds is changed to 10 semiannual periods.

Our computation is twofold: (1) find the present value of the $100,000 maturity payment and (2) find the present value of the series of 10 payments of $6,000 each; see Exhibit 17.9. These present values can be found by using present value tables. First, go to Table II.1 on row 10 and go across to the 5% column. The table value is 0.6139. Second, go to Table II.3 on row 10 and go across to the 5% column, where the table value is 7.7217. The bond price is computed by multiplying the cash flow amounts by their corresponding table values and adding them together. Exhibit 17.15 shows these computations.

Exhibit 17.15

Computing Hydro Quebec's Bond Price

Cash Flow	Table	Table Value	Amount	Present Value
$100,000 par value	II.1	0.6139	$100,000	$ 61,390
$6,000 interest payments	II.3	7.7217	6,000	46,330
Price of Bond				$107,720

This means if 5% is the semiannual market rate for Hydro Quebec bonds, the maximum price that buyers will pay is $107,720. This amount is also the minimum price the issuer will accept.

Flash back

Use this information to solve 7, 8, and 9: On December 31, 1999, a company issued 16%, 10-year bonds with a par value of $100,000. Interest is paid on June 30 and December 31. The bonds are sold to yield a 14% annual market rate at an issue price of $110,592.

7. Are these bonds issued at a discount or premium? Explain why.

8. Using the effective interest method of allocating bond interest expense, the issuer records the second interest payment (on December 31, 2000) with a debit to Premium on Bonds Payable in the amount of (a) $7,470, (b) $7,741, (c) $259, (d) $530, (e) $277.

9. How are the bonds reported in the long-term liability section of the issuer's balance sheet as of December 31, 2000?

10. On May 1, a company sells 9% bonds with a $500,000 par value that pays semiannual interest on each of January 1 and July 1. The bonds are sold at par value plus interest accrued since January 1. The bond issuer's entry to record the first semiannual interest payment on July 1 includes (a) a debit to Interest Payable for $15,000, (b) a debit to Bond interest expense for $22,500, (c) a credit to Interest Payable for $7,500.

Answers—p. 809

This section describes the retirement of bonds: (1) at maturity, (2) before maturity, and (3) by converting them to shares.

Bond Retirement at Maturity

The carrying value of bonds at maturity will always equal their par value. Both Exhibits 17.9 (a discount) and 17.13 (a premium) show the carrying value of these bonds at the end of their five-year life ($100,000) equals the bonds' par value.

The entry to record retirement of the Hydro Quebec bonds in Exhibit 17.12 at maturity, assuming interest is already paid and recorded, is:

2005			
Dec. 31	Bonds Payable	100,000	
	Cash		100,000
	To record retirement of bonds at maturity.		

Bond Retirement before Maturity

Companies sometimes wish to retire some or all of their bonds prior to maturity. For instance, if interest rates decline significantly, a company may wish to replace old high-interest paying bonds with new low-interest bonds. Two common ways of retiring bonds before maturity are to (1) exercise a call option or (2) purchase them on the open market.

In the first instance, a company can reserve the right to retire bonds early by issuing *callable bonds*. This means the bond indenture gives the issuing company an option to *call* the bonds before they mature by paying the par value plus a *call premium* to the bondholders. The second case is where the issuer retires bonds by repurchasing them on the open market at their current price. Whether bonds are called or repurchased, the issuer is unlikely to pay a price that exactly equals the bonds' carrying value. When there is a difference between the bonds' carrying value and the amount paid in a bond retirement transaction, the issuer records a gain or loss equal to the difference.

To illustrate the accounting for retiring callable bonds, let's assume a company has issued callable bonds with a par value of $100,000. The call option requires the issuer to pay a call premium of $3,000 to bondholders in addition to the par value. Immediately after the June 30, 2000, interest payment, the bonds have a carrying value of $104,500. On July 1, 2000, the issuer calls these bonds and pays $103,000 to bondholders. The issuer recognizes a $1,500 gain from the difference between the bonds' carrying value of $104,500 and the retirement price of $103,000. The entry to record this bond retirement is:

July 1	Bonds Payable	100,000	
	Premium on Bonds Payable	4,500	
	Gain on Retirement of Bonds		1,500
	Cash		103,000
	To record retirement of bonds before maturity.		

A company generally must call all of its bonds when it exercises a call option. But a company can retire as many or as few bonds as it desires through open market transactions. If it retires less than the entire set of bonds, it recognizes a gain or loss for the difference between the carrying value of those bonds retired and the amount paid to acquire them.

Flash back

11. Six years ago, a company issued $500,000 of 6%, eight-year bonds at a price of 95. The current carrying value is $493,750. The company retired 50% of the bonds by buying them on the open market at a price of $102\frac{1}{2}$. What is the amount of gain or loss on retirement of these bonds?

Answers—p. 809

Convertible Bond

Assets = Liabilities + Equity
$-100,000$ $+100,000$

Bond Retirement by Conversion of Shares

We described convertible bonds earlier in the chapter, and explained how bond-holders have the right to convert their bonds to common shares. When conversion occurs, the carrying value of bonds is transferred to contributed capital accounts and no gain or loss is recorded.

To illustrate, on January 1 the $100,000 par value bonds of **Converse**, with a carrying value of $100,000, are converted to 15,000 no-par value common shares. The entry to record this conversion is:

Jan. 1	Bonds Payable	100,000	
	Common Shares, no-par value		100,000
	To record retirement of bonds by *conversion into common shares.*		

The market prices of the bonds and shares are not part of this entry.

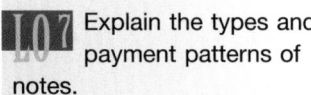

Did You Know?

Cruising with Convertibles
A convertible bond has both debt and equity features. The debt feature is the economic obligation to deliver cash or other assets. The equity feature is the call option granting the investor the right to convert to common shares of the issuer. When the share price is greater than the conversion price it is probable that the debt will not have to be repaid. For purposes of measuring a firm's ratio of debt to equity the convertible bond should be treated as equity. But when the share price is less than the conversion price and it is likely that conversion will not occur, the bond should be included as debt. The *CICA Handbook* provides guidelines on the presentation of financial instruments that contain both debt and equity features. These guidelines emphasize economic substance over form and will be dealt with in later accounting courses.

Long-Term Notes Payable

LO7 Explain the types and payment patterns of notes.

Like bonds, notes payable are issued to finance operations and borrow money. But, unlike a bond, signing a note payable is typically a transaction with a single lender such as a bank. A note is initially measured and recorded at its selling price. Selling price is the note's face value minus any discount or plus any premium. Over the life of a note, the amount of interest expense allocated to each period is computed by multiplying the interest rate at issuance of the note by the beginning-of-period balance of the note. The balance of a note at any point in time equals its face value minus any unallocated discount or plus any unallocated premium.[5]

---

[5] A note's balance at any date is also computed as the present value of all remaining future payments, discounted at the original interest rate.

Interest-Bearing Notes

Let's assume **Taco Bell** buys service equipment on January 2 with a fair market value of $45,000 by issuing an 8%, three-year note with a face value of $45,000. The company records the purchase with this entry:

Jan. 2	Service Equipment	45,000	
	Notes Payable		45,000
	Issued a $45,000, three-year, 8% note payable for equipment.		

Assets = Liabilities + Equity
+45,000   +45,000

The company (note issuer) reports annual interest expense equal to the original interest rate times each year's beginning balance of the note over the life of the note. Exhibit 17.16 shows this interest expense computation and allocation.

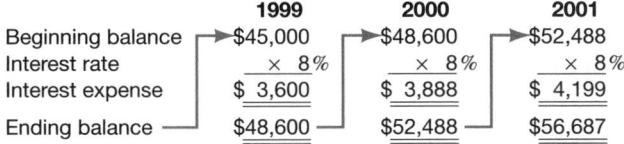

	1999	**2000**	**2001**
Beginning balance	$45,000	$48,600	$52,488
Interest rate	× 8%	× 8%	× 8%
Interest expense	$ 3,600	$ 3,888	$ 4,199
Ending balance	$48,600	$52,488	$56,687

Exhibit 17.16

Interest-Bearing Note—
Interest Paid at Maturity

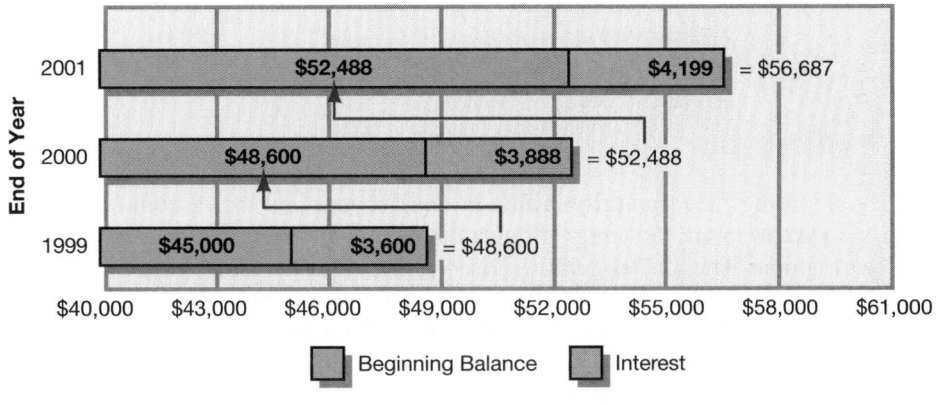

Interest is computed by multiplying each year's beginning balance by the original 8% interest rate. Interest is then added to the beginning balance to find the ending balance. A period's ending balance becomes next period's beginning balance. Because the balance grows by compounding, the amount of interest allocated to each year increases over the life of the note. The final ending balance of $56,687 equals the original $45,000 borrowed plus total interest of $11,687. A note that delays interest payments is more common for lower risk companies that wish to delay cash payments until some later period. It is often backed with assets as collateral.

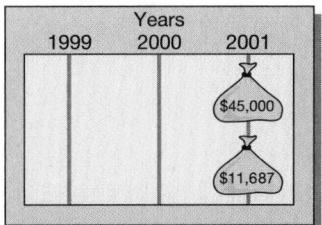

Retailer
You are a retailer in stereo components. You are planning a holiday sale on a quality stereo system requiring no payments for two years. At the end of two years, buyers must pay the full amount. Your normal selling price is $4,100, but you are willing to sell it today for $3,000 cash. What is your sale price if payment will not occur for two years and the market rate is 10%?

You Make the Call

Answer—p. 809

Non-interest-Bearing Notes

A *non-interest-bearing note* includes interest in its face (maturity) value. When a non-interest-bearing note is used to purchase an asset, the note's face value (because it includes interest) is greater than the asset's fair value. This type of note is desired by issuers who wish to avoid periodic interest payments. The asset and the note are recorded at a carrying value of either the asset's fair value or the note's fair value, whichever is more clearly determinable. A note's fair value, like that of a bond, is computed based on the market interest rate when it is issued. An asset's fair value is determined by current market transactions.

To illustrate, let's assume **Neptune Theatre** buys staging machinery on January 2, 1999, by issuing a non-interest-bearing, 5-year, $10,000 note payable. Exhibit 17.17 shows this note's cash flows.

Exhibit 17.17

Cash Flows of
Non-interest-Bearing Note

Neptune decides its estimate of the machinery's fair value is less reliable than the current 10% market interest rate available to Neptune. This note's fair value when issued is $6,209.[6] This also gives us the implied fair value of the machinery. The entry to record this purchase is:

Assets = Liabilities + Equity
+6,209   −3,791
         +10,000

1999			
Jan. 2	Machinery	6,209	
	Discount on Notes Payable	3,791	
	Long-Term Notes Payable		10,000
	Exchanged a five-year		
	non-interest-bearing note for machinery.		

By recording face (maturity) value in one account and the discount in a liability contra account, this entry follows the usual way of recording a non-interest-bearing note. The $3,791 debit to Discount on Notes Payable is the *total interest expense* to be allocated to the five years of the note's life.

Exhibit 17.18 shows each year's interest, the allocation of the discount, and the note balance. The note balance grows over the five years until it reaches its face value of $10,000. The discount balance decreases to $0 after five years, and reflects *amortizing the discount*. The process of computing each year's interest is the same as in the previous discussion of the interest-bearing note. The note balance at the beginning of each year is multiplied by the 10% interest rate to determine interest for that year.

The first year's interest expense and discount amortization are recorded when we make year-end adjusting entries as follows:

Assets = Liabilities + Equity
         +621   −621

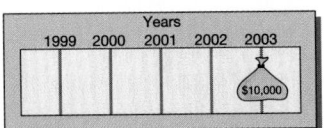

1999			
Dec. 31	Interest Expense	621	
	Discount on Notes Payable		621
	To record interest expense accrued on		
	non-interest-bearing note.		

Similar entries are recorded at the end of each year until the balance of the discount account equals $0 and the net liability balance equals $10,000.

---

[6] The note's fair value is computed as the present value of the $10,000 payment due after five years discounted at the market rate of 10%. Table II.1 in Appendix II shows the present value of 1 discounted at 10% for five years is 0.6209. The present (fair) value of the note is $6,209, computed as $10,000 × 0.6209.

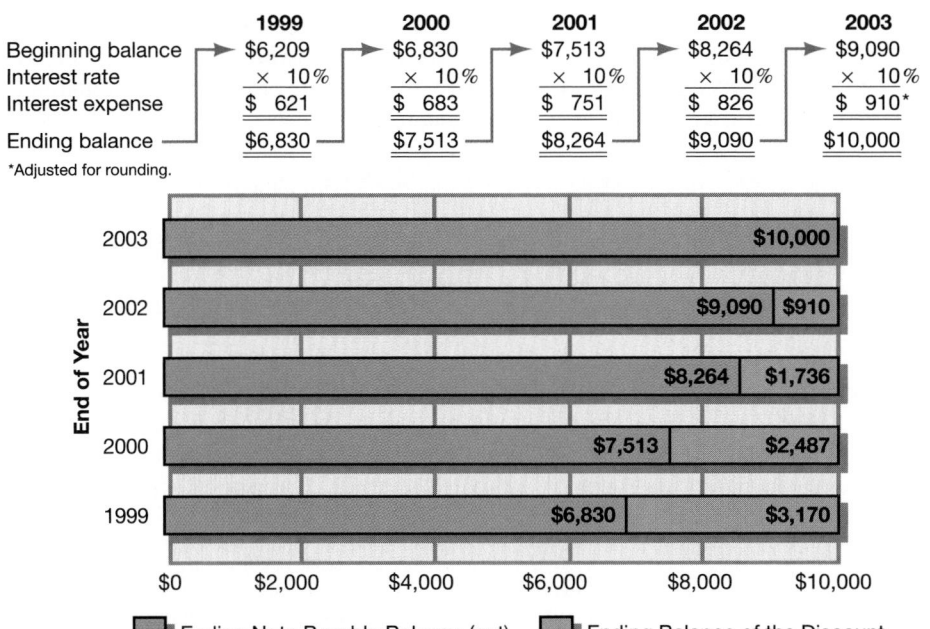

Exhibit 17.18

Non-interest-Bearing Note

When the note matures on January 2, 2004, the issuer records its payment with the entry:

2004			
Jan. 2	Long-Term Notes Payable	10,000	
	Cash		10,000
	Paid non-interest-bearing note.		

Assets = Liabilities + Equity
−10,000 −10,000

Flashback

12. On January 1, 1999, a company signs a $6,000 three-year note payable bearing 6% annual interest. The original principal and all interest is paid on December 31, 2001. Interest is compounded annually. How much interest is allocated to year 2000? (a) $0, (b) $360, (c) $381.60, or (d) $404.50.

13. A company promises to pay a lender $4,000 at the end of four years. The annual interest rate is 8% and interest is included in the $4,000 payments, meaning the note's fair value is $2,940. Record this note's issuance.

Answers—p. 809

Installment Notes

An **installment note** is an obligation requiring a series of periodic payments to the lender. Installments notes are common for franchises and other businesses where costs are large and the owner desires to spread these costs over several periods. When an installment note is used to borrow money or pay for assets, the borrower records the note with an entry similar to the one used for a single-payment note. This means the increase in cash or assets is recorded with a debit and the increase in the liability is recorded with a credit to Notes Payable.

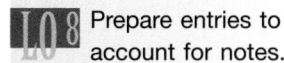 Prepare entries to account for notes.

To illustrate, let's assume **SuperBowl,** a bowling establishment, borrows $60,000 from a bank to purchase AMF and Brunswick bowling equipment. SuperBowl signs an 8% installment note with the bank requiring six annual payments. SuperBowl records the note's issuance as:

Assets   =   Liabilities = Equity
+60,000   +60,000

1999				
Dec. 31	Cash		60,000	
	Notes Payable			60,000
	Borrowed $60,000 by signing an 8%			
	installment note.			

SuperBowl might also issue a note directly to the seller of the bowling equipment. In this case, SuperBowl would record the bowling equipment received instead of cash. One of these sellers, **Brunswick Corp.,** often provides commitments to banks in event of a buyer's default. Brunswick's annual report states:

The company has entered into agreements ... that provide for the repurchase of its products from a financial institution in the event of repossession upon a dealer's default ... [And] provide limited recourse on marine and bowling capital equipment sales.

Payments on an installment note normally include the interest expense accruing to the date of the payment plus a portion of the amount borrowed (the *principal*). Generally, we can identify two types of payment patterns: (1) accrued interest plus equal principal payments, and (2) equal payments. The remainder of this section describes these two patterns and how we account for them.

Accrued Interest plus Equal Principal Payments

One payment pattern is accrued interest plus equal amounts of principal. This pattern creates cash flows that decrease in size over the life of the note. This decrease occurs because each payment reduces the note's principal balance, yielding less accrued interest expense for the next period.

To illustrate, let's assume the $60,000, 8% note signed by SuperBowl requires it to make six payments at the end of each year equal to *accrued interest plus $10,000 of principal*. Exhibit 17.19 describes these payments, interest, and changes in the balance of this note. Column A lists the note's beginning balance. Columns B, C, and D list each cash payment and how it is divided between interest and principal. Column B shows interest expense accruing in each year at 8% of the beginning balance. Column C shows each payment reduces principal with a $10,000 debit to the Notes Payable account. Column D is the total of B and C. Column E shows the ending balance of the note, which equals the beginning balance in column A minus the principal payment in column C.

We also include *debit* or *credit* in column headings to help understand their accounting effects. For instance, the credit to Cash equals the sum of debits to interest expense and principal. This table shows total interest expense is $16,800 and total principal is $60,000. This means total cash payments are $76,800. The graph in the lower portion of Exhibit 17.19 captures these effects and highlights the (1) decreasing total payment pattern, (2) decreasing accrued interest, and (3) constant principal payments of $10,000.

Period Ending	(A) Beginning Balance Prior (e)	Payments (B) Debit Interest Expense 8% × (A)	+	(C) Debit Notes Payable $60,000/6	=	(D) Credit Cash (B) + (C)	(E) Ending Balance (A) − (C)
Dec. 31/2000	$60,000	$ 4,800		$10,000		$14,800	$50,000
Dec. 31/2001	50,000	4,000		10,000		14,000	40,000
Dec. 31/2002	40,000	3,200		10,000		13,200	30,000
Dec. 31/2003	30,000	2,400		10,000		12,400	20,000
Dec. 31/2004	20,000	1,600		10,000		11,600	10,000
Dec. 31/2005	10,000	800		10,000		10,800	-0-
		$16,800		$60,000		$76,800	

Exhibit 17.19

Installment Note—Accrued Interest plus Equal Principal Payments

SuperBowl (borrower) records the effects of the first two payments with these entries:

2000			
Dec. 31	Interest Expense	4,800	
	Notes Payable	10,000	
	Cash		14,800
	To record first installment payment.		

Assets = Liabilities + Equity
−14,800   −10,000   −4,800

2001			
Dec. 31	Interest Expense	4,000	
	Notes Payable	10,000	
	Cash		14,000
	To record second installment payment.		

Assets = Liabilities + Equity
−14,000   − 10,000   − 4,000

After all six payments are recorded, the balance of the Notes Payable account is zero.

Installment Note—Equal
Total Payments

Equal Total Payments

Many installment notes require the borrower to make a series of equal payments. These payments consist of changing amounts of interest and principal.

To illustrate, let's assume the above $60,000 note requires SuperBowl (borrower) to make a series of six equal total payments of $12,979 at the end of each year.[7] Exhibit 17.20 shows the *equal total payments pattern* and its effects on the note balance. Each payment of $12,979 includes both interest and principal. See how the total amount of each payment is allocated between interest and principal.

		Payments			
	(A)	**(B)** Debit	**(C)** Debit	**(D)** Credit	**(E)**
Period Ending	**Beginning Balance Prior (e)**	**Interest Expense 8% × (A)**	+ **Notes Payable (B) − (D)**	= **Cash Computed**	**Ending Balance (A) − (C)**
Dec. 31/2000	$60,000	$ 4,800	$ 8,179	$12,979	$51,821
Dec. 31/2001	51,821	4,146	8,833	12,979	42,988
Dec. 31/2002	42,988	3,439	9,540	12,979	33,448
Dec. 31/2003	33,448	2,676	10,303	12,979	23,145
Dec. 31/2004	23,145	1,852	11,127	12,979	12,018
Dec. 31/2005	12,018	961	12,018	12,979	-0-
		$17,874	$60,000	$77,874	

Principal
Interest

Increasing Principal Amounts   Decreasing Accrued Interest   Equal Total Payments

End of Year	Payment Pattern
2005	$12,018 $961
2004	$11,127 $1,852
2003	$10,303 $2,676
2002	$9,540 $3,439
2001	$8,833 $4,146
2000	$8,179 $4,800

0   $2,500 $5,000 $7,500 $10,000 $12,500 $15,000
Payment Pattern

Exhibit 17.20 is very similar to Exhibit 17.19. Column A shows the note's beginning balance for each year. Column B shows accrued interest for each year at 8% of the beginning balance. Column C shows the change in the principal of the note, which equals the difference between the total payment in column D and the interest expense in column B. Column E shows the ending balance after each payment.

---

[7] The $60,000 equals the present value of an annuity of six annual payments of $12,979, discounted at 8% (we show this computation later in the section).

While all six payments are equal, the accrued interest decreases each year because the principal balance of the note is declining. As the amount of interest decreases each year, the amount applied to the principal increases. This pattern is graphed in the lower portion of Exhibit 17.20.

The amounts in Exhibit 17.20 are used to show how we record the first two payments toward this note with these journal entries:

2000			
Dec. 31	Interest Expense	4,800	
	Notes Payable	8,179	
	Cash		12,979
	To record first installment payment.		

Assets = Liabilities + Equity
−12,979   −8,179   −4,800

2001			
Dec. 31	Interest Expense	4,146	
	Notes Payable	8,833	
	Cash		12,979
	To record second installment payment.		

Assets = Liabilities + Equity
−12,979   −8,833   −4,146

The borrower records similar entries for each of the remaining payments. After six years, the Notes Payable account balance is zero.

It is interesting to compare the two payment patterns in Exhibits 17.19 and 17.20. The series of equal total payments leads to a greater amount of interest expense over the life of the note. This is because the first three payments in Exhibit 17.20 are smaller and do not reduce the principal as quickly as the first three payments in Exhibit 17.19.[8]

Mortgage Notes

A **mortgage** is a legal agreement that helps protect a lender if a borrower fails to make the required payments on bonds or notes. A mortgage gives the lender the right to be paid out of the cash proceeds from the sale of a borrower's specific assets identified in the mortgage. A separate legal document, called a *mortgage contract*, describes the terms of a mortgage.

Mortgage notes include a mortgage contract pledging title to specific assets as security for the note. While less common, there also exist *mortgage bonds* backed by assets of the issuer. A mortgage contract is given to the lender who accepts a note or to the trustee for the bonds. This contract usually requires the issuer (borrower) to pay all property taxes on the mortgaged assets, to maintain them properly, and to carry adequate insurance against fire and other types of losses. These requirements are designed to keep the property from losing value and avoid diminishing the lender's security. Mortgage notes are especially popular in the purchase of homes and in the acquisition of plant assets by companies. Accounting for mortgage notes and bonds is essentially the same as

---

[8] Table II.3 in Appendix II is used to compute the series of six payments equal to the present value of the initial note balance of $60,000 at 8% interest. We go to Table II.3 on row 6 and go across to the 8% column, where the table value is 4.6229. The present value is equal to the payment amounts multiplied by the table value as shown below:

Cash Flow	Table	Table Value	Amount	Present Value
$? interest payments	II.3	4.6229	?	60,000

We solve for the payment by dividing $60,000 by 4.6229. When a note requires a series of equal payments, we can compute the payment amount with a present value table or calculator.

accounting for unsecured notes and bonds. The primary difference is the mortgage agreement needs to be disclosed to users of financial statements

Some mortgage notes carry a variable interest rate, also called floating rate. The contract rate on these types of notes and bonds can be periodically adjusted according to changes in interest rates and terms of the contract.

Most mortgage contracts grant the lender the right to *foreclose* on the property if the borrower fails to pay in accordance with the terms of the debt agreement. If foreclosure occurs, a court either orders the property to be sold or simply grants legal title of the mortgaged property to the lender. If the property is sold, the proceeds are first applied to court costs and then to the claims of the mortgage holder. If there are any additional proceeds, the borrower is entitled to receive them depending on any claims from the borrower's unsecured creditors.

Flash back

14. Which of the following is true for an installment note requiring a series of equal payments?
   a. Payments consist of an increasing amount of interest and a decreasing amount of principal.
   b. Payments consist of changing amounts of principal, but the interest portion remains constant.
   c. Payments consist of a decreasing amount of interest and an increasing amount of principal.
15. How is the interest portion of an installment note payment computed?
16. When a borrower records a periodic interest payment on an installment note, how are the balance sheet and income statement affected?

Answers—p. 809

Pledged Assets to Secured Liabilities   USING THE INFORMATION

This section explains how lenders can reduce their risk of loss and how borrowers can achieve more favourable terms by entering into collateral agreements. We also describe an important measure of this risk.

Collateral Agreements for Bonds and Notes

LO 9 Explain collateral agreements and their effects on loan risk.

We already explained how some bonds are secured by collateral agreements. Other bonds, called *debentures*, are unsecured. We also explained how mortgage notes can be secured by collateral. Collateral agreements reduce the risk of loss for both bonds and notes. Unsecured bonds and notes are more risky because the issuer's obligation to pay interest and principal has the same priority as all other unsecured liabilities in the event of bankruptcy. If a company's financial troubles leave it unable to pay its debts in full, the unsecured creditors (including the holders of debentures) lose a proportion or all of their balances.

A company's ability to borrow money with or without collateral agreements depends on its credit rating. In some cases, debt financing is unavailable unless the borrower can provide security to creditors with a collateral agreement. Even if unsecured loans are available, the creditors are likely to charge a higher rate of interest to compensate for the added risk. To borrow funds at a more favourable rate, many bonds and notes are secured by collateral agreements in the form of mortgages.

Information about a company's security agreements with its lenders is important to users. Notes to financial statements sometimes describe the amounts of assets pledged as security against liabilities. We next describe a ratio used to assess a borrower's situation with respect to its security agreements.

Ratio of Pledged Assets to Secured Liabilities

Lenders reduce their risk with agreements that can force borrowers to sell specific assets to settle overdue debts. Buyers (investors) of a company's secured debt obligations need to determine whether the pledged assets of the debtor provide adequate security. One method of evaluating this is to compute the ratio of **pledged assets to secured liabilities.** This is computed by dividing the book value of the company's assets pledged as collateral by the book value of the liabilities secured by these collateral agreements as shown in Exhibit 17.21.

LO 10 Compute the ratio of pledged assets to secured liabilities and explain its use.

$$\text{Pledged assets to secured liabilities} = \frac{\text{Book value of pledged asset}}{\text{Book value of secured liabilities}}$$

Exhibit 17.21

Pledged Assets to Secured Liabilities

To illustrate how we use this ratio, let's assume a company owns assets with a book value of $230,000 pledged against loans with a balance of $100,000. The pledged assets to secured liabilities ratio is 2.3 (often expressed as "2.3 to 1") and is computed as $230,000/$100,000. While there are no exact guidelines for interpreting the values for this ratio, the 2.3 value is sufficiently high to provide secured creditors with some comfort that their loans are covered by the borrower's assets.

The pledging of assets for the benefit of secured creditors also affects unsecured creditors. As an increasing portion of the assets are pledged, the unsecured creditors are less likely to receive a full repayment. In evaluating their position, unsecured creditors also gain information from the ratio of pledged assets to secured liabilities. A high ratio suggests that unsecured creditors are at greater risk for two reasons. Namely, secured creditors often demand a high ratio when they perceive (1) the values of the assets in liquidation are low, and (2) the likelihood of the company to meet its obligations from operating cash flows is weak.

When we use this ratio we must be aware that reported book values of the company's assets are unlikely to exactly reflect their market values. This ratio is improved if we can determine the assets' current market values and then use them in the ratio instead of book values. Major lenders to a company can sometimes get this information directly by asking the borrower to provide recent appraisals or other evidence of the assets' market values. Many lenders do not have this option. Using the ratio also requires knowledge about secured liabilities and pledged assets—both how they're measured and reported. This requires analysis of information in both the financial statements and their notes.

Bond Investor

You are a bond investor. You're planning to purchase debenture bonds from one of two companies that operate in the same industry and are similar in size and performance. The first company has $350,000 of unsecured liabilities and $575,000 of secured liabilities. The book value of this company's pledged assets is $1,265,000. The second company has $1,200,000 of unsecured liabilities and $800,000 of secured liabilities, and its book value of pledged assets is $2,000,000. Using the ratio of pledged assets to secured liabilities, determine which company's debenture bonds are less risky.

You Make the Call

Answer—p. 809

Summary

LO 1 **Compare bond financing versus shares financing.** Bond financing is used to fund business activities. Advantages of bond financing versus common shares include (a) no effect on shareholders' control, (b) tax savings, and (c) increased earnings due to financial leverage. Disadvantages include (a) required interest and principal payments, and (b) decreased earnings when operations turn less profitable.

LO 2 **Explain the types of bonds and their issuing procedures.** An issuer's bonds usually are sold to many investors. Certain bonds are secured by the issuer's assets while other bonds, called *debentures*, are unsecured. Serial bonds mature at different points in time while term bonds mature at one time. Registered bonds have each bondholder's name and address recorded by the issuing company, while bearer bonds are payable to whoever holds the bonds. Convertible bonds are exchangeable by bondholders for shares of the issuing company's shares. Callable bonds can be retired by the issuer at a set price. Bonds are often issued by an underwriter, and a bond certificate is evidence of the issuer's obligation.

LO 3 **Prepare entries to record bond issuance and bond interest expense.** When bonds are issued at par, Cash is debited and Bonds Payable are credited for the bonds' par value. At the bonds' interest payment dates, Bond Interest Expense is debited and Cash credited for an amount equal to the bonds' par value multiplied by the bonds' contract rate. The cash paid to bondholders on semiannual interest payment dates is computed as one-half of the result of multiplying the par value of the bonds by their contract rate.

LO 4 **Compute and record amortization of bond discount.** The issue price of a bond is computed using the market rate in solving for the present values of the bonds' interest payments and their par value. Bonds are issued at a discount when the contract rate is less than the market rate. This is the same as saying the issue (selling) price is less than par. When this occurs, the issuer records a credit to Bonds Payable (at par) and debits both to Discount on Bonds Payable and to Cash. The amount of bond interest expense assigned to each period is computed using either the straight-line or effective interest method. Straight-line can only be used if the results are not materially different from the effective interest method. Bond interest expense using the effective interest method equals the bonds' beginning-of-period carrying value multiplied by the original market rate at time of issuance.

LO 5 **Compute and record amortization of bond premium.** Bonds are issued at a premium when the contract rate is higher than the market rate. This means the issue (selling) price is greater than par. When this occurs,

the issuer records a debit to Cash and credits both to Premium on Bonds Payable and to Bonds Payable (at par). The amount of bond interest expense assigned to each period is computed using either the straight-line or effective interest method. The balance of the Premium on Bonds Payable is allocated to reduce bond interest expense over the life of the bonds.

LO 6 **Record the retirement of bonds.** Bonds are retired at maturity with a debit to Bonds Payable and a credit to Cash for the par value of the bonds. Bonds can be retired early by the issuer by exercising a call option or by purchases on the open market. Alternatively, bondholders can retire bonds early by exercising a conversion feature on convertible bonds. The issuer recognizes a gain or loss for the difference between the amount paid out and the bonds' carrying value, unless the bonds are converted into shares in which case no gain or loss is recognized.

LO 7 **Explain the types and payment patterns of notes.** Notes are either interest-bearing or non-interest-bearing. Notes can require repayment of principal and interest (a) at the end of a period of time, or (b) gradually over a period of time in either equal or unequal amounts. Notes repaid over a period of time are called installment notes and usually follow one of two payment patterns: (a) decreasing payments of interest plus equal amounts of principal or (b) equal total payments.

LO 8 **Prepare entries to account for notes.** Interest is allocated to each period in a note's life by multiplying its carrying value by its market rate at issuance. If a note is repaid with equal payments, the amount of payment is computed by dividing the borrowed amount by the present value of an annuity number (taken from a present value table) using the market rate and the number of payments.

LO 9 **Explain collateral agreements and their effects on loan risk.** Some bonds and notes are secured by collateral agreements. Collateral agreements reduce the risk of loss for both bonds and notes. Unsecured bonds and notes are more risky because the issuer's obligation to pay interest and principal has the same priority as all other unsecured liabilities in the event of bankruptcy. To borrow funds at a more favourable rate, many bonds and notes are secured by collateral agreements called *mortgages*.

LO 10 **Compute the ratio of pledged assets to secured liabilities and explain its use.** Both secured and unsecured creditors are concerned about the relation between the amounts of assets owned by the debtor and the amounts of secured liabilities. Secured creditors are safer when the ratio of pledged assets to secured liabilities is larger. But the risks of unsecured creditors are often increased when this ratio is high because their claims to assets are secondary to secured creditors.

Guidance Answers to **You Make the Call**

Bond Rater

One factor in rating a bond is its payment pattern. Higher-risk bonds have longer repayment periods and smaller interest payments over the life of the bond. Another factor is the competitive position of the company. Higher-risk bonds are more likely issued by companies in financial difficulties or facing higher than normal uncertainties. Still another factor is the financial health of the company. Companies with higher than normal debt and with large fluctuations in earnings are considered of higher risk.

Retailer

This is a present value question where the market rate (10%) and present value ($3,000) are known, but the payment made two years later is not known. The amount we'd expect to receive at the end of two years is $3,630, computed as $3,000 × 1.10 × 1.10. (This is similar to the computation in Exhibit

17.16.) Therefore, your sale price is $3,630 with no payments for two years. This $3,630 received two years from today is equivalent to $3,000 cash today.

Bond Investor

The first company's ratio of pledged assets to secured liabilities is 2.2 ($1,265,000/$575,000), and for the second company it is 2.5 ($2,000,000/$800,000). This suggests that secured creditors of the second company are at less risk than secured creditors of the first company. But *debenture bonds are unsecured*. Therefore, since the first company has fewer secured liabilities, it is of lower risk for unsecured debenture bonds. In addition, the first company has fewer liabilities and, since the companies are of equal size, the liabilities of the first company make up a smaller portion of total assets. Consequently, as a buyer of unsecured debenture bonds, you prefer the first company.

Guidance Answers to

1. *b*

2. Multiply the par value of the bonds by the contract rate of interest.

3. The bonds sell at a premium, and the purchasers pay more than the par value of the bonds.

4. The bonds are issued at a discount, meaning issue price is less than par value. A discount occurs because the bonds' contract rate is less than their market rate.

5.

Cash	91,893	
Discount on Bonds Payable	8,107	
Bonds Payable		100,000

6. *a.* $3,811 (total interest equal to $38,107, or 10 payments of $3,000 plus the $8,107 discount, divided by 10 periods.)

b. $3,676 (beginning balance of $91,893 times 4% market interest rate.)

7. The bonds are issued at a premium, meaning issue price is greater than par value. A premium occurs because the bonds' contract rate is greater than their market rate.

8. *e.* (On June 30/2000: $110,592 × 7% = $7,741 bond interest expense; $8,000 − $7,741 = $259 premium amortization; $110,592 − $259 = $110,333 ending balance. On Dec. 31/2000: $110,333 × 7% = $7,723 bond interest expense; $8,000 − $7,723 = $277 premium amortiza-

9.

Bonds payable, 16%, due December 31, 2009	$100,000	
Plus premium on bonds payable .	10,056*	$110,056

*Beginning premium balance of $10,592 less $259 and $277 amortized on June 30/2000 and Dec. 31/2000.

10. *a*

11. $9,375 loss (difference between repurchase price of $256,250 [50% of ($500,000 × 102.5%)] and carrying value of $246,875 [50% of $493,750].)

12. *c* [$6,000 + ($6,000 × .06)] × .06 = $381.60

13.

Cash	2,940	
Discount on Notes Payable	1,060	
Long-Term Notes Payable . . .		4,000
Exchanged a four-year non-interest-bearing note for cash.		

14. *c*

15. The interest portion of an installment payment equals the beginning balance for the period multiplied by the original interest rate.

16. On the balance sheet, the balances of the liability and cash are decreased. On the income statement, interest expense is increased.

Demonstration Problem

The Staley Tile Company patented and successfully test-marketed a new product. However, to expand its ability to produce and market the product, the company needed to raise $800,000 of additional financing. On January 1, 1999, the company borrowed the money under these arrangements:

a. Staley signed a $400,000, 10% installment note that will be repaid with five equal annual installments. The payments will be made on December 31 of 1999 through 2003.

b. Staley issued five-year bonds with a par value of $400,000. The bonds have a 12% annual contract rate and pay interest on June 30 and December 31. The annual market interest rate for the bonds was 10% on January 1, 1999.

Required

1. For the installment note, (a) compute the size of each payment, (b) prepare an amortization table, and (c) present the entry for the first payment.

2. For the bonds, (a) estimate the issue price of the bonds, (b) present the January 1, 1999, entry to record issuing the bonds, (c) prepare an amortization table using the interest method, (d) present the June 30, 1999, entry to record the first payment of interest, and (e) present an entry to record retiring the bonds at the call price of $416,000 on January 1, 2001.

Planning the Solution

■ For the installment note, divide the borrowed amount by the annuity table factor (from Exhibit 17A.6) for 10% and five payments. Prepare a table similar to Exhibit 17.20 and use the numbers in the first line for the entry.

■ For the bonds, estimate the issue price by using the market rate to find the present values of the bonds' cash flows (use tables found in Appendix II). Then, use this result to record issuing the bonds. Next, develop an amortization table like Exhibit 17.8, and use it to get the numbers that you need for the journal entry. Finally, use the table to find the carrying value as of the date of the retirement of the bonds that you need for the journal entry.

Solution to Demonstration Problem

Part 1

Payment = Note balance/Table value = $400,000/3.7908 = $105,519
Table value is for five payments and an interest rate of 10%.

| | | Payments | | |
| | (a) | (b) | (c) | (d) | (e) |
Period Ending	Beginning Balance	Debit Interest Expense	Debit Notes Payable	Credit Cash	Ending Balance
1999	$400,000	$ 40,000	$ 65,519	$105,519	$334,481
2000	334,481	33,448	72,071	105,519	262,410
2001	262,410	26,241	79,278	105,519	183,132
2002	183,132	18,313	87,206	105,519	95,926
2003	95,926	9,593	95,926	105,519	-0-
Total		$127,595	$400,000	$527,595	

1999			
Dec. 31	Interest Expense	40,000	
	Notes Payable	65,519	
	Cash		105,519
	To record first installment payment.		

Part 2

Estimated issue price of the bonds:

Cash Flow	Table	Table Value	Amount	Present Value
Par value	App. II (PV of $1)	0.6139	$400,000	$245,560
Interest (annuity) ...	App. II (PV of annuity)	7.7217	24,000	185,321
Total				$430,881

Table value is for 10 payments and an interest rate of 5%.

1999			
Jan. 1	Cash	430,881	
	Premium on Bonds Payable		30,881
	Bonds Payable		400,000
	Sold bonds at a premium.		

Semiannual Interest Period	(A) Cash Interest Paid 6% × $400,000	(B) Interest Expense 5% × (E)	(C) Premium Amortization (A) − (B)	(D) Unamortized Premium	(E) Carrying Value
Jan. 1/99				$30,881	$430,881
Jun. 30/99	$ 24,000	$ 21,544	$ 2,456	28,425	428,425
Dec. 31/99	24,000	21,421	2,579	25,846	425,846
Jun. 30/2000	24,000	21,292	2,708	23,138	423,138
Dec. 31/2000	24,000	21,157	2,843	20,295	420,295
Jun. 30/2001	24,000	21,015	2,985	17,310	417,310
Dec. 31/2001	24,000	20,866	3,134	14,176	414,176
Jun. 30/2002	24,000	20,709	3,291	10,885	410,885
Dec. 31/2002	24,000	20,544	3,456	7,429	407,429
Jun. 30/2003	24,000	20,371	3,629	3,800	403,800
Dec. 31/2003	24,000	20,200*	3,800	-0-	400,000
Totals	$240,000	$209,119	$30,881		

*Adjusted for rounding.

1999			
June 30	Bond interest expense	21,544	
	Premium on Bonds Payable	2,456	
	Cash		24,000
	Paid semiannual interest on the bonds.		

2001			
Jan. 1	Bonds Payable	400,000	
	Premium on Bonds Payable	20,295	
	Cash		416,000
	Gain on Retirement of Bonds		4,295
	To record the retirement of bonds (carrying value determined as of December 31, 2000).		

Present Values of Bonds and Notes

Learning Objectives

 LO 11 Explain and compute the present value of an amount to be paid at a future date.

 LO 12 Explain and compute the present value of a series of equal amounts to be paid at future dates.

Accounting for long-term liabilities such as bonds and notes presents us with new challenges because of the extended time period until these obligations are settled. This appendix explains how we can apply present value techniques both to measure a long-term liability when it is created and to assign interest expense to the periods until it is settled. Appendix II provides additional discussion of present value concepts.

Present Value Concepts

 LO 11 Explain and compute the present value of an amount to be paid at a future date.

The concept of present value affects accounting for liabilities. A focus on liabilities leads to a focus on the present value of future cash outflows, payables, and interest expense. But present value concepts also apply to future cash inflows, receivables, and interest income. The basic present value concept is the idea that cash paid (or received) in the future has less value now than the same amount of cash paid (or received) today.

To illustrate, if we must pay $1 one year from now, its present value is less than $1. To see this, let's assume we borrow $0.9259 today for one year at 8% interest. Our interest expense for this loan is computed as $0.9259 x 8% or $0.0741. When the $0.0741 interest is added to the $0.9259 borrowed, we get the $1 payment necessary to repay our loan with interest. This is formally computed in Exhibit 17A.1.

Exhibit 17A.1

Components of a One-Year Loan

Amount borrowed	$0.9259
Interest for one year at 8%	0.0741
Amount owed after one year	$1.0000

The $0.9259 borrowed is the present value of the $1 future payment. More generally, an amount borrowed equals the present value of the future payment. This relation implies that a borrowed amount can yield interest at a given rate such that its future amount will repay the loan with interest.[9]

To extend this example, let's assume we must repay the $1 after two years instead of one, and the 8% interest is compounded annually. *Compounded* means

---

[9] This same interpretation applies to an investment. If $0.9259 is invested at 8%, it yields $0.0741 interest revenue in one year. This amounts to $1, made up of principal and interest.

interest during the second period is based on the total of the amount borrowed plus the interest accrued from the first period. The second period's interest is then computed as 8% multiplied by the sum of the amount borrowed plus interest earned in the first period.

What then is the present value of the $1 we must repay in two years? Exhibit 17A.2 shows how we compute this amount to be $0.8573. Note the first year's interest is added to the principal so that the second year's interest is based on $0.9259.[10]

Amount borrowed in first year	$0.8573
Interest for first year ($0.8573 × 8%)	0.0686
Amount borrowed in second year	$0.9259
Interest for second year ($0.9259 × 8%) . .	0.0741
Amount owed after 2 years	$1.0000

Exhibit 17A.2

Components of a Two-Year Loan

Present Value Tables

The present value of $1 that we must repay several periods into the future can be computed by using the formula: $1/(1 + i)^n$. The symbol i in the formula equation is the interest rate per period and n is the number of periods until the future payment must be made. Applying this formula to our two-year loan we get: $1/(1.08)^2$ or $0.8573. This is the same value shown in Exhibit 17A.2.

We can use this formula to find any present value. But simpler methods are available. Perhaps the easiest is for us to use electronic calculators that are preprogrammed with present value formulas. But we can also use a present value table. A *present value table* lists present values computed with the formula for various interest rates and time periods. Many people find it helpful in learning present value concepts to first work with the table and then move to using a calculator.

Exhibit 17A.3 shows a present value table for a future payment of $1 for up to 10

Periods	Rate			
	4%	6%	8%	10%
1	0.9615	0.9434	**0.9259**	0.9091
2	0.9246	0.8900	**0.8573**	0.8264
3	0.8890	0.8396	0.7938	0.7513
4	0.8548	0.7921	0.7350	0.6830
5	0.8219	0.7473	0.6806	0.6209
6	0.7903	0.7050	0.6302	0.5645
7	0.7599	0.6651	0.5835	0.5132
8	0.7307	0.6274	0.5403	0.4665
9	0.7026	0.5919	0.5002	0.4241
10	0.6756	0.5584	0.4632	0.3855

Exhibit 17A.3

Present Value of $1

periods at five different interest rates. Present values in this table are rounded to four decimal places.[11] This table is drawn from the larger and more complete Table II.1 in Appendix II at the end of the book.

Note the first value in the 8% column is 0.9259. This is the value we computed above for the present value of a $1 loan for 1-year at 8% (see Exhibit 17A.1). Go down one row in the same 8% column and we find the present value of $1 discounted at 8% for two years, or 0.8573. Again, this value means $0.8573 is the present value of our obligation to repay $1 after two periods at 8% interest (see Exhibit 17A.2).

---

[10] Benjamin Franklin is said to have described compounding as: "The money, money makes, makes more money."

[11] Four decimal places are sufficient for applications in this book. Some situations require more precision.

Applying a Present Value Table

Exhibit 17A.4

Present Value of a Series of Unequal Payments

To illustrate how we measure a liability using a present value table, let's assume a company plans to borrow cash and repay it as follows:

Payment after 1 year	$ 2,000
Payment after 2 years	3,000
Payment after 3 years	5,000
Total Payments	$10,000

How much does this company receive today if the interest rate is 10% on this loan? To answer this we need to compute the present value of the three future payments, discounted at 10%. This computation is shown in Exhibit 17A.4 using values from Exhibit 17A.3. It shows the company can borrow $8,054 at 10% in exchange for its promise to make three payments at the scheduled dates.

 Explain and compute the present value of a series of equal amounts to be paid at future dates.

Years from Now	Expected Payments	Present Value of $1 at 10%	Present Value of Expected Payments
1	$2,000	0.9091	$1,818
2	3,000	0.8264	2,479
3	5,000	0.7513	3,757
Present value of all payments			$8,054

Present Value of an Annuity

Exhibit 17A.5

Present Value of a Series of Equal Payments (Annuity) by Discounting Each Payment

The $8,054 present value of the loan in Exhibit 17A.4 equals the sum of the present values of the three payments. When payments are not equal, their combined present value is best computed by adding their individual present values as shown in Exhibit 17A.4. But sometimes payments follow an annuity. An **annuity** is a series of equal payments at equal time intervals. The present value of an annuity is readily computed.

To illustrate, let's take a company that must repay a 6% loan with a $5,000 payment at the end of each year for the next four years. The amount borrowed under this loan equals the present value of the four payments discounted at 6%. Exhibit 17A.5 shows how to compute its present value of $17,326 by multiplying each payment by its matching present value factor from Exhibit 17A.3.

Years from Now	Expected Payments	Present Value of $1 at 6%	Present Value of Expected payments
1	$5,000	0.9434	$ 4,717
2	5,000	0.8900	4,450
3	5,000	0.8396	4,198
4	5,000	0.7921	3,961
Present value of all payments . .		3.4651	$17,326

But since the series of $5,000 payments is an annuity, we can compute present value with either of two shortcuts. First, the third column of Exhibit 17A.5 shows the sum of the present values of $1 at 6% for period 1 through 4 equals 3.4651. The short-cut is to multiply this total of 3.4651 by the $5,000 annual payment to get the combined present value of $17,326. It requires one multiplication instead of four.

The second shortcut uses an *annuity table* such as the one shown in Exhibit 17A.6.[12] Exhibit 17A.6 is drawn from the more complete Table II.3 in Appendix II. Instead of having to take the sum of individual present values from Exhibit 17A.3, we go directly to the annuity table to get the present value factor for a specific number of payments and interest rate. We then multiply this factor by the amount of the payment to find the present value of the entire annuity.

Exhibit 17A.6

Present Value of an Annuity of $1

Periods	Rate			
	4%	6%	8%	10%
1	0.9615	0.9434	0.9259	0.9091
2	1.8861	1.8334	1.7833	1.7355
3	2.7751	2.6730	2.5771	2.4869
4	3.6299	**3.4651**	3.3121	3.1699
5	4.4518	4.2124	3.9927	3.7908
6	5.2421	4.9173	4.6229	4.3553
7	6.0021	5.5824	5.2064	4.8684
8	6.7327	6.2098	5.7466	5.3349
9	7.4353	6.8017	6.2469	5.7590
10	**8.1109**	7.3601	6.7101	6.1446

Specifically, we look at Exhibit 17A.6 to find the row for four periods and go across until we reach the column for 6%, where we find the factor 3.4651. This factor equals the present value of an annuity with four payments of $1, discounted at 6%. We then multiply 3.4651 times $5,000 to get the $17,326 present value of our annuity.

Compounding Periods Shorter Than a Year

Our present value examples all involved periods of a year. But in many situations, interest is compounded over shorter periods. For example, interest rate on bonds is usually stated as an annual rate but interest is often paid every six months. This means the present value of interest payments from these bonds must be computed using interest periods of six months.

To illustrate, let's assume a borrower wants to know the present value of a series of ten $4,000 *semiannual payments* made over five years at an *annual interest rate* of 8%. While the interest rate is stated as an annual rate of 8%, it is actually a rate of 4% per six-month interest period. To compute the present value of this series of $4,000 payments, enter Exhibit 17A.6 on row 10 and go across to the 4% column to find the factor 8.1109. The present value of this annuity is $32,444 (8.1109 × $4,000).

Note: We recommend reading Appendix II to learn more about present value concepts. This appendix includes more complete present value tables and also provides a discussion of future value concepts and tables. It includes exercises to help in understanding present value concepts.

---

[12] The formula for finding this table's values is: $\dfrac{1 - \dfrac{1}{(1+i)^n}}{i}$ The present values in Exhibit 17A.6 are also found by adding the values of the individual payments from Exhibit 17A.3. (Since only four decimal places are shown, there are some ±0.0001 rounding differences between them).

★**Flash back**

17. A company enters into an agreement to make four annual payments of $1,000 each, starting one year from now. The annual interest rate is 8%. The present value of these four payments is (a) $2,923, (b) $2,940, (c) $3,312, (d) $4,000, (e) $6,733.

18. Suppose a company has an option to pay either $10,000 after one year or $5,000 after six months and another $5,000 after one year. Which choice has the smaller present value?

Answers—p. 816

Summary of Appendix 17A

11. Explain and compute the present value of an amount to be paid at a future date. The basic concept of present value is that an amount of cash to be paid or received in the future is worth less than the same amount of cash to be paid or received today. Another important present value concept is that interest is compounded. This means interest is added to the balance and used to determine interest for succeeding periods. The present value of an amount is computed using the present value table for a single amount (or calculator).

12. Explain and compute the present value of a series of equal amounts to be paid at future dates. An annuity is a series of equal payments occurring at equal time intervals. The present value of an annuity can be computed as the sum of individual present values for each payment. Alternatively, and the preferred approach, is to compute the present value of the entire series using the present value table for an annuity (or calculator).

Guidance Answer to ★**Flash backs**

17. *c.* 3.3121 × $1,000 = $3,312

18. The option of paying $10,000 after a year always has a lower present value. In effect, it postpones paying the first $5,000 by six months. As a result, the present value of the delayed payment is always less.

Glossary

Annuity A series of annual payments at equal time intervals. (p. 814)

Bearer bonds Bonds that are made payable to whoever holds them (called the bearer); also called *unregistered bonds*. (p. 782)

Bond A written promise to pay an amount identified as the par value of the bond along with interest at a stated annual amount; usually issued in denominations of $1,000. (p. 780)

Bond certificate A document containing bond specifics such as the issuer's name, the bonds' par value, the contract interest rate, and the maturity date. (p. 783)

Bond indenture The contract between the bond issuer and the bondholders; it identifies the rights and obligations of the parties. (p. 783)

Callable bonds Bonds that give the issuer an option of retiring them at a stated dollar amount prior to maturity; also called *redeemable bonds*. (p. 782)

Carrying amount The net amount at which bonds are reflected on the balance sheet; equals the par value of the bonds less any unamortized discount or plus any unamortized premium; also called the *book value* of the bonds. (p. 786)

Contract rate The interest rate specified in the bond indenture; it is multiplied by the par value of the bonds to determine the amount of interest to be paid each year; also called the *coupon rate*, the *stated rate*, or the *nominal rate*. (p. 785)

Convertible bonds Bonds that can be exchanged by the bondholders for a fixed number of shares of the issuing company's common shares. (p. 782)

Coupon bonds Bonds that have interest coupons attached to their certificates; the bondholders detach the coupons when they mature and present them to a bank or broker for collection. (p. 782)

Discount on bonds payable The difference between the par value of a bond and its lower issue price that arises when the contract rate is lower than the market rate. (p. 786)

Effective interest method Allocates interest expense over the life of the bonds in a way that yields a constant rate of interest; interest expense for a period is found by multiplying the balance of the liability at the beginning of the period by the bonds' original market rate; also called *interest method.* (p. 788)

Installment note An obligation requiring a series of periodic payments to the lender. (p. 801)

Market rate The interest rate that borrowers are willing to pay and that lenders are willing to earn for a particular bond at its risk level. (p. 785)

Mortgage A legal agreement that protects a lender by giving the lender the right to be paid out of the cash proceeds from the sale of the borrower's specific assets identified in the mortgage. (p. 805)

Par value of a bond The amount that the bond issuer agrees to pay at maturity and the amount on which interest payments are based; also called the *face amount* or *face value.* (p. 780)

Pledged assets to secured liabilities The ratio of the book value of a company's pledged assets to the book value of its secured liabilities. (p. 808)

Premium on bonds The difference between the par value of a bond and its higher issue price that arises when the contract rate is higher than the market rate. (p. 790)

Redeemable Bonds See *callable bonds.* (p. 782)

Registered bonds Bonds owned by investors whose names and addresses are recorded by the issuing company; the interest payments are made with cheques to the registered owners. (p. 782)

Secured bonds Bonds that have specific assets of the issuing company pledged as collateral. (p. 781)

Serial bonds Bonds that mature at different dates with the result that the entire debt is repaid gradually over a number of years. (p. 782)

Sinking fund bonds Bonds that require the issuing company to make deposits to a separate pool of assets; the bondholders are repaid at maturity from the assets in this pool. (p. 782)

Straight-line method (interest allocation) A method that allocates an equal amount of interest to each accounting period in the life of bonds. (p. 787)

Term bonds Bonds that are scheduled for payment (mature) at a single specified date. (p. 782)

Unsecured bonds Bonds that are backed by the issuer's general credit standing; unsecured bonds are almost always more risky than unsecured bonds; also called *debentures.* (p. 781)

Questions

1. What is the difference between notes payable and bonds payable?

2. What is the primary difference between a share and a bond?

3. What is the main advantage of issuing bonds instead of obtaining funds from the company's owners?

4. What is a bond indenture? What provisions are usually included in an indenture?

5. What are the duties of a trustee for bondholders?

6. Why does a company that issues bonds between interest dates collect accrued interest from the bonds' purchasers?

7. What are the *contract* and *market interest rates* for bonds?

8. What factors affect the market interest rates for bonds?

9. If you know the par value of bonds, the contract rate and the market interest rate, how can you estimate the market value of the bonds?

10. Does the straight-line or interest method produce an allocation of interest that creates a constant rate of interest over a bond's life? Explain your answer.

11. What is the cash price of a $2,000 bond that is sold at $98\frac{1}{4}$? What is the cash price of a $6,000 bond that is sold at $101\frac{1}{2}$?

12. Describe two alternative payment patterns for installment notes.

13. Explain why unsecured creditors should be alarmed when the pledged assets to secured liabilities ratio for a borrower has grown substantially.

14. Refer to the annual report for **Alliance** presented in Appendix I. Is there any indication that the company has issued bonds?

15. Refer to the annual report for **Atlantis** presented in Appendix I. For the fiscal year ended December 31, 1997, did Atlantis have any outstanding mortgages payable. If so how were they secured?

16. What obligation does Yvette Bourque have to the investors who purchased $200,000 of bonds to finance her natural foods store?

Match the following terms and phrases by entering the letter of the phrase that best describes each term in the blank next to the term.

_____ **1.** debentures
_____ **2.** bearer bonds
_____ **3.** registered bonds
_____ **4.** bond indenture
_____ **5.** sinking fund bonds
_____ **6.** serial bonds
_____ **7.** secured bonds
_____ **8.** convertible bonds

Quick Study

QS 17-1
Bond terms and identifications

 LO 2

a. Issuer records the bondholders' names and addresses.

b. Unsecured; backed only by the issuer's general credit standing.

c. Varying maturity dates.

d. Identifies the rights and responsibilities of the issuer and bondholders.

e. Can be exchanged for shares of the issuer's common shares.

f. Unregistered; interest is paid to whoever possesses them.

g. Issuer maintains a separate pool of assets from which bondholders are paid at maturity.

h. Specific assets of the issuer are mortgaged as collateral.

QS 17-2

Quoted bond selling price and bond interest expense for bonds issued at a discount

 LO 4

Lyndon Industries issued 8%, 10-year bonds with a par value of $350,000 and semiannual interest payments. On the issue date, the annual market rate of interest for the bonds was 10%, and the selling price was 87.5. The straight-line method is used to allocate the interest.

a. What are the proceeds of the bond?

b. What is the total amount of bond interest expense that will be recognized over the life of the bonds?

c. What is the amount of bond interest expense recorded on the first interest payment date?

QS 17-3

Quoted bond selling price and bond interest expense for bonds issued at a premium

 LO 1,5

Top Notch, Inc., issued 10%, 15-year bonds with a par value of $120,000 and semiannual interest payments. On the issue date, the annual market rate of interest for the bonds was 8%, and they sold it at $117\frac{1}{4}$. The interest method is used to allocate the interest.

a. What are the proceeds of the Top Notch, Inc. bonds?

b. What is the total amount of bond interest expense that will be recognized over the life of the bonds?

c. What is the amount of bond interest expense recorded on the first interest payment date?

QS 17-4

Journalizing the issuance of bonds at a premium and discount

 LO 3

Journalize the bonds issued in QS 17-2 and QS 17-3. Assume that both bonds are issued on January 1, 1999.

QS 17-5

Calculating bond proceeds using present values

 LO 4,5

Using the facts in QS 17-2 and QS 17-3 confirm that the bond proceeds given in each problem are correct. Use the comprehensive present value tables in Appendix II.

QS 17-6

Issuing bonds between interest dates

 LO 3

Lafrentz Company issues bonds as of January 1, 1999. The total bond issue was $2,000,000 of 8% bonds. The company sold $1,800,000 of the bonds on the original issue date. The final $200,000 were sold at par on March 1, 1999. The bonds pay interest semiannually as of June 30 and December 31. Record the entry for the March 1 sale of bonds.

QS 17-7

Retiring bonds before maturity

 LO 6

On July 1, 1999, the Geiger Company exercises a $4,000 call option on its outstanding bonds that have a carrying value of $208,000 and par value of $200,000. The company exercises the call option immediately after the semiannual interest is paid on June 30, 1999. Record the journal entry to show retiring the bonds.

QS 17-8

Bond retirement by share conversion

 LO 6

On January 1, 1999, the $1,000,000 par value bonds of Stephens Company with a carrying value of $1,000,000 are converted to 500,000 shares of $0.50 par value common shares. Journalize the conversion of the bonds.

New West Corp. borrowed $170,000 from a bank and signed an installment note that calls for five annual payments of equal size, with the first payment due one year after the note was signed. Use Table 17.20 to compute the size of the annual payment for each of the following annual interest rates: (a) 4%, (b) 8%, (c) 12%.

QS 17-9
Installment note with equal payments
LO 3

Footnote 2 of the **Collins Industries'** annual report reads as follows:

QS 17-10
Collateral Agreements
LO 9

> The credit facility [line] is collateralized by receivables, inventories, equipment and certain real property. Under the terms of the Agreement, the Company is required to maintain certain financial ratios and other financial conditions. The Agreement also prohibits the Company from incurring certain additional indebtedness, limits certain investments, advances or loans and restricts substantial asset sales, capital expenditures and cash dividends. At October 31, 1997 and 1996 the Company was in compliance with all loan covenants.

What restrictions are placed on Collins Industry by the bank which has granted the company credit?

On January 1, 1999, The Deitrich Company borrowed $75,000 in exchange for an interest-bearing note. The note plus compounded interest at an annual rate of 8% is due on December 31, 2001. Determine the amount that Deitrich will pay on the due date. (Round to the nearest dollar.)

QS 17-11
Computing the amount due on an interest-bearing note
LO 7

Use the following information to compute the ratio of pledged assets to secured liabilities for both companies:

QS 17-12
Ratio of pledged assets to secured liabilities
LO 10

	Delta Co.	Sigma Co.
Pledged assets	$387,000	$172,000
Total assets	550,000	490,000
Secured liabilities	163,000	158,000
Unsecured liabilities	266,000	390,000

Which company appears to have the riskier secured debt?

When solving the following exercises, round all dollar amounts to the nearest whole dollar. Also assume that none of the companies use reversing entries.

Exercises

On January 1, 1999, Maverick Enterprises issued $1,700,000 of 20-year bonds, dated January 1, 1999. The bonds have a $1,700,000 par value, mature in 20 years, and pay 9% interest semiannually on June 30 and December 31. The bonds were sold to investors at their par value.

a. How much interest will Maverick pay to the holders of these bonds every six months?

b. Show the journal entries that Maverick would make to record (1) the issuance of the bonds on January 1, 1999, (2) the first interest payment on June 30, 1999, and (3) the second interest payment on December 31, 1999.

c. Assume the Maverick Enterprises bonds were sold at (1) 98 and (2) 102. Journalize the issuance of the bonds at 98 and 102.

Exercise 17-1
Journal entries for bond issuance and interest payments
LO 3

Exercise 17-2
Journal entries for bond issuance with accrued interest

LO 3

On May 1, 1999, Maverick Enterprises issued bonds dated January 1, 1999. The bonds have a $1,700,000 par value, mature in 20 years, and pay 9% interest semiannually on June 30 and December 31. The bonds were sold to investors at their par value plus the four months' interest that had accrued since the original issue date.

a. How much accrued interest was paid to Maverick by the purchasers of these bonds on May 1, 1999?

b. Show the journal entries that Maverick would make to record (1) the issuance of the bonds on May 1, 1999, (2) the first interest payment on June 30, 1999, and (3) the second interest payment on December 31, 1999.

Exercise 17-3
Computing the present value of a bond and recording the issuance

LO 4

The Kloss Company issued bonds with a par value of $600,000 on their initial issue date. The bonds mature in 10 years and pay 6% annual interest in two semiannual payments. On the issue date, the annual market rate of interest for the bonds turned out to be 8%.

a. What is the size of the semiannual interest payment for these bonds?

b. How many semiannual interest payments will be made on these bonds over their life?

c. Use the information about the interest rates to decide whether the bonds were issued at par, a discount, or a premium.

d. Estimate the market value of the bonds as of the date they were issued.

e. Present the journal entry that would be made to record the bonds' issuance.

Exercise 17-4
Straight-line allocation of interest for bonds sold at a discount

LO 4

Bailey's, Inc., issued bonds with a par value of $90,000 on January 1, 2000. The annual contract rate on the bonds is 8%, and the interest is paid semiannually on June 30 and December 31. The bonds mature after three years. The annual market interest rate at the date of issuance was 10%, and the bonds were sold for $85,431.

a. What is the amount of the original discount on these bonds?

b. How much total bond interest expense will be recognized over the life of these bonds?

c. Present an amortization table like Exhibit 17.7 for these bonds; use the straight-line method of allocating the interest and amortizing the discount.

Exercise 17-5
Interest method allocation of interest for bonds sold at a discount

LO 4

Profitt Corporation issued bonds with a par value of $250,000 on January 1, 2000. The annual contract rate on the bonds is 9%, and the interest is paid semiannually. The bonds mature after three years. The annual market interest rate at the date of issuance was 12%, and the bonds were sold for $231,570.

a. What is the amount of the original discount on these bonds?

b. How much total bond interest expense will be recognized over the life of these bonds?

c. Present an amortization table like Exhibit 17.8 for these bonds; use the interest method of allocating the interest and amortizing the discount.

Exercise 17-6
Computing the present value of a bond and recording the issuance

LO 5

Innovention, Inc., issued bonds with a par value of $75,000 on their initial issue date. The bonds mature in five years and pay 10% annual interest in two semiannual payments. On the issue date, the annual market rate of interest for the bonds turned out to be 8%.

a. What is the size of the semiannual interest payment for these bonds?

b. How many semiannual interest payments will be made on these bonds over their life?

c. Use the information about the interest rates to decide whether the bonds were issued at par, a discount, or a premium.

d. Estimate the market value of the bonds as of the date they were issued.

e. Present the journal entry that would be made to record the bonds' issuance.

Great Plains Power Company issued bonds with a par value of $800,000 on January 1, 2000. The annual contract rate on the bonds was 13%, and the interest is paid semiannually. The bonds mature after three years. The annual market interest rate at the date of issuance was 12%, and the bonds were sold for $819,700.

a. What is the amount of the original premium on these bonds?

b. How much total bond interest expense will be recognized over the life of these bonds?

c. Present an amortization table like Exhibit 17.12 for these bonds; use the interest method of allocating the interest and amortizing the premium.

Exercise 17-7
Interest method allocation of interest for bonds sold at a premium
LO 5

On January 1, 1999, AeroFab, Inc., issued $350,000 of 10%, 15-year bonds at a price of $97\frac{3}{4}$. Six years later, on January 1, 2005, the corporation retired 20% of these bonds by buying them on the open market at $104\frac{1}{2}$. All interest had been properly accounted for and paid through December 31, 2004, the day before the purchase. The straight-line method was used to allocate the interest and amortize the original discount.

a. How much money did the company receive when it first issued the entire group of bonds?

b. How large was the original discount on the entire group of bonds?

c. How much amortization did the company record on the entire group of bonds between January 1, 1999, and December 31, 2004?

d. What was the carrying value of the entire group of bonds as of the close of business on December 31, 2004? What was the carrying value of the retired bonds on this date?

e. How much money did the company pay on January 1, 2005, to purchase the bonds that it retired?

f. What is the amount of the gain or loss from retiring the bonds?

g. Provide the general journal entry that the company would make to record the retirement of the bonds.

Exercise 17-8
Retiring bonds payable
LO 6

Piccolo Corp. issued bonds with a par value of $50,000 and a four-year life on June 1, 1999. The contract interest rate is 7%. The bonds pay interest on November 30 and May 31. They were issued at a price of $47,974.

a. Prepare an amortization table (as shown in Exhibit 17.7) for these bonds that covers their entire life. Use the straight-line method of allocating interest.

b. Show the journal entries that the issuer would make to record the first two interest payments and to accrue interest as of December 31, 1999.

Exercise 17-9
Straight-line amortization table and accrued interest
LO 4

Kern Company acquired a machine on December 1 by giving a $60,000 non-interest-bearing note due in one year. The market rate of interest for this type of debt was 10%. Show the entries that would be made when the note (a) is created on December 1, 1999, (b) as of December 31, 1999, and (c) at maturity on December 1, 2000.

Exercise 17-10
Accounting for a non-interest-bearing note
LO 8

On December 31, 1999, JMS, Inc. borrowed $25,000 by signing a four-year, 7% installment note. The note requires annual payments of accrued interest and equal amounts of principal on December 31 of each year from 2000 through 2003.

a. How much principal will be included in each of the four payments?

b. Prepare an amortization table for this installment note like the one presented in Exhibit 17.19.

Exercise 17-11
Installment note with payments of accrued interest and equal amounts of principal
LO 7, 8

Exercise 17-12
Journal entries for an installment note with payments of accrued interest and equal amounts of principal
LO 7, 8

Use the data in Exercise 17-11 to prepare journal entries that JMS, Inc. would make to record the loan on December 31, 1999, and the four payments starting on December 31, 2000, through the final payment on December 31, 2003.

Exercise 17-13
Installment note with equal payments
LO 7, 8

On December 31, 1999, Volks Corp. borrowed $25,000 by signing a four-year, 7% installment note. The note requires four equal payments of accrued interest and principal on December 31 of each year from 2000 through 2003.

a. Compute the size of each of the four equal payments.

b. Prepare an amortization table for this installment note like the one presented in Exhibit 17.20.

Exercise 17-14
Journal entries for an installment note with equal payments
LO 7, 8

Use the data in Exercise 17-13 to prepare journal entries that Volks Corp. would make to record the loan on December 31, 1999, and the four payments starting on December 31, 2000, through the final payment on December 31, 2003.

Exercise 17-15
Computing the ratio of pledged assets to secured liabilities
LO 9, 10

An unsecured major creditor of Telstar Corporation has been monitoring the company's financing activities. Two years before, the ratio of its pledged assets to secured liabilities had been 1.7. One year ago, the ratio had climbed to 2.3, and the most recent financial report shows that the ratio value is now 3.1. Briefly describe what this trend may indicate about the company's activities, specifically from the point of view of this creditor.

Problems

When solving the following problems, round all dollar amounts to the nearest whole dollar. Also assume that none of the companies use reversing entries.

Problem 17-1
Computing bond prices and recording issuance with journal entries
LO 3, 4, 5

Check Figure Part 1, premium, $2,718

Abbey Research, Inc., issued bonds on January 1, 1999, that pay interest semiannually on June 30 and December 31. The par value of the bonds is $20,000, the annual contract rate is 10%, and the bonds mature in 10 years.

Required

For each of these three situations, (a) determine the issue price of the bonds and (b) show the journal entry that would record the issuance.

1. The market interest rate at the date of issuance was 8%.

2. The market interest rate at the date of issuance was 10%.

3. The market interest rate at the date of issuance was 12%.

Problem 17-2
Straight-line method of allocating interest amortizing a bond discount and a bond premium.
LO 3, 4, 5

The Scofield Corporation issued $2,000,000 of bonds that pay 6% annual interest with two semiannual payments. The date of issuance was January 1, 1999, and the interest is paid on June 30 and December 31. The bonds mature after 15 years and were issued at the price of $1,728,224.

Required

1. Prepare a general journal entry to record the issuance of the bonds.

2. Calculate the cash payment, discount amortization amount, and bond interest expense to be recognized every six months.

3. Determine the total bond interest expense that will be recognized over the life of these bonds.

4. Prepare the first two years of an amortization table like Exhibit 17.7 based on the straight-line method of allocating the interest.

5. Present the journal entries that Scofield would make to record the first two interest payments.

6. Assume that the proceeds of the bond are $2,447,990. Repeat requirements 1–5.

Check Figure Total bond interest expense, $2,071,776

Evans Materials Corp. issued $650,000 of bonds that pay 5% annual interest with two semi-annual payments. The date of issuance was January 1, 1999, and the interest is paid on June 30 and December 31. The bonds mature after four years and were issued at the price of $584,361. The market interest rate was 8%.

Problem 17-3
Interest method of allocating bond interest and amortizing a bond discount

LO 4

Required

Preparation component:

1. Prepare a general journal entry to record the issuance of the bonds.

2. Determine the total bond interest expense that will be recognized over the life of these bonds.

3. Prepare the first two years of an amortization table like Exhibit 17.8 based on the interest method.

4. Present the journal entries that Evans would make to record the first two interest payments.

Analysis component:

5. Now assume that the market interest rate on January 1, 1999, was 4% instead of 8%. Without presenting any specific numbers, describe how this change would affect the amounts presented on the Evans's financial statements.

Check Figure Total bond interest expense, $195,639

Phantom Industries issued $90,000 of bonds that pay 11% annual interest with two semi-annual payments. The date of issuance was January 1, 1999, and the interest is paid on June 30 and December 31. The bonds mature after three years and were issued at the price of $92,283. The market interest rate was 10%.

Problem 17-4
Interest method of amortizing bond interest, amortizing bond premium, and retiring bonds

LO 5, 6

Required

1. Prepare a general journal entry to record the issuance of the bonds.

2. Determine the total bond interest expense that will be recognized over the life of these bonds.

3. Prepare the first four lines of an amortization table like Exhibit 17.12 based on the interest method.

4. Present the journal entries that Phantom would make to record the first two interest payments.

5. Present the journal entry that would be made to record the retirement of these bonds on December 31, 2000, at a price of 98.

Check Figure Interest for period ending Jun 30/2000, $4,580

Ford Products, Inc., issued bonds with a par value of $500,000 and a five-year life on January 1, 1999. The bonds pay interest on June 30 and December 31. The contract interest rate is 6.5%. The bonds were issued at a price of $510,666. The market interest rate was 6% on the original issue date.

Problem 17-5
Bond premium amortization and finding the present value of remaining cash flows

LO 5

Required

1. Calculate the total bond interest expense over the life of the bonds.

2. Prepare an amortization table like Exhibit 17.12 for these bonds that covers their entire life. Use the interest method.

3. Show the journal entries that Ford Products would make to record the first two interest payments.

Check Figure Balance as of Jun 30/2001 $505,728

4. Use the original market interest rate to compute the present value of the remaining cash flows for these bonds as of December 31, 2001. Compare your answer with the amount shown on the amortization table as the balance for that date and explain your findings.

Problem 17-6
Installment notes
LO 7, 8

Check Figure Part 2, interest for period ending Oct. 31/2003, $14,292

On October 31, 1999, Borghese Ltd. borrowed $400,000 from a bank by signing a five-year installment note bearing interest at 8%. The terms of the note require equal payments each year on October 31.

Required

1. Compute the size of each installment payment.
2. Complete an installment note amortization schedule for this note similar to Exhibit 17.20.
3. Present the journal entries that Borghese would make to record accrued interest as of December 31, 1999 (the end of the annual reporting period), and the first payment on the note.
4. Now assume that the note does not require equal payments but does require four payments that include accrued interest and an equal amount of principal in each payment. Complete an installment note amortization schedule for this note similar to Exhibit 17.19. Present the journal entries that Borghese would make to record accrued interest as of December 31, 1999 (the end of the annual reporting period), and the first payment on the note.

Problem 17-7
Computing and analyzing ratio of pledged assets to secured liabilities
LO 9, 10

On January 1, 2000, Dailey Company issued at par 11%, four-year bonds with a $135,000 par value. The bonds are secured by a mortgage that specifies assets totalling $225,000 as collateral. On the same date, Weekley Company issued at par 11%, four-year bonds with a par value of $60,000. Weekley is securing its bonds with a mortgage that includes $150,000 of pledged assets. Following is December 31, 1999, balance sheet information for both companies:

	Dailey Co.	Weekley Co.
Total assets	$900,000*	$450,000**
Liabilities:		
Secured	$210,000	$ 75,000
Unsecured	150,000	165,000
Shareholders' equity	540,000	210,000
Total liabilities and shareholders' equity . .	$900,000	$450,000

* 43% pledged
**55% pledged

Required

Preparation component:

Check Figure Dailey, 1.8 to 1; Weekley, 2.9 to 1

1. Compute the ratio of pledged assets to secured liabilities for each company after January 1, 2000.

Analysis component:

2. Which company's bonds appear to offer the best security? What other information might be helpful in evaluating the risk of the bonds?

When solving the following alternate problems, round all dollar amounts to the nearest whole dollar. Also assume that none of the companies use reversing entries.

Alternate Problems

Strata Systems, Inc., issued a group of bonds on January 1, 1999, that pay interest semiannually on June 30 and December 31. The par value of the bonds is $45,000, the annual contract rate is 12%, and the bonds mature in five years.

Problem 17-1A
Computing bond prices and recording issuance with journal entries
LO 3, 4, 5

Required

For each of these three situations, (a) determine the issue price of the bonds and (b) show the journal entry that would record the issuance.
1. The market interest rate at the date of issuance was 10%.
2. The market interest rate at the date of issuance was 12%.
3. The market interest rate at the date of issuance was 14%.

The Poole Corporation issued $1,700,000 of bonds that pay 10% annual interest with two semiannual payments. The date of issuance was January 1, 1999, and the interest is paid on June 30 and December 31. The bonds mature after ten years and were issued at the price of $1,505,001.

Problem 17-2A
Straight-line method of allocating interest and amortizing a bond discount and a bond premium
LO 3, 4, 5

Required

1. Prepare a general journal entry to record the issuance of the bonds.
2. Calculate the cash payment, discount amortization amount, and bond interest expense to be recognized every six months.
3. Determine the total bond interest expense that will be recognized over the life of these bonds.
4. Prepare the first two years of an amortization table like Exhibit 17.7 based on the straight-line method of allocating the interest.
5. Present the journal entries that Poole would make to record the first two interest payments.
6. Assume that the proceeds on the bond are $2,096,466. Repeat requirements 1–5.

Joseph Manufacturing Corp. issued $120,000 of bonds that pay 6% annual interest with two semiannual payments. The date of issuance was January 1, 1999, and the interest is paid on June 30 and December 31. The bonds mature after 15 years and were issued at the price of $99,247. The market interest rate was 8%.

Problem 17-3A
Interest method of allocating interest and amortizing a bond discount
LO 4

Required

1. Prepare a general journal entry to record the issuance of the bonds.
2. Determine the total bond interest expense that will be recognized over the life of these bonds.
3. Prepare the first four lines of an amortization table like Exhibit 17.8 based on the interest method.
4. Present the journal entries that Joseph Manufacturing would make to record the first two interest payments.

Adams Brothers, Inc., issued $900,000 of bonds that pay 13% annual interest with two semiannual payments. The date of issuance was January 1, 1999, and the interest is paid on June 30 and December 31. The bonds mature after four years and were issued at the price of $987,217. The market interest rate was 10%.

Problem 17-4A
Interest method of allocating interest, amortizing bond premium and retiring bonds
LO 5, 6

Required

Preparation component:

1. Prepare a general journal entry to record the issuance of the bonds.
2. Determine the total bond interest expense that will be recognized over the life of these bonds.
3. Prepare the first two years of an amortization table like Exhibit 17.12 based on the interest method.

4. Present the journal entries that Adams Brothers would make to record the first two interest payments.

5. Present the journal entry that would be made to record the retirement of these bonds on December 31, 2000, at the price of 106.

Analysis component:

6. Instead of the facts described in the problem, assume that the market interest rate on January 1, 1999, was 14% instead of 10%. Without presenting any specific numbers, describe how this change would affect the amounts presented on the company's financial statements.

Problem 17-5A
Bond premium amortization and finding the present value of remaining cash flows

LO 5

LaRue Company issued bonds with a par value of $160,000 and a five-year life on January 1, 1999. The bonds pay interest on June 30 and December 31. The contract interest rate is 9%. The bonds were issued at a price of $166,494. The market interest rate was 8% on the original issue date.

Required

1. Calculate the total bond interest expense over the life of the bonds.

2. Prepare an amortization table like Exhibit 17.12 for these bonds that covers their entire life. Use the interest method.

3. Show the journal entries that LaRue would make to record the first two interest payments.

4. Use the original market interest rate to compute the present value of the remaining cash flows for these bonds as of December 31, 2001. Compare your answer with the amount shown on the amortization table as the balance for that date, and explain your findings.

Problem 17-6A
Installment notes

LO 7, 8

On September 30, 1999, Rome Enterprises borrowed $300,000 from a bank by signing a three-year installment note bearing interest at 10%. The terms of the note require equal payments each year on September 30.

Required

1. Compute the size of each installment payment.

2. Complete an installment note amortization schedule for this note similar to Exhibit 17.20.

3. Present the journal entries that Rome would make to record accrued interest as of December 31, 1999 (the end of the annual reporting period), and the first payment on the note.

4. Now assume that the note does not require equal payments but does require three payments that include accrued interest and an equal amount of principal in each payment. Complete an installment note amortization schedule for this note similar to Exhibit 17.19. Present the journal entries that Rome would make to record accrued interest as of December 31, 1999 (the end of the annual reporting period) and the first payment on the note.

Problem 17-7A
Computing and analyzing ratio of pledged assets to secured liabilities

LO 9, 10

On January 1, 2002, Spruce Company issued $45,000 of 12%, ten-year bonds secured by a mortgage that specifies assets totalling $120,000 as collateral. On the same date, Willow Company issued 12%, ten-year bonds on January 1, with a par value of $150,000. Willow's bonds are secured by a mortgage that includes $225,000 of pledged assets. Following is December 31, 2001, balance sheet information for both companies:

	Spruce Co.	Willow Co.
Total assets	$180,000*	$750,000**
Liabilities:		
Secured	$ 39,000	$ 57,000
Unsecured	42,000	505,500
Owners' equity	99,000	187,500
Total liabilities and owners' equity	$180,000	$750,000

*59% pledged
**10% pledged

Required

Preparation component:

1. Compute the ratio of pledged assets to secured liabilities for each company after January 1, 2002.

Analysis component:

2. Which company's bonds appear to offer the best security? What other information would be helpful in evaluating the risk of the bonds?

The accounts of Clues Corporation showed the following balances as of December 31, 1999:

Bonds Payable	$1,500,000
Bond Discount	$ 30,900

The 9%, 10-year bonds dated August 1, 1998, were issued on December 1, 1998, and the cash proceeds were $1,510,200. Interest is payable semiannually. Assume that bond discount is amortized on a straight-line basis over the bond's useful life.

Required

Reconstruct the entries pertaining to the bond issue that were made on the company's books during 1998 and 1999. Assume that the company's fiscal year coincides with the calendar year.

Analytical and Review Problem

A & R Problem 17-1

BEYOND THE NUMBERS

Refer to the financial statements and related information for **Alliance** in Appendix I. Answer the following questions by analyzing the information in the report:

1. Has Alliance issued any bonds or long-term notes payable?

2. What is the due date of the company's long-term loans payable?

3. Are any assets pledged as security for the long-term loans payable?

4. At whose option are the debentures convertible?

5. Obtain access to Alliance's annual report for fiscal years ending after March 31, 1997. Has Alliance issued additional long-term debt since the fiscal year ended May 31, 1997?

Reporting in Action

LO 1, 2

Both **NIKE** and **Reebok** design, produce, market and sell sports footwear and apparel. Key comparative figures ($ millions) for these two organizations follow:

Comparative Analysis

LO 10

Key Figures	NIKE 1997	Reebok 1996
Accounts receivable, net	$1,754	$591
Inventory	1,339	545
Property and equipment, net	922	186
Long-term debt (includes current portion)	298	907

* NIKE figures are from the annual report for the fiscal year ended May 31, 1997.
Reebok figures are from the annual report for the fiscal year ended December 31, 1996.

Required

1. Assume that both NIKE and Reebok have pledged substantially all of their accounts receivables, inventories, and property and equipment to collateralize their long-term debt. Compute the ratio of pledged assets to secured liabilities for both companies.

2. Using the ratio you computed in part 1 of this question, determine which company's long-term debt is less risky.

**Ethics
Challenge**

LO 1

A few years ago the politicians needed a new headquarters building for their municipal government. The price tag for the building approached $24 million. The politicians felt that it was unlikely that the voters would approve a bond issue to raise money for the headquarters since approving the bond issue would cause taxes to increase. The politicians opted for a different approach. They had a bank issue $24 million worth of securities to pay for the construction of the building. The municipality then agreed to make a yearly lease payment (comprised of repayment of principal and interest) to repay the obligation. Unlike conventional municipal bonds the lease payments are not binding obligations on the municipal government and, therefore, no voter approval is required.

Required

1. Do you think the actions of the politicians and the investment bankers were ethical in this situation?

2. How does the security issued to pay for the building compare in riskiness to a regular municipal bond issued by a municipal government?

**Communicating
in Practice**

LO 5

Your business associate mentioned he is considering investing in the corporate bond market. He recently sent you an e-mail to say he is considering investing in bonds currently selling at a premium. He says that since the bonds are selling at a premium, they are highly valued and his investment will yield more than the going rate of return for the risk involved. Reply via e-mail (or memo) to confirm or correct your associate's analysis.

**Taking It to the
Net**

LO 1

Visit the Canadian Bond Rating Service at **http://www.cbrs.com**.

Required

1. Click on Rating. Then click on rating methodology. What seven major areas does CBRS consider when rating a particular issuer?

2. Go back to the table of contents and click on CBRS rating scales. Describe the ratings for long-term debt.

3. Go back to the table of contents and click on ratings process. What factors make CBRS change a company rating?

**Teamwork in
Action**

LO 4,5

Let's work as a team to reinforce understanding of how to prepare an effective interest method amortization table for bond premiums and discounts.

1. Each member of the team is to independently prepare a blank table with the appropriate headings for amortization of bond premiums. When each member is done, compare tables and ensure all are in agreement.

Steps 2 and 3 require use of the following facts: January 1, 1999—Issued $100,000, 9%, five-year bonds at 104.1. Market rate at issue was 8%. Rates specified are annual rates and interest is to be paid semiannually on June 30 and December 31.

2. In rotation, *each* member of the team will fully explain how to complete *one* line of the table. Each member must completely verbalize any formula used and the specific numbers for their table line. (Round all amounts to the nearest dollar) All members are to fill in their tables during this process. You need not finish the table; stop when each member has an opportunity to explain a line.

3. In rotation, team members are to identify a column from which we can readily project the final number, explain what that number is, and how this number is known.

4. Come to a team consensus as to what the total bond interest expense on this bond issue would be if the bond is not retired before maturity.

5. As a team, you are to prepare a list of similarities and differences between the amortization table just prepared and the necessary table if the bond had been issued at a discount. You may again use a rotation system to identify these items.

Visit your local library. Ask a librarian to help you locate the recent financial records of your city or municipal government. Examine the records of the municipality you choose.

Required

1. Determine the amount of long-term debt in the form of bonds that the municipality currently has outstanding.
2. Read the supporting information to the financial statements and record:
   a. Interest rate the debt was issued at.
   b. When the debt will be retired.
   c. Whether the debt has received a rating from the Canadian Bond Rating Service, Moody's, Standard and Poor's, or another rating agency.

Read the article "The Bond Boom in the Former Soviet Bloc," in the September 15, 1997, issue of *Business Week*.

Required

1. Historically have companies in central and eastern Europe relied on debt financing?
2. How does the yield on a Eurobond issued by a Russian bank compare to comparable North American securities?
3. Do experts feel the yields on bonds issued in central Europe compensate investors for the risks?
4. Refer to the chart in the article and list the top five eastern and central European companies in terms of Eurobond amounts issued in 1997.

18

Long-Term Investments and International Accounting

A Look Back

Chapter 17 focused on a special group of long-term liabilities: notes payable and bonds. We described both of these liabilities and explained how they are both accounted for and reported.

A Look at This Chapter

This chapter emphasizes another special category, that of long-term investments in securities. We explain how to identify, account for, and report long-term investments in both debt and equity securities. We also introduce foreign exchange rates and describe accounting for transactions listed in a foreign currency.

A Look Forward

Chapter 19 focuses on reporting and analyzing a company's cash flows. Special emphasis is directed at the statement of cash flows.

Investing: The Next Generation

Bay Street, Toronto, ON—It was the worst day in Sara Brempong's young career as a financial analyst. She had just failed to land a major client and her boss removed her from a special analyst training program. Brempong's response? She quit. "Nothing fit," says Brempong. "Here I was, 23-years-old, in a stuffy old-boys' firm, advising clients twice my age on securities investments. I knew what I was doing, but no one believed in me."

That was five years ago. Today, Brempong is running her own investment firm, **Brempong & Brempong**. The other Brempong? "Well," laughs Brempong, "I asked my grandfather to sign on as joint partner because, like all the big firms, I thought I needed multiple names for the title of an investment firm." Adds Brempong, "Actually, he is the person who started me on my career. When he gave gifts to us grandchildren, he always tucked in some shares of the manufacturer."

Grandpa must now be proud, for Brempong's upstart firm pulled in over $485,000 in commissions and consulting revenues this past year. And the current year is running 28% ahead of last year. What's the secret? "Two things," says Brempong. "First, I work hard at knowing my investments and client needs. Second, I pursue a niche market for clients." What Brempong does is work tirelessly at attracting young investors, the twenty- and thirty-something crowd. "There is a large untapped market that I've only begun to break into," says Brempong. "Larger investment houses don't pursue these clients—I do." She also relies heavily on analysis of annual reports.

"My fundamental analysis is twofold," says Brempong. "I analyze the financial statements of potential investments to assess their strengths and weaknesses. Then I use their products and services, and ask others about them." Brempong also usually insists on visiting a company before she invests, or recommends investment, in it. "If I'm looking at a camera company, I use its cameras. I ask other people for their opinions too." Still, she cautions, "there is always a risk, but I try to minimize it through smart investing." Seems like grandpa was a good teacher.

Learning Objectives

LO 1 Distinguish long-term investments from temporary investments.

LO 2 Identify classes of securities in long-term investments.

LO 3 Account for debt securities held to maturity.

LO 4 Account for equity securities using the cost method.

LO 5 Account for equity securities having significant influence.

LO 6 Describe how equity securities having controlling influence are reported.

LO 7 Explain foreign exchange rates between currencies.

LO 8 Record transactions listed in a foreign currency.

LO 9 Compute and analyze the components of return on total assets.

CHAPTER PREVIEW

This chapter completes our study of assets by focusing on long-term investments. Many companies have long-term investments, and many of these are in the form of debt and equity securities issued by other companies. This chapter describes long-term investments in these securities and how they are accounted for. An increasing number of companies also invest in international operations. The financial statement effects of these investments are often very important. We explain how transactions listed in foreign currencies are accounted for and reported. Our understanding of the topics in this chapter are important in our ability to read and interpret financial statements. This knowledge is the type used by Sara Brempong as described in the opening article for investment decisions in shares and bonds.

Classifying Investments

This section explains how we classify investments. We first describe the distinction between short- and long-term investments. We then describe the different classification of long-term investments.

Temporary versus Long-Term

LO 1 Distinguish long-term investments from temporary investments.

We explained in Chapter 10 how to account for temporary investments in debt and equity securities. Temporary investments are usually held as an investment of cash for use in current operations. Temporary investments are current assets and must meet two requirements. First, they are expected to be converted into cash within one year or the current operating cycle of the business, whichever is longer. Second, they are readily convertible to cash, sometimes called *marketable*.[1]

Long-term investments are investments not meeting the two requirements for temporary investments. This means long-term investments include investments in bonds and shares that are not marketable or, if marketable, are not intended to be converted into cash in the short-term. Long-term investments also include funds earmarked for a special purpose. Examples are bond sinking funds, and investments in land or other assets not used in the company's operations. Long-term investments are reported in the noncurrent section of the balance sheet often in its own separate section titled *Long-term investments*.

Classes of Long-Term Investments

LO 2 Identify classes of securities in long-term investments.

Accounting for investments depends on several factors. One is whether securities are classified as (1) *trading* securities, (2) debt securities *held-to-maturity*, or (3) debt and equity securities *available-for-sale*. Investments in trading securities always are temporary investments and are reported as current assets. The other two classes of investments are either long-term or temporary depending on what the company intends to do with them. Another factor for equity securities is a company (investor's) percent ownership in the other company's (investee's) shares.

Exhibit 18.1 classifies long-term securities investments on these two factors. The four classifications shown are: (1) debt securities *held-to-maturity*, (2) debt and equity securities *available-for-sale*, (3) equity securities giving an investor a significant influence over an investee, and (4) equity securities giving an investor control over an investee. We next describe each of these four important classes of securities and how to account for them.

---

[1] It is helpful to review the section on temporary investments in Chapter 10 before studying this chapter.

Exhibit 18.1

Accounting for Long-Term Investments in Securities

Flash back

1. Give at least two examples of assets classified as long-term investments.
2. What are the requirements for a security to be classified as a long-term investment?

Answers—p. 848

Similar to the accounting for temporary investments, a long-term investment is recorded at cost when purchased. Cost is defined as all necessary expenditures to acquire the investment, including any commissions or brokerage fees paid. Recall that temporary investments are current assets; they are expected to be converted into cash within one year or the current operating cycle of the business, whichever is longer. In general, temporary investments such as T-bills and term deposits are those that are "capable of reasonably prompt liquidation."[2] Temporary investments either mature in one year or the current operating cycle or are easily sold and therefore qualify as *marketable*. Securites that do not qualify as current assets are called long-term investments. Long-term investments include investments in bonds and shares that are not marketable or that, although marketable, are not *intended* to serve as a ready source of cash. Long-term investments also include funds earmarked for a special purpose, such as bond sinking funds, and land or other assets owned but not used in the regular operations of the business. In general, these assets are reported on the balance sheet in a separate *Long-term investments* section. But after the purchase, the accounting treatment for long-term investments depends on the class of investments.

Investments in Debt Securities Held to Maturity

Long-term investments in *debt* securities are those that a company intends and is able to hold until maturity. Debt securities are recorded at cost when purchased. Also, long-term investments in debt securities require us to record interest revenue as it accrues.

Long-Term Investments in Securities

LO3 Account for debt securities held to maturity.

---

[2] *CICA Handbook*, par. 3010.02.

The cost of an investment in a long-term debt security can be either higher or lower than the maturity value of the debt security. When the investment is long-term, the difference between cost and maturity value is amortized over the remaining life of the security. Chapters 13 and 17 explain how we amortize this difference. For this chapter, *we assume for ease of computations that the cost of a debt security equals its maturity value.*

Illustration of a Debt Security Held-to-Maturity

Music City paid $29,500 plus a brokerage fee of $500 to buy Power Corp. 7% bonds payable with a $30,000 par value on August 31,1998. The bonds pay interest semiannually on August 31 and February 28. The amount of each interest payment is $1,050, computed as $30,000 face value × 7% interest × 6/12 year. Music City intends to hold the bonds until they mature on August 31, 2000. The entry to record this purchase is:

Assets = Liabilities + Equity
+30,000
−30,000

1998			
Aug. 31	Investment in Power Corp. Bonds	30,000	
	Cash		30,000
	Purchased bonds to be held to maturity.		

On December 31, 1998, at the end of its accounting period, Music City accrues interest receivable in the following entry:

Assets = Liabilities + Equity
+700   +700

Dec. 31	Interest Receivable	700	
	Interest Earned		700
	$1,050 × 4/6 = $700.		

The $700 reflects 4/6 of the semiannual cash receipt of interest. This is the portion earned by Music City. Music City's financial statements at December 31, 1998, are show in Exhibit 18.2.

Exhibit 18.2

Financial Statement Effects of Debt Securities

On the income statement for 1998:	
Interest earned	$ 700
On the December 31, 1998, balance sheet:	
Assets:	
Current Assets:	
Interest receivable	$ 700
Long-term investments:	
Investment in Power Corp. bonds	$30,000

On February 28, 1999, and each interest payment date thereafter, Music City records receipt of the semiannual interest as:

Assets = Liabilities + Equity
+1,050   +350
−700

1999			
Feb. 28	Cash	1,050	
	Interest Receivable		700
	Interest Earned		350
	Received six months' interest on Power		
	Corp. bonds.		

When the bonds mature, the entry to record proceeds from the matured bonds is:

Assets = Liabilities + Equity
+30,000
−30,000

2000			
Aug. 31	Cash	30,000	
	Investment in Power Corp. Bonds . . .		30,000
	Received cash from matured bonds.		

This illustration reflects the *cost method* for recording and reporting long-term investments in long-term debt securities. This method is required in practice.

Money Manager
You are a money manager for a company. You currently manage a fund with a large amount of investments in other companies' fixed-rate bonds and notes. You expect interest rates to both sharply fall within a few weeks and remain at this lower rate. What is the strategy for your investments in fixed-rate bonds and notes?

Answer—p. 847

Trading Secrets
Mutual fund companies keep secret their trading records for many reasons including regulatory requirements and potential lawsuits. But a mystery arose when top-secret trading records of the $55 billion **Fidelity Magellan** fund appeared in the *Washington Post*. This resulted in several lawsuits filed against Fidelity. Fidelity's fund managers have since been barred from talking about individual shares with the press, and the company has stopped its internal circulation of daily fund trading for security reasons.
[Source: *Business Week*, May 27, 1996.]

Did You Know?

Investments in Equity Securities

The accounting for long-term investments in portfolio securities is similar to accounting for temporary investments. First, these investments are recorded at cost. Second, dividends received are credited to Dividends Earned and reported in the income statement. Third, when the shares are sold, proceeds from the sale are compared with the cost of the investment and any gain or loss on the sale is reported in the income statement.

A portfolio investment could consist of the same securities as a temporary investment. The difference is that management intends not to dispose of the securities of a portfolio in the short term. Portfolio investments are held to generate investment income. For example, a company that holds shares of **B.C. Tel** with the intention of selling them within six months would classify this investment as temporary. If the intent were to hold on to these shares for the long-term the investment in B.C. Tel would be classified as long term. An important requirement for a security to be classified as a long-term portfolio investment in equity securities is that it must not enable its investor to have significant influence over the investee. This usually is interpreted as an investor who owns less than 20% of the investee company's voting shares.[3]

LO 4 Account for equity securities using the cost method.

Illustration of the Cost Method of Accounting for an Equity Security

Music City purchased 1,000 shares of **Intex's** common shares at its par value of $86,000 on October 10, 1998. The entry to record this purchase is:

Oct. 10	Investment in Intex Common Shares	86,000	
	Cash		86,000
	Purchased 1,000 shares.		

Assets = Liabilities + Equity
+86,000
−86,000

---

[3] The 20% limit is not an absolute rule. Other factors may overrule. See *CICA Handbook*, section 3050, "Long-term Investments," par. .04.

On November 2, Music City receives a $1,720 quarterly dividend on the Intex shares. The entry to record the dividend receipt is:

Assets = Liabilities + Equity
+1,720   +1,720

Nov. 2	Cash	1,720	
	Dividends Earned		1,720
	Received dividend of $1.72 per share.		

On December 20, Music City sells 500 of the Intex shares for $45,000. The entry to record this sale is:

Assets = Liabilities + Equity
+45,000   +2,000
−43,000

Dec. 20	Cash	45,000	
	Investment in Intex Common Shares .		43,000
	Gain on Sale of Long-Term Investment		2,000
	$86,000/2 = $43,000		

Reporting Long-Term Investments

Long-term investments are stated at cost with market value disclosed even if market value is below cost as long as the decline in value is temporary. However, when there has been a loss in value that is other than temporary, the investment is written down to recognize the loss.[4] The writedown (loss) would be included in determining net income. When a long-term investment has been written down to recognize the loss, the new carrying value is deemed to be the new cost basis for subsequent accounting purposes. A subsequent increase in value would be recognized only when realized, i.e., when the shares are sold. For purposes of calculating the gain or loss on sale of the investment, the cost of the investment sold should be calculated on the basis of the average carrying value (total cost of the shares ÷ number of shares held).[5]

Investment in Equity Securities with Significant Influence

LO 5 Account for equity securities having significant influence.

A long-term investment in **equity securities with significant influence** is defined as an investor who is able to exert significant influence over the investee. This is usually the result of an investor buying a large block of a company's voting shares. An investor who owns 20% or more (but not more than 50%) of a company's voting shares is usually presumed to have a significant influence over the investee. Yet there are cases where the 20% test of significant influence is overruled by other, more persuasive, evidence. This evidence can either lower the 20% requirement or increase it. According to section 3050.04 of the *CICA Handbook:*

> An investor may be able to exercise significant influence over strategic operating, investing and financing policies of an investee even though the investor does not control or jointly control the investee. The ability to exercise significant influence may be indicated by, for example, representation on the board of directors, participation in policy-making processes, material intercompany transactions, interchange of managerial personnel or provision of technical information. If the investor holds less than 20% of the voting interest in the investee, it is presumed that the investor does not have the ability to exercise significant influence, unless such influence is clearly demonstrated. On the other hand, the holding of 20% or more of the voting interest in the investee does not in itself confirm the ability to exercise significant influence. A substantial or majority ownership by another investor would not necessarily preclude an investor from exercising significant influence.

---

[4] Ibid., par. 3050.20.

[5] Ibid., par. 3050.27.

The **equity method** of accounting and reporting is used for long-term investments in equity securities with significant influence. We now illustrate this method.

Illustration of an Equity Security with Significant Influence.

This section illustrates the equity method of accounting for long-term investments in equity securities with significant influence. The investor records the purchase of these securities at cost when acquired. To illustrate, Micron Company purchased 3,000 shares (30%) of JVT common shares for a total cost of $70,650 on January 1, 1998. The entry to record this purchase on Micron's books is:

Jan. 1	Investment in JVT Common Shares	70,650	
	Cash		70,650
	Purchased 3,000 shares.		

Assets = Liabilities + Equity
+70,650
−70,650

Under the equity method, earnings of the investee (JVT) increase both the investee's net assets and the investor's (Micron) equity claims against the investee's assets. This means when the investee closes its books and reports its earnings, the investor records its share of those earnings in its investment account. JVT reported net income of $20,000 for 1998. Micron's entry to record its 30% share of these earnings is:

Dec. 31	Investment in JVT Common Shares	6,000	
	Earnings from Investment in JVT		6,000
	To record 30% equity in investee's		
	earnings of $20,000.		

Assets = Liabilities + Equity
+6,000   +6,000

The debit reflects the increase in Micron's equity in JVT. The credit means 30% of JVT's net income appears on Micron's income statement as earnings from the investment. As with all revenues, Micron closes these earnings to Income Summary.

If the investee incurs a net loss instead of a net income, the investor records its share of the loss and reduces (credits) its investment account. The investor closes a loss to Income Summary. For example assume that JVT had reported a loss of $15,000. The following entries would be made by Micron:

Dec. 31	Loss from Investment in JVT Common Shares	4,500	
	Investment in JVT		4,500
	To record 30% decrease in equity from		
	investee's loss of $15,000.		

Assets = Liabilities + Equity
−4,500   −4,500

Dec. 31	Income Summary	4,500	
	Loss from Investment in JVT Common Shares		4,500
	To close the loss from investments to		
	income summary.		

Assets = Liabilities + Equity
                      −4,500
                      +4,500

The receipt of cash dividends is not recorded as revenue when using the equity method. This is because the investor has already recorded its share of the earnings reported by the investee. Instead, dividends received from an investee convert the form of the investor's asset from a shares investment to cash. This means dividends reduce the balance of the investment account, but increase cash. To illustrate, JVT declared and paid $10,000 in cash dividends on its common shares. Micron's entry to record its 30% share of these dividends received on January 9, 1999 is:

Jan. 9	Cash	3,000	
	Investment in JVT Common Shares ..		3,000
	To record receipt of 30% of $10,000		
	dividend paid by JVT.		

Assets = Liabilities + Equity
+3,000
−3,000

The book value of an investment in equity securities when using the equity method is equal to the cost of the investment plus the investor's equity in the *undistributed* earnings of the investee. Once we record the above transactions for Micron, its investment account appears as in Exhibit 18.3.

Exhibit 18.3

Investment in JVT Common Shares Ledger Account

Date		Explanation	Debit	Credit	Balance
1998					
Jan.	1	Investment	70,650		70,650
Dec.	31	Share of earnings	6,000		76,650
1999					
Jan.	9	Share of dividend		3,000	73,650

Micron's account balance on January 9, 1999, for the Investment in JVT is $73,650. This is the investment's cost *plus* Micron's equity in JVT's earnings since its purchase *less* Micron's equity in JVT's cash dividends since its purchase.

When an investment in equity securities is sold, the gain or loss is computed by comparing proceeds from the sale with the book value of the investment on the date of sale. If Micron sells its JVT shares for $80,000 on January 10, 1999, the entry to record the sale is:

Assets = Liabilities + Equity
+80,000   +6,350
−73,650

Jan. 10	Cash	80,000	
	Investment in JVT Common Shares ..		73,650
	Gain on Sale of Investments		6,350
	Sold 3,000 shares for $80,000		

In most cases shares are purchased at amounts greater than their net book value. If the acquisition cost is greater than the book value at the date of acquisition the investor must adjust the earnings recorded by amortizing the excess of cost over book value. This added complexity is discussed in detail in intermediate accounting texts.

Did You Know?

Tinseltown Securities
Did you ever wish you could share in the profits of Hollywood films like *Independence Day*, *The Lost World*, *Titanic*, or *Speed*? Well, you can now. Both **Fox** and **Universal Studios** are selling equity shares in their upcoming movies to outside investors. **Citicorp**, who is handling these shares, forecasts a minimum annualized rate of return of 15%. But the possibility of big hits is what is drawing many investors. [Source: *Business Week*, August 11, 1997.]

Investment in Equity Securities with Controlling Influence

LO 6 Describe how equity securities having controlling influence are reported.

A long-term investment in **equity securities with controlling influence** is defined as an investor who is able to exert a controlling influence over the investee. An investor who owns more than 50% of a company's voting shares is presumed to have a controlling influence over the investee. This investor can dominate all other shareholders in electing the corporation's board of directors. This investor usually has control over the investee corporation's management. The controlling corporation (investor) is known as the **parent company** and the company whose shares are held by the parent (investee) is referred to as a **subsidiary.**

Many large companies are parents with subsidiaries. For example, **George Weston Limited** is the parent of several subsidiaries, including **Loblaw, Neilson/Cadbury, Zehrmart, E.B. Eddy Paper,** and **National Grocers.**

When a corporation owns all the outstanding shares of a subsidiary, it can take over the subsidiary's asssets, cancel the subsidiary's shares, and merge the

subsidiary into the parent
company. However, there
often are financial, legal,
and tax advantages if a
large business is operated
as a parent corporation
that controls one or more
subsidiary corporations.

Equity
Method with
Consolidation
(50%+)

Equity Method
(20%–50%)

Fair Market
Value Method
(Under 20%)

Exhibit 18.4

Accounting for Equity
Investments by Percent
of Ownership

In fact, many large companies are parent corporations that own one or more subsidiaries. A summary of accounting for equity investments by percent of ownership is provided in Exhibit 18.4.

When a business operates as a parent company with subsidiaries, separate accounting records are maintained by each corporation. From a legal viewpoint, the parent
and each subsidiary are still separate entitites with all the rights, duties, and responsibilities of individual corporations. However, investors in the parent company indirectly are investors in the subsidiaries. To evaluate their investments, parent company
investors must consider the financial status and operations of the subsidiaries as well
as the parent. This information is provided in consolidated financial statements.

Consolidated financial statements show the financial position, results of
operations, and cash flows of all companies under the parent's control, including all subsidiaries. These statements are prepared as if the company is organized as one entity. The parent uses the equity method in its accounts, but the
investment account is *not* reported on the parent's financial statements. Instead,
the individual assets and liabilities of the parent and its subsidiaries are combined on one balance sheet. Their revenues and expenses also are combined on
one income statement and their cash flows are combined on one statement of
changes in financial position. The detailed procedures for preparing consolidated
financial statements are included in advanced courses. Some of the basics procedures however are provided in the appendix at the end of this chapter.

Flashback

3. What are the three classes of long-term equity investments? Describe the criteria
for each class and the method used to account for each.

Answers—p. 848

The following transactions relate to Brown Company's long-term investment activities during 19X1 and 19X2. Brown did not own any long-term investments prior to
19X1. Show the appropriate journal entries and the portions of each year's balance
sheet and income statement that describe these transactions.

19X1

Sept. 9   Purchased 1,000 shares of **Packard, Inc.,** common shares for $80,000 cash.
            These shares represent 30% of Packard's outstanding shares.
Oct.   2   Purchased 2,000 shares of **MT&T** common shares for $60,000 cash. These
            shares represent less than a 1% ownership in MT&T.
       17   Purchased as a long-term investment 1,000 shares of **Four Seasons** com-
            mon shares for $40,000 cash. These shares are less than 1% of Four
            Seasons's outstanding shares.
Nov.   1   Received $5,000 cash dividend from Packard.
       30   Received $3,000 cash dividend from MT&T.
Dec.   15   Received $1,400 cash dividend from Four Seasons.
       31   Packard's 19X1 net income was $70,000.
       31   Market values for the investments in equity securities are Packard, $84,000;
            MT&T, $48,000; and Four Seasons Hotels, $45,000.

Mid-Chapter
Demonstration
Problem

19X2

Jan.	1	Packard, Inc., was taken over by other investors, and Brown sold its shares for $108,000 cash.
May	30	Received $3,100 cash dividend from MT&T.
June	15	Received $1,600 cash dividend from Four Seasons.
Aug.	17	Sold the MT&T shares for $52,000 cash.
	19	Purchased 2,000 shares of Loblaw common shares for $50,000 as a long-term investment. The shares represent less than a 5% ownership in Loblaw.
Dec.	15	Received $1,800 cash dividend from Four Seasons.
	31	Market values of the investments in marketable equity securities are Four Seasons, $39,000 and Loblaw, $48,000.

Planning the Solution

■ Account for the investment in Packard under the equity method.

■ Account for the investments in MT&T, Four Seasons, and Loblaw as long-term investments in securities.

■ Prepare the information for the two balance sheets by including the appropriate assets and shareholders' equity accounts.

Solution to Mid-Chapter Demonstration Problem

Journal Entries during 19X1

Assets = Liabilities + Equity
+80,000
−80,000

Sept. 9	Investment in Packard Common Shares . . .	80,000	
	Cash		80,000
	Acquired 1,000 shares representing a		
	30% equity in Packard, Inc.		

Assets = Liabilities + Equity
+60,000
−60,000

Oct. 2	Investment in MT&T Common Shares	60,000	
	Cash		60,000
	Acquired 2,000 shares as a long-term		
	investment in securities available for sale.		

Assets = Liabilities + Equity
+40,000
−40,000

17	Investment in Four Seasons Common Shares	40,000	
	Cash		40,000
	Acquired 1,000 shares as a long-term		
	investment in securities available for sale.		

Assets = Liabilities + Equity
+5,000
−5,000

Nov. 1	Cash	5,000	
	Investment in Packard Common Shares		5,000
	Received dividend from Packard, Inc.		

Assets = Liabilities + Equity
+3,000   +3,000

30	Cash	3,000	
	Dividends Earned		3,000
	Received dividend from MT&T		

Assets = Liabilities + Equity
+1,400   +1,400

Dec. 15	Cash	1,400	
	Dividends Earned		1,400
	Received dividend from Four Seasons.		

Assets = Liabilities + Equity
+21,000   +21,000

31	Investment in Packard Common Shares . . .	21,000	
	Earnings from Investment in Packard .		21,000
	To record our 30% share of Packard's		
	annual earnings of $70,000		

	Cost	Fair (Market) Value
MT&T	$ 60,000	$ 48,000
Four Seasons	40,000	45,000
Total	$100,000	$ 93,000

Given the usual fluctuations in market prices, it is reasonable to assume that the reduction is temporary. Therefore, no adjustment is necessary.

December 31, 19X1, Balance Sheet Items

Assets
Long-term investments:
   Equity securities, at cost (market value, $93,000) $100,000
Investment in Packard, Inc. (market value,$84,000)   96,000

   Total $196,000

Income Statement Items for the Year Ended December 31, 19X1

Dividends earned	$ 4,400
Earnings from equity method investment	21,000

Journal Entries during 19X2

Jan. 1	Cash	108,000		Assets = Liabilities + Equity
	Investment in Packard Common Shares		96,000	+108,000 +12,000
	Gain on Sale of Investments		12,000	−96,000
	Sold 1,000 shares for cash.			

May 30	Cash	3,100		Assets = Liabilities + Equity
	Dividends Earned		3,100	+3,100 +3,100
	Received dividend from MT&T.			

June 15	Cash	1,600		Assets = Liabilities + Equity
	Dividends Earned		1,600	+1,600 +1,600
	Received dividend from Four Seasons.			

Aug. 17	Cash	52,000		Assets = Liabilities + Equity
	Loss on Sale of Investments	8,000		+52,000 −8,000
	Investment in MT&T Common Shares .		60,000	+60,000
	Sold 2,000 shares for cash.			
19	Investment in Loblaw Common Shares	50,000		Assets = Liabilities + Equity
	Cash		50,000	+50,000
	Acquired 2,000 shares as a long-term			−50,000
	investment in securities available for sale.			

Dec. 15	Cash	1,800		Assets = Liabilities + Equity
	Dividends Earned		1,800	+1,800 +1,800
	Received dividend from Four Seasons.			

	Cost	Fair (Market) Value
Four Seasons	$ 40,000	$ 39,000
Loblaw	50,000	48,000
Total	$ 90,000	$ 87,000

December 31, 19X2, Balance Sheet Items

Assets
Long-term investments:
   Equity securities, at cost (market value, $87,000) $90,000

Income Statement Items for the Year Ended December 31, 19X2

Dividends earned	$ 6,500
Gain on sale of investments	12,000
Loss on sale of investments	(8,000)

Investments in International Operations

Many companies from small entrepreneurs to large corporations conduct business internationally. The operations of some large corporations take place in so many different countries that they are called **multinationals.** Many of us, for example, think of **Alcan** and **Bombardier** as primarily Canadian companies. Yet both companies earn over three-quarters of their sales from outside Canada. Other corporations such as **Magna, McCain Foods, CAE Electronics,** and **Molson's** are major players in the world of international business.

Two major accounting challenges arise when companies have international operations. Both relate to transactions that occur using more than one currency. The two challenges can be described as (1) accounting for sales or purchases listed in a foreign currency and (2) preparing consolidated financial statements with international subsidiaries. For ease in discussion of these challenges, we use companies with a base of operations in Canada and with a need to prepare financial statements in Canadian dollars. This means the *reporting currency* of these companies is the Canadian dollar.

Exchange Rates between Currencies

LO 7 Explain foreign exchange rates between currencies.

Markets for the purchase and sale of foreign currencies exist all over the world. In these markets, Canadian dollars can be exchanged for U.S. dollars, British pounds, French francs, Japanese yen, or any other legal currencies. The price of one currency stated in terms of another currency is called a **foreign exchange rate.**

Exhibit 18.5 lists foreign exchange rates for selected currencies at April 13, 1998. We see the exchange rate for British pounds and Canadian dollars is $2.3839 on January 1, 1998. This rate means one British pound can be purchased for $2.3839. On the same day, the exchange rate between German marks and Canadian dollars is $0.7822. This rate means one German mark can be purchased for $0.7822. Foreign exchange rates fluctuate due to changing economic and political conditions. These include the supply and demand for currencies and expectations about future events.

Exhibit 18.5

Foreign Exchange Rates for Selected Currencies*

Country (unit)	Price in $Can.	Country (unit)	Price in $Can.
Britain (pound)	$ 2.3839	U.S. (dollar)	$ 1.4212
Germany (mark)	0.7822	France (franc)	0.2334
Mexico (peso)	0.1680	Japan (yen)	0.0195
Taiwan (dollar)	0.0433	Europe (ECU)	1.5524

*Rates for April 13, 1998, **http://www.traveloco.com/index2.html?loco=/tools/currency**

Did You Know?

Sales or Purchases Listed in a Foreign Currency

When a Canadian company makes a credit sale to an international customer, accounting for the sale and the account receivable requires special treatment when the terms of the sale require payment in a foreign currency.

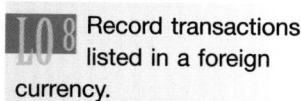

LO 8 Record transactions listed in a foreign currency.

Did You Know?

Consider the case of the Canadian-based manufacturer, **Quebec Company,** who makes credit sales to **London Outfitters,** a British retail company. A sale occurred on December 12, 1998, for a price of £10,000, payment due on February 10, 1999. Quebec Company keeps its accounting records in Canadian dollars. To record the sale, Canadian Company must translate the sales price from pounds to dollars. This is done using the exchange rate on the date of the sale. Assuming the exchange rate on December 12, 1998 is $2.36, Quebec records this sale as:

Dec. 12	Accounts Receivable — London Outfitters .	23,600	
	Sales (£10,000 × $2.36)		23,600
	To record a sale at £10,000, when the		
	exchange rate equals $2.36.		

Assets = Liabilities + Equity
+23,600   +23,600

Quebec Company prepares its annual financial statements on December 31, 1998. On that date, the current exchange rate increases to $2.38. This means the current dollar value of Quebec Company's receivable is $23,800 (10,000 × $2.38). This amount is $200 greater than the amount recorded on December 12. Accepted accounting principles require a receivable to be reported in the balance sheet at its current dollar value. Quebec Company must make the following entry to record the increase in the dollar value of this receivable:

Dec. 31	Accounts Receivable—London Outfitters ..	200	
	Foreign Exchange Gain or Loss		200
	To record the increased value of the British		
	pound on the receivable.		

Assets = Liabilities + Equity
+200   +200

Quebec Company receives London Outfitters' payment of £10,000 on February 10, 1999. Quebec Company immediately exchanges the pounds for Canadian dollars. On this date, the exchange rate for pounds is $2.35. This means Quebec Company receives only $23,500 (10,000 × $2.35). It records the cash receipt and the loss associated with the decline in the exchange rate as follows:

Assets = Liabilities + Equity
+23,500   −300
−23,800

Feb. 10	Cash	23,500	
	Foreign Exchange Gain or Loss	300	
	Accounts Receivable — London Outfitters		23,800
	Received foreign currency payment of an		
	account and converted it into dollars.		

Gains and losses from foreign exchange transactions are accumulated in the Foreign Exchange Gain or Loss account. After year-end adjustments, the balance in the Foreign Exchange Gain or Loss account is reported on the income statement and closed to the Income Summary account.

Accounting for credit purchases from an international supplier is similar to the case of a credit sale to an international customer. In particular, if the Canadian company is required to make payment in a foreign currency, the account payable must be translated into dollars before the Canadian company can record it. If the exchange rate is different when preparing financial statements and when paying for the purchase, the Canadian company must recognize an exchange gain or loss at those dates.

Home Builder
You are a Canadian home builder who regularly purchases lumber from mills in both the U.S. and Canada. Lumber prices have been similar across both countries. But today the price of the Canadian dollar in terms of the U.S. dollar jumped from U.S.$0.70 to U.S.$0.80. Are you now more or less likely to buy lumber from Canadian or U.S. mills?

Answer—p. 847

Consolidated Statements with International Subsidiaries

A second challenge in accounting for international operations involves preparing consolidated financial statements when the parent company has one or more international subsidiaries. Consider the Canadian-based company, **Classic Winery,** which owns a controlling interest in a French subsidiary. The reporting currency of the Canadian parent is the dollar. The French subsidiary maintains its financial records in francs. Before preparing consolidated statements, the parent must translate financial statements of the French company into Canadian dollars. After this translation is complete, we prepare consolidated statements the same as with domestic subsidiaries.[6]

Procedures for translating an international subsidiary's account balances depend on the nature of the subsidiary's operations. The process requires the parent company to select appropriate foreign exchange rates and to apply those rates to the account balances of the foreign subsidiary. This concept is introduced; however, it is beyond the scope of first year accounting.

---

[6] The problem is more challenging when the accounts of the French subsidiary are maintained in accordance with the French version of GAAP. The French statements then must be converted to Canadian GAAP before consolidation.

★Flashback

4. If a Canadian company makes a credit sale of merchandise to a French customer and the sales terms require payment in francs:

a. The Canadian company incurs an exchange loss if the foreign exchange rate between francs and dollars increases from $0.234 at the date of sale to $0.239 at the date the account is settled.

b. The French company may eventually need to record an exchange gain or loss.

c. The Canadian company may be required to record an exchange gain or loss on the date of the sale.

Answer—p. 848

Components of Return on Total Assets

USING THE INFORMATION

Chapter 1 described a company's *return on total assets* (or simply *return on assets*) and explained its importance in assessing financial performance. The **return on total assets** can be separated into two components to help us in this analysis. The two components are: net profit margin and total asset turnover. Net profit margin was explained in Chapter 4 and total asset turnover in Chapter 13. Exhibit 18.6 shows how these two components determine return on total assets.

 LO 9 Compute and analyze the components of return on total assets.

Return on Total Assets	=	Profit Margin	×	Total Asset Turnover
$\dfrac{\text{Net Income}}{\text{Average Total Assets}}$	=	$\dfrac{\text{Net Income}}{\text{Net Sales}}$	×	$\dfrac{\text{Net Sales}}{\text{Average Total Assets}}$

Exhibit 18.6

Components of Return on Total Assets

Net profit margin (net income / net sales) is the first component and reflects the percent of net income in each dollar of net sales. Total asset turnover (net sales / average total assets) is the second component and reflects a company's ability to produce net sales from total assets. All companies desire a high return on total assets. By looking at these two components, we can often discover strengths and weaknesses not revealed by return on total assets. This improves our ability to assess future performance and company strategy.

To illustrate, we look at return on total assets and its components for **Reebok** and **NIKE**. Reebok's return on total assets and its components are shown in Exhibit 18.7.

Year	Return on Total Assets	=	Profit Margin	×	Total Asset Turnover
1996	8.08%	=	3.99%	×	2.02
1995	9.98%	=	4.73%	×	2.11
1994	16.74%	=	7.76%	×	2.16

Exhibit 18.7

Reebok's Components of Return on Total Assets

At least three results emerge. First, Reebok's return on total assets declines from 1994 through 1996. Second, total asset turnover also declines over this period, but not significantly. And third, Reebok's net profit margin sharply falls between 1994 and 1996. These components show the dual role of net profit margin and total asset turnover for Reebok. More important, it shows the cause of Reebok's decline is not total asset turnover, but net profit margin. Reebok's costs and expenses have increased as a percent of sales, and cost management is necessary.

Generally, if a company is to maintain its return on total assets, then a decline in either profit margin or total asset turnover must be met with an increase in the other. If not, then return on assets will decline. Companies look at these components in planning future strategies. A component analysis can also reveal where a company is weak and where changes are needed.

We also look at these two components in comparing competitors. If asset turnover is lower than the industry norm, for instance, a company should focus on getting asset turnover at least up to the norm. The same applies to profit margin. Exhibit 18.8 shows NIKE's components for its fiscal year ending May 31, 1997.

Exhibit 18.8

NIKE's Components of
Return on Total Assets

Fiscal Year	Return on Total Assets	=	Profit Margin	x	Total Asset Turnover
1997	17.09%	=	8.66%	x	1.97

NIKE's most recent return on total assets is much higher than Reebok's. But the components show Reebok is as good and slightly better than NIKE on total asset turnover. This highlights Reebok's sharp decline in net profit margin in recent years. One potential cause is Reebok's increased Cost of Goods Sold and Selling, General and Administrative Expenses as a percent of net sales. Reebok should focus on reducing these expenditures as a percent of sales.[7]

You Make the Call

Retailer
You are an entrepreneur and owner of a retail sporting goods store. The store's recent year's performance reveals (industry norms in parenthesis): return on total assets = 11% (11.2%); profit margin = 4.4% (3.5%); and total asset turnover = 2.5 (3.2). What does your analysis of these figures suggest?

Answer—p. 847

Summary

LO 1 Distinguish long-term investments from temporary investments. Temporary investments in securities are current assets that meet two criteria. First, they are expected to be converted into cash within one year or the current operating cycle of the business, whichever is longer. Second, they are readily converted to cash, sometimes called marketable. All other investments in securities are long-term investments. Long-term investments also include assets not used in operations and those held for a special purpose such as land for expansion.

LO 2 Identify classes of securities in long-term investments. Long-term investments in securities are classified into one of four groups: (a) debt securities held-to-maturity, (b) debt and equity securities available-for-sale,

(c) equity securities where an investor has a significant influence over the investee, and (d) equity securities where an investor has a controlling influence over the investee.

LO 3 Account for debt securities held to maturity. Debt securities held-to-maturity are reported at cost when purchased. Interest revenue is recorded as it accrues. The cost of held-to-maturity securities is adjusted for amortization of any difference between cost and maturity value.

LO 4 Account for equity securities using the cost method. Debt and equity securities available-for-sale are recorded at cost when purchased. Available-for-sale securities are reported at their fair market values with unrealized holding gains or losses shown in the shareholders' equity section of

---

[7] Another base of comparison is to compute average figures for manufacturers of athletic footwear and apparel. Industry averages are available through publications such as Dun & Bradstreet's *Industry Norms and Key Ratios*.

the balance sheet. Gains and losses realized on the sale of these investments are reported in the income statement.

LO 5 Account for equity securities having significant influence. The equity method is used when an investor has a significant influence over an investee. This usually exists when an investor owns 20% or more of the investee's voting shares, but not exceeding 50% ownership. The equity method means an investor records its share of the investee's earnings with a debit to the investment account and a credit to a revenue account. Dividends received satisfy the investor's equity claims and reduce the investment account balance.

LO 6 Describe how equity securities having controlling influence are reported. If an investor owns more than 50% of another company's voting shares and controls the investee, the investor's financial reports are prepared on a consolidated basis. These reports are prepared as if the company is organized as one entity. The individual assets and liabilities of the parent and its subsidiaries are combined on one balance sheet. Similarly, their revenues and expenses are combined on one income statement and their cash flows are combined on one statement of changes in financial position.

LO 7 Explain foreign exchange rates between currencies. A foreign exchange rate is the price of one currency stated in terms of another. A company with transactions in a foreign currency when the exchange rate changes between the time of the transactions and its settlement will experience an exchange gain or loss.

LO 8 Record transactions listed in a foreign currency. When a company makes a credit sale to a foreign customer and sales terms call for payment in a foreign currency, the company must translate the foreign currency into dollars to record the receivable. If the exchange rate changes before payment is received, foreign exchange gains or losses are recognized in the year they occur. The same treatment is used when a company makes a credit purchase from a foreign supplier and is required to make payment in a foreign currency. Also, a company with a foreign subsidiary that maintains its accounts in a foreign currency must translate these account balances into dollars before they are consolidated with the parent's accounts.

LO 9 Compute and analyze the components of return on total assets. Return on total assets is made up of two components we can use to assess a company's ability in using its assets: net profit margin and total asset turnover. A decline in one component must be met with an increase in another if profits are to be maintained. The components are also helpful in assessing company performance compared to competitors. For instance, if one component is worse than the industry norm, then a company should focus on getting its performance on this component at least up to the industry norm.

Guidance Answers to **You Make the Call**

Money Manager

If you have investments in fixed-rate bonds and notes when interest rates fall, then the value of your investments increase. This is because the bonds and notes you hold continue to pay the same (high) rate while the market is demanding a new lower interest rate. Your strategy is to continue holding your investments in bonds and notes, and potentially to increase these holdings through additional purchases.

Home Builder

You are now more likely to buy Canadian lumber. This is because it takes more U.S. money to buy a Canadian dollar (and lumber). For instance, the purchase of lumber from a U.S. mill with a $1,000 (Canadian dollars) price cost the builder $700 (U.S. dollars, computed as C.$1,000 × U.S.$0.70) before the rate change and $800 (U.S. dollars, computed as C.$1,000 × U.S.$0.80) after the rate change.

Retailer

Your analysis of return on assets shows your store to be competitive. In particular, your store's return on assets is 11%, which is similar to the industry norm of 11.2%. However, disaggregation of return on assets reveals additional information. Your store's profit margin of 4.4% is much higher than the norm of 3.5%. But your total asset turnover of 2.5 is much lower than the norm of 3.2. These results suggest you are less efficient in using assets as compared with competitors. You need to focus on increasing sales or reducing your assets. You might wish to consider reducing prices to increase sales. You need to make sure such a strategy doesn't reduce your return on total assets. For instance, you could reduce your profit margin to 4% to increase sales. If total asset turnover increases to more than 2.75 when profit margin is lowered to 4%, then your return on total assets is improved.

Guidance Answers to Flashbacks

1. Long-term investments include funds earmarked for a special purpose, bonds and shares that do not meet the test of a current asset, and other assets that are not used in the regular operations of the business.
2. A shares investment is classified as a long-term investment if it is not marketable or, if marketable, it is not held as an available source of cash to meet the needs of current operations.
3. Long-term equity investments are placed in one of the following three categories and accounted for using the method indicated:

a. Available-for-sale (noninfluential, less than 20% of outstanding shares) — cost method.
b. Significant influence (20% to 50% of outstanding shares) — equity method.
c. Controlling influence (holding more than 50% of outstanding shares) — consolidation to report.
4. *a*

Demonstration Problem

Boudreau Co. is a Canadian corporation that has customers in several foreign countries. Following are some of Boudreau's 19X1 and 19X2 transactions:

19X1

Apr. 8   Sold merchandise to Lejeune Co. of France for 125,000 francs to be received in 60 days. The exchange rate for francs was $0.02822.

July 21   Sold merchandise for $8,880 cash to Vongurp Corp. of Germany. The exchange rate for marks was $0.5920 on this date.

Oct. 14   Received the Lejeune Company's payment for its purchase of Apr. 8 and exchanged the francs for dollars. The current foreign exchange rate for francs into dollars was $0.02840.

Nov. 18   Sold merchandise on credit to British Imports, Ltd., a company located in London, England. The price of 3,000 pounds was to be paid 90 days from the date of sale. On Nov. 18, the exchange rate for pounds into dollars was $1.7730.

Dec. 20   Sold merchandise for 350,000 yen to Yamoto Company of Japan;, payment in full to be received in 60 days. On this day, the foreign exchange rate for yen was $0.007710.

31   Prepared adjusting entries to recognize exchange gains or losses on the annual financial statements. Rates for exchanging foreign currencies on this day included the following:

Francs (Belgium)	$0.1335
Yen (Japan)	0.007897
Pounds (Britain)	1.7125
Marks (Germany)	0.5944

19X2

Jan. 12   Received full payment from British Imports, Ltd. for the sale of November 18 and immediately exchanged the pounds for dollars. The exchange rate for pounds was $1.7628.

19   Received Yamoto's full payment for the sale of December 20 and immediately exchanged the yen for dollars. The exchange rate for marks was $0.007779.

Required

1. Prepare general journal entries to account for these transactions on Boudreau's books.
2. Compute the foreign exchange gain or loss to be reported on Boudreau's 19X1 income statement.
3. What actions might Boudreau consider to reduce its risk of foreign exchange gains or losses?

Planning the Solution

■ Account for each transaction.

■ Calculate any foreign exchange gain or loss at year-end by multiplying the number of foreign currency units by the difference between the foreign exchange rate on the transaction date and the year-end foreign exchange rate.

■ Calculate any foreign exchange rate on the date cash is received by multiplying the number of foreign currency units by the difference between the foreign exchange rate on the cash collection date and the foreign exchange rate at the previous year-end.

Solution to Demonstration Problem

Part 1.

19X1			
Apr. 8	Accounts receivable/Lejeune	3,527.50	
	Sales (125,000 × $0.02822)		3,527.50

July 21	Cash	8,880.00	
	Sales		8,880.00

Oct. 14	Cash (125,000 × $0.028400)	3,550.00	
	Foreign exchange gain or loss		22.50
	Accounts receivable — Lejeune		3,527.50

Nov. 18	Accounts Receivable		
	British Imports (1.773 × 3,000)	5,319.00	
	Sales		5,319.00

Dec. 20	Accounts Receivable — Yomoto	2,698.50	
	Sales (350,000 × $0.007710)		2,698.50
31	Foreign Exchange Gain or Loss	181.50	
	Accounts Receivable — British Imp. ...		181.50
	Original measure =		
	(3,000 × $1.773) = $5,319.00		
	Year-end measure =		
	(3,000 × $1.7125) = 5,137.50		
	Loss for the period = $181.50		
31	Accounts Receivable — Yomoto	65.45	
	Foreign Exchange Gain or Loss		65.45
	Original measure =		
	(350,000 × $0.007710) = $2,698.50		
	Year-end measure =		
	(350,000 × $0.007897) = 2,763.95		
	Gain for the period = $65.45		

19X2			
Jan. 12	Cash (3,000 × $1.7628)	5,288.40	
	Accounts Receivable — British Imp.		
	($5,319.00 − $155.00)		5,164.00
	Foreign Exchange Gain or Loss		124.40
19	Cash (350,000 × $0.007779)	2722.65	
	Foreign Exchange Gain or Loss	41.30	
	Accounts Receivable—Yomoto		
	($2,698.50 + $65.45)		2,763.95

Part 2. Foreign exchange loss to be reported on the 19X1 income statement:

October 14	$ 22.50
December 31	(181.50)
December 31	65.45
Total	$ (93.55)

Part 3. To reduce the risk of foreign exchange gain or loss, Boudreau could attempt to negotiate foreign customer sales that are denominated in Canadian dollars. To accomplish this, Boudreau may be willing to offer favourable terms, such as price discounts or longer credit terms. Another possibility that may be of limited potential is for Boudreau to make credit purchases denominated in foreign currencies, planning the purchases so that the payables in foreign currencies match the foreign currency receivables in time and amount.

Parent and Subsidiary Corporations

Corporations commonly own shares in and may even control other corporations. For example, if Par Company owns more than 50% of the voting shares of Sub Company, Par company can elect Sub Company's board of directors and thus control its activities and resources. In this case, the controlling corporation, Par Company, is known as the *parent company*, and Sub Company is called the *subsidiary*.

When a corporation owns all the outstanding shares of a subsidiary, it can take over the subsidiary's assets, cancel its shares, and merge the subsidiary into the parent company. However, instead of operating the business as a single corporation, there often are financial, legal, and tax advantages if a large business is operated as a parent corporation that controls one or more subsidiary corporations. Actually, most large companies are parent corporations that own one or more subsidiaries.

When a business is operated as a parent company with subsidiaries, separate accounting records are kept for each corporation. Also, from a legal viewpoint, the parent and each subsidiary are separate entities with all the rights, duties, and responsibilities of a separate corporation. However, investors in the parent company depend on the parent to present consolidated financial statements. Consolidated statements show the financial position and results of all operations under the parent's control, including those of any subsidiaries. These statements are prepared as if the business were organized as a single company. In other words, the assets and liabilities of all affiliated companies are combined on a single balance sheet. Also, their revenues and expenses are combined on a single income statement and their cash flows are combined on a single income statement and their cash flows are combined on a single statement of cash flows. The relationships between the consolidated entity and the separate parent and subsidiary corporations is shown in the top portion of Exhibit 18A.1.

Learning Objectives

LO 10 Prepare consolidated balance sheets and explain how to report any excess of investment cost over book value or minority interests.

Consolidated Balance Sheets

The bottom portion of Exhibit 18A.1 shows the process of preparing a consolidated balance sheet from the separate balance sheets of the parent and the subsidiary. When parent and subsidiary balance sheets are consolidated, duplications in items are eliminated so that the combined figures do not show more assets and equities than actually exist. For example, a parent's investment in a subsidiary is evidenced by shares that are carried as an asset in the parent company's records. However, these shares actually represent an equity in the subsidiary's assets. Therefore, if the parent's investment in a subsidiary and the subsidiary's assets were both shown on the consolidated balance sheet, the same resource would be counted twice. To prevent this, the parent's investment and the subsidiary's capital accounts are offset and eliminated in preparing a consolidated balance sheet.

**A Consolidated Entity's
Relationship to the Parent
and Subsidiary Corporations**

Parent and subsidiary corporations

Consolidating the balance sheet of the parent and subsidiary corporations

Likewise, a single enterprise cannot owe a debt to itself. This would be like a student who "borrows" $20 for a date from funds saved for next semester's expenses and who then prepares a balance sheet that shows the $20 as both a receivable from himself and a payable to himself. To prevent such double counting, intercompany debts and receivables are also eliminated in preparing a consolidated balance sheet.

Balance Sheets Consolidated at Time of Acquisition

When a parent's and a subsidiary's assets are combined in the preparation of a consolidated balance sheet, a work sheet normally is used to organize the data. For example, Exhibit 18A.2 shows a work sheet to consolidate the accounts of Par Company and its subsidiary called Sub Company. In the work sheet, the account balances are on December 31, 1998, which was the day Par Company acquired Sub Company. On that day, Par Company paid cash to purchase all of Sub Company's outstanding common shares. The shares had a book value of $115,000, or $11.50 per share, on the books of Sub Company. In this first illustration, we assume that Par Company paid $115,000, or book value, for the outstanding shares.

In Exhibit 18A.2, notice that the eliminations columns include two sets of debts and credits. One set is identified by the letter (a), and the other set is identified by the letter (b).

Elimination (a)

On the day it acquired Sub Company, Par Company loaned Sub Company $10,000 to use in the subsidiary's operations. In exchange for the cash, Sub Company signed a promissory note to Par Company. This intercompany debt was in reality a transfer of funds within the consolidated entity. Therefore, since it did not increase the total assets and total liabilities of the affiliated companies, elimination (a) prevents these balances from appearing on the consolidated balance sheet. To understand this elimination, recall that the subsidiary's promissory note appears as a $10,000 debit in Par Company's Notes Receivable account. Then, observe that the first credit in the Eliminations column exactly offsets or eliminates this item. Next, recall that the subsidiary's note appears as a credit in its Notes Payable account. In the Eliminations columns, the $10,000 debit completes the elimination of this intercompany debt.

Par Company and Sub Company Work Sheet for a Consolidated Balance Sheet December 31, 1998					
	Par Company	Sub Company	Eliminations		Consolidated Amount
			Debit	Credit	
Assets					
Cash	5,000	15,000			20,000
Notes receivable	10,000			(a) 10,000	
Investment in Sub Company . . .	115,000			(b)115,000	
Other assets	190,000	117,000			307,000
	320,000	132,000			327,000
Liabilities and Equities					
Accounts payable	15,000	7,000			22,000
Notes payable		10,000	(a) 10,000		
Common shares	250,000	100,000	(b)100,000		250,000
Retained earnings	55,000	15,000	(b) 15,000		55,000
	320,000	132,000	125,000	125,000	327,000

Exhibit 18A.2

Consolidated Work Sheet
for 100% Owned
Subsidiary—Shares
Purchased at Book Value

Elimination (b)

When a parent company buys a subsidiary's shares, the investment is recorded in the accounts of the parent as an asset. This investment represents an equity in the subsidiary's net assets. However, you must not show both the subsidiary's (net) assets and the parent company's investment in the subsidiary on a consolidated balance sheet. To do so would be to double count those resources. On the work sheet, the credit portion of elimination (b) prevents double counting of Sub company's net assets.

Also, shareholders' equity accounts represent the equity of outside parties that own the company's shares. But from a consolidated point of view, there are no outside parties that own the subsidiary's shares. Therefore, the shareholders' equity account balances of Sub Company should not appear on a consolidated balance sheet. On the work sheet, the debits of elimination (b) prevent Sub Company's shareholders' equity balances from appearing on the consolidated balance sheet.

After the intercompany items are eliminated on a work sheet as in Exhibit 18A.2, the assets of the parent and the subsidiary and the remaining equities in these assets are combined and carried into the work sheet's last column. The combined amounts are then used to prepare a consolidated balance sheet that shows all the assets and equities of the parent and its subsidiary.

Parent Company Does Not Buy All of Subsidiary's Shares and Pays More Than Book Values

In the above example, Par Company purchased all of its subsidiary's shares and paid book value for it. However, a parent company often purchases less than 100% of a subsidiary's shares and commonly pays a price that is either more or less than book value. To illustrate, assume Par Company purchased only 80% of Sub Company's outstanding shares. Also assume that Par company paid $13 per share, a price that was $1.50 more than the shares's book value.

These new assumptions result in a more complicated work sheet entry to eliminate the parent's investment and the subsidiary's shareholders' equity accounts. The entry is complicated by (1) the minority interest in the subsidiary and (2) the excess over book value paid by the parent company for the subsidiary's shares.

Minority Interest

When a parent buys a controlling interest in a subsidiary, the parent company is the subsidiary's majority shareholder. However, when the parent owns less than 100% of the subsidiary's shares, the subsidiary has other shareholders who own a **minority interest** in its assets and share in its earnings.

When you prepare a consolidated work sheet for a parent and a subsidiary that has a minority interest, the equity of the minority interest must be recognized. This is done in the process of eliminating the shareholders' equity balances of the subsidiary, as shown in Exhibit 18A.3. In this case, the minority shareholders have a 20% interest in the subsidiary. Therefore, on the work sheet, 20% of the subsidiary' shareholders' equity amounts [($100,000 + $15,000) × 20% = $23,000] is reclassified as the minority interest.

Exhibit 18A.3

Consolidated Work Sheet—80% of Subsidiary Shares Purchased at More Than Book Value

Par Company and Sub Company
Work Sheet for a Consolidated Balance Sheet
December 31, 1998

	Par Company	Sub Company	Eliminations		Consolidated Amount
			Debit	Credit	
Assets					
Cash	16,000	15,000			31,000
Notes receivable	10,000			(a) 10,000	
Investment in Sub Company . . .	104,000			(b)104,000	
Other assets	190,000	117,000			307,000
Excess of cost over book Value .			(b) 12,000		12,000
	320,000	132,000			350,000
Liabilities and Equities					
Accounts payable	15,000	7,000			22,000
Notes payable		10,000	(a) 10,000		
Common shares	250,000	100,000	(b)100,000		250,000
Retained earnings	55,000	15,000	(b) 15,000		55,000
Minority interest				(b) 23,000	23,000
	320,000	132,000	137,000	137,000	350,000

Excess of Investment Cost over Book Value

In Exhibit 18A.3, we assume that Par Company paid $13 per share for its 8,000 shares of Sub Company. Therefore, the cost of these shares exceeded their book value by $12,000, calculated as follows:

Cost of shares (8,000 shares at $13 per share)	$104,000
Book value (8,000 shares at $11.50 per share)	92,000
Excess of cost over book value	$ 12,000

Now observe how in the process of eliminating the parent's investment in the subsidiary, this excess of cost over book value is set out on the work sheet. Then, it is carried into the Consolidated Amounts columns as an asset.

After the work sheet of Exhibit 18A.3 was completed, the consolidated amounts in the last column were used to prepare the consolidated balance sheet of Exhibit 18A.4. Note the treatment of the minority interest in the balance sheet. The minority shareholders have a $23,000 equity in the consolidated assets of the affiliated companies. Some accountants argue that this item should be disclosed in the shareholders' equity section. Others believe it should be shown in the long-term liabilities section. However, the minority interest usually is shown as a separate item between the liabilities and shareholders' equity sections, as shown in Exhibit 18A.4.

Par Company and Subsidiary Consolidated Balance Sheet December 31,1998		
Assets		
Cash		$ 31,000
Other assets		307,000
Goodwill from consolidation		12,000
Total assets		$ 350,000
Liabilities and Shareholders' Equity		
Liabilities:		
Accounts payable		$ 22,000
Minority interest		23,000
Shareholders' equity:		
Common shares	$250,000	
Retained earnings	55,000	
Total shareholders' equity		305,000
Total liabilities and shareholders' equity		$ 350,000

Exhibit 18A.4

Consolidated Balance Sheet of Par Company and Subsidiary

Next, observe that the $12,000 excess over book value that Par Company paid for Sub Company's shares appears on the consolidated balance sheet as an asset called "Goodwill from consolidation." There are several reasons why a parent might pay more than book value for its equity in a subsidiary. (1) One reason may be that certain of the subsidiary's assets are carried on the subsidiary's books at less than fair value. (2) Another reason may be that certain of the subsidiary's liabilities are carried at book values that are greater than fair values. (3) Also, the subsidiary's earnings prospects may be good enough to justify paying more than the net fair (market) value of its assets and liabilities. In this illustration, we assume that the book values of Sub Company's assets and liabilities are equal to their fair values. However, Sub Company's expected earnings justified paying $104,000 for an 80% equity in the subsidiary's net assets (assets less liabilities).

When a company pays more than book value because the subsidiary's assets are undervalued, the cost in excess of book value must be allocated to those assets and liabilities so that they are restated at fair values. After the subsidiary's assets and liabilities have been restated to reflect fair values, any remaining cost in excess of book value is reported on the consolidated balance sheet as "Goodwill from consolidation."

Occasionally, a parent company pays less than book value for its interest in a subsidiary. The probable reason for a price below book value is that some of the subsidiary's assets are carried on its books at amounts in excess of fair value. Therefore, the CICA ruled that the excess of book value over cost should be allocated to reduce the balance sheet valuations of the overvalued assets.

Earnings and Dividends of a Subsidiary

As you already learned, a parent uses the equity method in its books to account for its investment in a subsidiary. As a result, the parent's recorded net income and Retained Earnings account include the parent's equity in the net income earned by the subsidiary since the date of acquisition. Also, the balance of the parent's Investment in Subsidiary account increases (or decreases) each year by an amount equal to the parent's equity in the subsidiary's earnings (or loss) less the parent's share of any dividends paid by the subsidiary.

For example, assume that Sub Company earned $12,500 during 1999, its first year as a subsidiary, and at year-end paid out $7,500 in dividends. Par Company records its 80% equity in these earnings and dividends as follows:

Assets = Liabilities + Equity
+10,000   +10,000

Dec. 31	Investment in Sub Company	10,000	
	Earnings from Investment in Subsidiary		10,000
	To record 80% of the net income reported by Sub Company.		

Assets = Liabilities + Equity
+6,000
−6,000

31	Cash	6,000	
	Investment in Sub Company		6,000
	To record the receipt of 80% of the $7,500 Dividends paid by Sub Company.		

Consolidated Balance Sheets at a Date after Acquisition

Exhibit 18A.5 shows the December 31, 1999, work sheet to consolidate the balance sheets of Par Company and Sub Company. To simplify the illustration, it is assumed that Par Company had no transactions during the year other than to record its equity in Sub Company's earnings and dividends. Also, the other assets and liabilities of Sub Company did not change, and the subsidiary had not paid its note to Par Company.

Compare Exhibit 18A.5 with 18A.3 to see the changes in Par Company's balance sheet (the first column). Par Company's cash increased from $16,000 to $22,000 because of the dividends received from Sub Company. The Investment in Sub Company account increased from $104,000 to $108,000 as a result of the equity method entries during the year. Finally, Par Company's Retained Earnings increased by $10,000 which was the Parent's equity in the subsidiary's earnings.

Exhibit 18A.5

Work Sheet for a
Consolidated Balance Sheet,
One Year after Acquisition

Par Company and Sub Company
Work Sheet for a Consolidated Balance Sheet
December 31, 1999

	Par Company	Sub Company	Eliminations Debit	Eliminations Credit	Consolidated Amount
Assets					
Cash	22,000	20,000			42,000
Notes receivable	10,000			(a) 10,000	
Investment in Sub Company ...	108,000			(b) 108,000	
Other assets	190,000	117,000			307,000
Excess of cost over book value ..			(b) 12,000		12,000
	330,000	137,000			361,000
Liabilities and Equities					
Accounts payable	15,000	7,000			22,000
Notes payable		10,000	(a) 10,000		
Common shares	250,000	100,000	(b)100,000		250,000
Retained earnings	65,000	20,000	(b) 20,000		65,000
Minority interest				(b) 24,000	24,000
	330,000	137,000	142,000	142,000	361,000

In the second column of Exhibit 18A.5 note only two changes: (a) Sub Company's cash balance increased by $5,000, which is the difference between its $12,500 net income and $7,500 payment of dividends; and (2) retained earnings also increased from $15,000 to $20,000, which is explained by the $12,500 net income less $7,500 dividends. Note that the $20,000 balance is eliminated on the work sheet.

Two additional items need explanation. First, the minority interest set out on the December 31, 1999, work sheet (Exhibit 18A.3) is greater than on the December 31, 1998, work sheet. The minority shareholders have a 20% equity in Sub Company. So, the $24,000 shown on the December 31, 1999, work sheet is 20% of Sub Company's Common Shares and Retained Earnings balances on December 31, 1999. This $24,000 is $1,000 greater than the beginning-of-year minority interest because the subsidiary's retained earnings increased $5,000 during the year; the minority shareholder's share of this increase is 20%, or $1,000.

Second, the $12,000 excess cost over book value shown in Exhibit 18A.5 is unchanged from a year earlier. However, generally accounting principles require that this cost be amortized. The procedures of amortizing this cost are explained in a more advanced course.

Other Consolidated Statements

In addition to the balance sheet, the consolidated financial statements include a consolidated income statement, consolidated retained earnings statement, and consolidated statement of cash flows. However, you can have a general understanding of these statements without further discussion of the procedures to prepare them. At this point, you need only recognize that all duplications in items are eliminated. Also, when one affiliate records profit on sales to the other affiliate, the profit is eliminated in the consolidated statements. Finally, the amounts of net income and retained earnings that are reported in consolidated statements are equal to the amounts recorded by the parent under the equity method.

Summary of Appendix 18A

LO 10 **Prepare consolidated balance sheets and explain how to report any excess of investment cost over book value or minority interests.** Consolidated balance sheets are prepared by combining the accounts of the separate corporations as if they were a single entity. When the purchase price of a sub's identifiable assets exceed book values the book values should be revalued. Any remaining excess of the purchase price over the revalued net assets should be shown on the consolidated financial statements as goodwill. In combining these accounts the effects of intercompany transactions must be eliminated to avoid double counting. Since 100% of subsidiary net assets are reported on the consolidated balance sheet any claim not represented by the parent company is to be reported as minority interest.

Glossary

Consolidated financial statements Financial statements that show the results of all operations under the parent's control, including those of any subsidiaries; assets and liabilities of all affiliated companies are combined on a single balance sheet, revenues and expenses are combined on a single income statement, and cash flows are combined on a single statement of cash flows as though the business were in fact a single company. (p. 839)

Equity method An accounting method used for long-term investments when the investor has significant or controlling influence over the investee; the investment account is initially debited for cost and then is increased to reflect the investor's share of the investee's earnings and decreased to reflect the investor's receipt of dividends paid by the investee. (p. 837)

Equity securities with controlling influence The definition for a long-term investment when the investor is able to exert controlling influence over the investee; investors owning 50% or more of a company's voting shares are presumed to exert controlling influence over the investee. (p. 838)

Equity securities with significant influence The definition for a long-term investment when the investor is able to exert significant influence over the investee; usually investors owning 20% or more of a company's voting

shares are presumed to exert significant influence over the investee. (p. 836)

Foreign exchange rate The price of one currency stated in terms of another currency. (p. 842)

Long-term investments Investments in shares and bonds that are not marketable or, if marketable, are not intended to be converted into cash in the short-term; also funds earmarked for a special purpose, such as bond sinking funds, and land or other assets not used in the company's operations. (p. 832)

Minority interest The portion of a subsidiary company's shareholders' equity that is not owned by the parent corporation. (p. 854)

Multinational business A company that operates in a large number of different countries. (p. 842)

Parent company A corporation that owns a controlling interest in another corporation (more than 50% of the voting shares is required). (p. 838)

Return on total assets A measure of a company's operating efficiency, computed by expressing net income as a percentage of average total assets. (p. 845)

Subsidiary A corporation that is controlled by another corporation (the parent) because the parent owns more than 50% of the subsidiary's voting shares. (p. 838)

A superscript letter A identifies assignment material based on Appendix 18A.

Questions

1. Under what conditions should investments be classified as current assets? As long-term assets?

2. Identify the classes for long-term investments.

3. On a balance sheet, what valuation must be reported for debt securities held to maturity? How is interest recognized on these securities?

4. In accounting for common shares investments, when should the equity method be used?

5. Under what circumstances would a company prepare consolidated financial statements?

6. Under what circumstances are long-term investments in debt securities reported at their original cost adjusted for amortization of any difference between cost and maturity value?

7. What are two basic problems of accounting for international operations?

8. If a Canadian company makes a credit sale to a foreign customer and the customer is required to make payment in Canadian dollars, can the Canadian company have an exchange gain or loss as a result of the sale?

9. A Canadian company makes a credit sale to a foreign customer, and the customer is required to make payment in a foreign currency. The foreign exchange rate was $1.40 on the date of the sale and is $1.30 on the date the customer pays the receivable. Will the Canadian company record an exchange gain or an exchange loss?

10. Refer to the financial statements of **Alliance Company** in Appendix I. What percent of Alliance's other assets consists of long-term investments?

11. Refer to the 1997 financial statements of **Atlantis** in Appendix I. How much revenue is derived from non-Canadian sources?

12. In the chapter's opening scenario how does Brempong employ fundamental analysis of companies she invests in or makes recommendations on?

Fill in the blanks.

1. Trading securities are classified as _____ assets.

2. Equity securities giving an investor significant influence are accounted for using the _____ _____.

3. Debt securities held to maturity are presented on the balance sheet at _____ _____ _____.

4. Accrual of interest on bonds held as investments will require a credit to _____ _____.

5. The controlling investor is called the _____ _____ and the investee company is called the _____.

Quick Study

QS 18-1
Short and long-term
investments

LO 1, 2, 6

Which of the following are true of long-term investments?

a. They are held as an investment of cash available for current operations.

b. They may include debt securities held-to-maturity.

c. They may include bonds and shares that are not intended to serve as a ready source of cash.

d. They may include funds earmarked for a special purpose, such as bond sinking funds.

e. They may include investments in trading securities.

f. They are easily sold and therefore qualify as being marketable.

QS 18-2
Distinguishing short and
long-term investments

LO 1

On February 1, 19X1, Tom LeJeune purchased 6% bonds issued by Aberdeen Utilities Corp. at a cost of $30,000, which equals their par value. The bonds pay interest semiannually on July 31 and January 31. Prepare the entries to record the July 31 receipt of interest and the December 31 accrual.

QS 18-3
Debt securities

LO 3

On May 20, 19X1, Castle Co. paid $750,000 to acquire 25,000 (10%) of B&G Corp.'s outstanding common shares as a long-term investment. On August 5, 19X3, Castle sold half of the shares for $475,000. What method should be used to account for this shares investment? Prepare entries to record the acquisition and sale of the shares.

QS 18-4
Equity securities

LO 4

Assume the same facts as in QS 18-4, except assume that the shares acquired represented 40% of B&G Corp.'s outstanding shares. Also assume that B&G Corp. paid a $125,000 dividend on November 1, 19X1, and reported a net income of $550,000 for 19X1. Prepare the entry to record the receipt of the dividend and the year-end adjustment of the investment account.

QS 18-5
Equity method

LO 5

On March 1, 19X1, a Canadian company made a sale with credit terms requiring payment in 30 days to a German company, Bittner Corp. The amount of the sale was 20,000 marks. Assuming the exchange rate between German marks and Canadian dollars was $0.6811 on March 1 and $0.6985 on March 31, prepare the entries to record the sale and the cash receipt on March 31.

QS 18-6
Foreign currency
transactions

LO 8

A Canadian company sells a British company a product with the transaction listed in British pounds. On the date of the sale the transaction of $16,000 was billed as 10,000 pounds, reflecting an exchange rate of 2.20 (that is, $2.20 per pound). Show the entry to record the sale and also the receipt of the payment when the exchange rate has fallen to 2.10.

QS 18-7
Foreign currency
transactions

LO 8

QS 18-8
Return on total assets
LO 9

How is the return on total assets computed? What does this ratio evaluate?

QS 18-9
Disaggregated return on total assets
LO 9

State the formula to disaggregate the return on total assets. Explain how disaggregation of the return on total assets is useful to users of financial statements.

Exercises

Exercise 18-1
Transactions involving temporary and long-term investments
LO 1, 3, 4

Prepare general journal entries to record the following transactions involving the temporary and long-term investments of Morton Financial Corp., all of which occurred during 19X1. Use an account titled "Temporary Investments" for any transactions that you determine are short-term.

a. On February 15, paid $150,000 to purchase $150,000 of Canada General's 90-day short-term notes payable, which are dated February 15 and pay 10% interest.

b. On March 22, bought 700 shares of Royal Industries common shares at 25 1/2 plus a $250 brokerage fee.

c. On May 16, received a cheque from Canadian General in payment of the principal and 90 days' interest on the notes purchased in transaction a.

d. On July 30, paid $50,000 to purchase $50,000 of OMB Electronics' 8% notes payable, dated July 30, 19X1, and due January 30, 19X2.

e. On September 1, received a $0.50 per share cash dividend on the Royal Industries common shares purchased in transaction b.

f. On October 8, sold 350 shares of Royal Industries common shares for $32 per share, less a $175 brokerage fee.

g. On October 30, received a cheque from OMB Electronics for three months' interest on the notes purchased in transaction d.

Exercise 18-2
Classifying share investments
LO 2

During 19X1, GeoMass Company's investments in securities included five items. These securities, with their December 31, 19X1, market values, are as follows:

a. Weller Company bonds payable: $418,500 cost; $455,000 market value. GeoMass positively intends and is able to hold these bonds until they mature in 19X6.

b. BayShore common shares: 29,500 shares; $332,450 cost; $361,375 market value. GeoMass owns 32% of Bayshore's voting shares and has a significant influence over Bayshore.

c. Carrollton common shares: 12,000 shares; $169,750 cost; $183,000 market value. The goal of this investment, which amounts to 3% of Carrollton's outstanding shares, is to earn dividends over the next few years.

d. Zetech common shares: 18,000 shares; $95,300 cost; $93,625 market value. The goal of this investment is an expected increase in market value of the shares over the next three to five years. Zetech has 30,000 common shares outstanding.

e. Flavius common shares: 16,300 shares; $102,860 cost; $109,210 market value. These shares are marketable and are held as an investment of cash available for operations.

State whether each of these investments should be classified as a current asset or as a long-term investment. Also, for each of the long-term items, indicate in which of the four types of long-term investments the item should be classified. Assume that GeoMass had no long-term investments prior to 19X1. Show how the long-term investments would be reported in the year-end financial statements.

Vallejo Services began operations in 19X1 and regularly makes long-term investments in securities. The total cost and fair value of these investments at the end of several years were:

	Cost	Market Value
On December 31, 19X1	$374,000	$362,560
On December 31, 19X2	426,900	453,200
On December 31, 19X3	580,700	686,450
On December 31, 19X4	875,500	778,800

Prepare journal entries to record the lower of cost or market of Vallejo's investments at the end of each year.

Exercise 18-3
Investments in securities

LO 3

Prepare general journal entries to record the following events on the books of Kedgewick Co.:

19X1
Jan.   2   Purchased 30,000 shares of Lintex Co. common shares for $204,000 plus a broker's fee of $3,480. Lintex has 90,000 shares of common shares outstanding and has acknowledged the fact that its policies will be significantly influenced by Kedgewick.
Sept. 1   Lintex declared and paid a cash dividend of $3.10 per share.
Dec. 31   Lintex announced that net income for the year amounted to $624,900.

19X2
June   1   Lintex declared and paid a cash dividend of $3.60 per share.
Dec. 31   Lintex announced that net income for the year amounted to $699,750.
      31   Kedgewick sold 10,000 shares of Lintex for $162,500.

Exercise 18-4
Shares investment transactions; equity method

LO 5

On May 8, 19X1, Laurier Company (a Canadian company) made a credit sale to Devereaux (a French company). The terms of the sale required Devereaux to pay 800,000 francs on February 10, 19X2. Laurier prepares quarterly financial statements on March 31, June 30, September 30, and December 31. The foreign exchange rates for francs during the time the receivable was outstanding were:

May 8, 19X1	$ 0.1984
June 30, 19X1	0.2013
September 30, 19X1	0.2029
December 31, 19X1	0.1996
February 10, 19X2	0.2047

Compute the foreign exchange gain or loss that Jefferson should report on each of its quarterly income statements during the last three quarters of 19X1 and the first quarter of 19X2. Also compute the amount that should be reported on Jefferson's balance sheets at the end of the last three quarters of 19X1.

Exercise 18-5
Receivables listed in a foreign currency

LO 8

Red Rover of Calgary sells its products to customers in Canada and in Great Britain. On December 16, 19X1, Red Rover sold merchandise on credit to Bronson Ltd. of London, England, at a price of 17,000 pounds. The exchange rate on that day for 1 pound was $2.1838. On December 31, 19X1, when Red Rover prepared its financial statements, the exchange rate was 1 pound for $2.0890. Bronson paid its bill in full on January 15, 19X2, at which time the exchange rate was 1 pound for $2.1656. Red Rover immediately exchanged the 17,000 pounds for Canadian dollars. Prepare journal entries on December 16, December 31, and January 15, to account for the sale and account receivable on Red Rover's books.

Exercise 18-6
Foreign currency transactions

LO 8

Exercise 18-7
Return on total assets

LO 9

The following information is available from the financial statements of Rawhide Industries:

	19X1	19X2	19X3
Total assets, December 31	$190,000	$320,000	$750,000
Net income	28,200	36,400	58,300

Compute Rawhide's return on total assets for 19X2 and 19X3. (Round answers to one decimal place.) Comment on the company's efficiency in using its assets in 19X2 and 19X3.

Problems

Problem 18-1
Entries for long-term investments

LO 4

Franklin Security, Inc., has relatively large idle cash balances and invests them in common shares that it holds as a long-term investment. Following is a series of events and other facts relevant to the long-term investment activity of the company:

19X1

Jan. 20   Purchased 900 shares of **Magna** Corporation at 18 3/4 plus a $590 commission.
Feb. 9   Purchased 2,200 shares of **Sony** Corp. at 46 7/8 plus a $2,578 commission.
June 12   Purchased 500 shares of **Corel**, Inc., at 55 1/2 plus an $832 commission.
Dec. 31   These per share market values were known for the shares in the portfolio: Magna Corporation, 20 3/8; Corel, 57 1/4; Sony, 39. The losses are not considered permanent.

19X2

Apr. 15   Sold 900 shares of Magna Corporation at 21 3/4 less a $685 commission.
July 5   Sold 500 shares of Corel at 49 1/8 less a $491 commission.
      22   Purchased 1,600 shares of Microcel Corp. at 36 1/4 plus a $1,740 commission.
Aug. 19   Purchased 1,800 shares of Paragon Communications at 28 plus a $1,260 commission.
Dec. 31   These per share market values were known for the shares in the portfolio: **Paragon**, 31 3/4; **Microcel**, 30; **Sony**, 36 1/2.

19X3

Feb. 27   Purchased 3,400 shares of **Microsoft Corp.** at 23-5/8 plus a $1,606 commission.
June 21   Sold 2,200 shares of Sony at 40 less a $2,640 commission.
      30   Purchased 1,200 shares of **Canadian Tire Corp.** at 47 1/2 plus a $1,995 commission.
Aug   3   Sold 1,600 shares of Microcel at 31 1/4 less a $1,750 commission.
Nov. 1   Sold 1,800 shares of Paragon at 42 3/4 less a $2,309 commission.
Dec. 31   These per share market values were known for the shares in the portfolio: Canadian Tire, 56 1/2; Microsoft, 28.

Required

1. Prepare journal entries to record each of the above transactions.
2. For each year, prepare a schedule that shows the realized gains and losses included in earnings and the total unrealized gain or loss at the end of each year. Are the unrealized gains and losses recorded?

Problem 18-2
Accounting for share investments

LO 5

Hammerman Steel Works was organized on January 4, 19X1. The following investment transactions and events subsequently occurred:

19X1

Jan. 5   Hammerman purchased 30,000 shares (20%) of Falcon International's outstanding common shares for $780,000.
Oct. 23   Falcon declared and paid a cash dividend of $1.60 per share.
Dec. 31   Falcon announced that its net income for 19X1 was $582,000. Market value of the shares was $27.75 per share.

19X2

Oct. 15   Falcon declared and paid a cash dividend of $1.30 per share.
Dec. 31   Falcon announced that its net income for 19X2 was $738,000. Market value of the shares was $30.45 per share.

19X3
Jan.   2   Hammerman sold all of its investment in Falcon for $947,000 cash.

Part 1. Assume that Hammerman has a significant influence over Falcon because it owns 20% of the shares.

Required

1. Give the entries to record the preceding events in Hammerman's books.
2. Compute the carrying value per share of Hammerman's investment as reflected in the investment account on January 1, 19X3.
3. Compute the change in Hammerman's equity from January 5, 19X1, through January 2, 19X3, resulting from its investment in Falcon.

Check Figure
Carrying value per share, $31.90

Part 2. Assume that even though Hammerman owns 20% of Falcon's outstanding shares, a thorough investigation of the surrounding circumstances indicates that it does not have a significant influence over the investee.

Required

1. Give the entries to record the preceding events in Hammerman's books.
2. Compute the cost per share of Hammerman's investment as reflected in the investment account on January 1, 19X3.
3. Compute the change in Hammerman's equity from January 5, 19X1, through January 2, 19X3, resulting from its investment in Falcon.

Decker Manufacturing Co.'s long-term investment portfolio at December 31, 19X1, consisted of the following:

Problem 18-3
Accounting for long-term investments

LO 4

Securities Available-for-Sale	Cost	Fair Market Value
80,000 shares of Company A common shares	$1,070,600	$980,000
14,000 shares of Company B common shares	318,750	308,000
35,000 shares of Company C common shares	1,325,500	1,281,875

Decker had the following long-term investment transactions during 19X2:

Jan. 29   Sold 7,000 shares of Company B common shares for $158,375 less a brokerage fee of $3,100.
Apr. 17   Purchased 20,000 shares of Company W common shares for $395,000 plus a brokerage fee of $6,800. The shares represent a 30% ownership in Company W.
July   6   Purchased 9,000 shares of Company X common shares for $253,125 plus a brokerage fee of $3,500. The shares represent a 10% ownership in Company X.
Aug. 22   Purchased 100,000 shares of Company Y common shares for $750,000 plus a brokerage fee of $8,200. The shares represent a 45% ownership in Company Y.
Nov. 13   Purchased 17,000 shares of Company Z common shares for $533,800 plus a brokerage fee of $6,900. The shares represent a 5% ownership in Company Z.
Dec.   9   Sold 80,000 shares of Company A common shares for $1,030,000 less a brokerage fee of $8,200.
Dec. 31   Company W anounced a net loss of $15,000 and Company Y announced a net loss of $15,000.

The fair (market) values of Decker's investments at December 31, 19X2, are: B, $162,750; C, $1,220,625; W, $382,500; X, $236,250; Y, $562,500; Z, $557,600.

Required

1. Determine what amount should be reported on Decker's December 31, 19X2, balance sheet for its investments in equity securities.
2. What amount of gain or loss on those transactions relating to these securities should be reported on Decker's December 31, 19X2, income statement?

Check Figure
(2) Realized holding loss, ($52,900)

Problem 18-4
Foreign currency
transactions

Savannah Co. is a Canadian corporation that has customers in several foreign countries. Following are some of Savannah's 19X1 and 19X2 transactions:

19X1

Apr.   8   Sold merchandise to Salinas & Sons of Mexico for $7,938 cash. The exchange rate for pesos was $0.1323.

July 21   Sold merchandise on credit to Sumitomo Corp. located in Japan. The price of 1.5 million yen was to be paid 120 days from the date of sale. The exchange rate for yen was $0.009646 on this date.

Oct. 14   Sold merchandise for 19,000 pounds to Smithers Ltd. of Great Britain, payment in full to be received in 90 days. The exchange rate for pounds was $1.5181.

Nov. 18   Received Sumitomo's payment for its purchase of July 21, and exchanged the yen for dollars. The current foreign exchange rate for yen was $0.009575.

Dec. 20   Sold merchandise for 17,000 marks to Schmidt Haus of Germany, payment in full to be received in 30 days. On this day, the foreign exchange rate for marks was $0.6852.

      31   Prepared adjusting entries to recognize exchange gains or losses on the annual financial statements. Rates for exchanging foreign currencies on this day included the following:

Pesos (Mexico)	$0.1335
Yen (Japan)	0.009551
Pounds (Britain)	1.5235
Marks (Germany)	0.6807

19X2

Jan. 12   Received full payment from Smithers for the sale of October 14 and immediately exchanged the pounds for dollars. The exchange rate for pounds was $1.5314.

      19   Received Schmidt Haus's full payment for the sale of December 20 and immediately exchanged the marks for dollars. The exchange rate for marks was $0.6771.

Required

Preparation component:

1. Prepare general journal entries to account for these transactions on Savannah's books.

2. Compute the foreign exchange gain or loss to be reported on Savannah's 19X1 income statement.

Analysis component:

3. What actions might Savannah consider to reduce its risk of foreign exchange gains or losses?

Problem 18-5A
Consolidated statements,
at acquisition and one
year later

LO 4

On January 1, 1998, Northwood Company purchased 80% of Souther Company's outstanding shares at $48 per share. On that date, Northwood Company had retained earnings of $517,500. Souther Company had retained earnings of $135,000 and had 15,000 shares outstanding.

Part 1.

Required

1. Give the elimination entry to be used on a work sheet for a consolidated balance sheet dated January 1, 1998.

2. Determine the amount of consolidated retained earnings that should be shown on a consolidated balance sheet dated January 1, 1998.

Part 2. During the year December 31, 1998, Northwood Company paid cash dividends of $67,500 and earned net income of $127,500 excluding earnings from its investment in Souther Company. Souther Company earned net income of $63,000 and paid dividends of $30,000. Except for Northwood Company's Retained Earnings account and the Investment in Souther Company account, the balance sheet accounts for the two companies on December 31, 1998, are as follows:

Assets	Northwood Company	Souther Company
Cash	$157,800	$124,200
Notes receivable	54,000	
Merchandise	367,200	178,200
Building, net	348,000	216,000
Land	210,000	189,000
Investment in Souther Company	?	
Total assets	$?	$707,400
Liabilities and Shareholders' Equity		
Accounts payable	$439,500	$260,400
Note payable		54,000
Common shares	672,000	225,000
Retained earnings	?	168,000
Total liabilities and shareholders' equity	$?	$707,400

Northwood Company loaned $54,000 to Souther Company during 1998 for which Souther Company signed a note. On December 31, 1998, the note had not been repaid.

Required

1. Calculate the December 31, 1998, balances in Northwood Company's Investment in Souther Company account and Retained Earnings account.
2. Complete a work sheet to consolidate the balance sheets of the two companies.

The following items appeared in the first columns of a work sheet prepared to consolidate the balance sheets of Upper Company and Lower Company on the day Upper Company gained control of Lower Company by purchasing 6,375 of its common shares at $65 per share. Lower Company has a total of 7,500 shares outstanding.

Problem 18-6A
Consolidated work sheet
and balance sheet

LO 4

Assets	Upper Company	Lower Company
Cash	$ 28,125	$ 41,250
Note receivable, Lower Company	37,500	
Accounts receivable, net	105,000	90,000
Inventories	157,500	131,250
Investment in Lower Company	414,375	
Equipment, net	300,000	262,500
Buildings, net	318,750	
Land	75,000	
Total assets	$1,436,250	$525,000
Liabilities and Shareholders' Equity		
Accounts payable	$ 78,750	$ 37,500
Note payable, Upper Company		37,500
Common shares	937,500	375,000
Retained earnings	420,000	75,000
Total liabilities and shareholders' equity	$1,436,250	$525,000

At the time Upper Company acquired control of Lower Company, it took Lower Company's note in exchange for $37,500 in cash, and it sold and delivered $7,500 of equipment at cost to Lower Company on open account (account receivable). Both transactions are reflected in the foregoing accounts.

Required

1. Prepare a work sheet to consolidate the balance sheets of the two companies and prepare a consolidated balance sheet.

2. Under the assumption that Lower Company earned $37,500 during the first year after it was acquired by Upper Company, paid out $22,500 in dividends, and retained the balance of its earnings in its operations, give the entry to eliminate Upper Company's investment in the subsidiary and Lower Company's shareholders' equity accounts at the year's end

Alternate Problems

Problem 18-1A
Entries for long-term investments

LO 4

Dayton Enterprises has idle cash balances and invests them in common shares of Canadian and foreign companies as a long-term investment. Following is a series of events and other facts relevant to the long-term investment activity of the company:

19X1

Mar. 10   Purchased 2,400 shares of **Four Seasons Hotels**, at $33 1/4 plus $1,995 commission.
Apr. 7   Purchased 5,000 shares of **Royal Bank** at $17 1/2 plus $2,625 commission.
Sept. 1   Purchased 1,200 shares of **Polaroid Corp.** at $49 plus $1,176 commission
Dec. 31   These per share market values were known for the shares in the portfolio: Four Seasons, $35 1/2; Royal Bank, $17; Polaroid, $51 3/4.

19X2

Apr. 26   Sold 5,000 shares of Royal Bank at $16 3/8 less $2,237 commission.
June 2   Purchased 3,600 shares of **Duracell Int'l, Inc.**, at $18 7/8 plus $2,312 commission.
14   Purchased 900 shares of **Sears Canada Inc.** at 24 1/2 plus $541 commission.
Nov. 27   Sold 1,200 shares of Polaroid at $52 less $1,672 commission.
Dec. 31   These per share market values were known for the shares in the portfolio: Four Seasons, $36 1/4; **Duracell**, $18 1/8; Sears, $26.

19X3

Jan. 28   Purchased 2,000 shares of **Loblaw Co.** at $41 plus $3,280 commission.
Aug. 22   Sold 2,400 shares of Four Seasons at $29 3/4 less $2,339 commission.
Sept. 3   Purchased 1,500 shares of **Motorola, Inc.**, at $29 plus $870 commission.
Oct. 9   Sold 900 shares of Sears at $27 1/2 less $619 commission.
31   Sold 3,600 shares of Duracell at $16 5/8 less $1,496 commission
Dec. 31   These per share market values were known for the shares in the portfolio: Loblaw, $46 7/8; Motorola, $22 1/2.

Required

1. Prepare journal entries to record the events and any year-end adjustments needed to record the fair values of the long-term investments.

2. For each year, prepare a schedule that shows the realized gains and losses included in earnings and the total unrealized gain or loss at the end of each year. Are the unrealized gains and losses recorded?

Problem 18-2A
Accounting for share investments

LO 5

Main Street Company was organized on January 3, 19X1. The following investment transactions and events subsequently occurred:

19X1

Jan. 5   Main Street purchased 15,000 shares (25%) of Cornerstone Industries's outstanding common shares for $187,500.
Aug. 1   Cornerstone declared and paid a cash dividend of $0.95 per share.
Dec. 31   Cornerstone announced that its net income for 19X1 was $92,000. Market value of the shares was $12.90 per share.

19X2

Aug. 1   Cornerstone declared and paid a cash dividend of $1.25 per share.
Dec. 31   Cornerstone announced that its net income for 19X2 was $76,000. Market value of the shares was $13.55 per share.

19X3

Jan. 8   Main Street sold all of its investment in Cornerstone for $204,750 cash.

Part 1. Assume that Main Street has a significant influence over Cornerstone because it owns 25% of the shares.

Required

1. Give the entries to record the preceding events in Main Street's books.
2. Compute the carrying value per share of Main Street's investment as reflected in the investment account on January 7, 19X3
3. Compute the change in Main Street's equity from January 5, 19X1, through January 8, 19X3, resulting from its investment in Cornerstone.

Part 2. Assume that even though Main Street owns 25% of Cornerstone's outstanding shares, a thorough investigation of the surrounding circumstances indicates that it does not have a significant influence over the investee.

Required

1. Give the entries to record the preceding events in Main Street's books.
2. Compute the cost per share of Main Street's investment as reflected in the investment account on January 7, 19X3.
3. Compute the change in Main Street's equity from January 5, 19X1, through January 8, 19X3, resulting from its investment in Cornerstone.

Certifax Co.'s long-term investment portfolio at December 31, 19X1, consisted of the following:

Problem 18-3A
Accounting for long-term investments

LO 4

Securities Available-for-Sale	Cost	Fair (Market) Value
45,000 shares of Company R common shares	$1,118,250	$1,198,125
17,000 shares of Company S common shares	616,760	586,500
22,000 shares of Company T common shares	294,470	303,600

Certifax had the following long-term investment transactions during 19X2:

Jan. 13 Sold 4,250 shares of Company S common shares for $144,500 less a brokerage fee of $2,390.

Mar. 24 Purchased 31,000 shares of Company U common shares for $565,750 plus a brokerage fee of $9,900. The shares represent a 62% ownership in Company U.

Apr. 5 Purchased 85,000 shares of Company V common shares for $267,750 plus a brokerage fee of $4,500. The shares represent a 10% ownership in Company V.

Sept. 2 Sold 22,000 shares of Company T common shares for $313,500 less a brokerage fee of $5,400.

27 Purchased 5,000 shares of Company W common shares for $101,000 plus a brokerage fee of $2,100. The shares represent a 25% ownership in Company W.

Oct. 30 Purchased 10,000 shares of Company X common shares for $97,500 plus a brokerage fee of $2,340. The shares represent a 13% ownership in Company X.

The fair (market) values of Certifax's investments at December 31, 19X2, are: R, $1,136,250; S, $420,750; U, $545,600; V, $269,875; W, $109,375; X, 91,250.

Required

1. Determine what amount should be reported on Certifax's December 31, 19X2, balance sheet for its investments in equity securities.
2. Prepare a December 31, 19X2, adjusting entry, if necessary, to record the fair value adjustment of the long-term investments in securities available for sale.
3. What amount of gain or loss on those transactions relating to securities should be reported on Certifax's December 31, 19X2, income statement?

Problem 18-4A
Foreign currency
transactions

 LO 8

C. D. Howe Co. is a Canadian corporation that has customers in several foreign countries. Following are some of C. D. Howe's 19X1 and 19X2 transactions:

19X1

May 26 Sold merchandise for 6.5 million yen to **Fuji Company** of Japan, payment in full to be received in 60 days. On this day, the foreign exchange rate for yen was $0.009412.

June   1 Sold merchandise to Fordham Ltd. of Great Britain for $72,613 cash. The foreign exchange rate for pounds was $1.5277.

July 25 Received Fuji's payment for its purchase of May 26, and exchanged the yen for dollars. The current exchange rate for yen was $0.009368.

Oct. 15 Sold merchandise on credit to Martinez Brothers of Mexico. The price of 373,000 pesos was to be paid 90 days from the date of sale. On this date, the foreign exchange rate for pesos was $0.1341.

Dec.   6 Sold merchandise for 242,000 francs to LeFevre Company of France, payment in full to be received in 30 days. The exchange rate for francs was $0.1974.

     31 Prepared adjusting entries to recognize exchange gains or losses on the annual financial statements. Rates of exchanging foreign currencies on this day included the following:

Yen (Japan)	$0.009447
Pounds (Britain)	1.5318
Pesos (Mexico)	0.1562
Francs (France)	0.1998

19X2

Jan.   5 Received LeFevre's full payment for the sale of December 6, and immediately exchanged the francs for dollars. The exchange rate for francs was $0.2063.

     13 Received full payment from Martinez Brothers for the sale of October 15, and immediately exchanged the pesos for dollars. The exchange rate for pesos was $0.1419.

Required

Preparation component:

1. Prepare general journal entries to account for these transactions on C. D. Howe's books.

2. Compute the foreign exchange gain or loss to be reported on C. D. Howe's 19X1 income statement.

Analysis component:

3. What actions might C. D. Howe consider to reduce its risk of foreign exchange gains or losses?

Problem 18-5A^A
Consolidated statements,
at acquisition and one
year later

 LO 4

On January 1, 1998, Larger Company purchased 90% of Smaller Company's outstanding shares at $24 per share. On that date, Larger Company had retained earnings of $350,500. Smaller Company had retained earnings of $225,000 and had outstanding 20,000 common shares issued at $10 per share.

Part 1.

Required

1. Give the elimination entry to be used on a work sheet for a consolidated balance sheet dated January 1, 1998.

2. Determine the amount of consolidated retained earnings that should be shown on a consolidated balance sheet dated January 1, 1998.

Part 2. During the year ended December 31, 1998, Larger Company paid cash dividends of $45,000 and earned net income of $90,000 excluding earnings from its investment in Smaller Company. Smaller Company earned net income of $45,000 and paid dividends of

$25,000. Except for Larger Company's Retained Earnings account and the Investment in Smaller Company account, the balance sheet accounts for the two companies on December 31, 1998, are as follows:

Assets	Larger Company	Smaller Company
Cash	$140,200	$106,800
Notes receivable	45,000	
Merchandise	220,800	175,300
Building, net	284,250	240,000
Land	186,000	183,500
Investment in Smaller Company	?	
Total assets	$?	$705,600
Liabilities and Shareholders' Equity		
Accounts payable	$215,250	$215,600
Note payable		45,000
Common shares	675,000	200,000
Retained earnings	?	245,000
Total liabilities and shareholders' equity	$?	$705,600

Larger Company loaned $45,000 to Smaller Company during 1998, for which Smaller Company signed a note. On December 31, 1998, the note had not been repaid.

Required

1. Calculate the December 31, 1998, balances in Larger Company's Investment in Smaller Company account and Retained Earnings account.
2. Complete a work sheet to consolidate the balance sheets of the two companies.

The following items appeared in the first two columns of a work sheet prepared to consolidate the balance sheets of Parent Company and Subsidiary Company on the day Parent Company gained control of Subsidiary Company by purchasing 29,750 shares of its common stock at $13 per share. Subsidiary Company has a total of 35,000 common shares outstanding.

Problem 18-6A^A
Consolidated work sheet and balance sheet

LO 4

Assets	Parent Company	Subsidiary Company
Cash	$ 37,250	$ 72,500
Note receivable, Subsidiary Company	54,000	
Accounts receivable, net	110,000	80,000
Inventories	215,000	162,500
Investment in Subsidiary Company	386,750	
Equipment, net	461,250	257,500
Buildings, net	337,500	
Land	150,000	
Total assets	$1,751,750	$572,500
Liabilities and Shareholders' Equity		
Accounts payable	$ 257,500	$ 98,500
Note payable, Parent Company		54,000
Common shares	875,000	350,000
Retained earnings	619,250	70,000
Total liabilities and shareholders' equity	$1,751,750	$572,500

At the time Parent Company acquired control of Subsidiary Company, it took Subsidiary Company's note in exchange for $54,000 in cash, and it sold and delivered $3,000 of equipment at cost to Subsidiary Company on open account (account receivable). Both transactions are reflected in the foregoing accounts.

Required

1. Prepare a work sheet to consolidate the balance sheets of the two companies and prepare a consolidated balance sheet.
2. Under the assumption that Subsidiary Company earned $50,000 during the first year after it was acquired by Parent Company, paid out $32,500 in dividends, and retained the balance of its earnings in its operations, give the entry to eliminate Parent Company's investment in the subsidiary and Subsidiary Company's shareholders' equity accounts at the year's end.

Analytical and Review Problems

A & R Problem 18-1

On January 1, 1997, Tony Company purchases 40% of Danny Company's outstanding voting shares. On December 31, 1998, Tony Company's account Investment in Danny Company showed a balance of $400,000. Danny Company reported the following information for the years of 1997 and 1998:

	Net Income	Dividends Paid
1997	$150,000	$50,000
1998	200,000	50,000

Required

Calculate the purchase price paid by Tony Company for the Danny Company shares.

A & R Problem 18-2

The following is an excerpt from the notes to the financial statements if **ABC Sciences Ltd.**:

ABC Sciences holds a 35.4% interest in Halifax-based Eastern Laboratories which develops, manufactures, and distributes chemicals solely in the Canadian market. ABC Sciences accounts for its investment in Eastern Chemicals by the equity method. During 1998, Eastern had a strong year, with revenues increasing 79.6% while net income more than doubled to $7.6 million. ABC Science's share of this net income was . . .

Required

1. Is ABC Sciences using the cost or equity method to account for its investment in Eastern Chemicals? Support your answer.
2. Prepare the journal entry to record ABC Sciences's share of Eastern's net income.
3. If Eastern paid out 50% of its 1998 net income as cash dividends, what entry would ABC Sciences make to record the receipt of cash?

BEYOND THE NUMBERS

Refer to the financial statements and related information for **Alliance** in Appendix I. Answer the following questions by analyzing the information in Alliance's report:

1. Are Alliance's financial statements consolidated? How can you tell?
2. Does Alliance have more than one subsidiary? How can you tell?
3. Does Alliance have any foreign operations? How can you tell?
4. Is there a foreign exchange gain or loss on the income statement (consolidated statement of operations)? Describe what you find or do not find.
5. Compute Alliance's return on total assets for the year ended March 31, 1997.
6. Obtain access to Alliance's annual report for fiscal years ending after March 31, 1997. This access may be through a shrink-wrapped annual report included with your text or you may gain access to annual report information at Alliance's Web site: **http://info.Alliance.com/ar/contents.htm**. Recompute Alliance's return on total assets for the years subsequent to March 31, 1997 for which you have information.

Reporting in Action
LO 7, 10

Both **NIKE** and **Reebok** design, produce, market and sell sports footwear and apparel. Key comparative figures ($ millions) for these two organizations follow:

Comparative Analysis
LO 9

Key Figures	NIKE		Reebok	
	1997	**1996**	**1996**	**1995**
Net income	$ 796	$ 553	$ 139	$ 165
Net Sales	$9,187	$6,471	$3,479	$3,481
Total Assets	$5,361	$3,952	$1,786	$1,652

* NIKE figures are from the annual reports for the fiscal years ended May 31,1997, and 1996.
Reebok figures are from the annual reports for the fiscal years ended December 31, 1996, and 1995.

Required

1. Compute the return on total assets for NIKE as of May 31, 1997, and Reebok as of December 31, 1996.
2. Disaggregate the return on total assets computed in part 1 of this question for both companies according to the formula given in the chapter.
3. Which company has the higher return on total assets? The higher profit margin? The higher total asset turnover? Compare your answers to the chapter's discussion of return on total asset which compared NIKE and Reebok.

Jack Phelps is the controller for Jayhawk Company. Jayhawk has numerous long-term investments in debt securities. About 18 months ago the company had significant amounts of idle cash that were invested in 10-year bonds. Management's intent was to dispose of the bonds within two years from the date of purchase. Jack is preparing the year-end financial statements. In accounting for investments, he knows he must designate each investment as temporary or long-term. Since the bonds were purchased, interest rates have risen sharply meaning the market values of the bonds have declined significantly. Jack earns a bonus each year which is computed as a percent of the net income of the company.

Ethics Challenge
LO 1, 2

Required

1. Will Jack's bonus be dependent in any way on the classification of the debt securities?
2. What criteria must Jack consider to properly classify the securities as temporary or long-term?
3. Are there any likely checks in the company to review the classification that Jack chooses for the securities?

**Communicating
in Practice**
LO 4, 5, 6

You are the accountant for Jackson Company. The owner of the company, Abel Terrio, has finished reviewing the financial statements you prepared for 19X3 and questions the $6,000 loss reported on the company's sale of its investment in the common shares of Blackhawk Co. Jackson acquired 50,000 shares of Blackhawk's outstanding common shares on December 31, 19X1, at a cost of $500,000. This shares purchase represented a 40% interest in Blackhawk. The 19X2 income statement showed the investments made by Jackson proved very profitable, and the earnings from all investments were $126,000. On January 3, 19X3, Jackson Company sold the Blackhawk shares for $575,000. Blackhawk did not pay any dividends during 19X2 and reported a net income of $202,500 for the year. Terrio believes that because the purchase price of the Blackhawk shares was $500,000, and it was sold for $575,000, the 19X3 income statement should report a $75,000 gain on the sale.

Required

Draft a memo to Terrio explaining why the $6,000 loss on the sale of the Blackhawk shares is correctly reported.

**Taking It to
the Net**
LO 7

Visit the Web site **www.royalbank.com/travel/fxconvert.html**. The Web site affords the opportunity to convert over 40 different currencies into any one of the other currencies. Use the website's currency converter and convert the Canadian. dollar into five other currencies.

**Teamwork
in Action**
LO 1, 2, 6, 3, 4, 5

Each member of the team has the responsibility to become an expert on a specific classification of long-term investments. This expertise will be used to facilitate their teammates understanding of the concepts and procedures relevant to the classification they have chosen. Follow the procedure outlined below:

1. Each team member is to quickly select her or his area for expertise development by choosing one of the classifications of long-term investments listed below.
   a. Held-to-maturity debt securities
   b. Long-term investments in debt securities and equity securities without significant influence.
   c. Equity securities with significant influence
   d. Equity securities with controlling influence
2. Learning teams are to disburse and expert teams are to be formed. Expert teams are made up of students who all select the same area of expertise. The instructor will identify the location where each expert team will meet.
3. Using data below, expert teams will collaborate to develop a presentation following requirements listed below. Each student must write up the presentation in a format they can show to their learning teams in the next step in the activity.

Requirements for expert presentation:

   a. Write a transaction for the acquisition of this investment. The transaction narrative is to include all necessary data to reflect the chosen classification.
   b. Prepare the journal entry to record the acquisition.
      (Note: The expert team on "Equity securities with controlling influence" will substitute requirements e–f below with a discussion of the reporting phase when this type of investment is owned.)
   c. Identify information necessary to complete the end-of-period accounting for this investment.
   d. Design information that will allow your expert team to illustrate possible end-of-period accounting.
   e. Assuming this is the only investment your business owns, prepare any necessary year-end entries.
   f. Present relevant Balance Sheet section(s).
4. Re-form learning teams. In rotation, each expert is to present to the team the presentation he or she developed in 3. Experts are to encourage and respond to questions.

Assume that you are planning a spring break trip to Europe. Identify three different locations where you can find exchange rates for the dollar relative to European currencies.

**Hitting the
Road**

LO 7

Read the article "Uniquely Canadian Number Crunching" in *The Financial Post* weekend edition July 25–27, 1998.

1. What is the central concern of this article?

2. What are the reported earnings of **Bombardier Inc.** and **Doman Industries Ltd.** for 1997 under Canadian GAAP? What would be their bottom line figures if U.S. GAAP had been used?

3. How do the accounting rules for currency losses in Canada differ from those of other countries?

4. Is the CICA proposing any changes?

Business Break

LO 7

19

CHAPTER

Reporting and Analyzing Cash Flows

A Look Back

Chapter 18 focused on long-term investments in securities. We explained how to identify, account for, and report for them. We also described accounting for transactions listed in a foreign currency.

A Look at This Chapter

Chapter 19 focuses on reporting and analyzing cash inflows and cash outflows. We emphasize how to prepare and interpret the statement of cash flows.

A Look Forward

Chapter 20 focuses on tools to help us analyze financial statements. We describe comparative analysis and the application of ratios for financial analysis.

Chapter Outline

▶ **Basics of Cash Flow Reporting**
- Purpose of the Statement of Cash Flows
- Importance of Cash Flows
- Measuring Cash Flows
- Classifying Cash Flows
- Classification Issues
- Noncash Investing and Financing Activities
- Format of the Statement of Cash Flows
- Preparing the Statement of Cash Flows

▶ **Cash Flows from Operating Activities**
- Methods of Reporting Operating Cash Flows
- Direct Method of Reporting Operating Cash Flows
- Indirect Method of Reporting Operating Cash Flows

▶ **Cash Flows from Investing Activities**
- Capital Asset Transactions

▶ **Cash Flows from Financing Activities**
- Bonds Payable Transactions
- Common Shares Transactions
- Retained Earnings Transactions
- Proving Cash Balances

▶ **Using the Information—Cash Flow Analysis**
- Analyzing Cash Sources and Uses
- Cash Flow on Total Assets

▶ **Appendix 19A—Using a Spreadsheet to Prepare the Statements of Cash Flows**

Ginseng Rich, Cash Poor

Moncton, NB—Dennis Chen is a grower of ginseng, a herb whose root is valued for its health benefits. But this summer, high winds and hail swept through Chen's 20 hectare plot of ginseng. Chen needed lumber and screening to repair the covering that protected his ginseng capital from nature's elements. But he neither had cash, nor the sympathy of bankers.

"Every banker wanted to see my financial statements, especially my cash flows. But I tried to explain that I'd only been in business four years, and had never received any cash from any customer," says Chen. "The bankers just didn't understand." What they didn't understand is that ginseng takes about five years to mature from planting until harvest. And since Chen began his business only four years ago, all of his cash flows were negative and large.

"When I finally showed them my statement of cash flows, there was a look of disbelief on their faces," says Chen. "One banker told me flat out he wouldn't touch my loan with a ten-foot pole!" Chen's income statement didn't help much either. Most accounting professionals won't accept recognition of revenue for agricultural products in their growth stage. Especially when growth extends over five years or more. So Chen's prospects were fading.

"I was lucky," says Chen. "I got an appointment with a small town credit union. The loan officer grew up on a farm, and was familiar with ginseng. While it wasn't the best terms, I got it." What Chen got was cash to do the necessary repairs and save his ginseng and four years of work. Chen accepted a higher than average interest rate and a collateral agreement giving the credit union access to his ginseng if he defaulted.

"That loan officer really saved me," says Chen. "He looked beyond the numbers and the cash flows to see what was happening. I think it'll be a win-win situation for both of us." And ginseng lovers alike.

Learning Objectives

LO 1 Explain the purpose and importance of cash flow information.

LO 2 Distinguish among operating, investing, and financing activities.

LO 3 Identify and disclose noncash investing and financing activities.

LO 4 Describe the format of the statement of cash flows.

LO 5 Prepare a statement of cash flows.

LO 6 Compute cash flows from operating activities using the direct method.

LO 7 Compute cash flows from operating activities using the indirect method.

LO 8 Determine cash flows from both investing and financing activities.

LO 9 Analyze the statement of cash flows.

LO 10 Compute and apply the cash flow on total assets ratio.

CHAPTER PREVIEW

Profitability is a primary goal of most managers. But it is not the only goal. A company cannot achieve or maintain profits without careful management of cash. Managers and other users of information pay close attention to a company's cash position and the events and transactions affecting cash. Information about these events and transactions is reported in the statement of cash flows. This chapter explains how we prepare, analyze, and interpret a statement of cash flows. It also discusses the importance of cash flow information for predicting future performance and making managerial decisions. Understanding the statement of cash flows is especially important in obtaining a small business loan and one with favourable terms. Dennis Chen's experience with the importance of this statement as described in the opening article is common.

Basics of Cash Flow Reporting

This section describes the basics of cash flow reporting including its purpose, measurement, classification, format, and preparation.

Purpose of the Statement of Cash Flows (SCF)

LO1 Explain the purpose and importance of cash flow information.

The purpose of the **statement of cash flows** is to assist users of financial statements to evaluate the liquidity and solvency of an enterprise and to assess the enterprise's ability to generate cash from internal sources, to repay its liabilities, and to reinvest and to make distributions to owners.[1] The SCF provides details of the major items comprising cash receipts and cash payments during a period. This includes separately identifying the cash flows related to operating, investing, and financing activities.

The statement of cash flows does more than simply report changes in cash. It is the detailed disclosure of individual cash flows that makes this statement useful to users. Information in this statement helps users answer questions such as:

- How does a company obtain its cash?
- Where does a company spend its cash?
- What is the change in the cash balance?

The statement of cash flows addresses these important questions by summarizing, classifying, and reporting a company's periodic cash inflows and outflows.

Importance of Cash Flows

Information about cash flows, its sources and uses, can influence decision makers in important ways. For instance, we look more favourably at a company that is financing its expenditures with cash from operations than one that does it by selling its assets. Information about cash flows helps users decide whether a company has enough cash to pay its existing debts as they mature. It is also relied upon to evaluate a company's ability to meet unexpected obligations and pursue unexpected opportunities. External information users especially want to assess a company's ability to take advantage of new business opportunities. Internal users such as managers use cash flow information to plan day-to-day operating activities and make long-term investment decisions.

---

[1] *CICA Handbook*, section 1540.

There are many striking examples of how careful analysis and management of cash flows have lead to improved financial stability. **Kasten Chase Applied Research,** a company specializing in wireless technologies support, obtained temporary protection from bankruptcy in 1992 and desperately needed to improve its cash flows. It turned around its cash flows from operations from a deficit of $4.3 million in 1996 to $1.3 million in 1997. It did so by engaging in aggressive cost-cutting measures. Cash flows are important to businesses in all sectors. At the time of writing this chapter it is uncertain whether **Eaton's** will be successful in solving its cash flow problems with restructuring that involves closing down unprofitable stores and engaging in strategic planning that is more customer focused.

The case of **W. T. Grant Co.** is a classic North American example of why cash flow information is important in predicting a company's future performance and financial strength. Grant reported net income of more than $40 million per year for three consecutive years. At the same time, it was experiencing an alarming decrease in cash provided by operations. For instance, net cash *outflow* was more than $90 million by the end of that three-year period.[2] Grant soon was bankrupt. Users who relied solely on Grant's earnings numbers were unpleasantly surprised. This reminds us that cash flows as well as income statement and balance sheet information is crucial in making business decisions.

Cash Valuation

Financial analysts who value private companies sometimes do so on the basis of a multiple of operating cash flow. Medium-sized private companies usually sell for five to seven times operating cash flows. Larger companies can command higher multiples. Rules of thumb, however, should not be used as a primary valuation technique but can be used as a reasonableness test of value reached through the application of other more rigorous techniques. You will learn about these valuation techniques in more advanced courses.

Did You Know?

Measuring Cash Flows

Cash flows are defined to include both "cash and cash equivalents" in the statement of cash flows. This means the statement explains the difference between the beginning and ending balances of *cash and cash equivalents*. While we continue to use the term cash flows we must remember that cash flows include both cash and cash equivalents.

Cash and Cash Equivalents

As we discussed in Chapter 9, a cash equivalent is an investment that must satisfy two criteria:

1. It must be readily convertible to a known amount of cash.

2. It must be sufficiently close to its maturity date so its market value is not significantly affected by interest rate changes.

A new section on Cash Flow Statements was issued in August 1998 to replace *CICA Handbook* section 1540 on the Statement of Changes in Financial Position (SCFP). This chapter will reflect the new recommendations which are now in line with IASC and FASB standards. A cash flow statement is now

---

[2] J. Largay and C. Stickney, "Cash Flow, Ratio Analysis and the W. T. Grant Company Bankruptcy," *Financial Analysts Journal*, July–August 1980, pp. 51–56.

required in every set of GAAP financial statements. The definition of *cash equivalents* is changed to short-term, highly liquid investments that are readily convertible to known amounts of cash and are subject to an insignificant risk of changes in value. In most cases cash and cash equivalents would include cash and temporary investments[3] of three months or less from the date of acquisition. Equity investments are not included as cash equivalents. Classifying short-term, highly liquid investments as cash equivalents is based on the idea that companies make these investments to earn a return on idle cash balances.

Items meeting the criteria of cash equivalents are sometimes not held as temporary investments of idle cash. For instance, an investment company that specializes in the purchase and sale of securities often buys cash equivalents as part of its investing strategy. Companies in this situation are allowed to exclude these securities from the cash equivalents account. These companies must follow a clear policy for determining the items to include and not include. These policies are disclosed in notes to their financial statements and must be followed consistently from period to period. **Canadian Tire** defines its cash as:

...cash and short-term investments less bank indebtedness. Short-term investments held include Canadian and United States government securities and notes of other creditworthy parties within one year.

Under the new provisions of section 1540 of the *CICA Hanbook*, Canadian Tire will no longer deduct bank indebtedness.

Classifying Cash Flows

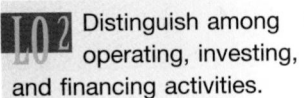

Distinguish among operating, investing, and financing activities.

Since we treat cash and cash equivalents as a single item on the statement of cash flows, transactions between cash and cash equivalents such as cash paid to purchase cash equivalents and cash received from selling cash equivalents are not reported in the statement. But all other cash receipts and payments are classified and reported on the statement as operating, investing, or financing activities. Individual cash receipts and payments within each of these three categories are labelled to identify their source transactions or events. Cash receipts and payments are then summarized for each category by netting them against each other. A net cash inflow (source) occurs when the receipts in a category exceed the payments. A net cash outflow (use) occurs when the payments in a category exceed receipts.

Operating Activities

Operating activities include the cash effects of transactions and events that determine net income. But remember that not all items in income such as unusual gains and losses are operating activities. We discuss these exceptions later in the chapter. Examples of operating activities are the production and purchase of merchandise, the sale of goods and services to customers, and expenditures toward administering the business. Exhibit 19.1 lists the more common cash inflows and outflows from operating activities.

---

[3] In recent years cash equivalents have been determined net of short-term borrowings. Short-term borrowings will no longer be deducted.

Exhibit 19.1

Cash Flows from Operating Activities

Investing Activities

Investing activities include the (a) purchase and sale of long-term assets, (b) the purchase and sale of short-term investments that are not cash equivalents, and (c) lending and collecting on loans other than those made by a financial institution. Exhibit 19.2 lists examples of cash flows from investing activities. Proceeds from collecting the principal amounts of loans deserve special attention. If the loan results from sales to customers, its cash receipts are classed as operating activities whether short-term or long-term. But if the loan results from a loan to another party, then its cash receipts from collecting the principal of the note is classed as an investing activity. Collection of interest on a loan is *not* part of investing activities but rather part of operating activities.

Exhibit 19.2

Cash Flows from Investing Activities*

* Investing activities exclude transactions in trading securities.

Financing Activities

Financing activities are those that result in changes in the size and composition of the equity capital and borrowings of the enterprise. They include (a) getting cash from issuing debt and repaying the amounts borrowed, and (b) getting cash from or distributing cash to owners. These activities all involve transactions with a company's owners and creditors. They also involve borrowing and repaying of principal amounts relating to both short- and long-term debt. But payments of interest expense are classified as operating activities. Also, cash payments to settle credit purchases of merchandise, whether on account or by note, are operating activities. Exhibit 19.3 lists examples of cash flows from financing activities.

Exhibit 19.3

Cash Flows from Financing
Activities

Classification Issues

Earlier in the chapter we classified dividends received as an operating cash flow. This seems logical because dividends received enter into the determination of net income. However, it is arguable that dividends received can also be classified as financing cash flows because they are a cost of obtaining funds or as investing cash flows because they reflect returns on investments made by the enterprise. Similar arguments can be made for interest received and paid. The *CICA Handbook* requires that interest and dividends received and paid that are included in the determination of net income should be classified as cash flows from operating activities. Alernative treatments, however, is permitted according to the nature of the transaction:

> Interest and dividends not included in the determination of net income should be classified according to their nature. Dividends and interest paid and charged to retained earnings should be presented separately as cash flows used in financing activities. Cash flows from dividends paid by subsidiaries to non-controlling interests should be presented separately as cash flows used in financing activities. (section 1540.35)

Noncash Investing and Financing Activities

There are often important investing and financing activities that do not affect cash receipts or payments. Yet because of their importance and the *full disclosure* principle, these important noncash investing and financing activities are disclosed in a note to the statement in a way that provides all the relevant information about these investing and financing activities. One example of such a transaction is the purchase of long-term assets by giving a long-term note payable. This transaction involves both investing and financing activities, but it does not affect any cash inflow and outflow and is not reported in any of the three sections of the statement of cash flows. Another example is where investing and financing activities involve cash receipts or payments but only for part of the entire transaction. The *CICA Handbook* includes the following examples: (a) acquisition of assets by assuming directly related liabilities or by means of a capital lease, (b) the acquisition of an enterprise in exchange for share of the acquirer and (c) the conversion of debt to equity.[4] A more exhaustive list is provided in Exhibit 19.4.

LO3 Identify and disclose
noncash investing
and financing activities.

---

[4] *CICA Handbook*, section 1540.47.

To illustrate, let's assume Burton purchases machinery for $12,000 by paying cash of $5,000 and trading in old machinery with a market value of $7,000. The statement of cash flows reports only the $5,000 cash outflow for purchase of machinery. This means the $12,000 investing transaction is only partially described in the body of the statement of cash flows. Yet this information is potentially important to users in that it changes the make up of assets. According to section 1540.46 of the *CICA Handbook:*

> Investing and financing transactions that do not require the use of cash or cash equivalents should be excluded from a cash flow statement. Such transactions should be disclosed elsewhere in the financial statements in a way that provides all the relevant information about these investing and financing activities.

Companies use one of two ways to disclose noncash investing and financing activities not reported in the body of the statement of cash flows. They must be disclosed in either (1) a note, or (2) a separate schedule attached to (often the bottom of) the statement. In the case of Burton, it could either describe the transaction in a note or include a small schedule at the bottom of its statement that lists the $12,000 asset investment along with financing of $5,000 and a $7,000 trade-in of old machinery. Union Camp provides an example of disclosure of noncash investing and financing activities as follows:

Fair value of assets acquired	$8,345
Less: cash paid	7,115
Liabilities incurred or assumed	$1,230

The Union Camp schedule attached to the statement describes an exchange of assets involving both cash and noncash aspects. The $7,115 cash payment is reported in Union Camp's statement of cash flows as an investing activity. But the note tells us that the purchase of certain assets involves a noncash aspect—that is, a liability to pay in the future. Exhibit 19.4 lists some transactions that are disclosed as noncash investing and financing activities.

- Retirement of debt by issuing equity securities.
- Conversion of preferred shares to common shares.
- Leasing of assets in capital lease transaction.
- Purchase of long-term asset by issuing note payable.
- Exchange of noncash assets for other noncash assets.
- Purchase of noncash assets by issuing equity or debt.

Exhibit 19.4

Examples of Noncash Investing and Financing Activities

Community Activist

You are a community activist trying to raise public awareness of pollution emitted by a local manufacturer. The manufacturer complains about the high costs of pollution controls and points to its recent $4 million annual loss as evidence. But you also know its net cash flows were a positive $8 million this past year. How are these results possible?

You Make the Call

Answer—p. 911

Format of the Statement of Cash Flows

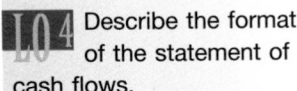 **Describe the format of the statement of cash flows.**

Accounting standards require companies to include a statement of cash flows in a complete set of financial statements. This statement must report information about a company's cash receipts and cash payments during the period.

Exhibit 19.5 shows us the usual format of the statement of cash flows. This exhibit shows that a company must report cash flows from three activities: operating, investing, and financing. Cash inflows and cash outflows are reported for each category. The statement explains how transactions and events impact the beginning-of-period cash (and cash equivalents) balance to produce its end-of-period balance.

Exhibit 19.5

Format of the Statement of Cash Flows

COMPANY NAME Statement of Cash Flows Period Covered	
Cash flows from operating activities:	
[List of individual inflows and outflows]	
Net cash provided (used) by operating activities	$ ###
Cash flows from investing activities:	
[List of individual inflows and outflows]	
Net cash provided (used) by investing activities	###
Cash flows from financing activities:	
[List of individual inflows and outflows]	
Net cash provided (used) in financing activities	###
Net increase (decrease) in cash	$ ###
Cash (and equivalents) balance at beginning of period	###
Cash (and equivalents) balance at end of period	$ ###

Note disclosure of "Noncash investing and financing transactions."

Flash back

1. Does a statement of cash flows disclose payments of cash to purchase cash equivalents? Does it disclose receipts of cash from selling cash equivalents?
2. Identify the categories of cash flows reported separately on the statement of cash flows.
3. Identify the category for each of the following cash flow activities: (a) purchase equipment for cash, (b) payment of wages, (c) sale of common shares for cash, (d) receipt of cash dividends from share investment, (e) cash collection from customers, (f) issuance of bonds for cash.

Answers—p. 911

Preparing the Statement of Cash Flows

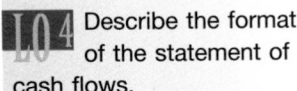 **Prepare a statement of cash flows.**

Preparation of a statement of cash flows involves five steps: (1) compute the net increase or decrease in cash, (2) compute and report net cash provided (used) by operating activities (using either the direct or indirect method—both are explained in this chapter), (3) compute and report net cash provided (used) by investing activities, (4) compute and report net cash provided (used) by financing activities, and (5) compute net cash flow by combining net cash provided (used) by operating, financing and investing activities and prove it by adding it to the beginning cash balance to show it equals the ending cash balance. Noncash investing and financing activities are disclosed in a note or a separate schedule to the statement.

The first step in preparing the statement—computing the net increase or decrease in cash—is a simple but crucial computation. It equals the current period's cash balance minus the prior period's cash balance. This is the "bottom line" figure for the statement of cash flows and is a helpful check on the accuracy of our work.

The information we need to prepare a statement of cash flows comes from a variety of sources. These include comparative balance sheets at the beginning and end of the period, an income statement for the period, and a careful analysis of each noncash balance sheet account in the general ledger. Because cash inflows and cash outflows are captured in our accounting system, we can also examine transactions affecting the Cash account.

The remaining sections of this chapter explain the important steps in preparing the statement of cash flows. But first we describe the two different approaches to preparing the statement: (1) analyzing the Cash account, and (2) analyzing noncash accounts.

Analyzing the Cash Account

All of a company's cash receipts and cash payments are recorded in the Cash account in the General Ledger. The Cash account is therefore a natural place to look for information about cash flows from operating, investing, and financing activities.

To illustrate, let's look at the summarized Cash account of **Genesis** in Exhibit 19.6.

Step 1: Compute net increase or decrease in cash

Step 2: Compute net cash from operating activities

Step 3: Compute net cash from investing activities

Step 4: Compute net cash from financing activities

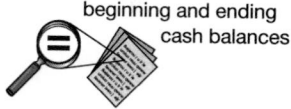
Step 5: Prove and report beginning and ending cash balances

Exhibit 19.6

Summarized Cash Account

Summarized Cash Account

Balance, Dec. 31/1999	12,000		
Receipts from customers	570,000	Payments for goods	319,000
Proceeds from asset sales	12,000	Payments for wages and	
Proceeds from share		operating expenses	218,000
issuance	15,000	Interest payments	8,000
		Tax payments	5,000
		Payments for assets	10,000
		Payments to retire bonds	18,000
		Dividend payments	14,000
Balance, Dec. 31/2000	17,000		

Individual cash transactions are summarized in this Cash account according to the major types of cash receipts and cash payments. For instance, only the total cash receipts from all customers is listed. Individual cash transactions underlying these totals can number into the thousands. Accounting software programs are available to provide us with summarized cash accounts similar to the one illustrated.

Preparing a statement of cash flows from Exhibit 19.6 requires us to determine whether the cash inflow or outflow is an operating, investing, or financing activity. We then list these individual cash flows according to their activity. This yields the statement shown in Exhibit 19.7.

Exhibit 19.7

Statement of Cash Flows—
Direct Method

| GENESIS |
| Statement of Cash Flows |
| For Year Ended December 31, 2000 |

Cash flows from operating activities:		
Cash received from customers	$570,000	
Cash paid for merchandise	(319,000)	
Cash paid for wages and other operating expenses .	(218,000)	
Cash paid for interest	(8,000)	
Cash paid for taxes	(5,000)	
Net cash provided by operating activities		$20,000
Cash flows from investing activities:		
Cash received from sale of capital assets	$ 12,000	
Cash paid for purchase of capital assets	(10,000)	
Net cash provided by investing activities		2,000
Cash flows from financing activities:		
Cash received from issuing shares	$ 15,000	
Cash paid to retire bonds	(18,000)	
Cash paid for dividends	(14,000)	
Net cash used in financing activities		(17,000)
Net increase in cash		$ 5,000
Cash balance at beginning of 2000		12,000
Cash balance at end of 2000		$17,000

Preparing the statement of cash flows from an analysis of the summarized Cash account presents two limitations. First, most companies have many individual cash receipts and payments making it difficult to review them all. While accounting software greatly minimizes this burden, it is still a task requiring professional judgment. Second, the Cash account does not usually carry a description of each cash transaction. This makes it difficult to assign cash transactions according to activity.

Analyzing Noncash Accounts

The second approach to preparing the statement of cash flows is based on analyzing noncash accounts. This approach uses the fact that when a company records cash inflows and outflows with debits and credits to the Cash account (as reflected in the prior section), it also records credits and debits in other noncash accounts. Many of these noncash accounts are balance sheet accounts. For instance, the sale of land for cash. Others are revenue and expense accounts that are closed to Retained Earnings, also a balance sheet account. For instance, the sale of services for cash yields a credit to services revenue that is closed to Retained Earnings. In sum, *all cash transactions eventually affect noncash balance sheet accounts.* This means we can determine cash inflows and cash outflows by analyzing changes in noncash balance sheet accounts. We are not limited to analyzing the Cash account.

Exhibit 19.8 uses the accounting equation to show the important relation between the Cash account and noncash balance sheet accounts.

Exhibit 19.8 starts with the familiar accounting equation at the top. We then expanded it in line (2) so that cash is separated from noncash asset accounts. Next, we move noncash asset accounts to the right-hand side of the equality in line (3) where they become a negative. This shows cash is equal to the sum of the liability and equity accounts minus the noncash asset accounts. Line (4) points out that *changes* in one side of the accounting equation are equal to changes on the other side. It also shows we can explain changes in cash by analyzing changes

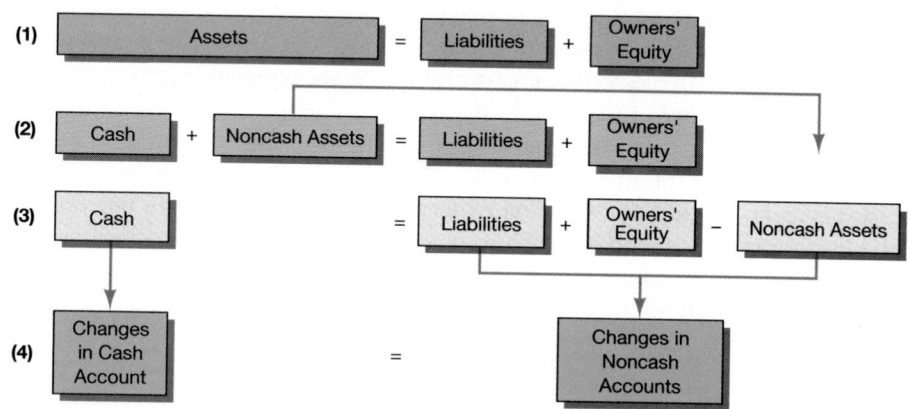

Exhibit 19.8

Relation between Cash and
Noncash Accounts

in the noncash accounts consisting of liabilities, equity accounts, and noncash assets. By analyzing all noncash balance sheet accounts and related income statement accounts, we have the information for preparing a statement of cash flows.

Information to Prepare the Statement

Information to prepare the statement of cash flows usually comes from three sources: (a) comparative balance sheets, (b) current income statement, and (c) additional information. Comparative balance sheets give us changes in noncash accounts from the beginning to the end of the period. The current income statement gives us details to help compute cash flows from operating activities. Additional information often includes details on transactions and events helping us explain both cash flows and noncash investing and financing activities.

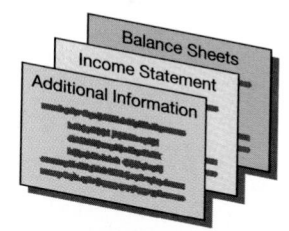

E-Cash

The electronic payment industry is advancing rapidly in Canada. Electronic cash or e-cash is based on smart card technology that makes use of a microcomputer chip embedded in a plastic card that allows a consumer to load digital cash and use the card to anonymously pay e-cash to retailers, banks, and even vending machines. However to gain mass market acceptance of this technology some kind of home-loading device probably needs to be developed.

Did You Know?

This section describes the reporting of cash flows from operating activities using two different methods: direct method and indirect method. These two different methods apply only to the operating activities section.

Cash Flows from Operating Activities

Methods of Reporting Operating Cash Flows

The net cash flows provided (used) by operating activities can be reported in one of two ways: the *direct method* or the *indirect method*. The direct method separately lists each major item of operating cash receipts (such as cash received from customers) and each major item of operating cash payments (such as cash paid for merchandise). The cash payments are subtracted from cash receipts to determine the net cash provided (used) by operating activities. The operating activities section of Exhibit 19.7 is an example of the direct method of reporting operating cash flows.

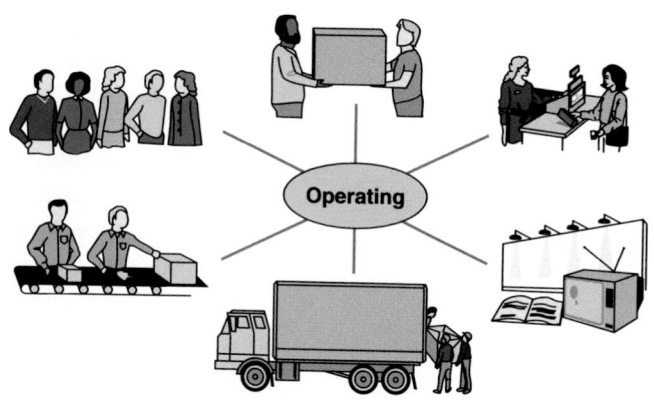

The **indirect method** reports net income and then adjusts it for items necessary to give us net cash provided (used) by operating activities. It does *not* report individual items of cash inflows and cash outflows from operating activities. Instead, the indirect method reports the necessary adjustments to reconcile net income to net cash provided (used) by operating activities. A common adjustment is an addition for amortization. Since amortization expense is not a current cash payment, we add amortization expense back to net income in our process of adjusting net income to net cash provided (used) by operating activities.

The operating activities section prepared under the indirect method appears as shown in Exhibit 19.9.

Exhibit 19.9

Operating Activities
Section—Indirect Method

Cash flows from operating activities:	
Net income	$38,000
Adjustments to reconcile net income to net cash provided by operating activities:	
Increase in accounts receivable	(20,000)
Increase in merchandise inventory	(14,000)
Increase in prepaid expenses	(2,000)
Decrease in accounts payable	(5,000)
Decrease in interest payable	(1,000)
Increase in income taxes payable	10,000
Amortization expense	24,000
Loss on sale of capital assets	6,000
Gain on retirement of bonds	(16,000)
Net cash provided by operating activities	$20,000

It is important to see that the amount of net cash provided by operating activities is *identical* under both the direct and indirect methods. This equality always exists. The difference in these methods is with computation of this amount.

The indirect method of reporting operating cash flows does not provide as much detailed information as the direct method. The direct method is *recommended* by the CICA. But since the direct method is not required and the indirect method is arguably easier to compute, companies are likely to continue reporting operating cash flows using the indirect method. We describe both methods in this chapter.

Since the direct method is the cash flow version of an income statement, many people find the direct method easier to understand when first learning about cash flow reporting. It allows decision makers to know how much of revenues and costs are actually received or paid in cash. It also follows the same format as the income statement. Many internal users such as managers and budget officers use the direct method to predict future cash requirements and availability.

To illustrate both methods, we prepare the operating activities section of the statement of cash flows for Genesis. The December 31, 1999, and 2000, balance sheets of Genesis along with its 2000 income statement are shown in Exhibit 19.10. Our objective is to prepare a statement of cash flows explaining the $5,000 increase in cash for year 2000 as seen from its balance sheets. This is computed as Cash of $17,000 at the end of year 2000 minus Cash of $12,000 at the end of 1999.

Genesis also discloses additional information about year 2000 transactions:

a. All accounts payable balances result from merchandise purchases.

b. Capital assets costing $70,000 are purchased by paying $10,000 cash and issuing $60,000 of bonds payable.

c. Capital assets with an original cost of $30,000 and accumulated amortization of $12,000 are sold for $12,000 cash. This yields a $6,000 loss.

d. Proceeds from issuing 3,000 common shares are $15,000.

e. Paid $18,000 to retire bonds with a book value of $34,000. This yields a $16,000 gain from bond retirement.

f. Cash dividends of $14,000 are declared and paid.

GENESIS Balance Sheet December 31, 2000 and 1999	2000	1999
Assets		
Current assets:		
Cash	$ 17,000	$ 12,000
Accounts receivable	60,000	40,000
Merchandise inventory	84,000	70,000
Prepaid expenses	6,000	4,000
Total current assets	$167,000	$126,000
Long-term assets:		
Capital assets	$250,000	$210,000
Less accumulated amortization	(60,000)	(48,000)
Total assets	$357,000	$288,000
Liabilities		
Current liabilities:		
Accounts payable	$ 35,000	$ 40,000
Interest payable	3,000	4,000
Income taxes payable	22,000	12,000
Total current liabilities	$ 60,000	$ 56,000
Long-term liabilities:		
Bonds payable	90,000	64,000
Total liabilities	$150,000	$120,000
Shareholders' Equity		
Contributed capital:		
Common shares, no-par value	$95,000	$80,000
Retained earnings	112,000	88,000
Total shareholders' equity	207,000	168,000
Total liabilities and shareholders' equity	$357,000	$288,000

GENESIS Income Statement For Year Ended December 31, 2000		
Sales		$590,000
Cost of goods sold	$300,000	
Wages and other operating expenses	216,000	
Interest expense	7,000	
Income taxes expense	15,000	
Amortization expense	24,000	(562,000)
Loss on sale of capital assets		(6,000)
Gain on retirement of debt		16,000
Net income		$ 38,000

Exhibit 19.10

Financial Statements

The next section describes the direct method. The section following this one describes the indirect method. An instructor may choose to cover one or the other in preparing a statement of cash flows. Neither section depends on the other.

Direct Method of Reporting Operating Cash Flows

Compute cash flows from operating activities using the direct method.

We compute cash flows from operating activities under the direct method by adjusting accrual-based income statement items to a cash basis. The usual approach is to adjust income statement accounts related to operating activities for changes in their related balance sheet accounts as follows:

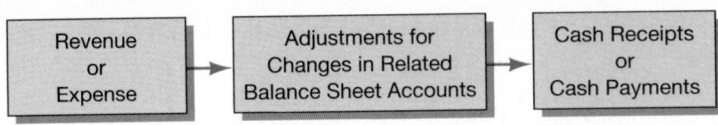

We follow this same approach in this section.

The framework for reporting major classes of cash receipts and cash payments is shown in Exhibit 19.11. This framework is for the operating section of the cash flow statement prepared using the **direct method.**

Exhibit 19.11

Major Classes of Operating Cash Flows

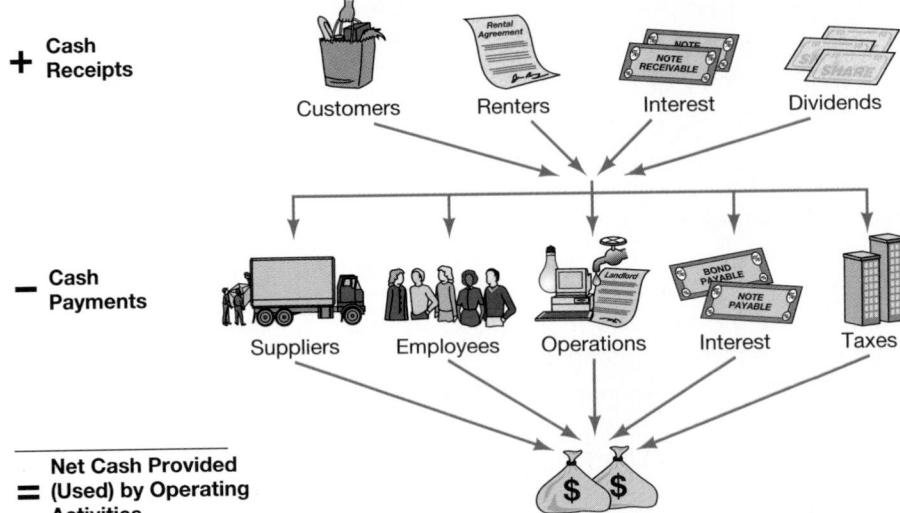

In preparing the operating section for Genesis, we first look at its cash receipts and then its cash payments.

Operating Cash Receipts

Exhibit 19.10 and the additional information from Genesis identifies only one potential cash receipt—that of sales to customers. This section takes sales from the accrual-based income statement and adjusts it as necessary to give us cash received from customers.

Cash Received from Customers

If all sales are for cash, the amount of cash received from customers is equal to sales. But when sales are on account, we must adjust the amount of sales revenue for the change in Accounts Receivable. It is often helpful to use *account analysis* for this purpose. This usually involves setting up a T-account and reconstructing its major entries, including its cash receipts and payments.

To illustrate, the T-account below reports accounts receivable balances on December 31, 1999, and 2000. The beginning balance is $40,000, and the ending balance is $60,000. The income statement shows sales is $590,000, and we enter it on the debit side of this account. With this information, we can reconstruct the Accounts Receivable account and determine the amount of cash received from customers.

Accounts Receivable			
Balance, Dec. 31/1999	40,000		
Sales	590,000	Collections =	570,000
Balance, Dec. 31/2000	60,000		

This T-account shows the balance of accounts receivable begins at $40,000 and increases to $630,000 from sales of $590,000. But then its ending balance is reported at only $60,000. This implies that cash receipts from customers are $570,000, computed as $40,000 + $590,000 − [?] = $60,000. This computation can be rearranged to express cash received as equal to sales of $590,000 minus a $20,000 increase in accounts receivable. This computation is summarized in Exhibit 19.12.

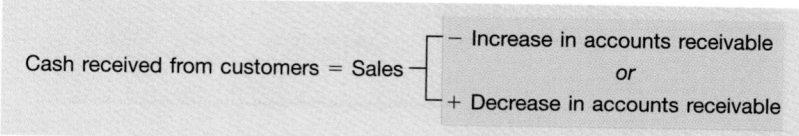

Cash received from customers = Sales
− Increase in accounts receivable
or
+ Decrease in accounts receivable

Exhibit 19.12

Formula to Compute Cash Received from Customers—Direct Method

The statement of cash flows for Genesis in Exhibit 19.7 shows the $570,000 cash received from customers as a cash inflow from operating activities.

Other Cash Receipts

While cash receipts of Genesis are limited to collections from customers, we sometimes see other types of cash receipts. The most common are cash receipts involving rent, interest, and dividends. We compute cash received from these items by subtracting an increase in their respective receivable account or adding a decrease. For instance, if rent receivable increases in the period, it implies cash received is less than rent revenue reported on the income statement. But if rent receivable decreases, it implies cash received is more than reported rent revenue. The same logic applies to interest and dividends. The formulas for these computations are summarized in Exhibit 19.16 later in this section.

Operating Cash Payments

Exhibit 19.10 and the additional information from Genesis identifies four operating expenses. We analyze each of these expenses to compute their operating cash payments for the statement of cash flows.

Cash Paid for Merchandise

We compute cash paid for merchandise by analyzing both cost of goods sold and merchandise inventory. If all merchandise purchases are for cash and the ending balance of Merchandise Inventory is unchanged from the beginning balance, then the amount of cash paid for merchandise equals cost of goods sold. But this situation is uncommon. We usually see some change in the Merchandise Inventory balance in a period. Also, merchandise purchases are often made on credit, and yield changes in the Accounts Payable balance.

When the balances of Merchandise Inventory and Accounts Payable change, we must adjust cost of goods sold for changes in both of these accounts to compute cash paid for merchandise. This adjustment has two steps. First, we use the change in the balance of Merchandise Inventory along with the amount of cost of goods sold to compute cost of purchases for the period. If inventory increases, it implies we bought more than was sold and we add the inventory change to cost of goods sold to compute cost of purchases. If inventory decreases, it implies we bought less than was sold and we subtract the inventory change from cost of goods sold to compute purchases.

The second step uses the change in the balance of Accounts Payable along with the amount of cost of purchases to compute cash paid for merchandise. If accounts payable decreases, it implies we paid for more goods than was acquired this period and we add the accounts payable change to cost of purchases to compute cash paid for merchandise. If accounts payable increases, it implies we paid less than was acquired and we subtract the accounts payable change from purchases to compute cash paid for merchandise.

We illustrate this two-step process for Genesis. First, we use account analysis of merchandise inventory to compute cost of purchases. We do this by reconstructing the Merchandise Inventory account:

Merchandise Inventory			
Balance, Dec. 31/1999	70,000		
Purchases =	314,000	Cost of goods sold	300,000
Balance, Dec. 31/2000	84,000		

The beginning balance is $70,000, and its ending balance is $84,000. The income statement shows cost of goods sold is $300,000, and we enter it on the credit side of this account. With this information, we can determine the amount for cost of purchases at $314,000. This computation can be rearranged to express cost of purchases as equal to cost of goods sold of $300,000 plus the $14,000 increase in inventory.

Our second step is to compute cash paid for merchandise by adjusting purchases for the change in accounts payable. This is done by reconstructing the Accounts Payable account:

Accounts Payable			
		Balance, Dec. 31/1999	40,000
Payments =	319,000	Purchases	314,000
		Balance, Dec. 31/2000	35,000

This account shows us that its beginning balance of $40,000 plus purchases of $314,000 minus an ending balance of $35,000 gives us cash paid of $319,000 (or $40,000 + $314,000 − [?] = $35,000). Alternatively, we can express cash paid for merchandise as equal to purchases of $314,000 plus the $5,000 decrease in accounts payable.

We summarize the two-step adjustment to cost of goods sold to compute cash paid for merchandise in Exhibit 19.13.

Exhibit 19.13

Two Steps to Compute Cash Paid for Merchandise—Direct Method

Step 1:

Purchases = Cost of goods sold
- + Increase in merchandise inventory
- or
- − Decrease in merchandise inventory

Step 2:

Cash paid for merchandise = Purchases
- + Decrease in accounts payable
- or
- − Increase in accounts payable

Exhibit 19.7 shows the $319,000 cash paid by Genesis for merchandise is reported on the statement of cash flows as a cash outflow for operating activities.

Cash Paid for Wages and Operating Expenses (Excluding Amortization)

The income statement of Genesis shows wages and other operating expenses of $216,000; see Exhibit 19.10. To compute cash paid for wages and other operating expenses, we adjust this amount for changes in their related balance sheet accounts.

We begin by looking for prepaid expenses and accrued liabilities relating to wages and other operating expenses in the beginning and ending balance sheets of Genesis in Exhibit 19.10. These balance sheets show Genesis has prepaid expenses but no accrued liabilities. This means its adjustment to this expense item is limited to the change in prepaid expenses. The amount of adjustment is computed by assuming all cash paid for wages and other operating expenses is initially debited to Prepaid Expenses. This assumption allows us to reconstruct the Prepaid Expenses account:

Prepaid Expenses			
Balance, Dec. 31/1999	4,000		
Payments =	218,000	Wages and other operating expenses	216,000
Balance, Dec. 31/2000	6,000		

This account shows prepaid expenses increase by $2,000 in the period. This means cash paid for wages and other operating expenses exceeded the reported expense by $2,000. Alternatively, we can express cash paid for wages and other operating expenses of Genesis as equal to its expenses of $216,000 plus the $2,000 increase in prepaid expenses.

Our analysis assumes all cash payments for wages and operating expenses are initially debited to Prepaid Expenses in reconstructing the Prepaid Expenses account. But this assumption is not necessary for our analysis to hold. If cash payments are debited directly to the expense account, the total amount of cash paid for wages and other operating expenses will still equal the $216,000 expense plus the $2,000 increase in prepaid expenses.

Exhibit 19.14 summarizes the adjustments to wages (including salaries) and other operating expenses. While the balance sheet of Genesis did not report accrued liabilities, we add these to the exhibit to explain the adjustment to cash when they do exist. If accrued liabilities decrease, it implies we paid for more goods or services than received this period, and we must add the change in accrued liabilities to the expense amount to get cash paid for these goods or services. If accrued liabilities increase, it implies we paid less than was acquired and we must subtract the change in accrued liabilities from the expense amount to get cash paid.

Exhibit 19.14

Formula to Compute Cash Paid for Wages and Operating Expenses—Direct Method

Cash Paid for Both Interest and Income Taxes

Our analysis for computing operating cash flows for interest and taxes is similar to that for operating expenses. Both require adjustments to their amounts on the income statement for changes in their related balance sheet accounts.

We begin with the income statement of Genesis showing interest expense of $7,000 and income taxes expense of $15,000. To compute the cash paid, we adjust interest expense for the change in interest payable and we adjust income taxes expense for the change in income taxes payable. These computations involve reconstructing both liability accounts:

Interest Payable		
	Balance, Dec.31/1999	4,000
Interest paid = 8,000	Interest expense	7,000
	Balance, Dec. 31/2000	3,000

Income Taxes Payable		
	Balance, Dec. 31/1999	12,000
Income taxes paid = 5,000	Income taxes expense	15,000
	Balance, Dec. 31/2000	22,000

These accounts reveal cash paid for interest of $8,000 and cash paid for income taxes of $5,000. The formulas to compute these amounts are shown in Exhibit 19.15.

Exhibit 19.15

Formulas to Compute Cash Paid for Both Interest and Taxes—Direct Method

Both of these cash payments are reported as operating cash outflows on the statement of cash flows for Genesis in Exhibit 19.7.

Analysis of Other Operating Expenses

Genesis has three other operating expenses reported on its income statement: amortization, loss on sale of assets, and gain on retirement of debt. We consider each of these for their potential cash effects.

Amortization Expense   Amortization expense for Genesis is $24,000. It is known as a *noncash expense* because there are no cash flows associated with amortization. Amortization expense is an allocation of the amortizable cost of a purchased asset. The cash outflow associated with an asset is reported as part of investing activities when it is paid for. This means amortization expense is *never* reported on a statement of cash flows using the direct method.

Loss on Sale of Assets   Sales of assets frequently result in gains and losses reported as part of net income. But the amount of recorded gain or loss does *not* reflect cash flows in these transactions. Asset sales result in cash inflow equal to the actual amount received, regardless of whether the asset was sold at a gain or a loss. This cash inflow is reported under investing activities. This means the loss or gain on a sale of assets is never reported on a statement of cash flows using the direct method.

Gain on Retirement of Debt   Retirements of debt usually yield gains and losses reported as part of net income. But the amount of recorded gain or loss does *not* reflect cash flows in these transactions. Debt retirement results in cash outflow equal to the actual amount paid to settle the debt, regardless of whether the debt was retired at a gain or loss. This cash outflow is reported under financing activities. This means the loss or gain from retirement of debt is never reported on a statement of cash flows using the direct method.

Summary of Adjustments for Direct Method

Exhibit 19.16 summarizes the adjustments to the revenues and expenses making up net income to give us net cash provided (used) by operating activities under the direct method.

Item	From Income Statement	Adjustments to Get Cash Flow Numbers
Receipts:		
From customers	Sales Revenue	+ Decrease in Accounts Receivable – Increase in Accounts Receivable
Of rent	Rent Revenue	+ Decrease in Rent Receivable – Increase in Rent Receivable
Of interest	Interest Revenue	+ Decrease in Interest Receivable – Increase in Interest Receivable
Of dividends	Dividend Revenue	+ Decrease in Dividends Receivable – Increase in Dividends Receivable
Payments:		
To suppliers	Cost of Goods Sold	+ Increase in Inventory + Decrease in Accounts Payable – Decrease in Inventory – Increase in Accounts Payable
For operations	Operating Expense	+ Increase in Prepaids + Decrease in Accrued Liabilities – Decrease in Prepaids – Increase in Accrued Liabilities
To employees	Wages (Salaries) Expense	+ Decrease in Wages (Salaries) Payable – Increase in Wages (Salaries) Payable
For interest	Interest Expense	+ Decrease in Interest Payable – Increase in Interest Payable
For income tax	Income Tax Expense	+ Decrease in Income Tax Payable – Increase in Income Tax Payable

Exhibit 19.16

Summary of Selected Adjustments for Direct Method

While computation for computing net cash provided (used) by operating activities is different for the direct and indirect methods, the result is identical. Both methods yield the same $20,000 amount for net cash provided (used) by operating activities; see Exhibits 19.7 and 19.17.

Direct Method Format of Operating Activities Section

Exhibit 19.7 shows the statement of cash flows for Genesis using the direct method. Major items of cash inflows and cash outflows are listed separately in the operating activities section. The format requires that operating cash outflows are subtracted from operating cash inflows to get net cash provided (used) by operating activities.

Flashback

4. Is the direct or indirect method of reporting operating cash flows more informative? Explain. Which method is more common in practice?

5. Net sales in a period are $590,000, beginning accounts receivable are $120,000, and ending accounts receivable are $90,000. What amount is collected from customers in the period?

6. The Merchandise Inventory account balance decreases in a period from a beginning balance of $32,000 to an ending balance of $28,000. Cost of goods sold for the period is $168,000. If the Accounts Payable balance increases $2,400 in the period, what is the amount of cash paid for merchandise?

7. Reported wages and other operating expenses incurred total $112,000. At the end of the prior year, prepaid expenses totalled $1,200, and this year the balance is $4,200. The current balance sheet shows wages payable of $5,600, whereas last year's did not show any accrued liabilities. How much is paid for wages and other operating expenses this year?

Answers—p. 911

Mid-Chapter Demonstration Problem

The following financial information refers to Mitchel Company:

MITCHELL COMPANY
Balance Sheets

Assets	Dec. 31, 1998	Dec. 31, 1999
Current Assets:		
Cash	$ 20,000	$ 15,000
Account receivable (net)	25,000	23,000
Inventory	34,000	37,000
Prepaid expenses	8,000	6,000
Total current assets	$ 87,000	$ 81,000
Long-term investments	40,000	37,000
Capital assets	170,000	191,000
Accumulated amortization	(25,000)	(31,000)
Total assets	$272,000	$280,000

Liabilities and Shareholders' Equity		
Current Liabilities:		
Accounts payable	$ 30,000	$ 38,000
Accrued liabilities	65,000	68,000
Total current liabilities	95,000	106,000
Bonds payable	90,000	100,000
Common shares	37,000	40,000
Retained earnings	50,000	34,000
	$272,000	$280,000

Income Statement
For Year Ended December 31, 1999

Sales	$250,000
Cost of goods sold	165,000
Gross margin	85,000
Operating expenses	40,000
Operating income before taxes	45,000
Gain on sale of investment	8,000
Income before taxes	53,000
Less income taxes	14,800
Net income	$ 38,200

Required

a. Calculate sales adjusted to a cash basis.

b. Calculate cost of goods sold adjusted to a cash basis.

c. How much cash was paid for operating expenses?

d. How much cash was provided by operating activities?

a.

Sales revenue reported per income statement	$250,000
Adjustments to cash basis:	
Decrease in accounts receivable	2,000 (source of cash)
Sales adjusted to a cash basis	$252,000

b.

Cost of goods sold per income statement	$165,000
Adjustments to a cash basis:	
Increase in inventory	3,000 (use of cash)
Increase in accounts payable	(8,000) (source of cash)
Cost of goods sold adjusted to a cash basis	$160,000

c.

Operating expenses per income statements	$ 40,000
Adjusted to a cash basis:	
Decrease in prepaid expenses	(2,000) (noncash expense)
Increase in accrued liabilities	(3,000) (increase in expense not using cash)
Amortization	(6,000) (noncash expense)
Cash paid for operating expenses	$ 29,000

d.

Sales adjusted to a cash basis	$525,000
Less: Cost of goods sold adjusted to a cash basis	160,000
Cash paid for operating expenses	29,000
Cash paid for income tax	14,800
Cash provided by operating activities	$ 48,200

Solution to Mid-Chapter Demonstration Problem

Indirect Method of Reporting Operating Cash Flows

We know net income is computed using accrual accounting. Accrual accounting recognizes revenues when earned and expenses when incurred. But revenues and expenses do not necessarily reflect the receipt and payment of cash. The indirect method of computing and reporting net cash flows from operating activities involves adjusting the net income figure to get the net cash provided (used) by operating activities. This includes subtracting noncash credits from net income and adding noncash charges back to net income.

We draw on the financial statements of Genesis in Exhibit 19.10 to illustrate application of the indirect method. The indirect method of reporting begins with net income of $38,000 for Genesis. Net income is then adjusted to give us net cash provided (used) by operating activities. Exhibit 19.17 shows the results of the indirect method of reporting operating cash flows for Genesis. The net cash provided by operating activities is $20,000. This amount is the same as that for the direct method of reporting operating cash flows; see Exhibit 19.7. *The two methods always yield the same net cash flow provided (used) by operating activities.* It is only the computations and presentation that are different.

The indirect method does not report individual operating cash inflows or cash outflows. Instead, the indirect method adjusts net income for three types of adjustments as shown in Exhibit 19.17. First, there are adjustments for changes in noncash current assets and current liabilities relating to operating activities (the first

LO7 Compute cash flows from operating activities using the indirect method.

6 items). Second, there are adjustments to income statement items involving operating activities that do not affect cash inflows or outflows in the period (amortization). Third, there are adjustments to eliminate gains and losses resulting from investing and financing activities (those not part of operating activities—the loss on sale of capital assets and gain on retirement of bonds). This section describes each of these three types of adjustments in applying the indirect method.

Exhibit 19.17

Statement of Cash Flows—
Indirect Method

GENESIS Statement of Cash Flows For Year Ended December 31, 2000		
Cash flows from operating activities:		
Net income	$38,000	
Adjustments to reconcile net income to net cash provided by operating activities:		
Increase in accounts receivable	(20,000)	
Increase in merchandise inventory	(14,000)	
Increase in prepaid expenses	(2,000)	
Decrease in accounts payable	(5,000)	
Decrease in interest payable	(1,000)	
Increase in income taxes payable	10,000	
Amortization expense	24,000	
Loss on sale of capital assets	6,000	
Gain on retirement of bonds	(16,000)	
Net cash provided by operating activities		$20,000
Cash flows from investing activities:		
Cash received from sale of capital assets	$12,000	
Cash paid for purchase of capital assets	(10,000)	
Net cash provided by investing activities		2,000
Cash flows from financing activities:		
Cash received from issuing shares	$15,000	
Cash paid to retire bonds	(18,000)	
Cash paid for dividends	(14,000)	
Net cash used in financing activities		(17,000)
Net increase in cash		$ 5,000
Cash balance at beginning of 1999		12,000
Cash balance at end of 2000		$17,000

Adjustments for Operating Items Not Providing or Using Cash

The income statement usually includes certain expenses that do not reflect cash outflows in the period. Examples are amortization of capital assets and amortization of bond discount. The indirect method for reporting operating cash flows requires that:

Expenses with no cash outflows are added back to net income

To see this logic, recall that items such as amortization of capital assets are recorded with debits to expense accounts and credits to noncash accounts. There is no cash effect in these entries. Yet because items such as amortization expense are proper deductions in computing accrual income, we need to add them back to net income when computing net cash flows from operations. Adding them back cancels their deductions.

Similarly, when net income includes revenues that do not reflect cash inflows in the period, the indirect method for reporting operating cash flows requires that:

Revenues with no cash inflows are subtracted from net income

Both types of adjustments to net income are a necessary part of the computations to get net cash provided by operating activities. We now look at the individual operating items of Genesis that fit this category and do not provide or use cash.

Amortization

Amortization expense is the only operating item for Genesis that does not affect cash flows in the period. Our discussion indicates we must add $24,000 amortization expense back to net income as part of our adjustments to get net cash provided by operating activities. Later in the chapter we explain that the cash outflow for a capital asset is reported as an investing activity on the statement of cash flows when paid.

Adjustments for Nonoperating Items

The income statement sometimes includes losses that are not part of operating activities, and are classified as either investing or financing activities. Examples are a loss from sale of a capital asset and a loss from retirement of a bond payable. Under the indirect method for reporting operating cash flows:

Nonoperating losses are added back to net income

To see the logic, consider that items such as a capital asset sale and bond retirement are normally recorded by recognizing the cash, removing all capital asset or bond accounts, and recognizing the loss or gain. The cash received or paid is not part of operating activities. Instead it is recorded under either investing or financing activities. There is *no* operating cash flow effect. But because the nonoperating loss is a deduction in computing accrual income, we need to add it back to net income when computing the net cash flow effect from operations. Adding it back cancels the deduction.

Similarly, when net income includes gains that are not part of operating activities, the indirect method for reporting operating cash flows requires:

Nonoperating gains are subtracted from net income

These net income adjustments are part of computations to get net cash provided by operating activities. We now look at the individual nonoperating items of Genesis.

Loss on Sale of Capital Assets

Genesis reports a $6,000 loss on sale of capital assets in its income statement. This loss is a proper deduction in computing net income, but it is *not part of operating activities*. Instead, a sale of capital assets is part of investing activities. This means the $6,000 nonoperating loss is added back to net income as part of our adjustments to get net cash provided by operating activities. Adding it back cancels the recorded loss. Later in the chapter we explain how the cash inflow from the capital asset sale is reported in investing activities.

Gain on Retirement of Debt

There is a $16,000 gain on retirement of debt reported in the income statement of Genesis. This gain is properly included in net income, but it is *not part of operating activities*. This means the $16,000 nonoperating gain is subtracted from net income as part of our adjustments to get net cash provided by operating activities. Subtracting it cancels the recorded gain. Later in the chapter we describe how the cash outflow to retire debt is reported in financing activities.

Adjustments for Changes in Current Assets and Current Liabilities

This section describes adjustments for changes in noncash current assets and current liabilities as part of the procedure for determining operating cash flows using the indirect method.

Adjustments for Changes in Noncash Current Assets

Changes in noncash current assets are normally the result of operating activities. Examples are sales affecting accounts receivable and use of rented assets affecting prepaid rent expense. Our adjustments to net income in computing operating cash flows must therefore include changes in noncash current assets. Under the indirect method for reporting operating cash flows:

> **Decreases in noncash current assets are added to net income**

To see this logic, consider that a decrease in a noncash current asset such as accounts receivable suggests more available cash at the end of the period compared to the beginning of the period. This is because a decrease in accounts receivable implies greater cash receipts. We add these greater cash receipts from decreases in noncash current assets to net income when computing net cash flow from operations.

Similarly, an increase in noncash current assets such as accounts receivable implies more credit sales than cash collections. An increase in prepaid rent expense suggests more cash was paid for rent than was deducted as rent expense. We must therefore subtract this increase in prepaid rent from net income in computing the amount of cash flow from operations. The indirect method for reporting operating cash flows requires:

> **Increases in noncash current assets are subtracted from net income**

These adjustments to net income are a necessary part of the computations to get net cash provided by operating activities. We now turn to the individual noncash current assets of Genesis as shown in Exhibit 17.10.

Accounts Receivable Accounts receivable of Genesis *increased* $20,000 in the period, from a beginning balance of $40,000 to an ending balance of $60,000. This increase implies Genesis collected less cash than its reported sales amount for this period. It also means some of these sales were in the form of accounts receivable, leaving accounts receivable with an increase. This lesser amount of cash collections compared with sales is reflected in the Accounts Receivable account as shown here:

Accounts Receivable			
Balance, Dec. 31/1999	40,000		
Sales, 2000	590,000	Collections =	570,000
Balance, Dec. 31/2000	60,000		

This $20,000 increase in accounts receivable is subtracted from net income as part of our adjustments to get net cash provided by operating activities. Subtracting it adjusts sales to the cash receipts amount.

Merchandise Inventory Merchandise inventory *increased* $14,000 in the period, from a beginning balance of $70,000 to an ending balance of $84,000. This increase implies Genesis had a greater amount of cash purchases than goods sold this period. This greater amount of cash purchases ended up in the form of inventory, resulting in an inventory increase. This greater amount of cash purchases compared to the amount subtracted from income as cost of goods sold is reflected in the Merchandise Inventory account increase:

Merchandise Inventory			
Balance, Dec. 31/1999	70,000		
Purchases =	314,000	Cost of goods sold	300,000
Balance, Dec. 31/2000	84,000		

The $14,000 increase in inventory is subtracted from net income as part of our adjustments to get net cash provided by operating activities.

Prepaid Expenses Prepaid expenses *increased* $2,000 in the period, from a beginning balance of $4,000 to an ending balance of $6,000. This increase implies Genesis' cash payments exceeded its operating expenses incurred this period. These larger cash payments ended up increasing the amount of prepaid expenses. This is reflected in the Prepaid Expenses account:

Prepaid Expenses			
Balance, Dec. 31/1999	4,000		
Payments =	218,000	Wages and other operating expenses	216,000
Balance, Dec. 31/2000	6,000		

This $2,000 increase in prepaid expenses is subtracted from net income as part of our adjustments to get net cash provided by operating activities. Subtracting it adjusts operating expenses to a cash payments amount.

Adjustments for Changes in Current Liabilities

Changes in current liabilities are normally the result of operating activities. An example is purchases affecting accounts payable. Our adjustments to net income in computing operating cash flows must therefore include changes in current liabilities. Under the indirect method for reporting operating cash flows:

Increases in current liabilities are added to net income

To see the logic, an increase in accounts payable suggests that cash payments are less than its related expense. As another example, an increase in wages payable implies that wages expense exceeded cash paid for the period. Because more was deducted as an expense than was paid in cash, we add the increase in wages payable to net income when computing net cash flow from operations.

Similarly, when current liabilities decrease in the period, the indirect method for reporting operating cash flows requires:

Decreases in current liabilities are subtracted from net income

These adjustments to net income are a necessary part of the computations to get net cash provided by operating activities. We now turn to the individual current liabilities of Genesis as shown in Exhibit 17.10.

Accounts Payable Accounts payable of Genesis *decreased* $5,000 in the period, from a beginning balance of $40,000 to an ending balance of $35,000. This decrease implies its cash payments exceeded its merchandise purchases by

$5,000 for the period. This larger amount for cash payments compared to purchases is reflected in the Accounts Payable account:

Accounts Payable			
		Balance, Dec. 31/1999	40,000
Payments =	319,000	Purchases	314,000
		Balance, Dec. 31/2000	35,000

The $5,000 decrease in accounts payable is subtracted from net income as part of our adjustments to get net cash provided by operating activities.

Interest Payable   Interest payable *decreased* $1,000 in the period, from a beginning balance of $4,000 to an ending balance of $3,000. This decrease indicates cash payments for interest exceeded interest expense for the period by $1,000. This larger cash payment compared to the reported interest expense is reflected in the Interest Payable account:

Interest Payable			
		Balance, Dec. 31/1999	4,000
Interest paid =	8,000	Interest expense	7,000
		Balance, Dec. 31/2000	3,000

The $1,000 decrease in interest payable is subtracted from net income as part of our adjustments to get net cash provided by operating activities.

Income Taxes Payable   Income taxes payable *increased* $10,000 in the period, from a beginning balance of $12,000 to an ending balance of $22,000. This increase implies the amount owed for income taxes exceeded the cash payments for the period by $10,000. This smaller cash payment compared to income taxes owed is reflected in the Income Taxes Payable account:

Income Taxes Payable			
		Balance, Dec. 31/1999	12,000
Income taxes paid =	5,000	Income taxes expense	15,000
		Balance, Dec. 31/2000	22,000

The $10,000 increase in income taxes payable is added to net income as part of our adjustments to get net cash provided by operating activities.

Did You Know?

Cash or Income
The difference between net income and operating cash flows can be large. As examples, Alcan reported a net income of $410 million and operating cash flows of $981 million in its 1996 annual report and CAE reported a net income of $60,276,000 and an operating cash outflow of $(44,485,000) in its 1997 annual report.

Summary of Adjustments for Indirect Method

Exhibit 19.18 summarizes the adjustments to net income to get net cash provided (used) by operating activities for the indirect method.

Net Income

　+ Amortization

　+ Loss on disposal of long-term asset

　+ Loss on retirement of debt

　− Gain on disposal of long-term asset

　− Gain on retirement of debt

　+ Decrease in noncash current asset

　− Increase in noncash current asset

　+ Increase in current liability*

　− Decrease in current liability*

Net cash provided (used) by operating activities

*Excludes current portion of long-term debt and any short-term notes payable if unrelated to sales. Both are financing activities.

Exhibit 19.18

Summary of Selected Adjustments for Indirect Method

While the computations in determining net cash provided (used) by operating activities is different for the direct and indirect methods, the result is identical. Both methods yield the same $20,000 figure for net cash provided (used) by operating activities; see Exhibits 19.7 and 19.17.

Flash back

8. Determine the net cash provided (or used) by operating activities using the following data:

Net income	$74,900
Decrease in accounts receivable	4,600
Increase in inventory	11,700
Decrease in accounts payable	1,000
Loss on sale of equipment	3,400
Payment of dividends	21,500

9. Why are expenses such as amortization added to net income when cash flow from operating activities is computed by the indirect method?

10. A company reports net income of $15,000 that includes a $3,000 gain on the sale of capital assets. Why is this gain subtracted from net income in computing cash flow from operating activities using the indirect method?

Answers—p. 911

Cash Flows from Investing Activities

The third step in preparing the statement of cash flows is to compute and report net cash flows from investing activities. Cash flows for investing activities reveal the extent to which expenditures have been made for the purpose of generating future income cash flows. We determine investing activities by identifying changes in all noncurrent asset accounts and both current and long-term notes receivable. These accounts include capital assets, investments, and notes. Changes in these accounts are then analyzed using available information to determine their effect, if any, on cash. Results of this analysis are reported in the investing activities section of the statement. *Reporting of investing activities is identical under the direct method and indirect method.*

Investing activities include transactions such as the (a) purchase and sale of property, plant and equipment, intangibles and other long-term assets, (b) lending and collecting on notes receivable, and (c) purchase and sale of debt or equity instruments other than those instruments considered to be cash equivalents. Information to compute cash flows from investing activities is usually taken from beginning and ending balance sheets and from the income statement. Information provided earlier in the chapter about the transactions of Genesis reveals it both purchased and sold capital assets during the period. Both transactions are investing activities.

L0 8 Determine cash flows from both investing and financing activities.

Capital Asset Transactions

We use a three-step process in determining net cash provided (used) by investing activities. (1) Identify changes in investing-related accounts. (2) Explain these changes using reconstruction analysis. (3) Report cash flow effects.

For capital assets, we need to deal with both the capital asset account and its related accumulated amortization account. Comparative balance sheet information for these accounts is in Exhibit 19.10. The first step reveals a $40,000 increase in capital assets from $210,000 to $250,000, and a $12,000 increase in accumulated amortization from $48,000 to $60,000. We need to explain these changes.

The second step begins by reviewing ledger accounts and any additional information at our disposal. A capital asset account is affected by both purchases and sales of capital assets. An accumulated amortization account is increased by additional amortization and reduced by removing accumulated amortization on asset disposals. Items (b) and (c) of the additional information reported on page 886 for Genesis are relevant for these accounts. To explain changes in these accounts and to help us understand the cash flows effects, we prepare *reconstructed entries*. A reconstructed entry is our reproduction of an entry from a transaction; *it is not the actual entry made by the preparer.* Item (b) reports Genesis purchased capital assets costing $70,000 by issuing $60,000 in bonds payable to the seller and paying $10,000 in cash. The reconstructed entry for our analysis of item (b) is:

Assets = Liabilities + Equity
+70,000   +60,000
−10,000

Capital Assets	70,000	
Bonds Payable		60,000
Cash		**10,000**

This entry reveals a $10,000 cash outflow for assets purchased. It also reveals a noncash investing and financing transaction involving $60,000 bonds given up for $60,000 of capital assets.

Item (c) reports Genesis sold capital assets costing $30,000 (with $12,000 of accumulated amortization) for cash received of $12,000, resulting in a loss of $6,000. The reconstructed entry for item (c) is:

Assets = Liabilities + Equity
+12,000   −6,000
−30,000
+12,000

Cash	**12,000**	
Accumulated Amortization	12,000	
Loss on Sale of Capital Assets	6,000	
Capital Assets		30,000

This entry reveals a $12,000 cash inflow for assets sold. Also, notice the $6,000 loss is computed by comparing the asset book value to the cash received, and does not reflect any cash inflow or outflow.

We can also reconstruct the entry for amortization expense using information from the income statement:

Assets = Liabilities + Equity
−24,000   −24,000

Amortization Expense	24,000	
Accumulated Amortization		24,000

This entry shows that amortization expense results in no cash flow effects.

These reconstructed entries are reflected in the ledger accounts for both capital assets and accumulated amortization.

Capital Assets			
Balance, Dec. 31/1999	210,000		
Purchase	70,000	Sale	30,000
Balance, Dec. 31/2000	250,000		

Accumulated Amortization, Capital Assets			
		Balance, Dec. 31/1999	48,000
Sale	12,000	Amort. expense	24,000
		Balance, Dec. 31/2000	60,000

In performing an actual cash flow analysis we have the entire ledger and additional information at our disposal. For brevity reasons, we are given the additional information for reconstructing accounts and verifying that our analysis of the investing-related accounts is complete.

The third step is to make the necessary disclosures on the statement of cash flows. Disclosure of the two cash flow effects in the investing section of the statement appears as (also see Exhibit 19.7 or 19.17):

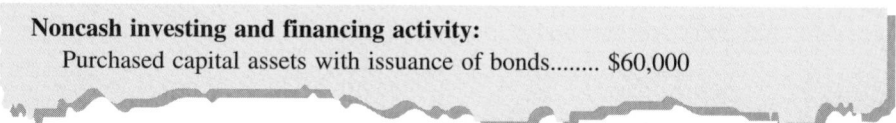

Cash flows from investing activities:
Cash received from sale of capital assets . . . . $ 12,000
Cash paid for purchase of capital assets . . . .   (10,000)

The $60,000 portion of the purchase described in item (b) and financed by issuance of bonds is a noncash investing and financing activity. This can be reported in a note to the statement as:

Noncash investing and financing activity:
Purchased capital assets with issuance of bonds........ $60,000

We have now reconstructed these accounts by explaining how the beginning balances of both accounts are affected by purchases, sales, and amortization in yielding their ending balances. For instance, the change in capital assets from $210,000 to $250,000 is fully explained by the $70,000 purchase and the $30,000 sale. Also, the change in accumulated amortization from $48,000 to $60,000 is fully explained by the sale of assets (with $12,000 of accumulated amortization) and $24,000 of amortization expense.

Flashback

11. Equipment costing $80,000 with accumulated amortization of $30,000 is sold at a loss of $10,000. What is the cash receipt from the sale? In what category of the statement of cash flows is it reported?

Answers—p. 911

Cash Flows from Financing Activities

The fourth step in preparing the statement of cash flows is to compute and report net cash flows from financing activities. We normally do this by identifying changes in all note payable (current and noncurrent), noncurrent liability, and equity accounts. These accounts include long-term debt, notes payable, bonds payable, owner's capital, common shares, and retained earnings. Changes in these accounts are then analyzed using available information to determine their effect, if any, on cash. Results of this analysis are reported in the financing activities section of the statement. *Reporting of financing activities is identical under the direct method and indirect method.*

Financing activities include transactions such as (a) receiving cash from issuing debt and repaying the amounts borrowed, and (b) receiving cash from or distributing cash to owners. Information provided earlier about the transactions of Genesis reveals four transactions involving financing activities. We already analyzed one of these, the $60,000 issuance of bonds payable to purchase capital assets as a noncash investing and financing activity. The remaining three transactions are retirement of bonds, issuance of common shares, and payment of cash dividends. We again use a three-step process in determining net cash provided (used) by financing activities. (1) Identify changes in financing-related accounts. (2) Explain these changes using reconstruction analysis. (3) Report cash flow effects.

Bonds Payable Transactions

Comparative balance sheet information from Exhibit 19.10 for bonds payable is our starting point. The first step reveals an increase in bonds payable from $64,000 to $90,000. We need to explain this change.

The second step is to review the bonds payable ledger account and any additional information available. Item (e) of the additional information given earlier for Genesis is relevant to bonds payable. Item (e) reports bonds with a carrying value of $34,000 are retired for $18,000 cash, resulting in a $16,000 gain. The reconstructed entry for our analysis of item (e) is:

Assets = Liabilities + Equity
−18,000　−34,000　+16,000

Bonds Payable	34,000	
Gain on retirement of debt		16,000
Cash		**18,000**

This entry reveals an $18,000 cash outflow for retirement of bonds. It also shows a $16,000 gain from comparing the bonds payable carrying value with the cash received. This gain does not reflect any cash inflow or outflow.

Item (b) also involves bonds payable. It reports Genesis purchased capital assets costing $70,000 by issuing $60,000 in bonds payable to the seller and paying $10,000 in cash. We already reconstructed its entry for our analysis of investing activities. Recall it increased bonds payable by $60,000 and is reported as a noncash investing and financing transaction. These reconstructed entries are reflected in the ledger account for bonds payable:

Bonds Payable			
		Balance, Dec. 31/1999	64,000
Retired bonds	34,000	Issued bonds	60,000
		Balance, Dec. 31/2000	90,000

The third step is to make the necessary disclosures on the statement of cash flows. Disclosure of the cash flow effect from the bond retirement in the financing section of the statement appears as (also see Exhibit 19.7 or 19.17):

Cash flows from financing activities:
Cash paid to retire bonds . . . .   (18,000)

We have now reconstructed the bonds payable account by explaining how its beginning balance is affected by a bond retirement and bond issuance in yielding its ending balance. In particular, the change in bonds payable from $64,000 to $90,000 is fully explained by the $34,000 retirement and the $60,000 issuance.

Common Shares Transactions

We use comparative balance sheet information from Exhibit 19.10 for the first step in analyzing the common shares account. This first step reveals an increase in common shares from $80,000 to $95,000. We need to explain this change.

Our second step is to review the common shares ledger account and any additional information available. Item (d) of the additional information given earlier for Genesis reports it issued 3,000 common shares for $5 per share. The reconstructed entry for our analysis of item (d) is:

Cash	**15,000**	
Common Shares		15,000

Assets = Liabilities + Equity
+15,000   +15,000

This entry reveals a $15,000 cash inflow from the issuance of shares. This reconstructed entry is reflected in the ledger account for common shares:

Common Shares		
	Balance, Dec. 31/1999	80,000
	Issued shares	15,000
	Balance, Dec. 31/2000	95,000

The third step is to make the necessary disclosure on the statement of cash flows. Disclosure of the cash flow effect from shares issuance in the financing section of the statement appears as (also see Exhibit 19.7 or 19.17):

Cash flows from financing activities:
Cash received from issuing shares . . . . $ 15,000

The $15,000 shares issue fully explains the change in the Common Shares account.

Retained Earnings Transactions

The first step in analyzing the Retained Earnings account is to review comparative balance sheet information from Exhibit 19.10. The first step reveals an increase in retained earnings from $88,000 to $112,000. We need to explain this change.

Our second step is to analyze the Retained Earnings account and any additional information available. Item (f) of the additional information given earlier for Genesis reports it paid cash dividends of $14,000. The reconstructed entry for our analysis of item (f) is:

Retained Earnings	14,000	
Cash		**14,000**

Assets = Liabilities + Equity
−14,000   −14,000

This entry reveals a $14,000 cash outflow to pay cash dividends. We must also remember retained earnings is affected by net income from the income statement. Net income was already dealt with under the operating section of the statement of cash flows. This reconstruction analysis is reflected in the ledger account for retained earnings:

Retained Earnings			
		Balance, Dec. 31/1999	88,000
Cash dividend	14,000	Net income	38,000
		Balance, Dec. 31/2000	112,000

The third step is to make the necessary disclosure on the statement of cash flows. Disclosure of the cash flow effect from the cash dividend appears in the financing section of the statement as (also see Exhibit 19.7 or 19.17):

Cash flows from financing activities:
Cash paid for dividends . . . .　(14,000)

The $14,000 dividend payment along with the reported net income of $38,000 fully explain the change in Retained Earnings.

Proving Cash Balances

We have now explained all of the cash inflows and outflows of Genesis, along with one noncash investing and financing transaction. Our analysis has reconciled changes in all noncash balance sheet accounts. The fifth and final step in preparing the statement is to report the beginning and ending cash balance and prove the *net change in cash* is explained by operating, investing, and financing net cash flows. This step is shown below for Genesis:

Net cash provided by operating activities	$20,000
Net cash provided by investing activities	2,000
Net cash used in financing activities	(17,000)
Net increase in cash and cash equivalents	$ 5,000
Cash and cash equivalents at beginning of 2000 .	12,000
Cash and cash equivalents at end of 2000	$17,000

This schedule shows the $5,000 net increase in cash from $12,000 at the beginning of the period to $17,000 at the end is reconciled by net cash flows from operating ($20,000 inflow), investing ($2,000 inflow), and financing ($17,000 outflow) activities. This is formally reported at the bottom of the statement of cash flows as shown in either Exhibit 19.7 or 19.17.

You Make the Call

Reporter
You are a newspaper reporter covering a workers' strike. Management grants you an interview and complains about recent losses and negative cash flows. It shows you financial numbers revealing a recent $600,000 net loss which included a $930,000 extraordinary loss. It also shows you the company's total net cash outflow of $550,000 which included net cash outflows of $850,000 for investing activities and $350,000 for financing activities. What is your initial reaction to management's complaints?

Answer—p. 911

Cash Flow Analysis

USING THE INFORMATION

Numerous ratios are used to analyze income statement and balance sheet data. By comparison, ratios related to the statement of cash flows are fewer in number. One of these ratios is cash flow per share. One must be careful not to interpret it as a measure of earnings performance.

Analyzing Cash Sources and Uses

Most managers stress the importance of understanding and predicting cash flows. Many business decisions are based on cash flow evaluations. For instance, creditors evaluate a company's ability to generate cash before deciding whether to loan money. Many investors make similar evaluations before buying shares. Specifically, information in the statement of cash flows helps us address questions such as:

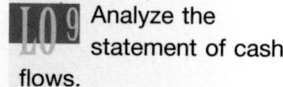 Analyze the statement of cash flows.

- How much cash is generated from or used in operations?
- What expenditures are made with cash from operations?
- How are dividends paid when losses occur?
- What is the source of cash for debt payments?
- What is the source of cash for distributions to owners?
- How is the increase in investments financed?
- What is the source of cash for new capital assets?
- Why is cash lower when income increased?
- What is the use of cash from financing?

While cash flows from investing and financing activities are important in these decisions, we pay special attention to operating cash flows. A statement of cash flows helps in this regard by separating investing, financing, and operating activities.

To illustrate the importance of separately analyzing cash flows by activities, we look at data from three different companies in Exhibit 19.19. These companies operate in the same industry and have been in business for several years.

(in thousands)	Foster	Smith	Tower
Cash provided (used) by operating activities	$90,000	$40,000	$(24,000)
Cash provided (used) by investing activities:			
Proceeds from sale of operating assets			26,000
Purchase of operating assets	(48,000)	(25,000)	
Cash provided (used) by financing activities:			
Proceeds from issuance of debt			13,000
Repayment of debt	(27,000)		
Net increase (decrease) in cash	$15,000	$15,000	$15,000

Exhibit 19.19

Cash Flows of Competitors

These three companies each generated a $15,000 net increase in cash flows. But their sources and uses of cash flows are very different. Foster's operating activities provided net cash flows of $90,000. This allowed it to purchase additional operating assets for $48,000 and repay $27,000 of debt. Smith's operating activities provided $40,000 of operating cash flows. This limited its purchase of operating assets to $25,000. Tower's net cash increase is due to selling operating assets and incurring additional debt. Its operating activities resulted in a net cash outflow of $24,000.

Our analysis of these cash flow data reveals that Foster is more capable of generating cash to meet its future obligations than is Smith or Tower. Also, the strong operating cash flows of Foster bode well for future performance, while Tower's operating outlook is poor. This evaluation is, of course, tentative and may be contradicted by other information, including data in the balance sheet or income statement.

Managers analyze cash flows for making many short-term and long-term decisions. A decision on the necessity of short-term borrowing is made using many of the procedures we discussed in this chapter. Short-term planning also can lead to decisions about investing idle cash balances. Managers' setting of sales prices is also influenced by cash flow data.

Managers' long-term decisions involving new investments are based on cash flow predictions. They estimate cash inflows and outflows over the life of the investment, often extending many years into the future. Other long-term decisions based on cash flow data include deciding whether a product is manufactured by the company or purchased from an outside supplier, and whether a product or a department is eliminated or retained.

Flash back

12. Refer to the statement of cash flows for **Atlantis** in Appendix I. What was the major investing activity that took place during the year ended December 31, 1997?

Answer—p. 911

Cash Flow on Total Assets

LO 10 Compute and apply the cash flow on total assets ratio.

We described the importance of return on total assets in both Chapters 1 and 18. Return on total assets is a valuable measure of financial performance and is computed as net income divided by average total assets. The numerator of return on total assets is net income based on accrual accounting. Accrual accounting records revenue when earned and expenses when incurred.

Cash flow accounting is different from accrual accounting. Cash flow accounting recognizes cash inflows when received (not necessarily earned) and cash outflows when paid (not necessarily incurred). While cash flow information has limitations, it can help us measure a company's ability to meet its obligations, pay dividends, expand operations, and obtain financing.

Because of the importance of cash flows, users often look at a cash-based measure called cash flow on total assets. It is somewhat similar to return on total assets, but its numerator is net cash flows from operating activities (not net income). Specifically, the *cash flow on total assets* is computed as shown in Exhibit 19.20.

Exhibit 19.20

Cash Flow on Total Assets

$$\text{Cash flow on total assets} = \frac{\text{Operating cash flows}}{\text{Average total assets}}$$

This ratio can add to our analysis of company performance. The cash flow on total assets ratio reflects actual cash flows and is not affected by the accounting constraints of recognition and measurement for net income. It is important for companies to recognize its cash flow amounts and patterns in planning and analyzing operating activities. The cash flow on total assets ratio is one measure to help us assess cash flows.

To illustrate, we look at the cash flow on total assets for **NIKE** at May 31, 1997. It is computed as ($ in thousands):

$$\text{Cash flow on total assets} = \frac{\$323{,}120}{(\$5{,}361{,}207 + \$3{,}951{,}628)/2} = 6.94\%$$

Is a 6.94% cash flow on total assets good or bad for NIKE? To help answer this question and others like it, we can compare NIKE's ratio with its prior performance, the ratios of competitors, and with ratios of other noncompeting companies. As a first step, we show NIKE's cash flow on total assets ratio for each of the prior three-years in the second column of Exhibit 19.21. Its return on total assets is provided for comparison purposes in the third column.

Year	Cash Flow on Total Assets	Return on Total Assets
1997	6.94%	17.09%
1996	9.58	15.60
1995	9.24	14.49

Exhibit 19.21

NIKE's Cash Flow on Total Assets

We see that NIKE's cash flow on total assets has declined steadily over the period 1995–97, while its return on total assets has slightly grown. This result suggests NIKE's *earnings quality* has declined over this period. This decline in earnings quality for NIKE means less of its earnings is realized in the form of cash.

We also compare NIKE's cash flow on total assets to some other companies including **PepsiCo, McDonald's, Wal-Mart,** and **Wendy's.** A bar chart of these results is shown in Exhibit 19.22.

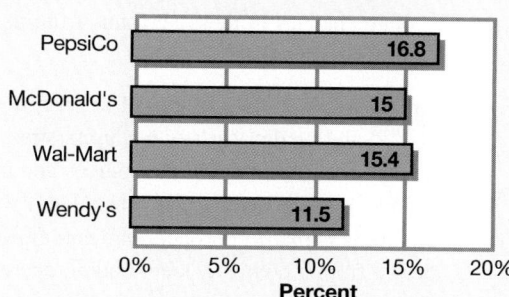

Exhibit 19.22

Cash Flow on Total Assets of Selected Companies

We see that NIKE's cash flow on total assets ratio is lower than the same ratio for these companies. This finding adds to our concern from the resulting decline in the cash flow on total assets ratio as evidenced in Exhibit 19.21.

Overall, the statement of cash flows is an important bridge between the income statement and balance sheet, and valuable in financial analysis. The cash flow on total assets ratio is a useful part of this analysis, and is used as an indicator of earnings quality.

Free Cash Flow

Free cash flow is a common term in financial analysis. It refers to operating cash flows available after allowing for investing and financing requirements. Free cash flow is usually defined as operating cash flows minus capital expenditures and cash dividends. Growth and financial flexibility depend on adequate free cash flow.

Did You Know?

Summary

LO1 **Explain the purpose and importance of cash flow information.** The main purpose of the statement of cash flows is to report the items comprising cash receipts and cash payments for a period. This includes identifying these cash flows as relating to either operating, investing, or financing activities. Many business decisions involve evaluating cash flows. Examples are investor and creditor decisions to invest in or loan money to a company. Users' evaluations include focusing on the activities that provide or use cash.

LO2 **Distinguish among operating, investing, and financing activities.** Operating activities include the cash effects of transactions and events that determine net income. Investing activities include the (a) purchase and sale of long-term assets, (b) the purchase and sale of short-term investments other than cash equivalents, and (c) lending and collecting on loans. Financing activities include (a) getting cash from issuing debt and repaying the amounts borrowed, and (b) obtaining cash from or distributing cash to owners and giving owners a return on investment.

LO3 **Identify and disclose noncash investing and financing activities.** For external reporting, a company must supplement its statement of cash flows with a description of its noncash investing and financing activities. These activities are disclosed in either a note to the statement or in a separate schedule usually reported at the bottom of the statement. Two examples of these activities are the retirement of debt by issuing equity securities and the exchange of a note payable for capital assets.

LO4 **Describe the format of the statement of cash flows.** The statement of cash flows reports cash receipts and disbursements into one of three categories: operating, investing, or financing activities. Cash inflows and cash outflows are reported for each category.

LO5 **Prepare a statement of cash flows.** Preparation of a statement of cash flows involves five steps: (1) compute the net increase or decrease in cash, (2) compute net cash provided (used) by operating activities [using either the direct or indirect method], (3) compute net cash provided (used) by investing activities, and (4) compute net cash provided (used) by financing activities. Noncash investing and financing activities are disclosed in either a note or in a separate schedule to the statement. (5) report the beginning and ending cash balance and prove it is explained by operating, investing and financing net cash flows.

LO6 **Compute cash flows from operating activities using the direct method.** The direct method for reporting net cash provided (used) by operating activities involves listing separately the major classes of operating cash inflows and outflows. The operating cash outflows are then subtracted from operating cash inflows to get the net inflow or outflow from operating activities. The direct method is recommended by the CICA. The direct method should also include a separate schedule reporting the reconciliation between net income and net cash provided (used) by operating activities.

LO7 **Compute cash flows from operating activities using the indirect method.** The indirect method for reporting net cash provided (used) by operating activities starts with net income and then adjusts it for three items: (1) revenues and expenses not providing (using) cash, (2) gains and losses from investing and financing activities, and (3) changes in noncash current assets and current liabilities related to operating activities.

LO8 **Determine cash flows from both investing and financing activities.** Cash flows from both investing and financing activities are determined by identifying the cash flow effects of transactions and events affecting each balance sheet account related to these activities. All cash flows from these activities are identified when we can explain changes in these accounts from the beginning to the end of the period.

LO9 **Analyze the statement of cash flows.** To understand and predict cash flows, users stress the importance of separately identifying the sources and uses of cash flows by operating, investing, and financing activities. Special emphasis is placed on operating cash flows since they derive from a company's continuing operations.

LO10 **Compute and apply the cash flow on total assets ratio.** The cash flow on total assets ratio is defined as operating cash flows divided by average total assets. Companies prefer to maintain a regular and positive level of net cash flows from operating activities, and analysis of current and past cash flow on total assets ratios is one measure of a company's success in achieving this goal. It is also viewed as a measure of earnings quality.

Guidance Answers to **You Make the Call**

Community Activist

Several reasons can explain an increase in net cash flows when a loss is reported. Possibilities include: (1) early recognition of expenses relative to revenues generated (research and development), (2) valuable long-term sales contracts not yet recognized in income, (3) issuances of debt or equity to finance expansion, (4) selling of assets, (5) delayed cash payments, and (6) prepayment on sales. Your analysis of this manufacturer needs to focus on the components of both net income and net cash flows, and their implications for future performance.

Reporter

Your initial course of action is to verify management's claims about poor performance. A $600,000 loss along with a $550,000 decrease in net cash flows seemingly supports its claim. But a closer scrutiny reveals a different picture. You compute its cash flow from operating activities at a positive $650,000, computed as [?] − $850,000 − $350,000 = ($550,000). You note also net income *before* the extraordinary loss is a positive $330,000, computed as [?] − $930,000 = ($600,000). This is powerful information to confront management. A serious and directed discussion is likely to reveal a far more positive picture of this company's financial performance.

Guidance Answers to Flash backs

1. No. The statement of cash flows reports changes in the sum of cash plus cash equivalents. It does not report transfers between cash and cash equivalents.

2. The three categories of cash inflows and outflows are operating activities, investing activities, and financing activities.

3. a. Investing
   b. Operating
   c. Financing
   d. Operating
   e. Operating
   f. Financing

4. The direct method is most informative because it separately lists each major item of operating cash receipts and each major item of operating cash payments. The indirect method is used most often.

5. $590,000 + ($120,000 − $90,000) = $620,000

6. $168,000 − ($32,000 − $28,000) − $2,400 = $161,600

7. $112,000 + ($4,200 − $1,200) − $5,600 = $109,400

8. $74,900 + $4,600 − $11,700 − $1,000 + $3,400 = $70,200

9. In the calculation of net income, expenses such as amortization are subtracted from revenue. These expenses do not require current cash outflows. Therefore, adding these expenses back to net income eliminates noncash items from the net income number, converting it to a cash basis.

10. In the process of reconciling net income to net cash provided (or used) by operating activities, a gain on the sale of capital assets is subtracted from net income because a sale of capital assets is not an operating activity; it is an investing activity.

11. $80,000 − $30,000 − $10,000 = $40,000

    The $40,000 cash receipt is reported as an investing activity.

12. Investing activities during the year ended December 31, 1997, showed that the largest use of cash was the completion of programs costing $129,945,000.

Demonstration Problem

Umlauf's beginning and ending balance sheet, income statement, and supplementary information follow.

Required

1. Prepare a statement of cash flows using the direct method for the year ended 2000.
2. Prepare a statement of cash flows using the indirect method for the year ended 2000.

UMLAUF COMPANY Balance Sheet December 31, 2000 and 1999		
	December 31	
	2000	1999
Assets		
Cash	$ 43,050	$ 23,925
Accounts receivable	34,125	39,825
Merchandise inventory	156,000	146,475
Prepaid expenses	3,600	1,650
Equipment	135,825	146,700
Accumulated amortization, equipment	(61,950)	(47,550)
Totals	$310,650	$311,025
Liabilities and Shareholders' Equity		
Accounts payable	28,800	33,750
Income taxes payable	5,100	4,425
Dividends payable	-0-	4,500
Bonds payable	-0-	37,500
Common shares no-par value	168,750	168,750
Retained earnings	108,000	62,100
Totals	$310,650	$311,025

An examination of the company's statements and accounts showed:

a. All sales were made on credit.
b. All merchandise purchases were on credit.
c. Accounts Payable balances resulted from merchandise purchases.
d. Prepaid expenses relate to other operating expenses.
e. Equipment costing $21,375 with accumulated amortization of $11,100 was sold for cash.
f. Equipment was purchased for cash.
g. The change in the balance of Accumulated Amortization resulted from amortization expense and from the sale of equipment.
h. The change in the balance of Retained Earnings resulted from dividend declarations and net income.

UMLAUF COMPANY Income Statement For Year Ended December 31, 2000		
Sales (see note 1)		$446,100
Cost of goods sold (see note 2)	$222,300	
Other operating expenses (see note 3)	120,300	
Amortization expense	25,500	
Income taxes expense (see note 4)	13,725	(381,825)
Loss on sale of equipment (see note 5)		(3,300)
Loss on retirement of bonds (see note 6)		(825)
Net income (See note 7)		$60,150

Planning the Solution

- ■ Prepare a blank statement of cash flows with sections for operating, investing, and financing activities using the direct method format.
- ■ Compute cash received from customers, cash paid for merchandise, cash paid for other operating expenses and taxes as illustrated in the chapter.
- ■ Compute the cash paid for equipment and the cash received from the sale of equipment according to the supplementary information provided, the amount for amortization expense, and the change in the balances of equipment and accumulated amortization. Use a T-account to help chart the effects of the sale and purchase of the equipment on the balances of the equipment account and the accumulated amortization account.
- ■ Calculate the effect of net income on the change in the retained earnings balance. Ascribe the difference between the change in retained earnings and the amount of net income to dividends declared. Adjust the dividends declared amount for the change in the dividends payable balance.
- ■ Enter the cash effects of the entry in the appropriate section of the statement,
- ■ Total each section of the statement, determine the total change in cash, and add the beginning balance to get the ending balance.
- ■ Now prepare a blank statement of cash flows with sections for operating, investing, and financing activities using the indirect method format.

Solution to Demonstration Problem

Notes:

(1)	Sales	$446,100
	Add decrease in accounts receivable	5,700
	Cash received from customers	$451,800
(2)	Cost of goods sold	$222,300
	Plus increase in merchandise inventory	9,525
	Purchases	231,825
	Plus decrease in accounts payable	4,950
	Cash paid for merchandise	$236,775
(3)	Other operating expenses	$120,300
	Plus increase in prepaid expenses	1,950
	Cash paid for other operating expenses	$122,250
(4)	Income taxes expense	$13,725
	Less increase in income taxes payable	(675)
	Payments of income taxes	$ 13,050
(5)	Cost of equipment sold	$21,375
	Accumulated amortization of equipment sold	(11,100)
	Book value of equipment sold	10,275
	Loss on sale of equipment	(3,300)
	Cash receipt from sale of equipment	$ 6,975
	Cost of equipment sold	$ 21,375
	Less decrease in the equipment account balance	(10,875)
	Cash paid for new equipment	$ 10,500

Equipment				Accumulated Amortization, Equipment			
Balance, Dec. 31/1999	146,700					Balance, Dec. 31/1999	47,550
Purchase	10,500	Sale	21,375	Sale	11,100	Amort. expense	25,500
Balance, Dec. 31/2000	135,825					Balance, Dec. 31/2000	61,950

(6) Loss on retirement of bonds		$ 825
Carrying value of bonds retired		37,500
Cash payment to retire bonds		$38,325
(7) Net income		$ 60,150
Less increase in retained earnings		45,900
Dividends declared		14,250
Plus decrease in dividends payable		4,500
Cash paid for dividends		$ 18,750

UMLAUF COMPANY Statement of Cash Flows (Direct Method) For Year Ended December 31, 2000		
Cash flows from operating activities:		
Cash received from customers	$451,800	
Cash paid for merchandise	(236,775)	
Cash paid for other operating expenses	(122,250)	
Cash paid for income taxes	(13,050)	
Net cash provided by operating activities		$79,725
Cash flows from investing activities:		
Cash received from sale of office equipment	$ 6,975	
Cash paid for store equipment	(10,500)	
Net cash used in investing activities		(3,525)
Cash flows from financing activities:		
Cash paid to retire bonds payable	$ (38,325)	
Cash paid for dividends	(18,750)	
Net cash used in financing activities		(57,075)
Net increase in cash		$19,125
Cash balance at beginning of year		23,925
Cash balance at end of year		$43,050

UMLAUF COMPANY
Statement of Cash Flows (Indirect Method)
For Year Ended December 31, 2000

Cash flows from operating activities:

Cash flows from operating activities:

Net income	$ 60,150	
Adjustments to reconcile net income to net cash provided by operating activities:		
Decrease in accounts receivable	5,700	
Increase in merchandise inventory	(9,525)	
Increase in prepaid expenses	(1,950)	
Decrease in accounts payable	(4,950)	
Increase in income taxes payable	675	
Amortization expense	25,500	
Loss on sale of capital assets	3,300	
Loss on retirement of bonds	825	
Net cash provided by operating activities		$79,725
Cash flows from investing activities:		
Cash received from sale of office equipment	$ 6,975	
Cash paid for store equipment	(10,500)	
Net cash used in investing activities		(3,525)
Cash flows from financing activities:		
Cash paid to retire bonds payable	$(38,325)	
Cash paid for dividends	(18,750)	
Net cash used in financing activities		(57,075)
Net increase in cash		$19,125
Cash balance at beginning of year		23,925
Cash balance at end of year		$43,050

19A

APPENDIX

Using a Spreadsheet to Prepare the Statement of Cash Flows

Learning Objective

LO 11   Illustrate use of a spreadsheet in preparing a statement of cash flows.

We compute net cash flows provided (or used) by operating activities under the indirect method by using balance sheets at the beginning and end of the period, the current period's income statement, and information about selected transactions. Exhibit 19.10 shows the income statement and balance sheet information for **Genesis.** Based on this information, Exhibit 19.17 presented the indirect method of reconciling net income to net cash provided by operating activities. This appendix explains how we can use a spreadsheet (work sheet) analysis to prepare the statement of cash flows using the indirect method.

Preparing the Indirect Method Spreadsheet

Analyzing noncash accounts can be challenging when a company has a large number of accounts and many operating, investing, and financing transactions. A *spreadsheet*, also called *working paper*, can help us organize the information needed to prepare a statement of cash flows. A spreadsheet also makes it easier to check the accuracy of our work.

To illustrate how we use this spreadsheet, we return to the comparative balance sheets and income statement shown in Exhibit 19.10. Information needed for the spreadsheet in preparing the statement of cash flows is listed below along with identifying letters:

a. Net income is $38,000.

b. Accounts receivable increases by $20,000.

c. Merchandise inventory increases by $14,000.

d. Prepaid expenses increases by $2,000.

e. Accounts payable decreases by $5,000.

f. Interest payable decreases by $1,000.

g. Income taxes payable increases by $10,000.

h. Amortization expense is $24,000.

i. Capital assets costing $30,000 with accumulated amortization of $12,000 are sold for $12,000 cash. Loss on sale of assets is $6,000.

j. Bonds with a book value of $34,000 are retired with a cash payment of $18,000. Gain on retirement of bonds is $16,000.

k. Capital assets costing $70,000 are purchased with a cash payment of $10,000 and an issuance of bonds payable for $60,000.

l. Issued 3,000 common shares for $15,000.

m. Paid cash dividends of $14,000.

Exhibit 19A.1 shows the indirect method spreadsheet for Genesis. Both beginning and ending balance sheets are recorded on the spreadsheet. We enter information in the Analysis of Changes columns for the cash flows from operating, investing, and financing activities. We also include information about noncash investing and financing activities near the bottom. The spreadsheet does not reconstruct the income statement. Instead, net income is entered as the first item used in computing the amount of cash flows from operating activities.

Exhibit 19A.1

Spreadsheet for Preparing Statement of Cash Flows—Indirect Method

GENESIS
Spreadsheet for Statement of Cash Flows—Indirect Method
For Year Ended December 31, 2000

	December 31, 1999	Analysis of Changes Debit	Analysis of Changes Credit	December 31, 2000
Balance sheet—debits:				
Cash	12,000			17,000
Accounts receivable	40,000	(b) 20,000		60,000
Merchandise inventory	70,000	(c) 14,000		84,000
Prepaid expenses	4,000	(d) 2,000		6,000
Capital assets	210,000	(k1)70,000	(i) 30,000	250,000
	336,000			417,000
Balance sheet — credits:				
Accumulated amortization	48,000	(i) 12,000	(h) 24,000	60,000
Accounts payable	40,000	(e) 5,000		35,000
Interest payable	4,000	(f) 1,000		3,000
Income taxes payable	12,000		(g) 10,000	22,000
Bonds payable	64,000	(j) 34,000	(k2)60,000	90,000
Common shares no-par value	80,000		(l) 15,000	95,000
Retained earnings	88,000	(m) 14,000	(a) 38,000	112,000
	336,000			417,000
Statement of cash flows:				
Operating activities:				
Net income		(a) 38,000		
Increase in accounts receivable			(b) 20,000	
Increase in merchandise inventory			(c) 14,000	
Increase in prepaid expenses			(d) 2,000	
Decrease in accounts payable			(e) 5,000	
Decrease in interest payable			(f) 1,000	
Increase in income taxes payable		(g) 10,000		
Amortization expense		(h) 24,000		
Loss on sale of capital assets		(i) 6,000		
Gain on retirement of bonds			(j) 16,000	
Investing activities:				
Receipts from sale of capital assets		(i) 12,000		
Payment for purchase of capital assets			(k1)10,000	
Financing activities:				
Payments to retire bonds			(j) 18,000	
Receipts from issuing shares		(l) 15,000		
Payments of dividends			(m) 14,000	
Noncash investing and financing activities				
disclosed in note:				
Purchase of capital assets				
financed by bonds		(k2)60,000	(k1) 60,000	
		337,000	337,000	

Entering the Analysis of Changes on the Spreadsheet

The following sequence of procedures are used to complete the spreadsheet after the balance sheet accounts are entered:

1. Enter net income as an operating cash inflow (debit) and as a credit to Retained Earnings.

2. In the statement of cash flows section, adjustments to net income are entered as debits if they increase cash inflows and as credits if they decrease cash inflows. Applying this rule, adjust net income for the change in each noncash current asset and current liability related to operating activities. For each adjustment to net income, the offsetting debit or credit helps reconcile the beginning and ending balances of a current asset or current liability.

3. Enter adjustments to net income for income statement items not providing or using cash in the period. For each adjustment, the offsetting debit or credit helps reconcile a noncash balance sheet account.

4. Adjust net income to eliminate any gains or losses from investing and financing activities. Because the cash from a gain must be excluded from operating activities, the gain is entered as a credit in the operating activities section. Losses are entered as debits. For each of these adjustments, the related debits and/or credits help reconcile balance sheet accounts and involve entries to show the cash flow from investing or financing activities.

5. After reviewing any unreconciled balance sheet accounts and related information, enter the reconciling entries for all remaining investing and financing activities. Examples are purchases of capital assets, issuances of long-term debt, sales of capital stock, and dividend payments. Some of these may require entries in the noncash investing and financing activities section of the spreadsheet.

6. Check accuracy by totalling the Analysis of Changes columns and by determining that the change in each balance sheet account has been explained.

We illustrate these steps in Exhibit 19A.1 for Genesis:

Step	Entries
1	(a)
2	(b) through (g)
3	(h)
4	(i) through (j)
5	(k) through (m)

Because adjustments *i*, *j*, and *k* are more challenging, we show them in the debit and credit format. *These entries are for purposes of our understanding—they are not the entries actually made in the journals.* The format we use is similar to the one used for general journal entries, except that changes in the Cash account are identified as sources or uses of cash.

i.	Loss from sale of capital assets	6,000	
	Accumulated amortization	12,000	
	Receipt from sale of capital assets		
	(source of cash)	12,000	
	Capital assets		30,000
	To describe sale of capital assets.		
j.	Bonds payable	34,000	
	Payments to retire bonds (use of cash)		18,000
	Gain on retirement of bonds		16,000
	To describe retirement of bonds.		

k1.	Capital assets	70,000	
	Payment to purchase capital assets		
	(use of cash)		10,000
	Purchase of capital assets financed		
	by bonds		60,000
	To describe purchase of capital assets,		
	cash payment, and use of noncash financing.		
k2.	Purchase of capital assets financed by bonds	60,000	
	Bonds payable		60,000
	To show issuance of bonds payable to		
	finance purchase of capital assets.		

Flash back

13. In using a spreadsheet for preparing the operating section of a statement of cash flows reported using the indirect method, which of the following is true?

a. Decrease in accounts receivable is analyzed with a debit in the statement of cash flows section and a credit in the balance sheet section.

b. Cash dividend paid is analyzed with a debit to retained earnings and a credit in the investing activities section.

c. Analysis of a cash payment to retire bonds payable at a loss requires one debit and two credits.

d. Amortization expense does not require analysis on the spreadsheet because there is no cash inflow or outflow.

Answers—p. 919

Summary of Appendix 19A

LO 11 **Illustrate use of a spreadsheet in preparing a statement of cash flows.** A spreadsheet is a useful tool in preparing a statement of cash flows. Six key steps (described in the Appendix) are applied when using the spreadsheet. The result is a properly classified statement of cash flows.

Guidance Anwser to *Flash backs*

13. *c*

Glossary

Direct method A calculation of the net cash provided or used by operating activities that lists the major classes of operating cash receipts, such as receipts from customers, and subtracts the major classes of operating cash disbursements, such as cash paid for merchandise. This method is recommended by the CICA. (p. 888)

Financing activities Transactions with a company's owners and creditors which include getting cash from issuing debt and repaying the amounts borrowed, and getting cash from or distributing cash to owners and giving owners a return on investments. (p. 879)

Indirect method A calculation that reports net income and then adjusts the net income amount by adding and subtracting items that are necessary to yield net cash provided or used by operating activities. (p. 886)

Investing activities The acquisition and disposal of long-term assets and other investments that are not classified as cash equivalents. (p. 879)

Operating activities The principal revenue-producing activities that are not investing or financing activities. Operating activities involve the production or purchase of merchandise and the sale of goods and services to cus-

tomers, including expenditures related to administering the business. (p. 878)

Statement of cash flows A financial statement that reports the cash inflows and outflows for an accounting period, and that classifies those cash flows as operating activities, investing activities, and financing activities. (p. 876)

A superscript letter A identifies questions based on Appendix 19A.

Questions

1. What are some examples of items reported on a statement of cash flows as investing activities?

2. What are some examples of items reported on a statement of cash flows as financing activities?

3. When a statement of cash flows is prepared by the direct method, what are some examples of items reported as cash flows from operating activities?

4. If a corporation pays cash dividends, where on the corporation's statement of cash flows should the payment be reported?

5. A company purchases land for $100,000, paying $20,000 cash and borrowing the remainder on a long-term note payable. How should this transaction be reported on a statement of cash flows?

6. What is the direct method of reporting cash flows from operating activities?

7. What is the indirect method of reporting cash flows from operating activities?

8. Is amortization a source of cash?

9. On June 3, a company borrowed $50,000 by giving its bank a 60-day, interest-bearing note. On the statement of cash flows, where should this item be reported?

10. If a company reports a net income for the year, is it possible for the company to show a net cash outflow from operating activities? Explain your answer.

11. Refer to **Alliance's** consolidated statement of changes in financial position shown in Appendix I. (a) Which method was used to compute net cash provided by operating activities? (b) Although the consolidated balance sheet shows that there was an increase in receivables from fiscal year 1996 to fiscal year 1997, why were receivables subtracted rather than added in the calculation of net cash provided by operating activities during the March 31, 1997, fiscal year-end as indicated in note 14?

12. Refer to **Atlantis's** consolidated statement of changes in financial position shown in Appendix I. How much cash was generated from interim financing in 1997, compared with 1996?

13. Refer to Alliance's consolidated statement of changes in financial position shown in Appendix I. What activities comprised the two largest investing activities resulting in cash outflows for the year ended March 31, 1997?

14. What do the loan terms given to Chen in the opening scenario suggest regarding the loan officer's risk assessment of the loan to the ginseng farm?

Quick Study

QS 19-1
Explaining statement of cash flows

Describe the content of a statement of cash flows.

QS 19-2
Classifying transactions by activity

Classify the following cash flows as operating, investing, or financing activities:

1. Issued common shares for cash.
2. Received interest on investment.
3. Paid interest on outstanding bonds.
4. Sold delivery equipment at a loss.
5. Paid property taxes on the company offices.

6. Collected proceeds from sale of long-term investments.

7. Received payments from customers.

8. Paid wages.

9. Purchased merchandise for cash.

10. Paid dividends.

List three examples of transactions that are noncash financing and investing transactions.

QS 19-3
Identifying noncash transactions
LO 2

Use the following information in QS 19-4 through QS 19-9.

QS 19-4
Computing cash from customers
LO 6

BRIGHTWELL CO., INC. Comparative Balance Sheet December 31, 2000 and 1999		
Assets	**2000**	**1999**
Cash	$ 95,800	$ 25,000
Accounts receivable (net)	42,000	52,000
Inventory	86,800	96,800
Prepaid expenses	6,400	5,200
Furniture	110,000	120,000
Accumulated amortization, furniture	(18,000)	(10,000)
Total assets	$323,000	$289,000
Liabilities and Shareholders' Equity		
Accounts payable	$ 16,000	$ 22,000
Wages payable	10,000	6,000
Income taxes payable	2,400	3,600
Notes payable (long-term)	30,000	70,000
Common shares no-par value	230,000	180,000
Retained earnings	34,600	7,400
Total liabilities and shareholders' equity	$323,000	$289,000

BRIGHTWELL CO., INC. Income Statement For Year Ended June 30, 2000		
Sales		$468,000
Cost of goods sold		312,000
Gross profit		$156,000
Operating expenses:		
Amortization expense	$ 38,600	
Other expenses	57,000	
Total operating expenses		95,600
Net income from operations		$ 60,400
Income taxes		24,600
Net income		$ 35,800

How much cash was received from customers during 2000?

Refer to the facts in QS 19-4. How much cash was paid for merchandise during 2000?

QS 19-5
Computing cash paid for merchandise
LO 6

QS 19-6

Computing cash paid for expenses

LO 6

Refer to the facts in QS 19-4. How much cash was paid for operating expenses during 2000?

QS 19-7

Computing cash from an asset sale

LO 3, 8

Refer to the facts in QS 19-4 and assume furniture that cost $54,000 is sold at its book value and all furniture acquisitions are for cash. What is the cash inflow related to the sale of furniture?

QS 19-8

Computing cash paid for dividends

LO 8

Refer to the facts in QS 19-4 and assume all shares are issued for cash. How much cash is paid for dividends?

QS 19-9

Computing cash from operations (indirect)

LO 7

Refer to the facts in QS 19-4. Using the indirect method, compute cash provided or used from operating activities.

QS 19-10

Analyzing sources and uses of cash

LO 9, 10

(in thousands)	Foxtail	Spiral	Tetris
Cash provided (used) by operating activities	$80,000	$70,000	$ (34,000)
Cash provided (used) by investing activities:			
Proceeds from sale of operating assets			36,000
Purchase of operating assets	(38,000)	(35,000)	
Cash provided (used) by financing activities:			
Proceeds from issuance of debt			33,000
Repayment of debt	(7,000)		
Net increase (decrease) in cash	$35,000	$35,000	$ 35,000
Average assets	$800,000	$650,000	$400,000

Required

1. Which of the three competitors is in the strongest position as indicted by their comparative cash flow statements?

2. Compare the strength of Foxtail's cash flow on total assets ratio to Spiral's.

QS 19-11A

Explaining noncash accounts on a spreadsheet

LO 5

When a spreadsheet for a statement of cash flows is prepared, all changes in noncash balance sheet accounts are explained using the spreadsheet. Explain how we can use noncash balance sheet accounts to account for cach.

The following events occurred during the year. Assuming that the company uses the direct method of reporting cash provided by operating activities, indicate the proper accounting treatment for each event by placing an *x* in the appropriate column.

Exercises

Exercise 19-1
Classifying transactions on statement of cash flows (direct)

LO 2, 3

	Statement of Cash Flows			Footnote Describing Noncash Investing and Financing Activities	Not Reported on Statement or in Footnote
	Operating Activities	Investing Activities	Financing Activities		
a. Borrowed cash from the bank by signing a nine-month note payable.					
b. Paid cash to purchase a patent.					
c. A six-month note receivable was accepted in exchange for a building that had been used in operations.					
d. Long-term bonds payable were retired by issuing common shares.					
e. Recorded amortization expense on all capital assets.					
f. A cash dividend that was declared in a previous period was paid in the current period.					
g. Surplus merchandise inventory was sold for cash.					

Use the following information about the 2000 cash flows of Ulrich Company to prepare a statement of cash flows using the direct method and a footnote describing noncash investing and financing activities.

Exercise 19-2
Organizing the statement of cash flows and supporting footnote

LO 2, 3, 4

Cash and cash equivalents balance, December 31, 1999	$25,000
Cash and cash equivalents balance, December 31, 2000	70,000
Cash received as interest	2,500
Cash paid for salaries	72,500
Bonds payable retired by issuing common shares	
(there was no gain or loss on the retirement)	187,500
Cash paid to retire long-term notes payable	125,000
Cash received from sale of equipment	61,250
Cash borrowed on six-month note payable	25,000
Land purchased and financed by long-term note payable	106,250
Cash paid for store equipment	23,750
Cash dividends paid	15,000
Cash paid for other expenses	40,000
Cash received from customers	485,000
Cash paid for merchandise	252,500

Exercise 19-3

Computing cash flows

LO 6

For each of the following cases, use the information provided about the 1999 operations of Milwood Company to compute the required cash flow information:

Case A: Compute cash paid for salaries:

Salaries expense	$ 51,000
Salaries payable, January 1	3,150
Salaries payable, December 31	3,750

Case B: Compute cash received from customers:

Sales revenue	$510,000
Accounts receivable, January 1	25,200
Accounts receivable, December 31	34,800

Case C: Compute cash paid for insurance:

Insurance expense	$ 68,400
Prepaid insurance, January 1	11,400
Prepaid insurance, December 31	17,100

Exercise 19-4

Computing cash flows

LO 6

In each of the following cases, use the information provided about the 1999 operations of Roche Company to compute the required cash flow information:

Case A: Compute cash received from interest:

Interest revenue	$ 34,000
Interest receivable, January 1	3,000
Interest receivable, December 31	3,600

Case B: Compute cash paid for rent:

Rent expense	$ 40,800
Rent payable, January 1	8,800
Rent payable, December 31	7,200

Case C: Compute cash paid for merchandise:

Cost of goods sold	$528,000
Merchandise inventory, January 1	159,600
Accounts payable, January 1	67,800
Merchandise inventory, December 31	131,400
Accounts payable, December 31	84,000

Exercise 19-5

Cash flows from operating activities (direct)

LO 6

Use the following income statement and information about changes in noncash current assets and current liabilities to present the cash flows from operating activities using the direct method:

RYLANDER COMPANY
Income Statement
For Year Ended December 31, 1999

Sales		$ 1,818,000
Cost of goods sold		891,000
Gross profit from sales		$ 927,000
Operating expenses:		
Salaries expense	$248,535	
Amortization expense	43,200	
Rent expense	48,600	
Amortization expense, patents	5,400	
Utilities expense	19,125	364,860
Total		$ 562,140
Gain on sale of equipment		7,200
Net income		$ 569,340

Changes in current asset and current liability accounts during the year, all of which related to operating activities, were as follows:

Accounts receivable	$40,500 increase
Merchandise inventory	27,000 increase
Accounts payable	13,500 decrease
Salaries payable	4,500 decrease

Refer to the information about Rylander Company presented in Exercise 19-5. Use the indirect method and compute the cash provided (or used) by operating activities.

Exercise 19-6
Cash flows from operating activities (indirect)

LO 7

Eden Company's 1999 income statement showed the following: net income, $364,000; amortization expense, building, $45,000; amortization expense, equipment, $8,200; and gain on sale of capital assets, $7,000. An examination of the company's current assets and current liabilities showed that the following changes occurred because of operating activities: accounts receivable decreased $18,100; merchandise inventory decreased $52,000; prepaid expenses increased $3,700; accounts payable decreased $9,200; other payables increased $1,400. Use the indirect method to compute the cash flow from operating activities.

Exercise 19-7
Cash flows from operating activities (indirect)

LO 7

The following events occurred during the year. Assuming that the company uses the indirect method of reporting cash provided by operating activities, indicate the proper accounting treatment for each event listed below by placing an *x* in the appropriate column.

Exercise 19-8
Classifying transactions on statement of cash flows (indirect)

LO 2, 7

	Statement of Cash Flows			Footnote Describing Noncash Investing and Financing Activities	Not Reported on Statement or in Footnote
	Operating Activities	Investing Activities	Financing Activities		
a. Sold capital equipment at a loss.	____	____	____	____	____
b. Recorded amortization expense.	____	____	____	____	____
c. Income taxes payable increased by 15% from prior year.	____	____	____	____	____
d. Declared and paid a cash dividend.	____	____	____	____	____
e. Paid cash to purchase merchandise inventory.	____	____	____	____	____
f. Land for a new plant was purchased by issuing common shares.	____	____	____	____	____
g. Accounts receivable decreased during the year.	____	____	____	____	____

Exercise 19-9
Preparation of statement of cash flows (direct)
LO 5, 6, 9

The following summarized journal entries show the total debits and credits to the Pyramid Corporation's Cash account for the year 2000.

Part 1. Use the information to prepare a statement of cash flows for the year 2000. The cash provided (or used) by operating activities should be presented according to the direct method. In the statement, identify the entry that records each item of cash flow. Assume that the beginning balance of cash was $133,200.

a.	Cash	1,440,000	
	Common Shares No-Par Value		1,440,000
	Issued common shares for cash.		
b.	Cash	2,400,000	
	Notes Payable		2,400,000
	Borrowed cash with a note payable.		
c.	Purchases	480,000	
	Cash		480,000
	Purchased merchandise for cash.		
d.	Accounts Payable	1,200,000	
	Cash		1,200,000
	Paid for credit purchases of merchandise.		
e.	Wages Expense	600,000	
	Cash		600,000
	Paid wages to employees.		
f.	Rent Expense	420,000	
	Cash		420,000
	Paid rent for buildings.		
g.	Cash	3,000,000	
	Sales		3,000,000
	Made cash sales to customers.		
h.	Cash	1,800,000	
	Accounts Receivable		1,800,000
	Collected accounts from credit customers.		
i.	Machinery	2,136,000	
	Cash		2,136,000
	Purchased machinery for cash.		
j.	Investments	2,160,000	
	Cash		2,160,000
	Purchased investments for cash.		
k.	Interest Expense	216,000	
	Notes Payable	384,000	
	Cash		600,000
	Paid notes and accrued interest.		
l.	Cash	206,400	
	Dividends Earned		206,400
	Collected dividends from investments.		
m.	Cash	210,000	
	Loss on Sale of Investments	30,000	
	Investments		240,000
	Sold investments for cash.		
n.	Cash	720,000	
	Accumulated Amortization, Machinery	420,000	
	Machinery		960,000
	Gain on Sale of Machinery		180,000
	Sold machinery for cash.		

o.	Common Dividend Payable	510,000	
	Cash		510,000
	Paid cash dividends to shareholders.		
p.	Income Taxes Payable	480,000	
	Cash		480,000
	Paid income taxes owed for the year.		
q.	Common Shares	228,000	
	Cash		228,000
	Purchased and retired common shares for cash.		

Part 2. Consult the statement of cash flows you have prepared for Part 1 and answer the following questions:

1. Of the three activity sections (operating, investing, or financing), which section shows the largest cash flow for the year?
2. What is the purpose of the largest investing cash outflow for the year?
3. Are the proceeds larger from issuing debt or equity for the year?
4. Did the company have a net cash inflow or outflow from borrowing activity in 2000?

Part 1. Use the Benton, Inc. financial statements and supplementary information given to prepare a statement of cash flows for the year ended June 30, 2000, using the direct method.

Exercise 19-10
Preparation of statement of cash flows (direct)

LO 5, 6, 10

BENTON INC. Comparative Balance Sheet June 30, 2000		
Assets	**2000**	**1999**
Cash	$ 85,800	$ 45,000
Accounts receivable (net)	70,000	52,000
Inventory	66,800	96,800
Prepaid expenses	5,400	5,200
Equipment	130,000	120,000
Accumulated amortization, furniture	(28,000)	(10,000)
Total assets	$330,000	$309,000
Liabilities and Shareholders' Equity		
Accounts payable	$ 26,000	$ 32,000
Wages payable	7,000	16,000
Income taxes payable	2,400	3,600
Notes payable (long-term)	40,000	70,000
Common shares, no-par value	230,000	180,000
Retained earnings	24,600	7,400
Total liabilities and shareholders' equity	$330,000	$309,000

Additional information follows:

a. The note is retired at carrying value.
b. The only changes affecting retained earning during 2000 are net income and cash dividends paid.
c. New equipment is acquired during 2000 for $58,600.
d. Sold equipment costing $48,600 for a $2,000 gain.
e. Prepaid expenses and wages expense affect other expenses on the Income Statement.
f. All sales and purchases of merchandise were on credit.

Part 2. Compute the cash flow on total assets ratio for Benton, Inc. for the fiscal year 2000.

BENTON INC. Income Statement For Year Ended June 30, 2000		
Sales		$668,000
Cost of goods sold		412,000
Gross profit		$256,000
Operating expenses:		
Amortization expense	$58,600	
Other expenses	67,000	
Total operating expenses		125,600
Net income from operations		$130,400
Income taxes		45,640
Gain on sale of equipment		2,000
Net income		$ 86,760

Problems

Problem 19-1
Statement of cash flows
(direct method)

LO 5, 6

Infinity Corporation's balance sheet and income statement are as follows:

INFINITY CORPORATION Comparative Balance Sheet December 31, 2000	December 31	
Assets	**2000**	**1999**
Cash	$ 174,000	$117,000
Accounts receivable	93,000	81,000
Merchandise inventory	609,000	534,000
Equipment	333,000	297,000
Accumulated amortization, equipment	(156,000)	(102,000)
Totals	$1,053,000	$927,000
Liabilities and Shareholders' Equity		
Accounts payable	$ 69,000	$ 96,000
Income taxes payable	27,000	24,000
Common shares, no-par value	780,000	720,000
Retained earnings	177,000	87,000
Totals	$1,053,000	$927,000

INFINITY CORPORATION Income Statement For Year Ended December 31, 2000		
Sales		$1,992,000
Cost of goods sold		1,194,000
Gross profit		$ 798,000
Operating expenses:		
Amortization expense	$ 54,000	
Other expenses	501,000	
Total operating expenses		555,000
Income from operations		$ 243,000
Income taxes		42,000
Net income		$ 201,000

Other information regarding Infinity: (1) all sales were credit sales, (2) all credits to accounts receivable in a period were receipts from customers, (3) all purchases of merchandise were on credit, (4) all debits to accounts payable in a period resulted from payments for merchandise, (5) other operating expenses were cash expenses, and (6) the decrease in income taxes payable was for payment of taxes.

Additional information regarding Infinity's activities during the year 2000:

a. Purchased equipment for $36,000 cash.

b. Issued 12,000 common shares at $5 per share.

c. Declared and paid $111,000 of cash dividends.

Required

Prepare a statement of cash flows that reports the cash inflows and outflows from operating activities according to the direct method. Show your supporting calculations.

Refer to Infinity Corporation's balance sheets presented in Problem 19-1.

Required

Prepare a statement of cash flows that reports the cash inflows and outflows from operating activities according to the indirect method.

Refer to the facts about Infinity Corporation presented in Problem 19-1.

Required

Prepare a statement of cash flows using a spreadsheet that follows the indirect method of computing cash flows from operating activities. Identify the debits and credits in the Analysis of Changes columns with letters that correspond to the following list of transactions and events:

a. Net Income is $201,000

b. Accounts receivable increased.

c. Merchandise inventory increased

d. Accounts payable decreased.

e. Income taxes payable increased

f. Amortization expense is $54,000.

g. Purchased equipment for $36,000.

h. Issued 12,000 shares at $5 per share.

i. Declared and paid $111,000 of cash dividends.

Comptex Company's balance sheet and income statement are as follows:

COMPTEX COMPANY
Comparative Balance Sheet
December 31, 2000

	December 31	
Assets	**2000**	**1999**
Cash	$ 53,875	$ 76,625
Accounts receivable	65,000	49,625
Merchandise inventory	273,750	252,500
Prepaid expenses	5,375	6,250
Equipment	159,500	110,000
Accumulated amortization, equipment	(34,625)	(44,000)
Totals	$522,875	$451,000
Liabilities and Shareholders' Equity		
Accounts payable	$ 88,125	$116,625
Short-term notes payable	10,000	6,250
Long-term notes payable	93,750	53,750
Common shares, no-par value	201,250	156,250
Retained earnings	129,750	118,125
Totals	$522,875	$451,000

Check Figure Net cash provided by operating activities, $144,000

Problem 19-2
Statement of cash flows (indirect method)
LO 5, 7

Check Figure Net cash provided by operating activities, $144,000

Problem 19-3A
Cash flows spreadsheet (indirect method)
LO 5, 7, 11

Check Figure Analysis of Changes column totals, $579,000

Problem 19-4
Statement of cash flows (direct method)
LO 5, 6, 9

COMPTEX COMPANY
Income Statement
For Year Ended December 31, 2000

Sales		$496,250
Cost of goods sold		250,000
Gross profit		$246,250
Operating expenses:		
Amortization expense	$ 18,750	
Other expenses	136,500	
Total operating expenses		155,250
Loss on sale of equipment		5,125
Income from operations		$ 85,875
Income taxes		12,125
Net income		$ 73,750

Comptex Company recently completed its year 2000 operations. Other information regarding Comptex: (1) all sales were credit sales, (2) all credits to accounts receivable in the period were receipts from customers, (3) purchases of merchandise were on credit, (4) all debits to accounts payable in the period resulted from payments for merchandise, (5) the income tax expenses were cash expenses, and (6) the other expenses were paid in advance and were initially debited to Prepaid expenses.

Additional information regarding Comptex's activities during 2000:

a. Loss on sale of equipment is $5,125.

b. Sold equipment costing $46,875, with accumulated amortization of $28,125, for $13,625.

c. Purchased equipment costing $96,375 by paying cash of $25,000 and signing a long-term note payable for the balance.

d. Borrowed $3,750 by signing a short-term note payable.

e. Paid $31,375 to reduce a long-term note payable.

f. Issued 2,500 common shares for cash at $18 per share.

g. Declared and paid cash dividends of $62,125.

Required

Preparation component:

1. Prepare a statement of cash flows that reports the cash inflows and outflows from operating activities according to the direct method. Show supporting calculations. Also prepare a footnote describing noncash investing and financing activities.

Analysis component:

2. Analyze and discuss the information contained in your answer to requirement 1, giving special attention to the wisdom of the dividend payment.

Refer to Comptex Company's balance sheets presented in Problem 19-4.

Required

Prepare a statement of cash flows that reports the cash inflows and outflows from operating activities according to the indirect method.

Check Figure Net cash provided by operating activities, $33,375

Problem 19-5
Statement of cash flows (indirect method)

LO 5, 7

Check Figure Net cash provided by operating activities, $33,375

Refer to the facts about Comptex Company presented in Problem 19-4 and Problem 19-5.

Required

Prepare a statement of cash flows spreadsheet that follows the indirect method of computing cash flows from operating activities. Identify the debits and credits in the Analysis of Changes columns with letters that correspond to the transactions presented in Problem 19-5.

Problem 19-6A
Cash flows spreadsheet
(indirect method)

LO 5, 7, 8, 11

Check Figure Analysis of
Changes column totals,
$515,375

Tanaka Company's balance sheet and income statement are as follows:

**Alternate
Problems**

Problem 19-1A
Statement of cash flows
(direct method)

LO 5, 6

TANAKA COMPANY
Comparative Balance Sheet
December 31, 2000

	December 31	
	2000	1999
Assets		
Cash	$ 53,925	$ 31,800
Accounts receivable	19,425	23,250
Merchandise inventory	175,350	139,875
Equipment	105,450	76,500
Accumulated amortization, equipment	(48,300)	(30,600)
Totals	$305,850	$240,825
Liabilities and Shareholders' Equity		
Accounts payable	$ 38,475	$ 35,625
Income taxes payable	4,500	6,750
Common shares, no-par value	207,000	165,000
Retained earnings	55,875	33,450
Totals	$305,850	$240,825

TANAKA COMPANY
Income Statement
For Year Ended December 31, 2000

Sales		$609,750
Cost of goods sold		279,000
Gross profit		$330,750
Operating expenses:		
Amortization expense	$ 17,700	
Other expenses	179,775	
Total operating expenses		197,475
Income from operations		$133,275
Income taxes		44,850
Net income		$ 88,425

Other information regarding Tanaka: (1) all sales were credit sales, (2) all credits to accounts receivable in the period were receipts from customers, (3) purchases of merchandise were on credit, (4) all debits to accounts payable in the period resulted from payments for merchandise, (5) the other operating expenses were cash expenses, and (6) the decrease in income taxes payable was for payment of taxes.

Additional information regarding Tanaka's activities during the year 2000:

a. Purchased equipment for $28,950 cash.

b. Issued 3,000 common shares at $14 per share.

c. Declared and paid $66,000 of cash dividends.

Required

Prepare a statement of cash flows that reports the cash inflows and outflows from operating activities according to the direct method. Show your supporting calculations.

Problem 19-2A
Statement of cash flows (indirect method)

LO 5, 7

Refer to Tanaka Company's balance sheets presented in Problem 19-1A.

Required

Prepare a statement of cash flows that reports the cash inflows and outflows from operating activities according to the indirect method.

Problem 19-3A^A
Cash flows spreadsheet (indirect method)

LO 7, 8, 11

Refer to the facts about Tanaka Company presented in Problem 19-1A.

Required

Prepare a statement of cash flows using a spreadsheet that follows the indirect method of computing cash flows from operating activities. Identify the debits and credits in the Analysis of Changes columns with letters that correspond to the following list of transactions and events:

a. Net income is $88,425
b. Accounts receivable increased.
c. Merchandise inventory increased.
d. Accounts payable decreased
e. Income taxes payable increased.

f. Amortization expense is $17,700.
g. Purchased equipment for $28,950.
h. Issued 3,000 shares at $14 per share.
i. Declared and paid $66,000 of cash dividends.

Problem 19-4A
Statement of cash flows (direct method)

LO 5, 6, 9

Kirby Corporation's balance sheet and income statement are as follows:

KIRBY CORPORATION Comparative Balance Sheet December 31, 2000		
	December 31	
	2000	**1999**
Assets		
Cash	$136,500	$ 71,550
Accounts receivable	74,100	90,750
Merchandise inventory	454,500	490,200
Prepaid expenses	17,100	19,200
Equipment	278,250	216,000
Accumulated amortization, equipment	(108,750)	(93,000)
Totals	$851,700	$794,700
Liabilities and Shareholders' Equity		
Accounts payable	$117,450	$123,450
Short-term notes payable	17,250	11,250
Long-term notes payable	112,500	82,500
Common shares, no-par value	483,000	450,000
Retained earnings	121,500	127,500
Totals	$851,700	$794,700

KIRBY CORPORATION Income Statement For Year Ended December 31, 2000		
Sales		$1,083,000
Cost of goods sold		585,000
Gross profit		$ 498,000
Operating expenses:		
Amortization expense	$ 36,600	
Other expenses	392,850	
Total operating expenses		429,450
Loss on sale of equipment		2,100
Income from operations		$ 66,450
Income taxes		9,450
Net income		$ 57,000

Kirby Company recently completed its year 2000 operations. Other information regarding Kirby: (1) all sales were credit sales, (2) all credits to accounts receivable in the period were receipts from customers, (3) purchases of merchandise were on credit, (4) all debits to accounts payable in the period resulted from payments for merchandise, (5) the decrease in income taxes payable resulted from cash payments (6) the other expenses were paid in advance and were initially debited to prepaid expenses.

Additional information regarding Kirby's activities during 2000:

a. Loss on sale of equipment is $2,100.

b. Sold equipment costing $51,000, with accumulated amortization of $20,850, for 28,050.

c. Purchased equipment costing $113,250 by paying cash of $38,250 and signing a long-term note payable for the balance.

d. Borrowed $6,000 by signing a short-term note payable.

e. Paid $45,000 to reduce a long-term note payable.

f. Issued 3,000 common shares for cash at $11 per share.

g. Declared and paid cash dividends of $63,000.

Required

Preparation component:

1. Prepare a statement of cash flows that reports the cash inflows and outflows from operating activities according to the direct method. Show supporting calculations. Also prepare a footnote describing noncash investing and financing activities.

Analysis component:

2. Analyze and discuss the information contained in your answer to requirement 1, giving special attention to the wisdom of the dividend payment.

Refer to Kirby Corporation's balance sheets presented in Problem 19-4A.

Problem 19-5A
Statement of cash flows
(indirect method)

LO 5, 7, 8

Required

Prepare a statement of cash flows that reports the cash inflows and outflows from operating activities according to the indirect method.

Refer to the facts about Kirby Corporation presented in Problem 19-4A and Problem 19-5A.

Problem 19-6AA
Cash flows spreadsheet
(indirect method)

LO 5, 7, 8, 11

Required

Prepare a statement of cash flows spreadsheet that follows the indirect method of computing cash flows from operating activities. Identify the debits and credits in the Analysis of Changes columns with letters that correspond to the transactions presented in Problem 19-5A.

Analytical and Review Problems

A & R 19-1

Morgan Corporation earned a $168,000 net income during 2000. Machinery was sold for $232,000 and a $48,000 loss on the sale was recorded. Machinery purchases totalled $660,000 including a July purchase for which a $160,000 promissory note was issued. Bonds were retired at their face value, and the issuance of new common shares produced an infusion of cash. Morgan's comparative balance sheets were as follows (in thousands):

MORGAN CORPORATION
Comparative Balance Sheet
December 31, 2000

	December 31	
	2000	1999
Assets		
Cash	$ 208	$ 168
Accounts receivable	392	444
Merchandise inventory	648	620
Machinery	2,700	2,520
Accumulated amortization, machinery	(380)	(420)
Totals	$3,568	$3,332
Liabilities and Shareholders' Equity		
Accounts payable	$ 476	$ 572
Notes payable	544	420
Dividends payable	64	40
Bonds payable	456	640
Common shares, no-par value	1,400	1,120
Retained earnings	628	540
Totals	$3,568	$3,332

1. What was Morgan's amortization expense in 2,000?
2. What was the amount of cash flow from operations?
3. What was the amount of cash flow from investing activities?
4. What was the amount of dividends declared? Paid?
5. By what amount would you expect the total sources of cash to differ from the total uses of cash?
6. What was the amount of cash flow from financing activities?

A & R 19-2

For each item, identify both the dollar amount and its classification—that is, whether it would appear as a positive or a negative adjustment to net income in the calculation of cash flow from operations or as some other source or use of cash.

1. Declared a $22,000 cash dividend; paid $19,000 during the year.
2. Sold land that cost $95,000 for $120,000 cash.
3. Sold for cash 2,000 shares for $14 a share.
4. Bought machinery for $37,000 in exchange for a note due in eight months.
5. Bought a computer that had a fair value of $140,000 by giving in exchange real estate that had cost $95,000 in an earlier period.
6. Equipment amortization, $56,000.
7. Issued for cash on December 31, 1998, 10-year, 10% $500,000 bonds at a $24,000 discount.
8. Bought its own shares for $13,500.
9. Paid a lawyer $13,500 for services performed, billed, and recorded correctly in 1997.
10. Reported net income of $86,000 for the year ended December 31, 1998.

BEYOND THE NUMBERS

Refer to the financial statements and related information for **Alliance** in Appendix I. Answer the following questions by analyzing the information in the report:

1. Alliance's annual report contains a consolidated statement of changes in financial position that reports cash flow information. Was this statement of cash flows prepared according to the direct method or the indirect method?

2. During each of the fiscal years 1997 and 1996 was cash provided by operating activities more or less than net income?

3. How much was Alliance's gain on sale of investments? How does it affect the reporting of cash flows?

4. What was the net amount spent on investing activities? How were these investments financed?

5. Obtain access to Alliance's annual report for fiscal years ending after March 31, 1997. This access may be through a securities investment firm or you may gain access to annual report information at the following Web site: **http://www.sedar.com**. Since March 31, 1997, what have been Alliance's largest cash outflows and inflows in the investing and financing sections of the cash flow statement?

Reporting in Action

LO 2, 6, 7, 9

Both **Atlantis** and **Alliance** are actively engaged in producing and broadcasting filmed entertainment. Key comparative figures ($ millions) for these two organizations follow:

Key Figures	Alliance		Atlantis	
	1997	**1996**	**1997**	**1996**
Operating cash flows	$240.7	$174.5	$136.9	$136.9
Total assets	$353.7	$238.8	$333.2	$334.8

* Alliance figures are from the annual reports for the fiscal years ended March 31,1997, and 1996.
Atlantis figures are from the annual reports for the fiscal years ended December 31, 1996, and 1995.

Comparative Analysis

LO 9, 10

Required

1. Compute the cash flow on total assets ratio for (a) Alliance for 1997 and (b) Atlantis for 1997.

2. What does the cash flow on total assets ratio measure?

3. Which company has the higher cash flow on total assets ratio?

4. Does the cash flow on total assets ratio provide any information as to the quality of earnings of a firm?

5. What are the two largest sources of cash for Alliance in 1997? For Atlantis in 1997?

Wendy Geiger is working late on a Friday night in preparation for a meeting with her banker early Monday morning. Her business is just finishing its fourth quarter. In the first year the business experienced negative cash flows from operations. In the second and third years, cash flows from operations turned positive. Unfortunately, her inventory costs rose significantly in year four and her net income will probably be down about 25% after this year's adjusting entries. Wendy is hoping to secure a line of credit from her banker which will be a nice financing buffer. From prior experience with her banker she knows a focus of the meeting on Monday will be cash flows from operations. The banker will scrutinize the cash flow numbers for years one through four and will want a projected number for year five. Wendy knows that a steady upward progression of cash flows in years one through four will really help her case for securing the line of credit. Wendy decides to use her discretion as owner of the business and proposes several adjusting entries and business actions which will help turn her cash flow number in year four from negative to positive.

Ethics Challenge

LO 9

Required

1. Identify three possible entries or business actions Wendy might use to improve the cash flow from operations number on the statement of cash flows for year four.

2. Comment on the ethics and possible consequences of Wendy's decision to propose the adjustments/actions for year four.

Communicating in Practice
LO 1, 4

Your friend, Maddy Massola, recently completed his second year in his own business. Maddy just received annual financial statements from his accountant. Maddy says he finds the income statement and balance sheet quite informative but he does not understand the statement of cash flows. He says the first section is particularly confusing and he cannot get much beyond it. He says it contains a lot of additions and subtractions that do not make sense to him. Maddy added "I'm not concerned. It's probably just one of those extra forms accountants are required to fill out. The Income Statement tells me the business was more profitable than last year and that is what's most important. If I want to know about cash or cash changes, I can look at the Balance Sheets from this year and last."

Required

Write a memo to your friend to explain the purpose of the statement of cash flows. Comment on why he found the first section so confusing and suggest what he might do to rectify this problem.

Taking It to the Net
LO 9

Use the Sedar database at **http://www.sedar.com** to access the December 31, 1997, annual report for **Canadian Pacific Corporation**. Locate this company's consolidated statement of changes in financial position for the years ended December 31, 1997, 1996, and 1995. (Note that under the current accounting recommendations this statement would be called a statement of cash flows.) Answer the following questions.

1. Which method, direct or indirect, does Canadian Pacific use to prepare a statement of cash flow?

2. What is the largest adjustment needed to reconcile cash flow from operations to net income in each of the two years?

3. What is the largest investment requiring cash in each of the three years presented?

4. For the fiscal year ended December 31, 1997, did Canadian Pacific issue a long-term debt? Was any long-term debt repaid during 1997?

Teamwork in Action
LO 1, 4, 9, 6, 7

The aim of this activity is to provide team support for "putting it all together" with the statement of cash flows. After completing *each* of the three sections below, members should report to the team. Team members are to confirm or correct teammate's responses.

1. Each member of the team is to prepare notes to present a response to one of the following questions about the statement of cash flows:
   a. What is this statement's reporting objectives?
   b. What methods or formats can be used to prepare it? Describe each by identifying their similarities and differences.
   c. What steps are followed to prepare it?
   d. What kinds of analysis are often made from its information?

2. Each member of the team is to prepare notes to identify *and explain* the formula for computing cash flows from operating activities using the direct method for one of the following items:
   a. Cash receipts from customers
   b. Cash paid for merchandise
   c. Cash paid for wages and operating expenses
   d. Cash paid for interest and taxes

3. Each member of the team is to prepare notes to identify *and explain* the adjustment from net income to cash flows from operating activities using the indirect method for one of the following items:

   a. Noncash operating revenues and expenses

   b. Gains and Losses

   c. Increases and decreases in current assets

   d. Increases and decreases in current liabilities

Visit the Motley Fool Investment Web site at **http://www.fool.com**. Click on the sidebar link entitled "School." Select the link "Valuation: Principles and Practice." How does the Fool's school define cash flow? Per the school's instruction why do analysts focus on earnings before interest and taxes (EBIT)? Visit other links at the Web site that may interest you such as "A Journey Through the Balance Sheet" or find out what the "Fool's Ratio" is.

Hitting the Road

LO 1

Read the article, "Are profits shakier than they look?" in the August 5, 1996, issue of *Business Week*.

Business Break

Required

1. How is the free cash flow number derived from cash flow from operations?

2. How does **Allied's** explanation of their cash concerns differ from the analyst Jeff Fotta's interpretation?

3. How does Fotta conduct the dual cash flow analysis?

20

Analyzing Financial Statements

▶ A Look Back

Chapter 19 focused on reporting and analyzing cash inflows and cash outflows. We explained how to prepare and interpret the statement of cash flows.

▶ A Look at This Chapter

This chapter emphasizes the analysis and interpretation of financial statement information. We learn to apply horizontal, vertical, and ratio analyses to better understand company performance and financial condition.

▶ A Look Forward

Chapter 21 introduces us to managerial accounting. We discuss its purposes, concepts, and roles in helping managers gather and organize information for decision making. Management principles are also explained.

Chapter Outline

▶ **Basics of Analysis**
- Purpose of Analysis
- Building Blocks of Analysis
- Information for Analysis
- Standards for Comparisons
- Tools of Analysis

▶ **Horizontal Analysis**
- Comparative Statements
- Trend Analysis

▶ **Vertical Analysis**
- Common-Size Statements
- Common-Size Graphics

▶ **Ratio Analysis**
- Liquidity and Efficiency
- Solvency
- Profitability
- Market
- Summary of Ratios
- Analysis Reporting

Say It Ain't So!

Beardstown—Is nothing sacred? The Beardstown Ladies, those home-spun, grandmotherly investors whose supposed success created a mini-industry, are being called frauds. The ladies may have fudged the figures.

With three books to their name in North American bookstores, the Beardstown Ladies are a fixture on the lecture circuit, riding a bull market in homespun advice. But their best advice might have been "Know your accounting." The ladies' *Common-Sense Investment Guide* claims an annual return of 23.4% over the decade covered in the book. But this return is computed by averaging the ladies two best years—1991 and 1992—and ignoring the other eight years.

Oops, that's not the way it's done. This would mean their total returns were nowhere near as great as claimed. The accounting firm Price Waterhouse, which did an audit of the ladies' books, says the actual return over the period covered in the book is 9.1%. This figure is well below the 23.4% claimed by the ladies, and less than the 15% return of the overall stock market for the same period.

Experts in accounting and analysis are not surprised. The ladies' investment strategy was simple and not fundamentally sound. They pooled their money and bought shares of big, low-risk companies, then watched as the share price rose with the general increase in the stock market. An index fund would have returned about double that of the ladies' return over the same period.

Still, their apparent success and their folksiness make them popular guests on television shows and brought some work as money manage-ment experts. Their first book sold more than 800,000 copies in Canada and the U.S. Senior partner Betty Sinnock says she is "just sick" about what's happened. A piece of homespun advice they didn't give—if it looks too good to be true, it probably is. Source: *Globe and Mail*, May 30, 1998; *Fortune* Web site (March 30, 1998), Paul Krugman "There'll Always Be a Soros"; CNN Web site, "Moneyweek" (Aired March 1, 1998); CNN Web site, "Your Money" (Aired February 28, 1998); *Wisconsin State Journal* (February 28, 1998) "Well! I never! Beardstown Ladies didn't mean to deceive"; and CNN Web site, "Moneyline" (Aired March 17, 1998).]

Learning Objectives

LO 1   Explain the purpose of analysis.

LO 2   Identify the building blocks of analysis.

LO 3   Describe standards for comparisons in analysis.

LO 4   Identify the tools of analysis.

LO 5   Explain and apply methods of horizontal analysis.

LO 6   Describe and apply methods of vertical analysis.

LO 7   Define and apply ratio analysis.

LO 8   Summarize and report results of analysis.

CHAPTER PREVIEW

This chapter shows us how to use the information in financial statements to evaluate the financial performance and condition of a company. We describe the purpose of analysis, its basic building blocks, the information available, standards for comparisons, and tools of analysis. Three major analysis tools are emphasized—horizontal analysis, vertical analysis, and ratio analysis. We illustrate the application of each of these tools using Ralco's financial statements. This chapter also expands and organizes the ratio analyses introduced at the end of each of the prior nineteen chapters. Understanding financial statement analysis is crucial to sound business decision making. Its proper application avoids our reliance on little old ladies from Beardstown.

Basics of Analysis

Financial statement analysis is the application of analytical tools to general-purpose financial statements and related *data* for making business decisions. It involves transforming data into useful information. Financial statement analysis reduces our reliance on hunches, guesses, and intuition. It reduces our uncertainty in decision making. But it does not lessen the need for expert judgment. Instead, it provides us an effective and systematic basis for business decisions. This section describes the purpose of financial statement analysis, its information sources, the use of comparisons, and some issues in computations.

Purpose of Analysis

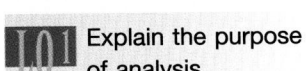 Explain the purpose of analysis.

The purpose of financial statement analysis is to help users make better business decisions. These users include decision makers both internal and external to the company.

Internal users of accounting information are those individuals involved in managing and operating the company. They include managers, officers, internal auditors, consultants, and many other important internal decision makers. Internal users make the strategic and operating decisions of a company. The purpose of financial statement analysis for these users is to provide information helpful in improving the company's efficiency or effectiveness in providing products or services.

External users of accounting information are *not* directly involved in running the company. They include shareholders, lenders, directors, customers, suppliers, regulators, lawyers, financial advisors, brokers and the press. Yet these users are affected by, and sometimes affect, the company's activities. External users rely on financial statement analysis to make better and more informed decisions in pursuing their own goals.

We can identify many examples of how financial statement analysis is used. Shareholders and creditors assess future company prospects for investing and lending decisions. A board of directors analyzes financial statements in monitoring management's decisions. Employees and unions use financial statements in labour negotiations. Suppliers use financial statements in establishing credit terms. Customers analyze financial statements in deciding whether to establish supply relationships. Public utilities set customer rates by analyzing financial statements. Auditors use financial statements in assessing the "fair presentation" of their clients' financial statement numbers. And analyst services such as *Dun & Bradstreet, Moody's,* and *Standard & Poor's* use financial statements in making buy-sell recommendations and setting credit ratings.

The common goal of all these users is to evaluate company performance. This includes evaluation of (1) past and current performance, (2) current financial position, and (3) future performance and risk.

Building Blocks of Analysis

Financial statement analysis focuses on one or more elements of a company's financial condition or performance. Our analysis emphasizes four areas of inquiry—with varying degrees of importance. These four areas are described and illustrated in this chapter and are considered the *building blocks* of financial statement analysis.

Identify the building blocks of analysis.

- *Liquidity and Efficiency*—ability to meet short-term obligations and to efficiently generate revenues.
- *Solvency*—ability to generate future revenues and meet long-term obligations.
- *Profitability*—ability to provide financial rewards sufficient to attract and retain financing.
- *Market*—ability to generate positive market expectations.

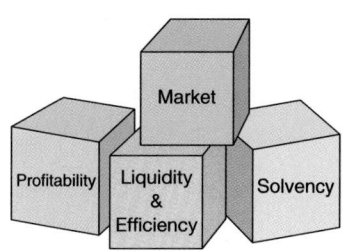

Applying the building blocks of financial statement analysis involves determining (1) the objectives of analysis, and (2) the relative emphasis among the building blocks. An investor, for instance, when evaluating the investment merit of common shares often emphasizes earnings and returns analyses. This involves assessing profitability and efficiency. But a thorough analysis requires an investor to assess other building blocks although with perhaps lesser emphasis. Attention to these other areas is necessary to assess risk exposure. This usually involves some analysis of liquidity and solvency. Further analysis can reveal important risks that outweigh earning power, and may lead to major changes in the financial statement analysis of a company.

We distinguish among these four building blocks to emphasize the different aspects of a company's financial condition or performance. Yet we must remember these areas of analysis are interrelated. For instance, a company's operating performance is affected by availability of financing and short-term liquidity conditions. Similarly, a company's credit standing is not limited to satisfactory short-term liquidity, but depends also on its profitability and efficiency in using assets. Early in our analysis, we need to tentatively determine the relative emphasis of each building block and their order of analysis. Emphasis and analysis can later change due to evidence collected.

Chips and Brokers
Blue chips is used to refer to shares of big, profitable companies. The term comes from poker—where the most valuable chips are the blue ones. *Brokers* execute orders to buy or sell shares. The term comes from wine retailers—individuals who broach (break) wine casks.

Did You Know?

Information for Analysis

We explained how decision makers such as managers, employees, directors, customers, suppliers, current and potential owners, current and potential lenders, brokers, regulatory authorities, lawyers, economists, labour unions, analysts, and consultants need to analyze financial statements. Some of these people such as managers and a few regulatory agencies are able to receive special financial reports prepared to meet their needs. But most must rely on general-purpose financial statements that companies publish periodically. **General-purpose financial statements** include the (1) income statement, (2) balance sheet, (3) statement of changes in shareholders' equity (or statement of retained earnings), (4) statement of cash flows, and (5) notes related to the statements.

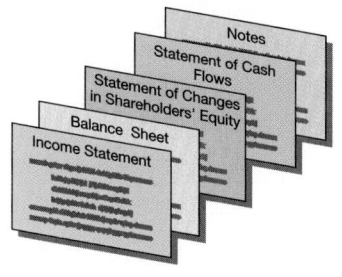

General-purpose financial statements are part of financial reporting. **Financial reporting** refers to the communication of relevant financial information to decision makers. It includes financial statements, but it also involves information from any filings with the securities commissions, news releases, shareholders' meetings, forecasts, management letters, auditor's report, and analyses published in annual reports. Financial reporting broadly refers to useful information for decision makers to make investment, credit, and other decisions. It should help users assess the amounts, timing, and uncertainty of future cash inflows and outflows.

One example of useful information outside the traditional financial statements is the Management Discussion and Analysis (MD&A) section. **Atlantis's** annual report in Appendix I provides us a typical example. The MD&A begins with a brief description of its television production and television distribution activities. It then proceeds with a discussion of operating results by summarizing its main revenues and expenses and net earnings. This is followed by a discussion of the company's financial position. The MD&A next examines liquidity and capital resources—roughly equivalent to investing and financing activities and ends with an outlook based on its positioning within the industry. While this analysis is not complete, it is an excellent starting point for us in understanding the business activities of a company.

Did You Know?

Data Web
Reviewing financial numbers used to involve mountains of paper in dark library basements. We can now do it from the convenience of our home via the Net. Many companies offer Web sites with free access and screening of numerous key financial numbers like earnings and sales. Most sites are updated daily with closing share prices. For instance, Standard & Poor's has information for more than 10,000 companies (**www.stockinfo.standardpoor.com**). [Source: *Business Week*, September 22, 1997.]

LO 3 Describe standards for comparisons in analysis.

Standards for Comparisons

When computing and interpreting analysis measures as part of our financial statement analysis, we need to decide whether these measures suggest good, bad, or average performance. To make these judgments, we need standards for comparisons. Standards for comparisons can include:

- *Intracompany.* The company under analysis provides standards for comparisons based on prior performance and relations between its financial items. **Atlantis's** current net income, for instance, can be compared with prior years' net income and its relation to revenues.
- *Competitor.* One or more direct competitors of the company under analysis can provide standards for comparisons. **Coca-Cola's** profit margin, for instance, can be compared with the profit margin of **PepsiCo.**
- *Industry.* Industry statistics can provide standards of comparisons. Published industry statistics are available from several services such as Dun & Bradstreet, Standard and Poor's, and Moody's.
- *Guidelines (Rules-of-Thumb).* General standards of comparisons can develop from past experiences. Examples are the 2 to 1 level for the current ratio or 1 to 1 level for the acid-test ratio. These guidelines, or rules-of-thumb, must be carefully applied since their context is often crucial.

All of these standards of comparisons are useful when properly applied. Yet analysis measures taken from a selected competitor or group of competitors are often the best standards of comparisons. Also, intracompany and industry measures are important parts of all analyses. Guidelines or rules-of-thumb should be applied with care, and then only if they seem reasonable in light of past experience and industry's norms.

> ## Flash back
>
> **1.** Who are the intended users of general-purpose financial statements?
> **2.** What statements are usually included in general-purpose financial statements published by corporations?
> **3.** Which of the following are not useful as a basis for comparison when analyzing ratios and turnovers? (a) companies operating in a different economy, (b) subjective standards from past experience, (c) rule-of-thumb standards, or (d) averages within a trade or industry.
> **4.** What basis of comparison for ratios is usually best?

Answers—pp. 968–969

Tools of Analysis

There are several tools of financial statement analysis. Three of the most common tools are:

 Identify the tools of analysis.

- ■ *Horizontal Analysis.* Tools comparing a company's financial condition and performance across time.
- ■ *Vertical Analysis.* Tools comparing a company's financial condition and performance to a base amount.
- ■ *Ratio Analysis.* Tools using key relations among financial statement items.

The remainder of this chapter describes these tools of analysis and how we apply them.

> **Ticker Prices**
> *Ticker prices* refer to a band of moving information on a computer or television screen carrying up-to-the-minute share prices. The terms comes from ticker tape—a one-inch wide strip of paper spewing share prices and transactions from a printer that ticked as it ran. While most of today's investors have never actually seen ticker tape, the term survives.

Did You Know?

Horizontal Analysis

Our analysis of a single financial item is important but is of limited value. Instead, important relations exist between items and across time, and our financial analysis needs to use this information. Much of financial statement analysis involves identifying and describing relations between items and groups of items and changes in those items. Horizontal analysis is a tool to evaluate changes in financial statement data *across time*.[1]

Comparative Statements

Our analysis of financial statement data is often helped by comparing amounts for two or more successive periods. **Comparative financial statements** are reports where financial amounts are placed side by side in columns on a single

Explain and apply methods of horizontal analysis.

---

[1] The term *horizontal analysis* arises from the left-to-right (or right-to-left) movement of our eyes as we review comparative financial statements across time.

statement for analysis purposes. Each financial statement can be presented in a *comparative format*. For instance, **Alliance's** *annual* report in Appendix I is a comparative statement based on three years of financial performance. This section explains how we compute dollar changes and percent changes in comparative statements and illustrates their application to the financial statements of **Ralco Corporation**.

Computation of Dollar Changes and Percent Changes

Comparing financial statements over relatively short time periods—two to three years—is often done by analyzing changes in line items. A change analysis usually includes an analysis of both changes in absolute dollar amounts as well as percent changes. Both analyses are relevant since dollar changes can sometimes yield large percent changes inconsistent with their importance. For instance, a 50% change from a base figure of $100 is less important than the same percent change from a base amount of $100,000 in the same statement. Reference to dollar amounts is necessary to retain a proper perspective and for assessing the importance of changes.

We compute the *dollar change* for a financial statement item as:

$$\text{Dollar change} = \text{Analysis period amount} - \text{Base period amount}$$

where *analysis period* is the point or period of time for the financial statements under analysis, and *base period* is the point or period of time for the financial statements used for comparison purposes. We commonly use the prior year as the base period.

We compute the *percent change* by dividing the dollar change by the base period amount, and then multiplying this quantity by 100:

$$\text{Percent change} = \frac{\text{Analysis period amount} - \text{Base period amount}}{\text{Base period amount}} \times 100$$

While we can always compute a dollar change, we must be aware of a few rules in working with percent changes. To illustrate, let's look at four separate cases in the chart below:

Case No.	Base Period	Analysis Period	Change Analysis Dollar	Change Analysis Percent
A	$(4,500)	$1,500	$6,000	—
B	2,000	(1,000)	(3,000)	—
C	—	8,000	8,000	—
D	10,000	-0-	(10,000)	(100%)

When a negative amount appears in the base period and a positive amount in the analysis period (or vice versa), we cannot compute a meaningful percent change; see cases A and B. Also, when there is no value in the base period, no percent change is computable; see case C. Finally, when an item has a value in the base period and zero in the next period, the decrease is 100 percent; see case D.

It is also common for horizontal analysis to compare amounts to average (or median[2]) values from prior periods. Comparing changes to average (or median)

---

[2] *Median* is the middle value in a group of numbers. For instance, if five prior years' incomes are (in 000s) $15, $19, $18, $20, and $22, their median value is $18. When there are two middle numbers, we can take their average. For instance, if four prior years' sales are (in 000s) $84, $91, $96, and $93, then the median is $92 (computed as the average of $91 and $93).

values computed over a number of years highlights unusual happenings, as average values smooth out erratic or unusual fluctuations. We also commonly round percents and ratios to one or two decimal places. But there is no uniform practice on this matter. Computations are as detailed as necessary. This is judged by whether or not they potentially affect users' decisions. Computations should not be excessively detailed so as to lose important relations among a mountain of decimal points.

Comparative Balance Sheet

One of the most useful comparative statements is the comparative balance sheet. It consists of amounts from two or more balance sheet dates arranged side by side. The usefulness of comparative financial statements is often improved by also showing each item's dollar change and percent change. This type of presentation highlights large dollar and percent changes for decision makers. Exhibit 20.1 shows the comparative balance sheet for Ralco.

Exhibit 20.1

Comparative Balance Sheet

RALCO CORPORATION **Comparative Balance Sheets** **Nov. 30, 19x8, and Nov. 30, 19x7**				
(in thousands)	**19X8**	**19X7**	**Amount of Increase or (Decrease) in 19X8**	**Percent of Increase or (Decrease) in 19X7**
Assets				
Current Assets:				
Cash and short-term investments ...	$ 85,618	$ 57,000	$28,618	50.2
Accounts receivable				
Trade	50,586	36,327	14,259	39.3
Other	2,264	2,185	79	3.6
Inventory	13,417	7,361	6,056	82.3
Prepaid expenses	1,348	812	536	66.0
Total current assets	153,233	103,685	49,548	47.8
Capital assets	38,189	28,605	9,584	33.5
Total assets	$191,422	$132,290	$59,132	44.7
Liabilities and Shareholders' Equity				
Current liabilities:				
Accounts payable	$ 8,487	$ 5,391	$ 3,096	57.4
Accrued liabilities	10,722	6,073	4,649	76.6
Income taxes payable	4,930	7,400	(2,470)	(33.4)
Total current liabilities	24,139	18,864	5,275	28.0
Deferred income taxes	2,330	2,192	$ 138	6.3
Total liabilities	26,469	21,056	5,413	25.7
Shareholders' equity:				
Common share capital	89,380	67,792	21,588	31.8
Contributed surplus	352	352	-0-	0.0
Foreign currency adjustment	372	(372)	(100.0)	
Retained earnings	75,221	42,718	32,503	76.1
Total shareholders' equity	164,953	111,234	53,719	48.3
Total liabilities and shareholders' equity	$191,422	$132,290	$59,132	44.7

Our analysis of comparative financial statements begins by focusing on items that show large dollar or percent changes. We then try to identify the reasons for these changes and, if possible, determine whether they are favourable or unfavourable. We also follow up on items with small changes when we expected the changes to be large.

Regarding Ralco's comparative balance sheet, its first line item, "Cash and short-term investments," in Exhibit 20.1 stands out and shows a $28.6 million increase (50.2%). To a large extent, this increase may be explained by the increase in two other items: the $21.6 million increase in share capital and the $32.5 million increase in Retained Earnings.

Note that Ralco's liabilities increased by $5.4 million. In light of this, the $28.6 million increase in Cash and short-term investments might appear to be an excessive investment in highly liquid assets that usually earn a low return. However the company's very strong and liquid financial position indicates an outstanding ability to respond to new opportunities such as the acquisition of other companies.

Comparative Income Statement

A comparative income statement is prepared similar to the comparative balance sheet. Amounts for two or more periods are placed side by side, with additional columns for dollar and percent changes. Exhibit 20.2 shows Ralco's comparative income statement.

Exhibit 20.2

Comparative Income Statements

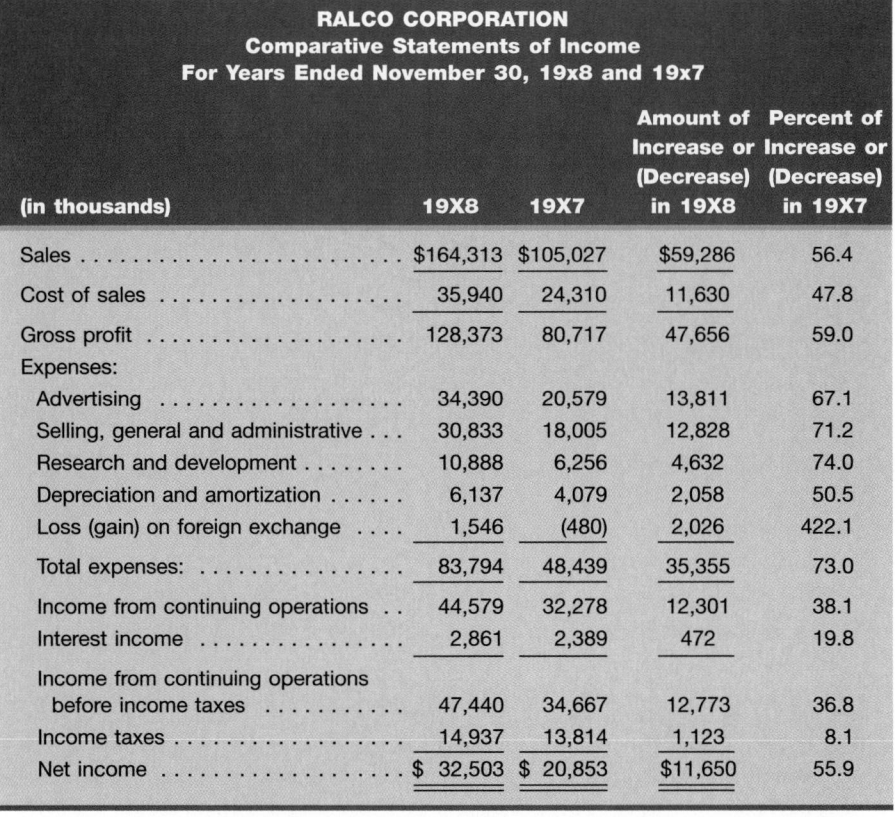

RALCO CORPORATION Comparative Statements of Income For Years Ended November 30, 19x8 and 19x7				
(in thousands)	19X8	19X7	Amount of Increase or (Decrease) in 19X8	Percent of Increase or (Decrease) in 19X7
Sales	$164,313	$105,027	$59,286	56.4
Cost of sales	35,940	24,310	11,630	47.8
Gross profit	128,373	80,717	47,656	59.0
Expenses:				
Advertising	34,390	20,579	13,811	67.1
Selling, general and administrative	30,833	18,005	12,828	71.2
Research and development	10,888	6,256	4,632	74.0
Depreciation and amortization	6,137	4,079	2,058	50.5
Loss (gain) on foreign exchange	1,546	(480)	2,026	422.1
Total expenses:	83,794	48,439	35,355	73.0
Income from continuing operations	44,579	32,278	12,301	38.1
Interest income	2,861	2,389	472	19.8
Income from continuing operations before income taxes	47,440	34,667	12,773	36.8
Income taxes	14,937	13,814	1,123	8.1
Net income	$ 32,503	$ 20,853	$11,650	55.9

All of the income statement items (except foreign exchange) reflect the company's rapid growth. The increases ranged from 67.1 to 19.8%. Expecially note the large $13.8 million or 67.1% increase in advertising. This suggests the company's leadership and strong response to competition in the software industry. Although the dollar increase in Interest income was only $.5 million, this amounted to a 19.8% increase. This is consistent with the increase in Cash and short-term investments reported in the balance sheet.

Output-Made-Easy
Today's accounting programs and spreadsheets can produce outputs with horizontal, vertical, and ratio analyses. These analyses include graphical depiction of financial relations. The key is being able to use this information properly and effectively for business decision making.

Did You Know?

Trend Analysis

Trend analysis, also called *trend percent analysis* or *index number trend analysis*, is used to reveal patterns in data covering successive periods. It involves computing trend percents for a series of financial numbers. This method of analysis is a variation on the use of percent changes for horizontal analysis. The difference is that trend analysis does not subtract the base period amount in the numerator. To compute trend percents we need to:

1. Select a *base period* and assign each item for the base period statement a weight of 100%.
2. Express financial numbers from other periods as a percent of its base period number.

Specifically, a *trend percent*, also called an *index number*, is measured as the amount in the analysis period divided by the amount of the same item in the base period, and then multiplying this quotient by 100 to get it in percent form:

$$\text{Trend percent} = \frac{\text{Analysis period amount}}{\text{Base period amount}} \times 100$$

To illustrate trend analysis, we use selected financial data of Ralco as shown in Exhibit 20.3.

	19X8	19X7	19X6	19X5	19X4
Revenues	$164,313	$105,027	$67,515	$52,242	$29,230
Costs of Sales	35,940	24,310	19,459	7,735	6,015
Gross profit	$128,373	$ 80,717	$48,056	$44,507	$23,215

Exhibit 20.3
Revenues and Expenses

We select 19X4 as the base period and compute the trend percent for each year and each item by dividing each year's dollar amount by its 19X4 dollar amount. For instance, the revenue trend percent for 19X7 is 359.3%, computed as $105,027/$29,230. The trend percents for the data from Exhibit 20.3 are shown in Exhibit 20.4.

	19X8	19X7	19X6	19X5	19X4
Revenues	562.1%	359.3%	231.0%	178.7%	100%
Costs of Sales	597.5	404.2	323.5	128.6	100
Gross Profit	553.0	347.7	207.0	191.7	100

Exhibit 20.4
Trend Percents of Revenues and Expenses

Our analysis of trend percents is often aided by graphical depictions. Exhibit 20.5 presents the trend percents from Exhibit 20.4 in a line graph. A *line graph* can help us identify trends and detect changes in direction or magnitude. For example, note that the gross profit line was bending upward from 19X4 to 19X5 but was essentially flat from 19X5 to 19X6. The gross profit increased

Exhibit 20.5

Trend Percent Lines for
Revenues and Selected
Expenses

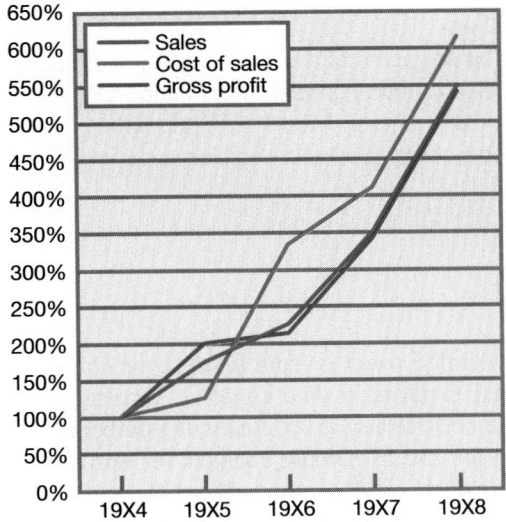

at a lower rate from 19X5 to 19X6 but then parallels the sales line from 19X6
to 19X8.

The line graph in Exhibit 20.5 also helps us understand the relationships
between items. For example, the graph in Exhibit 20.5 shows that through 19X7,
cost of sales increased at a rate that was somewhat more than the increase in
sales. Further, the differing trends in these two items had a clear effect on the
percentage changes in gross profit. That is, gross profit increased each year at a
somewhat slower rate than sales.

Trend analysis of financial statement items also can include comparisons of
relations between items on different financial statements. For instance, Exhibit
20.6 shows a comparison of Ralco's total assets and revenues.

Exhibit 20.6

Revenues and Total Assets
Data

	19X8	19X4	Trend Percent (19X8 vs 19X4)
Revenues	$164.3	$29.2	562.7%
Total assets (fiscal year-end)	191.4	41.9	456.8

The rate of increase in total assets was not quite as large as the increase in revenues. Is this change favourable? We cannot say for sure. It might suggest that
the company is no longer able to use assets as efficiently as in earlier years. On
the other hand, it might mean that the company can expect slower growth in
future years. Financial statement analysis often leads the analyst to ask questions, without providing one clear answer.

You Make the Call

Auditor
You are an auditor testing the "reasonableness" of a client's income. Your tests
reveal a 3% increase in sales from $200,000 to $206,000, and a 4% decrease in
expenses from $190,000 to $182,400. Both changes are within your
reasonableness criterion of ±5% and, therefore, you do not pursue additional tests
of the accounts. The partner in charge questions your lack of follow-up and notes
the *joint relation* between sales and expenses. What is the partner referring to?

Answer—p. 968

Vertical analysis is a tool to evaluate individual financial statement items or groups of items in terms of a specific base amount. This base amount is commonly defined as 100%. When analyzing financial statements, we usually define a key aggregate figure as the base. For instance, an income statement's base is usually revenue and a balance sheet's base is usually total assets. Since the sum of individual items in vertical analysis is 100%, this analysis is also called *common-size analysis*. This section explains vertical analysis and applies it to Ralco's statements.[3]

Vertical Analysis

Common-Size Statements

The comparative statements in Exhibits 20.1 and 20.2 show how each item has changed over time, but they do not emphasize the relative importance of each item. We use **common-size statements** to reveal changes in the relative importance of each financial statement item. All individual amounts in common-size statements are redefined in terms of common-size percents. A *common-size percent* is measured by taking each individual financial statement amount under analysis and dividing it by its base amount:

LO 6 Describe and apply methods of vertical analysis.

$$\text{Common-size percent} = \frac{\text{Analysis amount}}{\text{Base amount}} \times 100$$

Common-Size Balance Sheet

Common-size statements express each item as a percent of a *base amount*. The base amount for a common-size balance sheet is usually total assets. It is assigned a value of 100%. This also implies the total amount of liabilities plus shareholders' equity equals 100% since this amount equals total assets. Next, we compute a common-size percent for each asset, liability, and shareholders' equity item where the base amount is total assets. When we present a company's successive balance sheets in this way, changes in the mixture of assets, liabilities, and equity are more apparent.

For example, look at the common-size comparative balance sheet for Ralco in Exhibit 20.7. Note that Cash and short-term investments amounted to 43.1% of total assets at the end of 19X7 fiscal year. By comparison, they were 44.7% of total assets at the end of 19X8.

Common-Size Income Statement

Our analysis also usually benefits from an examination of a common-size income statement. In this case the amount of revenues is usually the base amount. It is assigned a value of 100%. Each common-size income statement item appears as a percent of revenues. If we think of the 100% revenues amount as representing one sales dollar, the remaining items show how each revenue dollar is distributed among costs, expenses, and profit.

Exhibit 20.8 shows the comparative income statement for each dollar of Ralco's revenues for 19X8 and 19X7. The exhibit shows expenses, as a percent of revenues, have increased from 46.1% to 51.0%. The largest change is an

---

[3] The term *vertical analysis* arises from the up-down (or down-up) movement of our eyes as we review common-size financial statements.

Exhibit 20.7

Common-Size Comparative
Balance Sheet

RALCO CORPORATION Common-Size Comparative Balance Sheet November, 19X8, and November, 19X7				
			Common-Size Percentages	
(in thousands)	19X8	19X7	19X8	19X7
Assets				
Current assets:				
Cash and short-term investments ...	$ 85,618	$ 57,000	44.7	43.1
Accounts receivable				
Trade	50,586	36,327	26.4	27.4
Other	2,264	2,185	1.2	1.7
Inventory	13,417	7,361	7.0	5.6
Prepaid expenses	1,348	812	0.7	0.6
Total current assets	153,233	103,685	80.0	78.4
Capital assets	38,189	28,605	20.0	21.6
Total assets	$191,422	$132,290	$100.0	100.0
Liabilities and Shareholders' Equity				
Current liabilities:				
Accounts payable	$ 8,487	$ 5,391	4.4	4.1
Accrued liabilities	10,722	6,073	5.6	4.6
Income taxes payable	4,930	7,400	2.6	5.6
Total current liabilities	24,139	18,864	12.6	14.3
Deferred income taxes	2,330	2,192	1.2	1.6
Total liabilities	26,469	21,056	13.8	15.9
Shareholders' equity				
Common share capital	89,380	67,792	46.7	51.2
Contribution surplus	352	352	0.2	0.3
Foreign currency adjustment		372		0.3
Retained earnings	75,221	42,718	39.3	32.3
Total shareholders' equity	164,953	111,234	86.2	84.1
Total liabilities and shareholders' equity	$191,422	$132,290	100.0	100.0

increase in selling and administrative expenses, from 17.1 cents on the dollar to 18.8 cents on the dollar. The only expense that decreased as a percentage of revenues is amortization which is a noncash expense.

One of the advantages of computing common-size percents for successive income statements is in helping us uncover potentially important changes in a company's expenses. For Ralco, the relative size of each expense changed very little from 19X7 to 19X8. Evidence of no changes is also valuable information for our analysis.

Common-Size Graphics

There are several tools of common-size analysis. Two of the most common are trend analysis of common-size statements and graphical analysis. The trend analysis of common-size statements is similar to the trend analysis of comparative statements discussed under vertical analysis. The only difference is the substitution of common-size percents for percent changes and, therefore, is not illustrated here. Instead, this section discusses graphical analysis of common-size statements.

RALCO CORPORATION Common-Size Comparative Income Statement For Years Ended November 30, 19X8 and 19X7				
			Common-Size Percentages	
(in thousands)	19X8	19X7	19X8	19X7
Sales	$164,313	$105,027	100.0	100.0
Cost of sales	35,940	24,310	21.9	23.1
Gross profit	128,373	80,717	78.1	76.9
Expenses:				
Advertising	34,390	20,579	20.9	19.6
Selling, general and administrative	30,833	18,005	18.8	17.1
Research and development	10.888	6,256	6.6	6.0
Depreciation and amortization	6,137	4,079	3.7	3.9
Loss (gain) on foreign exchange	1,546	(480)	0.9	(0.5)
Total expenses	83,794	48,439	51.0	46.1
Income from continuing operations	44,579	32,278	27.1	30.7
Interest income	2,861	2,389	1.7	2.3
Income from continuing operations before income taxes	47,440	34,667	28.9	33.0
Income taxes	14,937	13,814	9.1	13.2
Net income	$ 32,503	$ 20,853	19.8	19.8
Earnings per share	$ 0.63	$ 0.45		
Weighted-average share outstanding	51,768	46,146		

Exhibit 20.8

Common-Size Comparative Income Statement

An income statement readily lends itself to common-size graphical analysis. Revenues affect nearly every item in an income statement. It is also usually helpful for our analysis to know what portion of revenues is taken up by various geographical regions. Exhibit 20.9 shows Ralco's common-size income statement in graphical form. This pie chart highlights the contribution of each component of revenues.

Exhibit 20.9

Common-Size Graphic of Ralco's Income Statement

The pie chart on the left side of the illustration shows the sales generated by each of the company's geographic regions in 19X7. The pie chart on the right shows the revenues by sales by region for 19X8. In the annual report, the data for these charts did not appear in the financial statements. Instead they were included as part of the discussion and analysis by management.

Common-size financial statements are useful in comparing different companies. This is because financial statements of different companies are recast in common-size format. But common-size statements fail to reflect the relative sizes of companies under analysis. Comparison of a company's common-size statements with competitors' or industry common-size statistics alerts our attention to differences in the structure or distribution of its financials. Major differences should be explored and explained.

Flash back

5. On common-size comparative statements, which of the following is true? (a) Each item is expressed as a percent of a base amount. (b) Total assets is assigned a value of 100%. (c) Amounts from two or more successive periods are placed side by side. (d) All of the above are true.

6. What is the difference between the percents shown on a comparative income statement and those shown on a common-size comparative income statement?

7. Trend percents (a) are shown on comparative income statement and comparative balance sheet, (b) are shown on common-size comparative statements, or (c) are also called index numbers.

Answers—p. 969

Mid-Chapter Demonstration Problem

Use the financial Statements of Precision Company to satisfy the following requirements.

1. Prepare a comparative income statement showing the percent increase or decrease for 2000 over 1999.
2. Prepare a common-size comparative balance sheet for 2000 and 1999.

PRECISION COMPANY Comparative Income Statement For Years Ended December 31, 2000 and 1999	2000	1999
Sales	$2,486,000	$2,075,000
Cost of goods sold	1,523,000	1,222,000
Gross profit from sales	$963,000	$853,000
Operating expenses:		
Advertising expense	$ 145,000	$ 100,000
Sales salaries expense	240,000	280,000
Office salaries expense	165,000	200,000
Insurance expense	100,000	45,000
Supplies expense	26,000	35,000
Amortization expense	85,000	75,000
Miscellaneous expenses	17,000	15,000
Total operating expenses	$ 778,000	$ 750,000
Operating income	$ 185,000	$ 103,000
Less interest expense	44,000	46,000
Income before taxes	$ 141,000	$ 57,000
Income taxes	47,000	19,000
Net income	$ 94,000	$ 38,000
Earnings per share	$ 0.99	$ 0.40

PRECISION COMPANY
Comparative Balance Sheet
December 31, 2000, and December 31, 1999

	2000	1999
Assets		
Current assets:		
Cash	$ 79,000	$ 42,000
Short-term investment	65,000	96,000
Accounts receivable (net)	120,000	100,000
Merchandise inventory	250,000	265,000
Total current assets	$ 514,000	$ 503,000
Capital Assets:		
Store equipment (net)	$ 400,000	$ 350,000
Office equipment (net)	45,000	50,000
Buildings (net)	625,000	675,000
Land	100,000	100,000
Total capital assets	$1,170,000	$1,175,000
Total assets	$1,684,000	$1,678,000
Liabilities		
Current liabilities:		
Accounts payable	$ 164,000	$ 190,000
Short-term notes payable	75,000	90,000
Taxes payable	26,000	12,000
Total current liabilities	$ 265,000	$ 292,000
Long-term liabilities:		
Notes payable (secured by mortgage on building and land)	400,000	420,000
Total liabilities	$ 665,000	$ 712,000
Shareholders' Equity		
Contributed capital:		
Common shares no-par value	$ 475,000	$ 475,000
Retained earnings	544,000	491,000
Total shareholders' equity	$1,019,000	$ 966,000
Total liabilities and shareholders' equity.	$1,684,000	$1,678,000

Planning the Solution

- Set up a four-column income statement; enter the 2000 and 1999 amounts in the first two columns and then enter the dollar change in the third column and the percent change from 1999 in the fourth column.

- Set up a four-column balance sheet; enter the 2000 and 1999 amounts in the first columns and then compute and enter the amount of each item as a percent of total assets.

Solution to
Mid-Chapter
Demonstration
Problem

PRECISION COMPANY Comparative Income Statement For Years Ended December 31, 2000 and 1999				
			Increase (Decrease) in 2000	
	2000	**1999**	**Amount**	**Percent**
Sales	$2,486,000	$2,075,000	$411,000	19.8%
Cost of goods sold	1,523,000	1,222,000	301,000	24.6
Gross profit from sales	$963,000	$ 853,000	$110,000	12.9
Operating expenses:				
Advertising expense	$ 145,000	$100,000	$45,000	45.0
Sales salaries expense	240,000	280,000	(40,000)	(14.3)
Office salaries expense	165,000	200,000	(35,000)	(17.5)
Insurance expense	100,000	45,000	55,000	122.2
Supplies expense	26,000	35,000	(9,000)	(25.7)
Amortization expense	85,000	75,000	10,000	13.3
Miscellaneous expenses	17,000	15,000	2,000	13.3
Total operating expenses	$ 778,000	$ 750,000	$ 28,000	3.7
Operating income	$ 185,000	$ 103,000	$ 82,000	79.6
Less interest expense	44,000	46,000	(2,000)	(4.3)
Income before taxes	$ 141,000	$ 57,000	$ 84,000	147.4
Income taxes	47,000	19,000	28,000	147.4
Net income	$ 94,000	$ 38,000	$ 56,000	147.4
Earnings per share	$0.99	$0.40	$ 0.59	147.5

PRECISION COMPANY Common-Size, Comparative Balance Sheet December 31, 2000, and December 31, 1999				
			Common-Size Percents	
	2000	**1999**	**2000***	**1999***
Assets				
Current assets:				
Cash	$ 79,000	$ 42,000	4.7%	2.5%
Short-term investments	65,000	96,000	3.9	5.7
Accounts receivable (net)	120,000	100,000	7.1	6.0
Merchandise inventory	250,000	265,000	14.8	15.8
Total current assets	$ 514,000	$ 503,000	30.5	30.0
Capital Assets:				
Store equipment (net)	$ 400,000	$ 350,000	23.8	20.9
Office equipment (net)	45,000	50,000	2.7	3.0
Buildings (net)	625,000	675,000	37.1	40.2
Land	100,000	100,000	5.9	6.0
Total capital assets	$1,170,000	$1,175,000	69.5	70.0
Total assets	$1,684,000	$1,678,000	100.0	100.0

Liabilities				
Current liabilities:				
Accounts payable	$ 164,000	$ 190,000	9.7	11.3
Short-term notes payable ..	75,000	90,000	4.5	5.4
Taxes payable	26,000	12,000	1.5	0.7
Total current liabilities	$ 265,000	$ 292,000	15.7	17.4
Long-term liabilities:				
Notes payable (secured by mortgage on buildings and land)	400,000	420,000	23.8	25.0
Total liabilities	$ 665,000	$ 712,000	39.4	42.4
Shareholders' Equity				
Contributed capital:				
Common shares no-par value	$ 475,000	$ 475,000	28.2	28.3
Retained earnings	544,000	491,000	32.3	29.3
Total shareholders' equity	$1,019,000	$ 966,000	60.5	57.6
Total liabilities and equity	$1,684,000	$1,678,000	100.0	100.0

*Columns may not foot due to rounding.

Solution to Mid-Chapter Demonstration Problem

Ratio Analysis

Ratios are among the most popular and widely used tools of financial analysis. They provide us with clues and symptoms of underlying conditions. Ratios, properly interpreted, identify areas requiring further investigation. A ratio can help us uncover conditions and trends difficult to detect by inspecting individual components comprising the ratio. Ratios, like other analysis tools, are usually future oriented. This means they are often adjusted for their probable future trend and magnitude. In this sense ratios can be used to prepare forecasted financial statements. Usefulness of ratios depends on our skillful interpretation of them, and is the most challenging aspect of ratio analysis.

A ratio expresses a mathematical relation between two quantities. It can be expressed as a percent, rate, or proportion. For instance, a change in an account balance from $100 to $250 can be expressed as: (1) 250%, (2) 2.5 times, or (3) 2.5 to 1 [or 2.5:1]. While computation of a ratio is a simple arithmetic operation, its interpretation is not. To be meaningful, a ratio must refer to an economically important relation. For example, there is a direct and crucial relation between an item's sales price and its cost. Accordingly, the ratio of cost of goods sold to sales is a significant one. In contrast, there is no obvious relation between freight costs and the balance of temporary investments in securities.

This section describes an important set of financial ratios and shows how to apply them. The selected ratios are organized into the four building blocks of financial statement analysis: (1) liquidity and efficiency, (2) solvency, (3) profitability, and (4) market. All of these ratios have been previously explained at relevant points in prior chapters. The purpose here is to organize and apply them under a summary framework.

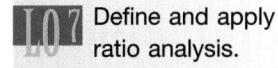 Define and apply ratio analysis.

Liquidity and Efficiency

Liquidity refers to the availability of resources to meet short-term cash requirements. A company's short-term liquidity is affected by the timing of cash inflows and outflows along with its prospects for future performance. Our analysis of liquidity is aimed at a company's capital requirements. **Efficiency** refers to how productive a company is in using its assets. Efficiency is usually measured relative to how much revenue is generated for a certain level of assets.

Both liquidity and efficiency are important and complementary in our analysis. If a company fails to meet its current obligations, its continued existence is doubtful. Viewed in this light, all other measures of analysis are of secondary importance. While accounting measurements assume indefinite existence (going-concern assumption) of the company, our analysis must always assess the validity of this assumption using liquidity measures. Efficiency is how well a company uses its assets. Inefficient use of assets can yield liquidity problems.

For users, a lack of liquidity often precedes lower profitability and opportunity. It can foretell a loss of owner control or loss of investment. When a company's owners possess unlimited liability (proprietorships and certain partnerships) a lack of liquidity endangers their personal assets. To creditors of a company, lack of liquidity can yield delays in collecting interest and principal payments or the loss of amounts due them. A company's customers and suppliers of goods and services are affected by short-term liquidity problems. Implications include a company's inability to execute contracts and potential damage to important customer and supplier relationships. This section describes and illustrates ratios relevant to accessing liquidity and efficiency.

Working Capital and Current Ratio

The amount of current assets less current liabilities is called **working capital** or *net working capital*. A company needs an adequate amount of working capital to meet current debts, carry sufficient inventories, and take advantage of cash discounts. A company that runs low on working capital is less likely to meet current obligations or continue operating.

When evaluating a company's working capital we must look beyond the dollar amount of current assets less current liabilities. We also need to consider the relation between the amounts of current assets and current liabilities. Recall from Chapter 5 that the *current ratio* describes a company's ability to pay its short-term obligations. The current ratio relates current assets to current liabilities as follows:

$$\text{Current ratio} = \frac{\text{Current assets}}{\text{Current liabilities}}$$

Drawing on information in Exhibit 20.1, Ralco's working capital amounts and current ratios for both 19X8 and 19X7 are shown in Exhibit 20.10

Exhibit 20.10

Working Capital and Current Ratio

(in millions)	Nov. 30, 19X8	Nov. 30, 19X7
Current assets	$153,233	$103,685
Current liabilities	24,139	18,864
Working capital	$129,094	$ 84,821
Current ratio:		
$153,233/$24,139	6.35 to 1	
$103,685/$18,864		5.50 to 1

A high current ratio suggests a strong liquidity position. A high ratio means a company should be able to meet its current obligations. But a company also can have a current ratio that is too high. An excessively high ratio means the company has invested too much in current assets compared to its current obligations. Since current assets do not normally generate much additional revenue, an excessive investment in current assets is not an efficient use of funds.

Many users apply a guideline of 2 to 1 for the current ratio in helping evaluate the debt-paying ability of a company. A company with a 2 to 1 or higher current ratio is generally thought to be a good credit risk in the short run. But this analysis is only one step in our process of assessing a company's debt-paying ability. We also need to analyze at least three additional factors:

1. Type of business.
2. Composition of current assets.
3. Turnover rate of current asset components.

Type of Business

The type of business a company operates affects our assessment of its current ratio. A service company that grants little or no credit and carries no inventories other than supplies can probably operate on a current ratio of less than 1 to 1 if its revenues generate enough cash to pay its current liabilities on time. On the other hand, a company selling high-priced clothing or furniture requires a higher ratio. This is because of difficulties in judging customer demand and other factors. For instance, if demands falls, this company's inventory may not generate as much cash as expected. A company facing these risks should maintain a current ratio of more than 2 to 1 to protect its creditors.

The importance of the type of business to our analysis implies an evaluation of a company's current ratio should include a comparison with ratios of other successful companies in the same industry. Another important part of our analysis is to observe how the current ratio changes over time. We must also recognize that the current ratio is affected by a company's accounting methods, especially choice of inventory method. For instance, a company using LIFO tends to report a smaller amount of current assets than if it uses FIFO when costs are rising. These factors should be considered before we decide whether a given current ratio is adequate.

Composition of Current Assets

The composition of a company's current assets is important to our evaluation of short-term liquidity. For instance, cash, cash equivalents, and temporary investments are more liquid than accounts and notes receivable. Also, receivables normally are more liquid than merchandise inventory. We know cash can be used to immediately pay current debts. But items such as accounts receivable and merchandise inventory must be converted into cash before payments can be made. An excessive amount of receivables and inventory weakens a company's ability to pay current liabilities. One way to take account of the composition of current assets is to evaluate the acid-test ratio. We discuss this in the next section.

Turnover Rate of Asset

Asset turnover measures the efficiency of a company's use of assets. One relevant measure of asset efficiency is the revenues generated. The general measure of asset turnover is revenues divided by total assets. But evaluation of turnover for individual assets is also useful in our analysis. We discuss total asset turnover along with both receivables and inventories turnover below.

Answer—p. 968

Banker

You are a banker, and a company calls on you for a one-year, $200,000 loan to finance expansion. This company's current ratio is 4:1 with current assets of $160,000. Key competitors carry a current ratio of about 1.9:1. Using this information, do you approve the loan application? Does your decision change if the application is for a 10-year loan?

Acid-Test Ratio

Chapter 6 introduced us to the *acid-test ratio*, also called *quick ratio*. This ratio focuses on current asset composition. Quick assets are cash, short-term investments, accounts receivable, and notes receivable. These are the most liquid types of current assets. We compute the acid-test ratio as:

$$\text{Acid-test ratio} = \frac{\text{Quick assets}}{\text{Current liabilities}}$$

Using information in Exhibit 20.1, we compute Ralco's acid-test ratios as shown in Exhibit 20.11.

Exhibit 20.11

Acid-Test Ratio

Ralco
Acid-Test Ratio = 5.64

(in millions)	November 30, 19X8	November 30, 19X7
Cash and short-term investments	$85,618	$57,000
Accounts receivable, trade	50,586	36,327
Total quick assets	$136,204	$93,327
Current liabilities	$ 24,139	$18,864
Acid-test ratio:		
$136,204/$24,139	5.64 to 1	
$93,327/$18,864		4.95 to 1

A traditional rule-of-thumb for an acceptable acid-test ratio is 1 to 1. Similar to our analysis of the current ratio, we need to consider other factors. For instance, the working capital requirements of a company are affected by how frequently the company converts its current assets into cash. This implies our analysis of the company's short-term liquidity should also include analysis of receivables and inventories. We next look at these analyses.

Accounts Receivable Turnover

We can measure how frequently a company converts its receivables into cash by computing *accounts receivable turnover*. As we explained in Chapter 10, this is computed as:

$$\text{Accounts receivable turnover} = \frac{\text{Net sales}}{\text{Average accounts receivable}}$$

While this ratio is called accounts receivable turnover, all short-term receivables (including notes receivable) from customers are normally included in the denominator amount along with accounts receivable. The numerator of this ratio is more precise if credit sales are used. But net sales (or revenues) is usually used by external users because information about credit sales is typically not reported. Ralco's 19X8 accounts receivable turnover is computed as:

$$\frac{\$164,313}{(\$50,586 + \$36,327)/2} = 3.78 \text{ times}$$

If accounts receivable are collected quickly, then accounts receivable turnover is high. A high turnover is favourable because it means the company need not commit large amounts of capital to accounts receivable. An accounts receivable turnover can be too high. This can occur when credit terms are so restrictive they negatively affect sales volume.

Ending accounts receivable is sometimes substituted for the average balance in computing accounts receivable turnover. This is acceptable if the difference between these figures is not material. Also, some users prefer using gross accounts receivable (before subtracting the allowance for doubtful accounts). But many balance sheets report only the net amount of accounts receivable.

Merchandise Inventory Turnover

Working capital requirements are affected by how long a company holds merchandise inventory before selling it. One measure of this effect is the *merchandise inventory turnover*, or simply *inventory turnover*. Merchandise turnover is defined in Chapter 7 as:

$$\text{Merchandise turnover} = \frac{\text{Cost of goods sold}}{\text{Average merchandise inventory}}$$

Using the costs of sales and inventories information in Exhibits 20.1 and 20.2, we compute Ralco's merchandise turnover for 19X8 as (cost of goods sold is called *costs of sales* on Ralco's income statement):

$$\frac{\$35,940}{(\$13,417 + \$7,361)/2} = 3.46 \text{ times}$$

Average inventory is estimated by averaging the beginning and the ending inventories for 19X8. If the beginning and ending inventories do not represent the amount normally on hand, an average of quarterly inventories may be used if available.

A company with a high turnover requires a smaller investment in inventory than one producing the same sales with a lower turnover. But merchandise turnover can be too high if a company keeps such a small inventory on hand that it restricts sales volume.

Days' Sales Uncollected

We already described how accounts receivable turnover can be used to evaluate how frequently a company collects its accounts. Another measure of this activity is *days' sales uncollected*. In Chapter 9 we defined it as:

$$\text{Days' sales uncollected} = \frac{\text{Accounts receivable}}{\text{Net sales}} \times 365$$

This formula takes the usual approach of placing accounts receivable in the numerator. Any short-term notes receivable from customers are also normally included in the numerator.

We illustrate this ratio's application by using Ralco's information in Exhibits 20.1 and 20.2. The days' sales uncollected on November 30, 19x8, is:

$$\frac{\$50,586}{\$164,313} \times 365 = 112.4 \text{ days}$$

Days' sales uncollected is more meaningful if we know the company's credit terms. A rough guideline is days' sales uncollected should not exceed one and one-third times the days in its: (a) credit period, if discounts are not offered; (b) discount period, if discounts are offered.

Days' Sales in Inventory

Chapter 7 explained how *days' sales in inventory* is a measure useful in evaluating the liquidity of a company's inventory. Days' sales in inventory is linked to inventory in a similar manner as days' sales uncollected is linked to receivables. Days' sales in inventory is computed as:

$$\text{Days' sales in inventory} = \frac{\text{Ending inventory}}{\text{Cost of goods sold}} \times 365$$

Applying this formula to Ralco's 19X8 financial statements, we compute days' sales in inventory as:

$$\frac{\$13,417}{\$35,940} \times 365 = 136.3 \text{ days}$$

If the products in Ralco's inventory are in demand by customers, this formula estimates that its inventory will be converted into receivables (or cash) in 136.3 days. If all of Ralco's sales are credit sales, the conversion of inventory to receivables in 136.3 days plus the conversion of receivables to cash in 112.4 days suggest that inventory will be converted to cash in about 248.7 days (136.3 + 112.4 = 248.7).

Total Asset Turnover

Total asset turnover describes the ability of a company to use its assets to generate sales. We explained in Chapter 13 that this ratio is computed as:

$$\text{Total asset turnover} = \frac{\text{Revenues}}{\text{Average total assets}}$$

In computing Ralco's total asset turnover for 19X8, we follow the usual practice of averaging total assets at the beginning and the end of the year. Taking the information from Exhibits 20.1 and 20.2, this computation is:

$$\frac{\$164,313}{(\$191,422 + \$132,290)/2} = 1.015 \text{ times}$$

Flash back

8. The following information is from the Dec. 31/2000 balance sheet of Paff Company: cash, $820,000; accounts receivable, $240,000; inventories, $470,000; capital assets, $910,000; accounts payable, $350,000; and income taxes payable, $180,000. Compute the (a) current ratio and (b) acid-test ratio.

9. On Dec. 31/1999, Paff Company (in prior question) had accounts receivable of $290,000 and inventories of $530,000. During 2000, net sales amounted to $2,500,000 and cost of goods sold was $750,000. Compute the (a) accounts receivable turnover, (b) days' sales uncollected, (c) merchandise turnover, and (d) days' sales in inventory.

Answers—p. 969

Solvency

Solvency refers to a company's long-run financial viability and its ability to cover long-term obligations. All business activities of a company—financing, investing, and operating—affect a company's solvency. One of the most important components of solvency analysis is the composition of a company's capital structure. *Capital structure* refers to a company's sources of financing.

Analyzing solvency of a company is different from analyzing short-term liquidity. Analysis of solvency is long-term and uses less precise but more encompassing measures. Analysis of capital structure is one key in evaluating solvency. Capital structure ranges from relatively permanent equity capital to more risky or temporary short-term financing. Assets represent secondary sources of security for lenders ranging from loans secured by specific assets to the assets available as general security to unsecured creditors. There are different risks associated with different assets and financing sources.

This section describes tools of solvency analysis. Our analysis is concerned with a company's ability to meet its obligations and provide security to its creditors over the long run. Indicators of this ability include *debt* and *equity* ratios, the relation between *pledged assets* and *secured liabilities*, and the company's capacity to earn sufficient income to *pay fixed interest charges*.

Debt and Equity Ratios

One element of solvency analysis is to assess the portion of a company's assets contributed by its owners and the portion contributed by creditors. This relation is reflected in the debt ratio described in Chapter 3. Recall the *debt ratio* expresses total liabilities as a percent of total assets. The **equity ratio** provides complementary information by expressing total shareholders' equity as a percent of total assets.

Ralco's debt and equity ratios are computed as:

	Nov.30, 19X8	Ratios	
Total liabilities	$ 26,469	13.8%	[Debt Ratio]
Total shareholders' equity	164,953	86.2	[Equity Ratio]
Total liabilities and shareholders' equity	$191,422	100.0%	

Ralco's financial statements reflect very little debt compared to most companies. The company has only one long-term liability and, at the end of 19X8, its liabilities provide only 13.8% of the total assets. A company is considered less risky if its capital structure (equity and long-term debt) is comprised more of equity. One source of this increased risk is the required payments under debt contracts for interest and principal amounts. Another factor is the amount of financing provided by shareholders. The greater is shareholder financing, the more losses a company can absorb through its shareholders before the remaining assets become inadequate to satisfy the claims of creditors.

From the shareholders' point of view, including debt in the capital structure of a company is desirable so long as risk is not too great. If a company earns a return on borrowed capital that is higher than the cost of borrowing, the difference represents increased income to shareholders. Because debt can have the effect of increasing the return to shareholders, the inclusion of debt is sometimes described as *financial leverage*. Companies are said to be highly leveraged if a large portion of their assets is financed by debt.

Pledged Assets to Secured Liabilities

We explained in Chapter 17 how we use the ratio of pledged assets to secured liabilities to evaluate the risk of nonpayment faced by secured creditors. This ratio also is relevant to unsecured creditors. The ratio is computed as:

$$\text{Pledged assets to secured liabilities} = \frac{\text{Book value of pledged assets}}{\text{Book value of secured liabilities}}$$

The information needed to compute this ratio is not usually reported in published financial statements. This means the ratio is used primarily by persons who have the ability to obtain information directly from the company such as bankers and certain lenders.

A generally agreed minimum value for this ratio is about 2 to 1. But the ratio needs careful interpretation because it is based on the *book value* of pledged assets. Book values are not necessarily intended to reflect amounts to be received for assets in event of liquidation. Also, the long-term earning ability of a company with pledged assets may be more important than the value of its pledged assets. Creditors prefer that a debtor be able to pay with cash generated by operating activities rather than with cash obtained by liquidating assets.

Times Interest Earned

Chapter 14 explained the *times interest earned ratio*. Its purpose is to reflect the riskiness of repayments with interest to creditors. The amount of income before the deduction of interest charges and income taxes is the amount available to pay interest charges. We compute this ratio as:

$$\text{Times interest earned} = \frac{\text{Income before interest and income taxes}}{\text{Interest expense}}$$

The larger this ratio, the less risky is the company for lenders. A guideline for this ratio says that creditors are reasonably safe if the company earns its fixed interest charges two or more times each year.

Exhibit 20.2 does not report interest expense as a separate item for Ralco. Apparently interest expense is not material; probably it is offset against interest income. Also, recall from Exhibit 20.1 that Ralco did not have any long-term debt. Furthermore, few if any of the company's current liabilities would be likely to generate interest expense. As a result, we are not able to calculate times interest earned for Ralco.

Did You Know?

Bears and Bulls
Bear market is a declining market. It comes from bear skin jobbers who often sold bear skins before the bears were caught. The term bear was then used to describe investors who sold shares they did not own in anticipation of a price decline. *Bull market* is a rising market. It comes from the once popular sport of bear and bull baiting. The term bull came to mean the opposite of bear.

Profitability

We are especially interested in the ability of a company to use its assets efficiently to produce profits (and positive cash flows). **Profitability** refers to a company's ability to generate an adequate return on invested capital. Return is judged by assessing earnings relative to the level and sources of financing. Profitability is also relevant to solvency.

This section describes profitability measures and their importance to financial statement analysis. We also explain variations in return measures and their interpretation. We analyze the components of return on invested capital for additional insights into company performance.

Profit Margin

The operating efficiency and profitability of a company can be expressed in two components. The first is the company's *profit margin*. We explained in Chapter 4 how profit margin reflects a company's ability to earn a net income from sales. It is measured by expressing net income as a percent of revenues (sales and revenues are treated as similar in ratio analysis). We can use the information in Exhibit 20.2 to compute Ralco's 19X8 profit margin as:

$$\text{Profit margin} = \frac{\text{Net income}}{\text{Revenues}} = \frac{\$32,503}{\$164,313} = 19.8\%$$

To evaluate the profit margin of a company, we must consider the industry in which it operates. For instance, a publishing company might be expected to have a profit margin between 10% and 15%, while a retail supermarket might have a normal profit margin of 1% or 2%.

The second component of operating efficiency is *total asset turnover*. We described this ratio earlier in this section. Both profit margin and total asset turnover make up the two basic components of operating efficiency. These ratios also reflect on management performance since managers are ultimately responsible for operating efficiency. The next section explains how we use both measures in analyzing return on total assets.

Return on Total Assets

The two basic components of operating efficiency, profit margin and total asset turnover, are used to compute a summary measure. This summary measure is the *return on total assets* we described in Chapters 1 and 18. It is computed as:

$$\text{Return on total assets} = \frac{\text{Net income}}{\text{Average total assets}}$$

Ralco's 19X8 return on total assets is:

$$\frac{\$32,503}{(\$191,422 + \$132,290)/2} = 20.1\%$$

Ralco's 20.1% return on total assets is favourable compared to most businesses; however, this is a risky industry and good times can turn into bad very quickly. The following computation shows the relation between profit margin, total asset turnover, and return on total assets:

$$\text{Profit margin} \times \text{Total asset turnover} = \text{Return on total assets}$$

or

$$\frac{\text{Net income}}{\text{Net sales}} \times \frac{\text{Net sales}}{\text{Average total assets}} = \frac{\text{Net income}}{\text{Average total assets}}$$

Notice that both profit margin and total asset turnover contribute to overall operating efficiency, as measured by return on total assets. If we apply this formula to Ralco we get:

$$19.8\% \times 1.015 = 20.1\%$$

Return on Common Shareholders' Equity

Perhaps the most important goal in operating companies is to earn net income for its owners. The *return on common shareholders' equity* measures the success of a company in reaching this goal. We explained in Chapter 2 how we compute this return measure:

$$\text{Return on common shareholders' equity} = \frac{\text{Net income} - \text{Preferred dividends}}{\text{Average common shareholders' equity}}$$

Recall from Exhibit 20.1 that Ralco did not have any preferred shares outstanding. As a result we determine Ralco's return as follows:

$$\frac{\$32,503 - \$0}{(\$164,953 + \$111,234)/2} = 23.5\%$$

The denominator in this computation is the book value of common shares. In the numerator, the dividends on cumulative preferred shares must be subtracted whether they are declared or are in arrears. If preferred is noncumulative, its dividends are subtracted only if declared.

Market

Market measures are useful when analyzing corporations having publicly traded shares. These market measures use share price in their computation. Share price reflects what the market (public) expectations are for the company. This includes both the return and risk characteristics of a company as currently perceived by the market.

Price-Earnings Ratio

We explained in Chapter 18 how the *price-earnings ratio* is computed as:

$$\text{Price-earnings ratio} = \frac{\text{Market price per share}}{\text{Earnings per share}}$$

We also described how the predicted earnings per share for the next period is often used in the denominator of this computation. But reported earnings per share for the most recent period is also commonly used. In both cases, the ratio is an indicator of the future growth of and risk related to a company's earnings as perceived by investors who establish the market price of the shares.

The market price of Ralco's common shares during 19X8 ranged from a low of $14.50 to a high of $23.25. Ralco's management reported that it did not expect 19X9 revenue growth rates to be as high as those for 19X8. Management also indicated that operating expenses as a percentage of revenues might increase. Nevertheless, the price earnings ratios are much higher than those of most companies. Using Ralco's $0.63 earnings per share that was reported at the end of 19X8, we compute its price-earnings ratios using both the low and high share prices:

$$\text{Low: } \frac{\$14.50}{\$0.63} = 23$$

$$\text{High: } \frac{\$23.25}{\$0.63} = 36.9$$

Ralco's higher ratios reflect the expectation of investors that the company will continue to grow at a rate faster than the normal company.

Dividend Yield

We explained in Chapter 16 how to use *dividend yield* as a means to compare the dividend-paying performance of different investment alternatives. Dividend yield is computed as:

$$\text{Dividend yield} = \frac{\text{Annual dividends per share}}{\text{Market price per share}}$$

Some companies decide not to declare dividends because they prefer to reinvest the cash. Ralco, for instance, does not pay cash dividends on its common shares.

Summary of Ratios

Exhibit 20.12 presents a summary of the major financial statement analysis ratios illustrated in this chapter and throughout the book. This summary includes each ratio's title, formula, and common use.

Exhibit 20.12

Financial Statement Analysis Ratios

Ratio	Formula	Measure of:
Liquidity and Efficiency		
Current ratio	$= \dfrac{\text{Current assets}}{\text{Current liabilities}}$	Short-term debt-paying ability
Acid-test ratio	$= \dfrac{\text{Cash} + \text{Temporary investments} + \text{Current receivables}}{\text{Current liabilities}}$	Immediate short-term debt-paying ability
Accounts receivable turnover	$= \dfrac{\text{Net sales}}{\text{Average accounts receivable}}$	Efficiency of collection
Merchandise turnover	$= \dfrac{\text{Cost of goods sold}}{\text{Average merchandise inventory}}$	Efficiency of inventory
Days' sales uncollected	$= \dfrac{\text{Accounts receivable}}{\text{Net sales}} \times 365$	Liquidity of receivables
Days' sales in inventory	$= \dfrac{\text{Ending inventory}}{\text{Cost of goods sold}} \times 365$	Liquidity of inventory
Total asset turnover	$= \dfrac{\text{Net sales}}{\text{Average total assets}}$	Efficiency of assets in producing sales
Solvency		
Debt ratio	$= \dfrac{\text{Total liabilities}}{\text{Total assets}}$	Creditor financing and leverage
Equity ratio	$= \dfrac{\text{Total shareholders' equity}}{\text{Total assets}}$	Owner financing
Pledged assets to secured liabilities	$= \dfrac{\text{Book value of pledged assets}}{\text{Book value of secured liabilities}}$	Protection to secured creditors
Times interest earned	$= \dfrac{\text{Income before interest and taxes}}{\text{Interest expense}}$	Protection in meeting interest payments

Exhibit 20.12

(Continued)

Ratio	Formula	Measure of:
Profitability		
Profit margin	$= \dfrac{\text{Net income}}{\text{Net sales}}$	Net income in each sales dollar
Gross margin	$= \dfrac{\text{Net sales} - \text{Cost of goods sold}}{\text{Net sales}}$	Gross margin in each sales dollar
Return on total assets	$= \dfrac{\text{Net income}}{\text{Average total assets}}$	Overall profitability of assets
Return on common shareholders' equity	$= \dfrac{\text{Net income} - \text{Preferred dividends}}{\text{Average common shareholders' equity}}$	Profitability of owner's investment
Book value per common share	$= \dfrac{\text{Shareholders' equity applicable to common shares}}{\text{Number of common shares outstanding}}$	Liquidation at reported amounts.
Basic earnings per share	$= \dfrac{\text{Net income} - \text{Preferred dividends}}{\text{Weighted-average common shares outstanding}}$	Net income on each common share
Market		
Price-earnings ratio	$= \dfrac{\text{Market price per common share}}{\text{Earnings per share}}$	Market value based on earnings
Dividend yield	$= \dfrac{\text{Annual dividends per share}}{\text{Market price per share}}$	Cash return to each common share

Flash back

10. Which ratio best reflects the ability of a company to meet immediate interest payments? (a) debt ratio, (b) equity ratio, (c) times interest earned, or (d) pledged assets to secured liabilities.

11. Which ratio measures the success of a company in earning net income for its owners? (a) profit margin, (b) return on common shareholders' equity, (c) price earnings ratio, or (d) dividend yield.

12. If a company has net sales of $8,500,000, net income of $945,000, and total asset turnover of 1.8 times, what is its return on total assets?

Answers—p. 969

Analysis Reporting

LO 8 Summarize and report results of analysis.

Understanding the purpose of our financial statement analysis is crucial to its quality. This understanding leads to efficiency of effort, effectiveness in application, and relevance in focus. Most analyses face constraints on availability of information and decisions must be made using incomplete or inadequate information.

A goal of most financial statement analyses is reducing uncertainty through a rigorous and sound evaluation. A *financial statement analysis report* helps by directly addressing the building blocks of analysis. It also helps identify weaknesses in inference by requiring explanation, and it forces us to organize our reasoning and to verify the flow and logic of analysis. A report serves as our communication device with readers. The writing process reinforces our judgments and vice versa. It helps us refine conclusions from evidence on key building blocks.

A good report separates interpretations and conclusions of analysis from the information underlying them. This separation enables readers to see our process and rationale of analysis. It also enables the reader to draw personal conclusions and make modifications as appropriate. A good analysis report often consists of six sections devoted to:

- ■ *Executive Summary.* The executive summary is brief and focuses on important analysis results and conclusions.
- ■ *Analysis Overview.* Background material on the company, its industry, and its economic environment.
- ■ *Evidential Matter.* Financial statements and information used in the analysis. This includes ratios, trends, comparisons, statistics, and all analytical measures assembled. Often organized under the building blocks of analysis.
- ■ *Assumptions.* Identification of important assumptions regarding a company's industry and economic environment, and other important assumptions for estimates.
- ■ *Important Factors.* Listing of important favourable and unfavourable factors, both quantitative and qualitative, for company performance—usually listed by areas of analysis.
- ■ *Inferences.* Includes forecasts, estimates, interpretations, and conclusions drawing on all sections of the report.

We must remember that "importance" is defined by the user. This means our analysis report should include a brief table of contents to help readers focus on those areas most relevant to their decisions. All irrelevant matter must be eliminated. For example, decades-old details of the beginnings of a company and a detailing of the miscues of our analysis are irrelevant. Ambiguities and qualifications to avoid responsibility or hedge inferences should be eliminated. Finally, writing is important. Mistakes in grammar and errors of fact compromise the credibility of our analysis.

Short Selling

Short selling refers to selling shares before you buy them. Here's an example of how it works: You borrow 100 **Atlantis** shares, sell them in the market at $40 each and receive money from their sale. You then wait. Your hope is that Atlantis's share price falls to say $35 each and you can replace the borrowed shares for less money than you sold them for—reaping a profit of $5 each less any transaction fees.

Did You Know?

Summary

LO1 Explain the purpose of analysis. The purpose of financial statement analysis is to help users make better business decisions. Internal users want information helpful in improving the company's efficiency or effectiveness in providing products or services. External users want information to make better and more informed decisions in pursuing their personal goals. The common goals of all users is to evaluate a company's (1) past and current performance, (2) current financial position, and (3) future performance and risk.

LO2 Identify the building blocks of analysis. Financial statement analysis focuses on mainly four areas of inquiry. These four areas are the building blocks of analysis: (1) liquidity and efficiency—ability to meet short-term obligations and to efficiently generate revenues; (2) solvency—ability to generate future revenues and meet long-term obligations; (3) profitability—ability to provide financial rewards sufficient to attract and retain financing; and (4) market—ability to generate positive market expectations.

LO 3 Describe standards for comparisons in analysis. To make conclusions from analysis we need standards for comparisons. Standards for comparisons include: (1) intracompany—prior performance and relations between financial items of company under analysis; (2) competitor—one or more direct competitors of the company under analysis provide standards for comparisons; (3) industry—industry statistics can provide standards of comparisons; and (4) guidelines (rules-of-thumb)—general standards of comparisons can develop from past experiences and personal judgments.

LO 4 Identify the tools of analysis. The three most common tools of financial statement analysis: (1) horizontal analysis—comparing a company's financial condition and performance across time; (2) vertical analysis—comparing a company's financial condition and performance to a base amount such as revenues or total assets; and (3) ratio analysis—using key relations among financial statement items.

LO 5 Explain and apply methods of horizontal analysis. Horizontal analysis is a tool to evaluate changes in financial statement data across time. Two important tools of horizontal analysis are comparative statements and trend analysis. Comparative statements show amounts for two or more successive periods, often with changes disclosed in both absolute and percent terms. Trend analysis is used to reveal important changes occurring from one period to the next.

LO 6 Describe and apply methods of vertical analysis. In common-size statements, each item is expressed as a percent of a base amount. The base amount for the balance sheet is usually total assets, and the base amount for the income statement is usually net sales. Vertical analysis is a tool to evaluate each financial statement item or group of items in terms of a specific base amount. This base amount is commonly defined as 100%. Two important tools of vertical analysis are common-size statements and graphical analyses.

LO 7 Define and apply ratio analysis. Ratio analysis provides clues and symptoms of underlying conditions. Ratios, properly interpreted, identify areas requiring further investigation. A ratio expresses a mathematical relation between two quantities such as a percent, rate, or proportion. Selected ratios are organized into the building blocks of analysis: (1) liquidity and efficiency, (2) solvency, (3) profitability, and (4) market.

LO 8 Summarize and report results of analysis. A financial statement analysis report is often organized around the building blocks of analysis. It serves as a communication device with readers. A good report separates interpretations and conclusions of analysis from the information underlying them. This separation enables readers to see the process and rationale of analysis. It also enables the reader to draw personal conclusions and make modifications as appropriate. An analysis report often consists of six sections: (1) executive summary; (2) analysis overview; (3) evidential matter; (4) assumptions; (5) important factors; and (6) inferences.

Guidance Answers to **You Make the Call**

Auditor

The *joint relation* referred to here is where the increase in sales and the decrease in expenses yield a greater than 5% increase in income. In particular, both *individual* accounts (sales and expenses) yielded percent changes within the ±5% acceptable range. However, a joint analysis suggests a different picture. For example, consider a joint analysis using the profit margin ratio (net income/sales). The client's profit margin is 11.46% ($206,000 – $182,400 / $206,000) for the current year compared with 5.0% ($200,000 – $190,000 / $200,000) for the prior year—a 129% increase in profit margin! This is what the partner is concerned with, and it suggests expanding audit tests to verify or refute the client's figures.

Banker

Your decision on the loan application is positive for at least two reasons. First, the current ratio suggests a strong ability to meet short-term obligations. Second, current assets of $160,000 and a current ratio of 4:1 imply current liabilities of $40,000 (one-fourth of current assets) and a working capital excess of $120,000. This working capital excess is 60% of the loan amount. However, if the application is for a 10-year loan, our decision is less optimistic. While the current ratio and working capital suggest a good safety margin, there are indications of inefficiency in operations. In particular, a 4:1 current ratio is more than double its competitors' ratio. This is characteristic of inefficient asset use.

Guidance Answers to Flashbacks

1. General-purpose financial statements are intended for the large variety of users who are interested in receiving financial information about a business but who do not have the ability to require the company to prepare specialized financial reports designed to meet their specific interests.

2. General-purpose financial statements include the income statement, balance sheet, statement of changes in shareholders' equity (or statement of retained earnings), and statement of cash flows, plus notes related to the statements.

3. *a*

4. Data from one or more direct competitors of the company under analysis are usually preferred for developing standards for comparisons.

5. *d*

6. Percents on a comparative income statement show the increase or decrease in each item from one period to the next. On a common-size comparative income statement, each item is shown as a percent of net sales for a specific period.

7. *c*

8. *a* ($820,000 + $240,000 + $470,000)/($350,000 + $180,000) = 2.9 to 1

b ($820,000 + $240,000)/($350,000 + $180,000) = 2 to 1

9. *a* $2,500,000/[($290,000 + $240,000)/2] = 9.43 times

b ($240,000/$2,500,000) × 365 = 35 days

c $750,000/[($530,000 + $470,000)/2] = 1.5 times

d ($470,000/$750,000) × 365 = 228.7 days

10. *c*

11. *b*

12. Profit margin × Total asset turnover = Return on total assets ($945,000/$8,500,000) × 1.8 = 20%

Demonstration Problem

Use the financial statements of Precision Company to satisfy the following requirements: Compute and identify the appropriate building block statement analysis for the following ratios as of December 31, 2000, or for the year ended December 31, 2000:

a. Current ratio
b. Acid-test ratio
c. Accounts receivable turnover
d. Days' sales uncollected
e. Merchandise turnover
f. Debt ratio

g. Pledged assets to secured liabilities
h. Times interest earned
i. Profit margin
j. Total asset turnover
k. Return on total assets
l. Return on common shareholders' equity

PRECISION COMPANY Comparative Income Statement For Years Ended December 31, 2000 and 1999		
	2000	**1999**
Sales	$2,486,000	$2,075,000
Cost of goods sold	1,523,000	1,222,000
Gross profit from sales	$ 963,000	$ 853,000
Operating expenses:		
Advertising expense	$ 145,000	$ 100,000
Sales salaries expense	240,000	280,000
Office salaries expense	165,000	200,000
Insurance expense	100,000	45,000
Supplies expense	26,000	35,000
Amortization expense	85,000	75,000
Miscellaneous expenses	17,000	15,000
Total operating expenses	$ 778,000	$ 750,000
Operating income	$ 185,000	$ 103,000
Less interest expense	44,000	46,000
Income before taxes	$ 141,000	$ 57,000
Income taxes	47,000	19,000
Net income	$ 94,000	$ 38,000
Earnings per share	$ 0.99	$ 0.40

PRECISION COMPANY Comparative Balance Sheet December 31, 2000, and December 31, 1999		
	2000	**1999**
Assets		
Current assets:		
Cash	$ 79,000	$ 42,000
Short-term investments	65,000	96,000
Accounts receivable (net)	120,000	100,000
Merchandise inventory	250,000	265,000
Total current assets	$ 514,000	$ 503,000
Capital Assets:		
Store equipment (net)	$ 400,000	$ 350,000
Office equipment (net)	45,000	50,000
Buildings (net)	625,000	675,000
Land	100,000	100,000
Total capital assets	$1,170,000	$1,175,000
Total assets	$1,684,000	$1,678,000
Liabilities		
Current liabilities:		
Accounts payable	$ 164,000	$ 190,000
Short-term notes payable	75,000	90,000
Taxes payable	26,000	12,000
Total current liabilities	$ 265,000	$ 292,000
Long-term liabilities:		
Notes payable (secured by mortgage on building and land)	400,000	420,000
Total liabilities	$ 665,000	$ 712,000
Shareholders' Equity		
Contributed capital:		
Common shares no-par value	$ 475,000	$ 475,000
Retained earnings	544,000	491,000
Total shareholders' equity	$1,019,000	$ 966,000
Total liabilities and shareholders' equity	$1,684,000	$1,678,000

Planning the Solution

■ Compute the given ratios using the provided numbers; be sure to use the average of the beginning and ending amounts where appropriate.

Solution to Demonstration Problem

Ratios for 2000:

a. Current ratio: $514,000/$265,000 = 1.9 to 1 (Liquidity and Efficiency)

b. Acid-test ratio: ($79,000 + $65,000 + $120,000)/$265,000 = 1.0 to 1 (Liquidity and Efficiency)

c. Average receivables: ($120,000 + $100,000)/2 = $110,000

Accounts receivable turnover: $2,486,000/$110,000 = 22.6 times (Liquidity and Efficiency)

d. Days' sales uncollected: ($120,000/$2,486,000) × 365 = 17.6 days (Liquidity and Efficiency)

e. Average inventory: ($250,000 + $265,000)/2 = $257,500

Merchandise turnover: $1,523,000/$257,500 = 5.9 times (Liquidity and Efficiency)

f. Debt ratio: $665,000/$1,684,000 = 39.5% (Solvency)

g. Pledged assets to secured liabilities: ($625,000 + $100,000)/$400,000 = 1.8 to 1 (Solvency)

h. Times interest earned: $185,000/$44,000 = 4.2 times (Solvency)

i. Profit margin: $94,000/$2,486,000 = 3.8% (Profitability)

j. Average total assets: ($1,684,000 + $1,678,000)/2 = $1,681,000

Total asset turnover: $2,486,000/$1,681,000 = 1.48 times (Liquidity and Efficiency)

k. Return on total assets: $94,000/$1,681,000 = 5.6% or 3.8% × 1.48 = 5.6% (Profitability)

l. Average total equity: ($1,019,000 + $966,000)/2 = $992,500

Return on common shareholders' equity: $94,000/$992,500 = 9.5% (Profitability)

Glossary

Common-size statements Comparative financial statements in which each amount is expressed as a percent of a base amount. In the balance sheet, the amount of total assets is usually selected as the base amount and is expressed as 100%. In the income statement, net sales is usually selected as the base amount. (p. 949)

Comparative financial statement A financial statement with data for two or more successive accounting periods placed in columns side by side, sometimes with changes shown in dollar amounts and percents. (p. 943)

Efficiency Refers to how productive a company is in using its assets; usually measured relative to how much revenue is generated for a certain level of assets. (p. 956)

Equity ratio The portion of total assets provided by shareholders' equity, computed as shareholders' equity divided by total assets. (p. 961)

Financial reporting The process of communicating information that is relevant to investors, creditors, and others in making investment, credit, and similar decisions. (p. 942)

Financial statement analysis The application of analytical tools to general-purpose financial statements and related data for making business decisions. (p. 940)

General-purpose financial statements Statements published periodically for use by a wide variety of interested parties; include the income statement, balance sheet, statement of changes in shareholders' equity (or statement of retained earnings), statement of cash flows, and notes related to the statements. (p. 941)

Liquidity Refers to the availability of resources to meet short-term cash requirements. (p. 956)

Profitability Refers to a company's ability to generate an adequate return on invested capital. (p. 962)

Solvency Refers to a company's long-run financial viability and its ability to cover long-term obligations. (p. 961)

Vertical analysis A tool to evaluate each financial statement item or group of items in terms of a specific base amount; the base amount is commonly defined as 100% and is usually revenue on the income statement and total assets on the balance sheet. (p. 949)

Working capital Current assets minus current liabilities. (p. 956)

Questions

1. Explain the difference between financial reporting and financial statements.

2. What is the difference between comparative financial statements and common-size comparative statements?

3. Which items are usually assigned a value of 100% on a common-size comparative balance sheet and a common-size comparative income statement?

4. Why is working capital given special attention in the process of analyzing balance sheets?

5. What are three factors that would influence your decision as to whether a company's current ratio is good or bad?

6. Suggest several reasons why a 2 to 1 current ratio may not be adequate for a particular company.

7. What does a relatively high accounts receivable turnover indicate about a company's short-term liquidity?

8. What is the significance of the number of days' sales uncollected?

9. Why does merchandise turnover provide information about a company's short-term liquidity?

10. Why is the capital structure of a company, as measured by debt and equity ratios, of importance to financial statement analysts?

11. Why must the ratio of pledged assets to secured liabilities be interpreted with caution?

12. Why would a company's return on total assets be different from its return on common shareholders' equity?

13. What ratios would you compute for the purpose of evaluating management performance?

14. Using the financial statements for Atlantis in Appendix I, compute Atlantis's return on total assets for the fiscal year ended December 31, 1997.

15. Refer to the financial statements for **Alliance** in Appendix I. Compute Alliance's equity ratio as of March 31, 1997.

16. Reread the chapter's opening article about the Beardstown Ladies. Identify three factors that impact the return computation for a group of shares and that may have contributed to the error made by Betty Sinnock.

Quick Study

QS 20-1
Building blocks of analysis

LO 2

Which of the following items are means of accomplishing the objective of financial reporting but are not included within general-purpose financial statements? (a) income statements, (b) company news releases, (c) balance sheets, (d) certain reports filed with the Ontario Securities and Exchange Commission, (e) statements of cash flows, or (f) management discussions and analyses of financial performance.

QS 20-2
Horizontal and vertical analysis

LO 5, 6

Given the following information for Heffington Corporation, determine (a) the common-size percents for gross profit from sales and (b) the trend percents for net sales, using 1999 as the base year.

	2000	1999
Net sales	$201,600	$114,800
Cost of goods sold	109,200	60,200

QS 20-3
Tools of analysis

LO 4

a. Which two short-term liquidity ratios measure how frequently a company collects its accounts?

b. Which two terms are used to describe the difference between current assets and current liabilities?

c. Which two ratios are the basic components in measuring a company's operating efficiency? Which ratio summarizes these two components?

QS 20-4
Standards for comparisons

LO 3

What are five possible standards of comparison you can use when analyzing financial statement ratios? Which of these is generally considered to be the most useful? Which one is least likely to provide a good basis for comparison?

QS 20-5
Purpose and tools of analysis

LO 1, 4

Match the ratio to the building block of financial statement analysis to which it relates:

A. Liquidity and efficiency
B. Solvency
C. Profitability
D. Market

_____ 1. Dividend yield
_____ 2. Return on total assets
_____ 3. Gross Margin
_____ 4. Acid-test ratio
_____ 5. Equity ratio

_____ 6. Times interest earned
_____ 7. Pledged assets to secured liabilities
_____ 8. Book value per common share
_____ 9. Days' sales in inventory
_____ 10. Accounts receivable turnover

For each ratio below identify whether the change in the ratio from 1999 to 2000 would generally be regarded as favourable or unfavourable.

QS 20-6
Define and apply ratio analysis
LO 5, 7

Ratio	2000	1999
1. Profit Margin	8%	6%
2. Debt Ratio	45%	40%
3. Gross Margin	33%	45%
4. Acid-test Ratio	.99	1.10
5. Accounts Receivable Turnover	5.4	6.6
6. Basic Earnings Per Share	$1.24	$1.20
7. Merchandise Turnover	3.5	3.3
8. Dividend Yield	1%	.8%

Compute trend percents for the following items, using 1998 as the base year. Then, state whether the situation shown by the trends appears to be favourable or unfavourable.

Exercises

Exercise 20-1
Computing trend percents
LO 5

	2002	2001	2000	1999	1998
Sales	$283,880	$271,800	$253,680	$235,560	$151,000
Cost of goods sold	129,200	123,080	116,280	107,440	68,000
Accounts receivable	19,100	18,300	17,400	16,200	10,000

Where possible, compute percents of increase and decrease for the following:

Exercise 20-2
Reporting percent changes
LO 5

	2000	1999
Temporary investments	$217,800	$165,000
Accounts receivable	42,120	48,000
Notes payable	57,000	-0-

Express the following income statement information in common-size percents and assess whether the situation is favourable or unfavourable.

Exercise 20-3
Computing common-size percents
LO 6

HARBISON CORPORATION Comparative Income Statement For Years Ended December 31, 2000, and 1999		
	2000	1999
Sales	$720,000	$535,000
Cost of goods sold	475,200	280,340
Gross profit from sales	$244,800	$254,660
Operating expenses	151,200	103,790
Net income	$ 93,600	$150,870

Exercise 20-4
Evaluating short-term liquidity

LO 7

Mixon Company's December 31 balance sheets included the following data:

	2001	2000	1999
Cash	$ 30,800	$ 35,625	$ 36,800
Accounts receivable, net	88,500	62,500	49,200
Merchandise inventory	111,500	82,500	53,000
Prepaid expenses	9,700	9,375	4,000
Capital assets,net	277,500	255,000	229,500
Total assets	$518,000	$445,000	$372,500
Accounts payable	$128,900	$ 75,250	$ 49,250
Long-term notes payable secured by mortgages on capital assets	97,500	102,500	82,500
Common shares, no-par value	162,500	162,500	162,500
Retained earnings	129,100	104,750	78,250
Total liabilities and shareholders' equity ...	$518,000	$445,000	$372,500

Required

Compare the short-term liquidity positions of the company at the end of 2001, 2000, and 1999 by computing: (a) the current ratio and (b) the acid-test ratio. Comment on any changes that occurred.

Exercise 20-5
Calculating common-size percentage

LO 6

Refer to Mixon Company's balance sheets in Exercise 20-4. Express the balance sheets in common-size percents. Round to the nearest tenth percent.

Exercise 20-6
Evaluating short-term liquidity

LO 7

Refer to the information in Exercise 20-4 about Mixon Company. The company's income statements for the years ended December 31, 2001, and 2000 included the following data:

	2001	2000
Sales	$672,500	$530,000
Cost of goods sold	$410,225	$344,500
Other operating expenses	208,550	133,980
Interest expense	11,100	12,300
Income taxes	8,525	7,845
Total costs and expenses	$638,400	$498,625
Net income	$ 34,100	$ 31,375
Earnings per share	$ 2.10	$ 1.93

Required

For the years ended December 31, 2001, and 2000, assume all sales were on credit and compute the following: (a) days' sales uncollected, (b) accounts receivable turnover, (c) merchandise turnover, and (d) days' sales in inventory. Comment on any changes that occurred from 2000 to 2001.

Refer to the information in Exercises 20-4 and 20-5 about Mixon Company. Compare the long-term risk and capital structure positions of the company at the end of 2001 and 2000 by computing the following ratios: (a) debt and equity ratios, (b) pledged assets to secured liabilities, and (c) times interest earned. Comment on any changes that occurred.

Exercise 20-7
Evaluating long-term risk and capital structure
LO 7

Refer to the financial statements of Mixon Company presented in Exercises 20-4 and 20-5. Evaluate the operating efficiency and profitability of the company by computing the following: (a) profit margin, (b) total asset turnover, and (c) return on total assets. Comment on any changes that occurred.

Exercise 20-8
Evaluating operating efficiency and profitability
LO 7

Refer to the financial statements of Mixon Company presented in Exercises 20-4 and 20-5. This additional information about the company is known:

Exercise 20-9
Evaluating profitability
LO 7

Common shares market price, December 31, 2001	$15.00
Common shares market price, December 31, 2000	14.00
Annual cash dividends per share in 2001	.30
Annual cash dividends per share in 2000	.15

Required

To evaluate the profitability of the company, compute the following for 2001 and 2000: (a) return on common shareholders' equity, (b) price-earnings ratio on December 31, and (c) dividend yield.

Common-size and trend percents for a company's sales, cost of goods sold, and expenses follow:

Exercise 20-10
Determining income effects from common-size and trend percents
LO 5,7

	Common-Size Percents			Trend Percents		
	2001	**2000**	**1999**	**2001**	**2000**	**1999**
Sales	100.0%	100.0%	100.0%	104.4%	103.2%	100.0%
Cost of goods sold	62.4	60.9	58.1	102.0	100.1	100.0
Expenses	14.3	13.8	14.1	94.0	90.0	100.0

Required

Determine whether the company's net income increased, decreased, or remained unchanged during this three-year period.

Huff Company and Mesa Company are similar firms that operate within the same industry. The following information is available:

Exercise 20-11
Evaluating short-term liquidity
LO 8

	Huff			Mesa		
	2001	**2000**	**1999**	**2001**	**2000**	**1999**
Current ratio	1.6	1.7	2.0	3.1	2.6	1.8
Acid-test ratio	.9	1.0	1.1	2.7	2.4	1.5
Accounts receivable turnover	29.5	24.2	28.2	15.4	14.2	15.0
Merchandise turnover . .	23.2	20.9	16.1	13.5	12.0	11.6
Working capital	$60,000	$48,000	$42,000	$121,000	$93,000	$68,000

Required

Write a brief essay comparing Huff and Mesa based on the preceding information. Your discussion should include their relative ability to meet current obligations and to use current assets efficiently.

Exercise 20-12
Analyze and report results
of analysis
LO 8

Kampa Company and Arbor Company are similar firms that operate within the same industry. Arbor began operations in 2005 and Kampa in 1999. In 2007, both companies paid 7% interest to creditors. The following information is available:

	KAMPA COMPANY			ARBOR COMPANY		
	2007	2006	2005	2007	2006	2005
Total asset turnover ...	3.0	2.7	2.9	1.6	1.4	1.1
Return on total assets .	8.9	9.5	8.7	5.8	5.5	5.2
Profit margin	2.3	2.4	2.2	2.7	2.9	2.8
Sales	$400,000	$370,000	$386,000	$200,000	$160,000	$100,000

Required

Write a brief essay comparing Kampa and Arbor based on the preceding information. Your discussion should include their relative ability to use assets efficiently to produce profits. Also comment on their relative success in employing financial leverage in 2007.

Problems

Problem 20-1
Computing ratios and
percents
LO 5, 6, 7

The condensed statements of Thornhill Company follow:

THORNHILL COMPANY
Comparative Income Statement ($000)
For Years Ended December 31, 2001, 2000, and 1999

	2001	2000	1999
Sales	$444,000	$340,000	$236,000
Cost of goods sold	267,288	212,500	151,040
Gross profit from sales	$176,712	$127,500	$ 84,960
Selling expenses	$ 62,694	$ 46,920	$ 31,152
Administrative expenses	40,137	29,920	19,470
Total expenses	$102,831	$ 76,840	$ 50,622
Income before taxes	$ 73,881	$ 50,660	$ 34,338
Income taxes	13,764	10,370	6,962
Net income	$ 60,117	$ 40,290	$ 27,376

THORNHILL COMPANY
Comparative Balance Sheet ($000)
December 31, 2001, 2000, and 1999

Assets	2001	2000	1999
Current assets	$ 48,480	$ 37,924	$ 50,648
Long-term investments	- 0 -	500	3,720
Capital assets	90,000	96,000	57,000
Total assets	$138,480	$134,424	$111,368
Liabilities and Shareholders' Equity			
Current liabilities	$ 20,200	$ 19,960	$ 19,480
Common shares	72,000	72,000	54,000
Other contributed capital	9,000	9,000	6,000
Retained earnings	37,280	33,464	31,888
Total liabilities and shareholders' equity ...	$138,480	$134,424	$111,368

Required

Preparation component:

1. Compute each year's current ratio.

2. Express the income statement data in common-size percents.

3. Express the balance sheet data in trend percents with 1999 as the base year.

Analysis component:

4. Comment on any significant relationships revealed by the ratios and percents.

Check Figure 2001, total assets, 124.34

The condensed comparative statements of Cohorn Company follow:

Problem 20-2
Calculation and analysis
of trend percents

LO 5

COHORN COMPANY Comparative Income Statement ($000) For Years Ended December 31, 2005–1999							
	2005	**2004**	**2003**	**2002**	**2001**	**2000**	**1999**
Sales	$1,594	$1,396	$1,270	$1,164	$1,086	$1,010	$ 828
Cost of goods sold	1,146	932	802	702	652	610	486
Gross profit from sales	$ 448	$ 464	$ 468	$ 462	$ 434	$ 400	$ 342
Operating expenses	340	266	244	180	156	154	128
Net income	$ 108	$ 198	$ 224	$ 282	$ 278	$ 246	$ 214

COHORN COMPANY Comparative Balance Sheet ($000) December 31, 2005–1999							
Assets	**2005**	**2004**	**2003**	**2002**	**2001**	**2000**	**1999**
Cash	$ 68	$ 88	$ 92	$ 94	$ 98	$ 96	$ 99
Accounts receivable, net	480	504	456	350	308	292	206
Merchandise inventory	1,738	1,264	1,104	932	836	710	515
Other current assets	46	42	24	44	38	38	19
Long-term investments	-0-	-0-	-0-	136	136	136	136
Capital assets, net	2,120	2,114	1,852	1,044	1,078	960	825
Total assets	$4,452	$4,012	$3,528	$2,600	$2,494	$2,232	$1,800
Liabilities and Equity							
Current liabilities	$1,120	$ 942	$ 618	$ 514	$ 446	$ 422	$ 272
Long-term liabilities	1,194	1,040	1,012	470	480	520	390
Common shares	1,000	1,000	1,000	840	840	640	640
Other contributed capital	250	250	250	180	180	160	160
Retained earnings	888	780	648	596	548	490	338
Total liabilities and equity	$4,452	$4,012	$3,528	$2,600	$2,494	$2,232	$1,800

Required

Preparation component:

1. Compute trend percents for the items of the statements using 1999 as the base year.

Analysis component:

2. Analyze and comment on the situation shown in the statements.

Check Figure 2005 total assets, 247.3

Problem 20-3
Calculation of financial
statement ratios

LO 7

The 2000 financial statements of Hoffman Corporation follow:

HOFFMAN CORPORATION Income Statement For Year Ended December 31, 2000		
Sales		$348,600
Cost of goods sold:		
Merchandise inventory, December 31, 1999	$ 32,400	
Purchases	227,900	
Goods available for sale	$260,300	
Merchandise inventory, December 31, 2000	31,150	
Cost of goods sold		229,150
Gross profit from sales		$119,450
Operating expenses		52,500
Operating income		$ 66,950
Interest expense		3,100
Income before taxes		$ 63,850
Income taxes		15,800
Net income		$ 48,050

HOFFMAN CORPORATION Balance Sheet December 31, 2000			
Assets		**Liabilities and Shareholders' Equity**	
Cash	$ 9,000	Accounts payable	$ 16,500
Temporary investments	7,400	Accrued wages payable	2,200
Accounts receivable, net	28,200	Income taxes payable	2,300
Notes receivable (trade)	3,500	Long-term note payable,	
Merchandise inventory	31,150	secured by mortgage on	
Prepaid expenses	1,650	capital assets	62,400
Capital assets, net	152,300	Common shares, no-par value	90,000
		Retained earnings	59,800
		Total liabilities and	
Total assets	$233,200	shareholders' equity	$233,200

Assume that all sales were on credit. On the December 31, 1999, balance sheet, the assets totalled $182,400, common shares were $90,000, and retained earnings amounted to $31,300.

Required

Compute the following: (a) current ratio, (b) acid-test ratio, (c) days' sales uncollected, (d) merchandise turnover, (e) days' sales in inventory, (f) ratio of pledged assets to secured liabilities, (g) times interest earned, (h) profit margin, (i) total asset turnover, (j) return on total assets, and (k) return on common shareholders' equity.

Two companies that compete in the same industry are being evaluated by a bank that can lend money to only one of them. Summary information from the financial statements of the two companies follows:

Problem 20-4
Comparative analysis of
financial statement ratios
LO 7

	Datatech Company	Sigma Company
Data from the current year-end balance sheets:		
Assets		
Cash	$ 18,500	$ 33,000
Accounts receivable	36,400	56,400
Notes receivable (trade)	8,100	6,200
Merchandise inventory	83,440	131,500
Prepaid expenses	4,000	5,950
Capital assets, net	284,000	303,400
Total assets	$434,440	$536,450
Liabilities and Shareholders' Equity		
Current liabilities	$ 60,340	$ 92,300
Long-term notes payable	79,800	100,000
Common shares, no-par value	175,000	205,000
Retained earnings	119,300	139,150
Total liabilities and shareholders' equity	$434,440	$536,450
Data from the current year's income statements:		
Sales	$660,000	$780,200
Cost of goods sold	485,100	532,500
Operating expenses	87,430	112,400
Interest expense	6,900	11,000
Income tax expense	12,800	19,300
Net income	67,770	105,000
Earnings per share	$ 1.94	$ 2.56
Beginning-of-year data:		
Accounts receivable, net	$ 28,800	$ 53,200
Notes receivable	-0-	-0-
Merchandise inventory	54,600	106,400
Total assets	388,000	372,500
Common shares, no par value	175,000	205,000
Retained earnings	94,300	90,600

Required

1. Compute the current ratio, acid-test ratio, accounts (including notes) receivable turnover, merchandise turnover, days' sales in inventory, and days' sales uncollected for the two companies. Then, identify the company that you consider to be the better short-term credit risk and explain why.

2. Compute the profit margin, total asset turnover, return on total assets, and return on common shareholders' equity for the two companies. Assuming that each company paid cash dividends of $1.50 per share and each company's shares can be purchased at $25 per share, compute their price-earnings ratios and dividend yields. Also, identify which company's shares you would recommend as the better investment and explain why.

Problem 20-5
Analysis of working capital

LO 7

Providence Corporation began the month of May with $650,000 of current assets, a current ratio of 2.5 to 1, and an acid-test ratio of 1.1 to 1. During the month, it completed the following transactions:

May 2 Bought $75,000 of merchandise on account. (The company uses a perpetual inventory system.)

8 Sold merchandise that cost $58,000 for $103,000.

10 Collected a $19,000 account receivable.

15 Paid a $21,000 account payable.

17 Wrote off a $3,000 bad debt against the Allowance for Doubtful Accounts account.

22 Declared a $1 per share cash dividend on the 40,000 shares of outstanding common shares.

26 Paid the dividend declared on May 22.

27 Borrowed $75,000 by giving the bank a 30-day, 10% note.

28 Borrowed $90,000 by signing a long-term secured note.

29 Used the proceeds from notes plus another $100,000 to buy additional machinery.

Check Figure May 29 working capital, $310,000

Required

Prepare a schedule showing Providence's current ratio, acid-test ratio, and working capital after each of the transactions. Round calculations to two decimal places.

Alternate Problems

Problem 20-1A
Computing ratios and percents

LO 5, 6, 7

The condensed statements of Temptron Corporation follow:

TEMPTRON CORPORATION Comparative Income Statement ($000) For Years Ended December 31, 2001, 2000, and 1999			
	2001	**2000**	**1999**
Sales	$199,800	$167,000	$144,800
Cost of goods sold	109,890	87,175	67,200
Gross profit from sales	$ 89,910	$ 79,825	$ 77,600
Selling expenses	$ 23,680	$ 20,790	$ 19,000
Administrative expenses	17,760	15,610	16,700
Total expenses	$ 41,440	$ 36,400	$ 35,700
Income before taxes	$ 48,470	$ 43,425	$ 41,900
Income taxes	5,050	4,910	4,300
Net income	$ 43,420	$ 38,515	$ 37,600

TEMPTRON CORPORATION Comparative Balance Sheet ($000) December 31, 2001, 2000, and 1999			
	2001	**2000**	**1999**
Assets			
Current assets	$ 55,860	$ 33,660	$ 37,300
Long-term investments	-0-	2,700	11,600
Capital assets	113,810	114,660	80,000
Total assets	$169,670	$151,020	$128,900
Liabilities and Shareholders' Equity			
Current liabilities	$ 23,370	$ 20,180	$ 17,500
Common shares	47,500	47,500	38,000
Other contributed capital	14,850	14,850	12,300
Retained earnings	83,950	68,490	61,100
Total liabilities and shareholders' equity	$169,670	$151,020	$128,900

Required

Preparation component:

1. Compute each year's current ratio.

2. Express the income statement data in common-size percents.

3. Express the balance sheet data in trend percents with 1999 as the base year.

Analysis component:

4. Comment on any significant relationships revealed by the ratios and percents.

The condensed comparative statements of Hensley Company follow:

Problem 20-2A
Calculation and analysis
of trend percents

LO 5

HENSLEY COMPANY Comparative Income Statement ($000) For Years Ended December 31, 2005–1999							
	2005	**2004**	**2003**	**2002**	**2001**	**2000**	**1999**
Sales	$660	$710	$730	$780	$840	$870	$960
Cost of goods sold . . .	376	390	394	414	440	450	480
Gross profit from sales .	$284	$320	$336	$366	$400	$420	$480
Operating expenses . . .	184	204	212	226	240	244	250
Net income	$100	$116	$124	$140	$160	$176	$230

HENSLEY COMPANY Comparative Balance Sheet ($000) December 31, 2005–1999							
	2005	**2004**	**2003**	**2002**	**2001**	**2000**	**1999**
Assets							
Cash	$34	$36	$42	$44	$50	$52	$58
Accounts receivable, net	120	126	130	134	140	144	150
Merchandise inventory .	156	162	168	170	176	180	198
Other current assets . .	24	24	26	28	28	30	30
Long-term investments	26	20	16	100	100	100	100
Capital assets, net	410	414	420	312	320	328	354
Total assets	$770	$782	$802	$788	$814	$834	$890
Liabilities and Equity							
Current liabilities	$138	$146	$176	$180	$200	$250	$270
Long-term liabilities . . .	82	110	132	138	184	204	250
Common shares	150	150	150	150	150	150	150
Other contributed capital	60	60	60	60	60	60	60
Retained earnings	340	316	284	260	220	170	160
Total liabilities and equity	$770	$782	$802	$788	$814	$834	$890

Required

Preparation component:

1. Compute trend percents for the items of the statements using 1999 as the base year.

Analysis component:

2. Analyze and comment on the situation shown in the statements.

Problem 20-3A
Calculation of financial
statement ratios

LO 7

The 2000 financial statements of Nowland Corporation follow:

NOWLAND CORPORATION
Income Statement
For Year Ended December 31, 2000

Sales		$215,500
Cost of goods sold:		
Merchandise inventory, December 31, 1999	$ 16,400	
Purchases	132,200	
Goods available for sale	$148,600	
Merchandise inventory, December 31, 2000	12,500	
Cost of goods sold		136,100
Gross profit from sales		$ 79,400
Operating expenses		50,200
Operating income		$ 29,200
Interest expense		1,200
Income before taxes		$ 28,000
Income taxes		2,200
Net income		$ 25,800

NOWLAND CORPORATION
Balance Sheet
December 31, 2000

Assets		Liabilities and Shareholders' Equity	
Cash	$5,100	Accounts payable	$10,500
Temporary investments	5,900	Accrued wages payable	2,300
Accounts receivable, net	11,100	Income taxes payable	1,600
Notes receivable (trade)	2,000	Long-term note payable,	
Merchandise inventory	12,500	secured by mortgage on capital assets	25,000
Prepaid expenses	1,000	Common shares, no-par value	41,000
Capital assets, net	72,900	Retained earnings	30,100
		Total liabilities and	
Total assets	$110,500	and shareholders' equity	$110,500

Assume that all sales were on credit. On the December 31, 1999, balance sheet, the assets totalled $95,900, common shares were $41,500, and retained earnings were $19,800.

Required

Compute the following: (a) current ratio, (b) acid-test ratio, (c) days' sales uncollected, (d) merchandise turnover, (e) days' sales in inventory, (f) ratio of pledged assets to secured liabilities, (g) times interest earned, (h) profit margin, (i) total asset turnover, (j) return on total assets, and (k) return on common shareholders' equity.

Two companies that operate in the same industry as competitors are being evaluated by a bank that can lend money to only one of them. Summary information from the financial statements of the two companies follows:

Problem 20-4A
Comparative analysis of
financial statement ratios

	Lutz Comapny	Highland Company
Data from the current year-end balance sheets		
Assets		
Cash	$ 22,000	$ 38,500
Accounts receivable	79,100	72,500
Notes receivable (trade)	13,600	11,000
Merchandise inventory	88,800	84,000
Prepaid expenses	11,700	12,100
Capital assets, net	178,900	254,300
Total assets	$394,100	$472,400
Liabilities and Shareholders' Equity		
Current liabilities	$ 92,500	$ 99,000
Long-term notes payable	95,000	95,300
Common shares, no-par value	135,000	143,000
Retained earnings	71,600	135,100
Total liabilities and shareholders' equity	$394,100	$472,400
Data from the current year's income statements		
Sales	$395,600	$669,500
Cost of goods sold	292,600	482,000
Operating expenses	51,550	97,100
Interest expense	7,900	12,400
Income tax expense	7,700	14,300
Net income	35,850	63,700
Earnings per share	$ 1.33	$ 2.23
Beginning-of-year data		
Accounts receivable, net	$ 74,200	$ 75,300
Notes receivable	-0-	-0-
Merchandise inventory	107,100	82,500
Total assets	385,400	445,000
Common shares, no-par value	135,000	143,000
Retained earnings	51,100	111,700

Required

1. Compute the current ratio, acid-test ratio, accounts (including notes) receivable turnover, merchandise turnover, days' sales in inventory, and days' sales uncollected for the two companies. Then, identify the company that you consider to be the better short-term credit risk and explain why.

2. Compute the profit margin, total asset turnover, return on total assets, and return on common shareholders' equity for the two companies. Assuming that each company paid cash dividends of $3 per share and each company's shares can be purchased at $25 per share, compute their price earnings ratios and dividend yields. Also, identify which company's shares you would recommend as the better investment and explain why.

Problem 20-5A
Analysis of working capital

Resource Corporation began the month of June with $280,000 of current assets, a current ratio of 2.80 to 1, and an acid-test ratio of 1.2 to 1. During the month, it completed the following transactions:

June 1 Sold merchandise that cost $62,000 for $101,000.
      3 Collected a $78,000 account receivable.
      5 Bought $130,000 of merchandise on account. (The company uses a perpetual inventory system.)
      7 Borrowed $90,000 by giving the bank a 60-day, 10% note.
   10 Borrowed $180,000 by signing a long-term secured note.
   12 Used $280,000 cash to buy additional machinery.
   15 Declared a $1 per share cash dividend on the 60,000 shares of outstanding common shares.
   19 Wrote off a $7,000 bad debt against Allowance for Doubtful Accounts.
   22 Paid a $11,000 account payable.
   31 Paid the dividend declared on June 15.

Required

Prepare a schedule showing the company's current ratio, acid-test ratio, and working capital after each of the transactions. Round to two decimal places.

Analytical and Review Problems

A & R 20-1

In your position as controller of Skinner Company, you are responsible for keeping the board of directors informed about the financial activities and status of the company. In preparing for the next board meeting, you have calculated the following ratios, turnovers, and percentages to enable you to answer questions:

Year	1998	1997	1996
Sales trend	137.00	125.00	100.00
Selling expenses to net sales	9.8%	13.7%	15.3%
Sales to capital assets	3.5 to 1	3.3 to 1	3 to 1
Current ratio	2.6 to 1	2.4 to 1	2.1 to 1
Acid-test ratio	0.8 to 1	1.1 to 1	1.2 to 1
Merchandise turnover	7.5 times	8.7 times	9.9 times
Accounts receivable turnover	6.7 times	7.4 times	8.2 times
Total asset turnover	2.6 times	2.6 times	3.0 times
Return on total assets	8.8 %	9.4%	10.1%
Return on shareholders' equity	9.75%	11.5%	12.25%
Profit margin	3.3%	3.5%	3.7%

Required

Using the preceding data, answer each of the following questions and explain your answers:

a. Is it becoming easier for the company to meet its current debts on time and to take advantage of cash discounts?

b. Is the company collecting its accounts receivable more rapidity?

c. Is the company's investment in accounts receivable decreasing?

d. Are dollars invested in inventory increasing?

e. Is the company's investment in capital assets increasing?

f. Is the shareholders' investment becoming more profitable?

g. Is the company using its assets efficiently?

h. Did the dollar amount of selling expenses decrease during the three-year period?

A & R 20-2

PETER LAU CORPORATION Balance Sheet December 31, 2000			
Assets		**Liabilities and Shareholders' Equity**	
Cash	$ ____	Current liabilities	$ ____
Accounts receivable, net	____	8% bonds payable	____
Merchandise inventory		Common shares, no-par value	$15,000
Capital assets, net . . .	____	Retained earnings	____
		Total liabilities and	
Total assets	$ ____	shareholders' equity.	$ ____

Sales (all credit)	$40,000
Cost of goods sold	24,000
Expenses	13,000
Income taxes	1,000
Net income	2,000
Net income/shareholders' equity	10%
Bonds payable/shareholders'equity	1 to 4
Inventory turnover	4 times
Accounts receivable collection period (360-day year)	45 days
Current ratio	2 to 1
Total asset turnover	1.25 times

Required

Complete the above balance sheet for Peter Lau Corporation.

A & R 20-3

A company began the month of May with $200,000 of current assets, a 2 to 1 current ratio, and a 1 to 1 acid-test (quick) ratio. During the month the following transactions were completed:

a. Bought $20,000 of merchandise on account.

b. Sold $25,000 of merchandise costing $15,000.

c. Collected an $8,500 account receivable.

d. Paid a $12,000 account payable.

e. Wrote off a $1,000 bad debt against the allowance account.

f. Declared a $1 per share cash dividend on the 10,000 common shares outstanding.

g. Paid the dividend declared in (f).

h. Borrowed $12,000 by giving the bank a 60-day, 10% note.

i. Borrowed $30,000 by placing a 10-year mortage on the capital assets.

j. Used $20,000 of proceeds of the mortgage to buy additional machinery.

Required

1. State the effect of each of the above transactions on working capital and on the current ratio. Give the effect in terms of increase, decrease or no effect. (Working capital is defined as "current assets minus current liabilities.")

2. For the end of May, calculate the
   i) current ratio
   ii) Acid-test ratio
   iii) Working capital

Reporting in Action

LO 5, 6

Refer to the financial statements and related information for **Alliance** in Appendix I. Answer the following questions by analyzing the available information.

1. Using 1995 as the base year, compute trend percents for 1995–1997 for revenues, gross profit, other expenses, income taxes, and net income. (Round to the nearest whole percent).

2. Compute common-size percents for 1997 and 1996 for the following categories of assets: (a) cash and short-term investments, (b) investment in film and television, (c) property and equipment, and (d) other assets. (Round to the nearest tenth percent).

3. Comment on any significant changes between years for the income statement trends and balance sheet percents.

4. Obtain access to Alliances's annual report for fiscal years ending after March 31, 1997. This access may be through alternative sources including the following Web site: **http:www.sedar.com.** Update your work for 1 and 2 above for any new information you have accessed.

Comparative Analysis

LO 6

Both **NIKE** and **Reebok** design, produce, market and sell sports footwear and apparel. Key comparative figures ($ thousands) for these two organizations follow:

Key Figures	NIKE 1997	Reebok 1996
Cash and equivalents	$445,421	$232,365
Accounts receivable	1,754,137	590,504
Inventory	1,338,640	544,522
Retained earnings	2,973,663	992,563
Cost of sales	5,502,993	2,144,422
Income taxes	499,400	84,083
Revenues (NIKE)	9,186,539	
Net sales (Reebok)		3,478,604
Total assets	5,361,207	1,786,184

* NIKE figures are from the annual report for the fiscal year ended May 31,1997.
Reebok figures are from the annual report for the fiscal year ended December 31, 1996.

Required

1. Compute common-size percents for the two companies for both years using the selected data provided.

2. Which company incurred a higher percent of their revenues or net sales as income tax expense?

3. Which company has retained a higher portion of total earnings in the company?

4. Which company has a higher gross margin on sales?

5. Which company is holding a higher percent of total assets as inventory?

In your position as controller of Tallman Company, you are responsible for keeping the board of directors informed about the financial activities and status of the company. At the board meeting you present the following report:

	2004	2003	2002
Sales trend	147.00	135.00	100.00
Selling expenses to net sales	10.1%	14.0%	15.6%
Sales to capital assets	3.8 to 1	3.6 to 1	3.3 to 1
Current ratio	2.9 to 1	2.7 to 1	2.4 to 1
Acid-test ratio	1.1 to 1	1.4 to 1	1.5 to 1
Merchandise turnover	7.8 times	9.0 times	10.2 times
Accounts receivable turnover	7.0 times	7.7 times	8.5 times
Total asset turnover	2.9 times	2.9 times	3.3 times
Return on total assets	9.1%	9.7%	10.4%
Return on shareholders' equity	9.75%	11.50%	12.25%
Profit margin	3.6%	3.8%	4.0%

After the meeting is over you overhear the company's CEO holding a press conference with analysts in which she mentions the following ratios.

	2004	2003	2002
Sales trend	147.00	135.00	100.00
Selling expenses to net sales	10.1%	14.0%	15.6%
Sales to capital assets	3.8 to 1	3.6 to 1	3.3 to 1
Current ratio	2.9 to 1	2.7 to 1	2.4 to 1

1. Why do think the CEO decided to report 4 ratios instead of the full 11 that you prepared?

2. Comment on the possible consequences of the CEO's decision.

The class should be divided into teams. Each team is to select a different industry, and each team member is to select a different company in that industry. Each team member is to acquire the annual report of the company selected. Annual reports can be obtained in many ways including the following Web site: **http://www.sedar.com.** Use the annual reports to analyze the company using at least one ratio from each of the four categories presented in this chapter. Where necessary use the financial press to determine the market price of the firm's shares. Communicate with teammates via a meeting, e-mail, or telephone to discuss how different companies compare to each other, and to industry norms. The team is to prepare a single memo reporting a comparison of the companies analyzed. The memo is also to present any conclusions reached from the comparison. Duplicate the memo and distribute it to the instructor and all classmates.

Taking It to the Net
LO 1, 4

A focus of both financial press and public is the TSE 100. While many people monitor the TSE 100 the majority of the public may not know what companies comprise the average. Visit the Web site **http://www.tse.com.**

1. Name five companies included as part of the TSE 100.
2. What are the stock symbols of the five companies you have chosen?
3. Click on "Quote look-up" on the top bar and search for any two of the five companies you have chosen. Report on the information retrieved by your search.

Teamwork in Action
LO 2, 4, 5, 6, 7

The aim of this activity is to provide team support for understanding the various approaches to analyzing information in financial statements.

A. After a team discussion of the meaning of horizontal and vertical analysis, write up a description of each that all team members agree with and understand. Illustrate each description with an example.

B. *Each* member of the team is to select *one* of the categories of ratio analysis listed below. Prepare notes to explain what the ratios in that category measure. Choose one specific ratio from the category selected. In your notes, present the formula for this ratio, and explain what it specifically measures.

1. Liquidity and Efficiency
2. Solvency
3. Profitability
4. Market

C. Each member is to report their notes from (B) to teammates. Team members are to confirm or correct teammate's presentation.

Hitting the Road
LO 1

This chapter and this course have given you tools to become a successful investor upon graduation. Devise a savings/investment strategy whereby you are able to accumulate $1,000,000 by age 65. Start by making some assumptions about your starting salary once you graduate from university or college. Next compute the percent of your salary that you will be able to save each year. If you will receive any lump-sum monies upon graduation you can also factor those amounts into your calculations. Historically, investments in shares have delivered average annual returns of 10–11%. Given this history you should probably not assume that you will earn above 10% on the money you invest. It is not necessary to specify in this assignment exactly what types of assets you will buy for your investments, just make an assumption about an interest rate that you expect to earn. Use the future value tables in Appendix II to calculate how your savings will grow. Experiment a bit with your figures to see how much less you have to save if you start at age 25 versus age 35 or 40. (For this assignment do not worry about factoring inflation into your calculations.)

Read the article, "Debt-to-equity ratio proves fundamental," in the July 25–27, 1998 weekend edition of *The Financial Post*.

Required

1. What is it that the article says is most often ignored during a rising stock market?
2. What surprises the author of this article about the performance of companies with high or low debt levels during a rising market?
3. How do companies with high dividend yields perform during a market correction (falling share prices) compared with the performance of firms with low debt ratios?
4. What problems can too much debt bring to a company? What first piece of advice does the author offer for the investor who desires to find companies that are less likely to fall apart during a downturn?

I APPENDIX

Financial Statement Information

This appendix includes financial statement information from (a) **Alliance Communications Corporation** and (b) **Atlantis Communications Inc.** All of this information is taken from their annual reports. An **annual report** is a summary of the financial results of a company's operations for the year and its future plans. It is directed at external users of financial information, but also affects actions of internal users.

An annual report is also used by a company to showcase itself and its products. Many include attractive pictures, diagrams and illustrations related to the company. But the *financial section* is its primary objective. This section communicates much information about a company, with most data drawn from the accounting information system.

The layout of the financial section of an annual report is fairly standard and usually includes:

■ Financial History and Highlights
■ Message to Shareholders
■ Management Discussion and Analysis
■ Management Report
■ Auditor's Report
■ Financial Statements
■ Notes to Financial Statements
■ List of Directors and Managers

This appendix provides most of this information for Alliance Communications Corporation and Atlantis Communications Inc. This appendix is organized as follows:

■ Alliance: I-1 to I-33
■ Atlantis: I-34 to I-60

Many assignments at the end of each chapter refer to information in this appendix. We encourage readers to spend extra time with these assignments as they are especially useful in reinforcing and showing the relevance and diversity of financial reporting.

ALLIANCE

CORPORATE PROFILE
Alliance Communications Corporation is a global producer, distributor and broadcaster of filmed entertainment. Headquartered in Toronto with offices in Montreal, Vancouver, Los Angeles, Paris and Shannon, Alliance shares trade in Toronto and Montreal under AAC, and on NASDAQ under the symbol ALLIF.

ALLIANCE

CORPORATE HIGHLIGHTS

CORPORATE STRUCTURE

Alliance Communications Corporation

Alliance Television Group   Alliance Motion Picture Group   Alliance Broadcasting Group   Alliance Multimedia Group   Alliance Equicap

REVENUES
in millions of dollars

Year	Value
1997	283
1996	269
1995	234
1994	109
1993	132

Scale: 50 | 100 | 150 | 200 | 250 | 300

CASH FLOW FROM OPERATIONS
in millions of dollars

Year	Value
1997	241
1996	175
1995	169
1994	111
1993	104

Scale: 50 | 100 | 150 | 200 | 250

EBITDA
in millions of dollars

Year	Value
1997	27
1996	19
1995	21
1994	12
1993	9

Scale: 5 | 10 | 15 | 20 | 25 | 30

INVESTMENTS IN FILM AND TELEVISION

Year	Value
1997	102
1996	63
1995	61
1994	51
1993	27

Scale: 20 | 40 | 60 | 80 | 100 | 120

NET EARNINGS
in millions of dollars

Year	Value
1997	18
1996	10
1995	13
1994	7
1993	5

Scale: 5 | 10 | 15 | 20

TOTAL ASSETS
in millions of dollars

Year	Value
1997	354
1996	239
1995	226
1994	186
1993	97

Scale: 50 | 100 | 150 | 200 | 250 | 300 | 350 | 400

BASIC EARNINGS PER COMMON SHARE
in dollars

Year	Value
1997	1.53
1996	1.05
1995	1.36
1994	1.01
1993	0.96

Scale: 0.20 | 0.40 | 0.60 | 0.80 | 1.00 | 1.20 | 1.40 | 1.60

SHAREHOLDERS' EQUITY
in millions of dollars

Year	Value
1997	150
1996	95
1995	84
1994	70
1993	13

Scale: 20 | 40 | 60 | 80 | 100 | 120 | 140 | 160

CORPORATE HIGHLIGHTS

AWARDS AND HONOURS

MOTION PICTURE AWARDS

Berlin Film Festival	C.I.C.A.E. Award	Welcome to the Dollhouse
Cannes International Film Festival	Special Jury Prize	Crash
Fantasporto, Portugal	Critics Award	Denise Calls Up
Fantasporto, Portugal	Audience Award	Denise Calls Up
Genie Awards	Best Achievement in Sound Editing	Crash
Genie Awards	Best Achievement in Film Editing	Crash
Genie Awards	Best Achievement in Art Direction	Lilies
Genie Awards	Best Achievement in Costume Design	Lilies
Genie Awards	Golden Reel Award	Crash
Genie Awards	Best Motion Picture	Lilies
Genie Awards	Best Overall Sound	Lilies
Genie Awards	Best Adapted Screenplay	Crash
Genie Awards	Best Achievement in Cinematography	Crash
Genie Awards	Best Achievement in Direction	Crash
Deauville Festival of American Cinema	Grand Prize	The Daytrippers
Sundance Film Festival	Filmmaker's Trophy Award	In the Company of Men

CANNES INTERNATIONAL FILM FESTIVAL AWARDS (MAY 1997)

Cannes International Film Festival	Grand Prix	The Sweet Hereafter
Cannes International Film Festival	International Critics Prize	The Sweet Hereafter
Cannes International Film Festival	Ecumenical Prize	The Sweet Hereafter

TELEVISION AWARDS

Banff International Television Festival	Best Continuing Series	Due South
Banff International Television Festiva	Best Animated Program	ReBoot
Golden Gates, San Francisco	Golden Gate Award	Due South
Worldfest Houston	Gold Award	Mirror Mirror
Worldfest Houston	Silver Award	Reboot
Gemini Awards	Chrysler Canada Award	Due South
Gemini Awards	Best Dramatic Series	Due South
Gemini Awards	Best Performance by an Actress	North of 60
Gemini Awards	Best Animated Program or Series	Reboot
Gemini Awards	Best Performance by a Supporting Actor	North of 60
Gemini Awards	Best Direction	Straight Up
Gemini Awards	Best Performance by an Actress	Mother Trucker: The Diana Kilmury Story
Worldfest Houston	Gold Special Jury Award	The Hunchback

PRIMETIME EMMY AWARDS NOMINATIONS (JULY 1997)

Outstanding Art Direction for a Miniseries or a Special	The Hunchback
Outstanding Costume Design for a Miniseries or a Special	The Hunchback
Outstanding Hairstyling for a Miniseries or a Special	The Hunchback
Outstanding Makeup for a Miniseries or a Special	The Hunchback
Outstanding Costume Design for a Miniseries or a Special	The Inheritance

SELECTED HIGHLIGHTS

May 20/96   Crash wins Special Jury Prize at Cannes Film Festival.

June 1/96   Diane Keaton signs first look deal with Alliance.

June 25/96   Alliance signs exclusive television deal with Director John Woo.

July 23/96   Crash becomes first Canadian motion picture to capture, in its opening week, first place at the French box office.

Aug. 22/96   Alliance completes cross border offering, realizing net proceeds of $32.9 million.

Sept. 4/96   Alliance wins coveted analog license to launch History Television.

Sept. 18/96   Alliance realizes profit in Mainframe investment and retains international distribution deal.

Sept. 19/96   Alliance forms Equicap Financial Corporation. Robert Beattie named division head.

Oct. 30/96   Principal photography begins on Atom Egoyan's The Sweet Hereafter.

Nov. 15/96   The English Patient opens in Canada culminating in $13 million at the box office.

Nov. 27/96   Crash wins 6 Genie awards including the Golden Reel Award for top grossing film. Lilies wins Genie award for Best Motion Picture.

Jan. 13/97   Alliance/Shaw Partnership files application for a national Video on Demand programming service.

Jan. 13/97   Alliance begins production with international partners on Captain Star, the Company's first conventional animation series.

Jan. 23/97   Alliance increases ownership in Showcase Television to 99%.

Jan. 23/97   Alliance acquires 20% interest in La Fete Group.

Feb. 27/97   Alliance forms joint venture with UK theatrical distributor, Electric Pictures.

Mar. 2/97   Alliance wins 7 Gemini Awards including Best Dramatic Series for Due South.

Mar. 4/97   Alliance begins principal photography on John Woo's Once a Thief, the series, for delivery on fiscal 1998.

Mar. 24/97   Films distributed in Canada by Alliance Releasing win 12 Academy Awards led by The English Patient.

ALLIANCE

MESSAGE TO SHAREHOLDERS

Fiscal 1997 was a year of success for Alliance. On the one hand, the company experienced earnings growth momentum, particularly in the core production, distribution and broadcasting businesses. On the other hand, Alliance's long term strategies began to bear fruit as the company achieved a number of its targeted objectives.

Robert Lantos
Chairman and
Chief Executive Officer

MESSAGE TO SHAREHOLDERS

We pursued our two-pronged strategy with determination and confidence:

1. TO MAXIMIZE OUR ACCESS TO THE MARKET BY BUILDING OUR DIRECT DISTRIBUTION REACH.

•We renewed long term Canadian distribution agreements with the two top US independent motion picture producers, Miramax and New Line.

•We successfully applied to the CRTC for a license to launch a new specialty network - History Television - a highly-prized and fiercely contested service which was awarded one of the last analog licenses and which will be launched on a new specialty tier by all major Canadian Cable Systems in September 1997.

•We consolidated our ownership of Showcase Television through the acquisition of most of the minority interest thereby increasing our equity from 55% to 99%.

•We ensured long term revenue growth for Showcase Television, obtaining the CRTC's approval to increase the service's permitted advertising time to 12 minutes per hour from its original 8 minute maximum.

•We expanded the reach of the now profitable Showcase Television to 3.5 million homes which will grow to 4 million in September 1997 through a new carriage agreement with Videotron and CF Cable in Montreal.

•Through a 50-50 joint venture with Shaw Communications, we applied for and received a license to launch a national Video-On-Demand service in English and French, a new distribution medium which we believe will have a significant long term impact on revenues.

•We entered the UK theatrical distribution market, teaming with distributor Electric Pictures.

•We expanded into the US first-run syndication market through distribution agreements with Polygram Filmed Entertainment.

•We acquired a 20% interest in Canada's leading childrens' film producer, Quebec's Les Productions La Fete, with an option to double our equity.

•We launched an in-house ad sales division in our Broadcasting Group, replacing the previous agency arrangements and resulting in immediate revenue growth.

•We acquired Canadian distribution rights to approximately 100 hours of drama from producer Telescene.

•We expanded our Canadian video operations into the distribution of non-theatrical product, including titles from Nelvana's animation catalogue.

Victor Loewy
President - Alliance Motion
Picture Distribution
Vice Chairman - Alliance
Communications Corporation

4

ALLIANCE

2. TO BUILD AND IMPROVE OUR CONTENT LIBRARY.

•We retain long term distribution rights by producing proprietary projects. We ensure continued production growth through increased investment in in-house development, exclusive deals with carefully targeted high profile talent, and by recruiting skilled creative executives.
This philosophy has already begun to yield dividends as highlighted in television by John Woo's *Once A Thief*, Diane Keaton's *Northern Lights* and Larry Gelbart's *Fast Track*, and in motion pictures by Atom Egoyan's *The Sweet Hereafter* and by the upcoming David Cronenberg's *eXistenZ*, Istvan Szabo's *Sunshine*, and Costa-Gavras' *No Other Life*.

Throughout the year, we continued our relentless pursuit of excellence. The quality of our product determines our stature in the industry and the prices we command in the international marketplace.

In turn, our peers rewarded us with some of the industry's highest laurels:

•Once again we won the top Canadian television and film honours. At the Gemini Awards, *Due South* was named Best Dramatic Series for the third consecutive year – the tenth time an Alliance produced series won this award. Also for the third time, *Due South* won the Chrysler Canada Award for Most Popular Television Program and *ReBoot* won the Gemini for Best Animated Program.

•*Crash* won a Special Jury Prize at the 1996 Cannes Film Festival.

•In May 1997, *The Sweet Hereafter*, the fourth Alliance collaboration with director Atom Egoyan, was the most decorated film at this year's Cannes Film Festival, winning three major awards including the Grand Prix. It is now three years in a row that an Alliance film has won an award in Cannes.

•Motion pictures acquired for Canada by Alliance such as *The English Patient, Shine, Secrets & Lies* and *Sling Blade* won 12 Academy Awards this year.

•In July 1997, Alliance received five prime time Emmy nominations, four for *The Hunchback* and one for *The Inheritance*.

Ultimately, our strategy is – to put it bluntly – to make money – which is exactly what we accomplished in fiscal 1997 with a 27% growth in earnings from $10.4 million to $13.2 million, a 42% growth in EBITDA from $18.8 million to $26.7 million, and a 66% growth in pre-tax earnings from $12.3 million to $20.4 million. (These results are exclusive of the Mainframe related gain). Our distribution-driven, diversified production strategy ensures that this growth will continue in fiscal 1998 and in the years to follow.

From left to right:
Atom Egoyan, director and producer of *The Sweet Hereafter*. **John Woo**, director and executive producer of *Once a Thief*, the movie. **David Cronenberg**, writer, director and producer of *Crash*. **Dianne Keaton**, executive producer and star of *Northern Lights*

ALLIANCE

MESSAGE TO SHAREHOLDERS

A report to our shareholders must be more than just corporate cheerleading. A critical analysis of the company must also take into account its vulnerabilities and unfulfilled expectations. This year at Alliance:

1. We targeted the UK market because, after the US, it is the world's strongest source of independent movies. To support the initiative we competed for a lottery franchise in order to better access British film subsidies.

We assembled a strong and diverse group of partners. Under the name Studio Pictures, we competed for a franchise award which, had it succeeded, would have triggered some $60 million of off-balance sheet production financing over five years.

Although we were not successful, we achieved our goal of expanding Alliance's production reach into the UK, forging an important tie with one of the UK's leading film production executives, George Faber, the former head of BBC Films. Mr. Faber's Company Pictures, in which Alliance is a shareholder, now has an overall production deal with Alliance. The British distributor Electric Pictures formed the platform for our move into the UK distribution market.

2. Our television production slate suffered from an imbalance between series and movies. With only two series in production, television movies dominated the slate. Movies are more costly per hour than series. This negatively impacted our gross margins. The imbalance has been addressed. Fiscal 1998 features our largest television production slate ever with 120 hours confirmed for delivery this year.

The slate is now dominated by series, with six in production and several pilots underway. Because we own extensive rights in perpetuity to all our productions, even the less profitable television movies are valuable additions to our library and will continue to generate revenues well beyond their amortization cycle.

3. In 1994, we invested in a start-up television station in Hungary, Budapest TV3. Our strategy was to create a new market for our library and, parallel with our investment, we entered into a long term product supply agreement with TV3.

The Company's diverse day to day business activities are managed by a Management Executive Committee comprised of Robert Lantos, Victor Loewy and shown here from left to right.

Roman Doroniuk
Chief Financial Officer,
George Burger
Executive Vice-President,
Jeff Rayman
Chairman,
Alliance Multimedia
President,
Alliance Equicap

ALLIANCE

While the station has been modestly successful, we are experiencing collection difficulties on our supply agreement which has now been suspended. Our investment in TV3 is not material (approximately $1.3 million) and we believe that its value is not at present impaired. With TV3 not proving to be of strategic value to our library sales, the Company may sell its interest in the station.

THE EQUICAP FACTOR

Our focus on expansion and the strengthening of our core businesses over the past three years has significantly reduced Equicap's share of the overall earnings picture of Alliance. The potential negative impact of ending Equicap's tax shelter activities on the Company's earnings has been minimized.

In fiscal 1997, Equicap's tax shelter business contributed approximately $4.5 million to our net earnings, or 34% excluding the Mainframe gain, down from 38% in fiscal 1996. Net earnings in our core businesses increased from 1996 to 1997 by 34%, excluding the Mainframe gain.

Our growing production slate, renewed distribution output deals, growth in our broadcasting business and revenues generated by our library will ensure that our overall earnings growth is not compromised by a reduced contribution from Equicap in fiscal 1998 and beyond. We are confident that we have successfully replaced Equicap's tax shelter earnings with valuable and predictable profits from our growing core activities.

While we anticipate no earnings from tax shelters in fiscal 1999, we do expect growing revenue and earning streams from Equicap's new ventures led by Equicap Financial Corporation.

HIDDEN ASSETS

A brief inventory of some extraordinary assets whose value is not fully reflected on the balance sheet:

1. We have amassed a world class library of movies, television drama and animation — the largest and most valuable library ever assembled by a Canadian company. It consists of over 1,000 hours of international rights and more than 8,000 hours of Canadian rights (including nearly 3,000 motion pictures). The growth of our international rights library is propelled by our philosophy to produce proprietary projects. Our Canadian rights library is the beneficiary of our strong theatrical distribution operation which consistently feeds our Canadian library with new titles.

NET EARNINGS
in millions of dollars

1997	4.5	13.2	18.2
1996	3.9	10.4	

Equicap Net Earnings
Consolidated Net Earnings (Excluding Mainframe Gain)
Consolidated Net Earnings

EBITDA
in millions of dollars

1997	8.2	26.7	34.3
1996	7.1	18.8	

Equicap EBITDA
Consolidated EBITDA (Excluding Mainframe Gain)
Consolidated EBITDA

ALLIANCE

In the business of filmed entertainment, library revenues are an essential pillar of strength. They represent a steadily increasing high margin income stream from off-balance sheet assets. For a library to generate meaningful revenues it has to achieve a certain critical mass and it must contain some highly desirable lead titles. Alliance's library has both. Since fiscal 1994, library revenues have grown at a compound annual rate of 42% from $4.5 million to $13.0 million and all of the titles in our library have been principally fully amortized. We define library revenues as sales of programs after their first cycle, typically three years after completion. There are more aggressive definitions practised in the industry which, in our opinion, mix library revenues with current revenues.

A major portion of Alliance's product is still in its first cycle of exploitation thus ensuring future growth in library revenue as these rights revert to the Company.

2. When we took Alliance public four years ago, we had no broadcast assets. Today, we have three specialty services:

I) Showcase Television, which is now generating operating revenue of $20 million with a subscriber growth rate of 20,000 households per month.

II) History Television, which even prior to its September 1997 launch, has begun to generate advertising sales.

The launching of History Television will bring economies of scale to Showcase Television as the two services share origination facilities, advertising sales force, administration and management.

One of the reasons we acquired the minority interests in Showcase Television was to be free to fully realize upon these efficiencies.

We consider Showcase Television and History Television to be "beachfront properties" as they are among the last specialty services to receive wide national cable carriage. With all analog slots now occupied, future specialty licences in English Canada will likely be issued on the basis of digital carriage only and will require a long period before achieving the level of consumer penetration necessary for profitability.

Our specialty networks have value beyond their earnings multiple. They are irreplaceable. Together with our strength in Canadian theatrical and home video distribution, our broadcast assets provide us with a uniquely diversified reach into the Canadian market.

LIBRARY REVENUE
in millions of dollars

Year	Value
1997	13.0
1996	10.4
1995	8.5
1994	4.5

2   4   6   8   10   12   14

III) Video-On-Demand (in partnership with Shaw Communications) which will bring the video store to the consumer's living room.

All three services are important new opportunities for Alliance's library.

3. In the years since our IPO, we have built a growing animation business from a start-up position. The two computer generated series which we co-produce with Mainframe and distribute world-wide, *ReBoot* and *Beast Wars*, are at the leading edge of CGI. They are widely sold internationally and are in the US market in first-run syndication. Both are ratings hits in Canada where they are among the top-rated shows on YTV.

Our first 2-D conventional animated series, *Captain Star*, is an international co-production with various European partners such as the UK's HTV.

It debuts in Canada in September on the new cartoon network, Teletoon.

An Alliance animation library is now beginning to take shape, containing 91 episodes of high-end animation to which we control international distribution rights.

Our 1994 investment in Mainframe Entertainment has strengthened our balance sheet with a ten-fold after tax cash return on our capital plus a 7% carried interest in the now publicly traded company. While we have reduced our equity position, we have maintained our principal strategic objective through a distribution agreement which provides us with international rights to Mainframe product.

Thanks to our strategic focus, we have carefully laid the groundwork for future growth. We have identified our weak spots and have replaced them with new building blocks, positioning the Company to focus on its strengths.

In closing, we record with great regret the passing of our friend and distinguished colleague, Andrew Sarlos, O.C., LL.D.(Hon), F.C.A., who served Alliance with distinction as a Director of the Company from 1992. He is greatly missed. At the same time, we record with pleasure the election to the Board in 1996 of Donald Sobey, Chairman of the Empire Group. We warmly welcome Mr. Sobey.

Robert Lantos

MANAGEMENTS DISCUSSION AND ANALYSIS
ALLANCE COMMUNICATIONS CORPORATION

RESULTS OF OPERATIONS

Fiscal 1997 marked renewed earnings growth with record net earnings, revenues and cash flow from operations.

Net earnings for the year ended March 31, 1997 increased 75.0% to $18.2 million compared to $10.4 million for the year ended March 31, 1996. Excluding the gain on sale of investment, net earnings in fiscal 1997 increased 26.9% to $13.2 million. EBITDA increased 42.0% to $26.7 million for the year ended March 31, 1997 from $18.8 million for the year ended March 31, 1996.

Revenues in fiscal 1997 increased 5.1% to $282.6 million compared to fiscal 1996 revenues of $268.9 million. Revenues increased in all businesses with the exception of Motion Pictures, where revenues declined due to the timing of the delivery of Alliance-produced motion pictures. Gross profit increased 16.2% to $68.8 million in fiscal 1997 from $59.2 million in fiscal 1996 while the gross margin increased to 24.3% in fiscal 1997 from 22.0% in fiscal 1996.

Cash flow from operations in fiscal 1997 increased 37.9% to $240.7 million from $174.5 million in fiscal 1996.

The following table presents a consolidated financial summary of the Company's businesses.

For the years ended March 31, 1997, March 31, 1996 and March 31, 1995
(In thousands of Canadian dollars)

	1997	%	1996	%	1995	%	% Increase (Decrease) 1997 over 1996	1996 over 1995
REVENUES BY BUSINESS:								
Alliance Television	$ 110,463	39.1	$ 104,676	38.9	$ 106,540	45.5	5.5	(1.7)
Alliance Motion Pictures	113,331	40.1	121,416	45.1	100,709	43.1	(6.7)	20.6
Alliance Equicap	24,967	8.8	23,204	8.6	23,582	10.1	7.6	(1.6)
Alliance Broadcasting	19,884	7.0	16,836	6.3	2,586	1.1	18.1	551.0
Alliance Multimedia	13,954	5.0	2,813	1.1	394	0.2	396.1	614.0
Total Revenues	$ 282,599	100.0	$ 268,945	100.0	$ 233,811	100.0	5.1	15.0
DIRECT OPERATING EXPENSES BY BUSINESS:								
Alliance Television	$ 88,699	80.3	$ 80,486	76.9	$ 83,282	78.2	10.2	(3.4)
Alliance Motion Pictures	90,762	80.1	109,331	90.0	87,743	87.1	(17.0)	24.6
Alliance Equicap	12,372	49.6	11,920	51.4	11,573	49.1	3.8	3.0
Alliance Broadcasting	11,218	56.4	7,299	43.4	827	32.0	53.7	782.6
Alliance Multimedia	10,765	77.1	753	26.8	260	66.0	1329.6	189.6
Total Direct Operating Expenses	$ 213,816	75.7	$ 209,789	78.0	$ 183,685	78.6	1.9	14.2
GROSS PROFIT BY BUSINESS:								
Alliance Television	$ 21,764	19.7	$ 24,190	23.1	$ 23,258	21.8	(10.0)	4.0
Alliance Motion Pictures	22,569	19.9	12,085	10.0	12,966	12.9	86.8	6.8
Alliance Equicap	12,595	50.4	11,284	48.6	12,009	50.9	11.6	(6.0)
Alliance Broadcasting	8,666	43.6	9,537	56.6	1,759	68.0	(9.1)	442.2
Alliance Multimedia	3,189	22.9	2,060	73.2	134	34.0	54.8	1,437.3
Total Gross Profit	$ 68,783	24.3	$ 59,156	22.0	$ 50,126	21.4	16.3	18.0

ALLIANCE

MANAGEMENTS DISCUSSION AND ANALYSIS
ALLIANCE COMMUNICATIONS CORPORATION

FISCAL 1997 COMPARED TO FISCAL 1996

Revenues in fiscal 1997 were $282.6 million, an increase of $13.7 million or 5.1%, compared to $268.9 million in fiscal 1996. This increase was due to revenue growth in all businesses, with the exception of a slight decline in Alliance Motion Pictures.

Alliance Television revenues in fiscal 1997 were $110.5 million, an increase of $5.8 million or 5.5%, compared to $104.7 million in fiscal 1996. This increase was due to an $8.1 million increase in production revenues, partially offset by a $2.3 million decrease in distribution revenues. In the current year, 56 hours of television production were delivered compared to 57 hours in the prior year. These hours were comprised of 35 hours of series delivered in fiscal 1997 compared to 46 hours in fiscal 1996, 18 hours of television movies delivered in fiscal 1997 compared to 10 hours in fiscal 1996 and three hours of television pilots delivered in fiscal 1997 compared to one hour in fiscal 1996. On average, therefore, the size of the average hourly production budget increased substantially over the prior year as television movie budgets per hour are generally much higher than television series' budgets per hour. The decreased distribution revenues were due to exceptional revenues being earned in the prior year on certain titles which was not repeated in the same magnitude in the current year.

Alliance Motion Pictures revenues in fiscal 1997 were $113.3 million, a decrease of $8.1 million or 6.7%, compared to $121.4 million in fiscal 1996. This decrease was due primarily to the production division where revenues decreased by $15.2 million over the prior year from $32.2 million in fiscal 1996 to $17.0 million in the current year. In the current year, the production division delivered one motion picture, Crash, whereas in the prior year three motion pictures were delivered. In Alliance Releasing, the Company's Canadian distribution business, revenues in fiscal 1997 were $82.0 million, an increase of $2.2 million or 2.8%, compared to $79.8 million in fiscal 1996. Within Alliance Releasing, theatrical revenues increased $1.4 million compared to the prior year, video revenues decreased $2.4 million compared to the prior year and television revenues increased $3.0 million compared to the prior year, due primarily to the timing of the releases in the various media formats. Theatrical successes in the current year included: The English Patient; Shine; Michael; and Trainspotting. Le Monde revenues were $11.7 million, an increase of $7.2 million or 160.0%, compared to $4.5 million in fiscal 1996 due to the growing library of titles. Top revenue performers in the current year included: Lethal Tender; Dead Silence; Hostile Intent; and Ravager. Alliance Independent Films' revenues of $2.7 million decreased $2.2 million or 44.9%, compared to $4.9 million in the prior year due to the decline in the amount of new product acquired and delivered in the current year. Deliveries in the current year included: Denise Calls Up; Welcome to the Dollhouse; and When Night is Falling.

Alliance Equicap revenues in fiscal 1997 were $25.0 million an increase of $1.8 million or 7.8%, compared to fiscal 1996 revenues of $23.2 million due primarily to the success of production services deals in the current year. In addition, the current year's revenues include Equicap Financial Corporation, which started up operations in the fall of 1996. Equicap Financial Corporation closed six deals in the period October 1996 to March 1997 for arrangement fee revenues and interest income of $0.6 million.

Alliance Broadcasting revenues in fiscal 1997 were $19.9 million, an increase of $3.1 million or 18.5%, compared to $16.8 million in fiscal 1996 due primarily to increased advertising sales. Cable revenues were slightly higher due to an increase in the subscriber base net of the impact of a lower average subscriber rate.

Alliance Multimedia revenues in fiscal 1997 were $14.0 million, an increase of $11.2 million or 400.0%, compared to $2.8 million in fiscal 1996. Distribution revenues of $12.0 million were recognized in fiscal 1997 as 26 episodes of Beastwars were delivered. TMP-The Music Publisher ("TMP") revenues increased to $2.0 million, an increase of $0.9 million or 81.8%, compared to $1.1 million in fiscal 1996 due to the timing of collections of foreign royalties and also from the successes of Amanda Marshall's debut album which contained five TMP songs and the TMP song "Heaven Help My Heart", recorded by both Wynonna Judd and Tina Arena.

Gross profit in fiscal 1997 was $68.8 million, an increase of $9.6 million or 16.2%, compared to $59.2 million in fiscal 1996. This increase was due primarily to Alliance Motion Pictures where the gross profit increased $10.5 million year-over-year. As a percentage of revenues, gross profit in fiscal 1997 was 24.3%, compared to 22.0% in fiscal 1996, due to increased margins in Alliance Motion Pictures and the change in the revenue mix, partially offset by decreased margins in Alliance Television. The increased margins in Alliance Motion Pictures were due primarily to an increased margin in the production division where the margin improved from - 11.8% on the motion pictures delivered in the prior year to 15.9% on Crash, which was delivered in the current year. The decreased margins in Alliance Television were due to the increased production costs per hour of delivering higher quality television movies in the current year such as: The Hunchback; The Inheritance and Toe Tags (pilot) as well as an increased proportion of television movies versus television series. Television series generally have better margins but accounted for a lower percentage of production in fiscal 1997.

Other operating expenses in fiscal 1997 were $42.0 million, an increase of $1.6 million or 4.0%, compared to $40.4 million in fiscal 1996. Other operating expenses as a percentage of revenues decreased slightly to 14.9% compared to 15.0% in fiscal 1996. Other operating expenses are comprised of corporate overhead and operating expenses other than direct operating expenses. These expenses include such items as general and administrative expenses, salaries and benefits, office rental, communications costs and professional fees. In fiscal 1997, $13.9 million of operating expenses related to corporate overhead, compared to $12.3 million in fiscal 1996. Corporate overhead included non-recurring charges of $2.1 million in fiscal 1997: $1 million relating to Equicap bonus costs; $600,000 relating to the Company's unsuccessful UK franchise bid; and $500,000 relating to head office moving costs, compared to $1.3 million in fiscal 1996: $800,000 relating to severance costs; and $500,000 relating to the Company's unsuccessful efforts to acquire the broadcast assets of John Labatt Limited. Before non-recurring charges, corporate overhead increased to $11.8 million in fiscal 1997 from $11.0 million in fiscal 1996. The increase in other operating expenses was primarily due to head count increases in new and expanding businesses such as Alliance Pictures International and Equicap Financial Corporation.

Net interest expense in fiscal 1997 was $1.3 million, an increase of $0.4 million or 44.4%, compared to $0.9 million in fiscal 1996, reflecting increased cash requirements in the current year, partially offset by the equity offering proceeds and lower interest rates.

The Company's effective tax rate for fiscal 1997 increased to 35.0% from 15.7% in fiscal 1996 due to a shift in the mix of earnings before income taxes to income tax jurisdictions with less favourable income tax rates. In addition, in the current year, the gain on sale of investment was taxed at approximately 34%.

Net earnings in fiscal 1997 were $18.2 million, an increase of $7.8 million or 75.0%, compared to $10.4 million in fiscal 1996.

MANAGEMENTS DISCUSSION AND ANALYSIS

ALLANCE COMMUNICATIONS CORPORATION

FISCAL 1996 COMPARED TO FISCAL 1995

Revenues in fiscal 1996 were $268.9 million, an increase of $35.1 million or 15.0%, compared to $233.8 million in fiscal 1995. This increase was due primarily to significant revenue growth in Alliance Motion Pictures, as well as the inclusion of revenues for a full year in Alliance Broadcasting, which started commercial operations in January 1995.

Alliance Television revenues in fiscal 1996 were $104.7 million, a decrease of $1.8 million or 1.7%, compared to $106.5 million in fiscal 1995. This decrease was due primarily to lower international revenues partially offset by higher North American revenues.

Alliance Motion Pictures revenues in fiscal 1996 were $121.4 million, an increase of $20.7 million or 20.6%, compared to $100.7 million in fiscal 1995. This increase was due primarily to increased revenues in Alliance Releasing, where revenues in fiscal 1996 were $79.8 million, an increase of $21.3 million or 36.4%, compared to $58.5 million in fiscal 1995. Within Alliance Releasing, this increase was due primarily to increased Canadian home video revenues as a result of a number of successful home video releases, including Pulp Fiction, Mortal Kombat, Don Juan DeMarco and Johnny Mnemonic, as well as the continued exploitation of Dumb and Dumber, The Swan Princess and The Mask, which were released theatrically in fiscal 1995. These increases were slightly offset by a $3.0 million decrease in Canadian theatrical revenues in fiscal 1996.

Alliance Equicap revenues in fiscal 1996 were $23.2 million which was approximately the same as fiscal 1995. In fiscal 1996, Equicap focused on structured production financings, which provided private investors with access to tax incentives provided by the Canadian government.

Alliance Broadcasting revenues in fiscal 1996 were $16.8 million, an increase of $14.2 million or 546.2%, compared to $2.6 million in fiscal 1995. This increase was due primarily to fiscal 1996 revenues reflecting the first full year of operations of Showcase, while the previous year reflected only one quarter of operations. Revenues were recognized in the first quarter of operations.

Alliance Multimedia revenues in fiscal 1996 were $2.8 million, an increase of $2.4 million or 600.0%, compared to $0.4 million in fiscal 1995. Distribution revenues of $1.7 million were recognized in fiscal 1996 as episodes of ReBoot were delivered to YTV. Fiscal 1996 also reflected the first full year of operations of TMP where revenues were $1.1 million, an increase of $0.7 million or 175.0%, compared to $0.4 million in fiscal 1995.

Gross profit in fiscal 1996 was $59.2 million, an increase of $9.1 million or 18.2%, compared to $50.1 million in fiscal 1995. This increase was due primarily to the inclusion of gross profit realized from Showcase Television's first full year of operations and distribution revenues realized upon the delivery of ReBoot. Gross profit in fiscal 1996 was 22.0%, compared to 21.4% in fiscal 1995, due to the change in the revenue mix and increased margins in Alliance Television, partially offset by decreased margins in Alliance Motion Pictures. Decreased margins in Alliance Motion Pictures were due primarily to an increase in the provision for investment in film and television programs in fiscal 1996. In addition, margins on films delivered in fiscal 1996 were not as favourable as the margins on films delivered in fiscal 1995.

Other operating expenses in fiscal 1996 were $40.4 million, an increase of $11.8 million or 41.3%, compared to $28.6 million in fiscal 1995. In fiscal 1996, $12.3 million of other operating expenses related to corporate overhead, compared to $11.7 million in fiscal 1995. Corporate overhead included non-recurring charges of $1.3 million in fiscal 1996 compared to $0.6 million in fiscal 1995. Before non-recurring charges, corporate overhead decreased to $11.0 million in fiscal 1996 from $11.1 million in fiscal 1995. The overall increase in other operating expenses was due to expansion of the Los Angeles office and international operations, increased expenses in Alliance Broadcasting associated with Showcase Television's first full year of operations, overall head count and wage increases and certain one-time expenditures, such as severance costs and costs associated with the company's unsuccessful efforts to acquire the broadcast assets of John Labatt Limited.

MANAGEMENTS DISCUSSION AND ANALYSIS
ALLANCE COMMUNICATIONS CORPORATION

Net interest expense in fiscal 1996 was $0.9 million, an increase of $0.6 million or 200.0%, compared to $0.3 million in fiscal 1995, reflecting increased interest costs as the opening cash balance was drawn down early in the fiscal year to finance production costs, acquisitions of distribution product and development costs.

The Company's effective tax rate for fiscal 1996 decreased to 15.7% from 22.0% in fiscal 1995 due to a shift in the mix of earnings before income taxes to non-Canadian operations with favourable income tax rates.

Net earnings in fiscal 1996 were $10.4 million, a decrease of $2.6 million or 20.0%, compared to $13.0 million in fiscal 1995.

LIQUIDITY AND CAPITAL RESOURCES

Cash flow from operations increased significantly during fiscal 1997 to $240.7 million from $174.5 million for fiscal 1996 and $169.1 million for fiscal 1995. Earnings before interest, provision for income taxes, depreciation, amortization and minority interest ("EBITDA") increased to $26.7 million during fiscal 1997 after dropping to $18.8 million in fiscal 1996 from $21.5 million in fiscal 1995.

Alliance has traditionally financed its working capital requirements principally through cash generated by operations, revolving bank credit facilities and sales of equity. The greatest demand for working capital exists in the start-up phase of production, which traditionally occurs in August and September, although it is progressively becoming less and less seasonal in nature as the company diversifies its business.

The nature of the Company's business is such that significant initial expenditures are required to produce and acquire television programs and films, while revenues from these television programs and films are earned over an extended period of time after their completion and acquisition. As Alliance's activities grow, its financing requirements are expected to grow. The Company believes it has sufficient resources to fund its operations through fiscal 1998 from cash generated by operations, existing bank facilities and the net proceeds of the U.S. equity offering in August 1996.

Alliance typically borrows from banks to provide interim production financing. All revenues associated with these productions are pledged as security for these loans. The majority of these borrowings relate specifically to television program and film production.

On October 28, 1994, prior to the reorganization of the share capital of the Company, the Company issued an unsecured, subordinated 6.5% convertible debenture maturing April 5, 2002 to Onex Corporation for $16.5 million cash. The debenture is convertible into common shares of the Company at any time at $19 per share. Interest is payable in cash or additional convertible debentures at the Company's option. Commencing October 28, 1999, the debenture or any portion thereof will be redeemable at the option of the Company, provided certain conditions are met, at the issue price, together with accrued and unpaid interest to the date of redemption. The debenture provides the Company with the option to pay for the redemption of the debenture by issuing common shares to the debenture holder at a price equal to 90% of the weighted average trading price of the common shares for the last 20 consecutive trading days prior to redemption or the maturity date.

ALLIANCE

In fiscal 1995, the Company obtained a $75 million credit facility from a Canadian chartered bank. The bank facility provided for a $20 million demand operating line, a $50 million term production financing facility and a $5 million facility to hedge foreign exchange exposure.

In August 1996, the Company completed a cross-border offering of 3,020,000 class B non-voting shares for net proceeds of $32.9 million.

In December 1996, the Company's bank facility was increased to $122 million to provide for a $65 million demand operating line, a $50 million term production financing facility, a $5 million facility to hedge foreign exchange exposure and a $2 million lease facility. As at March 31, 1997, the Company had loans outstanding under its term production facility on productions in progress in the amount of $15.9 million. The Company applied $12.5 million of its cash against the $15.9 million loans for net operating loan and bank indebtedness of $3.4 million as at March 31, 1997. See note 5 to the Consolidated Financial Statements.

In March 1997, Equicap Financial Corporation obtained a $25 million non-recourse revolving line of credit with a Canadian Chartered bank. The line of credit forms part of the funds made available for film projects financed by Equicap Financial Corporation.

RISKS AND UNCERTAINTIES

The Company capitalizes production and distribution costs as incurred to investment in film and television programs and such costs are amortized to direct operating expenses in accordance with SFAS 53. Under SFAS 53, all costs incurred in connection with an individual film or television program, including production costs, release prints and advertising costs, are capitalized as investment in film and television programs. These costs are stated at the lower of unamortized cost and estimated net realizable value. Estimated total production costs for an individual film or television program are amortized in the proportion that revenues realized relates to management's estimate of the total revenues expected to be received from such film or television program. As a result, if revenue estimates change with respect to a film or television program, the Company may be required to write down all or a portion of the unamortized costs of such film or television program. No assurance can be given that a write down will not have a significant impact on the Company's results of operations and financial condition.

Results of operations for any period are significantly dependent on the number and timing of television programs and films delivered or made available to various media. Consequently, the Company's results of operations may fluctuate materially from period to period and the results for any one period are not necessarily indicative of results for future periods. Ultimately, profitability depends not only on revenues but on the amount paid to acquire or produce the film or television program and the amount spent on the prints and advertising campaign used to promote it.

The Company currently finances a portion of its production budgets from Canadian governmental agencies and incentive programs, such as Telefilm Canada and federal and provincial tax credits, as well as international sources in the case of the Company's co-productions. There can be no assurance that local cultural incentive programs which the Company may access in Canada and internationally, will not be reduced, amended or eliminated. Any change in these incentive programs may have an adverse impact on the Company.

MANAGEMENTS DISCUSSION AND ANALYSIS
ALLANCE COMMUNICATIONS CORPORATION

A significant portion of the Company's revenues and expenses is in U.S. dollars, and therefore subject to fluctuation in exchange rates. There is risk that a significant fluctuation in exchange rates may have an adverse impact on the Company's results of operations.

Commissions earned by Alliance Equicap have been principally related to sales of limited partnership units to private investors in connection with structured production financings. Recent changes to Canadian income tax legislation have eliminated tax incentives available to investors in connection with certain financings. Consequently, it is expected that Alliance Equicap's revenues in fiscal 1998 will be substantially less than in fiscal 1997.

OUTLOOK

The Company achieved record results in fiscal 1997 and plans to continue to build on this success. The Company will continue to pursue its long term strategy of expanding its libraries and increasing its direct distribution reach. The Company's proven ability to deliver and distribute high quality product combined with its strong financial position, makes it well positioned to achieve its aggressive growth strategy.

QUARTERLY REVIEW

The business of the Company fluctuates during the year as indicated by the table below, which summarizes quarterly results for the fiscal year ended March 31, 1997:

(In thousands of Canadian dollars except share information)

	1st Qtr.	2nd Qtr.	3rd. Qtr.	4th Qtr.	Total
Revenues	$ 63,516	$ 54,617	$ 64,956	$ 99,510	$ 282,599
Gross Profit	12,402	15,688	16,066	24,627	68,783
EBITDA	3,026	3,529	6,850	13,341	26,746
Net Earnings	955	6,260	4,081	6,892	18,188
Basic Earnings Per Share	$ 0.10	$ 0.53	$ 0.32	$ 0.53	$ 1.53

ALLIANCE

AUDITORS' REPORT

ALLIANCE COMMUNICATIONS CORPORATION

To the shareholders of Alliance Communications Corporation:

We have audited the consolidated balance sheets of Alliance Communications Corporation as at March 31, 1997 and 1996 and the consolidated statements of earnings and retained earnings and changes in financial position for each of the years in the three year period ended March 31, 1997. These financial statements are the responsibility of the company's management. Our responsibility is to express an opinion on these financial statements based on our audits.

We conducted our audits in accordance with Canadian generally accepted auditing standards. Those standards require that we plan and perform an audit to obtain reasonable assurance whether the financial statements are free of material misstatement. An audit includes examining, on a test basis, evidence supporting the amounts and disclosures in the financial statements. An audit also includes assessing the accounting principles used and significant estimates made by management, as well as evaluating the overall financial statement presentation.

In our opinion, these consolidated financial statements present fairly, in all material respects, the financial position of the company as at March 31, 1997 and 1996 and the results of its operations and the changes in its financial position for each of the years in the three year period ended March 31, 1997 in accordance with Canadian generally accepted accounting principles.

Coopers & Lybrand

Chartered Accountants

North York, Ontario, Canada
May 30, 1997
(except as to note 21 which is as of June 17, 1997)

CONSOLIDATED BALANCE SHEETS

ALLIANCE COMMUNICATIONS CORPORATION

As at March 31, 1997 and March 31, 1996
(In thousands of Canadian dollars)

	1997	1996
ASSETS		
Cash and short-term investments	$ 10,777	$ 5,090
Accounts receivable	82,184	53,081
Distribution contracts receivable	76,272	64,948
Loans receivable	9,283	-
Investment in film and television programs (note 2)	101,531	63,274
Film and television programs in progress	22,955	22,398
Program exhibition rights	11,821	9,151
Development costs and investment in scripts	13,103	7,762
Property and equipment (note 3)	10,314	6,848
Broadcasting licences, net of accumulated amortization of $30 (1996 - $nil)	7,236	-
Other assets (note 4)	8,246	6,346
	$ 353,722	$ 238,898
LIABILITIES		
Operating loan and bank indebtedness (note 5)	$3,361	$ 5,617
Accounts payable and accrued liabilities	86,268	47,440
Distribution revenues payable	23,223	26,238
Loans payable (note 6)	-	2,083
Income taxes (note 12)	10,927	10,818
Deferred revenue	62,980	32,706
Convertible debenture (note 7)	16,500	16,500
Minority interest	39	2,116
	203,298	143,518
SHAREHOLDERS' EQUITY		
Capital stock (note 8)	88,836	52,295
Retained earnings	60,893	42,705
Cumulative translation adjustments	695	380
	150,424	95,380
	$ 353,722	$ 238,898

Signed on behalf of the Board,

David J Kassie
Director

Ellis Jacob
Director

The accompanying notes form an integral part of these financial statements.

CONSOLIDATED STATEMENTS OF EARNINGS AND RETAINED EARNINGS

ALLIANCE COMMUNICATIONS CORPORATION

For the years ended March 31, 1997, March 31, 1996 and March 31, 1995

(In thousands of Canadian dollars, except per share data)

	1997	1996	1995
REVENUES	$ 282,599	$ 268,945	$ 233,811
DIRECT OPERATING EXPENSES	213,816	209,789	183,685
GROSS PROFIT	68,783	59,156	50,126
OTHER EXPENSES			
Other operating expenses	42,037	40,363	28,643
Amortization	5,160	5,038	5,164
Interest (note 10)	1,296	893	282
Minority interest	(142)	562	(596)
	48,351	46,856	33,493
EARNINGS BEFORE UNDERNOTED	20,432	12,300	16,633
GAIN ON SALE OF INVESTMENT (NOTE 11)	7,544	-	-
EARNINGS BEFORE INCOME TAXES	27,976	12,300	16,633
PROVISION FOR INCOME TAXES (NOTE 12)	9,788	1,935	3,658
NET EARNINGS FOR THE YEAR	18,188	10,365	12,975
RETAINED EARNINGS, BEGINNING OF YEAR	42,705	32,340	19,365
RETAINED EARNINGS, END OF YEAR	$ 60,893	$ 42,705	$ 32,340
BASIC EARNINGS PER COMMON SHARE (NOTE 13)	$ 1.53	$ 1.05	$ 1.36

The accompanying notes form an integral part of these financial statements

CONSOLIDATED STATEMENTS OF CHANGES IN FINANCIAL POSITION

ALLIANCE COMMUNICATIONS CORPORATION

For the years ended March 31, 1997, March 31, 1996 and March 31, 1995
(In thousands of Canadian dollars)

	1997	1996	1995
CASH AND SHORT-TERM INVESTMENTS PROVIDED BY (USED IN):			
OPERATING ACTIVITIES			
Net earnings for the year	$ 18,188	$ 10,365	$ 12,975
Items not affecting cash:			
Amortization of investment in film and television programs	190,226	185,534	169,460
Amortization of program exhibition rights	9,363	6,807	-
Amortization of development costs and investment in scripts	2,351	1,800	1,342
Amortization of property and equipment and pre-operating costs	2,401	2,934	3,518
Amortization of broadcasting licences and goodwill	408	304	304
Gain on sale of investment (note 11)	(7,544)	-	-
Minority interest	(142)	562	(596)
Deferred income taxes	3,529	1,594	3,284
Net changes in other non-cash balances related to operations (note 14)	21,950	(35,373)	(21,173)
	240,730	174,527	169,114
INVESTING ACTIVITIES			
Investment in films and television programs	(228,483)	(188,156)	(177,414)
Film and television programs in progress	(557)	7,516	(5,328)
Program exhibition rights	(12,033)	(6,333)	(10,236)
Development costs and investment in scripts	(7,692)	(5,226)	(2,278)
Net additions to property and equipment	(5,237)	(2,973)	(6,280)
Net proceeds from sale of investment (note 11)	7,684	-	-
Business acquisitions	(9,425)	135	(2,765)
Cash balances of acquired businesses	-	-	4,308
Long-term investments	(2,219)	(992)	(617)
	(257,962)	(196,029)	(200,610)
FINANCING ACTIVITIES			
Operating loan and bank indebtedness	(2,256)	5,617	-
Increase in loans receivable	(9,283)	-	-
Increase (decrease) in loans payable	(2,083)	712	1,086
Issue of convertible debenture	-	-	16,500
Issue of common shares	36,541	1,403	21,818
Exercise of warrants	-	-	(20,984)
	22,919	7,732	18,420
INCREASE (DECREASE) IN CASH AND SHORT-TERM INVESTMENTS	5,687	(13,770)	(13,076)
CASH AND SHORT-TERM INVESTMENTS, BEGINNING OF YEAR	5,090	18,860	31,936
CASH AND SHORT-TERM INVESTMENTS, END OF YEAR	$ 10,777	$ 5,090	$ 18,860

The accompanying notes form an integral part of these financial statements

NOTES TO THE FINANCIAL STATEMENTS
ALLIANCE COMMUNICATIONS CORPORATION

Alliance Communications Corporation ("the Company") is a fully integrated global supplier of entertainment products whose origins are in television and motion picture production and distribution. The Company also has interests in broadcasting, computer generated animation facilities, music publishing and financing services.

1. SIGNIFICANT ACCOUNTING POLICIES

(a) Generally Accepted Accounting Principles

These consolidated financial statements have been prepared in accordance with Canadian generally accepted accounting principles ("Canadian GAAP"). These principles conform in all material respects with the accounting principles generally accepted in the United States ("U.S. GAAP") except as described in note 20.

(b) Principle of Consolidation

The consolidated financial statements include the accounts of Alliance Communications Corporation and all of its subsidiaries.

(c) Revenue Recognition

Revenue is derived from sale of distribution rights and equity in productions and theatrical or television exhibition. Revenue is recognized as earned when the film or television program is completed and delivered, when amounts are due from the exhibitor or when a contract is executed that irrevocably transfers distribution rights to a licensee or equity to an investor, and there is reasonable assurance of collectability of proceeds.

The Company recognizes as revenue only the net benefits from sales to limited partnerships when the investor has irrevocably committed to acquire the related equity.

Fees related to loan origination, including loan restructuring or renegotiating, are recognized as revenue over the expected term of the loan.

Cable service subscriber fee revenue is accrued as earned. Advertising revenue is recognized when advertisements are aired.

Revenue for music publishing is derived from the collection of royalties on the rights owned and is recognized when received.

Amounts received and receivable and not recognized as revenue are included in deferred revenue.

(d) Short-term Investments

Short-term investments are carried at the lower of cost and market value.

(e) Loans Receivable

Loans receivable are stated net of unearned income and an allowance for credit losses. An allowance for credit losses is maintained in an amount considered adequate to absorb estimated credit-related losses. The allowance is increased by provisions for credit losses which are charged to income, and reduced by write-offs net of expected recoveries. The Company conducts ongoing credit assessments of its loan portfolio on an account-by-account basis and establishes specific allowances when doubtful accounts are identified.

(f) Investment in Film and Television Programs

Investment in film and television programs represents the unamortized costs of motion picture and television programs which have been produced by the Company or for which the Company has acquired distribution rights. Such costs include all production, print and advertising costs which are expected to be recovered from future revenues, net of estimated future liabilities related to the product.

NOTES TO THE FINANCIAL STATEMENTS

ALLIANCE COMMUNICATIONS CORPORATION

Amortization is determined based on the ratio that current revenues earned from the film and television programs bear to expected gross future revenues. Based on management's estimates of gross future revenues as at March 31, 1997, it is expected that the investment in film and television programs will be absorbed principally over the next three years.

Investment in film and television programs is written down to the net recoverable amount if the investment is greater than the net recoverable amount. Net recoverable amount is defined as the total future revenues expected to be earned from film and television programs, net of future costs.

(g) Film and Television Programs in Progress

Film and television programs in progress represents the accumulated costs of uncompleted motion picture and television programs which are being produced by the Company.

(h) Program Exhibition Rights

Program exhibition rights represents the rights to various long-term contracts acquired from third parties to broadcast television programs and motion pictures. Program exhibition rights and corresponding liabilities are recorded at the time the Company becomes committed under a license agreement and the product is available for telecast. The carrying value of the program exhibition rights is amortized over the lesser of two years and the contracted exhibition period beginning in the month the film or television program is premiered.

(i) Development Costs and Investment in Scripts

Development costs and investment in scripts represents expenditures made on projects prior to production. Advances or contributions received from third parties to assist in development are deducted from these expenditures. Upon commencement of production, development costs and investment in scripts are charged to the production. Development costs and investment in scripts are amortized on the straight-line basis over three years commencing in the year following the year such costs are incurred when production has not commenced. Development costs and investment in scripts are written off when determined not to be recoverable.

(j) Government Financing and Assistance

The Company has access to several government programs that are designed to assist film and television production and distribution in Canada. Amounts received in respect of production assistance are recorded as revenue in accordance with the Company's revenue recognition policy for completed film and television programs. Government assistance with respect to distribution rights is recorded as a reduction of investment in film and television programs. Government assistance towards current expenses is included in net earnings for the year.

(k) Property and Equipment

Property and equipment are carried at cost less accumulated amortization. Amortization is provided, commencing in the year after acquisition, using the following rates and methods:

Computer hardware
- 30% principally by declining balance
Computer software
- 100% principally by declining balance
Furniture and fixtures
- 20% principally by declining balance
Equipment
- 30% principally by declining balance
Leasehold improvements
- straight-line over the lease term
Broadcast and transmission equipment
- straight-line over 5 years

NOTES TO THE FINANCIAL STATEMENTS
ALLIANCE COMMUNICATIONS CORPORATION

(l) Broadcasting Licences

In acquisitions involving broadcasting undertakings, fair value is assigned to the broadcasting licences acquired. Broadcasting licences are amortized on a straight-line basis over a period of forty years. When there is an expectation that the net carrying amount of the licence will not be recovered, the licence is written down to its net recoverable amount.

(m) Other Assets

Other assets include pre-operating costs related to the period before commencement of commercial operations of Showcase Television Inc. and other businesses. The amount is being amortized on a straight-line basis over a period of five years.

Other assets also include long-term investments which are accounted for at cost when the conditions for equity accounting are not present and goodwill which is amortized on a straight-line basis over a period of five years.

(n) Distribution Revenues Payable

Distribution revenues payable represents the excess of receipts from the distribution of film and television programs over commissions earned and distribution costs incurred and are payable to the licensor of the film or television program.

(o) Foreign Currency

Assets and liabilities denominated in currencies other than Canadian dollars are translated at exchange rates in effect at the balance sheet date. Revenue and expense items are translated at average rates of exchange for the year. Translation gains or losses are included in the determination of earnings except for gains or losses arising on the translation of the accounts of the foreign subsidiaries considered to be self-sustaining, which are deferred as a separate component of shareholders' equity.

(p) Non-Cash Balances Related to Operations

Non-cash balances related to operations are comprised of the aggregate of the following assets and liabilities: accounts receivable; distribution contracts receivable; other assets excluding long-term-investments and goodwill; accounts payable and accrued liabilities; distribution revenues payable; income taxes; deferred revenue; and cumulative translation adjustments.

(q) Use of Estimates

The preparation of financial statements in conformity with generally accepted accounting principles requires management to make estimates and assumptions that affect the reported amounts of assets and liabilities and disclosure of contingent assets and liabilities at the dates of the financial statements and the reported amounts of revenues and expenses during the reporting periods. Actual results could differ from those estimates.

(r) Comparative Amounts

Certain amounts presented in the prior period have been reclassified to conform with the presentation adopted in the current year.

2. INVESTMENT IN FILM AND TELEVISION PROGRAMS

(In thousands of Canadian dollars)

	1997	1996
Completed film and television programs produced, net of amortization	$ 37,218	$ 22,837
Film and television programs acquired, net of amortization	64,313	40,437
	$ 101,531	$ 63,274

23

NOTES TO THE FINANCIAL STATEMENTS
ALLIANCE COMMUNICATIONS CORPORATION

The Company expects that 92% of completed film and television programs produced, net of amortization, and 72% of acquisition costs related to film and television programs acquired, net of amortization, will be amortized during the three year period ending March 31, 2000.

The Company earns revenues from films and television programs which are fully amortized and are not valued in the accounts.

3. PROPERTY AND EQUIPMENT
(In thousands of Canadian dollars)

	1997		1996	
	Cost	Accumulated Amortization	Cost	Accumulated Amortization
Computer hardware and software	$ 5,243	$ 2,142	$ 4,040	$ 1,387
Furniture and fixtures	3,206	985	2,061	742
Equipment	1,438	975	1,316	704
Leasehold improvements	4,340	881	1,876	771
Broadcast and transmission equipment	1,570	500	1,482	323
	15,797	5,483	10,775	3,927
Net property and equipment		$ 10,314		$ 6,848

4. OTHER ASSETS
(In thousands of Canadian dollars)

	1997	1996
Pre-operating costs, net of accumulated amortization of $1,338 (1996 - $708)	$ 2,507	$ 2,231
Prepaid expenses	1,344	1,622
Long-term investments	3,688	1,609
Goodwill, net of accumulated amortization of $1,162 (1996 - $784)	707	884
	$ 8,246	$ 6,346

5. OPERATING LOAN AND BANK INDEBTEDNESS
(In thousands of Canadian dollars)

	1997	1996
Bank indebtedness - gross	$ 15,871	$ 18,760
Interest expense on bank indebtedness	$ 1,010	$ 961
Weighted average interest rate	6.09%	9.04%

Operating loan and bank indebtedness is netted on the balance sheet with cash and short-term investments to the extent a right of offset exists.

The Company's assets and the assets of its subsidiaries have been pledged as collateral for the bank indebtedness.

At March 31, 1997, the Company had unused credit facilities aggregating $131,729,000 (1996 - $61,240,000) subject to margin calculations. These facilities are primarily used for bridge financing of productions.

6. LOANS PAYABLE
(In thousands of Canadian dollars)

	1997	1996
Interest bearing loans at prime plus 1%, unsecured with no specific repayment date	$ nil	$ 2,083

ALLIANCE

NOTES TO THE FINANCIAL STATEMENTS

ALLIANCE COMMUNICATIONS CORPORATION

7. CONVERTIBLE DEBENTURE

On October 28, 1994, the Company issued a convertible, unsecured, subordinated debenture for $16,500,000 cash, bearing interest at 6.5% per year and maturing on April 5, 2002. The debenture is convertible at the option of the holder into common shares of the Company at any time after October 28, 1995 at a conversion price of $19 per share. Interest is payable in cash or additional convertible debentures at the Company's option.

Commencing October 28, 1999, the debenture will be redeemable at the option of the Company, provided certain conditions are met, at the issue price, together with accrued and unpaid interest to the date of redemption. The Company has the option to pay for the redemption of the debenture by issuing its own common shares to the debenture holder at a price equal to 90% of the weighted average trading price of the common shares for the last 20 consecutive trading days prior to redemption or the maturity date.

8. CAPITAL STOCK

a) The authorized capital stock of the Company consists of an unlimited number of common shares. The common shares are comprised of Class A Voting Shares (the "Voting Shares") and Class B Non-Voting Shares (the "Non-Voting Shares") which have identical attributes except that the Non-Voting Shares are non-voting and each of the Voting Shares is convertible at any time at the holder's option into one fully paid and non-assessable Non-Voting Share. The Non-Voting Shares may be converted into Voting Shares only in certain circumstances.

b) During fiscal 1997, the following transactions occurred:
In August 1996, 3,020,000 Non-Voting Shares were issued pursuant to a public offering at a gross price of US$8.50 per share for proceeds of CDN$32,920,000, net of issue expenses and income tax benefits;

In September 1996, 10,000 Non-Voting Shares were issued in connection with the acquisition of film and television programs at $13.62 per share for proceeds of $136,000;

In January 1997, 95,421 Non-Voting Shares were issued in connection with a long-term investment in another company at $11.79 per share for proceeds of $1,125,000;

In January and February 1997, 162,807 Non-Voting Shares were issued in connection with the acquisition of an additional 44% ownership interest in Showcase Television Inc. at $11.84 per share for proceeds of $1,927,000 (note 9); and

During fiscal 1997, 62,100 Voting Shares were converted into Non-Voting Shares. In addition, 37,020 employee stock options for 18,509 Voting Shares and 18,511 Non-Voting Shares were exercised pursuant to the Company stock option plan for proceeds of $433,000.

c) During fiscal 1996, the following transactions occurred:
On April 26, 1995, the Company reorganized its share capital and created the Voting Shares and Non-Voting Shares, converted each existing common share into one-half of a Voting Share and one-half of a Non-Voting Share, and cancelled all of the existing authorized and issued common shares; and

During fiscal 1996, 117,478 employee stock options were exercised pursuant to the Company stock option plan for proceeds of $1,403,000.

d) During fiscal 1995, the following transactions occurred:
In May 1994, 1,530,000 shares were issued pursuant to the exercise of 1,530,000 warrants to acquire common shares and the receipt of proceeds of $20,984,000 released from escrow net of issue expenses and income tax benefits;

NOTES TO THE FINANCIAL STATEMENTS
ALLIANCE COMMUNICATIONS CORPORATION

In October 1994, 13,900 shares were issued in connection with the purchase of a 75% interest in Partisan Music Productions Inc., carrying on business as TMP - The Music Publisher, at $16.33 per share for aggregate proceeds of $227,000; and

During fiscal 1995, 51,936 employee stock options were exercised pursuant to the Company stock option plan for proceeds of $607,700.

e) As a result, the issued capital stock is as follows:
(In thousands of Canadian dollars)

	1997	1996
Common shares:		
Voting Shares, 4,905,134 (1996 - 4,948,725)	$ 26,057	$ 26,169
Non-Voting Shares, 8,313,882 (1996 - 4,945,043)	62,779	26,126
	$ 88,836	$ 52,295

f) The Company has an Amended and Restated 1993 Employee Stock Option Plan which provides for the issuance of up to 1,750,000 common shares. These options generally vest in equal annual amounts over three to five years. No options are exercisable for periods of more than ten years after date of grant. Options granted under the plan may not have an option price less than the fair market value of the Non-Voting Shares on the date the option is granted.

Options outstanding were split 50% Voting Shares and 50% Non-Voting Shares on May 15, 1995. All new options granted after May 15, 1995 are options to purchase Non-Voting Shares.

Stock option activity for 1995, 1996 and 1997 is as follows:

(In thousands of Canadian dollars)

	Number of Shares			Weighted Average Exercise Price
	Voting	Non-Voting	Total	
Outstanding at March 31, 1994	360,633	360,633	721,266	$ 11.80
Granted	276,203	276,203	552,406	14.24
Exercised	(25,968)	(25,968)	(51,936)	13.29
Cancelled	(14,850)	(14,850)	(29,700)	11.34
Outstanding at March 31, 1995	596,018	596,018	1,192,036	12.88
Granted	-	537,520	537,520	14.75
Exercised	(58,739)	(58,739)	(117,478)	11.70
Cancelled	(99,409)	(99,416)	(198,825)	12.85
Outstanding at March 31, 1996	437,870	975,383	1,413,253	13.69
Granted	5,000	121,120	126,120	14.25
Exercised	(18,509)	(18,511)	(37,020)	11.71
Cancelled	(17,934)	(17,925)	(35,859)	12.85
Outstanding at March 31, 1997	406,427	1,060,067	1,466,494	$ 13.81
Exercisable at March 31, 1997	291,628	503,604	795,232	$ 13.20
Exercisable at March 31, 1996	216,962	216,962	433,924	12.47
Exercisable at March 31, 1995	172,943	172,944	345,887	11.78

At March 31, 1997, 1,466,494 options were outstanding with exercise prices ranging from $11.70 to $16.375 and with a weighted average remaining contractual life of 4.9 years.

NOTES TO THE FINANCIAL STATEMENTS

ALLIANCE COMMUNICATIONS CORPORATION

9. BUSINESS ACQUISITIONS

During fiscal 1997, the Company acquired an additional 44% ownership interest in Showcase Television Inc. for total consideration of $9,207,000. The consideration was in the form of $7,280,000 cash and 162,807 common shares of the Company. The fair value assigned to the broadcasting licence in this acquisition was $7,266,000. After completion of this acquisition, the Company had a 99% ownership interest in Showcase Television Inc.

10. INTEREST

(In thousands of Canadian dollars)

	1997	1996	1995
Interest expense on long-term debt	$ 1,073	$ 1,195	$ 476
Interest income	(1,282)	(1,550)	(359)
Other	1,505	1,248	165
	$ 1,296	$ 893	$ 282

Interest paid for the year ended March 31, 1997 amounted to $1,925,000 (1996 - $2,040,000, 1995 - $1,332,000).

11. GAIN ON SALE OF INVESTMENT

In September 1996, Mainframe Entertainment Inc. repurchased a portion of the Company's investment in Mainframe for net proceeds of $7,684,000 resulting in a pre-tax gain on sale of $7,544,000. The Company retained a 15% ownership interest in Mainframe (note 21).

12. INCOME TAXES

The differences between the effective tax rate reflected in the provision for income taxes and the Canadian statutory income tax rate are as follows:

	1997	1996	1995
Corporate statutory income tax rate	44.6%	44.6%	44.0%
Add (deduct) the income tax rate effect of:			
Foreign operations subject to different income tax rates	(11.9)	(31.9)	(24.6)
Expenses not deductible for income tax purposes	2.8	2.3	3.4
Other	(0.5)	0.7	(0.8)
	35.0%	15.7%	22.0%

The subsidiaries' non-capital tax losses are approximately $1,180,000, which are available for offset against those subsidiaries' future taxable income. The benefits of these losses, which have not been reflected in these accounts, expire in various years to fiscal 2002.

NOTES TO THE FINANCIAL STATEMENTS
ALLIANCE COMMUNICATIONS CORPORATION

Details of income taxes are as follows:

(In thousands of Canadian dollars)

	1997	1996
Depreciation	$ 388	$ 185
Financing fees	(1,803)	(995)
Prepaid royalties	5,217	20,067
Development costs	-	3,450
Investment in film and television programs	-	7,622
Other	1,719	1,927
Net operating loss carry-forwards	(2,822)	(21,438)
Deferred income taxes	2,699	10,818
Taxes payable	8,228	-
	$ 10,927	$ 10,818

13. EARNINGS PER SHARE

Earnings per common share is calculated on the basis of 11,919,000 (1996 - 9,840,000, 1995 - 9,543,000) weighted average common shares outstanding.

Fully diluted earnings per common share for 1997 is $1.44 (1996 - $0.99, 1995 - $1.31). This reflects the effects of employee stock options and convertible debenture outstanding as at March 31, 1997 and 1996 and 1995.

14. STATEMENT OF CHANGES IN FINANCIAL POSITION
(In thousands of Canadian dollars)

	1997	1996	1995
Cash provided by (used in):			
Accounts receivable and distribution contracts receivable	$ (40,427)	$ (26,569)	$ (22,388)
Accounts payable and accrued liabilities	38,828	(248)	5,551
Distribution revenue payable	(3,015)	(6,532)	13,223
Deferred revenue	30,274	(498)	(14,607)
Other	(3,710)	(1,526)	(2,952)
Net changes in non-cash working capital balances related to operations	$ 21,950	$ (35,373)	$ (21,173)

15. GOVERNMENT FINANCING AND ASSISTANCE

Revenues include $14,101,000 of production financing obtained from the government for the year ended March 31, 1997 (1996 - $13,824,000, 1995 - $8,881,000). This financing is repayable from distribution revenues in respect of which the financing was made. As revenues from these productions are not currently known, the amounts ultimately repayable to government agencies are not determinable. In addition, revenues include $2,290,000 of government grants (1995 - $693,000, 1994 - $2,406,000).

Investment in film and television programs includes a reduction of $10,291,000 (1996 - $10,810,000, 1995 - $10,209,000) with respect to government assistance for distribution of certain programs. In addition, revenues include $859,000 (1996 - $1,023,000, 1995 - $1,492,000) of government grants. Government assistance may be repayable in whole or in part depending upon future revenues generated by certain individual film and television programs. The potential amounts repayable are not determinable.

16. RELATED PARTY TRANSACTIONS

Included in accounts receivable is $218,000 (1996 - $nil) due from officers of the Company.

ALLIANCE

NOTES TO THE FINANCIAL STATEMENTS
ALLIANCE COMMUNICATIONS CORPORATION

17. COMMITMENTS AND CONTINGENCIES

a) The Company is committed with respect to operating leases for office premises and equipment expiring at various dates to May 2007. The future minimum payments under the terms of such leases are as follows:

(In thousands of Canadian dollars)

1998	$ 2,982
1999	1,679
2000	1,366
2001	1,423
2002	959
Thereafter	3,007
	$ 11,416

Rent expense for 1997 is $2,053,000 (1996 - $1,525,000, 1995 - $1,418,000).

b) The Company is involved in various legal actions. In the opinion of management, any resulting liability is not expected to have a material adverse effect on the Company's financial position.

c) The Company has a letter of credit of US$2,500,000 outstanding at March 31, 1997 (1996 - US$2,500,000, 1995 - US$2,500,000).

18. SEGMENTED INFORMATION

The Company is vertically integrated and operates exclusively in the production, distribution and structured production financing of television programs and motion pictures, broadcasting and music publishing industries, which are considered the dominant industry segments.

Revenues include $113,216,000 (1996 - $100,902,000, 1995 - $105,588,000) derived from foreign sources.

19. FINANCIAL INSTRUMENTS

Fair Value of Financial Instruments

The estimated fair values of financial instruments as at March 31, 1997 and March 31, 1996 are based on relevant market prices and information available at the time. The carrying value of cash and short-term investments, accounts receivable, loans receivable, long-term investments, operating loan and bank indebtedness, accounts payable and accrued liabilities, distribution revenues payable, loans payable, and convertible debenture approximates the fair value of these financial instruments. Financial instruments with a carrying value different from their fair value include:

(In thousands of Canadian dollars)

	1997		1996	
	Carrying Value	Fair Value	Carrying Value	Fair Value
Financial Assets:				
Assets for which fair value approximates carrying value	$ 105,932	$ 105,932	$ 59,780	$ 59,780
Distribution contracts receivable	76,272	74,066	64,948	63,283
Financial Liabilities:				
Liabilities for which fair value approximates carrying value	$ 129,352	$ 129,352	$ 97,878	$ 97,878

NOTES TO THE FINANCIAL STATEMENTS
ALLIANCE COMMUNICATIONS CORPORATION

The fair value of distribution contracts receivable is based on discounting future cash flows using rates currently available for similar instruments. The Company has not written these receivables down as it expects to recover their carrying amounts fully by holding them to maturity.

Concentration of Credit Risk

Accounts receivable from the federal government and a government agency in connection with production financing represents 41% of total accounts receivable at March 31, 1997. The Company believes that there is minimal risk associated with the collection of these amounts. The balance of accounts receivable and distribution contracts receivable is widely distributed amongst customers. Loans receivable include amounts due from a relatively small number of customers. The Company maintains an allowance for credit losses in an amount considered adequate to absorb estimated credit-related losses.

20. RECONCILIATION TO UNITED STATES GAAP

The consolidated financial statements of the Company have been prepared in accordance with Canadian GAAP. The following adjustments and/or additional disclosures, would be required in order to present the financial statements in accordance with U.S. GAAP, as required by the United States Securities and Exchange Commission.

Under U.S. GAAP, the net earnings and earnings per common share figures and shareholders' equity for the years ended March 31, 1997, 1996 and 1995 would be adjusted as follows:

(In thousands of Canadian dollars)

	Net Earnings			Shareholders' Equity	
	1997	1996	1995	1997	1996
Canadian GAAP	$ 18,188	$ 10,365	$ 12,975	$ 150,424	$ 95,380
Adjustment to development costs and investment in scripts net of income taxes of $92 (1996 - $648, 1995 - $447)(a)	115	808	(562)	(401)	(516)
Adjustment to operating expenses with respect to stock options (b)	(77)	90	(457)	(799)	(722)
Adjustment to revenue with respect to television license agreements net of income taxes of $662 (1996 - $90, 1995 - $243)(c)	(2,062)	(2,501)	(125)	(5,718)	(3,656)
Adjustment to income tax provision excluding cumulative effect adjustment noted below (d)	-	-	166	193	193
Adjustment to retained earnings with respect to stock options.	-	-	-	799	722
U.S. GAAP excluding cumulative effect adjustment	16,164	8,762	11,997	144,498	91,401
Cumulative effect of income tax adjustment for years prior to April 1, 1993 (d)	-	-	-	(285)	(285)
U.S. GAAP	$ 16,164	$ 8,762	$ 11,997	$ 144,213	$ 91,116
Earnings Per Common Share Based on U.S. GAAP(e)					
Primary	$ 1.35	$ 0.88	$ 1.23		
Fully Diluted	$ 1.30	$ 0.86	$ 1.17		

a) Accounting for Development Costs and Investment in Scripts

Under Statement of Financial Accounting Standards No. 53 "Financial Reporting by Producers and Distributors of Motion Picture Films" (SFAS 53), expenditures associated with the development of stories and scenarios are expensed as incurred while expenditures for properties such as film rights to books, stage plays, original screenplays, etc. are expensed if the property has been held for three years and has not been set for production. Under Canadian GAAP, development costs and investment in scripts is amortized over three years commencing in the year following the year such costs are incurred. The net difference of the two adjustments is disclosed as a U.S. GAAP reconciling item.

b) Accounting for Stock Options and Share Issuances

During fiscal 1997, the Company adopted the disclosure-only provisions of Statement of Financial Accounting Standards No. 123 "Accounting for Stock-Based Compensation" (SFAS 123) but, as permitted, continues to apply Accounting Principles Board Opinion No. 25 "Accounting for Stock Issued to Employees" (APB 25) in accounting for its employee stock option plan for U.S. GAAP reconciliation purposes.

For the year ended March 31, 1996, compensatory employee stock options were issued and vested in the year. In accordance with APB 25, the difference between the quoted market price and the option price is recorded as compensation expense over the vesting period.

For the years ended March 31, 1997 and 1995, no compensatory employee stock options were issued which resulted in a compensation expense, however, a compensatory expense was recognized for options issued in prior years as they vested in the year.

Under SFAS 123, the Company's pro forma net earnings for U.S. GAAP would be $15,123,000 (1996 - $8,459,000) and primary earnings per common share would be $1.26 (1996 - $0.85).

As the provisions of SFAS 123 have not been applied to options granted prior to January 1, 1995, the resulting pro forma compensation cost may not be representative of that to be expected in future years.

For disclosure purposes the fair value of each stock option grant is estimated on the date of grant using the Black-Scholes option pricing model with the following weighted average assumptions used for stock options granted in 1997 and 1996, respectively: expected dividend yields of 0.0% for both years, expected volatility of 41.4% and 39.9%, risk-free interest rate of 5.9% and 6.5% and expected life of 3 years for all grants. The weighted average fair value of the stock options granted in 1997 and 1996 was $4.77 and $5.30, respectively.

c) Revenue Recognition From Television License Agreements

Under Canadian GAAP, revenues from license agreements for television programs are recognized as earned when the television program is completed and delivered, when amounts are due from exhibitor or when a contract is executed that irrevocably transfers distribution rights to a licensee, and there is reasonable assurance of collectability of proceeds. Under SFAS 53, revenues from license agreements for television programs are recognized at the time the license periods commence instead of at the time the license agreements are executed.

NOTES TO THE FINANCIAL STATEMENTS
ALLIANCE COMMUNICATIONS CORPORATION

d) Accounting for Income Taxes

Effective April 1, 1993, the Company adopted Statement of Financial Accounting Standards No. 109 "Accounting for Income Taxes" (SFAS 109) for U.S. GAAP reconciliation purposes. The adoption of SFAS 109 changes the Company's method of accounting for income taxes from the deferral method to the asset and liability method. SFAS 109 requires recognition of deferred tax liabilities and assets for the expected future tax consequences of assets and liabilities that have been recognized in the financial statements.

As a result of the adoption of SFAS 109, the Company recognized an additional expense of $285,000, representing the cumulative effect of the change on results for year prior to April 1, 1993.

Under U.S. GAAP, the provision for income taxes for the year ended March 31, 1997 would be $9,218,000 (1996 - $2,493,000, 1995 - $2,802,000).

The application of SFAS 109 would increase broadcasting licences and income taxes by approximately $5,850,000 at March 31, 1997 (1996 - $nil).

e) Earnings per Common Share

Under Accounting Principles Board Opinion No. 15 "Earnings per Share" (APB 15), earnings per share is based on the weighted average number of common shares issued and outstanding and common stock equivalents, including stock options and warrants.

Certain stock options and shares are considered to have been outstanding from the beginning of the year for the earnings per common share calculations at March 31, 1997, 1996 and 1995. The treasury stock method was applied in the earnings per common share calculations.

Primary earnings per common share is calculated on the basis of 11,985,000 (1996 - 9,922,000, 1995 - 9,719,000) weighted average shares outstanding.

For U.S. GAAP disclosure purposes, the Company will adopt the new U.S. GAAP standard for computing earnings per share, Statement of Financial Accounting Standards No. 128 "Earnings Per Share" (SFAS 128) for the year ended March 31, 1998. The effect of applying SFAS 128 to years prior to March 31, 1998 does not produce a materially different earnings per share as computed under APB 15.

f) Consolidated Statements of Cash Flows

The Company's cash flows determined in accordance with U.S. GAAP would be as follows:

(In thousands of Canadian dollars)

	1997	1996	1995
Operating activities	$ 238,383	$ 174,282	$ 166,992
Investing activities	(252,676)	(195,037)	(198,479)
Financing activities	19,867	7,732	18,193
Effect of exchange rates on cash	113	(747)	218
Increase (decrease) in cash and cash equivalents	$ 5,687	($13,770)	$ (13,076)

21. SUBSEQUENT EVENT

On June 17, 1997, the Company sold a portion of its investment in Mainframe Entertainment Inc. in connection with Mainframe's initial public offering for net proceeds of $4,594,000 and realized a pre-tax gain on sale of $4,535,000. The Company retained a 7% ownership interest in Mainframe.

ATLANTIS

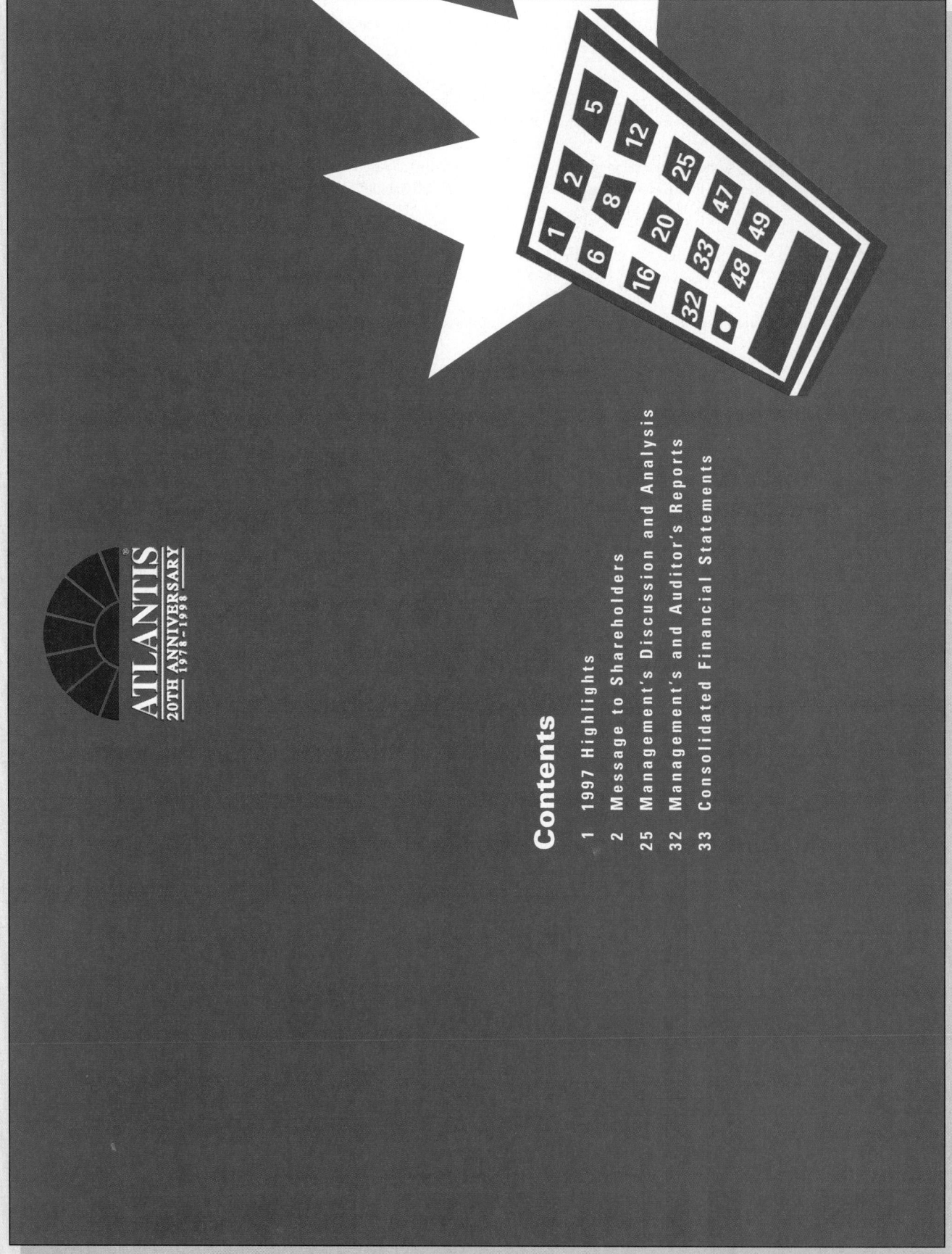

Contents

ATLANTIS

Net earnings before unusual items ($ millions): 1995: 1.5, 1996: 3.4, 1997: 5.6

Net earnings per share before unusual items ($): 1995: 0.15, 1996: 0.35, 1997: 0.55

Financial Highlights

For the years ended December 31
(in millions of dollars, except per share information)

	1997	1996	Change
Operating Results			
Revenue	$ 178	$ 138	29 %
Net earnings before unusual items	$ 5.6	$ 3.4	65 %
Net earnings	$ 5.6	$ 6.9 (1)	(19)%
Financial Position			
Completed programs	$ 46.9	$ 44.7	5 %
Cash, net of loans payable	$ 19.8	$ 3.1	539 %
Interim financing	$ 67.1	$ 27.2	147 %
Shareholders' equity	$ 97.1	$ 68.8	41 %
Per Share Information			
Net earnings before unusual items	$ 0.55	$ 0.35	57 %
Net earnings	$ 0.55	$ 0.72 (1)	(24)%
Book value	$ 7.82	$ 7.16	9 %
Shares Outstanding *(millions)*			
Average for the year	10.1	9.6	5 %
At year end	12.4 (2)	9.6	29 %

Note (1): 1996 Net earnings include the gain on sale of the Company's interest in VTV of $3.5 million or $0.37 per share.
(2): Includes the conversion into common shares of 2.3 million Special Warrants issued in December 1997.

1997 Highlights

★ ATLANTIS delivered 104 hours of original television drama, up 18 per cent from 1996, representing the renewal of four existing series, two new series and two television movies.

★ ATLANTIS' series *Gene Roddenberry's Earth: Final Conflict* ® was the highest-rated original one-hour series to have entered U.S. syndication in the past two years.

★ ATLANTIS' television movie *Borrowed Hearts: A Holiday Romance* was the highest-rated program on all of American television for the last week of November 1997, garnering 30 million viewers in the U.S. and Canada.

★ ATLANTIS acquired 50 per cent of Calibre Digital Pictures, a leading animation and digital effects company, and reached an agreement to acquire

Ironstar Communications, a Canadian distributor with a library of 300 hours.

★ ATLANTIS successfully launched Home & Garden Television (HGTV) Canada and imported the Food Network into over four million homes on October 17, 1997.

★ ATLANTIS applied to the CRTC (Canadian Radio-television and Telecommunications Commission) for five new Canadian cable channels: Food Network Canada, National Geographic Channel Canada, FIT TV Canada, Canada's Health Network and People Channel and is a minority partner in the CHAOS TV application.

★ ATLANTIS completed a successful $20 million equity offering in December 1997.

★ ATLANTIS' stock price closed the year at $10.50, a 50 per cent increase over the prior year.

ATLANTIS

Message to Shareholders

Nineteen ninety-seven was a year of operational, financial and strategic success for Atlantis Communications Inc. We achieved significant growth in revenues and net income and we did so in a manner that achieved our primary goal – to increase the ongoing sustainability and reliability of the growth in our operating results. The strategies we employed to achieve this primary goal in 1997 will be continued going forward.

Our first key strategy, given that the largest segment of our business is the production and distribution of original prime time television drama, was to increase the production of series that were renewable from year to year (as opposed to stand alone television movies). We wanted series that provide ongoing opportunities for future exploitation once a critical mass of episodes has been produced. We wanted series where Atlantis controlled major distribution rights.

All four of our one-hour series were renewed in 1997 – *Traders*, *PSI FACTOR®: Chronicles of the Paranormal*, *The Outer Limits* and *The Adventures of Sinbad*; as well, we launched two new series – *Cold Squad* and *Gene Roddenberry's Earth: Final Conflict®*. Importantly, the newer series – *Cold Squad*, *Gene Roddenberry's Earth: Final Conflict®* and *PSI FACTOR®: Chronicles of the Paranormal* – are all series where the Canadian and major international distribution rights are controlled by Atlantis.

Already, five of our series from 1997 have been renewed for 1998 and our two new series announced to date – *The World of*

Peter Cottontail and *Sixth Grade Alien* – are also series to which Atlantis controls Canadian and all international distribution rights.

Reliable and sustainable earnings are also created through "output" or "package" deals, whereby customers commit to acquire a certain volume of programming prior to the programs being produced or even identified. Atlantis recently entered into a major "package" deal with the leading European entertainment company, Endemol Entertainment of The Netherlands. Endemol agreed to license European, African and Middle Eastern rights to a number of television series and movies produced by Atlantis in 1998 and each of the next two years, as well as a selection of Atlantis' library catalogue. This arrangement will continue to increase the predictability of our growth and provide revenue to Atlantis of $115 million over the three years.

The second key strategy we employed last year was to leverage the strength of our distribution infrastructure to take advantage of Atlantis' knowledge of and relationships within the Canadian and international

Michael MacMillan, Chairman and Chief Executive Officer *(right)*; **Lewis Rose,** President *(left)*, on the set of *Traders*

2   Atlantis Communications Inc.

television marketplace. We sought to add additional product lines to be exploited by our distribution company, Atlantis Releasing, so that we could grow our sales with only modest incremental costs.

This is why we were pleased to be named the exclusive Canadian distributor of CBS television programming. The CBS appointment began in 1997 and has an initial three-year term. This means that Atlantis is the distributor in Canada of such shows as *Touched By An Angel, 60 Minutes* and *Brooklyn South*, among others.

Likewise, our recent purchase of Canadian distributor Ironstar Communications gives Atlantis access to Ironstar's program library for both Canadian and international exploitation.

It was for similar distribution leverage purposes that we decided to increase the children's program component of our catalogue. By adding animation and more live action children's series to our production activity we feed our established distribution strength while complementing our core prime time drama catalogue. Thus, in 1997, we acquired 50 per cent of Calibre Digital Pictures, a

successful Canadian animation company which creates all types of animation including leading edge computer generated animation. Calibre continues to grow under the leadership of its founder, Neil Williamson, and we intend to purchase the remainder of Calibre within two years.

In 1998 we are growing our animation and live action children's initiatives with success. We recently licensed two new series to YTV Canada, which we are currently placing with other buyers internationally. These are the live action series *Sixth Grade Alien*, based on new books by best selling children's author Bruce Coville and the animated series *The World of Peter Cottontail*, based on the celebrated books by author Thornton W. Burgess. We are fortunate to mark our entry into animation with a property as well known and popular as *The World of Peter Cottontail*.

The final key strategy for 1997 was to continue aggressively to develop our broadcasting activities. Last year we secured national analogue carriage of our new specialty channel Home & Garden

Television (HGTV) Canada, which launched on October 17, 1997. Already, HGTV Canada is attracting a positive viewer and advertiser response and we are optimistic for its continued growth and financial success.

On September 30, 1997 Atlantis applied to the CRTC for permission to launch five new specialty channels, controlled by Atlantis – People Channel, National Geographic Channel Canada, Food Network Canada, FIT TV Canada and Canada's Health Network. We believe that each of these concepts will, if approved by the CRTC, be an excellent complement to our two existing channels, Life Network and HGTV Canada.

As an interim measure, Atlantis is the exclusive agent for Food Network (U.S.), which we are currently importing into four million Canadian cable homes. Our agreement with the owners of Food Network (U.S.), E.W. Scripps Co. (the owner of HGTV in the U.S. and our partner in HGTV Canada), is that when the CRTC approves our Food Network Canada application, Food Network (U.S.) will voluntarily withdraw from Canada. Then, Food Network Canada, which Atlantis will control and manage, will replace it.

E.W. Scripps Co. will become a 29 per cent shareholder in the Canadian channel, and Shaw Communications will own 20 per cent.

In recognition of the importance of our broadcasting activities, in 1997 we created a new business unit called Atlantis Broadcasting, incorporating Life Network, HGTV Canada, Food Network and the pending applications. Juris Silkans, who has played a key role in the development of Life Network and HGTV Canada, now has an expanded leadership role as President of Atlantis Broadcasting.

The North American television marketplace continues to change substantially and quickly: viewers clearly enjoy having an increased choice of channels to watch. As well, they obviously enjoy watching "themed" channels where they reliably know the type of programming to be presented.

In Canada and the U.S., viewing of specialty and pay channels has now risen to approximately 30 per cent of total television viewing. This is astounding growth, particularly in the last few years. Television advertising revenue in North America has not yet caught up to reflect this fundamental shift in how viewers are using television. We believe that advertising spending will shift to reflect the trends in actual viewing; as such, specialty channels like ours have an exciting and substantial growth opportunity.

In 1998 our broadcasting focus will be to grow HGTV Canada through its first full year, while we prepare for the CRTC hearings on the new channel applications, anticipated to be in the first quarter of 1999. Meanwhile, we are pursuing other possibilities of expanding the "brand" value of our existing channels both within Canada and through international opportunities.

I am particularly pleased that the strategies and initiatives described here have also been reflected in increased shareholder value. The Atlantis stock price began 1997 at $7.00 and finished the year at $10.50 – an increase of exactly 50 per cent. In the first months of 1998 the price has continued to strengthen. We completed a successful equity issue in December 1997, raising approximately $20 million of equity at $9.00/share. That equity issue combined with the increase in share price has materially increased the size of our market capitalization.

This year marks the 20th anniversary of Atlantis and the theme of this year's annual report celebrates these two decades. We are very proud of what we have accomplished and created. The growth and success of Atlantis over these 20 years reflects the growth of our industry worldwide. When we started Atlantis there was no meaningful use of VCRs in homes; there was no significant pay television or specialty television; there was limited private ownership of television networks outside of North America. Atlantis' growth was possible, in part, because of the new methods of delivering filmed entertainment to viewers. Looking ahead, the methods of delivering entertainment and information will continue to diversify and evolve with the advent of the Internet, digital signals and other, still unknown, opportunities. As these new technologies become real, we will again be reminded that, as in the past, it is the content, not the hardware, which ultimately matters the most. That is where we come in.

To ensure that we participate fully in this exciting future we will need to continue to attract and retain the best and the brightest to our management team and attract the best creative talent to all of our productions. That, I believe, is how we arrived at our position today. Over the past few years we have significantly strengthened our management, both corporately and within each of our operating companies. Included in those positive moves was the 1997 appointment of Lewis Rose as President of Atlantis Communications Inc.

Looking forward to the next two decades I am particularly thankful for the continuing friendship and business partnership with Seaton McLean. Seaton co-founded Atlantis with Janice Platt and me, amongst others, in 1978. Seaton has provided Atlantis its inspiration and leadership every step of the way for each of those 20 years.

Similarly, I look forward to the ongoing and vital contributions and friendships with Ted Riley and Peter Sussman who have shared most of the past 20 years with us and who initiated and led our expansion internationally and into the U.S.

Atlantis has extremely talented and dedicated employees. The achievements of 20 years and the prospect for future growth would, clearly, never have been possible without our terrific team, both past and present.

I also offer a heartfelt thank you to our casts, crews, writers, directors and all those who participate in the production of our programs, including producers, suppliers, broadcast customers and financiers, as well as to our shareholders and our Board of Directors whose advice is always appreciated.

Atlantis begins its third decade with a clear sense of opportunity, excitement and growth. The best is yet to come.

Michael I.M. MacMillan
Chairman and
Chief Executive Officer

Management's Discussion and Analysis

The following discussion and analysis for the years ended December 31, 1997 and 1996 should be read in conjunction with the consolidated financial statements and the notes to the consolidated financial statements included in this annual report.

Atlantis Communications Inc. is a leading international producer, distributor and broadcaster of popular high-quality television programming for audiences worldwide. Television Production includes the production of television programs, as well as ownership and management of studios and post-production facilities. Television Distribution includes the licensing of both proprietary Atlantis-produced and third-party acquired television programming. Atlantis' Broadcasting interests include 100% of the specialty channel Life Network, and a controlling 67% interest in the specialty channel Home & Garden Television (HGTV) Canada. Atlantis Broadcasting also is the exclusive agent in Canada for Food Network, FiT TV and America's Health Network.

The impact of the two broad business areas, Television Production/Distribution and Broadcasting, on the Company's results and financial position is discussed below.

Operating Results

Revenue

The Company's total revenue of $178.0 million increased by $40.0 million (29%) in 1997. Revenue from the Production/Distribution business increased by $35.8 million (32%) to $149.4 million, while revenue from the Broadcasting business increased by $4.1 million (19%) to $26.0 million, and Other Revenue, primarily from investments, increased by $0.1 million to $2.6 million.

Production/Distribution Revenue

Production/Distribution revenue consists of program licence revenue, other program revenue, and post-production revenue. The results of the Production/ Distribution operations may vary significantly in any period depending on the number of hours of television programs delivered in

that period. As a result, the Company's earnings for any one period are not necessarily indicative of results for future periods.

Program Licence Revenue

Program licence revenue is comprised of pre-sale licencing revenue (licensing of Atlantis-produced programs prior to the delivery of the program) as well as after-sale licencing revenue (licensing of completed Atlantis-produced programs or completed programs acquired from third parties). Program licence revenue is recognized when a program is delivered, the licence period begins and the collectability of proceeds is reasonably assured. In the case of a television series, revenue is recognized on a pro-rata episodic basis.

Program licence revenue increased $45.8 million (50%) to $137.4 million, largely as a result of increased revenue from pre-sale licencing and after-sales of *Gene Rodden-*

Revenue Analysis

(millions)	1997		1996	
Production/Distribution Revenue				
▶ Program Licence	$ 137.4	77%	$ 91.6	66%
▶ Other Program	$ 10.9	6%	$ 20.8	15%
▶ Post-Production	$ 1.1	1%	$ 1.2	1%
	$ 149.4	84%	$ 113.6	82%
▲ Broadcast Revenue	$ 26.0	15%	$ 21.9	16%
△ Other Revenue	$ 2.6	1%	$ 2.5	2%
Total Revenue	**$ 178.0**	**100%**	**$ 138.0**	**100%**

berry's Earth: Final Conflict® and Cold Squad, two new series added to the Atlantis slate during 1997. An increase in the number of episodes delivered of both PSI FACTOR®: Chronicles of the Paranormal and The Adventures of Sinbad also contributed to the significant year over year increase in program licence revenue. The 1997 library revenues increased by $5.6 million (52%) to $16.3 million and included the sale of all 65 episodes of the family drama Neon Rider to Pax Net, the new Paxson Communications Network in the U.S.

Atlantis continues to generate the majority (89%) of its program licence revenues from outside Canada, with 47% (46% – 1996) from the United States and 42% (43% – 1996) from other markets around the world (see chart). This reflects the global appeal of Atlantis' programming.

Other Program Revenue

Other program revenue is comprised of revenue raised by the Company from third-party sources to fund production costs. This revenue includes non-recourse investments in programs by government agencies and broadcasters and financing from the Canada Television and Cable Production Fund in both years. During 1996, other program revenue also included interest income from limited partnership syndications and proceeds from the sale of copyright to limited partnership syndications. Other program revenue is recognized

when a program is delivered and the collectability of proceeds is reasonably assured. In the case of a television series, revenue is recognized on a pro-rata episodic basis.

Other program revenue declined by $9.9 million (48%) to $10.9 million. The decrease was due to the fact that 1996 was the final year in which the Company recognized revenue related to interest income and proceeds from sales of copyright to limited partnership syndications. The revenue recognized on these limited partnership syndications in 1996 was $11.9 million and related to purchase agreements entered into prior to December 31, 1995. During 1995, amendments to the Income Tax Act arising from the February 1995 Fed-

eral Budget were implemented to eliminate new limited partnership syndications of Canadian certified film and television productions effective December 31, 1995.

Other program revenue of $10.9 million in 1997, primarily represents financing from government incentive and regulatory programs, up from $8.9 million in 1996. In early 1998, the Federal government announced a three-year commitment for the CTCPF (Canada Television Cable Production Fund), but there is no assurance as to the eligibility criteria for programs, the funding caps, or the availability of funds for Atlantis programs given the first come first served nature of the Licence Fee Program.

The Company continues to emphasize the creation of more commercial, market-driven programming which can be increasingly financed by pre-sale licences from the international market, with reduced reliance on the domestic market and related government incentives.

Post-Production Revenue

Post-production revenue is comprised of revenue from sound mixing, picture editing, and sound editing services for both television and theatrical films provided by a wholly-owned subsidiary, Casablanca Sound & Picture Inc., and is recognized as services are performed. In 1997, post-production revenue was $1.1 million ($1.2 million – 1996) after elimination of $4.0 million ($2.8 million – 1996) in respect of services performed for production companies in the associated Atlantis group of companies.

Broadcast Revenue

Broadcast revenue in 1997 is derived from the operation of the Company's specialty television channels: Life Network and HGTV Canada. Broadcasting revenue is comprised of two principal sources: cable subscriber revenue and advertising revenue. Cable subscriber revenue increased by $0.4 million (3%) to $13.8 million as the number of households that receive Life Network increased by 300,000 to 5.7 million at December 31, 1997. The HGTV Canada signal

Program Licence Revenue – Geographic Analysis

(millions)	1997		1996	
▷ Canada	$ 15.5	11%	$ 10.1	11%
▷ United States	$ 64.1	47%	$ 42.3	46%
▷ Other Markets	$ 57.8	42%	$ 39.2	43%
Total Program Licence Revenue	$ 137.4	100%	$ 91.6	100%

was received by over 4.0 million households at December 31, 1997 and was still in the free preview period at that date.

Advertising, ancillary and other revenue increased by $3.7 million (44%) to $12.2 million in 1997. This increase was due to continued advertiser confidence in Life Network's ability to deliver significant ratings from a desirable audience demographic, together with the launch of HGTV Canada on October 17, 1997 which provided synergies for the sales effort. The results have been a continued increase in sales of commercial time at more favourable rates during 1997.

Amortization

Amortization of $150.1 million in 1997 ($116.1 million – 1996) was comprised of amortization of completed programs, costs of distributing programs, amortization of broadcast rights and development costs.

Amortization of Atlantis-produced programs as a percentage of Production/Distribution revenue was 88% in 1997, which compares to 87% in 1996.

The Company's completed program asset represents the original cost of completed programs, net of accumulated amortization. The completed program inventory contains 745 hours of Atlantis-produced programming, including 104 hours delivered in 1997.

1997 Production Activity

Production Initiated in 1997	Episode Length (hours)	Total Series/ Movie Budget ($ millions)	Number of Hours Delivered						Key Broadcasters
			Q1	Q2	Q3	Q4	1997	1998	
T.V. Series									
Gene Roddenberry's Earth: Final Conflict® I	1.0	37	—	—	3.0	10.0	**13.0**	9.0	Tribune Entertainment – U.S. Syndication, CTV/ Baton Broadcasting System
Cold Squad I	1.0	11	—	—	—	6.0	**6.0**	5.0	CTV/Baton Broadcasting System
Outer Limits IIIB	1.0	41	—	—	—	2.0	**2.0**	20.0	Showtime, MGM – U.S. Syndication, Global
PSI FACTOR®: Chronicles of the Paranormal II	1.0	23	—	1.0	6.0	9.0	**16.0**	6.0	EYEMARK Entertainment (CBS) – U.S. Syndication, Global
The Adventures of Sinbad II	1.0	31	—	—	5.0	8.0	**13.0**	9.0	All American – U.S. Syndication, Global
Traders III	1.0	18	—	—	4.0	10.0	**14.0**	8.0	Global, CBC
T.V. Movies									
Borrowed Hearts: A Holiday Romance	2.0	6	—	—	2.0	—	**2.0**	—	CBS, CTV/Baton Broadcasting System
The Return of Alex Kelly	2.0	7	—	—	—	2.0	**2.0**	—	CBS, CTV/Baton Broadcasting System
			—	1.0	20.0	47.0	**68.0**	57.0	

Production Initiated in 1996 and delivered in 1997	Episode Length (hours)	Total Series/ Movie Budget ($ millions)	Number of Hours Delivered							Key Broadcasters
			1996	Q1	Q2	Q3	Q4	1997	1998	
T.V. Series										
Flash Forward II	0.5	8	8.0	3.0	—	—	—	**3.0**	—	ABC, Disney Channel, Family Channel (Canada), Global
Outer Limits IIIA	1.0	41	5.0	7.0	8.0	2.0	—	**17.0**	—	Showtime, MGM – U.S. Syndication, Global, TMN, Superchannel
PSI FACTOR®: Chronicles of the Paranormal I	1.0	22	16.0	5.0	1.0	—	—	**6.0**	—	EYEMARK Entertainment (CBS) – U.S. Syndication, Global
The Adventures of Sinbad	1.0	32	12.0	7.0	3.0	—	—	**10.0**	—	All American – U.S. Syndication, Global
			41.0	22.0	12.0	2.0	—	**36.0**	—	
Total number of hours delivered				22.0	13.0	22.0	47.0	**104.0**	57.0	

In addition, the Atlantis library contains 362 hours of acquired programs (including 300 hours obtained in the Ironstar acquisition which closed in early 1998). Atlantis also represents other third-party programs such as the CBS catalogue.

The Company utilizes the individual film forecast computation method in amortizing its completed programs. Capitalized production and/or acquisition costs, together with the estimated total cost of any residual payments, or other participations related to a particular program, are amortized in the ratio that revenue generated by the program in a particular period bears to management's estimate of total gross revenue, to be realized from that program over the next four years. Although the value of the completed programs at December 31, 1997, is expected to be fully amortized by December 31, 2001, management is confident that the library will continue to generate revenue well beyond the amortization period.

At December 31, 1997, the Company had amortized 92% of the original cost of its completed programs. The Company anticipates that these programs will be fully amortized after four years.

Amortization is based on management's estimates of future revenues, and as such, any significant negative variation between the estimated revenue and the actual revenue realized over time in respect of a program may require a write-down of that program. Management controls this risk by periodically reviewing and updating the estimates and assumptions involved in the calculations used to amortize the program inventory in the context of a continually changing marketplace.

The Company has applied for tax credits under federal and provincial tax credit programs. This funding, along with government grants, has been reflected as a reduction to the cost of completed programs in the amount of $16.5 million ($9.9 million – 1996), and a reduction of $2.6 million ($2.5 million – 1996) to the cost of programs in process.

Amortization of Broadcast rights in 1997 was 60% of total Broadcast revenue, compared with 75% in 1996. The Company's Broadcast rights asset represents the original cost of broadcast programming net of accumulated amortization. The Broadcast rights are amortized over the exclusivity period of the contract, if applicable, or otherwise over one-half of the duration of the contract.

The decrease in the ratio of Broadcast rights amortization to total Broadcast revenue can be attributed to the change in the required level of spending on Canadian content as required by condition of licence between Life Network's first and second year of operation. In 1997, Life Network's conditions of licence required it to maintain Canadian program expenditures at a level equal to 65% of the previous year's revenue from regulated broadcast activities less a 5% allowable variance. In its first full year of operation, ended August 31, 1996, Life Network expended $15.2 million on Canadian program expenditures, which was within the 5% allowable variance of the initial year requirement of $16.0 million in Canadian program expenditures.

HGTV Canada's conditions of licence will require it to maintain Canadian program expenditures at a level equal to 50% of the previous year's revenue from regulated broadcast activities within a 5% allowable variance. For its first year of operation, an expenditure level was not established as part of the licence conditions. Management expects that both Life Network and HGTV Canada will continue to meet this condition of licence at future fiscal year ends.

Operating Expense

Operating expense, net of capitalized operating expenses which relate directly to programs and development projects, increased by $0.3 million (2%) to $14.1 million in 1997. Gross operating expenses increased by $3.3 million (17%) to $22.9 million.

The entire increase in gross operating expenses is attributable to the Broadcasting group where additional costs were incurred for the start-up of the HGTV Canada channel and to accommodate growth at Life Network. The Company capitalized $2.1 million of pre-operating expenses for HGTV Canada, which represented $3.0 million of operating expenses net of advertising and ancillary revenue of $0.9 million. These capitalized operating costs will be amortized over five years from the commencement of commercial operations.

While gross operating expenses of $13.0 million did not increase in the Television Production/Distribution area, additional operating costs were capitalized to reflect the increased level of production activity for television programming during 1997.

Depreciation

Depreciation includes depreciation expense for fixed assets and the amortization expense related to goodwill, deferred start-up costs and other assets.

Depreciation expense increased by $1.3 million to $3.0 million in 1997. The increase relates to the goodwill associated with the Life Network acquisition, amortization of deferred start-up costs associated with Life Network and additional depreciation on capital expenditures made during 1997. The majority of the capital expenditures of $5.7 million were for broadcasting equipment associated with the start-up of HGTV Canada ($3.6 million) and information technology and financial systems investment throughout the Company ($0.8 million).

Gain on Sale of Investment

On August 30, 1996, the Company sold its 28% interest in YTV for net proceeds of approximately $25 million. The Company accounted for its share of equity earnings from YTV, as well as for amortization of related goodwill incurred in connection with the acquisition of its interest in YTV, up until the date of disposition. The gain on the sale of this investment was $5.3 million before taxes ($3.5 million or $0.37 cents per share, on an after-tax basis). The proceeds of disposition were retained by the Company in general cash reserves and contributed to the increase in the Company's cash and marketable securities at December 31, 1996 and the reduction in the Company's interest expense in 1996.

Interest Expense

Interest expense decreased by approximately $0.4 million (29%) in 1997. This decrease was primarily due to an increase in the average cash position of the Company throughout 1997. Interest expense attributable to interim financing is included in the production costs of the particular program to which it relates, and therefore does not appear as interest expense on the Company's Consolidated Statement of Earnings.

EBITDA (Earnings before interest, taxes, depreciation and amortization)

EBITDA for 1997 increased by $5.7 million (71%) to $13.7 million. The improvement in EBITDA results from increased margin from the production, distribution and broadcast of television programs, partially offset by a slight increase in net operating expenses.

Net Earnings

Net earnings for 1997 were $5.6 million, compared with net earnings before unusual items of $3.4 million for 1996. The total 1996 net earnings of $6.9 million included an after-tax gain of $3.5 million, or $0.37 per share, on the sale of the Company's interest in YTV (see Gain on Sale of Investment).

Net earnings per share in 1997, before unusual items, increased by $0.20 or 57% from $0.35 in 1996. Total net earnings per share in 1997 were $0.55 compared with $0.72 in 1996, which included the $0.37 per share after-tax gain described above.

The 1997 per share calculation is based on a weighted average of 10,067,074 shares outstanding (1996 – 9,603,294 shares). There were 10,119,244 shares outstanding at December 31, 1997.

Income Taxes

The Company's effective income tax rate for 1997 was 43.7% of earnings before taxes (1996 – 34.7%). This effective tax rate reflects a 15.8% reduction in the effective income tax rate due to the utilization of loss carryforwards, an increase in the income tax rate due to non-deductible expenses (5.8%), an accrual for income tax contingencies (8.4%) and other adjustments (0.7%).

The Company is currently undergoing audits of the taxation years ended 1992 to 1994 by Revenue Canada and the taxation years ended 1993 to 1995 by the Ontario Ministry of Revenue. The Company has not been reassessed by either body, and as such, any reassessment may result in additional tax liability not currently reflected in the Company's financial statements.

before unusual items, is a result of the increased margin from the production, distribution and broadcast of television programs ($6.0 million), plus a reduction in interest expense ($0.4 million). The increase in earnings was partially offset by increases in operating expenses ($0.2 million) and depreciation ($1.3 million).

Liquidity and Capital Resources

Cash and Cash Equivalents

During 1997, the Company's cash and cash equivalents increased by $15.6 million to $29.7 million at December 31, 1997. Net cash (cash and cash equivalents less loans payable) increased by $16.7 million to $19.8 million at December 31, 1997. In addition to these cash reserves, the Company has unused operating lines of credit of $22.4 million with Canadian chartered banks, and separate interim financing arrangements for productions.

The Company also has financing commitments, from a Canadian chartered bank for $29.4 million, which support the applications for five new specialty channels. The financing will be available to fund the Company's investment and operating debts in the specialty channels, should licence(s) be awarded.

The Company is generally required to make significant initial expenditures either to produce its own television programs or to acquire programs from third parties. As the revenues from these programs are received by the Company over an extended period of time, the Company has traditionally financed its working capital requirements in this initial period through cash generated by operations and its lines of credit. In the case of television series, where cash flow requirements are more substantial, the Company uses self-liquidating interim financing loans, primarily from Canadian chartered banks.

Cash used in Operating Activities

During 1997, the Company had a net cash inflow of $133 million compared with $137 million in 1996. The net use of cash was to primarily finance accounts receivable associated with the increased production activity and interim funding of applications for federal and provincial tax credit programs for both the 1996 and 1997 programs. This use of cash was partially offset by an increase in gross margin from television production, distribution and broadcasting activity.

Cash used in Investing Activities

During 1997, the Company had a cash outflow from investing activity of $181 million compared with $128 million in 1996. The 1997 cash outflow included increased investments in programs in process and completed programs due to the

increased production activity ($30 million), increased expenditures for capital and other assets mainly associated with the start-up of HGTV Canada ($4 million) and the investment in Calibre Digital Pictures ($2 million).

The remaining variance results from activities in 1996, where the Company received proceeds of $25 million on the sale of its interest in YTV, partially offset by the purchase of the remaining 43% interest in the Life Network for $9 million.

Cash provided from Financing Activities

During 1997, the Company funded its operating and investment activities mainly through the use of interim financing and a private placement of Special Warrants that took place in December 1997. The cash provided from financing activities was $64 million for 1997 ($1 million – 1996).

Interim Financing

During 1997, the Company received $40 million of interim financing ($5 million – 1996) to support the increased production activity and the applications for tax credits under federal and provincial tax credit programs.

Interim financing on programs is debt which the Company raises in respect of a specific program in order to bridge the cash flow requirements of that program during its production. Interim

financing is generally 100% secured by assigned accounts receivable of the program to which it relates. As such, the debt is self-liquidating. Interest expense attributable to interim financing is included in the production costs of the particular program to which it relates, and therefore does not appear as interest expense on the Company's Consolidated Statement of Earnings.

During 1997, the Company actively financed its programs through the use of an interim $45 million Production Revolver Facility with the Royal Bank of Canada. During 1997, the Company re-negotiated the terms of this facility, in conjunction with its lines of credit to obtain a more favourable overall credit package which provides lower borrowing costs and more efficient administration. The overall average interest rate for interim financing during 1997 was 4.7%, compared with 7.3% during 1996. The lower rate for 1997 is a result of the improved borrowing terms of the Production Revolver Facility and a lower average Canadian prime borrowing rate during 1997.

Private Placement of Special Warrants

On December 23, 1997, the Company issued 2,292,400 Special Warrants for cash consideration of $20.6 million ($9 per share). The Company's share issue costs including the underwriters' fees and expenses totaled $1.9 million

($1.0 million after taxes). On February 9, 1998, all of the Special Warrants were converted into subordinate voting shares on a one-for-one basis. As at April 2, 1998, there were 8,180,645 subordinated voting shares outstanding (12,418,144 total shares).

Year 2000

The year 2000 poses a challenge to businesses that are reliant on computer systems or other equipment that use the last two digits to represent a year. The Company has performed an analysis of the risks and uncertainties arising from the year 2000 issue and developed a plan to address the risks and uncertainties. The plan is reviewed on an ongoing basis by executive management and the Board of Directors. The scope of the analysis includes all computer hardware products, computer software products, broadcasting, production, post-production, animation equipment, and general office equipment. This analysis will be expanded to include the systems of the Company's key suppliers, customers and bankers during 1998.

The Company's inventory of software includes mainly third-party products and some custom-developed applications. The custom-developed applications, which have been implemented recently, were designed with four digit date processing and are fully year 2000 compliant.

An inventory of substantially all third-party hardware and software products has been taken and the state of year 2000 readiness evaluated. A significant number of products are already year 2000 compliant and supplier certifications from other third-party vendors have been obtained or are being pursued as part of the implementation plan. The Year 2000 plan includes some limited testing of major systems to ensure year 2000 compliance, in addition to relying on supplier certifications and the experience of their clients who conduct tests on these products. Contingency plans will be developed for any product where supplier certification has not been provided during fiscal 1998.

The costs associated with the Year 2000 plan are mainly administrative costs and will be incurred by existing in-house staff from 1997 through the year 1999. These costs will be expensed as incurred and are not expected to be material. The Company's existing budget for information technology includes the replacement of desktop technology and key financial operating systems during fiscal 1998. The replacement products that have been selected for implementation during 1998 are year 2000 compliant.

The Company presently believes that through testing and upgrading its systems and working with third-party vendors, it will ensure a

smooth transition for the Company and its customers.

Outlook

The Company is committed to growth through excellence in television programming.

For 1998, five of the Company's six 1997 television series have been re-ordered for a further season of production, along with orders for two new children's television series, two series' pilots and one network movie. This totals over 125 hours of television production that is already committed and is expected to be delivered during 1998.

In an increasing global market for television programs, a significant amount of pre-sale revenue is required to create programs that are a high quality and meet the necessary commercial appeal in the marketplace. In order to secure substantial pre-sale revenue for many projects, the Company has entered into program package/output arrangements with key customers including Endemol Entertainment for Europe, Africa and the Middle East and TV3 for New Zealand. The Endemol arrangement, signed in April 1998, also included a significant sale of the available rights for Endemol's territories of a variety of Atlantis' drama programs from its library.

The television production and distribution industry is experienc-

ing consolidation both within Canada and North America and on a global basis, which may limit the number of customers and suppliers in the marketplace. In order to ensure that the Company remains competitive, it may from time to time pursue investment opportunities in the industry which expand its scale and scope in order to maximize its future growth and profit potential. During 1997, the Company acquired an interest in Calibre Digital Pictures to expand its capability in the area of animation and special effects. The investment opportunities will be carefully evaluated in terms of their overall strategic and financial value to the Company.

In 1997, the Company's broadcasting operation filed applications with the Canadian Radio-television and Telecommunications Commission ("CRTC") for five new specialty broadcasting services which Atlantis controls. They are: Food Network Canada, Canada's Health Network, People Channel, National Geographic Channel Canada and FIT TV Canada. In addition, the Company participated as a 20% shareholder in Shaw Communications Inc.'s application for CHAOS TV. Over the next fiscal year, no decisions from the CRTC are expected with regard to the specialty broadcasting applications. The Company expects that the CRTC will hold hearings regarding the applications during the first quarter of 1999 and is

optimistic that it will be successful in expanding its broadcasting operation beyond its current two channels, Life Network and HGTV Canada. Management believes that the addition of new broadcasting services to its existing operation will create synergies and improve overall operating results.

Management believes that the key events of 1997: continued development of a growing television program slate with international appeal; the significant growth in Life Network and the launch of HGTV Canada; the Company's entry into the animation and special effects business through the acquisition of Calibre Digital Pictures; coupled with the addition of new product lines such as the CBS representation agreement; and the application for five new specialty broadcast services, which Atlantis controls, are consistent with the Company's growth strategy to enhance shareholder value.

ATLANTIS

Management's Report

The accompanying financial statements and all information contained in this annual report of Atlantis Communications Inc. are the responsibility of Management and have been approved by the Board of Directors. Financial and operating data elsewhere in the annual report is consistent with the information contained in the financial statements. The financial statements and all other information have been prepared by Management in accordance with generally accepted accounting principles. The financial statements include some figures and assumptions based on Management's best estimates which have been derived with careful judgement.

In fulfilling its responsibilities, Management of the Company has developed and maintains a system of internal accounting controls. These controls ensure that the financial records are reliable for preparing the financial statements. The Board of Directors of the Company carries out its responsibility for the financial statements through its Audit Committee. The Audit Committee reviews the Company's annual consolidated financial statements and recommends their approval by the Board of Directors. The auditors have full access to the Audit Committee with and without Management present.

The financial statements have been audited by Deloitte & Touche Chartered Accountants, whose findings are contained in this annual report.

Michael I.M. MacMillan
Chairman and Chief Executive Officer

Lewis N. Rose
President

Kerri Golden
Chief Financial Officer

Auditors' Report

To the Shareholders of Atlantis Communications Inc.

We have audited the consolidated balance sheets of Atlantis Communications Inc. as at December 31, 1997 and 1996 and the consolidated statements of earnings and retained earnings and changes in financial position for the years then ended. These financial statements are the responsibility of the Company's management. Our responsibility is to express an opinion on these financial statements based on our audits.

We conducted our audits in accordance with generally accepted auditing standards. Those standards require that we plan and perform an audit to obtain reasonable assurance whether the financial statements are free of material misstatement. An audit includes examining, on a test basis, evidence supporting the amounts and disclosures in the financial statements. An audit also includes assessing the accounting principles used and significant estimates made by management, as well as evaluating the overall financial statement presentation.

In our opinion, these consolidated financial statements present fairly, in all material respects, the financial position of the Company as at December 31, 1997 and 1996 and the results of its operations and the changes in its financial position for the years then ended in accordance with generally accepted accounting principles.

Deloitte & Touche
Chartered Accountants

Toronto, Ontario
April 02, 1998

Consolidated Balance Sheets

As at December 31 (in thousands of Canadian dollars, except for per share information)

	1997	1996
Assets		
Cash and cash equivalents (Note 2)	$ 29,669	$ 14,099
Accounts receivable (Note 3)	145,611	75,645
Development costs	4,147	4,561
Programs in process	40,308	22,829
Completed programs (Note 4)	46,932	44,698
Broadcast rights (Note 5)	13,517	11,260
Notes receivable (Note 6)	20,526	140,673
Investments (Note 7)	3,513	1,500
Fixed assets (Note 8)	12,537	8,937
Deferred income taxes	4,284	—
Other assets (Note 9)	12,503	10,624
	$ 333,547	$ 334,826
Liabilities		
Accounts payable and accrued liabilities	$ 42,592	$ 24,591
Broadcast rights payable	4,457	5,043
Distribution revenue payable	10,996	9,419
Interim financing on programs (Note 10)	67,055	27,230
Loans payable (Note 11)	9,847	10,952
Deferred revenue	78,842	45,904
Notes payable (Note 6)	20,526	140,673
Deferred income taxes	—	2,186
Non-controlling interest	2,145	—
	236,460	265,998
Shareholders' Equity		
Capital stock (Note 12)	76,705	52,961
Retained earnings	20,382	15,867
	97,087	68,828
	$ 333,547	$ 334,826
Book value per share (Note 13)	$ 7.82	$ 7.16

See accompanying notes

On behalf of the Board:

Michael I.M. MacMillan
Director

Donald W. Paterson
Director

ATLANTIS

Consolidated Statements of Earnings and Retained Earnings

For the years ended December 31 (in thousands of Canadian dollars, except for per share information)

	1997	1996
Revenue	$ 177,960	$ 137,984
Expenses		
Amortization	150,101	116,134
Operating	14,129	13,856
Depreciation	3,029	1,694
	167,259	131,684
Earnings before undernoted	10,701	6,300
Gain on sale of investment (Note 9)	—	5,272
Earnings before interest and income taxes	10,701	11,572
Interest	947	1,339
Earnings before income taxes	9,754	10,233
Provision for (recovery of) income taxes (Note 14)		
Current	9,887	2,954
Deferred	(5,625)	593
	4,262	3,547
Earnings before equity earnings and non-controlling interest	5,492	6,686
Equity earnings from investment	73	318
Non-controlling interest	—	(138)
Net earnings for the year	5,565	6,866
Retained earnings, beginning of year	15,867	9,001
Share issue costs (Note 12)	(1,050)	—
Retained earnings, end of year	$ 20,382	$ 15,867
Earnings per share (Note 15)	$ 0.55	$ 0.72

See accompanying notes

Consolidated Statements of Changes in Financial Position

For the years ended December 31 (in thousands of Canadian dollars)

	1997	1996
Cash provided by (used in):		
Operating activities		
Net earnings for the year	$ 5,565	$ 6,866
Items not affecting cash		
Amortization and depreciation	153,130	117,828
Gain on disposition of an investment	—	(5,272)
Deferred income taxes	(5,625)	593
Non-controlling interest and equity earnings	(73)	(180)
	152,997	119,835
Changes in other non-cash balances	(19,842)	17,067
	133,155	136,902
Investing activities		
Development costs	(2,565)	(2,219)
Programs in process	(19,749)	(5,478)
Completed programs	(129,945)	(112,166)
Broadcast rights	(18,436)	(19,038)
Investments	(1,940)	(400)
Proceeds on sale of investment	—	25,145
Net additions to fixed assets	(5,755)	(1,831)
Acquisition of Life Network	—	(9,473)
Other assets	(2,754)	(2,899)
	(181,144)	(128,359)
Financing activities		
Notes receivable	120,148	(256)
Interim financing	39,825	5,097
Loans payable	(1,105)	(4,331)
Notes payable	(120,148)	256
Non-controlling interest	2,145	—
Capital stock issued	23,744	50
Share issue costs	(1,050)	—
	63,559	816
Increase in cash and cash equivalents	15,570	9,359
Cash and cash equivalents, beginning of year	14,099	4,740
Cash and cash equivalents, end of year	$ 29,669	$ 14,099

See accompanying notes

Atlantis Communications Inc.   35

ATLANTIS

ATLANTIS

Notes to Consolidated Financial Statements

December 31, 1997 and 1996 (in thousands of Canadian dollars, except for per share information)

ATLANTIS COMMUNICATIONS INC., together with its subsidiaries (the "Company") is an international producer, distributor and broadcaster of television programs.

1. Summary of Significant Accounting Policies

Generally accepted accounting principles

These consolidated financial statements have been prepared in accordance with generally accepted accounting principles.

The Company has adopted United States Financial Accounting Standards Board Statement No. 53 for revenue recognition and amortization of program costs, as there are no Canadian accounting standards specific to the television industry.

Principles of consolidation

These consolidated financial statements include the financial statements of the Company, its subsidiaries, an equity ownership in Calibre Digital Design Inc. ("Calibre"), and a 50% joint venture interest in Cinevillage Inc. ("Cinevillage"). Calibre is accounted for using the equity method. Cinevillage is accounted for using the proportionate consolidation method to reflect the Company's share of assets, liabilities, revenues and expenses in the joint venture.

Revenue recognition

The Company's primary sources of revenue are derived from the production and distribution of television programs, and revenue derived from broadcast activities. Production and distribution revenue is comprised of program licence revenue, other program revenue, and post-production revenue.

Program licence revenue is derived from licensing distribution rights to broadcasters and syndicators. The Company recognizes program licence revenue when the program is delivered, the licence period begins, and the collectability of the revenue is reasonably assured. In the case of a television series, revenue is recognized on a pro-rata episodic basis.

Other program revenue is comprised of non-recourse investments in programs by government agencies and broadcasters and financing from the Canada Television and Cable Production Fund. The Company recognizes other program revenue when a program is delivered and the collectability of the revenue is reasonably assured. In the case of a television series, revenue is recognized on a pro-rata episodic basis.

Broadcast revenue is derived from the operations of the Company's specialty cable television channel, Life Network Inc. ("Life Network"), and is comprised of two principal sources: cable subscriber revenue, and advertising revenue. Cable subscriber revenue is recognized as the services are provided. Advertising revenue is recognized when the commercials are aired. Revenue of Home & Garden Television Canada Inc. ("HGTV") has been deferred as the channel is in the pre-operating stage.

Development costs

The Company capitalizes costs, including related overhead, incurred with respect to literary works and other underlying rights it intends to adapt to adapt for production. Non-recourse development financing received by the Company has been offset against the related development costs. Development costs are assessed periodically on a project by project basis, and are written off when determined not to be recoverable.

Programs in process

Programs in process represent the costs incurred by the Company in the production of television programs where principal photography has commenced, but where the programs were not delivered at year end. These costs include production expenditures, interest and overhead, net of federal and provincial tax credits and grants. Programs in process are not amortized as no revenue has been recognized.

Completed programs

Completed programs represent the costs incurred by the Company in the production of television programs which have been produced and delivered, or for which the Company has acquired distribution rights from third parties. These costs include production expenditures, acquisition costs, interest, overhead, third-party participation and print and advertising costs, net of federal and provincial tax credits and grants.

Completed programs are stated at the lower of cost, net of amortization, and net realizable value. The net realizable value of a completed program is the Company's share of the estimated future revenue to be earned from the program, net of the estimated future costs.

The individual film forecast method is used to amortize the cost of completed programs. Amortization for each completed program is based on the ratio that current revenue earned from that program bears to estimated future revenue, including subsequent licensing periods.

Broadcast rights

Broadcast subsidiaries are committed, under various contracts, to pay for the rights to broadcast programming. Broadcast rights and corresponding liabilities are recorded when the licence period begins and the program becomes available for use. Broadcast rights are stated at the lower of cost, net of amortization, and net realizable value. The cost of each contract is amortized over the exclusivity period, if applicable, and otherwise over one-half of the duration of the contract.

Investments

Investments in shares of associated companies over which the Company has significant influence, are accounted for by the equity method. Other investments are carried at cost.

Fixed assets

Fixed assets are carried at cost less accumulated depreciation. Depreciation is provided using the following rates and methods:

Building	5% declining balance
Broadcast and production equipment	20 – 30% declining balance
Furniture and other equipment	20 – 30% declining balance
Leasehold improvements	20% straight-line
Vehicles	30% declining balance

Other assets

Other assets include pre-operating costs and goodwill. Pre-operating costs primarily relate to HGTV and Life Network. HGTV is currently in the pre-operating stage. All start-up costs incurred during the pre-operating stage are being capitalized and will be amortized over five years from commencement of commercial operations.

Life Network was in the pre-operating stage to December 31, 1994. All start-up costs related to the pre-operating stage are being amortized from the commencement of operations on January 1, 1995 over 56 months.

Goodwill represents the excess of the cost of investments over the assigned values of assets and liabilities acquired, and is amortized using the straight-line method over periods not exceeding 40 years. The balance is reviewed on an annual basis and, in the event of a permanent impairment to goodwill, such as material change in the business practices or significant operating losses, the Company will record a reduction in the unamortized portion of goodwill.

Distribution revenue payable

Distribution revenue payable represents amounts owing to investors, co-producers and other third-party participants.

Deferred revenue

Completed program revenue is deferred until the program is delivered. Program licence revenue is also deferred until the licence meets the revenue recognition criteria as described in this note.

Government financing, tax credits and grants

The Company has access to government financing that is designed to assist television production and distribution in Canada. Financing from government agencies is considered revenue, and is recognized in accordance with the Company's revenue recognition policy. Federal and provincial tax credits and grants related to programs in process and completed programs are recorded as a reduction in the cost of the respective program.

Use of estimates

The preparation of financial statements in conformity with generally accepted accounting principles requires management to make estimates and assumptions that affect the amounts reported in the financial statements. Actual results could differ from these estimates.

Amortization of completed programs is based on management's estimates of future revenue. Accordingly, any significant negative variation between the estimated revenue and the actual revenue realized over time in respect of a program, may require a write-down of that program. Due to a continually changing marketplace, management controls this risk by periodically reviewing and updating these estimates and assumptions.

The Company is currently undergoing audits by Revenue Canada and the Ontario Ministry of Revenue. As the result of these audits is unknown and as no reassessments have been made to date, a reassessment may result in additional tax liability not currently reflected in the Company's financial statements.

Income taxes

The Company accounts for income taxes using the deferral method.

2. Cash and Cash Equivalents

Bank demand loans have been netted against cash and marketable securities. The Company has unused operating lines of credit of $22,400 with Canadian chartered banks, secured by general security agreements over the Company and a first floating charge over the assets of certain subsidiaries. Outstanding borrowings of $1,350 ($Nil – 1996), are due upon demand and bear interest at prime.

3. Accounts Receivable

Accounts receivable includes $39,818 ($8,934 – 1996) of receivables which are non interest bearing and are due subsequent to December 31, 1998.

4. Completed Programs

	1997 value	%	1996 value	%
Original cost of completed programs	$ 596,786	100 %	$ 477,056	100 %
Less: accumulated amortization	(549,854)	(92)	(432,358)	(91)
Completed programs, net of accumulated amortization	$ 46,932	8 %	$ 44,698	9 %

As at December 31, 1997, the Company anticipates that approximately 99% of these original program costs will be amortized after three years and 100% after four years.

5. Broadcast Rights

	1997 value	%	1996 value	%
Original cost of broadcast rights	$ 28,789	100 %	$ 21,462	100 %
Less: accumulated amortization	(15,272)	(53)	(10,202)	(48)
Broadcast rights, net of accumulated amortization	$ 13,517	47 %	$ 11,260	52 %

6. Notes Receivable and Notes Payable

Notes receivable from limited partnerships become due on various dates up to January 15, 1999 and are exactly matched by dates and amounts of the Notes payable. These Notes receivable are secured by assignments of promissory notes from a financial corporation which are in turn secured by financial instruments and the promissory notes of the private investors in the limited partnerships.

7. Investments

	1997	1996
Calibre Digital Design Inc. – equity basis	$ 2,435	$ —
Other investments – at cost	1,078	1,500
	$ 3,513	$ 1,500

The Company's share of the difference between the replacement cost and the net book value of Calibre's assets at the date of purchase was $1,304. This difference is being amortized over a period of 60 months, beginning on June 1, 1997.

8. Fixed Assets

	1997		1996	
	Cost	Accumulated Depreciation	Cost	Accumulated Depreciation
Building (including land of $363)	$ 3,592	$ 1,266	$ 3,582	$ 1,171
Broadcast and production equipment	10,671	4,213	5,691	1,654
Furniture and other equipment	4,863	2,307	3,305	1,743
Leasehold improvements	2,193	1,062	1,738	835
Vehicles	82	16	29	5
	$ 21,401	$ 8,864	$ 14,345	$ 5,408
Net Book Value	$ 12,537		$ 8,937	

As at December 31, 1997, $3,219 ($3,620 – 1996) of the equipment described above, less accumulated depreciation of $1,275 ($1,202 – 1996), was subject to capital leases.

9. Acquisitions and Divestiture

Investment in Calibre Digital Design Inc.

On May 31, 1997, the Company acquired 50% of the voting shares (60% equity) of Calibre for $2,545, including $1,045 relating to restructuring and integration costs. This acquisition has been accounted for using the equity method.

Acquisition of 43% of Life Network

In 1996, the Company increased its ownership in Life Network from 57% to 100%. The Company acquired the remaining interest for aggregate consideration of $9,473 comprised of cash, rights and 474,981 treasury shares of the Company. Also included in this amount is approximately $2,000 relating to restructuring and integration costs. Part of the consideration, including the treasury shares, was paid subsequent to December 31, 1996 (see Note 12). The 43% interest in Life Network was acquired from related parties, including management and a significant shareholder of the Company.

The increase in ownership of Life Network was accounted for as a purchase. As a result of the acquisition, goodwill, included in other assets, increased by $6,466, and non-controlling interest decreased by $3,007.

Divestiture of 28% of YTV Canada, Inc.

In 1996, the Company sold its 28% interest in YTV Canada, Inc. for net proceeds of $25,145. The pre-tax gain on the sale of YTV amounted to $5,272, or $3,532 ($0.37 per share) on an after-tax basis.

10. Interim Financing on Programs

Interim financing on programs at December 31, 1997 bears interest at various rates up to U.S. prime rate plus 1.0% (U.S. prime rate plus 1.0% – 1996). Of the outstanding balance, $2,537 represents U.S. dollar borrowings. The loans are fully secured by direct assignments of accounts receivable.

The Company has available $45,000 under an interim production credit facility, secured by direct assignments of accounts receivable. Outstanding borrowings of $35,018 at December 31, 1997 ($Nil – 1996) bear interest at prime plus 5/8%.

11. Loans Payable

	1997	1996
Mortgages payable		
Bear interest from a fixed rate of 9.99% to 3.0% above average cost of funds to		
the mortgagee, secured by land and building, maturing at the latest October 2005	$ 3,421	$ 3,576
Bank term loans		
Bear interest at rates up to prime rate plus 1.5%, secured by various assets and		
distribution licencing agreements or territories, maturing at the latest November 2001	3,244	2,790
Other debt	1,581	2,580
Obligation under capital leases	1,601	2,006
	$ 9,847	$ 10,952

ATLANTIS

Principal payments are due as follows:

1998	$ 4,438
1999	1,548
2000	1,107
2001	244
2002	255
Thereafter	2,255
	$ 9,847

12. Capital Stock

	1997		1996	
	# of Shares	Value	# of Shares	Value
Authorized				
Multiple Voting Shares (MVS)	4,237,499		4,237,499	
Subordinate Voting Shares (SVS)	Unlimited		Unlimited	
Preference Shares	Unlimited		Unlimited	
Share Purchase Warrants (SPW)	2,292,400		—	
Issued and Outstanding				
Share Purchase Warrants	2,292,400	$ 20,631	—	$ —
Multiple Voting Shares (ten dollars book value)	4,237,499	—	4,237,499	—
Subordinate Voting Shares	5,881,745	56,074	5,371,550	52,961
Total Voting Shares	10,119,244	56,074	9,609,049	52,961
Total Capital Stock		$ 76,705		$ 52,961

The MVS carry 10 votes per share and SVS carry one vote per share. MVS are convertible into SVS on a one-for-one basis. The MVS and SVS rank equally with respect to dividends and capital distributions, however, there are restrictions on ownership and transfer of the MVS. The MVS and SVS are currently constrained to limit non-Canadian ownership to levels which will not adversely affect the Company in carrying on any regulated business. Currently the CRTC limits non-Canadian ownership to 33 1/3% of the Company's voting shares. The SVS are entitled to specific rights, including coattail provisions, in the event of a take-over bid.

On December 23, 1997, the Company issued 2,292,400 Special Warrants for cash consideration of $20,631 ($9 per share). The Company's share of issue costs including underwriters' fees and expenses totalled $1,895 ($1,050 net of related taxes). On February 9, 1998, all of the Special Warrants were converted into subordinate voting shares on a one-for-one basis. During 1997, the Company issued 13,414 SVS to the Directors as consideration for services in the amount of $99, and 15,600 SVS, with an ascribed value of $94, were issued in connection with 1996 bonuses payable. In addition, 6,200 options with a total value of $37 were exercised by option holders.

In 1997, the Company paid the consideration which was accrued at December 31, 1996 in conjunction with the acquisition of the remaining interest in Life Network (Note 9). In conjunction with this acquisition, the Company issued 474,981 SVS on January 20, 1997, with a total value of $2,850.

During 1996, the Company issued 7,405 SVS to the Directors as consideration for services in the amount of $50.

Options

As at December 31, 1997, there were 1,453,964 options (960,164 – 1996) authorized to purchase SVS, and 1,014,323 options (884,469 – 1996) to purchase SVS were outstanding at prices ranging from $5.95 to $14.50 per share with a weighted average price of $8.72 ($10.08 – 1996). These options vest over time and will expire, at the latest, by May 2002.

Subsequent to December 31, 1997, 76,500 options were issued at $10.25. These options vest over time and will expire, at the latest, by February 2003. Subsequent to December 31, 1997, 20,934 options were cancelled or expired, and 6,500 options were exercised.

13. Book Value Per Share

Book value per share represents the total of shareholders' equity divided by the number of shares and Special Warrants outstanding at year end.

14. Income Taxes

(a) The effective rates of income taxes provided in the statements of earnings vary from the rates specified in the tax statutes as follows:

	1997	1996
Combined basic federal and provincial income tax rate	44.6 %	44.6 %
Non-deductible expenses	5.8	—
Reduction due to income taxed in other jurisdictions	—	(4.6)
Gain on sale of investment taxed at capital gains rate	—	(5.7)
Use of loss carry-forwards	(15.8)	(3.5)
Increase in income tax accrual	8.4	—
Other	0.7	3.9
	43.7 %	34.7 %

During the year the Company accrued an additional amount for income tax contingencies.

(b) Loss carry-forwards of certain of the Company's subsidiaries, for which no benefit has been recognized, amount to $133 as at December 31, 1997 ($4,083 – 1996) and are available for utilization against future taxable income. As at December 31, 1997, the loss carry-forwards expire as follows:

2002	$ 35
2003	98
	$ 133

ATLANTIS

15. Earnings Per Share

	1997		1996	
	Basic	Fully Diluted	Basic	Fully Diluted
Operating earnings per share	$ 0.55	$ 0.52	$ 0.35	$ 0.34
Earnings per share from unusual items	—	—	0.37	0.33
Total earnings per share	$ 0.55	$ 0.52	$ 0.72	$ 0.67
Weighted average number of shares	10,067,074	11,195,706	9,603,294	10,844,792
Number of shares outstanding at December 31	10,119,244	13,425,967	9,609,049	10,493,518

Earnings per share from unusual items in 1996 represents the after-tax earnings per share from the gain on sale of YTV (see Note 9).

16. Government Financing, Tax Credits and Grants

Revenue includes $10,589 of government program financing for the year ended December 31, 1997 ($8,947 – 1996). A portion of this amount is repayable depending on the future revenue of the individual program, and therefore has been reflected in the determination of the net realizable value of the program as a future cost. Completed program costs for the year ended December 31, 1997 are net of $16,471 of federal and provincial tax credits and grants ($9,877 – 1996). Programs in process costs for the year ended December 31, 1997 are net of $2,591 of federal and provincial tax credits and grants ($2,493 – 1996).

17. Financial Instruments

Fair values

The estimated fair values of financial instruments as at December 31, 1997 and December 31, 1996 are based on the relevant market prices and information available at that time. The fair value estimates are not indicative of the amounts that the Company might receive or incur in actual market transactions.

	1997		1996	
	Book Value	Fair Value	Book Value	Fair Value
Financial assets				
Assets for which fair value approximates book value	$ 29,669	$ 29,669	$ 14,099	$ 14,099
Accounts receivable	145,611	142,843	78,448	78,061
Notes receivable	20,526	19,650	140,673	139,813
Financial liabilities				
Liabilities for which fair value approximates book value	$ 133,846	$ 133,846	$ 77,128	$ 77,128
Obligations under capital lease	1,601	1,549	—	—
Notes payable	20,526	19,650	140,673	139,813

Cash and marketable securities, accounts payable and accrued liabilities, broadcast rights payable, distribution revenue payable, loans payable and interim financing on programs are all short-term in nature and as such, their carrying value approximates fair value.

The fair value of accounts receivable on balances due subsequent to December 31, 1998, was estimated using discount rates based on an average of market interest rates.

The fair value of notes receivable and notes payable was estimated based on quoted market prices or discounted cash flows, using discount rates based on market interest rates. Amounts recorded as fair value relating to notes receivable and payable are based on amounts due and receivable subsequent to December 31, 1998. The terms of these instruments require the notes receivable to be matched with the notes payable.

Forward contracts

The Company has committed to the sale of 800 million Italian Lira on February 27, 1998, at an exchange rate of U.S. $0.00647.

The Company has committed to the sale of U.S. $31,786 under forward exchange contracts. The contracts are at rates of exchange ranging from Cdn. $1.3592 to $1.4205, and maturing at various dates to August 15, 2000.

The unrealized loss on forward exchange contracts at December 31, 1997 is $821. This loss has not been recorded as the contracts are considered to be hedges.

Concentration of credit risk

Accounts receivable from one customer, excluding receivables from government programs, represents 14% (24% – 1996) of total accounts receivable at December 31, 1997. The Company believes that there is no risk associated with the collection of this amount. The balance of accounts receivable are widely disbursed amongst customers.

18. Contingent Liabilities and Commitments

(a) In addition to the mortgage payable obligation (Note 11), the Company has jointly and severally guaranteed an additional $3,500 to a mortgagee of Cinevillage.

(b) The Company has entered into agreements with program investors on a number of projects under which the Company has guaranteed payments to such investors in aggregate of $297 as at December 31, 1997 ($2,357 – 1996). The Company anticipates that revenues from each of the programs in connection with which guarantees were given will meet or exceed obligations to respective program investors.

(c) The Company is committed to further payments totaling $1,500 related to marketing the launch of HGTV. These payments will be made during the current year.

(d) As at December 31, 1997 the Company is committed to future minimum operating lease payments as follows:

1998	$ 2,442
1999	2,215
2000	1,515
2001	492
2002	492
Thereafter	—
	$ 7,156

19. Segmented Information

(a) The Company's only significant activity is the production, distribution and broadcasting of television programs and ancillary rights.

(b) Revenue for the year ended December 31, 1997 includes $121,925 ($81,405 – 1996) derived from non-Canadian sources.

20. Supplementary Information

The Company has a 50% investment in Cinevillage. The Company's proportionate share in the assets, liabilities and net earnings from operations of Cinevillage is as follows:

	1997	1996
Assets, including fixed assets, at cost less accumulated depreciation of $1,398 ($1,275 – 1996)	$ 2,423	$ 2,548
Liabilities	3,532	3,708
Net income (loss)	$ 52	$ (258)

21. Comparative Figures

Certain comparative figures have been reclassified to conform with the current year's presentation.

Present and Future Values

II

Appendix Outline

▶ **Present and Future Value Concepts**

▶ **Present Value of a Single Amount**

▶ **Future Value of a Single Amount**

▶ **Present Value of an Annuity**

▶ **Future Value of an Annuity**

Learning Objectives

LO1 Describe the earning of interest and the concepts of present and future values.

LO2 Apply present value concepts to a single amount by using interest tables.

LO3 Apply future value concepts to a single amount by using interest tables.

LO4 Apply present value concepts to an annuity by using interest tables.

LO5 Apply future value concepts to an annuity by using interest tables.

A PPENDIX PREVIEW

The concepts of present value are described and applied in Chapter 17. This appendix helps to supplement that discussion with added explanations, illustrations, computations, present value tables, and additional assignments. We also give attention to illustrations, definitions, and computations of future values.

Present and Future Value Concepts

 Describe the earning of interest and the concepts of present and future values.

There's an old saying, *time is money*. This saying reflects the notion that as time passes, the assets and liabilities we hold are changing. This change is due to interest. *Interest* is the payment to the owner of an asset for its use by a borrower. The most common example of this type of asset is a savings account. As we keep a balance of cash in our accounts, it earns interest that is paid to us by the financial institution. An example of a liability is a car loan. As we carry the balance of the loan, we accumulate interest costs on this debt. We must ultimately repay this loan with interest.

Present and future value computations are a way for us to estimate the interest component of holding assets or liabilities over time. The present value of an amount applies when we either lend or borrow an asset that must be repaid in full at some future date, and we want to know its worth today. The future value of an amount applies when we either lend or borrow an asset that must be repaid in full at some future date, and we want to know its worth at a future date.

The first section focuses on the present value of a single amount. Later sections focus on the future value of a single amount, and then both present and future values of a series of amounts (or annuity).

Present Value of a Single Amount

Exhibit II.1

Present Value of a Single Amount

 Apply present value concepts to a single amount by using interest tables.

Exhibit II.2

Present Value of a Single Amount Formula

We graphically express the present value (*p*) of a single future amount (*f*) received or paid at a future date in Exhibit II.1.

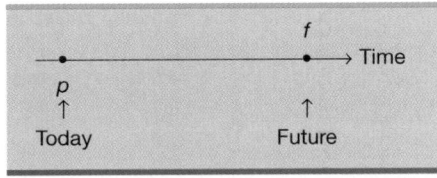

The formula to compute the present value of this single amount is shown in Exhibit II.2 where: *p* = present value; *f* = future value; *i* = rate of interest per period; and *n* = number of periods.

$$p = \frac{f}{(1 + i)^n}$$

To illustrate the application of this formula, let's assume we need $220 one period from today. We want to know how much must be invested now, for one period, at an interest rate of 10% to provide for this $220.[1] For this illustration the *p*, or present value, is the unknown amount. In particular, the present and future values, along with the interest rate, are shown graphically as:

$$f = \$220$$
$$(i = 0.10)$$
$$p = ?$$

Conceptually, we know *p* must be less than $220. This is obvious from the answer to the question: Would we rather have $220 today or $220 at some future date? If we had $220 today, we could invest it and see it grow to something more than $220 in the future. Therefore, if we were promised $220 in the future, we would take less than $220 today. But how much less?

---

[1] Interest is also called a *discount*, and an interest rate is also called a *discount rate*.

To answer that question we can compute an estimate of the present value of the $220 to be received one period from now using the formula in Exhibit II.2 as:

$$p = \frac{f}{(1 + i)^n} = \frac{\$242}{(1 + .10)^1} = \$200$$

This means we are indifferent between $200 today or $220 at the end of one period.

We can also use this formula to compute the present value for *any number of periods*. To illustrate this computation, we consider a payment of $242 at the end of two periods at 10% interest. The present value of this $242 to be received two periods from now is computed as:

$$p = \frac{f}{(1 + i)^n} = \frac{\$242}{(1 + .10)^2} = \$200$$

These results tells us we are indifferent between $200 today, or $220 one period from today, or $242 two periods from today.

The number of periods (n) in the present value formula does not have to be expressed in years. Any period of time such as a day, a month, a quarter, or a year can be used. But, whatever period is used, the interest rate (i) must be compounded for the same period. This means if a situation expresses n in months, and i equals 12% per year, then we can assume 1% of an amount invested at the beginning of each month is earned in interest per month and added to the investment. In this case, interest is said to be compounded monthly.

A present value table helps us with present value computations. It gives us present values for a variety of interest rates (i) and a variety of periods (n). Each present value in a present value table assumes the future value (f) is 1. When the future value (f) is different than 1, we can simply multiply present value (p) by that future amount to give us our estimate.

The formula used to construct a table of present values of a single future amount of 1 is shown in Exhibit II.3.

$$p = \frac{1}{(1 + i)^n}$$

Exhibit II.3

Present Value of 1 Formula

This formula is identical to that in Exhibit II.2 except that f equals 1. Table II.1 at the end of this appendix is a present value table for a single future amount. It is often called a **present value of 1 table.** A present value table involves three factors: p, i, and n.[2] Knowing two of these three factors allows us to compute the third. To illustrate, consider the three possible cases.

Case 1 (solve for p when knowing i and n). Our example above is a case in which we need to solve for p when knowing i and n. To illustrate how we use a present value table, let's again look at how we estimate the present value of $220 ($f$) at the end of one period (n) where the interest rate (i) is 10%. To answer this we go to the present value table (Table II.1) and look in the row for 1 period and in the column for 10% interest. Here we find a present value (p) of 0.9091 based on a future value of 1. This means, for instance, that $1 to be received 1 period from today at 10% interest is worth $0.9091 today. Since the future value is not $1, but is $220, we multiply the 0.9091 by $220 to get an answer of $200.

---

[2] A fourth is f, but as we already explained, we need only multiple the "1" used in the formula by f.

Case 2 (solve for *n* when knowing *p* and *i*). This is a case in which we have, say, a $100,000 future value (*f*) valued at $13,000 today (*p*) with an interest rate of 12% (*i*). In this case we want to know how many periods (*n*) there are between the present value and the future value. A case example is when we want to retire with $100,000, but have only $13,000 earning a 12% return. How long will it be before we can retire? To answer this we go to Table II.1 and look in the 12% interest column. Here we find a column of present values (*p*) based on a future value of 1. To use the present value table for this solution, we must divide $13,000 (*p*) by $100,000 (*f*), which equals 0.1300. This is necessary because a present value table defines *f* equal to 1, and *p* as a fraction of 1. We look for a value nearest to 0.1300 (*p*), which we find in the row for 18 periods (*n*). This means the present value of $100,000 at the end of 18 periods at 12% interest is $13,000 or, alternatively stated, we must work 18 more years.

Case 3 (solve for *i* when knowing *p* and *n*). This is a case where we have, say, a $120,000 future value (*f*) valued at $60,000 (*p*) today when there are nine periods (*n*) between the present and future values. Here we want to know what rate of interest is being used. As an example, suppose we want to retire with $120,000, but we only have $60,000 and hope to retire in nine years. What interest rate must we earn to retire with $120,000 in nine years? To answer this we go to the present value table (Table II.1) and look in the row for nine periods. To again use the present value table we must divide $60,000 (*p*) by $120,000 (*f*), which equals 0.5000. Recall this is necessary because a present value table defines *f* equal to 1, and *p* as a fraction of 1. We look for a value in the row for nine periods that is nearest to 0.5000 (*p*), which we find in the column for 8% interest (*i*). This means the present value of $120,000 at the end of nine periods at 8% interest is $60,000 or, in our example, we must earn 8% annual interest to retire in nine years.

Flash back

1. A company is considering an investment expected to yield $70,000 after six years. If this company demands an 8% return, how much is it willing to pay for this investment?

Answer—p. II-9

Future Value of a Single Amount

Exhibit II.4

Future Value of a Single Amount Formula

L03 Apply future value concepts to a single amount by using interest tables.

We use the formula for the present value of a single amount and modify it to obtain the formula for the future value of a single amount. To illustrate, we multiply both sides of the equation in Exhibit II.2 by $(1 + i)^n$. The result is shown in Exhibit II.4.

$$f = p \times (1 + i)^n$$

Future value (*f*) is defined in terms of *p*, *i*, and *n*. We can use this formula to determine that $200 invested for 1 period at an interest rate of 10% increases to a future value of $220 as follows:

$$f = p \times (1 + i)^n$$
$$= \$200 \times (1 + .10)^1$$
$$= \$220$$

This formula can also be used to compute the future value of an amount for *any number of periods* into the future. As an example, assume $200 is invested for three periods at 10%. The future value of this $200 is $266.20 and is computed as:

$$f = p \times (1 + i)^n$$
$$= \$200 \times (1 + .10)^3$$
$$= \$266.20$$

It is also possible to use a future value table to compute future values (*f*) for many combinations of interest rates (*i*) and time periods (*n*). Each future value in a future value table assumes the present value (*p*) is 1. As with a present value table, if the future amount is something other than 1, we simply multiply our answer by that amount. The formula used to construct a table of future values of a single amount of 1 is shown in Exhibit II.5.

$$f = (1 + i)^n$$

Exhibit II.5

Future Value of 1 Formula

Table II.2 at the end of this appendix shows a table of future values of a single amount of 1. This type of table is called a **future value of 1 table.**

It is interesting to point out some items in Tables II.1 and II.2. Note in Table II.2 for the row where $n = 0$, that the future value is 1 for every interest rate. This is because no interest is earned when time does not pass. Also notice that Tables II.1 and II.2 report the same information in a different manner. In particular, one table is simply the inverse of the other.

To illustrate this inverse relation let's say we invest $100 annually for a period of five years at 12% per year. How much do we expect to have after five years? We can answer this question using Table II.2 by finding the future value (*f*) of 1, for five periods from now, compounded at 12%. From the table we find $f = 1.7623$. If we start with $100, the amount it accumulates to after five years is $176.23 ($100 \times 1.7623$).

We can alternatively use Table II.1. Here we find the present value (*p*) of 1, discounted five periods at 12%, is 0.5674. Recall the inverse relation between present value and future value. This means $p = 1/f$ (or equivalently $f = 1/p$).[3] Knowing this we can compute the future value of $100 invested for five periods at 12% as:

$$f = \$100 \times (1 / 0.5674) = \$176.24$$

A future value table involves three factors: *f, i,* and *n*. Knowing two of these three factors allows us to compute the third. To illustrate, consider the three possible cases.

Case 1 (solve for *f* when knowing *i* and *n*). Our example above is a case in which we need to solve for *f* when knowing *i* and *n*. We found that $100 invested for five periods at 12% interest accumulates to $176.24.

Case 2 (solve for *n* when knowing *f* and *i*). This is a case where we have, say, $2,000 (*p*) and we want to know how many periods (*n*) it will take to accumulate to $3,000 (*f*) at 7% (*i*) interest. To answer this, we go to the future value table (Table II.2) and look in the 7% interest column. Here we find a column of future values (*f*) based on a present value of 1. To use a future value table, we must divide $3,000 (*f*) by $2,000 (*p*), which equals 1.500. This is necessary because a future value table defines *p* equal to 1, and *f* as a multiple of 1. We

---

[3] Proof of this relation is left for advanced courses.

look for a value nearest to 1.50 (f), which we find in the row for six periods (n). This means $2,000 invested for six periods at 7% interest accumulates to $3,000.

   Case 3 (solve for i when knowing f and n). This is a case where we have, say, $2,001 (p) and in nine years (n) we want to have $4,000 (f). What rate of interest must we earn to accomplish this? To answer this, we go to Table II.2 and search in the row for nine periods. To use a future value table, we must divide $4,000 (f) by $2,001 (p), which equals 1.9990. Recall this is necessary because a future value table defines p equal to 1, and f as a multiple of 1. We look for a value nearest to 1.9990 (f), which we find in the column for 8% interest (i). This means $2,001 invested for nine periods at 8% interest accumulates to $4,000.

Flash back

2. Assume you are a winner in a $150,000 cash sweepstakes. You decide to deposit this cash in an account earning 8% annual interest and you plan to quit your job when the account equals $555,000. How many years will it be before you can quit working?

Answers—p. II-9

Present Value of an Annuity

An annuity is a series of equal payments occurring at equal intervals. One example is a series of three annual payments of $100 each. The present value of an ordinary annuity is defined as the present value of equal payments at equal intervals as of one period before the first payment. An ordinary annuity of $100 and its present value (p) is illustrated in Exhibit II.6.

Exhibit II.6

Present Value of an Ordinary Annuity

LO4 Apply present value concepts to an annuity by using interest tables.

One way for us to compute the present value of an ordinary annuity is to find the present value of each payment using our present value formula from Exhibit II.3. We then would add up each of the three present values. To illustrate, let's look at three, $100 payments at the end of each of the next three periods with an interest rate of 15%. Our present value computations are:

$$p = \frac{\$100}{(1 + .15)^1} + \frac{\$100}{(1 + .15)^2} + \frac{\$100}{(1 + .15)^3} = \$228.32$$

This computation also is identical to computing the present value of each payment (from Table II.1) and taking their sum or, alternatively, adding the values from Table II.1 for each of the three payments and multiplying their sum by the $100 annuity payment.

   A more direct way is to use a present value of annuity table. Table II.3 at the end of this appendix is one such table. This table is called a **present value of an annuity of 1 table.** If we look at Table II.3 where n = 3 and i = 15%, we see the present value is 2.2832. This means the present value of an annuity of 1 for 3 periods, with a 15% interest rate, is 2.2832.

A present value of annuity formula is used to construct Table II.3. It can also be constructed by adding the amounts in a present value of 1 table.[4] To illustrate, we use Tables II.1 and II.3 to confirm this relation for the prior example: We can also use business calculators or spreadsheet computer programs to find the present value of an annuity.

From Table II.1		From Table II.3	
$i = 15\%$, $n = 1$	0.8696		
$i = 15\%$, $n = 2$	0.7561		
$i = 15\%$, $n = 3$	0.6575		
Total	2.2832	$i = 15\%$, $n = 3$	2.2832

Flash back

3. A company is considering an investment paying $10,000 every six months for three years. The first payment would be received in six months. If this company requires an annual return of 8%, what is the maximum amount they are willing to invest?

Answer—p. II-9

We can also compute the future value of an annuity. The future value of an *ordinary annuity* is the accumulated value of each annuity payment with interest as of the date of the final payment. To illustrate, let's consider the earlier annuity of three annual payments of $100. Exhibit II.7 shows the point in time for the future value (*f*). The first payment is made two periods prior to the point where future value is determined, and the final payment occurs on the future value date.

Future Value of an Annuity

Exhibit II.7

Future Value of an Ordinary Annuity

One way to compute the future value of an annuity is to use the formula to find the future value of *each* payment and add them together. If we assume an interest rate of 15%, our calculation is:

$$f = \$100 \times (1 + .15)^2 + \$100 \times (1 + .15)^1 + \$100 \times (1 + .15)^0 = \$347.25$$

L05 Apply future value concepts to an annuity by using interest tables.

---

[4] The formula for the present value of an annuity of 1 is:

$$p = \frac{1 - \dfrac{1}{(1 + i)^n}}{i}$$

This is identical to using Table II.2 and finding the sum of the future values of each payment, or adding the future values of the three payments of 1 and multiplying the sum by $100.

A more direct way is to use a table showing future values of annuities. Such a table is called a future value of an annuity of 1 table. Table II.4 at the end of this appendix is one such table. We should note in Table II.4 that when $n = 1$, the future values are equal to 1 ($f = 1$) for all rates of interest. That is because the annuity consists of only one payment and the future value is determined on the date of that payment — no time passes between the payment and its future value.

A formula is used to construct Table II.4.[5] We can also construct it by adding the amounts from a future value of 1 table. To illustrate, we use Tables II.2 and II.4 to confirm this relation for the prior example:

From Table II.2		From Table II.4	
$i = 15\%, n = 0$	1.0000		
$i = 15\%, n = 1$	1.1500		
$i = 15\%, n = 2$	1.3225		
Total	3.4725	$i = 15\%, n = 3$	3.4725

Note the future value in Table II.2 is 1.0000 when $n = 0$, but the future value in Table II.4 is 1.0000 when $n = 1$. Is this a contradiction? No. When $n = 0$ in Table II.2, the future value is determined on the date where a single payment occurs. This means no interest is earned, since no time has passed, and the future value equals the payment. Table II.4 describes annuities with equal payments occurring at the end of each period. When $n = 1$, the annuity has one payment, and its future value equals 1 on the date of its final and only payment. Again, no time passes from the payment and its future value date.

Flashback

4. A company invests $45,000 per year for five years at 12% annual interest. Compute the value of this annuity investment at the end of five years.

Answers—p. II-9

---

[5] The formula for the future value of an annuity of 1 is: $f = \dfrac{(1 + i)^n - 1}{i}$

Summary

L01 **Describe the earning of interest and the concepts of present and future values.** Interest is payment to the owner of an asset for its use by a borrower. Present and future value computations are a way for us to estimate the interest component of holding assets or liabilities over a period of time.

L02 **Apply present value concepts to a single amount by using interest tables.** The present value of a single amount to be received at a future date is the amount that can be invested now at the specified interest rate to yield that future value.

L03 **Apply future value concepts to a single amount by using interest tables.** The future value of a single

amount invested at a specified rate of interest is the amount that would accumulate at a future date.

L04 **Apply present value concepts to an annuity by using interest tables.** The present value of an annuity is the amount that can be invested now at the specified interest rate to yield that series of equal periodic payments.

L05 **Apply future value concepts to an annuity by using interest tables.** The future value of an annuity to be invested at a specific rate of interest is the amount that would accumulate at the date of the final equal periodic payment.

Guidance Answers to

1. $70,000 × 0.6302 = $44,114 (using Table II.1, $i = 8\%$, $n = 6$).

2. $555,000/$150,000 = 3.7000; Table II.2 shows this value is not achieved until after 17 years at 8% interest.

3. $10,000 × 5.2421 = $52,421 (using Table II.3, $i = 4\%$, $n = 6$).

4. $45,000 × 6.3528 = $285,876 (using Table II.4, $i = 12\%$, $n = 5$).

You are asked to make future value estimates using the future value of 1 table (Table II.2). Which interest rate column do you use when working with the following rates?

a. 8% compounded quarterly

b. 12% compounded annually

c. 6% compounded semiannually

d. 12% compounded monthly

Quick Study

QS II-1
Identifying interest rates in tables

L01

Flaherty is considering an investment which, if paid for immediately, is expected to return $140,000 five years hence. If Flaherty demands a 9% return, how much is she willing to pay for this investment?

QS II-2
Present value of an amount

L02

CII, Inc., invested $630,000 in a project expected to earn a 12% annual rate of return. The earnings will be reinvested in the project each year until the entire investment is liquidated 10 years hence. What will the cash proceeds be when the project is liquidated?

QS II-3
Future value of an amount

L03

Beene Distributing is considering a contract that will return $150,000 annually at the end of each year for six years. If Beene demands an annual return of 7% and pays for the investment immediately, how much should it be willing to pay?

QS II-4
Present value of an annuity

L04

QS II-5
Future value of an annuity

Claire Fitch is planning to begin an individual retirement program in which she will invest $1,500 annually at the end of each year. Fitch plans to retire after making 30 annual investments in a program that earns a return of 10%. What will be the value of the program on the date of the last investment?

QS II-6
Interest rate on an investment

Ken Francis has been offered the possibility of investing $2,745 for 15 years, after which he will be paid $10,000. What annual rate of interest will Francis earn? (Use Table II.1.)

QS II-7
Number of periods of an investment

L02

Megan Brink has been offered the possibility of investing $6,651. The investment will earn 6% per year and will return Brink $10,000 at the end of the investment. How many years must Brink wait to receive the $10,000? (Use Table II.1.)

Exercises

Exercise II-1
Using present and future value tables

L01

For each of the following situations identify (1) it as either (a) present or future value and (b) single amount or annuity case, (2) the table you would use in your computations (but do not solve the problem), and (3) the interest rate and time periods you would use.

a. You need to accumulate $10,000 for a trip you wish to take in four years. You are able to earn 8% compounded semiannually on your savings. You only plan on making one deposit and letting the money accumulate for four years. How would you determine the amount of the one-time deposit?

b. Assume the same facts as in (a), except you will make semiannual deposits to your savings account.

c. You hope to retire after working 40 years with savings in excess of $1,000,000. You expect to save $4,000 a year for 40 years and earn an annual rate of interest of 8%. Will you be able to retire with more than $1,000,000 in 40 years?

d. A sweepstakes agency names you a grand prize winner. You can take $225,000 immediately or elect to receive annual installments of $30,000 for 20 years. You can earn 10% annually on investments you make. Which prize do you choose to receive?

Exercise II-2
Number of periods of an investment

L02

Bill Thompson expects to invest $10,000 at 12% and, at the end of the investment, receive $96,463. How many years will elapse before Thompson receives the payment? (Use Table II.2.)

Exercise II-3
Interest rate on an investment

L02

Ed Summers expects to invest $10,000 for 25 years, after which he will receive $108,347. What rate of interest will Summers earn? (Use Table II.2.)

Exercise II-4
Interest rate on an investment

L04

Betsey Jones expects an immediate investment of $57,466 to return $10,000 annually for eight years, with the first payment to be received in one year. What rate of interest will Jones earn? (Use Table II.3.)

Keith Riggins expects an investment of $82,014 to return $10,000 annually for several years. If Riggins is to earn a return of 10%, how many annual payments must he receive? (Use Table II.3.)

Exercise II-5
Number of periods of an investment

L04

Steve Algoe expects to invest $1,000 annually for 40 years and have an accumulated value of $154,762 on the date of the last investment. If this occurs, what rate of interest will Algoe earn? (Use Table II.4.)

Exercise II-6
Interest rate on an investment

L05

Katherine Beckwith expects to invest $10,000 annually that will earn 8%. How many annual investments must Beckwith make to accumulate $303,243 on the date of the last investment? (Use Table II.4.)

Exercise II-7
Number of periods of an investment

L05

Sam Weber financed a new automobile by paying $6,500 cash and agreeing to make 40 monthly payments of $500 each, the first payment to be made one month after the purchase. The loan bears interest at an annual rate of 12%. What was the cost of the automobile?

Exercise II-8
Present value of an annuity

L04

Mark Welsch deposited $7,200 in a savings account that earns interest at an annual rate of 8%, compounded quarterly. The $7,200 plus earned interest must remain in the account 10 years before it can be withdrawn. How much money will be in the account at the end of the 10 years?

Exercise II-9
Future value of an amount

L03

Kelly Malone plans to have $50 withheld from her monthly paycheque and deposited in a savings account that earns 12% annually, compounded monthly. If Malone continues with her plan for 2 1/2 years, how much will be accumulated in the account on the date of the last deposit?

Exercise II-10
Future value of an annuity

L04

Spiller Corp. plans to issue 10%, 15-year, $500,000 par value bonds payable that pay interest semiannually on June 30 and December 31. The bonds are dated December 31, 1999, and are to be issued on that date. If the market rate of interest for the bonds is 8% on the date of issue, what will be the cash proceeds from the bond issue?

Exercise II-11
Present value of bonds

L02, 3

Starr Company has decided to establish a fund that will be used 10 years hence to replace an aging productive facility. The company will make an initial contribution of $100,000 to the fund and plans to make quarterly contributions of $50,000 beginning in three months. The fund is expected to earn 12%, compounded quarterly. What will be the value of the fund 10 years hence?

Exercise II-12
Future value of an amount plus an annuity

L03,5

McAdams Company expects to earn 10% per year on an investment that will pay $606,773 six years hence. Use Table II.1 to compute the present value of the investment.

Exercise II-13
Present value of an amount

L03

Exercise II-14
Future value of an amount
L03

Catten, Inc., invests $163,170 at 7% per year for nine years. Use Table II.2 to compute the future value of the investment nine years hence.

Exercise II-15
Present value of an amount and annuity
L02, 4

Compute the amount that can be borrowed under each of the following circumstances:

a. A promise to pay $90,000 in seven years at an interest rate of 6%.

b. An agreement made on February 1, 2000, to make three payments of $20,000 on February 1 of 2001, 2002, and 2003. The annual interest rate is 10%.

Exercise II-16
Present value of an amount
L02

On January 1, 2000, a company agrees to pay $20,000 in three years. If the annual interest rate is 10%, determine how much cash the company can borrow with this promise.

Exercise II-17
Present value of an amount
L02

Find the amount of money that can be borrowed with each of the following promises:

Case	Single Future Payment	Number of Years	Interest Rate
a.	$ 40,000	3	4%
b.	75,000	7	8%
c.	52,000	9	10%
d.	18,000	2	4%
e.	63,000	8	6%
f.	89,000	5	2%

Exercise II-18
Present values of annuities
L04

C&H Ski Club recently borrowed money and agreed to pay it back with a series of six annual payments of $5,000 each. C&H subsequently borrowed more money and agreed to pay it back with a series of four annual payments of $7,500 each. The annual interest rate for both loans is 6%.

a. Use Table II.1 to find the present value of these two annuities. (Round amounts to the nearest dollar.)

b. Use Table II.3 to find the present value of these two annuities.

Exercise II-19
Present value with semiannual compounding
L01, 4

Otto Co. borrowed cash on April 30, 2000, by promising to make four payments of $13,000 each on November 1, 2000, May 1, 2001, November 1, 2001, and May 1, 2002.

a. How much cash is Otto able to borrow if the interest rate is 8%, compounded semiannually?

b. How much cash is Otto able to borrow if the interest rate is 12%, compounded semiannually?

c. How much cash is Otto able to borrow if the interest rate is 16%, compounded semiannually?

Table II.1
Present Value of 1 Due in n Periods

Periods	Rate											
	1%	2%	3%	4%	5%	6%	7%	8%	9%	10%	12%	15%
1	0.9901	0.9804	0.9709	0.9615	0.9524	0.9434	0.9346	0.9259	0.9174	0.9091	0.8929	0.8696
2	0.9803	0.9612	0.9426	0.9246	0.9070	0.8900	0.8734	0.8573	0.8417	0.8264	0.7972	0.7561
3	0.9706	0.9423	0.9151	0.8890	0.8638	0.8396	0.8163	0.7938	0.7722	0.7513	0.7118	0.6575
4	0.9610	0.9238	0.8885	0.8548	0.8227	0.7921	0.7629	0.7350	0.7084	0.6830	0.6355	0.5718
5	0.9515	0.9057	0.8626	0.8219	0.7835	0.7473	0.7130	0.6806	0.6499	0.6209	0.5674	0.4972
6	0.9420	0.8880	0.8375	0.7903	0.7462	0.7050	0.6663	0.6302	0.5963	0.5645	0.5066	0.4323
7	0.9327	0.8706	0.8131	0.7599	0.7107	0.6651	0.6227	0.5835	0.5470	0.5132	0.4523	0.3759
8	0.9235	0.8535	0.7894	0.7307	0.6768	0.6274	0.5820	0.5403	0.5019	0.4665	0.4039	0.3269
9	0.9143	0.8368	0.7664	0.7026	0.6446	0.5919	0.5439	0.5002	0.4604	0.4241	0.3606	0.2843
10	0.9053	0.8203	0.7441	0.6756	0.6139	0.5584	0.5083	0.4632	0.4224	0.3855	0.3220	0.2472
11	0.8963	0.8043	0.7224	0.6496	0.5847	0.5268	0.4751	0.4289	0.3875	0.3505	0.2875	0.2149
12	0.8874	0.7885	0.7014	0.6246	0.5568	0.4970	0.4440	0.3971	0.3555	0.3186	0.2567	0.1869
13	0.8787	0.7730	0.6810	0.6006	0.5303	0.4688	0.4150	0.3677	0.3262	0.2897	0.2292	0.1625
14	0.8700	0.7579	0.6611	0.5775	0.5051	0.4423	0.3878	0.3405	0.2992	0.2633	0.2046	0.1413
15	0.8613	0.7430	0.6419	0.5553	0.4810	0.4173	0.3624	0.3152	0.2745	0.2394	0.1827	0.1229
16	0.8528	0.7284	0.6232	0.5339	0.4581	0.3936	0.3387	0.2919	0.2519	0.2176	0.1631	0.1069
17	0.8444	0.7142	0.6050	0.5134	0.4363	0.3714	0.3166	0.2703	0.2311	0.1978	0.1456	0.0929
18	0.8360	0.7002	0.5874	0.4936	0.4155	0.3503	0.2959	0.2502	0.2120	0.1799	0.1300	0.0808
19	0.8277	0.6864	0.5703	0.4746	0.3957	0.3305	0.2765	0.2317	0.1945	0.1635	0.1161	0.0703
20	0.8195	0.6730	0.5537	0.4564	0.3769	0.3118	0.2584	0.2145	0.1784	0.1486	0.1037	0.0611
25	0.7798	0.6095	0.4776	0.3751	0.2953	0.2330	0.1842	0.1460	0.1160	0.0923	0.0588	0.0304
30	0.7419	0.5521	0.4120	0.3083	0.2314	0.1741	0.1314	0.0994	0.0754	0.0573	0.0334	0.0151
35	0.7059	0.5000	0.3554	0.2534	0.1813	0.1301	0.0937	0.0676	0.0490	0.0356	0.0189	0.0075
40	0.6717	0.4529	0.3066	0.2083	0.1420	0.0972	0.0668	0.0460	0.0318	0.0221	0.0107	0.0037

Table II.2
Future Value of 1 Due in n Periods

Periods	Rate											
	1%	2%	3%	4%	5%	6%	7%	8%	9%	10%	12%	15%
0	1.0000	1.0000	1.0000	1.0000	1.0000	1.0000	1.0000	1.0000	1.0000	1.0000	1.0000	1.0000
1	1.0100	1.0200	1.0300	1.0400	1.0500	1.0600	1.0700	1.0800	1.0900	1.1000	1.1200	1.1500
2	1.0201	1.0404	1.0609	1.0816	1.1025	1.1236	1.1449	1.1664	1.1811	1.2100	1.2544	1.3225
3	1.0303	1.0612	1.0927	1.1249	1.1576	1.1910	1.2250	1.2597	1.2950	1.3310	1.4049	1.5209
4	1.0406	1.0824	1.1255	1.1699	1.2155	1.2625	1.3108	1.3605	1.4116	1.4641	1.5735	1.7490
5	1.0510	1.1041	1.1593	1.2167	1.2763	1.3382	1.4026	1.4693	1.5386	1.6105	1.7623	2.0114
6	1.0615	1.1262	1.1941	1.2653	1.3401	1.4185	1.5007	1.5869	1.6771	1.7116	1.9738	2.3131
7	1.0721	1.1487	1.2299	1.3159	1.4071	1.5036	1.6058	1.7138	1.8280	1.9487	2.2107	2.6600
8	1.0829	1.1717	1.2668	1.3686	1.4775	1.5938	1.7182	1.8509	1.9926	2.1436	2.4760	3.0590
9	1.0937	1.1951	1.3048	1.4233	1.5513	1.6895	1.8385	1.9990	2.1719	2.3579	2.7731	3.5179
10	1.1046	1.2190	1.3439	1.4802	1.6289	1.7908	1.9672	2.1589	2.3674	2.5937	3.1058	4.0456
11	1.1157	1.2434	1.3842	1.5395	1.7103	1.8983	2.1049	2.3316	2.5804	2.8531	3.4785	4.6524
12	1.1268	1.2682	1.4258	1.6010	1.7959	2.0122	2.2522	2.5182	2.8127	3.1384	3.8960	5.3503
13	1.1381	1.2936	1.4685	1.6651	1.8856	2.1329	2.4098	2.7196	3.0658	3.4523	4.3635	6.1528
14	1.1495	1.3195	1.5126	1.7317	1.9799	2.2609	2.5785	2.9372	3.3417	3.7975	4.8871	7.0757
15	1.1610	1.3459	1.5580	1.8009	2.0789	2.3966	2.7590	3.1722	3.6425	4.1772	5.4736	8.1371
16	1.1726	1.3728	1.6047	1.8730	2.1829	2.5404	2.9522	3.4259	3.9703	4.5950	6.1304	9.3576
17	1.1843	1.4002	1.6528	1.9479	2.2920	2.6928	3.1588	3.7000	4.3276	5.0545	6.8660	10.7613
18	1.1961	1.4282	1.7024	2.0258	2.4066	2.8543	3.3799	3.9960	4.7171	5.5599	7.6900	12.3755
19	1.2081	1.4568	1.7535	2.1068	2.5270	3.0256	3.6165	4.3157	5.1417	6.1159	8.6128	14.2318
20	1.2202	1.4859	1.8061	2.1911	2.6533	3.2071	3.8697	4.6610	5.6044	6.7275	9.6463	16.3665
25	1.2824	1.6406	2.0938	2.6658	3.3864	4.2919	5.4274	6.8485	8.6231	10.8347	17.0001	32.9190
30	1.3478	1.8114	2.4273	3.2434	4.3219	5.7435	7.6123	10.0627	13.2677	17.4494	29.9599	66.2118
35	1.4166	1.9999	2.8139	3.9461	5.5160	7.6861	10.6766	14.7853	20.4140	28.1024	52.7996	133.176
40	1.4889	2.2080	3.2620	4.8010	7.0400	10.2857	14.9745	21.7245	31.4094	45.2593	93.0510	267.864

Table II.3

Present Value of an Annuity of 1 per Period

Periods	Rate											
	1%	2%	3%	4%	5%	6%	7%	8%	9%	10%	12%	15%
1	0.9901	0.9804	0.9709	0.9615	0.9524	0.9434	0.9346	0.9259	0.9174	0.9091	0.8929	0.8696
2	1.9704	1.9416	1.9135	1.8861	1.8594	1.8334	1.8080	1.7833	1.7591	1.7355	1.6901	1.6257
3	2.9410	2.8839	2.8286	2.7751	2.7232	2.6730	2.6243	2.5771	2.5313	2.4869	2.4018	2.2832
4	3.9020	3.8077	3.7171	3.6299	3.5460	3.4651	3.3872	3.3121	3.2397	3.1699	3.0373	2.8550
5	4.8534	4.7135	4.5797	4.4518	4.3295	4.2124	4.1002	3.9927	3.8897	3.7908	3.6048	3.3522
6	5.7955	5.6014	5.4172	5.2421	5.0757	4.9173	4.7665	4.6229	4.4859	4.3553	4.1114	3.7845
7	6.7282	6.4720	6.2303	6.0021	5.7864	5.5824	5.3893	5.2064	5.0330	4.8684	4.5638	4.1604
8	7.6517	7.3255	7.0197	6.7327	6.4632	6.2098	5.9713	5.7466	5.5348	5.3349	4.9676	4.4873
9	8.5660	8.1622	7.7861	7.4353	7.1078	6.8017	6.5152	6.2469	5.9952	5.7950	5.3282	4.7716
10	9.4713	8.9826	8.5302	8.1109	7.7217	7.3601	7.0236	6.7101	6.4177	6.1446	5.6502	5.0188
11	10.3676	9.7868	9.2526	8.7605	8.3064	7.8869	7.4987	7.1390	6.8052	6.4951	5.9377	5.2337
12	11.2551	10.5753	9.9540	9.3851	8.8633	8.3838	7.9427	7.5361	7.1607	6.8137	6.1944	5.4206
13	12.1337	11.3484	10.6350	9.9856	9.3936	8.8527	8.3577	7.9038	7.4869	7.1034	6.4235	5.5831
14	13.0037	12.1062	11.2961	10.5631	9.8986	9.2950	8.7455	8.2442	7.7862	7.3667	6.6282	5.7245
15	13.8651	12.8493	11.9379	11.1184	10.3797	9.7122	9.1079	8.5595	8.0607	7.6061	6.8109	5.8474
16	14.7179	13.5777	12.5611	11.6523	10.8378	10.1059	9.4466	8.8514	8.3126	7.8237	6.9740	5.9542
17	15.5623	14.2919	13.1661	12.1657	11.2741	10.4773	9.7632	9.1216	8.5436	8.0216	7.1196	6.0472
18	16.3983	14.9920	13.7535	12.6593	11.6896	10.8276	10.0591	9.3719	8.7556	8.2014	7.2497	6.1280
19	17.2260	15.6785	14.3238	13.1339	12.0853	11.1581	10.3356	9.6036	8.9501	8.3649	7.3658	6.1982
20	18.0456	16.3514	14.8775	13.5903	12.4622	11.4699	10.5940	9.8181	9.1285	8.5136	7.4694	6.2593
25	22.0232	19.5235	17.4131	15.6221	14.0939	12.7834	11.6536	10.6748	9.8226	9.0770	7.8431	6.4641
30	25.8077	22.3965	19.6004	17.2920	15.3725	13.7648	12.4090	11.2578	10.2737	9.4269	8.0552	6.5660
35	29.4086	24.9986	21.4872	18.6646	16.3742	14.4982	12.9477	11.6546	10.5668	9.6442	8.1755	6.6166
40	32.8347	27.3555	23.1148	19.7928	17.1591	15.0463	13.3317	11.9246	10.7574	9.7791	8.2438	6.6418

 Table II.4

Future Value of an Annuity of 1 per Period

Periods	Rate											
	1%	2%	3%	4%	5%	6%	7%	8%	9%	10%	12%	15%
1	1.0000	1.0000	1.0000	1.0000	1.0000	1.0000	1.0000	1.0000	1.0000	1.0000	1.0000	1.0000
2	2.0100	2.0200	2.0300	2.0400	2.0500	2.0600	2.0700	2.0800	2.0900	2.1000	2.1200	2.1500
3	3.0301	3.0604	3.0909	3.1216	3.1525	3.1836	3.2149	3.2464	3.2781	3.3100	3.3744	3.4725
4	4.0604	4.1216	4.1836	4.2465	4.3101	4.3746	4.4399	4.5061	4.5731	4.6410	4.7793	4.9934
5	5.1010	5.2040	5.3091	5.4163	5.5256	5.6371	5.7507	5.8666	5.9847	6.1051	6.3528	6.7424
6	6.1520	6.3081	6.4684	6.6330	6.8019	6.9753	7.1533	7.3359	7.5233	7.7156	8.1152	8.7537
7	7.2135	7.4343	7.6625	7.8983	8.1420	8.3938	8.6540	8.9228	9.2004	9.4872	10.0890	11.0668
8	8.2857	8.5830	8.8923	9.2142	9.5491	9.8975	10.2598	10.6366	11.0285	11.4359	12.2997	13.7268
9	9.3685	9.7546	10.1591	10.5828	11.0266	11.4913	11.9780	12.4876	13.0210	13.5795	14.7757	16.7858
10	10.4622	10.9497	11.4639	12.0061	12.5779	13.1808	13.8164	14.4866	15.1929	15.9374	17.5487	20.3037
11	11.5668	12.1687	12.8078	13.4864	14.2068	14.9716	15.7835	16.6455	17.5603	18.5312	20.6546	24.3493
12	12.6825	13.4121	14.1920	15.0258	15.9171	16.8699	17.8885	18.9771	20.1407	21.3843	24.1331	29.0017
13	13.8093	14.6803	15.6178	16.6268	17.7130	18.8821	20.1406	21.4953	22.9534	24.5227	28.0291	34.3519
14	14.9474	15.9739	17.0863	18.2919	19.5986	21.0151	22.5505	24.2149	26.0192	27.9750	32.3926	40.5047
15	16.0969	17.2934	18.5989	20.0236	21.5786	23.2760	25.1290	27.1521	29.3609	31.7725	37.2797	47.5804
16	17.2579	18.6393	20.1569	21.8245	23.6575	25.6725	27.8881	30.3243	33.0034	35.9497	42.7533	55.7175
17	18.4304	20.012	21.7616	23.6975	25.8404	28.2129	30.8402	33.7502	36.9737	40.5447	48.8837	65.0751
18	19.6147	21.4123	23.4144	25.6454	28.1324	30.9057	33.9990	37.4502	41.3013	45.5992	55.7497	75.8364
19	20.8109	22.8406	25.1169	27.6712	30.5390	33.7600	37.3790	41.4463	46.0185	41.1591	63.4397	88.2118
20	22.0190	24.2974	26.8704	29.7781	33.0660	36.7856	40.9955	45.7620	51.1601	57.2750	72.0524	102.444
25	28.2432	32.0303	36.4593	41.6459	47.7271	54.8645	63.2490	73.1059	84.7009	98.3471	133.334	212.793
30	34.7849	40.5681	47.5754	56.0849	66.4388	79.0582	94.4608	113.283	136.308	164.494	241.333	434.745
35	41.6603	49.9945	60.4621	73.6522	90.3203	111.435	138.237	172.317	215.711	271.024	431.663	881.170
40	48.8864	60.4020	75.4013	95.0255	120.800	154.762	199.635	259.057	337.882	442.593	767.091	1,779.09

Accounting Concepts and Alternative Valuations

III

Chapter Outine

A PPENDIX PREVIEW

Accounting concepts are not laws of nature. They are broad ideas developed as a way of *describing* current accounting practices and *prescribing* new and improved practices. In this Appendix we explain the accounting concepts the CICA developed in an effort to guide future changes and improvements in accounting. We also discuss alternatives to the historical cost measurements reported in financial statements. Understanding these alternatives helps us with interpreting information in these statements.

▶ A Look At This Appendix

This appendix describes accounting concepts, how they are developed, and the conceptual framework in accounting. It also discusses alternative valuations to historical cost accounting.

Learning Objectives

LO 1 Explain both descriptive and prescriptive concepts and their development.

LO 2 Describe the financial statement concepts for accounting.

LO 3 Explain how price changes impact conventional financial statements.

LO 4 Discuss valuation alternatives to historical cost.

SECTION 1 ACCOUNTING CONCEPTS

Accounting Concepts and Principles

 LO1 Explain both descriptive and prescriptive concepts and their development.

Accounting *concepts* serve two main purposes. First, they provide descriptions of existing accounting practices. They act as guidelines that help us understand and use accounting information. Knowing how concepts are applied enables us to effectively use accounting information in different situations, and understanding accounting concepts is easier and more useful than memorizing a long list of procedures. Second, accounting concepts are important for the Accounting Standards Board (AcSB), which is charged with developing acceptable practices for financial reporting in Canada and with improving the quality of such reporting.

We defined and illustrated several important accounting *principles* in this book. Several of these major principles are listed in Exhibit III.1. Accounting principles describe in general terms the practices as currently applied.

We first explained these principles in Chapter 2, but we referred to them frequently in the book. The term *concepts* include both these principles as well as other general rules. The AcSB also uses the word *concepts* in this same way.

Exhibit III.1

Partial List of Accounting Principles

Business entity principle
Conservatism principle
Consistency principle
Cost principle
Full-disclosure principle
Going-concern principle
Matching principle
Materiality principle
Objectivity principle
Revenue recognition principle
Time period principle

As business practices evolved in recent years, accounting concepts were sometimes difficult to apply in dealing with new and different types of transactions. This occurs because they are intended as general descriptions of current accounting practices. They do not necessarily describe what should be done. Since concepts do not identify weaknesses in accounting practices, they do not lead to major changes or improvements in accounting practices.

The AcSB, however, is charged with improving financial reporting. It was generally agreed that a new set of concepts needed to be developed for this purpose. They also decided this new set of concepts should not merely *describe* what is being done in current practice. Instead, the new concepts should *prescribe* (or guide) what ought to be done to improve things. Before we describe the concepts developed by the AcSB, we look more closely at the differences between descriptive and prescriptive uses of accounting concepts.

Descriptive and Prescriptive Concepts

Exhibit III.2

"Bottom-Up" Development of Descriptive Concepts

Concepts differ in how they are developed and used. Generally, when concepts are intended to describe current practice, they are developed by looking at accepted practices and then making rules to encompass them. This bottom-up, or *descriptive*, approach is shown in Exhibit III.2.

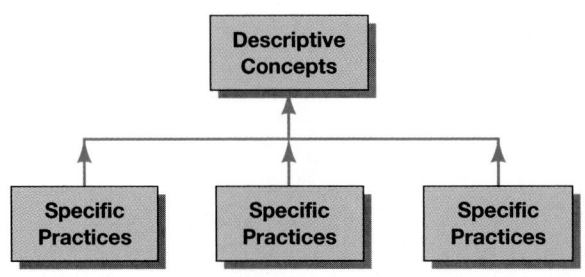

It shows arrows going from specific practices to concepts. The outcome of this process is a set of concepts that summarize practice. This process, for instance, leads us to the concept that asset purchases are recorded at cost.

But these concepts often fail to show how new problems might be solved. For example, the concept that assets are recorded at cost doesn't provide direct guidance for situations where assets have no cost because they are donated to a company by a local government. The bottom-up approach is based on the presumption that current practices are adequate. They don't lead to development of new and improved accounting methods. The concept that assets are initially recorded at cost doesn't encourage asking the question of whether they should always be carried at that amount.

Alternatively, when concepts are intended to *prescribe* (or guide) improvements in accounting practice, they are likely to be designed by a top-down approach as shown in Exhibit III.3.

The top-down approach starts with broad accounting objectives. The process then generates broad concepts about the types of information that should be reported. These concepts lead to specific practices that ought to be used. The advantage of this approach is that these concepts are good for solving new problems and evaluating old answers. Its disadvantage is the concepts may not be very descriptive of current practice. The suggested practices may not even be in current use.

Since the AcSB uses accounting concepts to prescribe accounting practices, the Board used a top-down approach. The Board's concepts are not necessarily more correct than others. But new concepts are intended to provide better guidelines for developing new and improved accounting practices. The AcSB continues to use them as a basis for future actions and already has used them to justify many important changes in financial reporting.

It is crucial in setting accounting standards that the issues be properly identified and described. Section 1000, "Financial Statement Concepts" of the *CICA Handbook* helps the AcSB do this by providing common objectives and terms. Section 1000 also helps the Board focus on the important factors in accounting standard setting and, hopefully, reduces some of the political aspects of policy making.

Exhibit III.3

"Top-Down" Development of Prescriptive Concepts

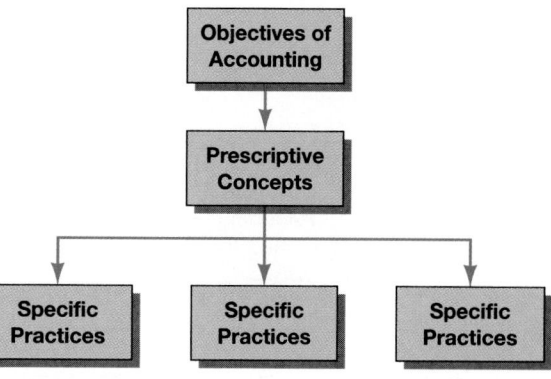

Flashback

III-1. What is the starting point in a top-down approach to developing accounting concepts?

III-2. What is the starting point in a bottom-up approach to developing accounting concepts?

Answers—p. III-9

During the 1970s the accounting profession in both Canada and the United States turned its attention to the apparent need for improvement in financial reporting. In 1980 *Corporate Reporting: Its Future Evolution,* a research study, was published by the Canadian Institute of Chartered Accountants, and in 1989 "Financial Statement Concepts," section 1000 of the *CICA Handbook,* was approved. In the United States the Financial Accounting Standards Board (FASB) published, in the 1978–85 period, six statements regarded as the most comprehensive pronouncement of the conceptual framework of accounting. FASB (SFAC 1) and Accounting Standards Board (*CICA Handbook,* section 1000) identified the broad objectives of financial reporting.

The Financial Accounting Standard Board's approach to developing a conceptual framework is diagrammed in Exhibit III.4. The Board has issued six

Financial Statement Concepts

LO2 Describe the financial statement concepts for accounting.

Statements of Financial Accounting Concepts (SFAC). These concepts statements are not the same as the FASB's *Statements of Financial Accounting Standards (SFAS).* The *SFASs* are authoritative statements of generally accepted accounting principles, whereas the *SFACs* are guidelines the Board uses in developing new standards. Accounting professionals are not required to follow the *SFACs* in practice.

Exhibit III.4

Conceptual Framework

Objectives of Financial Reporting

"Financial Statement Concepts" identified the broad objectives of financial reporting. The most general objective stated in the *CICA Handbook,* par. 1000.12, is to "communicate information that is useful to investors, creditors, and other users in making resource allocation decisions and/or assessing management stewardship." From this beginning point the Accounting Standards Board (AcSB) expressed other, more specific objectives. These objectives recognize that (1) financial reporting should help users predict future cash flow and (2) in making such predictions, information about a company's resources and obligations is useful if it possesses certain qualities. All of the concepts in the "Financial Statement Concepts" are intended to be consistent with these general objectives. Of course, present accounting practice already provides information about a company's resources and obligations. Thus, although the conceptual framework is intended to be prescriptive of new and improved practices, the concepts in the framework are also descriptive of many current practices.

Did You Know?

On-Line Concepts

The CICA has a Web site [www.cica.ca] where we can access exposure drafts and the latest news from the Accounting Standards Board. This site also provides access to many current standards and happenings in accounting.

Qualities of Useful Information

Exhibit III.4 shows the next step in the conceptual framework was to identify the qualities (or qualitative characteristics) that financial information should have if it is to be useful in decision making. The Board discussed the fact that information is useful only if it is understandable to users. But the Board assumed users have the training, experience, and motivation to analyze financial reports. With this decision, the Board indicated financial reporting should not try to meet the needs of unsophisticated or casual users.

In *Section 1000,* the Board stated information is useful if it is (1) relevant, (2) reliable, and (3) comparable. Information is *relevant* if it can make a difference in a decision. Information has this quality when it helps users predict the future or evaluate the past and is received in time to affect their decisions.

Information is *reliable* if users can depend on it to be free from bias and error. Reliable information is verifiable and faithfully represents what is intended to be described. Users can depend on information only if it is neutral. This means the rules used to produce information are not designed to lead users to accept or reject any specific decision.

Information is *comparable* if users can use it to identify differences and similarities between companies. Complete comparability is possible only if companies follow uniform practices. But even if all companies uniformly follow the same practices, comparable reports do not result if the practices are inappropriate. For example, comparable information is not provided if all companies ignored the useful lives of their assets and depreciate them over two years.

Comparability also requires consistency (see Chapter 7). This means a company should not change its accounting practices unless the change is justified as a reporting improvement. Another important concept discussed in *Section 1000* is materiality (see Chapter 10). An item is material if it affects decisions of users. Items not material are often accounted for in the easiest way possible using cost-benefit criteria.

Elements of Financial Statements

Exhibit III.4 shows an important part of the conceptual framework is the elements of financial statements. This includes defining the categories of information that are contained in financial statements. The Board's discussion of financial statement elements included defining important items such as assets, liabilities, equity, revenues, expenses, gains and losses. In earlier chapters, we drew on many of these definitions. Recently, the Board has issued recommendations for not-for-profit accounting entities.[1]

Recognition and Measurement

The Board has established concepts for deciding (1) when items should be presented (or recognized) in financial statements and (2) how to assign numbers to (or measure) those items. The Board generally concluded that items should be recognized in financial statements if they meet the following criteria:

Defined.	Item meets the definition of an element of financial statements.
Measurable.	Has a relevant attribute measurable with sufficient reliability.
Relevant.	Information about it is capable of making a difference in user decisions.
Reliable.	Information is representationally faithful, verifiable, and neutral.

The question of how an item is measured raises a fundamental question of whether financial statements should be based on cost or on current value. The Board's discussion of this issue is more descriptive of current practice than it is prescriptive of new measurement methods.

Paragraph 1000.04 of the *CICA Handbook* states that a full set of financial statements should show:

1. Balance Sheet (financial position at the end of the period.)
2. Income Statement (earnings for the period.)
3. Statement of Retained Earnings
4. Statement of Cash Flows (cash flows during the period.)
5. Notes to financial statements and supporting schedules to which the financial statements are cross-referenced are an integral part of such statements.

---

[1] *CICA Handbook,* sections 4400ff, "Not-for-Profit Organizations."

Flashback

III-3. The AcSB's financial statement concepts are intended to:

    a. Provide a historical analysis of accounting practice.

    b. Describe current accounting practice.

    c. Provide concepts that are prescriptive of what should be done in accounting practice.

III-4. The notion that accounting practices should be consistent from year to year most directly relates to the AcSB's concept that information reported in financial statements should be (a) relevant, (b) material, (c) reliable, or (d) comparable.

III-5. What characteristics of accounting information make it reliable?

III-6. What do the elements of financial statements refer to?

Answers—p. III-9

SECTION 2
ALTERNATIVE ACCOUNTING VALUATIONS

Historical Cost Accounting and Price Changes

Most agree that conventional (historical cost based) financial statements provide useful information to users. But many also believe conventional financial statements inadequately account for the impact of changing prices. When prices changes, users often look for alternative valuations along with the conventional statements when making decisions.

LO3 Explain how price changes impact conventional financial statements.

Impact of Price Changes on the Balance Sheet

Conventional financial statements reflect transactions recorded using historical costs. Amounts in statements are usually not adjusted even though subsequent price changes alter their values.[2] As an example, consider Company X who purchases 10 acres of land for $25,000. At the end of each accounting period, Company X reports a balance sheet showing "Land ... $25,000." Several years later, after sharp price increases, Company Y purchases 10 acres of land next to and nearly identical to Company X's land. But Company Y paid $60,000 for its land. Exhibit III.5 shows the conventional balance sheet disclosures for these two companies for the land account.

Exhibit III.5

Conventional Balance Sheet Comparison

	Company X	Company Y
Land	$25,000	$60,000

Absent the details, a user is likely to conclude that either Company Y has more land than Company X or that Company Y's land is more valuable. In reality, both companies own 10 acres that are identical. The difference is due to price changes.

---

[2] One exception to this is with the reporting of certain investments in debt and equity securities at their market values. We explained this exception in Chapters 10 and 17.

Impact of Price Changes on the Income Statement

The inability of a conventional balance sheet to reflect price changes also shows up in the income statement. As an example, consider two companies that purchase identical machines but at different times. Company A purchases the machine for $10,000 in 1998, while Company Z purchases the machine in 2000 when its price is $18,000. Both machines are depreciated on a straight-line basis over a 10-year period with no salvage value. Exhibit III.6 shows amortization expense in the conventional annual income statements for these two companies.

	Company A	Company Z
Amortization expense, machinery	$1,000	$1,800

Exhibit III.6

Conventional Income Statement Comparison

Although identical assets are being amortized, the income statements show a sharply higher amortization expense for Company Z.

This section discusses three alternatives to historical cost valuation for financial statements.

Valuation Alternatives to Historical Cost

LO 4 Discuss valuation alternatives to historical cost.

Constant Dollar Accounting

One alternative to conventional financial statements is to restate dollar amounts of cost incurred in earlier years for changes in the general price level. This means a specific dollar amount of cost in a previous year is restated as the number of dollars spent if the cost is paid with dollars having the current amount of purchasing power. Restating accounting numbers into dollars of equal purchasing power yields *constant dollar* financial statements. Constant dollar accounting changes the unit of measurement, but it is still based on historical cost.

Current Cost Accounting

All prices do not change at the same rate. When the general price level is rising, some specific prices may be falling. *Current cost* accounting measures financial statement elements at current values. It is not based on historical cost. The result of measuring expenses in current costs is that revenue is matched with current (at the time of the sale) costs of the resources used to earn the revenue. This means operating profit is not positive unless revenues are large enough to replace all of the resources consumed in the process of producing those revenues. Those who argue for current costs believe that operating profit measured in this fashion provides an improved basis for evaluating the effectiveness of operating activities. On the balance sheet, current cost accounting reports assets at amounts needed to purchase them as of the balance sheet date. Liabilities are reported at amounts needed to satisfy the liabilities as of the balance sheet date.

Mark-to-Market Accounting

We can also report assets (and liabilities) at current selling prices. On the balance sheet, this means assets are reported at amounts received if the assets were sold. Liabilities are reported at amounts needed to settle the liabilities. This method of valuation is called the current selling price method or, more commonly, *mark-to-market* accounting.

One argument supporting current selling prices of assets is that the alternative to owning an asset is to sell it. This means the sacrifice a business makes to hold an asset is the amount it would receive if the asset were sold. Also, the benefit derived from holding a liability is the amount the business avoids paying by not settling it. Shareholders' equity in this case represents the net amount of cash from liquidating the company. This net liquidation value is the amount that can be invested in other projects if the company were liquidated. It is a relevant basis for evaluating whether the income the company earns is enough to justify remaining in business.

Some proponents of current selling price believe it should be applied to assets but not liabilities. Others argue it applies equally well to both. Still others believe it should be applied only to assets held for sale. As Chapters 10 and 16 explain, companies use the current selling price approach to value some investments. Investments in trading securities are reported at their fair (market) values, with the related changes in fair values reported on the income statement. Investments in securities available for sale are also reported at their fair values, but the related changes in fair values are not reported on the conventional income statement. Instead, they are reported as part of shareholders' equity.

Summary

LO1 **Explain both descriptive and prescriptive concepts and their development.** Descriptive accounting concepts provide general descriptions of current accounting practices and are most useful in learning about accounting. Prescriptive accounting concepts guide us in the practices that should be followed. These prescriptive concepts are most useful in developing accounting procedures for new types of transactions and making improvements in accounting practice. A bottom-up approach to developing concepts begins by examining the practices currently in use. Then, concepts are developed that provide general descriptions of those practices. A top-down approach begins by stating the objectives of accounting. From these objectives, concepts are developed that guide us in identifying the types of accounting practices one should follow.

LO2 **Describe the financial statement concepts for accounting.** The CICA's Financial Statement Concepts begins by stating the broad objectives of financial reporting. Next, it identifies the qualitative characteristics accounting information should possess. The elements

contained in financial reports are then defined, followed by recognition and measurement criteria.

LO3 **Explain how price changes impact conventional financial statements.** Conventional financial statements report transactions in terms of historical dollars received or paid. The statements usually are not adjusted to reflect general price level changes or changes in the specific prices of the items reported. This can impact the statements with items not reflecting current values, which can lead to errors in judgment by users.

LO4 **Discuss valuation alternatives to historical cost.** Constant dollar accounting involves multiplying cost by a factor reflecting the change in the general price level since the cost was incurred. Current cost accounting involves reporting on the balance sheet the dollar amounts needed to purchase the assets at the balance sheet date, and on the income statement the amounts needed to acquire operating assets on the date they are used. Mark-to-market accounting involves reporting current selling prices of assets and liabilities.

Guidance Answers to Flash backs

III-1. A top-down approach to developing accounting concepts begins by identifying appropriate objectives of accounting reports.

III-2. A bottom-up approach to developing accounting concepts starts by examining existing accounting practices and determining the general features that characterize those procedures.

III-3. *c*

III-4. *d*

III-5. To have the qualitative characteristic of being reliable, accounting information should be free from bias and error, should be verifiable, should faithfully represent what is supposed to be described, and should be neutral.

III-6. The elements of financial statements are the objects and events that financial statements should describe; for example, assets, liabilities, revenues, and expenses.

Questions

1. Can a concept be used descriptively and prescriptively?
2. Which three qualitative characteristics of accounting information did the CICA identify as being necessary if the information is to be useful?
3. What is implied by saying that financial information should have the qualitative characteristic of relevance?
4. What are the four criteria an item should satisfy to be recognized in the financial statements?
5. Some people argue that conventional financial statements fail to adequately account for inflation. What general problem with conventional financial statements generates this argument?
6. What is the fundamental difference in the adjustments made under current cost accounting and under historical cost/constant dollar accounting?
7. What are three alternatives to historical cost valuation for financial statements?

Identify the following statements as true or false:

_____ 1. Accounting concepts are good examples of laws of nature.

_____ 2. There are really no viable alternatives to historical cost measurements for financial statement reporting.

_____ 3. Practices suggested by applying CICA's Financial Statement Concepts must be in current use in practice.

_____ 4. Accounting professionals are not required to follow the Financial Statement Concepts in practice.

_____ 5. Only the Financial Statement Concepts describe authoritative generally accepted accounting principles.

_____ 6. Relevance, as an important quality of financial information, is placed above reliability in the conceptual framework hierarchy.

_____ 7. When concepts are intended to prescribe improvements in accounting practice, they are likely to be designed by a top-down approach.

Quick Study

QS III-1
Accounting concepts

LO 1,2

Match the desired qualities of financial information to the proper descriptions of the qualities. Use the following codes:

A. Relevant

B. Reliable

C. Comparable

_____ 1. Timely

_____ 2. Neutral

_____ 3. Verifiable

_____ 4. Requires consistency

_____ 5. Makes a difference in decision making

_____ 6. Useful in identifying differences between companies

_____ 7. Faithful representation

_____ 8. Free from bias and error

_____ 9. Predictive

QS III-2
Qualities of accounting information

LO 2

Identify *four* accounts from the following list that you feel are most susceptible to changing prices.

a. Accounts receivable

b. Inventories

c. Land

d. Equipment

e. Accounts payable

QS III-3
Impact of price changes on the balance sheet

LO 3

f. Cash

g. Long-term equity investments

h. Prepaid expenses

i. Income taxes payable

Exercises

Exercise III-1
Review of accounting principles

Match the principle to its proper description

Principle

_____ **1.** Business Entity principle

_____ **2.** Going-concern principle

_____ **3.** Objectivity principle

_____ **4.** Revenue recognition principle

_____ **5.** Matching principle

_____ **6.** Time period principle

Decription

A. Requires that financial statement information be supported by something other than someone's opinion or imagination.

B. Requires that revenue be recognized at the same time that it is earned.

C. Assumes that the business will continue operating instead of being closed or sold.

D. Requires expenses to be reported in the same period as the revenues that were earned as the result of the expenses.

E. Requires every business to be accounted for separately and distinctly from its owners.

F. Requires identifying the activities of a business with specific time periods such as quarters or years.

Exercise III-2

Write a brief report explaining the difference between descriptive and prescriptive concepts. Indicate why the CICA's Financial Statement Concepts is designed to be prescriptive, and discuss the issue of whether specific concepts can be both descriptive and prescriptive.

Exercise III-3
Mark-to-market valuation

Review Alliance's balance sheet in Appendix I. Identify three account balances that would likely change if its balance sheet were prepared on a mark-to-market basis rather than using generally accepted accounting principles.

Exercise III-4
Mark-to-market valuation

Assume that your employer has asked you to prepare the company's balance sheet using mark-to-market accounting. You realize that some accounts have valuations that don't differ from the historical cost basis, such as cash, accounts receivable, accounts payable, and prepaid expenses. However, there are four accounts that you need to locate market values for. These accounts are inventory, land, equipment, and temporary investments. Identify possible sources you may need to consult for these market values.

Codes of Professional Conduct

Principles

Selections from the
ICAO Rules of
Professional Conduct[1]

- A member or student shall conduct himself or herself at all times in a manner which will maintain the good reputation of the profession and its ability to serve the public interest.
- A member or student shall perform his or her professional services with integrity and care and accept an obligation to sustain his or her professional competence by keeping himself or herself informed of, and complying with, developments in professional standards.
- A member who is engaged in an attest function such as an audit or review of financial statements shall hold himself or herself free of any influence, interest or relationship, in respect of his or her client's affairs, which impairs his or her professional judgement or objectivity or which, in the view of a reasonable observer, would impair the member's professional judgement or objectivity.
- A member or student has a duty of confidence in respect of the affairs of any client and shall not disclose, without proper cause, any information obtained in the course of his or her duties, nor shall he or she in any way exploit such information to his or her advantage.
- The development of a member's practice shall be founded upon a reputation for professional excellence. The use of methods of advertising which do not uphold professional good taste, which could be characterized as self-promotion, and which solicit, rather than inform, is not in keeping with this principle.
- A member shall act in relation to any member with the courtesy and consideration due between professional colleagues and which, in turn, he or she would wish to be accorded by the other member.

Standards of Conduct Affecting the Public Interest

201	Maintenance of reputation of profession
202	Integrity and due care
203	Professional competence

---

[1] ICAO, *Rules of Professional Conduct* (Toronto: Institute of Chartered Accountants of Ontario). Other provincial institutes have similar provisions.

Compliance with the ICAO Rules of Professional Conduct depends primarily on a member's understanding and voluntary actions. However, there are provisions for reinforcement by peers and the public through public opinion, and ultimately by disciplinary proceedings, where necessary. Adherence to the Rules helps ensure individual and collective ethical behaviour by CAs.

Selections from the Code of Professional Ethics for Management Accountants[2]

Introduction

- Professional Ethics is the behaviour of a professional toward peers, other professionals and members of the public. They concern the performance of professional duties in accordance with recognized standards of accounting and professional integrity.

- The codes of professional ethics vary from province to province in certain details in order to comply with provincial legislation and the by-laws of the provincial societies. The following discussion covers the elements common to these codes. Reference should be made to the relevant code of ethics for specific information.

- Every member of the Society is duty bound to uphold and increase the competence and prestige of the accounting profession. In keeping with high standards of ethical conduct, members will conduct their professional work with honesty, impartiality, courtesy, and personal honour. Any breach of the principles of professional ethics will constitute discreditable conduct. The offending member will be liable to disciplinary measures the by-laws of the Society consider appropriate.

- A professional approach to resolving a problem of ethics requires that the rules of behaviour establish minimum, not maximum standards. Where the rules are silent, an even greater burden of responsibility falls upon the member to ensure that the course of action followed is consistent with general standards established by the Society.

General

- Members shall, in exercising their professional responsibilities, subordinate personal interest to those of the public, the employer, the Society and the profession.

---

[2] The Society of Management Accountants of Ontario, *Management Accountants Handbook.* (Toronto: SMAC).

■ Any member convicted of any criminal offence or who has been a party to any fraud or improper business practice may be charged with professional misconduct and be required to appear before a Society disciplinary tribunal. If found quilty of such charges by the tribunal, the member may be subject to dismissal from membership in the Society and to forfeiture of the right to use the CMA designation, or to other penalties provided in the by-laws.

■ A certificate of conviction in any court in Canada shall be sufficient evidence of a criminal conviction.

■ No member shall report any false or misleading fact in a financial statement, or knowingly misrepresent any statement.

Relations with the Public

■ Subject to provincial legislation, a Certified Management Accountant may offer services to the public as a management or cost accountant or consultant with the status of proprietor, partner, director, officer, or shareholder of an incorporated company and may associate with non-members for this purpose. A member associated with any company must abide by the rules of professional conduct of the Society. Certified members may use the initials CMA on the letterhead, professional cards or announcement in any public forum of the businesses with which they are associated.

■ The right of Certified Management Accountants to sign an audit certificate or perform a review engagement varies from jurisdiction to jurisdiction across Canada. Members of the Society must comply with local legislation.

■ No person except a Certified member, shall on letterhead, nameplates, professional cards or announcements claim membership in the Society.

■ When practising as a management accountant in preparing or expressing an opinion on financial statements intended to inform the public or management, a member shall disclose all material facts, require all and sufficient information to warrant expression of opinion, and will report all material misstatements or departures from generally accepted accounting principles.

■ Improper use by a member of a client's or employer's confidential information or affairs is discreditable conduct.

■ The member will treat as confident any information obtained concerning a client's affairs. The member also has a duty to inform the client of any member interest, affiliation or other matter of which the client ought reasonably to be informed, or which might influence the member's judgement.

Relations with Employers

■ No member shall use an employer's confidential information or business affairs to acquire any personal interest, property or benefit.

■ A member shall treat as confidential any information, or documents concerning the employer's business affairs and shall not disclose or release such information or documents without the consent of the employer, or the order of lawful authority.

■ A member shall inform the employer of any business connections, affiliations or interests of which the employer might reasonably expect to be informed.

■ No member shall knowingly be a party to any unlawful act of the employer.

Relations with Professional Accountants

■ No member shall criticize the professional work of another professional accountant except with the knowledge of that accountant unless the member reviews the work of others as a normal responsibility.

■ Members will uphold the principle of appropriate and adequate compensation for work and will endeavour to provide opportunities for professional development and advancement for accountants employed by them or under their supervision.

Chart of Accounts

Assets

Current Assets

101 Cash
102 Petty Cash
103 Cash equivalents
104 Temporary investments
105 Allowance to reduce temporary investments to market
106 Accounts receivable
107 Allowance for doubtful accounts
108 Legal fees receivable
109 Interest receivable
110 Rent receivable
111 Notes receivable
115 Subscription receivable, common shares
116 Subscription receivable, preferred shares
119 Merchandise inventory
120 _____ inventory
121 _____ inventory
124 Office supplies
125 Store supplies
126 _____ supplies
128 Prepaid insurance
129 Prepaid interest
131 Prepaid rent
132 Raw materials inventory
133 Goods in process inventory, _____
134 Goods in process inventory, _____
135 Finished goods inventory

Long-Term Investments

141 Investment in _____ shares
142 Investment in _____ bonds
144 Investment in _____
145 Bond sinking fund

Capital Assets

151 Automobiles
152 Accumulated amortization, automobiles
153 Trucks
154 Accumulated amortization, trucks
155 Boats
156 Accumulated amortization, boats
157 Professional library
158 Accumulated amortization, professional library
159 Law library
160 Accumulated amortization, law library
161 Furniture
162 Accumulated amortization, Furniture
163 Office equipment
164 Accumulated amortization, office equipment
165 Store equipment
166 Accumulated amortization, store equipment
167 _____ equipment
168 Accumulated amortization, _____ equipment
169 Machinery
170 Accumulated amortization, machinery
173 Building _____
174 Accumulated amortization, building _____
175 Building _____
176 Accumulated amortization, building _____
179 Land improvements, _____
180 Accumulated amortization, land improvements _____
181 Land improvements _____
182 Accumulated amortization, land improvements _____
183 Land

Natural Resources

185 Mineral deposit
186 Accumulated depletion, mineral deposit

Intangible Assets

191 Patents
192 Leasehold
193 Franchise
194 Copyright
195 Leasehold improvements
196 Organization costs
197 Deferred income tax debits

Liabilities

Current Liabilities

201 Accounts payable
202 Insurance payable
203 Interest payable
204 Legal fees payable
205 Short-term notes payable
206 Discount on short notes payable
207 Office salaries payable
208 Rent payable
209 Salaries payable
210 Wages payable
211 Accrued payroll payable
214 Estimated warranty liability

215   Income taxes payable
216   Common dividends payable
217   Preferred dividends payable
218   UI payable
219   CPP payable
221   Employees' medical insurance payable
222   Employees' retirement program payable
223   Employees' union dues payable
224   PST payable
225   GST payable
226   Estimated vacation pay liability

Unearned Revenues

230   Unearned consulting fees
231   Unearned legal fees
232   Unearned property management fees
233   Unearned _____ fees
234   Unearned _____
235   Unearned janitorial revenue
236   Unearned _____ revenue
238   Unearned rent _____

Long-Term Liabilities

251   Long-term notes payable
252   Discount on notes payable
253   Long-term lease liability
254   Discount on lease liability
255   Bonds payable
256   Discount on bonds payable
257   Premium on bonds payable
258   Deferred income tax credit

Equity

Owners' Equity

301   _____ , capital
302   _____ , withdrawals
303   _____ , capital
304   _____ , withdrawals
305   _____ , capital
305   _____ , withdrawals

Corporate Contributed Capital

307   Common shares
309   Common shares subscribed
310   Common stock dividends distributable
313   Contributed capital from the retirement of common shares
315   Preferred shares
317   Preferred shares subscribed

Retained Earnings

318   Retained earnings
319   Cash dividends declared
320   Stock dividends declared

Revenues

401   _____ fees earned
402   _____ fees earned
403   _____ services revenue
404   _____ services revenue
405   Commission earned
406   Rent earned
407   Dividends earned
408   Earnings from investment in _____
409   Interest earned
410   Sinking fund earnings
413   Sales
414   Sales returns and allowances
415   Sales discounts

Cost of Sales

501   Amortization of patents
502   Cost of goods sold
503   Depletion of mine deposit
505   Purchases
506   Purchases returns and allowances
507   Purchases discounts
508   Transportation-in

Manufacturing Accounts

520   Raw materials purchases
521   Freight-in on raw materials
530   Factory payroll
531   Direct labour
540   Factory overhead
541   Indirect materials
542   Indirect labour
543   Factory insurance expired
544   Factory supervision
545   Factory supplies used
546   Factory utilities
547   Miscellaneous production costs
548   Property taxes on factory building
550   Rent on factory building
551   Repairs, factory equipment
552   Small tools written off
560   Amortization of factory equipment
561   Amortization of factory building

Standard Cost Variance Accounts

580   Direct material quantity variance
581   Direct material price variance
582   Direct labour quantity variance
583   Direct labour price variance
584   Factory overhead volume variance
585   Factory overhead controllable variance

Expenses

Amortization (Depreciation and Depletion Expenses)

601   Amortization expense, _____
602   Amortization expense, copyrights
603   Depletion expense, _____
604   Amortization expense, boats
605   Amortization expense, automobiles
606   Amortization expense, building _____
607   Amortization expense, building _____
608   Amortization expense, land improvements _____
609   Amortization expense, land improvements _____
610   Amortization expense, law library
611   Amortization expense, trucks
612   Amortization expense, _____ equipment
613   Amortization expense, _____ equipment
614   Amortization expense, _____
615   Amortization expense, _____

Employee Related Expense

620   Office salaries expense
621   Sales salaries expense
622   Salaries expense
623   _____ wages expense
624   Employees' benefits expense
625   Payroll taxes expense

Financial Expenses

630   Cash over and short
631   Discounts lost
633   Interest expense

Insurance Expenses

635   Insurance expense, delivery equipment
636   Insurance expense, office equipment
637   Insurance expense, _____

Rental Expenses

640   Rent expense
641   Rent expense, office space
642   Rent expense, selling space

643 Press rental expense
644 Truck rental expense
645 _____ rental expense

Supplies Expense

650 Office supplies expense
651 Store supplies expense
652 _____ supplies expense
653 _____ supplies expense

Miscellaneous Expenses

655 Advertising expense
656 Bad debts expense
657 Blueprinting expense
658 Boat expense
659 Collection expense
661 Concessions expense
662 Credit card expense
663 Delivery expense
664 Dumping expense
667 Equipment expense
668 Food and drinks expense
669 Gas, oil, and repairs expense
671 Gas and oil expense
672 General and administrative expense

673 Janitorial expense
674 Legal fees expense
676 Mileage expense
677 Miscellaneous expenses
678 Mower and tools expense
679 Operating expenses
681 Permits expense
682 Postage expense
683 Property taxes expense
684 Repairs expense, _____
685 Repairs expense, _____
687 Selling expenses
688 Telephone expense
689 Travel and entertaining expense
690 Utilities expense
691 Warranty expense
695 Income taxes expense

Gains and Losses

701 Gain on retirement of bonds
702 Gain on sale of machinery
703 Gain on sale of temporary investments
704 Gain on sale of trucks

705 Gain on _____
801 Loss on disposal of machinery
802 Loss on exchange of equipment
803 Loss on exchange of _____
804 Loss on market decline of temporary investments
805 Loss on retirement of bonds
806 Loss on sale of investments
807 Loss on sale of Machinery
808 Loss on sale of _____
809 Loss on _____
810 Loss or gain from liquidation

Clearing Accounts

901 Income summary
902 Manufacturing summary

Credits

Index

FUNDAMENTALS

① Accounting Equation

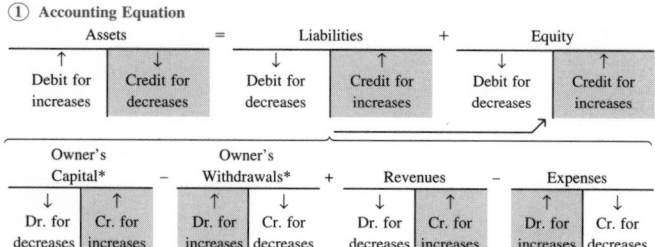

Assets = Liabilities + Equity

Assets		Liabilities		Equity	
Debit for increases	Credit for decreases	Debit for decreases	Credit for increases	Debit for decreases	Credit for increases

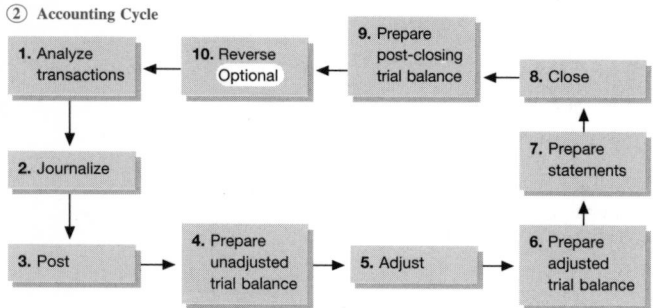

Owner's Capital*		– Owner's Withdrawals*		+ Revenues		– Expenses	
Dr. for decreases	Cr. for increases	Dr. for increases	Cr. for decreases	Dr. for decreases	Cr. for increases	Dr. for increases	Cr. for decreases

Indicates normal balance.

*Comparable corporate accounts are Contributed Capital and Cash Dividends.

② Accounting Cycle

1. Analyze transactions
2. Journalize
3. Post
4. Prepare unadjusted trial balance
5. Adjust
6. Prepare adjusted trial balance
7. Prepare statements
8. Close
9. Prepare post-closing trial balance
10. Reverse Optional

③ Adjustments and Entries

Type	Adjusting Entry	
Prepaid Expense	Dr. Expense	Cr. Asset
Depreciation	Dr. Expense	Cr. Contra-Asset
Unearned Revenues	Dr. Liability	Cr. Revenue
Accrued Expenses	Dr. Expense	Cr. Liability
Accrued Revenues	Dr. Asset	Cr. Revenue

④ 4-Step Closing Process

<1> Transfer revenue account balances to Income Summary.
<2> Transfer expense account balances to Income Summary.
<3> Transfer Income Summary balance to Owner's Capital.
<4> Transfer Withdrawals balance to Owner's Capital.

⑤ Accounting Concepts

Characteristics	Assumptions	Principles	Constraints
Relevance	Business entity	Historical cost	Cost-benefit
Reliability	Going concern	Revenue recognition	Materiality
Comparability	Monetary unit	Matching	Industry practice
Consistency	Periodicity	Full disclosure	Conservatism

⑥ Ownership of Inventory

	Ownership transfers when goods passed to	Transportation costs paid by
FOB Shipping Point	Carrier	Buyer
FOB Destination	Buyer	Seller

⑦ Inventory Costing Methods

Specific Identification
First-In, First-Out (FIFO)
Last-In, First-Out (LIFO)
Weighted-Average

⑧ Amortization

Straight-Line: $\dfrac{\text{Cost} - \text{Salvage value}}{\text{Useful life in periods}} \times \text{Periods expired}$

Units-of-Production: $\dfrac{\text{Cost} - \text{Salvage value}}{\text{Useful life in units}} \times \text{Units produced}$

Declining Balance: Rate* × Beginning of period book value
*Rate is often double the straight-line rate, or 2x(1/useful life)

Depletion: $\dfrac{\text{Cost} - \text{Salvage value}}{\text{Total capacity in units}} \times \text{Units extracted}$

⑨ Interest Computation

Interest = Principal (face) × Rate × Time

⑩ Costing Terminology

Variable cost: Cost changes in proportion to volume of activity.
Fixed cost: Cost does not change in proportion to volume of activity.
Direct cost: Cost incurred for the benefit of one cost object.
Indirect cost: Cost incurred for the benefit of more than one cost object.
Relevant cost: Cost that is pertinent to a decision.
Standard cost: Cost computed using standard price and standard quantity.
Budget: Formal statement of a company's future plans.

ANALYSES

① Liquidity and Efficiency

$\text{Current ratio} = \dfrac{\text{Current assets}}{\text{Current liabilities}}$

$\text{Acid-test ratio} = \dfrac{\text{Cash} + \text{Short-term investments} + \text{Current receivables}}{\text{Current liabilities}}$

$\text{Accounts receivable turnover} = \dfrac{\text{Net sales}}{\text{Average accounts receivable}}$

$\text{Merchandise turnover} = \dfrac{\text{Cost of goods sold}}{\text{Average merchandise inventory}}$

$\text{Days' sales uncollected} = \dfrac{\text{Accounts receivable}}{\text{Net sales}} \times 365$

$\text{Days' sales in inventory} = \dfrac{\text{Ending inventory}}{\text{Cost of goods sold}} \times 365$

$\text{Total asset turnover} = \dfrac{\text{Net sales}}{\text{Average total assets}}$

② Solvency

$\text{Debt ratio} = \dfrac{\text{Total liabilities}}{\text{Total assets}}$

$\text{Equity ratio} = \dfrac{\text{Total equity}}{\text{Total assets}}$

$\text{Pledged assets to secured liabilities} = \dfrac{\text{Book value of pledged assets}}{\text{Book value of secured liabilities}}$

$\text{Times interest earned} = \dfrac{\text{Income before interest and taxes}}{\text{Interest expense}}$

③ Profitability

$\text{Profit margin} = \dfrac{\text{Net income}}{\text{Net sales}}$

$\text{Gross margin} = \dfrac{\text{Net sales} - \text{Cost of goods sold}}{\text{Net sales}}$

$\text{Return on total assets} = \dfrac{\text{Net income}}{\text{Average total assets}}$

$\text{Return on common shareholders' equity} = \dfrac{\text{Net income} - \text{Preferred dividends}}{\text{Average common shareholders' equity}}$

$\text{Book value per common share} = \dfrac{\text{Shareholders' equity applicable to common shares}}{\text{Number of common shares outstanding}}$

$\text{Basic earnings per share} = \dfrac{\text{Net income} - \text{Preferred dividends}}{\text{Weighted-average common shares outstanding}}$

$\text{Cash flow on total assets} = \dfrac{\text{Operating cash flows}}{\text{Average total assets}}$

④ Market

$\text{Price-earnings ratio} = \dfrac{\text{Market price per common share}}{\text{Earnings per share}}$

$\text{Dividend yield} = \dfrac{\text{Annual dividends per share}}{\text{Market price per share}}$

⑤ Ratio Adjustments for Noncorporations*

$\text{Profit margin} = \dfrac{\text{Net income} - \text{Value of owner's efforts}}{\text{Net sales}}$

$\text{Return on total assets} = \dfrac{\text{Net income} - \text{Value of owner's efforts}}{\text{Average total assets}}$

$\text{Return on equity} = \dfrac{\text{Net income} - \text{Value of owner's efforts}}{\text{Average equity}}$

*Notes: 1. Taxes are zero for nearly all proprietorships and partnerships. 2. Sales are also called revenues. 3. Costs of goods sold are also called costs of sales.

⑥ Costing Ratios

Contribution margin ratio = (Sales − Variable costs)/Sales
Predetermined overhead rate = Estimated overhead costs/Estimated "factor" costs
Costs per unit = Material, labour, and overhead costs per unit

⑦ Planning and Control

Bread-even point = Fixed costs/Contribution margin per unit
Cost variance = Actual cost − Budgeted cost
Revenue variance = Actual sales − Budgeted sales
Payback period = Time expected to recover initial investment
Net present value = Present value of cash flows − Initial investment

REPORTS*

Income Statement For *period* Ended *date*		
Total net sales (revenues)		$ #
Cost of goods sold:		
Beginning inventory	$ #	
Cost of purchases	#	
Goods available for sale	$ #	
Ending inventory	#	
Cost of goods sold		#
Gross margin (gross profit)		$ #
Operating expenses:		
Examples: amortization, salaries, ...	$ #	
wages, rent, utilities, interest, ...	#	
advertising, taxes	#	
Total operating expenses		#
Nonoperating gains and losses		#
Net income (net profit or earnings)		$ #

*A chart of accounts near the end of the book classifies accounts by financial statement categories.